Colonial America

Colonial America

Essays in Politics
and Social Development

FIFTH EDITION

Stanley N. Katz
Princeton University

John M. Murrin
Princeton University

Douglas Greenberg
Survivors of the Shoah Visual History Foundation

Boston   Burr Ridge, IL   Dubuque, IA   Madison, WI   New York
San Francisco   St. Louis   Bangkok   Bogotá   Caracas   Kuala Lumpur
Lisbon   London   Madrid   Mexico City   Milan   Montreal   New Delhi
Santiago   Seoul   Singapore   Sydney   Taipei   Toronto

McGraw-Hill Higher Education

A Division of The McGraw-Hill Companies

COLONIAL AMERICA: ESSAYS IN POLITICS AND SOCIAL DEVELOPMENT
FIFTH EDITION

Published by McGraw-Hill, an imprint of The McGraw-Hill Companies, Inc., 1221 Avenue of the Americas, New York, NY 10020. Copyright © 2001, 1993, 1983 by The McGraw-Hill Companies, Inc. All rights reserved. No part of this publication may be reproduced or distributed in any form or by any means, or stored in a database or retrieval system, without the prior written consent of The McGraw-Hill Companies, Inc., including, but not limited to, in any network or other electronic storage or transmission, or broadcast for distance learning.

Some ancillaries, including electronic and print components, may not be available to customers outside the United States.

This book is printed on acid-free paper.

4 5 6 7 8 9 0 QPF/QPF 0 9 8 7 6

ISBN-13: 978-0-07-231740-4
ISBN-10: 0-07-231740-X

Vice president and editor-in-chief: *Thalia Dorwick*
Editorial director: *Jane E. Vaicunas*
Executive editor: *Lyn Uhl*
Developmental editor: *Kristen Mellitt*
Marketing manager: *Janise A. Fry*
Project manager: *Richard H. Hecker*
Production supervisor: *Kara Kudronowicz*
Design director: *Keith J. McPherson*
Cover designer: *Michael Warrell, Design Solutions*
Cover image: *Month of July from Father Abraham's Almanack for the year 1760.*
Courtesy, American Antiquarian Society
Compositor: *ElectraGraphics, Inc.*
Typeface: *10/12 Palatino*
Printer: *Quebecor World Fairfield Inc.*

Library of Congress Cataloging-in-Publication Data

Colonial America : essays in politics and social development / [edited by] Stanley N. Katz, John M. Murrin, Douglas Greenberg. — 5th ed.
    p. cm.
  Includes bibliographical references.
  ISBN 0–07–231740–X
  1. United States—Social conditions—To 1865. 2. United States—Politics and government—To 1775. I. Katz, Stanley Nider. II. Murrin, John M. III. Greenberg, Douglas.

HN57 .C584 2001
306'.0973—dc21

00–049558
CIP

www.mhhe.com

About the Editors

STANLEY N. KATZ was born in 1934 and received his B.A., M.A. and Ph.D. degrees, all in history, from Harvard University. He has taught at Harvard, Wisconsin, Chicago, Penn and Princeton, where from 1978–1986 he was the Class of 1921 Bicentennial Professor of the History of American Law and Liberty. From 1986 until 1997 he was President of the American Council of Learned Societies, and he is currently Lecturer with the rank of Professor at the Woodrow Wilson School, Princeton. He has published in the fields of early American history, American legal history, and the history of philanthropy.

JOHN M. MURRIN was born in Minneapolis in 1935 and received his degrees from the College (now University) of St. Thomas, the University of Notre Dame, and Yale University. He taught for ten years at Washington University, St. Louis, before moving to Princeton University in 1973 where he is professor of history. Active in both the Columbia Seminar in Early American History and the McNeil Center for Early American Studies, he has served on the editorial boards of the Omohundro Institute of Early American History and Culture, the *Journal of American History, New Jersey History,* and *Pennsylvania History.* He is co-author of *Liberty, Equality, Power: A History of the American People* (2nd edn., 1999), co-editor of *Saints and Revolutionaries: Essays in Early American History* (1983), and has published about four dozen essays on American history from the seventeenth to the nineteenth centuries. In 1998–99 he served as president of the Society for Historians of the Early American Republic.

DOUGLAS GREENBERG was born in Jersey City, New Jersey in 1947. He received his B.A. with Highest Distinction in History from Rutgers University and his M.A. and Ph.D. from Cornell University. He taught history at Lawrence and Princeton University, as well as at Rutgers. The author or editor of many books and articles on historical subjects, he has also written widely on the humanities, technology, and higher education in both scholarly and popular journals. Formerly Vice President of the American Council of Learned Societies, Greenberg has served on the Council of the American

Historical Association, among many other boards and advisory councils, including 10 years of service as a member and chairman of the New Jersey Historical Commission. From 1993 until 2000, he was President and CEO of the Chicago Historical Society. A member of the Executive Board of the Organization of American Historians, he now serves as President and CEO of Survivors of the Shoah Visual History Foundation in Los Angeles.

To the Memory of
LAWRENCE STONE (1919–1999)
An Historian of Immense Range and Depth
A Wonderful Colleague and True Friend

Contents

Part III
THE CLASH OF CULTURES IN AN AGE OF CRISIS

Part IV
PROVINCIAL AMERICA

Part V
MID-CENTURY CRISES AND TRANSFORMATIONS

Preface

ABOUT THE COLLECTION

This book, designed as supplementary reading for a colonial history course, makes a series of provocative and enlightening essays accessible to undergraduates and has also proved useful for graduate students. It provides a selection of readings out of which instructors can choose those that suit their own lectures and reading lists. The essays are distributed over the full time period covered in the course. Each is accompanied by an introduction that puts the essay in historical context and raises questions for the student to consider as he or she reads.

NEW TO THE FIFTH EDITION

We have increased the number of essays in this collection from twenty-four to twenty-five. Only eight carry over from the fourth edition, while seventeen are new. Only one survives from the first edition of the collection.

We are impressed by how rapidly the field of American colonial history has been changing. We have tried to reflect the evolving interests of early American historians, who are becoming both Atlantic and continentalist in their orientation. Our selections include major essays on the French and Spanish borderlands of the British mainland colonies while keeping, we hope, an appropriate balance among the diverse regions within the British colonies and continuing and broadening our earlier emphases on gender, family, Indians, and blacks. Other choices are oceanic in their orientation.

We have also made an important change to the essay introductions for this edition. The questions they include are now set off as bulleted lists, which will draw attention to them so that students will be more apt to keep the questions in mind as they read.

ACKNOWLEDGMENTS

We wish to thank instructors who reviewed the fourth edition and our proposed changes for the fifth edition for their many helpful suggestions for revision: Michael Andersen, Clarke College; Virginia DeJohn Anderson, University of Colorado; Stephen Aron, UCLA; Jennifer Baszile, University of Connecticut; Rosalind J. Beiler, University of Central Florida; S. Charles Bolton, University of Arkansas–Little Rock; Stephen R. Boyd, University of Texas–San Antonio; Miles L. Bradbury, University of Maryland; Louise A. Breen, Kansas State University; Joel A. Cohen, University of Rhode Island; Sheldon S. Cohen, Loyola University of Chicago; Edward Countryman, Southern Methodist University; J. Frederick Fausz, University of Missouri–St. Louis; James Haw, Indiana Purdue University at Fort Wayne; Katherine Hermes, Central Connecticut State University; Ruth Wallis Herndon, University of Toledo; David T. Konig, Washington University; Johanna Miller Lewis, University of Arkansas–Little Rock; Ann M. Little, University of Dayton; Peter C. Mancall, University of Kansas; Dane A. Morrison, Salem State College; Wendy Nicholson, Lawrence University; Oliver Rink, California State University–Bakersfield; Susanne M. Schick, Messiah College; Philip J. Schwarz, Virginia Commonwealth University; Stephen Stein, Indiana University–Bloomington; Paul E. Teed, Saginaw Valley State University; and Alan Watson, University of North Carolina–Wilmington. We are particularly grateful to Denver A. Brunsman, William C. Carter, Andrew Graybill, Evan P. Haefeli, and David J. Silverman for drafting the introductions to the seventeen new selections. Denver Brunsman has also given the entire volume a careful proofreading. We again welcome any comments or suggestions from those who use this collection.

Stanley N. Katz

John M. Murrin

Douglas Greenberg

PART I

A Global Perspective

Spacious Skies
and Tilted Axes

Jared Diamond

INTRODUCTION

Haunting the field of early American history in particular and of modern world history in general is the question of why peoples from Europe were so well equipped to dominate those of the Americas and Africa. If we accept that groups from different parts of the globe were and are of similar intelligence and equal abilities, how do we explain why those of the West became so disproportionately innovative and powerful? Intimidated by the immensity of the question and the tendency of such inquiry to fuel racist discourse, scholars have generally avoided this problem.

But not Jared Diamond. Demonstrating formidable interdisciplinary skills, Diamond tackles the question head-on, all the while refusing to give an inch to those who would ascribe the lopsided outcomes to biological difference. Among his several contributions is the following piece. Diamond argues that if one wants to understand how the West came to wield guns, the nastiest germs, and steel in its conquests, one must begin with the fact that Eurasia rests on an east-west axis, whereas Africa and America stretch along north-south axes. Humans most easily adopt new crops from peoples who live along the same latitude, because areas of similar latitudes, unlike those along the same longitudes, generally possess like climates and disease environments. Eurasia had the geographical benefit of an eight-thousand-mile latitudinal expanse relatively unhindered by geographical barriers. Over the course of several thousand years, this feature facilitated the spread of productive crops outward from a single zone, the "Fertile Crescent" (Southwestern Asia). Diffusion of other technologies, such as the wheel, metallurgy, writing, and domesticated animals as well as complex economic systems, centralized polities, and multistate religions traveled along paths blazed by the Eurasian crop diaspora. By contrast, Africa and the Americas had longitudinal orientations and were divided by large swaths

Jared Diamond in *Guns, Germs, and Steel: The Fates of the Human Societies*, pp. 176–191. Copyright © 1997 by Jared Diamond. Used by permission of W. W. Norton & Company, Inc.

of dry ground and rain forest, respectively, both of which discouraged such exchange. It is not that the people of these regions were biologically inca-pable of developing societies that could compete with Europe, but that they drew from a well of ideas and technologies limited by geographical circum-stance. So overwhelming were the Europeans' advantages that one might conclude their conquest of new worlds was all but ensured when they set foot on African and American shores.

Yet, as articles by Virginia DeJohn Anderson, Gregory E. Dowd, Ramón A. Gutiérrez, and John Thornton in this volume show, Indians and Africans did resist European colonizers.

- *To what extent was the success, or even failure, of these campaigns linked to native peoples' borrowing from those they warred against?*
- *Was there any real chance that such opposition would succeed over the long term, given the technological disparities highlighted by Diamond?*
- *If Diamond's work is the big picture, is it a political rather than historical exercise to highlight episodes of native resistance?*
- *What is gained and what is lost if one does not keep both perspectives in mind?*

On the map of the world [shown here], compare the shapes and orientations of the continents. You'll be struck by an obvious difference. The Americas span a much greater distance north-south (9,000 miles) than east-west: only 3,000 miles at the widest, narrowing to a mere 40 miles at the Isthmus of Panama. That is, the major axis of the Americas is north-south. The same is also true, though to a less extreme degree, for Africa. In contrast, the major

Major axes of the continents.

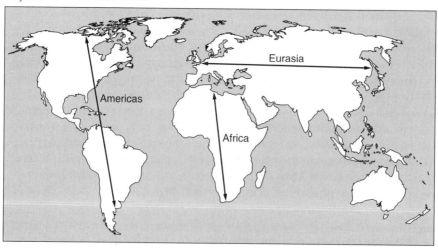

axis of Eurasia is east-west. What effect, if any, did those differences in the orientation of the continents' axes have on human history?

This chapter will be about what I see as their enormous, sometimes tragic, consequences. Axis orientations affected the rate of spread of crops and live-stock, and possibly also of writing, wheels, and other inventions. That basic feature of geography thereby contributed heavily to the very different experiences of Native Americans, Africans, and Eurasians in the last 500 years.

Food production's spread proves as crucial to understanding geographic differences in the rise of guns, germs, and steel as did its origins. . . . There were no more than nine areas of the globe, perhaps as few as five, where food production arose independently. Yet, already in prehistoric times, food production became established in many other regions besides those few areas of origins. All those other areas became food producing as a result of the spread of crops, livestock, and knowledge of how to grow them and, in some cases, as a result of migrations of farmers and herders themselves.

The main such spreads of food production were from Southwest Asia to Europe, Egypt and North Africa, Ethiopia, Central Asia, and the Indus Valley; from the Sahel and West Africa to East and South Africa; from China to tropical Southeast Asia, the Philippines, Indonesia, Korea, and Japan; and from Mesoamerica to North America. Moreover, food production even in its areas of origin became enriched by the addition of crops, livestock, and techniques from other areas of origin.

Just as some regions proved much more suitable than others for the origins of food production, the ease of its spread also varied greatly around the world. Some areas that are ecologically very suitable for food production never acquired it in prehistoric times at all, even though areas of prehistoric food production existed nearby. The most conspicuous such examples are the failure of both farming and herding to reach Native American California from the U.S. Southwest or to reach Australia from New Guinea and Indonesia, and the failure of farming to spread from South Africa's Natal Province to South Africa's Cape. Even among all those areas where food production did spread in the prehistoric era, the rates and dates of spread varied considerably. At the one extreme was its rapid spread along east-west axes: from Southwest Asia both west to Europe and Egypt and east to the Indus Valley (at an average rate of about 0.7 miles per year); and from the Philippines east to Polynesia (at 3.2 miles per year). At the opposite extreme was its slow spread along north-south axes: at less than 0.5 miles per year, from Mexico northward to the U.S. Southwest; at less than 0.3 miles per year, for corn and beans from Mexico northward to become productive in the eastern United States around A.D. 900; and at 0.2 miles per year, for the llama from Peru north to Ecuador. These differences could be even greater if corn was not domesticated in Mexico as late as 3500 B.C., as I assumed conservatively for these calculations, and as some archaeologists now assume, but if it was instead domesticated considerably earlier, as most archaeologists used to assume (and many still do).

There were also great differences in the completeness with which suites of crops and livestock spread, again implying stronger or weaker barriers to their spreading. For instance, while most of Southwest Asia's founder crops and livestock did spread west to Europe and east to the Indus Valley, neither of the Andes' domestic mammals (the llama/alpaca and the guinea pig) ever reached Mesoamerica in pre-Columbian times. That astonishing failure cries out for explanation. After all, Mesoamerica did develop dense farming populations and complex societies, so there can be no doubt that Andean domestic animals (if they had been available) would have been valuable for food, transport, and wool. Except for dogs, Mesoamerica was utterly without indigenous mammals to fill those needs. Some South American crops nevertheless did succeed in reaching Mesoamerica, such as manioc, sweet potatoes, and peanuts. What selective barrier let those crops through but screened out llamas and guinea pigs?

A subtler expression of this geographically varying ease of spread is the phenomenon termed preemptive domestication. Most of the wild plant species from which our crops were derived vary genetically from area to area, because alternative mutations had become established among the wild ancestral populations of different areas. Similarly, the changes required to transform wild plants into crops can in principle be brought about by alternative new mutations or alternative courses of selection to yield equivalent results. In this light, one can examine a crop widespread in prehistoric times and ask whether all of its varieties show the same wild mutation or same transforming mutation. The purpose of this examination is to try to figure out whether the crop was developed in just one area or else independently in several areas.

If one carries out such a genetic analysis for major ancient New World crops, many of them prove to include two or more of those alternative wild variants, or two or more of those alternative transforming mutations. This suggests that the crop was domesticated independently in at least two different areas, and that some varieties of the crop inherited the particular mutation of one area while other varieties of the same crop inherited the mutation of another area. On this basis, botanists conclude that lima beans *(Phaseolus lunatus)*, common beans *(Phaseolus vulgaris)*, and chili peppers of the *Capsicum annuum/chinense* group were all domesticated on at least two separate occasions, once in Mesoamerica and once in South America; and that the squash *Cucurbita pepo* and the seed plant goosefoot were also domesticated independently at least twice, once in Mesoamerica and once in the eastern United States. In contrast, most ancient Southwest Asian crops exhibit just one of the alternative wild variants or alternative transforming mutations, suggesting that all modern varieties of that particular crop stem from only a single domestication.

What does it imply if the same crop has been repeatedly and independently domesticated in several different parts of its wild range, and not just once and in a single area? We have already seen that plant domestication involves the modification of wild plants so that they become more useful to humans by virtue of larger seeds, a less bitter taste, or other qualities. Hence if a productive crop is already available, incipient farmers will surely proceed to grow it rather than start all over again by gathering its not yet so useful wild relative and redomesticating it. Evidence for just a single domestication thus suggests that, once a wild plant had been domesticated, the crop spread quickly to other areas throughout the wild plant's range, preempting the need for other independent domestications of the same plant. However, when we find evidence that the same wild ancestor was domesticated independently in different areas, we infer that the crop spread too slowly to preempt its domestication elsewhere. The evidence for predominantly single domestications in Southwest Asia, but frequent multiple domestications in the Americas, might thus provide more subtle evidence that crops spread more easily out of Southwest Asia than in the Americas.

Rapid spread of a crop may preempt domestication not only of the same wild ancestral species somewhere else but also of related wild species. If you're already growing good peas, it's of course pointless to start from scratch to domesticate the same wild ancestral pea again, but it's also pointless to domesticate closely related wild pea species that for farmers are virtually equivalent to the already domesticated pea species. All of Southwest Asia's founder crops preempted domestication of any of their close relatives throughout the whole expanse of western Eurasia. In contrast, the New World presents many cases of equivalent and closely related, but nevertheless distinct, species having been domesticated in Mesoamerica and South America. For instance, 95 percent of the cotton grown in the world today belongs to the cotton species *Gossypium hirsutum*, which was domesticated in prehistoric times in Mesoamerica. However, prehistoric South American farmers instead grew the related cotton *Gossypium barbadense*. Evidently, Mesoamerican cotton had such difficulty reaching South America that it failed in the prehistoric era to preempt the domestication of a different cotton species there (and vice versa). Chili peppers, squashes, amaranths, and chenopods are other crops of which different but related species were domesticated in Mesoamerica and South America, since no species was able to spread fast enough to preempt the others.

We thus have many different phenomena converging on the same conclusion: that food production spread more readily out of Southwest Asia than in the Americas, and possibly also than in sub-Saharan Africa. Those phenomena include food production's complete failure to reach some ecologically suitable areas; the differences in its rate and selectivity of spread; and the differences in whether the earliest domesticated crops preempted redomestications of the same species or domestications of close relatives. What

The spread of Fertile Crescent crops across western Eurasia

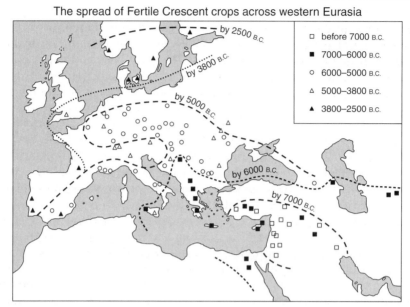

The symbols show early radiocarbon-dated sites where remains of Fertile Crescent crops have been found. □ = the Fertile Crescent itself (sites before 7000 B.C.). Note that dates become progressively later as one gets farther from the Fertile Crescent. This map is based on Map 20 of Zohary and Hopf's *Domestication of Plants in the Old World* but substitutes calibrated radiocarbon dates for their uncalibrated dates.

was it about the Americas and Africa that made the spread of food production more difficult there than in Eurasia?

To answer this question, let's begin by examining the rapid spread of food production out of Southwest Asia (the Fertile Crescent). Soon after food production arose there, somewhat before 8000 B.C., a centrifugal wave of it appeared in other parts of western Eurasia and North Africa farther and farther removed from the Fertile Crescent, to the west and east. I have redrawn the striking map [shown here] assembled by the geneticist Daniel Zohary and botanist Maria Hopf, in which they illustrate how the wave had reached Greece and Cyprus and the Indian subcontinent by 6500 B.C., Egypt soon after 6000 B.C., central Europe by 5400 B.C., southern Spain by 5200 B.C., and Britain around 3500 B.C. In each of those areas, food production was initiated by some of the same suite of domestic plants and animals that launched it in the Fertile Crescent. In addition, the Fertile Crescent package penetrated Africa southward to Ethiopia at some still-uncertain date. However, Ethiopia also developed many indigenous crops, and we do not yet know whether it was these crops or the arriving Fertile Crescent crops that launched Ethiopian food production.

Of course, not all pieces of the package spread to all those outlying areas: for example, Egypt was too warm for einkorn wheat to become established. In some outlying areas, elements of the package arrived at different times: for instance, sheep preceded cereals in southwestern Europe. Some outlying areas went on to domesticate a few local crops of their own, such as poppies in western Europe and watermelons possibly in Egypt. But most food production in outlying areas depended initially on Fertile Crescent domesticates. Their spread was soon followed by that of other innovations originating in or near the Fertile Crescent, including the wheel, writing, metalworking techniques, milking, fruit trees, and beer and wine production.

Why did the same plant package launch food production throughout western Eurasia? Was it because the same set of plants occurred in the wild in many areas, were found useful there just as in the Fertile Crescent, and were independently domesticated? No, that's not the reason. First, many of the Fertile Crescent's founder crops don't even occur in the wild outside Southwest Asia. For instance, none of the eight main founder crops except barley grows wild in Egypt. Egypt's Nile Valley provides an environment similar to the Fertile Crescent's Tigris and Euphrates Valleys. Hence the package that worked well in the latter valleys also worked well enough in the Nile Valley to trigger the spectacular rise of indigenous Egyptian civilization. But the foods to fuel that spectacular rise were originally absent in Egypt. The sphinx and pyramids were built by people fed on crops originally native to the Fertile Crescent, not to Egypt.

Second, even for those crops whose wild ancestor does occur outside of Southwest Asia, we can be confident that the crops of Europe and India were mostly obtained from Southwest Asia and were not local domesticates. For example, wild flax occurs west to Britain and Algeria and east to the Caspian Sea, while wild barley occurs east even to Tibet. However, for most of the Fertile Crescent's founding crops, all cultivated varieties in the world today share only one arrangement of chromosomes out of the multiple arrangements found in the wild ancestor; or else they share only a single mutation (out of many possible mutations) by which the cultivated varieties differ from the wild ancestor in characteristics desirable to humans. For instance, all cultivated peas share the same recessive gene that prevents ripe pods of cultivated peas from spontaneously popping open and spilling their peas, as wild pea pods do.

Evidently, most of the Fertile Crescent's founder crops were never domesticated again elsewhere after their initial domestication in the Fertile Crescent. Had they been repeatedly domesticated independently, they would exhibit legacies of those multiple origins in the form of varied chromosomal arrangements or varied mutations. Hence these are typical examples of the phenomenon of preemptive domestication that we discussed above. The quick spread of the Fertile Crescent package preempted any possible other attempts, within the Fertile Crescent or elsewhere, to domesticate the same wild ancestors. Once the crop had become available, there was no further need to gather it from the wild and thereby set it on the path to domestication again.

The ancestors of most of the founder crops have wild relatives, in the Fertile Crescent and elsewhere, that would also have been suitable for domestication. For example, peas belong to the genus *Pisum*, which consists of two wild species: *Pisum sativum*, the one that became domesticated to yield our garden peas, and *Pisum fulvum*, which was never domesticated. Yet wild peas of *Pisum fulvum* taste good, either fresh or dried, and are common in the wild. Similarly, wheats, barley, lentil, chickpea, beans, and flax all have numerous wild relatives besides the ones that became domesticated. Some of those related beans and barleys were indeed domesticated independently in the Americas or China, far from the early site of domestication in the Fertile Crescent. But in western Eurasia only one of several potentially useful wild species was domesticated—probably because that one spread so quickly that people soon stopped gathering the other wild relatives and ate only the crop. Again as we discussed above, the crop's rapid spread preempted any possible further attempts to domesticate its relatives, as well as to redomesticate its ancestor.

Why was the spread of crops from the Fertile Crescent so rapid? The answer depends partly on that east-west axis of Eurasia with which I opened this chapter. Localities distributed east and west of each other at the same latitude share exactly the same day length and its seasonal variations. To a lesser degree, they also tend to share similar diseases, regimes of temperature and rainfall, and habitats or biomes (types of vegetation). For example, southern Italy, northern Iran, and Japan, all located at about the same latitude but lying successively 4,000 miles east or west of each other, are more similar to each other in climate than each is to a location lying even a mere 1,000 miles due south. On all the continents the habitat type known as tropical rain forest is confined to within about 10 degrees latitude of the equator, while Mediterranean scrub habitats (such as California's chaparral and Europe's maquis) lie between about 30 and 40 degrees of latitude.

But the germination, growth, and disease resistance of plants are adapted to precisely those features of climate. Seasonal changes of day length, temperature, and rainfall constitute signals that stimulate seeds to germinate, seedlings to grow, and mature plants to develop flowers, seeds, and fruit. Each plant population becomes genetically programmed, through natural selection, to respond appropriately to signals of the seasonal regime under which it has evolved. Those regimes vary greatly with latitude. For example, day length is constant throughout the year at the equator, but at temperate latitudes it increases as the months advance from the winter solstice to the summer solstice, and it then declines again through the next half of the year. The growing season—that is, the months with temperatures and day lengths suitable for plant growth—is shortest at high latitudes and longest toward the equator. Plants are also adapted to the diseases prevalent at their latitude.

Woe betide the plant whose genetic program is mismatched to the latitude of the field in which it is planted! Imagine a Canadian farmer foolish enough to plant a race of corn adapted to growing farther south, in Mexico. The unfortunate corn plant, following its Mexico-adapted genetic program, would prepare to thrust up its shoots in March, only to find itself still buried under 10 feet of snow. Should the plant become genetically reprogrammed so as to germinate at a time more appropriate to Canada—say, late June—the plant would still be in trouble for other reasons. Its genes would be telling it to grow at a leisurely rate, sufficient only to bring it to maturity in five months. That's a perfectly safe strategy in Mexico's mild climate, but in Canada a disastrous one that would guarantee the plant's being killed by autumn frosts before it had produced any mature corn cobs. The plant would also lack genes for resistance to diseases of northern climates, while uselessly carrying genes for resistance to diseases of southern climates. All those features make low-latitude plants poorly adapted to high-latitude conditions, and vice versa. As a consequence, most Fertile Crescent crops grow well in France and Japan but poorly at the equator.

Animals too are adapted to latitude-related features of climate. In that respect we are typical animals, as we know by introspection. Some of us can't stand cold northern winters with their short days and characteristic germs, while others of us can't stand hot tropical climates with their own characteristic diseases. In recent centuries overseas colonists from cool northern Europe have preferred to emigrate to the similarly cool climates of North America, Australia, and South Africa, and to settle in the cool highlands within equatorial Kenya and New Guinea. Northern Europeans who were sent out to hot tropical lowland areas used to die in droves of diseases such as malaria, to which tropical peoples had evolved some genetic resistance.

That's part of the reason why Fertile Crescent domesticates spread west and east so rapidly: they were already well adapted to the climates of the regions to which they were spreading. For instance, once farming crossed from the plains of Hungary into central Europe around 5400 B.C., it spread so quickly that the sites of the first farmers in the vast area from Poland west to Holland (marked by their characteristic pottery with linear decorations) were nearly contemporaneous. By the time of Christ, cereals of Fertile Crescent origin were growing over the 10,000-mile expanse from the Atlantic coast of Ireland to the Pacific coast of Japan. That west-east expanse of Eurasia is the largest land distance on Earth.

Thus, Eurasia's west-east axis allowed Fertile Crescent crops quickly to launch agriculture over the band of temperate latitudes from Ireland to the Indus Valley, and to enrich the agriculture that arose independently in eastern Asia. Conversely, Eurasian crops that were first domesticated far from the Fertile Crescent but at the same latitudes were able to diffuse back to the

Fertile Crescent. Today, when seeds are transported over the whole globe by ship and plane, we take it for granted that our meals are a geographic mishmash. A typical American fast-food restaurant meal would include chicken (first domesticated in China) and potatoes (from the Andes) or corn (from Mexico), seasoned with black pepper (from India) and washed down with a cup of coffee (of Ethiopian origin). Already, though, by 2,000 years ago, Romans were also nourishing themselves with their own hodgepodge of foods that mostly originated elsewhere. Of Roman crops, only oats and poppies were native to Italy. Roman staples were the Fertile Crescent founder package, supplemented by quince (originating in the Caucasus); millet and cumin (domesticated in Central Asia); cucumber, sesame, and citrus fruit (from India); and chicken, rice, apricots, peaches, and foxtail millet (originally from China). Even though Rome's apples were at least native to western Eurasia, they were grown by means of grafting techniques that had developed in China and spread westward from there.

While Eurasia provides the world's widest band of land at the same latitude, and hence the most dramatic example of rapid spread of domesticates, there are other examples as well. Rivaling in speed the spread of the Fertile Crescent package was the eastward spread of a subtropical package that was initially assembled in South China and that received additions on reaching tropical Southeast Asia, the Philippines, Indonesia, and New Guinea. Within 1,600 years that resulting package of crops (including bananas, taro, and yams) and domestic animals (chickens, pigs, and dogs) had spread more than 5,000 miles eastward into the tropical Pacific to reach the islands of Polynesia. A further likely example is the east-west spread of crops within Africa's wide Sahel zone, but paleobotanists have yet to work out the details.

Contrast the ease of east-west diffusion in Eurasia with the difficulties of diffusion along Africa's north-south axis. Most of the Fertile Crescent founder crops reached Egypt very quickly and then spread as far south as the cool highlands of Ethiopia, beyond which they didn't spread. South Africa's Mediterranean climate would have been ideal for them, but the 2,000 miles of tropical conditions between Ethiopia and South Africa posed an insuperable barrier. Instead, African agriculture south of the Sahara was launched by the domestication of wild plants (such as sorghum and African yams) indigenous to the Sahel zone and to tropical West Africa, and adapted to the warm temperatures, summer rains, and relatively constant day lengths of those low latitudes.

Similarly, the spread southward of Fertile Crescent domestic animals through Africa was stopped or slowed by climate and disease, especially by trypanosome diseases carried by tsetse flies. The horse never became established farther south than West Africa's kingdoms north of the equator. The advance of cattle, sheep, and goats halted for 2,000 years at the northern edge of the Serengeti Plains, while new types of human economies and livestock breeds were being developed. Not until the period A.D. 1–200, some 8,000 years after livestock were domesticated in the Fertile Crescent, did cattle, sheep, and goats finally reach South Africa. Tropical African crops had their own difficulties spreading south in Africa, arriving in South Africa with black African farmers (the Bantu) just after those Fertile Crescent livestock did. However, those tropical African crops could never be transmitted across South Africa's Fish River, beyond which they were stopped by Mediterranean conditions to which they were not adapted.

The result was the all-too-familiar course of the last two millennia of South African history. Some of South Africa's indigenous Khoisan peoples (otherwise known as Hottentots and Bushmen) acquired livestock but remained without agriculture. They became outnumbered and were replaced northeast of the Fish River by black African farmers, whose southward spread halted at that river. Only when European settlers arrived by sea in 1652, bringing with them their Fertile Crescent crop package, could agriculture thrive in South Africa's Mediterranean zone. The collisions of all those peoples produced the tragedies of modern South Africa: the quick decimation of the Khoisan by European germs and guns; a century of wars between Europeans and blacks; another century of racial oppression; and now, efforts by Europeans and blacks to seek a new mode of coexistence in the former Khoisan lands.

Contrast also the ease of diffusion in Eurasia with its difficulties along the Americas' north-south axis. The distance between Mesoamerica and South America—say, between Mexico's highlands and Ecuador's—is only 1,200 miles, approximately the same as the distance in Eurasia separating the Balkans from Mesopotamia. The Balkans provided ideal growing conditions for most Mesopotamian crops and livestock, and received those domesticates as a package within 2,000 years of its assembly in the Fertile Crescent. That rapid spread preempted opportunities for domesticating those and related species in the Balkans. Highland Mexico and the Andes would similarly have been suitable for many of each other's crops and domestic animals. A few crops, notably Mexican corn, did indeed spread to the other region in the pre-Columbian era.

But other crops and domestic animals failed to spread between Mesoamerica and South America. The cool highlands of Mexico would have provided ideal conditions for raising llamas, guinea pigs, and potatoes, all domesticated in the cool highlands of the South American Andes. Yet the northward spread of those Andean specialties was stopped completely by the hot intervening lowlands of Central America. Five thousand years after llamas had been domesticated in the Andes, the Olmecs, Maya, Aztecs, and all other native societies of Mexico remained without pack animals and without any edible domestic mammals except for dogs.

Conversely, domestic turkeys of Mexico and domestic sunflowers of the eastern United States might have thrived in the Andes, but their southward spread was stopped by the intervening tropical climates. The mere 700 miles of north-south distance prevented Mexican corn, squash, and beans from reaching the U.S. Southwest for several thousand years after their domestication in Mexico, and Mexican chili peppers and chenopods never did reach it in prehistoric times. For thousands of years after corn was domesticated in Mexico, it failed to spread northward into eastern North America, because of the cooler climates and shorter growing season prevailing there. At some time between A.D. 1 and A.D. 200, corn finally appeared in the eastern United States but only as a very minor crop. Not until around A.D. 900, after hardy varieties of corn adapted to northern climates had been developed, could corn-based agriculture contribute to the flowering of the most complex Native American society of North America, the Mississippian culture—a brief flowering ended by European-introduced germs arriving with and after Columbus.

Recall that most Fertile Crescent crops prove, upon genetic study, to derive from only a single domestication process, whose resulting crop spread so quickly that it preempted any other incipient domestications of the same or related species. In contrast, many apparently widespread Native American crops prove to consist of related species or even of genetically distinct varieties of the same species, independently domesticated in Mesoamerica, South America, and the eastern United States. Closely related species replace each other geographically among the amaranths, beans, chenopods, chili peppers, cottons, squashes, and tobaccos. Different varieties of the same species replace each other among the kidney beans, lima beans, the chili pepper *Capsicum annuum/chinense,* and the squash *Cucurbita pepo.* Those legacies of multiple independent domestications may provide further testimony to the slow diffusion of crops along the Americas' north-south axis.

Africa and the Americas are thus the two largest landmasses with a predominantly north-south axis and resulting slow diffusion. In certain other parts of the world, slow north-south diffusion was important on a smaller scale. These other examples include the snail's pace of crop exchange between Pakistan's Indus Valley and South India, the slow spread of South Chinese food production into Peninsular Malaysia, and the failure of tropical Indonesian and New Guinean food production to arrive in prehistoric times in the modern farmlands of southwestern and southeastern Australia, respectively. Those two corners of Australia are now the continent's breadbaskets, but they lie more than 2,000 miles south of the equator. Farming there had to await the arrival from faraway Europe, on European ships, of crops adapted to Europe's cool climate and short growing season.

I have been dwelling on latitude, readily assessed by a glance at a map, because it is a major determinant of climate, growing conditions, and ease of spread of food production. However, latitude is of course not the only such determinant, and it is not always true that adjacent places at the same latitude have the same climate (though they do necessarily have the same day length).

Topographic and ecological barriers, much more pronounced on some continents than on others, were locally important obstacles to diffusion.

For instance, crop diffusion between the U.S. Southeast and Southwest was very slow and selective although these two regions are at the same latitude. That's because much of the intervening area of Texas and the southern Great Plains was dry and unsuitable for agriculture. A corresponding example within Eurasia involved the eastern limit of Fertile Crescent crops, which spread rapidly westward to the Atlantic Ocean and eastward to the Indus Valley without encountering a major barrier. However, farther eastward in India the shift from predominantly winter rainfall to predominantly summer rainfall contributed to a much more delayed extension of agriculture, involving different crops and farming techniques, into the Ganges plain of northeastern India. Still farther east, temperate areas of China were isolated from western Eurasian areas with similar climates by the combination of the Central Asian desert, Tibetan plateau, and Himalayas. The initial development of food production in China was therefore independent of that at the same latitude in the Fertile Crescent, and gave rise to entirely different crops. However, even those barriers between China and western Eurasia were at least partly overcome during the second millennium B.C., when West Asian wheat, barley, and horses reached China.

By the same token, the potency of a 2,000-mile north-south shift as a barrier also varies with local conditions. Fertile Crescent food production spread southward over that distance to Ethiopia, and Bantu food production spread quickly from Africa's Great Lakes region south to Natal, because in both cases the intervening areas had similar rainfall regimes and were suitable for agriculture. In contrast, crop diffusion from Indonesia south to southwestern Australia was completely impossible, and diffusion over the much shorter distance from Mexico to the U.S. Southwest and Southeast was slow, because the intervening areas were deserts hostile to agriculture. The lack of a high-elevation plateau in Mesoamerica south of Guatemala, and Mesoamerica's extreme narrowness south of Mexico and especially in Panama, were at least as important as the latitudinal gradient in throttling crop and livestock exchanges between the highlands of Mexico and the Andes.

Continental differences in axis orientation affected the diffusion not only of food production but also of other technologies and inventions. For example, around 3,000 B.C. the invention of the wheel in or near Southwest Asia spread rapidly west and east across much of Eurasia within a few centuries, whereas the wheels invented independently in prehistoric Mexico never spread south to the Andes. Similarly, the principle of alphabetic writing, developed in the western part of the Fertile Crescent by 1500 B.C., spread west to Carthage and east to the Indian subcontinent within about a thousand years, but the Mesoamerican writing systems that flourished in prehistoric times for at least 2,000 years never reached the Andes.

Naturally, wheels and writing aren't directly linked to latitude and day length in the way crops are. Instead, the links are indirect, especially via food production systems and their consequences. The earliest wheels were parts of ox-drawn carts used to transport agricultural produce. Early writing was restricted to elites supported by food-producing peasants, and it served purposes of economically and socially complex food-producing societies (such as royal propaganda, goods inventories, and bureaucratic record keeping). In general, societies that engaged in intense exchanges of crops, livestock, and technologies related to food production were more likely to become involved in other exchanges as well.

America's patriotic song "America the Beautiful" invokes our spacious skies, our amber waves of grain, from sea to shining sea. Actually, that song reverses geographic realities. As in Africa, in the Americas the spread of native crops and domestic animals was slowed by constricted skies and environmental barriers. No waves of native grain ever stretched from the Atlantic to the Pacific coast of North America, from Canada to Patagonia, or from Egypt to South Africa, while amber waves of wheat and barley came to stretch from the Atlantic to the Pacific across the spacious skies of Eurasia. That faster spread of Eurasian agriculture, compared with that of Native American and sub-Saharan African agriculture, played a role . . . in the more rapid diffusion of Eurasian writing, metallurgy, technology, and empires.

To bring up all those differences isn't to claim that widely distributed crops are admirable, or that they testify to the superior ingenuity of early Eurasian farmers. They reflect, instead, the orientation of Eurasia's axis compared with that of the Americas or Africa. Around those axes turned the fortunes of history.

PART II

The European Invasion of the Americas

Taking Possession and Reading Texts: Establishing the Authority of Overseas Empires

Patricia Seed

INTRODUCTION

The historiography of the Conquest has tended to stress the importance of political and intellectual developments in shaping the European invasion of the New World. Historian Patricia Seed, however, has adopted a different focus in her work, exploring instead the cultural factors that may have affected the encounter between the Old World and the New. In this essay, which captures the central argument of her book Ceremonies of Possession, *Seed explores the means by which European powers—specifically, England and Spain—established the right to rule over the lands and peoples of the New World, and what these practices reveal about differing European notions of empire.*

As Seed explains, English and Spanish methods of taking possession of alien lands stood in marked contrast to one another. English authority derived from letters patent, documents stating the sovereign's right to claim new territories, enacted and made inviolate simply by the occupation of the lands in question. Spanish explorers, on the other hand, performed elaborate

Patricia Seed, "Taking Possession and Reading Texts: Establishing the Authority of Overseas Empires," *William and Mary Quarterly,* 49 (1992), pp. 183–209. Reprinted by permission of Omohundro Institute of Early American History and Culture, Williamsburg, VA.

Patricia Seed is a member of the History Department, Rice University. Acknowledgments: My colleague Ira Gruber provided invaluable advice on colonial Anglo-America, as did in different areas Susan Deeds, Tamsyn Donaldson, Ranajit Guha, Peter Hulme, George E. Marcus, George Stocking, and John E. Wills, Jr. The Institute for Aboriginal Studies at Australian National University, Canberra, the History Department of Northern Arizona University, and the Getty Center for the History of Art and the Humanities have heard this article presented as a ceremonial speech. It is part of a work in progress on the comparative history of the politics and ceremony of European expansion in the New World.

19

rituals to solemnize their arrival, the most important of which was a manda-
tory reading of the Requirimento, *a religious decree commanding natives*
to submit to the authority of the Spanish crown. These differences, Seed ar-
gues, were neither insignificant nor coincidental. Rather, she insists that
they reflect the distinct colonial imperatives of both empires for the New
World: the English sought possession of the land, while Spaniards looked to
control its inhabitants.

Seed's work has provoked substantial debate among historians and has
raised important questions about the Conquest and the nature of European
claims in the Americas. Her essay also raises questions of its own.

- *Can we assume that the English and Spanish models that Seed describes,*
  devised at the very highest levels in European royal and legal courts, were
  implemented on the ground with the same spirit and intent?
- *Are the different forms of European conquest best explained by the concept*
  of "nation," or are other frames, such as varying economic objectives, more
  helpful?
- *Finally, to what extent do the postcontact histories of America's English*
  and Spanish colonies lend support to Seed's findings?

The Admiral [Christopher Columbus] went ashore in the armed launch, and
Martín Alonso Pinzón and his brother Vicente Yañes, who was captain of the
Niña. The Admiral brought out the royal banner and the captains [brought]
two flags of the green cross . . . with an F [Ferdinand] and a Y [Isabella], and
over each letter a crown, one [letter] on one side of the [cross], and the other
on the other [side]. . . . The Admiral called to the two captains and to the others who had jumped onto land, and to Rodrigo d'Escobedo, the notary and
registrar of the whole fleet, and to Rodrigo Sánchez de Segovia; and he said
that they should bear faith and witness [as to] how he, in the presence of all,
was going to take, and in fact, did take possession of said island for the king
and for the queen, his lords, making the solemn declarations required to preserve their rights, as is contained at greater length in the legal instruments of
proof made there in writing."[1] Columbus's son Fernando's version of the
events of October 12, 1492, is that "The Admiral . . . took possession of it in
the name of the Catholic Sovereigns *with appropriate ceremony and words.*"[2]

In 1583, Sir Humphrey Gilbert, in the first English effort at New World
settlement, at St. John's Harbor, gathered together the Portuguese, French,
and English merchants and shipmasters trading and fishing off the banks of

[1] *The* Diario *of Christopher Columbus's First Voyage to America 1492–1493; Abstracted by Fray Bar-*
tolomé de Las Casas, trans. Oliver Dunn and James E. Kelley, Jr. (Norman, Okla., 1989), 62, 64. I
have used their transcription of the Las Casas text rather than the translation. A *"protestación,"*
for example, in Spanish law is and was "a solemn declaration for the purpose of preserving
one's right;" *"testimonio,"* both "proof by witness" and "an instrument legalized by a notary."
[2] *The Life of the Admiral Christopher Columbus by his Son Ferdinand,* trans. Benjamin Keen (New
Brunswick, N. J., 1959), 59 (emphasis added).

Newfoundland and informed them of his written authorization to possess the territory for England. He then "had delivered unto him (after the custom of England) a rod [small twig] and a turf of the same soil."[3] No banners were unfurled, no elaborate ceremonies observed upon landing. Where Columbus declared the intent of the Spanish crown to remain by a solemn speech duly recorded by notaries, Gilbert indicated his intent to settle by having a twig and a piece of earth brought to him.

Even as the conquest of the New World was often accomplished by military means or by occupation, its authority—that is, the *right* to rule—was established by language and ceremony. For Columbus, it was the ritual landing of the royal banner and twin flags, together with the language of his well-witnessed solemn declarations, that established the right of the crown of Castile to this territory, later known as the New World. Columbus's first step was to mark his presence on the land—the customary first element in the Roman tradition of taking possession. Like Venetian John Cabot, who had planted a cross and two flags on the coast of Cape Breton only a few years later, Columbus borrowed the ceremonial elements marking his arrival in the New World from his Mediterranean seafaring predecessors.[4]

Ceremonies of arrival, marking physical presence on the land, no matter how compelling, frequently used, or well witnessed were only the first step. The second part of the Roman-derived conception of possession was manifesting intent to remain, which Columbus did, in his son's report, by "appropriate ceremony and words." Columbus's solemn declaration and due recording of the intent to claim the land were far from improvised. By the terms of his agreement with Ferdinand and Isabella, Columbus was required to make a grave declaration of the intent to remain and to record those words for posterity by writing them down.[5] The Spanish monarchs considered such statements critically important to establish their possession and rightful power.[6] No specific device or words need be employed. What mattered was the solemnity of the utterance.

[3] Richard Hakluyt, *Principal Navigations, Voyages, Traffiques, and Discoveries of the English Nation,* 12 vols., Hakluyt Society Publications, Extra Series (Glasgow, 1904), VIII, 53–54; "*Vortigerne be king Be-taehte heom al his lond ne bileafd him an heonde a turf of londe,*" *Lazamon's Brut or Chronicle of Britain* (ca. 1205), quoted in the *Oxford English Dictionary,* "Turf."
[4] Lorenzo Pasqualigo to his brother, Aug. 23, 1497, in Henry Harrisse, *Jean et Sébastian Cabot; leur origine et leurs voyages* (Amsterdam, 1968; orig. pub. 1882), 322; see also James A. Williamson, *The Cabot Voyages and Bristol Discovery under Henry VII* (Cambridge, 1962), 208. According to Harrisse, Cabot was Genoese by birth, like Columbus, but Venetian by adoption (pp. 1–41). The use of banners and insignia was also recommended in Henry VII's letter patent; Hakluyt, *Divers voyages touching the discoverie of America, and the Islands adjacent . . .* (1582), ed. John Winter-Jones (London, 1850), 21.
[5] "Carta de merced . . . a Cristóval Colón" in Antonio Rumeu de Armas, *Nueva Luz sobre las capitulaciones de Santa Fe de 1492 concertadas entre Los Reyes Católicos y Cristóbal Colón* (Madrid, 1985), 239–241.
[6] "*Seyendo por vos descubiertas e ganadas las dichas islas . . . e fecho por vos . . . el juramento e solemnidad que en tal caso se require.*" "Carta de merced . . . a Cristóval Colón," Rumeu de Armas, *Nueva Luz,* 239–241. See also Rafael Diego Fernández, *Capitulaciones Colombinas (1492–1506)* (Zamora, Méx., 1987).

Immediately after Columbus's return to Spain, the monarchs sought formal legal authorization for their title from the pope. For much of the sixteenth century, the Spanish crown's right to rule the New World was embedded in the 1493 donation of Pope Alexander VI and constituted by reading a text containing an account of that donation, called the Requirement.

For English monarchs the language used to constitute their right was also embedded in a written text (letters patent), but the right was executed in the act of settling on land in the New World. In June 1578, four years prior to the voyage to Newfoundland at which he received the "rod and turf," Sir Humphrey Gilbert received a royal patent authorizing him to "discover . . . such remote, barbarous, and heathen lands, countreis, and territories not possessed by any Christian prince or people nor inhabited by Christian people and the same to have, holde, occupy and enjoy." This patent was subsequently renewed on behalf of Gilbert's half-brother, Sir Walter Ralegh, and used to found the first semipermanent English settlement in the New World, the colony at Roanoke in the territory later known as Virginia.[7] By contrasting the language of the official authorizations for empire—the English letter patent and the Spanish papal bull—and their divergent forms of cultural expression—taking possession and reading texts—this article will contrast English and Spanish practices in establishing the authority of overseas empire.[8]

The word "patent" comes from the Latin *patente,* signifying "open." Letters patent are open letters, as distinguished from letters close, private letters closed up or sealed.[9] Letters patent came from a sovereign (or other person in authority) and were used to record an agreement, confer a right, title, or property, or authorize or command something to be done. Queen Elizabeth's letters patent to Gilbert and Ralegh authorized—that is, literally established the authority for—Englishmen to venture into the New World. From similar and sometimes identical patents in the next century came the authorizations for the settlement of Virginia, New England, Maryland, and the Carolinas.

The patent makes explicit what the queen legitimated. Her twin authorizations, on the one hand, to "discover, find, search out, and view" and, on the other, "to have, holde, occupy and enjoy" relate not to the peoples of the New World but to the lands, which are described as "remote, barbarous, and

---

[7] The text of two patents is in Hakluyt, *Principal Navigations,* VIII, 17–23 (Gilbert), 289–296 (Ralegh).

[8] In medieval times *imperium* (empire) was synonymous with the Holy Roman Empire, but in the 14th century it began to acquire in popular works the more general meaning of a great realm, a usage current in the period of European expansion; Richard Koebner, *Empire* (Cambridge, 1961), 46–47; Robert Folz, *The Concept of Empire in Western Europe from the Fifth to the Fourteenth Century,* trans. Sheila Ann Ogilvie (New York, 1969; orig. pub. 1953).

[9] S. R. Scargill-Bird, *A Guide to the Principal Classes of Documents Preserved in the Public Record Office,* 2d ed. (London, 1896), 34–35. Letters patent were first used in 1201; the forms became fixed early in the 13th century; minor modifications occurred between 1460 and 1482. By the early 16th century they replaced earlier forms of both the writ and the royal charter; Hubert Hall, *A Formula Book of English Official Historical Documents,* vol. 1 (Cambridge, 1908–1909), 24–25, 53–54.

[handwritten marginalia: How does Engl. mean? C Law ... what about Ireland? Wales?]

heathen." There is a critical elision at the core of this definition because, while land can be remote, it cannot be barbarous or heathen; only people can have these qualities. If, as is sometimes alleged, attributing a characteristic of a people to a place is common in English, this simply tells us that the language itself allows for suppressing knowledge of the existence of peoples. But far from being an insignificant or merely rhetorical feature of the English language, this omission of persons plays a central role within a crucial political document, the first formal authorization that actually led to English settlement in the New World and the model used for all subsequent English patents for occupying the New World.

Elizabeth's letters patent specify what Gilbert was entitled to "have, hold, occupy and enjoy," namely, "all the *soyle* of all such lands, countreis, and territories . . . and of all Cities, Castles, Towns and Villages, and *places* in the same."[10] The official authorization is limited to subduing space that is implicitly occupied but to whose inhabitants the patent does not refer. It is to the "soyle," not the people, that Gilbert and Ralegh were granted rights to hold and enjoy. The very definition of what is to be possessed elides—that is to say, suppresses by omission—the question of inhabitants by focusing on the "soyle." And it is possession of the soil that Gilbert then ceremonially enacted on the banks of Newfoundland in 1583.

Furthermore, the Gilbert and Ralegh patents both state, these lands were granted "with full power to dispose thereof, and of every part in fee simple or otherwise, according to the order of the lawes of England."[11] In other words, the land of the New World is given to use and to distribute "according to . . . the lawes of England," as though full title were already established by virtue of the royal patent.

In English law of the time, only the monarch enjoyed full dominion over land, and hence the ultimate authorization for control over land—including the power to dispose of it—had to originate there.[12] To justify the right to rule New World "soyle" in terms of England's legal code, official permission to distribute land had to be bestowed by the queen.

---

[10] Hakluyt, *Principal Navigations,* VIII, 18. Subsequent patents only expanded the basic idea of space—"lands, woods, soil, grounds, havens, ports, rivers, mines, minerals, marshes, waters, fishings, commodities, and hereditaments" (Virginia, Apr. 10, 1606), in Alexander Brown, *The Genesis of the United States* (New York, 1964; orig. pub. 1890), 54; "land, soyles, grounds, havens, ports, rivers, waters, fishing, mines and minerals" (Massachusetts, Mar. 4, 1628), "soil, lands, fields woods, mountains, fens, lakes, rivers, bays and inlets" (Lord Baltimore, June 28, 1632), "lands, tenements, or heridements" (Connecticut, Apr. 23, 1662), "tract or part of land" (William Penn, Feb. 28, 1681), in Samuel Lucas, *Charters of the Old English Colonies in America* (London, 1850), 32, 89, 48, 106.

[11] Maryland's charter (1632) reads "in fee simple or in fee tail or otherwise"; Connecticut's (1662) grants the right to "Lese, grant, demise, alien bargain, sell, dispose of, as our other liege people of this our realm of England"; Lucas, *Charters,* 89, 48.

[12] G. E. Aylmer, "The Meaning and Definition of 'Property' in Seventeenth-Century England," *Past and Present,* No. 86 (1980), 87–96.

By what right did Elizabeth I authorize Gilbert and Ralegh to "have, hold, occupy and enjoy" with the additional "full power to dispose thereof . . . according to . . . the lawes of England" territories that she did not actually own? The patent lays out two "reasons" (or rationalizations) justifying English dominion over the New World: the authority of the crown and the eminent domain of Christian princes.

The authority invoked by Elizabeth originated first, in the words of the patent, from her own "especial grace, certaine science, and mere motion." "Especial grace" designated the source of royal authority in medieval English thinking—the idea that royal authority derives from God and comes to the crown by grace. The queen's special grace is therefore a power that comes to her directly from God, a concept of kingship unique in Western Europe in medieval and early modern times.[13] Grace also signified favor or benignant regard on the part of a superior, as the ground of a concession (as opposed to a right or an obligation) or manifestation of favor. "Science" in the sixteenth century signified knowledge, but knowledge as a personal attribute. And "motion" was either moving, prompting, urging, instigating, or bidding—a ground or cause of action. The adjectives that qualify the three bases of royal authority are *special* (favor), *certain* (knowledge), and *mere* (motion), all personal: they depend solely on the distinctive qualities of the queen. The queen's authority derives from her direct and personal relationship with the ultimate source of power. Neither popes nor compacts with the people or commonwealth disturb the singular assertion of that authority in granting land.

The second source of the queen's authority is the absence of dominion over the lands by any other Christian ruler. Her grants are to those "lands, countreis, and territories not possessed by any Christian prince . . . nor inhabited by Christian people." Here, for the first and only time, the letters patent refer to human beings, but the word "people" only encompasses Christians: the presence of native peoples is still suppressed by omission. In making possession possible for Christian sovereigns, the letters patent tacitly acknowledge the legitimacy of dominion of other Christian (that is, European) rulers while passing over in silence the potential legitimacy of the New World's inhabitants. Although this right of other Europeans was not always respected in practice, it was at least enshrined in theory.[14]

The authorization to occupy lands not possessed by another Christian monarch suggests that Elizabeth's jurisdiction was also implicitly grounded

[13] Ernst H. Kantorowicz, *The King's Two Bodies: A Study in Mediaeval Political Theology* (Princeton, N. J., 1957), 48. "Special grace" was first used in letters patent in the first quarter of the 14th century during the reign of Edward II; Hall, *Formula Book*, 25.

[14] James I of England granted the Virginia Company five-sixths of the territory between 40° and 46° N, which Henry IV of France had already granted the Sieur de Monts. James I's grant (Apr. 10–20, 1606) came just 3 years after the Sieur de Monts's (Nov. 8, 1603). De Monts's first charter is in Marc Lescarbot, *Histoire de la Nouvelle-France* (Paris, 1866; orig. pub. 1611), bk. 4, chap. 1, vol. II, 408–414.

in the right of eminent domain of Christian rulers. While Anglican preachers such as Richard Hakluyt and Samuel Purchas and many Puritans advanced conversion as one reason for conquest,[15] the letters patent fail to make English occupation of the land contingent upon proselytizing Indians.[16] Only twice in subsequent patents did the crown make Christianization its goal. On both occasions, its aim was to solidify rule over its own subjects, not to assert authority over the Indians.[17] All other sixteenth-century patents— French, Spanish, and Portuguese alike—insisted that legitimacy, the right to rule or even be present in the New World, was contingent on evangelizing the natives.[18] In papal bulls and letters dating from as early as the fifteenth century, this was the condition of the right to conquer infidel or pagan territory accorded the crowns of Spain and Portugal.[19] For the English queen, rather than being an aim of conquest, religion legitimated the power of the state. It was the Christian (European) *prince* who had a right to the land. And the dominion of the Christian sovereign was justified simply by his or her possession of Christianity, not by the desire to spread it. In the constitution

---

[15] Hakluyt, "Dedication," *Divers Voyages,* 8–18. For other Anglicans, including the bishop of London, see Louis B. Wright, *Religion and Empire: The Alliance between Piety and Commerce in English Expansion, 1558–1625* (New York, 1965; orig. pub. 1943), 12, 53, 93, 124, 138–139. John Winthrop expressed this as "the propagation of the gospell to the Indians. . . . tendinge to the inlargement of the Kingdome of Jesus Christ"; *Winthrop's Conclusions for the Plantations in New England,* reprinted in *Old South Leaflets,* No. 50 (Boston, n.d.), 1; R. C. [Robert Cushman], "Reasons and Considerations Touching the Lawfulness of Removing out of England and into the Parts of America" (1621), in Alexander Young, *Chronicles of the Pilgrim Fathers of the Colony of Plymouth from 1602–1625* (Boston, 1844), 239–249.

[16] Some American historians have erroneously claimed that the letters patent express a desire to spread Christianity as an official goal of colonization. G. L. Beer, *The Origins of the British Colonial System, 1578–1660* (Gloucester, Mass., 1959; orig. pub. 1908), 29; Perry Miller, *Errand into the Wilderness* (Cambridge, Mass., 1956), 101. The actual wording of the letters patent on which Miller based his assertion is simply that the crown is "greatly commending, and graciously accepting of, *their* [the colonists'] desires . . . in propagating of Christian religion to such people" (emphasis added); Brown, *Genesis,* 53–54. The charters to Cecil Calvert (June 28, 1632) and William Penn (Feb. 28, 1681) similarly acknowledge the grantee's desire to convert the Indians, but religious dominion is not the crown's concern; Lucas, *Charters,* 100.

[17] "Our said people in inhabiting there may be so religiously, peaceably, and civilly governed, as theire goode life and orderly convrsation may winne and invite the natives of that countrey to the knowledge and obedience of the the onlly true God and Savior of mankind and the Christian faith, which in our royal intention and the adventurers' free profession is the principal end of this plantation," Massachusetts colony charter, Mar. 4, 1628, Lucas, *Charters,* 43. In the second Virginia charter, May 23, 1609, sec. 29, the reason is to exclude Spaniards from Virginia; Brown, *Genesis,* 236; Lucas, *Charters,* 18. Mention of Christianization was dropped from subsequent patents for these areas.

[18] François I's 1540 commissions to Jacques Cartier and the Seigneur de Roberval introduce the aim of French conquest—"to more easily bring the other peoples of these countries to believe in our Holy Faith." The authorization for Spain's declaration of war is the refusal of the natives to listen to the preaching of the priests. Roberval's commission is in *Collection de manuscrits contenant lettres, mémoires, et autres documents historiques relatifs à la Nouvelle-France,* vol. 1 (Quebec, 1883), 19, 30

[19] *Romanus pontifex,* Sept. 15, 1436, *Dudum cum ad nos,* Nov. 6, 1436, *Monumenta Henr*̇ (Coimbra, Port., 1962), 281–282, 347–349.

of English rule over the New World, religion functioned as a prop for the authority of the state but not as a means of controlling subjects.[20]

After obtaining the patent, the next step was for European adventurers to establish the authority articulated therein. Elizabeth's formula for instituting her authority was the phrase "to have, holde, occupy and enjoy," used synonymously with the phrase "to possess." The royal patent to Gilbert states that "Wee doe by these presents graunt, and declare, that all such countries so hereafter to be possessed and inhabited as aforesayd, from thesefoorth shall bee of the allegiance of us, our heires, and successours."[21] In other words, all that is necessary for the territories of the New World to belong to the queen, her heirs, and successors is that the authority of the letters patent be enacted by taking possession.

Possession in Roman law (from which English as well as Spanish law derives) signifies two things: physical presence and intention to hold the territory as one's own.[22] It is both an act and a mental process, an intention. Taking possession means establishing the intent to own and hence is incomplete or inchoate ownership. It is occupation on the way to ownership. Taking possession occurs at the moment when the authority created by the text of the letters patent is activated. The English style of taking possession was culturally distinctive. In the classic English legal treatise on possession, Frederick Pollock and Robert Samuel Wright declare that "in the eyes of [English] medieval lawyers, that possession largely usurped not only the substance but the name of property."[23] Not only was the authority in the New World over land, but, to the English, the concept of property (dominion over land) was synonymous with possession.

Another dimension of English thinking on possession is expressed most vividly in a popular version of the old legal proverb—"possession is nine-points of the law"[24]—meaning that possession constitutes nearly all of the legal claim to ownership. Pollock and Wright establish this principle succinctly: "possession is the root of title," and the right to ownership (unac-

---

[20] Neither the English nor the Dutch refer to Christianizing the natives as an authorization for their discovery or presence in the New World. See Arthur S. Keller et al., *Creation of Rights of Sovereignty through Symbolic Acts, 1400–1800* (New York, 1938), 134–135, and Allen W. Trelease, "Indian-White Contacts in Eastern North America: The Dutch in New Netherland," *Ethnohistory,* IX (1962), 137–146.

[21] Hakluyt, *Principal Navigations,* VIII, 20.

[22] John M. Lightwood, *A Treatise on Possession of Land* (London, 1894), 9; *The Digest of Justinian,* Latin text, ed. Theodor Mommsen, trans. Alan Watson (Philadelphia, 1985), sec. 41.2.3.

[23] Pollock and Wright, *An Essay on Possession in the Common Law* (Oxford, 1888), 5. For examples of the importance of possession in 16th- and 17th-century English law see the legal handbook *The Compleat Clerk . . .* (London, 1677), 98–104, 157–158, 316–318, 320–321, 742–744, 780–781, 867. Many of the formulas date from the reign of Elizabeth I.

[24] According to the *Oxford English Dictionary,* the 17th-century legal expression was: possession may be 11 points of the law (out of a total of 12 points), i.e., a majority of the points of law. For its subsequent legal use see James William Norton-Kyshe, *The Dictionary of Legal Quotations* (London, 1904).

companied by actual possession) is merely a right to sue the possessor.[25] Where Roman law distinguished possession from the right to possess, English law collapsed the two categories.[26] Thus in English law and, interestingly, in English law alone, the *fact* of ownership creates a virtually unassailable *right* to own as well.

For the most part, the act of taking possession in the English colonies was neither ritualized nor ceremonialized. Ceremonies of arrival are absent from English accounts of voyages to the New World. Neither the New England narratives of William Bradford and John Winthrop, nor the Virginia tales of John Smith and William Strachey, nor the report of the initial voyage of Philip Amadas and Arthur Barlowe describe a ritual of arrival.[27] Nor do most of them note a ceremony marking the transition of the land into the possession of the monarch. "English practice required no particular symbolic action or form of words, provided the intention was clearly expressed . . . and followed by actual entry," writes a prominent English authority on land laws.[28] Ceremonies were not necessary: the authority of England over the land was already created by the letters patent, and taking possession— the placing of the bodies of Englishmen on American soil with the intent to remain—was sufficient to activate that authority.

While Gilbert's reception of the twig and turf was the ceremonial declaration of the intent to remain—the second critical element of possession—it was rarely observed subsequently.[29] In the medieval Anglo-Saxon tradition, the intent to remain was most commonly established through occupation— the building of fences or other boundary markers—and the construction of permanent edifices on the land.[30] In the New World, building houses, forts,

[25] Pollock and Wright, *Essay on Possession*, 22. "It is one of the most general and long-settled rules of law that a person who is in apparent possession has all the rights, remedies and immunities of a possessor. . . . He cannot be disturbed except by another person who is able to show a present right to the possession" (p. 147). The "right to possession . . . is merely a right in one person to sue" (p. 145). For an example of this principle in colonial America see *The Colonial Laws of Massachusetts, Reprinted from the Edition of 1672* (Boston, 1890), 123–124.

[26] In Roman law the distinctions are *possidere* (a right) and *in possessium esse* (physical possession); Pollock and Wright, *Essay on Possession*, 47.

[27] One of the few other examples is Alexander Harris, ed., *A Relation of a Voyage to Guiana by Richard Harcourt, 1613* (London, 1928), 77.

[28] Pollock, *The Land Laws* (London, 1896), 75. Charters emerged later for the purpose of maintaining a record. In English law, recording was not an important part of either the ceremony of possession or the proof of ownership as it was in the Spanish world.

[29] Bradford, *History of Plymouth Plantation, 1620–1647*, 2 vols. (New York, 1968); Winthrop, *The History of New England from 1630 to 1645* (Boston, 1825); Smith, *A True Relation of . . . Virginia*, in Philip L. Barbour, ed., *The Complete Works of Captain John Smith (1580–1631)*, vol. 1 (Chapel Hill, N. C., 1986); Strachey, *Historie of Travaile into Virginia Britannia . . .* (London, 1849); "The Proceedings of the English Colony in Virginia" (1606–1610), in Samuel Purchas, *Hakluytus Posthumus, or Purchas His Pilgrimes . . .*, vol. 18 (Glasgow and New York, 1906), 459–540. Amadas and Barlow are the first to state they took possession of Virginia for the queen; "First Virginia Voyage, 1584," in Hakluyt, *Voyages to the Virginia Colonies* (London, 1986), 65–76.

[30] Lightwood, *Treatise on Possession*, 13.

or other property,[31] which the letters patent describe as habitation, was sufficient to prove possession. Building permanent dwelling places or boundary markers manifested the intention to remain that was essential to taking possession.

The culturally distinctive characteristics of the English act of taking possession become apparent when contrasted with the practices of other European powers. In the conquest of the New World, as well as in their expansion into Asia and Africa in the sixteenth century, European explorers used a variety of symbolic acts to mark their presence or their contact.[32] Beginning in 1483, Portuguese explorers placed *padrões* (pillars of stone) bearing the royal arms along the coasts of Africa, India, and Brazil. The first Portuguese to sail to Brazil in 1500 erected a cross similarly emblazoned.[33] A Dutch expedition to the East Indies landed on the uninhabited island of Mauritius, where the vice admiral nailed a wooden board bearing the arms of Holland, Amsterdam, and Zeeland to a tree.[34] Jacques Cartier raised a cross with a shield bearing the fleur-de-lis and the text "Vive le Roy de France" at Gaspé harbor on the St. Lawrence River in 1534. On the coast of Florida in 1562,

[31] Winthrop, *History*, I, 290; John Brereton, "Notes . . . out of a Tractate written by James Rosier to Sir Walter Raleigh" (1602), in Purchas, *Hakluytus Posthumus*, XVIII, 315.

[32] A study that fails to make the distinction between official and unofficial acts and often makes errors of fact but is nonetheless interesting is Keller et al., *Creation of Rights*. Henry R. Wagner, "Creation of Rights of Sovereignty through Symbolic Acts," *Pacific Historical Review*, IV (1938), 297–326, provides critical commentary on Keller but no footnotes. Francisco Morales Padrón, "Descubrimiento y toma de posesión," *Anuario de estudios americanos*, XII (1955), 321–380, contains several interesting descriptions of ceremonies but ignores the extensive 16th-century Spanish legal literature on discovery and possession (see n. 77). John T. Juricek, "English Territorial Claims in North America under Elizabeth and the Early Stuarts," *Terra Incognitae*, VII (1976), 7–22, unfortunately relies heavily on Morales Padrón.

[33] The first stone pillar was placed probably ca. May 1483 at the mouth of the Kongo River. António Baião, Hernani Cidade, and Manuel Múrias, eds., *Historia da expansão portuguesa no mundo*, 3 vols. (Lisbon, 1937–1940), I, 366. Notice of subsequent pillars is in ibid., 380 (Dias), II, 104 (Almeida), and Carlos Malheiro Dias ed., *Historia da colonização portuguesa no Brasil*, 3 vols. (Oporto, Port., 1924–1926), III, xxxi (Brazil). Fernão Lopes de Castanheda, *Historia do descobrimento e conquista da India pelos portugueses* (1551), 3d ed., 9 vols. (Coimbra, Port., 1924–1933), bk. 1, chap. 1, 1, 6; "Carta de Pedro Vaz de Caminha sobre o descobrimento da terra nova (o Brazil) que fez Pedro Alvarez Cabral," May 1, 1500, *Alguns documentos do archivo nacional da torre do Tombo acerca das navegações e conquistas portugesas* (Lisbon, 1892), 108–121, esp. 119.

[34] *The Journall or Dayly Register Containing a true manifestation, and historicall declaration of the voyage, accomplished by eight shippes of Amsterdam, under the conduct of Jacob Corneliszen Neck Admirall, Wybrandt van Warwick, vice Admirall, which sayled from Amsterdam the first day of March, 1598* . . . (Amsterdam, 1974; orig. pub. 1601). "In this Island, our Vice Admirall caused a shield of wood to be made & fastened to a tree, to the end that if any ships arrived at that place they might perceive that Christians had been there; & thereupon was carved these words 'Christians Reformados' reformed Christians, with the armes of Holland, Zealand, and Amsterdam" (p. 7). Dutch version in Isaäk Commelin, *Begin ende Voortang van de Vereenighde Nederlandtsche geoctroyeerde Oost-Indische Compagnie*, vol. 1 (Amsterdam, 1646), voyage no. 3, fol. 4. The previous Dutch voyage (under Cornelius Houtman) followed well-known routes and landed only in places well populated with other Europeans.

Jean Ribault set up pillars with the arms of the king of France.[35] Vasco Nuñez de Balboa built a pile of stones to note his sighting of the Pacific Ocean and carved the names of the kings of Castile on some tall trees.[36] Some of these devices were not related to formal acts of authority but were designed to ceremonialize the occasion. And when the discoveries were unexpected, as was Balboa's, the signs of possession—the stones and graffiti—were hastily improvised on the spot. But other actions, such as the placing of the stone pillars by the Portuguese, crosses by the Spanish, and wooden boards by the Dutch were regarded by their rulers as official acts indicating their dominion over the territory. The Portuguese saw the stone pillars as signaling their possession of territory following the Roman tradition of stone markers; the French and Spanish envisioned the cross as a sign of having taken possession of the territory;[37] and the Dutch similarly regarded nailing the arms of the States General to a tree.[38]

[35] Cartier, *A Shorte and Briefe Narration of the Two Navigations and Discoveries to the Northwest Partes called Newe France* (1580), trans. John Florio (Amsterdam, 1975), 21; for similar cross planting on Cartier's second voyage see Séraphin Marion, *Relations des voyageurs français en Nouvelle France au XVII siècle* (Paris, 1923), 5; "A notable historie containing foure voyages made by certaine French Captaines into Florida . . . by Rene Laudionniere," in Hakluyt, *Principal Navigations*, VII, 457, 462. In 1613 Samuel Champlain also placed a cross with the arms of France; *The Voyages and Explorations of Samuel de Champlain*, trans. Annie Nettleton Bourne (New York, 1922), II, 15, 34–35. Seventeenth-century French missionaries on the Mississippi appear not to have attached regal emblems to the crosses; John Gilmary Shea, *Discovery and Exploration of the Mississippi Valley*, 2d ed. (Albany, N. Y., 1903), 16.

[36] Bartolomé de Las Casas, *Historia de las Indias*, 3d ed., 3 vols. (México, D. F., 1986), lib. 3, cap. 48, II, 595. In the absence of trees, Francisco Cano in 1568 carved a cross into nopal cactuses; Morales Padrón, "Descubrimiento y toma de posesión," 362.

[37] For the French see above n. 35. On Roman stone markers in the Iberian peninsula see *The Visigothic Code*, trans. S. P. Scott (Boston, 1910), 348. "Instrucción que dió el Rey a Juan de Solis, Nov. 24, 1514," Martín Fernández Navarrete, *Colección de los Viages y Descubrimientos que hicieron por mar los españoles . . .* , 5 vols. (Buenos Aires, 1945–1946; orig. pub. 1825–1837), III, 149–150; "Instrucción de Don Antonio de Mendoza" (1539), *Colección de documentos ineditos relativos al descubrimiento . . . en América y Oceanía* (hereafter *CDI*), 43 vols. (Madrid, 1864–1884), III, 325–328; "Ordenanzas sobre descubrimiento nuevo y población" of Phillip II, July 13, 1563, ibid., 484–538, esp. 490. For examples of actions see "Testimonios de un auto de posesión que tomó el Gobernador Pedrarías Dávila, Jan. 27, 1519," ibid., II, 549–556; Hernando Grijalvo (1533), ibid., XIV, 134–135; "Relación y derroteo de una armada" and "Relación de Fray Marcos de Niza" (Culiacán, Mar. 7, 1539), ibid., III, 337; "Relación de Lope de Varillas sobre la conquista y población de Nueva Córdoba (Guyana, 1569), ibid., IV, 470; "Sumaria relación de Pedro Sarmiento de Gamboa, Gobernador y Capitán general del estrecho de Magallenes," Sept. 15, 1589, in ibid., V, 286ff., esp. 370–371; Domingo de Vera, Apr. 1593, in Hakluyt, *Principal Navigations*, X, 434–438. Ironically, when it came to the dispute between the Portuguese and the Spanish in the Moluccas, the Spanish argued a position closer to the English; Charles V to D. Jõao III, Dec. 18, 1523, in Navarrette, *Colección*, IV, 283–290.

[38] Adriaen Van der Donck, Jacob van Couwenhoven, and Jan Everts Bout, *Vertoogh van Nieuw Nederland, Weghens de Ghelegentheydt, Vruchtbaer heydt, en Soberen Staat desselfs* (1650) (Representation of New Netherland, Concerning its Location, Productiveness, and Poor Condition), in J. Franklin Jameson, ed., *Narratives of New Netherland 1609–1664* (New York, 1909), 293–354, esp. 309.

Because their concept of dominion was bound up with residence on the land and with the nearly synonymous use of "possession" and "property," the English believed that symbolic manifestations such as crosses, shields, and stone pillars functioned merely as mnemonic devices, or at best as navigational beacons.[39] And this is how such markers were seen by many of the earliest English explorers. A member of a 1580 expedition searching for a northeast passage to the Far East described a cross he left for a fellow explorer: "Upon the said crosse Master Pet did grave his name with the date of our Lourde . . . to the end that if the William did chaunce to come thither, they [sic] might have knowledge that wee had beene there."[40] During the voyage resulting in the memorable wreck of the *Sea-Venture* in Bermuda, the fleet that reached Virginia left a cross at Cape Henry to signal that it had sailed that way.[41] On occasion, the English planted crosses with the name of the monarch to replace those of other powers, as a sign of supersession. When the English attacked a French settlement at Saint Sauveur on Mount Desert Island, they took down the cross that the French fathers had erected and placed their own, inscribed with the name of James I.[42]

Placing a cross, even if ceremonial rather than official, was a political act directed not at the natives but at other Europeans. "And this we diligently observed," wrote Captain George Waymouth, "that in no place . . . wee could discerne any token or signe that ever any Christian had beene before; which either by cutting wood, digging for water, or setting up Crosses (a thing never omitted by any Christian travailours) wee should have perceived some mention [written or spoken commemoration]."[43] The Dutch carved the name of their religion *in Spanish* on a board in Mauritius, clearly warning Spaniards to stay away; Queen Isabella in 1501 ordered one of her subjects to "place landmarks with the coat of arms of their Highnesses, or with other known signs . . . in order to obstruct the *English* from discovery."[44] These

[39] This is also the argument that Cartier used in addressing the native leaders at Gaspé harbor. See Gian Battista Ramusio, *Navigationi et Viaggi*, 3 vols. (Amsterdam, 1967; orig. pub. 1556). *"Dipoi su mostrato con segni, che detta croce era stat piantata per sar dar segno, & cognoscenza come s'hauesse da entrar in detto portio,"* ibid., f. 375. The French original was discovered in 1867 and is reproduced in H. P. Biggar, *The Voyages of Jacques Cartier* (Ottawa, Can., 1924), 66. *"Et puis leurs monstrames par signe, que ladite croix avoit esté plantée pour faire merche et ballise, pur entrer dedans le hable."*
[40] "The discoverie made by M. Arthur Pet and M. Charles Jackman of the Northeast parts" (1580), Hakluyt, *Principal Navigations*, III, 288.
[41] "To sett up a cross upon the pointe . . . to signify our coming in [the harbor]." Governor and Council of Virginia to the Virginia Company of London, July 7, 1610, in Brown, *Genesis*, 402–413, quotation on 403.
[42] Champlain, *Voyages and Explorations*, I, 152.
[43] Waymouth, "Wee carried with us a Crosse to erect at that point," "Extracts of a Virginian Voyage made An. 1605 by Captaine George Waymouth . . . ," in Purchas, *Hakluytus Posthumus*, XVIII, 353. They are called "testimonies of Christians" in *A True and Sincere Declaration of the purpose and ends of the Plantation begun in Virginia set forth by the authority of the Governors and Councellors established for that Plantation* (1609), Brown, *Genesis*, 338–353, esp. 348–349.
[44] Real cédula, Queen Isabella to Alonso de Hojeda, June 8, 1501, in Navarrete, *Colección*, III, 100.

markers functioned in much the way that the placing of national flags on the North Pole, the South Pole, and the moon have functioned in the nineteenth and twentieth centuries.[45] The medium of the cross defined dominion over territory at a time when the dream of a universal Christian empire still prevailed; the additional decorations of the coats of arms of cities or kings symbolized the connection to secular power—the divisions within that dream.

Unlike other Europeans, the English rejected the idea that signs—markers, pillars, plaques, or piles of stone—could establish dominion over a territory or that anything other than "taking possession" (constructing permanent residences) constituted dominion. Where Portuguese sovereigns saw their stone pillars with crosses and royal arms "as a sign of how they saw said lands and islands . . . and acquired . . . dominion over them," the English refused to recognize anything other than occupation or settlement.[46] Because the concepts of what constituted possession were mutually exclusive and the respective imperial aims competitive, conflict over the meaning of sovereignty was inevitable.

In 1562 the Portuguese ambassador to Elizabeth's court lodged a formal protest against English trading in Guinea on the west coast of Africa, justifying an exclusive claim on the basis of Portugal's discovery, propagation of Christianity, and peaceful domination of the commerce of that territory for sixty years. He further complained that the English had placed an arbitrary interpretation on the concept of dominion and asked the queen to forbid her subjects to trade in Portuguese areas. "They [the English] decide that he [the Portuguese king] has no dominion but where he has forts and receives tribute . . . but as the words are doubtful, he desires her [Queen Elizabeth] . . . to change them into such others [words] as may comprehend all the land *discovered* by the Crown of Portugal."[47] The queen replied that "her meaning . . . is . . . to restrain her subjects from haunting [frequenting] . . . land . . . wherein the King of Portugal had obedience, dominion, and tribute, and *not* [to prevent their trading] from all places *discovered* whereof he had no superiority at all."[48] An annoyed ambassador responded that "his master *has* absolute dominion . . . over those lands already discovered."[49]

At the core of this exchange were two fundamental cultural and linguistic differences between Portuguese and English. First, to the Portuguese

---

[45] "Before we went from thence, our generall caused to be set up, a monument of our being there; as also of her majesties, and successors, right and title to that kingdome, namely, a plate of brasse, fast nailed to a great and firme post; whereon is engraven her graces name, and the day and yeare of our arrivall there, and of the free giving up, of the province and kingdome, both by the king and people, into her majesties hands"; Sir Francis Drake, *The World Encompassed* (London, 1628), 80.

[46] Julio Firmino Judice Biker, *Colecção de tratados e concertos des pazes que o estado da India portugueza fez com os reis e senhores . . . da Asia e Africae oriental . . .* (Lisbon, 1881), I, 55. See also n. 47.

[47] Replication of the Portuguese ambassador, June 7, 1562, in Joseph Stevenson, ed., *Calendar of State Papers, Foreign Series, of the Reign of Elizabeth, 1562 . . .* (London, 1867), 77 (emphasis added).

[48] Answer to the Portuguese ambassador, June 15, 1562, ibid., 95 (emphasis added).

[49] Second replication of the Portuguese ambassador, June 19, 1562, ibid., 106 (emphasis added).

ambassador "discovery" signified the establishment of legitimate dominion. For the Portuguese, the concept of "discovery" was linked to the technology and knowledge that they had pioneered. They had invented the navigational aids, found the most efficient sailing routes to west Africa, located the African groups willing to supply the goods most desired by the European market. Expressed in more modern terms, "discovery" was the insistence that the Portuguese held a patent on the technology—maps and sailing devices—and the knowledge of trading seaports, latitudes, and sea-lanes that they had acquired.[50] The English crown refused to consider discovery, so understood, as a legitimate source of the right to rule.[51]

A second and greater difference concerned the understanding of the word "possession." The phrase closest to the English "taking possession" that appears in Portuguese charters of exploration and discovery is *"tomar posse"* ("to hold something with the objective of taking some economic advantage from it"), a form of economic *jouissance.* Dom João III's 1530 instructions to Lopalverez, for example, ordered him to *"tomar posse"*—that is, "to hold with the intention of taking economic advantage, whatever land, places and islands which said captains . . . discover or see, to hold and thus in my name acquire dominion over said places, lands, and islands." After ordering his captains to *"tomar posse"* the lands that had been "discovered"—the territories to which the Portuguese had located the sea-lanes—João went on to specify how Portuguese dominion was to be exercised, the precise object of Portuguese "taking possession." João's captains were to "take with the intention of obtaining economic benefit the navigation, trade, and commerce of said lands, places and islands"—in other words, anything that could be reduced to money.[52] The principal object was not land, as for the English, but trade and commerce.

[50] The idea of "invention" continues to play a more important role in the meaning of discovery in Portuguese than in English. Contrast the *Oxford English Dictionary*'s definition of discovery with that of Luiz A. P. Victoria, *Pequeno Dicionário de Sinônimos* (Rio de Janeiro, 1970). The argument for invention or innovation did apply to the Portuguese South Atlantic voyages but was considerably more difficult to make for navigation in the Indian Ocean, which had been sailed for millennia. Luis Filipe Ferreira Reis Thomaz, "Estructura politica e administrativa do Estado da India no século XVI," in Luis de Albuquerque and Inácio Guerreiro, eds., *Actas do II seminario internacional de história Indo-Portuguesa* (Lisbon, 1985), 526.

[51] The debate about discovery seems, from 1940 to the early 1960s, to have focused primarily on the intention of the individual actor, rather than on imperial intention. Samuel Eliot Morison, *Portuguese Voyages to America in the Fifteenth Century* (Cambridge, Mass., 1940), 5–10; Marcel Bataillon and Edmundo O'Gorman, *Dos concepciones de la tarea histórica: con motivo de la ideal del descubrimiento de América* (México, D. F., 1955); O'Gorman, *The Invention of America: An Inquiry into the Historical Nature of the New World and the Meaning of its History* (Bloomington, Ind., 1961); Wilcomb E. Washburn, "The Meaning of 'Discovery,'" *American Historical Review,* LXVIII (1962), 1–21.

[52] "Tratado de paz entre El-Rey D. João II e os habitantes da ilha de Sunda, e auto de posse que se tomou en nome do dito Rey, da mesma ilha," Biker, *Colecção de tratados,* 55–57. The object of *posse* is still "anything that can be reduced to money" in contemporary Brazilian law. Tupinambá Miguel Castro do Nascimento, *Posse e propriedade* (Rio de Janeiro, 1986), 130–131.

[handwritten marginalia: "Portugese → trade = dominion / not law"]

In the Portuguese conception of dominion, imperial authority over the "important transactions, commerce and trade" was usually asserted either by a formal agreement such as a treaty with the native inhabitants, or by informal agreements that the Portuguese termed "introducing and maintaining the rules of prudence" (what we now call the market).[53] Portuguese authorities claimed to be bringing prudence and market discipline into communities they described as previously operating solely on individual greed.[54] No permanent physical presence or fixed dwellings were necessary for the Portuguese to assert dominion, only a set of contractual agreements or customary practices relating to trade. Portuguese dominion was that of a market economy.

The Portuguese ambassador further argued as evidence of his king's dominion over the commerce of the Guinea region the king's longtime peaceful possession of the title "Lord of Guinea, of the conquest and navigation and traffic of Ethiopia, Arabia, Persia, and the Indies." The title, which dated from news of Vasco de Gama's return in 1499, described the geographic reach of Portuguese vessels in the spice trade's sea-lanes and ports where vessels of other nations customarily sought Portuguese safe-conduct passes in order to navigate.[55] The failure of other powers to contest the monarch's use of that title constituted acceptance of his right to dominate the economic markets of the region.

The English responded by denying Portuguese dominion. Their arguments derived from differing cultural and linguistic conceptions of "discovery" and "taking possession."[56] The role of translation in fixing the meanings was critical, for in this dispute Robert Cecil read the ambassador's *"tomar posse"* as "taking possession," thereby imposing the English conception of possession as property (land) on the Portuguese conception of economic arrangements as the core of dominion.[57] Cecil's translation guaranteed that each side could remain convinced that the other was engaged in an outrageous violation of obvious

[53] For examples of the conditions of trade established in the treaties with India see Biker, *Colecção de tratados.*

[54] "*[São] gentes sem ley nem regras de prudencia, sômente se governava & regia pelo impeto da cobiça que cada huũtinha; nos o reduzinos & possemos em arte [do commerço] com regras universaes & particulares come tem toda las sciencias.*" João de Barros, *Asia, primeira decada* (1539), 4th ed., rev. António Baião (Coimbra, 1932; orig. pub. 1534), 10 decada 1, liv. 1, cap. 1.

[55] Barros elaborates the reasons for the title "Senhor da conquista, navegação, e comercio da Etiopia, Arabia, Persia e India"; ibid., liv. 6, cap. 1. Earlier the Portuguese envoy to Bengal in 1522 defended the title on grounds that "The King, our lord, is called by his titles. . . . [F]or this reason, where his ships sail, no others may sail without his permission [*seguros*]." For a modern critical history of safe-conduct passes see Thomaz, "Estructura politica," 522, 525.

[56] The only semiofficial enunciation of the Portuguese in terms of international law is by Justo Seraphim de Freitas, *De iusto imperio lusitanorvm asiatico* (Valladolid, Sp., 1625), a response to the publication of Hugo Grotius, *De mare liberum* (Leiden, Neth., 1609).

[57] Contrast the original version of the Portuguese ambassador's remarks in *Quadro elementar das relações politicas e diplomaticas de Portugal*, ed. Visconde de Santarem (Paris, 1854), XV, 128–134, 136–145, with William Cecil's translation in Stevenson, ed., *Calendar State Papers*, 41–42, 54–55, 75–79, 106–107.

principles. The act of translation was thus involved in shaping the political mis-conceptions of the sides in this cross-cultural dispute.

Nearly two decades later, a similar dispute erupted between England and Spain, turning on mutually exclusive concepts of the legitimate means of establishing political empire. In 1580, the Spanish ambassador protested Francis Drake's intrusions into territory claimed by Spain during his voyage around the world (1577–1580). The official chronicler of the reign of Queen Elizabeth, William Camden, reported that the queen responded by denying Spanish dominion over the territory in the following words: "[Spaniards] had touched here and there upon the Coasts, built Cottages, and given Names to a River or Cape which does not entitle them to ownership; . . . Pre-scription without possession is worth little."[58] Elizabeth was quoting a com-monplace of medieval English law: "A man cannot by prescription [that is, by declaration or decree] make title to land,"[59] an understanding, as already noted, not shared by Spaniards or indeed by any other European power of the time. Her observations on the lack of relationship between naming and the establishment of sovereignty denied legitimacy to Spanish cultural and linguistic conceptions of taking possession. These conceptions can be seen as early as the actions of Columbus during his first journey to the New World.

Fernando Colón's account of the events of October 12, 1492, begins with his father's going ashore bearing banners with a cross and the symbols of the crowns of Castile and Aragon. Before the solemn declarations that Ferdi-nand and Isabella had required of him in order to assure Spanish dominion and "after all had rendered thanks to Our Lord, kneeling on the ground and kissing it with tears of joy, . . . the Admiral [Columbus] arose and gave the island the name San Salvador." Beginning with this small strip of land, on his first voyage Columbus claimed to have named 600 islands, leaving 3,000 islands unnamed and thus unpossessed, only "scattered on the waves."[60] On

---

[58] "Nec alio quopiam jure quam quod Hispani hinc illinc appulerint, casulas posuerint, sslumen [sic] aut Promontorium denominaverint quae proprietatem acquirere non possunt . . . cum praescriptio sine pos-sessione haud valeat"; William Camden, Rerum Anglicarvm et hibernicarvm Annales regnante Elisa-betha (London, 1625), 328. The Latin text was translated by R. N., Gent., as Annals or a History of the Most Renowned and Victorious Princesse Elizabeth, Late Queene of England, 3d ed. (London, 1635). The widely cited 20th-century translation of this passage by Edward Cheyney, "Interna-tional Law under Queen Elizabeth," English Historical Review, XX (1905), 660, differs signifi-cantly from the 1635 English translation on several scores. Most important, Cheyney renders the final phrase categorically as "prescription without possession is not valid." R. N., historically closer to the Latin original, is more equivocal: "prescription without Possession is little worth"; he accepts symbolic acts as valid but demeans their importance.

[59] Thomas Arnold Herber, The History of the Law of Prescription in England (London, 1891), 2. Sim-ilar sentiments are expressed in Nova Britannia: Offring Most excellent fruites by Planting in Vir-ginia (London, 1609), excerpted in Brown, Genesis, 262.

[60] The Life of the Admiral . . . by his son Ferdinand, 59. Peter Martyr, De orbe novo de Pierre Martyr Anghiera, trans. Paul Gaffarel (Paris, 1907), dec. 1, chap. 3, 45. Martyr interviewed members of Columbus's expedition, including Columbus himself.

some days he plunged into what one commentator calls "a veritable naming frenzy."[61] At midnight on January 11, 1493, "he left the Rio de Gracia . . . [sailing] east four leagues as far as a cape that he called Bel Prado; and from there to the southeast is the mountain to which he gave the name Monte de Plata. . . . From there, 18 leagues east by south . . . is the cape the Admiral called Del Angel. . . . [f]our leagues to the east is a point which he named Del Hierro, and in the same direction four more leagues there is another point that he called Punta Seca. And from there in the same direction six more leagues is the cape that he named Redondo, and from there is Cabo Francés. . . . One league from there is Cabo del Buen Tiempo; from this [cape] south by southeast there is a cape called Tajado."[62]

Columbus's practice of naming or, more accurately, renaming rivers, capes, and islands as part of the ceremony of taking possession was repeated throughout the conquest of the New World and constituted one of the culturally specific acts of Spanish imperial authority.[63] The practice represents a form of ritual speech that undertakes a remaking of the land. Naming geographical features in effect converts them from their former status to a new European one: the external body of the land remains the same, but its essence is redefined by a new name. The use of ritual speech to name territory is analogous to the process of baptism practiced upon the peoples of the New World. These two key elements—the renaming of landmass and the ceremonial declarations—instituted Spanish colonial authority through an act of speaking, a dramatic enactment of belief in the power of words.

For the English, naming was merely symbolic, in the same category as planting crosses. George Percy, who visited the shores of the Virginia territory in 1606, described the conjunction between naming and placing a cross: "The ninth and twentieth day we set up a Crosse at Chesupioc Bay, and named that place Cape Henry."[64] Naming for the English had no connection with the establishment of the authority of empire. For the Spanish, it was critical.

Elizabeth, in this dispute, dismissed other components of Spanish possession as merely touching "here and there upon the Coasts," building

[61] Tzvetan Todorov, *The Conquest of America: The Questions of the Other*, trans. Richard Howard (New York, 1984), 27.

[62] *Diario*, ed. Dunn and Kelley, 322–325. I have worked from their transcription.

[63] "*Llegados allá con la buenaventura, lo primero que se ha de fazer es pone nombre general a toda la tierra general, a las ciudades e villa e logares.*" Ynstrucción para el Gobernador de Tierra Firme (Pedrarias Dávila), Aug. 4, 1513, in Manuel Serrano y Sanz, *Origenes de la Dominación española en América* (Madrid, 1916), I, 279–280, esp. 280. Bernal Díaz del Castillo cites literally hundreds of instances of renaming in *Historia verdadera de la Conquista de la Nueva España* (México, D. F., 1960; orig. pub. 1632), a point Ranajit Guha noted while reading Díaz for *An Indian Historiography of India* (Calcutta, 1988), personal communication.

[64] Percy, "Observations gathered out of a Discourse of the Plantation of the Southerne Colonie in Virginia by the English, 1606," in Purchas, *Hakluytus Posthumus*, XVIII, 409.

"cottages" as a substitute for setting up residence. Both rejections relate to the way in which Spaniards established a relation to land. In place of settling on the land they merely glanced off its fringes, "touched . . . upon the Coasts"; rather than erecting substantial buildings they constructed a few cottages.[65] Thus one part of Elizabeth's response stemmed from her objection to the Spanish understanding of "taking possession" as an essentially symbolic act, the other from the allegedly impermanent character of Spanish relationship to land.

Finally, a linguistic difference lay at the core of the misunderstandings between Spaniards and English in this dispute. By "taking possession" the English meant residing or inhabiting. When Spanish officials referred to settlement, they used the verb "to people" (*"poblar"*). But even this word bore connotations and significance that diverged sharply from the English word "habitation." *"Poblar"* defines the arrival of *people* rather than the construction of buildings or dwellings as the critical step in occupying a region. Furthermore, to the Spanish crown, peopling (*poblando*) did not establish the right to rule but was an activity sometimes taken after imperial authority had been established by naming and solemn declarations.[66] From the Spanish perspective, one shared by other European powers, the English had no respect for international conventions or rights but simply marched into a territory, settled, and declared it theirs.[67]

While described legally in the same Roman-inspired terms as the Spanish—placing a body over the land with the intention of remaining—the English customarily manifested *both* by erecting permanent dwelling places or homes. But even though sixteenth-century Englishmen denounced other nations for invoking mere "signs" or symbols to hold overseas territory, these same English failed to realize that their own belief in "taking possession" or the creation of rights to suzerainty through the construction of permanent buildings was itself a symbolic act, as culturally distinctive as that of any other European power of the time. The only difference was that the primary symbolism of the English conception of sovereignty was architectural.

At the core of the differences were incompatible cultural and linguistic concepts of what constituted the right to rule colonial territory: "posses-

[65] Spanish authorities would sometimes order erection of a symbolic house and gallows on a hill, visible from the ocean, in order to discourage other Europeans from entering the territory. See the instructions for Juan de Solís for Golden Castile and lands south (1514) in Navarrete, *Colección*, III, 149–150.
[66] On the subsidiary role of instructions to *"poblar"* even in early agreements see Fernández, *Capitulaciones colombinas*; for a later example (May 15, 1522) see Hernán Cortés, *Cartas de relación* (México, D. F., 1970), 165.
[67] "Instrucción que dió el Rey a Juan Díaz de Solís," Nov. 24, 1514, in Navarrete, *Colección*, III, 149–150. For French comments on English practices see Marion, *Relations des voyageurs français*, 38–39. Dutch observations are in David Pietersz. de Vries, *Korte historiael* (S'Gravenhage, Neth., 1911), 233, and Van der Donck et al., *Vertoogh van Nieuw Nederland* (1650), in Jameson, ed., *Narratives of New Netherland*, 309.

sion," "appropriate ceremony and words," or *"tomar posse."* Allied to these linguistically irreconcilable ideas about the basic nature of entitlement to overseas rule were incompatible cultural images of how such rights were ceremonially enacted over territory.

Like the English, the Spanish in the New World used a written document to ensure the legitimacy of imperial authority. For the English, authority was established by letters patent; for the Spaniards it was created by a papal bull. *Inter caetera* of Pope Alexander VI in 1493 gave Spain the exclusive right to present the Gospel to the natives of the New World and guaranteed Spain's right to rule the land in order to secure the right to preach.[68]

Alexander VI granted the New World on these terms: of his "own motion, mere liberality, certain science, and apostolic authority" *"motu proprio, mera liberalitate, et ex certa scientia, ad de Apostolicae potestatis"*—language near that used by Queen Elizabeth—"especial grace, certain science, mere motion."[69] The parallels are even greater than this. Not only the language but also the parchment form, scribal style, and great seals of Elizabethan patents are identical to those of medieval papal bulls. Finally, "letter patent" was the most common sixteenth-century English translation of the Latin *bula*. At the time, "bull" more often referred to the lead seal than to the document itself.[70]

Although Elizabeth's language in the royal patent differs only sightly from that of the papal bull, the differences are instructive as to the origins of both sources of authority. The word "grace" in Elizabeth's terms meant both a special authority from God and the queen's own freely bestowed favor—the latter being the exact sense of the papal "liberality." As for the "apostolic authority," by the mid-fifteenth century Edward IV was using the phrase "of our special grace, ful power, and authority royall" on royal charters, substituting "authority royall" for the papal "authority apostolic."[71] In using the

---

[68] *Bullarum diplomatum et privilegiorum sanctorum romanorum pontificum . . .* , vol. 5 (Rome, 1858), 361ff. Portugal received the same rights for Africa and Asia, as well as, it later turned out, a tiny portion of South America that was expanded into the territory now known as Brazil. For negotiations and intrigue surrounding the acquisition of these bulls see Manuel Giménez Fernández, "Las bulas alejandrinas de 1493 referentes a las Indias," *Anuario de estudios americanos,* I (1944), 171–430, and the critique by Alfonso García Gallo, "Las bulas de Alejandro VI y el ordenamiento de la expansión portuguesa y castellana en Africa e Indias," *Anuario de historia del derecho español,* XXVII–XXVIII (1958), 461–829.

[69] *Bullarum,* V, 361ff.

[70] *Dictionnaire de Theologie Catholique,* vol. 2, pt. 1 (Paris, 1910), 1255–1264; A. Amanieu, ed., *Dictionnaire de Droit Canonique . . .* , vol. 2 (Paris, 1925), 1126–1132; *A Treatyse of the Donation Gyven unto Sylvester Pope of Rome by Constayne* (Amsterdam, 1979; orig. pub. 1534). On the clerical origins of English charters generally see Hubert Hall, *Studies in English Official Historical Documents* (New York, 1969; orig. pub. 1908), 167–177.

[71] Charter of Edward IV, Apr. 16, 1462, in Hakluyt, *Principal Navigations,* II, 147–158. Cabot's patents use "grace especial" (Feb. 3, 1498) and "special goodness" and "own motion" (Mar. 19, 1501); Williamson, *Cabot Voyages,* 226, 243. The substitution of royal for apostolic authority was

formula of the Roman pontiff to establish authority over the New World, the queen implicitly asserted her authority as equal to his.

As did the English letters patent, the papal bull also granted Spaniards territory "not possessed by any Christian prince." (In many Spanish translations this is rendered as "the right that any Christian prince has gained," and "possession" is not used.) Just as the letters patent concede the authority to dispose of the New World, so did the bull give the New World to Spain "with free and absolute power, authority, and jurisdiction." But the English patent altered the papal formula to characterize the grant of absolute authority over the New World as decidedly English—"according to the lawes of England."

The most profound changes made by the English in the papal formula restricted the category of dominion to the "soyle" and added the phrase "remote, barbarous, and heathen lands" to characterize the object of English empire. These alterations to the papal format reveal English cultural biases regarding the target of imperial authority.

For the twenty years following Columbus's arrival in the New World, Spaniards employed the methods described above. Upon landing at or entering into a new territory (an enterprise they termed "discovery" or "entry"),[72] Spaniards ritually invoked the crown of Castile and the pope in a solemn fashion, often renaming the land as well.[73] Spanish officials did not require any specific language in the ceremonies that inaugurated their rule.[74] But while the practice of activating Spanish authority through ceremony and ritual speech continued to be followed throughout the colonial period, the speech itself was altered in the third decade of Spanish settlement in the New World.

Because the pope's grant was contingent upon conversion of natives, a challenge was not long in coming. It came from Dominicans newly arrived on the island of Hispaniola. In a December 1511 sermon, Father Antonio de Montesinos attacked Spanish officials on the island (including one of Columbus's sons) in a scathing critique focusing on their failure to convert the na-

---

common practice in other European courts. The Portuguese kings when making land grants used the phrase *"de nosso moto proprio, çierta çiencia, livre vomtade, poder reall e aussoluto."* Note, however, the omission of "special grace." "Carta de donação de El-Rei D. Manuel a Miguel Corte Real," Jan. 15, 1502, in *Alguns Documentos,* 131–132.

[72] Réal provision, Apr. 10, 1495, Navarrete, *Colección,* II, 196–199; real cédula, June 8, 1501, to Alonso de Hojeda, ibid., III, 99–102; June 12, 1523 to Lúcas Vásquez de Ayllón, ibid., 166–173; real carta, Queen to Juan de Agramonte, Oct. 1511, ibid., 137–140; instrucción to Ferdinand Magellan, May 8, 1519, ibid., IV, 123; Cortés, *Cartas,* 163. Pedrarias used a white banner; *CDI,* II, 549–556.

[73] See above nn. 61, 63. Also *CDI,* II, 558–567, III, 337, IV, 467–470, V, 211–215, 221–229, 370, X, 12–18; XIV, 128–135, XV, 306–307, 320–323, XVI, 165–373.

[74] For some examples of the variety of language used see Morales Padrón, "Descubrimiento y toma de posesión," 347–348. This often fascinating collection of ceremonies is marred by a misunderstanding of possession in 16th-century Spanish legal theory. An excellent English introduction to the subject is James Brown Scott, *The Spanish Origin of International Law: Francisco Vitoria and his Law of Nations* (Oxford, 1934), esp. 116–136.

tives.[75] The criticism found its mark, for the following year King Ferdinand ordered a reconsideration of the matter of Spanish title to the New World. He convened a commission to draw up new laws governing treatment and conversion of Indians (the Laws of Burgos) and asked a canonist and a jurist to consider how the authority of the Spanish empire might be better legitimated. The canonist was the Dominican Fray Matías de Paz of the University of Salamanca; the jurist, Juan López de Palacios Rubios.[76] Their treatises expanded and elaborated the reasons for the conquest. From Palacios Rubios's essay government officials extracted a portion that could be used to justify Spain's future conquests of New World peoples. This text became known as the *Requirimento* or Requirement; it required the natives to submit to the authority of the Spanish crown. Used in explorations of the Caribbean after 1512, it would be employed whenever Spaniards encountered people in the New World. It was invoked in the conquests of Mexico and Peru, as well as in hundreds of other encounters with hunter-gatherers and small agricultural and fishing communities.[77] The Requirement served to legitimate Spanish authority over the New World until it was replaced in 1573 by a revised, less demanding version, the Instrument of Obedience and Vassalage.[78]

In the instructions issued by the crown for discoveries and conquests after 1512, the Requirement was ordered to be read to the New World natives. In other words, from then on, the crown specified a ritual speech to be used in enacting the authority of its empire over people. No longer would any "appropriate ceremony and words," as employed by Columbus, be sufficient; the words had to be those of the Requirement.

Just as the English did, the Spanish claimed a right to rule based on their possession of Christianity, a (self-proclaimed) superior religion. But the relationship between religion and the power of the Christian state was delineated differently in the Requirement than in the English letters patent. The

[75] Las Casas, *Historia de las Indias*, bk. 3, caps. 3, 4, II, 440–442.

[76] Rafael Altamira, "El texto de las leyes de Burgos de 1512," *Revista de historia de América*, No. 4 (1938), 5–79; Palacios Rubios, *De las islas del mar océano*, and Paz, *Del dominio de los reyes de España sobre los indios*, trans. Augustín Millares Carlo. (México, D. F., 1954); Eloy Bullón y Fernández, "El problema jurídico de la dominación española en America antes de las Relecciones de Francisco Vitoria," *Anuario*, IV (1933), 99–128, esp. 104–105.

[77] Original rationales in Palacios Rubios, *De las islas*, 36–37, and Paz, *Del dominio*, 250–252. For examples of its use in small communities prior to the discoveries of Mexico and Peru see *CDI*, XX, 14–119; for examples of the Requirement as issued for Peru see Diego de Encinas, *Cedulario indiano*, vol. 4 (Madrid, 1945; orig. pub. 1596), 226–227; for Panama see Serrano y Sanz, *Dominación española*, I, 292–294, and Gonzalo Fernández de Oviedo, *Historia general y natural de las Indias*, vol. 7 (Asunción, Para., 1944), lib. 29, cap. 7; for Chile see José Toribio Medina, *El descubrimiento del Océano pacífico*, vol. 2 (Santiago, 1920), 287–289. Lewis Hanke, "A applicãçao do requerimento na America Hespanhola, 1526–1600," *Revista do Brasil*, 3d Ser. (1938), 231–248. When no people were encountered, no specific speech was required in possession ceremonies.

[78] Instrument of Obedience and Vassalage, *CDI*, XVI, 142–187. For examples of its use see ibid., IX, 30–45, XVI, 88ff, 188–207. One interpretation of the reasons for the shift is Hanke, *Aristotle and the American Indians: A Study in Race Prejudice in the Modern World* (London, 1959), 86–88.

opening phrases announce the status of the person reading as a messenger and servant of the king of Castile, whose sources of authority are provided by tracing a genealogy of power beginning with God and extending in an unbroken line to St. Peter, the pope, and finally to the papal donation made to Ferdinand and Isabella, by virtue of which "Their Highnesses are kings and lords of these islands and the mainland."[79]

The Requirement concludes by demanding two things: that the Indians recognize the genealogy of power and that they allow Christian priests to preach the faith. "Therefore, as best I can, I beg and *require* you to understand well what I have said . . . that it is just and that you recognize the Church as lady and superior of the universal world, and the Pontiff . . . in her name, and the King and the Queen our lords in his place as superiors and lords and monarchs of these islands and mainland . . . and that you consent . . . to having the religious fathers declare and preach to you on this subject."[80] If natives refused to acknowledge the papal donation and to admit preachers, the Spaniards considered themselves justified in commencing hostilities.

This document, according to Lewis Hanke, "was read to trees and empty huts. . . . Captains muttered its theological phrases into their beards on the edge of sleeping Indian settlements, or even a league away before starting the formal attack. . . . Ship captains would sometimes have the document read from the deck as they approached an island, and at night would send out enslaving expeditions, whose leaders would shout the traditional Castilian war cry 'Santiago!' rather than read the Requirement before they attacked."[81]

Gonzalo Fernández de Oviedo, an early sixteenth-century *conquistador* and chronicler of the conquest, wrote, "I would have preferred to make sure that they [the Indians] understood what was being said; but for one reason or another, that was impossible. . . . I afterwards asked Doctor Palacios Rubios, the author of the Requirement, whether the reading sufficed to clear the consciences of the Spaniards; he replied that it did."[82] No demonstration of understanding was required: rather, the issue of reception was studiously ignored. It was the *act of reading the text* that constituted the authority. The only other action needed to legitimate Spanish rule was to record that the act of reading had taken place. Just as Columbus had been required to register his solemn declarations in (written) legal instruments, the final step in implementing the Requirement and establishing its legality was the order that a notary preserve a record of this reading with "a signed testimony."

During the sixteenth-century debates over the Requirement, occasional consideration was given to the issue of translation.[83] But no deliberation was

[79] Serrano y Sanz, *Dominación española,* I, 293.
[80] Ibid., 294.
[81] Hanke, *The Spanish Struggle for Justice in the Conquest of America* (Philadelphia, 1949), 33–34.
[82] Oviedo, *Historia general y natural,* lib. 29, cap. 7, VII, esp. 131–132. The manner in which the Requirement was read appears at the start of cap. 7.
[83] Ibid., cap. 8.

given to the strangeness of the act of reading to people who had not only never read but had never seen the act of reading. We who have grown up with reading can only imagine the questions. Why is someone holding up an object (a written document) in front of himself and looking at it while he speaks? Is it an avoidance taboo? Is he afraid? ashamed? Why is the speaker's glance or gaze not directed at the listener but at the object he is holding? To New World societies with different body language conventions for speech, European reading (and even speaking) practices appeared strange.[84]

While most of the commentators on the Requirement, from Walter Ralegh and Bartolomé de Las Casas to modern historians, have interpreted it in a derisive or ironical way, there is more to it than simple absurdity.[85] First, it expressed a traditional European form of establishing authority (the letters patent or bull) derived from the practices of the papal chancery. Second, lest the idea that the act of reading to an uncomprehending audience seem a bizarre or unusual form of legitimizing power, it should be remembered that there are dozens of similar examples in contemporary American criminal and civil law. The most obvious instance is the United States Supreme Court's *Miranda* decision, which legitimates the authority of the American government over an often uncomprehending suspect when he is *read his rights*. The dominion of the American criminal justice system is also established by reading. What the act of reading accomplishes, in contradistinction to English architectural symbolism or Portuguese stone posts and flag planting, is the establishment of authority over *people*. The central, most important act legitimating Spanish rights over the New World articulated authority over persons rather than over land or commerce.

For the Spaniards, the principal target of imperial authority was people, and all the major institutions of the first century of Spanish colonial rule established public and private authority over people. In addition to slavery, the Spaniards brought with them two other institutions exerting authority

---

[84] On the strangeness to North American Indians of one form of European speech behavior (preaching) see Johannes Megapolensis, *Een kort Onwterp vande Mahakvase Indianen* (Aug. 26, 1644), "A Short Account of the Mohawk Indians," in Jameson, ed., *Narratives of New Netherland*, 177–178. On the reaction of the Peruvian Indians to writing see Patricia Seed, "'Failing to Marvel': Atahualpa's Encounter with the Word," *Latin American Research Review*, XXVI (1990), 7–32. Mexican pictographs appear to have been used as mnenomic devices that were "read" in the Western style. John B. Glass, "A Survey of Native Middle American Pictorial Manuscripts," in Robert Wauchope, ed., *Handbook of Middle American Indians*, vol. 14: *Guide to Ethnohistorical Sources*, pt. 3, ed. Howard F. Cline (Austin, Tex., 1975), 7–11; Charles Gibson, "Prose Sources in the Native Historical Tradition," in Wauchope, ed., *Handbook of Middle American Indians*, vol. 15: *Guide to Ethnohistorical Sources*, pt. 4, ed. Howard F. Cline (Austin, Tex., 1975), 313–315.

[85] Hanke, "The 'Requirimiento' and its Interpreters," *Revista de historia de América*, No. 1 (1938), 25–34; Hanke, "A aplicação"; Charles Verlinden, *The Beginnings of Modern Colonization* (Ithaca, N. Y., 1970), 41–42; Silvio A. Zavala, *Las instituciones jurídicas en la conquista de América*, 3d ed. (México, D. F., 1988), 78–81.

over persons. The *encomienda*, the principal reward sought by Spanish settlers in the New World, was a grant of Indian labor to private citizens; the *repartimiento* was a bureaucratic process for organizing rotating weekly pools of Indian workers. The major institutions of the first century of Spanish rule thus exerted authority over people. Grants of land (*mercedes de tierra*) came relatively late in the conquest and were subsidiary to grants of labor.[86]

It might be argued that the Spaniards came to rule over people, and the English over land, due to ecological exigencies rather than cultural predispositions: the English in North America encountered a lightly inhabited terrain, while the Spaniards encountered the most densely populated regions of the Americas. Several facts disturb this thesis.

First is the historical timing of the development of the Requirement and the institutions of Spanish rule over people. Indian slaving began with Columbus, and the New World *encomienda* originated in 1503.[87] The doctrine of the Requirement asserting imperial authority over people was created in 1512. Even by this late date, Spanish settlement was restricted to a few Caribbean islands no more densely populated than areas subsequently claimed by the English.[88] In other words, the institutions of rule over people were established long before the discovery of Central and South America with their sizable native populations.

Second is the timing of the English focus on land as their primary object. English concern with authority over land was apparent as early as the letter patent of 1578, *before* any expedition to settle the New World was launched, and it remained a constant feature of official authorizations thereafter. Furthermore, the English patents were issued after news of the Inca, Maya, and Nahua empires had spread throughout Europe, and there was the distinct (but unrealized) possibility that a similar empire would be found on the North American continent.

Finally, to the question of what the English might have done had they encountered such an empire, one can look to the eighteenth century, when they began to rule a continent more densely populated than central Mexico or highland Peru. In India, the first act of English officials was to *survey native land laws* and to try to organize a system of taxation based on ownership of land.[89] They subsequently invented the modern techniques of land survey

[86] Lesley Byrd Simpson, *The Encomienda in New Spain: Forced Native Labor in the Spanish Colonies, 1492–1550* (Berkeley, Calif., 1929); Zavala, *La encomienda indiana,* 2d ed. (México, D. F., 1973); William L. Sherman, *Forced Native Labor in Sixteenth-Century Central America* (Lincoln, Neb., 1979); Robert S. Chamberlain, "The Roots of Lordship: The *Encomienda* in Medieval Castile," in H. B. Johnson, Jr., ed., *From Reconquest to Empire: The Iberian Background to Latin American History* (New York, 1970), 124–147; *Colección de Documentos Inéditos . . . de Ultramar,* 25 vols. (Madrid, 1885–1932), I, 105–106.

[87] The *encomienda* received its first legal recognition in the instructions sent to Nicolás de Ovando, governor of Hispaniola in 1503; *CDI,* XXXI, 209–212.

[88] When the Requirement was promulgated there were Spanish settlements on only 3 Caribbean islands, Jamaica, Hispaniola, and Puerto Rico; Las Casas, *Historia de las Indias,* lib. 3, cap. 8, II, 456.

[89] Guha, *A Rule of Property for Bengal* (New Delhi, 1981).

in order to rule the Indian subcontinent.[90] Spanish officials in highland Peru and Mexico counted people, the English in India surveyed the land.[91] Spanish colonialism produced the census, British colonialism the map. It was not the ecology of peoples encountered, but cultural conceptions, that defined the central objects of European authority.

The Requirement officially ceased to be the means of enacting the authority of the Spanish empire overseas in 1573 when it was replaced by a new set of instructions called an "Instrument of Obedience and Vassalage." Eliminating reference to the papal bull, it described the king as "the only and singular defender of the Church." The Indians were invited to obey him, so that in exchange for protection from their enemies they might be beneficiaries of Spanish political and economic power. But although the source of authority was redefined, the method of enacting it was not. The Instrument of Obedience and Vassalage was still to be read to the natives, with the added provision that efforts be made to secure translators. In its new form, the Instrument was read not only to natives of the New World but also in the Philippines to legitimize Spanish conquest.[92] While the obvious implausibility of asserting a papal donation was eliminated in an era that had witnessed the end of papal universality, the method of implementation, reading, continued.

Each of these separate targets of imperial authority—land for the English, labor for the Spaniards—was also the principal focus of internal struggle and contention over the legitimacy of imperial rule. English and Anglo-American critics of English imperial policy such as Roger Williams and others attacked the means by which Englishmen acquired land. Their Spanish counterparts— Las Casas and Juan Zumárraga—criticized the means by which Spaniards acquired the right to Indian labor. Neither developed substantial critical assessments of the other empire's principal object. Enslavement of Indians never came in for the scathing critiques in England or Anglo-America that it received in the Spanish empire, nor did the gradual dispossession of native peoples from their lands receive the same attacks in Spain that it did in the English empire. Discourses critical of imperial authority centered on the aspects each culture defined as crucial. In English culture, what mattered was

[90] The modern land survey's origin in British India was acknowledged at length in the 1911 *Encyclopedia Britannica* but disappeared by mid-20th-century editions. In later encyclopedias, the actual colonial origin is concealed by descriptive language, e.g., "the land survey is."

[91] The remarkable *Suma de visitas*, the partial summaries in Juan López de Velasco's *Geografía y descripción universal de las Indias* and other counts of people are described in Peter Gerhard, *A Guide to the Historical Geography of New Spain* (Cambridge, 1972), 28–33. Similar reports exist from the reign in Peru of viceroy Francisco de Toledo; Noble David Cook, *Demographic Collapse in Indian Peru, 1520–1620* (Cambridge, 1981), 7. The English experience in North America did not place them in contact with sufficient numbers of people, so techniques of surveying remained relatively primitive; Douglas W. Marshall and Howard H. Peckham, *Campaigns of the American Revolution: An Atlas of Manuscript Maps* (Ann Arbor, Mich., 1976); J. B. Harley, Barbara B. Petchenik, and Lawrence W. Towner, *Mapping the American Revolution* (Chicago, 1978).

[92] Hanke, "A aplicação"; "*Traslado de la posesión que en nombre des su magestad tomó Don Joan de Oñate, de los reinos y provincias de la Nueva México,*" *CDI*, XVI, 88–142.

the title to land; in Spanish culture, the right to use labor. The difference centered on the priorities of the two societies: the conquest of land and the conquest of peoples.

What the differing constructions of the authority of empire additionally illuminate is the very different responses to the problem of native depopulation. For the crown of Spain, widespread deaths of natives from disease and other causes were evidence of God's disfavor. Charles V in 1523 ordered Hernán Cortés to take into consideration "the monumental harm and losses received by the said Indians through their deaths and dwindling numbers and the great diservice that Our Lord has received because of it."[93] In a similar royal order to Juan Ponce de Leon two years later Charles added: "not only has our duty to God Our Lord not been performed because such a multitude of souls have perished . . . but we ourselves [the crown] have been ill-served by it as well."[94] James I of England, on the other hand, in his 1620 patent for Plymouth Colony wrote: "Within this late yeares there hath by God's Visitation raigned a Wonderfull Plague . . . to the utter Destruction, Devastacion and Depopulation of the whole Territorye, so that there is not left for many Leagues together in a Manner any [person] that doe claim or challenge . . . Whereby We in our Judgment are persuaded and satisfied that the appointed Time is come in which the Almighty God in his great Goodness and Bountie towards Us and our People hath thought fitt and determined that those large and goodly Territoryes, deserted as it were by their naturall inhabitants should be possesed and enjoyed."[95] Massive numbers of native deaths are not to be mourned, nor are they to be taken as evidence of unjust and tyrannical conduct. Rather, they are proof of divine intervention on behalf of the English, "a Wonderfull Plague" demonstrating God's "great Goodness and Bountie towards Us and our People."

This sentiment was echoed by Puritan settlers as well as Catholic monarchs. John Winthrop suggested that the plague that hit the natives just before the Puritans arrived was evidence of God's hand in creating a vacant land. "God hath consumed the Natives with a great plague in those parts soe as there be few in-habitants left."[96] The Spanish critique of empire found its fulcrum in the devastating losses of people—losses that threatened the basis of the empire's wealth in human beings. For the English, native deaths were more than unproblematic; they were declared signs of divine favor.

[93] Real cédula a Hernán Cortés, Jun. 20, 1523, in Encinas, *Cedulario indiano,* II, 185.
[94] Ibid., 186.
[95] Ebenezer Hazard, *Historical Collections; Consisting of State Papers, and Other Authentic Documents* (Philadelphia, 1792), I, 105.
[96] Winthrop, *Conclusions,* 7. Similar sentiments were expressed by Edward Johnson in *Wonder-Working Providence, 1628–1651,* ed. Jameson (New York, 1937; orig. pub. 1654), 41, 79–80: "The Indians . . . began to quarrell with them [the English] about their bounds of Land, . . . but the Lord put an end to this quarrell also, by smiting the Indians with a sore disease. . . . Thus did the Lord allay their quarrelsome spirits, and made roome for the following part of his Army."

English and Spanish empires in the New World were Christian imperialisms, founded at the core on beliefs in the right of the religion of the West to rule the other religions of the world. For the English, religion functioned as a prop for the authority of the state; for the Spaniards it was a means of coercing Indians into European ways of thinking. In their invocation of Christian imperialism as the authority for expansion over the rest of the world, both English and Spanish empires addressed medieval tradition. The Spanish king appealed to the authority of the Roman papacy, and Elizabeth I similarly drew upon the same sources as the medieval Roman pontiffs in her letters patent. Their assertions were thus the last effort to claim a traditional medieval authority at the very newest moment, the start of the age of European expansion.

It is ironic that, by using letters patent, English rulers continued to invoke both the form and the substance of the medieval papal bull to legitimate rule over the New World through the middle of the seventeenth century. The English made little effort to alter their adaptation of the authority of the pontiff, even after Spain ceased to regard the bull as a legitimate source of authority.[97] While this can be seen partly as the result of the position of the English monarch as head of the church, its formulas were invoked unselfconsciously by Oliver Cromwell—no friend of the Church of England—to justify settlement of Nova Scotia.[98] Although the Spanish are often considered the most medieval of European powers, it was the English, whose formula for establishing empire became fixed in the late sixteenth century, who continued for the longest period to assert medieval concepts of sovereignty overseas. The language of Gilbert's 1578 patent was used for the last time in letters patent issued for Australia at the end of the eighteenth century.

Spanish imperial authority relied centrally upon articulating a relationship between Europeans and a living, breathing Other rather than simply demarcating space. It had to constitute its authority primarily through possession not of territory but of bodies and minds, by authority over persons rather than places. If possession in the medieval English world was synonymous with property, in the Spanish world it signified dominion over people. When the English conquered, they aimed to conquer territory, and when they took over an area, they sought to possess the land, not the people. Spanish authority was textual imperialism par excellence—the reading of a Western text to uncomprehending natives. Whereas the ultimate authority of each empire was founded on written language, that of the English empire in the New World was established by habitation, "taking possession," while that of the Spanish empire was enacted by reading.

---

[97] For its use by Oliver Cromwell, Aug. 6, 1656, see letters patent for Acadia and Nova Scotia in Hazard, *Historical Collections*, 616–617.
[98] "Concession faite par Cromwel," Aug. 6, 1656, ibid., 617–619.

Historical memories of the origins of these two empires have been built around the central aims of each. We commemorate the origins of English settlement in the New World by place: Plymouth Rock, Jamestown, even Roanoke. But we do not remember the start of the Spanish empire by a location. Exactly where Columbus landed is uncertain in our memories as well as in our scholarship. We do remember the date on which he made his solemn declarations, the ceremony, and the words. We mark the conquest of land by the place where it began; we remember the ceremonies that initiated the conquest of people by commemorating a day, October 12, and a year, 1492.

Conquistadores of the Spirit

David J. Weber

INTRODUCTION

Many historians have thought almost exclusively in terms of the thirteen English colonies in their studies of early America. As a result, the important contributions of other cultures during the colonial period have often received less attention than they merit. One scholar seeking to redress this imbalance is David Weber, a historian who has written extensively on America's Hispanic past, with particular emphasis on the U.S. Southwest. In his work, Weber has steered a careful course between the two dominant trends in the historiography of Spanish colonialism in America: the pro-Spanish romanticism of Herbert Bolton, the historian who shaped this field of study, and the antagonism of hispanophobic writers eager to vilify Spaniards and assail their legacy in America.

In the following selection, taken from his comprehensive survey of the Spanish frontier in North America, Weber examines the role played by Franciscan friars in the Spanish exploration and settlement of present-day New Mexico and Florida. Driven from central Mexico by the Crown's efforts to curb their influence, friars moved to the empire's peripheries in order to continue their missionary work with minimal government interference. Often working by themselves, priests established their presence in existing native villages, striving to remake Indian communities through religious conversion and the introduction of European farming and cultural practices. These efforts, performed with millennial zeal by the Franciscans, were frequently unwelcome in the native communities they transformed, a fact underscored by Ramón Gutierrez in his discussion of the Pueblo Revolt of 1680 later in this volume.

David J. Weber, "Conquistadors of the Spirit," *The Spanish Frontier in North America,* pp. 92–121. Copyright © 1992 Yale University Press. Reprinted with permission.

Beyond providing an intriguing point of comparison with English colonial practices, the religious component of Spanish settlement in America raises a host of important historical questions.

- *On the most basic level, how should we assess and interpret the religious "conversion" of natives by the friars, especially when one considers the political context and obvious cultural barriers?*
- *Furthermore, in reflecting on the ideas behind the Royal Orders of 1573, what should we make of the Franciscans' efforts in Florida and New Mexico?*
- *More broadly, what conclusions might we draw concerning the significance of spiritual imperatives to military and political conquest?*

If your highness may be pleased to have the Holy Gospel preached to the people in those provinces with the necessary zeal, God our Lord will be served and many idolatries and notable sins which the devil has implanted among the natives will be eradicated. Thus having succeeded in this holy purpose your royal crown will be served by an increase of vassals, tribute, and royal fifths.
—Baltasar Obregón to the king, Mexico City, 1584

It has been impossible to correct their concubinage, the abominable crime of idolatry, their accursed superstitions, idolatrous dances, and other faults.
—fray Nicolás de Freitas, New Mexico, 1660

On the feast of the Pentecost, June 3, 1629, a day in which Christians commemorate the descent of their Holy Spirit to the initial twelve apostles of the son of their god, fray Estevan de Perea led a group of thirty road-weary Spanish priests into the tiny, adobe town of Santa Fe. They had come to the end of a long and dangerous journey that had begun nine months before in Mexico City. A caravan of thirty-six heavily loaded oxcarts and a small military escort had brought the Spanish priests more than fifteen hundred miles to the dusty plaza of the most northerly Spanish community in the western hemisphere.[1] In New Mexico these holy men planned not only to minister to the fledgling colony that Juan de Oñate had founded in 1598, but to destroy the indigenous religion and replace it with their own.

These Spanish priests believed that Jesus Christ, who had lived some sixteen hundred years before, was the only son of the one true god. In the words of the Christians' creed, Jesus Christ "was crucified, died and was buried. He descended into hell; the third day He rose again from the dead;

[1] The caravan departed on Sept. 4 and arrived in Santa Fe on the seventh Sunday after Easter (June 3), according to fray Estevan de Perea's "True Report of the Great Conversion" (first published in 1632–33) in Bloom, ed. and trans., "Fray Estevan de Perea's *Relación*," 224–25. Thirty-one Franciscans left Mexico City (counting Perea), but one died on route and another four days after reaching Santa Fe (ibid.). On the long intervals between supply caravans, see Scholes, "Supply Service," 94–95.

He ascended into Heaven to sit at the right hand of God." The priests sought to convince the natives of the truth of this credo and of the efficacy of their god. The task must have seemed daunting, for tens of thousands of natives occupied the vastness that Spaniards called New Mexico, and there were few priests to convert them. The thirty new arrivals more than doubled the number already there, bringing the total to fifty.[2] Notwithstanding the odds against them, faith and reason told these conquistadores of the spirit that they would prevail.

Fray Estevan's tiny band wore no armor and carried no weapons. For inspiration, they looked to San Francisco rather than to Santiago, and they gave thanks to St. Francis upon reaching Santa Fe. Members of a religious order of celibate males founded in 1209 by Francis Bernardone of the Italian town of Assisi, Franciscans vowed not to possess private or community property. They lived only on alms, for which they begged or which the king or other patrons bestowed upon them. Like members of other mendicant brotherhoods, the friars, or brothers, wore the simple robe and cowl of an Italian peasant of St. Francis's day. In theory, if not always in practice, the Franciscans emulated peasants by walking rather than riding on horseback and by wearing sandals rather than shoes.[3] Instead of an isolated and contemplative monastic life, Franciscans ministered among the laity. Popes had sent them to convert pagans in central Asia and China, and in Spain Franciscan friars had sought to convert Muslims and Canary Islanders. The first Franciscans had come to America in 1493, on Columbus's second voyage; they had begun work in New Spain in 1523, on the heels of the Spanish conquest of the Aztec empire. As early as 1526, royal regulations required that at least two priests accompany all exploring parties. More than any other religious order, Franciscans rose to the task of serving as chaplains to explorers in North America. They accompanied expeditions such as those of Pánfilo de Narváez, Hernando de Soto, and Francisco Vázquez de Coronado—"that the conquest be a Christian apostolic one and not a butchery," as Mexico's first bishop explained.[4]

---

[2] Twenty friars were in New Mexico when the 1619 caravan arrived. By the end of the year, one had died and three had returned to Mexico, leaving a total of forty-six (Scholes and Bloom, "Friar Personnel," 70–71).

[3] Franciscans who worked in Spanish North America were Observant Franciscans, of the Order of Friars Minor, as opposed to the Discalced, "barefoot" Franciscans, or to Capuchins or Conventuals, who also belong to the so-called First Order of St. Francis (Habig, "Franciscan Provinces," 89). In practice, Franciscans on the frontier often found it expedient to ride horses.

[4] Bishop Juan de Zumárraga to his nephew, Aug. 23, 1539, speaking of Viceroy Mendoza's plans for the Coronado expedition, quoted in Rey, "Missionary Aspects," 23. Phelan, *Millennial Kingdom*, 29–38, is one of the finest accounts of early Franciscan activity written in English. The requirement that two priests accompany exploring parties appeared in the Ordenanzas de Granada of Nov. 17, 1526, described in Gómez Canedo, *Evangelización*, 75–76. The New Laws of 1542 repeated that requirement. Dominicans had also accompanied early expeditions, such as those of Lucas Vázquez de Ayllón and Hernando de Soto (O'Daniel, *Dominicans*).

Franciscans had come to America with a militant vision that rivaled the more worldly dreams of the conquistadores. Instead of cities of gold, however, the friars imagined a spiritual Antilia. The discovery of America seemed to provide a heaven-sent opportunity to rescue the spirits or souls of benighted aborigines and send them to the Christians' eternal paradise. Some Spaniards had doubted that Indians were human beings who possessed a soul, but in 1537 in a papal bull, Sublimis Deus, Pope Paul III put the question officially to rest by declaring that "Indians are truly men capable of understanding the catholic faith."[5] In addition to "saving" souls, most Franciscans also hoped to reshape the natives' cultures. At first, many Franciscans paternalistically and optimistically regarded Indians as pliable, childlike innocents, uncorrupted by Europeans—clay to be molded into ideal Christian communities. With communally owned property, communal labor, and representative government, these Indian communities would be heavenly cities of God on earth—utopian Christian republics. In such places, one sixteenth-century Franciscan noted, Indians might live "virtuously and peacefully serving God, as in a terrestrial paradise."[6]

In the decades following the fall of the Aztecs, Franciscans had worked with special urgency to construct an earthly paradise in central Mexico. The discovery of previously unknown pagans seemed to foretell the end of the world, predicted in early Christian writings, and this would be the friars' last opportunity to fulfill their destiny of converting all peoples of all tongues.[7] By their own accounts, the Franciscans achieved a series of stunning successes in saving the souls of the native Mexicans, but within two generations their future in New Spain looked bleak.

Although the apocalypse expected by the friars failed to arrive, the world of the Aztecs crumbled. Opportunities for Franciscans to make further conversions declined as European diseases consumed the natives. At the same time, the colonists' demands for the diminished supply of Indian laborers grew intense and put more pressure on missionaries to relinquish control over Indians. Finally, the Crown itself concluded that the Franciscans had outlived their usefulness in central Mexico. In an effort to cut government costs and to control the powerful and independent friars, the Crown took steps in 1572 to bring them under diocesan control. It began to replace the Franciscans in Mexico with their bitter rivals, the secular or diocesan clergy. *Doctrinas,* or Indian parishes, which had received support from the royal exchequer, were to become self-supporting diocesan parishes. Indian converts were to become tax-paying citizens whose labor could be more easily ex-

---

[5] Gibson, ed., *Spanish Tradition,* 104–5. For an example of the ongoing expression of doubt about whether or not Indians had a soul, see Poole, "War by Fire and Blood," 126.

[6] Gerónimo de Mendieta, quoted in Phelan, *Millennial Kingdom,* 69. See, too, Gibson, *Spain in America,* 68–74, and Parry, *Spanish Seaborne Empire,* 158–70, for good general discussions of Franciscan ideology and guides to the literature.

[7] Phelan, *Millennial Kingdom,* 7–21.

ploited than when they had been under the paternalistic care of the friars.[8] This so-called secularization of the missions, one historian has explained, left the mendicants with two alternatives: "to abandon their ministry and retire to their convents, or to undertake the conversion of remote pagan regions."[9] The friars chose the latter and discovered that whatever influence they had lost in their tawdry struggle with the diocesan branch of the church in central Mexico, they more than regained on the frontiers of the empire.

The decline of opportunities for mendicant missionaries in central Mexico coincided with issuance of the Royal Orders for New Discoveries of 1573, which gave missionaries the central role in the exploration and pacification of new lands. The Orders of 1573 reiterated the Crown's often expressed intention, that "preaching the holy gospel . . . is the principal purpose for which we order new discoveries and settlements to be made," and established stricter rules to assure that this pious wish would become a reality.[10] The Royal Orders prohibited conquest or violence against Indians for any reasons. Pacification rather than conquest would be the new order of the day. Missionaries, their expenses still paid by alms from the Crown, were to enter new lands before all others.[11]

[8] Francisco Morales, "Los Franciscanos en la Nueva España. La época de oro, siglo xvi," in Morales, ed., *Franciscan Presence in the Americas* (Potomac, Md.: Academy of American Franciscan History, 1983), 77–80, explains the Crown's economic motives more clearly than have previous writers. In 1572 Felipe II appointed a secular cleric to the archbishopric of New Spain, a position that regular clergy had held to that time, and the new archbishop moved quickly to bring the nettlesome missionaries under control and secularize their missions. To hasten the process, the first Jesuits, a non-mendicant religious order, arrived in Mexico in 1572, charged with the responsibility of improving the quality of the secular clergy. See, too, Stafford Poole, *Pedro Moya de Contreras: Catholic Reform and Royal Power in New Spain, 1571–1591* (Berkeley: University of California Press, 1987), 66–87; 163–67, and John Frederick Schwaller, *The Church and Clergy in Sixteenth-Century Mexico* (Albuquerque: University of New Mexico, 1987), 81–109, on the important *Ordenanza del Patronazgo*.

[9] Ricard, *Spiritual Conquest of Mexico*, 3, which remains the best single account in English of the mendicants' activities in central Mexico up to 1572. The process of secularization in the old Aztec realm was gradual and did not end until the nineteenth century. See Gibson, *Aztecs under Spanish Rule*, 110. For a more recent and succinct interpretive essay, see Liss, *Mexico under Spain*, 69–94.

[10] "Ordenanzas de su Magestad hechas para los nuevos descubrimientos, conquistas y pacificaciones," July 13, 1573, in *CDI*(1), 16: 149–52; the quote is on 154. Much has been written about the evolution of this policy and the significance of these famous orders. For a discussion of their relationship to missionary endeavors, see Gómez Canedo, *Evangelización*, 74–82.

[11] Gómez Canedo, *Evangelización*, 49–51, who explains this late sixteenth-century transition more clearly than other writers of whom I am aware, sees previous missionary efforts as located among Indians who had already been conquered. After 1573, he argues, missionaries would play the central role in conquest itself. A number of other writers see the mission as an institution that gained greater importance during the late 1500s. See, e.g., Bolton, "Mission as a Frontier Institution," 190–91, and Powell, *Soldiers, Indians, and Silver*, 188, 192–93, 208–9, 212. The view that the Orders of 1573 marked a radical change between an "encomienda-doctrina system" and a "new . . . mission system," as argued by Antonine S. Tibesar, "The Franciscan *doctrinero* versus the Franciscan *misionero* in Seventeenth-Century Peru," *The Americas* 14 (Oct. 1957): 117, does not seem sustained by the evidence. The Orders of 1573 permitted granting of more *encomiendas* and

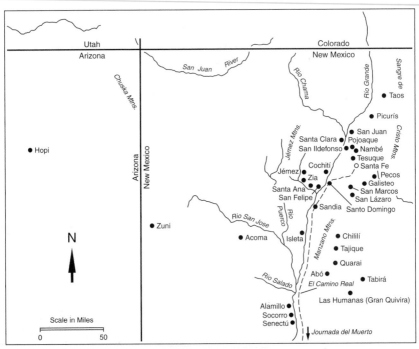

Pueblos in New Mexico, circa 1650.

On the frontiers, then, Franciscans could begin anew to build a terrestrial paradise. The fringes of empire beckoned especially to those Franciscans who had not lost their apocalyptic zeal for new conversions or their
taste for lives of personal deprivation. Those few moved quickly into North
America.[12] In 1573 friars began sustained missionary work in Florida. In
1581 fray Agustín Rodríguez, encouraged by the Royal Orders of 1573, had
rediscovered the Pueblos of New Mexico; by 1598 Franciscans had returned
to New Mexico with Juan de Oñate and had begun to build missions. Until
1821, when the Spanish empire in North America collapsed, members of the
Franciscan Order monopolized the missions along the Spanish rim from California to Florida. Only Jesuits, who had worked briefly in Florida (1566–72)
and whose missions among Pimas extended to the northern edge of Pimería
Alta into today's southern Arizona (1700–67), effectively challenged Franciscan control of the vast mission field of Spanish North America.

Franciscans who initially pushed the frontiers of Christianity into
Florida and New Mexico enjoyed more favorable conditions than they had
previously known in Mexico. In theory, the Royal Orders of 1573 assured

the essential features of the mission, as described in Ricard's *Spiritual Conquest of Mexico*, were
formed early in New Spain and transported to the frontier with little modification.
[12] Liss, *Mexico under Spain*, 87, and Gibson, *Spain in America*, 80.

them the opportunity to contend for the souls of Indians through friendly
persuasion rather than to minister to alienated peoples conquered by force.
Then, too, they could depend upon financial support from the government
so long as Spain relied upon missionaries to advance and hold its American
frontiers. Finally, in North America the padres moved into areas that were so
marginal to the economic life of the Spanish empire that they met less competition from civilians, secular priests, or members of other religious orders
who had been their chief rivals in core areas of the empire.[13] In this frontier
milieu, the missionaries made the most of their opportunities.

I

The Franciscan reinforcements who arrived in New Mexico with fray Estevan de Perea on the feast of the Pentecost in 1629 found their brethren had
made rapid progress in building missions among the Pueblo Indians. By that
year, according to one count, Franciscans had already overseen the construction of fifty churches and friaries (residences for priests) in New Mexico.[14] Under the friars' supervision, Pueblo women did the actual work of
building the walls, just as they constructed those of their own homes, while
Pueblo men apparently did much of the carpentry. The Pueblo communities,
as one Franciscan noted, spread out across New Mexico in the shape of a
huge cross, evocative of the crucified Christ, and the Franciscan missions followed that configuration.[15] The arms of the cross ran up the Rio Grande Valley, from the Piro pueblo of Socorro in the south to the Tiwa pueblo of Taos
in the north—over two hundred miles. The top of the cross extended eastward, from the Rio Grande to the pueblos of Pecos, Chililí, and Abó, where
Franciscans had also established missions. Work along the long western base
of the cross, however, had awaited the arrival of additional Franciscans.[16]

[13] Dominicans unsuccessfully sought permission to extend their activities to New Mexico.
[14] The number of "churches and monasteries [i.e., friaries]" is in Benavides, *Memorial . . . 1630,*
62, which contains a facsimile of the original edition of this memorial, published in Madrid in
1630 (164 of the Spanish facsimile corresponds to p. 62 of the translation). Earlier, Benavides also
mentions the figure of fifty, but applies it just to churches (p. 33, corresponding to 121 of the
Spanish facsimile). A more recent and smoother translation by Peter Forrestal, *Benavides' Memorial of 1630,* lacks the facsimile of the 1630 Spanish imprint. Riley, "Las Casas and the Benavides
Memorial," 209–22, is essential to understanding the concluding sections of the *Memorial . . .
1630.* For women building walls, see Kubler, *Religious Architecture of New Mexico,* 7.
[15] "The shape which all that which is settled has is that of a cross" (Fr. Juan de Pardo to the
viceroy, Convento of San Francisco, Mexico, Sept. 26, 1638, in Hackett, ed., *Historical Documents,*
3:107). I have supposed the length of Pardo's imaginary cross to run east and west, but if one
does not take the Hopi pueblos into account, fray Juan might have imagined the cross to have
its base in the south.
[16] The most detailed account of the first decades of missionary expansion among the Pueblos is
Scholes and Bloom, "Friar Personnel," 319–36; 58–62.

Resting for only three weeks after their 1,500-mile journey to Santa Fe, eight of the friars who arrived in 1629 completed the cross by establishing missions in the pueblos of the Acomas, Zunis, and Hopis—the latter some 250 miles west of the Rio Grande. Sixty-four-year-old Estevan de Perea, who had labored in New Mexico since 1609, led the priests. The governor, Francisco Manuel de Silva Nieto, and a small military escort accompanied them, promoting the friars' work with standard theater rather than force of arms. At Cíbola, for example, the largest of the Zuni pueblos, the governor and soldiers knelt before the Franciscans and kissed their feet, "in order," fray Estevan wrote, "to make these people understand the true veneration that they should show the friars whenever they met them." Through an interpreter, a priest announced that he had come to free natives "from the miserable slavery of the demon and from the obscure darkness of their idolatry . . . giving them to understand the coming of the Son of God to the World."[17] The Zunis had heard this message nearly a century before from Coronado's friars. They had rejected it then and the Spaniards had waged war on them. This time, rather than risk a similar fate, they, like the Acomas and the Hopis, tolerated the messengers of the new religion, if not the message, and allowed a Franciscan to remain among them.

The Franciscans' apparent success at Zuni occurred at the high point of Franciscan missionary expansion in New Mexico. In the late 1620s Franciscans basked in a moment of extraordinary optimism, when anything seemed possible. Astonishing events had occurred and the Franciscans' century-long dream of imposing their religion upon the Pueblos seemed within their grasp.

News of the natives' rapid and sometimes astounding conversions in New Mexico soon reached Mexico City and the capitals of Europe, carried by an eye witness, fray Alonso de Benavides. When the supply caravan that had brought fresh Franciscan recruits to Santa Fe in the spring of 1629 turned around that autumn to return to Mexico City, fray Alonso traveled with it. He had served in New Mexico since 1626 as the chief administrator, or *custodio*, of its missions. Leaving fray Estevan de Perea as the new custodio, fray Alonso journeyed to Mexico City and then to Spain, which he reached in 1630. In a report published in Madrid that year (and in French, Latin, Dutch, and German editions between 1631 and 1634), he described the progress of the disciples of St. Francis in a faraway corner of the world.[18]

Over and over again, as fray Alonso de Benavides recounted it, Franciscans had convinced natives to submit to a ritual known to Christians as baptism. They instructed Indians briefly, then used water and formulaic incantations to admit them to the Christian community and to enable their spirits to pass upon death into an eternal and paradisiacal afterlife. The Franciscans, he

[17] Both quotes in this paragraph are from Bloom, ed. and trans., "Fray Estevan de Perea's *Relación*," 229–30, who provides a firsthand account of the expedition to Acoma, Zuni, and the Hopi country.
[18] "Biography of Benavides," in Benavides, *Revised Memorial of 1634*, 1–17.

reported, had baptized 86,000 Indians in New Mexico, Apaches and Navajos as well as Pueblos. Most of the conversions were recent, but it seemed to fray Alonso as though the Pueblos in particular had been Christians for a hundred years. "If we go passing along the roads, and they see us from their pueblos or fields, they all come forth to meet us with very great joy, saying: Praised be our Lord Jesus Christ! Praise be the most holy Sacrament!"[19]

But, fray Alonso lamented, many Indian souls remained unconquered. He urged the Crown to undertake nothing less than the spiritual conquest of all of North America. The geographical scope of the friar's vision rivaled the expansive secular goals of the adelantados Menéndez and Oñate. Alonso de Benavides called for the conversion of Indians all the way to the Atlantic coast. This would not only "save" the souls of new converts, he argued, but it would protect those already converted in New Mexico from the contamination of heresies introduced by the Dutch and English, whom he believed were not far away. He estimated that the Spaniards had pacified over 500,000 Indians in New Mexico and on its vast peripheries, and those natives still needed baptism.[20]

The Franciscans' apparent conquest of the hearts and minds of Indians in New Mexico had occurred in no small part, in fray Alonso's view, as a result of divine intercession. Magical events, of the kind known to Christians as "miracles," had taken place. Baptismal waters, he said, had brought an Acoma infant back to life, a Christian cross had restored the eyesight of a Hopi boy, and a thunderbolt had struck a "sorceress" dead at Taos Pueblo. This powerful magic, fray Alonso reported, suggested to the Pueblos the power of the Christian god and facilitated the Franciscans' work. Although a number of Franciscans had won martyrdom in New Mexico, some enjoyed divine protection. Indians from Picurís Pueblo discovered this, according to fray Alonso, when they entered the room of a priest intending to kill him. The priest became "invisible" and the Indians fled in confusion.[21]

In Spain, Alonso de Benavides learned that one source of the unusual occurrences in New Mexico was a well-known mystic. Reports had it that a Franciscan nun of the order of Poor Clares of St. Francis, María de Jesús de Agreda, had made spiritual journeys to North America.[22] Eager to hear the story from her own lips, in the spring of 1631 fray Alonso journeyed to the

---

[19] Benavides, *Memorial . . . 1630,* 34.

[20] For the 500,000 figures, see Benavides, *Memorial . . . 1630,* 62. One of Benavides's more statistically minded brethren tallied up the baptismal registers, probably in 1626, and found that the Franciscans had baptized 34,650 persons, presumably among the Pueblos alone (Zárate Salmerón, *Relaciones,* 53). On the method of baptism at this time, including the need for preliminary instruction, see Ricard, *Spiritual Conquest,* 83–95. For the English-Dutch threat, see Benavides, *Revised Memorial of 1634,* 167, 197–98.

[21] Benavides, *Memorial . . . 1630,* 25. Fray Alonso describes the other miracles on 26–29.

[22] Much has been written about the life of María de Jesús. The best critical biography is Kendrick, *Mary of Agreda,* which should also serve as a guide to other sources. Kendrick takes the position that the story of María reached New Mexico in 1629, with the supply caravan (31). That position has been more fully explicated by Donahue, "Mary of Agreda," 294–95, but evidence is

nun's convent at Agreda, on the northern edges of Castile near the Ebro River. As he told it, the beautiful twenty-nine-year-old abbess revealed how, for the last decade, she had made flights to New Mexico. Delegations of Plains Indians, known to the Spaniards as Apaches and Jumanos, had told the Franciscans that a woman dressed like a nun had preached to them in their own language, but the friars had not known what to make of such a story. Now Benavides understood. María de Agreda had spoken to the natives, to whom she was visible, and urged them to seek the Franciscans, to whom she remained invisible.[23]

At the urging of fray Alonso, Sister María wrote a letter to the Franciscans in New Mexico. She recounted her numerous trips to New Mexico, "transported by the aid of the angels," and expressed admiration for the friars' work.[24] Fray Alonso forwarded a copy of the letter to New Mexico, along with his own enthusiastic interpretation of his conversation with the nun dressed in the Franciscan robes and blue cloak of her order.[25]

Two decades after Benavides's visit, by which time she had become one of the most eminent women in Spain, María de Agreda repudiated much of what she had told the priest from New Mexico. She burned a copy of her 1631 letter to the friars of New Mexico and claimed that she had been misunderstood and badgered by fray Alonso and the two Franciscans who accompanied him. "I have always doubted that it was my actual body that went," she wrote in 1650. But since fray Alonso had told her that Indians had seen her, she surmised that "it might have been an angel impersonating me."[26]

---

circumstantial and depends chiefly on Benavides, *Revised Memorial of 1634*, rather than on other contemporary evidence.

[23] Benavides, *Memorial . . . 1630*, 56–60, and Benavides, *Revised Memorial of 1634*, 92–96. In 1630, Benavides did not yet know the identity of the woman, dressed like a nun, who the Plains Indians said had preached to them.

[24] María de Agreda to the friars of New Mexico, May 15, 1631, in Benavides, *Revised Memorial of 1634*, appendix 11, 140.

[25] Benavides, *Revised Memorial of 1634*, 35 (also 99). Compare these passages to Benavides, *Memorial . . . 1630*, 62. With this firm evidence that God smiled on the Franciscans' work in New Mexico, Benavides traveled on to Rome. He revised and expanded his 1630 treatise on New Mexico, painting an even rosier picture. Instead of claiming 500,000 *potential* converts, for example, as he had done in 1630, Benavides now boasted that this number of "barbarous Indians have been converted to our holy Catholic faith." Benavides directed his revised treatise to Pope Urban VIII, whom he hoped to persuade to grant favors that would advance the missionary enterprise in New Mexico, elevate the province to the rank of a bishopric, and put Benavides in the new post (instead, Benavides received a bishopric for himself in Goa, Portuguese India).

[26] María de Jesús to fray Pedro Manero, quoted in Kendrick, *Mary of Agreda*, 43–44, who also noted that her spiritual journeys were limited to the years 1620–23. See, too, Kendrick's analysis (35–40), who dismisses María's 1631 statement, which she was forced to sign "under obedience" (38), as "preposterous nonsense." María's repudiation of much of what Benavides reported that she said has gone unnoticed by most other writers.

María de Agreda's repudiation of Alonso de Benavides's account was soon forgotten, but the memory of her miraculous visits to America endured. Across New Spain's far northern frontier, from Texas to Arizona, Franciscans continued until the end of the century to report meeting Indians who remembered a visit from a "Lady in Blue."[27] On at least three occasions in the next century, María de Agreda's 1631 letter was reprinted in New Spain,[28] and in 1769 when Junípero Serra began to build missions in Alta California, the Spanish Franciscans' last frontier in North America, he and his confrères continued to draw inspiration from the story of the Lady in Blue.[29] Today, those interested in explaining María de Agreda's behavior rather than in drawing inspiration from it might regard her visions as induced in part by the disease anorexia mirabilis—a "miraculous" loss of appetite apparently brought on by fasting in search of perfection of the spirit.[30] Its modern manifestation is, of course, anorexia nervosa—excessive fasting seemingly caused by an inordinate desire for perfection of the body.

Fray Alonso de Benavides never returned to New Mexico to implement his plan to convert all of the Indians of North America. Reports of *Grandiosa Conversion* of the Zunis and Hopis, written by fray Estevan de Perea, who died in 1638 after nearly three decades of missionary labor in New Mexico, were published in Seville in 1632 and 1633. After midcentury, in 1659, Franciscans established the mission of Nuestra Señora de Guadalupe de los Mansos in what is today downtown Ciudad Juárez across the river from present-day El Paso (then considered a part of New Mexico), but in the main the friars had reached the limits of their expansion into New Mexico in fray Alonso's day. Their spiritual conquest of the Pueblos had proceeded with remarkable speed, but with a thoroughness that would prove illusory.[31] Meanwhile, using Spain and the Antilles as their bases, Franciscans had begun a similar process of converting natives on the Atlantic coast, long before Benavides urged that strategy on the king.

[handwritten margin note: Natives act as if convert but not in reality]

[27] Donahue, "Mary of Agreda," 309–13, and Kendrick, *Mary of Agreda*, 46–55.
[28] See Wagner, *Spanish Southwest*, 2:342–56.
[29] Donahue, "Mary of Agreda," 313–14.
[30] Kendrick, *Mary of Agreda*, 19, mentions her early fasting and visions. See Rudolph M. Bell, *Holy Anorexia* (Chicago: University of Chicago Press, 1985), and Caroline Walker Bynum, *Holy Feast and Holy Fast: The Religious Significance of Food to Medieval Women* (Berkeley: University of California Press, 1987), which raises subtle questions about the relationship between anorexia and saintly behavior.
[31] Bloom, ed. and trans., "Fray Estevan de Perea's *Relación*," 223, 230; Timmons, *El Paso*, 15–16; Spicer, *Cycles of Conquest*, 158, 162. Franciscan historians regard the period 1625–40 as the "golden age" of the New Mexico missions (Espinosa, "Our Debt," 84). See, too, Lynch, "Introduction" to *Benavides' Memorial of 1630*, xx, who uses the term *golden age* for New Mexico in Benavides's time. Scholes, *Troublous Times*, 195, noted that "From 1632 on, there was a definitive slowing down of the mission program."

II

A generation before the Franciscans began to minister to the Pueblos of New Mexico, friars had already established themselves in southeastern America. In the humid, low-lying areas of what is today Florida, Georgia, South Carolina, and Alabama, but what was then known simply as Florida, Franciscans labored without noting the aid of a miraculous nun. They too, however, reported supernatural assistance, including the appearance of the Lady of the Rosary in the form of a bluish light. They also reported rapid success at mission building, and they continued to expand their operations in Florida long after the New Mexico enterprise had reached its peak.[32]

The first Franciscans arrived in Florida in 1573, the year after the Jesuits who came with Menéndez de Avilés had left.[33] Between 1566 and 1572, Florida had been the scene of the first Jesuit proselytizing in Spanish America. Jesuits had built ten missions at sites ranging from Virginia, near present Jamestown, to south Florida at present Miami, and up to Tampa on the Gulf coast, but they met such fierce Indian resistance that they gave up on the area as a lost cause.[34] The Franciscans persisted. Beginning a sustained, large-scale program in 1595, the friars' missions steadily expanded. As in central Mexico and New Mexico, the Franciscans established themselves in existing villages. By 1655, seventy Franciscans served in Florida (the high for that century), and ministered to 26,000 natives, a claim that some historians find exaggerated. Twenty years later, in 1675, the Franciscans reached the high point of their territorial expansion in Florida. Although the number of friars had diminished to forty, and they had retrenched on the Atlantic coast, the Florida missions extended westward over 250 miles beyond St. Augustine.[35]

By 1675, Spanish Florida had come to comprise four mission provinces: Guale, Timucua, Apalachee, and the short-lived Apalachicola.[36] Each province corresponded to the friars' understanding of a distinctive zone of Indian culture. Yet whatever differences the friars perceived, these native peoples seemed to share a great many characteristics common to southeastern Indians, including social organization, culture, and language (all, with

[32] For examples of padres' descriptions of magical events, see Oré, *Martyrs of Florida,* 102–3, 113–14, 115, and Covington, ed., *Pirates, Indians and Spaniards,* 130–31. The episode of the bluish light is in Bushnell, "Archaeology of Mission Santa Catalina."

[33] Geiger, *Franciscan Conquest of Florida,* 32–33.

[34] Zubillaga, *La Florida,* 388–90, gives Indians substantial credit for the Jesuit withdrawal.

[35] Matter, "Spanish Missions of Florida," 106, 117, 122, 345 *n.* 47, has made the most careful study of the statistics for these years yet finds them "confusing and incomplete." Most writers see 1675 as the high point of missionary activity in Florida (ibid., 340–41 *n.* 6); Gannon, *Cross in the Sand,* 57, 66–67.

[36] Wenhold, ed. and trans., *Letter of Gabriel Díaz,* contains a facsimile of the bishop's letter of 1675 to Queen Mariana, which is the source of much of the following description. Florida and New Mexico lacked resident bishops; none visited New Mexico until 1760; two bishops inspected Florida in the 1600s, the first in 1606.

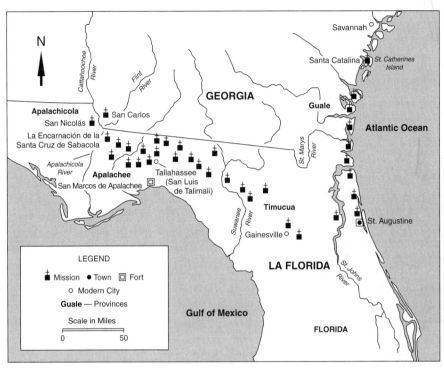

Missions in Spanish Florida, circa 1674–75.

the possible exception of the Timucuans, spoke Muskhogean languages, although those languages were mutually unintelligible).[37] Most lived in small,
scattered towns with circular public plazas that also served as ball courts.
These towns generally held a variety of circular buildings with dome-
shaped roofs of palm thatch: communal store houses, large public meeting
halls called *buhíos,* and private residences with their own outbuildings for
storage.[38] Most cultivated corn, beans, and other crops and supplemented
their diet by hunting, fishing, and gathering. The Guales, who had lived
along the inland waterway and sea islands of the Georgia and South Carolina coasts, and the coastal dwelling Timucuans may have reversed the emphasis, migrating seasonally to fish, hunt, and gather, and supplementing
those activities with farming.[39]

[37] On Muskhogean and the bewildering changes of nomenclature and ethnicity among Southeastern Indians, see Wright, *Creeks and Seminoles.* For the identity of Timucuan languages, see
Milanich, "Western Timucua," 61–62.
[38] Milanich and Fairbanks, *Florida Archaeology,* 216–30, provides an authoritative overview.
[39] Scholars once doubted that Indians in Guale dwelled in villages or engaged in significant agriculture, but current archaeological work has tended to place the Guale in the larger traditions that
I describe, although the extent of their sedentism remains uncertain. See Jones, "Ethnohistory of

In 1674–75, at this zenith of Franciscan expansion, Gabriel Díaz Vara Calderón, the bishop of Cuba under whose jurisdiction Florida fell, inspected Florida's four mission provinces. One leg of his arduous tour took him northward by sea from St. Augustine to the missions that dotted the coastal plain and islands of present-day Georgia—the Province of Guale. Franciscans had begun to evangelize among the Guale-speaking Indians in the 1570s. By the mid-seventeenth century they had expanded their mission chain beyond Guale into present South Carolina, which they called the Province of Orista. By 1660, however, Indians had forced the Franciscans to retreat from Orista to the south of the Savannah River, into Guale.[40] Traveling "among shoals, bars, and rivers," Bishop Díaz visited eight missions in Guale—two were in Timucua villages. European diseases had taken a toll. The largest of the missions, Santa Catalina, held 140 neophytes, but Christian Indians numbered only 40 in most of these missions.[41] On the surface, life in Guale seemed tranquil, and Spain had only token military force in the area. At the most northerly Guale village, on what is today Saint Catherine's Island, some 150 miles beyond St. Augustine and 25 miles south of present Savannah, Spain maintained a small garrison as well as the mission of Santa Catalina.[42]

Close to St. Augustine, Bishop Díaz toured the Province of Timucua. When Spaniards first encountered them, Timucuans comprised at least fifteen different tribes with communities scattered over a small portion of southeastern Georgia and the northern third of the Florida peninsula, westward nearly to the Gulf coast. Beginning in the 1570s Franciscans established several missions near St. Augustine among coastal-dwelling, or Eastern Timucuans, who had adapted to the coastal marshes, barrier islands, and pinewoods as far inland as the St. Johns River. In the early 1600s, beginning with the work of the vigorous fray Martín Prieto among the Potano peoples near present Gainesville, Franciscans became a permanent presence among the Western Timucuans of the forests and fields of central Florida.[43] By 1674,

the Guale Coast," 178–210. For recent archaeological advances in understanding what he terms "The Guale Problem" see Thomas, "Archaeology of Mission Santa Catalina de Guale," 57–64.

[40] Matter, "Spanish Missions of Florida," 108. Guale was the last province on the bishop's itinerary. To facilitate the reader's understanding of the chronological development of the missions, I have placed it first.

[41] Survey of Guale by Pedro de Arcos, in Boyd, trans. and ed., "Enumeration of Florida Spanish Missions," 182–84, which provide more specific population figures than did the bishop. Not all natives counted by Arcos were mission Indians. In several villages he distinguishes between "men, women and children and pagans."

[42] For the apparent tranquility of the Guale missions at this time, and their language differences, see Pearson, "Arguelles Inspection of Guale," 210–22. Lanning, *Spanish Missions of Georgia,* remains the standard account of the Georgia missions, but the subject merits a fresh study that will incorporate recent historical and archaeological research and move beyond Lanning's pro-Franciscan interpretation.

[43] Prieto's own account of these years is in Oré, *Martyrs of Florida,* 112–19. For the larger context, see Geiger, *Franciscan Conquest of Florida,* 227–29. Little is known about Prieto, and biographical

when Bishop Díaz made his inspection, a trail of eleven Franciscan Timucua missions extended west from St. Augustine along a trail that skirted swamps, crossed savannas, and penetrated forests of live oak draped with Spanish moss. But epidemics of European diseases had swept away most of the Timucuans. Perhaps as few as 1,330 remained in the missions in 1675.[44]

Beyond the westernmost Timucuan towns, Bishop Díaz pushed across the mosquito-infested peninsula, beyond the Aucilla River into the Florida panhandle and the lands of the Apalachee, known to Spaniards since Pánfilo de Narváez and Hernando de Soto had made themselves unwelcome visitors. An armed escort of Spanish infantry and two companies of Indians kept the bishop secure from Chiscas and Chichimecos—the latter a Mexican name that Spaniards appropriated and applied to marauding barbarians in northern Mexico as well as Florida.[45] These natives, the bishop believed, had little other ambition in life than to roast and eat hapless captives. Some 98 winding leagues (255 miles) from St. Augustine by his reckoning, the bishop arrived at the heartland of Apalachee—a fertile farmland of red clay hills that supported the most intensive native agriculture in Florida and the densest native population.[46] Near what is today Tallahassee, he found the great ceremonial center of the Apalachees—a people who spoke Hitchiti, a Muskhogean language that survives today among some Seminoles.

Franciscans had preached in Apalachee as early as 1608, when the peripatetic Martin Prieto visited this prosperous people, who were reputedly superb warriors. The first Franciscan visitors did little more than erect crosses in the natives' villages, however, and then move on. A shortage of missionaries and the problems of moving supplies across the peninsula from St. Augustine had discouraged the friars from establishing a permanent presence. So, too, had the absence of military support. "Moved by the devil," as Father Prieto put it, the Indians might mistreat the priests or "take away their lives," and the king would be "obliged" to punish them.[47] Not until 1633 did Franciscans take up permanent residence in Apalachee. Then, Spaniards hoped that the natives and the natives' prosperous farms would alleviate the chronic labor and food shortages at St. Augustine and offset the liabilities of such distant operations.

---

information regarding the padres who served in early Florida is scanty. Compare, e.g., the brief entries in Geiger, *Biographical Dictionary,* with the relatively full entries in Geiger's *Franciscan Missionaries.*

[44] Survey of the missions of Apalachee and Timucua by Juan Fernández de Florencia, in Boyd, trans. and ed., "Enumeration of Florida Spanish Missions," 186–88.

[45] Hann, *Apalachee,* 185 *n.* 6, 401–2.

[46] The Díaz league was 2.6 miles (Matter, "Spanish Missions of Florida," 348 *n.* 65). By what may be a more direct route, the distance today from St. Augustine to Tallahassee is 205 miles.

[47] Prieto in Oré, *Martyrs of Florida,* 118; Geiger, *Franciscan Conquest of Florida,* 229–30. The most authoritative account of the establishment of the *Apalachee* missions is Hann, *Apalachee,* 5–23.

By the 1670s the Apalachee missions seemed the most prosperous and populous of the Florida mission provinces, containing at least eight thousand baptized Indians—perhaps 75 percent of the mission Indian population in the four provinces of Florida.[48] Bishop Díaz inspected all eleven missions in Apalachee in 1674, and he himself founded two more. At the largest of the Apalachee mission towns, San Luis de Talimali, on a hilltop within the limits of present-day Tallahassee, the bishop entered a community of some fourteen hundred residents. At one end of the town a massive circular council house served as a place for public meetings and dances. As a public space, it dwarfed the nearby church—and every other church Spaniards built in Florida. San Luis, the bishop learned, also had a small garrison inhabited by a few soldiers and their families—the only Hispanic outpost west of St. Augustine in Spanish Florida. Nearby, in the late 1670s, Spaniards would build a rude fort, San Marcos de Apalachee, on the Gulf near the mouth of the St. Marks River where, a century and a half before, Cabeza de Vaca and the Narváez expedition had built their horsehide barges to flee the region. The fort of San Marcos de Apalachee was to protect the principal river route into Apalachee from pirates, but pirates soon destroyed it.[49]

Beyond Apalachee, Bishop Díaz traveled still farther west—some twenty-six leagues or sixty-eight miles—to inspect missions in Apalachicola, the most tenuous of the four Franciscan provinces of Florida. Missionary labors had begun there just months before, as Spanish officials sought to build a barrier against Englishmen pushing toward the Gulf of Mexico from their base in South Carolina. In 1674, in what is today southwestern Alabama and southeastern Georgia, above where the Chattahoochee and Flint rivers merge to form the Apalachicola River, Franciscans had built the missions of San Nicolás and San Carlos in two villages of Chacatos (whom Englishmen would call Choctaws). Nearby among the Apalachicolas (later known to the English as the Lower Creeks), Bishop Díaz established a third mission, La Encarnación de la Santa Cruz de Sabacola, in February 1675. Before the year was out, the Chacatos rebelled and abandoned their villages; two years later, Franciscans abandoned the mission that Bishop Díaz had founded.[50]

---

[48] Survey of the missions of Apalachee and Timucua by Juan Fernández de Florencia, in Boyd, trans. and ed., "Enumeration of Florida Spanish Missions," 184–86, suggests over eight thousand, but as Fernández noted, "I have not taken a census and they die daily, for which reason I have said a little more or less" (188). The figure may be much higher. Bushnell, "'That Demonic Game,'" 4, suggests ten thousand.

[49] San Luis de Talimali, 2.5 miles west of the State Capitol, is presently under excavation by the Florida Bureau of Archaeological Research and is open to the public. The diameter of the council house is 36 meters (Shapiro and Hann, "Documentary Image of the Council Houses," 519), while mission chapels did not exceed 26 by 13 meters (Jones and Shapiro, "Nine Mission Sites," 504, and Saunders, "Ideal and Innovation," 527–42). For San Marcos, see Bushnell, "How to Fight a Pirate."

[50] For the most up-to-date account of the founding and demise of these Apalachicola missions, see Hann, *Apalachee,* 47–50, 183–84.

The Franciscan failure in Apalachicola was not unusual. Attempts to convert Calusas, Tocobagas, and other tribes in the southern two-thirds of the peninsula had also failed—and would continue to fail, and north of the St. Augustine-Apalachee road the Chichimecos and Chiscas resisted conversion.[51] Nonetheless, the bishop must have been impressed that so few Franciscans had cut such a wide swath up the Atlantic coast and across Florida. Altogether during his ten-month tour of the four provinces of Florida, he had counted thirty-six churches staffed by some forty Franciscans. By his own reckoning, Bishop Díaz administered the rite of confirmation to 13,152 Indians.[52] He had found the converted Indians "weak and phlegmatic as regards work," but "clever and quick to learn." Like Benavides in New Mexico, he glowingly described the neophytes as devoted Christians who attended the ritual of the Mass on Sundays and all holy days and contributed to the support of the priest: "They are not idolaters, and they embrace with devotion the mysteries of our holy faith."[53] Unmolested by pagan Chiscas and Chichimecos, Bishop Díaz traveled back to St. Augustine the way he had come and then returned to Havana where he soon died. His strenuous journey, it was said, had weakened his health.

III

On the southern fringes of seventeenth-century North America, then, a small number of Spanish preachers—seldom exceeding fifty at a time in either Florida or New Mexico—made rapid inroads into the communal and individual lives of large numbers of natives.[54] Alone, or with the aid of a single companion and a small military escort, a Franciscan moved into an Indian community and persuaded the residents to construct a temple to an alien

---

[51] Matter, "Spanish Missions of Florida," 110–11, 116; Matter, "Missions in the Defense of Spanish Florida," 32. Sturtevant, "Last of the South Florida Aborigines," 141–62, recounts a Jesuit attempt to build a mission at present Miami in 1743.

[52] Since children did not usually receive this sacrament, the mission population of Florida may have exceeded this number. On the other hand, a rough estimate of the population of three main mission provinces (excluding Apalachicola), authorized by Gov. Pablo de Hita Salazar in 1675, suggested fewer Christian Indians—somewhat more than 10,000 (Boyd, trans. and ed., "Enumeration of Florida Spanish Missions," 182). Disparities between the statistics developed by Franciscans and civil officials were not unusual.

[53] Both quotes are in Wenhold, ed. and trans., *Letter of Gabriel Díaz*, 12.

[54] See, e.g., Spicer, *Cycles of Conquest*, 167, who compares the rapid imposition of the mission program on the Pueblos with the more gradual missionization in northwestern Mexico. The Crown apparently authorized as many as seventy friars for Florida, but the actual number usually stayed below fifty (Matter, "Spanish Missions of Florida," 417–18). In New Mexico, sixty-six was apparently the highest number authorized in the 1600s, a number seldom reached (Scholes, *Troublous Times*, 9).

god. Among the Pueblos of New Mexico and the natives of the four provinces of Florida, whose largest enclosed public spaces had been circular kivas or council houses, the Franciscans oversaw the construction of small, rectangular, fortress-like churches.

These foreign priests persuaded numerous Indians to participate in Christian rituals and, at the least, to take on some of the external attributes of Spanish Christians. At mission schools, adults and children learned the rudiments of Catholic doctrine—set prayers and rote answers to questions in a catechism. Some students reportedly learned so well that they, in turn, taught the catechism. Franciscans also instructed natives in the singing of Christian hymns and playing of European musical instruments in honor of the Christian's single deity. Indians learned to participate in the Catholic ceremony of the Mass, where Indian boys assisted the priests at the altar. In the earliest mission schools, some boys and girls as well as adults of both sexes apparently took instruction in reading and writing. A few became literate in Spanish and others in their own language. Like lower-class Spaniards of the era, however, most natives mastered the recitation of prayers without knowing how to read or write.[55]

Franciscans also altered native societies in ways that had nothing to do with Christianity but everything to do with living in civilized or European fashion—living *políticamente* as fray Alonso de Benavides and his contemporaries would have put it.[56] For many of the Spanish padres, like their English and French counterparts, it seemed plain that a people could not become Christians unless they also lived like Christians. Christian doctrine and social behavior were inextricably linked in the minds of Spaniards, who had also sought to make converts from Islam dress, cook, eat, walk, and talk like Spaniards. Only if natives lived like Spaniards would they move upward on the hierarchical scale of mankind, from barbarism to the apex that Europeans believed they occupied. Given that premise, missionaries concluded that they had "to deal a body-blow at the whole structure of native society," as one Franciscan historian has explained.[57] The Spanish Crown presented the scenario in the Royal Orders for New Discoveries of

---

[55] For the Provinces of Florida, reports of Indians adopting the outward manifestations of Christianity come from several sources, including Bishop Díaz, who was no friend of the Franciscans (Wenhold, ed. and trans., *Letter of Gabriel Díaz*, 14). See, too, the account of Francisco Pareja, ca. 1616, in Oré, *Martyrs of Florida*, 126–29. Barth, *Franciscan Education*, 135–57, sees a shift away from compulsory reading and writing toward more vocational education in eighteenth-century Texas and California. For prayer and literacy in Spain, see Bennassar, *Spanish Character*, 73.

[56] Benavides, *Memorial . . . 1630*, 19.

[57] Barth, *Franciscan Education*, 339. For the sixteenth-century development of the idea of a hierarchical classification of mankind see John Rowe, "Ethnography and Ethnology in the Sixteenth Century," *Kroeber Anthropology Society Papers* 30 (1964): 1–19; Elliott, "Discovery of America," 53.

1573. Indians who swore obedience to Spain and accepted missionaries were to be taught

> to live in a civilized manner, clothed and wearing shoes . . . given the use of bread and wine and oil and many other essentials of life—bread, silk, linen, horses, cattle, tools, and weapons, and all the rest that Spain has had. Instructed in the trades and skills with which they might live richly.[58]

Depending on climate, soils, and local needs, missionaries in Florida and New Mexico taught native converts to husband European domestic animals—horses, cattle, sheep, goats, pigs, and chickens; cultivate European crops, from watermelon to wheat; raise fruit trees, from peaches to pomegranates; use such iron tools as wheels, saws, chisels, planes, nails, and spikes; and practice those arts and crafts that Spaniards regarded as essential for civilization as they knew it.[59] Variations in native tolerance and the availability of goods from Spain helped determine the level and pace of instruction. A century after Franciscans had begun to preach in Florida, for example, Bishop Díaz counted no fewer than 4,081 neophyte women who still lacked "proper" clothing. They were "naked from the waist up and the knees down" and he ordered them to cover the rest of their bodies in a local fabric made of Spanish moss. The friars lacked not only the silks and linens that the Crown spoke of as "essentials of life," but cotton and weavers as well.[60]

Although the rate of success varied with time and place, it seems remarkable in retrospect that a small number of Franciscans managed to direct changes in the external and internal lives of many Indians. How does one account for the steady expansion of the friars' missionary programs in New Mexico and Florida? Perhaps, as Franciscans believed, divine intervention played a role, but more worldly explanations suggest themselves: the zeal and skill of the Franciscans, the powerful economic and bureaucratic

---

[58] "Ordenanzas . . . para los nuevos descubrimientos, conquistas y pacificaciones," July 13, 1573, in *CDI*(1), 16:183. The "civilizing function of typical Spanish mission" is a central theme in the seminal essay by Bolton, "Mission as a Frontier Institution," 206. Ricard, *Spiritual Conquest of Mexico*, 290, writing of the first decades of missionization in Mexico, notes that Franciscans "would not countenance any attempt to Hispanize or Europeanize the natives," but he means this in a very restricted way. The Crown and the Franciscans had a different agenda by the late sixteenth century.

[59] Schroeder, "Rio Grande Ethnohistory," 50; Kubler, *Religious Architecture of New Mexico*, 8; Milanich and Fairbanks, *Florida Archaeology*, 226; Hann, *Apalachee*, 239, 241–42. It is easy to overstate the extent of Franciscan instruction. Some writers, for example, have incorrectly credited friars with teaching Pueblos to make fireplaces, beehive ovens, and sun-dried adobe bricks; for a corrective, see Dozier, *Pueblo Indians*, 65.

[60] Wenhold, ed. and trans., *Letter of Gabriel Díaz*, 12. See, too, Benavides, *Memorial . . . 1630*, 20, 21, 22, 23. An Englishman whose ship was wrecked on the Florida coast described Indians at the mission of Santa Catalina on Amelia Island in 1696 wearing "gowns and petticoats" of Spanish moss, "which at a distance or in the night look very neat" (Andrews and Andrews, *Jonathan Dickinson's Journal*, 67). For the shortage of cotton and cotton cloth, see Hann, ed. and trans., "Alonso de Leturiondo's Memorial," 178.

apparatus of church and state that supported them, and the natives themselves, who decided when and how they would cooperate with the Christians.

IV

The Franciscans' work in North America coincided with a general decline in clerical fervor in the Hispanic world, but many of the missionaries who served on the fringes of Spain's empire, whatever their religious order, went prepared to make great sacrifices in the new lands. Some wore hair shirts, walked barefoot, or flagellated themselves. All sacrificed a way of life, "voluntarily depriving ourselves," as one Franciscan explained, "of our homes and loved ones in the solitude of the forest, destitute, without enjoyment, comforts, medical aid in sickness and accident, and without the company of others like us."[61] "Beyond a doubt they eat their bread in sorrow in these places," wrote one visitor to Florida.[62] Some preachers seemed eager to make the ultimate earthly sacrifice, believing that martyrdom would guarantee them a favorable place in an eternal afterlife. "The thought of dying for Jesus burned in his heart like a spark of fire," one Franciscan wrote of a colleague in Florida.[63] Some who sought martyrdom had their wish fulfilled.

Along with extraordinary dedication, Franciscans brought to North America a number of shrewd strategies for imposing Christianity upon native peoples. Refined through decades of experience, some of these strategies had proved so effective that the Crown had mandated their use in the Royal Orders for New Discoveries of 1573, and they remained popular with religious orders for over two centuries throughout the Spanish empire.[64]

[61] Matter, "Spanish Missions of Florida," 129, quoting a manuscript "Testimony and complaints by the provincial and definitors to the Governor of Florida," May-June, 1681. See, too, Oré, *Martyrs of Florida*, 130–31, and Benavides, *Memorial . . . 1630*, 66. Examples of Franciscan sacrifice abound; see the description of fray Blas de Montes in Oré, *Martyrs of Florida*, 66. For the decline in the vigor of the Church and the clergy, see Bennassar, *Spanish Character*, 80–85. That decline apparently contributed to the Franciscans' failure to fill the quota of seventy that the king provided for in Florida and was perhaps reflected, too, in a decline in the quality of Franciscans in Florida, as suggested by Matter, "Spanish Missions of Florida," 108–9, 118.

[62] Juan de las Cabezas, Bishop of Cuba, to the king, St. Augustine, Florida, June 24, 1606, in Cabezas, "First Episcopal Visitation," 457, who also alluded to scandalous conduct of some Franciscans.

[63] Covington, ed., *Pirates, Indians and Spaniards*, 126.

[64] "Ordenanzas . . . para los nuevos descubrimientos, conquistas y pacificaciones," July 1573, in *CDI*(1), 16:182–85, 186. For methods used by mendicants in New Spain in the first half century of missionization, see Ricard, *Spiritual Conquest*, 167–68, 176–93, and a Franciscan historian who draws many examples from New Spain, Gómez Canedo, *Evangelización*, 147–214: "Métodos y Medios de Evangelización." Borges, *Métodos misionales*, examined the methods of all religious orders in the sixteenth century. Notwithstanding the broad scope suggested by its title, Barth, another Franciscan historian, focuses largely on sixteenth-century New Spain in his *Franciscan Education*. The methods of converting Indians and maintaining them in missions that I describe here for Florida and New Mexico continued to be used in Alta California in the late eighteenth and early nineteenth centuries. See McGarry, "Educational Methods," 335–58. See, too, Polzer,

In the initial entrada or *misión* stage, Franciscans often sought to dazzle natives with showy vestments, music, paintings, statuary of sacred images, and ceremonies. They often won native people over with gifts, such as hawks' bells, glass beads, hatchets, knives, scissors, cloth, and clothing. As a missionary in Florida explained, "this world is the route to the other . . . gifts can break rocks." Gifts of food were especially effective and brought some Indians "like fish to the fish hook," one Franciscan in New Mexico exclaimed.[65] In many Indian societies, as among many Spaniards of that day, the acceptance of gifts established a sense of obligation and reciprocity.[66]

Once they won the confidence of a group of natives, Franciscans attempted to bring about conversions. In Florida and New Mexico in the seventeenth century, the friars concentrated on the time-honored strategy of insinuating themselves into existing communities of sedentary natives. In indigenous towns where they chose to reside, Franciscans persuaded the natives to build friaries or *conventos* for priests, and temples that the Christians called *iglesias* or churches. Urban centers gave Franciscans access to the greatest concentrations of natives, and they extended their influence to nearby towns by employing the *cabecera-visita* system that they used in central Mexico. Towns where friars resided became the head, or *cabecera*, of mission districts. Like later-day circuit riders, but often on foot, friars regularly toured nearby villages, which they termed *visitas*, thus increasing the scope of their native congregations, or *doctrinas*.[67]

Rules and Precepts, 39–58, who describes Jesuit methods, with some attention to Franciscans. The general strategy that he describes seems applicable to both orders. Spicer, *Cycles of Conquest*, 281–83, 288–98, 324–31, offers an interesting overview of missionary methods, contrasting the work of Jesuits in Pimería Alta and Franciscans in New Mexico, but it should be remembered that Jesuits began mission building in that area a century later than the Franciscans. Dominicans followed similar procedures. See, too, Felix M. Kesing, *The Ethnohistory of Northern Luzon* (Stanford: Stanford University Press, 1962), 224–26, 242–60.

[65] The first quote is from Dominican Gregorio Beteta, 1549, who accompanied Luis Cáncer to Florida, quoted in Quinn, ed., *New American World*, 2:192; the second from *Testimonio* of fray Salvador de Guerra, Jan. 23, 1668, in Scholes, ed. and trans., "Documents for the History of the New Mexican Missions," 199–200. Examples of gifts come from those distributed to the Hopis in 1629, Bloom, ed. and trans., "Fray Estevan de Perea's *Relación,*" 232, and from Wenhold, ed. and trans., *Letter of Gabriel Díaz,* 13. Beginning in the late 1700s, Franciscans in California took pains not to baptize more Indians than they could feed. See Coombs and Plog, "Conversion of the Chumash Indians," 309–28.

[66] Gutiérrez, *When Jesus Came,* 9; MacLachlin, *Spain's Empire,* 23.

[67] To avoid confusion for the modern reader, I have generally used the familiar term *mission* as a synonym for *doctrina*. In seventeenth-century Florida and New Mexico, the terms had different meanings. A *misión* represented the initial stage of evangelizing; a *doctrina* represented an established Indian parish, including both *cabecera* and *visita* and presided over by a Franciscan *doctrinero*. Polzer, *Rules and Precepts,* 4–5, 47, identifies three stages of a mission's development: *entrada, conversión,* and *doctrina,* culminating with a secular phase—the *parroquia* or parish. The terminology employed by contemporaries, however, changed over time. In the eighteenth century, missionaries avoided the term *doctrina,* for once a mission became classified as a doctrina, or an Indian parish, it had taken the first step toward secularization (wherein Indians were no longer exempt from paying tithes and would be brought under episcopal control). See, e.g., Guest, *Fermín Francisco de Lasuén,* 141–42. By the eighteenth century, fray Diego Bringas noted, a

The spiritual success of missions required that Indians live in towns, within the sound of the mission bell and the reach of the sacraments, and the "civilization" of Indians required that they follow the Spanish ideal of urban life.[68] In Florida and New Mexico, missionaries found ample Indians already living in towns. On occasion, the friars tried to relocate sedentary natives in order to increase the size of towns, make them more defensible, and minimize travel to distant visitas. In general, however, the Franciscans in Florida and New Mexico did not need to devote energy and resources to congregating or "reducing" dispersed natives into towns, or *reducciones*, as they had done earlier in the Caribbean and in central New Spain, and as they would do again in eighteenth-century Texas or California.[69]

In all stages of a mission's development, gifts, ceremony, and showy display remained important. Although most frontier churches were plain compared to their Gothic counterparts in the Caribbean and central Mexico, Franciscans in Florida and New Mexico adorned the interiors of their modest chapels with as much religious treasure as circumstances allowed. At its dedication in 1668, for example, the church of Nuestra Señora de Guadalupe in El Paso contained several paintings and statues, including one of the Virgin of Guadalupe, "dressed in flowered silk and a silver crown," and silver wine goblets, a silver plate and spoon, and three chalices probably made of precious metal.[70] In the Florida missions, an inventory taken in 1681 reveals an extraordinary quantity of costly solid silver vessels for a poor area and an excessive number of vestments, paintings, and statues by present-day standards. In Apalachee alone, religious articles valued 2,500 pesos per town by the 1680s—"more than a single Indian could earn in a lifetime of work at the king's wages," one historian has calculated.[71]

---

misión and a conversión had become "essentially the same institution" (Matson and Fontana, eds. and trans., *Friar Bringas*, 47, 43). Bringas also objected vigorously to reclassifying the Pimería Alta missions as doctrinas.

[68] Bushnell, "Sacramental Imperative," 475–90; Elliott, "Discovery of America," 54–55.

[69] Gannon, *Cross in the Sand*, 34–35; Zubillaga, *La Florida*, 378–80, and Oré, *Martyrs of Florida*, 119. Hann, "Demographic Patterns," 371, finds no evidence that friars used reducciones in Florida. Some entire towns, however, were moved to bring Indians nearer to the *camino real* (Spellman [pseud., Gannon], "'Golden Age' of the Florida Missions," 365). In New Mexico, Governor Peralta arrived with instructions in 1609 to concentrate Pueblos into fewer and larger villages, but this seems to have occurred only at Jémez (Scholes, *Church and State*, 20–21). Kubler, *Religious Architecture of New Mexico*, 16–17, is insightful on this point. In New Mexico, Franciscans tried but generally failed to missionize nomads in the seventeenth century (Gómez Canedo, *Evangelización*, 107–12).

[70] *Testimonio* of fray Salvador de Guerra, Jan. 23, 1668, in Scholes, ed. and trans., "Documents for the History of the New Mexican Missions," 198–99. See, too, the inventory of goods that the mission supply caravan brought to New Mexico in 1629, described in Bloom [ed. and trans.], "Fray Estevan Perea's *Relación*," 219–20.

[71] Bushnell, "Ruling 'the Republic of Indians,'" 142. For the 1681 inventory and an analysis of it, see Hann, "Church Furnishings," 147–64, and Hann, *Apalachee*, 213–16, who takes exception to Bushnell's calculations. Although one might quibble over the arithmetic, her point, I believe, is valid.

Extrapolating from their knowledge of European societies, Franciscans made a special effort to win the allegiance of native leaders, assuming that if they won over the "natural lord" of a native group they would also gain the loyalty of the lord's vassals. Thus, friars worked through the existing native power structure, including some women *caciques*, or chiefs, in Timucua and Guale. The friars replaced recalcitrant leaders with more pliant figures as the need arose and sought to put themselves at the apex of Indian political leadership—although they often failed to understand the nature of native politics.[72]

The opportunistic Franciscans also directed their attention to the conversion of children, whom they perceived to be more malleable than adults. Once the celibate missionary fathers had made Indian children their own, they enlisted their aid in converting others and in discrediting the beliefs and undermining the authority of obdurate members of the older generation, including native religious leaders. "Nourished by the milk of the gospel" as one Florida friar put it, young people often ridiculed their elders with enthusiasm.[73] As the elders lost influence and the native social structure began to fracture, the power of the padres and their youthful neophytes grew accordingly.[74]

As they had on earlier frontiers, many Franciscans became linguists and ethnographers in order to facilitate conversion and instruction and perhaps to fulfill the Crown's requirement that all missionaries learn native languages (a regulation that proved impossible to enforce).[75] Throughout Spain's long tenure in North America, some Franciscans recorded native languages and a few published the results. The linguistically talented Francisco de Pareja, for example, prepared a Castilian-Timucuan catechism and a confessional, both published in Mexico City. These imprints, the first of which appeared at least as early as 1612, may constitute "the earliest surviving texts in any North American Indian language" according to one study (Timucuan-speakers spoke different dialects but shared a common language, one that

[72] Gómez Canedo, *Evangelización*, 86–89; Bushnell, "Ruling 'the Republic of Indians,'" 139. For the use of women caciques, see Deagan, "Spanish-Indian Interaction," 299. Dozier, *Pueblo Indians*, 68, notes that the Pueblos established a "dual system of government," wherein "a set of secular officers served as a convenient facade behind which the more important and vital organization of native priests carried out the social and religious functions of the pueblo." Similarly in Florida, Hann, *Apalachee*, 101 n. 2, cites anthropologist Gary Shapiro's suggestion that the persons Spaniards believed were in charge were simply ambitious persons posing as leaders in order to advance their own interests. See, too, ibid., 110–12.

[73] Oré, *Martyrs of Florida*, 106.

[74] Richard C. Trexler, "From the Mouths of Babes: Christianization by Children in 16th Century New Spain," *Religious Organization and Religious Experience*, J. Davis, ed. (New York: Academic Press, 1982), 115–35, and for New Mexico, see Gutiérrez, *When Jesus Came*, 74–84. For Florida, see Pedro Menéndez Márques to the Audiencia of Santo Domingo, St. Augustine, Apr. 2, 1579, in Connor, ed., *Colonial Records of Spanish Florida*, 2:227.

[75] See, e.g., the law of Mar. 8, 1603, in the *Recopilación de leyes*, tomo I, lib. I, tit. XV, ley v, which makes it obligatory for doctrineros to learn Indian languages. See, too, Bolton, "Mission as a Frontier Institution," 203–4, and Schuetz, "Indians of the San Antonio Missions," 234.

remains poorly understood).⁷⁶ More important, these bilingual texts, which often reveal considerable knowledge of the beliefs and customs of Indian peoples, facilitated the Franciscans' efforts to enter into the private worlds of the natives without the intermediary of a translator—to redefine Indians' values and to alter their rituals and their sexual behavior. A priest using Pareja's *confesionario* could, for example, ask in Timucuan:

"Have you said suggestive words?"

"Have you shown some part of your body to arouse in some person desires of lust or to excite them?"

"Have you desired to . . . do some lewd act with some man or woman or kin?"

"Have you had intercourse with someone contrary to the ordinary manner?"⁷⁷

Father Pareja's bilingual catechism and *confesionario* were not unique in Spanish North America. Franciscans in Texas and California continued to produce religious primers in native languages until late in the eighteenth century. Few were printed, for the variety of native languages and the relatively small number of native speakers of any single language made publication impractical.⁷⁸ Published or in manuscript, however, these aids must have been highly valued by priests, and perhaps by a few laymen as well. By the 1630s an Indian trader in New Mexico, Nicolás de Aguilar, had acquired a copy of Pareja's Castilian-Timucuan catechism. Given the Spaniards' hazy knowledge of North American geography, it seems likely that Aguilar expected to find the Timucuan vocabulary useful should his business take him beyond the Great Plains into Florida.⁷⁹

⁷⁶ Milanich and Sturtevant, eds., *Pareja's 1613 Confessionario*, 15. The editors make it clear that Pareja was not the only Franciscan in Florida to record texts in Timucuan, and the work of at least one other padre has survived (7–8). By 1572 Franciscans in New Spain had prepared at least eighty literary works in native languages—catechisms, grammars, dictionaries (usually copied by hand rather than printed) (Ricard, *Spiritual Conquest of Mexico*, 48). For Timucuan, see Milanich, "Western Timucua," 61–62.
⁷⁷ Milanich and Sturtevant, eds., *Pareja's 1613 Confessionario*, 36, 38.
⁷⁸ For Texas, see García, *Manual para administrar los santos sacramentos*, a Castilian-Coauiltecan manual. For California, see Kelsey, ed. and trans., *Doctrina and Confesionario of Juan Cortés*, who cites four other bilingual manuscripts for California (3–4). No bilingual aid to instructing California natives appears to have been published at the time, but manuscript booklets such as that of Father Cortés (1798) probably existed at every mission, Kelsey believes. Among lists of extant books from New Mexico missions, no volume in a Pueblo language is cited. See, e.g., Adams and Scholes, "Books in New Mexico, 1598–1680," 226–70. Contemporaries in New Mexico, including one Franciscan, noted that written grammars did not exist for any of the languages of New Mexico. See the Testimony of fray Nicolás de Freitas, Feb. 21, 1661 [Mexico], and the Report of the Rev. Father Provincial of Santo Evangelio to the viceroy, Convent of San Francisco, March 1750, in Hackett, ed., *Historical Documents*, 3:136, 442, 445. The exception may be fray Gerónimo Zárate Salmerón. See Simmons, *Authors and Books*, 24.
⁷⁹ This was apparently Pareja's *Catecismo, en Lengua Castellana, y Timuquana*. See the first hearing of Nicolás Aguilar, Mexico, Apr. 12, 1663, in Hackett, ed., *Historical Documents*, 3:139.

Notwithstanding official injunctions to learn native languages, most Franciscans apparently failed to do so. Their enthusiasm for language study seems to have waned from a high point in the first half of the sixteenth century. Some Franciscans simply lacked the talent or energy for learning other languages—a task that may have seemed counterproductive in much of North America where native languages were so numerous and where the difficulty of crossing cultural barriers with language must have become painfully evident.[80] "Words, such as God, Trinity, Person, Blessed Sacrament," as one Franciscan in New Mexico noted, needed to be taught in Castilian because Indian languages did not have "equivalent terms." Those friars who did not know the language of their converts commonly used trained translators to hear confessions and otherwise communicate.[81]

Even as the Crown urged priests to learn native languages for more effective instruction, it also urged friars to teach Castilian to natives. This would not only rescue Indians from their barbarism by making them more like Spaniards but would reduce the babble of Spain's New World domain to a common language. Governor Pedro de Peralta, for example, arrived in New Mexico in 1609 with orders from the viceroy to encourage the padres to instruct the natives in Castilian. Effective administration of New Mexico required a common language, the viceroy told the governor, because "that land is populated by a variety of nations, with very few people in each one of them, who speak various difficult and barbarous languages."[82] The extent to which the friars complied with those instructions became a matter of contention between them and civil officials. Early on, in both Florida and New Mexico, some neophytes learned to use Castilian proficiently, some reading and writing as well as speaking it, but the majority probably used it only for ceremonial occasions and religious instruction. In New Mexico, after a century and a half of exposure, some Pueblos still spoke no Castilian. Most, however, spoke it poorly but well enough that it became a *lingua franca*. The extent to which

---

[80] Borges, *Métodos misionales*, 544–50; Hann, *Apalachee*, 251; Gómez Canedo, *Evangelización*, 154–62. Although the supply of Franciscans with talent and energy to learn native languages never reached the demand, it is clearly an exaggeration to suppose (as did Bowden, *American Indians and Christian Missions*, 45, 51) that Spanish Franciscans had ceased to learn native languages by the time they reached the area of present-day North America. See, for example, Zárate Salmerón, *Relaciones*, 26; Hackett, ed., *Historical Documents*, 3:163; Kelly, *Franciscan Missions of New Mexico*, 63–64. But Franciscans in New Mexico acquired a reputation, perhaps unfairly, for reticence to learn Pueblo languages. See Adams, ed. and trans., *Bishop Tamarón's Visitation*, 18, 31, 78, who was unfriendly to Franciscans. For a fascinating look at the failure of cross-cultural communication, see Vincente L. Rafael, *Contracting Colonialism: Translation and Christian Conversion in Tagalog Society under Early Spanish Rule* (Ithaca: Cornell University Press, 1988).

[81] The quote is from Vélez de Escalante, "Letter to the Missionaries of New Mexico," 323. See also Adams, "Passive Resistance," 77–91. For the use of translators: Bloom ed. and trans., "Fray Estevan de Perea's *Relación*," 235; Hann, *Apalachee*, 107–8, 112.

[82] Viceroy Martín López de Guana, Mar. 30, 1609, to Pedro de Peralta, in Bloom and Chaves, ed. and trans., "Ynstruccion a Peralta por Vi-Rey," 184 (the translation is defective at this place).

the Pueblos acquired Spanish due to the teaching of Franciscans, or as a result of exposure to Spanish settlers remains a matter of conjecture.[83]

Paradoxically, the same padres who sought to bring Spanish culture into every corner of native life also tried to insulate Indians from what they saw as the baneful influence of Spanish laymen. Pope Pius V had reminded Pedro Menéndez de Avilés that "there is nothing more important for the conversion of those idolatrous Indians than . . . to keep them from being scandalized by the vices and bad habits of those who go to those lands from Europe,"[84] and his concern was well founded. In New Mexico, one Franciscan reported, a Pueblo Indian had asked "if we who are Christians caused so much harm and violence, why should they become Christians?"[85] In variant forms, this question would echo across the next two centuries, asked by Indians from California to Florida.[86]

To shield Indians from Europeans, missionaries tried to maintain segregated communities. That policy coincided with the Crown's vision of Indians and non-Indians residing in separate spheres or "republics"—a Commonwealth of Indians and a Commonwealth of Spaniards. By law, mission Indians could not leave their village to travel to Hispanic towns such as St. Augustine or Santa Fe without a pass, and Europeans, mestizos, blacks, mulattos, and other non-Indians could not live in Indian villages or spend more than three days in one.[87] In New Mexico, demographic pressure and a shortage of secure, well-watered land, invited Hispanic colonists to encroach on Pueblos' lands, to the annoyance of natives and missionaries. In Florida, with its reduced Hispanic and Indian populations and more abundant grazing lands, it appears that colonists found government regulations easier to honor.[88]

[83] Hann, *Apalachee,* 250. Spicer, *Cycles of Conquest,* 425–27, takes a more negative view of the Pueblos' acquisition of Spanish than does Dozier, *Pueblo Indians,* 69. I have based my conclusion on Dozier and on the pueblo-by-pueblo survey reported in Adams and Chávez, eds. and trans., *Missions of New Mexico,* 51, 19, 71, 90, 98, 112ff. For critical views of the Franciscans' efforts see, e.g., Adams, ed. and trans., *Bishop Tamarón's Visitation,* 79, and the Report of the Rev. Father Provincial of the Province of El Santo Evangelio to the viceroy, Convent of San Francisco, Mar. 1750, in Hackett, ed., *Historical Documents,* 3:439. See, too, Kelly, *Franciscan Missions of New Mexico,* 63–64. A few Pueblos, such as the mixed-blood governor of the Pueblo of Santa Ana, Bartolomé de Ojeda, wrote Spanish well. See Espinosa, ed. and trans., *Pueblo Indian Revolt,* 240–41.

[84] Pius V to Menéndez, 1569, quoted in Gannon, *Cross in the Sand,* 34–35.

[85] Quoted by fray Francisco de Zamora in Hammond and Rey, eds. and trans., *Don Juan de Oñate,* 2:675. See this and the testimony taken under oath at the meeting of Sept. 7, 1601, ibid., 672–89.

[86] See, e.g., Geiger, ed. and trans., *Letter of Luís Jayme,* 42.

[87] "Republic" had not yet taken on its present meaning of a state in which power is vested in the people but referred rather to a community of people with a common interest. For background on this, see Gómez Canedo, *Evangelización,* 140–43; Ricard, *Spiritual Conquest,* 153, 290; Bushnell, "Ruling 'the Republic of Indians,'" 138. The idea of separate republics broke down in the eighteenth century. See, especially, Guest, "Mission Colonization and Political Control," 97–116.

[88] There are numerous examples of encroachment in New Mexico. See Jenkins, "Spanish Colonial Policy," 203. For the abundance of land in Florida, see Bushnell, "Ruling 'the Republic of Indians,'" 141.

V

The spiritual conquest of North American Indians moved forward on more than Franciscan zeal and technique. Franciscans also had behind them a sizable state apparatus. The Spanish Crown, which enjoyed patronage over the Catholic church in its American colonies and used the church as an instrument of conquest and consolidation, provided the friars with resources and military support that enabled them to impose their will by force upon certain natives.[89]

The mendicants who preached in remote North America received alms chiefly from the king's coffers. Through much of the seventeenth century, for example, government-financed caravans of large iron-tired wagons, each pulled by eight oxen, lumbered north from Mexico City every three years, heavy with supplies bound for New Mexico. That structures in the mission compound might be properly built, government wagons carried metal tools and other hardware—nails, hinges, and hook and eye latches. That Catholic rituals might be properly performed, the Crown sent sacramental wine and oil, candles and candle wax, candlesticks, bells, musical instruments, and other accoutrements. That the padres might live like Europeans, the Crown shipped sackcloth, sandals, stockings, hats, medicines, cooking utensils, and foods such as sweetmeats, raisins, almonds, flour, oysters, sugar, saffron, pepper, and cinnamon.[90] More accessible by sea and by relatively short overland routes, the Florida missions received supplies three times a year rather than every three years, as in New Mexico. In both places, when government support arrived late or inequities seemed to occur, the mendicants plied their trade with vigor. "The missionaries . . . kill me with petitions," one governor of Florida wrote to the king.[91]

Indirectly, the Crown's subsidy of the New Mexico and Florida missions also included maintaining officials and soldiers in provinces that existed primarily for the conversion of Indians. Over the course of the seventeenth century, New Mexico alone cost the Crown nearly 2,390,000 pesos, according to one estimate, with more than half, some 1,340,000 pesos, representing direct costs of maintaining missions and missionaries. Florida, with its permanent paid garrison, cost nearly three times as much as New Mexico where unpaid citizen-soldiers served, or were supposed to serve, the friars.[92]

[89] MacLachlin, *Spain's Empire*, 30.
[90] See the remarkably detailed list in the contract between the Crown and the Franciscans of 1631, translated in Scholes, "Supply Service," 100–105. For the wagons themselves, see Moorhead, *New Mexico's Royal Road*, 33. For the Florida missions, supplied more frequently than those of isolated New Mexico, see Bushnell, "Archaeology of Mission Santa Catalina de Guale."
[91] Damián de Vega Castro y Pardo, St. Augustine, July 9, 1643, in Arnade, ed. and trans., "Florida in 1643," 175.
[92] Bloom, "Spain's Investment in New Mexico," 13, whose estimate covers the period 1596–1697. With more documents available to him than were available to Bloom, Scholes calculated a deficit to the Crown of 1,759,268 pesos over a different time span (1586–1683) and estimated that 70

The Crown supported the Franciscans in North America for reasons both pious and practical. First, the papal bull of May 4, 1493, which was issued by Alexander VI and gave the Spanish monarchy title to the Indies, had obliged Spain's monarchs to convert native Americans. Franciscans, such as Alonso de Benavides, did not fail to remind the Crown of its responsibility.[93] Second, if missionaries succeeded in Hispanicizing natives, they would add to the number of laborers and taxpayers—an important consideration for a nation so small in relation to the size of its empire. Natives themselves, then, would become Hispanic residents of frontiers that might otherwise be neglected for lack of Spaniards.[94] Third, the government regarded support of missions as an investment in war and peace. Missionaries, it appeared, could pacify natives at less cost and with longer-lasting results than could soldiers.[95] "We are the ones who are subduing and conquering the land," fray Francisco Pareja wrote from Florida, where the Crown gave each Franciscan a soldier's annual wage and rations.[96] Indeed, well into the eighteenth century, the royal treasury debited the war fund for the expenses of missions. In general, missions in areas deemed strategically vital received more support than those that failed to serve the Crown's political ends.[97]

Franciscans, however, did not usually attempt a spiritual conquest without the aid of soldiers. The Royal Orders for New Discoveries of 1573 had prohibited military conquest as an instrument for pacifying frontiers, and some missionaries took the extreme view that North American natives were best converted in the complete absence of armed men. By the 1570s, however, most priests recognized the high risks of that strategy. Soldierless proselytizing by Dominican Luis Cáncer de Barbastro on the beaches of Florida in 1549 and the Jesuit Juan Baptista de Segura on the Chesapeake in 1570 had come to tragic ends; an elaborate plan for Franciscans to pacify North America from New Mexico to Florida without the aid of troops was never attempted. It seemed prudent to take minimal military precautions to avoid

percent of that sum went to support the missionaries ("Royal Treasury Records," 159–60). These figures are meant to be suggestive, since Scholes and Bloom based their calculations on incomplete documentation. Sluiter, *Florida Situado,* has made the fullest study of the Florida subsidy. He calculates 662,130 pesos for the decade 1611–1620, and 720,771 for the decade 1621–30 (6–9). According to Bloom's figures, the royal subsidy to New Mexico averaged 239,000 pesos per decade.

[93] Benavides, *Memorial . . . 1630,* 68.

[94] Bolton, "Mission as a Frontier Institution," 200.

[95] This had been the case since the Chichimeca Wars in northern New Spain in the last half of the sixteenth century, if not before. Powell, *Soldiers, Indians, and Silver,* 211, notes that in the late 1500s, funds to support Jesuits and Franciscans on the Chichimeca frontier came from the royal treasury and were labeled "gastos de la paz de chichimecas."

[96] Francisco Pareja, ca. 1616, quoted in Oré, *Martyrs of Florida,* 107; Matter, "Missions in the Defense of Spanish Florida," 27–29; Sluiter, *Florida Situado,* 6, 17–18.

[97] Bolton, "Mission as a Frontier Institution," 194–99.

failure and the senseless deaths of missionaries—especially as Indians obtained firearms and horses.[98]

In North America, soldiers accompanied Franciscans to ensure their
safety, but not to impose Christianity by force on unbelievers. Following a
brief period of theological dispute over the question, missionaries had rejected
forced conversion as bad theology and poor strategy. "With suavity and mildness an obstinate spirit can better be reclaimed than with violence and rigor,"
fray Estevan de Perea wrote from New Mexico.[99] Once natives consented to receive baptism of their own free will, however, Franciscans commonly relied
upon military force to prevent them from slipping back into apostasy. If new
converts could leave the missions, they might miss essential sacraments and
fall into the company of pagans who would surely lead them further into sin.
Franciscans turned to soldiers, then, to compel baptized Indians to remain in
mission communities, as Spanish law required, hunt down neophytes who
fled, and administer corporal punishment to natives who failed to live up to
the canons of their newly adopted faith or who continued religious practices
that Spaniards found loathsome.[100]

In the Florida missions, according to Bishop Díaz Vara Calderón, Franciscans appointed certain neophytes as spies, to "report to them all parishioners who live in evil."[101] Indians who failed to receive instruction or attend
Mass, or who committed what the padres regarded as sexual transgressions,
theft, or acts of idolatry were commonly placed in stocks, incarcerated, or
whipped—a punishment "so necessary to their good education and direction," as one Florida missionary put it.[102] Franciscans usually avoided applying the lash personally, delegating the task to a soldier or an Indian assistant (*a fiscal*) toward whom punished Indians could direct their anger.[103]
Occasionally, however, as in central Mexico, a few ill-tempered friars took it

[98] For Cáncer see O'Daniel, *Dominicans.* Vigil, "Bartolomé de las Casas," 45–47, describes a plan
of 1558 for the nonmilitary pacification by Franciscans of the area from Florida to New Mexico.
For the question of dependence upon soldiers, see especially Gómez Canedo, *Evangelización,*
xvi–xvii, 82–86; Bolton, "Mission as a Frontier Institution," 201–2, and Guest, "An Examination
of the Thesis of S. F. Cook," 57–59.
[99] Bloom, ed. and trans., "Fray Estevan de Perea's Relación," 228. See, too, fray Isidro Félix de
Espinosa, quoted in Gómez Canedo, *Evangelización,* 86.
[100] For an extended and somewhat apologetic discussion of these questions in one borderland
area, see Guest, "Examination of the Thesis of S. F. Cook," 1–77. Although the missions of Alta
California were not established until the late eighteenth century, Guest looks at sixteenth- and
seventeenth-century antecedents, especially in Appendix II. See, too, Phelan, *Millennial Kingdom,* 9–10, and Sabine MacCormack, "'The Heart Has Its Reasons': Predicaments of Missionary
Christianity in Early Colonial Peru," *HAHR* 65 (Aug. 1985): 443–66, with its fine discussion of
the theological questions surrounding the Christian tension between authority and reason.
[101] Wenhold, ed. and trans., *Letter of Gabriel Díaz,* 14.
[102] Unnamed Franciscan testimony of 1681, quoted in Matter, "Spanish Missions of Florida," 354
n. 9. See, too, ibid., 278–79.
[103] Much has been written on this subject. See, e.g., Gómez Canedo, *Evangelización,* 177–78; Polzer,
Rules and Precepts, 50. For New Mexico, see Scholes, *Troublous Times,* 11. For a sympathetic view

upon themselves to whip, strike, or verbally abuse neophytes, or smash offensive objects. On rare occasions they administered ghastly punishments. In New Mexico, fray Salvador de Guerra whipped Juan Cuna, a Hopi Indian suspected of idolatry, until he was covered with blood. The priest then smeared burning turpentine over the idolator's body. Juan Cuna died.[104]

Father Guerra's brutality was extraordinary, but whipping seemed an appropriate punishment to Franciscans reared in an era when the lash was commonly applied to Spanish miscreants from schoolchildren to soldiers. Until the end of the Spanish era in North America, the padres defended the practice of flogging disobedient Indians, and to atone for their sins they whipped themselves as well. "You Christians are so crazy . . . flogging yourselves like crazy people in the streets, shedding blood," one Jumano "wizard," or *hechicero*, told Father Benavides. Exclaiming that "he did not want to become crazy" like the Christians, the Jumano fled. The episode heartened Benavides, leaving him "persuaded that it was the Demon, who went fleeing."[105]

To many Franciscans, native religious beliefs seemed to mock Christianity and to represent the work of the devil, whose playground extended to the New World as well as the Old. "They adore the Devil," one Franciscan in Florida exclaimed.[106] Missionaries, then, sought to remove all traces of what they saw as satan-inspired caricatures of the True Faith. Initially, friars in North America fought the devil through persuasion and prayer. Father Benavides, for example, exorcised the churches in an effort "to conjure and banish the devil."[107] When exorcism, and other nonviolent means failed, however, Franciscans reached into their arsenal and made war.

---

of whipping as part of a system of rewards and punishments, see Keegan and Sanz, *Experiencia misionera*, 331–38.

[104] This brutal act, committed at Oraibi in 1655, is described by Scholes as "the most flagrant case on record during the entire seventeenth century" (*Troublous Times*, 11–12). For Florida, see Hann, *Apalachee*, 256–59, and Bushnell, "Archaeology of Mission Santa Catalina de Guale." In sixteenth-century Mexico, Indians found guilty of idolatry might suffer torture, lifetime imprisonment, or execution, but such stern measures seem to have lessened by the eighteenth century (Gibson, *Aztecs under Spanish Rule*, 117–18).

[105] Benavides, *Memorial . . . 1630*, 21 (see 102 for the Spanish version). Several Catholic historians have argued that whipping was mild and needed to be understood in the context of the times: Luzbetak, "If Junípero Serra Were Alive," 514; McGarry, "Educational Methods," 354–55; Guest, "Role of the Discipline," 1–68. Indians may not have shared this view—see Archibald, "Indian Labor at the California Missions," 172–82. Questions of morality and severity produced a lively debate in California in the 1980s: Costo and Costo, eds., *Missions of California* (a largely polemical work); Meighan, "Indians and California Missions," 187–201; and Sandos, "Junípero Serra's Canonization," 1253–69.

[106] The quote is from Covington, ed., *Pirates, Indians and Spaniards*, 142. Franciscans of that era commonly expressed this idea, and it is discussed in some of the secondary literature, such as Ricard, *Spiritual Conquest*, 284–90; Keegan and Tormo, *Experiencia misionera*, 325; and Polzer, *Rules and Precepts*, 44, who sees its strongest manifestation in missionary thought prior to the Enlightenment. Ricard, *Spiritual Conquest*, 286, notes that the friars "were particularly haunted . . . by the fear of a pagan-Christian syncretism."

[107] Benavides, *Revised Memorial of 1634*, 63.

In New Mexico and Florida, as they had done since the earliest stages of the conquest of America, the preachers smashed, burned, or confiscated objects sacred to the natives—what one friar in New Mexico described as "idols, offerings, masks, and other things of the kind which the Indians were accustomed to use in their heathenism."[108] Franciscans also tried to suppress native religious rituals and ceremonial dances because they saw them as expressions of "idolatry and worship of the devil."[109] In Florida, when they belatedly discovered what they perceived to be idolatrous symbolism and magic in a popular ball game, Franciscans banned the game. They ordered ball poles lowered in the plazas of Indian towns and crosses raised in their stead.[110]

Native spiritual leaders came under special attack by the friars.[111] Whatever similarity might have existed between native and Christian priests in their common roles as intercessors between man and the supernatural was disregarded by most Franciscans, who saw the sources of their respective powers as fundamentally at odds. In fact, native religions and Catholicism contained a number of compatible elements. Pueblos and Christians, for example, each believed in sacred places, a religious calendar that regulated community life, and ceremonies that used altars, ritual chants, and sacred utensils. Popular religion in Spain had a long tradition of devotion and prayer to a variety of saints and their images.[112] Like Pueblo deities, Spanish images of saints occupied sacred places and specialized in combating a variety of natural ills, from pestilence to locusts.[113] But the few Franciscans who argued for coexistence and gradual change lost out to those who advocated their rapid and violent eradication.[114]

Franciscans who defended the use of corporal punishment and force, did so on firm philosophical ground. First, as one padre claimed, only

---

[108] Fray Alonzo de Posadas to the Holy Office, May 23, 1661, in Hackett, ed., *Historical Documents*, 3:166, and Scholes, *Troublous Times*, 11. For New Spain, see Gómez Canedo, *Evangelización*, 162–69. For one example of the burning of idols in Florida, see fray Martin Prieto, in Oré, *Martyrs of Florida*, 115.

[109] Statement of Nicolás de Freitas, Mexico, Jan. 24, 1661, in Hackett, ed., *Historical Documents*, 3:158. Freitas was condemning the kachina dances. Many other priests expressed this view of them.

[110] Bushnell, "'That Demonic Game,'" 1–19.

[111] Loucks, "Political and Economic Interactions," 55.

[112] Bowden, *American Indians and Christian Missions*, 46–51, succinctly describes the similarities and differences between Catholicism and Pueblo religion.

[113] William A. Christian, Jr., *Local Religion in Sixteenth-Century Spain* (Princeton: Princeton University Press, 1981), 3, 22, 42–47, 55–56, 147.

[114] Inga Clendinnen, "Disciplining the Indians: Franciscan Ideology and Missionary Violence in Sixteenth-Century Yucatan," *Past and Present* 94 (Feb. 1982): 27–48; MacCormack, "Predicaments of Missionary Christianity in Early Colonial Peru," 451–52, 464. See, too, Henry Kamen, "Toleration and Dissent in Sixteenth-Century Spain: The Alternative Tradition," *Sixteenth-Century Journal* 19 (Spring 1988): 3–23, for a discussion of a long Spanish tradition, often a minority view, that coercion should not be used against unbelievers.

through forcible means could a people "of vicious and ferocious habits who know no law but force" be rescued from their own barbarism.[115] Second, schooled in a time and place where the good of the community prevailed over the rights of the individual, some Franciscans regarded it as their duty to punish individuals harshly lest they infect others with their wicked ways. Third, thoughtful Franciscans saw the use of force as essential to saving their own souls, for their theology suggested that "he who could prevent a given sin and failed to do so was actually cooperating in the offense committed against God and therefore shared in the guilt."[116] Finally, in a struggle with Satan, the end surely justified the means.

Even when the friars did not use force or unleash soldiers on the natives, the possibility of force must have persuaded some natives to accept baptism and cooperate. To suppose, for example, that Indians would have voluntarily performed such tasks as building churches because priests and soldiers were too few to compel them to work, misses an essential point. In the process of "pacifying" Florida and New Mexico, Spaniards had inflicted devastating punishment on Indians. "War by fire and blood" had probably served its intended purpose of breaking the will of some Indian communities to offer further resistance to missionaries accompanied by soldiers.[117]

As much as Franciscans depended upon soldiers to maintain the new order, their relationship with them remained ambivalent. Until the end of Spain's tenure in North America, friars deplored the scandalous behavior and immoral examples that military men set for neophytes. Many of the soldiers, one California friar wrote in 1772, "deserve to be hanged on account of the continuous outrages which they are committing in seizing and raping the women."[118] Antipathy toward soldiers ran so deeply that friars occasionally sought permission to found new missions without military protection and frequently opposed stationing troops near missions. They argued vigorously against the building of a blockhouse in Apalachee in 1657, for example, even

---

[115] The quote is from the "Refutation of Charges," by Fermín Francisco de Lasuén, Monterey, June 19, 1801, in Archibald, "Indian Labor at the California Missions," 176 (the entire document is in Kenneally, ed. and trans., *Writings of Fermín Francisco de Lasuén*, 2:194–234). Although it is a late colonial example, Lasuén's eloquent defense of the use of force seems representative of padres' views in other times and places as well. See also, Guest, "Examination of the Thesis of S. F. Cook," 61–62; Elliott, "Discovery of America," 57.

[116] Guest, "New Look at the California's Missions [sic]," 84, who examined what the friars read as well as what they wrote, is perhaps the finest examination of the mentalité of Spanish friars in North America.

[117] See, too, John, *Storms Brewed*, 30, and the view of the Spanish jurist Juan de Solórzano Pereira, noted in Guest, "Examination of the Thesis of S. F. Cook," 57. John Leddy Phelan, *The Hispanization of the Philippines: Spanish Aims and Filipino Responses, 1565–1700* (Madison: University of Wisconsin Press, 1959), 54, also saw the threat of force as assisting missionaries in the Philippines. For an example of the view that Indians cooperated voluntarily, see Kubler, *Religious Architecture*, 7.

[118] Geiger, ed. and trans., *Letter of Luís Jayme*, 38.

in the face of strong pressure from government officials. "The damned priests," wrote Florida's annoyed governor. On the other hand, when hostile Indians threatened their work, friars pleaded for troops.[119]

VI

Whatever skill, resources, and force the Franciscans brought to their struggle to extend Christianity to North American natives, they did not succeed unless Indians cooperated, and Indians cooperated only when they believed they had something to gain from the new religion and the material benefits that accompanied it, or too much to lose from resisting it.

Some natives welcomed missionaries, calculating that friendly relationships with friars would bring material benefits, such as gifts and access to Spanish trade goods.[120] Other natives saw the Franciscans as a key to defense against predatory Spaniards or predatory Indian neighbors. Natives often regarded priests as useful intermediaries between themselves and the potentially hostile Spanish soldiers. Indians, Viceroy Antonio de Mendoza reported, "welcome the friars, and where they flee from us like deer . . . they come to them."[121] Some natives saw an alliance with the friars as a way to shift the balance of power against enemies from other tribes. In the early stages of Franciscan missionary work in New Mexico, for example, growing pressure from Apaches appears to have driven a number of Pueblos to the friars—just as pressure from Comanches would later drive Apaches to seek missionaries.[122] Thus, natives sought to manipulate missionaries to promote their own security much as the Spanish Crown tried to use missionaries to secure its frontiers

[119] The quote is Diego de Rebolledo in Hann, ed. and trans., "Rebolledo's 1657 Visitation," 85. Matter, "Missions in the Defense of Spanish Florida," 19–27, summarizes the conflict in early Florida. New Mexico had no garrison in the seventeenth century, but Franciscans often called upon the governor to dispatch military escorts of settler-soldiers to accompany the padres in the founding of new missions, while at the same time Franciscans took measures that seemed designed to drive all Spaniards out of New Mexico (Scholes, *Church and State*, 23–24, 71–72, 80, 89, 108). For examples of missionaries opposing the use of soldiers in Texas, see John, *Storms Brewed*, 188, and Gómez Canedo, *Evangelización*, 86. For a call for soldiers, see fray Andrés Varo, 1751, quoted in fray Pedro Serrano to the viceroy, 1761 [sic], in Hackett, ed., *Historical Documents*, 3:496.

[120] Most authorities, and most Franciscans of the time, took the view that gifts and trade goods, such as iron tools, clothing, and ornaments, were powerful inducements. See, e.g., Hann, *Apalachee*, 123–33.

[121] Mendoza to the king, Jacona, Apr. 17, 1540, in Hammond and Rey, eds. and trans., *Coronado Expedition*, 161. There are many examples of natives appealing to friars for help. See, e.g., fray Juan Sanz de Lezaún, Nov. 14, 1760, "Account of Lamentable Happenings in New Mexico," in Hackett, ed., *Historical Documents*, 3:477.

[122] John, *Storms Brewed*, 56, suggests this possibility for the years 1607–8, when the Franciscans reported an unusual number of baptisms. See, too, ibid., 258–303.

from natives and imperial rivals. When conditions were right, the natives' tactics worked and enabled some of their societies to survive.[123]

Initially, at least, submission to the foreign priests also seemed to offer natives access to awesome spiritual power. To some Indians, Franciscans may have appeared to be "powerful witches" who needed to be appeased, or powerful shamans with whom it seemed wise to cooperate.[124] Like Christians, many North American Indians believed that priests and ceremonies had power to mediate between man and nature, and Franciscans claimed such power as they conjured cures, rain, and good harvests.[125] From the first, several signs of the friars' power were readily evident to Indians. Armed Spanish soldiers and splendidly attired government officials prostrated themselves before the unarmed, plain-robed friars. Franciscans introduced and controlled domestic animals, larger than the natives had previously known, and could thereby provide a steady supply of meat without hunting.[126] Strange diseases that took the lives of Indians spared Europeans who followed the Christian god. At first, then, natives had reason to believe that the foreign preachers possessed life-saving powers. The specter of death from mysterious maladies, rather than the apparition of the Lady in Blue, probably persuaded some tribes to request missionaries and some Indian mothers to seek baptism for their children.[127]

The extent to which Indians saw themselves as beneficiaries of relationships with missionaries was, in part, specific to the values of each native society. Franciscan celibacy may have seemed unremarkable to some natives, for example, but probably awed the Pueblos for whom, as one historian has put it, "coitus was the symbol of cosmic harmony."[128] Pueblo males believed that by abstaining from sexual activity for several days they achieved greater strength for the hunt, for curing, or for conjuring rain. What power might accrue to those friars who practiced lifelong sexual abstinence!

[123] A number of studies have reached this conclusion. See, e.g., Cushing, "Zuni and the Missionaries," 182, and Hu-DeHart, *Missionaries, Miners, and Indians*, 3. See also James Axtell, "Some Thoughts on the Ethnohistory of Missions," in Axtell, *After Columbus*, 51–52.

[124] The quote is from anthropologist Shipek, "California Indian Reactions," 485, who offers a delightful reconstruction of how Diegueño (Ipai) Indians probably responded to Franciscans. Native responses can only be reconstructed through an informed imagination, but on the points in these paragraphs, anthropologists seem to agree.

[125] For the Pueblos, see Dozier, *Pueblo Indians*, 50; Loucks, "Political and Economic Interactions," 28–31.

[126] Gutiérrez, *When Jesus Came*, 63, 77. See, too, Polzer, *Rules and Precepts*, 48. I do not mean to suggest that Indians preferred raising livestock to hunting, but only to suggest that the relative efficiency of keeping large animals contained may have impressed natives.

[127] Dobyns, *From Fire to Flood*, 54, suggests this in the case of the Pimas. See, too, Smith, *Archaeology of Aboriginal Culture Change*, 126. Reff, *Disease, Depopulation, and Culture Change*, 260, argues that Jesuits' presumed curative powers were more attractive to Indians than any other inducement the Jesuits offered.

[128] Gutiérrez, *When Jesus Came*, 71, 63. Like the Pueblos, Apalachees abstained from sexual activity to give them strength in warfare (Hann, *Apalachee*, 249).

Economic and environmental conditions also figured into the natives' calculations of costs and benefits. Nomads and seminomads, such as Apaches and Chiscas, succeeded in retaining their spiritual and physical independence for they could move beyond the Spanish sphere and leave behind little of value at traditional hunting or gathering places—a fact that Franciscans recognized.[129] Conversely, Franciscans in Florida and New Mexico made their earliest conversions among town-dwelling agriculturalists, who had the most to lose if antagonized Spaniards burned their villages and trampled their crops—the more so perhaps in arid New Mexico which offered few ecological niches to which native farmers might escape. Of course, some town-dwellers, protected from reprisal by distance or natural barriers, managed to retain a high degree of spiritual independence and physical freedom. Hopis, for example, submitted to missionaries in 1629, but regained their independence in 1680 and refused thereafter to permit a missionary to remain among them. "The religion of the Moqui [Hopi] today is the same as before they heard about the Gospel," lamented one Franciscan who visited their isolated mesa-top villages in 1775.[130]

Natives who decided to accept missions after weighing their apparent benefits and liabilities also determined which aspects of Christianity and European culture they would embrace and which they would reject. As a rule, those native societies that had not been vitiated by war or disease adopted from the friars what they perceived was both useful and compatible with their essential values and institutions. Ideally, they sought to add the new without discarding the old, or to replace elements in their culture with parallel elements from the new—as they had done long before the arrival of Europeans.[131] In the religious sphere, for example, many natives simply added Jesus, Mary, and Christian saints to their rich pantheons and welcomed the Franciscans into their communities as additional shamans. Guales who had previously carried offerings of food to mortuary temples now brought those offerings on the Day of the Dead; in place of shell gorgets, Guales wore religious medals.[132] Some Pueblos seem to have incorporated Franciscans, and perhaps even Jesus, into their cosmography as kachinas, or representatives of mythological

---

[129] For attempts to convert Apaches and other nomads in the 1600s, see, e.g., Forbes, *Apache, Navaho, and Spaniard*, 116–20, 128–29, 158, 159–60, and the episode recounted in John, *Storms Brewed*, 76. Four Franciscans to the Crown, Oct. 16, 1612, quoted in Bushnell, "Sacramental Imperative," 479–80.

[130] Fray Silvestre Vélez de Escalante's diary, quoted in Adams, "Fray Silvestre," 136. See also Adams, "Passive Resistance," 77–91.

[131] This is, of course, a universal tendency, and there is widespread agreement among scholars that a syncretic religion developed among most natives in Spanish America. See, e.g., Barth, *Franciscan Education*, 339, Gibson, *Aztecs under Spanish Rule*, 100–101, 134. For Spanish North America, see Deagan, "Cultures in Transition," 112–14; Spicer, *Cycles of Conquest*, 506–8, 567–72; Schroeder, "Shifting for Survival," 239. This was also true in English America; see Axtell, "Some Thoughts on the Ethnohistory of Missions," in Axtell, *After Columbus*, 54.

[132] Larson, "Historic Guale Indians," 135, and Thomas, "Saints and Soldiers," 119.

beings.[133] To cite other examples in the area of material culture, neophytes added foods to their diet without discarding the old, added metal to their hoes yet retained their way of farming, and used metal tools for carpentry but did not change radically the method of constructing their own buildings.[134]

However selectively neophytes adopted aspects of Christianity and Spanish culture, these borrowings began to transform their cultures—often in ways that neither they nor the missionaries intended.[135] Indians such as the Guales, for example, who had enjoyed a rich variety of foods from fishing, hunting, and gathering, experienced a decline in nutritional quality on the more restricted mission diet, making them more prone to disease, iron-deficiency anemia, and lower birthrates.[136] On the other hand, by cultivating certain European crops and raising European domestic animals, other natives enriched their diet, lengthened the growing season, deemphasized hunting in favor of agriculture, and made it possible for their villages to support denser populations. Their prosperity also made them more attractive targets for raids by nomads and forced them to devote more resources to defense.[137] To take still another example, the political structures and religious systems of some Indian communities fractured as leaders became bitterly divided between those who converted and those who did not. On occasion, factionalism (presumably a feature of precontact Indian societies, too) be-

[133] Gutiérrez, *When Jesus Came,* 163. For a modern reference to Jesus as a kachina, see Fergusson, *Dancing Gods,* 33. Among the Hopis, who resisted Christianity more staunchly than other Pueblos, Dockstader, *The Kachina and the White Man,* 11, found no case of a Kachina "taken over from white culture."

[134] Hann, *Apalachee,* 239, 241, 243. Deagan, "Cultures in Transition," 113–14; Dozier, *Pueblo Indians,* 65–67. For one aspect of this question in a broader context, see John Super, *Food, Conquest, and Colonization in Sixteenth-Century Spanish America* (Albuquerque: University of New Mexico Press, 1988). Archaeologists in Florida have been especially vigorous in addressing these questions. For their tentative conclusions and an introduction to the large literature, see Reitz, "Zooarchaeological Evidence," 543–54, and Ruhl, "Spanish Mission Paleoethnobotany," 555–80.

[135] See, e.g., Dozier, *Pueblo Indians,* 65, who probably understates the impact of material culture, but who notes that "the most tangible changes . . . affected the economy." For Florida, see the wide-ranging essay by Hilton, "El impacto español en la florida," 249–70. Hann, *Apalachee,* 237–63, devotes a chapter to "Indian and Spanish Interaction and Acculturation," much of which represented missionary and Indian interaction.

[136] Larsen et al., "Beyond Demographic Collapse," 409–28.

[137] Deagan, "Spanish-Indian Interaction," 302. Sheridan, "Kino's Unforeseen Legacy," 157–60, cogently discusses the indirect impact on the Pimas of accepting European domestic animals and winter wheat. For the Pueblos, see Ford, "New Pueblo Economy," 73–91, and John, *Storms Brewed,* 67. See, too, Larson, "Historic Guale Indians" 133. Reff, *Disease, Depopulation, and Culture Change,* 254–59, dismisses the importance of European "innovations" including livestock, but even if one accepts his argument, it may be specific to the region that he studied. Archaeological evidence suggests that Spanish trade goods were not abundant, especially in comparison to those available through the French and English. See, e.g., Larson, "Historic Guale Indians" 135–38, and Merritt, "Beyond the Walls," 146–47, but the few trade goods that Spaniards did offer, together with those animals and plants that reproduced themselves, seem to me to be of great significance.

came so bitter that it led to bloodshed.[138] Thus, in ways too numerous to enumerate, but that varied greatly among Indian peoples, acceptance of missionaries and European material goods transformed native economies, polities, social structure, and family life. Indians who had previously enjoyed independence found themselves reduced from the status of sovereign peoples to subject populations, occupying one of the lowest rungs on the socioeconomic ladder of the new social order.

The direct and indirect transformations effected by the missionary process notwithstanding, it appears that most natives successfully resisted the friars' efforts to eradicate or significantly transform their religious beliefs or cultural values. One cannot take as disinterested the effusive reports of fray Alonso de Benavides, Bishop Gabriel Díaz, or the optimism of a fray Juan de Prada, who announced from New Mexico in 1638 that "idolatry has been banished."[139] Fray Francisco de Jesús María Casañas was probably more on the mark when he wrote of the Pueblos in 1696, a century after Franciscans had begun their missionary labors: "They are still drawn more by their idolatry and infidelity than by the Christian doctrine."[140]

It is impossible, of course, to know the depth of change that Franciscans effected in the internal lives of numerous Indians. Some probably underwent profound and complete conversions, and others almost certainly found ways to synthesize old and new religions—much as their Christian contemporaries in Spain blended elements of pagan and Catholic belief and ritual. Then, too, some mission Indians made superficial adjustments to please the friars or to win the favor of the Christian god, such as participating in Catholic rituals or changing burial customs, while also continuing to practice the old religion.[141] Mission Indians did not survive long enough in Spanish Florida to provide testimony to the depth or manner of their conversions, but Pueblos did. Well into the twentieth century they simultaneously practiced Catholicism, through the intermediary of a Catholic priest, and indigenous religious traditions through native priests—"compartmentalizing" the two religions rather than synthesizing them.[142]

---

[138] Examples are numerous. For Florida, see Covington, ed., *Pirates, Indians and Spaniards,* 130–31, and for New Mexico, see the well-known episode at the Hopi Pueblo of Awatovi in 1700 (Cordell, *Prehistory of the Southwest,* 354–55).

[139] Fray Juan de Prada to the viceroy, Mexico, Sept. 26, 1638, in Hackett, ed., *Historical Documents,* 3:108. See, too, a similar comment by Francisco de Pareja, letter ca. 1616, in Oré, *Martyrs of Florida,* 106.

[140] To Gov. Diego de Vargas, Bernalillo, Apr. 18, 1696, in Espinosa, ed. and trans., *Pueblo Indian Revolt,* 228. See, too, fray Nicolás de Freitas to fray García de San Francisco, Cuarac, New Mexico, June 18, 1660, in Hackett, ed., *Historical Documents,* 3:150–51, quoted in the epigraph at the outset of this chapter.

[141] For changes in burial customs, see, e.g., Deagan, "Cultures in Transition," 114, and Larson, "Historic Guale Indians," 134.

[142] Spicer identified "compartmentalization" as specific to the Eastern Pueblos—a concept that has been well accepted but that did not occur among all native peoples for it depended upon

One can imagine many reasons why neophytes did not succumb so completely to the blandishments of the new religion that they rejected the old. One reason seems especially evident. The bright future that Franciscans offered at the outset of the courtship quickly lost its luster as the terms of exchange shifted against mission Indians. Along with gifts and access to trade goods had come demands for labor and resources, and those demands on individual neophytes increased as local Indian populations declined. Obedience to the Franciscans and their god did not stop the spread of diseases strange to the natives. The worlds of the natives continued to collapse. By 1680, the Pueblo population had declined by at least half, to some 17,000, since the Franciscans' arrival.[143] In Florida, the Eastern Timucuans had nearly disappeared by 1680; a Spanish census of 1675 reported that only 1,370 Timucuans remained, most of them west of the Suwannee River. Florida, as one historian has put it, "had become a hollow peninsula."[144] The Apalachees had declined from about 25,000, from their first contact with missionaries early in the 1600s, to some 10,000 by about 1680.[145] Enemy raids, desertions, movement into colonists' communities, and forced labor also diminished the numbers of Indians in missions, but epidemics of smallpox, measles, and other difficult-to-identify diseases appear to have been the principal cause of premature Indian deaths.[146]

The prayers of the padres did not shield the natives from European diseases or from other natural or man-made disasters. In the semiarid South-

---

the nature of indigenous society and the circumstances of contact with Spaniards ("Spanish-Indian Acculturation," 663–78). For a dissenting view, see Ellis's "Comment," *American Anthropologist* 56 (Aug. 1954): 678–80. Scholes, *Troublous Times*, 16, anticipated Spicer when he suggestively argued that in societies like those of the Pueblos, where "religion, village government, and social institutions were so closely interrelated . . . it was impossible to abolish any part without destroying the whole." For an extraordinary example of a Pueblo individual who publicly professed Catholicism, but who privately continued traditional practices, see Kessell, "Esteban Clemente," 16–17. Matter, "Mission Life," 418–20, provides a brief and balanced assessment of this question for Florida. For elements of syncretism in Spain, see William A. Christian, Jr., *Person and God in a Spanish Village* (New York: Seminar Press, 1972), and William A. Christian, Jr., *Local Religion in Sixteenth-Century Spain* (Princeton: Princeton University Press, 1981). See, too, James Axtell, "Were Indian Conversions *Bona Fide?*," in *After Columbus*, 100–121.

[143] The rate and percentage of decline of the Pueblo population over the course of the seventeenth century cannot be stated with accuracy because estimates of the base population in 1600 vary wildly. See Schroeder, "Pueblos Abandoned in Historic Times," 254. The decline of numbers of Pueblos and their towns may have occurred quite early in the century. See Forbes, *Apache, Navaho, and Spaniard*, 139, 175, and fray Juan de Pardo to the viceroy, Mexico, Sept. 26, 1638, who estimated the Pueblos had declined from 60,000 to 40,000 due to smallpox "and the sickness that the Mexicans call *cocolitzli*" (Hackett, ed., *Historical Documents*, 3:108).

[144] Bushnell, "'That Demonic Game,'" 4, provides a good, brief discussion of the complicated question of the population of the Florida provinces in 1675 and guidance to sources. Her figures do not include Apalachicola. On the Timucua, see Deagan, "Cultures in Transition," 89–90, 95. See, too, Milanich, "Western Timucua," 59–88.

[145] Hann, *Apalachee*, 163–66.

[146] Authorities agree on this point. See, e.g., Dozier, *Pueblo Indians*, 63; Hann, *Apalachee*, 175–78, 180.

west, years passed when little rain fell upon the land. Crops failed, hunger increased, and the surviving crops and livestock proved tempting targets for Apache raiders. In the Southeast, a skilled Indian labor force at the Spanish missions proved irresistible to English slave hunters by the late seventeenth century.

In such troubled times it must have seemed to Indian neophytes that Franciscan shamans had lost their magic, or that the Christian god did not have the strength of the old god. A story handed down among the Pueblos, originating perhaps at Zuni, tells of a struggle between the Christians' "God" and Poshaiyanyi, a Pueblo deity to whom the Pueblos would turn when they launched a full-scale offensive against the Spaniards in 1680.

> God and Poshaiyanyi were going to have a contest to see which one had the most power. They were going to shoot at a tree. God shot at it with a gun and cut a gash in the bark. Poshaiyanyi struck it with a bolt of lightning and split the trunk in half. Next they were going to see which one had the best things to eat. God had a table with lots of good things on it. Poshaiyanyi ate on the ground; he had some fat deer meat and some tortillas. God watched Poshaiyanyi eat for a while, then he got down on the ground and ate with him.[147]

To control the forces of the cosmos, which seemed to have deserted them, mission Indians turned more openly to traditional gods, such as Poshaiyanyi, and to prayers, ceremonies, and priests that had proved efficacious in the past.[148] Indians learned to their sorrow, however, that Christianity was incompatible with some of their most cherished values and institutions, and that their decision to accept baptism was irrevocable in the eyes of the friars. Mission Indians heard their traditional religious practices condemned as idolatrous by the padres, who quashed non-Catholic public religious ceremonies and who intruded into the most private aspects of natives' lives. Friars, for example, attempted to end polygamy among those natives who practiced it and to impose upon them indissoluble monogamy. In so doing, the friars often enraged and humiliated native males who lacked the Christian arithmetic that one wife was better than two or three. Timucuans, who explained to one priest that "they enjoyed their vice and therefore it must not be evil but good and just," received an unsympathetic hearing.[149] Among the Pueblos, where sexuality and sanctity were closely linked, the affront to their dignity must have been especially deep, and the hypocrisy of

[147] Part of a folktale from Santo Domingo that apparently originated at Zuni, told in Chávez "Pohé-Yemo's Representative," 115, who identifies this figure as *Pohé-Yemo*. In Tewa, the correct name is *P'ose yemu*—"he who scatters mist before him" (Ortiz, "Popay's Leadership," 21).

[148] There is substantial evidence of this among the Pueblos. See, e.g., Scholes, *Troublous Times*, 16, and Dozier, *Pueblo Indians*, 50.

[149] Covington, ed., *Pirates, Indians and Spaniards*, 133. See, too, Hann, *Apalachee*, 12–13, 184. See Oré, *Martyrs of Florida*, 101, and Matter, "Spanish Missions of Florida," 74, for other examples from Apalachee, Apalachicola, Timucua, and Guale respectively.

Christians (including some of the friars), who themselves engaged in sexual practices they sought to prohibit, could not have gone unnoticed.[150]

Oppressed in body and in spirit, many mission Indians sought ways to extricate themselves from the loving embrace of the sons of St. Francis. Strategies varied. Some individuals fled, as did entire communities on a few occasions. Others tried to rid themselves of individual priests by murdering them or by making their lives unpleasant (Pueblos at Taos served their padre corn tortillas laced with urine and mice meat).[151] Prior to their successful rebellions of the late 1600s, neophytes rebelled on a large-scale at least once in each of the four mission provinces of Florida, and on a number of occasions in New Mexico. Friars often understood these revolts as the work of the "devil," or as a sign of native ingratitude.[152] The actions of natives, however, who killed Franciscans, mocked their religion, and desecrated the friars' sacred objects and shrines, make it clear, at least in retrospect, that these rebellions represented efforts to achieve freedom of religious and cultural expression.[153] Franciscans met similar displays of resistance when they sought to extend the spiritual conquest to other North American peoples in the eighteenth and nineteenth centuries.[154]

VII

The Spanish Franciscans who contended with native religions on the seventeenth-century frontiers of North America both succeeded and failed, as would those friars who followed them on subsequent Spanish frontiers. By their own count, the friars succeeded when they tallied the numbers of souls saved through baptism and the number of mission communities where natives worshiped as Catholics and lived as Spaniards. From the missionaries' vantage point, and the viewpoints of historians sympathetic to their goals, their enterprises in North America represented a "triumph" and a "success," exemplifying "Spain's frontiering genius."[155] From the missionary perspective, even when native rebellions took the lives of missionaries their

[150] Foote and Schackel, "Indian Women of New Mexico," 26–29; Gutiérrez, *When Jesus Came,* 14–19. For sexual misconduct among priests and Hispanics in general, see my chapter 11.
[151] For an example of a village fleeing, see the case of a Guale village cited in Gannon, "Conflicto entre iglesia y estado en Florida," 232. Benavides, *Revised Memorial of 1634,* 97, told of the urine and mice meat at Taos (he reported this as a murder attempt, but taoseños certainly would have used more lethal substances if they intended to kill the priest) and of the death of a priest at the Hopi Pueblo of Awatovi from what he believed to be poison (77). Both Florida and New Mexico had a substantial number of martyrs, some of whom died rather mysteriously.
[152] Oré, *Martyrs of Florida,* 73.
[153] These rebellions are discussed in greater detail in the next chapter.
[154] For a fine case study from Alta California, see Sandos, *"Levantamiento!,"* 109–33.
[155] The quotes are respectively from Gannon, *Cross in the Sand,* 37, Espinosa, "Our Debt," 84, and Bolton, "Mission as a Frontier Institution," 211 (Gannon altered his view and offered a less glowing portrait in an article, Spellman [pseud., Gannon], "'Golden Age' of Florida Missions."

missions were not judged as failures. Overlooking the blood shed by Indians, one Jesuit historian has argued that "in mission history every page written with the blood of martyrs is glorious" and "would attract the blessings
of heaven for the conversion of natives."[156] Nor could the deaths of neophytes from European diseases inadvertently introduced by the friars be
considered a mark of failure. Franciscans not only regarded the deaths of Indians and non-Indians as manifestations of God's will but, as one historian
has noted, "missionaries would have philosophically preferred dead Christians to live pagans."[157]

At a less transcendental but more demonstrable level, the friars could
also count among their achievements the number of natives saved from extinction at the hands of unscrupulous Spanish settlers and soldiers.[158] The
Spanish missions, as one historian has argued, were designed "for the
preservation of the Indians, as opposed to their destruction, so characteristic
of the Anglo-American frontier."[159] It must be remembered, however, that
the friars intended to preserve the lives of Indian individuals and not the individual's Indian life.

Whatever they accomplished, the Franciscans recognized that they fell
short of their goal of weakening the indigenous religions and replacing them
with their own. After eighty years of missionary efforts among the Pueblos, for
example, one Spaniard complained that "most" of them "have never forsaken
idolatry, and they appear to be Christians more by force than to
be Indians who are reduced to the Holy Faith."[160] A true synthesis of the
belief systems of the natives and the Spanish intruders did not occur in
seventeenth-century North America any more than it had in sixteenth-century
New Spain. Rather, religions and values remained in lively contention with
one another. To the extent that the militant Franciscans persecuted native religious leaders and tried to impose religious orthodoxy by force, they drove true
believers into secret worship and provoked violent resistance.[161] Critics of the

---

For the identification of Gannon as Spellman, see Weber, "Blood of Martyrs; Blood of Indians,"
440 *n.* 7). The historical literature abounds with praise for the padres, describing them, for example, as carriers of "the light of Christianity and the comforts of civilization to the untutored
children of the forest. . . ." (Castañeda, "Sons of St. Francis," 289), and their work "one of the
brightest chapters in human history" (Alfaro, "Spirit of the First Franciscan Missionaries," 49).
[156] Zubillaga, *La Florida,* 430.
[157] Archibald, "Indian Labor at the California Missions," 180.
[158] For this argument, see, among others, Bolton, "Mission as a Frontier Institution," 211; Gómez
Canedo, *Evangelización,* 143; and Kelsey, "European Impact," 511, who comes to this conclusion
after describing the story of the missions as "a tale of disaster."
[159] Bolton, "Mission as a Frontier Institution," 211. For a similar comparison, see Cook, *Conflict,* 3–5.
[160] Declaration of Luís de Quintana, Dec. 22, 1681, quoted in Forbes, *Apache, Navaho, and
Spaniard,* 177; Dozier, *Pueblo Indians,* 50.
[161] For a succinct and insightful view of sixteenth-century precedent, see León-Portilla, "Spiritual Conquest," 55–83. By resorting to force, the Christian preachers, as one Pueblo scholar has
put it, "produced . . . a people hostile to Spanish Catholicism and civilization" (Dozier, *Pueblo
Indians,* 55).

missions have compared them to penal institutions and Indian neophytes to inmates, who suffered from pestilence, oppression, brutality, and "near-slavery."[162] Critics have questioned the right of missionaries "to invade the most sacred inner precincts of another man's being" and have charged the Franciscans with "religious persecution." They have asked: "If the Indian cultures are extinct is that success?"[163]

The friars also failed to achieve fully their goal of Hispanicizing Indians. In retrospect, it seems clear that they could not have done so in an institution that, in practice, isolated Indians from the larger Hispanic community and in which members of the recipient culture, apparently as dedicated to their own values as Spaniards were to theirs, so vastly outnumbered the missionaries who represented the donor culture.[164]

Finally, missions failed to serve the defensive function that the Crown envisioned. In Florida and New Mexico, native rebellions proved especially costly. They destroyed not only the missions but, as we shall see, rolled back the entire Spanish frontier. As one historian has argued, Spain's "fantasy" of relying on missionaries for Indian control had "helped to divert it from establishing realistic defenses."[165] In the late seventeenth century, reality intruded and the Crown began to abandon its excessive dependence on missions for frontier defense and relied more heavily on soldiers to advance and hold subsequent Spanish frontiers in North America. Nonetheless, even though the government sought to deemphasize them, missionaries would remain in the vanguard of Spanish expansion into Texas, Pimería Alta, and California in the eighteenth century.

Whatever their spiritual successes, then, missionaries failed to advance permanently, defend effectively, or Hispanicize deeply North American frontiers in the seventeenth century.[166] Although Franciscans succeeded ini-

---

[162] The quote is from Spellman [pseud., Gannon], "'Golden Age' of Florida Missions," 355, who argues that there was no golden age. There is no shortage of critical views by scholars. See, e.g., Bowden, *American Indians and Christian Missions,* xvi; Heizer, "Impact of Colonization," 121–39; Matter, "Mission Life," 402, 418–20.

[163] The first quote is from Matson and Fontana, eds. and trans., *Friar Bringas,* 31; the second is from Ortiz, "San Juan," 281, writing about seventeenth-century New Mexico; the third is from Fontana, "Indians and Missionaries," 58.

[164] Polzer, *Rules and Precepts,* 53–54, 58, suggests missionaries did not fail in this task, but rather that the racially stratified non-Indian world beyond the mission was "probably incapable of preparing and accepting Indians into the more advanced forms of frontier society" (55). His position, however, seems to beg the question. For the other viewpoint, see Ricard, *Spiritual Conquest,* 153–54, 288–95.

[165] Matter, "Missions in the Defense of Spanish Florida," 36, 32 *n.* 48, 37 *n.* 67, disagrees explicitly with Bolton on this point. See, too, Arnade, "Failure of Spanish Florida," 277.

[166] In his classic essay, "Mission as a Frontier Institution," Bolton acknowledged that "sometimes, and to some degree, they failed" (211), but in the main he concluded that the missions had succeeded in "extending, holding, and civilizing" the frontier (194). Bolton's conclusions need to be reexamined.

tially in pushing the edges of Christendom into parts of North America, natives pushed them back. Despite new safeguards that the Spanish Crown had built into the system in the late sixteenth century, friars and natives in seventeenth-century North America repeated a cycle that had played itself out a century before in other regions of Spanish America where natives' initial acceptance of missionaries had turned to disillusion, estrangement, and finally to resistance in its many forms, including rebellion.[167] The reasons for the missions' failures, however, lay only partially with Indians and missionaries, for missions represented but one of the oppressive frontier institutions of the Spanish state.

[167] Gibson, *Aztecs under Spanish Rule*, 111–12; Nancy M. Farriss, *Maya Society under Colonial Rule: The Collective Enterprise of Survival* (Princeton: Princeton University Press, 1984), 68–79; Murdo J. MacLeod, *Spanish Central America: A Socioeconomic History, 1520–1720* (Berkeley: University of California Press, 1973), 120–142; Steve J. Stern, *Peru's Indian Peoples and the Challenge of Spanish Conquest: Huamanga to 1640* (Madison: University of Wisconsin Press, 1982), 51–79; Eugene H. Korth, S. J., *Spanish Policy in Colonial Chile: The Struggle for Social Justice, 1535–1700* (Stanford: Stanford University Press, 1968), 51–52, 60, 84.

Reluctant Exiles: Emigrants from France in Canada before 1760

Peter N. Moogk

INTRODUCTION

At the time of the British conquest in 1760, the population of New France was dwarfed by that of its English neighbors. In this piece, Moogk tries to suggest why by presenting a striking counterimage to the familiar narratives of American colonialism. Instead of a land of opportunity and plenty, America is a cold, distant, dreary place. Moogk suggests that the rigors of Canadian life held little appeal for French people deeply attached to the culture of their homeland. New France was clearly very different from the English settler and plantation colonies. The question is, why?

In many circumstances, New France was not all that different from the English colonies. Disease, disastrous Indian wars, family ties, and return migration affected the English colonies as well. Canada's demographic profile is similar to that of the English Chesapeake colonies, which also depended heavily on young, predominantly male, servants. There too, demographic stability and growth only emerged at the turn of the seventeenth century, as the native-born population began to grow of its own accord. New England, with a very similar environment, only outgrew New France because it began with thousands more families than did New France. By the second half of the eighteenth century it had become a place more people emigrated from than to.

French people arrived in North America under rather different circumstances from those of their English counterparts. Most were laborers and artisans who otherwise would have been working in French towns and cities, not yeoman farmers looking for a homestead of their own.

Peter N. Moogk, "Reluctant Exiles: The Problem of Colonization in French North America," *William and Mary Quarterly* 46 (1989), pp. 463–505. Reprinted by permission of Omohundro Institute of Early American History and Culture, Williamsburg, VA.

Mr. Moogk is a member of the Department of History at the University of British Columbia. Acknowledgments: the research for this article was assisted by the Social Sciences and Humanities Research Council. The article has benefited greatly from the suggestions of James Axtell, W. J. Eccles, and Yves Landry.

- *What role did the shorter terms of French indenture contracts play?*
- *Does a man working for three years in a country develop less of an attachment to it than one working for seven years, frequently the term of service for English indentures?*
- *Could it be that French commoners had more say in shaping their colonial experience than the English did?*
- *Finally, should we perhaps be looking for another model to compare New France to other than the neighboring English colonies?*

For the ambitious government administrator, wholesale merchant, or regular army officer, service in the colony of New France was a painful route to a desirable position in the mother country. The colony was seldom accepted as a home; life there was described as an "exile" or "purgatory." In 1707 a military engineer bemoaned his sojourn in Canada, "a wretched place [*triste Endroit*] where I am spending the best years of my life imperceptibly [*Insensiblement*]."[1] Earlier, an intendant observed that "Canada has always been regarded as a country at the end of the world, and as an exile that might almost pass for a [sentence] of civil death."[2] The revulsion felt by these emissaries from the metropolis for the cold and remote North American colony is understandable. What is surprising is that their inferiors, such as indentured servants or soldiers, were just as eager to return to France. Their attitude was eloquently expressed by their actions; they, too, were reluctant exiles. Recently, Mario Boleda concluded that "at least 27,000 French people came to Canada during the French regime." Of these, only 31.6 percent became permanent residents. Over two-thirds of the migrants returned to France.[3]

This astonishing flight back to the homeland helps to explain why New France had no more than 62,000 European inhabitants in 1755. There never was a sustained or large-scale movement of people from France to Canada, and most of those who came did not stay. Indentured workers and subsidized

[1] Jacques Levasseur de Neré to the minister of maritime affairs, Nov. 12, 1707, MG 1, C11A series transcript, XXVII, p. 41, Public Archives of Canada.

[2] Memorial of Intendant Jacques de Meulles to the minister, c. 1684, F3 Moreau de St. Méry, II-1, f. 198, Archives des Colonies, Archives nationales de France, Paris. See also Jean Talon to Jean-Baptiste Colbert, Oct. 31, 1671, Archives nationales du Québec, *Rapport de l'Archiviste de la Province de Québec* (Quebec, 1921–),1930–1931, 150, hereafter cited as *Rapport de l'Archiviste*, in which he begs to be allowed to return to France after "mes travaux dans un païs aussy rude qu'estoit celuy cy dans ses commencemens." Similar sentiments were expressed by 18th-century writers in the French West Indies (Intercepted letters, H.C.A. 30, Public Record Office).

[3] Boleda, "Les Migrations au Canada sous le régime français" (Ph.D. diss., l'Université de Montréal, 1983), xxiv, 339. This estimate of the gross migration and the consequent deduction that about 70% of the migrants left the colony go beyond previous estimates. Hubert Charbonneau and Yves Landry speculate that 56% of all French emigrants to Canada in the 17th century became permanent residents ("La Politique démographique en Nouvelle-France," *Annales de Démographie historique* [1979], 29–57). Stanislas A. Lortie estimated 53.6%. See Hubert Charbonneau, *Vie et mort de nos ancêtres: Etude démographique* (Montreal, 1975), 39.

migrants were numerous in the 1650s and 1660s, but apart from the arrival of prisoners in the 1730s and the settlement of disbanded soldiers and Acadian refugees in the 1740s and 1750s, migrants were an incidental addition to the established population after 1673. There were rarely more than three hundred newcomers a year during the 1600s, and that number dwindled until the 1740s. It was natural increase, rather than migration, that increased the white population of the St. Lawrence Valley sevenfold between 1681 and 1765.

The total migration from France and then back home has been understated by historians of Canada, who relied on census returns and church registers. A "natural increase" was established by subtracting recorded deaths (including migrants) from the number of infant baptisms. The excess above this increase, recorded in censuses, was attributed to immigration. It was assumed that most migrants stayed. Thus traditional estimates of the migration from France between 1608 and 1760 varied from 7,500 to 12,000.[4]

The fitful, small-scale migration to Canada and the high rate of returns to France reveal the influence of cultural attitudes. Human migrations are not fully explained by identifying the "push" of uncomfortable conditions at home and the "pull" of a new land's attractions. Between the "push" and the "pull" there must be mediating factors to produce a large and sustained movement of people over a long distance to a place where they will make a new home. Those factors include communal traditions, an emigrant recruiting system, favorable publicity about the new land, and commercial carriers who will transport numerous passengers. From 1600 to 1760 there was sufficient "push" to dislodge people from France, and life for the lower classes in Canada was sufficiently good to provide the "pull." But because the elements of linkage were deficient, there was no mass migration to French North America.

This article will emphasize popular resistance in France to overseas resettlement; it will also draw attention to the unwillingness of eighteenth-century French shipowners and merchant brokers to assist a large-scale migration of free migrants. High-seas traders decided that the modest profit from indentured workers did not justify the trouble involved in recruiting them. French traders preferred to carry goods and, by the mid-1700s, black slaves. This preference had a cultural as well as a commercial dimension, since contemporary merchants from Rotterdam willingly carried thousands of contract workers to British North America. What might the Netherlanders have done for Canada had they not been excluded from French colonial trade in the eighteenth century?

Apart from the prejudices of potential emigrants and merchant-shipowners, there were other serious impediments to a large-scale, volun-

---

[4] Boleda discusses these estimates with critical comments ("Les Migrations au Canada," 41–55). The estimates, identified by author and date, were Edmé Rameau (1859)—9,700–10,000; Benjamin Sulte (1907)—8,000; Emile Chartier (1920)—12,012: Paul-Emile Renaud (1928)—10,126; Archange Godbout (1946)—7,498; and the Programme de Recherche en démographie historique (c. 1982)—8,527.

tary migration to Canada before 1760. Little reliable information on the colony's assets was available to the lower classes in France. The Atlantic passage was costly and dangerous, and the maritime traffic to Canada, which might have carried migrants, was small.

In France, popular knowledge of the colonies depended more on hearsay than on publications or private letters. What little was heard was damning. Even in the literature of the early 1600s, " 'Canada' was used only as a joke, a synonym for frightful exile."[5] In 1659, when the people of La Flèche heard that forty respectable women were departing for Canada, the townsfolk tried to prevent their departure because no one could believe that the women were going voluntarily. Pierre Boucher's *Histoire Véritable et Naturelle des Moeurs & Productions du Pays de la Nouvelle France* (1664) was expressly written to improve the reputation of Canada. Boucher denied that ne'er-do-wells *[garnemens]* and prostitutes were exiled to New France but conceded that the colony had four great *incommoditez:* mosquitoes, long winters, rattlesnakes, and "the Iroquois our enemies."[6]

There were compensatory advantages to life in Canada for able-bodied members of the lower classes: obtainable land and material independence. Under seigneurial land tenure, uncleared land could be had for the asking; it cost the would-be tenant nothing. No direct taxes were paid to the crown—a wondrous situation for the peasantry of France. Seventeenth-century authors, such as Samuel de Champlain and the Jesuit missionaries, described the fertile soil, abundance of water, ample resources, and variety of wild game (which commoners could hunt!) in New France. Boucher also extolled these benefits but compromised his role as a recruiter of emigrants. Wanting to show that the Iroquois must be conquered, as well as to gratify European curiosity about the "wild people" *[les sauvages]* of the Americas, he devoted a quarter of his book to the native Indians, with a chapter on Iroquoian ritual torture and the eating of captives. Stories about such horrors had already been conveyed to France.[7] The impression of Canada left in the minds of those who read Boucher's book or heard it read aloud would have been contradictory: it was a fruitful land inhabited by cruel and barbarous natives.

Boucher's book and the annual *Relations* published by the Jesuits probably reached few potential settlers. The publications cost more than a manual worker's daily wage. In the *Relation* of 1636, Father Paul Le Jeune acknowledged that landless and ambitious members of France's lower orders were

[5] Morris Bishop, *Champlain: The Life of Fortitude* (New York, 1948), 362.

[6] Boucher, *Histoire Véritable et Naturelle de Moeurs et Productions du Pays de la Nouvelle France . . .* (Paris, 1664), 149–155.

[7] Marriage of Jacques Chaigneau and Louise Forrestier, Jan. 7, 1657, Mariages et inhumations de la paroisse Saint-Nicolas de La Rochelle, 1654–1667, Registre 668, série E supplément, Archives de la Charente-Maritime. Witnesses in the French port testified beforehand that Chaigneau's first wife "had been killed by the Iroquois one league from Quebec."

not his readers: "But to whom do I speak? To people who cannot know what I am writing, unless more capable ones than they tell it to them. These I beg to do so, in the name of God and of the King; for the interests of both are involved in peopling this Country."[8]

There was nothing in France to match the single-minded, effusive literature of seventeenth-century England that promoted emigration to the New World. Potential emigrants in France relied on hearsay and chance to learn about the colonies: one literate man obtained information about Canada and Louisiana from sailors, while another was told about New France by an officer visiting Paris.[9]

British colonization was spurred on by an army of pamphleteers *and* by private letters sent home by the immigrants. By this transatlantic correspondence the hesitant were informed, reassured, and encouraged to follow those who had gone ahead. The letter writers were familiar and trusted informants who frequently offered to help those who followed them to the New World. Two-thirds of Scottish emigrants bound for the Carolinas in 1774, when interviewed by customs officials at Lerwick, said they were induced to emigrate by letters from friends and kin in North America, as well as by hardships at home.[10] There is no evidence of a comparable network of correspondence to attract and assist emigrants to New France. Mail delivery in the French empire was informal and risky, and barely half the migrants in Canada could sign their names.[11] Only one private letter to a relative recom-

---

[8] Paul Le Jeune, "Some Advice to Those Who Desire to Cross Over into New France [1636]," in Reuben Gold Thwaites, ed., *The Jesuit Relations and Allied Documents: Travels and Explorations of the Jesuit Missionaries in New France, 1610–1791*, 73 vols. (Cleveland, Ohio, 1896–1901), IX, 187, hereafter cited as *Jesuit Relations*. Le Jeune consistently promoted emigration to Canada. See his letter to Cardinal de Richelieu, Quebec, Aug. 1, 1635, *ibid.*, VII, 238–245; the 1635 Relation, chap. 3, "How it is a benefit to both Old and New France, to send colonies here," *ibid.*, VIII, 8–15; and the Relation for 1659–1660, chap. 1, *ibid.*, XLV, 189–195.

[9] In 1752 a man who joined the colonial troops recalled "I sought information about the best country to live in; about Louisiana and Canada. . . . The sailors told me that Canada was more healthy, although its climate was colder" (Sylvester K. Stevens *et al.*, eds., *Travels in New France by J.C.B.* [Harrisburg, Pa., 1941], 1–2). Inconsistencies in the story lead one to suspect that "J.C.B." was a transported convict and not a willing passenger. In a 1698 petition a servant at Quebec stated that at Paris, his birthplace, he met a minor port official from Quebec through a friend, "Et auroit pris Resolution Sur Le Recit que luy fit . . . De Ce Païs [Canada], dy passer" (Petition of Etienne Courtin to Quebec's *Lieutenant général civil et criminel*. 1698, 62e liasse, No. 3289, Collection de pièces judiciaires et notariales, Archives Nationales du Québec.

[10] "Motives for Scotch emigration to America (1774)," in Merrill Jensen, ed., *English Historical Documents: American Colonial Documents to 1776* (New York, 1955), IX, 469–476.

[11] The only way of measuring literacy in New France is by signatures on documents and by the legally required declaration that a party could not sign. Using this evidence, Marcel Trudel finds that 56.8% of the immigrants who came in 1632–1663 could sign, males being more literate than females (62.2% as opposed to 34.4%) (*Histoire de la Nouvelle France. Vol. III: La Seigneurie des Cent-Associés. 1627–1663.* Pt. 2: *La Société* [Montreal, 1983], 51, hereafter cited as Trudel, *Histoire—La Société*). Using parochial marriage registers from 1680–1699, Allan Greer finds that 44.1% of the male French immigrants could sign whereas 29% of the French-born females signed ("L'alphabétisation et son histoire au Québec: Etat de la question," in Yvan Lamonde, ed., *L'Imprimé*

mending the colony as a place for settlement is known to exist: it was sent in 1651 by a gentleman at Quebec to his brother-in-law at Tours.[12] As we shall see, the French migrants were more likely to receive appeals to return home than to invite others to join them.

Can the royal government of France be blamed for hindering a large migration to North America? Some historians have argued that official preference for Roman Catholic settlers deprived New France of the addition of Huguenot fugitives from France.[13] The royal administration also feared that France would be weakened militarily and economically by the loss of any part of its population. In 1665, when Intendant Jean Talon offered to prepare homesteads in Canada for more than that year's quota of three hundred assisted emigrants, Secretary of State Jean-Baptiste Colbert refused the offer. He told Talon that the king regarded the increase as impractical and believed that "it would not be prudent to depopulate his kingdom to populate Canada."[14] Colbert expected New France's European population to grow by natural increase, once a nucleus of colonists had been established. Despite official religious prejudices and concern for maintaining the population of France, the government did not impede migration to the colony. The formal exclusion of Protestants and Jews from the French colonies was not strictly enforced, despite appeals from the Roman Catholic clergy. In the eighteenth century the crown approved the emigration of German-speaking Protestants to Louisiana, Cayenne, and Saint-Domingue.[15]

---

au Québec: Aspects historiques (18–20e *siècles*) [Quebec, 1983], 42). It is evident from the crudeness of nearly a third of the signatures that signing one's name was the limit of the writer's literacy.
[12] Lucien Campeau, S.J., "Un Témoignage de 1651 sur la Nouvelle-France," *Revue d'Histoire de l'Amérique française.* XXIII (1970), 601–612. The author, Simon Denys, had come to Quebec from Acadia with his wife. He commended the fertility of the land and the virtues of the colonists. He too remarked on the prejudices in France: "Lorsqu'en France vous entendez parler du Canada, vous imaginez un désert inculte et plein d'horreur." As for him and his wife, they had decided to stay "sans renoncer toutefois à l'espérance de revoir la France" (*ibid.,* 609, 611). This hope of seeing France again was typical of most emigrants.
[13] Because the 1627 charter of the *Compagnie des Cent-Associés* specified that only Roman Catholic French subjects should be brought to New France, it has been suggested that the colony was deprived of a host of useful Protestant settlers by this requirement. This suggestion was first made by Louis-Armand de Lom d'Arce de Lahontan in 1703. See Reuben Gold Thwaites, ed., *New Voyages to North America, by the Baron de Lahontan.* 2 vols. (Chicago, 1905), I, 392–393. François-Xavier Garneau repeated this idea in *Histoire du Canada.* 5th ed. rev., 2 vols. (Paris, 1913–1920 [orig. publ. Quebec, 1845–1852]), I, 94.
[14] Talon to Colbert, Oct. 4, 1665, *Rapport de l'Archiviste.* 1930–1931, 36; Colbert to Talon, Jan. 5, 1666, *ibid.,* 41. In 1666 Talon acknowledged Colbert's belief "qu'il n'y a pas dans l'ancienne France assez de surnuméraires, et de sujets ynutils po. peupler La Nouvelle" (Talon to Colbert, Nov. 13, 1666, *ibid.,* 54).
[15] Marc André Bédard has shown that the exclusion did not prevent a few hundred Protestants from entering or settling in the colony ("La présence protestante en Nouvelle-France," *Revue d'Histoire, XXXI* [1977], 325–349). See his more detailed account, *Les Protestants en Nouvelle-France* (Quebec, 1978). In the more tolerant atmosphere of the 18th century, German-speaking Protestants were recruited by a private company as colonists for Louisiana in the 1720s and in 1765 Rhineland Germans were sent by the crown to Cayenne and Saint-Domingue. This underlines

The six-to-nine-week voyage from France to Quebec could have been a deterrent to migration. The passage was longer than that to the British North American colonies, and the hazards were much the same. Some deaths en route were to be expected. The misfortunes afflicting passengers from France befell other transatlantic migrants: shipwreck, contrary winds, storms, seasickness, water damage to clothes and possessions, a tedious diet, foul drinking water, ship fevers, and surly crew members. Before 1760, piracy or attack by foreign warships was an additional risk.

For civilian passengers to Canada, shipboard conditions were usually better than those endured on immigrant ships going to the British possessions, because passengers on French merchant vessels were a small addition to the crew. Humble voyagers slept in hammocks on the gun deck and ate with the sailors—a situation to be envied by British immigrants traveling in steerage. When a vessel was packed with people as well as cargo, the crowding and unsanitary conditions bred maladies. Fatal epidemics sometimes broke out on French warships and royal transports carrying scores of soldiers and prisoners in addition to the usual complement of officers, government officials, and religious personnel.[16]

At the beginning of the crown-subsidized migration in 1662–1671, royal transports carried hundreds of workers and settlers. Without experience in caring for so many passengers and in the absence of health regulations, these vessels were death traps. Thirty-three percent of the passengers died en route in 1662. Of 300 persons embarked in France in 1663, nearly 60 perished at sea and a dozen more died in Quebec's hospital after arrival.[17] Thereafter, recruiting and transportation of the royal levies were entrusted to merchants with experience in the delivery of indentured laborers. In 1664 Dutch vessels were chartered, possibly because the Netherlanders knew how to keep passengers alive as well as being cheap and efficient mariners. A Dutch ship was retained in 1665 when the *Compagnie des Indes Occidentales* assumed responsibility for the royal program. The people transported by private vessels arrived in good health, and the death rates of 1662–1663 were matched only in 1732, 1740, and 1757, when large numbers of soldiers, prisoners, and government workers were packed on royal vessels.[18]

---

the resistance of the native French to overseas migration. Protestants and Jews were also formally excluded from the French West Indies and there, too, secular officials quietly tolerated their presence. The Roman Catholic clergy, however, complained about heretics in the colonies. Mathé Allain, "Slave Policies in French Louisiana," *Louisiana History*, XXI (1980), 127–137.

[16] Gilles Proulx, *Entre France et Nouvelle-France* (Laprairie, Quebec, 1984), 107–113.

[17] *Jugements et Délibérations du Conseil souverain de la Nouvelle-France*, 6 vols. (Quebec, 1885–1891), I, 201–204; the passenger rolls appear in *Revue d'histoire*. VI (1952–1953), 392–396. In 1663 a Dutch ship *Le Phoenix [de Feniks]* of Flushing, had been used to deliver the first contingent of *filles du roi* to Canada.

[18] In 1740, just 81 of a complement of 270 on the king's ship *Le Rubis* arrived alive and well; 42 died en route to Canada. The passengers were military recruits, exiled prisoners, and workers

Danger in Canada and in route

Since religious and political dissidents from France tended to move to adjacent European countries rather than emigrate to the French colonies, secular migrants to Canada usually lacked ideological mettle to face the rigors of overseas settlement. Apprehension of the sea voyage and the Iroquois might explain the panic that swept one group. In the 1650s the *Société de Notre-Dame de Montréal* recruited batches of people in France for the Montreal Island settlement, which was frequently raided by the Iroquois. In 1653, 153 men were enticed to sign up for five years in the colony in return for good pay and a cash advance. Before boarding ship at Saint-Nazaire, 49 fled with the advance payment and one annulled his contract. The hulk bearing the remaining 103 took on so much seawater that it was forced back to France. The expedition's commander placed the migrant workers on an island off the French coast, "from which it was impossible to escape since, otherwise, not one of them would have remained." According to the same eyewitness, some were so desperate to escape that they jumped into the ocean to swim to the mainland "to save themselves, for they were like madmen and believed that they were being led to destruction."[19] That fear was vindicated: while crossing in a second ship, eight went to a watery grave and, in New France, another 24 were killed by Indians.

From this, it is evident that the "pull" of Canada was weak. The same could not be said of the "push" needed to dislodge people from home and familiar surroundings. If unemployment, famine, and hardship incline people to overseas migration, then France should have been an ideal recruiting ground for Canadian settlers. The entire seventeenth century and the early eighteenth century have been described as an era of crisis for all of France. In 1959, when Robert Mandrou sought the essence of Gabriel Debien's study of workers indentured at La Rochelle in 1634–1714 for service in the Americas, he saw an exact correlation between peaks in enlistments and periods of famine, hunger, and riot in western France. Mandrou concluded that "the emigration from La Rochelle is, therefore, largely due to misery . . . The indentured workers were only willing [to sign up] in the port . . . during difficult years. In ordinary times, it was necessary to appeal to them, to go out and seek them, and often from very far away."[20]

There were major grain famines in northwestern France in 1660–1662, 1675–1679, 1692–1694, 1698–1699, and in 1709, when an excessively cold

---

for the royal shipyard at Quebec (Charles de Beauharnias and Gilles Hocquart to the minister, Aug. 27, 1740, MG 1, C11A series transcript, LXXIII, p. 7, Public Archs. Canada).

[19] Etienne Michel Faillon, *Mémoires particuliers pour servir á l'Histoire de l'Eglise de l'Amérique du Nord . . . .* 4 vols. (Paris, 1853), I, 65. See also Roland J. Auger, *La Grande Recrue de 1653* (Montreal, 1955), 9–15. M. Auger introduced me to the genealogical sources that made it possible to trace the fate of individual immigrants.

[20] Robert Mandrou, "Vers les Antilles et le Canada au XVIIe siècle," *Annales, Economies, Sociétés, et Civilisations*, XIV (1959), 667–675. The book was Gabriel Debien, *Les Engagés pour les Antilles (1634–1715). Revue d'Histoire des Colonies*, XXXVIII (1951).

winter caused a general crop failure. Hunger and unemployment increased the wandering population. La Rochelle's civic authorities appointed archers in 1698 "to prevent itinerant beggars [gueux forains] and foreigners from entering the town."[21] Some of these starving wretches had traveled great distances: among the paupers who died at La Rochelle were a boy from Mons diocese, a young man from Maine province, a confectioner from Arles in Provence, as well as beggars from nearby Poitou.[22]

There was a connection between hard times in France and peaks in the recruiting of *engagés* (indentured workers) for the colonies. Famines in 1660–1662, 1698–1699, 1709–1710 and 1721–1723 aided recruiters in the ports of La Rochelle and Nantes.[23] There was *not*, however, *an exact correspondence* between acute distress in France and the scale of recruiting. By dealing with the "push" alone, Mandrou neglected the "pull" exerted by recruiters. The Montreal associates were responsible for the peaks in 1644 and 1659, and the royal program underlay the mass of contracts made in 1664–1665 . . . Some regions may have been sheltered from the major demographic crises in France,[24] but La Rochelle was not one of them. The poor soil of its hinterland produced little grain; some inferior wines from the district were distilled into brandy for export. Distress in a region linked by trade with the American colonies did not automatically produce a wave of voluntary emigrants for the overseas possessions, as the table shows. A famine in the area around La Rochelle might displace farm workers and town artisans, but it did not follow that they would resettle in the colonies.

Most French migrants to Canada came from Paris and surrounding Ile-de-France, Perche, and the coastal provinces of Saintonge, Aunis, Poitou, Brittany, and Normandy.[25] Recruiters concentrated on the hinterland of Atlantic seaports, such as St. Malo, Granville, and Dieppe. La Rochelle was the principal port of departure for New France during Louis XIV's reign. It was the natural outlet for Poitou, Aunis, Saintonge, and Angoumois, which,

---

[21] [Louis-Marie de] Meschinet de Richemond, *Inventaire sommaire des Archives départmentales antérieures à 1790: Série E Supplément (archives communales). Ville de La Rochelle* (La Rochelle, 1892), 22–23.

[22] Meschinet de Richemond, *Inventaire.* 277, 282, 290, 292, 326, 329, 450.

[23] See graph in Mandrou, "Vers les Antilles," *Annales*, XIV (1959), 671, covering indentures made for the West Indies as well as Canada. Gabriel Debien, "Les départs d'engagés par Nantes pour l'Amérique" (typescript, c. 1969), shows peaks in recruiting in 1698–1700, 1708, 1710, and 1713. Some of his findings are communicated in "les Engagés pour le Canada partis de Nantes (1725–1732)," *Revue d'Histoire*, XXXIII (1980), 583–586. Among 6,000 indentures made at Nantes in 1632–1732, he found just 18 contracts for Ile Royale and the St. Lawrence Valley.

[24] Pierre Goubert's *La Vie quotidienne des Pays francais au XVIIᵉ siècle* (Paris, 1982) describes regional economies within France that operated independently of one another.

[25] Observations made by Stanislas A. Lortie and Adjutor Rivard, *L'Origine et le Parler des Canadiens-français* (Paris, 1903) are confirmed by Mandrou, "Vers les Antilles," *Annales*, XIV (1959), 667–675, and by Hubert Charbonneau and Normand Robert in R. Cole Harris, ed., *Historical Atlas of Canada. Vol. I: From the Beginning to 1800* (Toronto, 1987), plate 45.

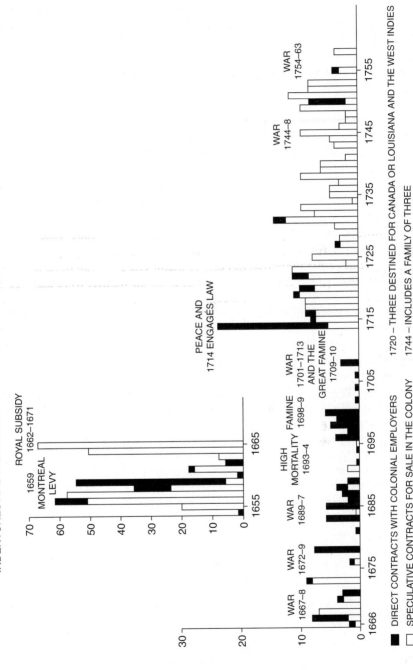

INDENTURES AT LA ROCHELLE FOR THE ST. LAWRENCE VALLEY, 1654–1760 (576 CONTRACTS)

ROYAL SUBSIDY
1662–1671

1659
MONTREAL
LEVY

WAR
1672–9

WAR
1667–8

WAR
1689–7

HIGH
MORTALITY
1693–4

FAMINE
1698–9

WAR
1701–1713
AND THE
GREAT FAMINE
1709–10

PEACE AND
1714 ENGAGÉS LAW

WAR
1744–8

WAR
1754–63

■ DIRECT CONTRACTS WITH COLONIAL EMPLOYERS
□ SPECULATIVE CONTRACTS FOR SALE IN THE COLONY

1720 – THREE DESTINED FOR CANADA OR LOUISIANA AND THE WEST INDIES
1744 – INCLUDES A FAMILY OF THREE

99

according to Stanislas A. Lortie and Adjutor Rivard, furnished 30 percent of Canada's French settlers in 1608–1700.[26] Thus La Rochelle is an appropriate choice for studying the migration from France to Canada.

The reluctance of the population to enroll for work in the colonies, even in times of distress, was common in France. Past overseas migration was geographically selective; regions accustomed to the departure of large portions of the population, whether as seamen or mercenary soldiers or migrant workers, always sent forth a disproportionately large number of emigrants. Areas of France that lost people by emigration, such as Normandy, lost them in internal migration to cities and other regions of France. Some wandered into neighboring European kingdoms. Only a few thousand chose permanent resettlement in a distant colony. With a population four times England's five million and a history of demographic disasters, France sent out a much smaller number of contract workers to the colonies.

Contemporaries remarked on the paradox of rural folk who preferred a miserable, precarious existence in France to material security abroad. After the famine of the 1630s, Father Paul Le Jeune marvelled that "there are so many strong and robust peasants in France who have no bread to put in their mouths; is it possible they are so afraid of losing sight of the village steeple, . . . that they would rather languish in their misery and poverty, than to place themselves some day at their ease among the inhabitants of New France?"[27]

The questions about Canada put to Pierre Boucher in the 1660s reveal that the enquirers were interested in emigration only if it allowed them to carry on their old way of life in greater comfort. Unlike the English Puritans, the French laity were seldom prepared to forego worldly comforts for spiritual ends. They were not escaping a detested liturgy and episcopacy to create a new Christian polity; they *had to be assured* that familiar religious institutions would be present. They also asked, "is wine dear there?, . . . are there horses in the country?," and, most often, "what profit can be made there?" Boucher affirmed that "the land is good, and capable of producing all sorts of things as in France."[28]

Self-financed, independent newcomers were so rare in New France that they were noted in administrative records and in official correspondence.[29]

---

[26] Lortie and Rivard, *L'Origine et le Parler des Canadiens-français*, II. Lortie made a meticulous study using Cyprien Tanguay's seven-volume digest of the surviving pre-1800 parish registers, *Dictionnaire généalogique des familles canadiennes depuis la fondation de la colonie jusqu'à nos jours* (Quebec, 1871–1880), as well as the bishop of Quebec's confirmations register to identify the origins of 4,894 French emigrants who settled in Canada in 1608–1700. Ile-de-France (including Paris) and Normandy accounted for 32.3% of the newcomers, exceeding the group from Poitou-Aunis-Saintonge-Angoumois.

[27] *Jesuit Relations*, IX, 187. In 1659–1660 Fr. Le Jeune answered his question in part by acknowledging that fear of the Iroquois forced settlers to leave their lands and seek refuge in the towns (*ibid.*, XIV, 191–199).

[28] Boucher, *Histoire Véritable*, 136–138.

[29] *Jugements et Délibérations*, I, 223; Talon to Colbert, Nov. 2, 1671, *Rapport de l'Archiviste*, 1930–1931, 154–155; Talon to the king, 9 March 1673, *ibid.*, 172.

expense

They were usually gentlemen-travelers spying out the land; their social inferiors needed help to get to Canada. The fare, rations included, for a lower-class passenger sailing to New France in the second half of the seventeenth century was sixty to eighty *livres*.[30] It would take a skilled craftsman a year to accumulate enough money for a single fare.[31] French shipowners did not compete in offering cheap passages to the New World. The only alternatives for humble folk were indentured labor or a redemption contract. In the system of indentured or bond labor, the sponsor offered a passage to North America and material benefits in return for a few years of work in the colonies. In the case of families, the sponsor might demand a promise of repayment for the costs of transportation. This was the "redemption" system that brought so many German-speaking families to British North America's Middle Colonies. The French knew about redemptioning; they sometimes used it but preferred to indenture individual workers. Before 1663, when the crown assumed direct administration of New France and ended the reign of the chartered companies, private interests sponsored the migration of most newcomers. Marcel Trudel estimates that 3,106 migrants had arrived in 1632–1676.[32]

In this period those making direct personal contracts with people in France were often recipients of seigneurial grants from *la Compagnie des Cent Associés*. Under its 1627 patent the company was to bring out 4,000

---

[30] Grand Livre: 1674–1687, MS C2, Archives du Séminaire de Québec. There are four cases in which the passage from La Rochelle to Quebec cost sixty *livres* (pp. 47–48, 188–189, 225, 242–243) and one in which the *engagé's* fare was 46 *livres*, 13 *sols*, 4 *deniers* (pp. 204–207); all are from the period 1675–1676.

In a 1653 court case at Trois-Rivières it was claimed that the cost of bringing out an *engagé* from France was 110 *livres tournois* in beaver pelts; a witness suggested that 80 *livres* was a more reasonable charge. See cahier 4, Nov. 20, 1653, MG 8, Di (Trois-Rivières), Public Archs. Canada.

In 1659 Jeanne Mance was charged 75 *livres* for the passage of each adult she had sponsored. Archange Godbout, *Les Passagers du Saint-André: La Recrue de 1659* (Montreal, 1964), 2. In peacetime, during the 1720s, the fare for those traveling on royal ships and eating with the crew, rather than at the captain's table, dropped to 30 *livres*. See Proulx, *Entre France et Nouvelle-France*, 108, and List of passengers embarked on the royal *flûte* Le Chameau, Nov. 2, 1724, série 1E, CV, p. 323, Archives du Port de Rochefort. In 1749 passengers sailing from Bayonne to Ile Royale paid 62 *livres* 10 *sols* "A la Ration ordinaire" or 150 *livres* to eat at the captain's table. See Bayonne: passengers for Ile Royale, 1749, série F5B, art. 38, nos. 1 and 2, Archs. des Colonies.

[31] In northwestern France in 1693 rural weavers earned five or six *sous* a day while a good weaver in Beauvais might command nine *sous*. Carpenters and locksmiths in Rouen earned as much as fifteen or thirty *sous* in the same period. Fernand Braudel and Ernest Labrousse, *Histoire économique et sociale de la France*, 3 vols. (Paris, 1970), II, 668–669. Allowing for compulsory days of rest, with no deduction for living expenses, even the Beauvais weaver would need almost a year to earn his passage to Canada.

Fares to British North America were slightly cheaper. According to Richard B. Morris, *Government and Labor in Early America* (New York, 1946), 319, in the 17th century "the average cost of transportation varied from £5 to £6 sterling."

[32] Trudel, *Histoire—La Société*, 11, 22.

emigrants over the next fifteen years.[33] English attacks on company ships and the loss of Quebec in 1629 so weakened the enterprise that it was unable to meet this requirement. After restoration of the colony to France in 1632, the company transferred part of its obligation to settle the land to those receiving estates from the venture. The recipients might be landless gentlemen or religious groups such as the pious founders of Montreal.

In 1634 the company granted Beauport seigneury to Robert Giffard, a surgeon from Mortagne in France. A condition of his grant was that "the men" he or his successors brought to Canada would be counted as part of the total the company had to transport to New France. In that year Giffard arranged to have forty-three people from the Mortagne district join his family in emigrating to the colony. A surviving contract made with a stonemason and a carpenter shows the high price he paid to overcome popular resistance to overseas migration. Giffard was to transport the two craftsmen to Canada and provide them with food, lodging, and maintenance "in all their necessities" during the three years they helped him to clear and cultivate land. In addition, they would receive half the lands they cleared, not as tenants but as subseigneurs, as well as another thousand acres of wild lands close to the river. Giffard was to bring out their families two years later and provide each family with two cows. The lord of Beauport kept his promise, but his ungrateful workers claimed in 1637 that *all* of the lands granted were noble estates and thus they owed him no tenants' dues. For the stonemason, these benefits and the presence of his children and fellow Percherons did not cure his homesickness; he waited twenty years before selling his house in Mortagne.[34]

Another colonizing seigneur, Noël Juchereau Des Chatelets, and his brothers who recruited some forty workers in Perche in 1646–1651, encountered the same reluctance to resettle permanently in Canada. All his recruits received, in addition to food and wages, *the promise of a prepaid passage home* at the end of their three or five years of service. Three made advance arrangements for that return, and one manservant asked that his salary be paid to his wife in France. Only a third of the workers became permanent residents of Canada.[35]

[33] *Edits, Ordonnances royaux, déclarations et Arrêts du Conseil d'Etat du Roi concernant le Canada* (Quebec, 1854), 6–7 ("Acte pour l'établissement de la Compagnie des Cent Associés pour le commerce du Canada . . . 29 avril 1627"). The king's acceptance in Mar. 1663 of the surrender of the company's charter claimed that the number of colonists established "étoit fort petit" (*ibid.,* 32). In fact, over 3,000 Europeans were living in New France in 1663.
[34] Alfred Cambray, *Robert Giffard, premier Seigneur de Beauport, et les origines de la Nouvelle-France* (Cap-de-la-Madeleine, Canada, 1932), 34–39, 73–77. The transcription of the contract on pp. 34–39 does not conform to the facsimile on the pages opposite. The stonemason was Jean Guion (1588–1663) whose six grown children were present when he dictated his will in 1663. Greffes des notaires du régime francais, G. Audouart, May 14, 1663, Archs. Nationales du Québec. For more information on Guion see *Bulletin des Recherches historiques,* XLIX (1943), 268–272, and J[ean]-B[aptiste] Ferland, *Notes sur les Registres de Notre-Dame de Québec* (Quebec, 1863), 64–67.
[35] Mme. Pierre Montagne, *Tourouvre et les Juchereau: Un chapitre de l'émigration percheronne au Canada* (Quebec, 1965), 31–86, lists contracts and provides additional information on these people.

The *Société de Montréal* was desperate to retain survivors of the 1653 levy in Canada; it offered them free land and settlement bounties to become colonists. Those who accepted the offer had their service contracts annulled in 1654 and were given credit and wages to assist their establishment, yet only forty workers accepted this generous proposal.[36]

Immediate land grants and family ties were seen as effective in keeping former indentured workers in the colony. The Montreal associates applied the lesson in 1659 when they recruited 109 persons in France; 40 were women (12 wives accompanied single women and a few nuns). Eight families had their passage paid in return for a redemption bond due in two years. Thanks to the presence of relatives and marriageable females, most of the 1659 recruits became *Canadiens*.[37] The value of bringing out entire families, as a sure way of fixing newcomers to the new land, was demonstrated. The evidence, alas, was ignored by later recruiters.

Coincidental with the making of direct, personal contracts with workers in France by colonial employers or their agents, was a speculative trade in impersonal contracts. From the mid-1650s, the merchants of La Rochelle and other trading cities hired large numbers of workers with the intention of selling the contracts in the Americas. The colonial buyer of the indenture acquired the stated rights and obligations of the master. Before 1663 the speculative trade brought 55 percent of the migrants to the St. Lawrence Valley—more than twice the number brought out by the *Cent Associés*.[38]

The trade in workers with Canada was a secondary branch of the large-scale West Indian commerce. This is revealed by contracts that described the laborer's destination as "the land of Canada in the said [Caribbean] islands"

[36] Auger, *La Grande Recrue*, 9–15; Gustave Lanctôt, *Montreal under Maisonneuve, 1642–1665*, trans. Alta Lind Cook (Toronto, 1969), 68–69.

[37] Of those presumed to be alive in 1663, 70.8% (68 out of 96) became permanent settlers. This information was extracted from Godbout, *Les Passagers du Saint-André*, 11, 13–48; E. Z. Massicotte, "Les Colons de Montréal de 1642 à 1667," *Memoirs of the Royal Society of Canada*, 1913, Section 1, pp. 16–22; and Masicotte, "Une recrue de Colons pour Montréal en 1659," *Canadian Antiquarian and Numismatic Journal*, 3d Ser., X (1913), 171–191.

The retention rate for the 1659 levy was exceptionally high. In *Habitants et Marchands de Montréal au XVIIᵉ siècle* (Paris, 1974) Louise Dechêne combines this group with the 1653 contingent to determine the proportion of survivors who became settlers. Her figure of 52% (pp. 74–75) only applies to this unusual sample and is atypical of the overall pattern for *engagés* going to 17th-century New France or even Montreal Island. Using other, equally limited samples of migrants from La Rochelle, Archange Godbout observes (without allowing for deaths in the colony) that "De 1642–1644, sur 147 engagés, . . . 15% s'établissent et . . . De 1655 a 1657, sur 42 engagés, . . . 12% s'établissent" ("Families venues de La Rochelle en Canada," *Rapport des Archives nationales du Québec*, XLVIII [1970], 119–126, quotation on p. 125). From my notes on 63 men indentured at La Rochelle for Canada in 1656–1657 before the notary P. Moreau (MSS 1845, ff. 56vo–109, and MSS 1846, ff. 45vo–121vo, Bibliothèque de la Rochelle), I found 14 or 22.2% still present in New France, according to the 1666–1667 censuses. It seems reasonable to assume that a quarter of the surviving, single male workers remained in the colony after their term of service during the 17th century.

[38] Trudel, *Histoire—La Société*, 22.

and by eighteenth-century accords providing a salary payable in sugar.[39] Over 900 people were indentured at La Rochelle for New France, yet there were five times as many hired for the French West Indies.[40] This matched the greater volume of maritime traffic between France and the Caribbean islands, which were probably a more profitable market for workers. By British North America's standard, it was still a small trade. Because of this dependency, the flow of indentured workers to Canada was influenced by the West Indian market for white labor.

From 1640 to 1670 the great demand in French America was for unskilled farm laborers; in Canada they were employed as land-clearers [défricheurs]. Among skilled occupations, the building trades attracted some interest.[41] By 1657 speculative contracts drawn up by French notaries no longer listed the worker's former trade; what counted were age and physique. Robust adult males were given a premium of ten to twenty *livres* above the base salary of sixty *livres* a year. Recruiters also began to restrict and then to omit the clause providing a prepaid return passage to France. This was an economy measure of employers, not an indication that *engagés* were willing to become colonists. The recruits still acted like mi-

[39] Greffe de Pierre Moreau, Bibliothèque de La Rochelle; The phrase "Pays de Canada aux dittes Isles" appears in three contracts: MSS 1845, f. 56vo, MSS 1846, ff. 118–118vo, and 121vo, *ibid*. The Caribbean standard for indentured service was invoked in 18th-century contracts for Canada: in 1716 a Rochelais captain hired men "aux conditions des îles" and three others enrolled in 1733 were to be "nourris, logés sur le pied des engagés des Îles." *Revue d'Histoire*, XIII (1959–1960), 255, XIV (1960–1961), 252.

[40] Relying on surviving notarial indentures made at La Rochelle in 1634–1716, there were 943 departures for New France, including Acadia, as opposed to 4,800 going to the West Indies. See Debien, "Les Engagés pour les Antilles," *Revue d'Histoire des Colonies*, XXXVIII (1951), 142. This sum includes 15 more indentures for what is now Canada that my wife Susan and I found at La Rochelle. These do not appear in the total found by Debien (928) and later researchers. Debien also stated that of some 6,000 *engagés* who sailed from Nantes in 1632–1732 only 18 went to Ile Royale and the St. Lawrence Valley (see above, n. 23). In the 18th century, Bordeaux became the principal port serving the American colonies and the contracts made there for overseas *engagés* have yet to be inventoried. It is unlikely, however, that they will reveal a large-scale traffic in workers for Canada.

[41] Occupational divisions among workers recruited for and resident in the St. Lawrence colony were as follows:

Sector	New France, 1663 (526 persons)	Direct Indentures Made at La Rochelle for Canada, 1641–1665 (224 contracts)
Agriculture and Domestic Service	30.3%	38.8%
Food Trades	7.4%	5.3%
Building Trades	23.7%	20.8%
Clothing Trades	6.8%	2.2%
Toolmaking	7.4%	0.0%
Metalwork	0.0%	5.8%

grant workers: fewer than a third of them became permanent residents of Canada.[42]

The program of subsidized emigration in 1662–1671 continued the older, speculative indenturing system under the king's auspices. Royal officials used merchants as recruiters, who probably employed the customary forms of publicity: posters and criers in public places directing volunteers to a well-known inn or tavern to be enrolled. Recruits were given an advance of thirty to thirty-five *livres* to buy clothes and other necessities before their departure. They were quartered in quayside inns until a ship was ready for boarding. Any delay in sailing increased the chance of desertions.[43]

Under the royal program, the crown paid merchant-recruiters for the indentured workers' transportation and for any cash advances. At Quebec the *Counseil souverain*, rather than the ship's master, arranged the sale of service contracts and the distribution of workers. Colonial employers of the king's *engagés* only had to pay the Quebec council for the advance given to the worker in France and, possibly, for his board in Canada if his indenture was not sold at once.[44]

Since the French crown bore the cost of the passage across the Atlantic, these workers were cheaper than those supplied by independent merchants. This undermined the trade in speculative contracts with Canada. A comparison of lists of the king's *engagés* sent out in 1664–1665 with the censuses of 1667–1668 reveals that *Conseil souverain* members used their control over the distribution of workers to supply themselves and their friends with cheap labor. Councillors, seigneurs, merchants, crown and company officials, as well as religious institutions, rather than simple colonists, profited from royal largesse.[45] Those who gained most from this program were the ones who had least need of a subsidy.

In the seventeenth century Boucher observed that "most of our settlers here [in Canada] are people who came as servants and, after serving a master for three years, set up for themselves."[46] The three-year term was just one

---

[42] The propensity of the single men hired by merchants under speculative contracts to go home is evident in Godbout's analysis of a 42 man sample from 1655–1657 ("Familles venues de La Rochelle," *Rapport des Archives nationales du Québec*, XLVIII [1970], 119–126).

[43] Debien, "Les Engagés pour les Antilles," *Revue d'Histoire des Colonies*, XXXVIII (1951), 69–72.

[44] *Jugements et Délibérations*, I, 190–191.

[45] Using the passenger roll for *Le Noir* in 1664 from Amirauté, B 5665, pièce 10, Archives de la Charente-Maritime (reprinted in *Revue d'Histoire*, VI [1952–1953], 392–393), I checked the names of 51 *engagés* listed against the nominal censuses of New France in 1666 and 1667. To make sure that the pattern for this group was not unique, I traced 66 other workers delivered by the other Dutch ship *Le Cat* (probably *De Kat*) in 1665, listed *ibid.*, 394–396, in the same fashion. After eliminating two duplications and one female, there remained 114 names. Of these, 57 could be found in the censuses; 38 were employed in Quebec town and the adjoining region. The masters were notable and wealthy colonials (23), tenant farmers (16), religious orders (10), and craftsmen (4). Ten indentured workers were employed as artisans, and 17 were living in towns.

[46] Boucher, *Histoire Véritable*, 161–162. He added: "Ordinarily, they have little of anything and they later marry a woman who has nothing more. However, in less than four or five years you

of the favorable conditions offered to the poor and unemployed of France to get them to enroll as *engagés*. There were suggestions that the term of service be reduced further, but the *Conseil souverain* insisted that every *engagé* must serve a full three years to learn all the skills needed for survival in Canada. Other evidence and the rapid adaptation of later British immigrants show this to be a self-serving argument of the workers' employers.[47]

Three years became the standard term of indentured workers, who were later called *"trente-six-mois."* This period was short in comparison with seventeenth-century English colonial servants' bonds, which ran from four to seven years—four being customary for adult males. French *engagés* worked for a *shorter* term *and received a salary*. An unskilled man received at least sixty *livres* a year, in addition to food, shelter, and some clothing. Granted, that salary was often a credit against which the worker received liquor, personal articles, and services from the master.[48] English indentured servants generally received no salary beyond "meat, drink, apparel, and lodging." "Freedom dues" were a rare privilege consisting of tools, clothes, perhaps some land, and occasionally a small amount of money.[49] This reward at the end of service was to discourage runaways and to hold the laborer for the full contractual period; it was not a salary.

---

will see them at their ease, if they are fairly hard-working people." According to Le Jeune in 1659–1660, many a diligent farmer with a family achieved self-sufficiency "in less than five or six years." *Jesuit Relations*, XLV, 191–193. In 1665 Mother Marie de l'Incarnation wrote "when a family commences to make a habitation, it needs two or three years before it has enough to feed itself, not to speak of clothing, furniture" (Joyce Marshall, trans. and ed., *Word from New France: The Selected Letters of Marie de l'Incarnation* [Toronto, 1967], 315).

[47] *Jugements et Délibérations*, I, 201–204. The hypocrisy of this claim is evident from the fact that 30% of the *engagés* were employed as servants in the towns, where life was little different from that in France. Moreover, in 1663 the council rejected a Sulpician priest's appeal that a former *engagé* who returned to New France on the king's ship be free to reenter the Sulpicians' service for a shorter term because "il ne seroit pas raisonnable qu'une personne qui auroit servy quatre ans dans le pais fust engagée comme les autres." The *engagé* had already been assigned to an officer and judge at Montreal. *Ibid.*, 30.

[48] Grand Livre: 1674–1687, MS C2 *passim*, and Grand Livre: 1688–1700, MS C4 *passim*. Archs. du Séminaire de Québec. These account books list debits and credits under each employee's name, although continuing entries jump several pages before resuming. Subsequent account books are rough ledgers listing each transaction as if happened, without consolidating the entries for different creditors and debtors. They cannot be used to evaluate the treatment of employees. From the 17th-century account books, it appears that the Quebec Seminary tried to make each worker's debts equal any credit due him as if to avoid cash payments. For example, of 15 *engagés* in 1674–1687, seven had no outstanding balance, five were owed amounts from 6 to 195 *livres*, and three owed the seminary amounts from 42 to 115 *livres*. Typically, Julien Brûlé, a shoemaker whose annual salary was 150 *livres*, had a credit of only 6 *livres*, 3 *sols* at the end of his first year's service. He used the amount to pay off a 7 *livres* debt to another person. See MS C2, pp. 250–251, *ibid*. His debts were for shoes, winter clothing, tobacco, beer, stockings, combs, fine shirts, a crucifix, laundry, and a tailor's services.

[49] Bernard Bailyn, *Voyagers to the West: A Passage in the Peopling of America on the Eve of the Revolution* (New York, 1986), 167; David W. Galenson, *White Servitude in Colonial America: An Eco-*

Indentured better in Canada than south a us

The benefits accorded a Canadian *"trente-six-mois"* did not end legal sub-jection. A governor defined an *engagé* as "a man obliged to go everywhere and to do whatever his master commanded like a slave."[50] Many were poorly fed and badly clothed. In 1737 a frozen body was identified as "a sailor or an *engagé*" because of its rough attire: brown vest and pants, gray outer vest, mittens, worn-out wool stockings, and sealskin moccasins.[51] In the brutal and exploited world of bond servants, however, the lot of the Canadian *engagé* was preferable to that of indentured workers in the British colonies; it was also superior to the fate of *engagés* in Louisiana and the French West Indies, where a white laborer's life was sickly and short.

Despite the advantages of service in Canada, recruiters never found vol-unteers in the numbers or of the quality desired. According to Quebec's *Conseil souverain*, those sent out by the crown in 1662–1663 included "several persons unsuited for work or the clearing of land, whether because of their advanced age, infirmities, illnesses or because of ill-usage and misconduct while coming on the said vessels. Among their number are some discharged soldiers, all of whom are now public charges. . . . It would be appropriate to send them back to France." The healthy and well-inclined servants were mostly "young clerks, schoolchildren, or of that nature; the best part of whom have never worked."[52] Many had to be clothed at the council's expense. In 1667 Intendant Talon com-plained about the levy delivered by the *Compagnie des Indes Occidentales*: "in-stead of four hundred good men . . . I have received only one hundred and twenty-seven, very weak, of low age, and of little service."[53] In future, he asked that "passengers for Canada" be between sixteen and forty years of age and that no "idiot, cripple, chronically ill person or wayward sons under arrest" be sent, since "they are a burden to the land and degrade it."[54] Despite Colbert's repeated assurances that every care would be taken in selecting men, the qual-ity of the king's *engagés* was never as good as in 1664, when nearly three hun-dred were delivered "ready to work upon landing."[55]

In 1682, a decade after the royal subsidy for transporting migrants to New France had lapsed, Intendant Jacques de Meulles asked for a restoration

---

nomic Analysis (Cambridge, 1981), 5–10, 102–113; Robert Owen Heavner, *Economic Aspects of In-dentured Servitude in Colonial Pennsylvania* (New York, 1978); Abbot Emerson Smith, *Colonists in Bondage: White Servitude and Convict Labor in America, 1607–1776* (Chapel Hill, N.C., 1947), 17; Warren B. Smith, *White Servitude in Colonial South Carolina* (Columbia, S.C., 1961), 72.

[50] Marginal note to Gov. Buade de Frontenac's memorial on illicit fur traders, 1681, in *Rapport de l'Archiviste*, 1926–1927, 123.

[51] Kenneth Donovan, "Tattered Clothes and Powdered Wigs: Case Studies of the Poor and Well-To-Do in Eighteenth-Century Louisbourg," in Donovan, ed., *Cape Breton at 200: Historical Essays in Honour of the Island's Bicentennial, 1785–1985* (Sydney, Nova Scotia, 1985), 7.

[52] *Jugements et Délibérations*, I, 29, 202.

[53] Talon to Colbert, Oct. 27, 1667, *Rapport de l'Archiviste*, 1930–1931, 81.

[54] Talon to Colbert, Oct. 29, 1667, *ibid.*, 87.

[55] *Jugements et Délibérations*, I, 201.

of the program since "we have an acute need for workers and day-laborers."[56] The result was disappointing: the intendant wrote that the sixty *engagés* who arrived in 1684 were "little children" aged twelve to fourteen, "fit, at most, to tend cows." He permitted an extension in their period of service to four and five years to dispose of them.[57] Few mature and able-bodied men, it appears, would volunteer to work for an unknown master in New France.

From 1662 to 1671 almost 200 *engagés* were brought to Canada at the king's expense each year, except in 1666 when none arrived. The *Compagnie de Indes Occidentales* delivered 978 "personnes" in 1665–1668; some were women. The crown brought out an additional 180 men in 1668. Funds were provided for sending 500 people of both sexes in 1669, but their arrival was not acknowledged. An allocation for 100 was made in 1670 and 49 arrived.[58] Assuming that a third of the 2,500 or more "personnes" delivered were females, the king's subsidy ought to have added 1,700 males to the colony's population. A worker delivered, however, was not a settler established.

On average, the program had cost the crown 25,000 *livres* a year; it did not produce a proportionate increase in the colonial population. By early 1666 the operation had transported 460 males to Canada, in addition to the workers hired by private individuals and religious orders. That year's census enumerated just 401 *engagés*. Colbert was surprised when the 1668 census of Canada listed only 1,568 males capable of bearing arms.[59] In 1676 the king ordered the head count to be redone, "being unable to persuade myself that there are but 7,832 persons . . . in the entire country, and having transported a larger number in the fifteen or sixteen years since I took charge."[60] This was an exaggeration, but the small number was remarkable since it included the native-born as well as settlers from other sources, such as the garrison troops. Marcel Trudel cautiously estimates that a third of all emigrants who came before 1660 re-embarked for France.[61] In the next decade that fraction increased as the proportion of single men whose contracts were to be sold to colonists grew. Over two-thirds of the king's *engagés* went home, just as the bachelors hired *en masse* by merchants had done.

Prevailing winds and the St. Lawrence River's current made it easier and cheaper to sail eastward to France than to come to Canada. Former indentured workers, if not tied to the colony by marriage or a land grant, were wanderers. Their inclination was to go home, but since a governor's permit was required to leave the colony, they were not free to depart. In 1658 the

[56] De Meulles to Colbert, Nov. 12, 1682, MG 1, C11A series transcript, VI, pp. 116–117, Public Archs. Canada. In a Nov. 4, 1682, dispatch de Meulles suggested that the holders of the export monopoly for beaver pelts be obliged to bring out fifty *engagés* yearly (*ibid.*, 289).
[57] De Meulles to Colbert, Nov. 12, 1684, serie C11A, VI, f. 399, Archs. des Colonies.
[58] Talon to Colbert, Nov. 2, 1671, *Rapport de l'Archiviste,* 1930–1931, 155.
[59] Colbert to Talon, Feb. 20, 1668, *ibid.*, 94.
[60] The king to Louis de Buade, Comte de Fontenac, Apr. 15, 1676, *ibid.,* 1926–1927, 87.
[61] Trudel, *Histoire—La Société,* 71–73.

governor noted with surprise that even workers whose services were in demand "all ask me for their permit [to leave]," once their contracts expired.[62]
Quebec's *Conseil souverain* recorded in 1663 that "there are many working
men who have served the time to which they are bound . . . [and] ask for the
right to return to France."[63]

Intendant Talon opposed the liberal distribution of departure permits
and warned Colbert that "while people return, this colony will scarcely grow
stronger, whatever pains you take to increase it. . . . Several people returned
this year, but a much larger number is still waiting to leave next year, thanks
to the liberality in giving out permits."[64] Talon suggested that only prominent persons and those with an established home or family in the colony be
allowed to leave "without difficulty," but that men who had just completed
their indentured service be charged the equivalent of one transatlantic fare.
An absolute denial would "dishearten those who might wish to come here
. . . with the thought . . . that one never leaves when one is once here." In the
meantime, Talon was endeavoring "to fix the single men and, by marriage,
attach them to some community and so oblige them to work at the cultivation of the land."[65]

Tying bachelors to the colony by marriage was easier said than done.
Eighty percent of the emigrants who arrived in 1632–1662 were males.[66] Few
European women were available as brides. In the 1660s there were more than
twelve unmarried males, aged 16 to 30, for every eligible female in the same
age group. This imbalance may have encouraged men to leave Canada. To
provide wives for the surplus of bachelors, the French crown assisted the emigration of 774 *"filles du roi"* in 1663–1673. These women came from a charitable hospice in Paris and, to a lesser extent, from the countryside. A quarter
were over age 25, when most women were already married, and more than
half had lost a parent.[67] For the *"filles du roi,"* overseas emigration led to marriage and, perhaps, a more honorable match than was possible at home. Unlike the *engagés,* these women were true *immigrants:* they came to Canada to
wed an established colonist and to stay. The royal administration also nursed
the hope that the missionaries' work would produce many Christian
Amerindian brides for French settlers, but this was a false expectation.

The *"filles du roi"* and punitive measures against bachelors, such as
Talon's 1670 interdict on trading and hunting by single men, did not eliminate by marriage the group that wanted to return to France. Devious methods were then used to hinder their departure. A dispatch in the king's name,

[62] Voyer d'Argenson to Baron de Fancamp, Sept. 5, 1658, quoted *ibid.,* 72.

[63] *Jugements et Délibérations,* I, 29.

[64] Talon to Colbert, Nov. 11, 1671, *Rapporte de l'Archiviste,* 1930–1931, 164.

[65] Memorial from Talon to Colbert, Nov. 2, 1671, *ibid.,* 152.

[66] Trudel, *Histoire—La Société,* 37.

[67] Silvio Dumas, *Les Filles du Roi en Nouvelle-France: Etude historique avec répertoire biographique*
(Quebec, 1972), 35–60.

sent to a governor in 1672, stated that "my intention is that you do not permit any Frenchman to return to my kingdom if he does not have a wife and children and a firm establishment in the said land of New France that will ensure his immediate return to the colony." The order was to be kept secret because, if widely known, it might discourage travel to Canada.[68] Migrant workers were to become settlers, whether they wished to or not. When the intendant was informed of this rule, he was advised to apply it discreetly, "it being important that the French should not feel themselves detained by force in the said country."[69]

Gentle firmness was again recommended to the governor of New France in 1675 when dealing with the persistent problem of people who wanted to leave the colony. "It would appear to me," wrote the king, "that a rather large number of residents, men and women, return to France. It is something you must prevent, as much as possible, by gentleness and by persuasion." Yet only those "who could never be suspected of deserting" would be permitted to leave Canada."[70] Unauthorized departures were indeed treated like military desertions. When one fugitive was sentenced to hang, the minister of maritime affairs reprimanded the governor for his excessive zeal.[71] If the rate of returns from New France was high, it would have been higher still had there been no restrictions on abandoning the colony.

The problem of retaining these unhappy exiles resulted from a shortsighted economy. Royal levies of migrants were recruited primarily from single males. In 1669 an official described the transportation of families as "a bad practice" since "one hundred persons, composing twenty-five families, will cost as much to the king as one hundred bachelors" who, presumably, would all be productive workers.[72] Bachelors' indentures would be easier to sell than contracts for families. The administration hoped that marriage *after* emancipation would convert migrant workers into settlers. In the seventeenth century, when voluntary civilian migration to the colony was greatest, most French *engagés* resisted settlement, whereas those coming with families almost always stayed in Canada.[73]

---

[68] The king to Frontenac, June 5, 1672, *Rapport de l'Archiviste*, 1926–1927, 8.

[69] Colbert to Talon, June 4, 1672, *ibid.*, 1930–1931, 169.

[70] The king to Frontenac, Apr. 22, 1675, *ibid.*, 1926–1927, 80. In a dispatch of Apr. 1676 the monarch told Frontenac that exit permits must be issued sparingly, because of the loss of colonists and "parce qu'ils n'y repassent que par inquietude et pour venir consommer leur bien dans un voyage inutile" (*ibid.*, 87).

[71] Jean-Baptiste Colbert, Marquis de Seignelay, to François Charon de La Barre, Apr. 10, 1684, in E. B. O'Callaghan, ed., *Documents Relative to the Colonial History of the State of New York*, 15 vols. (Albany, N.Y., 1853–1887), IX, 221. The same volume contains the king's 1684 ordinance against removing to English and Dutch settlements and an edict to punish those who attempt to do so (pp. 224–225).

[72] Acting Intendant Patoulet to Colbert, Nov. 11, 1669, série C11A, III, f. 61, Archs. des Colonies.

[73] Richard C. Harris, "The French Background of Immigrants to Canada before 1700," *Cahiers de Géographie du Québec*, XVI (1972), 313–324. The author, in using Fr. Archange Godbout's genealogical information published in *Rapport de l'Archiviste* from 1951 to 1965 under the title "Nos

Emigration does not work out well for everyone; invariably, some retrace their steps in disappointment. In the seventeenth century many New Englanders lost heart and returned to old England, but they were a small fraction of the total migration.[74] This was equally true during the Great Migration from Britain in 1815–1860. The numerous letters of their kin in Britain enquired about the prospects of life in North America. In the few hundred surviving letters to pre-1760 emigrants in French America, the theme is very different. Here we have evidence of a major cultural contrast; those left behind in France looked upon resettlement abroad as unnatural, even as selfish and immoral. Family obligations helped to call the emigrants home.

A worker hired in 1653 by the Montreal associates acquired land with the evident intention of becoming a colonist. In 1669 his distressed father wrote to remind the expatriate that filial duty and his material interests demanded his return to France. "I find it very strange," wrote the father, "to have a child whom I have cherished more than myself and who has no desire at all for me. I believed that I would have the happiness of seeing him within four or five years of his departure." Work in Canada was to be a temporary expedient, not a prelude to settlement there. In just three months, the son was told, he could be "in your good town of La Flèche, from which you come" and in possession of 800 *livres* from his late mother's estate, as well as "many other things that you only have to ask for." By the *droit de légitime*, every lawful child was assured of a share of the parental estate.[75] This may have enticed others home. As a final, persuasive flourish, the father conveyed the best wishes of the exile's kin "and all your good friends in this fine land of Anjou,

---

ancêtres au XVIIᵉ siècle," assumed that the progenitors of Canadian families were representative of the entire migration. The bias of the evidence resulted in an erroneous conclusion that "the immigrants sent to Canada after 1662 usually came alone, and *almost never returned to France.*" The propensity of single males to return to France is also neglected in Lucien Campeau, "Le peuplement de la Nouvelle-France, opération civilisée," in René Bouchard, ed., *La Vie quotidienne au Québec: Histoire, Métiers, Techniques et Traditions* (Sillery, Quebec, 1983), 107–123. Fr. Campeau has argued in this and in his previous work, *Les Cent-Associés et le peuplement de la Nouvelle-France (1633–1663)* (Montreal, 1974), that colonization before 1663 has been underestimated by historians whereas the contribution of Louis XIV, Colbert, and Talon to the colony's settlement has been exaggerated. His evidence is the rate of population growth in the decades before and after 1663. Although the high proportion of single males in the post-1663 migration is noted, their tendency to return home is not related to the slower rate of population growth. A lower proportion of the crown's recruits stayed in Canada *because* they were unmarried men.
[74] Everett Emerson, ed., *Letters from New England: The Massachusetts Bay Colony, 1629–1638* (Amherst, Mass., 1976), 65, 72. Those who returned are receiving scholarly attention; see Susan M. Hardman, "The Return of New England settlers to England, 1640–60" (Ph.D. diss., Kent University, forthcoming).
[75] Claude-Joseph de Ferrière, *Dictionnaire de Droit et de Pratique . . . .* 2 vols. (Toulouse, 1779 [orig. publ. 1740]), II, 104–106; *Ordonnance des Testamens du mois d'Août 1735. articles 51–53*, in [Jacques-Antoine] Salle. *L'Esprit des Ordonnances et des Principaux Edits et Déclarations de Louis XV* (Paris, 1771), 201–206.

where we drink good wine for a sou." The son returned to France for a decade, but then reappeared in Canada, where he married and died.[76]

Memories of friends and home were also skillfully evoked in 1756 for a Bayonne merchant living on Ile Royale (Cape Breton). "Come back to your homeland [*Patrie*]," he was told, "here fine grapes are eaten . . . Come and let us see if you have not lost your taste for them as well as for peaches, pears, and so on." The writer in France listed the daily amusements at Bayonne: skittles, *pelota,* and a card game for money. "This game, which will last all winter, will not ruin you," and "you might even win 800 *livres* for your bastard children while amusing yourself." The recipient in North America was addressed as "libertine" or "old sinner" and was advised that the "young lasses [*des jeunes tendrons*]" of Gascony would take his mind off his profits.[77]

One *fille du roi* sent to Canada to help secure the male population did the reverse. She married a Montreal joiner who, in 1680, unwisely let her depart with three of their children to visit her home in Paris. Once there, she begged him in letters to join her with the other children. "It is something absolutely necessary; that is why I beg you in God's name, my dearest husband, not to delay in coming as soon as you can." He was to sell their house and possessions in the colony and to smuggle large fur muffs with their clothing, because "beaver and marten fur are extremely valuable in Paris." The joiner was assured of employment in France.[78] Church registers testify that the entire family, save one grown-up son, moved to France and stayed there.[79]

In a society built on networks of kinship and patronage, successful and well-connected individuals were expected to assist less fortunate relations. The widowed sister-in-law of the king's engineer in Canada offered in 1755 to attend to his affairs in France if he would obtain a clerical position in a government ministry for his fatherless nephew, who was unemployed.[80] Female relatives expected succor. There are innumerable letters from women that pray for the emigrant's good health and express hopes for his early return or, failing that, a remittance to aid family members in France.[81] The aid

[76] Letter deposited in the file of the Montreal notary, Bénigne Basset, Mar. 25, 1670, in Auger, *La Grande Recrue de 1653,* 103–104.
[77] J. Barrère, cadet at Bayonne, to M. Laborde at Louisbourg, Oct. 23, 1756, H.C.A. 30/264, 194.
[78] Madeleine-Thérèse Sallé, Mme. Raimbault, at Paris to Claude Raimbault, master joiner at Montreal, Mar. 15, 1681, Centre régional de Montreal, Bailliages, feuillets séparés: 1681, Archs. Nationales du Québec. This letter is reprinted, with accents and punctuation added, in E. Z. Massicotte, "De l'usage du manchon autrefois," *Bulletin des Recherches historiques* XXXIII (1927), 325–327.
[79] The makeup of the family and its members' fate are revealed by Tanguay, *Dictionnaire généalogique,* I, 507–508, VI, p. 500; by E. Z. *Massicotte in Bulletin des Recherches historiques* XXI (1915), 78–81; and by Robert Lahaise in *Dictionary of Canadian Biography* (Toronto, 1969), II, 541–542.
[80] Irène Chaussegros, in France, to her brother-in-law, Joseph Gaspard Chaussegros de Léry, at Quebec, May 13, 1755, Author's Collection.
[81] In addition to the letters referred to in notes 78, 80, 82, and 84, see Maria Pasqual to her father, Martin Pasqual, carpenter at Louisbourg, Mar. 12, 1757 (H.C.A. 30/264, 126); Catherine Valentin to Antoine Valentin, carpenter at Cap Français, Nov. 12, 1757, in which she assures him that upon

expected by relatives was best provided when the giver was in his place of birth; transatlantic communications were uncertain.

It was made emphatically clear to one absentee that the welfare of his widowed mother and unmarried sister demanded his return from New France; sending money was not enough. When this ship's captain married at Louisbourg, suggesting a desire to stay in North America, it was reported by a parish priest in France that the captain's mother "was excessively afflicted to the point of dissolving into tears and of shrieking [*à jetter des hauts cris*] when she was given the news of your marriage at Louisbourg, but her pain ebbed slightly after receiving your two letters that inform her of your reasons binding you to establish yourself in this land [Gascony-Navarre] and, finally, she was almost entirely consoled upon learning that you had married a young lady of merit." In short, the girl had property and respectable parents. Now that the captain and his bride had told the mother of their wish to come home "and live with her, she gives you both her blessing." The priest assured the newlyweds that "she . . . only sighs . . . to see you and embrace you. Therefore, come . . . as soon as you can; come to console her and give her the satisfaction of spending her last days with you. Natural impulses, sentiments of honor and religion, gratitude for all the kind acts and for all the pains she took for your education—all cry out for that; all of them call you to her side." By corollary, his settlement in North America would be dishonorable, impious, ungrateful, and immoral. The *curé* suggested that the captain send some money to his mother and sister immediately "to ease thereby their discomfort."[82] An uncle made a similar suggestion.[83] The sickly sister informed the emigrant that her initial distress upon hearing of his marriage had been eclipsed by a belief that "my poor mother will have a

---

his return "vous Seres Contan Come un Roy pour votre etat et vous metre[z] mon esprit an Repos" (H.C.A. 30/265, 57), as well as a mother at Marseilles to Joseph Danillon at Cap Saint-Marc, Oct. 20, 1757 (*ibid.*, 58); Mme. Audileort at Aix to Joseph Audileort at Moka Neuf, Cap Français, July 12, 1757 (a mother's appeal to a military deserter to come home under an amnesty and restore "la tranquilité d'une pauvre mere qui ne feroit que plurer") (*ibid.*, 63); Catherine Detchegaray at Ascain to Pierre Detchevery, shipbuilder on Martinique, Mar. 22, 1757 (*ibid.*, 68); and *passim*. A sixth of the letters to Ile Royale are in Euzkara/Basque, and seem to follow the same pattern. See Martin Larralde de Bastidaguerre at Saint-Pée to his nephew Saint-Martin de Duronea at Louisbourg, Mar. 16, 1757, in which he seeks aid for the recipient's mother (H.C.A. 30/264, 68). Maria Urquidi of Vancouver translated this letter and the few other texts in Euzkara.
[82] Father Behola at Saint Pée to St. Martin Duronea at Louisbourg, Feb. 14, 1757 (H.C.A. 30/264, 122). A sailor from Saint-Jean de Luz, who had stayed on at Louisbourg, received a similar appeal from his mother in 1757: "Je suis Baucop [*sic*] Entristé de Votre part . . . Je suis dans un age Comme Vous scavez La grasse que Je vous demande [est] de vous Retirer ché Vous Mon cher fils pour Lamour de moy dans Letat que Vous Etes cet [*sic*] La grasse que Je demande avant ma mort que Je vous puisse vous Voir une fois au moins apres que Je vous E [*sic*] veu une fois Je ceRais content de moury." Here was a mother who knew how to exploit her son's conscience! Mariya Delapits at Saint-Jean de Luz to Pierre Laborde at Louisbourg, Apr. 2, 1757, *ibid.*, 130.
[83] St. Jean Mornigust at Ciboure to St. Martin Duronea, Mar. 17, 1757, *ibid.*, 95.

peaceful and secure old age and I [will have] all the help and advantages that I ought to expect from a brother I love tenderly."[84] Such a consensus made establishment abroad impossible. If this were typical of the social pressure exerted on emigrants, one can readily understand their urge to return home.

The unwillingness of the French to come to New France and stay persisted after the danger of Iroquois attacks receded and the imbalance of the sexes was corrected. The 1701 peace treaty with the Five Nations Iroquois ended the threat of murderous incursions that had alarmed colonists.[85] By 1698, males no longer outnumbered females in the European population of Canada. This demographic change affected the market for indentured workers and reduced the flow of migrants from France. When it was easier to find a wife, concession farms became family-run operations. They produced enough to feed and maintain the family, with a small surplus to be bartered for manufactured goods. Canadian farms were not commercial enterprises; family self-sufficiency was all that was desired. Married tenant farmers did not want the costly services of an *engagé*. The potential employers of indentured workers were seigneurs with large demesnes, the administrative and mercantile elite, and religious houses. They still wanted cheap manual laborers and lamented the disappearance of the king's *engagés*.[86]

The market for indentured workers in Canada became more selective as well as smaller. Population growth and economic diversification produced skilled craftsmen who formerly had to be imported. The character of colonial workers was known, and they could be dismissed without financial loss if no longer wanted. For cheap domestic servants, *Canadiens* turned to the children of the poor, who would be bound until adulthood for their maintenance

---

[84] Marie Martin Duronea to St. Martin Duronea, Feb. 12, 1757, *ibid.*, 104.

[85] François Dupont, in a contract passed before the Quebec notary Guillaume Audouart, Aug. 24, 1661, sold his land to return to France because in Canada he was "sans assurance contre les incursions des Iroquois" (quoted in Trudel, *Histoire—La Société*, 72. Cyprien Tanquay, *A travers les Registres* (Montreal, 1886), 36–90, 262–263, shows that attacks intensified in 1660–1662, 1667, and reached a peak in 1687–1694. John A. Dickinson, "La guerre iroquoise et la mortalité en Nouvelle-France, 1608–1666," *Revue d'Histoire*, XXXVI (1982), 31–47, argues that since some 190 colonists were killed by the Iroquois in this period and more people died by accident or by drowning, the murderous reputation of the Iroquois is undeserved. Perceived danger is not always based on statistical probabilities. The shocking and unusual nature of the killings would have made a greater impression on the colonists than a drowning.

[86] Jean Bochart de Champigny to the minister, 1699, MG 1, C11A series transcript, XVII, p. 108, Public Archs. Canada. See also résumé of a letter from Mme. Vaudreuil to the minister, *Rapport de l'Archiviste*, 1942–1943, 415–416. Gedéon de Catalogne added his voice to the chorus in 1712; see his report of Nov. 7, 1712, in William Bennett Munro, ed., *Documents Relating to the Seigniorial Tenure in Canada, 1598–1854* (Toronto, 1908), 145, 149.

A 1687 memorial on the advantages that *engagés* would bring to neglected Acadia suggests that this region of New France no longer received indentured workers. Advantages to the state and to trade . . . to be procured by a company on the coast and land of Acadia, série C11D, II, ff. 67–75, Archs. des Colonies.

alone.[87] The cost of an indentured worker could be reduced by leasing the *engagé* out to other employers or by selling the contract before the term had expired, but hiring a stranger in Europe was a risky and expensive business. The cost and risk became less tolerable as the colony's labor supply developed.

After 1671 the flow of voluntary emigrants to Canada declined. Royal subsidies for transporting workers ended in 1672 when Louis XIV's war against the Low Countries diverted funds from colonial development. With the crown gone as a competitor, La Rochelle's merchant-shipowners resumed speculation in contract labor for the colonies but abandoned this commerce after 1673. In the French West Indies the shift to black slave labor explains the declining interest in European manual workers. Once again, the Caribbean trade may have determined the fate of commerce with Canada, but there were good local reasons for the decline in speculative contracts in the late seventeenth century . . .

Direct personal contracts with workers in France continued on a reduced scale. Colonial employers were always more selective than merchant-speculators; increasingly, they wanted skilled and experienced craftsmen. But such artisans were even more reluctant than unskilled youths to go overseas. In 1687 Canada's senior administrators were told that royal officials at La Rochelle had taken "all the pains in the world to find the [skilled] workers . . . asked for; there being scarcely one of them who would wish to leave his establishment to go to a country like Canada without some certainty of earning his living more richly than in France." The colonial officials were advised to keep the few being sent fully occupied and to pay them everything that had been promised, since it was agreed that the craftsmen "could return to France at any time they might please."[88]

Thirty years later, in an era of peace, the situation was no better. In 1720 Jean-Antoine, comte d'Agrain was commissioned to hire forty-eight masons, carpenters, and stonecutters to work on the fortifications of Ile Royale and the Windward Islands. He traveled over 300 kilometers from Rochefort to the Auvergne, where, even with help, he obtained only twenty-five artisans, two of whom were limeburners accepted for want of the desired craftsmen. The workers insisted on a yearly salary, rather than payment by piecework, and a free return passage to France. All were given a cash advance and a travel allowance to get to the port of embarkation. One ingrate then tried to

---

[87] Peter Moogk, "Les Petits Sauvages: The Children of Eighteenth-Century New France," in J. Parr, ed., *Childhood and Family in Canadian History* (Toronto, 1982), 17–43.

[88] Minister to de Champigny, Apr. 9, 1687, B series transcript, XIII, pp. 172–173, Public Archs. Canada. A letter of the same date to Gov. Jacques-René de Brisay de Denonville repeats this statement with the variation "pour aller dans un pais aussy esloigné que le Canada" (série B, XIII, f. 58, Archs. des Colonies). This letter mentions the right of the workers to return whenever they please. In 1719 the king's engineer at Louisbourg noted "les bons ouvriers qui connoissent les Isles [American colonies] par experience ou par reputation demandent aujourd'huy 80#. de gages par mois" M. de Verville to the maritime council, Aug. 10, 1719, série C11B, IV, f. 235, *ibid.*

desert.[89] This affair led the maritime council to observe that it was very hard to find craftsmen for the colonies; it directed the intendant at Rochefort to keep all workers subsequently hired on Oléron Island "so they cannot escape."[90]

The Quebec Seminary's unhappy experiences with contract workers from France brought about a change in hiring policy. The seminary still wanted skilled specialists from France but had difficulty finding reliable and competent workers. When a brickmaker was wanted, the seminary's Paris agent (a priest) asked a brickyard owner, who came for confession, to find the craftsman. Months passed with no result. "I did not want one from the provinces, such as Normandy or elsewhere," wrote the agent, "but no one wanted to go to Canada. . . . It is no small difficulty to find a faithful and industrious man who is not immoral and who has a fear of God." A visiting builder-architect from Quebec considered himself "too great a lord to involve himself in this search" and refused to help.[91]

Qualified craftsmen, apart from textile workers and shoemakers, commanded yearly salaries of 75–120 *livres*. In addition, a man's food and lodgings cost the employer another 90–180 *livres* a year. There was also an initial expenditure of 70 or more *livres* to recruit and transport a worker from France. An employer counted on three years of labor to justify these expenses. Unfortunately for the seminary, some recruits turned out to be idlers, bunglers, drunkards, and runaways. Of thirty-two workers hired in France in 1671–1676, seven had to be sent back before completing their term of service.[92] A gardener enrolled in 1673 for 75 *livres* a year was given clothing, a knife, and a comb on credit. After seven and a half months at Quebec he ran away. When he returned, he was sent to a new master on a distant estate. After a second flight, the seminary's account book recorded that the gardener was "sent back to France after five months in prison where he was fed [by the seminary] out of charity."[93]

Such experiences led the seminary's proctor to recommend in 1682 that, henceforth, colonial workers be hired "even if they are more costly . . . since

[89] The story of d'Agrain's recruiting expedition comes from série B, XLII-1, ff. 58–58vo, 201vo–202, XLII-2, ff. 468–469, 485vo, Archs. des Colonies, and from série IE (correspondence between the maritime council and the intendant at Rochefort), XCIV, pp. 501–503, 621–625, XCV, pp. 11–15, 57–58, C, p. 61. Archs. du Port de Rochefort. The crown paid out 2,675 *livres* in expenses for the expedition; it gave the count a 400 *livres* bonus as well as a free passage with rations for eight workers destined for his Ile Royale estate. These men murdered d'Agrain because of maltreatment and inadequate food. See série G2, CLXXVIII, ff. 78–85, Archs. des Colonies.
[90] Maritime council to the intendant at Rochefort, Jan. 22, 1721, série IE, XCVI, pp. 69–70, Archs. du Port de Rochefort.
[91] Abbé Tremblay to François de Laval, June 15, 1703, Lettres, Carton N, No. 121, Archs. du Séminaire de Québec.
[92] Grand Livre: 1674–1687, pp. 41–412, MS C2, *ibid.* In 1634 a Jesuit father at Quebec reported, "Last year they sent us a man as a carpenter who was not one" (*Jesuit Relations*, VI, 71).
[93] MS C2, p. 47 [Jean Dubosq], Archs. du Séminaire de Québec.

one is often deceived in those who are sent from France" and because the value of the French *engagés'* work in the first year barely exceeded the cost of obtaining them.[94] From 1675 onward, the seminary relied increasingly on local men hired by the year or by the month. Some French recruits were kept at Paris for a probationary period to assess their nature because, as the bishop of Quebec observed in 1685, "it is very difficult to judge the character of all these people."[95]

Given the more selective market in Canada for French contract workers and their continuing reluctance to be enrolled, indentures for resale in the colony might have disappeared entirely. The absence of speculative contracts from 1696 to 1713 . . . did not result solely from the buyers' wariness; the War of the Spanish Succession (1701–1713) choked off the flow of workers, for the French navy was unable to protect merchant vessels in the colonial trade. The consequent shortage of laborers and servants inconvenienced Canada's gentry. In letters and memorials sent to the government in France, the colony's notables asked for a revival of the royal subsidy for *engagés*.[96] But because of the crown's indebtedness at the end of Louis XIV's reign, the encouragement for sending workers to Canada would have to be legislative rather than financial.

Precedents existed for compelling shipowners or outfitters to carry workers on vessels sent to New France. The *Compagnie des Cent Associés* had a quota of one man for so many tons of cargo, and in 1664 the Quebec *Conseil souverain* wanted to insert a similar stipulation in its proposed landing permits.[97] The large number of workers then arriving in the colony made this provision unnecessary. In the West Indian trade, ships were obliged to carry a quota of specified commodities, livestock, or men, and one item could be substituted for another. By the 1680s blacks outnumbered Europeans on the French Caribbean islands, and the government became more insistent on the transportation of white workers because it feared a slave insurrection against the European minority. Indentured servants had to be carried on all ships sailing to "the American islands" and royal ordinances in 1699 and 1707 set minimum standards for the age and height of these men, who were

---

[94] M. Dudouyt at Paris to Mgr. de Laval at Quebec, Mar. 9. 1682, Lettres, Carton N, No. 61, p. 10, *ibid.*
[95] Mgr. de Laval at Paris to the gentlemen of the Quebec Seminary, May 1685, *Rapport de l'Archiviste*, 1939–1940, 263–265.
[96] See above, n. 86.
[97] *Jugements et Délibérations.* I, 269, and Gabriel Debien, "Engagés pour le Canada au XVIIᵉ siècle vus de la Rochelle," *Revue d'Histoire*, VI (1952–1953), 190. François Ruette d'Auteuil attributed the regulation that shipowners carry one man for every ten tons of cargo destined for Quebec to "le Conseil établi ensuite à Québec" (memorial of Dec. 12, 1715, in *Rapport de l'Archiviste*, 1922–1923, 62–63). Paul-Emile Renaud, *Les Origines économiques du Canada: l'oeuvre de la France* (Mamers, 1928), 237, rephrases this as an enactment by "le Conseil qui fut alors institué à Québec (1647)" that shipowners must embark "un homme pour chaque tonneau [sic] de fret." Debien and later authors accepted Renaud's faulty paraphrase as a reference to a law made in 1647. D'Auteuil was referring to the Aug. 1664 proposal of the *Conseil souverain*.

to be inspected by admiralty officers. A wartime ordinance of 1706 allowed ship outfitters the option of paying a sixty *livres* fine for each worker not embarked, since recruits were difficult to find.[98] These provisions were incorporated into laws for vessels trading with Canada.

A royal ordinance of March 20, 1714, extended the requirement for carrying indentured servants to vessels sailing for France's North American colonies. The preamble spoke of the need of "the inhabitants of New France . . . [for] *Engagés* to aid them . . . whether for the cultivation of the land as well as for other tasks." Henceforth, passports would be issued to ships bound for Canada only on condition "that three indentured workers are carried there on those vessels of sixty tons or less; four for those ships of sixty to one hundred tons; and six for those over one hundred tons." The workers were to be "at least eighteen years old, and they cannot be older than forty, and they will be, at least, four *pieds* [four feet, four inches] tall." Port officials were to examine the men to see that they met these standards and were "of good complexion."[99] Shipowners were given the option of carrying two recruits for the colonial troops in place of each required *engagé*, and the ministry expected some captains to take this option, although there would be no indenture to be sold to pay for transportation costs.[100] More attractive was the provision of the 1714 ordinance allowing one craftsman to take the place of two unskilled laborers "in consideration of their [the artisans'] usefulness to the colony."

The La Rochelle indentures and official correspondence indicate that the 1714 ordinance was enforced and obeyed in that year and the following six. The merchant-shipowners' compliance was deceptively gratifying. When peace returned in 1713, the colonial market for workers was good because of the wartime interruption of trade. After a few years, however, merchants were trying to evade this new obligation. The profit in carrying *engagés* to New France was small in comparison with the gains to be made from delivering slaves to the West Indies. The overseas traders had frustrated an unpopular law in the past. To overcome the reluctance of workers in France to go to remote lands such as the Americas, Colbert in 1670 had unilaterally reduced the duration of unskilled *engagés'* contracts to eighteen months. Recruiters and employers ignored this law and had notaries draw up indentures for three years, as before. The administration backed down and reinstated the customary minimum term in 1672.[101]

[98] Debien, "Les Engagés pour les Antilles," *Revue d'Histoire des Colonies*, XXXVIII (1951), 23–24; Lawrence C. Wroth and G. L. Annan, *Acts of French Royal Administration concerning Canada, Guiana, the West Indies, and Louisiana, prior to 1791* (New York, 1930), 36, 40.
[99] Ordinance compelling captains of merchant vessels to transport indentured workers to New France, Mar. 20, 1714, série B, XXXVI, ff. 336vo–337vo, Archs. des Colonies.
[100] Minister to Beauharnais, Mar. 28, 1714, *ibid.*, f. 149vo; the king to Vaudreuil and Michel Bégon, Mar. 19, 1714, *ibid.*, ff. 338–341.
[101] Athanase Jourdan *et al.*, eds., *Recueil Général des Anciennes Lois Françaises depuis l'an 420 jusqu'à la révolution de 1789*, 29 vols. (Paris, 1821–1833), XVIII, 370; Debien, "Les Engagés pour les Antilles," *Revue d'Histoire des Colonies*, XXXVIII (1951), 64.

After 1714, captains sailing to Canada declared that all the indentured workers on board were artisans, thereby cutting their quota in half. Merchants, familiar with their impecunious and extortionate government, regarded the sixty *livres* fine as a new tax. Since the mandatory *engagés* had been introduced into the West Indian trade as an alternative to certain goods, the merchants claimed that their obligation to transport workers had ended in February 1716, when the requirement to carry the enumerated commodities was lifted. A ruling of November 16, 1716, removed this misconception and identified the craftsmen who would be accepted in place of any two unskilled men: "mason, stonecutter, blacksmith, locksmith, joiner, cooper, carpenter, caulker, and other trades that can be useful in the colonies."[102] Textile workers were not listed, possibly because their products would reduce the colonial market for French cloth.

Between royal administration and merchants there was a recurrent cycle of a new legal imposition, evasion or noncompliance, followed by reassertion of the more precisely defined law. Merchants from Nantes, La Rochelle, and Bordeaux complained that it was difficult to find potential *engagés* and pleaded that they sometimes failed to meet the quota because hired men jumped ship before sailing. The government took them at their word. To ship outfitters *[armateurs]*, a royal ordinance of January 1721 offered imprisoned "defrauders of the king's [fiscal] rights, vagabonds and others" to replace voluntary bond servants. The petty criminals would go to colonial employers for the cost of the passage. The malefactors' exile was not to end after three to five years of servitude; it was to be permanent. As for alleged escapes, a ship's crew was believed to be capable of preventing them, and, now, for every prisoner who fled, the shipowner would have to take on *two* more convicts as well as paying a sixty *livres* fine.[103] A supplementary ordinance granted exemptions—say, for fishing vessels—and allowed ships unable to meet the quota, when no prisoners were available, to sail after payment of the fines.[104]

There were always some petty criminals among the voluntary contract workers. Seventeenth-century writers noted the presence of fugitive rogues

---

[102] Ruling . . . concerning the *engagés* and muskets that must be carried to the French American colonies, Nov. 16, 1716, série A2, Art. 23, ff. 634–643, Archives de la Marine, Archs. Nationales. An earlier dispatch to the intendant of New France told him that the required *engagés* would be craftsmen and that he and the port captain were not to interfere in the sale of the workers' contracts. The freedom of ships' captains to sell to anyone at whatever price they pleased was said to be an established practice in the West Indies. Maritime council to Intendant Bégon, June 16, 1716, MG 1, B series transcript, XXXVIII-2, p. 379, Public Archs. Canada.

[103] Royal ordinance concerning the prisoners who will replace the *engagés* to be transported to the colonies, Jan. 14, 1721, série B, XLIV, ff. 130–130vo, Archs. des Colonies. Wroth and Annan, *Acts of French Royal Administration*, 53–54, lists a decree of Jan. 8, 1719, authorizing the dispatch of "les condamnés aux Galères, les Bannis, les Vagabons & les Gens sans aveu" to the colonies as *engagés*.

[104] Royal ordinance concerning indentured workers, May 20, 1721, série B, XLIV, ff. 161vo–162vo, Archs. des Colonies. Ships of the *Compagnie des Indes* going to Louisiana and those destined for Ile Saint-Jean were also exempted.

and villains among the *engagés*.[105] Villainy past and present brought an indentured journeyman-carpenter to the attention of Louisbourg's *Conseil supérieur* in September 1725. This eighteen-year-old was charged with stealing a piece of cloth from a merchant's garden. He admitted to the theft and said "his intention was to sell it [the cloth] to obtain some bread; that he had not eaten a full meal for four days." When asked "by what occasion had he come to this port?," the *engagé* replied that while

> working at his trade of joiner and turner in his father's house—his father being a [shipyard] foreman for the king at Brest—he unfortunately took from an adjoining storehouse . . . two cotton handkerchiefs that belonged to a merchant. The maidservant saw him and stopped him and, after having taken back the handkerchiefs, she and the merchant complained to the father of the accused. The father was outraged by this act. Since he [the son] was a wastrel *[libertain]*, his father had him put on board the king's ship *Le Jason* to send him to this island. He arrived here in July of this year and was delivered by the ship's captain . . . to Mr. de Bourville, the Town Major, to be employed at his trade for three years, and to be kept longer if he did not become well-behaved.

When asked "why would he wish to buy food, since he was fed at the major's house?, he replied that he was only given Canadian biscuits and some soup to eat."[106]

Like this joiner, most exiled prisoners were delivered to the colonies on the king's ships. French merchants were no more willing to transport petty criminals than the required *engagés*. In July 1721 the maritime council offered *to pay* shipowners sixty *livres* a head as well as a daily allowance for every prisoner carried in excess of the legal quota. La Rochelle's merchants promptly rejected this generous proposition.[107] After 1721, when the quota could be filled with involuntary exiles, French merchants still did not comply with the laws. In 1722 Louisbourg's administrators reported that "of all

---

[105] Intendant de Meulles to the minister, Nov. 4, 1683, MG 1, C11A series transcript, VI, pp. 290–291, Public Archs. Canada. Dom Guy Oury, ed., *Marie de l'Incarnation, Ursuline (1599–1672): Correspondance* (Solesmes, France, 1971), 863.

Bishop de Laval described one case in 1687 when he sent a joiner to the Quebec Seminary. The joiner was a family man, and a decent person *(honnête)*, but was obliged to leave France "à cause d'un accident qui luy est arrivé d'avoir frappé un monopolier d'un coup de pierre dont il est mort" (Mgr. de Laval to the directors of the Quebec Seminary, June 9, 1687, in *Rapport de l'Archiviste*, 1939–1940, 279).

[106] Interrogation of Jean Legouel in prison, Sept. 20, 1725, série G2 (Conseil supérieur de Louisbourg), CLXXVIII, ff. 831–835, Archs. des Colonies.

[107] Série B, XLIV, ff. 56vo–57, 191–191vo, 196vo–197, *ibid.* The per diem allowance was seven *sols*. In June 1721 printed copies of the offer were sent to Calais, Dieppe, Le Havre, Rouen, Honfleur, Saint-Malo, Morlaix, Brest, Nantes, La Rochelle, Bordeaux, Bayonne, and Marseille; these ports and Certe were the only ones authorized in 1717 to trade with the colonies. The resistance of La Rochelle's merchants was acknowledged in August and the council decided that acceptance of the prisoners would be voluntary: "l'Intention du Conseil n'est pas de les y contraindre" (*ibid.*, f. 197).

the ships that came last year . . . there was just one from Nantes that brought
engagés." Other ships' captains pleaded ignorance of the 1721 ordinance.[108]
There was no excuse in 1723, when only eight of thirty-five trading vessels
brought indentured servants to Ile Royale.[109]

The king's ordinance of February 15, 1724, chronicled the deceptions
used in France to evade the laws. "Most of the outfitters," it said, presented
for the mandatory review "individuals that they would pass off as *engagés*
. . . and whom they dismiss after having presented them for inspection. To
discharge themselves [from responsibility], they content themselves with
bringing back certificates of desertion." As a result, "not a third of the indentured workers who were embarked in any one port of France went to the
colonies last year." Moreover, "some of these outfitters presented people
they said were craftsmen, even though they had no trade." Thereafter, documentary proof of desertions would not be accepted; there would be an au-
tomatic fine for each worker for whom there was no "certificate of delivery"
to a colony. The fine for a missing craftsman was 120 *livres*, and those presented as artisans required a certificate of competence from a master craftsman chosen by the administration.[110] A November 1728 ruling restated the
1716 regulations, but the official restatements, amplifications, and clarifica-
tions merely testify to the merchants' dogged resistance to carrying contract
workers to the Americas.

Faced with this resistance, port officials lost heart and enforcement of the
laws became haphazard. Exemptions were granted and fines accepted to
allow ships to sail without *engagés*.[111] In 1742 Louisbourg's civil administrator reported that only vessels from Havre de Grace brought the required
complement of workers; "those of Bordeaux and Nantes sometimes carry
some, and those coming from other ports do not carry any at all."[112] The rarity of adult male servants at Quebec in 1744, in contrast to the numerous female and juvenile domestics, indicates that few *engagés* were arriving in that
port too.[113] The number of imported workers would never have been great.

[108] Maritime council to the intendant at Rochefort, Apr. 9, 1722, série IE, XCIX, pp. 381–382, Archs. du Port de Rochefort.
[109] Jacques-Ange Le Normant de Mézy to the minister, Dec. 28, 1723, série C11B, VI, ff. 257–257vo, Archs. des Colonies.
[110] Royal ordinance concerning indentured servants, Feb. 15, 1724, série A1, Art. 62, piece 11, Archs. de la Marine.
[111] Maurice Filion, *La Pensée et L'Action coloniales de Maurepas vis-à-vis du Canada: 1723–1749* (Montreal, 1972), 376.
[112] François Bigot to the minister, Sept. 29, 1742, série C11B, XXIV, ff. 103–103vo, Archs. des Colonies. See also Bigot to the minister, Oct. 7, 1744, *ibid.*, XXVI, ff. 101–102vo, when he antici-pated the wartime suspension of the regulations, which happened in 1748.
[113] "Le recensement de Québec, en 1744," *Rapport de l'Archiviste*, 1939–1940, 3–153, shows that in the town there were 27 white male *domestiques or ouvriers*, older than 19 years, as opposed to 137 miscellaneous female servants and 89 juvenile or adolescent male servants, including slaves. There may have been more adult male *engagés* in the rural areas, even though craftsmen tended

For 1713–1743, yearly arrivals from France at Quebec averaged nine or ten vessels. Although this traffic doubled and tripled in the next two decades,[114] full compliance with the regulations would have delivered fewer than one hundred craftsmen to Quebec annually. Had there been a great demand for passages and had shipowners seen a good profit in the passenger traffic, the number of vessels would have increased further. It did not.

War in 1744–1748 led to a suspension of these laws and, when peace returned, merchants acted as if the regulations were still suspended. The intendant of New France had to ask for their formal reinstatement. Direct personal indentures were now rare, and speculative indentures for resale in New France were barely kept alive by the laws. Merchants were now able to obtain men for yearly salaries of fifty *livres* or less, indicating a willingness among the poor to come to the St. Lawrence Valley. It was now the shipowners' reluctance to carry *engagés* that prevented a substantial migration. Ile Royale's administrators were more interested in the enforcement of these laws than were the officials at Quebec, and in 1751 the island's governor wrote that "most of the outfitters coming here from France greatly neglect the obligation they are under to bring us indentured workers or *trente-six-mois*. Nevertheless, we have great need of them in this colony."[115]

Surviving embarkation lists give the impression that there was a steady flow of passengers, including *engagés*, to French North America. The 1749–1758 register for Bayonne, a major port for the Ile Royale and Newfoundland fishery, names seventy-four indentured workers who—if we believe it—went to Ile Royale and Quebec.[116] The precision of the list, which gives age and occupation, makes it plausible evidence. Those familiar with French administration in the old regime, however, will be wary of any official's record of his fulfillment of royal directives.[117]

Chance revealed the falsity of this document. In March 1757 it recorded that, in compliance with the laws, a blacksmith and a joiner were taken on

---

to work in the towns. The use of indirect evidence is necessary because the Quebec admiralty registers have been lost and there are few sales of French *engagés'* contracts in the files of Canadian notaries. Greffes des notaires, L. Chambalon, contains one such sale (Aug. 12, 1715), and some other possible sales (Dec. 20, 1693, Mar. 29, 1701, Oct. 30, 1706, Aug. 10, 1713), Archs. Nationales du Québec.

[114] James S. Pritchard, "The Pattern of French Colonial Shipping to Canada before 1760," *Revue française d'Histoire d'Outre-Mer*, LXIII (1976), 189–210. In 1853 Quebec received 1,351 ships of 570,738 tons in total; in 1753 only 25 vessels of 4,959 tons left France for Quebec.

[115] Jean Louis, Comte de Raymond to the minister, Nov. 4, 1751, série C11B, XXXI, ff. 50vo–51, Archs. des Colonies.

[116] Classes: Bayonne, Passengers going to the colonies, 1749–1777, f. 72 (Mar. 2, 1757: *La Louise*), série F5B, Art. 30, *ibid.* Previous voyages of this schooner are noted on ff. 53–54, 58, and a later trip on f. 75.

[117] On the deliberate falsification of statistics by government officials see Peter Moogk, "Beyond the C11 Series: Approaches and Sources for the Social History of New France," *Archivaria*, No. 14 (1982), 53–62.

board the schooner *La Louise* as *engagés* for the colonies. The two artisans did not reach New France. The truth is revealed by one private letter among many from French vessels captured by the British and now in the Public Record Office at London. A Bayonne merchant wrote to his partner on Ile Royale about *La Louise*'s cargo, which was to be sold for their joint profit. "Observe," wrote the merchant, "that there are two *Engagés* with trades on the crew list who will not be making the voyage at all. Do not fail to have them discharged on the roll as being disembarked, to avoid paying a fine of 80 *écus*." Another captain in their employ had returned to France without delivery receipts for his mythical workers; "I was obliged to pay that [fine] on your behalf" complained the writer.[118] This frank discussion about evading the laws indicates that there were admiralty officers who cooperated in the deception, undoubtedly for a consideration. Thus embarkation lists should be treated with caution. British reports on the personnel found aboard French ships captured in the 1740s and 1750s reveal that even notarial indentures and ships' rolls were falsified to appear to conform with the laws.[119]

What can be deduced from the reliable evidence on voluntary migration from France to Canada? Of those lay persons who could afford a transatlantic fare, fewer than 300 settled in the St. Lawrence Valley. Independent emigrants who paid their own way were always rare. The colonization of New France depended on sponsored emigrants such as indentured servants. From the 1640s to the 1670s, commercial companies, seigneurs, religious groups, merchant-outfitters, and the crown brought out about 4,000 persons, male and female. Seventeenth-century recruiters met popular resistance to overseas emigration. They had to offer wages, a short period of service, and

[118] B. Duvergé at Bayonne to M. Imbert at Louisbourg, Mar. 10, 1757, H.C.A. 30/264, 186.

[119] Dale Miquelon found that the rolls of vessels contracted to Dugard of Rouen in 1731–1755 carefully listed *engagés* and muskets carried in compliance with the laws (private correspondence.) Series H.C.A. 32 (papers of prize vessels) in the Public Record Office provides an opportunity to compare the numbers of crewmen and indentured workers on the ships' rolls with the number of men found on board by British captors. Evidence that *La Louise* was not the sole delinquent is contained in the following examples: 1744: *Le Saint Marc* of Olonne via Bordeaux destined for Canada, crew 15, no *engagés* carried (Box 130-1); 1745: *La Gracieuse* of Bayonne, 122 tons, destined for Quebec, crew 22 with 3 *engagés* aged 32, 29 and 22; when captured, the ship had 23 mariners and 4 "boys" on board (Box 113-1); 1747: *La Fleur du Jour* of La Rochelle, 102 tons, destined for Quebec, 12 crew on roll, one extra sailor found on board when captured but not the 3 *engagés* declared upon departure (Box 112-1); 1747: *Le Fortuné* of Bordeaux, 200 tons, destined for Quebec, crew 28 with one shoemaker-*engagé* in place of the required four by special permission of the admiralty. English captors reported that the ship had 26 live crewmen and two dead on board when taken (Box 112-2); 1757: *L'Acadie* of Bordeaux, 160 tons, destined for Quebec and the West Indies, crew 22 and 3 *engagés;* the English report reads "there was Twenty Two Mariners officers included on board" (Box 161-1); and 1757: *L'Aigle* of Bordeaux, 200 tons, destined for the West Indies, crew 33 and 2 *engagés* (in place of 3), had 36 persons aboard when captured! (Box 161-1). There were indentures for *engagés* among the ship's papers of *La Fleur du Jour* and *L'Acadie* but none on board *L'Aigle*, which shows that false contracts were made to satisfy the authorities.

even prepaid return passages to obtain volunteers. Free emigrants, apart from women, were still reluctant to make a permanent home in Canada. Rough living conditions, the Iroquois threat, the shortage of marriageable European women, and strong ties to family and place of birth led most to abandon the colony. Over two-thirds of the single men brought out by merchant-speculators and the crown returned home, and more would have gone if colonial officials had not hindered departures.

After the 1670s the shipowners' and outfitters' dislike for the trade in *engagés* meant that few workers' contracts were made for resale. Speculative indentures for the Americas were kept alive from 1699 onward by the force of law. The indentures' terms show that there was less popular resistance to overseas emigration in the 1700s. The merchants' attitude was now the major obstruction, but no document explains their disdain for the traffic in *engagés*. The merchants simply evaded the legal obligation to carry contract workers to the American colonies. Servants' indentures delivered thousands of potential settlers to British North America; they were unable to perform the same service for French North America in the eighteenth century.[120] After the 1670s most arrivals in New France were involuntary or unwitting immigrants.

Among the involuntary immigrants, the exiled petty criminals known as *faux-sauniers* have already been mentioned: about 720 poachers, smugglers, sellers of untaxed salt, and other minor offenders were exiled to Canada from 1721 to 1749. Only healthy men with useful skills were to be dispatched,[121] and most were countryfolk suited to farm work. In the 1720s some were *"fils de famille,"* wayward sons sent abroad to save their families further embarrassment. Like the seventeenth-century *engagés*, the transported criminals tried to leave the colony: some fled to the English colonies

---

[120] Jack and Marion Kaminkow, *A List of Emigrants from England to America 1718–1759* (Baltimore, 1964), names 3,122 persons indentured at London for service in the British American colonies. Galenson's *White Servitude in Colonial America* is based on a sample of 16,847 indentured servants going to the British American colonies in 1654–1775. Morris speaks of 10,000 emigrants from the port of Bristol alone, and of 6,000 leaving England from Dec. 1773 to Oct. 1775; he also quotes an estimate of 43,720 departing from five Irish ports in 1769–1774 (*Government and Labor*, 315, n. 2).

[121] President of the maritime council to Gov. Beauharnais and Intendant Hocquart in Canada, May 8, 1743, série B, LXXVI, ff. 70–70vo, Archs. des Colonies. In 1731 these officials expressed satisfaction with the *faux-sauniers* as useful workers and potential settlers, in contrast to the worthless characters sent in the previous year. See série C11A, LII, ff. 83–85, LIV, ff. 77–78vo, *ibid.* The idea of exiling petty criminals to New France had been discussed in 1715–1716 but was put off without explanation. See MG 1, B Series transcript, XXXVIII-2, p. 356, Public Archs. Canada. Série B, XLIV, ff. 130–267vo, Archs. des Colonies, contains letters and documents about the first shipment of petty criminals in 1721. The difficulty of preventing escapes by *faux-sauniers* is mentioned in 1735 in Beauharnais and Hocquart to the minister, Oct. 5, 1735, MG 1, C11A series transcript, LXIII, pp. 18–19, Public Archs. Canada. In that year 54 men arrived in Canada of whom five joined the troops and the remainder were distributed to colonists to work for 100 *livres* a year (*ibid.*, LXIII, pp. 26–27, 89–93).

while others stowed away on ships returning to France.[122] Gérard Malche-losse's careful study of the prisoners in the St. Lawrence Valley concludes that, "like the prisoners and *fils de famille* of 1723–1729, a very small number of the faux sauniers who came to Canada from 1730 to 1743 became estab-lished colonists." Of 648 *faux-sauniers* sent out in 1730–1749, only 106 were noted in the colony's parish registers.[123]

Speaking of involuntary immigrants, let us not forget the 320 black slaves brought to the St. Lawrence settlement from the French West Indies and the British colonies. There were twice as many Amerindian slaves in the colony. Most slaves arrived in the eighteenth century, long after the decline of colonial service indentures made in France, so there is no clear link be-tween the appearance of slaves and the waning of white servitude.[124]

As numerous as these one thousand slaves, and equally unwilling im-migrants, were the British captives seized by French and Indian raiding par-ties or taken off captured ships. Half were repatriated, and several hundred chose to remain in New France. The 126 who were granted French letters of naturalization in 1710–1714 came primarily from New England and New York; some were Irish, and a few had German or Dutch surnames.[125] Hun-dreds more were brought to Canada during the War of the Austrian Succes-sion (1744–1748).[126] Over five hundred former captives elected to stay in

---

[122] A royal ordinance to prevent the return to France or escape to the English colonies of "faux sauniers et Contrebandiers déserteurs" exiled to Canada and Ile Royale, dated May 25, 1742, is in série A1, Art. 78, pièce 44, Archs. de la Marine, and also in série B, LXXIV, ff. 538–538vo, *ibid.* The continuing escapes on English colonial ships are mentioned in a dispatch from Jean-Baptiste-Louis Le Prévost Duquesnel and Bigot to the minister, Oct. 14, 1742, série B, XXIV, ff. 22–22vo, Archs. des Colonies.

[123] Malchelosse, "Faux sauniers, prisonniers et fils de famille en Nouvelle-France au XVIIIᵉ siè-cle," *Cahiers des Dix.* IX (1944), 161–197. See also his "Les Fils de famille en Nouvelle-France, 1720–1750," *ibid.,* XI (1946), 261–311, in which he says that only 10 out of 68 *fils de famille* became permanent settlers.

[124] Marcel Trudel, *L'esclavage au Canada français: Histoire et conditions de l'esclavage* (Quebec, 1960).

[125] Pierre-Georges Roy, "Les Lettres de Naturalité sous le régime français," *Bulletin des Recherches historiques.* XXX (1924), 225–232. One hundred twenty-six letters are listed in Pierre-Georges Roy, ed., *Inventaire des insinuations du Conseil souverain de la Nouvelle-France* (Beauceville, 1921), 119–121. In 1705–1707 there was a long correspondence about a list of "Anglais, Ambourgois et Flamans qui sont establis en ce pays" who desired letters of naturalization as well as many fe-male converts to Roman Catholicism who wanted to remain in Canada (*Rapport de l'Archiviste,* 1938–1939, 83, 110, 158, 169, 1939–1940, 366). This may be the origin of the large number of let-ters of naturalization in 1710–1713. Since the letters cost 100 *livres* after 1722 (while also requir-ing proof of Catholicity), they are not a complete record of those who stayed in Canada.

[126] See a 1747 report on those who returned to Boston and on those left behind in Emma Lewis Coleman, *New England Captives Carried to Canada between 1677 and 1670 during the French and In-dian Wars,* 2 vols. (Portland, Maine, 1925), I, 107. More captives were taken before the war ended. For example, 20 Irish and Scottish girls destined for Virginia were captured with a prize vessel in 1748 and became domestic servants in Canada. See O'Callaghan, ed., *Documents,* X, 172. After the war 33 "English deserters" also chose to remain in New France. Jacques-Pierre de Taffanel de La Jonquière and Bigot to the minister, Oct. 23, 1750, série C11A, XCV, ff. 102–103,

New France, while one hundred other British subjects willingly removed to the French colony.[127]

The largest group of North American immigrants to Canada is the least documented one; they were indisputably reluctant exiles. When administrators in the British colony of Nova Scotia began to expel the French-speaking, Roman Catholic Acadians in 1755, many fled overland to the St. Lawrence Valley settlements. After British forces captured Ile Royale and Ile Saint-Jean [Prince Edward Island] in 1758, mass deportations followed. Nearly two thousand Acadians sought refuge in Canada in the late 1750s.[128] At the 1760 capitulation of Montreal, Gen. Jeffrey Amherst refused the French governor's request that the refugees be safeguarded from a further expulsion.[129] Justifiably fearful of the British conquerors, the *Acadiens* submerged themselves in the Canadian population.

Last, there were soldiers sent to New France who chose to remain there; they were unwitting immigrants. Military garrisons in the French colonies were long regarded as a source of settlers. Beginning with the Carignan-Salières Regiment in 1665, soldiers who volunteered to become colonists were discharged and given settlement grants. From 1683 onward, the *Compagnies franches de la marine* were the garrison troops for the North American colonies and, in turn, provided settlers. Quartering soldiers in private homes and hiring them out to civilian employers helped to introduce the newcomers into colonial society. After 1698 a soldier marrying a woman of the colony was entitled to a discharge, his clothing, a year's pay, and land.[130] Over a

---

Archs. des Nationales. James Axtell, *The Invasion Within: The Contest of Cultures in Colonial North America* (New York, 1985), 289–292, gives a total of 1,641 for persons captured between 1675 and 1763 and analyzes the nature of those who remained in Canada.

[127] Maritime council to M. Dupuy, May 14, 1728, B series transcript, L-2, p. 79 (ff. 498–498vo), Public Archs. Canada, mentions the "great number of Englishmen" living at Montreal said to be smugglers posing as merchants, craftsmen, or settlers. The activities of "the great number of English artizans, merchants and others established at Montreal" was also discussed in 1727 in the light of a law forbidding intercolonial trade by foreigners. O'Callaghan, ed., *Documents*, IX, 985. In 1753 the "prodigious number of English deserters" being maintained at French posts on the frontiers of Canada was reduced by shipping off 45 to France. The governor complained that deserters employed as servants were more adept at thievery than honest labor. Ange Duquesne de Menneville to the minister, Aug. 18, 1753, série C11A, XCIX, ff. 7–9, Archs. des Colonies.

[128] Michel Roy estimates that 1,800 fled to New France (*L'Acadie des origines à nos jours: Essai de synthèse historique* [Montreal, 1981], 133). Some estimates are higher and, indeed, a higher estimate is justified if we add fugitives from Ile Royale and Ile Saint-Jean.

[129] Adam Shortt and Arthur G. Doughty, eds., *Documents Relating to the Constitutional History of Canada, 1759–1791* (Ottawa, 1907), 27. See articles 38, 39, and 41 of the 1760 capitulation.

[130] Ordinance of May 21, 1698, série B, XXVII (Canada, 1706), ff. 89vo–90, Archs. des Colonies. The law's text did not reach New France until 1706 and war delayed its implementation. In 1716 the intendant's subdelegate on Ile Royale was told not to hinder soldiers' marriages "dans une Colonie qu'il faut peupler et surtout dans les Commencemens." Maritime council to de Soubras, Apr. 22, 1716, MG1, B series transcript, XXXVIII-2, p. 556, Public Archs. Canada. The secondary role of the French soldiers as settlers is evident in the king's instructions not to accept *Canadiens*

thousand soldier-settlers made a home in New France during the seventeenth century, and more followed their example in the next century.

The marine soldiers enlisted for service in French ports, on ships, or in the overseas territories; they did not choose to come to Canada. According to one official, recruiting men for colonial garrisons was hindered by a popular belief in France that the soldiers never came home again.[131] Many were unemployed textile and clothing workers. To fill the ranks, standards were lowered, deceptive enlistments were used, and prisoners were conscripted.[132] The soldiers may have been social outcasts, but they, too, responded to the call of the homeland. In 1698 an intendant wrote of "the ardor that the greater part have to return to France in the hope of greater freedom."[133] A later memorialist regretted that too many soldiers were allowed to go home "under various specious pretexts."[134]

Despite opposition from the governors and military officers to a scheme that drew seasoned soldiers from the garrison troops and produced few good farmers,[135] soldiers were the principal source of immigrants for Canada

---

into the ranks of the garrison troops. That would deprive the colony of "des hommes capables de contribuer a Son Etablissement." Memorial of the king to Beauharnais and Hocquart, May 31, 1743, série B, LXXVI, ff. 95vo–96, Archs. des Colonies.

[131] In 1753 Gov. Raymond of Ile Royale wrote that it was widely believed in France that "lorsqu'un Soldat . . . est engagé [pour les colonies], il n'en peut plus revenir." This quotation from série C11B, XXXIII, f. 89, Archs. des Colonies, appears in T. A. Crowley, "The Forgotten Soldiers of New France: The Louisbourg Example," French Colonial Historical Society, *Proceedings of the Third Annual Meeting* (Athens, Ga., 1978), 55.

[132] These points are made by Crowley in "Forgotten Soldiers," French Col. Hist. Soc., *Procs. of 3d Annual Mtg.*, 52–69, and by Allan Greer, "Mutiny at Louisbourg, December 1744," in *Histoire sociale/Social History,* X (1977), 20, 305–336. Although it is not possible to measure the moral quality of the recruits, the physical standards were certainly low. Looking at a list of 585 recruits on the Ile de Ré in 1753, I found that 170 were under the minimum height of "5. pieds 2. pouces" and "Sans Espérance de croistre." See Review of recruits destined for the colonies, Ile de Ré citadel, Feb. 1753, série 1R, No. 20, Archs. du Port de Rochefort. Although recruits were described in 1685 and 1698 as being very young and of deplorable quality, in 1706 and 1728 officials praised the soldiers received. See série B, XI, f. 3, Archs. des Colonies, and MG 1, C11A series transcript, XV, 38, XXIV, 8, L, 114, Public Archs. Canada.

[133] Intendant Bochart de Champigny, Oct. 14, 1698, quoted in Dechêne, *Habitants et Marchands.* 87.

[134] Ruette d'Auteuil, 1715, *Rapport de l'Archiviste*, 1922–1923, 64.

[135] The process by which experienced soldiers were released to marry and were replaced by new recruits, leaving many unfit soldiers in the ranks, was described by Chaussegros de Léry in Oct. 1720, in Pierre-Georges Roy, ed., *Inventaire des Papiers de Léry.* 3 vols. (Quebec, 1939–1940), I, 62.

Gov. Duquesne claimed that soldiers married sluts and wine-sops in order to get a settler's discharge and that these men were more likely to become tavern-keepers rather than successful farmers. Duquesne to the minister, Oct. 26, 1753, série C11A, XCIX, f. 98vo, Archs. des Colonies. On Ile Royale it was alleged that, except for the Germans [Swiss?] who were "plus laborieux et plus patiens Cultivateurs," soldiers were hopeless as farmers. See Augustin de Boschenry de Drucour to the minister, June 27, 1756, série C11B, XXXVI, ff. 61vo–62, *ibid.* An earlier dispatch argued that to expect a soldier to become a farmer was unrealistic: "aussytost qu'il a gousté La vie du Soldat jl n'est plus propre a labourer la terre." See Joseph de Mombeton de Saint-Ovide de Brouillon and Le Normant de Mézy to the minister, Nov. 28, 1726, *ibid.*, VIII, ff. 16vo–17.

in the eighteenth century. The exact number is open to conjecture. Yves Landry estimates that the battalions of French regulars sent out in the 1750s supplied 500 to 700 soldier-colonists.[136] The importance of military immigrants is evident in Mario Boleda's estimate of the gross recorded migration [l'immigration observée] from France to the St. Lawrence Valley: Soldiers— 13,076; Engagés—3,900; Women—1,797; Prisoners—716; Male clergy—721. The net migration [l'immigration fondatrice] of those who settled permanently was said to be precisely 8,527, although the varying retention rates for each category are not suggested.[137]

All estimates are open to dispute; for example, the figure for indentured servants is probably too high.[138] The exclusive focus on migrants from France and the implicit assumption that they were culturally French is also misleading. The soldiers and workers contained a seasoning of Flemings, Germans, Swiss, Italians, and Iberians. A more comprehensive estimate of the migrants who made a permanent home in Canada before 1760 would be: Soldiers—3,300; Acadians—1,800; Women from France—1,500; Indentured workers—1,200; Slaves—900; British subjects—600; Male clergy—500; Self-financed migrants—250; Transported prisoners—200. Soldiers supplied a third of the estimated 10,250 colonists; their prominence was recognized by a writer in 1709 who grandly asserted that "soldiers populated this country," along with the women sent out by the crown. This fact, he wrote, explained the "excessive pride and idleness" of the Canadiens.[139] The emphasis on the filles du roi was warranted. What this writer and subsequent historians failed to mention is that most of those who came to Canada did so unwillingly and with no intention of making a home there.

[136] Landry, "Mortalité, nuptialité et canadianisation des troupes françaises de la guerre de Sept Ans," Histoire sociale/Social History. XII (1979), 298–315.
[137] Boleda, "Les Migrations au Canada," 112, 339. This hypothetical total and a conjectural breakdown of net migration from France by decades is presented as fact in Harris, ed., Historical Atlas of Canada, plate 45.
[138] Mario Boleda reached the figure of 3,900 for indentured workers by deducing that La Rochelle supplied 23.1% of the engagés for New France and then by multiplying the 922 indentures for "Canada" found by Debien and others by 4.23 to achieve a total number of engagés sent from France. The problems with this computation are that La Rochelle was probably the port of departure for at least 30% of all indentured workers going to New France, the figure 922 (which misses some deeds) is for "Canada" in the modern sense (including Acadia and French settlements on the Atlantic coast and Gulf of St. Lawrence), and no allowance is made for fraudulent indentures after 1716. There are at least 709 indentures made at La Rochelle for the St. Lawrence Valley and, allowing for a loss of a fifth of the indentures as well as falsification of a tenth of the post-1716 contracts, one comes up with 820 for La Rochelle and a possible total of 2,733 coming from all French ports to the St. Lawrence Valley. A cautious estimate might be 3,000. Boleda's total figure for female migrants is a compromise between four different estimates by earlier researchers. See Boleda, "Les Migrations au Canada," 105.
[139] Camille de Rochemonteix, ed., Relation par Lettres de l'Amérique Septentrionale (Paris, 1904), 4. The author is probably the co-Indendant Antoine-Denis Raudot.

A study of migrants from France to Canada before 1760 reveals that large-scale emigration is not a simple mechanical process. The "push" of hardship at home, whether physical or mental, does not suffice to produce an overseas movement of humanity. The "pull" of opportunities in the New World must be publicized in print, through private letters or by emigrant recruiters. There was no effective campaign in France to counteract the colonies' low reputation in popular lore. Attractive publicity was one mediating factor needed to make a connection between the "push" and "pull." Other mediating factors were the volume of shipping, active recruitment, and the willingness of shipowners to transport large numbers of people paying low fares or traveling as redemptioners and indentured workers.

After the 1670s, French merchant-shipowners were indifferent to the passenger trade with Canada, and in the eighteenth century they evaded their legal obligation to carry a small quota of *engagés*. French skippers and *armateurs* were no longer willing to provide the transportation link required for an overseas exodus from France. As carriers of humans, they sought greater profits in the slave trade.

There was internal migration in France, some of it from the countryside to cities.[140] The origins of indentured workers and of beggars show that there was a large wandering population.[141] French artisans sought work in adjacent European states. Paul Le Jeune observed that "every year a great number of people leave France, and cast themselves, some here, some there, among foreigners, because they have no employment in their own country. I have been told . . . that a large part of the artisans in Spain are Frenchmen."[142] France's army, which expanded from 20,000 in 1661 to 300,000 in 1710,[143] absorbed large numbers of unemployed craftsmen. Overseas emigration was not a popular answer to hardship. Despite the larger number of *engagés* going to Saint-Domingue, that French colony had only 20,000 white settlers in 1740. France's most valuable possession in the Americas seems to have been affected by the same reluctance to emigrate and the same resistance to resettlement. More needs to be known about the alternatives in old

---

[140] Migration within France and into its neighbors is described in Michael W. Flinn, *The European Demographic System, 1500–1820* (Baltimore, 1981), chap. 5, "The Movement of Population."

[141] Two-thirds of the men indentured at La Rochelle for Canada before 1716 came from this port, its immediate neighborhood, and the provinces of Aunis and Saintonge. The balance, and especially the unskilled men hired speculatively by merchants, came from distant cities. The patterns for all the men indentured at La Rochelle for the Americas are discussed in Debien, *Les Engagés pour les Antilles, Revue d'Histoire des Colonies*, XXXVIII (1951), chap. 4, and are displayed on the maps accompanying Mandrou, "Vers les Antilles," *Annales*. XIV (1959), 667–675.

[142] *Jesuit Relations*. VII, 243; this observation is confirmed in Fernand Braudel, *Civilization and Capitalism, 15th–18th Century*. Vol. I: *The Structures of Everyday Life: The Limits of the Possible*, trans. Siân Reynolds (New York, 1981), 54–55, which mentions the migration from France into Spain, which is the subject of J. Nadal, *La Population catalane de 1553 à 1717: L'immigration française et les autres facteurs de son développement* (Paris, 1960).

[143] André Corvisier, *Armies and Societies in Europe, 1494–1789* (Bloomington, Ind., 1979), 113.

regime France to permanent relocation overseas. To say that because migration to Canada was so small, living conditions in France cannot have been bad, flies in the face of evidence of severe famines, unemployment, oppressive taxation, and social conflict during this period. Group migrations abroad are the result of a host of variable factors, such as religion, politics, historical experience, community traditions, recruiting, available information, financial assistance, and transportation facilities. To emphasize one impersonal factor, such as the land tenure system,[144] and to ignore cultural forces is to willfully misunderstand human behavior because it is culture that shapes our choices.

There was nothing uniquely French in the reluctance to emigrate because the diverse subjects of His Most Christian Majesty were not yet a cultural nation. It would be anachronistic to refer to Bretons, Basques, Flemings. Alsatians, Provençaux and speakers of French dialects as "the French people." The resistance to overseas emigration was probably normal for most peoples; willingness to relocate across the ocean was unusual, something that might develop over time with encouragement.

This account has emphasized the need for communities that are resigned to the continual and permanent departure of some members, who willingly accept settlement abroad as a prerequisite for a substantial, voluntary emigration. The emigrants to Canada left few literary sources, yet their behavior makes it plain that most were reluctant expatriates from their provincial homeland or *patrie*. Single males left France unwillingly and with no intention of staying abroad. The high rate of returns from Canada proves this. Unlike the indentured workers going to the British colonies, the *engagés* were migrant workers rather than intending colonists. Soldiers stationed in the French colonies had the same outlook: they too were reluctant exiles. Nothing need be said about the intentions of the exiled prisoners and slaves; they had no choice in the matter. Only the families that came before 1663, the female migrants, and a handful of self-financed arrivals could be described as true immigrants—that is, people who intended to settle abroad and establish a new home. The rest of the migrants, the majority, saw absence from their birthplace as a banishment and yearned to return to their families and to France.

---

[144] Roberta Hamilton argues that the small migration to New France, which she underestimates at 10,000, was due to the "feudal" nature of French society, which gave the peasant more secure land tenure than was known in rural England. As "the world's first capitalist country," England had "a surplus population [displaced by commercial farming], surplus capital accumulated through capitalist agriculture, rapidly expanding internal markets, and the potential for the development of external markets." These, she says, were the preconditions for successful, large-scale colonization. *(Feudal Society and Colonization: The Historiography of New France* [Ganonoque, 1988], 59). This is a rhetorical argument drawing on secondary studies and theoretical works; it is not based on the primary evidence and ignores the problem of emigrants who returned to France.

From Servant to Freeholder: Status Mobility and Property Accumulation in Seventeenth-Century Maryland

Russell R. Menard

INTRODUCTION

We tend to think of Southern colonial history as the story of plantation society, the history of plantation owners and Negro slaves. We have always known, of course, that not all whites were slave owners, nor were all blacks slaves. The group least prominent in the historical record has been poorer whites, since they have not left behind the rich literary evidence that has familiarized us with their "betters." Russell Menard and his co-workers in the Chesapeake school of colonial historians have mined the quantitative evidence available in Maryland and Virginia and have thereby begun to build up a picture of the totality of colonial society. Their results have been particularly revealing for the seventeenth century, which has been much more difficult to analyze by traditional historical methods. The results are important and surprising.

In this essay, Menard analyzes that majority of immigrants to seventeenth-century Maryland who came as servants in order to pay their passage to the New World. It has always been tempting to look forward from the vantage point of eighteenth-century plantation life to the origins of that "mature" form of Southern colonial life, but Menard suggests that we will understand plantation society better if we begin from the beginning.

He finds two phases in the social history of the servant class in seventeenth-century Maryland. In the first, from about 1640 to 1660,

Russell R. Menard, "From Servant to Freeholder: Status Mobility and Property Accumulation in Seventeenth-Century Maryland," *William and Mary Quarterly*, 3rd ser., XXX (1973), 37–64. Reprinted by permission of Omohundro Institute of Early American History and Culture, Williamsburg, VA.

immigrants approximated the general American myth of socioeconomic mobility. Servants were treated well, worked out their indentures, moved from renting to landowning, and frequently rose to positions of wealth and power. In the second, however, during the last decades of the century, the story of servant life history was not so happy. These men tended to remain dependent on others. They were rather less likely than earlier immigrants to become landowners, even if they successfully worked out their indentures. Nor did they come to play significant roles in political society.

Why were the sons less upwardly mobile than their fathers? Menard believes that the key was a dramatic rise in Maryland population after 1660, which increased the numbers of those competing for land and power. This demographic revolution was accompanied by rising land prices and falling tobacco prices, both of which made it difficult for small farmers to achieve yeoman status. Thus a combination of physical and economic forces dramatically altered the prospects for success of servants and petty farmers during the course of the seventeenth century and altered the nature of indentured servitude as a labor system to the disadvantage of immigrants and the native poor and to the advantage of landowners.

Menard thus reasons from a painstaking analysis of local records to a systematic interpretation of Maryland social and economic life.

- *Can these records tell us, however, how clear this pattern was to contemporaries?*
- *Were servants and petty farmers conscious of the fact that their chances were declining?*
- *How would we expect poor whites in the seventeenth century to react to such a perception?*
- *Was such a development inevitable, given the economic environment of Maryland, or can it be attributed to political decisions consciously taken?*
- *How aware were Marylanders of the existence of a labor "system"?*

Whatever your answers to these questions, it should be clear that Menard and his colleagues are providing us with powerful tools and critically important information for understanding how colonists actually lived.

Miles Gibson, Stephen Sealus, and William Scot all arrived in Maryland as indentured servants in the 1660s. They completed their terms and soon accumulated enough capital to purchase land. Thereafter, their careers diverged sharply. Gibson, aided by two good marriages, gained a place among the local gentry and served his country as justice of the peace, burgess, and sheriff. At his death in 1692, he owned more than two thousand acres of land and a personal estate appraised at over six hundred pounds sterling, including nine slaves.[1] Sealus's career offers a sharp contrast to that of his highly successful contemporary. He lost a costly court case in the mid-1670s and apparently was forced to sell his plantation to cover the expenses. He spent the rest of his days working other men's land. By 1691, Sealus was reduced to petitioning the county court for relief. He was "both weake and lame," he pleaded, "and not able to worke whereby to maintaine himselfe nor his wife." His petition was granted, but the Sealus family remained poor. Stephen died in 1696, leaving an estate appraised at £18 6s.[2] William Scot did not approach Gibson's success, but he did manage to avoid the dismal failure of Sealus. He lived on his small plantation for nearly forty years, served his community in minor offices, and slowly accumulated property. In his will, Scot gave all seven of his sons land of their own and provided his three daughters with small dowries.[3] Although interesting in themselves, these brief case histories do not reveal very much about the life chances of servants in the seventeenth century. They do suggest a range of accomplishment, but how are we to tell whether Scot, Sealus, or Gibson is most typical, or even if any one of them represents the position that most servants attained? Did servitude offer any hard-working Englishman without capital a good chance of becoming, like Miles Gibson, a man of means and position in a new community? Or did servitude only offer, as it finally offered Stephen Sealus, a chance to live in poverty in another place? Perhaps Scot was more typical. Did servitude promise poor men a chance to obtain moderate prosperity and respectability for themselves and their families? How much property and status mobility did most servants manage to achieve in the seventeenth century? This essay examines the careers of a group of men who immigrated to Maryland in the seventeenth century in order to provide some of the data needed for answers to such questions.[4]

[1] Baltimore County Land Records, IR#PP, 64 (all manuscript sources cited in this essay are in the Maryland Hall of Records, Annapolis, Md.); Patents, XII, 269, 283; IB&IL#C, 22, 29, 44, 63, 65; Testamentary Proceedings, 15C, 51; Kenneth L. Carroll, "Thomas Thurston, Renegade Maryland Quaker," *Maryland Historical Magazine,* LXII (1967), 189; William Hand Browne *et al.,* eds., *Archives of Maryland . . .* (Baltimore, 1883–), VII, 349; XV, 253; XVII, 142; Inventories and Accounts, XII, 152–153; XIIIA, 53–58; XX, 208–209.

[2] Patents, XI, 334, 573; XII, 342, 427; *Md. Arch.,* LXVI, 18–19, 138–139; Dorchester County Land Records, Old#3, 101–103; Old#4½, 121; Inventories and Accounts, XIV, 67.

[3] Somerset County Judicials, DT7, 146; SC, 134; Somerset County Land Records, L, 22; Patents, XXII, 59, 77; XIX, 562; Rent Roll, IX, 15; Somerset Wills, Box 2, folder 50; Inventories and Accounts, XXXIV, 159–160; XXXV, 280.

[4] Useful studies of indentured servants in colonial history include Thomas J. Wertenbaker, *The Planters of Colonial Virginia* (Princeton, 1922); Richard B. Morris, *Government and Labor in Early America* (New York, 1946); Abbot Emerson Smith, *Colonists in Bondage: White Servitude and Convict Labor in America, 1607–1776* (Chapel Hill, 1947); Marcus Wilson Jernegan, *Laboring and Dependent Classes in Colonial America, 1607–1783* (Chicago, 1931); Mildred Campbell, "Social Origins of Some Early Americans," in James Morton Smith, ed., *Seventeenth-Century America: Essays in Colonial History* (Chapel Hill, 1959), 63–89.

The study of mobility requires an assessment of a man's position in so-ciety for at least two points in his career, a task that the general absence of census materials, tax lists, and assessment records makes difficult. Never-theless, a study of mobility among servants is possible because we know their place in the social structure at the beginning of their careers in the New World. Servants started at the bottom of white society: they entered the colonies with neither freedom nor capital. Since we can define their position on arrival, measuring the degree of success they achieved is a fairly simple task. We can, as the capsule biographies of Gibson, Sealus, and Scot demon-strate, describe their progress in the New World. A study of the fortunes of indentured servants and the way those fortunes changed over time provides a sensitive indicator of the opportunities available within colonial society.

The broadest group under study in this essay consists of 275 men who entered Maryland as servants before the end of 1642, although the main con-cern is with 158 for whom proof exists that they survived to be freemen.[5] Not all the men who came into Maryland as servants by 1642 are included in the 275. No doubt a few servants escape any recorded mention, while others ap-pear who are not positively identified as servants. One large group falling into this latter category included 66 men, not specifically called servants, who were listed in the proofs of headrights as having been transported into the colony at the expense of someone else to whom they were not related. It is probable that all of these men emigrated under indentures, but since proof was lacking they have been excluded from the study.[6]

The mortality rate among these servants was probably high. One hun-dred and seventeen of the 275—more than 40 percent—did not appear in the records as freemen. The deaths of 14 of the missing are mentioned,[7] but we can only speculate on the fate of most of the servants who disappeared. Some may have been sold out of the province before their terms were com-pleted, and some may have run away, while others may have left Maryland immediately after becoming freemen. A majority probably died while still servants, victims of the unusual climate, poor food, ill housing, hard work, or an occasional cruel master, before they had a chance to discover for them-selves if America was a land of opportunity.

---

[5] The period could have been extended to include those arriving as late as 1644 or 1645, but this seemed pointless. It was only necessary to have a group large enough so that an occasional error would not alter percentages drastically; 158 seemed adequate for that purpose.

[6] The terms servant and servitude covered a wide variety of men and situations in the 17th cen-tury and the terms of the contracts the men in this sample served under are not known. How-ever, I am confident that the men under study shared three characteristics: first, they did not pay their own passage; second, they arrived in Maryland without capital; third, they were bound in service for a term of years. As a means of determining whether the selection process contained any significant bias, the careers of the 66 transportees were also studied. Including them would have slightly strengthened the argument presented in this essay.

[7] *Md. Arch.*, I, 17; IV, 22–23, 49, 52–53; V, 192, 197; Raphael Semmes, "Claiborne vs. Clobery et als. in the High Court of Admiralty," *Md. Hist. Mag.*, XXVII (1933), 181, 185–186.

For the 158 who definitely survived the rigors of servitude, opportunity was abundant. Seventy-nine to 81 (identification is uncertain in two cases) of the survivors, about 50 percent, eventually acquired land in Maryland. To be properly interpreted, however, this figure must be understood within the context of the careers of those who failed to acquire land. Fourteen of those who survived servitude but did not acquire land in Maryland died within a decade of completing their terms. Another 25 left before they had lived in the colony for ten years as freemen. These figures are conservative, for they include only those for whom death or migration can be proven. Twenty-five of the 158 survivors appear only briefly in the records and then vanish without a trace, presumably among the early casualties or emigrants. Furthermore, there is no reason to believe that those who left were any less successful than those who remained. At least 11 of the 25 known emigrants became landowners in Virginia. Only 13 to 15 of the 158 servants who appeared in the records as freemen (less than 10 percent) lived for more than a decade in Maryland as freemen without becoming landowners.[8]

Those who acquired land did so rapidly. The interval between achieving freedom and acquiring land, which was discovered in forty-six cases, ranged from two years for Richard Nevill and Phillip West to twelve for John Norman and Walter Walterlin. Francis Pope, for whom the interval was seven years, and John Maunsell, who took eight, came closer to the median of seven and one-half years.

The holdings of the vast majority of those who acquired land were small. Most lived as small planters on tracts ranging in size from fifty acres to four hundred acres, although fourteen former servants managed to become large landowners, possessing at least one thousand acres at one time in their lives. Zachary Wade, who owned over four thousand acres at his death in 1678 and about five thousand acres in the early 1670s, ranked with the largest landowners in Maryland.[9]

Inventories of personal estates, taken at death, have survived for 31 of the 158 former servants. Analysis of the inventories reinforces the conclusion that most of these men became small planters. About 60 percent of the inventories show personal property appraised at less than one hundred pounds sterling.[10] Men whose estates fell into this range led very simple

---

[8] The figure of 10% may be too high. A few of the men who do not appear as landowners may have held freeholds on one of the private manors for which we do not have records.

[9] For a list of Wade's land at his death, see his will in Charles County Wills, 1665–1708, 54–56.

[10] The use of £100 as a cutoff point is derived from Aubrey Land, "Economic Base and Social Structure: The Northern Chesapeake in the Eighteenth Century," *Journal of Economic History*, XXV (1965), 642. There is no way of determining whether these inventories constitute a representative sample. My impression is that they are biased in favor of the wealthiest and that a more complete series would show 75 to 80% of the estates worth less than £100. Prior to the early 1680s, estates were appraised in tobacco. I have translated them into sterling according to the average price of tobacco in the year the inventory was taken. See Russell R. Menard, "Farm Prices of Maryland Tobacco, 1659–1710," *Md. Hist. Mag.*, forthcoming, for details.

lives. In most cases, livestock accounted for more than half the total value of their personal possessions. At best their clothing and household furnishings were meager. They either worked their plantations themselves or with the help of their wives and children, for few of these small planters owned servants and even fewer owned slaves. In Aubrey Land's apt phrase, they led lives of "rude sufficiency."[11] But they fared no better than if they had remained in England.

Not all former servants remained small planters. Twelve of the thirty-one left estates appraised at more than one hundred pounds. Men such as John Halfhead, Francis Pope, and James Walker could be described as substantial planters. Their life style was not luxurious, but their economic position was secure and their assets usually included a servant or two and perhaps even a slave.[12] Two men, Zachary Wade and Henry Adams, gained entry into the group of planter-merchants who dominated the local economy in the seventeenth century. Wade, whose estate was appraised at just over four hundred pounds, was wealthier than 95 percent of his contemporaries, while Adams left an estate valued at £569 15s. ld. when he died in 1686.[13]

There are still other measures of mobility which confirm the picture of abundant opportunity for ex-servants that the study of property accumulation has indicated. Abbot E. Smith has estimated that only two of every ten servants brought to America in the seventeenth century became stable and useful members of colonial society, but if we take participation in government as indicative of stability and usefulness, the careers of the 158 men who survived servitude demonstrate that Smith's estimates are much too low, at least for the earlier part of the century.[14]

Former servants participated in the government of Maryland as jurors, minor office holders, justices of the peace, sheriffs, burgesses, and officers in the militia. Many also attended the Assembly as freemen at those sessions at which they were permitted. The frequency with which responsible positions were given to ex-servants testifies to the impressive status mobility they achieved in the mid-seventeenth century. Seventy-five or seventy-six of the survivors—just under 50 percent—sat on a jury, attended an Assembly session, or filled an office in Maryland. As was the case with landholding, this

[11] Land, "Northern Chesapeake," *Journal Econ. Hist.*, XXV (1965), 642.
[12] Testamentary Proceedings, V, 363–365; Inventories and Accounts, I, 394–397, 500–503; III, 63–65.
[13] Inventories and Accounts, V, 197–203; VIII, 389; IX, 239–244. The statement on Wade's relative wealth is based on an analysis of all inventories filed in the 1670s.
[14] Smith, *Colonists in Bondage*, 299–300. In an earlier essay Smith used an estimate of 8% and explained this low figure by reference to the "at best irresponsible, lazy, and ungoverned, and at worst frankly criminal" character of the typical servant! "The Indentured Servant and Land Speculation in Seventeenth Century Maryland," *American Historical Review*, XL (1934–1935), 467–472.

figure must be understood in light of the careers of those who failed to participate. Fourteen of the nonparticipants died within a decade of becoming freemen; another twenty-seven left the province within ten years of completing their terms. There is no reason to assume that those who left did not participate in their new homes—two of the twenty-seven, John Tue and Mathew Rhodan, became justices of the peace in Virginia, while two others, Thomas Yewell and Robert Sedgrave, served as militia officer and clerk of a county court respectively.[15] If we eliminate the twenty-five who appeared but fleetingly in the records, only sixteen or seventeen (slightly more than 10 percent) lived for more than a decade in the province as freemen without leaving any record of contribution to the community's government.[16]

For most former servants participation was limited to occasional service as a juror, an appointment as constable, or service as a sergeant in the militia. Some compiled remarkable records in these minor positions. William Edwin, who was brought into the province in 1634 by Richard Gerard and served his time with the Jesuits, sat on nine provincial court juries and served a term as constable.[17] Richard Nevill, who also entered Maryland in 1634, served on six provincial court juries and was a sergeant in the militia.[18] A former servant of Gov. Leonard Calvert, John Halfhead, served on eleven juries and attended two sessions of the Assembly.[19] John Robinson managed, in five years before his death in 1643, to attend two Assemblies, sit on three provincial court juries, and serve as constable and coroner of St. Clement's Hundred.[20]

A high percentage of the 158 survivors went beyond service in these minor posts to positions of authority in the community. Twenty-two of them served the province as justice of the peace, burgess, sheriff, councillor, or officer in the militia. They accounted for four of Maryland's militia officers, twelve burgesses, sixteen justices, seven sheriffs, and two members of the Council.

For nine of the twenty-two former servants who came to hold major office in Maryland, tenure was brief. They served for a few years as an officer in the militia or as a county justice, or sat as burgess in a single session of the Assembly. During most of John Maunsell's twenty years in Maryland, participation was limited to occasional service as a juror. In 1649, he was returned as

[15] Lyon G. Tyler, "Washington and His Neighbors," *William and Mary Quarterly,* 1st Ser., IV (1895–1896), 41, 75; Charles Arthur Hoppin, "The Good Name and Fame of the Washingtons," *Tylers Quarterly Historical and Genealogical Magazine,* IV (1922–1923), 350; *Md. Arch.,* IV, 540–541.
[16] The figure of 10% is probably too high. The absence of county court records for St. Mary's and Calvert counties and the partial loss of those for Kent—three of the four counties in which most of the men lived—make a complete study of participation impossible. Undoubtedly some of the men counted as nonparticipants sat on juries for which the records are lost.
[17] Patents, I, 20, 38; AB&H, 5; *Md. Arch.,* IV, 33, 260, 403; X, 74, 134, 143, 273, 295; XLI, 119, 340.
[18] Patents, I, 20, 38; AB&H, 244; II, 79; *Md. Arch.,* IV, 238, 240, 444; X, 54, 116, 525; XLI, 340.
[19] Patents, I, 121; II, 579; *Md. Arch.,* I, 72, 116; IV, 9, 21, 180, 237, 240, 349, 409, 447; LVII, 309.
[20] *Md. Arch.,* I, 120; III, 89; IV, 9, 21, 176.

burgess from St. Mary's County.[21] Daniel Clocker, who started out in Maryland as a servant to Thomas Cornwallis, compiled an impressive record of minor office holding. He sat on numerous provincial court juries, served St. Mary's County as overseer of the highways, and was named to the Common Council of St. Mary's City in 1671. In 1655, when many more qualified men (Clocker was illiterate) were barred from office because of their Catholicism or suspect loyalty, he was appointed justice in St. Mary's County, a post he held for three years at most. Clocker was appointed militia officer by the rebellious Governor Josias Fendall in 1660, but again his taste of power was brief.[22] John Cage, also a former servant to Cornwallis, was appointed to the Charles County bench in April 1660, but sat for only six months. Although Cage lived in Maryland for eighteen years after his brief term as justice, his participation was limited to infrequent jury duty.[23] James Walker sat as justice in Charles County for a little more than two years. He lived in Maryland for more than thirty years, but this is the only recorded instance of his holding office.[24]

Thirteen of the twenty-two men who acquired office could count themselves among Maryland's rulers in the first few decades following the founding of the province. Two even reached the Council, although neither became a major figure in the provincial government. John Hatch first participated as a provincial court juror in February 1643. By December 1647, he had been appointed sheriff of St. Mary's County. He was elected to the Assembly from St. George's Hundred in 1650 and from Charles County in 1658 and 1660. Hatch also sat as justice in Charles County from 1658 to 1661. He was appointed to the Council in 1654 and served until 1658. His son-in-law, Governor Fendall, again elevated him to the Council in 1660 during the rebellion against Lord Baltimore. Although after 1661 he was excluded from major office because his loyalty to the proprietor was suspect, he did manage to compile an impressive record of accomplishment for a man who entered Maryland as a servant.[25] Robert Vaughan also entered Maryland as a servant, probably to Lord Baltimore. Vaughan attended the 1638 session of the Assembly as a freeman. He must have been an able man, for he was already both a sergeant in the militia and constable of St. George's Hundred. In 1640, he was returned as burgess from St. Clement's Hundred. He moved to Kent Island in 1642, probably at the urging of Governor Calvert, who sorely needed loyal supporters on the island which was a hotbed of opposition to his interests. Vaughan sat as justice of Kent for twenty-six years before he died in 1668 and served as an officer in the militia for at least that long. He was a member of the Council in 1648.[26]

[21] *Ibid.*, I, 237.
[22] Patents, AB&H, 36, 244; *Md. Arch.*, IV, 230, 539; X, 295, 413; XLI, 427; XLIX, 29, 206; LI, 387; LVII, 597.
[23] Patents, II, 570; AB&H, 244; *Md. Arch.*, IV, 213; LIII, 69, 92, 363, 502, 543.
[24] *Md. Arch.*, XLI, 87–88.
[25] *Ibid.*, I, 249–261, 380; III, 311–314; IV, 181, 349; XLI, 62, 87–88; LIII, 76.
[26] Patents, I, 99; *Md. Arch.*, 1, 2, 85, 125, 259–261, 426; III, 124–127, 211–213.

Although Hatch and Vaughan were the only former servants to reach positions of importance in the provincial government, eleven others became men of real weight in their counties of residence. These eleven averaged more than ten years on the bench, more than three sessions as burgess, and just under two years as sheriff. Zachary Wade, formerly a servant to Margaret Brent, was returned to the Assembly from St. Mary's County in 1658 and from Charles County from 1660 to 1666. He sat as justice of Charles County in 1660 and was reappointed in 1663. Wade served on the bench for a year and then stepped down to take a term as sheriff. He returned to the bench in 1667 and sat until his death in 1678.[27] Henry Adams was brought into Maryland in 1638 and served his time with Thomas Greene, who later became governor. He was first appointed to the Charles County bench in 1658 and served continuously as justice until his death in 1686, with the exception of one year, 1665–1666, during which he was sheriff. Adams also represented Charles County in the Assembly in 1661, 1663–1664, and in every session from 1671 to 1684, when illness prevented him from assuming his seat.[28] Nicholas Gwyther started out in Maryland as a servant to Thomas Cornwallis. Although he was never appointed justice and sat only once in the Assembly, his seven years as sheriff of St. Mary's County and three years as sheriff of Charles County made him one of the mainstays of Maryland's county government.[29]

The significant role played by former servants in Maryland's government in the mid-seventeenth century and the opportunities available to industrious men can also be seen in an examination of the officials of Charles County in the years immediately following its establishment in 1658. Six justices were appointed to the Charles County bench by a commission dated May 10, 1658. Four of them—John Hatch, James Lindsey, Henry Adams, and James Walker—began their careers in Maryland as servants. In the next three years, four more ex-servants—John Cage, James Langworth, Francis Pope, and Zachary Wade—were appointed justices. Hatch, Wade, and Adams also represented the county in the Assembly in this period. Nicholas Gwyther, another former servant, was Charles County's first sheriff; four of the five men who immediately succeeded Gwyther were former servants. In the late 1650s and early 1660s, Charles County was governed by men who had entered the province under indentures.[30]

The accomplishments of those former servants who were especially successful were recognized by the community through the use of titles of distinction. At least 19 of the 158 survivors acquired the title of mister, gentleman, or esquire and retained it until they died. The 13 men who achieved positions of importance in the colony's government were all honored in this

[27] Patents, II, 575; *Md. Arch.*, I, 380–383, 426; II, 8; III, 492; V, 21; XLI, 62; LIII, 76.
[28] Patents, I, 18; AB&H, 377; *Md. Arch.*, I, 396; III, 424, 519; XIII, 54; XLI, 87–88.
[29] Patents, AB&H, 60; *Md. Arch.*, I, 369, 460; X, 124; XLI, 88.
[30] *Md. Arch.*, I, 380–383, 396, 426, 451, 460; II, 8; III, 481, 492, 519; XLI, 87–88; LIII, 69, 76.

fashion. Office was not, however, the only path to a title. John Courts, for example, rode to distinction on his son's coattails. Although his father acquired a substantial landed estate, John Courts, Jr., started from humble beginnings, nevertheless married well, and, perhaps as a result of his father-in-law's influence, gained appointment to the Charles County bench in 1685. He represented the county in the Associator's Assembly and was appointed to the Council in 1692, a position he held until he died ten years later as one of Maryland's wealthiest men, leaving an estate worth over £1,800, including thirty slaves and six servants. John Courts, Sr., was regularly addressed as mister after his more illustrious son was appointed to the Council.[31] A few other men were honored with titles for part of their lives, but lost them before they died, as in the case of John Cage, who was only called mister during his brief tenure as justice.[32]

Although the personal history of each of these 158 men is unique, common patterns may be discerned. We can construct a career model for indentured servants in Maryland in the middle of the seventeenth century which should reveal something about the way opportunity was structured and what options were open to men at various stages in their lives. We can also identify some of the components necessary for constructing a successful career in Maryland.

As a group, the indentured servants were young when they emigrated. While they ranged in age from mere boys such as Ralph Hasleton to the "old and decripit" Original Browne, the great majority were in their late teens and early twenties. Age on arrival was determined in thirty-six cases with a median of nineteen.[33] Probably most were from English families of the "middling sort," yeomen, husbandmen, and artisans, men whose expectations might well include the acquisition of a freehold or participation in local government.[34]

The careers of these men suggest that a few had formal education. Robert Vaughan and Robert Sedgrave both served as clerks in county court, a position requiring record-keeping skills.[35] Cuthbert Fenwick was attorney to Thomas Cornwallis, who was probably the wealthiest man in Maryland in the 1630s and 1640s. It seems unlikely that Cornwallis would have allowed a man without education to manage his estate during his frequent absences

---

[31] *Ibid.*, XVII, 380; Charles County Inventories, 1673–1717, 143–148, 311; Charles County Accounts, 1708–1735, 47–49, 51–54, 72–73; David W. Jordan, "The Royal Period of Colonial Maryland, 1689–1715" (Ph.D. diss., Princeton University, 1966), 351, 352.

[32] *Md. Arch.*, X, 160; LIII, 69, 92, 318.

[33] Patents, AB&H, 151; *Md. Arch.*, X, 192; Semmes, "Claiborne vs. Clobery," *Md. Hist. Mag.*, XXVIII (1933), 184.

[34] Campbell, "Social Origins," in Smith, ed., *Seventeenth-Century America*, 63–89.

[35] *Md. Arch.*, IV, 540–541; Donnell MacClure Owings, *His Lordship's Patronage: Offices of Profit in Colonial Maryland* (Baltimore, 1953), 146.

from the province.[36] These men were, however, not at all typical, for most of the 158 survivors were without education. Total illiterates outnumbered those who could write their names by about three to two, and it is probable that many who could sign their names could do little more.[37]

A servant's life was not easy, even by seventeenth-century standards. Probably they worked the ten to fourteen hours a day, six days a week, specified in the famous Elizabethan Statute of Artificers. Servants could be sold, and there were severe penalties for running away. They were subject to the discipline of their masters, including corporal punishment within reason. On the other hand, servants had rights to adequate food, clothing, shelter, and a Sunday free from hard labor. Servants could not sue at common law, but they could protest ill-treatment and receive a hearing in the courts. Cases in this period are few, but the provincial court seems to have taken seriously its obligation to enforce the terms of indentures and protect servants' rights.[38] No instances of serious mistreatment of servants appear in the records in the late 1630s and early 1640s. Servants were worked long and hard, but they were seldom abused. Moreover, the servant who escaped premature death soon found himself a free man in a society that offered great opportunities for advancement.[39]

None of the indentures signed by these servants has survived, but it is possible to offer some reasonable conjecture concerning the terms of their service. John Lewger and Jerome Hawley, in their *Relation of Maryland*, offered some advice to men thinking of transporting servants into the province and they also printed a model indenture. A servant was to work at whatever his master "shall there imploy him, according to the custome of the Countrey." In return, the master was to pay his passage and provide food, lodging, clothing,

---

[36] *Md. Arch.*, I, 85.

[37] Determining literacy was difficult because there are few original papers. It was assumed that if a clerk recorded a man's mark, that man was illiterate, and that if a clerk recorded a signature when transcribing a document that also contained the mark of another man, the man whose signature was recorded could sign his name. This method is not foolproof, but it seems the best available given the limitations of the data. There were 37 illiterates and 24 who could write their names.

[38] A bill considered but not passed by the 1639 Assembly describes rules governing master-servant relations that were probably followed in practice. *Ibid.*, I, 52–54. For a revealing example of the provincial court's concern for the rights of servants, see *ibid.*, IV, 35–39. For discussions of the legal status of indentured servants, see Lois Green Carr, "County Government in Maryland, 1689–1709" (Ph.D. diss., Harvard University, 1968), 315–319, 583–584; and Morris, *Government and Labor*, 390–512.

[39] Edmund S. Morgan presents an understanding of the treatment of servants in Virginia just before the settlement of Maryland that differs sharply from the one offered here in "The First American Boom: Virginia 1618 to 1630," *WMQ*, 3d Ser., XXVIII (1971), 195–198. Even if servants were as abused and degraded as Morgan suspects, consideration of the opportunities available to ex-servants in Virginia in the 1620s and 1630s might alter his perspective on the institution. For evidence of extensive mobility among former servants in early Virginia, see Wertenbaker, *Planters of Colonial Virginia*, 60–83.

and other "necessaries" during the servant's term "and at the end of the said term, to give him one whole yeeres provision of Corne, and fifty acres of Land, according to the order of the countrey."[40] The order or custom of the country was specified in an act passed by the October 1640 session of the Assembly. Upon completion of his term the servant was to receive "one good Cloth Suite of Keirsey or Broadcloth a Shift of white linen one new pair of Stockins and Shoes two hoes one axe 3 barrels of Corne and fifty acres of land five whereof at least to be plantable." The land records make it clear that the requirement that masters give their former servants fifty acres of land cannot be taken literally. In practice, custom demanded only that a master provide a servant with the rights for fifty acres, an obligation assumed by the proprietor in 1648. If a servant wished to take advantage of this right and actually acquire a tract, he had to locate some vacant land and pay surveyor's and clerk's fees himself.[41]

The usual term of service, according to Lewger and Hawley, was five years. However, they suggested, "for any artificer, or one that shall deserve more than ordinary, the Adventurer shall doe well to shorten that time . . . rather then to want such usefull men."[42] A bill considered but not passed by the 1639 Assembly would have required servants arriving in Maryland without indentures to serve for four years if they were eighteen years old or over and until the age of twenty-four if they were under eighteen.[43] The gap between time of arrival and first appearance in the records as freemen for the men under study suggests that the terms specified in this rejected bill were often followed in practice.

Servants were occasionally able to work out arrangements with their masters which allowed them to become freemen before their terms were completed. John Courts and Francis Pope purchased their remaining time from Fulke Brent, probably arranging to pay him out of whatever money they could earn by working as freemen. Thomas Todd, a glover, was released from servitude early by his master, John Lewger. In return, Todd was to dress a specified number of skins and also to make breeches and gloves to Lewger. George Evelin released three of his servants, Philip West, William Williamson, and John Hopson, for one year, during which they were to provide food, clothing, and lodging for themselves and also pay Evelin one thousand pounds of tobacco each.[44] Such opportunities were not available to all servants, however, and most probably served full terms.

[40] *A Relation of Maryland* . . . (1635), in Clayton Colman Hall, ed., *Narratives of Early Maryland, 1633–1684*, Original Narratives of Early American History (New York, 1910), 99. On the authorship of this pamphlet, see L. Leon Bernard, "Some New Light on the Early Years of the Baltimore Plantation," *Md. Hist. Mag.*, XLIV (1947), 100.
[41] *Md. Arch.*, I, 97; III, 226; Patents, I, 27, 99; AB&H, 101, 102. A 50-acre warrant could be purchased for 100 pounds of tobacco or less. *Md. Arch.*, IV, 319, 328.
[42] *Relation of Maryland*, in Hall, ed., *Narratives of Early Maryland*, 100.
[43] *Md. Arch.*, I, 80.
[44] *Ibid.*, IV, 27, 283; V, 183; Patents, II, 509.

On achieving freedom there were three options open to the former servant: he could either hire out for wages, lease land and raise tobacco on his own, or work on another man's plantation as a sharecropper. Although custom demanded that servants be granted the rights to fifty acres of land on completing their terms, actual acquisition of a tract during the first year of freedom was simply impracticable, and all former servants who eventually became freeholders were free for at least two years before they did so. To acquire land, one had to either pay surveyor's and clerk's fees for a patent or pay a purchase price to a landholder. The land then had to be cleared and housing erected. Provisions had to be obtained in some way until the crop was harvested, for a man could not survive a growing season on a mere three barrels of corn. Tools, seed, and livestock were also necessary. All this required capital, and capital was precisely what servants did not have.[45] Wage labor, sharecropping, and leaseholding all offered men a chance to accumulate enough capital to get started on their own plantations and to sustain themselves in the meantime.

Wages were high in mid-seventeenth-century Maryland, usually fifteen to twenty pounds of tobacco per day for unskilled agricultural labor and even higher for those with much needed skills. These were remarkable rates given the fact that a man working alone could harvest, on the average, no more than fifteen hundred to two thousand pounds of tobacco a year.[46] Thirty-two of the 158 survivors were designated artisans in the records: 11 carpenters, 4 blacksmiths, 5 tailors, 4 sawyers, 2 millwrights, a brickmason, mariner, cooper, glover, and barber-surgeon. These men probably had little trouble marketing their skills. At a time when labor was scarce, even men who had nothing but a strong back and willing hands must have found all the work they wanted. However, few of the 158 men devoted themselves to full time wage labor for extended periods. Instead, most worked their own crop and only hired out occasionally to supplement their planting income.

Nevertheless, some men did sign contracts or enter into verbal agreements for long-term wage labor. There were some differences between their status and that of indentured servants. They probably could not be sold, they could sue at common law for breach of covenant, and they may have possessed some political privileges.[47] There were severe restrictions on their

[45] According to John Hammond, some masters did permit their servants to accumulate capital while still under indenture. *Leah and Rachel, or, the Two Fruitfull Sisters Virginia and Mary-land* (1656), in Hall, ed., *Narratives of Early Maryland*, 292. However, there is no evidence to support Hammond's assertion that this practice was extensive.

[46] Manfred Jonas, "Wages in Early Colonial Maryland," *Md. Hist. Mag.*, LI (1956), 27–38. For the amount of tobacco a man could produce in a year, see Lewis Cecil Gray, *History of Agriculture in the Southern United States to 1860*, I (Washington, D.C., 1932), 218–219; Carr, "County Government in Maryland," appendix IV, 94–96; Arthur Pierce Middleton, *Tobacco Coast: A Maritime History of Chesapeake Bay in the Colonial Era* (Newport News, Va., 1953), 103.

[47] For an exception to the general rule that men with long-term wage contracts could not be sold, see *Md. Arch.*, IV, 173–174. For purposes of taxation, wage laborers were considered freemen,

personal freedom, however, and their daily life must have been similar to a servant's. Wages ranged from eleven hundred to fifteen hundred pounds of tobacco a year plus shelter, food, and clothing. Ex-servants occasionally hired out for long terms, perhaps because of heavy indebtedness or lack of alternative opportunities, or perhaps because of the security such contracts afforded. Recently freed servants may have found long-term wage contracts an attractive means of making the transition from indentured laborer to free colonist.[48] While long-term wage labor was, in a sense, a prolongation of servitude, it could also serve as a means of capital accumulation and an avenue of mobility.

The records reveal little of the extent or conditions of sharecropping in the 1640s, but it is clear that several of the 158 former servants did work on another man's plantation for a share of the crop.[49] By the 1660s—and there seems no reason to assume that this was not also the case in the earlier period—working for a "share" meant that a man joined other workers on a plantation in making a crop, the size of his share to be determined by dividing the total crop by the number of laborers. Contracts often required the plantation owner to pay the cropper's taxes and provide diet, lodging, and washing, while obliging the cropper to work at other tasks around the plantation.[50] The status of such sharecroppers seems indistinguishable from that of wage laborers on long-term contracts.

Most of the 158 former servants established themselves as small planters on leased land immediately after they had completed their terms. There were two types of leases available to ex-servants, leaseholds for life or for a long term of years and short-term leaseholds or tenancies at will. Although these forms of leaseholding differed in several important respects, both allowed the tenant to become the head of a household. As householders, former bondsmen achieved a degree of independence and a measure of responsibility denied to servants, wage laborers, and sharecroppers. Heads of households were masters in their own families, responsible for the discipline, education, and maintenance of their subordinates. They formed the backbone of the political community, serving on juries, sitting in Assembly, and filling the minor offices. The favorable man/land ratio in early Maryland made the formation

---

but it is not certain that for political purposes they were counted among the freemen of the province. See *ibid.*, I, 123. Biographical studies suggest that, in general, political participation was limited to heads of households.

[48] *Ibid.*, I, 166, 173–174, 201, 286, 468. John Hammond recommended that immigrants without capital sign year-long wage contracts when they arrived in the colonies. *Leah and Rachel*, in Hall, ed., *Narratives of Early Maryland*, 293.

[49] Patents, III, 18; *Md. Arch.*, X, 208.

[50] For examples of sharecropping arrangements, see Talbot County Court Proceedings, 1685–1689, 287; Charles County Court and Land Records, H#1, 160–162; *Md. Arch.*, XLIX, 326–327.

of new households a fairly easy task and servants usually became householders soon after completing their terms.[51]

In many ways there was little difference between land held in fee simple
and a lease for life or for a long term of years. Such leases were inheritable
and could be sold; they were usually purchased for a lump sum and yearly
rents were often nominal. Terms varied considerably, but all long-term leaseholds provided the tenant a secure tenure and a chance to build up equity in
his property. Such leases were not common in seventeenth-century Maryland, although a few appear on the private manors in St. Mary's County in
the 1640s. Probably men were reluctant to purchase a lease when they could
acquire land in fee simple for little additional outlay.[52]

Tenancies at will or short-term leaseholds, usually running for no more
than six or seven years, were undoubtedly the most common form of tenure
for recently freed servants. In contrast to long-term leases, short-term leaseholds offered little security, could not be sold or inherited, and terminated at
the death of either party to the contract. Their great advantage was the absence of an entry fee, a feature particularly attractive to men without capital.
Since land was plentiful and labor scarce, rents must have been low, certainly
no higher than five hundred pounds of tobacco a year for a plantation and
perhaps as low as two hundred pounds. Rent for the first year, furthermore,
was probably not demanded until after the crop was in. No contracts for the
1640s have survived, but later in the century tenants were often required to
make extensive improvements on the plantation. Although tenure was inse-
cure, short-term leaseholding afforded ample opportunity for mobility as
long as tobacco prices remained high. In the 1640s and 1650s, leaseholding
benefited both landlord and tenant. Landlords had their land cleared, housing erected, and orchards planted and fenced while receiving a small rental
income. Tenants were able to accumulate the capital necessary to acquire a
tract of their own.[53]

Prior to 1660, small planters, whether leaseholders or landowners, frequently worked in partnership with another man when attempting to carve
new plantations out of the wilderness. Much hard work was involved in
clearing land, building shelter, and getting in a crop; men who could not afford to buy servants or pay wages often joined with a mate. Partners Joseph
Edlow and Christopher Martin, John Courts and Francis Pope, John Shirt-
cliffe and Henry Spinke, and William Brown and John Thimbelly were all
former servants who arrived in Maryland before the end of 1642. They must

---

[51] For some indication of the status of heads of households in early Maryland, see *Md. Arch.,* I,
123, 197.
[52] For examples of long-term leases, see *ibid.,* LIII, 127; LX, 51–52; Baltimore County Deeds,
RM#HS, 218–219.
[53] For examples of short-term leases, see *Md. Arch.,* LX, 305; LIV, 12–13, 79–80, 244–245; Charles
County Court and Land Records, I#1, 41; K#1, 33–34.

have found their "mateships" mutually beneficial, since, except for Martin who died in 1641, all eventually became landowners.[54]

Some men—about 10 percent of those former servants who lived in Maryland for more than a decade as freemen—did not manage to escape tenancy. Rowland Mace, for example, was still a leaseholder on St. Clement's Manor in 1659, after which he disappeared from the records.[55] The inventory of the estate of Charles Steward, who lived on Kent Island as a freeman for more than forty years and was frequently called planter, indicates that he was operating a plantation when he died in 1685, but Steward failed to acquire freehold title to a tract of his own.[56] A few others acquired land, held it briefly, and then returned to leaseholding arrangements. John Maunsell had some prosperous years in Maryland. He arrived in the province in 1638 as a servant to William Bretton and served about four years. He patented one hundred acres in 1649 and added five hundred more in 1651, but he could not hold the land and in 1653 sold it all to William Whittle. He then moved to St. Clement's Manor, where he took up a leasehold, and was still a tenant on the manor when he died in 1660.[57] John Shanks, although he too suffered fluctuations in prosperity, ended his career on a more positive note. Entering Maryland in 1640 as a servant to Thomas Gerard, he must have been quite young when he arrived, for he did not gain his freedom until 1648. In 1652 he patented two hundred acres and also purchased the freedom of one Abigail, a servant to Robert Brooke, whom he soon married. He sold his land in 1654, and, following Maunsell's path, took up a leasehold on St. Clement's Manor. Shanks, however, managed to attain the status of a freeholder again, owning three hundred acres in St. Mary's County when he died in 1684. His inventory—the estate was appraised at just under one hundred pounds—indicates that Shanks ended life in Maryland as a fairly prosperous small planter.[58]

Most of the 158 former servants, if they lived in Maryland for more than ten years as freemen, acquired land and held it for as long as they remained in the province. Almost any healthy man in Maryland in the 1640s and 1650s, if he worked hard, practiced thrift, avoided expensive lawsuits, and did not suffer from plain bad luck, could become a landowner in a short time. Tobacco prices were relatively high, and, while living costs may also have been high, land was not expensive. Even at the highest rates a one hundred-acre tract could be patented for less than five hundred pounds of tobacco, and even the lowest estimates indicate that a man could harvest twelve hundred pounds in a year.[59] Again barring ill-health and misfortune, retaining land

[54] Patents, II, 534, 550; III, 6–7; *Md. Arch., IV,* 92–93.

[55] *Md. Arch.,* LIII, 627.

[56] Inventories and Accounts, VIII, 373.

[57] Patents, I, 68–69; II, 438; AB&H, 373, 380, 421; *Md. Arch.,* LIII, 627, 630.

[58] Patents, AB&H, 15, 78, 101, 232, 319–320, 411; *Md. Arch.,* LIII, 627, 633, 635; Wills, IV, 91; Inventories and Accounts, VIII, 373–375; IX, 83.

[59] *Md. Arch.,* I, 163.

once acquired must not have been too difficult a task, at least before tobacco prices fell after the Restoration.

Hard work and thrift were, of course, not the only paths to landowner- ship. For some the fruits of office cleared the way. William Empson, for ex- ample, was still a tenant to Thomas Baker in 1658, after ten years of freedom. In 1659, Nicholas Gwyther employed him as deputy sheriff, and in the next year Empson was able to purchase a plantation from his former landlord.[60] Others charmed their way to the status of freeholder. Henry Adams married Mary Cockshott, daughter of John Cockshott and stepdaughter of Nicholas Causine, both of whom were substantial Maryland planters. To the historian, though perhaps not to Adams, Miss Cockshott's most obvious asset was twelve hundred acres of land which her mother had taken up for her and her sister Jane in 1649.[61]

For most former servants progress stopped with the acquisition of a small plantation. Others managed to go beyond small planter status to be- come men of wealth and power. What was it that distinguished the 13 for- mer servants who became men of importance in Maryland politics from the other 145 who survived servitude?

Education was one factor. We have already seen that a few of the 158 prob- ably possessed some formal training. Early colonial Maryland did not have enough educated men to serve as justices or sheriffs, perform clerical and sur- veying functions, or work as attorneys in the courts. Under such conditions, a man proficient with the pen could do quite well for himself. Men such as Cuthbert Fenwick, Robert Vaughan, and Robert Sedgrave found their educa- tion valuable in making the transition from servant to man of consequence. While approximately 60 percent of the 158 who survived servitude were to- tally illiterate, only 2 of the 13 who came to exercise real power in Maryland and only 7 of the 22 who held major office were unable to write their names.

Marriage played a role in some of the most impressive success stories. Henry Adams's marriage has already been mentioned. Zachary Wade mar- ried a niece of Thomas Hatton, principal secretary of Maryland in the 1650s.[62] James Langsworth married a Gardiner, thereby allying himself with a very prominent southern Maryland family.[63] Cuthbert Fenwick married at least twice. We know nothing of his first wife, but Fenwick found fame and fortune by marrying in 1649 Jane Moryson, widow of a prominent Virginian, a niece of Edward Eltonhead, one of the masters of chancery, and a sister of William Eltonhead, who sat on the Maryland Council in the 1650s.[64]

---

[60] *Ibid.*, XLI, 344; LIII, 26, 74–75.
[61] Patents, II, 535; *Md. Arch.*, XLI, 169–174.
[62] Carr, "County Government in Maryland," appendix IV, 371–373.
[63] Wills, I, 133–141.
[64] Harry Wright Newman, *The Flowering of the Maryland Palatinate . . .* (Washington, D.C., 1961), 280–290; Patents, III, 413–414.

It would be a mistake, however, to overestimate the significance of education and marriage in the building of a successful career. Certainly they helped, but they were not essential ingredients. Nicholas Gwyther became a man of consequence in Maryland, but married a former servant.[65] John Warren served as justice of St. Mary's County for nine years, but could not write his name.[66] Daniel Clocker and John Maunsell both held major office in Maryland. Both were illiterate and both married former servants.[67] Clearly, Maryland in the middle of the seventeenth century was open enough to allow a man who started at the bottom without special advantages to acquire a substantial estate and a responsible position.

It seems probable that Maryland continued to offer ambitious immigrants without capital a good prospect of advancement throughout the 1640s and 1650s. But there is evidence to suggest that opportunities declined sharply after 1660. True, the society did not become completely closed and some men who started life among the servants were still able to end life among the masters. Miles Gibson is a case in point, and there were others. Philip Lynes emigrated as a servant in the late 1660s and later became a member of the Council and a man of considerable wealth.[68] Christopher Goodhand, who also entered Maryland as a servant in the late 1660s, later served as justice of Kent County and left an estate appraised at nearly six hundred pounds.[69] However, in the latter part of the century men such as Gibson, Goodhand, and Lynes were unusual; at mid-century they were not.

TABLE 1 Servant Officer Holders, 1634–1689
(Former servants serving as burgess, justice of the peace, and sheriff in Charles, Kent, and St. Mary's counties, Maryland, 1634–1689, by date of first appointment.)

	New Officials	Servants	
		NUMBER	PERCENT
1634–1649	57	11–12	19.3–22.8
1650–1659	39	12	30.8
1660–1669	64	9	14.1
1670–1679	44	4–5	9.1–11.4
1680–1689	46	4	8.7

[65] *Md. Arch.*, X, 32.

[66] *Ibid.*, V, 33; LXVI, 5.

[67] Patents, II, 581; AB&H, 35, 150; *Md. Arch.*, XLIX, 29, 290.

[68] Patents, XVI, 411; XVIII, 110; *Md. Arch.*, XXVII, 181; Inventories and Accounts, XXX, 280; XXXIIB, 128; Wills, XII, 151A.

[69] Patents, XV, 379; XVII, 65; *Md. Arch.*, XVII, 379; Inventories and Accounts, WB#3, 542; XXVI, 326.

As Table 1 illustrates, the chances that a former servant would attain an office of power in Maryland diminished sharply as the century progressed.[70]

This reduction in the proportion of former servants among Maryland's rulers is directly related to basic demographic processes that worked fundamental changes in the colony's political structure. The rapid growth in the population of the province during the seventeenth century affected the life chances of former servants in at least two ways. First, there was a reduction in the number of offices available in proportion to the number of freemen, resulting in increased competition for positions of power and profit. Secondly, there was an increase in the number of men of wealth and status available to fill positions of authority. In the decades immediately following the founding of the province there were simply not enough men who conformed to the standards people expected their rulers to meet. As a consequence, many uneducated small planters of humble origins were called upon to rule. Among the immigrants to Maryland after the Restoration were a number of younger sons of English gentry families and an even larger number of merchants, many of whom were attracted to the Chesapeake as a result of their engagement in the tobacco trade. By the late seventeenth century, these new arrivals, together with a steadily growing number of native gentlemen, had created a ruling group with more wealth, higher status, and better education than the men who had ruled earlier in the century. As this group grew in size, poor illiterate planters were gradually excluded from office. Table 2,

TABLE 2 Illiterate Office Holders, 1634–1689
(Illiterates serving as burgess, justice of the peace, and sheriff in Charles, Kent, and St. Mary's counties, Maryland, 1634–1689, by date of first appointment.)

	New Officials	Illiterates	
		NUMBER	PERCENT
1634–1649	57	16	28.1
1650–1659	39	9	23.1
1660–1669	64	17	26.6
1670–1679	44	1	2.3
1680–1689	46	4	8.7

[70] This is not intended to exclude the possibility of cyclical fluctuations similar to those identified by P. M. G. Harris in "The Social Origins of American Leaders: The Demographic Foundations," *Perspectives in American History*, III (1969), 159–344. Biographies of the men who held major office in Maryland from 1634 to 1692 do not reveal any obvious cyclical patterns, but this is not a long enough period to provide a fair test for Harris's hypotheses. It may be that further research will reveal cyclical changes within this long-term decline. This issue is discussed more fully in my dissertation, "Politics and Social Structure in Seventeenth Century Maryland," to be submitted to the University of Iowa.

which focuses on the educational levels of all major office holders by measuring literacy, demonstrates the degree and rate of change.[71]

Former servants also found that their chances of acquiring land and of serving as jurors and minor office holders were decreasing. Probably the movement of prices for tobacco and land was the most important factor responsible for this decline of opportunity. During the 1640s and 1650s, the available evidence—which, it must be admitted, is not entirely satisfactory—indicates that farm prices for Chesapeake tobacco fluctuated between one and one-half and three pence per pound.[72] After 1660, prices declined due to overproduction, mercantilist restrictions, and a poorly developed marketing system that allowed farm prices to sink far below those justified by European price levels.[73] By using crop appraisals and other data from estate inventories, it is possible to construct a fairly dependable series for farm prices of Maryland tobacco from 1659 to 1710. In the 1660s, prices averaged 1.3d. per pound. For the 1670s, the average was just over a penny. During each of the next three decades the average price was less than a penny per pound.[74] Falling tobacco prices were not, however, the only obstacle to land acquisition, for while tobacco prices were going down, land prices were going up. V. J. Wyckoff has argued that the purchase price of land increased by 135 percent from 1663 to 1700.[75]

One consequence of these price changes was a change in the nature and dimensions of short-term leaseholding. In the 1640s and 1650s, tenancy was a typical step taken by a man without capital on the road to land acquisition. However, falling tobacco prices and rising land prices made it increasingly difficult to accumulate the capital necessary to purchase a freehold. In the 1660s fragmentary results suggest that only 10 percent of the householders in Maryland were established on land they did not own. By the end of the century the proportion of tenants had nearly tripled. Tenancy was no longer a transitory status; for many it had become a permanent fate.[76]

---

[71] The argument in this paragraph is a major theme of my dissertation. See also Jordan, "Royal Period of Colonial Maryland," and Bernard Bailyn, "Politics and Social Structure in Virginia," in Smith, ed., *Seventeenth-Century America*, 90–115.

[72] Gray, *History of Agriculture*, I, 262–263; Wertenbaker, *Planters of Colonial Virginia*, 66.

[73] Jacob M. Price, "The Tobacco Adventure to Russia: Enterprise, Politics, and Diplomacy in the Quest for a Northern Market for English Colonial Tobacco, 1676–1722," American Philosophical Society, *Transactions*, N.S., LI (1961), 5–6; Wertenbaker, *Planters of Colonial Virginia*, 88–96.

[74] Menard, "Farm Prices of Maryland Tobacco," *Md. Hist. Mag.*, forthcoming.

[75] "Land Prices in Seventeenth-Century Maryland," *American Economic Review*, XXVIII (1938), 81–88. It seems reasonable to assume that rents rose with land prices.

[76] These assertions concerning tenancy are based on Carr's work on Prince George's County in the early 18th century (see "County Government in Maryland," 605), on Carville Earle's work on Anne Arundel, and on my research on Charles, St. Mary's, and Somerset counties. The work on Charles and St. Mary's is summarized in Menard, "Population Growth and Land Distribution in St. Mary's County, 1634–1710" (unpubl. report prepared for the St. Mary's City Commission, 1971). A copy of this report is available at the Maryland Hall of Records.

A gradual constriction of the political community paralleled the rise in tenancy. In years immediately following settlement, all freemen, whether or not they owned land, regularly participated in government as voters, jurors, and minor office holders.[77] At the beginning of the eighteenth century a very different situation prevailed. In a proclamation of 1670, Lord Baltimore disfranchised all freemen who possessed neither fifty acres of land nor a visible estate worth forty pounds sterling. This meant, in effect, that short-term leaseholders could no longer vote, since few could meet the forty pounds requirement.[78] Furthermore, by the early eighteenth century landowners virtually monopolized jury duty and the minor offices.[79] In the middle of the seventeenth century, most freemen in Maryland had an ample opportunity to acquire land and participate in community government; by the end of the century a substantial portion of the free male heads of households were excluded from the political process and unable to become landowners.

Evidence for this general constriction of opportunity can be seen in the careers of the children of the 158 survivors. No attempt was made at a systematic survey of the fortunes of the second generation, but enough information was gathered in the course of research to support some generalizations. In only one family did the children clearly outdistance the accomplishments of their father. John Courts's son, John Jr., became a member of the Council, while his daughter, Elizabeth, married James Keech, later a provincial court justice.[80] Of the 22 former servants who came to hold major office in Maryland, only 6 either left sons who also held major office or daughters who married men who did so. The great leap upward in the histories of these families took place in the first generation. If the immigrants managed to become small, landowning planters, their children maintained that position but seldom moved beyond it. If the immigrants were somewhat more successful and obtained offices of power, their children sometimes were able to maintain the family station but often experienced downward mobility into small planter status.

In order to provide more direct evidence that opportunities for men who entered Maryland without capital were declining, an effort was made to study the careers of a group of servants who arrived in the 1660s and 1670s. The problems encountered were formidable. The increase in population and the fact that by this time servants could end up in any one of ten counties in

[77] For example, 34 men sat on the first three juries convened in the provincial court in 1643. Twenty-three of them did not own land, and nonlandowners were a majority on all three. *Md. Arch.*, IV, 176–177, 180, 191.
[78] Charles M. Andrews, *The Colonial Period of American History*, II (New Haven, 1936), 339–340; Carr, "County Government in Maryland," 608. Inventories were found for 17 nonlandowners who died in Somerset County in the period 1670–1690. Only three had estates worth more than £40, and two of those three had sources of income other than planting.
[79] Carr, "County Government in Maryland," 606. My research in Somerset County confirms Carr's findings.
[80] Wills, XII, 215–217. See also n. 31 above.

Maryland made simple name correlation from headright entries unreliable. To surmount this difficulty an alternative approach was developed. In 1661, in order to regulate the length of service for those servants brought into the colony without indentures, the Assembly passed an act requiring that masters bring their servants into the county courts to have their ages judged and registered.[81] Using a list of names from this source simplified the problem of identification by placing the servants geographically and providing precise information about their age and length of service. Even with these additional aids, career-line study of obscure men proved difficult and the sample disappointingly small. However, the results did confirm inferences drawn from data about price changes and tenancy and offered support for the argument that as the century progressed, servants found it increasingly difficult to acquire land and participate in government.

From 1662 to 1672, 179 servants were brought into the Charles County Court to have their ages judged.[82] Only 58 of the 179 definitely appeared in the records as freemen, a fact which in itself suggests declining opportunities, since there does seem to be a relationship between a man's importance in the community and the frequency of his appearance in the public records.[83] Of the 58 of whom something could be learned, only 13 to 17—22 to 29 percent—eventually became landowners. Furthermore, none acquired great wealth. Mark Lampton, who owned 649 acres in the early 1690s, was the largest landowner in the group and the only one who owned more than 500 acres. Robert Benson, whose estate was appraised at just over two hundred pounds, left the largest inventory. Lampton was the only other one of the 58 whose estate was valued at more than one hundred pounds.[84]

A study of the participation of these men in local government indicates that opportunities in this field were also declining. Only twenty-three to twenty-five of the fifty-eight sat on a jury or filled an office, and the level at which they participated was low. Only one, Henry Hardy, who was appointed to the Charles County bench in 1696, held major office.[85] A few oth-

---

[81] *Md. Arch.,* I, 409–419.

[82] Charles County was chosen for two reasons. First, many of the servants who arrived by 1642 settled there, so it provides geographical continuity; second, there are exceptionally good 17th-century records for the county.

[83] In this connection, in a similar study of 116 servants brought into Prince George's County from 1696 to 1706, only 5 to 8 appeared as heads of households on a nearly complete tax list of 1719, so the project was abandoned.

[84] Patents, NS#2, 34; Charles County Court and Land Records, Q#1, 120–121; S#1, 343–344; Wills, XI, 200; Inventories and Accounts, 19½B, 136–138; XXI 292–293.

[85] Hardy was also the only one of the 58 to acquire a title of distinction. Charles County Court and Land Records, V#1, 20–21. It is probable that the Richard Gwin who was appointed justice in Baltimore County in 1685 is identical with the Richard Gwin brought into Charles County Court to have his age judged by Francis Pope in 1664. Gwin was "living in Adultry" and was not allowed to sit on the bench. *Md. Arch.,* V, 524–525; XVII, 380; LIII, 451; Baltimore County Court Proceedings, 1682–1686, 358.

ers compiled impressive records as minor office holders. Mathew Dike, for example, sat on eight juries and served as overseer of the highways and constable, while Robert Benson was twice a constable and fourteen times a juryman.[86] For most of these men, however, occasional service as a juror was the limit of their participation. Five of the twenty-three known participants served only once as a juror, while another six only sat twice.

The contrast between the careers of these 58 men and the 158 who entered Maryland before 1642 is stark. At least 46 of the 58 lived in the province as freemen for over a decade. In other words, 50 to 57 percent lived in Maryland as freemen for more than ten years and did not acquire land, while 36 to 40 percent did not participate in government. Only about 10 percent of the 158 who arrived in the earlier period and lived in the colony for a decade as freemen failed to become landowners and participants.[87]

How successful, then, in the light of these data, was the institution of servitude in seventeenth-century Maryland? The answer depends on perspective and chronology. Servitude had two primary functions. From the master's viewpoint its function was to supply labor. From the point of view of the prospective immigrant without capital, servitude was a means of mobility, both geographic and social; that is, it was a way of getting to the New World and, once there, of building a life with more prosperity and standing than one could reasonably expect to attain at home. Its success in performing these two quite different functions varied inversely as the century progressed. Prior to 1660, servitude served both purposes well. It provided large planters with an inexpensive and capable work force and allowed poor men entry into a society offering great opportunities for advancement. This situation in which the two purposes complemented each other did not last, and the institution gradually became more successful at supplying labor as it became less so at providing new opportunities. Some men were always able to use servitude as an avenue of mobility, but, over the course of the century, more and more found that providing labor for larger planters, first as servants and later as tenants, was their permanent fate.

[86] Charles County Court and Land Records, H#1, 338; I#1, 176; K#1, 384; M#1, 208, 223; N#1, 166, 323; P#1, 7; Q#1, 27; R#1, 136, 237, 369, 482; S#1, 2, 28, 247, 275, 279; V#1, 62, 133, 210, 241, 333, 351.

[87] There are two possible objections to this comparison. Although I do not think either is valid, both are difficult to refute. First, it could be argued that the quality of servants declined over the course of the century. Mildred Campbell, however, noticed no such change in the status of servants leaving Bristol from 1654 to 1685. "Social Origins," in Smith, ed., *Seventeenth-Century America*, 63–89. Secondly, although the first group includes servants in general and the second only redemptioners, it does not follow that there are significant differences between the two categories. Both groups consisted largely of poor, illiterate farmers and artisans; both also included a few poor but educated men. Henry Hardy, for example, seems to have had some education, while the three Dulany brothers arrived in Maryland as redemptioners. Aubrey C. Land, *The Dulanys of Maryland: A Biographical Study of Daniel Dulany, the Elder (1685–1753), and Daniel Du-*

The Planter's Wife: The Experience of White Women in Seventeenth-Century Maryland

Lois G. Carr and Lorena S. Walsh

INTRODUCTION

For about a decade beginning in the mid-1960s, most studies of colonial families concentrated on New England with a strong emphasis on males— fathers and sons. This essay by Lois Carr and Lorena Walsh reminds us how much we miss through such an approach. The role and behavior of women underscore some of the most significant social differences between the early Chesapeake colonies and New England. While most Puritan females traveled as part of organized families, a great majority of the women who reached Virginia and Maryland arrived as unmarried servants, not wives or daughters of other settlers. About half of them either bore bastard children or were pregnant at marriage, but these rates then fell dramatically for their native-born daughters. Because life expectancy was much shorter than in New England, the family was brittle, orphanhood became the eventual experience of most surviving children, and the larger society somehow had to adjust to these realities.

Some important questions remain unanswered.

- *What kinds of women were likely to accept indentured bondage thousands of miles from home and family?*
- *How desperate did they have to be to venture alone into the terrifying world of an oceanic vessel with its crew of irreverent and salacious sailors?*

Lois G. Carr and Lorena S. Walsh, "The Planter's Wife: The Experience of White Women in Seventeenth-Century Maryland," *William and Mary Quarterly*, 3rd ser., XXXIV (1977), 542–571. Reprinted by permission of Omohundro Institute of Early American History and Culture, Williamsburg, VA.

154

- *In short, did the women of the early Chesapeake colonies probably come from farther down the social scale than did their male counterparts?*
- *If so, did they have better chances than the men did for dramatic upward mobility?*
- *Finally, did removal to America enhance a woman's chances to achieve social respectability for herself and her daughters?*
- *Ought we perhaps to seek social idealism in the early South more among its women than its men?*

Four facts were basic to all human experience in seventeenth-century Maryland. First, for most of the period the great majority of inhabitants had been born in what we now call Britain. Population increase in Maryland did not result primarily from births in the colony before the late 1680s and did not produce a predominantly native population of adults before the first decade of the eighteenth century. Second, immigrant men could not expect to live beyond age forty-three, and 70 percent would die before age fifty. Women may have had even shorter lives. Third, perhaps 85 percent of the immigrants, and practically all the unmarried immigrant women, arrived as indentured servants and consequently married late. Family groups were never predominant in the immigration to Maryland and were a significant part for only a brief time at mid-century. Fourth, many more men than women immigrated during the whole period.[1] These facts—immigrant predominance, early death, late marriage, and sexual imbalance—created circumstances of social and demographic disruption that deeply affected family and community life.

We need to assess the effects of this disruption on the experience of women in seventeenth-century Maryland. Were women degraded by the hazards of servitude in a society in which everyone had left community and kin behind and in which women were in short supply? Were traditional restraints on social conduct weakened? If so, were women more exploited or more independent and powerful than women who remained in England? Did any differences from English experience which we can observe in the experience of Maryland women survive the transformation from an immigrant to a predominantly native-born society with its own kinship networks and community traditions? The tentative argument put forward here is that the answer to all these questions is Yes. There were degrading aspects of servitude, although

---

[1] Russell R. Menard, "Economy and Society in Early Colonial Maryland" (Ph.D. diss., University of Iowa, 1975), 153–212, and "Immigrants and Their Increase: The Process of Population Growth in Early Colonial Maryland," in Aubrey C. Land, Lois Green Carr, and Edward C. Papenfuse, eds., *Law, Society, and Politics in Early Maryland* (Baltimore, 1977), 88–110, hereafter cited as Menard, "Immigrants and Their Increase"; Lorena S. Walsh and Russell R. Menard, "Death in the Chesapeake: Two Life Tables for Men in Early Colonial Maryland," *Maryland Historical Magazine*, LXIX (1974), 211–227. In a sample of 806 headrights Menard found only two unmarried women who paid their own passage ("Economy and Society," 187).

these probably did not characterize the lot of most women; there were fewer restraints on social conduct, especially in courtship in England; women were less protected but also more powerful than those who remained at home; and at least some of these changes survived the appearance in Maryland of New World creole communities. However, these issues are far from settled, and we shall offer some suggestions as to how they might be further pursued.

Maryland was settled in 1634, but in 1650 there were probably no more than six hundred persons and fewer than two hundred adult women in the province. After that time population growth was steady; in 1704 a census listed 30,437 white persons, of whom 7,163 were adult women.[2] Thus in discussing the experience of white women in seventeenth-century Maryland we are dealing basically with the second half of the century.

Marylanders of that period did not leave letters and diaries to record their New World experience or their relationships to one another. Nevertheless, they left trails in the public records that give us clues. Immigrant lists kept in England and documents of the Maryland courts offer quantifiable evidence about the kinds of people who came and some of the problems they faced in making a new life. Especially valuable are the probate court records. Estate inventories reveal the kinds of activities carried on in the house and on the farm, and wills, which are usually the only personal statements that remain for any man or woman, show something of personal attitudes. This essay relies on the most useful of the immigrant lists and all surviving Maryland court records, but concentrates especially on the surviving records of the lower Western Shore, an early-settled area highly suitable for tobacco. Most of this region comprised four counties: St. Mary's, Calvert, Charles, and Prince George's (formed in 1696 from Calvert and Charles). Inventories from all four counties, wills from St. Mary's and Charles, and court proceedings from Charles and Prince George's provide the major data.[3]

Because immigrants predominated, who they were determined much about the character of Maryland society. The best information so far available comes from lists of indentured servants who left the ports of London, Bristol, and Liverpool. These lists vary in quality, but at the very least they distinguish immigrants by sex and general destination. A place of residence in England is usually given, although it may not represent the emigrant's place of origin; and age and occupation are often noted. These lists reveal several characteristics of immigrants to the Chesapeake and, by inference, to Maryland.[4]

[2] Menard, "Immigrants and Their Increase," Fig. 1; William Hand Browne et al., eds., Archives of Maryland (Baltimore, 1883–   ), XXV, 256, hereafter cited as Maryland Archives.

[3] Court proceedings for St. Mary's and Calvert counties have not survived.

[4] The lists of immigrants are found in John Camden Hotten, ed., The Original Lists of Persons of Quality; Emigrants; Religious Exiles; Political Rebels; . . . and Others Who Went from Great Britain to the American Plantations, 1600–1700 (London, 1874); William Dodgson Bowman, ed., Bristol and America: A Record of the First Settlers in the Colonies of North America, 1654–1685 (Baltimore, 1967)

Servants who arrived under indenture included yeomen, husbandmen, farm laborers, artisans, and small tradesmen, as well as many untrained to any special skill. They were young: over half of the men on the London lists of 1683–1684 were aged eighteen to twenty-two. They were seldom under seventeen or over twenty-eight. The women were a little older; the great majority were between eighteen and twenty-five, and half were aged twenty to twenty-two. Most servants contracted for four or five years of service, although those under fifteen were to serve at least seven years.[5] These youthful immigrants represented a wide range of English society. All were seeking opportunities they had not found at home.

However, many immigrants—perhaps about half[6]—did not leave England with indentures but paid for their passage by serving according to the custom of the country. Less is known about their social characteristics, but some inferences are possible. From 1661, customary service was set by Maryland laws that required four-year (later five-year) terms for men and women who were twenty-two years or over at arrival and longer terms for those who were younger. A requirement of these laws enables us to determine something about age at arrival of servants who came without indentures. A planter who wished to obtain more than four or five years of service had to take his servant before the county court to have his or her age judged and a written record made. Servants aged over twenty-one were not often registered, there being no incentive for a master to pay court fees for those who would serve the minimum term. Nevertheless, a comparison of the ages of servants under twenty-two recorded in Charles County, 1658–1689, with those under twenty-two on the London list is revealing. Of Charles County

---

[orig. publ. London, 1929]; [C. D. P. Nicholson, comp., *Some Early Emigrants to America* (Baltimore, 1965)]; Michael Ghirelli, ed., *A List of Emigrants to America, 1682–1692* (Baltimore, 1968); and Elizabeth French, ed., *List of Emigrants to America from Liverpool, 1697–1707* (Baltimore, 1962) [orig. publ. Boston, 1913]. Folger Shakespeare Library, MS, V.B. 16 (Washington, D.C.), consists of 66 additional indentures that were originally part of the London records. For studies of these lists, see Mildred Campbell, "Social Origins of Some Early Americans," in James Morton Smith, ed., *Seventeenth-Century America: Essays in Colonial History* (Chapel Hill, N.C., 1959), 63–89; David W. Galenson, "'Middling People' or 'Common Sort'?: The Social Origins of Some Early Americans Reexamined," *William and Mary Quarterly* (forthcoming). See also Menard, "Immigrants and Their Increase," Table 4.1, and "Economy and Society," Table VIII–6; and Lorena S. Walsh, "Servitude and Opportunity in Charles County," in Land, Carr, and Papenfuse, eds., *Law, Society and Politics in Early Maryland,* 112–114, hereafter cited as Walsh, "Servitude and Opportunity."

[5] Campbell, "Social Origins of Some Early Americans," in Smith, ed., *Seventeenth-Century America,* 74–77; Galenson, "'Middling People' or 'Common Sort'?" *WMQ* (forthcoming). When the ages recorded in the London list (Nicholson, comp., *Some Early Emigrants*) and on the Folger Library indentures for servants bound for Maryland and Virginia are combined, 84.5% of the men (N = 354) are found to have been aged 17 to 30, and 54.9% were 18 through 22. Of the women (N = 119), 81.4% were 18 through 25; 10% were older, 8.3% younger, and half (51.2%) immigrated between ages 20 and 22. Russell Menard has generously lent us his abstracts of the London list.

[6] This assumption is defended in Walsh, "Servitude and Opportunity," 129.

male servants (N = 363), 77.1 percent were aged seventeen or under, whereas on the London list (N = 196), 77.6 percent were eighteen or over. Women registered in Charles County court were somewhat older than the men, but among those under twenty-two (N = 107), 5.5 percent were aged twenty-one, whereas on the London list (N = 69), 46.4 percent had reached this age. Evidently, some immigrants who served by custom were younger than those who came indentured, and this age difference probably characterized the two groups as a whole. Servants who were not only very young but had arrived without the protection of a written contract were possibly of lower social origins than were servants who came under indenture. The absence of skills among Charles County servants who served by custom supports this supposition.[7]

Whatever their status, one fact about immigrant women is certain: many fewer came than men. Immigrant lists, headright lists, and itemizations of servants in inventories show severe imbalance. On a London immigrant list of 1634–1635 men outnumbered women six to one. From the 1650s at least until the 1680s most sources show a ratio of three to one. From then on, all sources show some, but not great, improvement. Among immigrants from Liverpool over the years 1697–1707 the ratio was just under two and one half to one.[8]

Why did not more women come? Presumably, fewer wished to leave family and community to venture into a wilderness. But perhaps more important, women were not as desirable as men to merchants and planters who were making fortunes raising and marketing tobacco, a crop that requires large amounts of labor. The gradual improvement in the sex ratio among servants toward the end of the century may have been the result of a change in recruiting the needed labor. In the late 1660s the supply of young men willing to emigrate stopped increasing sufficiently to meet the labor demands of a growing Chesapeake population. Merchants who recruited servants for planters turned to other sources, and among these sources were women. They did not crowd the ships arriving in the Chesapeake, but their numbers did increase.[9]

To ask the question another way, why did women come? Doubtless, most came to get a husband, an objective virtually certain of success in a

---

[7] *Ibid.*, 112–114, describes the legislation and the Charles County data base. There is some reason to believe that by 1700, young servants had contracts more often than earlier. Figures from the London list include the Folger Library indentures.

[8] Menard, "Immigrants and Their Increase," Table I.

[9] Menard, "Economy and Society, 336–356; Lois Green Carr and Russell R. Menard, "Servants and Freedmen in Early Colonial Maryland," in Thad W. Tate and David A. Ammerman, eds., *Essays on the Chesapeake in the Seventeenth Century* (Chapel Hill, N.C., forthcoming); E. A. Wrigley, "Family Limitation in Pre-Industrial England," *Economic History Review,* 2d Ser., XIX (1966), 82–109; Michael Drake, "An Elementary Exercise in Parish Register Demography," *ibid.,* XIV (1962), 427–445; J. D. Chambers, *Population, Economy, and Society in Pre-Industrial England* (London, 1972).

land where women were so far outnumbered. The promotional literature, furthermore, painted bright pictures of the life that awaited men and women once out of their time; and various studies suggest that for a while, at least, the promoters were not being entirely fanciful. Until the 1660s, and to a less degree the 1680s, the expanding economy of Maryland and Virginia offered opportunities well beyond those available in England to men without capital and to the women who became their wives.[10]

Nevertheless, the hazards were also great, and the greatest was untimely death. Newcomers promptly became ill, probably with malaria, and many died. What proportion survived is unclear; so far no one has devised a way of measuring it. Recurrent malaria made the woman who survived seasoning less able to withstand other diseases, especially dysentery and influenza. She was especially vulnerable when pregnant. Expectation of life for everyone was low in the Chesapeake, but especially so for women.[11] A woman who had immigrated to Maryland took an extra risk, though perhaps a risk not greater than she might have suffered by moving from her village to London instead.[12]

The majority of women who survived seasoning paid their transportation costs by working for a four- or five-year term of service. The kind of work depended on the status of the family they served. A female servant of a small planter—who through about the 1670s might have had a servant[13]—probably worked at the hoe. Such a man could not afford to buy labor that would not help with the cash crop. In wealthy families women probably were household servants, although some were occasionally listed in inventories of well-to-do planters as living on the quarters—that is, on plantations other than the dwelling plantation. Such women saved men the jobs of preparing food and washing linen but doubtless also worked in the fields.[14] In middling households experience must have varied. Where the number of people to feed and wash for was large, female servants would have had little time to tend the crops.

[10] John Hammond, *Leah and Rachel, or, the Two Fruitful Sisters Virginia and Maryland . . .* , and George Alsop, *A Character of the Province of Mary-land. . . .* , in Clayton Colman Hall, ed., *Narratives of Early Maryland, 1633–1684*, Original Narratives of Early American History (New York, 1910), 281–308, 340–387; Russell R. Menard, P. M. G. Harris, and Lois Green Carr, "Opportunity and Inequality: The Distribution of Wealth on the Lower Western Shore of Maryland, 1638–1705," *Md. Hist. Mag.*, LXIX (1974), 169–184; Russell R. Menard, "From Servant to Freeholder: Status Mobility and Property Accumulation in Seventeenth-Century Maryland," *WMQ*, 3d Ser., XXX (1973), 37–64; Carr and Menard, "Servants and Freedmen," in Tate and Ammerman, eds., *Essays on the Chesapeake*; Walsh, "Servitude and Opportunity," 111–133.

[11] Walsh and Menard, "Death in the Chesapeake," *Md. Hist. Mag.*, LXIX (1974), 211–227; Darrett B. and Anita H. Rutman, "Of Ages and Fevers: Malaria in the Early Chesapeake," *WMQ*, 3d Ser., XXXIII (1976), 31–60.

[12] E. A. Wrigley, *Population and History* (New York, 1969), 96–100.

[13] Menard, "Economy and Society," Table VII-5.

[14] Lorena, S. Walsh, "Charles County, Maryland, 1658–1705: A Study in Chesapeake Political and Social Structure" (Ph.D. diss., Michigan State University, 1977), chap. 4.

Tracts that promoted immigration to the Chesapeake region asserted that female servants did not labor in the fields, except "nasty" wenches not fit for other tasks. This implies that most immigrant women expected, or at least hoped, to avoid heavy field work, which English women—at least those above the cottager's status—did not do.[15] What proportion of female servants in Maryland found themselves demeaned by this unaccustomed labor is impossible to say, but this must have been the fate of some. A study of the distribution of female servants among wealth groups in Maryland might shed some light on this question. Nevertheless, we still would not know whether those purchased by the poor or sent to work on a quarter were women whose previous experience suited them for field labor.

An additional risk for the woman who came as a servant was the possibility of bearing a bastard. At least 20 percent of the female servants who came to Charles County between 1658 and 1705 were presented to the county court for this cause.[16] A servant woman could not marry unless someone was willing to pay her master for the term she had left to serve.[17] If a man made her pregnant, she could not marry him unless he could buy her time. Once a woman became free, however, marriage was clearly the usual solution. Only a handful of free women were presented in Charles County for bastardy between 1658 and 1705. Since few free women remained either single or widowed for long, not many were subject to the risk. The hazard of bearing a bastard was a hazard of being a servant.[18]

This high rate of illegitimate pregnancies among servants raises lurid questions. Did men import women for sexual exploitation? Does John Barth's Whore of Dorset have a basis outside his fertile imagination?[19] In our opinion, the answers are clearly No. Servants were economic investments on the part of planters who needed labor. A female servant in a household where there were unmarried men must have both provided and faced temptation, for the pressures were great in a society in which men outnumbered women by three to one. Nevertheless, the servant woman was in the household to work—to help feed and clothe the family and make tobacco. She was not primarily a concubine.

[15] Hammond, *Leah and Rachel*, and Alsop, *Character of the Province*, in Hall, ed., *Narratives of Maryland*, 281–308, 340–387; Mildred Campbell, *The English Yeoman Under Elizabeth and the Early Stuarts*, Yale Historical Publications (New Haven, Conn., 1942), 255–261; Alan Everitt, "Farm Labourers," in Joan Thirsk, ed., *The Agrarian History of England and Wales, 1540–1640* (Cambridge, 1967), 432.
[16] Lorena S. Walsh and Russell R. Menard are preparing an article on the history of illegitimacy in Charles and Somerset counties, 1658–1776.
[17] Abbott Emerson Smith, *Colonists in Bondage: White Servitude and Convict Labor in America, 1607–1776* (Chapel Hill, N.C., 1947), 271–273. Marriage was in effect a breach of contract.
[18] Lois Green Carr, "County, Government in Maryland, 1689–1709" (Ph.D. diss., Harvard University, 1968), text, 267–269, 363. The courts pursued bastardy offenses regardless of the social status of the culprits in order to ensure that the children would not become public charges. Free single women were not being overlooked.
[19] John Barth, *The Sot-Weed Factor* (New York, 1960), 429.

This point could be established more firmly if we knew more about the fathers of the bastards. Often the culprits were fellow servants or men recently freed but too poor to purchase the woman's remaining time. Sometimes the master was clearly at fault. But often the father is not identified. Some masters surely did exploit their female servants sexually. Nevertheless, masters were infrequently accused of fathering their servants' bastards, and those found guilty were punished as severely as were other men. Community mores did not sanction their misconduct.[20]

A female servant paid dearly for the fault of unmarried pregnancy. She was heavily fined and if no one would pay her fine, she was whipped. Furthermore, she served an extra twelve to twenty-four months to repay her master for the "trouble of his house" and labor lost, and the fathers often did not share in this payment of damages. On top of all, she might lose the child after weaning unless by then she had become free, for the courts bound out bastard children at very early ages.[21]

English life probably did not offer a comparable hazard to young unmarried female servants. No figures are available to show rates of illegitimacy among those who were subject to the risk,[22] but the female servant was less restricted in England than in the Chesapeake. She did not owe anyone for passage across the Atlantic; hence it was easier for her to marry, supposing she happened to become pregnant while in service. Perhaps, furthermore, her temptations were fewer. She was not 3,000 miles from home and friends, and she lived in a society in which there was no shortage of women. Bastards were born in England in the seventeenth century, but surely not to as many as one-fifth of the female servants.

Some women escaped all or part of their servitude because prospective husbands purchased the remainder of their time. At least one promotional

---

[20] This impression is based on Walsh's close reading of Charles County records, Carr's close reading of Prince George's County records, and less detailed examination by both of all other 17th-century Maryland court records.

[21] Walsh, "Charles County, Maryland," chap. 4; Carr, "County Government in Maryland," chap. 4, n. 269. Carr summarizes the evidence from Charles, Prince George's, Baltimore, Talbot, and Somerset counties, 1689–1709, for comparing punishment of fathers and mothers of bastards. Leniency toward fathers varied from county to county and time to time. The length of time served for restitution also varied over place and time, increasing as the century progressed. See Charles County Court and Land Records, MS, L#1, ff. 276–277, Hall of Records, Annapolis, Md. Unless otherwise indicated, all manuscripts cited are at the Hall of Records.

[22] Peter Laslett and Karla Osterveen have calculated illegitimacy ratios—the percentage of bastard births among all births registered—in 24 English parishes, 1581–1810. The highest ratio over the period 1630–1710 was 2.4. Laslett and Osterveen, "Long Term Trends in Bastardy in England: A Study of the Illegitimacy Figures in the Parish Registers and in the Reports of the Registrar General, 1561–1960," *Population Studies*, XXVII (1973), 267. In Somerset County, Maryland, 1666–1694, the illegitimacy ratio ranged from 6.3 to 11.8. Russell R. Menard, "The Demography of Somerset County, Maryland: A Preliminary Report" (paper presented to the Stony Brook Conference on Social History, State University of New York at Stony Brook, June 1975), Table XVI. The absence of figures for the number of women in these places of childbearing age but with no living husband prevents construction of illegitimacy rates.

pamphlet published in the 1660s described such purchases as likely, but how often they actually occurred is difficult to determine.[23] Suggestive is a 20 percent difference between the sex ratios found in a Maryland headright sample, 1658–1681, and among servants listed in lower Western Shore inventories for 1658–1679.[24] Some of the discrepancy must reflect the fact that male servants were younger than female servants and therefore served longer terms; hence they had a greater chance of appearing in an inventory. But part of the discrepancy doubtless follows from the purchase of women for wives. Before 1660, when sex ratios were even more unbalanced and the expanding economy enabled men to establish themselves more quickly, even more women may have married before their terms were finished.[25]

Were women sold for wives against their wills? No record says so, but nothing restricted a man from selling his servant to whomever he wished. Perhaps some women were forced into such marriages or accepted them as the least evil. But the man who could afford to purchase a wife—especially a new arrival—was usually already an established landowner.[26] Probably most servant women saw an opportunity in such a marriage. In addition, the shortage of labor gave women some bargaining power. Many masters must have been ready to refuse to sell a woman who was unwilling to marry a would-be purchaser.

If a woman's time was not purchased by a prospective husband, she was virtually certain to find a husband once she was free. Those famous spinsters, Margaret and Mary Brent, were probably almost unique in seventeenth-century Maryland. In the four counties of the lower Western Shore only two of the women who left a probate inventory before the eighteenth century are known to have died single.[27] Comely or homely, strong or weak, any young woman was too valuable to be overlooked, and most could find a man with prospects.

The woman who immigrated to Maryland, survived seasoning and service, and gained her freedom became a planter's wife. She had consider-

---

[23] Alsop, *Character of the Province*, in Hall, ed., *Narratives of Maryland*, 358.

[24] Maryland Headright Sample, 1658–1681 (N = 625); 257.1 men per 100 women; Maryland Inventories, 1658–1679 (N = 584); 320.1 men per 100 women. Menard, "Immigrants and Their Increase," Table I.

[25] A comparison of a Virginia Headright Sample, 1648–1666 (N = 4,272) with inventories from York and Lower Norfolk counties, 1637–1675 (N = 168) shows less, rather than more, imbalance in inventories as compared to headrights. This indicates fewer purchases of wives than we have suggested for the period after 1660. However, the inventory sample is small.

[26] Only 8% of the tenant farmers who left inventories in four Maryland counties of the lower Western Shore owned labor, 1658–1705. St. Mary's City Commission Inventory Project, "Social Stratification in Maryland, 1658–1705" (National Science Foundation Grant GS-32272), hereafter cited as "Social Stratification." This is an analysis of 1,735 inventories recorded from 1658 to 1705 in St. Mary's, Calvert, Charles, and Prince George's counties, which together constitute most of the lower Western Shore of Maryland.

[27] Sixty women left inventories. The status of five is unknown. The two who died single died in 1698. Menard, "Immigrants and Their Increase," Table I.

able liberty in making her choice. There were men aplenty, and no fathers or brothers were hovering to monitor her behavior or disapprove her preference. This is the modern way of looking at her situation, of course. Perhaps she missed the protection of a father, a guardian, or kinfolk, and the participation in her decision of a community to which she felt ties. There is some evidence that the absence of kin and the pressures of the sex ratio created conditions of sexual freedom in courtship that were not customary in England. A register of marriages and births for seventeenth-century Somerset County shows that about one-third of the immigrant women whose marriages are recorded were pregnant at the time of the ceremony—nearly twice the rate in English parishes.[28] There is no indication of community objection to this freedom so long as marriage took place. No presentments for bridal pregnancy were made in any of the Maryland courts.[29]

The planter's wife was likely to be in her mid-twenties at marriage. An estimate of minimum age at marriage for servant women can be made from lists of indentured servants who left London over the years 1683–1684 and from age judgments in Maryland county court records. If we assume that the 112 female indentured servants going to Maryland and Virginia whose ages are given in the London lists served full four-year terms, then only 1.8 percent married before age twenty, but 68 percent after age twenty-four.[30] Similarly, if the 141 women whose ages were judged in Charles County between 1666 and 1705 served out their terms according to the custom of the country, none married before age twenty-two, and half were twenty-five or over.[31] When adjustments are made for the ages at which wives may have been purchased, the figures drop, but even so the majority of women waited until at least age twenty-four to marry.[32] Actual age at marriage in Maryland can be

[28] Menard, "Demography of Somerset County," Table XVII; Daniel Scott Smith and Michael S. Hindus, "Premarital Pregnancy in America, 1640–1971: An Overview," *Journal of Interdisciplinary History,* V (1975), 541. It was also two to three times the rate found in New England in the late 17th century.

[29] In Maryland any proceedings against pregnant brides could have been brought only in the civil courts. No vestries were established until 1693, and their jurisdiction was confined to the admonishment of men and women suspected of fornication unproved by the conception of a child. Churchwardens were to inform the county clerk of bastardies. Carr, "County Government in Maryland," text, 148–149, 221–223.

[30] The data are from Nicholson, comp., *Some Early Emigrants.*

[31] Charles County Court and Land Records, MSS, C #1 through B #2.

[32] Available ages at arrival are as follows:

Age	under 12	13	14	15	16	17	18	19	20	21	22	23	24	25	26	27	28	29	30
Indentured (1682–1687)			1	1	6	2	9	9	8	29	19	6	5	6	2	3	1	2	3
Unindentured (1666–1705)	8	5	12	4	7	18	16	13	34	9	11	2	1	1					

Terms of service for women without indentures from 1666 on were 5 years if they were aged 22 at arrival; 6 years if 18–21; 7 years if 15–17; and until 22 if under 15. From 1661 to 1665 these terms were shorter by a year, and women under 15 served until age 21. If we assume that

found for few seventeenth-century female immigrants, but observations for
Charles and Somerset counties place the mean age at about twenty-five.[33]

Because of the age at which an immigrant woman married, the number
of children she would bear her husband was small. She had lost up to ten
years of her childbearing life[34]—the possibility of perhaps four or five children, given the usual rhythm of childbearing.[35] At the same time, high mortality would reduce both the number of children she would bear over the
rest of her life and the number who would live. One partner to a marriage
was likely to die within seven years, and the chances were only one in three
that a marriage would last ten years.[36] In these circumstances, most women
would not bear more than three or four children—not counting those stillborn—to any one husband, plus a posthumous child were she the survivor.
The best estimates suggest that nearly a quarter, perhaps more, of the children born alive died during their first year and that 40 to 55 percent would
not live to see age twenty.[37] Consequently, one of her children would probably die in infancy, and another one or two would fail to reach adulthood.
Wills left in St. Mary's County during the seventeenth century show the results. In 105 families over the years 1660 to 1680 only twelve parents left
more than three children behind them, including those conceived but not yet
born. The average number was 2.3, nearly always minors, some of whom
might die before reaching adulthood.[38]

---

(1) indentured women served 4 years; (2) they constituted half the servant women; (3) women
under age 12 were not purchased as wives; (4) 20% of women aged 12 or older were purchased;
and (5) purchases were spread evenly over the possible years of service, then from 1666, 73.9%
were 23 or older at marriage, and 66.0% were 24 or older; 70.8% were 23 or older from 1661 to
1665, and 55.5% were 24 or older. Mean ages at eligibility for marriage, as calculated by dividing person-years by the number of women, were 24.37 from 1666 on and 23.42 from 1661 to
1665. All assumptions except (3) and (5) are discussed above. The third is made on the basis that
native girls married as young as age 12.

[33] Walsh, "Charles County, Maryland," chap. 2; Menard, "Demography of Somerset County,"
Tables XI, XII.

[34] The impact of later marriages is best demonstrated with age-specific marital fertility statistics.
Susan L. Norton reports that women in colonial Ipswich, Massachusetts, bore an average of 7.5
children if they married between ages 15 and 19; 7.1 if they married between 20 and 24; and 4.5
if they married after 24. Norton, "Population Growth in Colonial America: A Study of Ipswich,
Massachusetts," *Pop. Studies*, XXV (1971), 444. Cf. Wrigley, "Family Limitation in Pre-Industrial
England," *Econ. Hist. Rev.* 2nd Ser., XIX (1966), 82–109.

[35] In Charles County the mean interval between first and second and subsequent births was 30.8,
and the median was 27.3 months. Walsh, "Charles County, Maryland," chap. 2. Menard has
found that in Somerset County, Maryland, the median birth intervals for immigrant women between child 1 and child 2, child 2 and child 3, child 3 and child 4, and child 4 and child 5 were
26, 26, 30, 27 months, respectively ("Demography of Somerset County," Table XX).

[36] Walsh, "Charles County, Maryland," chap. 2.

[37] Walsh and Menard, "Death in the Chesapeake," *Md. Hist. Mag.*, LXIX (1974), 222.

[38] Menard, using all Maryland wills, found a considerably lower number of children per family
in a similar period: 1.83 in wills probated 1660–1665; 2.20 in wills probated 1680–1684 ("Economy and Society," 198). Family reconstitution not surprisingly produces slightly higher figures,

For the immigrant woman, then, one of the major facts of life was that although she might bear a child about every two years, nearly half would not reach maturity. The social implications of this fact are far-reaching. Because she married late in her childbearing years and because so many of her children would die young, the number who would reach marriageable age might not replace, or might only barely replace, her and her husband or husbands as child-producing members of society. Consequently, so long as immigrants were heavily predominant in the adult female population, Maryland could not grow much by natural increase.[39] It remained a land of newcomers.

This fact was fundamental to the character of seventeenth-century Maryland society, although its implications have yet to be fully explored. Settlers came from all parts of England and hence from different traditions—in types of agriculture, forms of landholding and estate management, kinds of building, construction, customary contributions to community needs, and family arrangements, including the role of women. The necessities of life in the Chesapeake required all immigrants to make adaptations. But until the native-born became predominant, a securely established Maryland tradition would not guide or restrict the newcomers.

If the immigrant woman had remained in England, she would probably have married at about the same age or perhaps a little later.[40] But the social consequences of marriage at these ages in most parts of England were probably different. More children may have lived to maturity, and even where mortality was as high newcomers are not likely to have been the main source of population growth.[41] The locally born would still dominate the community, its social organization, and its traditions. However, where there were exceptions, as perhaps in London, late age at marriage, combined with high mortality and heavy immigration, may have had consequences in some ways similar to those we have found in Maryland.

---

since daughters are often underrecorded in wills but are recorded as frequently as sons in birth registers. In 17th-century Charles County the mean size of all reconstituted families was 2.75. For marriages contracted in the years 1658–1669 (N = 118), 1670–1679 (N = 79), and 1680–1689 (N = 95), family size was 3.15, 2.58, and 2.86 respectively. In Somerset County, family size for immigrant marriages formed between 1665 and 1695 (N = 41) was 3.9. Walsh, "Charles County, Maryland," chap. 2; Menard, "Demography of Somerset County," Table XXI.

[39] For fuller exposition of the process see Menard, "Immigrants and Their Increase."

[40] P. E. Razell, "Population Change in Eighteenth-Century England. A Reinterpretation," *Econ. Hist. Rev.*, 2nd Ser., XVIII (1965), 315, cites mean age at marriage as 23.76 years for 7,242 women in Yorkshire, 1662–1714, and 24.6 years for 280 women of Wiltshire, Berkshire, Hampshire, and Dorset, 1615–1621. Peter Laslett, *The World We Have Lost: England before the Industrial Age*, 2nd ed. (London, 1971), 86, shows a mean age of 23.58 for 1,007 women in the Diocese of Canterbury, 1619–1690. Wrigley, "Family Limitation in Pre-Industrial England," *Econ. Hist. Rev.*, 2nd Ser., XIX (1966), 87, shows mean ages at marriage for 259 women in Colyton, Devon, ranging from 26.15 to 30.0 years, 1600–1699.

[41] For a brief discussion of Chesapeake and English mortality see Walsh and Menard, "Death in the Chesapeake," *Md. Hist. Mag.*, LXIX (1974), 224–225.

A hazard of marriage for seventeenth-century women everywhere was death in childbirth, but this hazard may have been greater than usual in the Chesapeake. Whereas in most societies women tend to outlive men, in this malaria-ridden area it is probable that men outlived women. Hazards of childbirth provide the likely reason that Chesapeake women died so young. Once a woman in the Chesapeake reached forty-five, she tended to outlive men who reached the same age. Darrett and Anita Rutman have found malaria a probable cause of an exceptionally high death rate among pregnant women, who are, it appears, peculiarly vulnerable to that disease.[42]

This argument, however, suggests that immigrant women may have lived longer than their native-born daughters, although among men the opposite was true. Life tables created for men in Maryland show that those native-born who survived to age twenty could expect a life span three to ten years longer than that of immigrants, depending upon the region where they lived. The reason for the improvement was doubtless immunities to local diseases developed in childhood.[43] A native woman developed these immunities, but, as we shall see, she also married earlier than immigrant women usually could and hence had more children.[44] Thus she was more exposed to the hazards of childbirth and may have died a little sooner. Unfortunately, the life tables for immigrant women that would settle this question have so far proved impossible to construct.

However long they lived, immigrant women in Maryland tended to outlive their husbands—in Charles County, for example, by a ratio of two to one. This was possible, despite the fact that women were younger than men at death, because women were also younger than men at marriage. Some women were widowed with no living children, but most were left responsible for two or three. These were often tiny, and nearly always not yet sixteen.[45]

This fact had drastic consequences, given the physical circumstances of life. People lived at a distance from one another, not even in villages, much

[42] George W. Barclay, *Techniques of Population Analysis* (New York, 1958), 136n; Darrett B. and Anita H. Rutman, "'Now-Wives and Sons-in-Law': Parental Death in a Seventeenth-Century Virginia County," in Tate and Ammerman, eds., *Essays on the Chesapeake;* Rutman and Rutman, "Of Agues and Fevers," *WMQ,* 3d Ser., XXXIII (1976), 31–60. Cf. Peter H. Wood, *Black Majority: Negroes in Colonial South Carolina from 1670 through the Stono Rebellion* (New York, 1974), chap. 3.
[43] Walsh and Menard, "Death in the Chesapeake," *Md. Hist. Mag.,* LXIX (1974), 211–227; Menard, "Demography of Somerset County."
[44] In Charles County immigrant women who ended childbearing years or died before 1705 bore a mean of 3.5 children (N = 59); the mean for natives was 5.1 (N = 42). Mean completed family size in Somerset County for marriages contracted between 1665 and 1695 was higher, but the immigrant-native differential remains. Immigrant women (N = 17) bore 6.1 children, while native women (N = 16) bore 9.4. Walsh, "Charles County, Maryland," chap. 2; Menard, "Demography of Somerset County," Table XXI.
[45] Among 1735 decedents who left inventories on Maryland's lower Western Shore, 1658–1705, 72% died without children or with children not yet of age. Only 16% could be proved to have a child of age. "Social Stratification."

less towns. The widow had left her kin 3,000 miles across an ocean, and her husband's family was also there. She would have to feed her children and make her own tobacco crop. Though neighbors might help, heavy labor would be required of her if she had no servants, until—what admittedly was usually not difficult—she acquired a new husband.

In this situation dying husbands were understandably anxious about the welfare of their families. Their wills reflected their feelings and tell something of how they regarded their wives. In St. Mary's and Charles counties during the seventeenth century, little more than one-quarter of the men left their widows with no more than the dower the law required—one-third of his land for her life, plus outright ownership of one-third of his personal property. (See Table 1.) If there were no children, a man almost always left his widow his whole estate. Otherwise there were a variety of arrangements. (See Table 2.)

TABLE 1 Bequests of Husbands to Wives, St. Mary's and Charles Counties, Maryland, 1640 to 1710

		Dower or Less	
	N	N	%
1640s	6	2	34
1650s	24	7	29
1660s	65	18	28
1670s	86	21	24
1680s	64	17	27
1690s	83	23	28
1700s	74	25	34
Totals	402	113	28

Source: Wills, I–XIV, Hall of Records, Annapolis, Md.

TABLE 2 Bequests of Husbands to Wives with Children, St. Mary's and Charles Counties, Maryland, 1640 to 1710

	N	All Estate		All or Dwelling Plantation for Life		All or Dwelling Plantation for Widowhood		All or Dwelling Plantation for Minority of Child		More Than Dower in Other Form		Dower or Less or Unknown	
		N	%	N	%	N	%	N	%	N	%	N	%
1640s	3	1	33									2	67
1650s	16	1	6	2	13	1	6	1	6	4	25	7	44
1660s	45	8	18	8	18	2	4	3	7	9	20	15	33
1670s	61	4	7	21	34	2	3	3	5	13	21	18	30
1680s	52	5	10	19	37	2	4	2	4	11	21	13	25
1690s	69	1	1	31	45	7	10	2	3	10	14	18	26
1700s	62			20	32	6	10	2	3	14	23	20	32
Totals	308	20	6	101	33	20	6	13	4	61	20	93	30

Source: Wills, I–XIV.

During the 1660s, when testators begin to appear in quantity, nearly a fifth of the men who had children left all to their wives, trusting them to see that the children received fair portions. Thus in 1663 John Shircliffe willed his whole estate to his wife "towards the maintenance of herself and my children into whose tender care I do Commend them Desireing to see them brought up in the fear of God and the Catholick Religion and Chargeing them to be Dutiful and obedient to her."[46] As the century progressed, husbands tended instead to give the wife all or a major part of the estate for her life, and to designate how it should be distributed after her death. Either way, the husband put great trust in his widow, considering that he knew she was bound to remarry. Only a handful of men left estates to their wives only for their term of widowhood or until the children came of age. When a man did not leave his wife a life estate, he often gave her land outright or more than her dower third of his movable property. Such bequests were at the expense of his children and showed his concern that his widow should have a maintenance which young children could not supply.

A husband usually made his wife his executor and thus responsible for paying his debts and preserving the estate. Only 11 percent deprived their wives of such powers.[47] In many instances, however, men also appointed overseers to assist their wives and to see that their children were not abused or their property embezzled. Danger lay in the fact that a second husband acquired control of all his wife's property, including her life estate in the property of his predecessor. Over half of the husbands who died in the 1650s and 1660s appointed overseers to ensure that their wills were followed. Some trusted to the overseers' "Care and good Conscience for the good of my widow and fatherless children." Others more explicitly made overseers responsible for seeing that "my said child . . . and the other [expected child] (when pleases God to send it) may have their right Proportion of my Said Estate and that the said Children may be bred up Chiefly in the fear of God."[48] A few men—but remarkably few—authorized overseers to remove children from households of stepfathers who abused them or wasted their property.[49] On the whole, the absence of such provisions for the protection of the children points to the husband's overriding concern for the welfare of his widow and to his confidence in her management, regardless of the certainty of her remarriage. Evidently, in the politics of family life women enjoyed great respect.[50]

---

[46] Wills I, 172.

[47] From 1640 to 1710, 17% of the married men named no executor. In such cases, the probate court automatically gave executorship to the wife unless she requested someone else to act.

[48] Wills, I, 96, 69.

[49] *Ibid.*, 193–194, 167, V, 82. The practice of appointing overseers ceased around the end of the century. From 1690 to 1710, only 13% of testators who made their wives executors appointed overseers.

[50] We divided wills according to whether decedents were immigrants, native born, or of unknown origins, and found no differences in patterns of bequests, choice of executors, or tendency

We have implied that this respect was a product of the experience of immigrants in the Chesapeake. Might it have been instead a reflection of English culture? Little work is yet in print that allows comparison of the provisions for Maryland widows with those made for the widows of English farmers. Possibly, Maryland husbands were making traditional wills which could have been written in the communities they left behind. However, Margaret Spufford's recent study of three Cambridgeshire villages in the late sixteenth century and early seventeenth century suggests a different pattern. In one of these villages, Chippenham, women usually did receive a life interest in the property, but in the other two they did not. If the children were all minors, the widow controlled the property until the oldest son came of age, and then only if she did not remarry. In the majority of cases adult sons were given control of the property with instructions for the support of their mothers. Spufford suggests that the pattern found in Chippenham must have been very exceptional. On the basis of village censuses in six other counties, dating from 1624 to 1724, which show only 3 percent of widowed people heading households that included a married child, she argues that if widows commonly controlled the farm, a higher proportion should have headed such households. However, she also argues that widows with an interest in land would not long remain unmarried.[51] If so, the low percentage may be deceptive. More direct work with wills needs to be done before we can be sure that Maryland husbands and fathers gave their widows greater control of property and family than did their English counterparts.

Maryland men trusted their widows, but this is not to say that many did not express great anxiety about the future of their children. They asked both wives and overseers to see that the children received "some learning." Robert Sly made his wife sole guardian of his children but admonished her "to take due Care that they be brought up in the true fear of God and instructed in such Literature as may tend to their improvement." Widowers, whose children would be left without any parent, were often the most explicit in prescribing their upbringing. Robert Cole, a middling planter, directed that his children "have such Education in Learning as [to] write and read and Cast accompt I mean my three Sonnes my two daughters to learn to read and sew with their needle and all of them to be kept from Idleness but not to be kept as Comon Servants." John Lawson required his executors to see that his two daughters be reared together, receive learning and sewing instruction, and be "brought up to huswifery."[52] Often present was the fear that orphaned children would be treated as servants and trained only to

---

to appoint overseers. No change occurred in 17th-century Maryland in these respects as a native-born population began to appear.

[51] Margaret Spufford, *Contrasting Communities: English Villagers in the Sixteenth and Seventeenth Centuries* (Cambridge, 1974), 85–90, 111–118, 161–164.

[52] Wills, I, 422, 182, 321.

work in the fields.[53] With stepfathers in mind, many fathers provided that their sons should be independent before the usual age of majority, which for girls was sixteen but for men twenty-one. Sometimes fathers willed that their sons should inherit when they were as young as sixteen, though more often eighteen. The sons could then escape an incompatible stepfather, who could no longer exploit their labor or property. If a son was already close to age sixteen, the father might bind him to his mother until he reached majority or his mother died, whichever came first. If she lived, she could watch out for his welfare, and his labor could contribute to her support. If she died, he and his property would be free from a stepfather's control.[54]

What happened to widows and children if a man died without leaving a will? There was great need for some community institution that could protect children left fatherless or parentless in a society where they usually had no other kin. By the 1660s the probate court and county orphan's courts were supplying this need.[55] If a man left a widow, the probate court—in Maryland a central government agency—usually appointed her or her new husband administrator of the estate with power to pay its creditors under court supervision. Probate procedures provided a large measure of protection. These required an inventory of the movable property and careful accounting of all disbursements, whether or not a man had left a will. William Hollis of Baltimore County, for example, had three stepfathers in seven years, and only the care of the judge of probate prevented the third stepfather from paying the debts of the second with goods that had belonged to William's father. As the judge remarked, William had "an uncareful mother."[56]

Once the property of an intestate had been fully accounted and creditors paid, the county courts appointed a guardian who took charge of the property and gave bond to the children with sureties that he or she would not waste it. If the mother were living, she could be the guardian, or if she had remarried, her new husband would act. Through most of the century bond was waived in these circumstances, but from the 1690s security was required of all guardians, even of mothers. Thereafter the courts might actually take away an orphan's property from a widow or stepfather if she or he could not find sureties—that is, neighbors who judged the parent responsible and hence were willing to risk their own property as security. Children without any parents were assigned new families, who at all times found surety if there were property to manage. If the orphans inherited land, English common law allowed them to choose guardians for themselves at age fourteen—

[53] For example, *ibid.*, 172, 182.
[54] Lorena S. Walsh, "'Till Death Do Us Part': Marriage and Family in Charles County, Maryland, 1658–1705," in Tate and Ammerman, eds., *Essays on the Chesapeake.*
[55] The following discussion of the orphans' court is based on Lois Green Carr, "The Development of the Maryland Orphans' Court, 1654–1715," in Land, Carr, and Papenfuse, eds., *Law, Society, and Politics in Early Maryland,* 41–61.
[56] Baltimore County Court Proceedings, D, ff. 385–386.

another escape hatch for children in conflict with stepparents. Orphans who had no property, or whose property was insufficient to provide an income that could maintain them, were expected to work for their guardians in return for their maintenance. Every year the county courts were expected to check on the welfare of orphans of intestate parents and remove them or their property from guardians who abused them or misused their estates. From 1681, Maryland law required that a special jury be impaneled once a year to report neighborhood knowledge of mistreatment of orphans and hear complaints.

This form of community surveillance of widows and orphans proved quite effective. In 1696 the assembly declared that orphans of intestates were often better cared for than orphans of testators. From that time forward, orphans' courts were charged with supervision of all orphans and were soon given powers to remove any guardians who were shown false to their trusts, regardless of the arrangements laid down in a will. The assumption was that the deceased parent's main concern was the welfare of the child, and that the orphans' court, as "father to us poor orphans," should implement the parent's intent. In actual fact, the courts never removed children—as opposed to their property—from a household in which the mother was living, except to apprentice them at the mother's request. These powers were mainly exercised over guardians of orphans both of whose parents were dead. The community as well as the husband believed the mother most capable of nurturing his children.

Remarriage was the usual and often the immediate solution for a woman who had lost her husband.[57] The shortage of women made any woman eligible to marry again, and the difficulties of raising a family while running a plantation must have made remarriage necessary for widows who had no son old enough to make tobacco. One indication of the high incidence of remarriage is the fact that there were only sixty women, almost all of them widows, among the 1,735 people who left probate inventories in four southern Maryland counties over the second half of the century.[58] Most other women must have died while married and therefore legally without property to put through probate.

One result of remarriage was the development of complex family structures. Men found themselves responsible for stepchildren as well as their own offspring, and children acquired half-sisters and half-brothers. Sometimes a woman married a second husband who himself had been previously married, and both brought children of former spouses to the new marriage. They then produced children of their own. The possibilities for conflict over the upbringing of children are evident, and crowded living conditions,

---

[57] In 17th-century Charles County two-thirds of surviving partners remarried within a year of their spouse's death. Walsh, "Charles County, Maryland," chap. 2.
[58] See n. 26.

found even in the households of the wealthy, must have added to family tensions. Luckily, the children of the family very often had the same mother. In Charles County, at least, widows took new husbands three times more often than widowers took new wives.[59] The role of the mother in managing the relationships of half-brothers and half-sisters or stepfathers and stepchildren must have been critical to family harmony.

Early death in this immigrant population thus had broad effects on Maryland society in the seventeenth century. It produced what we might call a pattern of serial polyandry, which enabled more men to marry and to father families than the sex ratios otherwise would have permitted. It produced thousands of orphaned children who had no kin to maintain them or preserve their property, and thus gave rise to an institution almost unknown in England, the orphans' court which was charged with their protection. And early death, by creating families in which the mother was the unifying element, may have increased her authority within the household.

When the immigrant woman married her first husband, there was usually no property settlement involved, since she was unlikely to have any dowry. But her remarriage was another matter. At the very least, she owned or had a life interest in a third of her former husband's estate. She needed also to think of her children's interests. If she remarried, she would lose control of the property. Consequently, property settlements occasionally appear in the seventeenth-century court records between widows and their future husbands. Sometimes she and her intended signed an agreement whereby he relinquished his rights to the use of her children's portions. Sometimes he deeded to her property which she could dispose of at her pleasure.[60] Whether any of these agreements or gifts would have survived a test in court is unknown. We have not yet found any challenged. Generally speaking, the formal marriage settlements of English law, which bypassed the legal difficulties of the married woman's inability to make a contract with her husband, were not adopted by immigrants, most of whom probably came from levels of English society that did not use these legal formalities.

The wife's dower rights in her husband's estate were a recognition of her role in contributing to his prosperity, whether by the property she had brought to the marriage or by the labor she performed in his household. A woman newly freed from servitude would not bring property, but the benefits of her labor would be great. A man not yet prosperous enough to own a servant might need his wife's help in the fields as well as in the house, especially if he were paying rent or still paying for land. Moreover, food preparation was so time-consuming that even if she worked only at household duties, she saved him time he needed for making tobacco and corn. The corn, for example, had to be pounded in the mortar or ground in a handmill before it could be used to make bread, for there were very few water mills in seventeenth-century

---

[59] Walsh, "'Till Death Do Us Part,'" in Tate and Ammerman, eds., *Essays on the Chesapeake.*
[60] *Ibid.*

Maryland. The wife probably raised vegetables in a kitchen garden; she also milked the cows and made butter and cheese, which might produce a salable surplus. She washed the clothes, and made them if she had the skill. When there were servants to do field work, the wife undoubtedly spent her time entirely in such household tasks. A contract of 1681 expressed such a division of labor. Nicholas Maniere agreed to live on a plantation with his wife and child and servant. Nicholas and the servant were to work the land; his wife was to "Dresse the Victualls milk the Cowes wash for the servants and Doe allthings necessary for a woman to doe upon the s[ai]d plantation."[61]

We have suggested that wives did field work; the suggestion is supported by occasional direct references in the court records. Mary Castleton, for example, told the judge of probate that "her husband late Deceased in his Life time had Little to sustaine himselfe and Children but what was produced out of ye ground by ye hard Labour of her the said Mary."[62] Household inventories provide indirect evidence. Before about 1680 those of poor men and even middling planters on Maryland's lower Western Shore—the bottom two-thirds of the married decedents—[63] show few signs of household industry, such as appear in equivalent English estates.[64] Sheep and woolcards, flax and hackles, and spinning wheels all were a rarity, and such things as candle molds were nonexistent. Women in these households must have been busy at other work. In households with bound labor the wife doubtless was fully occupied preparing food and washing clothes for family and hands. But the wife in a household too poor to afford bound labor—the bottom fifth of the married decedent group—might well tend tobacco when she could.[65] Eventually, the profits of her labor might enable the family to buy a servant, making greater profits possible. From such beginnings many families climbed the economic ladder in seventeenth-century Maryland.[66]

[61] *Maryland Archives*, LXX, 87. See also *ibid.*, XLI, 210, 474, 598, for examples of allusions to washing clothes and dairying activities. Water mills were so scarce that in 1669 the Maryland assembly passed an act permitting land to be condemned for the use of anyone willing to build and operate a water mill. *Ibid.*, II, 211–214. In the whole colony only four condemnations were carried out over the next 10 years. *Ibid.*, LI, 25, 57, 86, 381. Probate inventories show that most households had a mortar and pestle or a hand mill.

[62] Testamentary Proceedings, X, 184–185. Cf. Charles County Court and Land Records, MS, I #1, ff. 9–10, 259.

[63] Among married decedents before 1680 (N = 308), the bottom two-thirds (N = 212) were those worth less than £150. Among all decedents worth less than £150 (N = 451), only 12 (about 3%) had sheep or yarn-making equipment. "Social Stratification."

[64] See Everitt, "Farm Labourers," in Thirsk, ed., *Agrarian History of England and Wales*, 422–426, and W. G. Hoskins, *Essays in Leicestershire History* (Liverpool, 1950), 134.

[65] Among married decedents, the bottom fifth were approximately those worth less than £30. Before 1680 these were 17% of the married decedents. By the end of the period, from 1700 to 1705, they were 22%. Before 1680, 92% had no bound labor. From 1700 to 1705, 95% had none. Less than 1% of all estates in this wealth group had sheep or yarn-making equipment before 1681. "Social Stratification."

[66] On opportunity to raise from the bottom to the middle see Menard, "From Servant to Freeholder," WMQ, 3d Ser., XXX (1973), 37–64; Walsh, "Servitude and Opportunity," 111–133; and Menard, Harris, and Carr, "Opportunity and Inequality," *Md. Hist. Mag.*, LXIX (1974), 169–184.

The proportion of servantless households must have been larger than is suggested by the inventories of the dead, since young men were less likely to die than old men and had had less time to accumulate property. Well over a fifth of the households of married men on the lower Western Shore may have had no bound labor. Not every wife in such households would necessarily work at the hoe—saved from it by upbringing, ill-health, or the presence of small children who needed her care—but many women performed such work. A lease of 1691, for example, specified that the lessee could farm the amount of land which "he his wife and children can tend."[67]

Stagnation of the tobacco economy, beginning about 1680, produced changes that had some effect on women's economic role.[68] As shown by inventories of the lower Western Shore, home industry increased, especially at the upper ranges of the economic spectrum. In these households women were spinning yarn and knitting it into clothing.[69] The increase in such activity was far less in the households of the bottom fifth, where changes of a different kind may have increased the pressures to grow tobacco. Fewer men at this level could now purchase land, and a portion of their crop went for rent.[70] At this level, more wives than before may have been helping to produce tobacco when they could. And by this time they were often helping as a matter of survival, not as a means of improving the family position.

[67] Charles County Court and Land Records, MS, R #1, f. 193.

[68] For 17th-century economic development see Menard, Harris, and Carr, "Opportunity and Inequality," Md. Hist. Mag., LXIX (1974), 169–184.

[69] Among estates worth £150 or more, signs of diversification in this form appeared in 22% before 1681 and in 67% after 1680. Over the years 1700–1705, the figure was 62%. Only 6% of estates worth less than £40 had such signs of diversification after 1680 or over the period 1700–1705. Knitting rather than weaving is assumed because looms were very rare. These figures are for all estates. "Social Stratification."

[70] After the mid-1670s information about landholdings of decedents becomes decreasingly available, making firm estimates of the increase in tenancy difficult. However, for householders in life cycle 2 (married or widowed decedents who died without children of age) the following table is suggestive. Householding decedents in life cycle 2 worth less than £40 (N = 255) were 21% of all decedents in this category (N = 1,218).

	£0–19				£20–39			
	DECE-DENTS N	LAND UNKN. N	WITH LAND N	WITH LAND %	DECE-DENTS N	LAND UNKN. N	WITH LAND N	WITH LAND %
To 1675	10	0	7	70	34	2	29	91
1675 on	98	22	40	53	113	16	64	66

In computing percentages, unknowns have been distributed according to knowns.

A man who died with a child of age was almost always a landowner, but these were a small proportion of all decedents (see n. 45).

Several studies provide indisputable evidence of an increase in tenancy on the lower Western Shore over the period 1660–1706. These compare heads of households with lists of landowners compiled from rent rolls made in 1659 and 1704–1706. Tenancy in St. Mary's and Charles

So far we have considered primarily the experience of immigrant women. What of their daughters? How were their lives affected by the demographic stresses of Chesapeake society?

One of the most important points in which the experience of daughters differed from that of their mothers was the age at which they married. In this woman-short world, the mothers had married as soon as they were eligible, but they had not usually become eligible until they were mature women in their middle twenties. Their daughters were much younger at marriage. A vital register kept in Somerset County shows that some girls married at age twelve and that the mean age at marriage for those born before 1670 was sixteen and a half years.

Were some of these girls actually child brides? It seems unlikely that girls were married before they had become capable of bearing children. Culturally, such a practice would fly in the face of English, indeed Western European, precedent, nobility excepted. Nevertheless, the number of girls who married before age sixteen, the legal age of inheritance for girls, is astonishing. Their English counterparts ordinarily did not marry until their mid- to late twenties or early thirties. In other parts of the Chesapeake, historians have found somewhat higher ages at marriage than appear in Somerset, but everywhere in seventeenth-century Maryland and Virginia most native-born women married before they reached age twenty-one.[71] Were such early marriages a result of the absence of fathers? Evidently not. In Somerset County, the fathers of very young brides—those under sixteen—were usually living.[72] Evidently, guardians were unlikely to allow such marriages, and this fact suggests that they were not entirely approved. But the shortage of women imposed strong pressures to marry as early as possible.

Not only did native girls marry early, but many of them were pregnant before the ceremony. Bridal pregnancy among native-born women was not as common among immigrants. Nevertheless, in seventeenth-century Somerset County 20 percent of native brides bore children within eight and one-half months of marriage. This was a somewhat higher percentage than has been reported from seventeenth-century English parishes.[73]

These facts suggest considerable freedom for girls in selecting a husband. Almost any girl must have had more than one suitor, and evidently

counties in 1660 was about 10%. In St. Mary's, Charles, and Prince George's counties, 1704–1706, 30–35% of householders were tenants. Russell R. Menard, "Population Growth and Land Distribution in St. Mary's County, 1634–1710" (ms. report, St. Mary's City Commission, 1971, copy on file at the Hall of Records); Menard, "Economy and Society," 423; Carr, "County Government in Maryland," text, 605.

[71] Menard, "Immigrants and Their Increase," Table III; n. 40 above.
[72] Menard, "Demography of Somerset County," Table XIII.
[73] *Ibid.*, Table XVII; P. E. H. Hair, "Bridal Pregnancy in Rural England in Earlier Centuries," *Pop. Studies*, XX (1966), 237; Chambers, *Population, Economy, and Society in England*, 75; Smith and Hindus, "Premarital Pregnancy in America," *Jour. Interdisciplinary Hist.*, V (1975), 537–570.

many had freedom to spend time with a suitor in a fashion that allowed her to become pregnant. We might suppose that such pregnancies were not incurred until after the couple had become betrothed, and that they were consequently an allowable part of courtship, were it not that girls whose fathers were living were usually not the culprits. In Somerset, at least, only 10 percent of the brides with fathers living were pregnant, in contrast to 30 percent of those who were orphans.[74] Since there was only about one year's difference between the mean ages at which orphan and non-orphan girls married, parental supervision rather than age seems to have been the main factor in the differing bridal pregnancy rates.[75]

Native girls married young and bore children young; hence they had more children than immigrant women. This fact ultimately changed the composition of the Maryland population. Native-born females began to have enough children to enable couples to replace themselves. These children, furthermore, were divided about evenly between males and females. By the mid-1680s, in all probability, the population thus began to grow through reproductive increase, and sexual imbalance began to decline. In 1704 the native-born preponderated in the Maryland assembly for the first time and by then were becoming predominant in the adult population as a whole.[76]

This appearance of a native population was bringing alterations in family life, especially for widows and orphaned minors. They were acquiring kin. St. Mary's and Charles counties wills demonstrate the change.[77] (See Table 3.) Before 1680, when nearly all those who died and left families had

---

[74] Menard, "Demography of Somerset County," Table XVIII.

[75] Adolescent subfecundity might also partly explain lower bridal pregnancy rates among very young brides.

[76] Menard develops this argument in detail in "Immigrants and Their Increase." For the assembly see David W. Jordan, "Political Stability and the Emergence of a Native Elite in Maryland, 1660–1715," in Tate and Ammerman, eds., *Essays on the Chesapeake.* In Charles County, Maryland, by 1705 at least half of all resident landowners were native born. Walsh, "Charles County, Maryland," chaps. 1, 7.

[77] The proportion of wills mentioning non-nuclear kin can, of course, prove only a proxy of the actual existence of these kin in Maryland. The reliability of such a measure may vary greatly from area to area and over time, depending on the character of the population and on local inheritance customs. To test the reliability of the will data, we compared them with data from reconstituted families in 17th-century Charles County.

These reconstitution data draw on a much broader variety of sources and include many men who did not leave wills. Because of insufficient information for female lines, we could trace only the male lines. The procedure compared the names of all married men against a file of all known county residents, asking how many kin in the male line might have been present in the county at the time of the married man's death. The proportions for immigrants were in most cases not markedly different from those found in wills. For native men, however, wills were somewhat less reliable indicators of the presence of such kin; when non-nuclear kin mentioned by testate natives were compared with kin found by reconstitution, 29% of the native testators had non-nuclear kin present in the county who were not mentioned in their wills.

TABLE 3   Resident Kin of Testate Men and Women Who Left Minor
Children, St. Mary's and Charles Counties, 1640 to 1710

A.

	FAMILIES N	NO KIN % FAMILIES	ONLY WIFE % FAMILIES	GROWN CHILD % FAMILIES	OTHER KIN % FAMILIES
1640–1669	95	23	43	11	23
1670–1679	76	17	50	7	26
1700–1710	71	6	35[a]	25	34[b]

B.

1700–1710					
Immigrant	41	10	37	37	17
Native	30		33[c]	10	57[d]

Notes: [a] If information found in other records is included, the percentage is 30.
[b] If information found in other records is included, the percentage is 39.
[c] If information found in other records is included, the percentage is 20.
[d] If information found in other records is included, the percentage is 70.
For a discussion of wills as a reliable source for discovery of kin see n. 78. Only 8 testators were natives of Maryland before 1680s; hence no effort has been made to distinguish them from immigrants.
Source: Wills, I–XIV.

been immigrants, three-quarters of the men and women who left widows and/or minor children made no mention in their wills of any other kin in Maryland. In the first decade of the eighteenth century, among native-born testators, nearly three-fifths mention other kin, and if we add information from sources other than wills—other probate records, land records, vital registers, and so on—at least 70 percent are found to have had such local connections. This development of local family ties must have been one of the most important events of early Maryland history.[78]

Historians have only recently begun to explore the consequences of the shift from an immigrant to a predominantly native population.[79] We would like to suggest some changes in the position of women that may have resulted from this transition. It is already known that as sexual imbalance disappeared, age at

[78] Not surprisingly, wills of immigrants show no increase in family ties, but these wills mention adult children far more often than earlier. Before 1680, only 11% of immigrant testators in St. Mary's and Charles counties mention adult children in their wills; from 1700 to 1710, 37% left adult children to help the family. Two facts help account for this change. First, survivors of early immigration were dying in old age. Second, proportionately fewer young immigrants with families were dying, not because life expectancy had improved, but because there were proportionately fewer of them than earlier. A long stagnation in the tobacco economy that began about 1680 had diminished opportunities for freed slaves to form households and families. Hence, among immigrants the proportion of young fathers at risk to die was smaller than in earlier years. In the larger population of men who left inventories, 18.2% had adult children before 1681, but in the years 1700–1709, 50% had adult children. "Social Stratification."
[79] Examples of some recent studies are Carole Shammas, "English-Born and Creole Elites in Turn-of-the-Century Virginia," in Tate and Ammerman, eds., *Essays on the Chesapeake;* Jordan,

first marriage rose, but it remained lower than it had been for immigrants over the second half of the seventeenth century. At the same time, life expectancy improved, at least for men. The results were longer marriages and more children who reached maturity.[80] In St. Mary's County after 1700, dying men far more often than earlier left children of age to maintain their widows, and widows may have felt less inclination and had less opportunity to remarry.[81]

We may speculate on the social consequences of such changes. More fathers were still alive when their daughters married, and hence would have been able to exercise control over the selection of their sons-in-law. What in the seventeenth century may have been a period of comparative independence for women, both immigrant and native, may have given way to a return to more traditional European social controls over the creation of new families. If so, we might see the results in a decline in bridal pregnancy and perhaps a decline in bastardy.[82]

We may also find the wife losing ground in the household polity, although her economic importance probably remained unimpaired. Indeed, she must have been far more likely than a seventeenth-century immigrant woman to bring property to her marriage. But several changes may have caused women to play a smaller role than before in household decisionmaking.[83] Women became proportionately more numerous and may have lost

---

"Political Stability and the Emergence of a Native Elite in Maryland," *ibid.*; Lois Green Carr, "The Foundations of Social Order: Local Government in Colonial Maryland," in Bruce C. Daniels, ed., *Town and Country: Essays on the Structure of Local Government in the American Colonies* (Middletown, Conn., forthcoming); Menard, "Economy and Society," 396–440.

[80] Allan Kulikoff has found that in Prince George's County the white adult sex ratio dropped significantly before the age of marriage rose. Women born in the 1720s were the first to marry at a mean age above 20, while those born in the 1740s and marrying in the 1760s, after the sex ratio neared equality, married at a mean age of 22. Marriages lasted longer because the rise in the mean age at which men married—from 23 to 27 between 1700 and 1740—was more than offset by gains in life expectancy. Kulikoff, "Tobacco and Slaves: Population, Economy, and Society in Eighteenth-Century Prince George's County, Maryland" (Ph.D. diss., Brandeis University, 1976), chap. 3; Menard, "Immigrants and Their Increase."

[81] Inventories and related biographical data have been analyzed by the St. Mary's City Commission under a grant from the National Endowment for the Humanities, "The Making of a Plantation Society in Maryland" (R 010585-74-267). From 1700 through 1776 the percentage of men known to have had children, and who had an adult child at death, ranged from a low of 32.8% in the years 1736–1738 to a high of 61.3% in the years 1707–1709. The figure was over 50% for 13 out of 23 year-groups of three to four years each. For the high in 1707–1709 see comments in n. 78.

[82] On the other hand, these rates may show little change. The restraining effect of increased parental control may have been offset by a trend toward increased sexual activity that appears to have become general throughout Western Europe and the United States by the mid-18th century. Smith and Hindus, "Premarital Pregnancy in America," *Jour. Interdisciplinary Hist.*, V (1975), 537–570; Edward Shorter, "Female Emancipation, Birth Control, and Fertility in European History," *American Historical Review*, LXXVIII (1973), 605–640.

[83] Page Smith has suggested that such a decline in the wife's household authority had occurred in the American family by—at the latest—the beginning of the 19th century (*Daughters of the Promised Land: Women in American History* [Boston, 1970], chaps. 3, 4).

bargaining power.[84] Furthermore, as marriages lasted longer, the proportion of households full of stepchildren and half-brothers and half-sisters united primarily by the mother must have diminished. Finally, when husbands died, more widows would have had children old enough to maintain them and any minor brothers and sisters. There would be less need for women to play a controlling role, as well as less incentive for their husbands to grant it. The provincial marriage of the eighteenth century may have more closely resembled that of England than did the immigrant marriage of the seventeenth century.

If this change occurred, we should find symptoms to measure. There should be fewer gifts from husbands to wives of property put at the wife's disposal. Husbands should less frequently make bequests to wives that provided them with property beyond their dower. A wife might even be restricted to less than her dower, although the law allowed her to choose her dower instead of a bequest.[85] At the same time, children should be commanded to maintain their mothers.

However, St. Mary's County wills do not show these symptoms. (See Table 4.) True, wives occasionally were willed less than their dower, an arrangement that was rare in the wills examined for the period before 1710. But there was no overall decrease in bequests to wives of property beyond their dower, nor was there a tendency to confine the wife's interest to the term of her widowhood or the minority of the oldest son. Children were not exhorted to help their mothers or give them living space. Widows evidently received at least enough property to maintain themselves, and husbands saw no need to ensure the help of children in managing it. Possibly, then, women did not lose ground, or at least not all ground, within the family polity. The demographic disruption of New World settlement may have given women power which they were able to keep even after sex ratios became balanced and traditional family networks appeared. Immigrant mothers may have bequeathed their daughters a legacy of independence which they in turn handed down, despite pressures toward more traditional behavior.

It is time to issue a warning. Whether or not Maryland women in a creole society lost ground, the argument hinges on an interpretation of English behavior that also requires testing. Either position supposes that women in seventeenth-century Maryland obtained power in the household which wives of English farmers did not enjoy. Much of the evidence for Maryland

---

[84] There is little doubt that extreme scarcity in the early years of Chesapeake history enhanced the worth of women in the eyes of men. However, as Smith has observed, "the functioning of the law of supply and demand could not in itself have guaranteed status for colonial women. Without an ideological basis, their privileges could not have been initially established or subsequently maintained" (*ibid.*, 38–39). In a culture where women were seriously undervalued, a shortage of women would not necessarily improve their status.
[85] Acts 1699, chap. 41, *Maryland Archives*, XXII, 542.

TABLE 4   Bequests of Husbands to Wives with Children, St. Mary's County, Maryland, 1710 to 1776

	N	All Estate %	All or Dwelling Plantation for Life %	All or Dwelling Plantation for Widow- Hood %	All or Dwelling Plantation for Minority of Child %	More Than Dower in Other Form %	Dower or Less or Un- Known %	Mainte- nance or House Room %
1710–1714	13	0	46	0	0	23	31	0
1715–1719	25	4	24	4	0	28	36	4
1720–1724	31	10	42	0	0	28	23	3
1725–1729	34	3	29	0	0	24	41	3
1730–1734	31	6	16	13	0	29	35	0
1735–1739	27	0	37	4	4	19	37	0
1740–1744	35	0	40	0	3	23	34	0
1745–1749	39	3	31	8	0	31	28	0
1750–1754	43	2	35	7	0	16	40	0
1755–1759	34	3	41	3	0	41	12	0
1760–1764	48	2	46	10	2	13	27	0
1765–1769	45	4	27	11	2	18	33	4
1770–1774	46	4	26	7	0	37	26	0
1775–1776	19	5	32	26	0	5	32	0
Totals	470	3	33	7	1	24	31	1

Source: Wills, XIV–XLI.

is drawn from the disposition of property in wills. If English wills show a similar pattern, similar inferences might be drawn about English women. We have already discussed evidence from English wills that supports the view that women in Maryland were favored; but the position of seventeenth-century English women—especially those not of gentle status—has been little explored.[86] A finding of little difference between bequests to women in England and in Maryland would greatly weaken the argument that demographic stress created peculiar conditions especially favorable to Maryland women.

If the demography of Maryland produced the effects here described, such effects should also be evident elsewhere in the Chesapeake. The four characteristics of the seventeenth-century Maryland population—immigrant predominance, early death, late marriage, and sexual imbalance—are to be

[86] Essays by Cicely Howell and Barbara Todd, printed or made available to the authors since this article was written, point out that customary as opposed to freehold tenures in England usually gave the widow the use of the land for life, but that remarriage often cost the widow this right. The degree to which this was true requires investigation. Howell, "Peasant Inheritance in the Midlands, 1280–1700," in Jack Goody, Joan Thirsk, and E. P. Thompson, eds., *Family and Inheritance: Rural Society in Western Europe, 1200–1800* (Cambridge, 1976), 112–155; Todd, "'In Her Free Widowhood': Succession to Property and Remarriage in Rural England, 1540–1800" (paper delivered to the Third Berkshire Conference of Women Historians, June 1976).

found everywhere in the region, at least at first. The timing of the disappearance of these peculiarities may have varied from place to place, depending on date of settlement or rapidity of development, but the effect of their existence upon the experience of women should be clear. Should research in other areas of the Chesapeake fail to find women enjoying the status they achieved on the lower Western Shore of Maryland, then our arguments would have to be revised.[87]

Work is also needed that will enable historians to compare conditions in Maryland with those in other colonies. Richard S. Dunn's study of the British West Indies also shows demographic disruption.[88] When the status of wives is studied, it should prove similar to that of Maryland women. In contrast were demographic conditions in New England, where immigrants came in family groups, major immigration had ceased by the mid-seventeenth century, sex ratios balanced early, and mortality was low.[89] Under these conditions, demographic disruption must have been both less severe and less prolonged. If New England women achieved status similar to that suggested for women in the Chesapeake, that fact will have to be explained. The dynamics might prove to have been different[90]; or a dynamic we have not identified, common to both areas, might turn out to have been the primary engine of change. And, if women in England shared the status—which we doubt—conditions in the New World may have had secondary importance. The Maryland data establish persuasive grounds for a hypothesis, but the evidence is not all in.

[87] James W. Deen, Jr., "Patterns of Testation: Four Tidewater Counties in Colonial Virginia," *American Journal of Legal History*, XVI (1972), 154–176, finds a life interest in property for the wife the predominant pattern before 1720. However, he includes an interest for widowhood in life interest and does not distinguish a dower interest from more than dower.

[88] Richard S. Dunn, *Sugar and Slaves: The Rise of the Planter Class in the English West Indies, 1624–1713* (Chapel Hill, N.C., 1972), 326–334. Dunn finds sex ratios surprisingly balanced, but he also finds very high mortality, short marriages, and many orphans.

[89] For a short discussion of this comparison see Menard, "Immigrants and Their Increase."

[90] James K. Somerville has used Salem, Massachusetts, wills from 1660 to 1770 to examine women's status and importance within the home ("The Salem [Mass.] Woman in the Home, 1660–1770," *Eighteenth-Century Life*, I [1974], 11–14). See also Alexander Keyssar, "Widowhood in Eighteenth-Century Massachusetts: A Problem in the History of the Family," *Perspectives in American History*, VIII (1974), 83–119, which discusses provisions for 22 widows in 18th-century Woburn, Massachusetts. Both men find provisions for houseroom and care of the widow's property enjoined upon children proportionately far more often than we have found in St. Mary's County, Maryland, where we found only five instances over 136 years. However, part of this difference may be a function of the differences in age at widowhood in the two regions. Neither Somerville nor Keyssar gives the percentage of widows who received a life interest in property, but their discussions imply a much higher proportion than we have found of women whose interest ended at remarriage or the majority of the oldest son.

The African Experience of the "20. and Odd Negroes" Arriving in Virginia in 1619

John Thornton

INTRODUCTION

Historians have long regarded the origins of European immigrants to America as important, and for a while now they have spoken with specificity about various Native American groups. Historians study European and Native American history before contact to better understand the subsequent encounters and history of the Americas. Similar thorough studies have not been undertaken on Africans or African history. American historians have been content with ascribing origins to West or Central Africa and have remained virtually ignorant of African history. This approach seemed justified by the argument that African cultures were so thoroughly disrupted by the middle passage, the scattering of cultural groups, and the harshness of slavery that coherent cultures failed to survive the Atlantic crossing, leaving only a generalized African influence. Specific African cultures and histories, then, were thought to have had little impact on the subsequent history of the Americas. John Thornton challenges this argument in his two essays in this volume and in his recent book Africa and Africans in the Making of the Atlantic World, 1400–1800. *Only by improving our understanding of African cultures and history in the early modern era can we hope to better understand the contributions that Africans have made to New World societies. After the efforts of John Thornton, no historian of early America can remain ignorant of Africa in good conscience.*

In this essay, Thornton describes in detail the likely origins of the "20. and Odd Negroes" who arrived in Virginia in 1619. In some respects, this

John Thornton, "The African Experience of the '20 and Odd Negroes' Arriving in Virginia in 1619," *William and Mary Quarterly*, 47 (1990), pp. 477–502. Reprinted by permission of Omohundro Institute of Early American History and Culture, Williamsburg, VA.

John Thornton is professor of history at Millersville University of Pennsylvania. I would like to thank Linda Heywood for her advice and commentary on the article and Joseph C. Miller, Douglas Chambers, and an anonymous reader for their help in clarifying details of the paper.

group had unusual origins (in that they came from a single region and were captured in the same war), but many aspects of their experience can be generalized. Slavery had deep roots in western and central Africa; elsewhere, Thornton argues that ownership of slaves was the principal measure of wealth in these regions (as opposed to land ownership in Europe). Thornton also argues elsewhere that Africans retained control of both the slave trade and encounters with Europeans generally.

- *Do these generalizations hold in the example described here?*
- *Which groups exert a greater control over events, the various Portuguese factions or the various African groups?*

   This example is also interesting because it runs counter to our stereotyped expectations. The slaves who arrived in Virginia came from an urban area; they went from being city dwellers in Africa to rural laborers in Virginia. They may also have had greater contact with Christianity in Africa than they did in Virginia.

- *How might the experiences of slaves in Africa and in the Americas differ?*
- *Which slave system was more harsh?*

   Thornton provides no answers for these questions here, so make your own guesses based on this reading.

Engel Sluiter's recent note on the origins of the Africans brought to Virginia in 1619 to work as laborers in the emerging English colony serves as an opportunity to explore the background of the best known of the "founders" of African America.[1] Thanks to documentary records uncovered by Sluiter, we now know that the "20. and odd Negroes" that arrived at Point Comfort in August had been taken on the high seas from the *São João Bautista*. This ship was a Portuguese slaver captained by Manuel Mendes da Cunha bound from Luanda, Angola, to Vera Cruz carrying slaves in conformity with an *asiento*, a contract to deliver slaves to Spanish colonies. Sluiter thus establishes that they were not seasoned slaves of many origins brought from the Caribbean, as was previously accepted by most historians, but probably a much more ethnically coherent group just recently enslaved in Africa.[2] The information on the time and place of their enslavement in Africa allows us to present them in their own historic context and not simply that of their owners-to-be.

[1] They were not the first, for the presence of some 32 Afro-Virginians was already noted 5 months earlier in a census; William Thorndale, "The Virginia Census of 1619," *Magazine of Virginia Genealogy,* 33 (1995), 155–70.
[2] Sluiter, "New Light on the '20. and Odd Negroes' Arriving in Virginia, August 1619," *William and Mary Quarterly,* 3d Ser., 54 (1997), 396–98. I have changed the ship's and its captain's names to reflect Portuguese orthography rather than the Spanish of the documents.

Knowing that these Africans came from Luanda, the recently established capital of the Portuguese colony of Angola, allows us to estimate their ethnic background and the likely conditions of their enslavement. In those days the colony of Angola was a sliver of land extending inland from Luanda and along the Kwanza River until its confluence with the Lukala River and not the larger country of the late twentieth century. Some of the cargo of the *São João Bautista* and the twenty-odd negroes may have been enslaved in the Kingdom of Kongo, the Portuguese colony's northern neighbor, or by its eastern neighbors. Portugal had been exporting slaves from Kongo sources since the early sixteenth century, primarily through the port of Mpinda on the Zaire River. When the colony of Angola was founded, many traders shifted their export operations southward, and, by the end of the century, Luanda-based merchants had developed a series of trading networks east across Kongo to the Maleba Pool area.[3] At the time, King Álvaro III of Kongo was involved in a complex dispute with his uncles, and, although this seems to have entailed little bloodshed, it had generated one major war against the duke of Nsundi sometime between 1616 and 1619 as well, perhaps, as some judicial enslavement.[4] Alternatively, the Africans may have come from beyond Kongo's eastern or northern frontier and been enslaved under circumstances that are beyond the reach of our documentation. It is quite possible, then, that among the slaves who boarded the *São João Bautista* in 1619 there were those who spoke the Kikongo language and were enslaved in Kongo's province of Nsundi or the land lying just beyond Kongo's eastern frontier.

It is also possible that some of those who left Luanda in 1619 were captured or otherwise enslaved in the lands south of the Portuguese colony, across the Kwanza River. Since the late sixteenth century the Portuguese had been buying slaves there who probably spoke the Kimbundu and Umbundu languages and transporting them to Luanda for shipment abroad. Wars, especially those of a marauding group of mercenary soldiers known as Imbangala, had disrupted the region greatly. In 1618, the Imbangala had just left the region, and the area was so devastated that it is unlikely that any more captives could have come from those districts, at least for a time.

---

[3] A good survey of these routes and the merchants involved in the late 16th century can be found in Arquivo Nacional de Torre do Tombo, Lisbon, Inquisição de Lisboa, 159/7/877, "Visita a Angola," esp. fols. 23–23v, 28v, 54v–55v, 64–64v, 82–83, 102v–103v. These were traders denounced to the Inquisition, mostly for being secret Jews. For a fuller treatment of the Portugal-Konga connection in this period see John Thornton, "Angola," in *O Império Africano*, vol. 9 of Joel Serrão and A. H. de Oliveira Marques, gen. eds., *Nova História da Expansão Portuguesa* (Lisbon, 1992–); on the life of these merchants see José da Silva Horta, "Africanos e Portugueses na Documentação Inquisitorial, de Luanda a Mbanza Kongo" (1596–1598), and Rosa Cruz e Silva, "As Feiras do Ndongo: A Outra Vertente do Comércio no Século XVII," in Comissão Nacional para as Comemorações dos Descobrimentos Portugueses, *Actas do Seminário: Encontro de Povos e Culturas em Angola (Luanda, April 3–6, 1995)* (Lisbon, 1997), 301–22, 405–22.

[4] Manuel Bautista Soares, "Relação," in António Brásio, ed., *Monumenta Missionaria Africana*, 1st Ser., 15 vols. (Lisbon, 1952–1988), 6:375.

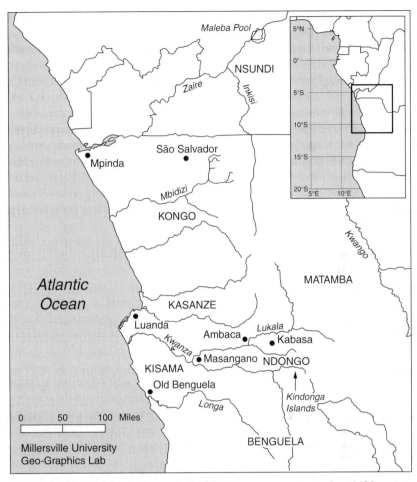

Angola in West Africa in the period of Portuguese conquest, circa 1620.

The most important military and enslavement operations in Angola, however, were the large and complex military campaigns waged in 1618–1620 under Portuguese leadership against the Kingdom of Ndongo, during which thousands of its Kimbundu-speaking subjects were captured and deported.[5] Given the significance and size of this war, most if not all of

[5] For a general English-language overview of Angolan history see David Birmingham, *Trade and Conflict in Angola: The Mbundu and Their Neighbours under the Influence of the Portuguese, 1483–1790* (Oxford, 1966); for detailed chronology of this period the best work is Beatrix Heintze, "Das Ende des Unabhängigen Staats Ndongo (Angola): Neue Chronologie und Rein-terpretation (1617–1630)," *Paideuma,* 27 (1981), 197–273; a revised version without full annota-tion is found in Heintze, *Studien zur Geschichte Angolas im 16. und 17. Jahrhundert. Ein Lesebuch* (Cologne, 1996), 111–68.

the slaves of the *São João Bautista* were very likely captured in these engagements. The Portuguese governor Luis Mendes de Vasconçelos, who arrived in the colony of Angola in 1617 and served as governor until 1621, led the campaigns. In the three years of his tenure, Angola exported about 50,000 slaves, far more than were exported before or would be again for some decades.[6]

A self-confident man, Mendes de Vasconçelos had served in Flanders as a soldier and had even written a treatise on the art of war.[7] He was sure that he could break through the military and diplomatic stalemate that had halted Portuguese advance in Angola since their decisive defeat at the Battle of Lukala on December 29, 1589, by a coalition of the Kingdoms of Matamba and Ndongo.[8] Indeed, he was so confident that, on receiving nomination as governor, he submitted a memorandum to the king announcing his intention to conquer the lands from one coast to the other and to join Angola with the equally new and uncertain Portuguese colony in what became Mozambique, thus opening a new route to India. In exchange, he proposed that he receive a variety of privileges and honors, including the title "Viceroy of Ethiopia" for his efforts.[9]

Mendes de Vasconçelos suggested that he would achieve these goals by his own skill as a soldier (and some 1,000 additional infantry and 200 cavalry he thought the crown should give him from Portugal). Instead, he arrived with very few reinforcements and immediately became aware of the generally unfavorable military situation. Since the beginning of the "conquest" of Angola, the Portuguese had relied on an assortment of military assets: soldiers from metropolitan Portugal, a few more from the island colony of São Tomé in the Gulf of Guinea, and personal slaves of those people armed for war. But they mainly depended on the supply of soldiers provided by African rulers (*sobas*) who submitted to Portuguese authority. *Sobas* were petty local nobles whose domains usually covered a few villages and who raised taxes and soldiers from among their subjects. Larger kingdoms such as Ndongo comprised dozens of these local vassals, who accepted the overlordship of larger powers while maintaining control in their local areas.

[6] On this interpretation see Heintze, "Ende des Unabhängigen Staats Ndongo" (*Paideuma* version, 206–09; *Studien zur Geschichte Angolas* version, 115, 119–20).

[7] António de Oliveira de Cadornega, *História geral das guerras angolanas (1680–81)* (1940–1942), ed. José Matias Delgado and Manuel Alves da Cunha, 3 vols. (Lisbon, 1972), 1:83. These notes were collected from recollections of contemporaries by the soldier-chronicler who arrived in Angola in 1639 and wrote his chronicle in 1680–1681. Although based on original materials, early portions of Cadornega's chronicle are sometimes garbled and contain errors of chronology. The treatise by Mendes de Vasconçelos, no longer extant, is cited in Cadornega.

[8] The best account of the battle is in Pero Rodrigues, "História da residência dos Padres da Companhia de Jesus em Angola, e cousas tocantes ao reino, e Conquista" (May 1, 1594), in Brásio, ed., *Monumenta Missionaria Africana*, 4:574–76.

[9] Mendes des Vasconçelos, "Adbierte de las cosas de que tiene falta el gouierno de Angola" (1616), in Brásio, ed., *Monumenta Missionaria Africana*, 6:263–70.

The soldiers provided by the *sobas*, known as the "black army" or *guerra preta*, composed most of the troops in all Portuguese military efforts.[10]

Nevertheless, *guerra preta* had proven unreliable, for the *sobas* were playing a diplomatic game in which they balanced submission between one or another of the greater African powers. They might claim obedience to the Kingdom of Kongo to the north or the Kingdom of Ndongo to the east, or alternatively swear vassalage to Portugal, since 1580 under the rule of the king of Spain. Slight changes in the military balance might bring disastrous results, so when the Portuguese lost at the Lukala, there were massive defections of the *sobas*.[11] Likewise, *sobas* sometimes changed sides without informing the Portuguese, also with catastrophic consequences for Portuguese policy.[12]

Portuguese inability to maintain an effective military force had compelled them to accept a status quo treaty (in 1599) with Ndongo, their principal African rival, after the Battle of Lukala. They had to content themselves with small-scale (and not always successful) raids against weaker polities to the north and south. The slave trade, which was the mainstay of Angola's international commerce, came to rely more on trading in the interior markets for people enslaved in surrounding countries than on direct capture in wars led by Portuguese officers. The Jesuit chronicler Pero Rodrigues wrote in 1594 that the numbers of "slaves taken in war are nothing compared to those bought at feiras [markets], at these feiras the kings and lords and all Ethiopia sell slaves," which were acquired in wars by the kings themselves or from among that portion of their population that was already enslaved.[13]

In the early years of the seventeenth century, help from an unexpected quarter allowed the Portuguese not only to break out of the military standoff but also to acquire thousands of slaves through direct capture. In those years, Portuguese merchants developing contacts south of their original colony, then known as the Kingdom of Benguela, first encountered the Imbangala, who would aid them and change the history of Angola fundamentally for the next half century.

The Imbangala are a mysterious group, and their origins have aroused much debate.[14] Although Portuguese officials of the time routinely called

[10] On the military situation see Thornton, "The Art of War in Angola, 1575–1680," *Comparative Studies in Society and History*, 30 (1988), 360–78.

[11] Rodrigues, "História da residência dos Padres da Companhia de Jesus em Angola," 570–71.

[12] *Ibid.*, 573–74; Baltasar Barreira, letter, May 14, 1586, in Brásio, ed., *Monumenta Missionaria Africana*, 3:328–30.

[13] Rodrigues, "História da residência dos Padres da Companhia de Jesus em Angola," 561.

[14] Although I use the word here (and previously) as an ethnonym, since it is so used today, its noun class suggests that it was not originally an ethnonym. Membership in this noun class (Bantu class 7/8, sing. *ki-*, plu. *i-* or *yi-*) is more likely to link it to a trait or characteristic than an ethnonym. Therefore, because in general I pluralize Kimbundu words by adding "s" to the singular and treat ethnonyms by ignoring class prefixes, I should make this term either "Kimbangalas" (a noun that is not an ethnonym) or "Mbangalas" (an ethnonym without a class marker).

them "Jagas" and linked them vaguely with a group that had invaded the Kingdom of Kongo in the 1570s, modern historians deny that connection and place their immediate origins in the central highlands of Angola in the region containing the modern cities of Huambo and Lubango.[15] They are described for the first time in the historical record by Andrew Battell, a captured English sailor forced to serve the Portuguese. In an account of his sixteen-months' stay with an Imbangala band led by Imbe Kalandula in about 1599 to 1601, Battell does not characterize the Imbangala as an ethnic or folk group (though some of their descendants became one in the late seventeenth century and persist today). Rather, the Imbangala were a company, or several independent companies, of soldiers and raiders who lived entirely by pillage.

The Imbangala seem to have been a quasi-religious cult dedicated to evil in the central African sense of violent greed and selfishness. They allowed no children in their camp, killing all newborn babies by burying them alive, according to Battell, and reinforcing themselves and replacing their casualties by recruiting adolescent boys from among their captives. These boys were made to wear a distinctive collar until they had learned the art of war and had killed someone, when they were admitted to full membership in the group. Imbe Kalandula's band had recruited so many of its people by this method that only the senior officers were said to be members of his original company; the rest had been recruited through capture.[16] Their penchant for

---

However, in my view the term Imbangala, used as an ethnonym, is too well fixed in the lexicon of central Africa to be handled this way, so I have retained what is now traditional usage, treating the word as both singular and plural.

[15] Earlier theories connected all the "Jagas" of 17th-century sources and linked them in turn with movements from the Lunda areas of modern-day Congo-Kinshasa. Joseph C. Miller, "The Imbangala and the Chronology of Early Central African History," *Journal of African History*, 13 (1972), 549–74, separates them from the Jagas who invaded Kongo. Miller initially thought that the Imbangala of Angola might have risen from a folk movement from Lunda, as he argued in *Kings and Kinsmen: Early Mbundu States in Angola* (Oxford, 1976), esp. 128–75. Thornton, "The Chronology and Causes of the Lunda Expansion to the West c. 1700 to 1852," *Zambia Journal of History*, 1 (1981), 1–5, attacked the folk movement idea in favor of a purely local origin in the central highlands. Miller has subsequently modified his argument, linking it to a movement of titles and ideas from the east (but not necessarily migrations from Lunda) in a local situation of ecological and political crisis; see Miller, "The Paradoxes of Impoverishment in the Atlantic Zone," in Birmingham and Phyllis M. Martin, eds., *History of Central Africa*, 2 vols. (London, 1983), 1:139–43, and seconded by Jan Vansina, "Population Movements and Emergence of New Socio-Political Forms in Africa," *UNESCO General History of Africa*, 8 vols. (Los Angeles, 1981–1993), 5:60–61.

[16] Battell, "The Strange Adventures of Andrew Battel of Leigh in Essex," in Samuel Purchas, *Purchas, His Pilgrimes* (London, 1625), vol. 6; mod. ed. E. G. Ravenstein, *The Strange Adventures of Andrew Battel, of Leigh, in Angola and the Adjoining Regions* (London, 1901; reprinted 1967), 21, 32–33. See also the "quixilla laws" that the founder of the Jagas gave her followers, as reported in the 1660s by Giovanni Antonio Cavazzi da Montecuccolo, "Missione Evangelica al regno de Congo," MSS Araldi (ca. 1668), vol. A, bk. 26.

cannibalism and human sacrifice was apparently rooted in beliefs about witchcraft. The Imbangala actively assumed the role of witches, whose fundamental characteristic was that they killed and ate their victims.[17] That they were viewed as fighting in the cause of profound evil is revealed by a folk belief recorded a half century later. According to this tale, the protective deities of the Gangela region were so terrified by the Imbangala that they went and hid in the lakes and rivers, only to reemerge when time had caused the Imbangala to soften their ways.[18] The Imbangala eschewed the cult of the protective deities (*kilundas*), who promoted peace and concord, in favor of their own ancestors, who were themselves selfish and bloody individuals and kept these characteristics in the Other World when they died.[19]

This radical devotion to evil was confirmed by their exploitative economy. Battell noted that "[they] doe reap thier Enemies Corne, and take their Cattell. For they will not sowe, nor plant, nor bring up any Cattell, more then they take by Warres." Their favorite pillage was palm wine taken from cultivated trees. Instead of tapping the trees and drawing small quantities of sap for oil or to ferment for wine, they cut down the whole tree. It gave no yield for ten days, then a small hole was drilled into the heart of the tree, which would yield about two quarts of sap a day for twenty-six days, when it dried up. By this method they destroyed all the palm trees in a region, and when all had been used up they moved on.[20]

The Portuguese from the colony of Angola took an interest in the Imbangala to their south largely because the marauders were prepared to sell their captives as slaves to Portuguese buyers. In the late 1590s, a group of Portuguese merchants had organized four voyages that included Battell to the area for the express purpose of buying captives for export. These merchants assisted Imbe Kalandula in crossing the River Kuvo to attack the Kingdom of Benguela.[21]

The Imbangala generally made a large encampment in the country they intended to pillage, often arriving near harvest time. They forced the local authorities either to fight them outright or to withdraw into fortified locations, leaving the fields for the Imbangala to harvest. Once their enemies

---

[17] The most systematic later account is that of Cavazzi da Montecuccolo, an Italian Capuchin priest who spent more than a dozen years in the region and collected their traditions and observed their life. His original account is found in the "Missione Evangelica al regno de Congo," vol. A, bk. 1, pp. 1–44, much of which found its way into the published edition cited in note 16. For a modern interpretation see Miller, *Kings and Kinsmen*; for linkages with witchcraft and evil see Thornton, "Cannibals and Slave Traders in the Atlantic World," paper presented at the conference "More than Cool Reason: Black Responses to Enslavement, Exile, and Resettlement," Haifa, Israel, Jan. 18–20, 1998.

[18] Cavazzi da Montecuccolo, "Missione Evangelica al regno de Congo," vol. A, bk. 1, 97.

[19] Cadornega, *História geral das guerras angolas*, 3:223–35. I have pluralized all Kimbundu nouns according to English usage; the Kimbundu plural of *kilunda* is *ilunda*.

[20] Battell, in Ravenstein, ed., *Strange Adventures of Andrew Battel*, 30–31.

[21] *Ibid.*, 17–21.

were weakened by fighting or lack of food, they could make a final assault on their lands and capture them. The presence of Portuguese slave buyers, who also provided firearms, made raiding people as profitable or even more profitable as raiding food and livestock had been before. Battell joined the group that entered the Kingdom of Benguela, and after their first successful battles they remained in that region for five months (during which time the Portuguese freighted three voyages with captives). Then, because they "wanted palm trees," they marched five days inland to an unidentifiable place named Kali ka Nsamba, where they remained pillaging for another four months. This band, which valued Battell and his musket, traveled steadily eastward just north of the great highlands for sixteen months, almost as far as the southward bend of the Kwanza River. In general, they took about four to five months to waste completely each country in which they stayed.[22] Whether because of the large size of their fighting force (which Battell estimated at 16,000) or the terror they spread through rumors of their ruthless evil and cannibalism, they seemed to have been uniformly successful, overcoming the determined resistance of country after country.

The ruined Kingdom of Benguela was so stripped of people, cattle, and palm trees by the Imbangala whom Battell and his associates assisted that when Manuel Cerveira Pereira went to the country in 1617 to become governor of a new Portuguese colony of Benguela, which initially was planned to be built around the abandoned commercial settlement of Benguela, he was unable to find enough people and economic activity to justify his efforts and moved farther south.[23] By the start of the second decade of the seventeenth century, much of the land south of the Kwanza River (more or less the southern border of Portuguese control) had been demolished and destroyed by Imbangala activity. For this reason, few people from this region probably found their way onto the *São João Bautista* in 1619.

Portuguese private merchants, such as those whom Battell was forced to serve about 1598, hoped to continue what for them was a profitable enterprise in the north. At some point they began to introduce Imbangala bands north of the river into lands under Portuguese authority. Royal governors, especially Pereira (1615–1617) and Antonio Gonçalvez Pita (1617), made this unofficial practice official. They did so in large measure because governors could benefit more from leading military campaigns that took slaves directly than they could from their salaries, which derived from taxing exports at markets or the coast. The Portuguese crown, however, instructed its governors to promote peaceful trade and frowned on practices such as recruiting Imbangala raiders. Local Portuguese settlers, for their part, commonly pre-

---

[22] *Ibid.*, 21–28.
[23] Pereita, according to Mendes de Vasconçelos to king of Portugal, Aug. 28, 1617, in Brásio, ed., *Monumenta Missionaria Africana*, 6:284.

ferred the crown's policy of staying clear of wars because they could acquire slaves by trade and conflict disrupted that trade.[24]

When Mendes de Vasconçelos arrived in Angola, then, despite his desire to conquer straight across Africa to Mozambique, he echoed the crown's concerns (and his own instructions) about the use of Imbangala by renouncing employment of those "who sustain themselves on human flesh and are enemies of all living things and thieves of the lands where they enter." Not only had they destroyed lands, but the government could no longer collect its tribute from the area, and even the markets were in ruins, thanks to Imbangala depredations. His predecessors' employment of them was a mistake, he argued, or even a crime, punishable by death and confiscation.[25] When Mendes de Vasconçelos took his first military action in the projected conquest of Ndongo, however, he quickly found he needed the Imbangala as allies.

An attack on Ndongo was inviting because the kingdom was undergoing a domestic political crisis. According to traditions collected about forty years later, the ruler of Ndongo, Mbandi Ngola Kiluanji, allowed the brothers of his wife to commit many crimes that outraged the nobility of the country, who, probably early in 1617, joined together, lured him into an ambush at the lands of a rebel *soba*, Kavulo ka Kabasa, near the Lukala, and overthrew him.[26]

Mbandi Ngola Kiluanji's son and successor, Ngola Mbandi, was not yet secure on his throne, and the coalition of *sobas* who had overthrown his father not yet fully loyal when Mendes de Vasconçelos arrived in August 1617. The new governor soon moved the Portuguese *presidio* of Hango eastward along the Lukala River to Ambaca, a point much closer to the court of Ndongo, but the new fort, probably a simple palisade mounting a few pieces of artillery, was soon besieged by the local ruler, Kaita ka Balanga, "a favorite of the King of Angola."[27] In this predicament, Mendes found the Imbangala useful allies. Consequently, as Bishop Manuel Bautista Soares of Kongo wrote to Lisbon in 1619, "in place of leaving off with the Jagas, he embraced them, and he has gone to war with them for two years, killing with them and

[24] For an overview and chronology see Heintze, "Ende des Unabhängigen Staats Ndongo," 202–09 *(Paideuma)*; 114–20 *(Studien zur Geschichte Angolas)*.
[25] Mendes de Vasconçelos to king of Portugal, Aug. 28, Sept. 9, 1617, in Brásio, ed., *Monumenta Missionaria Africana*, 6:283–85, 286.
[26] Cavazzi da Montecuccolo, "Missione Evangelica al regno de Congo" (ca. 1665, updated to 1668), vol. A, bk. 2, 11–15; for the interpretation of these highly politicized and manipulated sources see Thornton, "Legitimacy and Political Power: Queen Njinga, 1624–1663," *J. African Hist.*, 32 (1991), 27–40.
[27] The *presidio* was moved sometime before 1618, when Baltasar Rebelo de Aragão, one of the original conquerors of Angola, wrote his memoirs (a date established by Brásio as being 25 years after his arrival in 1593); Rebelo de Aragão to king of Portugal [?], 1618, in Brásio, ed., *Monumenta Missionaria Africana*, 6:334 (date on 343).

capturing innumerable innocent people, not only against the law of God but also against the expressed regulations of Your Majesty."[28]

To start his campaign Mendes de Vasconçelos brought three Imbangala bands across the Kwanza to assist him. He had two of them baptized as João Kasanje and João Kasa ka Ngola, although the third, Donga, apparently declined to be baptized.[29] Thanks to their assistance, in the campaign season of 1618 Mendes de Vasconçelos was able to defeat completely the forces of the *soba* Kaita ka Balanga and break out of the siege. His opponents were probably already mobilized at the start of the campaign.

Mobilization in Ndongo began, according to late sixteenth-century witnesses, by the sounding of the *ngongo,* a double clapperless bell used for war calls in all the settlements of the area, followed by the cry, in Kimbundu, *"Ita! Ita!"* (War! War!). Old people, some women, and most children were ordered to retire to hills or other inaccessible places until the fighting was over, while the men prepared for battle. Some took up arms, mostly bows and arrows but also crescent-shaped axes and lances; others carried supplies. Some women accompanied the armies to cook for and comfort the soldiers. These militia soldiers were not expected to remain in position beyond the initial shock of battle, which progressed quickly. At some point the soldiers' nerves broke, and they retreated so rapidly that sometimes the front ranks hacked their way through the rearward soldiers who did not flee fast enough.[30] Although they might reform later, even within a few days, they left strategic positions undefended, and the remaining civilians who had not taken adequate shelter in hills or forests were vulnerable to enslavement.

The Portuguese-Imbangala forces capitalized on their victory by attacking the now undefended royal palace in the city of Kabasa, taking "many captives," who represented the real fruit of the war. The army "wintered" in the city but suffered a great deal from sicknesses common to the central African rainy season (September 1618 to March 1619). Falling ill himself, Mendes de Vasconçelos withdrew his forces to Hango and returned to Luanda, entrusting the new army to his nineteen-year-old son, João. In 1619, João returned to the field, defeated and killed the *soba* Kaita ka Balanga and

[28] Soares, "Copia dos excessos que se cometem no gouerno de Angola que o bispo deu a V. Magestade pedindo remedio delles de presente, e de futuro," Sept. 7, 1619, in Brásio, ed., *Monumenta Missionaria Africana,* 6:368. If the "two years" in this statement is taken literally, Mendes de Vasconçelos would have begun the Imbangala alliance virtually on the same day as he wrote his letters to Lisbon denouncing their use by his predecessors, which strikes me as unlikely.
[29] Fernão de Sousa, "Guerras do Reino de Angola," ca. 1630, fol. 217, in Heintze, ed., *Fontes para a História de Angola do século XVII,* 2 vols. (Stuttgart, 1985–1988), 1:212. This rather late source (de Sousa came to Angola only in 1624 but had access to official documents filed there) is the only one to name the Imbangala bands or to give details about their origins.
[30] For military culture and the role of noncombatants see Thornton, "Art of War," and Rodrigues, "História da residência dos Padres da Companhia de Jesus em Angola," 562–64.

ninety-four other nobles, attacked Kabasa, and drove out Ngola Mbandi, leaving his mother and wives, in the words of a contemporary Portuguese chronicler, "in our power, who with many prisoners and slaves were carried away as captives."[31] The bishop wrote in September 1619 that the dead from this campaign had infected the rivers, and "a great multitude of innocent people had been captured without cause."[32] The demographic impact of this war was starkly obvious when the campaign was resumed the next year; the army "met no resistance in any part of the back-country [Sertão], these provinces having become destitute of inhabitants."[33] Although many people had been killed or enslaved, others simply fled the region—either hiding in the hills or the bush or following the king to his new headquarters on the Kindonga Islands in the Kwanza River.

The stunning military success was largely the work of the Imbangala allies. As the bishop noted, "as he had Jagas [Imbangala], the wars were without any danger [to them] but with discredit to the Portuguese."[34] Although Mendes de Vasconçelos was a soldier experienced in European wars and thus thought himself capable of great achievements in Africa, his initial approach to warfare in Angola was flawed. According to later accounts, he endangered his troops in their first actions by mustering them into tight formations, and only after suffering losses did he accept the wisdom of African methods of warfare, which included the use of Imbangala expertise and prowess.[35]

The military forces unleashed by Mendes de Vasconçelos got far out of hand. The Imbangala bands broke free from Portuguese alliance and began a long campaign of freebooting in lands formerly under Ndongo's rule: one band, led by João Kasa ka Ngola, ended up entering the king of Ndongo's service against the Portuguese. The bishop maintained that some 4,000 baptized

[31] Manuel Severim da Faria, "História portugueza e de outras provincias do occidente desde o anno de 1610 até o de 1640 . . . ," Biblioteca Nacional de Lisboa, MS 241, fol. 163v, under date Mar. 1, 1619, to end of Feb. 1620, but related to material of a year earlier (1618–1619), quoted in Cadornega, *História geral das guerras angolas,* ed. Delgado, 1:88–90 n. 1. The formation of the Imbangala alliance and movement of the presidio is given as 1618 in Manuel Vogado Sotomaior, "Papel sobre as cousas de Angola" (undated, but probably around 1620), in Brásio, ed., *Monumenta Missionaria Africana,* 15:476 (date on 480).

[32] Soares, "Copia dos excessos," Sept. 7, 1619, in Brásio, ed., *Monumenta Missionaria Africana,* 6:369–70. Vogado Sotomaior, then holding the position of ouvidor geral de Angola, noted that the city of Angola (Kabasa) was "sacked in such a way that many thousand souls were captured, eaten and killed" and all the palm trees were cut down (in Imbangala fashion) so that the area was effectively barren of them; "Papel," ibid., 15:476.

[33] Manuel Severim da Faria, "História portugueza e de outras provincias," fol. 174v, Mar. 1621 to Feb. 1622, but relating to 1620–1621, quoted in Cadornega, *História geral das guerras angolas,* ed. Delgado, 1:90 n. 1.

[34] Soares, "Copia dos excessos," Sept. 7, 1619, in Brásio, ed., *Monumenta Missionaria Africana,* 6:370.

[35] Cadornega, *História geral das guerras angolas,* ed. Delgado, 1:83. For a fuller discussion of the art of war in Angola see Thornton, "Art of War in Angola," 360–78.

Christians from the Portuguese baggage train, some free, some enslaved, had been captured illegally by rampaging Imbangalas in the 1619 campaign.[36] Beyond that, the king of Kongo also protested on behalf of his own Kimbundu-speaking subordinates north of Ndongo who had also been attacked and closed the border to trade. A number of Portuguese settlers and the bishop protested vigorously as well, because they were all but ruined by the Imbangala raids on their lands and also saw their trade disrupted. But their protests were to no avail, for Mendes de Vasconçelos served out his three-year term and returned to Portugal, wealthier by far.[37]

So many people were captured and designated for sale abroad during this brief time that they overwhelmed the capacities of Luanda to manage them. During the confusion, thousands of slaves escaped to Kisama south of the city or to the swampy Kasanze region to the north, forming runaway communities that required an entire military campaign to round up two years later.[38] Shipping was probably inadequate to transport all the slaves captured in 1618 who remained imprisoned in the city in makeshift and not always secure pens, to be joined by the flood arriving from the more successful and devastating campaign of 1619. The *São João Bautista* was one of thirty-six slave ships that left Luanda for Brazil or ports of the Spanish Indies in 1619.[39]

The people enslaved by Mendes de Vasconçelos's army and his Imbangala allies were from the narrow corridor of land about thirty miles broad and some fifty miles deep between the Lukala and Lutete Rivers, a cool plateau region mostly over 4,000-foot elevation. Within this larger region most of the enslaved came from the royal district of Ndongo, the target of both the 1618 and 1619 campaigns and the heartland of the area. As such, they were probably from urban backgrounds. Kabasa, the royal court, and nearby settlements formed a dense complex of towns in a thickly populated countryside. The royal district was not much different in 1618 than it had been in 1564 when it was first visited by Portuguese who described the nucleated town of Angoleme as being as large as the Portuguese city of Évora. Aligned along streets inside a stockade interwoven with grasses were 5,000–6,000 thatched dwellings that probably housed 20,000–30,000 people. There were several such enclosed towns in close proximity in the royal district as well as a rural population tightly settled between them. Central

---

[36] Soares, "Copia dos excessos," Sept. 7, 1619, in Brásio, ed., *Monumenta Missionaria Africana,* 6:370.

[37] *Ibid.,* 369–71; Vogado Sotomaior, "Papal sobre as cousas de Angola," *ibid.,* 15:476–77.

[38] On the general problem of slave flight see Heintze, "Gefährdetes Asyl. Chancen und Konsequenzen der Flucht angolanischer Skalven im 17. Jahrhundert," *Paideuma,* 39 (1993), 321–41, and revised but unannotated version of the same article in *Studien zur Geschichte Angolas,* 232–520. For details about the specific campaigns of 1621–1622 see Heintze, "Ende des Unabhängigen Staats Ndongo," 112–26 (*Studien zur Geschichte Angolas*).

[39] Heintze, "Ende des Unabhängigen Staats Ndongo," 115 (*Studien zur Geschichte Angolas*).

African cities were more rural than European ones, so there was a great deal of farming going on nearby, and many urban residents raised food crops and even domestic animals. Yet the rural areas formed a continuous landscape of settlement, so that when a fire broke out in Angoleme in 1564 the destruction of proximate houses spread for miles and was said to have displaced 100,000 people—clearly an exaggeration but suggestive of the size and density of the general region.[40]

The rural people of the district as well as many of the town dwellers raised millet and sorghum (American crops like manioc and maize had not yet become popular) to make into *funji*, a stiff porridge, that would be eaten along with *nicefo* (a banana) and a palm oil-based gravy. They also tended large herds of cattle and raised smaller stocks of goats, chicken, and guinea fowl in their fields and pastures. They dressed in cloth made locally from tree bark and cotton or imported from as far away as Kongo. They attended regular markets in their own district and regional markets to obtain what they did not produce—iron and steel from favored regions in an area famous for its steel production or salt from the region south of the Kwanza.[41]

The captives of Mendes de Vasconçelos's campaigns probably had a stronger sense of a common identity than was typical of single cargoes at other times or places, who might have come from diverse origins and have been acquired through wide-ranging trade routes, wars, or other means of enslavement. But because such a large number of captives in that year were taken from this single campaign, most of the people awaiting export in Luanda in 1619 must have come from a relatively small area.

People in seventeenth-century Ndongo had primary political loyalties connected to local territories, called *xi* in Kimbundu, which were ruled by the *sobas*. Within the area of the 1618–1619 campaigns, people in the royal district considered themselves "people of the court" (thus serving the king as a *soba*), which is more or less what Kabasa means, and subjects of Ndongo, whereas those living farther away, in Kaita ka Balanga, for instance, might have taken their loyalty to that *soba* as equally important as their loyalty to the king.[42] In Kimbundu, *xi* represented geographically and juridically

---

[40] Francisco de Gouveia to Jesuit General, Nov. 1, 1564, in Brásio, ed., *Monumenta Missionaria Africana*, 15:230–31. This is the original version of a text printed from a copy *ibid.*, 2:528. Although the text is from more than 50 years before, it is the only description of the capital of Ndongo available to us. For a description of Kongo's capital and central African cities in general see Thornton, "Mbanza Kongo/São Salvador: Kongo's Holy City," in Richard Rathbone and Andrew Roberts, eds., *Africa's Urban Past* (London, forthcoming).

[41] Heintze, "Unbekanntes Angola: Der Staat Ndongo im 16. Jahrhundert," *Anthropos*, 72 (1977), 771–76; a revised but reduced version, "Der Staat Ndongo im 16. Jahrhundert," is in Heintze, *Studien zur Geschichte Angolas*, 74–75.

[42] For detailed consideration of these elements of their identity see Virgilio Coelho, "Em busca de Kábàsà: Um tentativa de explicação da estrutura politico-administrativo do 'Reino de Ndongo,'" in Comissão Nacional para as Comemorações dos Descobrimentos Portugueses, *Actas do Seminário: Encontro de Povos e Culturas em Angola (Luanda, Apr. 3–6, 1995)* (Lisbon, 1997), 443–78.

defined communities such as the royal district or the lands of the *soba* Kaita ka Balanga. In the Kimbundu catechism of 1642, the primary text for the seventeenth-century language (probably first composed within five years of the great wars of 1618–1620), Jerusalem was defined as a *xi*, and Pontius Pilate was *"tandala ya xi imoxi ailûca'Ierusalem"* or "governor of one xi known as Jerusalem."[43] By contrast, in giving an example from local experience, the Portuguese version of the catechism notes that "in the Kingdom of Ndongo, when a vassal is a traitor," whereas the Kimbundu text simply reads *"co Ndongo"* ("in Ndongo") and omits any term for kingdom or territory. At another point, where the Portuguese refers to the "kings and lords who govern," the text produces *"o Michino, no gingâna ginêne jâbata o xi gicalacalà,"* literally, "the kings, the great lords of villages and countries *[xi]* of all sorts."[44] These units were defined by clear boundaries *(mbande),* a term so widely used that it had entered Angolan Portuguese by the 1620s.[45]

These terms defined political loyalty, not necessarily ethnic sense. Although people surely had a parochial identification with their *xi,* in a region like that between the Lukala and Kwanza Rivers, which was integrated economically thanks to the presence of the court and its settlements and ruled politically by the king, they were likely to have a regional identity defined by the kingdom itself. Each person was, as the catechism notes, *mucu Ndongo* (a person from that place, that is, Ndongo).[46] In modern Kimbundu, the *mukwa*-prefix (plural *akwa-*) is the normal way to express membership in an ethnic group that combines the personal class prefix with the locative prefix *ku-;* this is thus a second way of describing ethnic identity with a geographical place.[47] In the end, they also had a larger and vaguer identity as those who spoke Kimbundu. The "Ambundu language" *(lingua ambunda)* was a term for Kimbundu so widely used in Portuguese documents that Governor Fernão de Sousa, writing in 1626, told his subordinate to "make announcements in every *quilombo* [military camp] in Portuguese and Ambundo."[48]

---

[43] Francesco Paccoino, *Gentio de Angola sufficimente instruido . . .* , ed. António do Couto (Lisbon, 1642), 4:2. The catechism was probably first composed by a native-speaking Kimbundu priest named Dionisio de Faria Barreto in the mid-1620s, though Paccoino, a long-serving Italian Jesuit, undoubtedly produced the finishing touches, returning with the text to Lisbon where he died in 1641 before bringing it to press. The final editor, do Couto, was from Kongo, born in its capital city São Salvador and probably a mulatto. Héli Chatelain, the Swiss Protestant missionary who did much to define modern Kimbundu with his grammar, collection of folklore, and other texts, praised this catechism for its rigor and fidelity to the language; see Chatelain, ed., *Folk-Tales of Angola* (New York, 1894). In this and following translations, I have made my translation directly from the Kimbundu and not from the accompanying Portuguese text.
[44] Paccoino, *Gentio de Angola sufficimente instruido,* fol. 55v (Portuguese on facing page, 56).
[45] See this usage in the Fernão de Sousa correspondence in Heintze, *Fontes para a História de Angola do século XVII.*
[46] Paccoino, introduction, *Gentio de Angola sufficimente instruido,* ed. do Couto, unpaged.
[47] Chatelain, *Grammatica Elementar do Kimbundu ou Lingua de Angola* (1888–1889), (Ridgewood, N. J., 1964), xii.
[48] Regimento of Fernão de Sousa to Bento Banha Cardoso, ca. Jan. 1626, *ibid.,* 1:205.

Kimbundu speakers used this term when speaking of themselves, as the "Ambundu people."[49] Thus a certain ethnic identity extended beyond the barriers of an individual *soba*'s territories and provided even stronger ethnic glue to people from the area when their removal and transportation to America made political identities and loyalties irrelevant. In America, when Kimbundu-speaking people were able to communicate and visit each other, a sense of an "Angola Nation" emerged. It was certainly observable in Spanish America, if not yet at the very beginnings of English-speaking Virginia's reception of Africans.

The Mbundus of the capital region followed the local religion, but Portuguese law required all African slaves to be baptized and made Christian before their arrival in America. By 1619, a Kimbundu-speaking Christian community existed in Angola, with its own informal catechismal literature, delivered by the Jesuit priests who had accompanied the first conquerors in 1575. The basic catechism, for those captives awaiting embarkation or on board ship, probably followed the outlines set down in a late sixteenth-century text, though undoubtedly delivered in Kimbundu.[50] Such a rudimentary instruction was probably oriented to the syncretic practice of the Angolan church, which followed patterns already a century old from the Kongo church that had originally fertilized it.[51] Thus early seventeenth-century Spanish Jesuits, conducting an investigation of the state of knowledge of the Christian religion among newly arrived slaves, found that, for all the problems they noted, the Angolan slaves seemed to have adequate understanding of the faith by the time they arrived.[52] Quite possibly then those slaves who ended up in Virginia instead of Vera Cruz had at least been introduced to the Christian faith, though Virginia slave holders, with their fear that Christianity would make slaves free, would have been reluctant to admit it, had they known.

If the victims of Mendes de Vasconçelos's war were among the twenty slaves brought to Virginia in 1619, they did not conform to the stereotyped, parochial image of Africans from precolonial villages. They were more likely from an urban or at least urbanized area (though they probably knew how to raise crops and domestic animals), and they had learned the rudiments of Christianity. It is probable that, in the decades that followed, those who

[49] The catechism, for instance, notes that "Negroes of Angola who have not received baptism" (in the Portuguese text) were *"Ambundo carià mongoaùa Nzambi"* in Kimbundu or "Mbundus who have not eaten the salt of God." Paccointo, *Gentio de Angola sufficimente instruido,* ed. do Couto, fol. 65. In this Kimbundu text, *Ambundu* is a plural form (hence my translation as *Mbundus*).

[50] "Practica para bautizar as adultos de gentio dos R[ein]os de Angola" (undated but apparently late 16th or early 17th century), MS, Biblioteca Pública e Arquivo Distrial de Évora.

[51] For more on the theology of these syncretic churches see Thornton, "Afro-Christian Syncretism in Central Africa," *Plantation Societies* (forthcoming).

[52] Alonso de Sandoval, *Naturaleza, policia sagrada i profana, costumbres i ritos . . . de todos Etiopes* (Seville, 1627); mod. ed. Angel Valtierra, *De instauranda Aethiopum salute: el mundo de la esclavitud en América* (Bogotá, 1956), 372–77, 380.

survived the first year in Virginia eventually encountered more Angolans from their homeland or from the nearby Kongo, brought especially to New York by Dutch traders and resold to Virginia colonists.[53] They may even have met up with the slaves that one Captain Guy (or Gay) took from a ship off the Angolan coast and exchanged for tobacco in Virginia in 1628.[54] At that time, a series of wars in the region around the Kindonga Islands between Ndongo's new and vigorous Queen Njinga (ruled 1624–1663) and a Portuguese-assisted rival for her throne led to the enslavement of thousands.[55] These new captives perhaps gave a certain Angolan touch to the early Chesapeake. Significantly, the grandson of one of their contemporaries, who had arrived in 1621, in 1677 named his Eastern Shore estate "Angola."[56]

[53] T. H. Breen and Stephen Innes, 'Myne Owne Ground': Race and Freedom on Virginia's Eastern Shore, 1640–1676 (New York, 1980), 70–71.

[54] Alden T. Vaughan, "Blacks in Virginia: A Note on the First Decade," WMQ, 3d Ser., 29 (1972), 477.

[55] Heintze, "Ende des Unabhängigen Staats Ndongo" (Paideuma version, 216–53: Studien version, 127–55).

[56] Breen and Innes, "Myne Owne Ground," 17.

Family Structure in Seventeenth-Century Andover, Massachusetts

Philip J. Greven, Jr.

INTRODUCTION

Like Menard, Carr and Walsh, and Barry Levy (see later in this volume), Philip Greven is another of the prominent demographic historians of colonial America. Greven's Andover was a very static community in which children married late, lived close to the homes of their parents, and were quite mature before they owned farms of their own. It was a patriarchal society in which first-generation males held onto control of their families, lands, and town government, and in which continuity was fostered by a self-conscious system of arranged marriages. There seems to have been little immigration into Andover or emigration from the town.

"Family structure" is a relatively novel concept in historical analysis, but Greven uses it to show how sociological categories can provide fresh historical insights. His implicit contention is that until we understand precisely how people behaved, we shall not be able to find out why they acted as they did. His essay attempts to demonstrate how very broad conclusions can be drawn from masses of very minute bits of evidence, however, and he suggests that many questions about the New England town remain unanswered. One obvious problem is why Andover should have been so different from the early Chesapeake colonies and Pennsylvania. Might the answers lie outside the scope of demographic inquiry?

Surprisingly little is known at present about family life and family structure in the seventeenth-century American colonies. The generalizations about colonial family life embedded in textbooks are seldom the result of studies of the extant source materials, which historians until recently have tended to ignore.[1]

Philip J. Greven, Jr., "Family Structure in Seventeenth-Century Andover, Massachusetts" from *William and Mary Quarterly*, XXXIII (1966), pp. 234–256. Reprinted by permission of the author.

[1] Two notable exceptions to this generalization are Edmund S. Morgan, *The Puritan Family* . . . (Boston, 1956), and John Demos, "Notes on Life in Plymouth Colony," *William and Mary Quarterly*, 3d Ser., XXII (1965), 264–286.

Genealogists long have been using records preserved in county archives, town halls, churches, and graveyards as well as personal documents to compile detailed information on successive generations of early American families. In addition to the work of local genealogists, many communities possess probate records and deeds for the colonial period. A study of these last testaments and deeds together with the vital statistics of family genealogies can provide the answers to such questions as how many children people had, how long people lived, at what ages did they marry, how much control did fathers have over their children, and to what extent and under what conditions did children remain in their parents' community. The answers to such questions enable an historian to reconstruct to some extent the basic characteristics of family life for specific families in specific communities. This essay is a study of a single seventeenth-century New England town, Andover, Massachusetts, during the lifetimes of its first and second generations—the pioneers who carved the community out of the wilderness, and their children who settled upon the lands which their fathers had acquired. A consideration of their births, marriages, and deaths, together with the disposition of land and property within the town from one generation to the next reveals some of the most important aspects of family life and family structure in early Andover.

The development of a particular type of family structure in seventeenth-century Andover was dependent in part upon the economic development of the community during the same period. Andover, settled by a group of about eighteen men during the early 1640s and incorporated in 1646, was patterned at the outset after the English open field villages familiar to many of the early settlers. The inhabitants resided on house lots adjacent to each other in the village center, with their individual holdings of land being distributed in small plots within two large fields beyond the village center. House lots ranged in size from four to twenty acres, and subsequent divisions of land within the town were proportionate to the size of the house lots. By the early 1660s, about forty-two men had arrived to settle in Andover, of whom thirty-six became permanent residents. During the first decade and a half, four major divisions of the arable land in the town were granted. The first two divisions established two open fields, in which land was granted to the inhabitants on the basis of one acre of land for each acre of house lot. The third division, which provided four acres of land for each acre of house lot, evidently did not form another open field, but was scattered about the town. The fourth and final division of land during the seventeenth century occurred in 1662, and gave land to the householders at the rate of twenty acres for each acre of their house lots. Each householder thus obtained a minimum division allotment of about eighty acres and a maximum allotment of about four hundred acres. Cumulatively, these four successive divisions of town land, together with additional divisions of meadow and swampland, provided each of the inhabitants with at least one hundred acres of land for farming, and as much as six hundred acres. During the years following these substantial grants of land, many of the families in the town removed their habitations from the house lots in the town center onto their distant, and extensive, farm lands, thus altering the character of the community through the establishment of independent family farms and scattered residences. By the 1680s, more than half the families in Andover lived outside the original center of the town on their own ample farms. The transformation of the earlier open field village effectively recast the basis for family life within the community.[2]

An examination of the number of children whose births are recorded in the Andover town records between 1651 and 1699 reveals a steady increase in the number of children being born throughout the period. (See Table 1.)[3] Between 1651 and 1654, 28 births are recorded, followed by 32 between 1655 and 1659, 43 between 1660 and 1664, 44 between 1665 and 1669, 78 between 1670 and 1674, and 90 between 1675 and 1679. After 1680, the figures rise to more than one hundred births every five years. The entire picture of population growth in Andover, however, cannot be formed from a study of the town records alone since these records do not reflect the pattern of generations within the town. Looked at from the point of view of the births of the children of the first generation of settlers who arrived in Andover between the first settlement in the mid-1640s and 1660, a very different picture emerges, hidden within the entries of the town records and genealogies.[4] The majority of the second-generation children were born during the two decades of the 1650s and the 1660s. The births of 159 second-generation children were distributed in decades as follows: 10 were born during the 1630s, either in England or in the towns along the Massachusetts coast where their parents first settled; 28 were born during the 1640s; 49 were born during the 1650s; 43 were born during the 1660s; declining to 21 during the 1670s, and falling to only 8 during the 1680s. Because of this pattern of births, the second generation of Andover children, born largely during the 1650s and the 1660s, would mature during the late 1670s and the 1680s. Many of the developments of the second half of

---

[2] For a full discussion of the transformation of 17th-century Andover, see my article, "Old Patterns in the New World: The Distribution of Land in 17th Century Andover," *Essex Institute Historical Collections*, CI (April 1965), 133–148. See also the study of Sudbury, Mass., in Sumner Chilton Powell, *Puritan Village: The Formation of a New England Town* (Middletown, Conn., 1963).

[3] The figures in Table 1 were compiled from the first MS book of Andover vital records. A Record of Births, Deaths, and Marriages, Begun 1651 Ended 1700, located in the vault of the Town Clerk's office, Town Hall, Andover, Mass. For a suggestive comparison of population growth in a small village, see W. G. Hoskins, "The Population of an English Village, 1086–1801: A Study of Wigston Magna," *Provincial England: Essays in Social and Economic History* (London, 1963), 195–200.

[4] The most important collection of unpublished genealogies of early Andover families are the typed MSS of Charlotte Helen Abbott, which are located in the Memorial Library, Andover. The two vols. of *Vital Records of Andover, Massachusetts, to the End of the Year 1849* (Topsfield, Mass., 1912) provide an invaluable and exceptionally reliable reference for vital statistics of births, marriages, and deaths.

TABLE 1   The Number of Sons and Daughters Living at the Age of 21 in Twenty-Nine First-Generation Families

Sons	0	1	2	3	4	5	6	7	8	9	10
Families	1	2	7	1	6	6	3	3	0	0	0
Daughters	0	1	2	3	4	5	6	7	8	9	10
Families	0	2	7	6	11	2	0	0	0	1	0

the seventeenth century in Andover, both within the town itself and within the families residing there, were the result of the problems posed by a maturing second generation.

For the records which remain, it is not possible to determine the size of the first-generation family with complete accuracy, since a number of children were undoubtedly stillborn, or died almost immediately after birth without ever being recorded in the town records. It is possible, however, to determine the number of children surviving childhood and adolescence with considerable accuracy, in part because of the greater likelihood of their names being recorded among the children born in the town, and in part because other records, such as church records, marriage records, tax lists, and wills, also note their presence. Evidence from all of these sources indicates that the families of Andover's first settlers were large, even without taking into account the numbers of children who may have been born but died unrecorded. An examination of the families of twenty-nine men who settled in Andover between 1645 and 1660 reveals that a total of 247 children are known to have been born to these particular families. Of these 247 children whose births may be ascertained, thirty-nine, or 15.7 percent, are known to have died before reaching the age of 21 years.[5] A total of 208 children or 84.3 percent of the number of children known to be born thus reached the age of 21 years, having survived the hazards both of infancy and of adolescence. This suggests that the number of deaths among children and adolescents during the middle of the seventeenth century in Andover was lower than might have been expected.

In terms of their actual sizes, the twenty-nine first-generation families varied considerably, as one might expect. Eleven of these twenty-nine families had between 0 and 3 sons who survived to the age of 21 years; twelve families had either 4 or 5 sons surviving, and six families had either 6 or 7 sons living to be 21. Eighteen of these families thus had four or more sons to provide with land or a trade when they reached maturity and wished to marry, a fact of considerable significance in terms of the development of family life in Andover

---

[5] While this figure is low, it should not be discounted entirely. Thomas Jefferson Wertenbaker, *The First Americans, 1607–1690* (New York, 1929), 185–186, found that, "Of the eight hundred and eight children of Harvard graduates for the years from 1658 to 1690, one hundred and sixty-two died before maturity. This gives a recorded child mortality among this selected group of *twenty* percent." Italics added.

during the years prior to 1690. Fewer of these twenty-nine families had large numbers of daughters. Fifteen families had between 0 and 3 daughters who reached adulthood, eleven families had 4 daughters surviving, and three families had 5 or more daughters reaching the age of 21. In terms of the total number of their children born and surviving to the age of 21 or more, four of these twenty-nine first-generation families had between 2 and 4 children (13.8 percent), eleven families had between 5 and 7 children (37.9 percent), and fourteen families had between 8 and 11 children (48.3 percent). Well over half of the first-generation families thus had 6 or more children who are known to have survived adolescence and to have reached the age of 21. The average number of children known to have been born to these twenty-nine first-generation families was 8.5, with an average of 7.2 children in these families being known to have reached the age of 21 years.[6] The size of the family, and particularly the number of sons who survived adolescence, was a matter of great importance in terms of the problems which would arise later over the settlement of the second generation upon land in Andover and the division of the estates of the first generation among their surviving children. The development of a particular type of family structure within Andover during the first two generations depended in part upon the number of children born and surviving in particular families.

Longevity was a second factor of considerable importance in the development of the family in Andover. For the first forty years following the settlement of the town in 1645, relatively few deaths were recorded among the inhabitants of the town. Unlike Boston, which evidently suffered from smallpox epidemics throughout the seventeenth century, there is no evidence to suggest the presence of smallpox or other epidemical diseases in Andover prior to 1690. With relatively few people, many of whom by the 1670s were scattered about the town upon their own farms, Andover appears to have been a remarkably healthy community during its early years. Lacking virulent epidemics, the principal hazards to health and to life were birth, accidents, non-epidemical diseases, and Indians. Death, consequently, visited relatively few of Andover's inhabitants during the first four decades following its settlement. This is evident in the fact that the first generation of Andover's settlers was very long lived. Prior to 1680, only five of the original settlers who came to Andover before 1660 and established permanent residence there had died; in 1690, fifteen of the first settlers (more than half of the original group) were still alive, forty-five years after the establishment of their town. The age at death of thirty men who settled in Andover prior to 1660 can be

---

[6] Comparative figures for the size of families in other rural New England villages are very rare. Wertenbaker, *First Americans*, 182–185, suggested that families were extremely large, with 10 to 20 children being common, but his data for Hingham, Mass., where he found that 105 women had "five or more children," with a total of 818 children "giving an average of 7.8 for each family," is in line with the data for Andover. The figures for seventeenth-century Plymouth are also remarkably similar. See Demos, "Notes on Life in Plymouth Colony," 270–271.

TABLE 2   Second-Generation Ages at Death

	Males		Females	
AGES	NUMBERS	PERCENTAGES	NUMBERS	PERCENTAGES
20–29	10	7.3	4	6.1
30–39	9	6.5	4	6.1
40–49	6	4.3	6	9.1
50–59	16	11.5	10	15.2
60–69	26	18.8	13	19.7
70–79	42	30.4	16	24.2
80–89	25	ss18.1	8	12.1
90–99	4	3.1	5	7.5
Total	138	100.0%	66	100.0%

determined with a relative degree of accuracy. Their average age at the time of their deaths was 71.8 years. Six of the thirty settlers died while in their fifties, 11 in their sixties, 3 in their seventies, 6 in their eighties, 3 in their nineties, and 1 at the advanced age of 106 years.[7] The longevity of the first-generation fathers was to have great influence on the lives of their children, for the authority of the first generation was maintained far longer than would have been possible if death had struck them down at an early age. The second generation, in turn, was almost as long lived as the first generation had been. The average age of 138 second-generation men at the time of their deaths was 65.2 years, and the average age of sixty-six second-generation women at the time of their deaths was 64.0 years. (See Table 2.)[8] Of the 138 second-generation men who reached the age of 21 years and whose lifespan is known, only twenty-five or 18.1 percent, died between the ages of 20 and 49. Forty-two (30.3 percent) of these 138 men died between the ages of 50 and 69; seventy-one (51.6 percent) died after reaching the age of 70. Twenty-five

[7] The town of Hingham, according to the evidence in Wertenbaker, *First Americans,* 181–186, was remarkably similar to Andover, since the life expectancy of its inhabitants during the 17th century was very high. "Of the eight hundred and twenty-seven persons mentioned as belonging to this period [17th century] and whose length of life is recorded, one hundred and five reached the age of eighty or over, nineteen lived to be ninety or over and three . . . attained the century mark."

[8] Since the size of the sample for the age of women at the time of their death is only half that of the sample for men, the average age of 64.0 may not be too reliable. However, the evidence for Hingham does suggest that the figures for Andover ought not to be dismissed too lightly. "The average life of the married women of Hingham during the seventeenth century," Wertenbaker noted, "seems to have been 61.4 years." He also found that for their 818 children, the average age at the time of death was 65.5 years. "These figures," he added, "apply to one little town only, and cannot be accepted as conclusive for conditions throughout the colonies, yet they permit of the strong presumption that much which has been written concerning the short expectation of life for women of large families is based upon insufficient evidence." *Ibid.,* 184. The observation remains cogent. For the longevity of Plymouth's settlers, see Demos, "Notes on Life in Plymouth Colony," 271.

TABLE 3   Second-Generation Female Marriage Ages

AGE	NUMBERS	PERCENTAGES			
Under 21	22	33.3	24 & under	=	69.7%
21–24	24	36.4	25 & over	=	30.3%
25–29	14	21.2	29 & under	=	90.9%
30–34	4	6.1	30 & over	=	9.1%
35–39	1	1.5			
40 & over	1	1.5			
			Average age	=	22.8 years
	66	100.0%			

second-generation men died in their eighties, and four died in their nineties. Longevity was characteristic of men living in seventeenth-century Andover.

The age of marriage often provides significant clues to circumstances affecting family life and to patterns of family relationships which might otherwise remain elusive.[9] Since marriages throughout the seventeenth century and the early part of the eighteenth century were rarely fortuitous, parental authority and concern, family interests, and economic considerations played into the decisions determining when particular men and women could and would marry for the first time. And during the seventeenth century in Andover, factors such as these frequently dictated delays of appreciable duration before young men, especially, might marry. The age of marriage both of men and of women in the second generation proved to be much higher than most historians hitherto have suspected.[10]

Traditionally in America women have married younger than men, and this was generally true for the second generation in Andover. Although the assertion is sometimes made that daughters of colonial families frequently married while in their early teens, the average age of sixty-six second-generation daughters of Andover families at the time of their first marriage was 22.8 years. (See Table 3). Only two girls are known to have married at 14 years, none at 15, and two more at 16. Four married at the age of 17, with a

[9] The most sophisticated analyses of marriage ages and their relationship to the social structure, family life, and economic conditions of various communities have been made by sociologists. Two exceptionally useful models are the studies of two contemporary English villages by W. M. Williams: *Goeforth: The Sociology of an English Village* (Glencoe, Ill., 1956), esp. pp. 45–49, and *A West Country Village, Ashworthy: Family, Kinship, and Land* (London, 1963), esp. pp. 85–91. Another useful study is Conrad M. Arensberg and Solon T. Kimball, *Family and Community in Ireland* (Cambridge, Mass., 1940). For the fullest statistical and historiographical account of marriage ages in the United States, see Thomas P. Monahan, *The Pattern of Age at Marriage in the United States*, 2 vols. (Philadelphia, 1951).

[10] In Plymouth colony during the seventeenth century, the age of marriage also was higher than expected. See Demos, "Notes on Life in Plymouth Colony," 275. For a discussion of various historians' views on marriage ages during the colonial period, see Monahan, *Pattern of Age at Marriage*, I, 99–104.

TABLE 4   Second-Generation Male Marriage Ages

AGE	NUMBERS	PERCENTAGES			
Under 21	4	4.3	24 & under	=	39.4%
21–24	33	35.1	25 & over	=	60.6%
25–29	34	36.2	29 & under	=	75.6%
30–34	16	17.2	30 & over	=	24.4%
35–39	4	4.3			
40 & over	3	2.9			
			Average age	=	27.1 years
	94	100.0%			

total of twenty-two of the sixty-six girls marrying before attaining the age of 21 years (33.3 percent). The largest percentage of women married between the ages of 21 and 24, with twenty-four or 36.4 percent being married during these years, making a total of 69.7 percent of the second-generation daughters married before reaching the age of 25. Between the ages of 25 and 29 years, fourteen women (21.2 percent) married, with six others marrying at the age of 30 or more (9.1 percent). Relatively few second-generation women thus married before the age of 17, and nearly 70 percent married before the age of 25. They were not as young in most instances as one might have expected if very early marriages had prevailed, but they were relatively young nonetheless.

The age of marriage for second-generation men reveals a very different picture, for instead of marrying young, as they so often are said to have done, they frequently married quite late. (See Table 4.) The average age for ninety-four second-generation sons of Andover families at the time of their first marriages was 27.1 years. No son is known to have married before the age of 18, and only one actually married then. None of the ninety-four second-generation men whose marriage ages could be determined married at the age of 19, and only three married at the age of 20. The contrast with the marriages of the women of the same generation is evident, since only 4.3 percent of the men married before the age of 21 compared to 33.3 percent of the women. The majority of second-generation men married while in their twenties, with thirty-three of the ninety-four men marrying between the ages of 21 and 24 (35.1 percent), and thirty-four men marrying between the ages of 25 and 29 (36.2 percent). Nearly one quarter of the second-generation men married at the age of 30 or later, however, since twenty-three men or 24.4 percent delayed their marriages until after their thirtieth year. In sharp contrast with the women of this generation, an appreciable majority of the second-generation men married at the age of 25 or more, with 60.6 percent marrying after that age. This tendency to delay marriages by men until after the age of 25, with the average age being about 27 years, proved to be characteristic of male marriage ages in Andover throughout the seventeenth century.

Averages can sometimes obscure significant variations in patterns of behavior, and it is worth noting that in the second generation the age at which
particular sons might marry depended in part upon which son was being
married. Eldest sons tended to marry earlier than younger sons in many
families, which suggests variations in their roles within their families, and
differences in the attitudes of their fathers towards them compared to their
younger brothers. For twenty-six eldest second-generation sons, the average
age at their first marriage was 25.6 years. Second sons in the family often met
with greater difficulties and married at an average age of 27.5 years, roughly
two years later than their elder brothers. Youngest sons tended to marry later
still, with the average of twenty-two youngest sons being 27.9 years. In their
marriages as in their inheritances, eldest sons often proved to be favored by
their families; and family interests and paternal wishes were major factors in
deciding which son should marry and when. More often than not, a son's
marriage depended upon the willingness of his father to allow it and the
ability of his father to provide the means for the couple's economic independence. Until a second-generation son had been given the means to support a wife—which in Andover during the seventeenth century generally
meant land—marriage was virtually impossible.

Marriage negotiations between the parents of couples proposing marriage and the frequent agreement by the father of a suitor to provide a house
and land for the settlement of his son and new bride are familiar facts.[11] But
the significance of this seventeenth-century custom is much greater than is
sometimes realized. It generally meant that the marriages of the second generation were dependent upon their fathers' willingness to let them leave
their families and to establish themselves in separate households elsewhere.
The late age at which so many sons married during this period indicates that
the majority of first-generation parents were unwilling to see their sons married and settled in their own families until long after they had passed the age
of 21. The usual age of adulthood, marked by marriage and the establishment of another family, was often 24 or later. Since 60 percent of the second-
generation sons were 25 or over at the time of their marriage and nearly one
quarter of them were 30 or over, one wonders what made the first generation so reluctant to part with its sons?

At least part of the answer seems to lie in the fact that Andover was largely
a farming community during the seventeenth century, structured, by the time
that the second generation was maturing, around the family farm which stood
isolated from its neighbors and which functioned independently. The family

---

[11] See especially Morgan, *Puritan Family*, 39–44. For one example of marriage negotiations in
Andover during this period, see the agreement between widow Hannah Osgood of Andover
and Samuel Archard, Sr., of Salem, about 1660 in the *Records and Files of the Quarterly Courts of
Essex County, Massachusetts* (Salem, 1912–21), III, 463, cited hereafter as *Essex Quarterly Court*.
Also see the negotiations of Simon Bradstreet of Andover and Nathaniel Wade of Ipswich, *New
England Historical and Genealogical Register*, XIII, 204, quoted in Morgan, *Puritan Family*, 41.

farm required all the labor it could obtain from its own members, and the sons evidently were expected to assist their fathers on their family farms as long as their fathers felt that it was necessary for them to provide their labor. In return for this essential, but prolonged, contribution to their family's economic security, the sons must have been promised land by their fathers when they married, established their own families, and wished to begin their own farms. But this meant that the sons were fully dependent upon their fathers as long as they remained at home. Even if they wanted to leave, they still needed paternal assistance and money in order to purchase land elsewhere. The delayed marriages of second-generation men thus indicate their prolonged attachment to their families, and the continuation of paternal authority over second-generation sons until they had reached their mid-twenties, at least. In effect, it appears, the maturity of this generation was appreciably later than has been suspected hitherto. The psychological consequences of this prolonged dependence of sons are difficult to assess, but they must have been significant.

Even more significant of the type of family relationships emerging with the maturing of the second generation than their late age of marriage is the fact that paternal authority over sons did not cease with marriage. In this community, at least, paternal authority was exercised by the first generation not only prior to their sons' marriages, while the second generation continued to reside under the same roof with their parents and to work on the family farm, and not only at the time of marriage, when fathers generally provided the economic means for their sons' establishment in separate households, but also *after* marriage, by the further step of the father's withholding legal control of the land from the sons who had settled upon it.[12] The majority of first-generation fathers continued to own the land which they settled their sons upon from the time the older men received it from the town to the day of their deaths. All of the first-generation fathers were willing to allow their sons to build houses upon their land, and to live apart from the paternal house after their marriage, but few were willing to permit their sons to become fully independent as long as they were still alive. By withholding deeds to the land which they had settled their sons upon, and which presumably would be theirs to inherit someday, the first generation successfully assured the continuity of their authority over their families long after their sons had become adults and had gained a nominal independence.[13] Since the

[12] Similar delays in the handing over of control of the land from one generation to the next are discussed by W. M. Williams in his study of Ashworthy, *West Country Village*, 84–98. Williams noted (p. 91) that "the length of time which the transference of control takes is broadly a reflection of the degree of patriarchalism within the family: the more authoritarian the father, the longer the son has to wait to become master."

[13] The use of inheritances as a covert threat by the older generation to control the younger generation is revealed only occasionally in their wills, but must have been a factor in their authority over their sons. One suggestive example of a threat to cut off children from their anticipated inheritances is to be found in the will of George Abbot, Sr., who died in 1681, about 64 years old. Prior to his death, his two eldest sons and one daughter had married, leaving at home five

second generation, with a few exceptions, lacked clear legal titles to the land which they lived upon and farmed, they were prohibited from selling the land which their fathers had settled them upon, or from alienating the land in any other way without the consent of their fathers, who continued to own it. Being unable to sell the land which they expected to inherit, second-generation sons could not even depart from Andover without their fathers' consent, since few had sufficient capital of their own with which to purchase land for themselves outside of Andover. The family thus was held together not only by settling sons upon family land in Andover, but also by refusing to relinquish control of the land until long after the second generation had established its nominal independence following their marriages and the establishment of separate households. In a majority of cases, the dependence of the second-generation sons continued until the deaths of their fathers. And most of the first generation of settlers was very long lived.

The first generation's reluctance to hand over the control of their property to their second-generation sons is evident in their actions.[14] Only three first-generation fathers divided their land among all of their sons before their deaths and gave them deeds of gift for their portions of the paternal estate. All three, however, waited until late in their lives to give their sons legal title to their portions of the family lands. Eleven first-generation fathers settled all of their sons upon their family estates in Andover, but gave a deed of gift for the land to only one of their sons; the rest of their sons had to await their fathers' deaths before inheriting the land which they had been settled upon. Ten of the settlers retained the title to all of their land until their deaths, handing over control to their sons only by means of their last wills and testaments. For the great majority of the second generation, inheritances constituted the principal means of transferring the ownership of land from one generation to the next.[15] The use of partible inheritances in Andover is

---

unmarried sons and two unmarried daughters with his widow after his death. Abbot left his entire estate to his wife except for the land which he had already given to his eldest son. At her death, he instructed, his wife was to divide the estate with the advice of her sons and friends, and all the children, except the eldest, who had already received a double portion, were to be treated equally unless "by their disobedient carige" towards her "there be rasen to cut them short." Widow Abbot thus had an effective means for controlling her children, the oldest of whom was 24 in 1681. George Abbott, MS will, Dec. 12, 1681, Probate File 43, Probate Record Office, Registry of Deeds and Probate Court Building, Salem, Mass.

[14] For deeds of gift of first-generation Andover fathers to their second-generation sons, see the following deeds, located in the MSS volumes of Essex Deeds, Registry of Deeds and Probate Court Building, Salem, Mass.: Richard Barker, v. 29, pp. 115–116; Hannah Dane (widow of George Abbot), v. 94, pp. 140–141; Edmund Faulkner, v. 39, p. 250; John Frye, v. 9, pp. 287–288; Nicholas Holt, v. 6, pp. 722–723, 814–821; v. 7, pp. 292–296; v. 9, p. 12; v. 32, pp. 130–131; v. 34, pp. 255–256; Henry Ingalls, v. 14, pp. 40–41; John Lovejoy, v. 33, pp. 40–41.

[15] The intimate relationship between inheritance patterns and family structure has been noted and examined by several historians and numerous sociologists. George C. Homans, in his study of *English Villagers of the Thirteenth Century* (New York, 1960), 26, pointed out that "differences in customs of inheritance are sensitive signs of differences in traditional types of family organization."

evident in the division of the estates of the first generation.[16] Twenty-one of twenty-two first-generation families which had two or more sons divided all of their land among all of their surviving sons. Out of seventy-seven sons who were alive at the time their fathers either wrote their wills or gave them deeds to the land, seventy-two sons received some land from their fathers. Out of a total of sixty-six sons whose inheritances can be determined from their fathers' wills, sixty-one or 92.4 percent received land from their fathers' estates in Andover. Often the land bequeathed to them by will was already in their possession, but without legal conveyances having been given. Thus although the great majority of second-generation sons were settled upon their fathers' lands while their fathers were still alive, few actually owned the land which they lived upon until after their fathers' deaths. With their inheritances came ownership; and with ownership came independence. Many waited a long time.

The characteristic delays in the handing over of control of the land from the first to the second generation may be illustrated by the lives and actions of several Andover families. Like most of the men who wrested their farms and their community from the wilderness, William Ballard was reluctant to part with the control over his land. When Ballard died intestate in 1689, aged about 72 years, his three sons, Joseph, William, and John, agreed to divide their father's estate among themselves "as Equally as they could."[17] They

---

See Homans' discussions of inheritance in England, chs. VIII and IX. H. J. Habakkuk, in his article, "Family Structure and Economic Change in Nineteenth-Century Europe," *The Journal of Economic History*, XV (1955), 4, wrote that "inheritance systems exerted an influence on the structure of the family, that is, on the size of the family, on the relations of parents to children and between the children. . . ." Very little, however, has been written about the role of inheritance in American life, or of its impact upon the development of the American family. One of the few observers to perceive the importance and impact of inheritance customs upon American family life was the shrewd visitor, Alexis de Tocqueville. See, for instance, his discussion of partible inheritance in *Democracy in America*, ed. Phillips Bradley (New York, 1956), I, 47–51.

[16] For further details, see the following wills: George Abbot, Probate File 43; Andrew Allen, Probate File 370; John Aslett, *Essex Quarterly Court*, IV, 409; William Ballard, Administration of Estate, Probate Record, Old Series, Book 4, vol. 304, pp. 388–389; Richard Barker, Probate File 1708; Samuel Blanchard, Probate File 2612; William Blunt, Probate File 2658; Thomas Chandler, Probate File 4974; William Chandler, Probate File 4979; Rev. Francis Dane, Probate File 7086; John Farnum, Probate File 9244; Thomas Farnum, Probate File 9254; Edmund Faulkner, Probate File 9305; Andrew Foster, Probate Record, Old Series, Book 2, vol. 302, pp. 136–137 (photostat copy); John Frye, Probate File 10301; Henry Ingalls, Probate File 14505; John Lovejoy, Probate File 17068; John Marston, Probate File 17847; Joseph Parker, *Essex Quarterly Court*, VII, 142–144; Andrew Peters, Probate File 21550; Daniel Poor, Probate Record, vol. 302, pp. 196–197; John Russ, Probate File 24365; John Stevens, *Essex Quarterly Court*, II, 414–416; and Walter Wright, Probate File 30733. The Probate Files of manuscript wills, inventories, and administrations of estates, and the bound Probate Records, are located in the Probate Record Office, Registry of Deeds and Probate Court Building, Salem, Mass.

[17] MS Articles of Agreement, Oct. 23, 1689, Probate Records, Old Series, Book 4, vol. 304, pp. 388–389 (photostat copy). For genealogical details of the Ballard family, see Abbott's Ballard genealogy, typed MSS, in the Memorial Library, Andover.

also agreed to give their elderly mother, Grace Ballard, a room in their father's house and to care for her as long as she remained a widow, thus adhering voluntarily to a common practice for the provision of the widow. The eldest son, Joseph, had married in 1665/6, almost certainly a rather young man, whereas his two brothers did not marry until the early 1680s, when their father was in his mid-sixties. William, Jr., must have been well over 30 by then, and John was 28. Both Joseph and William received as part of their division of their father's estate in Andover the land where their houses already stood, as well as more than 75 acres of land apiece. The youngest son, John, got all the housing, land, and meadow "his father lived upon except the land and meadow his father gave William Blunt upon the marriage with his daughter," which had taken place in 1668. It is unclear whether John lived with his wife and their four children in the same house as his parents, but there is a strong likelihood that this was the case in view of his assuming control of it after his father's death. His two older brothers had been given land to build upon by their father before his death, but no deeds of gift had been granted to them, thus preventing their full independence so long as he remained alive. Their family remained closely knit both by their establishment of residences near their paternal home on family land and by the prolonged control by William Ballard over the land he had received as one of the first settlers in Andover. It was a pattern repeated in many families.

There were variations, however, such as those exemplified by the Holt family, one of the most prominent in Andover during the seventeenth century. Nicholas Holt, originally a tanner by trade, had settled in Newbury, Massachusetts, for nearly a decade before joining the group of men planting the new town of Andover during the 1640s. Once established in the wilderness community, Holt ranked third among the householders, with an estate which eventually included at least 400 acres of land in Andover as a result of successive divisions of the common land.[18] At some time prior to 1675, he removed his family from the village, where all the original house lots had been located, and built a dwelling house on his third division of land. Although a small portion of his land still lay to the north and west of the old village center, the greatest part of his estate lay in a reasonably compact farm south of his new house. Holt owned no land outside of Andover, and he acquired very little besides the original division grants from the town. It was upon this land that he eventually settled all his sons. In 1662, however, when Nicholas Holt received the fourth division grant of 300 acres from the town, his eldest son, Samuel, was 21 years old, and his three other sons were 18, 15, and 11. The fifth son was yet unborn. His four sons were thus still

[18] For Nicholas Holt's land grants in Andover, see the MS volume, A Record of Town Roads and Town Bounds, 18–19, located in the vault of the Town Clerk's office, Andover, Mass. For genealogical information on the Holt family, see Daniel S. Durrie, *A Genealogical History of the Holt Family in the United States* . . . (Albany, N.Y., 1864), 9–16.

adolescents, and at ages at which they could provide the physical labor needed to cultivate the land already cleared about the house, and to clear and break up the land which their father had just received. The family probably provided most of the labor, since there is no evidence to indicate that servants or hired laborers were numerous in Andover at the time. With the exception of two daughters who married in the late 1650s, the Holt family remained together on their farm until 1669, when the two oldest sons and the eldest daughter married.

By 1669, when Holt's eldest son, Samuel, finally married at the age of 28, the only possible means of obtaining land to settle upon from the town was to purchase one of the twenty-acre lots which were offered for sale. House-lot grants with accommodation land had long since been abandoned by the town, and Samuel's marriage and independence therefore depended upon his father's willingness to provide him with sufficient land to build upon and to farm for himself. Evidently his father had proved unwilling for many years, but when Samuel did at last marry, he was allowed to build a house for himself and his wife upon his father's "Three-score Acres of upland," known otherwise as his third division.[19] Soon afterwards, his second brother, Henry, married and also was given land to build upon in the third division. Neither Samuel nor Henry was given a deed to his land by their father at the time he settled upon it. Their marriages and their establishment of separate households left their three younger brothers still living with their aging father and step-mother. Five years passed before the next son married. James, the fourth of the five sons, married in 1675, at the age of 24, whereupon he, too, was provided with a part of his father's farm to build a house upon.[20] The third son, Nicholas, Jr., continued to live with his father, waiting until 1680 to marry at the late age of 32. His willingness to delay even a token independence so long suggests that personal factors must have played an important part in his continued assistance to his father, who was then about 77 years old.[21] John Holt, the youngest of the sons, married at the age of 21, shortly before his father's death.

For Nicholas Holt's four oldest sons, full economic independence was delayed for many years. Although all had withdrawn from their father's house and had established separate residences of their own, they nonetheless were settled upon their father's land not too far distant from their family homestead, and none had yet been given a legal title to the land where he lived. Until Nicholas Holt was willing to give his sons deeds of gift for the lands where he had allowed them to build and to farm, he retained all legal rights to his estate and could still dispose of it in any way he chose. Without his consent, therefore, none of his sons could sell or mortgage the land where

---

[19] Essex Deeds, v. 32, p. 130.
[20] *Ibid.*, v. 7, pp. 292–296.
[21] See *ibid.*, v. 6, pp. 814–815.

he lived since none of them owned it. In the Holt family, paternal authority rested upon firm economic foundations, a situation characteristic of the majority of Andover families of this period and these two generations.

Eventually, Nicholas Holt decided to relinquish his control over his Andover property by giving to his sons, after many years, legal titles to the lands which they lived upon. In a deed of gift, dated February 14, 1680/1, he conveyed to his eldest son, Samuel, who had been married almost twelve years, one half of his third division land, "the Said land on which the said Samuels House now Stands," which had the land of his brother, Henry, adjoining on the west, as well as an additional 130 acres of upland from the fourth division of land, several parcels of meadow, and all privileges accompanying these grants of land.[22] In return for this gift, Samuel, then forty years old, promised to pay his father for his maintenance so long as his "naturall life Shall Continue," the sum of twenty shillings a year. Ten months later, December 15, 1681, Nicholas Holt conveyed almost exactly the same amount of land to his second son, Henry, and also obligated him to pay twenty shillings yearly for his maintenance.[23] Prior to this gift, Nicholas had given his fourth son, James, his portion, which consisted of one-third part of "my farme" including "the land where his house now stands," some upland, a third of the great meadow, and other small parcels. In return, James promised to pay his father three pounds a year for life (three times the sum his two elder brothers were to pay), and to pay his mother-in-law forty shillings a year when she should become a widow.[24] The farm which James received was shared by his two other brothers, Nicholas and John, as well. Nicholas, in a deed of June 16, 1682, received "one third part of the farme where he now dwells," some meadow, and, most importantly, his father's own dwelling house, including the cellar, orchard, and barn, which constituted the principal homestead and house of Nicholas Holt, Sr.[25] In "consideration of this my fathers gift . . . to me his sone," Nicholas, Junior, wrote, "I doe promise and engage to pay yearly" the sum of three pounds for his father's maintenance. Thus Nicholas, Junior, in return for his labors and sacrifices as a son who stayed with his father until the age of 32, received not only a share in the family farm equal to that of his two younger brothers, but in addition received the paternal house and homestead. The youngest of the five Holt sons, John, was the only one to receive his inheritance from his father by deed prior to his marriage. On June 19, 1685, Nicholas Holt, Sr., at the age of 83, gave his "Lovinge" son a parcel of land lying on the easterly side of "my now Dwelling house," some meadow, and fifteen acres of upland "as yett unlaid out."[26] One month later, John married, having already built himself a

---

[22] *Ibid.*, v. 32, pp. 130–131.
[23] *Ibid.*, v. 34, pp. 255–256.
[24] *Ibid.*, v. 7, pp. 292–296.
[25] *Ibid.*, v. 6, pp. 814–816.
[26] *Ibid.*, v. 9, p. 12.

house upon the land which his father promised to give him. Unlike his older brothers, John Holt thus gained his complete independence as an exceptionally young man. His brothers, however, still were not completely free from obligations to their father since each had agreed to the yearly payment of money to their father in return for full ownership of their farms. Not until Nicholas Holt's death at the end of January 1685/6 could his sons consider themselves fully independent of their aged father. He must have died content in the knowledge that all of his sons had been established on farms fashioned out of his own ample estate in Andover, all enjoying as a result of his patriarchal hand the rewards of his venture into the wilderness.[27]

Some Andover families were less reluctant than Nicholas Holt to let their sons marry early and to establish separate households, although the control of the land in most instances still rested in the father's hands. The Lovejoy family, with seven sons, enabled the four oldest sons to marry at the ages of 22 and 23. John Lovejoy, Sr., who originally emigrated from England as a young indentured servant, acquired a seven-acre house lot after his settlement in Andover during the mid-1640s, and eventually possessed an estate of over 200 acres in the town.[28] At his death in 1690, at the age of 68, he left an estate worth a total of £327.11.6, with housing and land valued at £260.00.0, a substantial sum at the time.[29] Although he himself had waited until the age of 29 to marry, his sons married earlier. His eldest son, John, Jr., married on March 23, 1677/8, aged 22, and built a house and began to raise crops on land which his father gave him for that purpose. He did not receive a deed of gift for his land, however; his inventory, taken in 1680 after his premature death, showed his major possessions to consist of "one house and a crope of corn" worth only twenty pounds. His entire estate, both real and personal, was valued at only £45.15.0, and was encumbered with £29.14.7 in debts.[30] Three years later, on April 6, 1683, the land which he had farmed without owning was given to his three-year-old son by his father, John Lovejoy, Sr. In a deed of gift, the elder Lovejoy gave his grandson, as a token of the love and affection he felt for his deceased son, the land which John, Junior, had had, consisting of fifty acres of upland, a piece of meadow, and a small parcel of another meadow, all of which lay in Andover.[31] Of the surviving Lovejoy sons only the second, William, received a deed of gift from

---

[27] For an example of a first-generation father who gave a deed of gift to his eldest son only, letting his five younger sons inherit their land, see the MS will of Richard Barker, dated Apr. 27, 1688, Probate File 1708. The deed to his eldest son is found in the Essex Deeds, v. 29, pp. 115–116. All of Barker's sons married late (27, 31, 35, 28, 28, and 25), and all but the eldest continued to be under the control of their father during his long life.

[28] For John Lovejoy's Andover land grants, see the MS volume, A Record of Town Roads and Town Bounds, 96–98.

[29] See John Lovejoy's MS inventory in Probate File 17068.

[30] For the inventory of the estate of John Lovejoy, Jr., see *Essex Quarterly Court*, VIII, 56.

[31] Essex Deeds, v. 33, pp. 40–41.

the elder Lovejoy for the land which he had given them.[32] The others had to await their inheritances to come into full possession of their land. In his will dated September 1, 1690, shortly before his death, Lovejoy distributed his estate among his five surviving sons: Christopher received thirty acres together with other unstated amounts of land, and Nathaniel received the land which his father had originally intended to give to his brother, Benjamin, who had been killed in 1689. Benjamin was 25 years old and unmarried at the time of his death, and left an estate worth only £1.02.8, his wages as a soldier.[33] Without their father's land, sons were penniless. The youngest of the Lovejoy sons, Ebenezer, received his father's homestead, with the house and lands, in return for fulfilling his father's wish that his mother should "be made comfortable while she Continues in this world."[34] His mother inherited the east end of the house, and elaborate provisions in the will ensured her comfort. With all the surviving sons settled upon their father's land in Andover, with the residence of the widow in the son's house, and with the fact that only one of the sons actually received a deed for his land during their father's life-time, the Lovejoys also epitomized some of the principal characteristics of family life in seventeenth-century Andover.

Exceptions to the general pattern of prolonged paternal control over sons were rare. The actions taken by Edmund Faulkner to settle his eldest son in Andover are instructive precisely because they were so exceptional. The first sign that Faulkner was planning ahead for his son came with his purchase of a twenty-acre lot from the town at the annual town meeting of March 22, 1669/70.[35] He was the only first-generation settler to purchase such a lot, all of the other purchasers being either second-generation sons or newcomers, and it was evident that he did not buy it for himself since he already had a six-acre house lot and more than one hundred acres of land in Andover.[36] The town voted that "in case the said Edmond shall at any time

[32] This deed from John Lovejoy, Sr., to his son, William, is not recorded in the Essex Deeds at the Registry of Deeds, Salem, Mass. The deed, however, is mentioned in his will, Probate File 17068, wherein he bequeathed to William the lands which he already had conveyed to his son by deed. It was customary for such deeds to be mentioned in wills, since they usually represented much or all of a son's portion of a father's estate.

[33] For the inventory to Benjamin Lovejoy's estate, see the Probate File 17048,

[34] *Ibid.*, 17068. Provision for the widow was customary, and is to be found in all the wills of first-generation settlers who left their wives still alive. Generally, the son who inherited the paternal homestead was obligated to fulfill most of the necessary services for his mother, usually including the provision of firewood and other essentials of daily living. Provision also was made in most instances for the mother to reside in one or two rooms of the paternal house, or to have one end of the house, sometimes with a garden attached. Accommodations thus were written into wills to ensure that the mother would be cared for in her old age and would retain legal grounds for demanding such provisions.

[35] Andover, MS volume of Ancient Town Records, located in the Town Clerk's office, Andover.

[36] For Edmund Faulkner's land grants in Andover, see the MS Record of Town Roads and Town Bounds, 52–53.

put such to live upon it as the town shall approve, or have no just matter against them, he is to be admitted to be a townsman." The eldest of his two sons, Francis, was then a youth of about nineteen years. Five years later, January 4, 1674/5, Francis was admitted as a townsman of Andover "upon the account of the land he now enjoyeth," almost certainly his father's twenty acres.[37] The following October, aged about 24, Francis married the minister's daughter. A year and a half later, in a deed dated February 1, 1676/7, Edmund Faulkner freely gave his eldest son "one halfe of my Living here at home" to be "Equally Divided between us both."[38] Francis was to pay the town rates on his half, and was to have half the barn, half the orchard, and half the land about his father's house, and both he and his father were to divide the meadows. Significantly, Edmund added that "all my Sixscore acres over Shawshinne river I wholly give unto him," thus handing over, at the relatively young age of 52, most of his upland and half of the remainder of his estate to his eldest son. The control of most of his estate thereby was transferred legally and completely from the first to the second generation. Edmund's second and youngest son, John, was still unmarried at the time Francis received his gift, and waited until 1682 before marrying at the age of 28. Eventually he received some land by his father's will, but his inheritance was small compared to his brother's. Edmund Faulkner's eagerness to hand over the control of his estate to his eldest son is notable for its rarity and accentuates the fact that almost none of his friends and neighbors chose to do likewise.[39] It is just possible that Faulkner, himself a younger son of an English gentry family, sought to preserve most of his Andover estate intact by giving it to his eldest son. If so, it would only emphasize his distinctiveness from his neighbors. For the great majority of the first-generation settlers in Andover, partible inheritances and delayed control by the first generation over the land were the rule. Faulkner was the exception which proved it.

Embedded in the reconstructions of particular family histories is a general pattern of family structure unlike any which are known or suspected to have existed either in England or its American colonies during the seventeenth century. It is evident that the family structure which developed during the lifetimes of the first two generations in Andover cannot be classified satisfactorily according to any of the more recent definitions applied to types of family life in the seventeenth century. It was not simply a "patrilineal

---

[37] Town meeting of Jan. 4, 1674/5, Andover, Ancient Town Records.

[38] Essex Deeds, v. 39, p. 250. Only one other instance of the co-partnership of father and son is to be found in the wills of seventeenth-century Andover, but not among the men who founded the town. See the MS will of Andrew Peters, Probate File 21550.

[39] The only instance of impartible inheritance, or primogeniture, to be found in the first generation of Andover's settlers occurred within the first decade of its settlement, before the extensive land grants of 1662 had been voted by the town. See John Osgood's will, dated Apr. 12, 1650, in *Essex Quarterly Court*, I, 239. Osgood left his entire Andover estate to the eldest of his two sons.

group of extended kinship gathered into a single household,"[40] nor was it simply a "nuclear independent family, that is man, wife, and children living apart from relatives."[41] The characteristic family structure which emerged in Andover with the maturing of the second generation during the 1670s and 1680s was a combination of both the classical extended family and the nuclear family. This distinctive form of family structure is best described as a *modified extended family*—defined as a kinship group of two or more generations living within a single community in which the dependence of the children upon their parents continues after the children have married and are living under a separate roof. This family structure is a *modified* extended family because all members of the family are not "gathered into a single household," but it is still an *extended* family because the newly created conjugal unit of husband and wife live in separate households in close proximity to their parents and siblings and continue to be economically dependent in some respects upon their parents. And because of the continuing dependence of the second generation upon their first-generation fathers, who continued to own most of the family land throughout the better part of their lives, the family in seventeenth-century Andover was *patriarchal* as well. The men who first settled the town long remained the dominant figures both in their families and their community. It was their decisions and their actions which produced the family characteristic of seventeenth-century Andover.

One of the most significant consequences of the development of the modified extended family characteristic of Andover during this period was the fact that remarkably few second-generation sons moved away from their families and their community. More than four fifths of the second-generation sons lived their entire lives in the town which their fathers had wrested from

[40] Bernard Bailyn, *Education in the Forming of American Society: Needs and Opportunities for Study* (Chapel Hill, 1960), 15–16. "Besides children, who often remained in the home well into maturity," Bailyn adds, the family "included a wide range of other dependents: nieces and nephews, cousins, and, except for families at the lowest rung of society, servants in filial discipline. In the Elizabethan family the conjugal unit was only the nucleus of a broad kinship community whose outer edges merged almost imperceptibly into the society at large." For further discussions of the extended family in England, see Peter Laslett, "The Gentry of Kent in 1640," *Cambridge Historical Journal*, IX (1948), 148–164; and Peter Laslett's introduction to his edition of *Patriarcha and Other Political Works of Sir Robert Filmer* (Oxford, 1949), esp. 22–26.

[41] Peter Laslett and John Harrison, "Clayworth and Cogenhoe," in H. E. Bell and R. L. Ollard, eds., *Historical Essays, 1660–1750, Presented to David Ogg* (London, 1963), 168. See also H. J. Habakkuk, "Population Growth and Economic Development," in *Lectures on Economic Development* (Istanbul, 1958), 23, who asserts that "from very early in European history, the social unit was the nuclear family—the husband and wife and their children—as opposed to the extended family or kinship group." See also Robin M. Williams, Jr., *American Society: A Sociological Interpretation*, 2d ed. rev. (New York, 1963), 50–57. For a contrasting interpretation of family structure in other 17th-century New England towns, see Demos, "Notes on Life in Plymouth Colony," 279–280.

the wilderness.[42] The first generation evidently was intent upon guaranteeing the future of the community and of their families within it through the settlement of all of their sons upon the lands originally granted to them by the town. Since it was quite true that the second generation could not expect to acquire as much land by staying in Andover as their fathers had by undergoing the perils of founding a new town on the frontier, it is quite possible that their reluctance to hand over the control of the land to their sons when young is not only a reflection of their patriarchalism, justified both by custom and by theology, but also of the fact that they could not be sure that their sons would stay, given a free choice. Through a series of delays, however, particularly those involving marriages and economic independence, the second generation continued to be closely tied to their paternal families. By keeping their sons in positions of prolonged dependence, the first generation successfully managed to keep them in Andover during those years in which their youth and energy might have led them to seek their fortunes elsewhere. Later generations achieved their independence earlier and moved more. It remains to be seen to what extent the family life characteristic of seventeenth-century Andover was the exception or the rule in the American colonies.

[42] Out of a total of 103 second-generation sons whose residences are known, only seventeen or 16.5 percent, departed from Andover. Five left before 1690, and twelve left after 1690. The majority of families in 17th-century Andover remained closely knit and remarkably immobile.

The Devil, the Body, and the Feminine Soul in Puritan New England

Elizabeth Reis

INTRODUCTION

In this piece, Elizabeth Reis suggests a compelling new explanation for a very old dilemma: why did New Englanders associate witchcraft so closely with women? Elsewhere, for example in Eastern Europe and New France, witchcraft allegations tended to fall much more evenly on men and women alike. Earlier explanations of this problem focused on the vulnerable position of women in the intensely patriarchal society of early New England. Here, Reis raises the possibility that the reason may be intimately entwined with the gendered dynamics of Puritan spirituality in which men and women shared equally, albeit distinctly.

Reis outlines a notable difference in the way women and men experienced and practiced witchcraft. Women's relationships with Satan centered on their bodies and their sexuality, whereas for men the relationships turned on material feats of strength and destruction of property. In other words, witchcraft affected the souls of their respective social identities. By drawing our attention to Puritan spirituality, Reis forces us to confront the question of what made New England Puritans so peculiar, their "Puritanism" or the society they had constructed in New England? Theologically, the Puritans shared much with other European Calvinists. Likewise, their gendered attitudes toward the soul and the body could be found across Christian Europe.

Elizabeth Reis, "The Devil, the Body, and the Feminine Soul in Puritan New England," in *Journal of American History,* 82 (1995), pp. 15–36. Copyright ©1995 Organization of American Historians. Reprinted with permission.

Elizabeth Reis is a visiting research fellow at the Center for the Study of American Religion at Princeton University, 1994–1995.

She would like to thank Matthew Dennis, Karen Kupperman, David D. Hall, Robert Middlekauff, Michael McGiffert, John Murrin, Carla Pestana, Richard Godbeer, Stephen Aron, Anita Tien, John Theibault, Cornelia Dayton, James F. Cooper, Jr., Margaret Masson, the Center for the Study of American Religion at Princeton University, and anonymous reviewers at the *Journal of American History.*

• *Was there something about life in small, intensely religious agricultural villages dominated by long-lived patriarchs that transformed these common Christian attitudes into a distinctly Puritan paranoia?*

Puritans regarded the soul as feminine and characterized it as insatiable, as consonant with the supposedly unappeasable nature of women. If historians have noticed the New England Puritans' feminized representation of the soul, they have failed to comment or to accord the matter much significance. Yet such representation is crucial to understanding how the soul could unite with Christ upon regeneration or, alternatively, with the devil through sin.[1]

The body, for its part, also entangled women. Puritans believed that Satan attacked the soul by assaulting the body, and that because women's bodies were weaker, the devil could reach women's souls more easily, breaching these "weaker vessels" with greater frequency. Not only was the body the means toward possessing the soul, it was the very expression of the devil's attack. Among witches, the body clearly manifested the soul's acceptance of the diabolical covenant.

Women were in a double bind during witchcraft episodes. Their souls, strictly speaking, were no more evil than those of men, but the representation of the vulnerable, unsatisfied, and yearning female soul, passively waiting for Christ but always ready to succumb to the devil, inadvertently implicated corporeal women themselves.[2] The representation of the soul in terms of worldly gender arrangements, and the understanding of women in terms of the characteristics of the feminine soul, in a circular fashion led Puritans to imagine that women were more likely than men to submit to Satan. A woman's feminine soul, jeopardized in a woman's feminine body, was frail, submissive, and passive—qualities that most New Englanders thought would allow her to become either a wife to Christ or a drudge to Satan.

---

[1] Scholars have studied the Puritan conception of the soul, but none has commented on gender distinctions. See, for example, Sargent Bush, Jr., ed., *The Writings of Thomas Hooker: Spiritual Adventure in Two Worlds* (Madison, 1980); Charles Lloyd Cohen, *God's Caress: The Psychology of Puritan Religious Experience* (New York, 1986); Edmund S. Morgan, *The Puritan Family: Religion and Domestic Relations in Seventeenth-Century New England* (New York, 1944); Kathleen Verduin, "'Our Cursed Natures': Sexuality and the Puritan Conscience," *New England Quarterly*, 56 (June 1983), 220–37; and Margaret W. Masson, "The Typology of the Female as a Model for the Regenerate: Puritan Preaching, 1690–1730," *Signs*, 2 (Winter 1976), 304–15.

[2] Since both men and women possessed feminine souls, ministers would have contended that the sexes were spiritually equal. Yet Carol F. Karlsen has shown that women's discontent with their lot in life opened them to witchcraft accusations. She has demonstrated that the sins for which women were punished—pride, deceit, envy—signified overall unhappiness, and as the minister John Davenport suggested, Puritans knew that "a froward discontented frame of spirit was a subject fitt for the Devill to work upon." See Carol F. Karlsen, *The Devil in the Shape of a Woman: Witchcraft in Colonial New England* (New York, 1987), esp. 125.

But was this a different view: than in Europe?

Witches, unlike commonplace sinners, took a further damning step. Their feminine souls made an explicit and aggressive choice to conjoin with the devil. By defining a witch as a person whose (feminine) soul covenanted with Satan by signing a devil's pact rather than quiescently waiting for Christ, Puritans effectively demonized the notion of active female choice. A woman risked being damned either way: If her soul waited longingly for salvation in Christ, such female yearning could conjure up images of unsatisfied women vulnerable to Satan; if, on the contrary, that soul acted assertively rather than in passive obedience, by definition it chose the devil overtly. Thus, although in Puritan theory women were not inherently more evil than men, they became so labeled during the practical process of defining women's souls and bodies in the context of Puritan New England.[3]

This essay examines the cultural construction of gender in early America in order to understand the intersection of Puritan theology, Puritan evaluations of womanhood, and the seventeenth-century witchcraft episodes, in which 78 percent of the accused were women. The Puritans' earthly perception of women's bodies and souls corresponded to their otherworldly belief concerning Satan's powers. New Englanders considered women more vulnerable to Satan because their image of the soul and its relationship to the body allowed them to associate womanhood with evil and sin. During the witchcraft episodes, the learned and the common people alike molded belief and interpreted circumstances, in the end cooperating in the construction of their natural and supernatural world. Of course, this seventeenth-century world was influenced by considerations of gender. Not only did Puritans' understanding of women's and men's bodies and souls reflect the gendered nature of their social universe, but the supernatural behaviors and powers that they believed the devil conferred on his female and male witches echoed the more mundane gender arrangements of colonial New England.[4]

Lay and clerical views of the tortures that Satan's victims endured during the witchcraft episodes paralleled the sermon literature on the relationship between the body, the soul, and Satan. The body was the most vulnerable part of one's total being, its Achilles' heel. Succumbing to Satan's assaults and temptations, the body could become the Puritan man or woman's own

[3] For the prevailing European view that women were more evil than men, see the influential 1486 work: Heinrich Institorus, *The Malleus Maleficarum of Heinrich Kramer and James Sprenger,* trans. Montague Summers (New York, 1971), esp. 41–47. The book appeared in various languages in almost thirty editions.
[4] Approximately 78% of the seventeenth-century witches who could be identified by sex were female. See Karlsen, *Devil in the Shape of a Woman,* 48; and John Putnam Demos, *Entertaining Satan: Witchcraft and the Culture of Early New England* (New York, 1982). On the relationship of lay and clerical thought, see David D. Hall, *Worlds of Wonder, Days of Judgment: Popular Religious Belief in Early New England* (New York, 1989), esp. 3–20. See also Richard Godbeer, *The Devil's Dominion: Magic and Religion in Early New England* (Cambridge, Eng., 1992), 154–57.

worst enemy. It was the primary battleground in the struggle between the devil and individual souls. The Reverend Henry Smith characterized the body as a betrayer. He lamented, "So soon as we rise in the morning, we go forth to fight with two mighty giants, the world and the devil; and whom do we take with us but a traitor, this brittle flesh, which is ready to yield up to the enemy at every assault?" Sinful temptations devised by Satan, such as carnality, drunkenness, and licentiousness, provoked the body and threatened to lead it astray, thus allowing Satan an inroad into the soul.[5]

Puritan sermons asserted that the body and the soul were both essential to human beings; each had its specific purpose, though the soul reigned supreme. The Reverend Samuel Willard explained that all the various parts of the body were made "to be at the Command and under the Government of the Nobler Part [the soul]." For example, "Here are the *Hands,* Organs suited to perform the Devices of the Soul, wherewith many Works are wrought. . . . And here are the *Feet* which carry the Body according to the Direction of the Soul." The body did the soul's bidding; a weak body, one that could not withstand the devil's attacks or seductions, rendered the soul vulnerable to Satan's extortion. The Reverend Joshua Moodey referred to the body as "A close Enemy because within thee, and the more dangerous because so close . . . , an Enemy that lurks in thine own bosome, and thence is advantaged to do thee the more harm."[6]

It seems ironic that Puritans envisioned the body protecting the soul rather than the reverse, so that a strong body rendered a person's soul less vulnerable to Satan's exertions. The body, after all, was usually seen as the weaker link in the soul/body relationship. However, in a seemingly illogical but nonetheless common way, the body became the path to the soul. A stronger body was less likely to submit to the devil's temptations and thus better protected the soul from the devil's domination.

The body was supposed to protect the soul, but more often than not it failed. Clergy and laity alike knew all too well that the body's lustful desires frequently overwhelmed the will, which resided in the soul. And although the body may have perpetrated the particular sins, ultimately the soul bore the responsibility. It was the soul that Satan held in bondage. "It is true, the body is employed in it, and all the members of it are engaged in this drudgery," Willard admitted, "but the bondage of it lies on the inward man."[7]

---

[5] On the struggle between body and soul, see John Downame, *The Christian Warfare Against the Devil, World and Flesh* (London, 1634). Thomas Fuller, ed., *The Works of Henry Smith; including Sermons, Treatises, Prayers, and Poems* (2 vols., Edinburgh, 1867), II, 18.

[6] Samuel Willard, *The Compleat Body of Divinity* (Boston, 1726), 123; Joshua Moodey, *Souldiery Spiritualized, or the Christian Souldier Orderly, and Strenuously Engaged in the Spiritual Warre, and So fighting the Good Fight* (Cambridge, Mass., 1674), 8.

[7] Willard, *Compleat Body of Divinity,* 229. On the relationship between the understanding, the will, the body, and the soul, see Cohen, *God's Caress,* 34–46. On the will and the soul, see also Perry Miller, *The New England Mind: The Seventeenth Century* (Cambridge, Mass., 1939), 181–85, 256–66.

Willard's use of the term "inward man" as a synonym for the (feminine) soul drew on biblical precedent and Puritan speculation that used the names of bodily things to designate spiritual entities. The metaphor carried more connotation of femininity in the seventeenth century than it earlier did. Quoting the source of the trope, the seventeenth-century English minister Richard Sibbes blurred the lines between the physical and the spiritual, writing that the heart is not "the inward material and fleshy part of the body; but that spiritual part, the soul and affections thereof . . . all the powers of the soul, the inward man, as Paul calleth it, 2 Cor. iv. 16, is the heart." Paul's phrase gained new significance from seventeenth- and eighteenth-century ideas of physical anatomy that perceived women's sexual organs as the same as men's, except insofar as they were contained *within* rather than outside the body. If inwardness meant femaleness, the term suggests that the soul was feminine; it, or "she," ultimately carried the burden of the body's weaknesses.[8]

Puritans conceived of body and soul as integral parts of the self, yet distinguished in function and prestige. As a result of the Fall, the body and soul suffered punishments that had to be endured. Willard explained the distinction to his congregation. Although the body was merely the instrument of the soul, he preached, the pair fit together to form a complete person, and so the body as well as the soul had to suffer for sin. The suffering, Willard reasoned, came in two forms, "privative" and "positive." Creatures could be denied things that would have made their lives more comfortable, or they could undergo manifest miseries, both emotional and physical.[9]

As a consequence of original and subsequent sin, the body endured ill health as its punishment. The privative suffering manifested itself in a lack of vivacity and a disposition to illness; the positive suffering in physical ailments that afflicted the human body. "These evils," according to Willard, "meet the man in the womb before he is born, and they follow him to his grave; and every affliction gives a chop at the tree of the life of the outward man, till at last it falls, and he dies."[10]

And yet, "if a man had a thousand bodies," postulated Willard, "he had better lose them all, than one soul." Willard admitted that a person could endure all sorts of corporal miseries and still be content; spiritual punishment mattered more. Spiritual miseries, Willard explained, included "all those evils to which the Soul is subjected in this life." The soul constituted "the most excellent part in Man," and so the miseries it suffered had to be

---

[8] Cohen, *God's Caress,* esp. 37, 39. On ideas of the equivalence of male and female sexual organs, see Thomas Laqueur, "Orgasm, Generation, and the Politics of Reproductive Biology," *Representations,* 14 (Spring 1986), esp. 5, 14–16. On how two genders corresponded to one sex—the male—see Thomas Laqueur, *Making Sex: Body and Gender from the Greeks to Freud* (Cambridge, Mass., 1990).

[9] Willard, *Compleat Body of Divinity,* 224–28.

[10] *Ibid.,* 224.

significantly greater.[11] A strong body could endure enormous suffering, but the agony of the soul imposed a more lasting effect on a person's life.

The soul's most excruciating misery resulted when the divine union with Christ, expected upon conversion, was cruelly subverted and instead a diabolical union was concluded with the devil as a result of sin. Puritans believed that this was exactly the devil's intention; Satan aggressively pursued souls, persuading them to join his minions. Deodat Lawson (preaching in the midst of the 1692 witchcraft crisis in Salem) proclaimed, "when [Satan] *touches* the life of the Body, he *Aims* at the Life of the Soul." Willard (in more ordinary times) warned his congregation, "It is the Soul[']s destruction the Devil mainly aims at: it is the precious Soul that he hunts for." Both Lawson and Willard illustrated their point with the biblical example of Job; the devil tortured Job's body, but his aim was to devastate the soul. "He [the devil] little regards the Body in comparison of that," said Willard. Cotton Mather made the same point. The devil's goal, he wrote, was to "seduce the souls, torment the bodies."[12]

Prior to conversion, the soul, corrupt and degenerate in its natural state, inevitably succumbed to Satan's wily ways and surrendered to his domination. Upon conversion the soul cleaved to Christ, "as moulded into one loafe."[13] The regenerate souls of both men and women were united with Christ as if in a marriage. Paradoxically, this matrimony with Christ constituted a heterosexual union for both men and women. Both Satan and Christ could possess the soul in this sexually specific way because, as we shall see below, for Puritans, the soul, as distinct from the body, was inherently feminine. Whether the soul fell victim to Satan's temptations or instead enjoyed Christ's protection upon conversion, the bond remained heterosexual because it was literally the soul, and only metaphorically the body, that Puritans believed converged with either Christ or the devil.

The marriage between God and a believer was the most common metaphor of regeneration because it closely approximated the relationship between husband and wife, the most important human relationship. Puritan ministers drew on a long Christian tradition in describing the union, in which the soul took the place of the wife, and Christ that of the husband. Thomas Shepard explained, "The soul hence gives itself, like one espoused to her husband, to the Lord Jesus." The betrothal metaphor took on a concrete expression when ministers urged that such sacred marriages, like profane ones, required consummation. Increase Mather argued, "In this Life Believers are Espoused to Christ. At his Second coming will be the Consummation of the Marriage. Christ will then come as a Bridegroom." Jonathan Mitchel described the union that

---

[11] *Ibid.*, 227.
[12] Deodat Lawson, *Christ's Fidelity the Only Shield Against Satan's Malignity* (Boston, 1704), 23; Willard, *Compleat Body of Divinity,* 229; Samuel Drake, ed., *The Witchcraft Delusion in New England,* vol. I: *The Wonders of the Invisible World* [1693], by Cotton Mather (Roxbury, Mass., 1866), 101.
[13] John Cotton, *The Way of Life* (London, 1634), 375.

would occur on Judgment Day: "our present state is but an Espousal, the consummation of the Marriage is at the day of Judgment; thence follows the full enjoyment each of other in Heaven, when Christ hath carried his Spouse home to his Father's house." The layman John Winthrop wrote, "God brought me by that occasion in to such a heavenly meditation of the love betweene Christ and me, as ravished my heart with unspeakable ioye [joy]; methought my soule had as familiar and sensible society with him as my wife could have with the kindest husbande." The mystical union between the believer and Christ was analogous, consummation and all, to the relationship between wife and husband, female and male. In both men and women, the soul was the female part that bonded spiritually, emotionally, and physically with Christ.[14]

If the feminine soul was to merge with Christ upon regeneration, then it must possess attributes that prepared it for this union. The historian Margaret W. Masson has described the Puritans' image of the regenerate Christian as a passive and submissive convert who exemplified "wifely" traits. The convert was supposed to wait patiently for Christ's overtures of grace. According to Shepard, the soul had an obligation to be quiescent. When the lover is Christ, said Shepard, "it is no presumption now, but duty to give *her* consent." Upon regeneration, Cotton Mather exhorted, "in this Act of *Resignation* there must and will be nothing less than thy very *All* included. *Resign* thy *Spirit* unto Him, and say, *O my SAVIOUR, I desire that all the Faculties of my Soul may be filled with thee, and used for thee. Resign* thy *Body* unto Him." The convert's object was to surrender completely to Christ's domination.[15]

---

[14] John Albro, ed., *The Works of Thomas Shepard* (1853; 3 vols., New York, 1967), II, 31: Increase Mather, *Practical Truths Plainly Delivered* (Boston, 1718), 54; Jonathan Mitchel, *A Discourse of the Glory to Which God hath Called Believers by Jesus Christ* (London, 1677), 30; Robert C. Winthrop, *Life and Letters of John Winthrop* (2 vols., Boston, 1869), I, 105. On the role of Puritan women as wives and mothers, see Amanda Porterfield, *Female Piety in Puritan New England: The Emergence of Religious Humanism* (New York, 1992). See also Morgan, *Puritan Family,* esp. chapter 7. On the medieval tradition of matrimonial and sexual imagery, see Caroline Walker Bynum, *Fragmentation and Redemption: Essays on Gender and the Human Body in Medieval Religion* (New York, 1991), 151–79; and Ann E. Matter, *The Voice of My Beloved: The Song of Songs in Western Medieval Christianity* (Philadelphia, 1990). On the metaphor of maternal love, see Caroline Walker Bynum, *Jesus as Mother: Studies in the Spirituality of the High Middle Ages* (Berkeley, 1982), 110–69. For the Puritan understanding of marriage, see John Cotton, *A Meet Help: Or, a Wedding Sermon, Preached at NewCastle in New England, June 19, 1694* (Boston, 1699); Willard, *Compleat Body of Divinity,* 610–20; Benjamin Wadsworth, *The Well-Ordered Family* (Boston, 1712); Alexander Niccholes, *A Discourse of Marriage and Wiving* (London, 1615); Thomas Gataker, *Marriage Duties* (London, 1620). For the historians' view of the relationship between men and women in marriage, see Morgan, *Puritan Family,* 29–64; James T. Johnson, "The Covenant Idea and the Puritan View of Marriage," *Journal of the History of Ideas,* 32 (Jan.–March 1971), 107–18; Karlsen, *Devil in the Shape of a Woman,* 160–68; and Laurel Thatcher Ulrich, *Good Wives: Image and Reality in the Lives of Women in Northern New England, 1650–1750* (New York, 1980), 35–50.

[15] Albro, ed., *Works of Thomas Shepard,* I, 197 (emphasis added). See also Verduin, "'Our Cursed Natures,'" 220–37; Cotton Mather, *Glorious Espousal: A Brief Essay to Illustrate and Prosecute the Marriage, Wherein Our Great Saviour Offers to Espouse unto Himself the Children of Men* (Boston, 1719), 26. See Masson, "Typology of the Female as a Model for the Regenerate," 304–15; and

Masson investigated an apparent paradox. Conversion required men to act in a contradictory manner; their position as dominant and assertive husbands ran counter to their role as passive "female" converts. Masson argued that men were able to assume such passive qualities because the fluid gender identities of the seventeenth and eighteenth centuries allowed men to adopt typically female attributes while retaining their masculinity. She contended that the more rigid sexual differentiation characteristic of the nineteenth century had not yet emerged, thus permitting this apparent role ambiguity. I argue that the gender role fluidity was made possible by the gendered split between the body and the soul. Men were not required to adopt outwardly feminine traits and risk compromising their masculinity, but man's soul, his inner self, could safely display female virtues. Passivity and receptivity to Christ's advances resided in men's souls, but their bodies—and sense of themselves—remained masculine.[16]

The ministers' use of the marriage metaphor to explain the bond between Christ and saints imposed worldly gender divisions on the most important spiritual process. The matrimony analogy worked so well to explain the bond between Christ and a believer precisely because the institution was so basic. Puritan women and men understood what was expected of them in a marriage. Because the sacred marriage metaphor reflected many of the components of profane marriage, the metaphor and the institution reinforced one another. The wife submitted to her husband, just as a female soul gave herself up to Christ. Indeed, the feminine soul's very happiness depended on Christ's protection, just as a woman's contentedness was thought to depend, ideally, on her providential betrothal.[17]

The relationship between the unregenerate soul and the devil paralleled the conjugality between the regenerate soul and Christ, although in submitting to Satan, men and women were enslaved rather than joined in a respectful and benevolent, if necessarily hierarchical, relationship. Slavery rather than matrimony characterized the possession. Both institutions implied perpetual and powerful connections, and, interestingly, ministers described the bond between participants and Christ as well as that between people and Satan by the metaphor of possession. Thus, the minister William Adams could declare:

> If thou art none of Christs, thou art the Devils. The possession of men in the world is divided betwixt *Christ* and *Satan*. What *Christ* possesses not are

David Leverenz, *The Language of Puritan Feeling: An Exploration in Literature, Psychology, and Social History* (New Brunswick, 1980), 148–56.

[16] Masson, "Typology of the Female as a Model for the Regenerate," 313–15. Perhaps notions of masculinity were changing even earlier than Masson suggested; men's increasing reluctance to convert in the late seventeenth and early eighteenth centuries may reflect an avoidance of the "feminine qualities" required of conversion. This issue needs further exploration.

[17] Ulrich, *Good Wives*, 110–23.

under *Satans power* and tyranny. Know therefore that if Christ hath no possession of thee, thou art possessed of the Devil.

Christ and the devil possessed converted and unregenerate souls, respectively, but the nature of the possession differed. Possession by Christ assured freedom and salvation; possession by the devil meant perpetual terror and degradation.[18]
Ministers preached that Satan held the unconverted soul in bondage; natural man came completely under Satan's control. Jonathan Mitchel urged his congregation to come out of the corrupt state of nature, "wherein men are before conversion, which is here said to be a state of darkness & bondage to Satan & consequently of perdition." Samuel Willard likewise equated Satan's possession with man's natural state. "The first possession of the heart is held by the Strong man," explained Willard, "whether by him we understand Satan, who is called the God of the world, and rules in the Children of disobedience; or the *body of death*, or the corrupt nature in man." "How fearfull a thing is it to be serving the devill!" exclaimed the minister Robert Baylie. Those who resisted God in sin "lie captive like Gally-slaves," remaining separate from God "with their master for ever in his horrible portion."[19]
The analogy to slavery allowed ministers to speak of the devil's lure as complete and inextricable. Thomas Hooker said of the wicked, "the Devill rules in them; he speaks their tongues, and works by their hands, and thinks and desires by their minds, and walks by their feete." The union, like the matrimony between Christ and the converted, merged the devil with the soul. Unlike the regenerate soul, which could expect marital bliss upon its

[18] William Adams, *The Necessity of the Pouring Out of the Spirit from on High Upon a Sinning Apostatizing People, set under Judgment, in order to their Merciful Deliverance and Salvation* (Boston, 1979), 38; Mary Beth Norton, *Liberty's Daughters: The Revolutionary Experience of American Women, 1750–1800* (Boston, 1980), 41–51. The metaphor of possession is a reminder that, although Puritan marriages may have aspired to spiritual equality, the reality dictated a power imbalance between husband and wife. In some marriages, at least, the wife felt herself to be a virtual slave to her husband. The legal relationship between husbands and wives connoted possession. When a woman married she became a *feme covert*, who could not own property or sign contracts and did not legally own any wages she earned. In 1694 in London, Mary Astell anonymously published *Reflections upon Marriage*. She bemoaned the fate of "poor Female Slaves" who "groan under Tyranny" and would grow unavoidably weary of the "matrimonial yoke." See Margaret George, "From 'Goodwife' to 'Mistress': The Transformation of the Female in Bourgeois Culture," *Science and Society*, 37 (Summer 1973), 152–77. On the legal status of wives, see Norton, *Liberty's Daughters*, 45–47; Marylynn Salmon, *Women and the Law of Property in Early America* (Chapel Hill, 1986); Joan R. Gundersen and Gwen Victor Gampel, "Married Women's Legal Status in Eighteenth-Century New York and Virginia," *William and Mary Quarterly*, 39 (Jan. 1982), 114–34; and Norma Basch, *In the Eyes of the Law: Women, Marriage, and Property in Nineteenth-Century New York* (Ithaca, 1982), 19–26.
[19] Jonathan Mitchel, "From the Power of Satan unto God," sermon, Aug. 15, 1655 (Massachusetts Historical Society, Boston, Mass.). See also Edward Trefz, "Satan as the Prince of Evil," *Boston Library Quarterly*, 7 (Jan. 1955), 3–22. Willard, *Compleat Body of Divinity*, 170; Robert Baylie, *Satan the Leader in Chief to all who Resist the Reparation of Sion* (London, 1643), 37.

union with Christ, the soul possessed by Satan remained forever unhappy. Willard stated unequivocally "That this slavery is a Soul misery."[20]

Implicitly this connubiality presumed an unregenerate feminine soul and an unrelenting masculine devil. Though they rarely drew explicit attention to the female character of the soul, clergy and laity used feminine adjectives, such as barren or fecund, to describe it and overtly referred to the soul using the feminine pronoun, "she." The soul was also described as insatiable, a negative characterization more often ascribed to women than to men; the soul was forever seeking happiness that it could never attain unaided. Indeed, the minister Urian Oakes spoke of the natural propensity to sin, original sin, in feminine terms. "Indwelling sin," he explained, was a "home-bred enemy, that *mother* of all the abominations that are brought forth in the lives of men, that adversary that is ever molesting the peace, disturbing the quiet, and endangering the people of GOD."[21] Bearing within it the "mother" of all sin, the unregenerate, natural soul submitted willingly to Satan's domination.

John Cotton described the unrepentant soul as a feminine entity. Depicting the "ungracious frame of nature" with which humankind entered the world, Cotton recounted the process of regeneration: "So as now the poor soule begins presently to stand amazed at *her* former condition, and looks at it as most dangerous and desperate; and now the soule begins to loathe itself, and to abhor itselfe, and to complaine and confesses its wickednesse before God."[22] Cotton's soul is thus ungracious, wicked, self-hating, and female—as the possessive pronoun implies. She is enveloped in Satan's embrace, yet eager to confess so that she can instead be coupled with Christ.

Feminine images of the soul punctuate Puritan sermon literature. In 1679 William Adams described the minister's work in preparing souls for conversion as "travailing in birth with Souls till Christ be formed in them." He likened the soul in its natural state to a wilderness, "barren and unfruitful, bringing forth no fruit to God, but wild fruits of sin." Once these unregenerate souls shifted their devotion from Satan to Christ upon conversion, they would "be changed, tilled, converted and made fruitful, to bring forth fruits of holiness unto God." "Fertile and fruitful" described the converted soul; the reprobate soul, possessed by Satan, remained "barren of all grace and goodness."[23]

---

[20] Thomas Hooker, *The Soules Humiliation* (London, 1637), 35; Willard, *Compleat Body of Divinity*, 229.

[21] Urian Oakes, *The Unconquerable, All Conquering and More than Conquering Souldier: or the successful warre which a believer wageth with the enemies of his soul* (Boston, 1674), 2 (emphasis added).

[22] Cotton, *Way of Life*, 5 (emphasis added).

[23] Adams, *Necessity of the Pouring Out of the Spirit*, A4, 4, 18. For other uses of the metaphor of birth, including one quoted from a layman, see Willard, *Compleat Body of Divinity*, 230; and George Selemant and Bruce C. Woolley, eds., *Thomas Shepard's* Confessions (Boston, 1981), 61. On descriptions of landscape in terms of female sexuality and motherhood, see Annette Kolodny, *The Lay of the Land: Metaphor as Experience and History in American Life and Letters* (Chapel Hill, 1975).

The representation of the soul as a woman invited metaphors of fecundity and sexuality. The poet Anne Bradstreet portrayed the eyes and ears as the doors of the soul, "through which innumerable objects enter," but the soul is never satisfied. Borrowing an image from the biblical book of Proverbs, she imagined the soul as "like the daughters of the horseleach"; it "cries, 'Give, give'; and which is most strange, the more it receives, the more empty it finds itself and sees an impossibility ever to be filled but by Him in whom all fullness dwells."[24] In Bradstreet's eyes, the feminine soul needed a virile Christ to satisfy her otherwise insatiable desires.

An English minister, the Reverend Mr. Simmons, similarly described the soul using sexual imagery. Like Bradstreet, he conceived of the eyes as the "port-holes" of the soul, through which "sin and Satan creep in at." He cautioned, "If those doors stand wide open for all comers and goers, either your soul, Dinah-like, will be gadding out, or Satan will be getting in, by which the poor soul will be defiled and defloured." Simmons recalled Dinah, the biblical daughter of Jacob, who left the protection of her father and brothers and was raped by Shechem, son of Hamor the Hivite.[25] Like Dinah, the soul, left unguarded, would fall victim to Satan's invasion; his potent intrusion was best described in sexual terms, as the rape of the feminine soul.

The feminine soul thus was insatiable, driven by almost physical desires, as Samuel Willard argued in his *Sacramental Meditations:* "The soul of man must have something to live upon, that is the great want, and for this want the creature hath no supply." Like a growling stomach, Thomas Shepard suggested, the soul "must have something to quiet and comfort it." Ironically, the active pursuit of sustenance and spiritual fulfillment was not only futile, given the soul's unrelenting appetite, but it invited Satan's abuse, conceived as rape and possession.[26]

In the battle between God and the devil, both Christ and Satan stood as aggressively masculine warriors, battling for the feminine soul's fidelity. Unconverted souls, ministers warned, unwittingly conspired with the forces of Satan and "spen[t] all their days in *Continual Rebellions* against [God]." But

---

[24] Anne Bradstreet, "Meditations Divine and Moral," in *The Works of Anne Bradstreet,* ed. Jeannine Hensley (Cambridge, Mass., 1967), 282. See Prov. 30:15 Revised Standard Version: "The leech has two daughters;/'Give', says one, and 'Give', says the other./Three things there are which will never be satisfied,/four which never say, 'Enough!'/The grave and a barren womb,/ a land thirsty for water/and fire that never says, 'Enough!'"

[25] Rev. Mr. Simmons, "How may we get rid of spiritual sloth, and know when our activity in duty is from the spirit of God?," in *Puritan Sermons, 1659–1680: Being the Morning Exercises at Cripplegate, St. Giles in the Fields, and in Southwark by Seventy-Five Ministers of the Gospel In or Near London,* ed. James Nichols (6 vols., Wheaton, Ill., 1981), I, 434–57, esp. 439. For a similar description of the relation of eyes and soul, see Willard, *Compleat Body of Divinity,* 123. For the Dinah story, see Gen. 34 RSV.

[26] Samuel Willard, *Some Brief Sacramental Meditations, Preparatory for Communion, at the Great Ordinance of the Supper* (Boston, 1711), 21–22; Albro, ed., *Works of Thomas Shepard,* II, 28. On the nearly physical desires of the soul, see Verduin, "'Our Cursed Natures,'" 236.

in his generalship, Satan showed little regard or mercy for his own troops. The soul thus occupied a dangerous position; even if she was an unwitting conscript in Satan's legion, she had to defend herself against the devil himself. As Bradstreet and Simmons cautioned, the soul had to shield herself from Satan's advances so that she would not be "defiled and defloured."[27]

During the witchcraft trials the unfulfilled feminine soul, quick to succumb to the devil's possession, became equated with discontented women, subjects primed for the devil's intrusion. The ministers taught that Satan tortured and weakened the body in order to dominate the soul, and the laity interpreted the message quite literally; that interpretation affected the understanding of sin, the soul, and the body in unanticipated ways. To lay people's minds, the weaker bodies of women rendered their souls more accessible to Satan. The clergy did not disagree. The minister John Cotton had succinctly described the relationship between sin, the soul, and Satan: "When a man wittingly and willingly commits any knowne sinne, he doth as actually give his Soule to the Devill, as a Witch doth her body and soule; we thereby renounce the covenant of God, and Satan takes Possession of us."[28] Cotton made a distinction between sinners and witches; Satan possessed the souls of all sinners alike, but witches, whom Cotton assumed were women, compounded their crime.

The witch's surrender was explicit; not only did her body falter and her soul submit but the witch also explicitly enlisted to promote the devil's purpose. The witch acted aggressively. Her soul specifically chose the devil, rather than passively waiting for Christ, and she purposefully allowed the devil to use her body. She presumably gave the devil permission to commandeer her body—her shape—to recruit more witches and perform *maleficium*. Thus, the witch acted assertively, while the sinner, after falling, suffered passively.

In both old and New England, Puritans conceived of women as the weaker sex. In seventeenth-century England some debated whether that weakness extended to women's spiritual or moral state as well. Joseph Swetnam argued in *The Arraignment of Lewd, Idle, Froward and Unconstant Women* that women were inherently evil. He wrote, "Then who can but say, that Women spring from the Devil, whose heads, hands, hearts, minds, and souls are evil?" His book came under attack, but it went through six editions between 1615 and 1702. Meric Casaubon, an English scholar with a special interest in witchcraft and possession, disagreed. He contended that women were not evil but, rather, that their brains were weaker, and so they were more likely to be caught in Satan's traps. He wrote of women, "all men know [them] to be naturally weaker of brain, and easiest to be infatuated and deluded." Swetnam blamed all of woman—not only her body but her soul—

[27] Cotton Mather, "Triparadisus," [1712–1726], pt. III, sect. VIII, octavo vol. 49, Mather Family Papers, 1613–1819 (American Antiquarian Society, Worcester, Mass.). On the date of this work, see Reiner Smolinski, "An Authoritative Edition of Cotton Mather's Unpublished Manuscript 'Triparadisus'" (Ph.D. diss., Pennsylvania State University, 1987).
[28] Cotton, *Way of Life*, 5.

for her evil nature' Casaubon blamed strictly woman' physical limitations. A weaker brain was quite different from an evil soul; seventeenth-century opinion considered the brain a part of the physical anatomy, like the liver or the spleen, while the soul was an immortal entity.[29]

New Englanders may have shared Swetnam's sentiments, but publicly they confined their notions of women's weakness to their physical states. The colonists shared with their English brethren the belief that women's bodies were physically weaker than men's and subject to more debilitating illness. An English midwife, Jane Sharp, wrote in a 1671 midwifery manual "that the Female sex are subject to more diseases by odds than the Male Kind are, and therefore it is reason that great care should be had for the cure of that sex that is the weaker and most subject to infirmities in some respects above the other." New Englanders concurred. Cotton Mather explained in *The Angel of Bethesda,* the only complete colonial medical guide, that "the Sex that is called, *The Weaker Vessel,* has not only a share with us, in the most of our Distempers, but also is liable to many that may be called, Its *Peculiar Weaknesses.*" He reported that a "Variety of Distempers" afflicted women's "Tender and Feeble Constitutions."[30]

As we have seen, the feminine souls of women and men were responsible for sinfulness, and both were all too likely to fall into Satan's deadly embrace. However, during the witchcraft episodes, the devil consistently and disproportionately seemed to torture women, trying to obtain their signatures in his black book, win their souls, and use their bodies to molest and recruit others. Given the gendered social and theological arrangements of seventeenth-century New England, we should not find this bias surprising.

Applying the teachings of their ministers rather literally, the laity, I believe, expected that women's weaker bodies would suffer more severely than men's in a world besieged by Satan's wrath. Because women's bodies lacked the strength and vitality of men's, according to popular thought, the devil could more frequently and successfully enter and possess women's souls, thus bringing them, according to the minister Deodat Lawson, "into *full* Submission, and entire *Resignation* to [Satan's] Hellish Designs."[31]

[29] For Joseph Swetnam's statement, see Antonia Fraser, *The Weaker Vessel* (New York, 1984), 2. Meric Casaubon, *A Treatise Concerning Enthusiasme, As it is an Effect of Nature: but is Mistaken by Many for Either Divine Inspiration, or Diabolical Possession* (London, 1655), 119. See also Cohen, *God's Caress,* 39.
[30] Jane Sharp, *The Midwives Book. Or the Whole Art of Midwifry Discovered. Directing Childbearing Women how to Behave Themselves In their Conception, Breeding, Bearing, and Nursing of Children* (London, 1671), 250; Cotton Mather, *The Angel of Bethesda* (1725; Barr, Mass., 1972), 233. It is estimated that one woman died for every 150 births until as late as 1930. Today one woman dies for every 10,000 births. See Laurel Thatcher Ulrich, "'The Living Mother of a Living Child': Midwifery and Mortality in Post-Revolutionary New England," *William and Mary Quarterly,* 46 (Jan. 1989), 27–48. See also Laurel Thatcher Ulrich, *A Midwife's Tale: The Life of Martha Ballard, Based on Her Diary, 1785–1812* (New York, 1990).
[31] Lawson, *Christ's Fidelity the Only Shield Against Satan's Malignity,* 27.

The devil pursued souls with particular vigor and success during witch-craft outbreaks, yet he did not display any new methods or depart significantly from his well-known devices. Satan perhaps asserted himself more physically and immediately in these incidents. Indeed, the evocative language that the clergy used to describe God's wrath toward those who refused to convert may have led the laity to interpret God's anger and the devil's torments so literally. But the powers of Satan still corresponded to those detailed by Puritan ministers.[32] The laity saw Satan in various guises, often in the accused witch's bodily shape. These specters, as they were called, were the focus of debate. Civic and religious leaders disputed whether the appearance of a specter indicated that the individual impersonated had actually made a compact granting Satan permission to appear in her or his shape and to torment others or whether Satan could appear in the bodily shape of an innocent person. Either way, the clergy and the laity believed that when the devil appeared in any form, his goal was to molest the bodies of potential recruits in order to capture their souls.

Anxious to dominate their souls, Satan harrassed his victims' bodies first. The language of the indictments brought against the accused witches illustrates the extent of the agonies inflicted by the devil. The indictments read that the victims were "Tortured Afflicted Consumed pined Wasted and Tormented." Presumably, Satan already possessed the body and soul of his primary victim, the witch, and so with her permission, and through her body, he attacked yet more victims. The accused witch Mary Bridges testified that "the way of her afflicting was by sticking pins into things and Clothes & think of hurting them."[33]

The victims described their tortures more graphically. One woman, Mary Walcott, swore that the apparition of Goody Buckly came and "hurt me and tortord me most dreadfully by pinching and choaking of me and twesting of my nick several times" to convince her to sign a covenant with Satan and renounce God. Likewise, Susannah Sheldon told the court that "I have very often ben most greviously tortored by Apperishtion of Sarah Good who has most dreadfully afflected me by bitting pricking and pinching me and allmost choaking me to death." Sheldon recalled that on June 26, 1692, Good "most violently pulled down my head behind a Cheast and tyed my hands together with a whele band & allmost Choaked me to death." The court records abound with women's testimony that the devil, usually but not always in the shape of the accused, brutally tormented their bodies and tempted them to sign his book in blood, signifying his possession of their souls.[34]

---

[32] Adams, *Necessity of the Pouring Out of the Spirit,* 10.

[33] Paul Boyer and Stephen Nissenbaum, eds., *The Salem Witchcraft Papers: Verbatim Transcripts of the Legal Documents of the Salem Witchcraft Outbreak of 1692* (3 vols., New York, 1977), I, 57, 135. The quoted indictment is found in most of the trials.

[34] *Ibid.,* I, 149, II, 374.

The devil's victims usually sought to endure his torture of their bodies and to resist relinquishing their souls, though with mixed results. Mercy Lewis told the court that the devil in the shape of the accused, George Jacobs, Sr., came to her and urged her to join his minions. "Because I would not yeald to his hellish temtations," she surmised, "he did tortor me most cruelly . . . and allmost redy to pull all my bones out of joynt . . . but being up held by an Allmighty hand . . . I indured his tortors that night." The devil could damage her body but not ultimately master it, and so he would not have her soul. The possessed Mary Warren owned that she "yeilded," and that she "was undon body and soul," and that she did it "for eas to her body; not for any good of her soul."[35]

Once the witch inscribed the pact with the devil, Puritans believed, she could no longer keep Satan's possession a secret; her soul had willfully joined the devil's camp. The devil often appeared directly to witches, and he could be so persuasive that some women confessed to giving themselves completely to him. Sarah Bridges testified that "the Divel Came Sometimes like a bird Som times like abare Sometimes like aman," and she admitted "Renouncing God and Christ & Gave her Soul & Body to the Devil." Bridges acknowledged that the devil had threatened to kill her if she confessed, but still she told the court that she used to "afflict persons by Squezing her hands & Sticking pins in her Clothes." Mary Barker also confessed that she was "afrayd She has Given up her Self Soul & body to the Divel." These two confessors, like many others, admitted that the devil had urged them to inscribe his book and that they had capitulated. By signing they renounced baptism. The pact created the same bond between the signers and Satan as the baptized had with Christ; its significance rested on its voluntary nature. Upon signing over their souls, they were expected to inflict harm on others, while the devil seized their shapes to attack, entrap, and recruit additional witches for his service. Becoming the devil's victim meant enduring affliction, either from the devil directly or from the shape of a witch.[36]

Women served the devil in ways particular to their sex. It was not unusual for a witch who had given herself body and soul to Satan to suckle familiars, or imps, Puritans believed. These little creatures, often animals or small, strange beasts, were thought to receive nourishment in the form of blood from the witch's body. Often the familiars sucked at the breasts, but they were as likely to latch onto any unusual marking, or witches' teat. The West Indian woman Tituba told the court that she saw a small yellow bird "suck [Sarah]

[35] *Ibid.*, II, 483, III, 797.

[36] *Ibid.*, I, 139, 141, 60. As far as we know, no one actually signed a devil's book in blood. Indeed, modern historians can hardly entertain such a notion. Yet many of the accused admitted doing so. See Elizabeth Reis, "Witches, Sinners, and the Underside of Covenant Theology," *Essex Institute Historical Collections,* 129 (Jan. 1993), 103–18. Giving oneself "soul and body" did not necessarily have a sexual meaning, although the devil was considered capable of using the witch's body sexually.

Good betwene the fore finger & Long finger upon the Right Hand." She added that sometimes she saw a cat with the bird and that she once noticed Good with two bizarre creatures. One, who had wings and two legs and a head like a woman, subsequently turned into a woman; the other was "a thing all over hairy, all the face hayry & a long nose & I don't know how to tell how the face looks w'th two Leggs, itt goeth upright & is about two or three foot high & goeth upright like a man." In Connecticut, the authorities searched the body of Mercy Disbrough and found "on her secret parts growing within ye lep of ye same a los [loose] pees of skin and when puld it is near an Inch long somewhat in form of ye fingar of a glove flatted."[37]

The creatures signified that the devil had taken possession of these women's bodies, and now they, as well as the devil himself, had the right to suck their blood. Susannah Sheldon, an eyewitness against Bridget Bishop, testified that Bishop "puled out her breast and the black man gave her a thing like a blake pig it had no haire on it and shee put it to her breast and gave it suck and when it had sucked on brest shee put it the other and gave it suck their then she gave it to the blak man." Although Sheldon saw this creature suckle at Bishop's breasts, Bishop still underwent a court-appointed search for likely spots where an imp might nurse. Five women found on her body "a preternathurall Excresence of flesh between the pudendum and Anus much like to Tetts & not usuall in women." Because Bishop's body was seen suckling the devil's familiar and because her shape was seen tormenting several victims, the court assumed that Bishop's soul also belonged to Satan. Despite her repeated protestations of innocence, Bishop was hanged; according to the court she had given the devil both her body and her soul and had become a witch.[38]

For the witch, sacrificing her soul to Satan could mean yielding her body sexually to his imps. In medieval folklore, the witch's familiar, or incubus, had intercourse with the witch. The learned tracts on witchcraft written in the colonies, for example, Increase Mather's, were skeptical about the possibility of the devil's familiars having sexual relations with the witches. Increase Mather wrote, "What fables are there concerning *incubi* and *succubae* and of men begotton by daemons! No doubt but the devil may delude the fancy, that one of his vassals shall think (as the witch at Hartford did) that he has carnal and cursed communion with them beyond what is real." On the other hand, Mather went on to admit, "Nor is it impossible for him [the devil] to assume a dead body, or to form a lifeless one out of the elements, and therewith to make his witches become guilty of sodomy." Even on this

---

[37] Boyer and Nissenbaum, eds., *Salem Witchcraft Papers,* III, 752; John Taylor, *The Witchcraft Delusion in Connecticut, 1647–1697* (New York, 1908), 45. On the relationship between the humoral theory of medicine and the understanding of breastfeeding during the colonial period, see Paula A. Treckel, "Breastfeeding and Maternal Sexuality in Colonial America," *Journal of Interdisciplinary History,* 20 (Summer 1989), 25–51. For the argument that the witch and her imp presented a perverted picture of human motherhood, see Demos, *Entertaining Satan,* 179–81.
[38] Boyer and Nissenbaum, eds., *Salem Witchcraft Papers,* I, 106, 107.

last point, Mather was ambiguous. Later in the text he concluded, "But to imagine that spirits shall really generate bodies, is irrational." In the colonial witchcraft trials, this traditional element was not emphasized, although the possibility of such behavior was certainly intimated. The creatures that sucked at women's breasts and at other sexually sensitive areas of their bodies may have been sucking for sexual pleasure rather than nourishment.[39]

Witches' bodies no longer belonged to themselves; Satan could take them wherever he pleased to use as he pleased. The devil appeared in the forms of both men and women witches, but when a specter assaulted a victim in a sexual way, it was always in the shape of a woman. Most often a male victim (though occasionally a female one) recounted awaking at night to find the specter of a witch sitting on top of him in bed. References to sexual activity were veiled but unmistakable. Samuel Gray reported that he woke up to see Bridget Bishop's apparition standing between the baby's cradle and his bed. He testified that

> he said to her in the name of God what doe you come for. then she vanished away soe he Locked the dore againe & went to bed and between sleeping & wakeing he felt some thing Come to his mouth or lipes cold, & there upon started & looked up & againe did see the same woman.

In a similarly suggestive tale, Bernard Peach claimed that Susannah Martin "drew up his body into a heape and Lay upon him about an hour and half or 2 hours, in all which taim this deponent coold not stir nor speake." New Englanders did not typically interpret the devil's intrusion in sexual terms, yet they sometimes understood his use of women witches in light of the witches' sexuality and their female bodies.[40]

Satan also tried to capture men's souls, but his torture of their bodies was markedly different and less drastic. Men were not as likely to be seen suckling imps, although their bodies were searched during the trials and the investigations occasionally found evidence of the potential for such activity. During the examination of two accused witches, George Burroughs and George Jacobs, both of whom were eventually hanged, the examiners found nothing unusual upon Burroughs's body, but Jacobs was not so lucky. The four men reported "3. tetts w'ch according to the best of our Judgement wee think is not naturall for wee run a pinn through 2 of them and he was not sinceible of it." As far as the court was concerned, the three abnormal markings, one in Jacobs's mouth, one on his shoulder blade, and one on his hip, signified the devil's possession of his body and soul.[41]

But the devil's possession of men contrasted with his domination of women because New Englanders expected that men's heartier bodies were

---

[39] Increase Mather, *Remarkable Providences Illustrative of the Earlier Days of American Colonisation* (Boston, 1684), 124–25.
[40] Boyer and Nissenbaum, eds., *Salem Witchcraft Papers*, I, 94, II, 562.
[41] *Ibid.*, I, 159.

more difficult and less tempting objects of the devil's attacks. The assumption that the devil had a different relationship with men was never explicitly articulated, but the incidents recounted at the trials can provide us with insights into Puritans' thinking about gender and the affliction of evil. First, witches were less likely to seduce men than women into the devil's service.[42] And when men told of their encounters with the accused witches, their testimony centered on bizarre acts of maleficence attributed to the accused, rather than on the physical harm caused by the witches' shape. Samuel Endicott charged Mary Bradbury with selling the captain of his ship butter that turned rancid after he and his crew were at sea for three weeks. Either the heedlessness of the sale, calculated fraud, or her magical ability to transform good butter into bad implicated her, and he did not doubt that she was a witch. As additional evidence, Endicott described a violent storm that cost the ship its mainmast, its rigging, and fifteen horses. The ship sprang a leak and took on four feet of water, and its crew was forced to unload the cargo. When they came upon land, Endicott saw "the appearance of a woman from her middle upwards, haveing a white Capp and white neck-cloth on her, w'ch then affrighted him very much."[43] Bradbury's shape frightened Endicott, and her misdeeds plagued him, but he was not subject to her direct, violent, physical abuse.

Often male victims' complaints against an accused witch centered on the harm inflicted on their personal property, rather than on the bodily pain they endured themselves. Samuel Abbey told the court that after the accused witch Sarah Good left his house, he began to lose cattle "after an unusuall Manner, in drupeing Condition." He lost seventeen cattle in two years, in addition to sheep and hogs, and he held the devil and Sarah Good responsible. John Roger testified that after an argument with Martha Carrier seven years earlier, two of his sows were lost and one of them was found dead near the Carriers' house with both of its ears cut off.[44]

Even more often men suffered through miseries visited on weaker members of their families, their wives and their children. Although William Beale testified that he awoke one morning because "A very greate & wracking paine had seized uppon my body," his primary evidence against the accused Philip English was that his son, who had been expected to recover from smallpox, died later that day, after Beale saw English's shape on the chimney. Samuel Perley complained that Elizabeth Howe stuck his ten-year-old daughter and his wife with pins. Astonished at the brutality to which they were subject, he claimed, "i could never aflict a dog as goode how aflicts mi

---

[42] Carol Karlsen noticed that 86% of possession cases in colonial New England involved women but did not explain why. See Karlsen, *Devil in the Shape of a Woman,* 135.
[43] Boyer and Nissenbaum, eds., *Salem Witchcraft Papers,* I, 122–23.
[44] *Ibid,* II, 368, I, 190.

wife." Perley's daughter "Pine d a wai [pined away] to skin and bone and ended her sorrowful life." The devil, in the shapes of the accused, tortured these two men, but not by destroying their own bodies.[45]

When men were direct victims of physical violence at the hands of the possessed, the scenes were far less dramatic. Samuel Smith, for example, heeded a threat from the accused witch Mary Easty, and as he walked past a stone wall on his way home, he "Received a little blow on my shoulder with I know not what and the stone wall rattleed very much which affrighted me."[46] That same threat might have caused a woman untold bodily fits and injuries.

On the rare occasions when male victims complained of severe physical abuse, it was always at the hands of another man, an accused male witch. Apparently, even with the aid of the devil, women were not physically capable of doing great harm to the bodies of men. When Beale told the court of the great pain that seized his body, he claimed that his attacker was the accused witch Philip English. Similarly, Benjamin Gould testified that Giles Cory, who was later pressed to death, induced "shuch a paine in one of my feet that I Cold not ware my shoe for 2: or 3.days." Eighty-one-year-old Bray Wilkins likewise was convinced that the accused witch John Willard had brought on a painful urinary tract obstruction. He told the court, "I continued so in greivous pain & my water much stopt till s'd Willard was in chains." However, after Willard pleaded innocence, Wilkins testified, he "was taken in the sorest distress & misery my water being turned into real blood, or of a bloody colour & the old pain returned excessively as before."[47]

Characteristically, Satan granted extraordinary power to his accomplices, either clairvoyance or great bodily strength.[48] In keeping with seventeenth-century notions of women's physical limitations, Satan bestowed unequal powers on men and women. He endowed his male witches with unusual strength and so made even other men vulnerable to the male witches' physical violence. Satan empowered women's bodies with only enough strength to torture their female victims successfully; often, ostensibly through their mere presence and without any particular bodily force, they produced fits of agony in those afflicted. Female witches seemed able to abuse only other women, while male witches could torture naturally weaker women as well as typically robust and potent men.

---

[45] *Ibid.*, I, 317–18, II, 439. A few men testified to bodily harm. Benjamin Abbott, for example, suffered a painful sore and was scheduled to have it lanced by a doctor, but it disappeared when the accused woman, Martha Carrier, was led away by the constable. See *ibid.*, I, 189.

[46] *Ibid.*, I, 301.

[47] *Ibid.*, I, 244, III, 848.

[48] On the powers that Satan bestowed, see D. P. Walker, *Unclean Spirits: Possession and Exorcism in France and England in the Late Sixteenth and Early Seventeenth Centuries* (Philadelphia, 1981), 9–17. See also Increase Mather, *Cases of Conscience Concerning Evil Spirits* (Boston, 1693); and Increase Mather, *Remarkable Providences.*

George Burroughs, a former minister at Salem and a condemned witch, epitomized the strength that Satan could contribute to male collaborators. During Burroughs's trial, all of the male eyewitnesses told the court that they had seen the accused exhibiting enormous force, much more than was characteristic of an ordinary man; his unusual strength could only have come with the devil's assistance, they believed. Thomas Greenslit, for example, say Burroughs "lift and hold Out a gunn of Six foot barrell or thereabouts putting the forefinger of his right hand into the Muzle of s'd gunn and So held it Out at Armes End Only with that finger." Simon Willard concurred with this report; he claimed that "s'd gun was about or near seven foot barrill: and very hevie: I then tryed to hold out s'd gun with both hands: but could not do it long enough to take sight." Four additional male witnesses saw Burroughs carry a barrel of molasses with only two fingers for some distance without putting it down.[49]

Interestingly, only the male witnesses offered Burroughs's unusual strength as evidence that he had colluded with Satan and had become a witch; his terrible strength, in sharp contrast to their own limited abilities, resonated with their notions of manliness and their expectations about how the devil might empower witches who were male. The women who testified against Burroughs were victims of physical violence, but their afflictions were similar to those that women victims typically received from women witches. The devil needed to provide extra strength to his male witches only when they afflicted other men.

Since Puritans believed that Satan designed his attacks according to his quarry, it made sense that the women and men victims whom the witches tried to lure into Satan's web perceived Satan's tortures differently. Just as female victims were more likely to be physically tormented, the women witches themselves—the majority of the accused—also experienced greater bodily distress than did men as Satan destroyed their bodies to capture their souls. Though men's bodies were hardly invulnerable, in women the devil sought easier marks.

Curiously, while a weak body and a vulnerable soul left one open to Satan, they might also encourage one's faith in God. Indeed, Cotton Mather and other ministers suggested that the frailty of women's bodies, compounded by the dangers of childbirth, gave women more reason to seek the Lord since death was more immediate. Anne Bradstreet, bemoaning an illness that had plagued her for months, hoped that her soul would gain some advantage while her body was faltering. Believing that God inflicted bodily illness only for the good of the soul, she mused, "I hope my soul shall flourish while my body decays, and the weakness of this outward man shall be a means to strengthen my inner man." Echoing Samuel Willard's biological reference to the soul, Bradstreet called her soul the "inner man" and tried to

[49] Boyer and Nissenbaum, eds., *Salem Witchcraft Papers,* I, 160–78, esp. 160–61.

dissociate its spiritual strength from her body's physical weaknesses. She cultivated resignation: "And if He knows that weakness and a frail body is the best to make me a vessel fit for His use why should I not bear it, not only willingly but joyfully." Bradstreet went so far as to suggest that good health might divert her from the Lord. She wrote, "The Lord knows I dare not desire that health that sometimes I have had, lest my heart should be drawn from Him, and set upon the world."[50]

Perhaps women's weaker bodies brought them closer to God, as Bradstreet hoped. Women, then, had a particular potential for goodness. But women's more fragile bodies also exposed them to Satan, perhaps encouraging a peculiar potential for evil—Eve's legacy. In the context of the witchcraft outbreaks, a time of extraordinary uncertainty and fear, New Englanders focused on the darker side of womanhood, emphasizing the vulnerability of women's bodies and souls to the devil, rather than their openness to regeneration. Women as witches were so threatening because their souls had made a conscious decision to ally with Satan. Too impatient or too weak to wait passively for Christ's advance, witches allowed their bodies and souls to choose, actively, the seductions of the devil. In the course of living their errand in the North American wilderness, Puritans thus constructed a gendered ideology and society that made women, ironically, closer both to God and to Satan.

---

[50] Cotton Mather's suggestion may help explain why more women than men became church members, especially late in the seventeenth century. See Cotton Mather, *Ornaments for the Daughters of Zion* (Boston, 1692); and Benjamin Colman, *The Honour and Happiness of the Vertuous Woman* (Boston, 1716). Bradstreet did not consistently refer to the body as male. In "The Flesh and the Spirit," she posited the body and the soul as feuding twin sisters. See Hensley, ed., *Works of Anne Bradstreet*, 255, 254, 216. On the colonists' attitude toward illness and prayer, see Hall, *Worlds of Wonder, Days of Judgment*, 198–210.

" 'Tender Plants':
Quaker Farmers and Children in the Delaware Valley, 1681–1735"

Barry J. Levy

INTRODUCTION

The social history of the Middle Colonies has lagged behind studies of New England and the Chesapeake, but Barry Levy has done much to narrow this gap. His study of Quaker families in southeastern Pennsylvania is all the more useful for the direct comparisons he makes with Philip Greven's Andover. Quaker parents accumulated far more land for their offspring than Puritans did, kept their children at home longer, treated them with greater affection, and granted them much fuller autonomy at marriage. As Levy shows, "holy conversation," or disciplined Quaker behavior, required a considerable base in material possessions to perpetuate itself from one generation to the next. Poor Quakers often could not meet these standards.

Can we explain these different patterns of behavior in material terms alone, or must we first understand the unique religious dynamic that distinguished Quakers from Puritans? Puritans saw their children as sinners who had to be converted or suffer inevitable damnation. Quakers regarded their offspring as innocents who had to be shielded from the corruptions of a hostile world.

- *How important were these underlying religious attitudes in shaping such apparently unrelated matters as landholding patterns?*
- *Why should parents who believed their children innocent acquire more land than parents who saw children as sinners?*
- *What is "modern" about Quaker families, and what is not?*

Barry Levy, " 'Tender Plants': Quaker Farmers and Children in the Delaware Valley, 1681–1735," in *Journal of Family History*, 3 (1978), 116–135. Copyright © 1978 by the National Council of Family Relations. Reprinted with permission.

"And whoso shall receive one such little child in my name, receiveth me. But whoso shall offend one of these little ones which believe in me, it were better for him that a millstone were hanged about his neck, and that he were drowned in the depth of the sea" (Matthew 18:5–6).

I

In the late seventeenth and early eighteenth centuries, the settlers of Chester and the Welsh Tract, bordering Philadelphia, devoted themselves to their children, and the results were economically impressive but socially ambiguous. The settlers were under the influence of a difficult religious doctrine, which can be called "holy conversation," institutionalized in their Monthly Meetings and practiced in their households. "Holy conversation" dictated that implicit instruction by loving parents, not coercion or stern discipline, would lead to the child's salvation. The farmers thus used the resources of the Delaware Valley to create environments for children and young adults, accumulating vast amounts of land, limiting the type of labor they brought into their households, and devising intricate, demanding strategies to hand out land and money to children. They directed intense attention to marriage and the conjugal household and spoke endlessly in their Meetings about "tenderness" and "love." These families, however, were religious, not affectionate, sentimental, or isolated. It was their religious conception of the child that both inspired and clearly limited the development of these adults and their society forming in the Delaware Valley.

The settlers were able, middling people from remote parts of Great Britain. The Welsh came from varying social backgrounds; they included eight gentlemen (the Welsh gentry was not wealthy as a rule) and twenty-five yeomen and husbandmen. The Chester settlers were mostly yeomen and artisans from Cheshire and surrounding counties in northwest England. Most settlers in both groups arrived in nuclear families having two or more children. Approximately seventy-five such Welsh Quaker and seventy-eight Cheshire Quaker families settled between 1681 and 1690 along the Schuylkill and Delaware Rivers near Philadelphia (Browning, 1912:1–29; Glenn, 1970:1–72).

The farmers clearly thought the spiritual fate of their children a vital reason for their coming to Pennsylvania. Each settler carried a removal certificate of about two hundred words describing his or her character. Much of the discussion in these documents concerned children and parenthood. One Welsh Meeting, for example, wrote of David Powell that "he hath hopeful children, several of them having behaved themselves well in Friends' services where they lived and we hope and desire the Lords presence may go along with them" [Friends Historical Library, Radnor Monthly Meeting Records (henceforth RMMR), 3/23/1690]. The only thing said of Griffith John, a poor farmer, was that "all his endeavor hath been to bring up his children in the fear of the Lord according to the order of Truth" (RMMR

4/22/1690). Sina Pugh was a "good, careful, industrious woman in things relating to her poor small children" (RMMR 2/5/1684). The Welsh Meetings acted *in loco parentis* for children left without parents and sent the orphans to Pennsylvania: the Tuddr orphans, for example, "were under the tuition of Friends since their parents deceased and we found them living and honest children; and we did what we could to keep them out of the wicked way and to preserve their small estate from waste and confiscation" (RMMR 2/3/1689). Meetings often referred to children as "tender," "sweet," and "loving," virtues which typified the descriptions of adult Friends with the most praised behavior. The metaphor most often used by the Welsh farmers when describing children was "tender plants growing in the Truth."

Two Welsh Tract leaders, John Bevan and Thomas Ellis, thought that the need to protect children from corruption explained the Quakers' emigration to Pennsylvania. Barbara Bevan persuaded her husband John Bevan to come to Pennsylvania for the sake of their children. "Some time before the year 1683," he later wrote, "I had heard that our esteemed Friend William Penn had a patent from King Charles the Second for the Province in America called Pennsylvania, and my wife had a great inclination to go thither and thought it might be a good place to train up children amongst sober people and to prevent the corruption of them here by the loose behavior of youthes and the bad example of too many of riper years." Bevan did not want to go, "but I was sensible her aim was an upright one, on account of our children, I was willing to weigh the matter in a true balance." He found that he could keep his three Welsh farms and still buy land in Pennsylvania (a member of the gentry in Treverig, near Cardiff, Bevan was the only settler not to sell his British property). Bevan returned to Wales in 1704 with his wife and favorite daughter because "we stayed there (Pennsylvania) many years, and had four of our children married with our consent, and they had several children, and the aim intended by my wife was in good measure answered" (Bevan, 1709). Bevan clearly saw Pennsylvania as a place best suited for rearing children.

In 1684 on arrival in Haverford, Thomas Ellis, a Welsh Quaker minister, prayed in a poem, "Song of Rejoicing," that "In our bounds, true love and peace from age to age may never cease" . . . when "trees and fields increase" and "heaven and earth proclaim thy peace" (Smith, 1862:492). Children were implicit in his vision. When on a return trip to England in 1685, after he noted that many English Quakers were suspicious of the large emigration of Friends to Pennsylvania, he wrote to George Fox stressing the relationship between children and wealth: "I wish those that have estates of their own and to leave fullness in their posterity may not be offended at the Lord's opening a door of mercy to thousands in England especially in Wales who have no estates either for themselves or children . . . nor any visible ground of hope for a better condition for children or children's children when they were gone hence." Ellis's argument rested on the promise of Quaker life in the new world. In Pennsylvania, Ellis showed, land could combine fruitfully with community life:

> About fifteen families of us have taken our land together and there are to be eight more that have not yet come, who took (to begin) 30 acres apiece with which we build upon and do improve, and the other land we have to range for our cattle, we have our burying place where we intend our Meeting House, as near as we can to the center, our men and women's Meeting and other Monthly Meetings in both week dayes unto which four townships at least belongs. And precious do we find other opportunities that are given as free will offering unto the Lord in evenings, some time which not intended but Friends coming simply to one another and setting together the Lord appears to his name be the Glory (Ellis, June 13, 1685).

With land broadly distributed for children to inherit, settlers like Ellis could hope to permanently realize their goals.

The attention and worry that the Welsh Meetings, John Bevan, and Thomas Ellis directed to children stemmed from the Quakers' world view which made child-rearing difficult and important. By dividing the human behavior into two "languages"—"holy conversation" leading to salvation, and "carnal talk" leading to corruption and death—Quakers had no choice but to secure environments of "holy conversation" for their children. Quakers thought that the Word was communicated only spontaneously in human relations, that all set forms of speech were ineffective. They thus challenged the Puritan view that God's reality was set forth solely in the Bible and that grace could only be received by listening and responding to ministers' explications of the Biblical text. In his *Journal* George Fox always called the Puritans "professors" in order to stigmatize them as people who only professed their faith in response to sermons they had heard. Quakers, on the other hand, lived their faith, they claimed, becoming virtually embodiments of the Word. Quakers found appropriate means of expressing the Word in their communities. In the worship meeting, after a period of silence, the Word was communicated through a "minister's" words, he or she being a conduit of the Word, or by spontaneous, nonverbal communication between attenders. In society the Word was to be communicated almost all the time by a man or woman's "conversation" (Haller, 1957; Hill, 1967; Nuttal, 1946; Kibbey, 1973; Bauman, 1974).

"Conversation" was defined in the seventeenth century, accounting to the *Oxford English Dictionary*, as the "manner of conducting oneself in the world or in society." The Quakers' concept of "conversation" included the idea that it was reflective of a person's inner being and that it communicated meaning, as suggested in the King James and Geneva Bibles ["Only let your conversation be as becometh Gospel" (Phil. 1:27), "Be an example of believers in conversation in purity" (1 Tim. 4:12), "they may also be won by the conversation of their wives" (1 Pet. 3:1)]. "Conversation" thus included not only speech but also behavior and non-verbal communication. Human communication, as Dell Hymes has argued, includes not just written and spoken words, but all "speech events," events that a culture regards as having a clear human message (Hymes, 1972; Hymes, 1974). Quakers posited in effect "languages"* underlying all formal languages and gesture: "holy conversation," the language of the Word, and "carnal conversation," the language of pride and of the world.

The emigrants' removal certificates into Pennsylvania described the settlers' "conversation" and give some idea of the qualities that made up the charismatic presence of the converted Friend. Thirty-six different adjectives or adjectival phrases described the adults in these sixty-two certificates. The adjectives most often used were "honest" (thirty-three), "blameless" (fourteen), "loving, (thirteen), "tender" (nine), "savory" (nine), "serviceable" (nine), "civil" (eight), "plain" (seven), and "modest" (five). Except for three cases—two cases of "industriousness," and one case of "punctual"—the adjectives related to Christlike qualities.

Almost all the adjectives had Biblical origins. "Holy conversation" was the language and behavior of both the Apostles and of the Quakers, who both claimed direct knowledge of Christ. All Quaker testimonies and practices were defended by Biblical reference. Fox, Barclay, Pennington, Naylor, and other Quaker ministers had interlarded their texts with Biblical quotation. Friends used "thee and thou" instead of "you" because it was the pronoun which Quaker ministers thought Christ and the Apostles used. As was the case in the Genevan Bible, Quakers avoided the use of pagan names for months and days, and refused to use titles, even Mr. and Mrs. Refusal to give that honor, refusal to take oaths, pacifism, non-violence, and special dress were all vocabulary in "holy conversation." The Bible (as well as the leadership of the Monthly, Quarterly and Yearly Meetings), though not the source of Truth for Friends, provided an anchor against what easily could become the anarchy of revelation (Levy, 1976:35–45).

The removal certificates discussed the relationship between "holy conversation" and children's spiritual development. Children were born with both Adam's sin and Christ's redeeming Seed. Which developed as the major principle in their lives depended greatly on the environment in which they grew, and particularly important was the character of their parents (Frost, 1973). The Merionth Meeting said of William Powell, for example:

> His conversation since [his conversion] hath been honest and savory in so much that his wife came soon to be affected with the Truth, and became a good example to her children by which means they also became affected with Truth, innocency, and an innocent conversation to this day (RMMR, 1686).

---

* "Language" is used here metaphorically to represent a whole communicative system. The Quakers, particularly George Fox, were hostile to "language" in its usual sense.

The Tyddyn Gareg Meeting said of the children of Griffith John: "As for their honesty and civility and good behavior we have not anything to say to the contrary but they behaved themselves very well as they came from a very honest family" (RMMR, 1686). Virtually all the children were discussed in these terms. Bachelors and spinsters, moreover, were also "hopeful" when like Elizabeth Owen, they came from "good and honest parentage" (RMMR, 1686). No belief developed in these Meetings similar to the idea which Edmund Morgan has shown developed among Massachusetts' ministers in the late seventeenth century who believed that the children of church members, being part of Abraham's Seed, were virtually assured justification (Morgan, 1966:161–186). Quaker members were known only by their "conversation" and children were only "hopeful" because of their parents' conversation.

By 1680 the guiding institution of Quaker life was the Monthly Meeting, whose purpose was, as George Fox said, "that all order their conversation aright, that they may see the salvation of God; they may all see and know, possess and partake of, the government of christ, of the increase of which there is no end" (Fox, 1963:152). The men's and women's Monthly Meetings in Chester and the Welsh Tract, like those elsewhere, encouraged "holy conversation" by identifying and disowning carnal talk and by organizing life for the rule of the Word. Their aim was, in a sense, to construct an ideal speech community, where the Word would constantly be exchanged in human relations. Newcomers would not be recognized as members unless they presented a removal certificate, an informed discussion of their spiritual personality, vouching for the high quality of their "conversation." The term is centrally mentioned in ninety-five percent of all the Welsh certificates from 1680 to 1694 (65) and eighty-seven percent of those fully recorded for Quakers within the jurisdiction of the Chester and the Welsh Tract they had their "clearness and conversation" inspected, and when disowned, they were denounced for "scandalous," "disorderly," "indecent," or "worldly" "conversation."

The primary support of the Quakers' social design was their elaborate marriage discipline, which controlled the establishment of new households. Most of the business that came before the Welsh Tract and Chester Men's and Women's Meetings directly concerned marriage. In the Welsh Tract, in the Men's Monthly Meeting (1683–1709) forty-six percent of the business dealt with marriages; the next largest category of business, administrative concerns, like building burial grounds and arranging worship meetings, included only seventeen percent of the itemized business. In the Women's Monthly Meeting marriages took fifty-four percent of the business and charity nineteen percent. In Chester the Men's and Women's Meeting sat together until 1705. Between 1681 and 1705, forty-three percent of the business concerned marriages; the next largest category, discipline, accounted for fourteen percent of the business. These figures do not account for the fact that marriage infractions composed the majority of discipline cases. In the

Welsh Tract between 1684 and 1725, eighty-two percent of all condemnations involved young men and women and seventy-eight percent marriage or fornication (fornication without marriage was rare, involving only four percent of the cases). Jack Marietta found similar figures for a number of other Pennsylvania Monthly Meetings, and Susan Forbes found that over seventy-five percent of the disownments in another Chester County meeting, New Garden, related to marriage (Marietta, 1968; Forbes, 1972; Radnor Men's and Women's Monthly Meeting Minutes, 1684–1725; Chester Men's and Women's Monthly Meetings Minutes, 1681–1725).

The Quaker marriage procedure was time-consuming, thorough, and intrusive. A prospective marriage couple had first to obtain permission for both courtship and then marriage from all the parents or close relatives involved. They then had to announce their intention of marriage before both the Men's and Women's Monthly Meetings. After hearing the announcement, the Meetings appointed two committees, each composed of two well established Friends, in order to investigate the "clearness" from prior ties and particularly the "conversation" of the man and woman (two women investigated the woman, two men the man). The man and woman would appear at the next Monthly Meeting to hear the verdict, which was usually favorable, since the Meetings warned off Friends with problems. After the second visit to the Monthly Meetings the marriage ceremony took place usually in the Meeting house of the woman's family. The Quakers married directly before God, the guests and attendants served as witnesses, signing the marriage certificate. The precedent for this type of ceremony was, according to George Fox, the marriage of Adam and Eve in the Garden. The couple had thus to be restored to the sinless state of Adam and Eve before the Fall in order for the ceremony to be meaningful (Fox, 1663; Fox, 1911:II, 154; Braithwaite, 1919:262). Not all Pennsylvania Friends conformed to Fox's spiritually pure concept of marriage. Both Meetings allowed a few questionable men and women to marry "out of tenderness to them" if they sincerely promised to reform and live as Friends. Two officials from the Monthly Meeting closely watched the ceremony to assure that it was conducted according to "Gospel Order." A committee of "weighty" Friends also visited the new couple (along with other families in these communities) at least four times a year in order to see that they were living according to the standards of "holy conversation." The Quaker marriage discipline and ritual aimed to insure that every Quaker spouse was sustained by another Quaker and that every Quaker child grew up under converted parents in a sustaining, religious environment.

In order to enhance the religious tone of the family, despite the control exercised by parents and Meetings, Friends wanted couples to love one another before they wed. Quaker writers stressed that this was to be a virtuous, Christian love, not romantic lust. It is of course impossible to know what quality of love these Friends expected, demanded, or actually received. Nevertheless, the idea was taken seriously; the Monthly Meetings record a number of Friends, mostly women, rejecting their male Friends at the last minute before the ceremony. After laboriously inspecting and approving one marriage in 1728, for example, the men of Chester were surprised to discover that the marriage had not taken place. The investigating committee reported "that the said Jane Kendal signified to them that she doth not love him well enough to marry him." Similarly in 1705 at Chester, Thomas Martin gained approval to marry Jane Hent, but next month "the above marriage not being accomplished, two Friends—Alice Simcock and Rebecca Faucit—spoke to Jane Hent to know the reason thereof and her answer was that she could not love him well enough to be her husband." Two other cases of this type occurred in Chester and the Welsh Tract between 1681 and 1750. The annoyed Meetings always deferred to the young people (Friends Historical Library, Chester Men's Monthly Meeting Minutes, 10/30/1728, 5/30/1705, 9/6/1705, 4/9/1730, 4/10/1708).

The marriage discipline, despite such responsiveness, was an obstacle to many Quaker children. Many went to a "priest" or magistrate in Philadelphia to marry. Sometimes they had married a non-Quaker but more often Quaker children would avoid the marriage procedure and their parents' approval by eloping to Philadelphia, often after sexual intimacy. Over one half of the offenders were disowned. The rest "acknowledged" their sin and after a period of spiritual probation were accepted fully as Friends.

Institutional surveillance could only go so far; Quaker families also needed wealth to assure that their children would live their lives among people of "holy conversation." In England and Wales farms were typically from forty to forty-five acres; farmers could rarely keep their children from service or from leaving for the city, particularly London (Hoskins, 1963:151–160; Campbell, 1942:chap. 3,4). For this reason William Penn wanted Pennsylvania settlers to form townships, "for the more convenient bringing up of youth . . . ," of 5000 acres with each farmer having ample, contiguous holdings of from one hundred to five hundred acres. The Quaker proprietor believed that farming was the least corrupting employment and that in England parents were too "addicted to put their children into Gentlemen's service or send them to towns to learn trades, that husbandry is neglected; and after a soft and delicate usage there, they are unfitted for the labor of farming life" (Penn, 1681, Lemon, 1972:98–99). An analysis of removal certificates and tax lists from Chester and Radnor indeed shows that youth did leave and work at home.

The Welsh Tract and Chester settlers accumulated more land than William Penn proposed. By the late 1690s the mean holding of the seventy resident families in the Welsh Tract was 332 acres. In the towns comprising the Chester Monthly Meeting, the mean holding of seventy-six families was 337 acres. Only six men had holdings of under one hundred acres, and eighty percent held over 150 acres. The Chester and Welsh settlers continued

TABLE 1   Welsh Tract and Chester
Settlers' Land Held at Death or
Distributed to Their Children
before Death, 1681–1735

Acres	Percentages of Settlers (n)	
50–199	9%	(5)
200–399	19	(10)
400–599	21	(11)
600–799	21	(11)
800–999	15	(8)
1000+	15	(8)
	100%	(53)

Source: Philadelphia City Hall, Philadelphia County Deeds,
Philadelphia County Wills and Inventories; Chester County
Court House, Chester County Deeds, Chester County Wills
and Inventories.

to buy land after 1699 as appears from a comparison of the landholdings of
fifty-three Chester and Welsh Quaker settlers in 1699 and the land which
they described to their children or sold at death. In the 1690s these men had
an average of 386 acres, about the same average as the general population of
landowners. They gave or sold to their children, however, an average of 701
acres, an average increase of 315 acres from 1690. Seventy percent of the settlers gave 400 acres or more (see Table 1) (Land Bureau, Harrisburg, Land
Commissioner's Minutes of the Welsh Tract, 1702; Chester County Historical
Society, Chester County Treasurer's Book, 1685–1716). The settlers bought
land as their families grew. A correlation exists between the number of sons
families had and the amount of land they held. Between the 1690s and the
end of their lives, the three men without sons did not increase their acreage;
those with one son increased their acreage an average of 135 acres; those
with two sons increased their acreage an average of 242 acres; those with
three an average of 309 acres; and those with four or more an average of 361
acres. Sons received over two hundred acres on an average, and daughters
received the equivalent in Pennsylvania currency.
     The settlers bought land almost exclusively for their children. The fifty-
three men gave away or sold a total of 160 parcels during their lives, a third
of these to their children. Six men engaged in forty-six percent of the sales,
however. These men were land speculators, though this role combined with
serving as middle men between William Penn and arriving colonists. They
were active members of their Monthly Meetings, acquaintances of William
Penn, and first purchasers. Most settlers did not engage in land speculation.
Thirty-nine of the forty-one wills existing for the fifty-three settlers show
large quantities of unused land which was later bequeathed to children.
Joseph Baker, for example, besides his plantation in Edgemount, bequeathed
a 200 acre tract in Thornberry to his son. Francis Yarnell, beside his planta-

tion in Willistown, bequeathed a 120 acre tract in Springfield. Only three men worked their additional land and only two men had tenants (Chester County Court House, Chester County Deeds, 1681–1790; Philadelphia City Hall, Philadelphia County Deeds, 1681–1790; Chester County Court House, Chester County Wills, August 25, 1724: A-155, 6/6/1721:A-124).

A study of these families' inventories confirms the child-centered use of land. Of the forty-one inventories, twenty-seven of these men at the time of their death already portioned at least two of their children. Seven of these men were nearly retired, though they still used their farms. The rest (fourteen) had portioned only one child or none at the time of their death, so they were probably near the height of productivity. The average farmer had a small herd of animals (six cows, four steers, six horses, fourteen sheep, and eight pigs) and was cultivating between forty and fifty acres for wheat, barley, and corn. The rule of thumb in eighteenth-century farming was three acres for one cow (this was the practice in Cheshire), so the cows and steers would require at least thirty acres. The six horses would need about six acres and grain, and the thirteen sheep about two acres a year. This gives a figure of, at least, eighty acres in use for the average farmer who had about 700 acres. The additional 620 acres awaited children (Chester County Court House, Chester County Inventories, 1681–1790; Philadelphia City Hall Annex, Philadelphia County Inventories, 1681–1776).

The land use pattern of Edmund Cartledge was typical, although he used more land than most. He had a personal estate of £377, including £63 worth of crops, mostly wheat, and £90 worth of livestock. In the "house chamber" and "in the barn" Cartledge had about 115 bushels of wheat, which was the harvest of about ten to fifteen acres. "In the field" he had twenty acres of wheat and rye (worth about £30) and ten acres of summer corn, barley, and oats (£18). He had in all at least forty to fifty acres under cultivation. "In the yard" were a large number of cows, pigs, and horses and in the field a flock of sheep. According to the usual feed requirements, he used from fifty to fifty-five acres for these animals. For both livestock and crops, he used about one hundred acres. His inventory describes his farm as "250 acres of land, buildings, orchards, garden, fences, wood, and meadows," evaluated at £400. From 1690 to 1710 ten inventories show the evaluation of improved land was £2:3:6 per acre and unimproved land was at £0:6:7 per acre. A comparison of his evaluation with the general evaluations of improved and unimproved lands tends to confirm that he used about one-half to two-thirds of his plantation. At his death, he also had 100 acres in Springfield and 1,107 acres in Plymouth at a low evaluation of £300, indicating that they were unimproved. Like the other Quaker farmers, Cartledge bought land to farm and more land to settle his children upon (Chester County Court House, Chester County Inventories, 2/2/1703:143).

Although individual farmers and planters in early America had more land than the average Quaker in the Delaware Valley, few seventeenth- or eighteenth-century communities appear collectively to have had such a high mean acreage, such a broad distribution of land, or a land distribution so generously devoted to children. James Henretta has argued that northern farmers accumulated land to pay off their sons' and daughters' labor and to secure their aid when old (Henretta, 1978:3–32). These Quaker accumulations roughly fit such an economic model, though they exceed the average needs of a young farmer. An average young man might need forty to one hundred acres of land to begin a family, not two or three hundred acres. Most fathers, moreover, did not need their sons' economic assistance in old age. A large percentage of sons bought their land from their fathers, who retired on interest from bonds.* To a large degree, the Quaker farmers were responding to the requirements, as they perceived them, of "holy conversation." Three hundred acres could seem to insure a new household's protection from the world.

II

In order to buy land Quaker farmers often needed to take "strangers" into their household as laborers. However, laborers brought into the household who fostered ungodly relationships could ruin the whole purpose of insulating the family from evil influences. These rural Quakers had few slaves or servants. Of the forty-one men who left inventories, among those families that were reconstructed, only nine recorded servants or slaves (twenty-five percent) and four had slaves (five percent) or about one in every twenty families. The fertile but inexpensive land of the Valley allowed rural Friends—unlike those in the city—to keep the use of servants to a minimum. At the same time, the wealth derived from the Valley allowed many Friends to afford slaves. The restriction of slavery was therefore partly the response to an explicitly expressed self-conscious policy.

Chester County Friends clearly remained sensitive to evidence of carnal talk or exotic people in their households. Robert Pyle, a prosperous Concord farmer writing in 1698, testified that he bought a slave because of the scarcity of white domestic labor. Pyle, however, felt the threat of contamination and had bad dreams:

> I was myself and a Friend going on a road, and by the roadside I saw a black pot, I took it up, the Friend said give me part, I said not, I went a little further and I saw a great ladder standing exact upright, reaching up to heaven, up which I must go to heaven with the pot in my hand intending to carry

---

* The economy of these farmers was relatively sophisticated. Over fifty percent of the farmers, according to their inventories, held bonds of over £100. The money was lent to other farmers. Older men had the most bonds and were clearly living on the income (Levy, 1976:145–150).

the black pot with me, but the ladder standing so upright, and seeing no man holding of it up, it seemed it would fall upon me; at which I stepped down, laid the pot at the foot of the ladder, and said them that take it might, for I found work enough for both hands to take hold of this ladder (Cadbury, ed., 1937:492–493).

Pyle concluded that "self must be left behind, and to let black Negroes or pots alone." To purify his household and himself, Pyle manumitted his black slave. Cadwallader Morgan of the Welsh Tract bought a Negro in 1698 so he could have more time to go to Meetings. But Morgan realized that greed was his real aim, that the slave symbolized the rule of the self over the Word. Pyle and Morgan also worried over the social and familial problems attending slavery. Pyle projected that Quakers might be forced to take up arms, if Negroes became too numerous in their communities. Morgan saw a host of problems for quaker families. "What," Morgan asked, "if I should have a bad one of them that must be corrected, or would run away, or when I went from home and leave him with a woman or maid, and he should desire to commit wickedness." Fearing many varieties of corruption, Morgan manumitted his slave and testified against slavery (Cadbury, ed., 1942:213; Drake, 1941:575–576).

Such fears were widespread. The Chester Quarterly and Monthly Meetings issued five letters or messages to the Philadelphia Yearly Meeting between 1690 and 1720, requesting a testimony against buying or importing slaves. The Chester Monthly Meeting in 1715 recorded that "it is the unanimous sense of this Meeting that Friends should not be concerned hereafter in the importation thereof nor buy any, and we request the concurrence of the Quarterly Meeting." The Philadelphia Quarterly Meeting in the same year chided Chester Friends for acting prejudicially against slave owners in their Meeting by excluding them from positions of authority (Turner, 1911:60–75; Davis, 1966:315).

Holy conversation and child-centeredness also brought these Friends using white, indentured servants problems. Friendly "conversation" conflicted with the need of keeping servants diligently at work. The Chester Meeting called John Worral before them in 1693 for whipping one of his male servants. He condemned his act "for the reputation of Truth" but said the fellow was "worthless" and "deserved to be beaten" (Historical Society of Pennsylvania, Chester Monthly Meeting Acknowledgments, 10/2/1693). By placing a lazy woman servant in a "noxious hole," Thomas Smedley thought he had found the alternative to whipping and beating, but the Chester Monthly Meeting thought his solution unseemly, and he had to condemn it (Historical Society of Pennsylvania, Chester Monthly Meeting Acknowledgments, 1/3/1740). In 1700 the Welsh Tract Monthly Meeting established a "committee to maintain good order," which recommended "that Friends be watchful over their families and that they should be careful what persons they brought or admitted to their families, whether servants or others, lest they should be hurt by them." The committee devised techniques for disciplining servants without flogging them. When their terms expired, masters were to write "certificates . . . concerning their behavior according to their deserts." No credit or jobs were to be extended to ex-servants unless they had such references. The Meeting established a public committee to "deal hard with servants" and to hear their complaints about their masters. No evidence exists as to what techniques the committee used to handle unruly servants, but they were probably non-violent. Because of their ideas about purified households, these rural Friends discouraged bringing blacks into the house and invented gentler ways of disciplining labor.

III

Controlling their children as they passed from youth to adulthood presented the final challenge for Chester and Welsh Tract parents. Quaker doctrine demanded that children be guided, not coerced into Quakerism. The choice to preserve the Light had to be a free one. There was very little evidence of disinheritance among Chester and Welsh Tract families.* The choosing of a mate involved parental approval and direction, but also courtship and free choice. The Meetings asked couples when announcing their proposed marriage to face both the Men's and Women's Meeting alone. A youth, as it has been seen, could call off his or her marriage at any time before the ceremony. Parents, however, still had to make new households Quakerly and substantial. For Quaker parents "holy conversation" meant establishing all their children on decently wealthy farms, married to Friends of their own choosing, with parental approval—a difficult job.

In Andover, Massachusetts in the seventeenth and early eighteenth centuries, parents had more implements to accomplish a similar task. Puritan parents shared responsibility with the local minister for their children's conversions, they had baptism, an intellectual regimen (sermons and Bible reading) and by the 1690s a general belief that the children of church members were likely to be justified (Morgan, 1966:65–86; Axtell, 1976:160–200). They also had power. Quaker parents had environments, wealth, and their own example. As Philip Greven has shown, during the seventeenth and early eighteenth century in Andover, Massachusetts, it was common for parents to allow sons to marry, live on their fathers' land and yet not own the land until their fathers died. According to Greven's description, "although the great majority of second generation sons were settled upon their father's land while their fathers were still alive, only about a quarter of them actually owned the land they lived upon until after their father's death." The proximity of the fa-

* A collation of wills and deeds of families whose children married out shows that there was seldom any economic penalty. Male children who married out were often not deeded land. They got land when their father died (Levy, 1976:121–123).

ther to the households of his married sons reinforced this pattern of economic dependency and patriarchy. Seventy-five percent of the sons of the first generation settled in the closely packed township of Andover. Well into the middle of the eighteenth century, "many members of families lived within reasonably short distances of each other," as Greven describes it, "with family groups often concentrated together in particular areas of the town." This strong system of parental power, as Greven argued, changed only slowly during the eighteenth century in the town (Greven, 1970:72–99, 139).

Delaware Valley families were similar in structure to those in Andover. Because Quaker birth and death records were poorly kept, it is possible only to estimate what health conditions were like in the seventeenth century along the Schuylkill and Delaware Rivers. Twenty-five Quaker settlers, traced through the Quaker registers in England and America, had an average age at death of sixty-seven years, with only four men dying in their forties, and four in their fifties. The survival rate of children also supports the view that conditions were fairly healthy. Based on a total of seventy-two reconstructed families in the first generation, the average number of children per family to reach twenty-one years of age was 4.73 in the Welsh Tract and 5.65 in Chester. In the Welsh Tract and Chester, based on ninety-three reconstructions of second generation families, the average number of children to reach twenty-one was 5.53. These families were smaller than those of 7.2 children to reach twenty-one which Greven found for early eighteenth-century Andover families whose children were born in the 1680s and 1690s (Greven, 1970:111).

Compared to the Andover settlers and descendants, the Delaware Valley settlers consistently had more land (see Table 2). Andover, moreover, began

TABLE 2 Land Distribution of Chester, Welsh Tract, and Andover Settlers

Acres	Welsh Tract and Chester First Generation Percent Settlers (N)		Andover First Generation Percent Settlers (N)	
0–99	0%	(0)	0%	(0)
100–199	10	(5)	67	(27)
200–299	15	(8)	18	(7)
300–399	2	(1)	8	(3)
400–499	6	(3)	2.5	(1)
500–599	15	(8)	2.5	(1)
600–699	10	(5)	0	(0)
700+	42	(22)	2.5	(1)
	100%	(52)	100.5%	(40)

Source: Philadelphia City Hall, Philadelphia County Deeds, Philadelphia County Wills and Inventories; Chester County Court House, Chester County Deeds, Chester County Wills and Inventories. Greven, 1970:58.

in a remote wilderness where it took many years to develop a cash economy. Throughout much of the lives of the founding generation, as Greven noted, both grain and livestock were being used in lieu of cash in exchange for hard goods from Salem merchants. A lack of specie, cash, or credit is suggested by the fact that sons did not regularly purchase land from their fathers until after 1720, eighty years after settlement. The fertile land of the Delaware Valley was more conducive to lucrative farming than the rocky soil of Andover. The settlers enjoyed the fast growing market in Philadelphia under the control of able Quaker merchants with connections in the West Indies. One thousand Finnish and Swedish farmers, who had been living modestly along the Delaware River for over fifty years, helped provide the settling Quakers with provisions. Cash and credit existed in Pennsylvania, as attested by the frequent and early purchasing of estates by sons. As early as 1707, twenty-six years after settlement, Ralph Lewis sold over one hundred acres to his son Abraham for £60, and after 1709 deeds of purchase were more frequently given than deeds of gift (Bridenbaugh, 1976:170; Chester County Court House, Chester County Deeds, April 15, 1707:B-86; Greven, 1970:68).

Begging the question of the typicality of Andover as a New England town, it is clear that the road to an independent household (independent from kin, not from community) was smoother in the Welsh Tract and Chester communities than it was in Andover. The economy of the Delaware Valley was more conducive to the setting up of independent households than that of Andover. Quaker families were also smaller. The older marriage ages of the Quakers strongly suggests, however, that religious community also played some role in creating a different pattern in Pennsylvania. The settlers in the Welsh Tract and Chester carefully helped establish their childrens' new households by providing sufficient material wealth, even if it meant making children wait a long time before marriage. The community closely watched new households. Yet, in contrast to Andover, Quaker parents tended to make their children financially independent at marriage or soon after marriage. They also set up their sons further from home.

Fifty-four of the settlers' sons received deeds in Chester and the Welsh Tract; and seventy-three percent (40) received them either before marriage or in one year after marriage. Fifty-nine of the eighty-four sons who received land from wills also received their land before marriage. Among all the second generation sons in the Delaware Valley whose inheritance, deeds of gift and purchase, and date of marriage can be known (139), seventy-one percent received land before, at, or within two years of marriage without restrictions. In Andover when a father gave a deed to a son he usually placed restrictions upon the gift. Most sons shared the experience of Stephen Barker, who received a deed of gift from his father for a homestead and land, provided "that he carefully and faithfully manure and carry on my whole living yearly." His father also retained the right to any part of his son's land "for my comfortable maintenance." Thomas Abbot of Andover sold his homestead, land, and buildings to the eldest of his three sons in 1723 for £20, but reserved for himself the right to improve half the land and to use half the buildings during his lifetime (Greven, 1970:144, 145). Only one Welsh Tract or Chester deed from the first to second generations contained a restrictive clause, and no Quaker deeds from the second to third generations contained such clauses. Once established, three quarters of the new households in the Welsh Tract and Chester were independent.*

Typical of the Quaker father was Thomas Minshall, whose son Isaac married Rebecca Owen in 1707. That same year, three months after the marriage, Thomas Minshall "for natural love and affection" gave Isaac gratis the "380 acres in Neither Providence where he now dwelleth." A younger son, Jacob, married at the age of twenty-one in 1706 to Sarah Owen and that year received gratis five hundred acres of land and a stone dwelling house. The Minshalls were among the wealthiest families in Chester and Radnor Meetings. Poorer families also granted independence to their married children. Ralph Lewis, who came over as a servant to John Bevan, gave deeds to three of his sons before or just after marriage. In 1707 he sold to his son Abraham at marriage a 200 acre tract for £60. Samuel Lewis, another son, bought 250 acres from his father for £60 in 1709. A deed three years later, shows that his debt to his father was paid off in 1712, the year he married (Philadelphia City Hall, Philadelphia County Deeds, 2/3/1706:A-203, 8/23/1707:A-172; Chester County Court House, Chester County Deeds, October 6, 1709:B-342, 3/2/1712:C-326).

In contrast to the situation in Andover, moreover, most second generation Delaware Valley sons did not live in the same townships as their fathers. Forty-five percent of the sons (71) of the first generation Welsh Tract and Chester families settled in the same township as their fathers, but a majority fifty-five percent (88) did not. Most sons (65) lived in other townships because their fathers bought land for them there. Francis Yarnell of Willistown, for example, found land for five of his sons in Willistown (his own town) and one in Springfield and one in Middletown. Andrew Job bought two of his sons land in Virginia. Indeed eleven of the second generation Delaware Valley sons moved outside southeastern Pennsylvania to Maryland, Virginia, North Carolina, and Long Island onto land purchased by their fathers. John Bevan who moved to Wales never saw his American sons again. Quaker fathers often sacrificed control for "holy conversation" and land.

The tendency of fathers to give away land to their sons and money to their daughters, when they married, left many of these fathers bereft of power. Quaker fathers took to giving exhortations, some of which have survived. Edward Foulke, the richest Quaker farmer in Gwynedd, left an exhortation to his children written just before his death in 1741. He gave all four of his sons

---

* John Waters found differences between inheritance patterns of Quakers and Puritans in seventeenth-century Barnstable similar to the differing patterns between Andover and Delaware Valley families (Waters, 1976).

land near the time of their marriages. Evan Foulke, for example, received 250 acres in Gwynedd at his marriage in 1725 (Philadelphia City Hall, Philadelphia County Deeds, December 15, 1725:I-14-248). But Foulke worried. He urged his children and grandchildren not to let business take priority over attending week-day Meetings. He noted that business carried out at such a time "did not answer my expectation of it in the morning." He worried also about his child-rearing practices: "It had been better for me, if I had been more careful, in sitting with my family at meals with a sober countenance because children, and servants have their eyes and observations on those who have command and government over them." This, he wrote, "has a great influence on the life and manners of youth" (Historical Society of Pennsylvania, Cope Collection, 1740:F-190). Another exhortation was left by Walter Faucit of Chester in 1704 who was nervous about his wealthy grown son's spiritual and economic future, "If thou refuse to be obedient to God's teachings and do thy own will and not His than thou will be a fool and a vagabound" (Historical Society of Pennsylvania, Cope Collection, 1704:F-23). Greven found no exhortations in Andover and most likely they did not exist. Seventeenth- and early eighteenth-century rural Puritan fathers left land, not advice, to obedient, married sons.

The mutual obligations in the Quaker family system show that the Welsh Tract and Chester families were nonetheless both well organized and demanding. The case of a family of comfortable means gives an idea of how independent households in the Delaware Valley were created. In the family of Philip Yarnell, almost all the sons received land for a price, and the time between marriage and receiving a deed was a time for sons to work the land in order to pay off their father. The purchase price would be returned to the family kitty in order to help portion the other children. Among the Yarnells' nine children, six sons and three daughters, their eldest son married at the age of twenty-six in 1719 and completed purchase of the land in 1725, when he received 200 acres and a farm house for £60 Pennsylvania currency from his father. Their second son also married in 1719 and bought his land from his father in 1724, a year earlier than his brother. He received a similar amount of land and also paid £60. The purchase price was about half the actual market value of the land. Yarnell's fifth son, Nathan, married in 1731 at the age of twenty-four and three years later received his land free in Philip Yarnell's will. Yarnell's third, unmarried son, Job, had a different role. In Philip's will he received "all my land in Ridley township," but had to pay £80 to daughter Mary Yarnell, half at eighteen and half at the age of twenty. Mary was then only ten years old, so Job had eight years to raise the first payment. He never married. Though the Yarnells were one of the wealthiest families in the Chester Meeting, they managed a vulnerable economic unit. Their children tended to mary by inclination, not in rank order. When a son or daughter married, his or her work and the land given was lost to the other children. Like most Quaker families, the Yarnells made the family into a revolving fund; new households became independent relatively soon after marriage, and with the returned money the other children became attractive marriage partners, and the parents bought bonds for their retirement (Chester County Court House, the Chester County Deeds, December 8, 1724: f-43, February 27, 1725:E-513; Chester County Court House, Chester County Wills, 6/14/1733:A-414).*

This demanding family system explains why the settlers' children married relatively late in life, despite the settlers' large landholdings. Although the Quaker families had fewer children and over twice the farm land, their children married later than the Andover settlers' children and also later than the third generation in Andover, who matured between 1705 and 1735, coeval to the second generation in Chester and the Welsh Tract. The marriage ages of quaker men were older than those of men in Andover in both the second and third generations, and the marriage ages of Quaker women were older than those of Andover women in the second generation, though slightly lower than Andover women in the third generation (see Table 3). While bachelors and spinsters were rare in New England towns, at least 14.4 percent of the Chester and Welsh Tract youth did not marry (see Table 4).

TABLE 3 Age at Marriage: Delaware Valley Quakers and Andover

Age at Marriage	Quakers (Chester, Welsh Tract) N	Percent	Andover (Second Generation) N	Percent	Andover (Third Generation) N	Percent
Men						
Under 21	5	5	5	5	6	3
21–24	35	32	36	35	72	32
25–29	30	27	39	38	87	39
30–34	26	23	17	16	39	17
35–39	9	8	4	4	12	5
40 and over	6	5	3	3	8	4
	111	100	104	101	224	100
29 and under	70	63	80	77	165	74
30 and over	41	37	24	23	59	26
Women						
Under 21	7	37	29	36	58	28
21–24	22	30	32	40	74	35
25–29	15	20	14	17	48	23
30–34	5	7	3	4	12	6
35–39	2	3	2	3	10	5
40 and over	3	4	1	1	8	4
	54	101	81	101	210	101
24 and under	49	66	61	75	132	63
25 and over	25	34	20	25	78	37

Source: Friends Historical Library, Radnor Monthly Meeting Records, Chester Monthly Meeting Records; Greven, 1970:31–37, 119, 121.

* The "revolving fund" method was used by all but the wealthiest and poorest Quaker families. For other examples see (Levy, 1976: 210–214).

TABLE 4 Wealth, Marriage and Discipline

Average Rate in Pounds	Number of Families	Number of Children	Number Married Out	Number and (Percent) Disowned	Number Single	Mean Marriage Age—Men	Mean Marriage Age—Women
90–100	19	101	3	1 (1%)	15	23	23
70–89	12	76	5	2 (3%)	5	27	24
50–69	11	45	3	2 (4%)	5	27	23
40–49	12	58	15	12 (20%)	9	26	23
30–39	18	81	21	17 (20%)	18	30	28
	72	361	47	34	52		

Source: Friends Historical Library, Radnor Men's and Women's Monthly Meeting Minutes, 1681–1745, Chester Men's and Women's Monthly Meeting Minutes, 1681–1745; Historical Society of Pennsylvania, Chester County Tax Lists, 1715–1765.

TABLE 5 Marriage Portions and Discipline

	Women		
Pounds (Pennsylvania)	Married In	Spinster	Married Out
80–150	10	1	0
40–79	9	1	1
20–39	30	0	1
0–19	7	9	12

	Men		
Land		Bachelor	
300 acres+	17	3	1
200 acres+	40	0	3
100 acres+	4	3	13

Source: Philadelphia City Hall, Philadelphia County Wills, 1681–1776, Philadelphia County Deeds, 1681–1776; Chester County Court House, Chester County Wills, 1681–1765, Chester County Deeds, 1681–1765.

Another symptom of economic pressure upon families was a competitive marriage market in which poorer Friends and their children tended to fail as Quakers. In Chester and the Welsh Tract poorer children had to control (or appear to control) their sexual impulses longer than wealthier children. Among the poorer families the mean marriage age was seven years older for men and almost six years older for women than for the children of the wealthiest families. The children of Ellis Ellis, for example, a relatively poor Welsh Tract farmer, all married in the Radnor Meeting, but his two sons married at the ages of forty and thirty-four, and his three daughters at the ages of twenty-nine, thirty-three, and thirty-one. John Bevan's son Evan, on the other hand, who inherited over one thousand acres, married at nineteen years of age and John Bevan's three daughters married at the ages of twenty, twenty, and eighteen. Poorer Friends also married out more often. Only fifteen percent of the children of the first generation in Chester and the Welsh Tract married out of discipline, and virtually all of these came from the poorer families (see Tables 4 and 5). The wealthiest families like the Simcocks, Bevans, Worrals, and Owens had among one hundred and one children only three children who married out of discipline. Two of the nineteen wealthiest families had children who broke the discipline, compared to fourteen of thirty-four families evaluated at £30 and £40 in Philadelphia and Chester County tax assessments.

IV

The distribution of prestige confirmed and reinforced the economic and religious pressures on parents to perform their tasks well. In these communities successful parents received not only Quakerly children but also religious status and self-assurance. Participation in the Monthly Meeting was broad, but not all Friends participated equally. In the Welsh Tract (1683–1689, 1693–1695) twenty men and women, for example, shared a majority of the tasks of the Monthly Meetings. These Friends dominated virtually all the differing categories of tasks assigned to the Meeting, including the arbitration of disputes, discipline, marriage investigations, and visiting families. Quakers described their leaders in terms of spiritual achievement: honorific terms included "elder," "ancient Friend"; or they were familial: John and Barbara Bevan were a "nursing father and mother to some weak and young amongst us." The Meetings expected leaders, more than others, to express "holy conversation." An elder in Radnor in 1694 allowed his daughter to marry a first cousin, an act against the discipline. It is a "scandal upon the Truth and Friends," the Meeting decided, "that he being looked upon as an elder should set such a bad example" (Friends Historical Library, Radnor Men's Monthly Meeting Minutes, 2/3/1694). These men and women were supposed to provide the same charismatic, loving authority for Quaker adults as Quaker parents provided for their children.

Approximately seventy percent of the Welsh leaders came from gentry families, but so did eighteen percent of the less active, and thirty percent of the leaders were yeomen and artisans. Although some significant correlation existed between land and leadership (see Table 6), the high standard deviations show that wealth was not the sole determinant of leadership. Among the men in the fifty-three reconstructed families, those who were leaders were in fact more distinguished by their Quakerly children than by their wealth. Though above average in wealth, the leaders were not consistently the wealthiest men. On the other hand, their families were twice as well disciplined as the remaining families (see Table 7).

TABLE 6   Real Property and Meeting Influence Among Welsh Tract Men, 1683–1695

Percentile Men	Percent Positions	Mean Acreage	Standard Deviation
10	45	745	25
20	67	356	189
30	78	395	570
40	86	312	240
50	91	227	119
60	94	280	482
70	97	233	60
80	98	160	34
90	99	212	32
100 (87)	100	325	211

Kendat Tau Beta: +.486

Source: Friends Historical Library, Radnor Men's Monthly Meeting Minutes, 1683–1689, 1693–1695; Bureau of Land Records, Harrisburg, Pennsylvania, Land Commissioner's Minutes of the Welsh Tract, 1702.

TABLE 7 Meeting Positions, Wealth, and Children's Behavior

	N	N Jobs	Percentage Jobs	Average Acreage	Percent of Children Who Married Out
			Welsh Tract		
Top quartile	6	178	64%	750	1 of 17 (5%)
2nd quartile	6	66	87%	829	4 of 29 (13%)
3rd quartile	6	26	97%	555	4 of 40 (10%)
4th quartile	6	4	100%	327	6 of 24 (25%)
	24	274			
			Chester Tract		
Top quartile	6	408	67%	585	5 of 47 (11%)
2nd quartile	6	146	91%	553	10 of 40 (25%)
3rd quartile	6	50	99%	600	8 of 40 (20%)
4th quartile	5	3	100%	435	6 of 32 (18%)

Source: Friends Historical Society, Radnor Men's Monthly Meeting Minutes, 1681–1715, Chester Men's Monthly Meeting Minutes, 1681–1715.

The religious standing of the men in chester and the Welsh Tract clearly hinged on family events. Those who could not control their own family had no claim to honor. The Meetings did not usually penalize a parent if only one child married out. Randal Malin, for example, held ninety-eight positions in the Chester Meeting between 1681 and 1721, more than the other Friends studied, despite his daughter marrying out in 1717 (as did another in 1721, after Malin's death) (Friends Historical Society, Chester Women's Monthly Meeting Minutes, 2/30/1716, Chester Men's Monthly Meeting Minutes, 10/29/1717, 3/29/1721). Richard Ormes, however, stumbled from leadership when his pregnant daughter got married in Meeting in 1715 after fooling the female inspectors. Ormes had been a fully recognized minister, sent by the Meeting on trips to Maryland, and an Elder, holding about five Meeting positions a year. Between 1693 and 1715 the Radnor Monthly Meeting sent him to the Quarterly Meeting five times. After his daughter's case, however, Ormes did not serve the Meeting again until 1720, five years later (Friends Historical Library, Radnor Men's Monthly Meeting Minutes, 9/3/1701, 7/2/1716). Neither Ormes nor Malin cooperated with their wayward children. If a father did cooperate, he was disciplined and dropped from leadership instantly. Howell James held four positions between 1693 and 1697, but in the latter year went to his son's Keithian wedding. He acknowledged his mistake but never served the Meeting again (Friends Historical Library, Radnor Men's Monthly Meeting Minutes, 6/27/1716).

When more than one child married out, even if a father did not cooperate, the man lost prestige and often was subjected to the attention of the Meeting. Edward Kinneson held twenty-four Meeting positions in Chester and Goshen between 1709 and 1721, when his daughter Mary married out. He continued to be appointed at nearly the same rate until 1726, when his son Edward married out, and then he was dropped from leadership. Although he did nothing to encourage the marriage or cooperate with his son, the Meeting decided to "treat with his father Edward who appears to have been remiss in endeavoring to prevent the marriage." When his daughter Hannah married out in 1732, the Meeting decided that "her father has been more indulgent therein than is agreeable with the testimony of Truth." In 1733, James Kinneson, Edward's last son, married out. The Meeting treated Kinneson gently: "Considering his age and weakness [we are] willing to pass by his infirmity." Though he remained a Friend until he died in 1734, his wife Mary responded to his humiliation. In 1741 the Goshen Meeting got the word "that Mary Kinneson, widow of Edward, who some time since removed herself into the colony of Virginia hath forsaken our Society and joined herself to the Church of England" (Friends Historical Library, Goshen Men's Monthly Meeting Minutes, 3/21/1733, 6/21/1732, 9/4/1726, 8/19/1741). A source of Kinneson's problem was clearly his relative poverty. He had only two hundred acres of land. His children all married in their early twenties; they most likely would have waited to marry or might not have married at all, if they had confined themselves to the Quaker marriage market.

In these communities the assessment of spiritual and social honor depended heavily then on having a successful Quaker household, and wealth helped to achieve this standard. Wealth reduced marriage ages and helped keep sons and daughters isolated from the world. Insufficient wealth increased the age at marriage and increased the contacts likely between Quaker children and carnal talkers. Wealth was not monopolized nor simply emblematic of a social or political upper class. It was regarded as necessary for full participation in the Quaker community. The cheap land of the Delaware Valley helped create this situation, but it was legitimized and partly formed by "holy conversation" and the settlers' Quakerly devotion to their children.

Religious ideas about children, not pure affection, dominated the families of the Welsh Tract and Chester Quaker communities in the late seventeenth and early eighteenth centuries. Though many Quaker doctrines approached those of the sentimental, domesticated family, doctrines such as the emphasis on household environments, childrens' rights to choose their own marriage partners, and the independence of conjugal units, Quaker doctrine often strongly directed families away from affection, emotion, and eroticism. Late marriage ages and celibacy among poorer families—"poor" relative only to other Quakers—show the constraints on emotion imposed by the Quakers' discipline. The intense "holy watching" in both Chester and the Welsh Tract shows clearly that Quaker families were subordinated to demanding communal ideas of "holy conversation." Only on the fringes of these communities, among the children who married out and the disowned and humiliated fathers and mothers who cooperated with them, does the isolated affectionate nuclear family appear. Such families may have been as numerous as those who retained full loyalty to the Quakers' world view, but they could not match the organization, power, or authority of the Quaker tribe in the Delaware Valley.

V

For the Quakers, their religious view of the world was crucial and demanding. Their impulse originated in the 1650s in England and Wales. The First Publishers of Truth (the original core of Quaker ministers), revitalized by their conversions in the 1650s, had become like joyous, unpredictable, fearless children themselves; but by the 1680s the Quaker farmers of Chester and the Welsh Tract had real children of their own. No longer joyous children themselves, beset with responsibilities and exhausted by persecution and poverty, the Quaker settlers became responsible, hard-working adults sustained by their belief that, if protected and nurtured with "holy conversation" in the rich, isolated lands of Pennsylvania, the innocent child would spring to life among their own children. In this way they began the development of what would become a privatistic, middle-class social order in the Delaware Valley.

Bibliography

Axtell, James (1974). The School Upon a Hill: Education and Society in Colonial New England. New Haven: Yale University Press.

Bauman, Richard (1974). "Speaking in the Light: the Role of the Quaker Minister." In Richard Bauman and Joel Sherzer, eds., Explorations in the Ethnography of Speaking. New York: Cambridge University Press.

Bevan, John (1709). "John Bevan's Narrative." In James Levick, ed., Pennsylvania Magazine of History and Biography. XVII: 235–245.

Braithwaite, William Charles (1919). The Second Period of Quakerism. Cambridge, England: Cambridge University Press.

Bridenbaugh, Carl (1976). "The Old and New Societies of the Delaware Valley in the Seventeenth Century." Pennsylvania Magazine of History and Biography. 2:143–172.

Browning, Charles (1912). Welsh Settlement of Pennsylvania. Philadelphia: William Campbell.

Bureau of Land Record, Harrisburg, Pennsylvania Land Commissioner's Minutes of the Welsh Tract, 1702.

Campbell, Mildred (1942). The English Yeomen under Elizabeth and the Early Stuarts. New Haven: Yale University Press.

Chester County Court House, West Chester, Pennsylvania Chester County Deeds, 1681–1776. Chester County Wills and Inventories 1681–1776.

Chester County Historical Society, West Chester, Pennsylvania Chester County Treasurer's Book, 1681–1760.

Davis, David Brion (1966). The Problem of Slavery in Western Culture. Ithaca, New York: Cornell University Press.

Drake, Thomas (1950). Quakers and Slavery. New Haven: Yale University Press.

Ellis, Thomas (1685). "Thomas Ellis to George Fox, 13 June, 1685." Journal of Friends Historical Society. 6:173–175.

Forbes, Susan (1972). "Twelve Candles Lighted." Ph.d. dissertation: University of Pennsylvania.

Fox, George (1911). The Journal of George Fox. ed. Norman Penny. Cambridge, England: Cambridge University Press.

(1663). Concerning Marriage. London: n.p.

Friends Historical Library, Swarthmore, Pennsylvania

    Chester Men's Monthly Meeting Minutes, 1681–1760.

    Chester Monthly Meeting Records: Births, Deaths, Removals, 1681–1760.

    Chester Women's Monthly Meeting Minutes, 1705–1760.

    Radnor Men's Monthly Meeting Minutes, 1681–1778.

    Radnor Monthly Meeting Records (RMMR): Births, Deaths, Removals, 1681–1770.

    Radnor Women's Monthly Meeting Minutes, 1683–1765.

Frost, J. William (1973). The Quaker Family in Colonial America. New York: St. Martin's Press.

Glenn, Thomas Allen (1970). Merion in the Welsh Tract. Baltimore: Genealogical Publishing Company.

Greven, Philip J. (1970). Four Generations: Population, Land, and Family in Colonial Andover, Massachusetts. Ithaca, New York: Cornell University Press.

Haller, William (1957). The Rise of Puritanism. New York: Harper and Row.

Henretta, James (1978). "Families and Farms: *Mentalité* in Pre-Industrial America." William and Mary Quarterly. 1:3–32.

Hill, Christopher (1967). Society and Puritanism in Pre-Revolutionary England. New York: Schocken.

Historical Society of Pennsylvania

    Chester County Tax Lists, 1715–1776.

    Cope Collection, Volumes 1–95, 1681–1790.

Hoskins, W. G. (1963). Provincial England: Essays in Social and Economic History. London: Cromwell.

Hymes, Dell (1972). "Toward Ethnographies of Communication: The Analysis of Communicative Events." In Peter Paolo Giglioni, ed., Language and Social Context. London: Penguin.

(1974). Foundations in Sociolinguistics: An Ethnographic Approach. Philadelphia: University of Pennsylvania Press.

Kibbey, Ann (1973). "Puritan Beliefs about Language and Speech." Paper given before the American Anthropological Association, New Orleans, 30 Dec., 1973.

Marietta, Jack B. (1968). "Ecclesiastical Discipline in the Society of Friends, 1685–1776." Ph.d. dissertation: Stanford University.

Morgan, Cadwallader (1770). "Morgan's Testimony." In Henry Cadbury, ed., "Another Early Quaker Anti-Slavery Document." Journal of Negro History. 27:213.

Morgan, Edmund S. (1966). The Puritan Family: Religion and Domestic Relations in Seventeenth Century New England. New York: Harper and Row.

Nuttal, Geoffrey (1946). The Holy Spirit in Puritan Faith Experience. Oxford, England: Blackwell.

Penn, William (1681). "Some Account of the Province of Pennsylvania." In Albert Cook Meyers, ed., Narratives of Early Pennsylvania, West New Jersey and Delaware 1630–1707. New York: Barnes and Noble.

Philadelphia City Hall
   Philadelphia County Deeds 1681–1776. Philadelphia County Wills and Inventories 1681–1765.

Pyle, Robert (1698). "Robert Pyle's Testimony." In Henry J. Cadbury, ed., "An Early Quaker Anti-Slavery Statement." Journal of Negro History. 22:492–493.

Smith, George (1862). History of Delaware County. Philadelphia: Ashmead.

Turner, Edward (1911). The Negro in Pennsylvania: Slavery, Freedom 1639–1861. New York: Arno Press.

Vann, Richard (1969). The Social Development of English Quakerism, 1655–1755. Cambridge: Harvard University Press.

Warner, Sam Bass (1968). The Private City: Philadelphia in Three Periods of Its Growth. Philadelphia: University of Pennsylvania Press.

Waters, John (1976). "The Traditional World of the New England Peasants: A View From Seventeenth Century Barnstable." The New England Historical and Genealogical Register. 130:19.

Wolf, Stephanie (1976). Urban Village: Population, Community, and Family Structure in Germantown, Pennsylvania 1683–1800. Princeton: Princeton University Press.

PART III

The Clash of Cultures in an Age of Crisis

War and Culture:
The Iroquois Experience

Daniel K. Richter

INTRODUCTION

Settlers, Africans, and Indians all faced major crises and transformations in the last three decades of the seventeenth century. The expansion of the colonies led to brutal wars with Indians in New England and the Chesapeake in 1675–1676, and this struggle touched off Bacon's Rebellion in Virginia, a major theme in Edmund S. Morgan's essay in this section. All colonies faced new pressures from the growing imperial demands of the English state, as John Murrin's essay on New York makes clear. Africans learned that their ambiguous status in the colonies, somewhere between servitude and slavery, was rapidly becoming hereditary slavery. Yet Indians faced the most appalling menace of all, the very real possibility of utter extinction through exposure to European diseases.

Daniel K. Richter studies the response of the Iroquois Five Nations (Mohawks, Oneidas, Onondagas, Cayugas, and Senecas) to this danger. The Confederation survived the threat of depopulation by drastically intensifying the traditional institution of the "mourning war," through which one or more nations would replace a dead person by capturing and adopting someone else. At first firearms gave the Iroquois a decisive advantage over their Indian neighbors, but as these nations also acquired such weapons and proved able to fight back, often with French assistance, the Five Nations began to lose rather than gain population through these military efforts. In response to this crisis, the Confederation in 1701 chose neutrality with its immediate neighbors (French, English, and Indian), an arrangement that English officials usually tried to construe as an alliance. The Confederation continued to wage mourning wars against more distant enemies to the south and west, such as the Catawbas who are discussed in the following essay.

Daniel K. Richter, "War and Culture: The Iroquois Experience," in *William and Mary Quarterly*, XL (1983), 528–559. Reprinted by permission of the author.

*As Richter's essay and other studies show, Indians made war from mo-
tives quite different from those that drove Europeans into armed conflict.
Even the Iroquois, who often did act as intermediaries in the beaver trade,
seldom fought for territory or commerce. Most of the time they accepted
combat to gain live captives, some of whom were tortured to death while
others were adopted (or, later, ransomed).*

- *How likely were settlers to appreciate Indian motives for conflict, or Indians to understand why settlers, when they went to war, preferred to kill
  large numbers of people, often including women and children as* preferred
  *targets, at a single battle site, such as an Indian village whose warriors
  were off campaigning somewhere else?*

"The character of all these [Iroquois] Nations is warlike and cruel," wrote Jesuit missionary Paul Le Jeune in 1657. "The chief virtue of these poor Pagans
being cruelty, just as mildness is that of Christians, they teach it to their children from their very cradles, and accustom them to the most atrocious car-
nage and the most barbarous spectacles."[1] Like most Europeans of his day,
Le Jeune ignored his own countrymen's capacity for bloodlust and attributed the supposedly unique bellicosity of the Iroquois to their irreligion and
uncivilized condition. Still, his observations contain a kernel of truth often
overlooked by our more sympathetic eyes: in ways quite unfamiliar and
largely unfathomable to Europeans, warfare was vitally important in the cultures of the seventeenth-century Iroquois and their neighbors. For generations of Euro-Americans, the significance that Indians attached to warfare
seemed to substantiate images of bloodthirsty savages who waged war for
mere sport. Only in recent decades have ethnohistorians discarded such
shibboleths and begun to study Indian wars in the same economic and
diplomatic frameworks long used by students of European conflicts. Almost
necessarily, given the weight of past prejudice, their work has stressed similarities between Indian and European warfare.[2] Thus neither commonplace
stereotypes nor scholarly efforts to combat them have left much room for serious consideration of the possibility that the non-state societies of aboriginal North America may have waged war for different—but no less rational
and no more savage—purposes than did the nation-states of Europe.[3]

---

[1] Reuben Gold Thwaites, ed., *The Jesuit Relations and Allied Documents: Travels and Explorations of
the Jesuit Missionaries in New France, 1610–1791* (Cleveland, Ohio, 1896–1901), XLIII, 263, hereafter cited as *Jesuit Relations.*
[2] See, for example, George T. Hunt, *The Wars of the Iroquois: A Study in Intertribal Trade Relations*
(Madison, Wis., 1940); W. W. Newcomb, Jr., "A Re-Examination of the Causes of Plains Warfare," *American Anthropologist*, N.S., LII (1950), 317–330; and Francis Jennings, *The Invasion of
America: Indians, Colonialism, and the Cant of Conquest* (Chapel Hill, N.C., 1975), 146–170.
[3] While anthropologists disagree about the precise distinctions between the wars of state-
organized and non-state societies, they generally agree that battles for territorial conquest, economic monopoly, and subjugation or enslavement of conquered peoples are the product of the

This article explores that possibility through an analysis of the changing role of warfare in Iroquois culture during the first century after European contact.

The Iroquois Confederacy (composed, from west to east, of the Five Nations of the Seneca, Cayuga, Onondaga, Oneida, and Mohawk) frequently went to war for reasons rooted as much in internal social demands as in external disputes with their neighbors. The same observation could be made about countless European states, but the particular internal motives that often propelled the Iroquois and other northeastern Indians to make war have few parallels in Euro-American experience. In many Indian cultures a pattern known as the "mourning-war" was one means of restoring lost population, ensuring social continuity, and dealing with death.[4] A grasp of the changing role of this pattern in Iroquois culture is essential if the seventeenth- and early eighteenth-century campaigns of the Five Nations—and a vital aspect of the contact situation—are to be understood. "War is a necessary exercise for the Iroquois," explained missionary and ethnologist Joseph François Lafitau, "for, besides the usual motives which people have in declaring it against troublesome neighbours . . . , it is indispensable to them also because of one of their fundamental laws of being."[5]

I

Euro-Americans often noted that martial skills were highly valued in Indian societies and that, for young men, exploits on the warpath were important determinants of personal prestige. This was, some hyperbolized, particularly true of the Iroquois. "It is not for the Sake of Tribute . . . that they make War," Cadwallader Colden observed of the Five Nations, "but from the Notions of Glory, which they have ever most strongly imprinted on their

---

technological and organizational capacities of the state. For overviews of the literature see C. R. Hallpike, "Functionalist Interpretations of Primitive Warfare, *Man*, N.S., VIII (1973), 451–470, and Andrew Vayda, "Warfare in Ecological Perspective," *Annual Review of Ecology and Systematics*, V (1974), 183–193.

[4] My use of the term *mourning-war* differs from that of Marian W. Smith in "American Indian Warfare," New York Academy of Sciences, *Transactions*, 2d Ser., XIII (1951), 348–365, which stresses the psychological and emotional functions of the mourning-war. As the following paragraphs seek to show, the psychology of the mourning-war was deeply rooted in Iroquois demography and social structure; my use of the term accordingly reflects a more holistic view of the cultural role of the mourning-war than does Smith's. On the dangers of an excessively psychological explanation of Indian warfare see Jennings, *Invasion of America*, 159; but see also the convincing defense of Smith in Richard Drinnon, "Ravished Land," *Indian Historian*, IX (Fall 1976), 24–26.

[5] Joseph François Lafitau, *Customs of the American Indians Compared with the Customs of Primitive Times*, ed. and trans. William N. Fenton and Elizabeth L. Moore (Toronto, 1974, 1977 [orig. publ. Paris, 1724]), II, 98–99.

Minds."[6] Participation in a war party was a benchmark episode in an Iroquois youth's development, and later success in battle increased the young man's stature in his clan and village. His prospects for an advantageous marriage, his chances for recognition as a village leader, and his hopes for eventual selection to a sachemship depended largely—though by no means entirely—on his skill on the warpath, his munificence in giving war feasts, and his ability to attract followers when organizing a raid.[7] Missionary-explorer Louis Hennepin exaggerated when he claimed that "those amongst the *Iroquoise* who are not given to War, are had in great Contempt, and pass for Lazy and Effeminate People," but warriors did in fact reap great social rewards.[8]

The plaudits offered to successful warriors suggest a deep cultural significance; societies usually reward warlike behavior not for its own sake but for the useful functions it performs.[9] Among the functions postulated in recent studies of non-state warfare is the maintenance of stable population levels. Usually this involves—in more or less obvious ways—a check on excessive population growth, but in some instances warfare can be, for the victors, a means to increase the group's numbers.[10] The traditional wars of the Five Nations served the latter purpose. The Iroquois conceptualized the process of population maintenance in terms of individual and collective spiritual power. When a person died, the power of his or her lineage, clan, and nation was diminished in proportion to his or her individual spiritual strength.[11] To replenish the depleted power the Iroquois conducted "requickening" ceremonies at which the deceased's name—and with it the social role and duties it represented—was transferred to a successor. Vacant positions in Iroquois families and villages were thus both literally and symbolically filled, and the

[6] Cadwallader Colden, *The History of the Five Indian Nations of Canada, Which Are Dependent on the Province of New-York in America, and Are the Barrier between the English and French in That Part of the World* (London, 1747), 4, hereafter cited as Colden, *History* (1747).

[7] Gabriel Sagard, *The Long Journey to the Country of the Hurons*, ed. George M. Wrong and trans. H. H. Langton (Toronto, 1939 [orig. publ. Paris, 1632]), 151–152; *Jesuit Relations*, XLII, William N. Fenton, ed., "The Hyde Manuscript: Captain William Hyde's Observations of the 5 Nations of Indians at New York, 1698," *American Scene Magazine*, VI (1965), [9]; Bruce G. Trigger, *The Children of Aataentsic: A History of the Huron People to 1660* (Montreal, 1976), I, 68–69, 145–147.

[8] Hennepin, *A New Discovery of a Vast Country in America . . .* , 1st English ed. (London, 1698), II, 88.

[9] Newcomb, "Re-Examination of Plains Warfare," *Am. Anthro.*, N.S., LII (1950), 320.

[10] Andrew P. Vayda, "Expansion and Warfare among Swidden Agriculturalists," *Am. Anthro.*, N.S., LXIII (1961), 346–358; Anthony Leeds, "The Functions of War," in Jules Masserman, ed., *Violence and War, with Clinical Studies* (New York, 1963), 69–82; William Tulio Divale and Marvin Harris, "Population, Warfare, and the Male Supremacist Complex," *Am. Anthro.*, N.S., LXXVIII (1976), 521–538.

[11] J. N. B. Hewitt, "Orenda and a Definition of Religion," *Am. Anthro.*, N.S., IV (1902), 33–46; Morris Wolf, *Iroquois Religion and Its Relation to Their Morals* (New York, 1919), 25–26; Alvin M. Josephy, Jr., *The Indian Heritage of America* (New York, 1968), 94; Ake Hultkrantz, *The Religions of the American Indians*, trans. Monica Setterwall (Berkeley, Calif., 1979), 12.

continuity of Iroquois society was confirmed, while survivors were assured that the social role and spiritual strength embodied in the departed's name had not been lost.[12] Warfare was crucial to these customs, for when the deceased was a person of ordinary status and little authority the beneficiary of the requickening was often a war captive, who would be adopted "to help strengthen the familye in lew of their deceased Freind."[13] "A father who has lost his son adopts a young prisoner in his place," explained an eighteenth-century commentator on Indian customs. "An orphan takes a father or mother; a widow a husband; one man takes a sister and another a brother."[14]

On a societal level, then, warfare helped the Iroquois to deal with deaths in their ranks. On a personal, emotional level it performed similar functions. The Iroquois believed that the grief inspired by a relative's death could, if uncontrolled, plunge survivors into depths of despair that robbed them of their reason and disposed them to fits of rage potentially harmful to themselves and the community. Accordingly, Iroquois culture directed mourners' emotions into ritualized channels. Members of the deceased's household, "after having the hair cut, smearing the face with earth or charcoal and gotten themselves up in the most frightful negligence," embarked on ten days of "deep mourning," during which "they remain at the back of their bunk, their face against the ground or turned towards the back of the platform, their head enveloped in their blanket which is the dirtiest and least clean rag that they have. They do not look at or speak to anyone except through necessity and in a low voice. They hold themselves excused from every duty of civility and courtesy."[15] For the next year the survivors engaged in less intense formalized grieving, beginning to resume their daily habits but continuing to disregard their personal appearance and many social amenities. While mourners thus channeled their emotions, others hastened to "cover up" the grief of the bereaved with condolence rituals, feasts, and presents (including the special variety of condolence gift often somewhat misleadingly described as *wergild*). These were designed to cleanse sorrowing hearts and to ease the return to normal life. Social and personal needs converged at the culmination of these ceremonies, the "requickening" of the deceased.[16]

[12] *Jesuit Relations,* XXIII, 165–169; Lafitau, *Customs of American Indians,* ed. and trans. Fenton and Moore, I, 71; B. H. Quain, "The Iroquois," in Margaret Mead, ed., *Cooperation and Competition among Primitive Peoples* (New York, 1937), 276–277.

[13] Fenton, ed., "Hyde Manuscript," *Am. Scene Mag.,* VI (1965), [16].

[14] Philip Mazzei, *Researches on the United States,* ed. and trans. Constance B. Sherman (Charlottesville, Va., 1976 [orig. publ. Paris, 1788]), 349. See also P[ierre] de Charlevoix, *Journal of a Voyage to North-America . . .* (London, 1761 [orig. publ. Paris, 1744]), I, 370–373, II, 33–34, and George S. Snyderman, "Behind the Tree of Peace: A Sociological Analysis of Iroquois Warfare," *Pennsylvania Archaeologist,* XVIII, nos. 3–4 (1948), 13–15.

[15] Lafitau, *Customs of American Indians,* ed. and trans. Fenton and Moore, II, 241–245, quotation on p. 242.

[16] *Jesuit Relations,* X, 273–275, XIX, 91, XLIII, 267–271, LX, 35–41. On *wergild* see Lewis H. Morgan, *League of the Ho-dé-no-sau-nee, or Iroquois* (Rochester, N.Y., 1851), 331–333, and Jennings,

But if the mourners' grief remained unassuaged, the ultimate socially sanctioned channel for their violent impulses was a raid to seek captives who, it was hoped, would ease their pain. The target of the mourning-war was usually a people traditionally defined as enemies; neither they nor any-one else need necessarily be held directly responsible for the death that pro-voked the attack, though most often the foe could be made to bear the blame.[17] Raids for captives could be either large-scale efforts organized on village, nation, or confederacy levels or, more often, attacks by small parties raised at the behest of female kin of the deceased. Members of the dead per-son's household—presumably lost in grief—did not usually participate di-rectly. Instead, young men who were related by marriage to the bereaved women but who lived in other longhouses were obliged to form a raiding party or face the matrons' accusations of cowardice.[18] When the warriors re-turned with captured men, women, and children, mourners could elect a prisoner for adoption in the place of the deceased or they could vent their rage in rituals of torture and execution.[19]

Invasion of America, 148–149. The parallel between Iroquois practice and the Germanic tradition of blood payments should not be stretched too far; Iroquois condolence presents were an inte-gral part of the broader condolence process.

[17] Smith, "American Indian Warfare," N.Y. Acad. Sci., *Trans.*, 2d Ser., XIII (1951), 352–354; An-thony F. C. Wallace, *The Death and Rebirth of the Seneca* (New York, 1970), 101. It is within the con-text of the mourning-war that what are usually described as Indian wars for revenge or blood feuds should be understood. The revenge motive—no doubt strong in Iroquois warfare—was only part of the larger complex of behavior and belief comprehended in the mourning-war. It should also be noted that raids might be inspired by *any* death, not just those attributable to murder or warfare and for which revenge or other atonement, such as the giving of condolence presents, was necessary. Among Euro-American observers, only the perceptive Lafitau seems to have been aware of this possibility (*Customs of American Indians*, ed. and trans. Fenton and Moore, II, 98–102, 154). I have found no other explicit contemporary discussion of this phe-nomenon, but several accounts indicate the formation of war parties in response to deaths from disease or other nonviolent causes. See H. P. Biggar *et al.*, eds. and trans., *The Works of Samuel de Champlain* (Toronto, 1922–1936), II, 206–208, hereafter cited as *Works of Champlain; Jesuit Rela-tions*, LXIV, 91; Jasper Dankers [Danckaerts] and Peter Sluyter, *Journal of a Voyage to New York and a Tour in Several of the American Colonies in 1679–80*, trans. and ed. Henry C. Murphy (Long Is-land Historical Society, *Memoirs*, I [Brooklyn, N.Y., 1867]), 277; and William M. Beauchamp, ed., *Moravian Journals Relating to Central New York, 1745–66* (Syracuse, N.Y., 1916), 125–126, 183–186.

[18] *Jesuit Relations*, X, 225–227; E. B. O'Callaghan *et al.*, eds., *Documents Relative to the Colonial His-tory of the State of New-York . . .* (Albany, N.Y., 1856–1887), IV, 22, hereafter cited as *N.-Y. Col. Docs.*; Lafitau, *Customs of American Indians*, ed. and trans. Fenton and Moore, II, 99–103; Snyderman, "Behind the Tree of Peace," *Pa. Archaeol.*, XVIII, nos. 3–4 (1948), 15–20.

[19] The following composite account is based on numerous contemporaneous reports of Iroquois treatment of captives. Among the more complete are *Jesuit Relations*, XXII, 251–267, XXXIX, 57–77, L, 59–63, LIV, 25–35; Gideon D. Scull, ed., *Voyages of Peter Esprit Radisson: Being an Account of His Travels and Experiences among the North American Indians, from 1652 to 1684* (Boston, 1885), 28–60; and James H. Coyne, ed. and trans., "Exploration of the Great Lakes, 1660–1670, by Dol-lier de Casson and de Bréhant de Galinée," Ontario Historical Society, *Papers and Records*, IV

The rituals began with the return of the war party, which had sent word ahead of the number of captives seized. Most of the villagers, holding clubs, sticks, and other weapons, stood in two rows outside the village entrance to meet the prisoners. Men—but usually not women or young children—received heavy blows designed to inflict pain without serious injury. Then they were stripped and led to a raised platform in an open space inside the village, where old women led the community in further physical abuse, tearing out fingernails and poking sensitive body parts with sticks and firebrands.[20] After several hours, prisoners were allowed to rest and eat, and later they were made to dance for their captors while their fate was decided. Headmen apportioned them to grieving families, whose matrons then chose either to adopt or to execute them.[21] If those who were adopted made a sincere effort to please their new relatives and to assimilate into village society, they could expect a long life; if they displeased, they were quietly and unceremoniously killed.

A captive slated for ritual execution was usually also adopted and subsequently addressed appropriately as "uncle" or "nephew," but his status was marked by a distinctive red and black pattern of facial paint. During the next few days the doomed man gave his death feast, where his executioners saluted him and allowed him to recite his war honors. On the appointed day he was tied with a short rope to a stake, and villagers of both sexes and all ages took turns wielding firebrands and various red-hot objects to burn him systematically from the feet up. The tormenters behaved with religious solemnity and spoke in symbolic language of "caressing" their adopted relative with their firebrands. The victim was expected to endure his sufferings stoically and even to encourage his torturers, but this seems to have been ideal rather than typical behavior. If he too quickly began to swoon, his ordeal briefly ceased and he received food and drink and time to recover somewhat before the burning resumed. At length, before he expired, someone scalped him, another threw hot sand on his exposed skull, and finally a warrior dispatched him with a knife to the chest or a hatchet to the neck.

(1903), 31–35. See also the many other portrayals in *Jesuit Relations;* the discussions in Lafitau, *Customs of American Indians,* ed. and trans. Fenton and Moore, II, 148–172; Nathaniel Knowles, "The Torture of Captives by the Indians of Eastern North America," American Philosophical Society, *Proceedings,* LXXXII (1940), 181–190; and Wallace, *Death and Rebirth of the Seneca,* 103–107.

[20] The gauntlet and the public humiliation and physical abuse of captives also served as initiation rites for prospective adoptees; see John Heckewelder, "An Account of the History, Manners, and Customs of the Indian Nations Who Once Inhabited Pennsylvania and the Neighbouring States," Am. Phil. Soc., *Transactions of the Historical and Literary Committee,* I (1819), 211–213. For a fuller discussion of Indian methods of indoctrinating adoptees see James Axtell, "The White Indians of Colonial America," *William and Mary Quarterly,* 3d Ser., XXXII (1975), 55–88.

[21] Usually only adult male captives were executed, and most women and children seem to have escaped physical abuse. Occasionally, however, the Iroquois did torture and execute women and children. See Scull, ed., *Voyages of Radisson,* 56, and *Jesuit Relations,* XXXIX, 219–221, XLII, 97–99, LI, 213, 231–233, LII, 79, 157–159, LIII, 253, LXII, 59, LXIV, 127–129, LXV, 33–39.

Then the victim's flesh was stripped from his bones and thrown into cooking kettles, and the whole village feasted on his remains. This feast carried great religious significance for the Iroquois, but its full meaning is irretrievable; most European observers were too shocked to probe its implications.[22]

Mourners were not the only ones to benefit from the ceremonial torture and execution of captives. While grieving relatives vented their emotions, all of the villagers, by partaking in the humiliation of every prisoner and the torture of some, were able to participate directly in the defeat of their foes. Warfare thus dramatically promoted group cohesion and demonstrated to the Iroquois their superiority over their enemies. At the same time, youths learned valuable lessons in the behavior expected of warriors and in the way to die bravely should they ever be captured. Le Jeune's "barbarous spectacles" were a vital element in the ceremonial life of Iroquois communities.[23]

The social demands of the mourning-war shaped strategy and tactics in at least two ways. First, the essential measure of a war party's success was its ability to seize prisoners and bring them home alive. Capturing of enemies was preferred to killing them on the spot and taking their scalps, while none of the benefits European combatants derived from war—territorial expansion, economic gain, plunder of the defeated—outranked the seizure of prisoners.[24] When missionary Jérôme Lalemant disparaged Iroquoian warfare as "consisting of a few broken heads along the highways, or of some captives brought into the country to be burned and eaten there," he was more accurate than he knew.[25] The overriding importance of captive taking set Iroquois warfare dramatically apart from the Euro-American military experience. "We are not like you CHRISTIANS for when you have taken Prisoners of one another you send them home, by such means you can never rout one another," explained the Onondaga orator Teganissorens to Gov. Robert Hunter of New York in 1711.[26]

The centrality of captives to the business of war was clear in pre-combat rituals: imagery centered on a boiling war kettle; the war feast presaged the

[22] Several authors—from James Adair and Philip Mazzei in the 18th century to W. Arens in 1979—have denied that the Iroquois engaged in cannabalism (Adair, *The History of the American Indians* . . . [London, 1775], 209; Mazzei, *Researches,* ed. and trans. Sherman, 359; Arens, *The Man-Eating Myth: Anthropology & Anthropophagy* [New York, 1979] 127–129). Arens is simply wrong, as Thomas S. Abler has shown in "Iroquois Cannibalism: Fact Not Fiction," *Ethnohistory,* XXVII (1980), 309–316. Adair and Mazzei, from the perspective of the late 18th century, were on firmer ground; by then the Five Nations apparently had abandoned anthropophagy. See Adolph B. Benson, ed., *Peter Kalm's Travels in North America* (New York, 1937), 694.
[23] Robert L. Rands and Carroll L. Riley, "Diffusion and Discontinuous Distribution," *Am. Anthro.,* N.S., LX (1958), 284–289; Maurice R. Davie, *The Evolution of War: A Study of Its Role in Early Societies* (New Haven, Conn., 1929), 36–38; Hennepin, *New Discovery,* II, 92.
[24] *Jesuit Relations,* LXII, 85–87, LXVII, 173; Knowles, "Torture of Captives," Am. Phil. Soc., *Procs.,* LXXXII (1940), 210–211.
[25] *Jesuit Relations,* XIX, 81.
[26] *N.-Y. Col. Docs.,* V, 274.

future cannibalistic rite; mourning women urged warriors to bring them prisoners to assuage their grief; and, if more than one village participated in the campaign, leaders agreed in advance on the share of captives that each town would receive.[27] As Iroquois warriors saw it, to forget the importance of captive taking or to ignore the rituals associated with it was to invite defeat. In 1642 missionary Isaac Jogues observed a ceremony he believed to be a sacrifice to Areskoui, the deity who presided over Iroquois wars. "At a solemn feast which they had made to two Bears, which they had offered to their demon, they had used this form of words: 'Aireskoi, thou dost right to punish us, and to give us no more captives' (they were speaking of the Algonquins, of whom that year they had not taken one . . .) 'because we have sinned by not eating the bodies of those whom thou last gavest us; but we promise thee to eat the first ones whom thou shalt give us, as we now do with these two Bears.' "[28]

A second tactical reflection of the social functions of warfare was a strong sanction against the loss of Iroquois lives in battle. A war party that, by European standards, seemed on the brink of triumph could be expected to retreat sorrowfully homeward if it suffered a few fatalities. For the Indians, such a campaign was no victory; casualties would subvert the purpose of warfare as a means of restocking the population.[29] In contrast to European beliefs that to perish in combat was acceptable and even honorable, Iroquois beliefs made death in battle a frightful prospect, though one that must be faced bravely if necessary. Slain warriors, like all who died violent deaths, were said to be excluded from the villages of the dead, doomed to spend a roving eternity seeking vengeance. As a result, their bodies were not interred in village cemeteries, lest their angry souls disturb the repose of others. Both in burial and in the afterlife, a warrior who fell in combat faced separation from his family and friends.[30]

Efforts to minimize fatalities accordingly underlay several tactics that contemporary Euro-Americans considered cowardly: fondness for ambushes and surprise attacks; unwillingness to fight when outnumbered; and avoidance of frontal assaults on fortified places. Defensive tactics showed a similar emphasis on precluding loss of life. Spies in enemy villages and an extensive network of scouts warned of invading war parties before they could harm Iroquois villagers. If intruders did enter Iroquoia, defenders attacked from ambush, but only if they felt confident of repulsing the enemy without too many losses of their own. The people retreated behind palisades or, if the enemy appeared too strong to resist, burned their own villages and fled—

[27] *Works of Champlain,* IV, 330; Charlevoix, *Voyage to North-America,* I, 316–333.
[28] *Jesuit Relations,* XXXIX, 221.
[29] *Works of Champlain,* III, 73–74; *Jesuit Relations,* XXXII, 159.
[30] *Jesuit Relations,* X, 145, XXXIX, 29–31; J. N. B. Hewitt, "The Iroquoian Concept of the Soul," *Journal of American Folk-Lore,* VIII (1895), 107–116.

warriors included—into the woods or to neighboring villages. Houses and corn supplies thus might temporarily be lost, but unless the invaders achieved complete surprise, the lives and spiritual power of the people remained intact. In general, when the Iroquois were at a disadvantage, they preferred flight or an insincerely negotiated truce to the costly last stands that earned glory for European warriors.[31]

That kind of glory, and the warlike way of life it reflected, were not Iroquois ideals. Warfare was a specific response to the death of specific individuals at specific times, a sporadic affair characterized by seizing from traditional enemies a few captives who would replace the dead, literally or symbolically, and ease the pain of those who mourned. While war was not to be undertaken gladly or lightly, it was still "a necessary exercise for the Iroquois,"[32] for it was an integral part of individual and social mourning practices. When the Iroquois envisioned a day of no more wars, with their Great League of Peace extended to all peoples, they also envisioned an alternative to the mourning functions of warfare. That alternative was embodied in the proceedings of league councils and Iroquois peace negotiations with other peoples, which began with—and frequently consisted entirely of—condolence ceremonies and exchanges of presents designed to dry the tears, unstop the mouths, and cleanse the hearts of bereaved participants.[33] Only when grief was forgotten could war end and peace begin. In the century following the arrival of Europeans, grief could seldom be forgotten.

II

After the 1620s, when the Five Nations first made sustained contact with Europeans, the role of warfare in Iroquois culture changed dramatically. By 1675, European diseases, firearms, and trade had produced dangerous new patterns of conflict that threatened to derange the traditional functions of the mourning-war.

Before most Iroquois had ever seen a Dutchman or a Frenchman, they had felt the impact of the maladies the invaders inadvertently brought with

[31] Sagard, *Long Journey*, ed. Wrong and trans. Langton, 152–156; *Jesuit Relations*, XXII, 309–311, XXXII, 173–175, XXXIV, 197, LV, 79, LXVI, 273; Hennepin, *New Discovery*, II, 86–94; Patrick Mitchell Malone, "Indian and English Military Systems in New England in the Seventeenth Century" (Ph.D. diss., Brown University, 1971), 33–38.
[32] Lafitau, *Customs of American Indians*, ed. and trans. Fenton and Moore, II, 98.
[33] Paul A. W. Wallace, *The White Roots of Peace* (Philadelphia, 1946); A. F. C. Wallace, *Death and Rebirth of the Seneca*, 39–48, 93–98; William M. Beauchamp, *Civil, Religious and Mourning Councils and Ceremonies of Adoption of the New York Indians*, New York State Museum Bulletin 113 (Albany, N.Y., 1907). For a suggestive discussion of Indian definitions of peace see John Phillip Reid, *A Better Kind of Hatchet: Law, Trade, and Diplomacy in the Cherokee Nation during the Early Years of European Contact* (University Park, Pa., 1976), 9–17.

them.³⁴ By the 1640s the number of Iroquois (and of their Indian neighbors) had probably already been halved by epidemics of smallpox, measles, and other European "childhood diseases," to which Indian populations had no immunity.³⁵ The devastation continued through the century. A partial list of plagues that struck the Five Nations includes "a general malady" among the Mohawk in 1647; "a great mortality" among the Onondaga in 1656–1657; a smallpox epidemic among the Oneida, Onondaga, Cayuga, and Seneca in 1661–1663; "a kind of contagion" among the Seneca in 1668; "a fever of . . . malignant character" among the Mohawk in 1673; and "a general Influenza" among the Seneca in 1676.³⁶ As thousands died, ever-growing numbers of captive adoptees would be necessary if the Iroquois were even to begin to replace their losses; mourning-wars of unprecedented scale loomed ahead. Warfare would cease to be a sporadic and specific response to individual deaths and would become instead a constant and increasingly undifferentiated symptom of societies in demographic crisis.

At the same time, European firearms would make warfare unprecedentedly dangerous for both the Iroquois and their foes, and would undermine traditional Indian sanctions against battle fatalities. The introduction of guns, together with the replacement of flint arrowheads by more efficient iron, copper, and brass ones that could pierce traditional Indian wooden armor, greatly increased the chances of death in combat and led to major changes in Iroquois tactics. In the early seventeenth century Champlain had observed mostly ceremonial and relatively bloodless confrontations between large Indian armies, but with the advent of muskets—which Europeans had designed to be fired in volleys during just such battles—massed confrontations became, from the Indian perspective, suicidal folly. They were quickly abandoned in favor of a redoubled emphasis on small-scale raids and ambushes, in which Indians learned far sooner than Euro-Americans how to aim cumbersome muskets accurately at individual targets.³⁷ By the early

³⁴ On the devastating impact of European diseases—some Indian populations may have declined by a factor of 20 to 1 within a century or so of contact—see the works surveyed in Russell Thornton, "American Indian Historical Demography: A Review Essay with Suggestions for Future Research," *American Indian Culture and Research Journal*, III, No. 1 (1979), 69–74.
³⁵ Trigger, *Children of Aataentsic*, II, 602; Cornelius J. Jaenen, *Friend and Foe: Aspects of French Amerindian Cultural Contact in the Sixteenth and Seventeenth Centuries* (New York, 1976), 100. Most of the early Iroquois epidemics went unrecorded by Europeans, but major smallpox epidemics are documented for the Mohawk in 1634 and the Seneca in 1640–1641; see [Harmen Meyndertsz van den Bogaert], "Narrative of a Journey into the Mohawk and Oneida Country, 1634–1635," in J. Franklin Jameson, ed., *Narratives of New Netherland, 1609–1664* (New York, 1909), 140–141, and *Jesuit Relations*, XXI, 211.
³⁶ *Jesuit Relations*, XXX, 273, XLIV, 43, XLVII, 193, 205, XLVIII, 79–83, L, 63, LIV, 79–81, LVII, 81–83, LX, 175.
³⁷ *Works of Champlain*, II, 95–100; Malone, "Indian and English Military Systems," 179–200; Jennings, *Invasion of America*, 165–166. After the introduction of firearms the Iroquois continued to raise armies of several hundred to a thousand men, but they almost never engaged them in set

1640s the Mohawk were honing such skills with approximately three hundred guns acquired from the Dutch of Albany and from English sources. Soon the rest of the Five Nations followed the Mohawk example.[38]

Temporarily, the Iroquois' plentiful supply and skillful use of firearms gave them a considerable advantage over their Indian enemies: during the 1640s and 1650s the less well armed Huron and the poorly armed Neutral and Khionontateronon (Petun or Tobacco Nation) succumbed to Iroquois firepower. That advantage had largely disappeared by the 1660s and 1670s, however, as the Five Nations learned in their battles with such heavily armed foes as the Susquehannock. Once muskets came into general use in Indian warfare, several drawbacks became apparent: they were more sluggish than arrows to fire and much slower to reload; their noise lessened the capacity for surprise; and reliance on them left Indians dependent on Euro-Americans for ammunition, repairs, and replacements. But there could be no return to the days of bows and arrows and wooden armor. Few Iroquois war parties could now expect to escape mortal casualties.[39]

While European diseases and firearms intensified Indian conflicts and stretched the mourning-war tradition beyond previous limits, a third major aspect of European contact pushed Iroquois warfare in novel directions. Trade with Europeans made economic motives central to American Indian conflicts for the first time. Because iron tools, firearms, and other trade goods so quickly became essential to Indian economies, struggles for those items and for furs to barter for them lay behind numerous seventeenth-century wars. Between 1624 and 1628 the Iroquois gained unimpeded access to European commodities when Mohawk warriors drove the Mahican to the east of the Hudson River and secured an open route to the Dutch traders of Albany.[40] But obtaining the furs to exchange for the goods of Albany was a problem not so easily solved. By about 1640 the Five Nations perhaps had

---

battles. Large armies ensured safe travel to distant battlegrounds and occasionally intimidated outnumbered opponents, but when they neared their objective they usually broke into small raiding parties. See Daniel Gookin, "Historical Collections of the Indians in New England" (1674), Massachusetts Historical Society, *Collections,* I (1792), 162, and Cadwallader Colden, *The History of the Five Indian Nations Depending on the Province of New-York in America* (New York, 1727), 8–10, hereafter cited as Colden, *History* (1727).

[38] *N.-Y. Col. Docs.,* I, 150; "Journal of New Netherland, 1647," in Jameson, ed., *Narratives of New Netherland,* 274; *Jesuit Relations,* XXIV, 295; Carl P. Russell, *Guns on the Early Frontiers: A History of Firearms from Colonial Times through the Years of the Western Fur Trade* (Berkeley, Calif., 1957), 11–15, 62–66.

[39] *Jesuit Relations,* XXVII, 71, 205–207; Elisabeth Tooker, "The Iroquois Defeat of the Huron: A Review of Causes," *Pa. Archaeol.,* XXXIII (1963), 115–123; Keith F. Otterbein, "Why the Iroquois Won: An Analysis of Iroquois Military Tactics," *Ethnohistory,* XI (1964), 56–63; John K. Mahon, "Anglo-American Methods of Indian Warfare, 1676–1794," *Mississippi Valley Historical Review,* XLV (1958), 255.

[40] Bruce G. Trigger, "The Mohawk-Mahican War (1624–28): The Establishment of a Pattern," *Canadian Historical Review,* LII (1971), 276–286.

exhausted the beaver stock of their home hunting territories; more important, they could not find in relatively temperate Iroquoia the thick northern
pelts prized by Euro-American traders.[41] A long, far-flung series of "beaver
wars" ensued, in which the Five Nations battled the Algonquian nations of
the Saint Lawrence River region, the Huron, the Khionontateronon, the Neutral, the Erie, and other western and northern peoples in a constant struggle
over fur supplies. In those wars the Iroquois more frequently sought dead
beavers than live ones: most of their raids were not part of a strategic plan to
seize new hunting grounds but piratical attacks on enemy canoes carrying
pelts to Montreal and Trois-Rivières.[42]

The beaver wars inexorably embroiled the Iroquois in conflict with the
French of Canada. Franco-Iroquois hostilities dated from the era of Champlain, who consistently based his relations with Canada's natives upon
promises to aid them in their traditional raids against the Five Nations. "I
came to the conclusion," wrote Champlain in 1619, "that it was very necessary to assist them, both to engage them the more to love us, and also to provide the means of furthering my enterprises and explorations which apparently could only be carried out with their help."[43] The French commander
and a few of his men participated in Indian campaigns against the Five Nations in 1609, 1610, and 1615, and encouraged countless other raids.[44] From
the 1630s to the 1660s, conflict between the Five Nations and Canadian Indians intensified, and Iroquois war parties armed with guns frequently blockaded the Saint Lawrence and stopped the flow of furs to the French settlements. A state of open war, punctuated by short truces, consequently
prevailed between New France and various members of the Five Nations,
particularly the Mohawk. The battles were almost exclusively economic
and geopolitical—the Iroquois were not much interested in French
captives—and in general the French suffered more than the Iroquois from

[41] Harold A. Ennis, *The Fur Trade in Canada: An Introduction to Canadian Economic History* (New
Haven, Conn., 1930), 1–4, 32–33; Hunt, *Wars of the Iroquois*, 33–37; John Witthoft, "Ancestry of
the Susquehannocks," in John Witthoft and W. Fred Kinsey III, eds., *Susquehannock Miscellany*
(Harrisburg, Pa., 1959), 34–35; Thomas Elliott Norton, *The Fur Trade in Colonial New York,
1686–1776* (Madison, Wis., 1974), 9–15.

[42] The classic account of the beaver wars is Hunt, *Wars of the Iroquois*, but three decades of sub-
sequent scholarship have overturned many of that work's interpretations. See Allen W. Trelease,
"The Iroquois and the Western Fur Trade: A Problem in Interpretation," *MVHR*, XLIX (1962),
32–51; Raoul Naroll, "The Causes of the Fourth Iroquois War," *Ethnohistory*, XVI (1969), 51–81;
Allan Forbes, Jr., "Two and a Half Centuries of Conflict: The Iroquois and the Laurentian Wars,"
Pa. Archaeol., XL, nos. 3–4 (1970), 1–20; William N. Fenton, "The Iroquois in History," in Eleanor
Burke Leacock and Nancy Oestreich Lurie, eds., *North American Indians in Historical Perspective*
(New York, 1971), 139–145; Karl H. Schlesier, "Epidemics and Indian Middlemen: Rethinking
the Wars of the Iroquois, 1609–1653," *Ethnohistory*, XXIII (1976), 129–145; and Trigger, *Children of
Aataentsic*, esp. II, 617–664.

[43] *Works of Champlain*, III, 31–32; see also II, 118–119, 186–191, 246–285, III, 207–228.

[44] *Ibid.*, II, 65–107, 120–138, III, 48–81.

the fighting.[45] Finally, in 1666, a French army invaded Iroquoia and burned the Mohawks' fortified villages, from which all had fled to safety except a few old men who chose to stay and die. In 1667, the Five Nations and the French made a peace that lasted for over a decade.[46]

While the fur trade introduced new economic goals, additional foes, and wider scope to Iroquois warfare, it did not crowd out older cultural motives. Instead, the mourning-war tradition, deaths from disease, dependence on firearms, and the trade in furs combined to produce a dangerous spiral: epidemics led to deadlier mourning-wars fought with firearms; the need for guns increased the demand for pelts to trade for them; the quest for furs provoked wars with other nations; and deaths in those conflicts began the mourning-war cycle anew. At each turn, fresh economic and demographic motives fed the spiral.

Accordingly, in the mid-seventeenth-century Iroquois wars, the quest for captives was at least as important as the quest for furs. Even in the archetypal beaver war, the Five Nations–Huron conflict, only an overriding—even desperate—demand for prisoners can explain much of Iroquois behavior. For nearly a decade after the dispersal of the Huron Confederacy in 1649, Iroquois war parties killed or took captive every starving (and certainly peltry-less) group of Huron refugees they could find. Meanwhile, Iroquois ambassadors and warriors alternately negotiated with, cajoled, and threatened the Huron remnants living at Quebec to make them join their captive relatives in Iroquoia. Through all this, Mohawks, Senecas, and Onondagas occasionally shed each other's blood in arguments over the human spoils. Ultimately, in 1657, with French acquiescence, most of the Huron refugees filed away from Quebec—the Arendaronon nation to the Onondaga country and the Attignawantan nation to the Mohawk country.[47]

Judging by the number of prisoners taken during the Five Nations' wars from the 1640s to the 1670s with their other Iroquoian neighbors—the Neutral,

---

[45] *Jesuit Relations*, XXI-L, *passim*; Robert A. Goldstein, *French-Iroquois Diplomatic and Military Relations, 1609–1701* (The Hague, 1969), 62–99. The actual Canadian death toll in wars with the Iroquois before 1666 has recently been shown to have been quite low. Only 153 French were killed in raids while 143 were taken prisoner (perhaps 38 of those died in captivity); John A. Dickinson, "La guerre iroquoise et la mortalité en Nouvelle-France, 1608–1666," *Revue d'histoire de l'amérique française*, XXXVI (1982), 31–54. On 17th-century French captives of the Iroquois see Daniel K. Richter, "The Iroquois Melting Pot: Seventeenth-Century War Captives of the Five Nations" (paper presented at the Shelby Cullom Davis Center Conference on War and Society in Early America, Princeton University, March 11–12, 1983), 18–19.

[46] *Jesuit Relations*, L, 127–147, 239; *N.-Y. Col. Docs.*, III, 121–127; A. J. F. van Laer, trans. and ed., *Correspondence of Jeremias van Rensselaer, 1651–1674* (Albany, N.Y., 1932), 388.

[47] *Jesuit Relations*, XXXV, 183–205, XXXVI, 177–191, XLI, 43–65, XLIII, 115–125, 187–207, XLIV, 69–77, 165–167, 187–191; A. J. F. van Laer, trans. and ed., *Minutes of the Court of Fort Orange and Beverwyck, 1657–1660*, II (Albany, N.Y., 1923), 45–48; Scull, ed., *Voyages of Radisson*, 93–119; Nicholas Perrot, "Memoir on the Manners, Customs, and Religion of the Savages of North America" (c. 1680–1718), in Emma Helen Blair, ed. and trans., *The Indian Tribes of the Upper Mississippi Valley and Region of the Great Lakes . . .* (Cleveland, Ohio, 1911), I, 148–193.

Khionontateronon, Erie, and Susquehannock—these conflicts stemmed from a similar mingling of captive-taking and fur trade motives. Like the Huron, each of those peoples shared with the Iroquois mixed horticultural and hunting and fishing economies, related languages, and similar beliefs, making them ideal candidates for adoption. But they could not satisfy the spiraling Iroquois demand for furs and captives; war parties from the Five Nations had to range ever farther in their quest. In a not atypical series of raids in 1661–1662, they struck the Abenaki of the New England region, the Algonquians of the subarctic, the Siouans of the Upper Mississippi area, and various Indians near Virginia, while continuing the struggle with enemies closer to home.[48] The results of the mid-century campaigns are recorded in the *Jesuit Relations*, whose pages are filled with descriptions of Iroquois torture and execution of captives and note enormous numbers of adoptions. The Five Nations had absorbed so many prisoners that in 1657 Le Jeune believed that "more Foreigners than natives of the country" resided in Iroquoia.[49] By the mid-1660s several missionaries estimated that two-thirds or more of the people in many Iroquois villages were adoptees.[50]

By 1675 a half-century of constantly escalating warfare had at best enabled the Iroquois to hold their own. Despite the beaver wars, the Five Nations still had few dependable sources of furs. In the early 1670s they hunted primarily on lands north of Lake Ontario, where armed clashes with Algonquian foes were likely, opportunities to steal peltries from them were abundant, and conflict with the French who claimed the territory was always possible.[51] Ironically, even the Franco-Iroquois peace of 1667 proved a mixed blessing for the Five Nations. Under the provisions of the treaty, Jesuit priests, who had hitherto labored in Iroquois villages only sporadically and at the risk of their lives, established missions in each of the Five Nations.[52] The Jesuits not only created Catholic converts but also generated strong Christian and traditionalist factions that brought unprecedented disquiet to Iroquois communities. Among the Onondaga, for example, the Christian sachem Garakontié's refusal to perform his duties in the traditional manner disrupted such important ceremonies as dream guessings, the roll call of the chiefs, and healing rituals.[53] And in 1671, traditionalist Mohawk women excluded at least one Catholic convert from her rightful seat on the council of matrons because of her faith.[54] Moreover, beginning in the late 1660s, missionaries encouraged increasing numbers of Catholic Iroquois—particularly Mohawks

[48] *Jesuit Relations*, XLVII, 139–153.

[49] *Ibid.*, XLIII, 265.

[50] *Ibid.*, XLV, 207, LI, 123, 187.

[51] *N.-Y. Col. Docs.*, IX, 80; Victor Konrad, "An Iroquois Frontier: The North Shore of Lake Ontario during the Late Seventeenth Century," *Journal of Historical Geography*, VII (1981), 129–144.

[52] *Jesuit Relations*, LI, 81–85, 167–257, LII, 53–55.

[53] *Ibid.*, LV, 61–63, LVII, 133–141, LVIII, 211, LX, 187–195.

[54] *Ibid.*, LIV, 281–283.

and Oneidas—to desert their homes for the mission villages of Canada; by the mid-1670s well over two hundred had departed.[55] A large proportion of those who left, however, were members of the Five Nations in name only. Many—perhaps most—were recently adopted Huron and other prisoners, an indication that the Iroquois were unable to assimilate effectively the mass of newcomers their mid-century wars had brought them.[56]

Problems in incorporating adoptees reflected a broader dilemma: by the late 1670s the mourning-war complex was crumbling. Warfare was failing to maintain a stable population; despite torrents of prisoners, gains from adoption were exceeded by losses from disease, combat, and migrations to Canada. Among the Mohawk—for whom more frequent contemporary population estimates exist than for the other nations of the confederacy—the number of warriors declined from 700 or 800 in the 1640s to approximately 300 in the late 1670s. Those figures imply that, even with a constant infusion of captive adoptees, Mohawk population fell by half during that period.[57] The Five Nations as a whole fared only slightly better. In the 1640s the confederacy, already drastically reduced in numbers, had counted over 10,000 people. By the 1670s there were perhaps only 8,600.[58] The mourning-war, then, was not discharging one of its primary functions.

[55] *Ibid.*, LVI, 29, LVIII, 247–253, LX, 145–147, LXI, 195–199, LXIII, 141–189.

[56] *Ibid.*, LV, 33–37, LVIII, 75–77.

[57] E. B. O'Callaghan, ed., *The Documentary History of the State of New-York*, octavo ed. (Albany, N.Y., 1849–1851), I, 12–14; *Jesuit Relations,* XXIV, 295. Reflecting the purposes of most Euro-Americans who made estimates of Indian population, figures are usually given in terms of the number of available fighting men. The limited data available for direct comparisons of estimates of Iroquois fighting strength with estimates of total population indicate that the ratio of one warrior for every four people proposed in Sherburne F. Cook, "Interracial Warfare and Population Decline among the New England Indians," *Ethnohistory,* XX (1973), 13, applies to the Five Nations. Compare the estimates of a total Mohawk population of 560–580 in William Andrews to the Secretary of the Society for the Propagation of the Gospel in Foreign Parts, Sept. 7, 1713, Oct. 17, 1715, Records of the Society for the Propagation of the Gospel, Letterbooks, Ser. A, VIII, 186, XI, 268–269, S.P.G. Archives, London (microfilm ed.), with the concurrent estimates of approximately 150 Mohawk warriors in Bernardus Freeman to the Secretary of S.P.G., May 28, 1712, *ibid.*, VII, 203; Peter Wraxall, *An Abridgement of the Indian Affairs . . . Transacted in the Colony of New York, from the Year 1678 to the Year 1751,* ed. Charles Howard McIlwain (Cambridge, Mass., 1915), 69; *N.-Y. Col. Docs.,* V, 272; and Lawrence H. Leder, ed., *The Livingston Indian Records, 1666–1723* (Gettysburg, Pa., 1956), 220.

[58] The estimate of 10,000 for the 1640s is from Trigger, *Children of Aataentsic,* I, 98; the figure of 8,600 for the 1670s is calculated from Wentworth Greenhalgh's 1677 estimate of 2,150 Iroquois warriors, in O'Callaghan, ed., *Documentary History,* I, 12–14. Compare the late 1670s estimate in Hennepin, *New Discovery,* II, 92–93, and see the tables of 17th- and 18th-century Iroquois warrior population in Snyderman, "Behind the Tree of Peace," *Pa. Archaeol.,* XVIII, nos. 3–4 (1948), 42; Bruce G. Trigger, ed., *Northeast,* in William C. Sturtevant, ed., *Handbook of North American Indians,* XV (Washington, D.C., 1978), 421; and Gunther Michelson, "Iroquois Population Statistics," *Man in the Northeast,* No. 14 (1977), 3–17. William Starna has recently suggested that all previous estimates for 1635 and earlier of Mohawk—and by implication Five Nations—population are drastically understated ("Mohawk Iroquois Populations: A Revision," *Ethnohistory,* XXVII [1980], 371–382).

Meanwhile, ancient customs regarding the treatment of prisoners were decaying as rituals degenerated into chaotic violence and sheer murderous rage displaced the orderly adoption of captives that the logic of the mourning-war demanded. In 1682 missionary Jean de Lamberville asserted that Iroquois warriors "killed and ate . . . on the spot" over six hundred enemies in a campaign in the Illinois country; if he was even half right, it is clear that something had gone horribly wrong in the practice of the mourning-war. The decay of important customs associated with traditional warfare is further indicated by Lamberville's account of the return of that war party with its surviving prisoners. A gauntlet ceremony at the main Onondaga village turned into a deadly attack, forcing headmen to struggle to protect the lives of the captives. A few hours later, drunken young men, "who observe[d] no usages or customs," broke into longhouses and tried to kill the prisoners whom the headmen had rescued. In vain leaders pleaded with their people to remember "that it was contrary to custom to ill-treat prisoners on their arrival, when They had not yet been given in the place of any person . . . and when their fate had been left Undecided by the victors."[59]

Nevertheless, despite the weakening of traditional restraints, in the 1670s Iroquois warfare still performed useful functions. It maintained a tenuous supply of furs to trade for essential European goods; it provided frequent campaigns to allow young men to show their valor; and it secured numerous captives to participate in the continual mourning rituals that the many Iroquois deaths demanded (though there could never be enough to restock the population absolutely). In the quarter-century after 1675, however, the scales would tip: by 1700 the Anglo-French struggle for control of the continent would make warfare as the Five Nations were practicing it dangerously dysfunctional for their societies.

III

During the mid-1670s the Five Nations' relations with their Indian and European neighbors were shifting. In 1675 the Mohawk and the Mahican made peace under pressure from Albany and ended—except for a few subsequent skirmishes—over a decade of conflict that had cost each side heavily.[60] In the same year the long and destructive war of the Oneida, Onondaga, Cayuga, and Seneca against the Susquehannock concluded as the latter withdrew from Pennsylvania to Maryland. The end of hostilities with the Mahican and Susquehannock allowed the Iroquois to refocus westward their quest for

[59] *Jesuit Relations,* LXII, 71–95, quotation on p. 83.
[60] Leder, ed., *Livingston Indian Records,* 35–38; Allen W. Trelease, *Indian Affairs in Colonial New York: The Seventeenth Century* (Ithaca, N.Y., 1960), 229–230; Francis Jennings, "Glory, Death, and Transfiguration: The Susquehannock Indians in the Seventeenth Century," Am. Phil. Soc., *Procs.,* CXII (1968), 15–53.

furs and captives. In the late 1670s and early 1680s conflicts with the Illinois, Miami, and other western peoples intensified, while relations with the Wyandot (composed of remnants of the Huron and other Iroquoian groups forced to the west in earlier wars with the Five Nations) and with various elements of the Ottawa alternated between skirmishes and efforts to cement military alliances against other enemies of the Iroquois.[61] As the Onondaga orator Otreouti (whom the French called *La Grande Gueule*, "Big Mouth") explained in 1684, the Five Nations "fell upon the *Illinese* and the *Oumamies* [Miami], because they cut down the trees of Peace that serv'd for limits or boundaries to our Frontiers. They came to hunt Beavers upon our Lands; and contrary to the custom of all the Savages, have carried off whole Stocks, both Male and Female."[62] Whether those hunting grounds actually belonged to the Five Nations is questionable, but the importance of furs as an Iroquois war aim is not. And captives were also a lucrative prize, as the arrival in 1682 of several hundred Illinois prisoners demonstrated.[63] But this last of the beaver wars—which would melt into the American phase of the War of the League of Augsburg (King William's War)—was to differ devastatingly from earlier Iroquois conflicts. At the same time that the Five Nations began their fresh series of western campaigns the English and French empires were also beginning to compete seriously for the furs and lands of that region. The Iroquois would inevitably be caught in the Europeans' conflicts.[64]

Until the mid-1670s the Five Nations had only to deal, for all practical purposes, with the imperial policies of one European Power, France. The vital Iroquois connection with the Dutch of New Netherland and, after the 1664 conquest, with the English of New York had rested almost solely on trade. But when the English took possession of the province for the second time in 1674, the new governor, Sir Edmund Andros, had more grandiose designs for the Iroquois in the British American empire. He saw the Five Nations as the linchpin in his plans to pacify the other Indian neighbors of the English colonies; he hoped to make the Five Nations a tool in his dealings with the Calverts of Maryland; and he sought an opportunity to annex land to New York from Connecticut by encouraging the Iroquois to fight alongside New

[61] *Jesuit Relations*, LVI, 43–45, LIX, 251, LX, 211, LXII, 185; Hennepin, *New Discovery*, I, 100–295. Although the western nations had been included in the Franco-Iroquois peace of 1667, skirmishing in the west had never totally ceased; see *Jesuit Relations*, LIII, 39–51, LIV, 219–227, and *N.-Y. Col. Docs.*, IX, 79–80.

[62] Baron [de] Lahontan, *New Voyages to North-America . . .* (London, 1703), I, 41.

[63] *Jesuit Relations*, LXII, 71.

[64] For fuller accounts of the complex diplomacy, intrigue, trade wars, and military conflicts concerning the west between 1675 and 1689 touched on in the following paragraphs see, from a Canadian perspective, W. J. Eccles, *Frontenac: The Courtier Governor* (Toronto, 1959), 99–229, and, from a New York perspective, Trelease, *Indian Affairs in Colonial New York*, 204–301. A brief discussion of the Iroquois role is Richard Aquilla, "The Iroquois Restoration: A Study of Iroquois Power, Politics, and Relations with Indians and Whites, 1700–1744" (Ph.D. diss., Ohio State University, 1977), 16–29.

England in its 1675–1676 war on the Wampanoag Metacom ("King Philip") and his allies.[65] After Andros, New York–Iroquois relations would never be the same, as successors in the governor's chair attempted to use the Five Nations for imperial purposes. Thomas Dongan, who assumed the governorship in 1683, tried to strengthen New York's tenuous claims to suzerainty over the Five Nations—in 1684 he ceremoniously distributed the duke of York's coat of arms to be hung in their villages—and he directly challenged French claims in the west by sending trading parties into the region.[66]

Meanwhile the French had begun their own new westward thrust. In 1676 Canadian governor Louis de Buade de Frontenac established a post at Niagara and a few years later René-Robert Cavelier de La Salle began to construct a series of forts in the Illinois country. The French had long trodden a fine line in western policy. On the one hand, Iroquois raids in the west could not be allowed to destroy Indian allies of New France or to disrupt the fur trade, but, on the other hand, some hostility between the Iroquois and the western Indians helped prevent the latter from taking their furs to Albany markets. In the late 1670s and the 1680s Frontenac, and especially the governors during the interval between his two tenures, Joseph-Antoine Le Febvre de La Barre and Jacques-René de Brisay de Denonville, watched that policy unravel as they noted with alarm New York trading expeditions in the west, Iroquois raids on Indian hunters and *coureurs de bois*, Iroquois negotiations with the Wyandot and Ottawa, and the continual flow of firearms from Albany to the Five Nations.[67] As Iroquois spokesmen concisely explained to Dongan in 1684, "The French will have all the Bevers, and are angry with us for bringing any to you."[68]

French officials, faced with the potential ruin of their western fur trade, determined to humble the Five Nations. For over a decade, Canadian armies repeatedly invaded Iroquoia to burn villages, fields, and corn supplies. Although the first French attempt, led by La Barre against the Seneca in 1684, ended in ignoble failure for the French and diplomatic triumph for the

---

[65] *N.-Y. Col. Docs.*, III, 254–259; Francis Paul Jennings, "Miquon's Passing: Indian-European Relations in Colonial Pennsylvania, 1674 to 1755" (Ph.D. diss., University of Pennsylvania, 1965), 10–50; Douglas Edward Leach, *Flintlock and Tomahawk: New England in King Philip's War* (New York, 1958), 59–60, 176–177.

[66] O'Callaghan, ed., *Documentary History*, I, 391–420; Wraxall, *Abridgement of Indian Affairs*, ed. McIlwain, 10; Helen Broshar, "The First Push Westward of the Albany Traders," *MVHR*, VII (1920), 228–241; Henry Allain St. Paul, "Governor Thomas Dongan's Expansion Policy," *Mid-America*, XVII (1935), 172–184, 236–272; Gary B. Nash, "The Quest for the Susquehanna Valley: New York, Pennsylvania, and the Seventeenth-Century Fur Trade," *New York History*, XLVIII (1967), 3–27; Daniel K. Richter, "Rediscovered Links in the Covenant Chain: Previously Unpublished Transcripts of New York Indian Treaty Minutes, 1677–1691," American Antiquarian Society, *Proceedings*, XCII (1982), 63–66.

[67] Hennepin, *New Discovery*, I, 20–144; Lahontan, *New Voyages*, I, 269–274; *Jesuit Relations*, LXII, 151–165; *N.-Y. Col. Docs.*, IX, 296–303.

[68] *N.-Y. Col. Docs.*, III, 417.

Iroquois, later invasions sent the Five Nations to the brink of disaster. In 1687 La Barre's successor, Denonville, marched against Iroquoia with an army of over 2,000 French regulars, Canadian militia, and Indian warriors. Near Fort Frontenac his troops kidnapped an Iroquois peace delegation and captured the residents of two small villages of Iroquois who had lived on the north shore of Lake Ontario for nearly two decades. Denonville sent over thirty of the prisoners to France as slaves for the royal galleys, and then proceeded toward the Seneca country. After a brief but costly skirmish with Seneca defenders who hid in ambush, the invaders destroyed what was left of the Seneca villages, most of which the inhabitants had burned before fleeing to safety. Six years later, after war had been declared between France and England, the Canadians struck again. In January 1693, 625 regulars, militia, and Indians surprised the four Mohawk villages, captured their residents, and burned longhouses and stores of food as they retreated. Then, in 1696, the aged Frontenac—again governor and now carried into the field on a chair by his retainers—led at least 2,000 men to Onondaga, which he found destroyed by the retreating villagers. While his troops razed the ripening Onondaga corn, he received a plea for negotiation from the nearby Oneida village. The governor despatched Philippe de Rigaud de Vaudreuil and a detachment of 600 men, who extracted from the few Oneida who remained at home a promise that their people would soon move to a Canadian mission. Vaudreuil burned the village anyway.[69]

The repeated French invasions of Iroquoia took few lives directly—only in the campaign against the Mohawk in 1693 did the invaders attack fully occupied villages—but their cumulative effect was severe. One village or nation left homeless and deprived of food supplies could not depend on aid from the others, who faced similar plights. And as the Five Nations struggled to avoid starvation and to rebuild their villages, frequent raids by the Indian allies of the French levied a heavy toll in lives. In December 1691 a Mohawk-Oneida war party sustained fifteen deaths in an encounter on Lake George—losses significant beyond their numbers because they included all of the two nations' war chiefs and contributed to a total of 90 Mohawk and Oneida warriors killed since 1689. The Mohawk, who in the late 1670s had fielded approximately 300 warriors, in 1691 could muster only 130.[70] Combat fatalities, the continued exodus of Catholic converts to Canada, and the invasion of 1693 had, lamented a Mohawk orator, left his nation "a mean poor people," who had "lost all by the Enemy."[71] Fighting in the early 1690s had considerably weakened the three western Iroquois nations as well. In

[69] N.-Y. Col. Docs., IX, 234–248, 358–369, 550–561, 639–656; Jesuit Relations, LXIII, 269–281, LXIV, 239–259, LXV, 25–29; Lahontan, New Voyages, I, 29–45, 68–80; Francis Parkman, Count Frontenac and New France under Louis XIV (Boston, 1877), 89–115, 139–157, 309–316, 410–417.
[70] N.-Y. Col. Docs., III, 814–816.
[71] Ibid., IV, 38–39.

February 1692, for example, 50 Iroquois encountered a much larger French and Indian force above Montreal, and 40 suffered death or capture; a month later, 200 met disaster farther up the Saint Lawrence, when many were "captured, killed and defeated with loss of their principal chiefs."[72] Through the mid-1690s sporadic raids in and around Iroquoia by Canada's Indian allies kept the Five Nations on the defensive.[73]

The Five Nations did not meekly succumb. In 1687, soon after Denonville's capture of the Iroquois settled near Fort Frontenac and his invasion of the Seneca country, a Mohawk orator declared to Governor Dongan his people's intention to strike back at the French in the tradition of the mourning-war. "The Governor of Canada," he proclaimed, "has started an unjust war against all the [Five] nations. The Maquase [Mohawk] does not yet have any prisoners, but that Governor has taken a hundred prisoners from all the nations to the West. . . . Therefore the nations have desired to revenge the unjust attacks."[74] Iroquois raids for captives kept New France in an uproar through the early 1690s.[75] The warriors' greatest successes occurred during the summer of 1689. That June a Mohawk orator, speaking for all Five Nations, vowed "that the Place where the French Stole their Indians two years ago should soon be cut off (meaning Fort Frontenac) for to steal people in a time of Peace is an Inconsiderate work."[76] Within two months the Iroquois had forced the temporary abandonment of Frontenac and other French western posts, and, in an assault at Lachine on Montreal Island, had killed twenty-four French and taken seventy to ninety prisoners.[77]

Later in the 1690s, however, as the Five Nations' losses mounted, their capacity to resist steadily diminished. They repeatedly sought military support from governors of New York, but little was forthcoming. "Since you are a Great People & we but a small, *you will protect us from the French*," an Iroquois orator told Dongan in 1684. "We have put *all our Lands & ourselves*, under the Protection of the Great Duke of york."[78] Yet as long as the crowns of England and France remained at peace, the duke's governors largely ignored their end of the

---

[72] *Ibid.*, IX, 531–535, quotation on p. 531.

[73] Leder, ed., *Livingston Indian Records*, 172–174; *N.-Y. Col. Docs.*, IX, 599–632; Colden, *History* (1747), 180–181.

[74] Leder, ed., *Livingston Indian Records*, 136–137.

[75] *Ibid.*, 139–140; *Jesuit Relations*, LXIII, 279, 287–289, LXIV, 249–259, LXV, 29; *N.-Y. Col. Docs.*, IX, 503–504, 538, 554–555.

[76] Treaty Minutes, June 17, 1689, untitled notebooks, Indians of North America, Miscellaneous Papers, 1620–1895, Manuscript Collections, American Antiquarian Society, Worcester, Mass.

[77] Richard A. Preston, trans., and Leopold Lamontagne, ed., *Royal Fort Frontenac* (Toronto, 1958), 175–180; Lahontan, *New Voyages*, I, 98–102, 147–151; *N.-Y. Col. Docs.*, IX, 434–438; Eccles, *Frontenac*, 186–197. English sources claimed 200 French deaths and 120 captures at Lachine (Trelease, *Indian Affairs in Colonial New York*, 297–298).

[78] Treaty Minutes, Aug. 2, 1684, untitled notebook, Indians of North America, Miscellaneous Papers, 1620–1895, Manuscript Collections, AAS.

bargain. England's subsequent declaration of war against France coincided with the Glorious Revolution of 1688, which unleashed in New York the period of political chaos known as Leisler's Rebellion. In 1689 Mohawks visiting Albany witnessed firsthand the turmoil between Leislerians and anti-Leislerians, and soon the Iroquois observed the resulting English military impotence. In February 1690, a few miles from the easternmost Mohawk village, a party of French and their Indian allies destroyed the sleeping town of Schenectady, whose Leislerian inhabitants had ignored warnings from anti-Leislerian authorities at Albany to be on guard.[79] Soon after the attack, the Mohawk headmen visited Albany to perform a condolence ceremony for their neighbors' losses at Schenectady. When they finished, they urged prompt New York action against the French. But neither then nor during the rest of the war did the Iroquois receive a satisfactory response. New York's offensive war consisted of two ill-fated and poorly supported invasions of Canada: the first, in 1690, was a dismal failure, and the second, in 1691, cost nearly as many English casualties as it inflicted on the enemy.[80] After 1691 New York factional strife, lack of aid from England, and the preoccupation of other colonies with their own defense prevented further commitments of English manpower to support the Iroquois struggle with the French. The Five Nations received arms and ammunition from Albany—never as much or as cheap as they desired—and little else.[81]

What to the Five Nations must have seemed the most typical of English responses to their plight followed the French invasion of the Mohawk country in 1693. Though local officials at Albany and Schenectady learned in advance of the Canadian army's approach and provided for their own defense, they neglected to inform the Mohawk. In the wake of the attack, as approximately 300 Mohawk prisoners trooped toward Canada, Peter Schuyler assembled at Schenectady a force of 250 New Yorkers and some Mohawks who had escaped capture, but he was restrained from immediate pursuit by his vacillating commander, Richard Ingoldsby. At length Schuyler moved on his own initiative and, reinforced by war parties from the western Iroquois nations, overtook the French army and inflicted enough damage to force the release of most of the captive Mohawk. Meanwhile, when word of the invasion reached Manhattan, Gov. Benjamin Fletcher mustered 150 militia and sailed to Albany in the unprecedented time of less than three days; nevertheless, the fighting was already over. At a conference with Iroquois headmen a few days later, Fletcher's rush upriver earned him the title by which he would henceforth be known to the Five Nations: Cayenquiragoe, or "Great Swift

---

[79] O'Callaghan, ed., *Documentary History*, I, 284–319, II, 130–132; Leder, ed., *Livingston Indian Records*, 158–160.

[80] O'Callaghan, ed., *Documentary History*, II, 164–290; *N.-Y. Col. Docs.*, III, 800–805, IV, 193–196, IX, 513–515, 520–524.

[81] *N.-Y. Col. Docs.*, III, 836–844; Leder, ed., *Livingston Indian Records*, 165–166; O'Callaghan, ed., *Documentary History*, I, 323–325, 341–345; Herbert L. Osgood, *The American Colonies in the Eighteenth Century*, I (New York, 1924), 228–265.

Arrow." Fletcher took the name—chosen when the Iroquois learned that the word *fletcher* meant arrowmaker—as a supreme compliment. But, in view of the Mohawk's recent experience with the English—receiving no warning of the impending invasion, having to cool their heels at Schenectady while the enemy got away and Schuyler waited for marching orders, and listening to Fletcher rebuke them for their lax scouting and defense—the governor's political opponent Peter De La Noy may have been right to claim that Cayenquiragoe was a "sarcasticall pun" on Fletcher's name, bestowed for a showy effort that yielded no practical results.[82]

Yet if the English had been unable—or, as the Iroquois undoubtedly saw it, unwilling—to give meaningful military aid to the Five Nations, they were able to keep the Indians from negotiating a separate peace with the French that might leave New York exposed alone to attack. Although after 1688 ambassadors from several Iroquois nations periodically treated with the Canadians, New Yorkers maintained enough influence with factions among the Five Nations to sabotage all negotiations.[83] New York authorities repeatedly reminded their friends among the Iroquois of past French treacheries. At Albany in 1692, for example, Commander-in-Chief Ingoldsby warned the ambassadors of the Five Nations "that the Enemy has not forgot their old tricks." The French hoped "to lull the Brethren asleep and to ruine and distroy them at once, when they have peace in their mouths they have warr in their hearts."[84] Many Iroquois heeded the message. Lamberville complained in 1694 that "the english of those quarters have so intrigued that they have ruined all the hopes for peace that we had entertained."[85] The repeated failure of negotiations reinforced Canadian mistrust of the Iroquois and led French authorities to prosecute the war with more vigor. By the mid-1690s, with talks stymied, all the Five Nations could do was to accept English arms and ammunition and continue minor raids on their enemies while awaiting a general peace.[86]

For the Iroquois that peace did not come with the Treaty of Ryswick in 1697. At Ryswick, the European powers settled none of the issues that had provoked the conflict, yet they gained a respite that allowed each side to regroup. Paradoxically, however, a truce between the empires precluded an end to conflict between the French and the Five Nations; jurisdiction over the Iroquois and their territory was one of the sticking points left unsettled. Accordingly, Frontenac and his successor, Louis-Hector de Callière, refused to consider the Iroquois—whom they called unruly French subjects—to be included in the treaty with England and insisted that they make a separate peace with New France. Fletcher and his successor, Richard Coote, earl of

[82] *N.-Y. Col. Docs.,* IV, 6–7, 14–24, 222; Colden, *History* (1747), 142–150.

[83] *N.-Y. Col. Docs.,* IX, 384–393, 515–517, 565–572, 596–599; *Jesuit Relations,* LXIV, 143–145.

[84] *N.-Y. Col. Docs.,* III, 841–844; see also *ibid.,* IV, 77–98, 279–282.

[85] *Jesuit Relations,* LXIV, 259.

[86] *N.-Y. Col. Docs.,* IX, 601–671.

nt, argued equally strenuously that the Iroquois were compre-
hen... in the treaty as English subjects. Thus they tried to forbid direct
Franco-Iroquois negotiations and continued to pressure their friends among
the Five Nations to prevent serious talks from occurring.[87] While Iroquois
leaders struggled to escape the diplomatic bind, the Indian allies of New
France continued their war against their ancient Iroquois enemies. In the late
1690s the Ojibwa led a major western Indian offensive that, according to
Ojibwa tradition, killed enormous numbers of Seneca and other Iroquois.
Euro-American sources document more moderate, yet still devastating, fatalities: the Onondaga lost over ninety men within a year of the signing of
the Treaty of Ryswick, and the Seneca perhaps as many. Such defeats continued into 1700, when the Seneca suffered over fifty deaths in battles with
the Ottawa and Illinois. All along at Albany, authorities counseled the Five
Nations not to strike back, but to allow Bellomont time to negotiate with Callière on their behalf.[88]

IV

By 1700 Iroquois warfare and culture had reached a turning point. Up to
about 1675, despite the impact of disease, firearms, and the fur trade, warfare still performed functions that outweighed its costs. But thereafter the
Anglo-French struggle for control of North America made war disastrous for
the Five Nations. Conflict in the west, instead of securing fur supplies, was
cutting them off, while lack of pelts to trade and wartime shortages of goods
at Albany created serious economic hardship in Iroquoia.[89] Those problems
paled, however, in comparison with the physical toll. All of the Iroquois nations except the Cayuga had seen their villages and crops destroyed by invading armies, and all five nations were greatly weakened by loss of members to captivity, to death in combat, or to famine and disease. By some
estimates, between 1689 and 1698 the Iroquois lost half of their fighting
strength. That figure is probably an exaggeration, but by 1700 perhaps 500 of
the 2,000 warriors the Five Nations fielded in 1689 had been killed or captured or had deserted to the French missions and had not been replaced by
younger warriors. A loss of well over 1,600 from a total population of approximately 8,600 seems a conservative estimate.[90]

[87] Trelease, *Indian Affairs in Colonial New York*, 323–342; *N.-Y. Col. Docs.*, IV, 367–374, 402–409.
[88] Leroy V. Eid, "The Ojibwa-Iroquois War: The War the Five Nations Did Not Win," *Ethnohistory*, XXVI (1979), 297–324; Wraxall, *Abridgement of Indian Affairs*, ed. McIlwain, 29–30; *N.-Y. Col.
Docs.*, IX, 681–688, 708–709.
[89] Aquila, "Iroquois Restoration," 71–79.
[90] A 1698 report on New York's suffering during the War of the League of Augsburg states that
there were 2,550 Iroquois warriors in 1689 and only 1,230 in 1698. The report probably contains
some polemical overstatement: the first figure seems too high and the second too low. By

At the turn of the century, therefore, the mourning-war was no longer even symbolically restocking the population. And, far from being socially integrative, the Five Nations' current war was splitting their communities asunder. The heavy death toll of previous decades had robbed them of many respected headmen and clan matrons to whom the people had looked for guidance and arbitration of disputes. As a group of young Mohawk warriors lamented in 1691 when they came to parley with the Catholic Iroquois settled near Montreal, "all those . . . who had sense are dead."[91] The power vacuum, war weariness, and the pressures of the imperial struggle combined to place at each other's throats those who believed that the Iroquois' best chance lay in a separate peace with the French and those who continued to rely on the English alliance. "The [Five] Nations are full of faction, the French having got a great interest among them," reported the Albany Commissioners for Indian Affairs in July 1700. At Onondaga, where, according to Governor Bellomont, the French had "full as many friends" as the English, the situation was particularly severe. Some sachems found themselves excluded from councils, and factions charged one another with using poison to remove adversaries from the scene. One pro-English Onondaga headman, Aquendero, had to take refuge near Albany, leaving his son near death and supposedly bewitched by opponents.[92] Their politics being ordered by an interlocking structure of lineages, clans, and moieties, the Iroquois found such factions, which cut across kinship lines, difficult if not impossible to handle. In the 1630s the Huron, whose political structure was similar, never could manage the novel factional alignments that resulted from the introduction of Christianity. That failure perhaps contributed to their demise at the hands of the Five Nations.[93] Now the Iroquois found themselves at a similar pass.

As the new century opened, however, Iroquois headmen were beginning to construct solutions to some of the problems facing their people. From 1699 to 1701 Iroquois ambassadors—in particular the influential Onondaga Teganissorens—threaded the thickets of domestic factionalism and shuttled between their country and the Euro-American colonies to negotiate what

---

comparison, 2,050 Iroquois warriors were estimated by Denonville in 1685, 1,400 by Bellomont in 1691, 1,750 by Bernardus Freeman in 1700, and 1,200 by a French cabinet paper in 1701 (*N.-Y. Col. Docs.*, IV, 337, 768, IX, 281, 725; Freeman to the Secretary, May 28, 1712, Records of S.P.G., Letterbooks, Ser. A, VII, 203). If the figure of 1,750 warriors cited by Freeman—a minister who worked with the Mohawk—is correct, the total Iroquois population in 1700 was approximately 7,000, calculated by the ratio in note 57.

[91] *Jesuit Relations*, LXIV, 59–61.

[92] *N.-Y. Col. Docs.*, IV, 648–661, 689–690.

[93] Trigger, *Children of Aataentsic*, II, 709–724. See also the discussions of Indian factionalism in Robert F. Berkhofer, Jr., "The Political Context of a New Indian History," *Pacific Historical Review*, XL (1971), 373–380; and Edward H. Spicer, *Cycles of Conquest: The Impact of Spain, Mexico, and the United States on the Indians of the Southwest, 1533–1960* (Tucson, Ariz., 1962), 491–501.

one scholar has termed "The Grand Settlement of 1701."[94] On August 4, 1701, at an immense gathering at Montreal, representatives of the Seneca, Cayuga, Onondaga, and Oneida, also speaking for the Mohawk, met Governor Callière and headmen of the Wyandot, Algonquin, Abenaki, Nipissing, Ottawa, Ojibwa, Sauk, Fox, Miami, Potawatomi, and other French allies. The participants ratified arrangements made during the previous year that provided for a general peace, established vague boundaries for western hunting territories (the Iroquois basically consented to remain east of Detroit), and eschewed armed conflict in favor of arbitration by the governor of New France. A few days later, the Iroquois and Callière reached more specific understandings concerning Iroquois access to Detroit and other French western trading posts. Most important from the French standpoint, the Iroquois promised neutrality in future Anglo-French wars.[95]

A delegation of Mohawks arrived late at the Montreal conference; they, along with ambassadors from the western Iroquois, had been at Albany negotiating with Lt. Gov. John Nanfan, who had replaced the deceased Bellomont. The Five Nations' spokesmen had first assured Nanfan of their fidelity and told him that the simultaneous negotiations at Montreal were of no significance. Then they had agreed equivocally to perpetuate their military alliance with the English, reiterated that trade lay at the heart of Iroquois–New York relations, consented to the passage through Iroquoia of western Indians going to trade at Albany, and granted the English crown a "deed" to the same western hunting territories assured to the Five Nations in the Montreal treaty. In return, Nanfun promised English defense of Iroquois hunting rights in those lands. Meanwhile, at Philadelphia, yet a third series of negotiations had begun, which, while not usually considered part of the Grand Settlement, reflected the same Iroquois diplomatic thrust; by 1704 those talks would produce an informal trade agreement between the Five Nations and Pennsylvania.[96]

On one level, this series of treaties represented an Iroquois defeat. The Five Nations had lost the war and, in agreeing to peace on terms largely dictated by Callière, had acknowledged their inability to prevail militarily over their French, and especially their Indian, enemies.[97] Nevertheless, the Grand

[94] Anthony F. C. Wallace, "Origins of Iroquois Neutrailty: The Grand Settlement of 1701," *Pennsylvania History*, XXIV (1957), 223–235. The best reconstruction of the Iroquois diplomacy that led to the Grand Settlement is Richard L. Haan, "The Covenant Chain: Iroquois Diplomacy on the Niagara Frontier, 1697–1730" (Ph.D. diss., University of California, Santa Barbara, 1976), 64–147.
[95] Bacqueville de La Potherie, *Histoire de l'Amérique Septentrionale*, IV (Paris, 1722), *passim; N.-Y. Col. Docs.*, IX, 715–725.
[96] *N.-Y. Col. Docs.*, IV, 889–911; *Minutes of the Provincial Council of Pennsylvania*, II (Harrisburg, Pa., 1838), 142–143; William M. Beauchamp, *A History of the New York Iroquois, Now Commonly Called the Six Nations*, New York State Museum Bulletin 78 (Albany, N.Y., 1905), 256; Jennings, "Miquon's Passing," 118–121.
[97] Eid, "Ojibwa–Iroquois War," *Ethnohistory*, XXVI (1979), 297–324.

Settlement did secure for the Iroquois five important ends: escape from the devastating warfare of the 1690s; rights to hunting in the west; potentially profitable trade with western Indians passing through Iroquoia to sell furs at Albany; access to markets in New France and Pennsylvania as well as in New York; and the promise of noninvolvement in future imperial wars. The Grand Settlement thus brought to the Five Nations not only peace on their northern and western flanks but also a more stable economy based on guaranteed western hunting territories and access to multiple Euro-American markets. Henceforth, self-destructive warfare need no longer be the only means of ensuring Iroquois economic survival, and neither need inter-Indian beaver wars necessarily entrap the Five Nations in struggles between Euro-Americans.[98] In 1724, nearly a generation after the negotiation of the Grand Settlement, an Iroquois spokesman explained to a delegation from Massachusetts how the treaties, while limiting Iroquois diplomatic and military options, nevertheless proved beneficial. "Tho' the Hatchett lays by our side yet the way is open between this Place and Canada, and trade is free both going and coming," he answered when the New Englanders urged the Iroquois to attack New France. "If a War should break out and we should use the Hatchett that lays by our Side, those Paths which are now open wo[u]ld be stopped, and if we should make war it would not end in a few days as yours doth but it must last till one nation or the other is destroyed as it has been heretofore with us[.] . . . [W]e know what whipping and scourging is from the Governor of Canada."[99]

After the Grand Settlement, then, Iroquois leaders tried to abandon warfare as a means of dealing with the diplomatic problems generated by the Anglo-French imperial rivalry and the economic dilemmas of the fur trade. Through most of the first half of the eighteenth century the headmen pursued a policy of neutrality between the empires with a dexterity that the English almost never, and the French only seldom, comprehended. At the same time the Iroquois began to cement peaceful trading relationships with the western nations. Sporadic fighting continued in the western hunting grounds through the first decade and a half of the eighteenth century, as the parties to the 1701 Montreal treaty sorted out the boundaries of their territories and engaged in reciprocal raids for captives that were provoked by contact between Iroquois and western Indian hunters near French posts. Iroquois headmen quickly took advantage of Canadian arbitration when such quarrels arose, however, and they struggled to restrain young warriors from campaigning in the west.[100] As peace took hold, Alexander Montour, the son

[98] Aquila, "Iroquois Restoration," 109–171; Richard Haan, "The Problem of Iroquois Neutrality: Suggestions for Revision," *Ethnohistory,* XXVII (1980), 317–330.
[99] *N.-Y. Col. Docs.,* V, 724–725.
[100] Leder, ed., *Livingston Indian Records,* 192–200; *N.-Y. Col. Docs.,* IX, 759–765, 848–849, 876–878; Yves F. Zoltvany, "New France and the West, 1701–1713," *Can. Hist. Rev.,* XLVI (1965), 315–321.

of a French man and an Iroquois woman, worked to build for the Iroquois a thriving trade between the western nations and Albany.[101]

The new diplomatic direction was tested between 1702 and 1713, when the imperial conflict resumed in the War of the Spanish Succession (Queen Anne's War). Through crafty Iroquois diplomacy, and thanks to the only halfhearted effort each European side devoted to the western theater, the Five Nations were able to maintain their neutrality and avoid heavy combat losses. Only between 1709 and 1711 did the imperial struggle again threaten to engulf the Five Nations. In 1709 Vaudreuil, now governor of New France, ordered the murder of Montour to prevent further diversion of French western trade to the Iroquois and the English. As a result, many formerly pro-French Iroquois turned against the Canadians, and most Mohawk and Oneida warriors, with many Onondagas and Cayugas, joined in the plans of Samuel Vetch and Francis Nicholson for an intercolonial invasion of Canada. Only the Senecas, who were most exposed to attack by Indian allies of the French, refused to participate.[102] The army of colonists and Iroquois, however, never set foot in Canada because Whitehall reneged on its promise of a fleet that would simultaneously attack Canada from the east. After the 1709 fiasco, Iroquois-French relations continued to deteriorate. The Seneca determined on war with the French in 1710, when they were attacked by western Indians apparently instigated by the Canadians. Then, in the spring of 1711, a party of French came to Onondaga and, spouting threats about the consequences of further Iroquois hostility, attempted to build a blockhouse in the village. When Vetch and Nicholson planned a second assault on Canada in the summer of 1711, large war parties from all Five Nations eagerly enlisted. Once more, however, the seaborne wing of the expedition failed, and the land army returned home without seeing the enemy.[103] The debacles of 1709 and 1711 confirmed the Iroquois in their opinion of English military impotence and contributed to a chill in Anglo-Iroquois relations that lasted for the rest of the decade.[104] Iroquois leaders once again steered a course of neutrality between the empires, and after the peace of Utrecht trade once again flourished with the western Indians.[105]

In addition to its diplomatic benefits, the Grand Settlement of 1701 provided a partial solution to Iroquois factionalism. Iroquoian non-state politi-

---

[101] Wraxall, *Abridgement of Indian Affairs*, ed. McIlwain, 44–67; "Continuation of Colden's History of the Five Indian Nations, for the Years 1707 through 1720," New-York Historical Society, *Collections*, LXVIII (1935), 360–367, hereafter cited as Colden, "Continuation"; Haan, "Covenant Chain," 152–153.

[102] Wraxall, *Abridgement of Indian Affairs*, ed. McIlwain, 64–69; *N.-Y. Col. Docs.*, IX, 902; Leder, ed., *Livingston Indian Records*, 207–210; Colden, "Continuation," 370–380.

[103] Colden, "Continuation," 398–409; *N.-Y. Col. Docs.*, V, 242–249, 267–277; G. M. Waller, "New York's Role in Queen Anne's War, 1702–1713," *New York History*, XXXIII (1952), 40–53; Bruce T. McCully, "Catastrophe in the Wilderness: New Light on the Canada Expedition of 1709," *WMQ*, 3d Ser., XI (1954), 441–456; Haan, "Covenant Chain," 148–198.

[104] *N.-Y. Col. Docs.*, V, 372–376, 382–388, 437, 484–487; Wraxall, *Abridgement of Indian Affairs*, ed. McIlwain, 98–105.

[105] *N.-Y. Col. Docs.*, V, 445–446, 584; Colden, "Continuation," 414–432; Haan, "Problem of Iroquois Neutrality," *Ethnohistory*, XXVII (1980), 324.

cal structures could not suppress factional cleavages entirely, and in the
years after 1701 differences over relations with the French and the English
still divided Iroquois communities, as each European power continued to
encourage its friends. Interpreters such as the Canadian Louis-Thomas
Chabert de Joncaire and the New Yorker Lawrence Claeson (or Claes) struggled to win the hearts of Iroquois villagers; each side gave presents to its
supporters; and on several occasions English officials interfered with the selection of sachems in order to strengthen pro-English factions. As a result,
fratricidal disputes still occasionally threatened to tear villages apart.[106] Still,
in general, avoidance of exclusive alliances or major military conflict with either European power allowed Iroquois councils to keep factional strife
within bounds. A new generation of headmen learned to maintain a rough
equilibrium between pro-French and pro-English factions at home, as well
as peaceful relations with French and English abroad. Central to that strategy was an intricate policy that tried to balance French against English fortified trading posts, Canadian against New York blacksmiths, and Jesuit
against Anglican missionaries. Each supplied the Iroquois with coveted aspects of Euro-American culture—trade goods, technology, and spiritual
power, respectively—but each also could be a focus of factional leadership
and a tool of Euro-American domination. The Grand Settlement provided a
way to lessen, though hardly eliminate, those dangers.[107]

The Iroquois balancing act was severely tested beginning in 1719, when
Joncaire persuaded pro-French elements of the Seneca to let him build a
French trading house at Niagara. Neither confederacy leaders nor Senecas opposed to the French encroachment attempted to dislodge the intruders
forcibly, as they had done in the previous century at Fort Frontenac. Instead,
Iroquois headmen unsuccessfully urged New York authorities to send troops
to destroy the post, thus hoping to place the onus on the British while avoiding an open breach between pro-French and pro-English Iroquois. But New
York Gov. William Burnet had other plans. In 1724 he announced his intention
to build an English counterpart to Niagara at Oswego. With the French beginning to fortify Niagara, league headmen reluctantly agreed to the English
proposals. In acquiescing to both forts, the Iroquois yielded a measure of sovereignty as Europeans defined the term; yet they dampened internal strife,
avoided exclusive dependence on either European power, and maintained
both factional and diplomatic balance.[108]

---

[106] *N.-Y. Col. Docs.*, V, 545, 569, 632, IX, 816; Thomas Barclay to Robert Hunter, Jan. 26, 1713 (extract), Records of S.P.G., Letterbooks, Ser. A, VIII, 251–252. For examples of Claeson's and Joncaire's activities see Colden, "Continuation," 360–363,   432–434, and *N.-Y. Col. Docs.*, V, 538,
562–569, IX, 759–765, 814, 876–903.

[107] *N.-Y. Col. Docs.*, V, 217–227; Colden, "Continuation," 408–409; Wraxall, *Abridgement of Indian
Affairs*, ed. McIlwain, 79n–80n.

[108] The evolution of Iroquois, French, and English policies concerning Niagara and Oswego may
be followed in *N.-Y. Col. Docs.*, V, *passim*, IX, 897–1016; Jennings, "Miquon's Passing," 256–274;
and Haan "Covenant Chain," 199–237.

The years following the Grand Settlement also witnessed the stabilization of Iroquois population. Though the numbers of the Iroquois continued to decline gradually, the forces that had so dramatically reduced them in the seventeenth century abated markedly after 1701. The first two decades of the eighteenth century brought only one major epidemic—smallpox in 1716[109]—while the flow of Catholic converts to Canadian missions also slowed. The missions near Montreal had lost much of the utopian character that had previously attracted so many Iroquois converts. By the early eighteenth century, drunkenness, crushing debts to traders, and insults from Euro-American neighbors were no less characteristic of Iroquois life in Canada than in Iroquoia, and the Jesuit priests serving the Canadian missions had become old, worn-out men who had long since abandoned dreams of turning Indians into Frenchmen.[110]

As the population drain from warfare, disease, and migration to mission villages moderated, peaceful assimilation of refugees from neighboring nations helped to replace those Iroquois who were lost. One French source even claimed, in 1716, that "the five Iroquois nations . . . are becoming more and more formidable through their great numbers."[111] Most notable among the newcomers were some 1,500 Tuscaroras who, after their defeat by the English and allied Indians of the Carolinas in 1713, migrated north to settle on lands located between the Onondaga and Oneida villages. They were adopted as the sixth nation of the Iroquois Confederacy about 1722. There are indications that the Tuscarora—who, according to William Andrews, Anglican missionary to the Mohawk, possessed "an Implacable hatred against Christians at Carolina"—contributed greatly to the spirit of independence and distrust of Europeans that guided the Six Nations on their middle course between the imperial powers. The Tuscarora, concluded Andrews, were "a great Occasion of Our Indians becoming so bad as they are, they now take all Occasions to find fault and quarrel, wanting to revolt."[112]

V

The first two decades of the eighteenth century brought a shift away from those aspects of Iroquois warfare that had been most socially disruptive. As the Iroquois freed themselves of many, though by no means all, of the demographic, economic, and diplomatic pressures that had made seventeenth-

---

[109] Andrews to the Secretary, Oct. 11, 1716, Records of S.P.G., Letterbooks, Ser. A, XII, 241; N.-Y. Col. Docs., V, 484–487, IX, 878.
[110] Jesuit Relations, LXVI, 203–207, LXVII, 39–41; N.-Y. Col. Docs., IX, 882–884; George F. G. Stanley, "The Policy of 'Franciscation' as Applied to the Indians during the Ancien Regime," Revue d'histoire de l'amérique française, III (1949–1950), 333–348; Cornelius J. Jaenen, "The Frenchification and Evanglization of the Amerindians in the Seventeenth Century New France" (sic), Canadian Catholic Historical Association, Study Sessions, XXXV (1969), 57–71.
[111] Jesuit Relations, LXVII, 27.
[112] Andrews to the Secretary, Apr. 20, 1716, Apr. 23, 1717, Records of S.P.G., Letterbooks, Ser. A, XI, 319–320, XII, 310–312.

century warfare so devastating, the mourning-war began to resume some of its traditional functions in Iroquois culture.

As the Five Nations made peace with their old western and northern foes, Iroquois mourning-war raids came to focus on enemies the Iroquois called "Flatheads"—a vague epithet for the Catawba and other tribes on the frontiers of Virginia and the Carolinas.[113] Iroquois and Flathead war parties had traded blows during the 1670s and 1680s, conflict had resumed about 1707, and after the arrival of the Tuscarora in the 1710s Iroquois raiding parties attacked the Flatheads regularly and almost exclusively.[114] The Catawba and other southeastern Indians sided with the Carolinians in the Tuscarora War of 1711–1713, bringing them into further conflict with warriors from the Five Nations, who fought alongside the Tuscarora.[115] After the Tuscarora moved north, Iroquois–Flathead warfare increased in intensity and lasted—despite several peace treaties—until the era of the American Revolution. This series of mourning-wars exasperated English officials from New York to the Carolinas, who could conceive no rational explanation for the conflicts except the intrigues of French envoys who delighted in stirring up trouble on English frontiers.[116]

Canadian authorities did indeed encourage Iroquois warriors with arms and presents. The French were happy for the chance to harass British settlements and to strike blows against Indians who troubled French inhabitants of New Orleans and the Mississippi Valley.[117] Yet the impetus for raiding the Flatheads lay with the Iroquois, not the French. At Onondaga in 1710, when emissaries from New York blamed French influence for the campaigns and presented a wampum belt calling for a halt to hostilities, a Seneca orator dismissed their arguments: "When I think of the Brave Warriours that hav[e] been slain by the Flatheads I can Govern my self no longer. . . . I reject your Belt for the Hatred I bear to the Flatheads can never be forgotten."[118] The Flatheads were an ideal target for the mourning-wars demanded by Iroquois women and warriors, for with conflict channeled southward, warfare with northern and western nations that, in the past, had brought disaster could be avoided. In addition, war with the Flatheads placated both Canadian

---

[113] Henry R. Schoolcraft, *Notes on the Iroquois: Or, Contributions to the Statistics, Aboriginal History, Antiquities and General Ethnology of Western New York* (New York, 1846), 148–149; Fenton, "Iroquois in History," in Leacock and Lurie, eds., *North American Indians*, 147–148; Beauchamp, *History of New York Iroquois*, 139.

[114] On Iroquois–Flathead conflicts before 1710 see Colden, *History* (1727), 30–71, and "Continuation," 361–363, and Wraxall, *Abridgement of Indian Affairs*, ed. McIlwain, 50–61. References to raids after 1710 in Colden, *N.-Y. Col. Docs.*, and other sources are too numerous to cite here; a useful discussion is Aquila, "Iroquois Restoration," 294–346.

[115] Wraxall, *Abridgement of Indian Affairs*, ed. McIlwain, 94–96; *N.-Y. Col. Docs.*, V, 372–376, 382–388, 484–493; Verner W. Crane, *The Southern Frontier, 1670–1732* (Durham, N.C., 1928), 158–161.

[116] *N.-Y. Col. Docs.*, V, 542–545, 562–569, 635–640.

[117] *Ibid.*, IX, 876–878, 884–885, 1085, 1097–1098.

[118] Colden, "Continuation," 382–383, brackets in original.

authorities and pro-French Iroquois factions, since the raids countered a pro-English trade policy with a military policy useful to the French. And, from the perspective of Iroquois–English relations, the southern campaigns posed few risks. New York officials alternately forbade and countenanced raids against southern Indians as the fortunes of frontier war in the Carolinas and the intrigues of intercolonial politics shifted. But even when the governors of the Carolinas, Virginia, Pennsylvania, and New York did agree on schemes to impose peace, experience with English military impotence had taught the Iroquois that the governors could do little to stop the conflict.[119]

While the diplomatic advantages were many, perhaps the most important aspect of the Iroquois–Flathead conflicts was the partial return they allowed to the traditional ways of the mourning-war. By the 1720s the Five Nations had not undone the ravages of the preceding century, yet they had largely extricated themselves from the socially disastrous wars of the fur trade and of the European empires. And though prisoners no longer flowed into Iroquois villages in the floods of the seventeenth century, the southern raids provided enough captives for occasional mourning and condolence rituals that dried Iroquois tears and reminded the Five Nations of their superiority over their enemies. In the same letter of 1716 in which missionary Andrews noted the growing independence of the Iroquois since the Tuscarora had settled among them and the southern wars had intensified, he also vividly described the reception recently given to captives of the Onondaga and Oneida.[120] Iroquois warfare was again binding Iroquois families and villages together.

---

[119] For examples of shifting New York policies regarding the Iroquois southern campaigns see *N.-Y. Col. Docs.*, V, 446–464, 542–545, and Wraxall, *Abridgement of Indian Affairs,* ed. McIlwain, 123.
[120] Andrews to the Secretary, Apr. 20, 1716, Records of S.P.G., Letterbooks, Ser. A., XI, 320.

The Indians' New World: The Catawba Experience

James H. Merrell

INTRODUCTION

The Indians encountered by British voyagers to the Americas have always been important players in the drama of early American history. For as long as scholars have been writing on the subject, they have acknowledged that the first Europeans to arrive in any part of the hemisphere had to confront the natives and deal with them. From the European point of view this confrontation was often made easier by epidemic disease. Despite this long-standing awareness of the presence of other people on the land that the British soldiers and settlers wished to conquer and exploit, however, a sensitive history of relationships between the arriving Europeans and particular Indian cultural groups has only recently begun to emerge in the historical literature. In part, this failing can be explained by the difficulty involved in identifying appropriate sources, and in part it can be attributed to ethnocentrism and insensitivity.

Whatever the cause, the absence of genuinely bilateral histories of Indian-white encounters is now being brilliantly corrected by a younger generation of scholars of whom James H. Merrell is one of the most talented. Merrell's basic insight—that the arrival of Europeans marked the emergence of a "new" world for Indians as well as for whites—may seem so obvious as barely to merit notice. Yet it is a point that turns out to have startling explanatory power because it redirects the focus of research and interpretation in a way that grants to Indians (in this case the Catawbas) a distinctive historical experience that previous historians had unthinkingly denied them.

Merrell's interpretation should be compared with Daniel Richter's essay on the Iroquois because they exhibit many of the same virtues. Both the Iroquois and the Catawbas survived the perils of contact by aggressively incorporating neighboring peoples, a common experience that did not

James H. Merrell, "The Indians' New World: The Catawba Experience," in *William and Mary Quarterly*, 41, 1984, pp. 537–565. Reprinted by permission of the author.

*prevent them from hating each other. In addition, Merrell's focus on mat-
ters of trade and economic relations should remind us that in many respects
Indians and British settlers found ways to accommodate themselves to each
other's presence and even to gain from the connection.*

*At the same time, Merrell does not allow us to forget that Indian life
was unalterably transformed by the arrival of white men and that, although
gradual, change inevitably came to Catawba life.*

- *Has Merrell added an important new dimension to our understanding of
early American history, or has he merely added detail to a story whose
tragic conclusion was foreordained?*
- *Were the Catawbas really the formidable force he portrays them to be, or has
he inflated their role in order to make a point?*

In August 1608 John Smith and his band of explorers captured an Indian
named Amoroleck during a skirmish along the Rappahannock River. Asked
why his men—a hunting party from towns upstream—had attacked the
English, Amoroleck replied that they had heard the strangers "were a people come from under the world, to take their world from them."[1] Smith's
prisoner grasped a simple yet important truth that students of colonial
America have overlooked: after 1492 native Americans lived in a world
every bit as new as that confronting transplanted Africans or Europeans.

The failure to explore the Indians' new world helps explain why, despite
many excellent studies of the native American past,[2] colonial history often
remains "a history of those men and women—English, European, and
African—who transformed America from a geographical expression into a
new nation."[3] One reason Indians generally are left out may be the apparent
inability to fit them into the new world theme, a theme that exerts a powerful hold on our historical imagination and runs throughout our efforts to in-

[1] Edward Arber and A. G. Bradley, eds., *Travels and Works of Captain John Smith . . .* , II (Edinburgh, 1910), 427.
[2] Bernard W. Sheehan, "Indian-White Relations in Early America: A Review Essay," *William and
Mary Quarterly*, 3d Ser., XXVI (1969), 267–286; James Axtell, "The Ethnohistory of Early Amer-
ica: A Review Essay," *ibid.*, XXXV (1978), 110–144.
[3] Benjamin W. Labaree, *America's Nation-Time: 1607–1789* (New York, 1976), cover, see also xi.
Two exceptions are Gary B. Nash, *Red, White, and Black: The Peoples of Early America* (Englewood
Cliffs, N. J., 1974), and Mary Beth Norton *et al.*, *A People and a Nation: A History of the United
States* (Boston, 1982), I. For analyses of the scholarly neglect of Indians in colonial America see
Thad W. Tate, "The Seventeenth-Century Chesapeake and Its Modern Historians," in Tate and
David L. Ammerman, eds., *The Chesapeake in the Seventeenth Century: Essays on Anglo-American
Society* (Chapel Hill, N. C., 1979), 30–32; Douglas Greenberg, "The Middle Colonies in Recent
American Historiography," WMQ, 3d Ser., XXXVI (1979), 415–416; and Neal Salisbury, *Manitou
and Providence: Indians, Europeans, and the Making of New England, 1500–1643* (New York, 1982),
3–7.

terpret American development. From Frederick Jackson Turner to David Grayson Allen, from Melville J. Herskovits to Daniel C. Littlefield, scholars have analyzed encounters between peoples from the Old World and conditions in the New, studying the complex interplay between Europeans or African cultural patterns and the American environment.[4] Indians crossed no ocean, peopled no faraway land. It might seem logical to exclude them.

The natives' segregation persists, in no small degree, because historians still tend to think only of the new world as the New World, a geographic entity bounded by the Atlantic Ocean on the one side and the Pacific on the other. Recent research suggests that process was as important as place. Many settlers in New England recreated familiar forms with such success that they did not really face an alien environment until long after their arrival.[5] Africans, on the other hand, were struck by the shock of the new at the moment of their enslavement, well before they stepped on board ship or set foot on American soil.[6] If the Atlantic was not a barrier between one world and another, if what happened to people was more a matter of subtle cultural processes than mere physical displacements, perhaps we should set aside the maps and think instead of a "world" as the physical and cultural milieu within which people live and a "new world" as a dramatically different milieu demanding basic changes in ways of life.[7] Considered in these terms, the experience of natives was more closely akin to that of immigrants and slaves,

---

[4] Turner, "The Significance of the Frontier in American History," American Historical Association, *Annual Report for the Year 1893* (Washington, D. C., 1984), 199–227; Allen, *In English Ways: The Movement of Societies and the Transferal of English Local Law and Custom to Massachusetts Bay in the Seventeenth Century* (Chapel Hill, N. C., 1981); Herskovits, *The Myth of the Negro Past* (New York, 1941); Littlefield, *Rice and Slaves: Ethnicity and the Slave Trade in Colonial South Carolina* (Baton Rouge, La., 1981).

[5] Allen, *In English Ways;* T. H. Breen, "Persistent Localism: English Social Change and the Shaping of New England Institutions," *WMQ,* 3d Ser., XXXII (1975), 3–28, and "Transfer of Culture: Chance and Design in Shaping Massachusetts Bay, 1630–1660," *New England Historical and Genealogical Register,* CXXXII (1978), 3–17.

More generally, others have argued that the European settlement of America marked an expansion of the Old World rather than a separation from it, "an extension of Europe rather than a wholly new world" (G. R. Elton, "Contentment and Discontent on the Eve of Colonization," in David B. Quinn, ed., *Early Maryland in a Wider World* (Detroit, Mich., 1982), 117–118; quotation from Quinn, "Why They Came," *ibid.,* 143).

[6] Sidney W. Mintz and Richard Price, *An Anthropological Approach to the Afro-American Past: A Caribbean Perspective* (Philadelphia, 1976), 22; Nathan Irvin Huggins, *Black Odyssey: The Afro-American Ordeal in Slavery* (New York, 1977), 25–34.

[7] While never thoroughly examined, the term has often been used this way by students of Indian history and others. For example, see Elizabeth A. H. John, *Storms Brewed in Other Men's Worlds: The Confrontation of Indians, Spanish, and French in the Southwest, 1540–1795* (College Station, Tex., 1975); Carolyn Gilman, *Where Two Worlds Meet: The Great Lakes Fur Trade* (St. Paul, Minn., 1982); Peter Laslett, *The World We Have Lost,* 2d ed. (New York, 1973); Edgar P. Richardson, Brooke Hindle, and Lillian B. Miller, *Charles Willson Peale and His World* (New York, 1982); and Irving Howe, *World of Our Fathers* (New York, 1976).

and the idea of an encounter between worlds can—indeed, must—include the aboriginal inhabitants of America.

For American Indians a new order arrived in three distinct yet overlapping stages.[8] First, alien microbes killed vast numbers of natives, sometimes before the victims had seen a white or black face. Next came traders who exchanged European technology for Indian products and brought natives into the developing world market. In time traders gave way to settlers eager to develop the land according to their own lights.[9] These three intrusions combined to transform native existence, disrupting established cultural habits and requiring creative responses to drastically altered conditions. Like their new neighbors, then, Indians were forced to blend old and new in ways that would permit them to survive in the present without forsaking their past. By the close of the colonial era, native Americans as well as whites and blacks had created new societies, each similar to, yet very different from, its parent culture.

The range of native societies produced by this mingling of ingredients probably exceeded the variety of social forms Europeans and Africans developed.[10] Rather than survey the broad spectrum of Indian adaptations, this article considers in some depth the response of natives in one area, the southern piedmont (see map). Avoiding extinction and eschewing retreat, the Indians of the piedmont have been in continuous contact with the invaders from across the sea almost since the beginning of the colonial period, thus permitting a thorough analysis of cultural intercourse.[11] Moreover, a regional approach embracing groups from South Carolina to Virginia can transcend narrow (and still poorly understood) ethnic or "tribal" boundaries without sacrificing the richness of detail a focused study provides.

Indeed, piedmont peoples had so much in common that a regional perspective is almost imperative. No formal political ties bound them at the

---

[8] See T. J. C. Brasser, "Group Identification along a Moving Frontier," *Verhandlungen des XXXVIII Internationalen Amerikanistenkongresses,* II (Munich, 1970), 261–262.

[9] Salisbury divides the course of events into two phases, the first including diseases and trade goods, the second encompassing settlement (*Manitou and Providence,* 12).

[10] For the societies created by Europeans and Africans see James A. Henretta, *The Evolution of American Society, 1700–1815: An Interdisciplinary Analysis* (Lexington, Mass., 1973), esp. 112–116; Jack P. Greene, "Society and Economy in the British Caribbean during the Seventeenth and Eighteenth Centuries," *American Historical Review,* LXXIX (1974), 1515–1517; and Ira Berlin, "Time, Space, and the Evolution of Afro-American Society on British Mainland North America," *ibid.,* LXXXV (1980), 44–78.

[11] Among some Indian peoples a fourth stage, missionaries, could be added to the three outlined above. These agents did not, however, play an important part in the piedmont (or in most other areas of the southeast) during the colonial period. Lack of evidence precludes discussion of native religion among upland communities or the changes in belief and ceremony that occurred after contact. It is clear, however, that Indians there opposed any systematic efforts to convert them to Christianity. See Hugh Jones, *The Present State of Virginia: From Whence Is Inferred a Short View of Maryland and North Carolina,* ed. Richard L. Morton (Chapel Hill, N. C., 1956), 59.

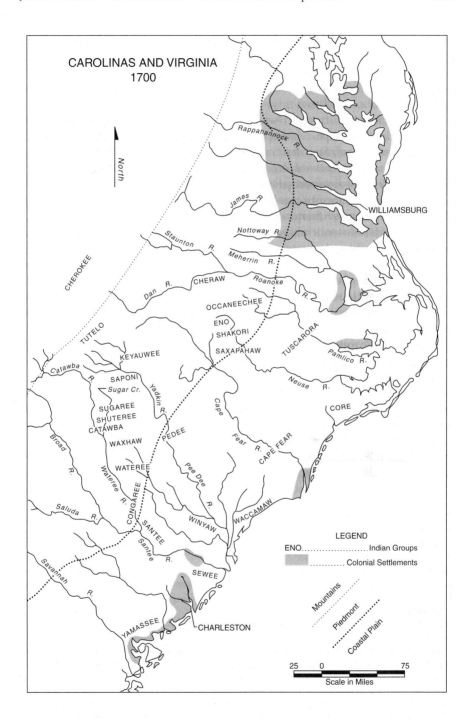

CAROLINAS AND VIRGINIA
1700

North

CHEROKEE

TUTELO

Catawba R.

SAPONI

Sugar Cr.

SUGAREE
SHUTEREE
CATAWBA

WAXHAW

WATEREE

Broad R.

Wateree R.

CONGAREE

Saluda R.

Savannah R.

SANTEE

Santee R.

SEWEE

YAMASSEE   CHARLESTON

WINYAW   WACCAMAW

Pee Dee R.

PEDEE

KEYAUWEE

Yadkin R.

Cape Fear R.   CAPE FEAR

CORE

Rappahannock R.

James R.

WILLIAMSBURG

Nottoway R.

Staunton R.

Meherrin R.

Dan R.   CHERAW

Roanoke R.

OCCANEECHEE

ENO
SHAKORI
SAXAPAHAW

TUSCARORA

Pamlico R.

Neuse R.

LEGEND

ENO .... Indian Groups

.... Colonial Settlements

Mountains

Piedmont

Coastal Plain

25   0   75

Scale in Miles

onset of European contact, but a similar environment shaped their lives, and their adjustment to this environment fostered cultural uniformity. Perhaps even more important, these groups shared a single history once Europeans and Africans arrived on the scene. Drawn together by their cultural affinities and their common plight, after 1700 they migrated to the Catawba Nation, a cluster of villages along the border between the Carolinas that became the focus of native life in the region. Tracing the experience of these upland communities both before and after they joined the Catawbas can illustrate the consequences of contact and illuminate the process by which natives learned to survive in their own new world.[12]

For centuries, ancestors of the Catawbas had lived astride important aboriginal trade routes and straddled the boundary between two cultural traditions, a position that involved them in a far-flung network of contacts and affected everything from potting techniques to burial practices.[13] Nonetheless, Africans and Europeans were utterly unlike any earlier foreign visitors to the piedmont. Their arrival meant more than merely another encounter with outsiders; it marked an important turning point in Indian history. Once these newcomers disembarked and began to feel their way across the continent, they forever altered the course and pace of native development.

Bacteria brought the most profound disturbances to upcountry villages. When Hernando de Soto led the first Europeans into the area in 1540, he found large towns already "grown up in grass" because "there had been a

[12] Catawbas and their Indian neighbors have been objects of much study and considerable disagreement. Because these peoples lived away from areas of initial European settlement, detailed records are scarce, and archaeologists are only beginning to help fill the gaps in the evidence. Important questions—the linguistic and political affiliations of some groups, their social structures, the degree of influence exerted by powerful societies to the east, west, and south, even their population—remain unanswered. But there are many reasons to argue for a fundamental cultural uniformity in this area beyond a common environment, hints of similar cultural traits, and the shared destiny of the region's inhabitants. Although these scattered villages fought with outsiders from the coast and the mountains, the north and the south, there is a distinct lack of recorded conflict among peoples in the piedmont itself. Peaceful relations may have been reinforced by a sense of common origin, for some (if not all) of these groups—including Saponis, Tutelos, Occaneechees, Catawbas, and Cheraws—spoke variant forms of the Siouan language and were descended from migrants who entered the area some seven centuries before Columbus arrived in America. Finally, other natives were cognizant of connections among these far-flung towns. The Iroquois, for example, called natives from the Catawbas to the Tutelos by the collective name "Toderichroone." For studies of these peoples see James Mooney, *The Siouan Tribes of the East*, Smithsonian Institution, Bureau of American Ethnology, Bulletin 22 (Washington, D. C., 1894); Joffre Lanning Coe, "The Cultural Sequence of the Carolina Piedmont," in James B. Griffin, ed., *Archeology of Eastern United States* (Chicago, 1952), 301–311; Douglas Summers Brown, *The Catawba Indians: The People of the River* (Columbia, S. C., 1966); Charles M. Hudson, *The Catawba Nation* (Athens, Ga., 1970); and James H. Merrell, "Natives in a New World: The Catawba Indians of Carolina, 1650–1800" (Ph.D. diss., The Johns Hopkins University, 1982).
[13] Coe, "Cultural Sequence," in Griffin, ed., *Archeology of Eastern U. S.*, 301–311; Hudson, *Catawba Nation*, 11–17; William E. Myer, "Indian Trails of the Southeast," Bureau of American Ethnology, *Forty-Second Annual Report* (Washington, D. C., 1928), plate 15.

pest in the land" two years before, a malady probably brought inland by natives who had visited distant Spanish posts.[14] The sources are silent about other "pests" over the next century, but soon after the English began colonizing Carolina in 1670 the disease pattern became all too clear. Major epidemics struck the region at least once every generation—in 1698, 1718, 1738, and 1759—and a variety of less virulent illnesses almost never left native settlements.[15]

Indians were not the only inhabitants of colonial America living—and dying—in a new disease environment. The swamps and lowlands of the Chesapeake were a deathtrap for Europeans, and sickness obliged colonists to discard or rearrange many of the social forms brought from England.[16] Among native peoples long isolated from the rest of the world and therefore lacking immunity to pathogens introduced by the intruders, the devastation was even more severe. John Lawson, who visited the Carolina upcountry in 1701, when perhaps ten thousand Indians were still there, estimated that "there is not the sixth Savage living within two hundred Miles of all our Settlements, as there were fifty Years ago." The recent smallpox epidemic "destroy'd whole Towns," he remarked, "without leaving one *Indian* alive in the Village."[17] Resistance to disease developed with painful slowness; colonists reported that the outbreak of smallpox in 1759 wiped out 60 percent of the natives, and, according to one source, "the woods were offensive with the

---

[14] "True Relation of the Vicissitudes That Attended the Governor Don Hernando De Soto and Some Nobles of Portugal in the Discovery of the Province of Florida Now Just Given by a Fidalgo of Elvas," in Edward Gaylord Bourne, ed., *Narratives of the Career of Hernando de Soto . . .* , I (New York, 1904), 66. See also John Grier Varner and Jeannette Johnson Varner, trans. and eds., *The Florida of the Inca . . .* (Austin, Tex., 1951), 298, 315, and Henry F. Dobyns, *Their Number Become Thinned: Native American Population Dynamics in Eastern North America* (Knoxville, Tenn., 1983), 262–264.

[15] South Carolina Council to Lords Proprietors, Apr. 23, 1698, in Alexander S. Salley, ed., *Commissions and Instructions from the Lords Proprietors of Carolina to Public Officials of South Carolina, 1685–1715* (Columbia, S. C., 1916), 105; Alexander Spotswood to the Board of Trade, Dec. 22, 1718, C.O. 5/1318, 590, Public Record Office (Library of Congress transcripts, 488); *South Carolina Gazette* (Charleston), May 4, 11, 25, June 29, Oct. 5, 1738. Catawba losses in this epidemic were never tabulated, but fully half of the Cherokees may have died (see John Duffy, *Epidemics in Colonial America* [Baton Rouge, La., 1953], 82–83; Catawbas to the governor of South Carolina, Oct. 1759, William Henry Lyttelton Papers, William L. Clements Library, Ann Arbor, Mich.; and *S.C. Gaz.*, Dec. 15, 1759). Dobyns constructs epidemic profiles for the continent and for Florida that offer a sense of the prevalence of disease (*Their Number Become Thinned,* essays, 1, 6).

[16] See Edmund S. Morgan, *American Slavery, American Freedom: The Ordeal of Colonial Virginia* (New York, 1975), chaps. 8–9; Darrett B. Rutman and Anita H. Rutman, "Of Agues and Fevers: Malaria in the Early Chesapeake," *WMQ*, 3d Ser., XXXIII (1976), 31–60; and several of the essays in Tate and Ammerman, eds., *Seventeenth-Century Chesapeake.*

[17] Lawson, *A New Voyage to Carolina,* ed. Hugh Talmage Lefler (Chapel Hill, N. C., 1967), 232. See also 17, 34. The population figure given here is a very rough estimate. Lawson reckoned that Saponis, Tutelos, Keyauwees, Occaneechees, and Shakoris numbered 750 and that Catawbas (he called them "Esaws") were "a very large Nation containing many thousand People" (pp. 242, 46). Totals for other groups in the piedmont are almost nonexistent.

dead bodies of the Indians; and dogs, wolves, and vultures were . . . busy for months in banqueting on them."[18]

Survivors of these horrors were thrust into a situation no less alien than what European immigrants and African slaves found. The collected wisdom of generations could vanish in a matter of days if sickness struck older members of a community who kept sacred traditions and taught special skills. When many of the elders succumbed at once, the deep pools of collective memory grew shallow, and some dried up altogether. In 1710, Indians near Charleston told a settler that "they have forgot most of their traditions since the Establishment of this Colony, they keep their Festivals and can tell but little of the reasons: their Old Men are dead."[19] Impoverishment of a rich cultural heritage followed the spread of disease. Nearly a century later, a South Carolinian exaggerated but captured the general trend when he noted that Catawbas "have forgotten their ancient rites, ceremonies, and manufactures."[20]

The same diseases that robbed a piedmont town of some of its most precious resources also stripped it of the population necessary to maintain an independent existence. In order to survive, groups were compelled to construct new societies from the splintered remnants of the old. The result was a kaleidoscopic array of migrations from ancient territories and mergers with nearby peoples. While such behavior was not unheard of in aboriginal times, population levels fell so precipitously after contact that survivors endured disruptions unlike anything previously known.

The dislocations of the Saponi Indians illustrate the common course of events. In 1670 they lived on the Staunton River in Virginia and were closely affiliated with a group called Nahyssans. A decade later Saponis moved toward the coast and built a town near the Occaneechees. When John Lawson came upon them along the Yadkin River in 1701, they were on the verge of banding together in a single village with Tutelos and Keyauwees. Soon thereafter Saponis applied to Virginia officials for permission to move to the Meherrin River, where Occaneechees, Tutelos, and others joined them. In 1714, at the urging of Virginia's Lt. Gov. Alexander Spotswood, these groups settled at Fort Christanna farther up the Meherrin. Their friendship with

---

[18] Philip E. Pearson, "Memoir of the Catawbas, furnished Gov. Hammond," MS (1842?), Wilberforce Eames Indian Collection, New York Public Library (typescript copy in the York County Public Library, Rock Hill, S. C.). For estimates of population losses see *S.C. Gaz.*, Dec. 15, 1759; Arthur Dobbs to the secretary of the Society for the Propagation of the Gospel in Foreign Parts, Apr. 15, 1760, in William L. Saunders, ed., *The Colonial Records of North Carolina*, 10 vols. (Raleigh, N. C., 1886–1890), VI, 235, hereafter cited as *N.C. Col. Recs.*

[19] Francis Le Jau to the secretary, June 13, 1710, in Frank J. Klingberg, ed., *The Carolina Chronicle of Dr. Francis Le Jau, 1706–1717* (Berkeley, Calif., 1956), 78.

[20] John Drayton to Dr. Benjamin Smith Barton, Sept. 9, 1803, Correspondence and Papers of Benjamin S. Barton, Historical Society of Pennsylvania, Philadelphia. I am indebted to Maurice Bric for this reference.

Virginia soured during the 1720s, and most of the "Christanna Indians" moved to the Catawba Nation. For some reason this arrangement did not satisfy them, and many returned to Virginia in 1732, remaining there for a decade before choosing to migrate north and accept the protection of the Iroquois.[21]

Saponis were unusual only in their decision to leave the Catawbas. Enos, Occaneechees, Waterees, Keyauwees, Cheraws, and others have their own stories to tell, similar in outline if not in detail. With the exception of the towns near the confluence of Sugar Creek and the Catawba River that composed the heart of the Catawba Nation, piedmont communities decimated by disease lived through a common round of catastrophes, shifting from place to place and group to group in search of a safe haven. Most eventually ended up in the Nation, and during the opening decades of the eighteenth century the villages scattered across the southern upcountry were abandoned as people drifted into the Catawba orbit.

No mere catalog of migrations and mergers can begin to convey how profoundly unsettling this experience was for those swept up in it. While upcountry Indians did not sail away to some distant land, they, too, were among the uprooted, leaving their ancestral homes to try to make a new life elsewhere. The peripatetic existence of Saponis and others proved deeply disruptive. A village and its surrounding territory were important elements of personal and collective identity, physical links in a chain binding a group to its past and making a locality sacred. Colonists, convinced that Indians were by nature "a shifting, wandring People," were oblivious to this, but Lawson offered a glimpse of the reasons for native attachment to a particular locale. "In our way," he wrote on leaving an Eno-Shakori town in 1701, "there stood a great Stone about the Size of a large Oven, and hollow; this the *Indians* took great Notice of, putting some Tobacco into the Concavity, and spitting after it. I ask'd them the Reason of their so doing, but they made me no Answer."[22] Natives throughout the interior honored similar places— graves of ancestors, monuments of stones commemorating important events—that could not be left behind without some cost.[23]

---

[21] Christian F. Feest, "Notes on Saponi Settlements in Virginia Prior to 1714," Archaeological Society of Virginia, *Quarterly Bulletin*, XXVIII (1974), 152–155; William Byrd, "The History of the Dividing Line betwixt Virginia and North Carolina Run in the Year of Our Lord 1728," in Louis B. Wright, ed., *The Prose Works of William Byrd of Westover: Narratives of a Colonial Virginian* (Cambridge, Mass., 1966), 315; H. R. McIlwaine *et al.*, eds., *Executive Journals of the Council of Colonial Virginia*, 6 vols. (Richmond, Va., 1925–1966), IV, 269, hereafter cited as *Va. Council Jours.*; "A List of all the Indian names present at the Treaty held in Lancaster in June 1744," in Samuel Hazard, ed., *Pennsylvania Archives Selected and Arranged from Original Documents . . .* , 1st Ser., I (Philadelphia, 1852), 657.

[22] Lawson, *New Voyage*, ed. Lefler, 173, 63.

[23] Edward Bland, "The Discovery of New Brittaine, 1650," in Alexander S. Salley, ed., *Narratives of Early Carolina, 1650–1708* (New York, 1911), 13–14; William P. Cumming, ed., *The Discoveries of John Lederer . . .* (Charlottesville, Va., 1958), 12, 17, 19–20; John Banister, "Of the Natives," in

The toll could be physical as well as spiritual, for even the most un-eventful of moves interrupted the established cycle of subsistence. Belong-ings had to be packed and unpacked, dwellings constructed, palisades raised. Once migrants had completed the business of settling in, the still more arduous task of exploiting new terrain awaited them. Living in one place year after year endowed a people with intimate knowledge of the area. The richest soils, the best hunting grounds, the choicest sites for gathering nuts or berries—none could be learned without years of experience, tested by time and passed down from one generation to the next. Small wonder that Carolina Indians worried about being "driven to some unknown Coun-try, to live, hunt, and get our Bread in."[24]

Some displaced groups tried to leave "unknown Country" behind and make their way back home. In 1716 Enos asked Virginia's permission to set-tle at "Enoe Town" on the North Carolina frontier, their location in Lawson's day.[25] Seventeen years later William Byrd II came upon an abandoned Cheraw village on a tributary of the upper Roanoke River and remarked how "it must have been a great misfortune to them to be obliged to abandon so beautiful a dwelling." The Indians apparently agreed: in 1717 the Virginia Council received "Divers applications" from the Cheraws (now living along the Pee Dee River) "for Liberty to Seat themselves on the head of Roanoke River."[26] Few natives managed to return permanently to their homelands. But their efforts to retrace their steps hint at a profound sense of loss and tes-tify to the powerful hold of ancient sites.

Compounding the trauma of leaving familiar territories was the neces-sity of abandoning customary relationships. Casting their lot with others tra-ditionally considered foreign compelled Indians to rearrange basic ways of ordering their existence. Despite frequent contacts among peoples, native life had always centered in kin and town. The consequences of this deep-seated localism were evident even to a newcomer like John Lawson, who in 1701 found striking differences in language, dress, and physical appearance among Carolina Indians living only a few miles apart.[27] Rules governing be-havior also drew sharp distinctions between outsiders and one's own "Country-Folks." Indians were "very kind, and charitable to one another,"

Joseph Ewan and Nesta Ewan, eds., *John Banister and His Natural History of Virginia, 1678–1692* (Urbana, Ill., 1970), 377; William J. Hinke, trans. and ed., "Report of the Journey of Francis Louis Michel from Berne, Switzerland, to Virginia, October 2, 1701—December 1, 1702," *Virginia Mag-azine of History and Biography*, XXIV (1916), 29; Lawson, *New Voyage*, ed. Lefler, 50; David I. Bush-nell, Jr., "'The Indian Grave'—a Monacan Site in Albemarle County, Virginia," *WMQ*, 1st Ser., XXIII (1914), 106–112.

[24] Lawson, *New Voyage*, ed. Lefler, 214.

[25] Council Journals, Aug. 4, 1716, *N.C. Col. Recs.*, II, 242–243.

[26] William Byrd, "Journey to the Land of Eden, Anno 1733," in Wright, ed., *Prose Works*, 398; *Va. Council Jours.*, III, 440.

[27] Lawson, *New Voyage*, ed. Lefler, 35, 233.

Lawson reported, "but more especially to those of their own Nation."[28] A visitor desiring a liaison with a local woman was required to approach her relatives and the village headman. On the other hand, "if it be an *Indian* of their own Town or Neighbourhood, that wants a Mistress, he comes to none but the Girl."[29] Lawson seemed unperturbed by this barrier until he discovered that a "Thief [is] held in Disgrace, that steals from any of his Country-Folks," "but to steal from the *English* [or any other foreigners] they reckon no Harm."[30]

Communities unable to continue on their own had to revise these rules and reweave the social fabric into new designs. What language would be spoken? How would fields be laid out, hunting territories divided, houses built? How would decisions be reached, offenders punished, ceremonies performed? When Lawson remarked that "now adays" the Indians must seek mates "amongst Strangers," he unwittingly characterized life in native Carolina.[31] Those who managed to withstand the ravages of disease had to redefine the meaning of the term *stranger* and transform outsiders into insiders.

The need to harmonize discordant peoples, an unpleasant fact of life for all native Americans, was no less common among black and white inhabitants of America during these years. Africans from a host of different groups were thrown into slavery together and forced to seek some common cultural ground, to blend or set aside clashing habits and beliefs. Europeans who came to America also met unexpected and unwelcome ethnic, religious, and linguistic diversity. The roots of the problem were quite different; the problem itself was much the same. In each case people from different backgrounds had to forge a common culture and a common future.

Indians in the southern uplands customarily combined with others like themselves in an attempt to solve the dilemma. Following the "principle of least effort," shattered communities cushioned the blows inflicted by disease and depopulation by joining a kindred society known through generations of trade and alliances.[32] Thus Saponis coalesced with Occaneechees and Tutelos—nearby groups "speaking much the same language"[33]—and Catawbas became a sanctuary for culturally related refugees from throughout the region. Even after moving in with friends and neighbors, however, natives tended to cling to ethnic boundaries in order to ease the transition. In 1715 Spotswood noticed that the Saponis and others gathered at Fort

[28] *Ibid.*, 184.
[29] *Ibid.*, 190.
[30] *Ibid.*, 184, 212, 24.
[31] *Ibid.*, 193.
[32] Robert A. LeVine and Donald T. Campbell, *Ethnocentrism: Theories of Conflict, Ethnic Attitudes, and Group Behavior* (New York, 1972), 108.
[33] Spotswood to the bishop of London, Jan. 27, 1715, in R. A. Brock, ed., *The Official Letters of Alexander Spotswood, Lieutenant-Governor of the Colony of Virginia, 1710–1722* (Virginia Historical Society, *Collections*, N.S., II [Richmond, Va., 1885]), 88, hereafter cited as Brock, ed., *Spotswood Letters*. See also Byrd, "History," in Wright, ed., *Prose Works*, 314.

Christanna were "confederated together, tho' still preserving their different Rules."[34] Indians entering the Catawba Nation were equally conservative. As late as 1743 a visitor could hear more than twenty different dialects spoken by peoples living there, and some bands continued to reside in separate towns under their own leaders.[35]

Time inevitably sapped the strength of ethnic feeling, allowing a more unified Nation to emerge from the collection of Indian communities that occupied the valleys of the Catawba River and its tributaries. By the mid-eighteenth century, the authority of village headmen was waning and leaders from the host population had begun to take responsibility for the actions of constituent groups.[36] The babel of different tongues fell silent as *"Kàtahba,"* the Nation's "standard, or court-dialect," slowly drowned out all others.[37] Eventually, entire peoples followed their languages and their leaders into oblivion, leaving only personal names like Santee Jemmy, Cheraw George, Congaree Jamie, Saponey Johnny, and Eno Jemmy as reminders of the Nation's diverse heritage.[38]

No European observer recorded the means by which nations became mere names and a congeries of groups forged itself into one people. No doubt the colonists' habit of ignoring ethnic distinctions and lumping confederated entities together under the Catawba rubric encouraged amalgamation. But Anglo-American efforts to create a society by proclamation were invariably unsuccessful[39]; consolidation had to come from within. In the

[34] Brock, ed., *Spotswood Letters,* 88.

[35] Samuel Cole Williams, ed., *Adair's History of the American Indians* (Johnson City, Tenn., 1930), 236; The Public Accounts of John Hammerton, Esq., Secretary of the Province, in Inventories, LL, 1744–1746, 29, 47, 51, South Carolina Department of Archives and History, Columbia, hereafter cited as Hammerton, Public Accounts; "Sketch Map of the Rivers Santee, Congaree, Wateree, Saludee, &c., with the Road to the Cuttauboes [1750?]," Colonial Office Library, Carolina 16, P.R.O. (copy in Brown, *Catawba Indians,* plate 6, between pp. 32–33); "Cuttahbaws Nation, men fit for warr 204 In the year 1756," Dalhousie Muniments, General John Forbes Papers, Document #2/104 (copy in S.C. Dept. Archs. and Hist.).

[36] J. H. Easterby, ed., *The Colonial Records of South Carolina: The Journal of the Commons House of Assembly, November 10, 1736–June 7, 1739* (Columbia, S. C., 1951), 481–482. Compare this to the Catawbas' failure to control Waccamaws living in the Nation a decade before (Journals of the Upper House of Assembly, Sept. 13, 1727, C.O. 5/429, 176–177 [microfilm, British Manuscripts Project, D 491]).

[37] Williams, ed., *Adair's History,* 236.

[38] Catawba Indians to Gov. Lyttelton, June 16, 1757, Lyttelton Papers (Santee Jemmy); Rev. William Richardson, "An Account of My Proceedings since I accepted the Indian mission in October 2d 1758 . . . ," Wilberforce Eames Indian Collection, entry of Nov. 8, 1758 (Cheraw George). South Carolina Council Journals (hereafter cited as S. C. Council Jours.), May 5, 1760, in William S. Jenkins, comp., Records of the States of the United States, microfilm ed. (Washington, D. C., 1950) (hereafter cited as Records of States), SC E.1p, Reel 8, Unit 3, 119 (Congaree Jamie); John Evans to Gov. James Glen, Apr. 18, 1748, in S. C. Council Jours., Apr. 27, 1748, Records of States, SC E.1p, 3/4 233 (Saponey Johnny); Hammerton, Public Accounts, 29, 51 (Eno Jemmy).

[39] See, for example, Spotswood's efforts to persuade some tributary groups to join the piedmont Indians at Fort Christanna. *Va. Council Jours.,* III, 367; Spotswood to bishop of London, Jan. 27, 1715, in Brock, ed., *Spotswood Letters,* II, 88.

absence of evidence, it seems reasonable to conclude that years of contacts paved the way for a closer relationship. Once a group moved to the Nation, intermarriages blurred ancient kinship networks, joint war parties or hunting expeditions brought young men together, and elders met in a council that gave everyone some say by including "all the Indian Chiefs or Head Men of that [Catawba] Nation and the several Tribes amongst them together."[40] The concentration of settlements within a day's walk of one another facilitated contact and communication. From their close proximity, common experience, and shared concerns, people developed ceremonies and myths that compensated for those lost to disease and gave the Nation a stronger collective consciousness.[41] Associations evolved that balanced traditional narrow ethnic allegiance with a new, broader, "national" identity, a balance that tilted steadily toward the latter. Ethnic differences died hard, but the peoples of the Catawba Nation learned to speak with a single voice.

Muskets and kettles came to the piedmont more slowly than smallpox and measles. Spanish explorers distributed a few gifts to local headmen, but inhabitants of the interior did not enjoy their first real taste of the fruits of European technology until Englishmen began venturing inland after 1650. Indians these traders met in upcountry towns were glad to barter for the more efficient tools, more lethal weapons, and more durable clothing that colonists offered. Spurred on by eager natives, men from Virginia and Carolina quickly flooded the region with the material trappings of European culture. In 1701 John Lawson considered the Wateree Chickanees "very poor in *English* Effects" because a few of them lacked muskets.[42]

Slower to arrive, trade goods were also less obvious agents of change. The Indians' ability to absorb foreign artifacts into established modes of existence hid the revolutionary consequences of trade for some time. Natives leaped the technological gulf with ease in part because they were discriminating shoppers. If hoes were too small, beads too large, or cloth the wrong color, Indian traders refused them.[43] Items they did select fit smoothly into existing ways. Waxhaws tied horse bells around their ankles at ceremonial dances, and some of the traditional stone pipes passed among the spectators at these dances had been shaped by metal files.[44] Those who could not afford a European weapon fashioned arrows from broken glass. Those who could went to great lengths to "set [a new musket] streight, sometimes shooting

[40] Easterby, ed., *Journal of the Commons House, 1736–1739*, 487.

[41] See Brasser, "Group Identification," *Verhandlungen*, II (1970), 261–265.

[42] Lawson, *New Voyage*, ed. Lefler, 38.

[43] William Byrd to [Arthur North?], Mar. 8, 1685/6, in Marion Tinling, ed., *The Correspondence of the Three William Byrds of Westover, Virginia, 1684–1776*, I (Charlottesville, Va., 1977), 57, Byrd to Perry and Lane, July 8, 1686, 64, Byrd to [Perry and Lane?], Mar. 20, 1685, 30, Byrd to North, Mar. 29, 1685, 31.

[44] Lawson, *New Voyage*, ed. Lefler, 44–45; George Edwin Stuart, "The Post-Archaic Occupation of Central South Carolina" (Ph.D. diss., University of North Carolina, 1975), 133, fig. 72, B.

away above 100 Loads of Ammunition, before they bring the Gun to shoot according to their Mind."[45]

Not every piece of merchandise hauled into the upcountry on a trader's packhorse could be "set streight" so easily. Liquor, for example, proved both impossible to resist and extraordinarily destructive. Indians "have no Power to refrain this Enemy," Lawson observed, "though sensible how many of them (are by it) hurry'd into the other World before their Time."[46] And yet even here, natives aware of the risks sought to control alcohol by incorporating it into their ceremonial life as a device for achieving a different level of consciousness. Consumption was usually restricted to men, who "go as solemnly about it, as if it were part of their Religion," preferring to drink only at night and only in quantities sufficient to stupefy them.[47] When ritual could not confine liquor to safe channels, Indians went still further and excused the excesses of overindulgence by refusing to hold an intoxicated person responsible for his actions. "They never call any Man to account for what he did, when he was drunk," wrote Lawson, "but say, it was the Drink that caused his Misbehaviour, therefore he ought to be forgiven."[48]

Working to absorb even the most dangerous commodities acquired from their new neighbors, aboriginal inhabitants of the uplands, like African slaves in the lowlands, made themselves at home in a different technological environment. Indians became convinced that "Guns, and Ammunition, besides a great many other Necessaries, . . . are helpful to Man"[49] and eagerly searched for the key that would unlock the secret of their production. At first many were confident that the "*Quera*, or good Spirit," would teach them to make these commodities "when that good Spirit sees fit."[50] Later they decided to help their deity along by approaching the colonists. In 1757, Catawbas asked Gov. Arthur Dobbs of North Carolina "to send us Smiths and other Tradesmen to teach our Children."[51]

It was not the new products themselves but the Indians' failure to learn the mysteries of manufacture from either Dobbs or the *Quera* that marked the real revolution wrought by trade. During the seventeenth and eighteenth

---

[45] Lawson, *New Voyage*, ed. Lefler, 33, 63. Archaeologists have uncovered these arrowheads. See Tommy Charles, "Thoughts and Records from the Survey of Private Collections of Prehistoric Artifacts: A Second Report," Institute of Archaeology and Anthropology, University of South Carolina, *Notebook*, XV (1983), 31.

[46] Lawson, *New Voyage*, ed. Lefler, 211, 18.

[47] *Ibid.*, 211; Robert Beverley, *The History and Present State of Virginia*, ed. Louis B. Wright (Chapel Hill, N. C., 1947), 182.

[48] Lawson, *New Voyage*, ed. Lefler, 210. See also Craig MacAndrew and Robert B. Edgerton, *Drunken Comportment: A Social Explanation* (New York, 1969), chap. 5.

[49] Lawson, *New Voyage*, ed. Lefler, 220.

[50] *Ibid.* One Santee priest claimed he had already been given this power by "the white Man above, (meaning God Almighty)" (*ibid.*, 26–27).

[51] Catawba Nation to Gov. Dobbs, Oct. 5, 1757, encl. in Dobbs to Lyttelton, Oct. 24, 1757, Lyttelton Papers.

centuries, everyone in eastern North America—masters and slaves, farmers near the coast and Indians near the mountains—became producers of raw materials for foreign markets and found themselves caught up in an international economic network.[52] Piedmont natives were part of this larger process, but their adjustment was more difficult because the contrast with previous ways was so pronounced. Before European contact, the localism characteristic of life in the uplands had been sustained by a remarkable degree of self-sufficiency. Trade among peoples, while common, was conducted primarily in commodities such as copper, mica, and shells, items that, exchanged with the appropriate ceremony, initiated or confirmed friendships among groups. Few, if any, villages relied on outsiders for goods essential to daily life.[53]

Intercultural exchange eroded this traditional independence and entangled natives in a web of commercial relations few of them understood and none controlled. In 1670 the explorer John Lederer observed a striking disparity in the trading habits of Indians living near Virginia and those deep in the interior. The "remoter Indians," still operating within a precontact framework, were content with ornamental items such as mirrors, beads, "and all manner of gaudy toys and knacks for children." "Neighbour-Indians," on the other hand, habitually traded with colonists for cloth, metal tools, and weapons.[54] Before long, towns near and far were demanding the entire range of European wares and were growing accustomed—and even addicted—to them. "They say we English are fools for . . . not always going with a gun," one Virginia colonist familiar with piedmont Indians wrote in the early 1690s, "for they think themselves undrest and not fit to walk abroad, unless they have their gun on their shoulder, and their shot-bag by their side."[55] Such an enthusiastic conversion to the new technology eroded ancient craft skills and hastened complete dependence on substitutes only colonists could supply.

By forcing Indians to look beyond their own territories for certain indispensable products, Anglo-American traders inserted new variables into the aboriginal equation of exchange. Colonists sought two commodities from

[52] Immanual Wallerstein, *The Modern World-System: Capitalist Agriculture and the Origins of the European World-Economy in the Sixteenth Century* (New York, 1974), esp. chap. 6.

[53] Harold Hickerson, "Fur Trade Colonialism and the North American Indians," *Journal of Ethnic Studies*, I (1973), 18–22; Charles Hudson, *The Southeastern Indians* (Knoxville, Tenn., 1976), 65–66, 316. Salt may have been an exception to this aboriginal self-sufficiency. Even here, however, Indians might have been able to get along without it or find acceptable substitutes. See Gloria J. Wentowski, "Salt as an Ecological Factor in the Prehistory of the Southeastern United States" (M.A. thesis, University of North Carolina, 1970). For substitutes see Lawson, *New Voyage*, ed. Lefler, 89; Banister, "Of the Natives," in Ewan and Ewan, eds., *Banister and His History*, 376; Beverley, *History*, ed. Wright, 180.

[54] Cumming, ed., *Discoveries of Lederer*, 41–42.

[55] Banister, "Of the Natives," in Ewan and Ewan, eds., *Banister and His History*, 382.

Indians—human beings and deerskins—and both undermined established relationships among native groups. While the demand for slaves encouraged piedmont peoples to expand their traditional warfare, the demand for peltry may have fostered conflicts over hunting territories.[56] Those who did not fight each other for slaves or deerskins fought each other for the European products these could bring. As firearms, cloth, and other items became increasingly important to native existence, competition replaced comity at the foundation of trade encounters as villages scrambled for the cargoes of merchandise. Some were in a better position to profit than others. In the early 1670s Occaneechees living on an island in the Roanoke River enjoyed power out of all proportion to their numbers because they controlled an important ford on the trading path from Virginia to the interior, and they resorted to threats, and even to force, to retain their advantage.[57] In Lawson's day Tuscaroras did the same, "hating that any of these Westward *Indians* should have any Commerce with the *English,* which would prove a Hinderance to their Gains."[58]

Competition among native groups was only the beginning of the transformation brought about by new forms of exchange. Inhabitants of the piedmont might bypass the native middleman, but they could not break free from a perilous dependence on colonial sources of supply. The danger may not have been immediately apparent to Indians caught up in the excitement

[56] "It is certain the Indians are very cruel to one another," Rev. Francis Le Jau wrote his superiors in England in April 1708, "but is it not to be feared some white men living or trading among them do foment and increase that Bloody Inclination in order to get Slaves?" (Le Jau to the secretary, Apr. 22, 1708, in Klingberg, ed., *Carolina Chronicle,* 39). Over the summer his worst fears were confirmed: "It is reported by some of our Inhabitants lately gone on Indian Trading that [Carolina traders] excite them to make War amongst themselves to get Slaves which they give for our European Goods" (Le Jau to the secretary, Sept. 15, 1708, *ibid.,* 41). For an analysis of the Indian slave trade see J. Leitch Wright, Jr., *The Only Land They Knew: The Tragic Story of the American Indians in the Old South* (New York, 1981), chap. 6. General studies of Indian warfare in the Southeast are John R. Swanton, *The Indians of the Southeastern United States,* Smithsonian Institution, Bureau of American Ethnology, Bulletin 137 (Washington, D. C., 1946), 686–701, and Hudson, *Southeastern Indians,* 239–257.

Evidence of an escalation in competition for hunting territories is sparse. But in 1702, only a year after Lawson noted that deer were scarce among the Tuscaroras, Indians in Virginia complained that Tuscarora hunting parties were crossing into the colony in search of game and ruining the hunting grounds of local groups. See Lawson, *New Voyage,* ed. Lefler, 65, and *Va. Council Jours.,* II, 275. It seems likely that this became more common as pressure on available supplies of game intensified.

[57] "Letter of Abraham Wood to John Richards, August 22, 1674," in Clarence Walworth Alvord and Lee Bidgood [eds.], *First Explorations of the Trans-Allegheny Region by the Virginians, 1650–1674* (Cleveland, Ohio, 1912), 211, 215–217, 223–225; "Virginias Deploured Condition: Or an Impartiall Narrative of the Murders comitted by the Indians there, and of the Sufferings of his Maties. Loyall Subjects under the Rebellious outrages of Mr. Nathaniell Bacon Junr. to the tenth day of August A. o Dom 1676," Massachusetts Historical Society, *Collections,* 4th Ser., IX (Boston, 1871), 167.

[58] Lawson, *New Voyage,* ed. Lefler, 64.

of acquiring new and wonderful things. For years they managed to dictate the terms of trade, compelling visitors from Carolina and Virginia to abide by aboriginal codes of conduct and playing one colony's traders against the other to ensure an abundance of goods at favorable rates.[59] But the natives' influence over the protocol of exchange combined with their skill at incorporating alien products to mask a loss of control over their own destiny. The mask came off when, in 1715, the traders—and the trade goods—suddenly disappeared during the Yamassee War.

The conflict's origins lay in a growing colonial awareness of the Indians' need for regular supplies of European merchandise. In 1701 Lawson pronounced the Santees "very tractable" because of their close connections with South Carolina. Eight years later he was convinced that the colonial officials in Charleston "are absolute Masters over the *Indians* . . . within the Circle of their Trade."[60] Carolina traders who shared this conviction quite naturally felt less and less constrained to obey native rules governing proper behavior. Abuses against Indians mounted until some men were literally getting away with murder. When repeated appeals to colonial officials failed, natives throughout Carolina began to consider war. Persuaded by Yamassee ambassadors that the conspiracy was widespread and convinced by years of ruthless commercial competition between Virginia and Carolina that an attack on one colony would not affect relations with the other, in the spring of 1715 Catawbas and their neighbors joined the invasion of South Carolina.[61]

The decision to fight was disastrous. Colonists everywhere shut off the flow of goods to the interior, and after some initial successes Carolina's native enemies soon plumbed the depths of their dependence. In a matter of months, refugees holed up in Charleston noticed that "the Indians want ammunition and are not able to mend their Arms."[62] The peace negotiations that ensued revealed a desperate thirst for fresh supplies of European wares. Ambassadors from piedmont towns invariably spoke in a single breath of restoring "a Peace and a free Trade," and one delegation even admitted that its people "cannot live without the assistance of the English."[63]

---

[59] See Cumming, ed., *Discoveries of Lederer,* 41; Lawson, *New Voyage,* ed. Lefler, 210; and Merrell, "Natives in a New World," 74–77. For the competition between colonies see Verner W. Crane, *The Southern Frontier, 1670–1732* (New York, 1981 [orig. publ. Durham, N. C., 1928]), 153–157, and Merrell, "Natives in a New World," 136–147.

[60] Lawson, *New Voyage,* ed. Lefler, 23, 10.

[61] The best studies of this conflict are Crane, *Southern Frontier,* chap. 7; John Phillip Reid, *A Better Kind of Hatchet: Law, Trade, and Diplomacy in the Cherokee Nation during the Early Years of European Contact* (University Park, Pa., 1976), chaps. 5–7; and Richard L. Haan, "The 'Trade Do's Not Flourish as Formerly': The Ecological Origins of the Yamassee War of 1715," *Ethnohistory,* XXVIII (1981), 341–358. The Catawbas' role in the war is detailed in Merrell, "Natives in a New World," chap. 4.

[62] Le Jau to [John Chamberlain?], Aug. 22, 1715, in Klingberg, ed., *Carolina Chronicle,* 162.

[63] *Va. Council Jours.,* III, 406, 412, 422.

Natives unable to live without the English henceforth tried to live with them. No upcountry group mounted a direct challenge to Anglo-America after 1715. Trade quickly resumed, and the piedmont Indians, now concentrated almost exclusively in the Catawba valley, briefly enjoyed a regular supply of necessary products sold by men willing once again to deal according to the old rules. By mid-century, however, deer were scarce and fresh sources of slaves almost impossible to find. Anglo-American traders took their business elsewhere, leaving inhabitants of the Nation with another material crisis of different but equally dangerous dimensions.[64]

Indians casting about for an alternative means of procuring the commodities they craved looked to imperial officials. During the 1740s and 1750s native dependence shifted from colonial traders to colonial authorities as Catawba leaders repeatedly visited provincial capitals to request goods. These delegations came not to beg but to bargain. Catawbas were still of enormous value to the English as allies and frontier guards, especially at a time when Anglo-America felt threatened by the French and their Indian auxiliaries. The Nation's position within reach of Virginia and both Carolinas enhanced its value by enabling headmen to approach all three colonies and offer their people's services to the highest bidder.

The strategy yielded Indians an arsenal of ammunition and a variety of other merchandise that helped offset the declining trade.[65] Crown officials were especially generous when the Nation managed to play one colony off against another. In 1746 a rumor that the Catawbas were about to move to Virginia was enough to garner them a large shipment of powder and lead from officials in Charleston concerned about losing this "valuable people."[66] A decade later, while the two Carolinas fought for the honor of constructing a fort in the Nation, the Indians encouraged (and received) gifts symbolizing good will from both colonies without reaching an agreement with either. Surveying the tangled thicket of promises and presents, the Crown's superintendent of Indian affairs, Edmond Atkin, ruefully admitted that "the People of both Provinces . . . have I beleive [sic] tampered too much on both sides with those Indians, who seem to understand well how to make their Advantage of it."[67]

By the end of the colonial period delicate negotiations across cultural boundaries were as familiar to Catawbas as the strouds they wore and the

---

[64] Merrell, "Natives in a New World," 280–300, 358–359.

[65] For an example of the gifts received by Catawbas see the list of goods delivered to the Catawba Indians at the Congaree Fort, Feb. 14, 1752, in William L. McDowell, ed., *The Colonial Records of South Carolina: Documents Relating to Indian Affairs, May 21, 1750–August 7, 1754, Ser. 2, The Indian Books* (Columbia, S. C., 1958), 217–218, hereafter cited as *Indian Affairs Docs.*

[66] J. H. Easterby, ed., *The Colonial Records of South Carolina: Journals of the Commons House of Assembly, September 10, 1745–June 17, 1746* (Columbia, S. C., 1956), 132, 141, 173; George Haig to Gov. James Glen, Mar. 21, 1746, S. C. Council Jours., Mar. 27, 1746, Records of States, SC E.1p. 3/2, 74–75.

[67] Atkin to Gov. William Henry Lyttelton, Nov. 23, 1757, Lyttelton Papers.

muskets they carried. But no matter how shrewdly the headmen loosened provincial purse strings to extract vital merchandise, they could not escape the simple fact that they no longer held the purse containing everything needed for their daily existence. In the space of a century the Indians had become thoroughly embedded in an alien economy, denizens of a new material world. The ancient self-sufficiency was only a dim memory in the minds of the Nation's elders.[68]

The Catawba peoples were veterans of countless campaigns against disease and masters of the arts of trade long before the third major element of their new world, white planters, became an integral part of their life. Settlement of the Carolina uplands did not begin until the 1730s, but once underway it spread with frightening speed. In November 1752, concerned Catawbas reminded South Carolina governor James Glen how they had "complained already . . . that the white People were settled too near us."[69] Two years later five hundred families lived within thirty miles of the Nation and surveyors were running their lines into the middle of native towns.[70] "[T]hose Indians are now in a fair way to be surrounded by White People," one observer concluded.[71]

Settlers' attitudes were as alarming as their numbers. Unlike traders who profited from them or colonial officials who deployed them as allies, ordinary colonists had little use for Indians. Natives made poor servants and worse slaves; they obstructed settlement; they attracted enemy warriors to the area. Even men who respected Indians and earned a living by trading with them admitted that they made unpleasant neighbors. "We may observe of them as of the fire," wrote the South Carolina trader James Adair after considering the Catawbas' situation on the eve of the American Revolution, "'it is safe and useful, cherished at proper distance; but if too near us, it becomes dangerous, and will scorch if not consume us.'"[72]

A common fondness for alcohol increased the likelihood of intercultural hostilities. Catawba leaders acknowledged that the Indians "get very Drunk with [liquor] this is the Very Cause that they oftentimes Commit those Crimes that is offencive to You and us."[73] Colonists were equally prone to bouts of drunkenness. In the 1760s the itinerant Anglican minister, Charles Woodmason, was shocked to find the citizens of one South Carolina upcountry

---

[68] Treaty between North Carolina Commissioners and the Catawba Indians, Aug. 29, 1754, *N. C. Col. Recs.*, V, 144a.

[69] Catawba King and Others to Gov. Glen, Nov. 21, 1752, *Indian Affairs Docs.*, 361.

[70] Mathew Rowan to the Board of Trade, June 3, 1754, *N. C. Col. Recs.*, V, 124; Samuel Wyly to clerk of Council, Mar. 2, 1754, in S. C. Council Jours., Mar. 13, 1754, Records of States, SC E.1p, 6/1, 140.

[71] Wilbur R. Jacobs, ed., *Indians of the Southern Colonial Frontier: The Edmond Atkin Report and Plan of 1755* (Columbia, S. C., 1954), 46.

[72] Williams, ed., *Adair's History*, 235.

[73] Treaty between North Carolina and the Catawbas, Aug. 29, 1754, *N. C. Col. Recs.*, V, 143. See also conference held with the Catawbas by Mr. Chief Justice Henley at Salisbury, May 1756, *ibid.*,

community "continually drunk." More appalling still, after attending church services "one half of them got drunk before they went home."[74] Indians sometimes suffered at the hands of intoxicated farmers. In 1760 a Catawba woman was murdered when she happened by a tavern shortly after four of its patrons "swore they would kill the first Indian they should meet with."[75]

Even when sober, natives and newcomers found many reasons to quarrel. Catawbas were outraged if colonists built farms on the Indians' doorstep or tramped across ancient burial grounds.[76] Planters, ignorant of (or indifferent to) native rules of hospitality, considered Indians who requested food nothing more than beggars and angrily drove them away.[77] Other disputes arose when the Nation's young men went looking for trouble. As hunting, warfare, and other traditional avenues for achieving status narrowed, Catawba youths transferred older patterns of behavior into a new arena by raiding nearby farms and hunting cattle or horses.[78]

Contrasting images of the piedmont landscape quite unintentionally generated still more friction. Colonists determined to tame what they considered a wilderness were in fact erasing a native signature on the land and scrawling their own. Bridges, buildings, fences, roads, crops, and other "improvements" made the area comfortable and familiar to colonists but uncomfortable and unfamiliar to Indians. "The Country side wear[s] a New face," proclaimed Woodmason proudly[79]; to the original inhabitants, it was a grim face indeed. "His Land was spoiled," one Catawba headman told British officials in 1763. "They have spoiled him 100 Miles every way."[80] Under these circumstances, even a settler with no wish to fight Indians met opposition to his fences, his outbuildings, his very presence. Similarly, a Catawba on a routine foray into traditional hunting territories had his weapon destroyed, his goods confiscated, his life threatened by men with different notions of the proper use of the land.[81]

581, 583; Matthew Toole to Glen, Oct. 28, 1752, *Indian Affairs Docs.*, 359; Catawbas to Lyttelton, June 16, 1757, Lyttelton Papers; and James Adamson to Lyttelton, June 12, 1759, *ibid.*

[74] Richard J. Hooker, ed., *The Carolina Backcountry on the Eve of the Revolution: The Journal and Other Writings of Charles Woodmason, Anglican Itinerant* (Chapel Hill, N. C., 1953), 7, 12. See also 30, 39, 53, 56, 97–99, 128–129.

[75] S. C. Council Jours., May 5, 1760, Records of States, SC E.1p, 8/3, 119.

[76] Robert Stiell to Gov. Glen, Mar, 11, 1753, *Indian Affairs Docs.*, 371; Gov. Thomas Boone to the Lords Commissioners of Trade and Plantations, Oct. 9, 1762, in W. Noel Sainsbury, comp., Records in the British Public Record Office Relating to South Carolina, 1663–1782, 36 vols., microfilm ed. (Columbia, S. C., 1955), XXIX, 245–246, hereafter cited as Brit. Public Recs., S. C.

[77] Treaty between North Carolina and the Catawbas, Aug. 29, 1754, *N. C. Col. Recs.*, V, 142–143; Council Journal, Mar. 18, 1756, *ibid.*, 655; Samuel Wyly to Lyttelton, Feb. 9, 1759, Lyttelton Papers.

[78] See, for example, Treaty between North Carolina and the Catawbas, Aug, 29, 1754, *N. C. Col. Recs.*, V, 142–143, and Catawbas to Lyttelton, June 16, 1757, Lyttelton Papers.

[79] Hooker, ed., *Carolina Backcountry*, 63.

[80] Augusta Congress, Nov. 1763, in Brit. Public Recs., S. C., XXX, 84.

[81] Robert Stiell to Gov. Glen, Mar. 11, 1753, *Indian Affairs Docs.*, 371; Inhabitants of the Waxhaws to Samuel Wyly, Apr. 15, 1759, encl. in Wyly to Lyttelton, Apr. 26, 1759, Lyttelton Papers

culture conflicts

To make matters worse, the importance both cultures attached to personal independence hampered efforts by authorities on either side to resolve conflicts. Piedmont settlers along the border between the Carolinas were "people of desperate fortune," a frightened North Carolina official reported after visiting the area. "[N]o officer of Justice from either Province dare meddle with them."[82] Woodmason, who spent even more time in the region, came to the same conclusion. "We are without any Law, or Order," he complained; the inhabitants' "Impudence is so very high, as to be past bearing."[83] Catawba leaders could have sympathized. Headmen informed colonists that the Nation's people "are oftentimes Cautioned from . . . ill Doings altho' to no purpose for we Cannot be present at all times to Look after them." "What they have done I could not prevent," one chief explained.[84]

Unruly, angry, intoxicated—Catawbas and Carolinians were constantly at odds during the middle decades of the eighteenth century. Planters who considered Indians "proud and deveilish" were themselves accused by natives of being "very bad and quarrelsome."[85] Warriors made a habit of "going into the Settlements, robbing and stealing where ever they get an Oppertunity."[86] Complaints generally brought no satisfaction—"they laugh and makes their Game of it, and says it is what they will"—leading some settlers to "whip [Indians] about the head, beat and abuse them."[87] "The white People . . . and the Cuttahbaws, are Continually at varience," a visitor to the Nation fretted in June 1759, "and Dayly New Animositys Doth a rise Between them which In my Humble oppion will be of Bad Consequence In a Short time, Both Partys Being obstinate."[88]

The litany of intercultural crimes committed by each side disguised a fundamental shift in the balance of physical and cultural power. In the early years of colonization of the interior the least disturbance by Indians sent scattered planters into a panic. Soon, however, Catawbas were few, colonists many, and it was the natives who now lived in fear. "[T]he white men [who] Lives Near the Neation is Contenuely asembleing and goes In the [Indian] towns In Bodys . . . ," worried another observer during the tense summer of 1759. "[T]he[y] tretton the[y] will Kill all the Cattabues."[89]

(colonists attacked). S. C. Council Jours., Feb. 6, 1769, Records of States, SC E.1p, 10/3, 9; King Frow to the governor, Mar. 15, 1770, in S. C. Council Jours., Mar. 27, 1770, *ibid.*, SC E.1p, 10/4, 56; "At a Meeting Held with the Catabaws," Mar. 26, 1771, Joseph Kershaw Papers, South Caroliniana Library, University of South Carolina, Columbia (Indians attacked).

[82] Information of John Frohock and others, Oct. 10, 1762, *N. C. Col. Recs.*, VI, 794–795.

[83] Hooker, ed., *Carolina Backcountry*, 45, 52.

[84] Treaty between North Carolina and the Catawbas, Aug. 29, 1754, *N. C. Col. Recs.*, V, 143; Catawbas to Glen, Nov. 21, 1752, *Indian Affairs Docs.*, 361.

[85] Waxhaw inhabitants to Wyly, Apr. 15, 1759, encl. in Wyly to Lyttelton, Apr. 26, 1759, Lyttelton Papers; Meeting between the Catawbas and Henley, May 1756, *N. C. Col. Recs.*, V, 581.

[86] Toole to Glen, Oct. 28, 1752, *Indian Affairs Docs.*, 358.

[87] *Ibid.*, 359; Meeting between the Catawbas and Henley, May 1756, *N. C. Col. Recs.*, V, 581.

[88] John Evans to Lyttelton, June 20, 1759, Lyttelton Papers.

[89] Adamson to Lyttelton, June 12, 1759, *ibid.*

The Indians would have to find some way to get along with these unpleasant neighbors if the Nation was to survive. As Catawba population fell
below five hundred after the smallpox epidemic of 1759 and the number of
colonists continued to climb, natives gradually came to recognize the futility
of violent resistance. During the last decades of the eighteenth century they
drew on years of experience in dealing with Europeans at a distance and
sought to overturn the common conviction that Indian neighbors were
frightening and useless.

This process was not the result of some clever plan; Catawbas had no
strategy for survival. A headman could warn them that "the White people
were now seated all round them and by that means had them entirely in
their power."[90] He could not command them to submit peacefully to the invasion of their homeland. The Nation's continued existence required countless individual decisions, made in a host of diverse circumstances, to complain rather than retaliate, to accept a subordinate place in a land that once
was theirs. Few of the choices made survive in the record. But it is clear that,
like the response to disease and to technology, the adaptation to white settlement was both painful and prolonged.

Catawbas took one of the first steps along the road to accommodation in
the early 1760s, when they used their influence with colonial officials to acquire a reservation encompassing the heart of their ancient territories.[91] This
grant gave the Indians a land base, grounded in Anglo-American law, that prevented farmers from shouldering them aside. Equally important, Catawbas
now had a commodity to exchange with nearby settlers. These men wanted
land, the natives had plenty, and shortly before the Revolution the Nation was
renting tracts to planters for cash, livestock, and manufactured goods.[92]

---

[90] Meeting between the Catawbas and Henley, May 1756, *N. C. Col. Recs.*, V, 582.

[91] The Indians lobbied for this land beginning in 1757. Crown officials finally reserved it to them
in Nov. 1763 and surveyed it in Feb. 1764. See Catawbas to Lyttelton, June 16, 1757, Lyttelton Papers; *S. C. Gaz.*, Aug. 9, 1760; S. C. Council Jours., May 15, 1762, Records of States, SC E.1p, 8/6,
497; Augusta Congress, Nov. 1763, Brit. Public Recs., S. C., XXX, 84, 104–106, 112–113; and "A
Map of the Catawba Indians Surveyed agreeable to a Treaty Entered into with Them At Augusta
in Georgia on the tenth Day of November 1763 . . . Executed, Certified and Signed by me the
22nd Day of February Anno Domini 1764, Sam[ue]l Wyly D[eputy] S[urveyo]r," Miscellaneous
Records, H, 460, S. C. Dept. Archs. and Hist.

[92] Brown, *Catawba Indians*, 283–284. For contemporary accounts, see Thomas Coke, *Extracts of the
Journals of the Rev. Dr. Coke's Five Visits to America* (London, 1793), 148–149; "Travel Diary of Marshall and Benzien from Salem to South Carolina, 1790 . . . ," in Adelaide L. Fries *et al.*, eds.,
Records of the Moravians in North Carolina, 11 vols. (Raleigh, N. C., 1922–1969), V, 1997; David
Hutchison, "The Catawba Indians. By Request," *Palmetto-State Banner* (Columbia), Aug. 30, 1849
(copy in the Draper Manuscript Collection, Ser. U, vol. 10, Doc. #100 [Wisconsin State Historical Society, Madison]), hereafter cited as Hutchison, "Catawba Indians."
    This land system broke down in 1840 when the Catawbas ceded their lands to South Car-
olina in exchange for promises of money and land to be purchased for them in North Carolina.
By that time, the Nation's place in South Carolina society was secure enough to survive the

Important as it was, land was not the only item Catawbas began trading to their neighbors. Some Indians put their skills as hunters and woodsmen to a different use, picking up stray horses and escaped slaves for a reward.[93] Others bartered their pottery, baskets, and table mats.[94] Still others traveled through the upcountry, demonstrating their prowess with the bow and arrow before appreciative audiences.[95] The exchange of these goods and services for European merchandise marked an important adjustment to the settlers' arrival. In the past, natives had acquired essential items by trading peltry and slaves or requesting gifts from representatives of the Crown. But piedmont planters frowned on hunting and warfare, while provincial authorities—finding Catawbas less useful as the Nation's population declined and the French threat disappeared—discouraged formal visits and handed out fewer presents. Hence the Indians had to develop new avenues of exchange that would enable them to obtain goods in ways less objectionable to their neighbors. Pots, baskets, and acres proved harmless substitutes for earlier methods of earning an income.

Quite apart from its economic benefits, trade had a profound impact on the character of Catawba-settler relations. Through countless repetitions of the same simple procedure at homesteads scattered across the Carolinas, a new form of intercourse arose, based not on suspicion and an expectation of conflict but on trust and a measure of friendship. When a farmer looked out his window and saw Indians approaching, his reaction more commonly became to pick up money or a jug of whiskey rather than a musket or an axe. The natives now appeared, the settler knew, not to plunder or kill but to peddle their wares or collect their rents.[96]

---

economic and social shock of losing its land base. When plans to live in North Carolina fell through and the Indians drifted back to their ancient territory, no one forced them to leave. Instead, the state of South Carolina purchased a small reservation for them, a tract of land that has been the core of Catawba life ever since. See Brown, *Catawba Indians,* chaps. 13–14.

[93] Affidavit of John Evans, S. C. Council Jours., Nov. 6, 1755, Records of States, SC E.1p, 7/2, 439; Affidavit of Liddy, Jan. 1, 1784, Kershaw Papers (horses). Report of the South Carolina Committee of Council, Apr. 19, 1769, Brit. Public Recs., S. C., XXX, 145–146; Hutchison, "Catawba Indians" (slaves).

[94] John F. D. Smyth, *A Tour in the United States of America . . . ,* I (London, 1784), 193–194; Lucius Verus Bierce, "The Piedmont Frontier, 1822–23," in Thomas D. Clark, ed., *South Carolina: The Grand Tour, 1780–1865* (Columbia, S. C., 1973), 64; William Gilmore Simms, "Caloya; Or, The Loves of the Driver," in his *The Wigwam and the Cabin* (New York, 1856), 361–363.

[95] Frank G. Speck, *Catawba Hunting, Trapping, and Fishing,* Joint Publications, Museum of The University of Pennsylvania and The Philadelphia Anthropological Society, No. 2 (Philadelphia, 1946), 10; Thomas J. Kirkland and Robert M. Kennedy, *Historic Camden,* I: *Colonial and Revolutionary* (Columbia, S. C., 1905), 58–59.

[96] Compare, for example, the bitterness whites expressed to Adair before the Revolution (Williams, ed., *Adair's History,* 234) with the bemused tolerance in Simms's 19th-century fictional account of Catawbas and planters ("Caloya," in his *Wigwam and Cabin,* 361–429).

The development of new trade forms could not bury all of the differences between Catawba and colonist overnight.[97] But in the latter half of the eighteenth century the beleaguered Indians learned to rely on peaceful means of resolving intercultural conflicts that did arise. Drawing a sharp distinction between "the good men that have rented Lands from us" and "the bad People [who] has frequently imposed upon us," Catawbas called on the former to protect the Nation from the latter.[98] In 1771 they met with the prominent Camden storekeeper, Joseph Kershaw, to request that he "represent us when [we are] a grieved."[99] After the Revolution the position became more formal. Catawbas informed the South Carolina government that, being "destitute of a man to take care of, and assist us in our affairs," they had chosen one Robert Patten "to take charge of our affairs, and to act and do for us."[100]

Neither Patten nor any other intermediary could have protected the Nation had it not joined the patriot side during the Revolutionary War. Though one scholar has termed the Indians' contribution to the cause "rather negligible,"[101] they fought in battles throughout the southeast and supplied rebel forces with food from time to time.[102] These actions made the Catawba heroes and laid a foundation for their popular renown as staunch patriots. In 1781 their old friend Kershaw told Catawba leaders how he welcomed the end of "this Long and Bloody War, in which You have taken so Noble a part and have fought and Bled with your white Brothers of America."[103] Grateful Carolinians would not soon forget the Nation's service. Shortly after the Civil War an elderly settler whose father had served with the Indians in the Revolution echoed Kershaw's sentiments, recalling that "his father never communicated much to him [about the Catawbas], except that all the tribe . . . served the entire war . . . and fought most heroically."[104]

Catawbas rose even higher in their neighbors' esteem when they began calling their chiefs "General" instead of "King" and stressed that these men

---

[97] Besides the conflicts over hunting noted above, see Hooker, ed., *Carolina Backcountry*, 20; Lark E. Adams, ed., *The State Records of South Carolina: Journals of the House of Representatives, 1785–1786* (Columbia, S. C., 1979), 511–512; Journals of the House of Representatives, Dec. 5, 1792, Records of States, SC A.1b, 23/1, 83.

[98] Catawba petition "To the Honourable the Legislature of the State of South Carolina now assembled at Charlestown," Feb. 13, 1784(?), Kershaw Papers. The Indians had made this distinction earlier. See S. C. Council Jours., Oct. 8, 1760, Records of States, SC E.1p, 8/5, 36.

[99] "At a Meeting Held with the Catabaws," Mar. 26, 1771, Kershaw Papers.

[100] Catawba Petition to S. C. Legislature, Feb. 13, 1784(?), *ibid.*

[101] Hudson, *Catawba Nation*, 51.

[102] The story of the Indians' service is summarized in Brown, *Catawba Indians*, 260–271.

[103] "To the Brave Genl New River and the rest of the Headmen Warriers of the Catawba Nation," 1771 (misdated), Kershaw Papers.

[104] A. Q. Bradley to Lyman C. Draper, May 31, 1873, Draper MSS, 14VV, 260. For other expressions of this attitude see J. F. White to Draper, n.d., *ibid.*, 15VV, 96; T. D. Spratt to Draper, May 7, 1873, *ibid.*, 107–108; Ezekiel Fewell to Draper, n.d., *ibid.*, 318–319; and David Hutchison, "Catawba Indians."

were elected by the people.[105] The change reflected little if any real shift in the Nation's political forms,[106] but it delighted the victorious Revolutionaries. In 1794 the Charleston *City Gazette* reported that during the war "King" Frow had abdicated and the Indians chose "General" New River in his stead. "What a pity," the paper concluded, "certain people on a certain island have not as good optics as the Catawbas!" In the same year the citizens of Camden celebrated the anniversary of the fall of the Bastille by raising their glasses to toast "King Prow [*sic*]—may all kings who will not follow his example follow that of Louis XVI."[107] Like tales of Indian patriots, the story proved durable. Nearly a century after the Revolution one nearby planter wrote that "the Catawbas, emulating the examples of their white brethren, threw off regal government."[108]

The Indians' new image as republicans and patriots, added to their trade with whites and their willingness to resolve conflicts peacefully, brought settlers to view Catawbas in a different light. By 1800 the natives were no longer violent and dangerous strangers but what one visitor termed an "inoffensive" people and one group of planters called "harmless and friendly" neighbors.[109] They had become traders of pottery but not deerskins, experts with a bow and arrow but not hunters, ferocious warriors against runaway slaves or tories but not against settlers. In these ways Catawbas could be distinctively Indian yet reassuringly harmless at the same time.

The Nation's separate identity rested on such obvious aboriginal traits. But its survival ultimately depended on a more general conformity with the surrounding society. During the nineteenth century both settlers and Indians owned or rented land. Both spoke proudly of their Revolutionary heritage and their republican forms of government. Both drank to excess.[110] Even the fact that Catawbas were not Christians failed to differentiate them sharply

[105] Brown, *Catawba Indians*, 276.
[106] The Nation's council "elected" headmen both before and after 1776, and kinship connections to former rulers continued to be important. For elections see S. C. Council Jours., Feb. 20, 1764, Records of States, SC E.1p, 9/2, 40–41; Nov. 9, 1764, *ibid.*, 354; Feb. 12, 1765, *ibid.*, 9/3, 442–443; S. C. Commons House Jours., Jan. 27, 1767, *ibid.*, SC A.1b, 8/1, n. p. For later hereditary links to former chiefs see John Drayton, *A View of South Carolina As Respects Her Natural and Civil Concerns* (Spartanburg, S. C., 1972 [orig. publ., 1802]), 98; Spratt to Draper, Jan. 12, 1871, Draper MSS, 15VV, 99–100.
[107] *City Gazette* (Charleston), Aug. 14, 1794, quoted in Kirkland and Kennedy, *Historic Camden*, 320, 319.
[108] Spratt to Draper, Jan. 12, 1871, Draper MSS, 15VV, 99. See also Hutchison, "Catawba Indians."
[109] Smyth, *Tour*, I, 192: Report of the Commissioners Appointed to Treat with the Catawba Indians, Apr. 3, 1840, in A. F. Whyte, "Account of the Catawba Indians," Draper MSS, 1OU, 112.
[110] W. J. Rorabaugh, *The Alcoholic Republic: An American Tradition* (New York, 1979), chap. 1. For reports of excessive drinking by whites along the Catawba River see Records of the General Assembly, Petitions, N.D. (#1916), 1798 (#139), S. C. Dept. Archs. and Hist.; Journals of the Senate, Dec. 11, 1819, Records of States, SC A.1a, 25/3, 57; Journals of the House of Representatives, Nov. 23, 1819, Nov. 21, 1827, Records of States, SC A.1b, 28/1, 8, 29/5, 15, 24.

from nearby white settlements, where, one visitor noted in 1822, "little attention is paid to the sabbath, or religeon."[111]

In retrospect it is clear that these similarities were as superficial as they were essential. For all the changes generated by contacts with vital Euro-American and Afro-American cultures, the Nation was never torn loose from its cultural moorings. Well after the Revolution, Indians maintained a distinctive way of life rich in tradition and meaningful to those it embraced. Ceremonies conducted by headmen and folk tales told by relatives continued to transmit traditional values and skills from one generation to the next. Catawba children grew up speaking the native language, making bows and arrows or pottery, and otherwise following patterns of belief and behavior derived from the past. The Indians' physical appearance and the meandering paths that set Catawba settlements off from neighboring communities served to reinforce this cultural isolation.[112]

The natives' utter indifference to missionary efforts after 1800 testified to the enduring power of established ways. Several clergymen stopped at the reservation in the first years of the nineteenth century; some stayed a year or two; none enjoyed any success.[113] As one white South Carolinian noted in 1826, Catawbas were "Indians still."[114] Outward conformity made it easier for them to blend into the changed landscape. Beneath the surface lay a more complex story.

Those few outsiders who tried to piece together that story generally found it difficult to learn much from the Indians. A people shrewd enough to discard the title of "King" was shrewd enough to understand that some things were better left unsaid and unseen. Catawbas kept their Indian names, and sometimes their language, a secret from prying visitors.[115] They echoed the racist attitudes of their white neighbors and even owned a few slaves, all the time trading with blacks and hiring them to work in the Nation, where the laborers "enjoyed considerable freedom" among the

---

[111] Bierce, "Piedmont Frontier," in Clark, ed., *Grand Tour,* 66.

[112] The story of the Catawbas' cultural persistence may be found in Merrell, "Natives in a New World," chap. 9, and "Reading 'an almost erased page': A Reassessment of Frank G. Speck's Catawba Studies," American Philosophical Society, *Proceedings,* CXXVII (1983), 248–262. For an interesting comparison of cultural independence in the slave quarter and the Indian reservation see Thomas L. Webber, *Deep Like the Rivers: Education in the Slave Quarter Community, 1831–1865* (New York, 1978), chap. 18.

[113] Hutchison, "Catawba Indians"; Daniel G. Stinson to Draper, July 4, 1873, Draper MSS, 9VV, 274–277.

[114] Robert Mills, *Statistics of South Carolina . . .* (Charleston, S. C., 1826), 773. See also the annual reports of the Catawba Agent to the Governor and State Legislature of South Carolina, 1841, 1842, 1848, 1849, 1860–1864, in Legislative Papers, Indian Affairs, Governors' Correspondence, S. C. Dept. Archs. and Hist.

[115] See Merrell, "Reading 'an almost erased page,'" Am. Phil. Soc., *Procs.,* CXXVII (1983), 256 (names). Smyth, *Tour,* I, 185; Coke, *Extracts,* 149; "Letter from the Country Landsford, S. C., September 6, 1867," in *Courier* (Charleston), Sept. 12, 1867, 3 (language).

natives.[116] Like Afro-Americans on the plantation who adopted a happy, childlike demeanor to placate suspicious whites, Indians on the reservation learned that a "harmless and friendly" posture revealing little of life in the Nation was best suited to conditions in post-Revolutionary South Carolina.

Success in clinging to their cultural identity and at least a fraction of their ancient lands cannot obscure the cost Catawba peoples paid. From the time the first European arrived, the deck was stacked against them. They played the hand dealt them well enough to survive, but they could never win. An incident that took place at the end of the eighteenth century helps shed light on the consequences of compromise. When the Catawba head-man, General New River, accidentally injured the horse he had borrowed from a nearby planter named Thomas Spratt, Spratt responded by "banging old New River with a pole all over the yard." This episode provided the set-tler with a colorful tale for his grandchildren; its effect on New River and his descendants can only be imagined.[117] Catawbas did succeed in the sense that they adjusted to a hostile and different world, becoming trusted friends in-stead of feared enemies. Had they been any less successful they would not have survived the eighteenth century. But poverty and oppression have plagued the Nation from New River's day to our own.[118] For a people who had once been proprietors of the piedmont, the pain of learning new rules was very great, the price of success very high.

On that August day in 1608 when Amoroleck feared the loss of his world, John Smith assured him that the English "came to them in peace, and to seeke their loves."[119] Events soon proved Amoroleck right and his captor wrong. Over the course of the next three centuries not only Amoroleck and other piedmont Indians but natives throughout North America had their world stolen and another put in its place. Though this occurred at different times and in different ways, no Indians escaped the explosive mixture of deadly bacteria, material riches, and alien peoples that was the invasion of America. Those in the southern piedmont who survived the onslaught were ensconced in their new world by the end of the eighteenth century. Popula-tion levels stabilized as the Catawba peoples developed immunities to once-lethal diseases. Rents, sales of pottery, and other economic activities proved adequate to support the Nation at a stable (if low) level of material life. Fi-nally, the Indians' image as "inoffensive" neighbors gave them a place in South Carolina society and continues to sustain them today.

[116] Catawba-black relations are analyzed in Merrill, "The Racial Education of the Catawba Indi-ans," *Journal of Southern History*, L (1984), 363–384.

[117] Thomas Dryden Spratt, "Recollections of His Family, July 1875," unpubl. MS, South Car-oliniana Lib., 62.

[118] See H. Lewis Scaife, *History and Condition of the Catawba Indians of South Carolina* (Philadel-phia, 1896), 16–23, and Hudson, *Catawba Nation*, chaps. 4–6.

[119] Arber and Bradley, eds., *Works of Smith*, II, 427.

Vast differences separated Catawbas and other natives from their colonial contemporaries. Europeans were the colonizers, Africans the enslaved, Indians the dispossessed: from these distinct positions came distinct histories. Yet once we acknowledge the differences, instructive similarities remain that help to integrate natives more thoroughly into the story of early America. By carving a niche for themselves in response to drastically different conditions, the peoples who composed the Catawba Nation shared in the most fundamental of American experiences. Like Afro-Americans, these Indians were compelled to accept a subordinate position in American life yet did not altogether lose their cultural integrity. Like settlers of the Chesapeake, aboriginal inhabitants of the uplands adjusted to appalling mortality rates and wrestled with the difficult task of "living with death."[120] Like inhabitants of the Middle Colonies, piedmont groups learned to cope with unprecedented ethnic diversity by balancing the pull of traditional loyalties with the demands of a new social order. Like Puritans in New England, Catawbas found that a new world did not arrive all at once and that localism, self-sufficiency, and the power of old ways were only gradually eroded by conditions in colonial America. More hints of a comparable heritage could be added to this list, but by now it should be clear that Indians belong on the colonial stage as important actors in the unfolding American drama rather than bit players, props, or spectators. For they, too, lived in a new world.

---

[120] Morgan, *American Slavery, American Freedom,* chap. 8.

King Philip's Herds: Indians, Colonists, and the Problem of Livestock in Early New England

Virginia DeJohn Anderson

INTRODUCTION

When one is asked to identify the shock troops of Euro-American settlement, what usually comes to mind are missionaries, fur traders, and squatters, but not cattle and hogs. Yet Virginia DeJohn Anderson argues that in seventeenth-century New England, disputes over livestock blazed the path toward King Philip's War of 1675–76, a bloody conflict that ultimately broke the back of Indian power in the region. In the decades preceding hostilities, the settlers' free-ranging livestock regularly wandered into native villages and feasted on Indian corn. Hogs dug up Indian clam banks and competed with deer and other game for food. When Indians responded to these encroachments by killing the beasts, the English held Indian sachems, or chiefs, responsible, demanding that they pay heavy fines and even threatening violence. Sometimes colonial officials addressed Indian complaints about livestock encroachment with laws that, in theory, required settlers to control their animals, but in fact little was done to enforce these statutes.

Virginia DeJohn Anderson, "King Phillip's Herds: Indians, Colonists, and the Problem of Livestock" from *William and Mary Quarterly*, 49 (1992), pp. 183–209. Reprinted by permission of Omohundro Institute of Early American History and Culture, Williamsburg, VA.

Ms. Anderson is a member of the Department of History, University of Colorado, Boulder. She thanks Fred Anderson, James Axtell, Bernard Bailyn, Barbara DeWolfe, Ruth Helm, Stephen Innes, Karen Kupperman, Gloria Main, Daniel Mandell, George Phillips, Neal Salisbury, Richard White, and Anne Yentsch for their helpful comments. She also thanks participants at seminars held at the Charles Warren Center at Harvard University, the American Antiquarian Society, and the Massachusetts Historical Society for their responses to earlier drafts of this essay. Generous support was received from a Charles Warren Center fellowship, a National Endowment for the Humanities Summer Stipend, and a grant-in-aid from the University of Colorado Council on Research and Creative Work.

Anderson shows that natives were infuriated not only by the indifference of colonial livestock to Indian boundaries or by English disrespect for Indian jurisdiction, but also by colonial restrictions on Indian animal husbandry. Missionaries such as John Eliot incessantly pressured their Indian charges to adopt the English economic model, and yet when native converts raised livestock for sale in Boston, Puritan authorities passed laws specifically designed to discourage Indians from competing in the English market. Despite such measures, eventually some non-Christian Indians from the Wampanoag heartland, most notably King Philip, joined the converts' "experiment to acculturation" by also acquiring hogs and perhaps cattle, only to find that colonial neighbors aimed to make this transition as difficult as possible by restricting native grazing rights. Anderson argues that rather than alleviating tensions with the settlers, native acculturation only compounded hostility between natives and newcomers. The English liked Indians less the more they adopted colonial practice. From the Indian perspective, this response made the colonists appear all the more like hypocrites. The mix was right for war.

Anderson's article represents a trend in which Indians appear more culturally flexible, more willing to experiment with English ways, than in earlier histories. Nevertheless, Anderson is careful to note that Indians who raised domestic animals were engaged in selective borrowing; they did not adopt colonial customs according to English dictate, even with regard to animal husbandry, but took on new behaviors on a limited, as-needed basis. Anderson also carefully notes that English settlers disparaged Indians for their lack of domestic stock in part because they deemed animal husbandry a culturally superior activity; it promoted sedentarism, permanent buildings, and private property.

- *Might it be that colonists hated Indians who experimented in animal husbandry in part because the Indians were sending a cultural message that they, and only they, would decide to what extent and when they would adopt English practices?*
- *What if the Wampanoags had adopted the English economic model more wholesale?*
- *What if they had more vigorously built up their herds and fences so that they could lay a greater claim to contested land?*

Finally, note that it was Philip's people, non-Christians, who struck the first blow against the colonists, not the praying Indians of Natick or Hassanamesitt, who lived closer to the English, suffered more from their wandering herds, and bore the brunt of hypocritical restrictions on native livestock sales. Given Anderson's argument that such irritations were the major impetus for war, how do we account for this contrast?

On a late spring day in 1669, the ambitious younger son of a prominent Rhode Island family received a letter from the town clerk of Portsmouth. Like many of his neighbors, the young man raised livestock and followed the common practice of placing his pigs on a nearby island where they could forage safe from predators. But that was what brought him to the attention of Portsmouth's inhabitants, who ordered the clerk to reprimand him for "intrudeinge on" the town's rights when he ferried his beasts to "hog-Island." The townsmen insisted that he remove "Such Swine or other Catle" as he had put there, on pain of legal action. They took the unusual step of instructing the clerk to make two copies of the letter and retain the duplicate—in effect preparing their legal case even before the recipient contested their action.[1]

It was by no means unusual for seventeenth-century New Englanders to find themselves in trouble with local officials, particularly when their search for gain conflicted with the rights of the community. But this case was different. We can only wonder what Metacom, whom the English called King Philip, made of the preemptory directive from the Portsmouth town clerk— for indeed it was to him, son of Massasoit and now sachem of the Wampanoags himself, that the letter was addressed. Because the records (which directed no comparable order to any English swine owner) do not mention the outcome of the dispute, we may suppose that Philip complied with the town's demand. The episode was thus brief, but it was no less important for that, because it involved the man whose name would soon be associated with what was, in proportion to the populations involved, the most destructive war in American history.[2]

For three centuries, historians have depicted Philip in many ways—as a savage chieftain, an implacable foe of innocent Christian settlers, and a doomed victim of European aggressors—but never as a keeper of swine. Although the Hog Island episode may seem unrelated to the subsequent horrors of King Philip's War, the two events were in fact linked. Philip resorted to violence in 1675 because of mounting frustrations with colonists, and no problem vexed relations between settlers and Indians more frequently in the years before the war than the control of livestock.[3] English colonists imported thousands of cattle, swine, sheep, and horses (none of which is native

---

[1] Clarence S. Brigham, ed., *The Early Records of the Town of Portsmouth* (Providence, R. I., 1901), 149–150. On the use of islands for grazing see Carl Bridenbaugh, *Fat Mutton and Liberty of Conscience: Society in Rhode Island, 1636–1690* (Providence, R. I., 1974), 16–17.

[2] Douglas Edward Leach, *Flintlock and Tomahawk: New England in King Philip's War* (New York, 1958), 243–244; for a detailed account of the impact of the war on one town see Richard I. Melvoin, *New England Outpost: War and Society in Colonial Deerfield* (New York, 1989), 92–128.

[3] Historians, when they have investigated livestock at all, have generally done so from an ecological perspective; see, for instance, William Cronon, *Changes in the Land: Indians, Colonists, and the Ecology of New England* (New York, 1983), and Alfred W. Crosby, *Ecological Imperialism: The Biological Expansion of Europe, 900–1900* (New York, 1986).

to North America) because they considered livestock essential to their survival, never supposing that the beasts would become objectionable to the Indians. But the animals exacerbated a host of problems related to subsistence practices, land use, property rights and, ultimately, political authority. Throughout the 1660s, Philip found himself caught in the middle, trying to defend Indian rights even as he adapted to the English presence. The snub delivered by Portsmouth's inhabitants showed him the limits of English flexibility, indicating that the colonists ultimately valued their livestock more than good relations with his people. When Philip recognized that fact, he took a critical step on the path that led him from livestock keeper to war leader.

Successful colonization of New England depended heavily on domestic animals. Nowhere is this better seen than in the early history of Plymouth Colony. Not until 1624—four years after the *Mayflower's* arrival—did Edward Winslow bring from England "three heifers and a bull, the first beginning of any cattle of that kind in the land." This date, not coincidentally, marked the end of the Pilgrims' "starving times" as dairy products and meat began to supplement their diet. By 1627, natural increase and further importations brought the Plymouth herd to at least fifteen animals, whose muscle power increased agricultural productivity.[4] The leaders of Massachusetts Bay Colony, perhaps learning from Plymouth's experience, brought animals from the start. John Winthrop regularly noted the arrival of settlers and livestock during the 1630s, often recording levels of shipboard mortality among animals as well as people. Edward Johnson estimated that participants in the Great Migration spent £12,000 to transport livestock across the ocean, not counting the original cost of the animals.[5]

Early descriptions often focused on the land's ability to support livestock. John Smith noted that in New England there was "grasse plenty, though very long and thicke stalked, which being neither mowne nor eaten, is very ranke, yet all their cattell like and prosper well therewith." Francis Higginson informed English friends that the "fertility of the soil is to be admired at, as appeareth in the abundance of grass that groweth everywhere." "It is scarce to be believed," he added, "how our kine and goats, horses, and hogs do thrive and prosper here and like well of this country." Colonists preferred to settle in areas with ample natural forage. Salt marshes attracted set-

[4] William Bradford, *Of Plymouth Plantation, 1620–1647,* ed. Samuel Eliot Morison (New York, 1952), 141; Nathaniel Shurtleff and David Pulsifer, eds., *Records of the Colony of New Plymouth in New England,* 12 vols. (Boston, 1855–1861), XII, 9–13. See also Darrett B. Rutman, *Husbandmen of Plymouth: Farms and Villages in the Old Colony, 1620–1692* (Boston, 1967), 6, 14–15.
[5] John Winthrop, *The History of New England from 1630 to 1649,* ed. James Savage, 2 vols. (Boston, 1825–1826), I, passim; Edward Johnson, *Johnson's Wonder-Working Providence, 1628–1651,* ed. J. Franklin Jameson, Original Narratives of Early American History (New York, 1910), 54.

tlers to Hampton, New Hampshire, and Sudbury's founders valued their town's riverside fresh meadow. Haverhill's settlers negotiated with the colony government for a large tract for their town in order to satisfy their "over-weaning desire . . . after Medow land." Most inland clearings bore mute witness to recent habitation by Indians, whose periodic burnings kept the areas from reverting to forest.[6]

The size of a town's herds soon became an important measure of its prosperity. As early as 1634, William Wood noted that Dorchester, Roxbury, and Cambridge were particularly "well stored" with cattle. Other commentators added to the list of towns with burgeoning herds. In 1651, Edward Johnson tallied the human and livestock populations for several communities as a measure of divine favor. His enumeration revealed that towns with three or four dozen families also contained several hundred head of livestock.[7] Like Old Testament patriarchs, New England farmers counted their blessings as they surveyed their herds.

Their interest in livestock grew in part from their English experience. Many settlers came from England's wood-pasture region, where they had engaged in a mixed husbandry of cattle and grain. In New England, the balance in that agrarian equation tipped toward livestock because the region's chronic labor shortage made raising cattle a particularly efficient use of resources. Selectmen usually hired one or two town herdsmen, freeing other livestock owners to clear fields, till crops, and construct buildings and fences. Until settlers managed to plant English hay, livestock foraged on the abundant, though less nutritious, native grasses, converting otherwise worthless herbage into milk and meat for consumption and sale. Livestock were so important to survival that New Englanders reversed the usual English fencing practices. English law required farmers to protect their crops by confining livestock within fenced or hedged pastures, but New England

---

[6] John Smith, "Advertisements for the unexperienced Planters of New-England, or any where . . ." (1631), in Massachusetts Historical Society, *Collections*, 3d Ser., III (1833), 37; Higginson to His Friends at Leicester, Sept. 1629, in Everett Emerson, ed., *Letters from New England: The Massachusetts Bay Colony, 1629–1638* (Amherst, Mass., 1976), 31; *Johnson's Wonder-Working Providence*, ed. Jameson, 188–189, 195–196, quotations on 234–235. See also William Wood, *New England's Prospect*, ed. Alden T. Vaughan (Amherst, Mass., 1977; orig. pub. 1634), 33–34. For the choice of Indian clearings for English settlement, see Howard S. Russell, *A Long, Deep Furrow: Three Centuries of Farming in New England* (Hanover, N. H., 1976), 22.

[7] Wood, *New England's Prospect*, ed. Vaughan, 58–60; Samuel Maverick, *A Briefe Discription of New England and the Severall Townes Therein Together with the Present Government Thereof* (1660), (Boston, 1885), 8–15; Paul J. Lindholdt, ed., *John Josselyn, Colonial Traveler: A Critical Edition of "Two Voyages to New-England"* (Hanover, N. H., 1988), 110–119, 138–141; *Johnson's Wonder-Working Providence*, ed. Jameson, 68–69, 72, 110, 188–189, 195–197. In Cape Cod towns during the 17th century, a majority of householders owned cattle and swine; see Anne E. Yentsch, "Farming, Fishing, Whaling, Trading: Land and Sea as Resource on Eighteenth-Century Cape Cod," in Mary C. Beaudry, ed., *Documentary Archaeology in the New World* (New York, 1988), Table 13.8, 149.

farmers were enjoined to construct and maintain sufficiently sturdy fences around cornfields to keep their peripatetic beasts out.[8]

Raising livestock had cultural as well as economic ramifications. For colonists, the absence of indigenous domestic animals underscored the region's essential wildness. "The country is yet raw," wrote Robert Cushman in 1621, "the land untilled; the cities not builded; the cattle not settled." The English saw a disturbing symmetry between the savagery of the land and its human and animal inhabitants. America, noted Cushman, "is spacious and void," and the Indians "do but run over the grass, as do also the foxes and wild beasts."[9] Such evaluations ultimately fueled colonists' own claims to the land. The "savage people," argued John Winthrop, held no legitimate title "for they inclose no ground, neither have they cattell to maintayne it, but remove their dwellings as they have occasion." Winthrop's objection to the Indians' seminomadic habits stemmed from a cultural assumption that equated civilization with sedentarism, a way of life that he linked to the keeping of domesticated animals. Drawing on biblical history, Winthrop argued that a "civil" right to the earth resulted when, "as men and cattell increased, they appropriated some parcells of ground by enclosing and peculiar manurance." Subduing—indeed, domesticating—the wilderness with English people and English beasts thus became a cultural imperative. New England could become a new Canaan, a land of milk and honey, only if, Thomas Morton wryly observed, "the Milke came by the industry" of its civilizing immigrants and their imported livestock.[10]

Accordingly, only those Indians who submitted to "domestication" could live in the New England Canaan. They had to accept Christianity, of course; in addition, colonists insisted that they adopt English ways entirely, including the keeping of domestic animals. Roger Williams urged natives to move "from Barbarism to Civilitie, in forsaking their filthy nakednes, in keeping some kind of Cattell."[11] John Eliot offered livestock, among other

[8] Virginia DeJohn Anderson, *New England's Generation: The Great Migration and the Formation of Society and Culture in the Seventeenth Century* (New York, 1991), 30–31, 151–152, 154–156; Russell, *Long, Deep Furrow*, chap. 4; Cronon, *Changes in the Land*, 141–142; Rutman, *Husbandmen of Plymouth*, 17–19; David Thomas Konig, *Law and Society in Puritan Massachusetts: Essex County, 1629–1692* (Chapel Hill, N. C., 1979), 118–119.

[9] Cushman, "Reasons and Considerations Touching the Lawfulness of Removing Out of England into the Parts of America" and "Of the State of the Colony, and the Need of Public Spirit in the Colonists," in Alexander Young, ed., *Chronicles of the Pilgrim Fathers of the Colony of Plymouth, From 1602 to 1625*, 2d ed. (Boston, 1844), 265, 243.

[10] Allyn B. Forbes et al., eds., *Winthrop Papers, 1498–1654*, 6 vols. (Boston, 1929–1992), II, 120; Thomas Morton, *New English Canaan or New Canaan . . .* (1637), ed. Charles Francis Adams, Jr., *Publications of the Prince Society*, XIV (Boston, 1883), 230. The honey for the New England Canaan would also be an import, since honeybees are not native to America; see Crosby, *Ecological Imperialism*, 188–189. English concern about sedentarism and the connection to property rights is addressed in Cronon, *Changes in the Land*, 130, and Neal Salisbury, *Manitou and Providence: Indians, Europeans, and the Making of New England, 1500–1643* (New York, 1982), 176–177.

[11] Glenn W. LaFantasie, ed., *The Correspondence of Roger Williams*, 2 vols. (Hanover, N. H., and London, 1988), II, 413.

material incentives, to entice Indians to become civilized. He admonished one native audience; "if you were more wise to know God, and obey his Commands, you would work more then [*sic*] you do." Labor six days a week, as God commanded and the English did, and, Eliot promised, "you should have cloths, houses, cattle, riches as they have, God would give you them."[12]

To assist Indians in making this transformation, Puritan officials established fourteen "praying towns" where they could proceed toward conversion as they earned the material rewards Providence would bestow. The inhabitants of these communities not only would learn to worship God as the English did but also would wear English clothes, live in English framed houses, and farm with English animals. Among the goods sent from England to support this civilizing program were seven bells for oxen, to be distributed to Indian farmers who exchanged their traditional hoe agriculture for the plow.[13] Soon the increase in livestock became as much a hallmark of the success of the praying towns as it was of English communities. Daniel Gookin reported in 1674 that the praying town of Hassanamesitt (Grafton) was "an apt place for keeping of cattle and swine; in which respect this people are the best stored of any Indian town of their size." He went on to observe, however, that though these natives "do as well, or rather better, than any other Indians" in raising crops and animals, they "are very far short of the English both in diligence and providence."[14]

Praying Indians raised livestock as participants in what may be called an experiment in acculturation. By moving to places such as Natick or Hassanamesitt, they announced their intention to follow English ways—including animal husbandry—in hopes of finding favor with the Christian God.[15] But the praying towns never contained more than a tiny minority of the native population; most Indians rejected the invitation to exchange their ways for English ones. For the vast majority, the cattle and swine that served as

---

[12] Letter from Eliot in Thomas Shepard, "The Clear Sun-shine of the Gospel Breaking Forth upon the Indians in New-England . . ." (1648), MHS, *Colls.*, 3d Ser., IV (1834), 57–58.

[13] William Kellaway, *The New England Company, 1649–1776: Missionary Society to the American Indians* (New York, 1961), 69.

[14] Gookin, "Historical Collections of the Indians in New England" (1674), MHS, *Colls.*, 1st Ser., I (1792), 185; see also 184, 189, and Lindholdt, ed., *John Josselyn, Colonial Traveler*, 105. On the establishment of the praying towns see James Axtell, *The Invasion Within: The Contest of Cultures in Colonial North America* (New York, 1985), chap. 7; Francis Jennings, *The Invasion of America: Indians, Colonialism, and the Cant of Conquest* (Chapel Hill, N. C., 1975), chap. 14; Salisbury, "Red Puritans: The 'Praying Indians' of Massachusetts Bay and John Eliot," *William and Mary Quarterly*, 3d Ser., XXXI (1974), 27–54; and James P. Ronda, "Generations of Faith: The Christian Indians of Martha's Vineyard," ibid., XXXVIII (1981), 369–394.

[15] The praying Indians never fully adopted the English program for their cultural transformation; see Harold W. Van Lonkhuyzen, "A Reappraisal of the Praying Indians: Acculturation, Conversion, and Identity at Natick, Massachusetts, 1646–1730," *New England Quarterly*, LXIII (1990), 396–428, and Kathleen J. Bragdon, "The Material Culture of the Christian Indians of New

emblems of the praying Indians' transformation had a very different mean-ing. They became instead a source of friction, revealing profound differences between Indians and colonists.

As Indians encountered these unfamiliar animals, they had to decide what to call them. Williams reported that the Narragansetts first looked for similarities in appearance and behavior between an indigenous animal and one of the new beasts and simply used the name of the known beast for both animals. Thus *ockqutchaun-nug,* the name of a "wild beast of a reddish haire about the bignesse of a Pig, and rooting like a Pig," was used for English swine. Finding no suitable parallels for most domestic animals, however, the Narragansetts resorted to neologisms such as "cowsnuck," "goatesuck," and eventually "hogsuck" or "pigsuck." The "termination *suck,* is common in their language," Williams explained, "and therefore they adde it to our Eng-lish Cattell, not else knowing what names to give them."[16]

Giving these animals Indian names in no way implied that most Indians wanted to own livestock. In fact, contact with domestic animals initially pro-duced the opposite reaction, because livestock husbandry did not fit easily with native practices. Indians could hardly undertake winter hunting expeditions accompanied by herds of cattle that required shelter and fodder to survive the cold weather. Swine would compete with their owners for nuts, berries, and roots, and the presence of livestock of any kind tended to drive away deer.[17] Moreover, the Indians, for whom most beasts were literally fair game, strug-gled with the very notion of property in animals. They assumed that one could own only dead animals, which hunters shared with their families.[18]

Further, the adoption of livestock would alter women's lives in crucial ways by affecting the traditional gender-based division of labor. Would women, who were mainly responsible for agricultural production, assume new duties of animal husbandry? If not, how would men's involvement with livestock rearing alter women's powerful role as the primary suppliers of food? Who would protect women's crops from the animals? How would the very different temporal cycle of livestock reproduction and care be rec-onciled with an Indian calendar that identified the months according to stages in the planting cycle?[19]

England, 1650–1775," in Beaudry, ed., *Documentary Archaeology,* 126–131. Their attempts to bal-ance English prescriptions with native preferences suffered heavily after King Philip's War; see Daniel Mandell, "'To Live More Like My Christian English Neighbors': Natick Indians in the Eighteenth Century," *WMQ,* 3d Ser., XLVIII (1991), 552–579.

[16] Williams, *A Key into the Language of America,* ed. John J. Teunissen and Evelyn J. Hinz (Detroit, Mich., 1973), 173–175. An *"ockqutchaun"* was a woodchuck; I am grateful to James Baker of Plimoth Plantation for this information.

[17] Cronon, *Changes in the Land,* 101, 108; M. K. Bennett, "The Food Economy of the New England Indians, 1605–75," *Journal of Political Economy,* LXIII (1955), 369–397.

[18] Cronon, *Changes in the Land,* 129–130.

[19] Van Lonkhuyzen, "Reappraisal of the Praying Indians," 412–413; Joan M. Jensen, "Native American Women and Agriculture: A Seneca Case Study," *Sex Roles: A Journal of Research,* III

Animal husbandry also challenged native spiritual beliefs and practices. Because their mental universe assumed no rigid distinction between human and animal beings, the Indians' hunting rituals aimed to appease the spirits of creatures that were not so much inferior to, as different from, their human killers. Such beliefs helped to make sense of a world in which animals were deemed equally rightful occupants of the forest and whose killing required an intimate knowledge of their habits. Would Indians be able to apply these ideas about animals as *manitous,* or other-than-human persons, to domestic beasts as well? Or would those beasts' English provenance and dependence on human owners prohibit their incorporation into the spiritual world with bears, deer, and beaver?[20]

Finally, a decision to keep livestock ran counter to a powerful hostility toward domestic animals that dated from the earliest years of English settlement. Because colonists often established towns on the sites of former Indian villages depopulated by the epidemics that preceded their arrival, no line of demarcation separated English from Indian habitation. Native villages and colonial towns could be quite close together, and the accident of propinquity made for tense relations. At least at first, friction between these unlikely neighbors grew less from the very different ideas that informed Indian and English concepts of property than from the behavior of livestock. Let loose to forage in the woods, the animals wandered away from English towns into Indian cornfields, ate their fill, and moved on.

Indians, who had never had to build fences to protect their fields, were unprepared for the onslaught. Even their underground storage pits proved vulnerable, as swine "found a way to unhinge their barn doors and rob their garners," prompting native women to "implore their husbands' help to roll the bodies of trees" over the pits to prevent further damage.[21] Hogs attacked another important food source when they "watch[ed] the low water (as the Indian women do)" along the shoreline and rooted for clams, making themselves "most hatefull to all Natives," who called them "filthy cut throats, &c."[22] In Plymouth Colony, settlers in Rehoboth and their Indian neighbors

(1977), 423–441; Salisbury, *Manitou and Providence,* 36. For an example of the way in which the adoption of domesticated animals—in this case, the horse—disturbed the gender-based division of labor in an Indian society see Richard White, "The Cultural Landscape of the Pawnees," *Great Plains Quarterly,* II (1982), 31–40. I thank George Phillips for this reference.

[20] Kenneth M. Morrison, *The Embattled Northeast; The Elusive Ideal of Alliance in Abenaki-Euramerican Relations* (Berkeley, Calif., 1984), chap. 2; Gregory Evans Dowd, *A Spirited Resistance: The North American Indian Struggle For Unity, 1745–1815* (Baltimore, 1992), chap. 1; Salisbury, *Manitou and Providence,* 35–36; Elisabeth Tooker, ed., *Native North American Spirituality of the Eastern Woodlands: Sacred Myths, Dreams, Visions, Speeches, Healing Formulas, Rituals, and Ceremonials* (New York, 1979), 11–29.

[21] Nathaniel B. Shurtleff, ed., *Records of the Governor and Company of the Massachusetts Bay in New England,* 5 vols. (Boston, 1853–1854), I, 102, 121, 133; John Noble, ed., *Records of the Court of Assistants of the Colony of the Massachusetts Bay, 1630–1692,* 3 vols. (Boston, 1901–1928), II, 46, 49; quotation from Wood, *New England's Prospect,* ed. Vaughan, 113.

[22] Williams, *Key into the Language of America,* ed. Teunissen and Hinz, 182.

engaged in a long-running dispute over damages from trespassing animals. At first, in 1653, the colonists claimed to "know nothing of" the Indian complaints. By 1656, settlers had erected a fence along the town boundary, but because a stream—across which livestock were "apte to swime"—also separated English and native lands, the animals still made their way into Indian cornfields, Four years later, Philip's older brother Wamsutta, known to the English as Alexander, was still bringing the Indians' complaints to the attention of Plymouth authorities.[23]

English livestock also proved to be a nuisance as they roamed through the woods. Cattle and swine walked into deer traps, and the English held the Indians liable for any injuries they sustained.[24] Similarly, in 1638, when William Hathorne of Salem found one of his cows stuck with an arrow, he insisted on restitution. Salem officials demanded the exorbitant sum of £100 from local Indians at a time when a cow was generally valued at about £20. Roger Williams pleaded the natives' case with John Winthrop, explaining that the colonists had charged the wrong Indians and that the sachems were outraged because the English held them personally responsible for the fine levied for their subjects' purported offense. "Nor doe they believe that the English Magistrates doe so practice," Williams reported, "and therefore they hope that what is Righteous amongst our Selves we will accept of from them."[25]

Williams went on to observe that "the Busines is ravelld and needes a patient and gentle hand to rectifie Misunderstanding of Each other and misprisions." He foresaw that endless recriminations would flow from colonists' attempts to raise livestock in the same space where Indians hunted. Native leaders, finding Williams a sympathetic listener, informed him of the "feares of their Men in hunting or travelling," for they had reason to believe they would be held responsible for every domestic animal found hurt or dead in the woods. Williams urged Winthrop to work with the Indians to contrive an equitable procedure to be followed in similar cases so that Indian hunters would not feel so much at risk from the rigors of a judicial system that appeared biased against them.[26]

Instead of recognizing the fundamental incompatibility of English and Indian subsistence regimes, colonial authorities repeatedly permitted joint use of land.[27] In so doing, they assumed that Indians would agree that the

---

[23] Shurtleff and Pulsifer, eds., *Plym. Col. Recs.*, III, 21, 106, 119–120, 167, 192.

[24] See, for instance, Shurtleff, ed., *Mass. Bay Recs.*, I, 143; Charles J. Hoadly, ed., *Records of the Colony and Plantation of New Haven*, 2 vols. (Hartford, Conn., 1857–1858), I, 150. For a description of Indian hunting techniques see Williams, *Key into the Language of America*, ed. Teunissen and Hinz, 224–225.

[25] LaFantasie, ed., *Correspondence of Williams*, I, 192.

[26] Ibid., I, 193, quotations on 192.

[27] On the problems of joint use see Peter A. Thomas, "Contrastive Subsistence Strategies and Land Use as Factors for Understanding Indian-White Relations in New England," *Ethnohistory*, XXIII (1976), 1–18.

colonists' livestock had, in effect, use rights to the woods and fields too. Indians could hunt on lands claimed by the English only if they accepted certain restrictions on their activities. Indians who set traps within the town of Barnstable, for instance, had "fully and dilligenttly" to visit their traps daily to check for ensnared livestock and, if any were found, "thaye shall speedyli lett them out."[28] The Connecticut government imposed stricter limits on Indian hunters when the town of Pequot was founded in 1649. Uncas, the Mohegan sachem, was instructed "that no trapps [should] bee sett by him or any of his men" within the town, although colonial officials saw no reason completely "to prohibitt and restraine Uncus and his men from hunting and fishing" unless they did so on the Sabbath. Connecticut authorities acquired meadow land from the Tunxis Indians in 1650 and similarly recognized native rights of hunting, fishing, and fowling on the property so long as such activities "be not dun to the breach of any orders in the country to hurt cattle."[29] As late as 1676, in the aftermath of King Philip's War, Connecticut officials allowed "friendly" Indians "to hunt in the conquered lands in the Narrogancett Country, provided they sett not traps to prejudice English cattell."[30]

Joint use was doomed to failure, not by Indian unwillingness to comply with English conditions, but by the insurmountable problems that arose from grazing livestock on hunting lands. Accidental injuries were bound to occur and to disturb colonists, while Indians resented the damage done by domestic animals wandering out of the woods and into their cornfields. The behavior of livestock—creatures as indispensable to the English as they were obnoxious to the Indians—undermined the efforts of each group to get along with the other. Attempts to resolve disputes stemming from trespassing livestock led only to mutual frustration.

The Indians were doubtless the first to recognize the difficulties inherent in the joint use of land and the unrestricted foraging of colonists' animals. One Connecticut sachem actually attempted to restrict the *settlers'* use of land that he was willing to grant them outright. When Pyamikee, who lived near Stamford, negotiated with town officials, he tried to make the English agree not to put their livestock on the tract, for he knew that "the English hoggs would be ready to spoyle their [the Indians'] corne" in an adjacent field, "and that the cattell, in case they came over the said five mile river,"

---

[28] Shurtleff and Pulsifer, eds., *Plym. Col. Recs.,* II, 130–131.
[29] Quotation in Kenneth L. Feder, " 'The Avaricious Humour of Designing Englishmen': The Ethnohistory of Land Transactions in the Farmington Valley," *Bulletin of the Archaeological Society of Connecticut,* No. 45 (1982), 36.
[30] J. Hammond Trumbull et al., eds., *The Public Records of the Colony of Connecticut . . . ,* 15 vols. (Hartford, Conn., 1850–1890), II, 289. Colonial officials eventually prohibited Indians from firing the woods in the autumn—a procedure that killed undergrowth and thus facilitated hunting—because of danger to the colonists' haystacks; Shurtleff, ed., *Mass. Bay Recs.,* V, 230–231.

would do likewise. But the colonists would only assure Pyamikee that live-stock would always travel under the supervision of a keeper.[31]

In another case, in 1648 in Rhode Island, an unfortunate Shawomet In-dian spent five days chasing swine from his cornfields, only to be confronted by an Englishman, armed with a cudgel, who "asked the Indian in a rage whie he drove out the Swine." When he replied, "because they dide eate the Corne," the Englishman "ran upon the Indian," and a melee ensued among the disputants' companions. An attempt to adjudicate the case led to further complications, for the Englishmen involved were Rhode Islanders whereas the land where the incident occurred was claimed by Plymouth. Skeptical of his chances for a fair hearing in the Plymouth court, Pumham, a Shawomet sachem acting on behalf of the aggrieved Indians, asked to have the case tried in Massachusetts.[32]

It might seem remarkable that Pumham trusted the English judicial sys-tem at all. Yet like Pumham, many Indians used colonial courts to seek re-dress for damage caused by trespassing livestock. English authorities, in turn, often recognized the legitimacy of such complaints and granted resti-tution, as in 1632 when the Massachusetts General Court ordered Sir Richard Saltonstall to "give Saggamore John a hogshead of corne for the hurt his cat-tell did him in his corne."[33] Trespass complaints were so frequent, however, that colonial governments instructed individual towns to establish proce-dures for local arbitration lest the courts be overwhelmed. In Plymouth Colony, the task of reviewing such cases fell either to town selectmen or to ad hoc committees. If the livestock owner ignored their orders to pay dam-ages, the aggrieved Indian could "repaire to some Majestrate for a warrant to recover such award by distraint."[34] Massachusetts and Connecticut adopted similar measures.[35]

But the colonists were less accommodating than they seemed. They in-sisted that Indians resort to an English court system that was foreign to them, the proceedings of which were conducted in an incomprehensible lan-guage necessitating the use of not-always reliable translators. (In the case de-

[31] Hoadly, ed. *New Haven Recs.,* II, 104–107.

[32] Forbes et al., eds., *Winthrop Papers,* V, 246–247. Pumham had established connections with the Bay Colony 6 years earlier, when he sold land to settlers from Massachusetts; Salisbury, *Mani-tou and Providence,* 230.

[33] Shurtleff, ed., *Mass. Bay Recs.,* I, 102. For similar instances of town and colony authorities granting restitution to Indians see ibid., I, 121, 133; Trumbull et al., eds., *Public Recs. of Conn.,* II, 165; III, 81; Shurtleff and Pulsifer, eds., *Plym. Col. Recs.,* III, 132; IV, 68; Howard M. Chapin, ed., *The Early Records of the Town of Warwick* (Providence, R. I., 1926), 89; and Leonard Bliss, Jr., *The History of Rehoboth, Bristol County, Massachusetts . . .* (Boston, 1836), 44. See also Yasuhide Kawashima, *Puritan Justice and the Indian: White Man's Law in Massachusetts, 1630–1763* (Mid-dletown, Conn., 1986), chap. 7.

[34] Shurtleff and Pulsifer, eds., *Plym. Col. Recs.,* V, 62; IX, 143 (quotation), 219.

[35] Shurtleff, ed., *Mass. Bay Recs.,* I, 293–294; Trumbull et al., eds., *Public Recs. of Conn.,* III, 42–43.

scribed above, one of Pumham's objections to using the Plymouth court was his mistrust of the court interpreters.) Moreover, the English soon required Indians to fence their cornfields before they could seek reparations. As early as 1632, Sagamore John, who received the award of damages from Saltonstall, had to promise "against the next yeare, & soe ever after" to fence his fields.[36] In 1640 Massachusetts law required settlers to help their Indian neighbors "in felling of Trees, Ryving & sharpning railes, and holing of posts" for fences, but this friendly gesture was coupled with stern provisos. Any Indian who refused to fence his fields after such help was offered forfeited his right to sue for damages. In addition, Indian complainants had to identify which beasts had trampled their corn—an impossible task if the animals had come and gone before the damage was discovered.[37] Beginning in the 1650s, Plymouth magistrates allowed Indians to impound offending beasts, but this meant either that they had to drive the animals to the nearest English pound or construct one on their own land and walk to the nearest town to give "speedy notice" of any animals so confined.[38]

Even if they complied with English conditions, Indians could not depend on the equitable enforcement of animal trespass laws. The coercive power of colonial governments was limited—magistrates could hardly march off to view every downed fence and ruined field—and reliance on local adjudication meant that townsmen had to police themselves. New England colonists were notoriously litigious, but it was one thing to defend against the charges of an English neighbor and quite another to judge impartially an Indian's accusations of trespass. When problems arose near the centers of colonial government, Indians could generally get a fair hearing, as did Sagamore John near Boston. But the enforcement of animal trespass laws became more haphazard toward the edges of settlement. Indians in the praying town of Okommakamesit (Marlborough)—thirty miles from Boston—abandoned a 150-acre tract with an apple orchard for "it brings little or no profit to them, nor is ever like to do; because the Englishmen's cattle, &c. devour all in it, because it lies open and unfenced," and they clearly expected no redress.[39] Along the disputed border between Rhode Island and Plymouth, settlers could scarcely agree among themselves who was in charge. Under such circumstances, as Pumham and his fellow Shawomets discovered, cudgel-wielding Englishmen all too easily took the law into their own

[36] Shurtleff, ed., *Mass. Bay Recs.*, I, 99.

[37] William H. Whitmore, ed., *The Colonial Laws of Massachusetts, Reprinted from the Edition of 1660, with the supplements to 1672, Containing Also, the Body of Liberties of 1641* (Boston, 1889), 162. In 1662 Plymouth Colony law required settlers to help Indians build fences; see Shurtleff and Pulsifer, eds., *Plym. Col. Recs.*, XI, 137–138.

[38] Trumbull et al., eds., *Public Recs. of Conn.*, III, 42–43; Shurtleff and Pulsifer, eds., *Plym. Col. Recs.*, III, 106, 192, XI, 123, 137–138.

[39] Gookin, "Historical Collections of the Indians in New England," 220.

hands. Farther away—in Maine, for example—even the pretense of due process could vanish. In 1636, Saco commissioners empowered one of their number to "excecut any Indians that ar proved to have killed any swyne of the Inglishe" and ordered all settlers summarily to "apprehend, execut or kill any Indian that hath binne known to murder any English, kill ther Cattell or any waie spoyle ther goods or doe them violence."[40]

Given the deficiencies of the colonial legal system, it is not surprising that many Indians dealt with intrusive livestock according to their own notions of justice. Indians who stole or killed livestock probably committed such deeds less as acts of wanton mischief, as the English assumed, than in retribution for damages suffered. In their loosely knit village bands, Indians placed a premium on loyalty to kin rather than to the larger social group. The strength of these kinship bonds at once limited the authority of sachems (a point lost on the magistrates who had ordered sachems to pay for Hathorne's cow) and sanctioned acts of violence undertaken in revenge for wrongs done to family members.[41] English authorities did not bother to inquire into Indian motives for theft and violence toward animals. But when, for instance, Pumham and other Shawomets—who had previously encountered irascible colonists and ineffective courts—were later charged with "killing cattle, and forceable entry" on settlers' lands, it takes little imagination to suspect that they were exacting their own retributive justice.[42]

Once they took matters into their own hands, Indians could be charged with theft and destruction of property with the full force of English law turned against them. The penalties for such offenses further corroded relations between the groups. Unable to pay the requisite fines—often levied in English money—Indians found themselves imprisoned or sentenced to corporal punishment.[43] Thus their options shrank even as livestock populations grew. Retaliation against the animals brought severe sanctions from the English, while efforts to accommodate the beasts on English terms required unacceptable alterations in Indian agriculture and the virtual abandonment of hunting. By the middle of the seventeenth century it was clear to the Indians that the English and their troublesome animals would not go away. The English, for their part, assumed that the solution was for Indians to abandon their ways and become livestock keepers themselves.

[40] Charles Thornton Libby et al., eds., *Province and Court Records of Maine,* 5 vols. (Portland, Me., 1928–1960), I, 2–4.

[41] Salisbury, *Manitou and Providence,* 41–42; Kawashima, *Puritan Justice and the Indian,* chap 1.

[42] John Russell Bartlett, ed., *Records of the Colony of Rhode Island and Providence Plantations, in New England,* 10 vols. (New York, 1968; orig. pub. 1856–1865), I, 391.

[43] For instances of Indian depredations against livestock see Trumbull et al., eds., *Public Recs. of Conn.,* I, 226; Hoadly, ed., *New Haven Recs.,* II, 361; Shurtleff, ed., *Mass. Bay Recs.,* I, 87, 88; IV, pt. 2, 54, 361; Shurtleff and Pulsifer, eds., *Plym. Col. Recs.,* IV, 92–93, 190–191, V, 80, IX, 111, 209; and Samuel Eliot Morison, ed., *Records of the Suffolk County Court, 1671–1680,* Colonial Society of Massachusetts, *Publications* (Boston, 1933), XXIX, 404.

*   *   *

Some Indians—most notably King Philip—adopted livestock husbandry, though not in capitulation to English example and exhortation. Their adaptation was not a step, either intentional or inadvertent, toward acculturation, for they refused to make the complete transformation advocated by Englishmen who linked animal husbandry to the acquisition of civilized ways. The natives' decision instead fit into a broader pattern of intercultural borrowing that formed an important theme in Anglo-Indian relations during the first decades of contact. Much as settlers incorporated native crops and farming techniques into their agricultural system, Indians selected from an array of English manufactures such items as guns, cloth, and iron pots that were more efficient substitutes for bows and arrows, animal skins, and earthenware. Neither group forfeited its cultural identity in so doing, and when some Indians began to raise livestock—again largely for practical considerations—they deliberately selected the English beast that would least disrupt their accustomed routines.

Indians who raised livestock overwhelmingly preferred hogs.[44] More than any other imported creatures, swine resembled dogs, the one domesticated animal that Indians already had. Both species scavenged for food and ate scraps from their owners' meals. Although hogs also competed with humans for wild plants and shellfish and could damage native cornfields, these disadvantages were offset by the meat they supplied and the fact that Indians could deal with their own swine however they wished. Like dogs, swine aggressively fended off predators, such as wolves. Roger Williams recorded an instance of "two English Swine, big with Pig," driving a wolf from a freshly killed deer and devouring the prey themselves. Hogs could also be trained like dogs to come when called, a useful trait in an animal that foraged for itself in the woods.[45]

Swine keeping required relatively few adjustments to native subsistence routines—far fewer than cattle rearing would have involved. It made minimal demands on labor, rendering moot the issue of who—men or women—would bear primary responsibility for their care. Keeping cattle would have either dramatically increased women's work loads or involved men in new types of labor tying them more closely to the village site. Cattle needed nightly feeding, and cows had to be milked daily. Most male calves would have had to be castrated, and the few bulls required careful handling. Since cattle needed fodder and shelter during the winter, Indians would have had to gather and

---

[44] Virtually all references to Indian ownership of livestock specify hogs; see Chapin, ed., *Early Recs. of Warwick*, 102; Shurtleff and Pulsifer, eds., *Plym. Col. Recs.*, IV, 66; V, 6, 11–12, 22, 85; Bartlett, ed., *R. I. Col. Recs.*, II, 172–173; Brigham, ed., *Early Recs. of Portsmouth*, 149–150; and Trumbull et al., ed., *Public Recs. of Conn.*, III, 55. See also Robert R. Gradie, "New England Indians and Colonizing Pigs," in William Cowan, ed., *Papers of the Fifteenth Algonquian Conference* (Ottawa, 1984), 147–169; I thank Barbara DeWolfe for this reference.

[45] Juliet Clutton-Brock, *Domesticated Animals from Early Times* (Austin, Tex., 1981), 73, 74; Williams, *Key into the Language of America*, ed. Teunissen and Hinz, 226.

dry hay and build and clean barns—activities that infringed on their mobility during the hunting season. Some members of each village would have had to become herdsmen. Losing a cow in the woods was a more serious matter than losing a pig, for pigs had a far higher rate of reproduction.[46]

In return for a limited investment in labor, native hog keepers acquired a year-round supply of protein that replaced the meat they could no longer get from a dwindling deer population. These Indians may in fact have enjoyed an improved diet, avoiding the seasonal malnutrition resulting from their former dependence on corn and game.[47] Swine also provided products that replaced items formerly obtained from wild animals. Gookin noted in 1674 that Indians "used to oil their skins and hair with bear's grease heretofore, but now with swine's fat." And in at least one instance, Indians fashioned moccasins from "green hogs skinns" in place of deerskin. Settlers, in contrast, valued cattle for reasons that had little appeal for Indians. They plowed with oxen, but Indians who farmed with hoes did not need them. Colonists also prized the meat and dairy products supplied by their herds; although Indians would eat beef, most native adults were physiologically unable to digest lactose except in tiny amounts and would have learned to avoid milk products.[48]

Settlers raised hogs and ate pork, but they did not share the Indians' preference for swine over cattle. Cattle were docile and, to the English mind, superior beasts. Swine, on the contrary, were slovenly creatures that wallowed in mud, gobbled up garbage, and were rumored to kill unwary children. Colonists named their cows Brindle and Sparke and Velvet; no one named pigs. The English kept swine as if on sufferance, tolerating their obnoxious behavior in order to eat salt pork, ham, and bacon. Most of all, swine keeping did not promote hard work and regular habits so well as cattle rearing did. Writers who extolled the civilizing benefits of livestock husbandry doubtless envisioned sedentary Indian farmers peacefully gathering hay and tending herds of cattle alongside their English neighbors, but the reality was hardly so bucolic.[49]

---

[46] Clutton-Brock, *Domesticated Animals*, 68, 73; Russell, *Long, Deep Furrow*, 35, 88; Percy Wells Bidwell and John I. Falconer, *History of Agriculture in the Northern United States, 1620–1860* (Washington, D. C., 1925; repr. New York, 1941), 25, 31–32.

[47] The evidence is sketchy but suggestive. One archaeological study of a Narragansett cemetery dating from the mid-17th century (roughly the time and location corresponding to historical evidence of Indian swine keeping) finds that the Indian skeletons show a surprising lack of iron deficiency anemia as well as little evidence of seasonal malnutrition. Such characteristics resulted from an improved diet, and although the specific content of that diet cannot be recovered, it is possible that the consumption of pork was an important factor. See Marc A. Kelley, Paul S. Sledzik, and Sean P. Murphy, "Health, Demographics, and Physical Constitution in Seventeenth-Century Rhode Island Indians," *Man in the Northeast*, No. 34 (1987), 1–25.

[48] Gookin, "Historical Collections of the Indians in New England," 153; Shurtleff, ed., *Mass. Bay Recs.*, IV, pt. 2, 360. On Indians' lactose intolerance see Crosby, *Ecological Imperialism*, 27.

[49] For contemporary English attitudes toward domestic animals see Keith Thomas, *Man and the Natural World: A History of the Modern Sensibility* (New York, 1983), 54, 64, 95, 96. These attitudes persisted into the 19th century; see Harriet Ritvo, *The Animal Estate: The English and Other Crea-*

Settlers instead encountered Indians who lived much as they always had, but who now had swine wandering across their lands—and occasionally into English cornfields.[50] The colonists recognized only grudgingly the Indians' property in animals and usually assumed that the natives' hogs were stolen. In 1672, Bay Colony officials insisted that Indians pilfered swine although they acknowledged that "it be very difficult to proove" that they had done so. Other explanations—that the Indians had captured feral animals or had purchased hogs from settlers—were seldom advanced. The fact that "the English, especially in the inland plantations, . . . loose many swine" and that Indians had hogs invited suspicion.[51]

To discourage the theft of animals among themselves and to identify strays, settlers used earmarks. Each owner had a distinctive mark that was entered in the town records, to be checked when an animal was reported stolen or a stray was found. The proliferation of town and colony orders requiring earmarks, as well as the increasing intricacy of the marks themselves—a mixture of crops, slits, "forks," "half-pennies," and so on—provides as good a measure as any of the growing livestock population. The earmark itself became a form of property handed down) from one generation to the next.[52] Instead of assigning earmarks to native owners, however, magistrates ordered that "no Indians shall give any ear mark to their Swine, upon the penalty of the forfeiture" of the animal. An Indian who wished to sell a hog had to bring it with its ears intact; if he sold pork, he had to produce the unmarked ears from the carcass. This practice made native purchases of English hogs problematic, for the animals would already have marked ears. Should the Indian subsequently desire to sell such an animal, he could be required to "bring good Testimonies that he honestly obtained such Swine so marked, of some English." Moreover, Indian owners were at the mercy of unscrupulous settlers who might steal their animals and mark them as their own. Colonists did not prohibit Indian ownership of swine, but they denied Indians the acknowledged symbol of legitimate possession.[53]

---

tures in the Victorian Age (Cambridge, Mass., 1987), 21. Colonists concurred with the assessment of the danger of swine to children; see City of Boston, Second Report of the Record Commissioners (Boston Town Records, 1634–1660), (Boston, 1877), 145. For naming of cattle see, for instance, George Francis Dow, ed., Records and Files of the Quarterly Courts of Essex County, 9 vols. (Salem, Mass., 1911–1975), III, 361, 428.

[50] Trumbull et al., eds., Public Recs. of Conn., III, 55n.

[51] Shurtleff, ed., Mass. Bay Recs., IV, pt. 2, 512.

[52] For ordinances requiring earmarks see, for example, Trumbull et al., eds., Public Recs. of Conn., I, 118, 517; Shurtleff, ed., Mass. Bay Recs., IV, pt. 2, 512–513; and Brigham, ed., Early Recs. of Portsmouth, 72–73, and for descriptions of earmarks see, for instance, ibid., 261–286, 288–295, 320–322. Cattle and horses were usually branded, and owners often entered complete descriptions of the animals in town books; see Whitmore, ed., Col. Laws of Mass., 158, 258, and City of Boston, Fourth Report of the Record Commissioners (Dorchester Town Records), 2d ed. (Boston, 1883), 35–36.

[53] John D. Cushing, ed., The Laws of the Pilgrims: A Facsimile Edition of "The Book of the General Laws of the Inhabitants of the Jurisdiction of New-Plimouth, 1672 & 1685" (Wilmington, Del., 1977), 44; see also Shurtleff, ed., Mass. Bay Recs., IV, pt. 2, 512–513.

The Indians' selective involvement with animal husbandry scarcely improved relations between natives and colonists. To the previous list of problems new and equally vexing issues were added, including trespasses by Indian animals, theft, and difficulties with proving ownership of animal property. For settlers, probably the least welcome change appeared when enterprising Indians started selling swine and pork in competition with English producers of the same commodities. Many orders pertaining to earmarks begin with a preamble that assumes that native competition went hand in hand with native dishonesty. In the Bay Colony, there was "ground to suspect that some of the Indians doe steale & sell the English mens swine;" in Plymouth, settlers complained "of Indians stealing of live Hogs from the English, and selling them." Thus magistrates urged colonists to mark their animals to protect their property from native thieves. In fact, the charges of theft were not substantiated; the real problem was commercial, not criminal. Earmark regulations aimed at least as much to make Indian sales difficult as to make Indians honest.[54]

Competition with Indians was more than colonists had bargained for. In 1669—just six years before the start of King Philip's War—the Plymouth General Court proposed to license certain colonists "to trade powder, shott, guns, and mony (now under prohibition) with the Indians" as a means of discouraging the local Indians' pork trade. The magistrates complained that "a greate parte of the porke that is now carryed by the Indians to Boston" was "sold there at an under rate," hurting Plymouth pork sellers. The court felt no need to make explicit connections between its proposal to sell arms and its complaint about competition, but the likeliest explanation is that Plymouth Indians were using the proceeds of their Boston pork sales to purchase guns from licensed Bay Colony sellers, tapping into an arms trade that the Massachusetts General Court had established in the previous year. If the Indians could obtain arms from Plymouth suppliers, they presumably would cede the Boston pork trade to Old Colony producers. The court expressed no particular interest in helping out Boston consumers who spurned the wares of their fellow Englishmen in order to buy cheaper meat; its explicit aim was to ensure that the pork trade would "fall into the hands of some of our people, and soe the prise may be kept up."[55]

The Plymouth government's concern in this instance testifies to a remarkable set of native adaptations. If the Indians indeed brought pork and not live animals to the Bay Colony, they had learned to preserve meat in a way that appealed to English consumers. Some colonists, noting native ignorance of salting techniques, had assumed that Indians did not know how

---

[54] Shurtleff, ed., *Mass. Bay Recs.*, IV, pt. 2, 512; Cushing, ed., *Laws of the Pilgrims*, 44.

[55] Shurtleff and Pulsifer, eds., *Plym. Col. Recs.*, V, 11–12. On the colonial arms trade see Patrick M. Malone, *The Skulking Way of War: Technology and Tactics Among the New England Indians* (Lanham, Md., 1991), 49.

to preserve food.[56] We do not know whether Plymouth Indians had learned to salt as well as to sell pork, but there is no doubt that they had identified Boston as New England's most lucrative food market. Almost from the start, Boston merchants and shopkeepers vied with farmers over the relatively scarce amount of land on the small peninsula occupied by the town. As early as 1636, officials prohibited families from grazing more than two cows on the peninsula itself, and in 1647, the town herd was fixed at seventy beasts.[57] By 1658, swine had become such a public nuisance that Boston officials required owners to keep them "in their owne ground," effectively limiting the number of hogs each family could maintain.[58] Given these restrictions, many Bostonians apparently gave up raising animals and bought meat from livestock producers in nearby towns, who were also raising stock for the West Indies market.[59] Did the Plymouth Indians know this when they went to Boston? Their business acumen should not be underestimated. Although he did not refer specifically to the meat trade, Williams noticed that Indian traders "will beate all markets and try all places, and runne twenty thirty, yea forty mile, and more, and lodge in the Woods, to save six pence." Ironically, native enterprise met with suspicion rather than approbation from colonists who liked the Indians less the more like the English they became.[60]

The extent of native livestock husbandry is difficult to measure because colonial records mainly preserve instances in which animals became a source of conflict. The evidence does suggest that Indians residing near English settlements had a greater tendency to raise domestic animals than did those farther away. The Wampanoags, living in the Mount Hope area between Plymouth Colony and Rhode Island, apparently began to raise hogs by the middle of the seventeenth century, after some thirty years of contact with English settlers.[61] The location and timing of their adaptation were scarcely accidental.

The Wampanoags had close contact with settlers and, accordingly, a greater need for livestock than did native peoples living elsewhere. The

---

[56] Morton, *New English Canaan,* ed. Adams, 161.

[57] Darrett B. Rutman, *Winthrop's Boston: A Portrait of a Puritan Town, 1630–1649* (Chapel Hill, N. C., 1965), 206.

[58] City of Boston, *Second Report of the Record Commissioners,* 145.

[59] A partial Boston tax valuation for 1676 indicates that fewer than half of household heads owned cattle or swine; see City of Boston, *First Report of the Record Commissioners of the City of Boston* (Boston, 1876), 60–70. On the development of a domestic and foreign market in livestock and meat see Karen J. Friedmann, "Victualling Colonial Boston," *Agricultural History,* XLVII (1973), 189–205, and Darrett B. Rutman, "Governor Winthrop's Garden Crop: The Significance of Agriculture in the Early Commerce of Massachusetts Bay," *WMQ,* 3d Ser., XX (1963), 396–415.

[60] Williams, *Key into the Language of America,* ed. Teunissen and Hinz, 218.

[61] Montauk Indians living on the eastern end of Long Island also raised hogs in the 17th century. Like the Wampanoags on the mainland, the Montauks lived in an area surrounded by English settlement and had been in contact with settlers for decades. See Jasper Dankers and Peter Sluyter, "Journal of a Voyage to New York in 1679–80," *Memoirs of the Long Island Historical Society,* I (1867), 126.

ecological changes caused by English settlers steadily converting woodland into fenced fields and open meadows around Mount Hope reduced the deer population on which the Wampanoags depended; their swine keeping substituted one form of protein for another. Their trade in hogs and pork may also have been intended to offer a new commodity to settlers as other trade items disappeared or diminished in value. By the 1660s, the New England fur trade had ended with the virtual extinction of beaver. At the same time, English demand for wampum sharply declined as an improving overseas trade brought in more hard currency and colonies ceased accepting wampum as legal tender.[62] But hogs and pork failed as substitutes for furs and wampum. Most colonists owned swine themselves and—as the response of the Plymouth magistrates in 1669 suggests—evidently preferred to limit the market in animals to English producers.

Wampanoag swine keeping also contributed to growing tensions with colonists over land, creating disputes that were even harder to resolve than those concerning trade. Land that diminished in usefulness to Indians as it ceased to support familiar subsistence activities regained value for raising hogs; indeed, such places as offshore islands held a special attraction to keepers of swine. The Wampanoags' desire to retain their land awakened precisely when settlers evinced an interest in acquiring it. By the 1660s, a younger generation of settlers had reached maturity and needed farms. In Plymouth Colony, bounded on the north by the more powerful Bay Colony and on the west by an obstreperous Rhode Island, aggressive settlers eyed the lands of their Wampanoag neighbors. During the 1660s, new villages were formed at Dartmouth, Swansea, and Middleborough, while established towns such as Rehoboth and Taunton enlarged their holdings—and in effect blockaded the Wampanoags on Mount Hope peninsula.[63]

No man was harder pressed by these developments than King Philip. As sachem of the Wampanoags since 1662, he had tried to protect his people and preserve their independence in the face of English intrusion. Over time, his tasks became far more difficult. The number of occasions when the interests of Indians and settlers came into conflict grew as his ability to mediate diminished. Since Wampanoag land bordered on Massachusetts, Rhode Island, and Plymouth, Philip had to contend at various times with three, often competing, colonial governments. Even more problematic were his relations with neighboring towns, whose inhabitants pursued their economic advantage with little fear of intervention from any colony government and no regard for how their actions would affect Indian welfare.

[62] Cronon, *Changes in the Land,* 101; Salisbury, "Indians and Colonists in Southern New England after the Pequot War: An Uneasy Balance," in Laurence M. Hauptman and James D. Wherry, eds., *The Pequots in Southern New England: The Fall and Rise of an American Indian Nation* (Norman, Okla., 1990), 90–91.
[63] On the expansion of Plymouth settlement see Rutman, *Husbandmen of Plymouth,* 21.

Philip confronted the implications of New England localism most directly in cases of trespass. Colonial governments ordered towns to address Indian grievances but could not or would not enforce compliance. For six years, beginning in the mid-1650s, Rehoboth's inhabitants virtually ignored complaints from nearby Indians about damage from livestock, despite orders from the Plymouth court to solve the problem. In 1664, more than a decade after the issue first arose, Philip himself appeared at court—this time to complain about Rehoboth men trespassing on Wampanoag land to cut timber—and even then he may have hoped for a favorable outcome.[64] But if he did, the court soon compounded his problems by deciding to refer trespass cases to the selectmen of the towns involved. From then on, Philip and his people would have to seek justice at the hands of the very people who might well own the offending beasts.[65]

The Wampanoag leader's problems in dealing with townsmen whose attitudes ranged from unsympathetic to hostile worsened after the colony government declared its hands-off policy on trespass and reached a low point in 1671, when Plymouth officials charged Philip with stockpiling arms and conspiring with other Indian groups to attack the colonists. He denied the charges and appealed to Bay Colony magistrates to confirm his innocence. But Plymouth threatened coercion if he did not submit to its authority, and Philip signed a compact that further eroded his ability to safeguard Wampanoag interests. This agreement compelled him to seek Plymouth's approval before he disposed of any native territory, but colony officials were not similarly constrained by the need for Philip's permission before they approached Indians to purchase land. He also agreed that differences between natives and settlers would be referred to the colony government for resolution, although the magistrates' record in dealing even with straightforward cases of trespass gave little cause for optimism.[66]

The Plymouth court intended to subvert Philip's authority over his people in order to facilitate the acquisition of Wampanoag land by a new generation of colonists who would, in turn, raise new generations of livestock. As early as 1632, William Bradford recognized that settlers who owned animals required a lot of land to support their beasts. He complained when families abandoned Plymouth to form new towns where meadow was available, but he could not stop them. Instead, he could only lament that "no man now thought he could live except he had cattle and a great deal of ground to keep them."[67] Expansion accelerated during the 1660s and early 1670s, once again fueled by a burgeoning livestock population. During the two decades before

[64] Shurtleff and Pulsifer, eds., *Plym. Col. Recs.*, III, 21, 167, IV, 54.
[65] The law requiring town selectmen to decide trespass cases was passed in the mid-1660s; the record contains no specific date. See Shurtleff and Pulsifer, eds., *Plym. Col. Recs.*, XI, 143.
[66] Ibid., V, 79.
[67] Bradford, *Of Plymouth Plantation*, ed. Morison, 253.

King Philip's War, Plymouth officials approached local Indians at least twenty-three times to purchase land, often mentioning a specific need for pasture. Sometimes they only wanted "some small parcells"; on other occasions they desired "all such lands as the Indians can well spare."[68]

The need to sustain their herds drove the English to seek Indian land, and their expansionary moves collided with an urgent Wampanoag need to preserve what remained of their territory. Joint use of land, although fraught with problems, at least recognized mutual subsistence needs; by the 1660s, however, the practice had greatly diminished. Now the English not only wanted more land but demanded exclusive use of it. They asserted their property rights even in situations when accommodating Indian interests would have presented little threat. Allowing Philip to put his swine on Hog Island probably would not have harmed Portsmouth's inhabitants and might have improved relations between Indians and settlers. But what was Philip to think of the townsmen's summary refusal to share land, even when he proposed to use it for precisely the same purpose as they did? In that spring of 1669, Philip personally experienced the same English intransigence that he encountered as the representative of his people. After the Hog Island episode, and even more after his forced submission to Plymouth in 1671, he could not fail to see that while the colonists insisted that he yield to them, they would not yield in any way to him.

In an atmosphere of increasing tension, trespass assumed new significance. As colonists moved closer to native villages, the chances that livestock would stray onto Indian lands multiplied. With both groups competing for a limited supply of land, colonists did not restrain their animals from grazing wherever they could, while Indians grew ever more sensitive to such intrusions. Whenever livestock were concerned, the English ignored the Indians' property rights, while demanding that the natives recognize English rights. Indians resented encroachment by beasts that usually presaged the approach of Englishmen requesting formal ownership of land that their animals had already informally appropriated. Faced with the manifest inability—or unwillingness—of New England towns to solve the problem of trespass, and discouraged from seeking help from colony governments, Indians often resorted to their own means of animal control; they killed the offending beasts. This response would once have landed Indians in court, but by 1671 they faced far more serious consequences.

In that year, a group of angry colonists living near Natick very nearly attacked the Wampanoags of Mount Hope for killing livestock that had trespassed on Indian land. Interceding on behalf of the Indians, the Bay Colony's Indian commissioner, Daniel Gookin, begged for forbearance from the settlers, arguing that it was not worth *"fighting with Indians about horses*

---

[68] Shurtleff and Pulsifer, eds., *Plym. Col. Recs.*, III, 84, 104, 123, 142, 216–217, IV, 18, 20, 45, 70, 82, 97, 109, 167, V, 20, 24, 24–25, 95, 96, 97–98, 98–99, 109, 126, 151.

and hogs, as matters too low to shed blood." He urged the settlers to keep their animals on their own land; if any strayed into native territory and were killed, the owners should make a record of the fact, presumably to facilitate legal recovery.[69] War was averted, but this incident nonetheless showed that tension over livestock had reached dangerously high levels.

Both sides now understood that disputes over trespassing animals epitomized differences so profound as to defy peaceful solution. Whenever Indians killed livestock that had damaged their cornfields, colonists denounced such acts as willful violations of English property rights—rights that some settlers wanted to defend by force of arms. For Indians, trespassing animals constituted an intolerable violation of *their* sovereign rights over their land. The problem intensified by the early 1670s, for the English were determined to deprive Philip of all means of ensuring the integrity of the shrinking tracts of Wampanoag land, even as they refused effectively to control their beasts. The issue of trespassing livestock generated such tension precisely because it could not be separated from fundamental questions of property rights and authority.

When war broke out in 1675, the Indians attacked first, but the underlying causes resembled those that had provoked English belligerence four years earlier. John Easton, a Rhode Island Quaker, sought out Philip early in the conflict to ask why he fought the colonists; Philip's response indicated that intermingled concerns about sovereignty, land, and animals had made war inevitable. He supplied Easton with a litany of grievances that recalled past confrontations with the English and particularly stressed intractable problems over land and animals. He complained that when Indian leaders agreed to sell land, "the English wold say it was more than thay agred to and a writing must be prove [proof] against all them." If any sachem opposed such sales, the English would "make a nother king that wold give or seell them there land, that now thay had no hopes left to kepe ani land." Even after they sold land, Indians suffered from English encroachments, for "the English Catell and horses still incresed that when thay removed 30 mill from wher English had anithing to do"—impossible for the native inhabitants of Mount Hope—"thay Could not kepe ther coren from being spoyled." The Indians had expected that "when the English boft [bought] land of them that thay wold have kept ther Catell upone ther owne land."[70]

Because livestock had come to symbolize the relentless advance of English settlement, the animals were special targets of native enmity during the

---

[69] Gookin's comments were paraphrased in a letter to him from Gov. Thomas Prince of Plymouth. Gookin had heard a rumor that he was accused of inciting Philip to fight against the English; Prince's letter aimed to reassure him that that was not the case; see MHS, *Colls.,* 1st Ser., VI (1799; repr. 1846), 200–201.

[70] "A Relacion of the Indyan Warre, by John Easton, 1675," in Charles H. Lincoln, ed., *Narratives of the Indian Wars, 1675–1699,* Original Narratives of Early American History (New York, 1913), 11.

war. Colonel Benjamin Church, who led colonial forces in several campaigns, reported that Indians "began their hostilities with plundering and destroying cattle."[71] In an attack near Brookfield, Indians burned dwellings and "made great spoyle of the cattel belonging to the inhabitants." At Rehoboth "they drove away many cattell & h[ors]es"; at Providence they "killd neer an hundred cattell"; in the Narragansett country they took away "at the least a thousand horses & it is like two thousan Cattell And many Sheep."[72] As the human toll also mounted in the summer of 1675, English forces failed to stop Philip from slipping away from Mount Hope and only managed to capture "six, eight, or ten young Pigs of King Philip's Herds."[73]

The livestock on which colonists depended exposed them to ambush. Early in the war, Indians attacked "five Men coming from Road-Island, to look up their Cattel upon Pocasset Neck." Settlers sought refuge in garrison houses and secured their cattle in palisaded yards but could not provide enough hay to sustain them for long. Sooner or later they had to drive the creatures out to pasture or bring in more hay. Philip and his forces—who had a keen understanding of the voraciousness of English livestock—would be waiting. Near Groton in March 1676 "a Parcel of Indians . . . laid an Ambush for two Carts, which went from the Garison to fetch in some Hay." At about the same time at Concord, "two men going for Hay, one of them was killed." Settlers counted themselves lucky when they escaped, even if their animals fell victim. When Hatfield inhabitants let their livestock out to graze in May 1676, they lost the entire herd of seventy cattle and horses to Indians who had anticipated the move.[74]

The Indians seized and killed cattle mainly to deprive the colonists of food, but some of their depredations also suggest an intense animosity

---

[71] Church, *Diary of King Philip's War, 1675–1676*, ed. Alan and Mary Simpson (Chester, Conn., 1975), 75; see also William Hubbard, *The History of the Indian Wars in New England from the First Settlement to the Termination of the War with King Philip, in 1677*, ed. Samuel G. Drake (New York, 1969; orig. pub. 1865), 64.

[72] "Capt. Thomas Wheeler's Narrative of an Expedition with Capt. Edward Hutchinson into the Nipmuck Country, and to Quaboag, now Brookfield, Mass., first published 1675," *Collections of the New-Hampshire Historical Society*, II (1827), 21; Douglas Edward Leach, ed., *A Rhode Islander Reports on King Philip's War: The Second William Harris Letter of August, 1676* (Providence, R. I., 1963), 44, 46, 58. For other descriptions of attacks on livestock see Church, *Diary of King Philip's War*, ed. Simpson and Simpson, 172; Samuel G. Drake, *The Old Indian Chronicle; Being a Collection of Exceeding Rare Tracts, Written and Published in the Time of King Philip's War . . .* (Boston, 1836), 13, 35, 58; and Hubbard, *History of the Indian Wars*, 164, 192, 234, 242.

[73] Drake, *Old Indian Chronicle*, 10; the anonymous author of this account subsequently refers to the capture of Philip's "Cattel and Hogs," although there is no corroborating evidence that Philip owned cattle; see p. 11. He did own a horse, given to him by the Plymouth General Court in 1665; see Shurtleff and Pulsifer, eds., *Plym. Col. Recs.*, IV, 93.

[74] Quotations from Hubbard, *History of the Indian Wars*, 83, 195–196, 222; for the Hatfield raid see George W. Ellis and John E. Morris, *King Philip's War, Based on the Archives and Records of Massachusetts, Plymouth, Rhode Island and Connecticut, and Contemporary Letters and Accounts* (New York, 1906), 227–228, and Melvoin, *New England Outpost*, 101, 107.

toward the animals themselves. One contemporary reported that "what cattle they took they seldom killed outright: or if they did, would eat but little of the flesh, but rather cut their bellies, and letting them go several days, trailing their guts after them, putting out their eyes, or cutting off one leg, &c."[75] Increase Mather described an incident near Chelmsford when Indians "took a Cow, knocked off one of her horns, cut out her tongue, and so left the poor creature in great misery."[76] Such mutilations recalled the tortures more often inflicted on human victims and perhaps similarly served a ritual purpose.[77] Certainly when Indians—who found a use for nearly every scrap of dead game animals—killed cattle "& let them ly & did neither eat them nor carry them away," they did so deliberately to send a message of terror to their enemies.[78]

Symbolic expressions of enmity, however, were a luxury that the Indians generally could not afford. As the war progressed, with cornfields ruined and hunting interrupted, Indians often needed captured livestock for food. When Church and his troops came upon an abandoned Indian encampment in an orchard, they found the apples gone and evidence of "the flesh of swine, which they had killed that day." At another site, colonial forces "found some of the English Beef boiling" in Indian kettles. In Maine, where fighting dragged on for months after Philip's death in August 1676, the "English took much Plunder from the Indians, about a thousand Weight of dried Beef, with other Things."[79] Edward Randolph, sent by the crown to investigate New England affairs in the summer of 1676, reported to the Council of Trade on the devastation caused by the war. He estimated that the settlers had lost "eight thousand head of Cattle great and small"—a tremendous reduction in the livestock population but not enough to starve the colonists into defeat or sustain the Indians to victory.[80]

The presence of livestock in New England was not the sole cause of the deterioration in relations between Indians and settlers. But because of their ubiquity and steady increase, domestic animals played a critical role in the larger, tragic human drama. The settlers had never been able to live without

[75] Quotation from an anonymous narrative of their war reprinted in Drake, *Old Indian Chronicle,* 102.

[76] Increase Mather, *A Brief History of the War with the Indians in New-England . . .* (1676), ed. Samuel G. Drake (Boston, 1862), 132.

[77] On Indian use of torture see Jennings, *Invasion of America,* 160–164.

[78] Leach, ed., *A Rhode Islander Reports on King Philip's War,* 46.

[79] Church, *Diary of King Philip's War,* ed. Simpson and Simpson, 133; Hubbard, *History of the Indian Wars,* 276, pt. 2, 223.

[80] Randolph's report is in Nathaniel Bouton et al., eds., *Provincial Papers: Documents and Records Relating to the Province of New-Hampshire,* vol. 1 (Concord, N. H., 1867), 344. Christian Indians also suffered losses to their livestock during the war; see Gookin, "An Historical Account of . . . the Christian Indians in New England . . . ," American Antiquarian Society, *Archaelogical Americana,* II (1836), 451, 504, 512.

livestock, but as the animal population grew, Indians found it increasingly difficult to live with them. Both sides threatened violence over the issue of livestock—the English in 1671 and the Indians, who made good on the threat, in 1675. The cultural divide separating Indians and colonists would have existed without the importation to America of domestic animals. But the presence of livestock brought differences into focus, created innumerable occasions for friction, tested the limits of cooperation—and led, in the end, to war.

Slavery and Freedom: The American Paradox

Edmund S. Morgan

INTRODUCTION

In this presidential address to the Organization of American Historians, Edmund Morgan confronts the central paradox of our history: Americans have created the freest society the modern world has known, and yet they have also constructed a massive slave labor system that has left behind it a heritage of racial prejudice. For two centuries historians have tried either to justify or to explain the coexistence of these seemingly incompatible social systems. Morgan's provocative answer is that, at least in Virginia, American freedom could not have existed without American slavery; the two systems were symbiotic rather than antagonistic.

Part of the argument is easy to understand. It has become almost commonplace to argue that the existence of black servitude helped placate the underclass of propertyless whites, for whom racial status was arguably more significant than economic status. So long as poor whites could lord it over black slaves, the expected status anxiety of the poor was supplanted by identification with the plantation-owning elite.

Morgan thinks that it was precisely the reverse sort of status anxiety that encouraged the creation of the slave labor system. The colonists had emigrated from Elizabethan England at a time when the principal fear was that overpopulation would lead to a rootless, propertyless class of vagabonds who might undermine the social fabric. One solution was to send the poor to the colonies, where they might prosper or at least be removed as a threat to social order in the mother country. As life expectancy in the Tidewater South increased and as land prices rose while tobacco prices fell, the southern colonies came, by the late seventeenth century, to resemble the perilous condition of preemigration England. This situation evoked comparable fears of social unrest, which were confirmed by the

Edmund S. Morgan, " 'Slavery and Freedom' The American Paradox," *Journal of American History,* 59 (June 1972), 5–29. Copyright © 1972 Organization of American Historians. Reprinted with permission.

violence of Bacon's Rebellion and other disruptions. The answer (which Morgan thinks was unconscious) was to supplant the white laboring force with an enslaved black labor force. This solution not only provided a more easily controlled labor supply, but it also created the economic conditions in which poor whites could improve themselves and, for the most part, exist on the fringe of the slave-owning class. It created a situation in which certain aspects of Virginia government were conceded to yeomen farmers. With slavery, that is, came freedom and republican government for all whites.

Morgan's thesis is elegantly argued, and it certainly provides a satisfying answer to the paradox of the coexistence of slavery and freedom. It does, however, raise some difficult questions.

- *Does this argument account for the existence of slavery in the northern colonies?*
- *If not, can it be considered an explanation of "American" freedom?*
- *More narrowly, why should the emergence of the slave system have improved the lot of propertyless whites in the seventeenth century?*
- *What has slavery to do with Jeffersonian fears of an urban proletariat?*

You might consider some of these questions in the light of the demographic evidence presented by Russell Menard (see earlier in this volume).

- *Would you expect Menard to agree with Morgan?*
- *Most important, if the creation of slavery was not a conscious response to the fears of wealthy Southerners for the security of their society, should we consider their republican ideas more than a rationalization for the cultivation of an evil social system?*

American historians interested in tracing the rise of liberty, democracy, and the common man have been challenged in the past two decades by other historians, interested in tracing the history of oppression, exploitation, and racism. The challenge has been salutary, because it has made us examine more directly than historians have hitherto been willing to do, the role of slavery in our early history. Colonial historians, in particular, when writing about the origin and development of American institutions have found it possible until recently to deal with slavery as an exception to everything they had to say. I am speaking about myself but also about most of my generation. We owe a debt of gratitude to those who have insisted that slavery was something more than an exception, that one fifth of the American population at the time of the Revolution is too many people to be treated as an exception.[1]

---

[1] Particularly Staughton Lynd, *Class Conflict, Slavery, and the United States Constitution: Ten Essays* (Indianapolis, 1967).

We shall not have met the challenge simply by studying the history of that one fifth, fruitful as such studies may be, urgent as they may be. Nor shall we have met the challenge if we merely execute the familiar maneuver of turning our old interpretations on their heads. The temptation is already apparent to argue that slavery and oppression were the dominant features of American history and that efforts to advance liberty and equality were the exception, indeed no more than a device to divert the masses while their chains were being fastened. To dismiss the rise of liberty and equality in American history as a mere sham is not only to ignore hard facts, it is also to evade the problem presented by those facts. The rise of liberty and equality in this country was accompanied by the rise of slavery. That two such contradictory developments were taking place simultaneously over a long period of our history, from the seventeenth century to the nineteenth, is the central paradox of American history.

The challenge, for a colonial historian at least, is to explain how a people could have developed the dedication to human liberty and dignity exhibited by the leaders of the American Revolution and at the same time have developed and maintained a system of labor that denied human liberty and dignity every hour of the day.

The paradox is evident at many levels if we care to see it. Think, for a moment, of the traditional American insistence of freedom of the seas. "Free ships make free goods" was the cardinal doctrine of American foreign policy in the Revolutionary era. But the goods for which the United States demanded freedom were produced in very large measure by slave labor. The irony is more than semantic. American reliance on slave labor must be viewed in the context of the American struggle for a separate and equal station among the nations of the earth. At the time the colonists announced their claim to that station they had neither the arms nor the ships to make the claim good. They desperately needed the assistance of other countries, especially France, and their single most valuable product with which to purchase assistance was tobacco, produced mainly by slave labor. So largely did that crop figure in American foreign relations that one historian has referred to the activities of France in supporting the Americans as "King Tobacco Diplomacy," a reminder that the position of the United States in the world depended not only in 1776 but during the span of a long lifetime thereafter on slave labor.[2] To a very large degree it may be said that Americans bought their independence with slave labor.

The paradox is sharpened if we think of the state where most of the tobacco came from. Virginia at the time of the first United States census in 1790 had 40 percent of the slaves in the entire United States. And Virginia

---

[2] Curtis P. Nettels, *The Emergence of a National Economy 1775–1815* (New York, 1962), 19. See also Merrill Jensen, "The American Revolution and American Agriculture," *Agricultural History*, XLIII (Jan. 1969), 107–24.

produced the most eloquent spokesmen for freedom and equality in the entire United States: George Washington, James Madison, and above all, Thomas Jefferson. They were all slaveholders and remained so throughout their lives. In recent years we have been shown in painful detail the contrast between Jefferson's pronouncements in favor of republican liberty and his complicity in denying the benefits of that liberty to blacks.[3] It has been tempting to dismiss Jefferson and the whole Virginia dynasty as hypocrites. But to do so is to deprive the term "hypocrisy" of useful meaning. If hypocrisy means, as I think it does, deliberately to affirm a principle without believing it, then hypocrisy requires a rare clarity of mind combined with an unscrupulous intention to deceive. To attribute such an intention, even to attribute such clarity of mind in the matter, to Jefferson, Madison, or Washington is once again to evade the challenge. What we need to explain is how such men could have arrived at beliefs and actions so full of contradiction.

Put the challenge another way: how did England, a country priding itself on the liberty of its citizens, produce colonies where most of the inhabitants enjoyed still greater liberty, greater opportunities, greater control over their own lives than most men in the mother country, while the remainder, one fifth of the total, were deprived of virtually all liberty, all opportunities, all control over their own lives? We may admit that the Englishmen who colonized America and their revolutionary descendants were racists, that consciously or unconsciously they believed liberties and rights should be confined to persons of a light complexion. When we have said as much, even when we have probed the depths of racial prejudice, we will not have fully accounted for the paradox. Racism was surely an essential element in it, but I should like to suggest another element, that I believe to have influenced the development of both slavery and freedom as we have known them in the United States.

Let us begin with Jefferson, this slaveholding spokesman of freedom. Could there have been anything in the kind of freedom he cherished that would have made him acquiesce, however reluctantly, in the slavery of so many Americans? The answer, I think, is yes. The freedom that Jefferson spoke for was not a gift to be conferred by governments, which he mistrusted at best. It was a freedom that sprang from the independence of the individual. The man who depended on another for his living could never be truly free. We may seek a clue to Jefferson's enigmatic posture toward slavery in his attitude toward those who enjoyed a seeming freedom without the independence needed to sustain it. For such persons Jefferson harbored a profound distrust, which found expression in two phobias that crop up from time to time in his writings.

[3] William Cohen, "Thomas Jefferson and the Problem of Slavery," *Journal of American History*, LVI (Dec. 1969), 503–26; D. B. Davis, *Was Thomas Jefferson An Authentic Enemy of Slavery?* (Oxford, 1970); Winthrop D. Jordan, *White over Black: American Attitudes Toward the Negro, 1550–1812* (Chapel Hill, 1968), 429–81.

The first was a passionate aversion to debt. Although the entire colonial economy of Virginia depended on the willingness of planters to go into debt and of British merchants to extend credit, although Jefferson himself was a debtor all his adult life—or perhaps because he was a debtor—he hated debt and hated anything that made him a debtor. He hated it because it limited his freedom of action. He could not, for example, have freed his slaves so long as he was in debt. Or so at least he told himself. But it was the impediment not simply to their freedom but to his own that bothered him. "I am miserable," he wrote, "till I shall owe not a shilling. . . ."[4]

The fact that he had so much company in his misery only added to it. His Declaration of Independence for the United States was mocked by the hold that British merchants retained over American debtors, including himself.[5] His hostility to Alexander Hamilton was rooted in his recognition that Hamilton's pro-British foreign policy would tighten the hold of British creditors, while his domestic policy would place the government in the debt of a class of native American creditors, whose power might become equally pernicious.

Though Jefferson's concern with the perniciousness of debt was almost obsessive, it was nevertheless altogether in keeping with the ideas of republican liberty that he shared with his countrymen. The trouble with debt was that by undermining the independence of the debtor it threatened republican liberty. Whenever debt brought a man under another's power, he lost more than his own freedom of action. He also weakened the capacity of his country to survive as a republic. It was an axiom of current political thought that republican government required a body of free, independent, property-owning citizens.[6] A nation of men, each of whom owned enough property to support his family, could be a republic. It would follow that a nation of debtors, who had lost their property or mortgaged it to creditors, was ripe for tyranny. Jefferson accordingly favored every means of keeping men out of debt and keeping property widely distributed. He insisted on the abolition of primogeniture and entail; he declared that the earth belonged to the living and should not be kept from them by the debts or credits of the dead; he would have given fifty acres of land to every American who did not have it—all because he believed the citizens of a republic must be free from the

---

[4] Julian P. Boyd, ed., *The Papers of Thomas Jefferson* (18 vols., Princeton, 1950–   ), X, 615. For other expressions of Thomas Jefferson's aversion to debt and distrust of credit both private and public, see *ibid.*, II, 275–76, VIII, 398–99, 632–33, IX, 217–18, 472–73, X, 304–05, XI, 472, 633, 636, 640, XII, 385–86.

[5] Jefferson's career as an ambassador to France was occupied very largely by unsuccessful efforts to break the hold of British creditors on American commerce.

[6] See Caroline Robbins, *The Eighteenth-Century Commonwealthman: Studies in the Transmission, Development and Circumstance of English Liberal Thought from the Restoration of Charles II until the War with the Thirteen Colonies* (Cambridge, Mass., 1959); J. G. A. Pocock, "Machiavelli, Harrington, and English Political Ideologies in the Eighteenth Century," *William and Mary Quarterly*, XXII (Oct. 1965), 549–83.

control of other men and that they could be free only if they were economically free by virtue of owning land on which to support themselves.[7]

If Jefferson felt so passionately about the bondage of the debtor, it is not surprising that he should also have sensed a danger to the republic from another class of men who, like debtors, were nominally free but whose independence was illusory. Jefferson's second phobia was his distrust of the landless urban workman who labored in manufactures. In Jefferson's view, he was a free man in name only. Jefferson's hostility to artificers is well known and is generally attributed to his romantic preference for the rural life. But both his distrust for artificers and his idealization of small landholders as "the most precious part of a state" rested on his concern for individual independence as the basis of freedom. Farmers made the best citizens because they were "the most vigorous, the most independant, the most virtuous. . . ." Artificers, on the other hand, were dependent on "the casualties and caprice of customers." If work was scarce, they had no land to fall back on for a living. In their dependence lay the danger. "Dependance," Jefferson argued, "begets subservience and venality, suffocates the germ of virtue, and prepares fit tools for the designs of ambition." Because artificers could lay claim to freedom without the independence to go with it, they were "the instruments by which the liberties of a country are generally overturned."[8]

In Jefferson's distrust of artificers we begin to get a glimpse of the limits—and limits not dictated by racism—that defined the republican vision of the eighteenth century. For Jefferson was by no means unique among republicans in his distrust of the landless laborer. Such a distrust was a necessary corollary of the widespread eighteenth-century insistence on the independent, property-holding individual as the only bulwark of liberty, an insistence originating in James Harrington's republican political philosophy and a guiding principle of American colonial politics, whether in the aristocratic South Carolina assembly or in the democratic New England town.[9] Americans both before and after 1776 learned their republican lessons from the seventeenth- and eighteenth-century British commonwealthmen; and the commonwealthmen were uninhibited in their contempt for the masses who did not have the propertied independence required of proper republicans.

John Locke, the classic explicator of the right of revolution for the protection of liberty, did not think about extending that right to the landless poor.

---

[7] Boyd, ed., *Papers of Thomas Jefferson*, I, 344, 352, 362, 560, VIII, 681–82.

[8] *Ibid.*, VIII, 426, 682; Thomas Jefferson, *Notes on the State of Virginia*, William Peden, ed. (Chapel Hill, 1955), 165. Jefferson seems to have overlooked the dependence of Virginia's farmers on the casualties and caprice of the tobacco market.

[9] See Robbins, *The Eighteenth-Century Commonwealthmen*; Pocock, "Machiavelli, Harrington, and English Political Ideologies," 549–83; Michael Zuckerman, "The Social Context of Democracy in Massachusetts," *William and Mary Quarterly*, XXV (Oct. 1968), 523–44, Robert M. Weir, " 'The Harmony We Were Famous For': An Interpretation of Pre-Revolutionary South Carolina Politics," *ibid.*, XXVI (Oct. 1969), 473–501.

Instead, he concocted a scheme of compulsory labor for them and their children. The children were to begin at the age of three in public institutions, called working schools because the only subject taught would be work (spinning and knitting). They would be paid in bread and water and grow up "inured to work." Meanwhile the mothers, thus relieved of the care of their offspring, could go to work beside their fathers and husbands. If they could not find regular employment, then they too could be sent to the working school.[10]

It requires some refinement of mind to discern precisely how this version of women's liberation from child care differed from outright slavery. And many of Locke's intellectual successors, while denouncing slavery in the abstract, openly preferred slavery to freedom for the lower ranks of laborers. Adam Ferguson, whose works were widely read in America, attributed the overthrow of the Roman republic, in part at least, to the emancipation of slaves, who "increased, by their numbers and their vices, the weight of that dreg, which, in great and prosperous cities, ever sinks, by the tendency of vice and misconduct to the lowest condition."[11]

That people in the lowest condition, the dregs of society, generally arrived at that position through their own vice and misconduct, whether in ancient Rome or modern Britain, was an unexamined article of faith among eighteenth-century republicans. And the vice that was thought to afflict the lower ranks most severely was idleness. The eighteenth-century's preferred cure for idleness lay in the religious and ethical doctrines which R. H. Tawney described as the New Medicine for Poverty, the doctrines in which Max Weber discerned the origins of the spirit of capitalism. But in every society a stubborn mass of men and women refused the medicine. For such persons the commonwealthmen did not hesitate to prescribe slavery. Thus Francis Hutcheson, who could argue eloquently against the enslavement of Africans, also argued that perpetual slavery should be "the ordinary punishment of such idle vagrants as, after proper admonitions and tryals of temporary servitude, cannot be engaged to support themselves and their families by any useful labours."[12] James Burgh, whose *Political Disquisitions* earned the praises of many American revolutionists, proposed a set of press gangs "to seize all idle and disorderly persons, who have been three times complained of before a magistrate, and to set them to work during a certain time, for the benefit of great trading, or manufacturing companies, &c."[13]

[10] C. B. Macpherson, *The Political Theory of Possessive Individualism* (Oxford, 1962), 221–24; H. R. Fox Bourne, *The Life of John Locke* (2 vols., London, 1876), II, 377–90.
[11] Adam Ferguson, *The History of the Progress and Termination of the Roman Republic* (5 vols., Edinburgh, 1799), I, 384. See also Adam Ferguson, *An Essay on the History of Civil Society* (London, 1768), 309–11.
[12] Francis Hutcheson, *A System of Moral Philosophy* (2 vols., London, 1755), II, 202; David B. Davis, *The Problem of Slavery in Western Culture* (Ithaca, 1966), 374–78. I am indebted to David B. Davis for several valuable suggestions.
[13] James Burgh, *Political Disquisitions: Or, An ENQUIRY into public Errors, Defects, and Abuses . . .* (3 vols., London, 1774–1775), III, 220–21. See the proposal of Bishop George Berkeley that "sturdy

The most comprehensive proposal came from Andrew Fletcher of Saltoun. Jefferson hailed in Fletcher a patriot whose political principles were those "in vigour at the epoch of the American emigration [from England]. Our ancestors brought them here and they needed little strengthening to make us what we are. . . ."[14] Fletcher, like other commonwealthmen, was a champion of liberty, but he was also a champion of slavery. He attacked the Christian church not only for having promoted the abolition of slavery in ancient times but also for having perpetuated the idleness of the freedmen thus turned loose on society. The church by setting up hospitals and almshouses had enabled men through the succeeding centuries to live without work. As a result, Fletcher argued, his native Scotland was burdened with 200,000 idle rogues, who roamed the country, drinking, cursing, fighting, robbing, and murdering. For a remedy he proposed that they all be made slaves to men of property. To the argument that their masters might abuse them, he answered in words which might have come a century and a half later from a George Fitzhugh: that this would be against the master's own interest, "That the most brutal man will not use his beast ill only out of a humour; and that if such Inconveniences do sometimes fall out, it proceeds, for the most part, from the perverseness of the Servant."[15]

In spite of Jefferson's tribute to Fletcher, there is no reason to suppose that he endorsed Fletcher's proposal. But he did share Fletcher's distrust of men who were free in name while their empty bellies made them thieves, threatening the property of honest men, or else made them slaves in fact to anyone who would feed them. Jefferson's own solution for the kind of situation described by Fletcher was given in a famous letter to Madison, prompted by the spectacle Jefferson encountered in France in the 1780s, where a handful of noblemen had engrossed huge tracts of land on which to hunt game, while hordes of the poor went without work and without bread. Jefferson's proposal, characteristically phrased in terms of natural right, was for the poor to appropriate the uncultivated lands of the nobility. And he drew for the United States his usual lesson of the need to keep land widely distributed among the people.[16]

Madison's answer, which is less well known than Jefferson's letter, raised the question whether it was possible to eliminate the idle poor in any country as fully populated as France. Spread the land among them in good republican fashion and there would still be, Madison thought, "a great sur-

beggars should . . . be seized and made slaves to the public for a certain term of years." Quoted in R. H. Tawney, *Religion and the Rise of Capitalism: A Historical Essay* (New York, 1926), 270.

[14] E. Millicent Sowerby, ed., *Catalogue of the Library of Thomas Jefferson* (5 vols., Washington, 1952–1959), I, 192.

[15] Andrew Fletcher, *Two Discourses Concerning the Affairs in Scotland; Written in the Year 1698* (Edinburgh, 1698). See second discourse (separately paged), 1–33, especially 16.

[16] Boyd, ed., *Papers of Thomas Jefferson*, VIII, 681–83.

plus of inhabitants, a greater by far than will be employed in cloathing both themselves and those who feed them. . . ." In spite of those occupied in trades and as mariners, soldiers, and so on, there would remain a mass of men without work. "A certain degree of misery," Madison concluded, "seems inseparable from a high degree of populousness."[17] He did not, however, go on to propose, as Fletcher had done, that the miserable and idle poor be reduced to slavery.

The situation contemplated by Madison and confronted by Fletcher was not irrelevant to those who were planning the future of the American republic. In a country where population grew by geometric progression, it was not too early to think about a time when there might be vast numbers of landless poor, when there might be those mobs in great cities that Jefferson feared as sores on the body politic. In the United States as Jefferson and Madison knew it, the urban labor force as yet posed no threat, because it was small; and the agricultural labor force was, for the most part, already enslaved. In Revolutionary America, among men who spent their lives working for other men rather than working for themselves, slaves probably constituted a majority.[18] In Virginia they constituted a large majority.[19] If Jefferson and Madison, not to mention Washington, were unhappy about that fact and yet did nothing to alter it, they may have been restrained, in part at least, by thoughts of the role that might be played in the United States by a large mass of free laborers.

When Jefferson contemplated the abolition of slavery, he found it inconceivable that the freed slaves should be allowed to remain in the country.[20] In this attitude he was probably moved by his or his countrymen's racial prejudice. But he may also have had in mind the possibility that when slaves ceased to be slaves, they would become instead a half million idle poor, who would create the same problems for the United States that the idle poor of Europe did for their states. The slave, accustomed to compulsory labor, would not work to support himself when the compulsion was removed. This was a commonplace among Virginia planters before the creation of the republic and long after. "If you free the slaves," wrote Landon Carter, two days after the Declaration of Independence, "you must send them out of the country or they must steal for their support."[21]

[17] *Ibid.*, IX, 659–60.
[18] Jackson Turner Main, *The Social Structure of Revolutionary America* (Princeton, 1965), 271.
[19] In 1755, Virginia had 43,329 white tithables and 60,078 black. Tithables included white men over sixteen years of age and black men and women over sixteen. In the census of 1790, Virginia had 292,717 slaves and 110,936 white males over sixteen, out of a total population of 747,680. Evarts B. Greene and Virginia D. Harrington, *American Population before the Federal Census of 1790* (New York, 1932), 150–55.
[20] Jefferson, *Notes on the State of Virginia*, 138.
[21] Jack P. Greene, ed., *The Diary of Colonel Landon Carter of Sabine Hall, 1752–1778* (2 vols., Charlottesville, 1965), II, 1055.

Jefferson's plan for freeing his own slaves (never carried out) included an interim education period in which they would have been half-taught, half-compelled to support themselves on rented land; for without guidance and preparation for self support, he believed, slaves could not be expected to become fit members of a republican society.[22] And St. George Tucker, who drafted detailed plans for freeing Virginia's slaves, worried about "the possibility of their becoming idle, dissipated, and finally a numerous banditti, instead of turning their attention to industry and labour." He therefore included in his plans a provision for compelling the labor of the freedmen on an annual basis. "For we must not lose sight of this important consideration," he said, "that these people must be *bound* to labour, if they do not *voluntarily* engage therein. . . . In absolving them from the yoke of slavery, we must not forget the interests of society. Those interests require the exertions of every individual in some mode or other; and those who have not wherewith to support themselves honestly without corporal labour, whatever be their complexion, ought to be compelled to labour."[23]

It is plain that Tucker, the would-be emancipator, distrusted the idle poor regardless of color. And it seems probable that the Revolutionary champions of liberty who acquiesced in the continued slavery of black labor did so not only because of racial prejudice but also because they shared with Tucker a distrust of the poor that was inherent in eighteenth-century conceptions of republican liberty. Their historical guidebooks had made them fear to enlarge the free labor force.

That fear, I believe, had a second point of origin in the experience of the American colonists, and especially of Virginians, during the preceding century and a half. If we turn now to the previous history of Virginia's labor force, we may find, I think, some further clues to the distrust of free labor among Revolutionary republicans and to the paradoxical rise of slavery and freedom together in colonial America.

The story properly begins in England with the burst of population growth there that sent the number of Englishmen from perhaps three million in 1500 to four-and-one-half million by 1650.[24] The increase did not occur in response to any corresponding growth in the capacity of the island's economy to support its people. And the result was precisely that misery which Madison pointed out to Jefferson as the consequence of "a high degree of populousness." Sixteenth-century England knew the same kind of unemployment and poverty that Jefferson witnessed in eighteenth-century France and Fletcher in seventeenth-century Scotland. Alarming numbers of idle and

[22] Boyd, ed., *Papers of Thomas Jefferson*, XIV, 492–93.
[23] St. George Tucker, *A Dissertation on Slavery with a Proposal for the Gradual Abolition of It, in the State of Virginia* (Philadelphia, 1796). See also Jordan, *White over Black*, 555–60.
[24] Joan Thrisk, ed., *The Agrarian History of England and Wales*, Vol. IV: *1500–1640* (Cambridge, England, 1967), 531.

hungry men drifted about the country looking for work or plunder. The government did what it could to make men of means hire them, but it also adopted increasingly severe measures against their wandering, their thieving, their roistering, and indeed their very existence. Whom the workhouses and prisons could not swallow the gallows would have to, or perhaps the army. When England had military expeditions to conduct abroad, every parish packed off its most unwanted inhabitants to the almost certain death that awaited them from the diseases of the camp.[25]

As the mass of idle rogues and beggars grew and increasingly threatened the peace of England, the efforts to cope with them increasingly threatened the liberties of Englishmen. Englishmen prided themselves on a "gentle government,"[26] a government that had been releasing its subjects from old forms of bondage and endowing them with new liberties, making the "rights of Englishmen" a phrase to conjure with. But there was nothing gentle about the government's treatment of the poor; and as more Englishmen became poor, other Englishmen had less to be proud of. Thoughtful men could see an obvious solution: get the surplus Englishmen out of England. Send them to the New World, where there were limitless opportunities for work. There they would redeem themselves, enrich the mother country, and spread English liberty abroad.

The great publicist for this program was Richard Hakluyt. His *Principall Navigations, Voiages and Discoveries of the English nation*[27] was not merely the narrative of voyages by Englishmen around the globe, but a powerful suggestion that the world ought to be English or at least ought to be ruled by Englishmen. Hakluyt's was a dream of empire, but of benevolent empire, in which England would confer the blessings of her own free government on the less fortunate peoples of the world. It is doubtless true that Englishmen, along with other Europeans, were already imbued with prejudice against men of darker complexions than their own. And it is also true that the principal beneficiaries of Hakluyt's empire would be Englishmen. But Hakluyt's dream cannot be dismissed as mere hypocrisy any more than Jefferson's affirmation of human equality can be so dismissed. Hakluyt's compassion for the poor and oppressed was not confined to the English poor, and in Francis Drake's exploits in the Caribbean Hakluyt saw, not a thinly disguised form of piracy, but a model for English liberation of men of all colors who labored under the tyranny of the Spaniard.

Drake had gone ashore at Panama in 1572 and made friends with an extraordinary band of runaway Negro slaves. "Cimarrons" they were called, and

---

[25] See Edmund S. Morgan, "The Labor Problem at Jamestown, 1607–18," *American Historical Review*, 76 (June 1971), 595–611, especially 600–06.

[26] This is Richard Hakluyt's phrase. See E. G. R. Taylor, ed., *The Original Writings & Correspondence of the Two Richard Hakluyts* (2 vols., London, 1935), I, 142.

[27] Richard Hakluyt, *The Principall Navigations, Voiages and Discoveries of the English nation . . .* (London, 1589).

they lived a free and hardy life in the wilderness, periodically raiding the Spanish settlements to carry off more of their people. They discovered in Drake a man who hated the Spanish as much as they did and who had the arms and men to mount a stronger attack than they could manage by themselves. Drake wanted Spanish gold, and the Cimarrons wanted Spanish iron for tools. They both wanted Spanish deaths. The alliance was a natural one and apparently untroubled by racial prejudice. Together the English and the Cimarrons robbed the mule train carrying the annual supply of Peruvian treasure across the isthmus. And before Drake sailed for England with his loot, he arranged for future meetings.[28] When Hakluyt heard of this alliance, he concocted his first colonizing proposal, a scheme for seizing the Straits of Magellan and transporting Cimarrons there, along with surplus Englishmen. The straits would be a strategic strong point for England's world empire, since they controlled the route from Atlantic to Pacific. Despite the severe climate of the place, the Cimarrons and their English friends would all live warmly together, clad in English woolens, "well lodged and by our nation made free from the tyrannous Spanyard, and quietly and courteously governed by our nation."[29]

The scheme for a colony in the Straits of Magellan never worked out, but Hakluyt's vision endured, of liberated natives and surplus Englishmen, courteously governed in English colonies around the world. Sir Walter Raleigh caught the vision. He dreamt of wresting the treasure of the Incas from the Spaniard by allying with the Indians of Guiana and sending Englishmen to live with them, lead them in rebellion against Spain, and govern them in the English manner.[30] Raleigh also dreamt of a similar colony in the country he named Virginia. Hakluyt helped him plan it.[31] And Drake stood ready to supply Negroes and Indians, liberated from Spanish tyranny in the Caribbean, to help the enterprise.[32]

Virginia from the beginning was conceived not only as a haven for England's suffering poor, but as a spearhead of English liberty in an oppressed world. That was the dream; but when it began to materialize at Roanoke Island in 1585, something went wrong. Drake did his part by liberating Spanish Caribbean slaves, and carrying to Roanoke those who wished to join him.[33] But the English settlers whom Raleigh sent there proved unworthy of

[28] The whole story of this extraordinary episode is to be found in I. A. Wright, ed., *Documents Concerning English Voyages to the Spanish Main 1569–1580* (London, 1932).

[29] Taylor, ed., *Original Writings & Correspondence*, I, 139–46.

[30] Walter Raleigh, *The Discoverie of the large and bewtiful Empire of Guiana*, V. T. Harlow, ed. (London, 1928), 138–49; V. T. Harlow, ed., *Ralegh's Last Voyage: Being an account drawn out of contemporary letters and relations . . .* (London, 1932), 44–45.

[31] Taylor, ed., *Original Writings & Correspondence*, II, 211–377, especially 318.

[32] Irene A. Wright, trans. and ed., *Further English Voyages to Spanish America, 1583–1594: Documents from the Archives of the Indies at Seville . . .* (London, 1951), lviii, lxiii, lxiv, 37, 52, 54, 55, 159, 172, 173, 181, 188–89, 204–06.

[33] The Spanish reported that "Although their masters were willing to ransom them the English would not give them up except when the slaves themselves desired to go." *Ibid.*, 159. On Walter Raleigh's later expedition to Guiana, the Spanish noted that the English told the natives "that

the role assigned them. By the time Drake arrived they had shown themselves less than courteous to the Indians on whose assistance they depended. The first group of settlers murdered the chief who befriended them, and then gave up and ran for home aboard Drake's returning ships. The second group simply disappeared, presumably killed by the Indians.[34]

What was lost in this famous lost colony was more than the band of colonists who have never been traced. What was also lost and never quite recovered in subsequent ventures was the dream of the Englishman and Indian living side by side in peace and liberty. When the English finally planted a permanent colony at Jamestown they came as conquerors, and their government was far from gentle. The Indians willing to endure it were too few in numbers and too broken in spirit to play a significant part in the settlement.

Without their help, Virginia offered a bleak alternative to the workhouse or the gallows for the first English poor who were transported there. During the first two decades of the colony's existence, most of the arriving immigrants found precious little English liberty in Virginia.[35] But by the 1630s the colony seemed to be working out, at least in part, as its first planners had hoped. Impoverished Englishmen were arriving every year in large numbers, engaged to serve the existing planters for a term of years, with the prospect of setting up their own households a few years later. The settlers were spreading up Virginia's great rivers, carving out plantations, living comfortably from their corn fields and from the cattle they ranged in the forests, and at the same time earning perhaps ten or twelve pounds a year per man from the tobacco they planted. A representative legislative assembly secured the traditional liberties of Englishmen and enabled a larger proportion of the population to participate in their own government than had ever been the case in England. The colony even began to look a little like the cosmopolitan haven of liberty that Hakluyt had first envisaged. Men of all countries appeared there: French, Spanish, Dutch, Turkish, Portuguese, and African.[36] Virginia took them in and began to make Englishmen out of them.

---

they did not desire to make them slaves, but only to be their friends; promising to bring them great quantities of hatchets and knives, and especially if they drove the Spaniards out of their territories." Harlow, ed., *Ralegh's Last Voyage*, 179.

[34] David Beers Quinn, ed., *The Roanoke Voyages 1584–1590* (2 vols., London, 1955).

[35] Morgan, "The Labor Problem at Jamestown, 1607–18," pp. 595–611; Edmund S. Morgan, "The First American Boom: Virginia 1618 to 1630," *William and Mary Quarterly*, XXVIII (April 1971), 169–98.

[36] There are no reliable records of immigration, but the presence of persons of these nationalities is evident from county court records, where all but the Dutch are commonly identified by name, such as "James the Scotchman," or "Cursory the Turk." The Dutch seem to have anglicized their names at once and are difficult to identify except where the records disclose their naturalization. The two counties for which the most complete records survive for the 1640s and 1650s are Accomack-Northampton and Lower Norfolk. Microfilms are in the Virginia State Library, Richmond.

It seems clear that most of the Africans, perhaps all of them, came as slaves, a status that had become obsolete in England, while it was becoming the expected condition of Africans outside Africa and of a good many inside.[37] It is equally clear that a substantial number of Virginia's Negroes were free or became free. And all of them, whether servant, slave, or free, enjoyed most of the same rights and duties as other Virginians. There is no evidence during the period before 1660 that they were subjected to a more severe discipline than other servants. They could sue and be sued in court. They did penance in the parish church for having illegitimate children. They earned money of their own, bought and sold and raised cattle of their own. Sometimes they bought their own freedom. In other cases, masters bequeathed them not only freedom but land, cattle, and houses.[38] Northampton, the only county for which full records exist, had at least ten free Negro households by 1668.[39]

As Negroes took their place in the community, they learned English ways, including even the truculence toward authority that has always been associated with the rights of Englishmen. Tony Longo, a free Negro of Northampton, when served a warrant to appear as a witness in court, responded with a scatological opinion of warrants, called the man who served it an idle rascal, and told him to go about his business. The man offered to go with him at any time before a justice of the peace so that his evidence could be recorded. He would go with him at night, tomorrow, the next day, next week, any time. But Longo was busy getting in his corn. He dismissed all pleas with a "Well, well, Ile goe when my Corne is in," and refused to receive the warrant.[40]

The judges understandably found this to be contempt of court; but it was the kind of contempt that free Englishmen often showed to authority, and it was combined with a devotion to work that English moralists were

---

[37] Because the surviving records are so fragmentary, there has been a great deal of controversy about the status of the first Negroes in Virginia. What the records do make clear is that not all were slaves and that not all were free. See Jordan, *White over Black*, 71–82.

[38] For examples, see Northampton County Court Records, Deeds, Wills, etc., Book III, f. 83, Book V, ff. 38, 54, 60, 102, 117–19; York County Court Records, Deeds, Orders, Wills, etc., no. 1, ff. 232–34; Surry County Records, Deeds, Wills, etc., no. 1, f. 349; Henrico County Court Records, Deeds and Wills 1677–1692, f. 139.

[39] This fact has been arrived at by comparing the names of householders on the annual list of tithables with casual identifications of persons as Negroes in the court records. The names of householders so identified for 1668, the peak year during the period for which the lists survive (1662–1677) were: Bastian Cane, Bashaw Ferdinando, John Francisco, Susan Grace, William Harman, Philip Mongum, Francis Pane, Manuel Rodriggus, Thomas Rodriggus, and King Tony. The total number of households in the county in 1668 was 172; total number of tithables 435; total number of tithable free Negroes 17; total number of tithable unfree Negroes 42. Thus nearly 29 percent of tithable Negroes and probably of all Negroes were free; and about 13.5 percent of all tithables were Negroes.

[40] Northampton Deeds, Wills, etc., Book V, 54–60 (Nov. 1, 1654).

doing their best to inculcate more widely in England. As England had absorbed people of every nationality over the centuries and turned them into Englishmen, Virginia's Englishmen were absorbing their own share of foreigners, including Negroes, and seemed to be successfully moulding a New World community on the English model.

But a closer look will show that the situation was not quite so promising as at first it seems. It is well known that Virginia in its first fifteen or twenty years killed off most of the men who went there. It is less well known that it continued to do so. If my estimate of the volume of immigration is anywhere near correct, Virginia must have been a death trap for at least another fifteen years and probably for twenty or twenty-five. In 1625 the population stood at 1,300 or 1,400; in 1640 it was about 8,000.[41] In the fifteen years between those dates at least 15,000 persons must have come to the colony.[42] If so, 15,000 immigrants increased the population by less than 7,000. There is no evidence of a large return migration. It seems probable that the death rate throughout this period was comparable only to that found in Europe during the peak years of a plague. Virginia, in other words, was absorbing England's surplus laborers mainly by killing them. The success of those who survived and rose from servant to planter must be attributed partly to the fact that so few did survive.

After 1640, when the diseases responsible for the high death rate began to decline and the population began a quick rise, it became increasingly difficult for an indigent immigrant to pull himself up in the world. The population

[41] The figure for 1625 derives from the census for that year, which gives 1,210 persons, but probably missed about 10 percent of the population. Morgan, "The First American Boom," 170n–71n. The figure for 1640 is derived from legislation limiting tobacco production per person in 1639–1640. The legislation is summarized in a manuscript belonging to Jefferson, printed in William Waller Hening, *The Statutes at Large; Being a Collection of All the Laws of Virginia, from the First Session of the Legislature, in the Year 1619* (13 vols., New York, 1823), I, 224–25, 228. The full text is in "Acts of the General Assembly, Jan. 6, 1639–40," *William and Mary Quarterly*, IV (Jan. 1924), 17–35, and "Acts of the General Assembly, Jan. 6, 1639–40," *ibid.* (July 1924), 159–62. The assembly calculated that a levy of four pounds of tobacco per tithable would yield 18,584 pounds, implying 4,646 tithables (men over sixteen). It also calculated that a limitation of planting to 170 pounds per poll would yield 1,300,000, implying 7,647 polls. Evidently the latter figure is for the whole population, as is evident also from Hening, *Statutes*, I, 228.

[42] In the year 1635, the only year for which such records exist, 2,010 persons embarked for Virginia from London alone. See John Camden Hotten, ed., *The Original Lists of Persons of Quality* . . . (London, 1874), 35–145. For other years casual estimates survive. In February 1627/8 Francis West said that 1,000 had been "lately receaved." Colonial Office Group, Class 1, Piece 4, folio 109 (Public Record Office, London). Hereafter cited CO 1/4, f. 109. In February 1633/4 Governor John Harvey said that "this yeares newcomers" had arrived "this yeare." Yong to Sir Tobie Matthew, July 13, 1634, "Aspinwall Papers," *Massachusetts Historical Society Collections*, IX, (1871), 110. In May 1635, Samuel Mathews said that 2,000 had arrived "this yeare." Mathews to ? , May 25, 1635, "The Mutiny in Virginia, 1635," *Virginia Magazine of History and Biography*, I (April 1894), 417. And in March 1636, John West said that 1,606 persons had arrived "this yeare." West to Commissioners for Plantations, March 28, 1636, "Virginia in 1636," *ibid.*, IX (July 1901), 37.

probably passed 25,000 by 1662,[43] hardly what Madison would have called a high degree of populousness. Yet the rapid rise brought serious trouble for Virginia. It brought the engrossment of tidewater land in thousands and tens of thousands of acres by speculators, who recognized that the demand would rise.[44] It brought a huge expansion of tobacco production, which helped to depress the price of tobacco and the earnings of the men who planted it.[45] It brought efforts by planters to prolong the terms of servants, since they were now living longer and therefore had a longer expectancy of usefulness.[46]

It would, in fact, be difficult to assess all the consequences of the increased longevity; but for our purposes one development was crucial, and that was the appearance in Virginia of a growing number of freemen who had served their terms but who were now unable to afford land of their own except on the frontiers or in the interior. In years when tobacco prices were especially low or crops especially poor, men who had been just scraping by were obliged to go back to work for their larger neighbors simply in order to stay alive. By 1676 it was estimated that one fourth of Virginia's freemen were without land of their own.[47] And in the same year Francis Moryson, a member of the governor's council, explained the term "freedmen" as used in Virginia to mean "persons without house and land," implying that this was now the normal condition of servants who had attained freedom.[48]

Some of them resigned themselves to working for wages; others preferred a meager living on dangerous frontier land or a hand-to-mouth exis-

[43] The official count of tithables for 1662 was 11,838. Clarendon Papers, 82 (Bodleian Library, Oxford). The ratio of tithables to total population by this time was probably about one to two. (In 1625 it was 1 to 1.5; in 1699 it was 1 to 2.7.) Since the official count was almost certainly below the actuality, a total population of roughly 25,000 seems probable. All population figures for seventeenth-century Virginia should be treated as rough estimates.

[44] Evidence of the engrossment of lands after 1660 will be found in CO 1/39, f. 196; CO 1/40, f. 23; CO 1/48; f. 48; CO 5/1309, numbers 5, 9, and 23; Sloane Papers, 1008, ff. 334–35 (British Museum, London). A recent count of headrights in patents issued for land in Virginia shows 82,000 headrights claimed in the years from 1635 to 1700. Of these nearly 47,000 or 57 percent (equivalent to 2,350,000 acres) were claimed in the twenty-five years after 1650. W. F. Craven, *White, Red, and Black: The Seventeenth-Century Virginian* (Charlottesville, 1971), 14–16.

[45] No continuous set of figures for Virginia's tobacco exports in the seventeenth century can now be obtained. The available figures for English imports of American tobacco (which was mostly Virginian) are in United States Bureau of the Census, *Historical Statistics of the United States, Colonial Times to 1957* (Washington, D. C., 1960), series Z 238–240, p. 766. They show for 1672 a total of 17,559,000 pounds. In 1631 the figure had been 272,300 pounds. Tobacco crops varied heavily from year to year. Prices are almost as difficult to obtain now as volume. Those for 1667–1675 are estimated from London prices current in Warren Billings, "Virginia's Deploured Condition, 1660–1676: The Coming of Bacon's Rebellion" (doctoral dissertation, Northern Illinois University, 1969), 155–59.

[46] See below.

[47] Thomas Ludwell and Robert Smith to the king, June 18, 1676, vol. LXXVII, f. 128, Coventry Papers Longleat House, American Council of Learned Societies British Mss. project, reel 63 (Library of Congress).

[48] *Ibid.*, 204–05.

tence, roaming from one county to another, renting a bit of land here, squatting on some there, dodging the tax collector, drinking, quarreling, stealing hogs, and enticing servants to run away with them.

The presence of this growing class of poverty-stricken Virginians was not a little frightening to the planters who had made it to the top or who had arrived in the colony already at the top, with ample supplies of servants and capital. They were caught in a dilemma. They wanted the immigrants who kept pouring in every year. Indeed they needed them and prized them the more as they lived longer. But as more and more turned free each year, Virginia seemed to have inherited the problem that she was helping England to solve. Virginia, complained Nicholas Spencer, secretary of the colony, was "a sinke to drayen England of her filth and scum."[49]

The men who worried the uppercrust looked even more dangerous in Virginia than they had in England. They were, to begin with, young, because it was young persons that the planters wanted for work in the fields; and the young have always seemed impatient of control by their elders and superiors, if not downright rebellious. They were also predominantly single men. Because the planters did not think women, or at least English women, fit for work in the fields, men outnumbered women among immigrants by three or four to one throughout the century.[50] Consequently most of the freedmen had no wife or family to tame their wilder impulses and serve as hostages to the respectable world.

Finally, what made these wild young men particularly dangerous was that they were armed and had to be armed. Life in Virginia required guns. The plantations were exposed to attack from Indians by land and from privateers and petty-thieving pirates by sea.[51] Whenever England was at war with the French or the Dutch, the settlers had to be ready to defend themselves. In 1667 the Dutch in a single raid captured twenty merchant ships in the James River, together with the English warship that was supposed to be defending them; and in 1673 they captured eleven more. On these occasions Governor William Berkeley gathered the planters in arms and at least prevented the enemy from making a landing. But while he stood off the Dutch he worried about the ragged crew at his back. Of the able-bodied men in the colony he estimated that "at least one third are Single freedmen (whose

[49] Nicholas Spencer to Lord Culpeper, Aug. 6, 1676, *ibid.,* 170. See also CO 1/49, f 107.
[50] The figures are derived from a sampling of the names of persons for whom headrights were claimed in land patents. Patent Books I–IX (Virginia State Library, Richmond). Wyndham B. Blanton found 17,350 women and 75,884 men in "a prolonged search of the patent books and other records of the times . . . ," a ratio of 1 woman to 4.4 men. Wyndham B. Blanton "Epidemics, Real and Imaginary, and other Factors Influencing Seventeenth Century Virginia's Population," *Bulletin of the History of Medicine,* XXXI (Sept.–Oct. 1957), 462. See also Craven, *White, Red, and Black,* 26–27.
[51] Pirates were particularly troublesome in the 1680s and 1690s. See CO 1/48, f. 71; CO 1/51, f. 340; CO 1/52, f. 54; CO 1/55, ff. 105–106; CO 1/57, f. 300; CO 5/1311, no. 10.

Labour will hardly maintaine them) or men much in debt, both which wee may reasonably expect upon any Small advantage the Enemy may gaine upon us, wold revolt to them in hopes of bettering their Condicion by Share-ing the Plunder of the Country with them."[52]

Berkeley's fears were justified. Three years later, sparked not by a Dutch invasion but by an Indian attack, rebellion swept Virginia. It began almost as Berkeley had predicted, when a group of volunteer Indian fighters turned from a fruitless expedition against the Indians to attack their rulers. Bacon's Rebellion was the largest popular rising in the colonies before the American Revolution. Sooner or later nearly everyone in Virginia got in on it, but it began in the frontier counties of Henrico and New Kent, among men whom the governor and his friends consistently characterized as rabble.[53] As it spread eastward, it turned out that there were rabble everywhere, and Berkeley understandably raised his estimate of their numbers. "How miser-able that man is," he exclaimed, "that Governes a People wher six parts of seaven at least are Poore Endebted Discontented and Armed."[54]

Virginia's poor had reason to be envious and angry against the men who owned the land and imported the servants and ran the government. But the rebellion produced no real program of reform, no ideology, not even any rev-olutionary slogans. It was a search for plunder, not for principles. And when the rebels had redistributed whatever wealth they could lay their hands on, the rebellion subsided almost as quickly as it had begun.

It had been a shattering experience, however, for Virginia's first families. They had seen each other fall in with the rebels in order to save their skins or their possessions or even to share in the plunder. When it was over, they eyed one another distrustfully, on the lookout for any new Bacons in their midst, who might be tempted to lead the still restive rabble on more plundering ex-peditions. When William Byrd and Laurence Smith proposed to solve the problems of defense against the Indians by establishing semi-independent buffer settlements on the upper reaches of the rivers, in each of which they would engage to keep fifty men in arms, the assembly at first reacted favor-ably. But it quickly occurred to the governor and council that this would in fact mean gathering a crowd of Virginia's wild bachelors and furnishing them with an abundant supply of arms and ammunition. Byrd had himself led such a crowd in at least one plundering foray during the rebellion. To put him or anyone else in charge of a large and permanent gang of armed men was to invite them to descend again on the people whom they were supposed to be protecting.[55]

---

[52] CO 1/30, ff. 114–115.
[53] CO 1/37, ff. 35–40.
[54] Vol. LXXVII, 144–46, Coventry Papers.
[55] Hening, *Statutes*, II, 448–54; CO 1/42, f. 178; CO 1/43, f. 29; CO 1/44, f. 398; CO 1/47, ff. 258–260, 267; CO 1/48, f. 46; vol. LXXVIII, 378–81, 386–87, 398–99, Coventry Papers.

The nervousness of those who had property worth plundering continued throughout the century, spurred in 1682 by the tobacco-cutting riots in which men roved about destroying crops in the fields, in the desperate hope of producing a shortage that would raise the price of the leaf.[56] And periodically in nearby Maryland and North Carolina, where the same conditions existed as in Virginia, there were tumults that threatened to spread to Virginia.[57]

As Virginia thus acquired a social problem analogous to England's own, the colony began to deal with it as England had done, by restricting the liberties of those who did not have the proper badge of freedom, namely the property that government was supposed to protect. One way was to extend the terms of service for servants entering the colony without indentures. Formerly they had served until twenty-one; now the age was advanced to twenty-four.[58] There had always been laws requiring them to serve extra time for running away; now the laws added corporal punishment and, in order to make habitual offenders more readily recognizable, specified that their hair be cropped.[59] New laws restricted the movement of servants on the highways and also increased the amount of extra time to be served for running away. In addition to serving two days for every day's absence, the captured runaway was now frequently required to compensate by labor for the loss to the crop that he had failed to tend and for the cost of his apprehension, including rewards paid for his capture.[60] A three week's holiday might result in a year's extra service.[61] If a servant struck his master, he was to serve another year.[62] For killing a hog he had to serve the owner a year and the informer another year. Since the owner of the hog, and the owner of the servant, and the informer were frequently the same man, and since a hog was worth at best less than one tenth the hire of a servant for a year, the law was very profitable to masters. One Lancaster master was awarded six years extra service from a servant who killed three of his hogs, worth about thirty shillings.[63]

The effect of these measures was to keep servants for as long as possible from gaining their freedom, especially the kind of servants who were most likely to cause trouble. At the same time the engrossment of land was driving many back to servitude after a brief taste of freedom. Freedmen who engaged to work for wages by so doing became servants again, subject to most of the same restrictions as other servants.

---

[56] CO 1/48 *passim.*

[57] CO 1/43, ff. 359–365; CO 1/44, ff. 10–62; CO 1/47, f. 261; CO 1/48, ff. 87–96, 100–102, 185; CO 5/1305, no. 43; CO 5/1309, no. 74.

[58] Hening, *Statutes,* II, 113–14, 240.

[59] *Ibid.,* II, 266, 278.

[60] *Ibid.,* II, 116–17, 273–74, 277–78.

[61] For example, James Gray, absent twenty-two days, was required to serve fifteen months extra. Order Book 1666–1680, p. 163, Lancaster County Court Records.

[62] Hening, *Statutes,* II, 118.

[63] Order Book 1666–1680, p. 142, Lancaster County Court Records.

Nevertheless, in spite of all the legal and economic pressures to keep men in service, the ranks of the freedmen grew, and so did poverty and discontent. To prevent the wild bachelors from gaining an influence in the government, the assembly in 1670 limited voting to landholders and householders.[64] But to disfranchise the growing mass of single freemen was not to deprive them of the weapons they had wielded so effectively under Nathaniel Bacon. It is questionable how far Virginia could safely have continued along this course, meeting discontent with repression and manning her plantations with annual importations of servants who would later add to the unruly ranks of the free. To be sure, the men at the bottom might have had both land and liberty, as the settlers of some other colonies did, if Virginia's frontier had been safe from Indians, or if the men at the top had been willing to forego some of their profits and to give up some of the lands they had engrossed. The English government itself made efforts to break up the great holdings that had helped to create the problem.[65] But it is unlikely that the policy makers in Whitehall would have contended long against the successful.

In any case they did not have to. There was another solution, which allowed Virginia's magnates to keep their lands, yet arrested the discontent and the repression of other Englishmen, a solution which strengthened the rights of Englishmen and nourished their attachment to liberty which came to fruition in the Revolutionary generation of Virginia statesmen. But the solution put an end to the process of turning Africans into Englishmen. The rights of Englishmen were preserved by destroying the rights of Africans.

I do not mean to argue that Virginians deliberately turned to African Negro slavery as a means of preserving and extending the rights of Englishmen. Winthrop Jordan has suggested that slavery came to Virginia as an unthinking decision.[66] We might go further and say that it came without a decision. It came automatically as Virginians bought the cheapest labor they could get. Once Virginia's heavy mortality ceased, an investment in slave labor was much more profitable than an investment in free labor; and the planters bought slaves as rapidly as traders made them available. In the last years of the seventeenth century they bought them in such numbers that slaves probably already constituted a majority or nearly a majority of the labor force by 1700.[67] The demand was so great that traders for a time found

---

[64] Hening, *Statutes,* II, 280. It had been found, the preamble to the law said, that such persons "haveing little interest in the country doe oftner make tumults at the election to the disturbance of his majesties peace, then by their discretions in their votes provide for the conservasion thereof, by makeing choyce of persons fitly qualifyed for the discharge of soe greate a trust. . . ."

[65] CO 1/39, f. 196; CO 1/48, f. 48; CO 5/1309, nos. 5, 9, 23; CO 5/1310, no. 83.

[66] Jordan, *White over Black,* 44–98.

[67] In 1700 they constituted half of the labor force (persons working for other men) in Surry County, the only county in which it is possible to ascertain the numbers. Robert Wheeler, "Social Transition in the Virginia Tidewater, 1650–1720: The Laboring Households as an Index," paper delivered at the Organization of American Historians' meeting, New Orleans, April 15, 1971. Surry County was on the south side of the James, one of the least wealthy regions of Virginia.

a better market in Virginia than in Jamaica or Barbados.[68] But the social benefits of an enslaved labor force, even if not consciously sought or recognized at the time by the men who bought the slaves, were larger than the economic benefits. The increase in the importation of slaves was matched by a decrease in the importation of indentured servants and consequently a decrease in the dangerous number of new freedmen who annually emerged seeking a place in society that they would be unable to achieve.[69]

If Africans had been unavailable, it would probably have proved impossible to devise a way to keep a continuing supply of English immigrants in their place. There was a limit beyond which the abridgement of English liberties would have resulted not merely in rebellion but in protests from England and in the cutting off of the supply of further servants. At the time of Bacon's Rebellion the English commission of investigation had shown more sympathy with the rebels than with the well-to-do planters who had engrossed Virginia's lands. To have attempted the enslavement of English-born laborers would have caused more disorder than it cured. But to keep as slaves black men who arrived in that condition *was* possible and apparently regarded as plain common sense.

The attitude of English officials was well expressed by the attorney who reviewed for the Privy Council the slave codes established in Barbados in 1679. He found the laws of Barbados to be well designed for the good of his majesty's subjects there, for, he said, "although Negros in that Island are punishable in a different and more severe manner than other Subjects are for Offences of the like nature; yet I humbly conceive that the Laws there concerning Negros are reasonable Laws, for by reason of their numbers they become dangerous, and being a brutish sort of People and reckoned as goods and chattels in that Island, it is of necessity or at least convenient to have Laws for the Government of them different from the Laws of England, to prevent the great mischief that otherwise may happen to the Planters and Inhabitants in that Island."[70] In Virginia too it seemed convenient and reasonable to have different laws for black and white. As the number of slaves increased, the assembly passed laws that carried forward with much greater severity the trend already under way in the colony's labor laws. But the new severity was reserved for people without white skin. The laws specifically exonerated the master who accidentally beat his slave to death, but they placed new limitations on his punishment of "Christian white servants."[71]

---

[68] See the letters of the Royal African Company to its ship captains, Oct. 23, 1701; Dec. 2, 1701; Dec. 7, 1704; Dec. 21, 1704; Jan. 25, 1704/5, T70 58 (Public Record Office, London).
[69] Abbot Emerson Smith, *Colonists in Bondage: White Servitude and Convict Labor in America 1607–1776* (Chapel Hill, 1947), 335. See also Thomas J. Wertenbaker, *The Planters of Colonial Virginia* (Princeton, 1922), 130–31, 134–35; Craven, *White, Red, and Black,* 17.
[70] CO 1/45, f. 138.
[71] Hening, *Statutes,* II, 481–82, 492–93; III, 86–88, 102–03, 179–80, 333–35, 447–62.

Virginians worried about the risk of having in their midst a body of men who had every reason to hate them.[72] The fear of a slave insurrection hung over them for nearly two centuries. But the danger from slaves actually proved to be less than that which the colony had faced from its restive and armed freedmen. Slaves had none of the rising expectations that so often produce human discontent. No one had told them that they had rights. They had been nurtured in heathen societies where they had lost their freedom; their children would be nurtured in a Christian society and never know freedom.

Moreover, slaves were less troubled by the sexual imbalance that helped to make Virginia's free laborers so restless. In an enslaved labor force women could be required to make tobacco just as the men did; and they also made children, who in a few years would be an asset to their master. From the beginning, therefore, traders imported women in a much higher ratio to men than was the case among English servants,[73] and the level of discontent was correspondingly reduced. Virginians did not doubt that discontent would remain, but it could be repressed by methods that would not have been considered reasonable, convenient, or even safe, if applied to Englishmen. Slaves could be deprived of opportunities for association and rebellion. They could be kept unarmed and unorganized. They could be subjected to savage punishments by their owners without fear of legal reprisals. And since their color disclosed their probable status, the rest of society could keep close watch on them. It is scarcely surprising that no slave insurrection in American history approached Bacon's Rebellion in its extent or in its success.

---

[72] For example, see William Byrd II to the Earl of Egmont, July 12, 1736, in Elizabeth Donnan, ed., *Documents Illustrative of the History of the Slave Trade to America* (4 vols., Washington, 1930–1935), IV, 131–32. But compare Byrd's letter to Peter Beckford, Dec. 6, 1735, "Letters of the Byrd Family," *Virginia Magazine of History and Biography*, XXXVI (April 1928), 121–23, in which he specifically denies any danger. The Virginia assembly at various times laid duties on the importation of slaves. See Donnan, ed., *Documents Illustrative of the History of the Slave Trade*, IV, 66–67, 86–88, 91–94, 102–17, 121–31, 132–42. The purpose of some of the acts was to discourage imports, but apparently the motive was to redress the colony's balance of trade after a period during which the planters had purchased far more than they could pay for. See also Wertenbaker, *The Planters of Colonial Virginia*, 129.

[73] The Swiss traveler Francis Ludwig Michel noted in 1702 that "Both sexes are usually bought, which increase afterwards." William J. Hinke, trans. and ed., "Report of the Journey of Francis Louis Michel from Berne Switzerland to Virginia, October 2, (1) 1701–December 1, 1702: Part II," *Virginia Magazine of History and Biography*, XXIV (April 1916), 116. A sampling of the names identifiable by sex, for whom headrights were claimed in land patents in the 1680s and 1690s shows a much higher ratio of women to men among blacks than among whites. For example, in the years 1695–1699 (Patent Book 9) I count 818 white men and 276 white women, 376 black men and 220 black women (but compare Craven, *White, Red, and Black*, 99–100). In Northampton County in 1677, among seventy-five black tithables there were thirty-six men, thirty-eight women, and one person whose sex cannot be determined. In Surry County in 1703, among 211 black tithables there were 132 men, seventy-four women, and five persons whose sex cannot be determined. These are the only counties where the records yield such information. Northampton County Court Records, Order Book 10, 189–91; Surry County Court Records, Deeds, Wills, etc., No. 5, part 2, 287–90.

Nor is it surprising that Virginia's freedmen never again posed a threat to society. Though in later years slavery was condemned because it was thought to compete with free labor, in the beginning it reduced by so much the number of freedmen who would otherwise have competed with each other. When the annual increment of freedmen fell off, the number that remained could more easily find an independent place in society, especially as the danger of Indian attack diminished and made settlement safer at the heads of the rivers or on the Carolina frontier. There might still remain a number of irredeemable, idle, and unruly freedmen, particularly among the convicts whom England exported to the colonies. But the numbers were small enough, so that they could be dealt with by the old expedient of drafting them for military expeditions.[74] The way was thus made easier for the remaining freedmen to acquire property, maybe acquire a slave or two of their own, and join with their superiors in the enjoyment of those English liberties that differentiated them from their black laborers.

A free society divided between large landholders and small was much less riven by antagonisms than one divided between landholders and landless, masterless men. With the freedman's expectations, sobriety, and status restored, he was no longer a man to be feared. That fact, together with the presence of a growing mass of alien slaves, tended to draw the white settlers closer together and to reduce the importance of the class difference between yeoman farmer and large plantation owner.[75]

The seventeenth century has sometimes been thought of as the day of the yeoman farmer in Virginia; but in many ways a stronger case can be made for the eighteenth century as the time when the yeoman farmer came into his own, because slavery relieved the small man of the pressures that had been reducing him to continued servitude. Such an interpretation conforms to the political development of the colony. During the seventeenth century the royally appointed governor's council, composed of the largest property-owners in the colony, had been the most powerful governing body.

[74] Virginia disposed of so many this way in the campaign against Cartagena in 1741 that a few years later the colony was unable to scrape up any more for another expedition. Fairfax Harrison, "When the Convicts Came," *Virginia Magazine of History and Biography,* XXX (July 1922), 250–60, especially 256–57; John W. Shy, "A New Look at Colonial Militia," *William and Mary Quarterly,* XX (April 1963), 175–85. In 1736, Virginia had shipped another batch of unwanted freedmen to Georgia because of a rumored attack by the Spanish. Byrd II to Lord Egmont, July 1736, "Letters of the Byrd Family," *Virginia Magazine of History and Biography,* XXXVI (July 1928), 216–17. Observations by an English traveler who embarked on the same ship suggest that they did not go willingly: "our Lading consisted of all the Scum of Virginia, who had been recruited for the Service of Georgia, and who were ready at every Turn to mutiny, whilst they belch'd out the most shocking Oaths, wishing Destruction to the Vessel and every Thing in her." "Observations in Several Voyages and Travels in America in the Year 1736," *William and Mary Quarterly,* XV (April 1907), 224.
[75] Compare Lyon G. Tyler, "Virginians Voting in the Colonial Period," *William and Mary Quarterly,* VI (July 1897), 7–13.

But as the tide of slavery rose between 1680 and 1720 Virginia moved toward a government in which the yeoman farmer had a larger share. In spite of the rise of Virginia's great families on the black tide, the power of the council declined; and the elective House of Burgesses became the dominant organ of government. Its members nurtured a closer relationship with their yeoman constituency than had earlier been the case.[76] And in its chambers Virginians developed the ideas they so fervently asserted in the Revolution: ideas about taxation, representation, and the rights of Englishmen, and ideas about the prerogatives and powers and sacred calling of the independent, property-holding yeoman farmer—commonwealth ideas.

In the eighteenth century, because they were no longer threatened by a dangerous free laboring class, Virginians could afford these ideas, whereas in Berkeley's time they could not. Berkeley himself was obsessed with the experience of the English civil wars and the danger of rebellion. He despised and feared the New Englanders for their association with the Puritans who had made England, however briefly, a commonwealth.[77] He was proud that Virginia, unlike New England, had no free schools and no printing press, because books and schools bred heresy and sedition.[78] He must have taken satisfaction in the fact that when his people did rebel against him under Bacon, they generated no republican ideas, no philosophy of rebellion or of human rights. Yet a century later, without benefit of rebellions, Virginians had learned republican lessons, had introduced schools and printing presses, and were as ready as New Englanders to recite the aphorisms of the commonwealthmen.

It was slavery, I suggest, more than any other single factor, that had made the difference, slavery that enabled Virginia to nourish representative government in a plantation society, slavery that transformed the Virginia of Governor Berkeley to the Virginia of Jefferson, slavery that made the Virginians dare to speak a political language that magnified the rights of freemen, and slavery, therefore, that brought Virginians into the same commonwealth political tradition with New Englanders. The very institution that was to divide North and South after the Revolution may have made possible their union in a republican government.

Thus began the American paradox of slavery and freedom, intertwined and interdependent, the rights of Englishmen supported on the wrongs of Africans. The American Revolution only made the contradictions more glaring, as the slaveholding colonists proclaimed to a candid world the rights not simply of Englishmen but of all men. To explain the origin of the contra-

[76] John C. Rainbolt, "The Alteration in the Relationship between Leadership and Constituents in Virginia, 1660 to 1720," *William and Mary Quarterly,* XXVII (July 1970), 411–34.
[77] William Berkeley to Richard Nicholls, May 20, 1666, May 4, 1667, Additional Mss. 28, 218, ff. 14–17 (British Museum, London).
[78] Hening, *Statutes,* II, 517.

dictions, if the explanation I have suggested is valid, does not eliminate them or make them less ugly. But it may enable us to understand a little better the strength of the ties that bound freedom to slavery, even in so noble a mind as Jefferson's. And it may perhaps make us wonder about the ties that bind more devious tyrannies to our own freedoms and give us still today our own American paradox.

The Menacing Shadow
of Louis XIV and
the Rage of Jacob Leisler:
The Constitutional Ordeal
of Seventeenth-Century
New York

John M. Murrin

INTRODUCTION

*New York was a complex colony with a tortured history of imperial wars
and bitter factional struggles. For many years, historians looked for explanations of colonial events such as Leisler's Rebellion in the local landscape.
The Leislerian/Anti-Leislerian split has been characterized as a division of
the lower orders against the upper classes, merchants against landowners,
resentful Dutchmen against their English overlords, or simply as a number of self-interested factions competing for power and status. In this mas-
terful analysis, John Murrin takes what now might be called an "Atlantic"
approach, interpreting the event within the context of contemporary religious and political struggles in Europe.*

*Paradoxically, although the conflict Murrin describes revolved around
ideas about "English rights," it was waged within a largely Dutch political*

John M. Murrin, "The Menacing Shadow of Louis XIV and the Rage of Jacob Leisler: The Constitutional Ordeal of Seventeenth-Century New York," in Stephen L. Schechter and Richard B.
Bernstein, eds., *New York and the Union: Contributions to the American Constitutional Experience*
(Albany: New York State Commission on the Bicentennial of the United States Constitution,
1990), pp. 29–71. Reprinted by permission of the New York State Museum, Albany, New York.

Revised version of a lecture co-sponsored by the New York State Commission on the Bicentennial of the United States Constitution and The New Netherland Project, Twelfth Rensse-
laerswyck Seminar, Albany, New York, September 23, 1989.

context. Leisler's fear of Catholics and Louis XIV reminds us that many colonists saw themselves as part of an international historical drama. The fates of Dutch and English Protestants had been linked since the early years of the Reformation. The Glorious Revolution pulled them together into what became two decades of almost continuous warfare against the shared French Catholic enemy. Yet in New York, the one truly Anglo-Dutch society in the Atlantic world, the Glorious Revolution brought only strife and bitterness.

Murrin's analysis uncovers the various religious and political traditions that late-seventeenth-century New Yorkers had to cope with. Their divisions were not inevitable outcomes of their different cultures, he argues, but the result of several contingent and very human factors, most notably of all, Leisler himself. New England and the south made an easy transition from King James to King William and Queen Mary because their societies were far less diverse.

- *What, then, did pluralism do to New York society?*
- *And how does ethnicity figure into the mix?*

The constitutional struggles of seventeenth-century New York may seem remote today. Even from an eighteenth-century perspective they were quite unusual. For Virginia, Massachusetts, and Pennsylvania, we can tell a relatively clean story about the early acceptance of representative institutions and their evolution over time into the era of the American Revolution, the adoption of new state constitutions between 1776 and 1780, and the drafting of the United States Constitution in 1787.

New Yorkers lived through a different history. They had to fight about what others usually took for granted. The ethnic and religious diversity of the population made these struggles quite complex, sometimes as baffling to contemporaries as to later historians who have tried to sort them out. New Yorkers went through a constitutional ordeal in a pluralistic environment. Their experience in the seventeenth century reminds us of other options and other possibilities open to the men and women who settled the mainland colonies. Events did not lead smoothly from the first settlements to 1776 and 1787. This essay explores major aspects of that discontinuity.

I

Jacob Leisler's Rebellion ought to be a simple matter, but it never has been. In June 1689 he assumed the leadership of those New Yorkers who insisted that the colony's government had to repudiate the Roman Catholic Stuart king of England, James II (1685–88), and proclaim its loyalty to James's son-in-law and daughter, the Protestant William, Prince of Orange, and his wife Mary.

News of their coronation as King William III (1689–1702) and Queen Mary II (1689–94) would soon reach the province. While in power, Leisler never lost sight of his highest priority—to hold the colony for William and the Protestant cause. Because of William's triumph in England, the story ought to have a happy ending. Surely the new monarch would be able to distinguish his friends from his enemies in New York and would name a governor who would recognize and accept what the Leislerians had done. Instead, William appointed a government dominated by men who had supported James well into the spring of 1689 and had then been displaced by Leisler. In 1691, these angry and vengeful people returned to New York, resumed office, and hanged Leisler for treason.[1]

If we place these events in an intercolonial context, the puzzle only deepens. In April 1689, Boston set the pace for all other colonies when the town overthrew the autocratic government of Sir Edmund Andros and the Dominion of New England. After a few weeks of hesitation, Massachusetts resumed the forms of its charter government, which James II had superseded with the Dominion in 1686. The other New England colonies soon followed this example. In England William and Mary acquiesced in the resumption of charter government by Connecticut and Rhode Island. They also agreed to accept the legitimacy of the previous history of Massachusetts Bay by negotiating a new charter for that province, which went into effect in 1692 and which recognized the validity of such distinctive institutions as the New England town and the land system. Massachusetts retained an elective assembly and won the right to elect its upper house indirectly. The Crown appointed the governor, all judges, and militia officers. The colony also had to grant religious toleration to all Protestants and could no longer restrict the suffrage to full members of the Congregational Church. Although this new regime would be quite different from the Puritan commonwealth of the seventeenth century, it retained many of its traditional privileges. Maryland, the last colony to overturn its government in 1689, also won approval in England for this political upheaval. It became a royal colony in 1692. Its Catholic dynasty, the Calvert family of lords proprietors, lost power until 1716 when the conversion of an heir to Protestantism prompted the Crown to restore the proprietary regime.

In short, New York really stood out. Its rebellion had close parallels elsewhere. Its result was unique. Only in New York did the English state deliberately crush the very people who had struggled to make the Glorious Revolution a success in the colony. New York got its religious and constitutional moorings thoroughly tangled between 1689 and 1691, with very serious consequences for the colony's later history.[2]

---

[1] For the most recent study of Leisler's Rebellion, see David William Voorhees, " 'In Behalf of the True Protestants Religion': The Glorious Revolution in New York" (Ph.D. dissertation: New York University, 1988).

[2] Important general histories of the Glorious Revolution in America include David S. Lovejoy, *The Glorious Revolution in America* (New York: Harper & Row, Publishers, 1972); and J. M. Sosin,

II

Because Leisler's Rebellion was a major governmental crisis for New York, we must try to sort out the constitutional ideas or assumptions of the major participants. New York was a highly pluralistic society in 1689. Founded as the Dutch colony of New Netherland, it had been conquered by England in 1664. The constitutional traditions of both countries affected the internal development of the province. So also, to a remarkable degree, did events in France.

For much of the seventeenth century, France was the most tolerant country in Western Europe. Only in France did the law protect the public worship of both Catholics and Protestants (Huguenots). By contrast, England persecuted both Protestant dissenters and Catholics for most of the same period, while the Dutch republic usually left Protestant dissenters alone and "connived" at the private—but not public—worship of peaceable Catholics. Most apologists for the French state believed that only royal absolutism made these arrangements possible, and on varying grounds the French monarchy found many admirers and defenders, both Catholic and Protestant. Charles and James, the two sons of King Charles I of England, came to manhood while in exile in France following their father's execution. They both brought back a softened attitude toward the Catholic Church and a deep respect for absolutism and broad religious toleration. Although no informed Protestant could forget the horrors of St. Bartholomew's Day in August 1572, when furious Catholic mobs had tried to exterminate Protestants in Paris and other French cities, Huguenots and Dutch Protestants generally regarded the French state as a political ally in the seventeenth century, at least until the 1670s. Its intervention against Spain in the Thirty Years' War had been decisive, and in the mid-1660s France had aligned with the Dutch republic against England. Even though the political privileges of Huguenots were restricted in the 1620s, they continued to worship freely and openly well into the 1670s, despite some less visible disabilities and pressures to conform.

These French achievements had a potent impact on Protestants in France and elsewhere. They strongly colored even the political thought of French Huguenots and Dutch Protestants, most of whom were quite eager to placate moderate Catholics in France and reluctant—unlike some radical Protestants in England and Scotland—to justify political resistance by the whole body of the people, as against duly constituted magistrates. While it

---

English America and the Revolution of 1688: Royal Administration and the Structure of Provincial Government (Lincoln, Neb.: University of Nebraska Press, 1982). For more specific studies, see Richard R. Johnson, *Adjustment to Empire: The New England Colonies, 1675–1715* (New Brunswick, N.J.: Rutgers University Press, 1981); and Lois Green Carr and David William Jordan, *Maryland's Revolution of Government, 1689–1692* (Ithaca, N.Y.: Cornell University Press, 1974).

lasted, French toleration moderated the demands of Huguenot and Dutch political thinkers and prompted the English court after 1660 to implement something similar to the French model, first in New York, later in England. New York may well have been a testing ground for policies too dangerous to attempt at home. And, when French support for the Dutch republic turned suddenly to war and aggression in 1672, and when French toleration died swiftly and brutally in the 1680s, the consequences in The Netherlands, England, and New York would be dramatic and extremely important. Leisler's Rebellion was only one aspect of a broader transatlantic response to the changing policies of Louis XIV (1642–1715).[3]

Both Leislerians and Anti-Leislerians were Anglo-Dutch coalitions. Both had several contemporary models to draw upon, Dutch and English. Within the seven United Provinces of The Netherlands, the central political tension pitted the regent class against the House of Orange. The regents were an oligarchy of merchant families who dominated the public life of Amsterdam and other major cities and usually controlled the governments of the more commercial provinces and the States General of the republic. By the middle of the seventeenth century, they had developed a coherent ideology of "true liberty." It extolled the benefits of decentralized government and broad religious toleration, even of Roman Catholics. It encouraged the maximum exploitation of commercial markets abroad, mostly by eliminating any regulations that hindered the expansion of trade, and it sought to maintain peaceful relations within Europe. Opposed to the regent class, especially in time of war, stood the House of Orange, whose princes had served for generations as the chief military officer of the republic, the *stadholder* of Holland, the wealthiest province in The Netherlands. Or, to give the office its closest equivalent title in the English world, the prince of Orange was the captain-general of Holland and any other province that similarly honored him.

Since the 1560s the princes of Orange had been a rallying point for international Calvinism under siege from hostile Catholic forces, marshalled first by Spain, later (after 1670) by France. Orthodox Calvinists supported the princes of Orange, demanded the suppression of Catholics at home (and sometimes Protestant dissenters as well), and supported an active war effort against the encircling Catholic powers. As late as the 1660s, Dutch Calvinists knew how to justify their ancestors' revolt against Spain, but they still routinely idealized monarchical over republican forms of government, and they had generated no coherent rationale for defending the peculiar mixture of institutions and practices that the United Provinces had become. Regents suspected that, if the Orangists ever got their way completely, they would turn the stadholderate into an authoritarian Protestant monarchy similar to

---

[3] See Joseph Lecler, *Toleration and the Reformation* (New York: Association Press, 1960), II, 5–323, 475–506; and Quentin Skinner, *The Foundations of Modern Political Thought* (Cambridge: Cambridge University Press, 1978), II, Chaps. 7–9.

those that had already emerged in the Lutheran states of Germany. For that reason the States General, under intense pressure from Oliver Cromwell in England, excluded William III (then a small boy) from the office of *stadholder* in 1654, and the province of Holland abolished the office itself in 1667.

Twice in the seventeenth century, militant Orangists killed the leader of the regent class as a way of reasserting their power. In 1618–19, just as the Thirty Years' War was getting under way and the famous Synod of Dort was defining orthodoxy for Calvinists everywhere, Prince Maurice of Nassau arrested the Grand Pensionary of Holland, Johan van Oldenbarneveldt, accused him of collusion with Spain, tried him for treason, and executed him. In 1672 an angry Orange mob attacked Jan de Witt and his brother Cornelis in The Hague, killed both, desecrated the bodies, and even cannibalized parts of them. On that occasion, the Orangists suspected the De Witts of sympathy for France at a time when the armies of Louis XIV threatened to overrun the republic, and they did succeed in restoring the office of *stadholder* to youthful William III, who had just come of age. Partly because popular elections had no role in the politics of the Dutch republic, mobs provided a quasi-legitimate way of expressing public discontent, usually on behalf of the House of Orange. Dutch New Yorkers, and probably many of the English as well, understood the significance of these chronic struggles between Orangists and regents. By the mid-1670s, William III had indeed become the Protestant world's most powerful symbol of resistance to Catholicism.[4]

England also provided conflicting constitutional models growing out of the era of civil wars and the interregnum between 1640 and 1660. The resistance of the Long Parliament to Charles I became an open war by 1642 and led to the king's execution in 1649. English Puritans, or strict Calvinists (Presbyterians and Congregationalists), and Protestant radicals (Baptists, Quakers, Seekers, Ranters, Muggletonians, Fifth Monarchy Men, and others) strongly supported Parliament while virtually all defenders of episcopacy backed the Crown and the traditional Church of England. Those who resisted the Crown suspected the royal family of absolutist ambitions, something

---

[4] For general studies of The Netherlands, see Simon Schama, *The Embarrassment of Riches: An Interpretation of Dutch Culture in the Golden Age* (New York: Alfred A. Knopf, 1987), esp. Chap. 2; and Pieter Geyl, *The Netherlands in the Seventeenth Century*, 2 vols. (New York: Barnes & Noble Inc., 1961–64). More specialized studies include Jan den Tex, *Oldenbarnevelt*, 2 vols. (Cambridge, Eng.: Cambridge University Press, 1973), esp. II, Chap. 15; Herbert H. Rowen, *John de Witt, Grand Pensionary of Holland, 1625–1672* (Princeton: Princeton University Press, 1978), esp. Chaps. 2, 11, 19, 41; Stephen B. Baxter, *William III and the Defense of European Liberty, 1650–1702* (New York: Harcourt, Brace and World, Inc., 1966); Douglas Nobbs, *Theocracy and Toleration: A Study of the Disputes in Dutch Calvinism from 1600 to 1650* (Cambridge, Eng.: Cambridge University Press, 1938); E. H. Kossmann, "The Development of Dutch Political Theory in the Seventeenth Century," in J. S. Bromley and E. H. Kossman, eds., *Britain and the Netherlands: Papers delivered to the Oxford–Netherlands Historical Conference, 1959* (London: Chatto & Windus, 1960), 91–110; Kossmann, *In Praise of the Dutch Republic: Some Seventeenth-Century Attitudes* (London: Inaugural Lecture, University College, London, May 13, 1963).

that even many royalists feared. The Restoration of Charles II in 1660 complicated these alignments in several ways. By then, Charles and his brother James, duke of York (King James II from 1685 to 1688) preferred religious toleration for both Catholics and Protestant dissenters. Most dissenters favored toleration only of all Protestants. The strongly Anglican Parliament tried to suppress both Catholics and dissenters.[5]

These tensions affected New York more acutely than any other colony because in 1664 Charles II made his brother James lord proprietor of the whole area between the Delaware and Connecticut rivers and dispatched a naval force to the Hudson, which compelled the government of New Netherland to surrender to the invading English. James did in New York what the royal family did not dare attempt in England. Influenced by the example of the French state, he created an absolutist government designed to rule through a fixed code of laws without an elective assembly. And, drawing somewhat more loosely upon French experience, he promised toleration to all Christians.[6]

New York's constitutional struggles became violent and extremely complex after 1664 because of the differing expectations and associations that Dutch and English settlers brought to the colony. Within The Netherlands the forces of dynasticism were Orangist and intolerant. In England the Stuart dynasty favored a broader toleration than did virtually anyone else except the Quakers, but even intolerant Anglicans demanded a continuing role for Parliament in the government of the realm. Dutch Calvinists, while committed to the triumph of militant Protestantism, had no experience with representative government in the way that most English settlers understood that term. But English Puritans had learned to place careful limits on the powers of the monarchy. In America they created colonial governments that lodged ultimate power in the legislature, not the governor.

Within New York, even a simple word like "liberty" could thus mean very different things to different groups. To most Englishmen it included some role for an elective assembly. To most Dutchmen it did not. It suggested generous toleration to the duke's men, most merchants, the Catholic minority, and even many of the Yankees who had left orthodox New England to settle on western Long Island (renamed Queens in 1638). To ortho-

---

[5] For a strong introduction to a vast literature, see J. R. Jones, *Country and Court: England 1658–1714* (Cambridge, Mass.: Harvard University Press, 1978). See also Anne Whiteman, "The Restoration of the Church of England"; Geoffrey F. Nuttall, "The First Nonconformists"; and Roger Thomas, "Comprehension and Indulgence," in Geoffrey F. Nuttall and Owen Chadwick, eds., *From Uniformity to Unity 1662–1962* (London: S.P.C.K., 1962), 19–88, 149–87, and 189–253.

[6] See Michael Kammen, *Colonial New York: A History* (New York: Charles Scribner's Sons, 1975); Oliver A. Rink, *Holland on the Hudson: An Economic and Social History of Dutch New York* (Ithaca, N.Y.: Cornell University Press, 1986); Robert C. Ritchie, *The Duke's Province: A Study of New York Politics and Society, 1664–1691* (Chapel Hill: University of North Carolina Press, 1977); and Joyce D. Goodfriend, "'Too Great a Mixture of Nations': The Development of New York City Society in the Seventeenth Century" (Ph.D. dissertation: University of California at Los Angeles, 1975).

dox Calvinists, Dutch and English, it still implied freedom for the true church to impose its will on the community.

For the first decade after the English conquest, the biggest problem faced by the new government was the loyalty of its population. Governor Richard Nicolls arranged an understanding with Governor John Winthrop, Jr., of Connecticut in which New York tacitly abandoned its claim to the Connecticut River as its eastern boundary while asserting control over all of Long Island, the eastern half of which had been under Connecticut's jurisdiction. These Yankees were used to government by an elective assembly and could not be talked out of their convictions. Nicolls also made ambitious plans to settle English colonists on the mainland south and west of Manhattan, only to learn that James had just given the region between the coast and the Delaware River to two courtiers, John Lord Berkeley and Sir George Carteret, who promptly organized their grant as the colony of New Jersey. This arrangement struck all New York governors as particularly troublesome. As a part of New York, the Jersey hinterland would strengthen the whole colony by attracting English newcomers and expanding trade. As a separate province, it would draw English settlers out of New York and magnify greatly the security problems of the duke's colony.[7]

Their anxieties were not misplaced. When England joined France in attacking The Netherlands in 1672, the Dutch responded by sending a major naval expedition into American waters in 1673. After raiding the tobacco fleet in Chesapeake Bay, it turned north and demanded the surrender of poorly defended Fort James. To the jubilation of the Dutch population, the English garrison gave up as easily as the Dutch had in 1664. The invaders restored New Netherland and renamed the city New Orange and its fortifications Fort Willem Hendrik, both after Prince William. They expelled English settlers unwilling to be loyal to the restored Dutch regime and established a stern, Calvinist government. Then, to the consternation of the population, the Dutch States General returned the province to England at the Treaty of Westminster in 1674. For the second time, New Netherland and its capital city became New York, and Fort William was once again Fort James.[8]

James ruled a Dutch population that did not wish to be English and an English population that desired to be freer than he cared to permit. It was not an auspicious formula for success. In no other part of the English Empire would the Glorious Revolution carry a higher and more ambiguous symbolic impact. In 1688–89, James and William, the two men for whom the fort had been twice named and renamed, were contesting for nothing less than the throne of England.

---

[7] For a strong intercolonial perspective on these events, see Wesley Frank Craven, *The Colonies in Transition, 1660–1713* (New York: Harper & Row, Publishers, 1968), Chaps. 2–3.

[8] Donald G. Shomette and Ronald D. Haslach, *Raid on America: The Dutch Naval Campaign of 1672–1674* (Columbia: University of South Carolina Press, 1988).

III

Before 1689, most of the important constitutional and legal decisions in New York had been made by men who would become Anti–Leislerians. What precedents had they set? What form of government did they prefer? What anxieties did they arouse?

They were, of course, a diverse coalition. The most important elements of it were the duke's men (people who owed their careers to James), a group of wealthy and interrelated Dutch mercantile families, and a growing number of English merchant newcomers who began to achieve prominence in New York City after 1674. Although they worked together as Anti–Leislerians after 1689, these factions reflected a broad spectrum of ideas about government and constitutionalism, and they clashed frequently with one another before the Glorious Revolution.

The duke's men consisted mostly of soldiers, although they also included some civil officials such as Councillors Mathias and William Nicolls and Collector Matthew Plowman. A fair number of them were Roman Catholics, including Plowman, Lieutenant Governor Anthony Brockholls, and Governor Thomas Dongan (1638–88). They believed they had a mandate to maintain order, secure the duke's (later the king's) revenues, and—somewhat more ambiguously—enforce the English Navigation Acts. So long as James demanded autocratic rule, they were prepared to enforce his will. Yet nearly all of them found this role unappealing and disquieting— perhaps even Sir Edmund Andros, governor of the colony from 1674 to 1680 and of the Dominion of New England from 1686 to 1689. In 1675 he may have tried—without success—to persuade the duke to grant an elective assembly to the colony. Brockholls presided over New York's government from 1681 to 1683 when the court of assizes, which had been designed as the principal bulwark of absolutist rule, demanded and finally got an elective assembly. Dongan implemented this concession, and William Nicolls sat in the first assembly. Even after James revoked this concession by 1686, Dongan kept the assembly alive by successive prorogations until 1687, apparently with the hope that he might yet receive permission to summon a new session. From this perspective the absolutism of James was a policy without a constituency. Even the men who implemented it did not believe in it, and on several occasions they sanctioned efforts to transform it in more conventional directions. Yet James's autocratic principles continued to affect New Yorkers in profound ways.[9]

---

[9] The Andros letter to James is not extant, but see duke of York to Edmund Andros, April 6, 1675, in Edmund Bailey O'Callaghan, ed., *Documents relative to the Colonial History of the State of New York* (Albany: Weed, Parsons and Co., 1856–87), III, 230 (hereafter cited as *NY Col. Docs.*). James commended Andros for not encouraging the settlers in their desire for an assembly. I suspect that Andros raised the question with James in the hope of finding greater flexibility.

The crisis of 1689 would force these men to decide to what or whom they were loyal. Their attachment to James was real enough, for they owed him their careers. But as the crisis deepened, they began to realize that they might have to choose between James and the English state. Their natural instinct was to avoid any decision of this kind as long as possible. Both Andros in Boston and Captain Francis Nicholson, his lieutenant governor in New York, first tried to suppress the news that William had landed in England. Boston overthrew Andros before he could reverse himself. Nicholson reacted somewhat differently.

On March 1, Nicholson learned from Philadelphia that William had landed in England, that James had tried to flee to France, and that London had welcomed the prince of Orange. He passed on the news to Andros and tried to suppress it in New York. Neither man yet knew what constitutional decisions were being made in England or that James had actually reached France in a second escape attempt. Who was king? Had perhaps a regency been established to rule in James's name while preserving the succession unaltered? To make a wrong choice on this extremely sensitive issue could ruin a man's career. It seemed far wiser to do nothing irrevocable until the situation became clearer.[10]

After the overthrow of Andros in Boston, Nicholson made his own decision. A loyal servant of James would have prepared for another Anglo–Dutch war (the fourth since 1652). The earliest news of William's invasion stimulated some talk of this kind. Stephanus Van Cortlandt, a member of the council and mayor of New York City, expected war with The Netherlands as of January 1689.[11] As late as April, Robert Livingston, somewhat isolated in the upper Hudson valley, told Albany Sheriff Richard Pretty that "there was a p'sell of Rebels gon out of Holland into England, & the prince of orringe was the hed of them & he might see how [he] got out a gaine, & should come to same end as Mulmoth [i.e., James, duke of Monmouth] did."[12] By late April, a servant of the English state would have

---

[10] See the deposition of Zechariah Whitpaine before the Pennsylvania council, February 24, 1688/89, in *Minutes of the Provincial Council of Pennsylvania from the Organization to the Termination of the Proprietary Government* (Philadelphia: John Stevens & Co., 1852–53), I, 245–47 (this series is often cited by the binding title, *Colonial Records of Pennsylvania*). Whitpaine left England just after hearing of James's capture during his first attempt to flee. In the late 1640s, Charles I had been held captive for more than a year before his trial and execution by the army and the Rump Parliament. The implications of James's capture had to seem extremely murky to officials in the colonies, such as Nicholson when he received a copy of Whitpaine's deposition on March 1. New-York Historical Society, *Collections* (1868), 241–43. (Hereafter cited as NYHS *Coll.*)

[11] Stephanus Van Cortlandt to Maria Van Rensselaer, January 21, 1688/89, in Albert J. F. Van Laer, ed., *Correspondence of Maria Van Rensselaer, 1669–1689* (Albany: University of the State of New York, 1935), 188–89.

[12] Richard Pretty to Jacob Milborne, January 15, 1689–90, in Edmund Bailey O'Callaghan, ed., *Documentary History of the State of New York*, octavo edn. (Albany: Weed, Parsons and Co., 1849–51), II, 60. (Hereafter cited as *NY Doc. Hist.*) In 1685 James II had crushed the rising of the duke of Monmouth, a bastard son of Charles II who had considerable support among radical Whigs.

expected war with France, not The Netherlands. Spurred to action by a rising of the New England settlers in Suffolk County on eastern Long Island,
Nicholson tried to prepare New York for a conflict with France, informed the
English secretary of state (rather than someone still in direct contact with
James II) what he was doing and why, and created an expanded council of
civil and military officers to give him advice and support and to preserve the
peace during the crisis.[13]

But, having secured this support at the end of April, Nicholson and three
councillors continued to make nearly all important decisions themselves
during the critical month of May while the ferment began to spread from
Long Island into the city. When Collector Plowman became an issue, they
pledged that all revenues paid to him would be used to strengthen the city's
defense. Their credibility disintegrated anyway, partly because they never
formally proclaimed William and Mary, partly because they could not regard
the New England uprising as anything less than rebellion and made open efforts to keep in touch with Andros. To suspicious opponents, these attitudes
had to seem pro-French. To Nicholson and his followers, hesitation was mere
prudence. They would act to proclaim someone when the English government so ordered and not before. They were not about to repudiate Andros,
who in their eyes was still governor of the Dominion of New England, of
which New York was but one portion.

With three centuries of hindsight on their predicament, we can understand both their caution and their rage when finally challenged. Nicholson invited the city militia to share with his soldiers the responsibility for guarding
Fort James at the southern tip of Manhattan. But when the militia continued
to make other demands that seemed to question the loyalty of the garrison,
Nicholson made a fatal error. The twenty-eight-year-old commander lost his
temper in front of a fifty-two-year-old Dutch militia lieutenant, Hendrik
Cuyler, and threatened to burn down the city if the militia did not stop pes-
tering him. Because Nicholson had been part of the English garrison of Tangiers that had burned the city before withdrawing a few years before, this
outburst had to seem terrifying. Within days, Nicholson's power collapsed,
and the militia took complete charge of the fort. Most of the city refused to believe that anyone appointed by James had really abandoned his cause.[14]

---

[13] See "Declaration of the Freeholders of Suffolk county, Long Island," May 3, 1689, in
O'Callaghan, ed., *NY Col. Docs.* III, 577. They sent a deputation of three men to the city "to demand the Fort to be delivered into the hands of such persons as the country shall chose." For
the government's actions from April 26 to May 15, 1689, see NYHS *Coll.* (1868), 244–62, especially the letter "to the principall secretary off State and the Secretary off plantacons" on May
15, pp. 259–62.

[14] For the Leislerian version of this incident, see O'Callaghan, ed., *NY Doc. Hist.* II, 10–13. Nichol-
son denied that he threatened to burn the city, but he probably did say, "I rather would see the
Towne on fire than to be commanded by you." Stephanus Van Cortlandt to Sir Edmund Andros,
July 9, 1689, in O'Callaghan, *NY Col. Docs.* III, 593–94. For a study of Nicholson including the

Prominent Dutch mercantile families also formed part of the Anti–Leislerian coalition. They resembled the regent class of The Netherlands in their preference for the broadest possible commercial opportunities and full religious toleration. They did not hesitate to work closely with the Roman Catholics in the duke's service. Probably they were more interested in the liberties of the cities of New York and Albany than in any larger questions about the desirability of representative institutions for the province as a whole. Although they never shed many of their underlying Dutch values, these families—the Philipse, Van Cortlandt, Bayard, Schuyler, and Van Rensselaer clans stood out—were anglicizers, people of Dutch background who were quite prepared to accept the social and political demands of English rule. Because of their behavior during the Dutch reconquest of 1673, they knew that they had to demonstrate their complete loyalty to the English state. They tried to master the conquerors' language and teach it to their children. Their religious commitments were rather flexible. When Anglicans finally organized Trinity Church in the 1690s, Nicholas Bayard, Tunis DeKey, Brandt Schuyler, and Stephanus Van Cortlandt were among those who joined. Such men were willing to serve autocratic regimes under both the Dutch and the English. They also held office from 1683 to 1685 and after 1691 when the colony had a representative assembly. In short, they seemed to take it for granted that they had a right to rule and reacted ferociously when that claim was challenged, especially by lesser Dutchmen.[15]

The least-studied portion of the Anti–Leislerian coalition was a bloc of English newcomers who entered the province in the 1670s and 1680s. Most of them were merchants, although some became lawyers or bookkeepers, and eventually many of them bought land outside the city. Other than Lewis Morris and George Heathcote, few of them have aroused the curiosity of anyone besides genealogists. Yet such men as William Pinhorne, Edward Antill, and John Robinson played important roles in the politics of the era. They believed that New York would never thrive until it guaranteed traditional English liberties to all settlers. Above all, they demanded an assembly and insisted on the principle of no taxation without representation. Without concessions of this kind, they feared, New York might suffer a fatal drain of scarce Englishmen to the freer societies then taking shape in East and West New Jersey and Pennsylvania. In 1676 twenty-five of them threatened to leave the province when New York City imposed a municipal tax upon them.[16] When Andros returned to England in January 1681 after neglecting

---

Tangiers incident, see Stephen Saunders Webb, "The Strange Career of Francis Nicholson," *William and Mary Quarterly*, 3rd ser., 23 (1966): 513–48.

[15] See Randall H. Balmer, *A Perfect Babel of Confusion: Dutch Religion and English Culture in the Middle Colonies* (New York: Oxford University Press, 1989), esp. Chap. 2.

[16] Herbert L. Osgood, ed., *Minutes of the Common Council of the City of New York, 1675–1776* (New York: Dodd, Mead and Company, 1905), I, 25–26.

to renew a revenue act that had expired in November, the merchants led a well-organized tax strike and won the support of the duke's own court of assizes, which sent James a formal petition for an assembly. As of 1681 these reformers still regarded the anglicizing Dutch elite as their principal enemies, families who monopolized too many offices and somehow managed to keep the colony's trade oriented toward Amsterdam instead of England. But by 1683 the duke's men, the anglicizing Dutch elite, and the English merchants were all willing to support the reform program adopted by the province's first elective legislature when it met in October of that year.[17]

IV

The reformers of 1683 had important political allies who would favor the overthrow of Nicholson in 1689, indeed serve as the principal catalyst to that upheaval—the New England population of Long Island and what is now Westchester and The Bronx. These people had been agitating for an assembly since the English conquest of 1664, and their town meetings joined lustily in this call during the turbulent year of 1681.[18]

By then they had more leverage than ever. The duke, who no longer made any effort to deny his conversion to Rome, was in deep political trouble in England where the newly organized Whig party was trying to bar him from succession to the throne. Within the colony prospects began to seem truly alarming between 1680 and 1683. Before leaving the colony, Andros tried to reassert New York's power over East New Jersey by arresting Governor Philip Carteret and trying him in New York for usurping the duke's authority. To the mortification of Andros, the largely English jury of the court of assizes acquitted Carteret in 1680 at about the same time that a Whig attorney general in England upheld important claims of West New Jersey settlers against the duke and his New York governor.[19]

---

[17] Robert C. Ritchie, "London Merchants, the New York Market, and the Recall of Sir Edmund Andros," *New York History*, 57 (1976): 5–30; Peter R. Christoph and Florence A. Christoph, eds., *Records of the Court of Assizes for the Colony of New York, 1665–1682* (Baltimore: Genealogical Publishing Co., Inc., 1983), 271–77. (Hereafter cited as *Recs. Ct. of Assizes.*)

[18] For an interpretation of the period that makes the Long Island towns and their demands the center of the story, see Jerome R. Reich, *Leisler's Rebellion: A Study of Democracy in New York, 1664–1720* (Chicago: University of Chicago Press, 1953), esp. Chaps. 1–2.

[19] William A. Whitehead, ed., *Documents relating to the Colonial History of the State of New Jersey*, 1st ser. (Newark: Daily Journal Establishment; Trenton: The John L. Murphy Publishing Company, 1880–1949), I, 292–319, 323–24 (hereafter cited as *NJ Archives*); Christoph and Christoph, eds., *Recs. Ct. of Assizes*, 260–66. See also John E. Pomfret, *The Province of East New Jersey 1609–1702: The Rebellious Proprietary* (Princeton: Princeton University Press, 1962), Chap. 6. On James's political difficulties in England, see J. R. Jones, *The First Whigs: The Politics of the Exclusion Crisis, 1678–1683* (London: Oxford University Press, 1961).

The Quakers knew how to use this opportunity, and their actions transformed the political climate of the Middle Atlantic colonies. In 1674 John Lord Berkeley, one of the New Jersey proprietors, sold his claim to a group of Quakers, who then arranged with Sir George Carteret, the other original proprietor, to divide the province into two distinct colonies, Carteret's East New Jersey and the Quakers' West New Jersey. The families settling West New Jersey next began to implement, by stages, their Concessions and Agreements of 1677, the most radical constitutional system put into practice in any English colony before the American Revolution. This document lodged most political power in a legislature of one hundred delegates, who in turn would choose a weak plural executive of ten men. In the court system, juries were to decide both fact and law while judges merely presided and responded to queries, when anybody bothered to put one to them. The Concessions imposed no military obligations on the settlers, guaranteed full toleration, and offered land on generous terms.[20]

In 1681, William Penn, one of the West Jersey proprietors, intensified the pressure on New York when he obtained his proprietary charter for a colony on the west bank of the Delaware and put an enormous amount of energy into drafting the First Frame of Government for the province. It was less bracing than the West Jersey Concessions, but it still had plenty of potential for enticing Englishmen away from New York. Penn agreed to modifications in early 1683 that became known as the Second Frame of Government, or Charter of Liberties. Meanwhile, Quakers had also gained control of the proprietary claim to East New Jersey, for which they drafted a text, called the Fundamental Constitutions, in 1683. Since the conquest, New York's governors had always worried about the superior liberties of New Englanders as a source of potential discontent within New York. Now the province was surrounded on three sides by much freer societies.[21]

This intercolonial context explains the utter collapse of the duke's absolutist regime almost as soon as Andros left the colony in early 1681. Nobody in authority did anything to punish merchants who refused to pay customs duties. Instead the court of assizes tried and convicted the duke's collector for insisting upon their payment, and then it joined in the popular demand

---

[20] The only accurate modern text of the West Jersey Concessions is in Mary Maples Dunn, Richard S. Dunn, *et al.*, eds., *The Papers of William Penn* (Philadelphia: University of Pennsylvania Press, 1981–86), I, 387–416. See also John E. Pomfret, *The Province of West Jersey, 1609–1702: A History of the Origins of an American Colony* (Princeton: Princeton University Press, 1956), esp. Chaps. 6–7; and *The West Jersey Concessions and Agreements of 1676/77: A Round Table of Historians*, New Jersey Historical Commission, *Occasional Papers Number 1* (Trenton, 1979).

[21] See Jean R. Soderlund, ed., *William Penn and the Founding of Pennsylvania, 1680–1684: A Documentary History* (Philadelphia: University of Pennsylvania Press, 1983), especially 37–50, 93–140, 265–74; and Aaron Learning and Jacob Spicer, eds., *The Grants, Concessions, and Original Constitutions of the Province of New Jersey . . .* , 2d edn. (Somerville, N.J.: Honeyman and Company, 1881), 153–66.

for an assembly. New York thus became swept into the extraordinary ferment of constitutional experimentation that threatened to intoxicate the entire Middle Atlantic region. The immediate result was the summoning of a
legislature to draft and implement the province's own Charter of Liberties in
1683.[22]

Governor Dongan issued election writs shortly after his arrival in August 1683. They called for the choice of eighteen representatives, nine to be
elected directly, nine indirectly. Oddly, in the predominantly Dutch portions
of the province where the settlers had little familiarity with English general
elections by the assembled freeholders and freemen, eight representatives
were chosen directly by the free holders, four indirectly by committeemen
selected in their individual towns, who then met to name representatives. In
the heavily English constituencies, five were selected indirectly, only one directly. Quite possibly Dongan was trying to expand English influence within
such heavily Dutch communities as New York City and Esopus, where in
fact at least three of those elected were English, and to reduce the impact of
ordinary New Englanders from Long Island and Westchester. When the as-
semblymen finally convened in late October, their first item of legislation
was New York's Charter of Liberties. The second, James's price for the Charter of Liberties, was a permanent revenue act designed to meet all ordinary
costs of government.[23]

This achievement ended absolutism in New York, at least for a heady
two-year period, but the Charter of Liberties was a much more cautious document than its counterparts in the Jerseys and Pennsylvania. Unlike the annual elections held in New England (semi-annual in Connecticut), West Jersey, and Pennsylvania, or the staggered triennial elections mandated for East
Jersey, the New York Charter of Liberties required only that a *session* of the
assembly meet every three years. Although it gave the choice of future as-
semblymen to the freeholders and freemen of the colony, it said nothing
about the frequency of elections. Yet it did include strong guarantees for
such civil liberties as trial by jury, equality before the law, and a ban against
quartering soldiers in private homes during peacetime. Some provisions, including a clause protecting the dower rights of women, were copied directly
from an East Jersey statute of the same year.

---

[22] See Christoph and Christoph, eds., *Recs. Ct. of Assizes*, 271–77.

[23] Indirect elections prevailed in the three ridings of Long Island and Westchester, among the
communities along the Esopus River, and on Martha's Vineyard and its dependencies. Direct
elections occurred in New York City, Staten Island, Albany, Schenectady, and Pemaquid. For the
writs, see *NY Col. Docs.* XIV, 770–71. For an attempt to reconstruct the membership of the assembly, see John M. Murrin, "English Rights as Ethnic Aggression: The English Conquest, the
Charter of Liberties of 1683, and Leisler's Rebellion in New York," in William Pencak and Conrad Edick Wright, eds., *Authority and Resistance in Early New York* (New York: New-York Historical Society, 1988), 56–94. See also Charles Z. Lincoln, ed., *The Colonial Laws of New York from the
Year 1664 to the Revolution* (Albany: James B. Lyon, State Printer, 1894–96), I, 111–21.

The charter became most innovative in defining the religious rights of settlers. All Christians received the freedom to worship with their coreligionists. Subject to approval by two-thirds of the voters, any town on Long Island could levy a tax for the support of the ministry. Religious minorities on Long Island, and all Christian denominations elsewhere in the province, could establish legally enforceable contractual relations between a congregation and its minister. In effect, the government was willing to underwrite the support of any minister whose congregation so desired, a system likely to antagonize only Quakers and Jews, and then only if they lived on Long Island. In full operation it would have anticipated freedom of religion as practiced in modern Canada, rather than the separation of church and state that finally took hold in the United States.[24]

The assembly met again in 1684 and, after new elections occasioned by the death of Charles II, also in 1685. The 1685 choices marked the only true general election in the colony's entire history before the Glorious Revolution—the only occasion, that is, on which freeholders and freemen in all constituencies had an opportunity to vote directly for their representatives. In their three meetings, Dongan's assemblies passed an ambitious legislative program that included a generous present to Dongan and the full imposition of English law even upon the most heavily Dutch portions of the colony. Dongan also granted corporate charters to the cities of New York and Albany in 1686, empowering them to elect their aldermen and common councilmen.[25]

Only after the assembly session of 1685 did the colony learn that James, now king, had approved the permanent revenue act but disallowed the Charter of Liberties. New York's reformers had asked to be as free as their neighbors in other English colonies. As the grand jury at the court of assizes put it in June 1681, New Yorkers wished to be placed "upon Equall Ground with our Fellow Brethren and Subjects of the Realme of England In our Neighbouring Plantacons."[26] James had another idea. He made the province's neighbors as unfree as New Yorkers had been before 1683. The Dominion of New England, which by 1688 included New York and both Jerseys, drew directly upon the absolutist principles in use in New York before the tax strike of 1681 and brought in Andros, a former New York governor, to implement them.

---

[24] See John M. Murrin, ed., "The New York Charter of Liberties, 1683 and 1691," in Stephen L. Schechter, ed., *Roots of the Republic* (Madison, Wis.: Madison House, for New York State Commission on the Bicentennial of the United States Constitution, 1990). Although the Charter of Liberties did not officially recognize the religious rights of Jews, they too enjoyed toleration under James.

[25] For all of Dongan's legislation, see Lincoln, ed., *The Colonial Laws of New York* I, 111–77. See also Mrs. Schuyler Van Rensselaer, *History of the City of New York in the Seventeenth Century* (New York: The Macmillan Company, 1909), II, Chap. 23. For the Albany charter, see Joel Munsell, *Annals of Albany* (Albany: J. Munsell, 1850–59), II, 62–87.

[26] Christoph and Christoph, eds., *Recs. Ct. of Assizes*, 275.

Nevertheless, one huge fact does stand out about the men who agitated for, passed, and implemented the Charter of Liberties. New Englanders aside, virtually none of them would support Jacob Leisler in 1689.

V

The Leislerians were in no sense an organized group in New York before 1689. If we ask what stand future Leislerians had taken during the province's long struggle between absolutism and participatory government, the most interesting finding is that they had not taken part in the contest. They erupted on the scene in May 1689 as angry and frightened supporters of William and the Protestant cause. In trying to prevent subversion by dangerous papist forces, they played the classic Dutch role of an Orange party in New York politics. They soon had their local *stadholder*, too—Captain Jacob Leisler, a wealthy merchant, ship captain, and former army officer from a distinguished Continental European family of renowned ministers, bankers, and lawyers.[27]

Leisler was the highest ranking militia officer willing to assume command of Fort James, which was once again renamed Fort William. Within New York City and western Long Island, those who rallied to Leisler were disproportionately Dutch, the sort of people that the reformers of 1683 had hoped to transform into Englishmen or swamp with English newcomers attracted by the guarantees of the Charter of Liberties. As of June 1689, some of them—but not Leisler—hoped that the Glorious Revolution would lead to a full restoration of Dutch rule in New York.[28] Like his principal opponents, he too chose to be loyal to the English state—they despite the triumph of William of Orange, he because of it.

The English population of New York City overwhelmingly sided against Leisler. Virtually all of the exceptions were men who had chosen to support the restored Dutch regime in 1673–74.[29] The fondness of English merchants for English liberty had not abated. As early as May 1689, several weeks before the militia took over the fort, some of them refused to pay "any Customs and other duties, as illegally establised [*sic*]," Nicholson reported to England.[30] At the end of the month, Leisler also refused to pay customs, but his motive was different. He was willing "to pay the Customs to such as should be legally qualified to receive them, which the Papist Plowman was not."[31] He objected to the religion of the collector, not to taxation without consent.

[27] David William Voorhees, "European Ancestry of Jacob Leisler," *New York Genealogical and Biographical Record*, 120 (1989): 193–202.
[28] Nicholas Bayard's journal for June 3, 1689, in O'Callaghan, ed., *NY Col. Docs.* III, 639.
[29] For a fuller development of this point, see Murrin, "English Rights as Ethnic Aggression."
[30] Nicholson and the New York Council to the Lords ("Board") of Trade, May 15, 1689, in O'Callaghan, ed., *NY Col. Docs.* III, 575.
[31] *Loyalty Vindicated from the Reflections of a Virulent Pamphlet* . . . (1698), in Charles M. Andrews, ed., *Narratives of the Insurrections, 1675–1690* (New York: Charles Scribner's Sons, 1915), 380–81.

Yet Leisler clearly hoped to unite sincere English Protestants behind his leadership. As he explained in July, his own militia company of one hundred men had been so worked upon by their opponents that by May 31 when they seized the fort their strength had fallen to about forty—a highly cosmopolitan forty. Twenty-five had been born in New York, presumably in the 1660s or earlier and were no doubt mostly Dutch. Eight were born in England, two were French Huguenots, two were Swiss, four were Hollanders, "and I a germane." He then related a most revealing incident:[32]

> here is one merchant borne in old England Joint with us & chosen by one company to represent them, they have stopt his horse & threatened his persone that our burgers will not trust him to their mercy but watches his house with one centry, which is s[ai]d high treason by them [Leisler's opponents], they have scattered them to all parts to incense the people with abominable lees [i.e., lies] making them beleeve that the people are abused by the dutch[,] that i have the fort for the french[,] have listed [i.e., mustered] 25 french[,] that I & my officers are continually drunk & in drunken fitts commits a great dale of insolvency.

This incident requires amplification. Despite Leisler's attempt to unite all Protestants regardless of ethnic background, and despite the explicit effort of one company to use an English merchant as its spokesman, the militia of the city at large would not let the man function in that capacity. The English merchants, who all along had been the city's most consistent advocates of English constitutional liberties, were alienated at the very start of the upheaval, not through any design of Leisler's but through pressures and resentments welling up from below among the Dutch militiamen. Whatever Leisler wished the struggle to be, the English merchants saw it as an ethnic explosion in which they were likely to become the most conspicuous victims. When Leisler challenged a group of them in late June 1689, "threatning before a weeke was to an end to secure them all," his outburst "occasioned severall English merchants & Gentlemen for safety of their lives to depart this Citty."[33] The refusal of some of them to pay customs in the spring of 1689 suggests that they could have been mobilized in a broad coalition designed to resist the Dominion of New England. Ethnic antagonisms made such unity impossible. This perception drove them into alliance with their enemies of the 1670s, James's officeholding clique and the anglicizing Dutch elite.

In expelling the English merchants from their coalition, the Leislerians were also cutting themselves off from the best possible sources available to

---

Although this explanation was made public nine years after the event, I see no reason to doubt it. In one of Leisler's earliest justifications of his actions, he complained that although Plowman "is a rank papist, I cannot get the other Captanes to resolve to turne him out but acts still as before." Leisler to the governor and committee of safety at Boston, June 4, 1689, in O'Callaghan, ed., *NY Doc. Hist.* II, 3–4.

[32] Leisler to William Jones of New Haven, July 10, 1689, in O'Callaghan, ed., *NY Doc. Hist.* II, 9.

[33] Nicholas Bayard's journal, in O'Callaghan, ed., *NY Col. Docs.* III, 601–02.

them for one critical task. Somebody had to present an effective defense of the New York revolution in England. Who else could do it? Leisler never sponsored any but the briefest justifications in the first year of the upheaval. Even though his competence with the English language has been underrated by most historians, he was not fluent enough to become a serious polemicist. Of the other militia captains, Charles Lodwyck was a highly anglicized Dutch merchant who had recently moved to New York from London. He commanded the English language well enough to prepare a paper for the Royal Society in London a few years later, and like Leisler he tried to stamp out expressions of ethnic contempt in his militia company. He also had a real interest in preserving traditional English liberties. In an effort to discredit the arbitrary rule of Nicholson's regime, he provided the revolutionary government in July 1689 with a sworn deposition. He had heard Nicholson claim, he testified, that New Yorkers "could but account ourselves as a conquered people, and therefore we could not so much claim rights and privileges as Englishmen in England but that the prince might lawfully govern us by his own will and appoint what laws he pleases among us." By emphasizing this critical item in the argument for absolutism, Lodwyck indicated that he probably understood English law somewhat better than Leisler. Yet by early 1690 at the latest, he transferred his loyalties to the Anti–Leislerians.[34]

Leisler's most prominent English officeholder was Samuel Edsall, four of whose sons-in-law were important Leislerians. Although Edsall began his career as a hatmaker, he was wealthy by 1689 and owned property in Hackensack, Queens, and New York City. He had also shown strong signs of assimilating into the Dutch community. He acquired burgher rights in New Amsterdam years before the English conquest, and when the English fleet arrived in 1664, it treated him as a Dutchman. He supported the restored

[34] Lodwyck was admitted to the Dutch Reformed Church in New York City in 1685 by transfer from the Dutch Church in London. After a long career in New York, he died in London about 1724. *New York Genealogical and Biographical Record* 59 (1928), 71; *id.* 40 (1909), 125. On May 31, 1689, his role in the uprising rivalled Leisler's. He was the captain who demanded and received the keys to Fort James from Nicholson. Stephanus Van Cortlandt to Sir Edmund Andros, July 9, 1689, in O'Callaghan, ed., *NY Col. Docs.* III, 594. In the next few days he was systematically collecting news as it arrived from abroad and sat with Leisler to sift through this information and interrogate newcomers. *Ibid.*, 586, 587. In July 1689, his militia company agreed to fine any member "who shall rail at any one or make any distinction in Nationality or otherwise." NYHS *Coll.* (1868), 294. For his deposition of July 25, 1689, against Nicholson, see *ibid.*, 295. Yet by early 1690 he was in Boston where on January 25 he joined with the moderate royalists of Massachusetts, many of whom were Anglicans, in petitioning William for a royal government. Robert E. Moody and Richard C. Simmons, eds., *The Glorious Revolution in Massachusetts: Selected Documents, 1689–1692* (Boston: Colonial Society of Massachusetts, 1988), 406–07. At least from that point on, his political affiliation remained Anti–Leislerian, prompting Jacob Milborne to question Lodwyck's religious orthodoxy. William Milborne, Jacob's brother and a Baptist minister in Boston, replied that Lodwyck was sound. William Milborne to Jacob Milborne, February 17, 1689/90, in O'Callaghan, ed., *NY Doc. Hist.* II, 72. Lodwyck's contribution to the Royal Society has been published as "New York in 1692," NYHS *Coll.*, 2nd ser., 2 (1849): 241–50.

Dutch regime in 1673–74. At least two of his four wives were Dutch, and most of his children were raised in the Dutch Reformed Church. No doubt he was thoroughly bilingual by 1689. Yet his political actions before that year made him an extremely awkward spokesman for English constitutional principles. In the public life of East New Jersey, he had consistently supported authoritarian policies and the proprietary governor against the assembly, especially in the dramatic confrontations of 1672 and 1681. The very assembly of 1683 that approved the East Jersey Fundamental Constitutions also demanded Edsall's arrest and trial for "evil and illegal practices" that tended to disturb the public peace. Although the charges were eventually dropped, the assembly clearly regarded him as a menace to the constitutional liberties of the province and hoped to bar him and his associates from office for life. Edsall's prominence on Leisler's council could in no way reassure settlers interested in securing their English liberties.[35]

One other Englishman, Jacob Milborne, might have acted as a Leislerian spokesman in England. After serving as an apprentice in Hartford and Barbados (where he met Lewis and Richard Morris before they moved to New York), he worked from 1668 to 1672 as a bookkeeper to Thomas Delavall, a prominent New Yorker who sat on the provincial council for several years. Milborne became a merchant, and on at least one occasion he represented a client as an attorney before the court of assizes. In 1676, he joined Leisler's fight to guarantee the orthodoxy of the Dutch Reformed Church of Albany against the interference of Andros. Two years later, Andros arrested him for refusing to report to the governor after returning to the colony from a business trip. Milborne pursued Andros to London, sued him for false arrest in 1681, and collected £45. That activity kept him out of the colony during the tax strike that led to the summoning of the 1683 assembly, but Milborne returned to New York about that time and married Samuel Edsall's daughter Johanna before sailing for Rotterdam in 1686. His family had taken radical political stands in England during the civil wars, and his brother William was accused of treason in Bermuda in 1678.

Jacob Milborne probably could have defended the New York revolution in London, and his family contacts may even have been strong enough to get him a hearing. But he was still in Rotterdam on business when the uprising

[35] See especially the genealogy of Samuel Edsall by Thomas Henry Edsall in *New York Genealogical and Biographical Record* 13 (1882), 191–96. See also NYHS *Coll.* 18 (1885), 23 (his burgher rights in New Amsterdam, 1657); O'Callaghan, ed., *NY Col. Docs.* III: 75 (Edsall required to take an oath of allegiance to the conquering English in 1664); *Records of the Reformed Dutch Churches of Hackensack and Schraanlenburgh, New Jersey,* I, Pt. 1 (New York: Holland Society of New York, 1891), *passim;* Whitehead, ed., *NJ Archives,* 1st ser., XIII, 53. Edsall's East Jersey career can be traced through Pomfret, *The Province of East New Jersey.* A Connecticut deputation to New York, which commended "Loyall Mr. Samuell Edsall & other good worthy and Loyall gentlemen," obviously had a favorable opinion of him but probably knew little or nothing about his public actions in East New Jersey, Connecticut delegates to Jacob Leisler, June 26, 1689, in O'Callaghan, ed., *NY Doc. Hist.* II, 17.

occurred and did not reach New York until August 25, 1689, a few days after
Joost Stol sailed for England as the agent of the committee of safety. Leisler
did select Milborne as his agent of choice in 1690, once he realized that Stol's
mission had failed, but events in Albany seemed so pressing that Leisler decided to keep him in the province, a change that permitted the recently widowed Milborne to marry Leisler's daughter Mary. Instead of explaining New
York's revolution to London, he spent much of 1689 and 1690 debating it
with the burghers of Albany.[36]

Leisler himself wrote to the king several times in 1689 to explain events
in New York. The letters reflect a confident tone that the king would approve
what the Leislerians did in the province on his behalf, but in fact William
never replied. As the news filtering back from England became more ominous in 1690, Leisler wrote to Bishop Gilbert Burnet and the earl of Shrewsbury to enlist their support, but he received only one reply that we know of,
and it was not very helpful. It instructed him to turn over to the incoming
governor copies of all papers relating to the proposals carried to England by
a second Leislerian agent in 1690. Presumably he would make all appropriate decisions. Although interesting on other grounds, none of these communications tells us anything new about Leisler's constitutional preferences.[37]

What then were the constitutional ideas of the Leislerians? They said little
on the subject and were often maddeningly vague, especially in comparison
with New Englanders defending their own overthrow of Andros. In an early
statement, for example, the Massachusetts revolutionaries denounced the "Illegal and Arbitrary Power" embodied in the Dominion government and asked
William and Mary that they not be "left without our share in that Universal
Restoration of Charters and English Liberties; Which the whole Nation is at
this Day made Happy withall."[38] In a word, they expected the restoration of

[36] The fullest autobiographical statement of Milborne's that has yet come to light is "The Information of Jacob Milborne of London Merchant," January 6, 1679/80, Rawlinson Mss A, 175, fol.
83, Bodleian Library, Oxford University. My thanks to Robert C. Ritchie for pointing it out to me
and providing me with a copy. See also, Christoph and Christoph, eds., *Recs. Ct. of Assizes*, 127;
O'Callaghan, ed., *NY Col. Docs.* III, 300–01; and Voorhees, "'In Behalf of the True Protestants Religion,'"450–52. For Leisler's intention to send Milborne to England in 1690, see Leisler to the
earl of Shrewsbury, June 23, 1690; and Leisler and the council to same, October 20, 1690, in
O'Callaghan, ed., *NY Col Docs.* III, 733, 751.
[37] Leisler to William and Mary, August 20, 1689; to the king, January 7, 1689/90; to Bishop
Gilbert Burnet, January 7, 1689/90; to the king, March 3, 1689/90; to Burnet, March 3, 1689/90;
to the earl of Shrewsbury, June 23, 1690; to the king, October 20, 1690; to Shrewsbury, October
20, 1690, in O'Callaghan, ed., *NY Col. Docs.* III, 614–16, 653–54, 654–57, 700, 700–02, 731–33, 751,
751–54. For the response of the English government, see lords of the council to Governor Henry
Sloughter, October 17, 1690, *ibid.*, 750; and the petition of Jacob Leisler and others to Governor
Sloughter, n.d. (probably March 1691), in O'Callaghan, ed., *NY Doc. Hist.* II, 360. The English
privy councillors almost certainly did not realize that they were authorizing Leisler's execution
by conferring full discretionary powers on Sloughter.
[38] Massachusetts Council of Safety to the King and Queen, May 20, 1689, in Moody and Simmons, eds., *The Glorious Revolution in Massachusetts*, 77–79.

the Massachusetts Charter of 1629, which had been abrogated by court action in England in 1684. In pursuit of this objective they made strenuous efforts to mobilize public opinion on their behalf on both sides of the Atlantic.[39]

In sharp contrast to the Boston pattern, at no point did the Leislerians request the New York equivalent of the restoration of the Massachusetts charter, which would have meant a return to government under the Charter of Liberties. Instead their enemies began to make these demands, and in 1691 they would try to carry them out.

Yet the Leislerians did issue a few statements about the kind of political future they desired for New York. The militia, in its first pronouncement on May 31 right after taking possession of Fort James, complained of living "thes many years under a wicked arbitrarie Power execissed by our Late popish governr Coll Dongan & severall of his wicked Creaturs and Pensionaris" and affirmed their dedication to "our Libertie, propertie and ye Laws." But the statement drew only one negative conclusion—that the militia were "Entirely Opposed to papists and their Religion"—and affirmed one positive commitment—that they would hold the fort until they could deliver it to any Protestant sent by William to take command of it. They made no request for any specific form of constitutional government.[40]

The militia's address to William and Mary a few days later amplified these demands without clarifying them. They complained that they had been governed "in a most arbitrary way [that has] subverted our ancient priviledges making us in effect slaves . . . contrary to the laws of England." They denounced Nicholson as a "pretended protestant" and affirmed "our Religion liberty and property," now about to be gloriously restored under the new monarchs.

What exactly did they mean? An elective assembly was not part of the political heritage of Continental Protestants, who made up most of the militia. In denouncing arbitrary power, such men usually meant something else—governing contrary to established law. Nor was an elective assembly an "ancient priviledge" of New Yorkers, who had enjoyed one for only three years in the colony's entire history of more than sixty years under Dutch and English rule. Were the militia demanding an assembly? I believe they were. But they hardly made their case clear, and most of them were probably thinking in terms of a simple duality that pitted good Protestants against bad Catholics, not in constitutional generalities.[41]

---

[39] Besides the material in Mody and Simmons, eds., *The Glorious Revolution in Massachusetts,* see also W. H. Whitmore, ed., *The Andros Tracts,* 3 vols., Publications of the Prince Society, V–VII (Boston, 1868–74). The sheer volume of this material is striking.

[40] O'Callaghan, *NY Doc. Hist.* II, 10–11.

[41] Address of the New York militia to William and Mary, June 1689, in O'Callaghan, *NY Col. Docs.* III, 583–84. This document gives no specific date, but it was undoubtedly written shortly after news reached New York from Barbados on June 3 that William and Mary had been proclaimed king and queen in February. See the deposition of John Dischington, June 5, 1689, in *ibid.,* 586.

Leisler has left us a few glimpses of his own thoughts on these questions. On June 8, an extemporized committee of safety named him commander of the fort until relieved by William and Mary, and a few days later Leisler wrote to the government of Connecticut. The seizure of the fort, he reported, was in the process of being ratified or upheld by local committees throughout the province. He remarked on the importance of sending "one trusted man . . . to procure in England some privileges." Did he mean a charter? Or less formal concessions? He did not say, but he did add one important explanation (or was it an alternative?): "I wish we may have parte in your Charter, being as I understand in the latitude. If possible I could be informed of the said Charter and priviledges it would be great satisfaction." His own preference, in short, was for a government similar to those of New England. He had no clear idea of exactly what those privileges were, but apparently he had heard about the clause in the Connecticut charter extending its western boundary to the Pacific Ocean. He was willing to explore the possibility of using that provision as a legal basis for merging the two provinces under the Connecticut charter and government.[42]

Later that summer, the Leislerians did send Ensign Joost Stol as their emissary to England. He was a terrible choice. In explaining to the English government what had happened in New York in May and June, he represented himself as the prime mover at every important juncture. Joost Stol organized the militia to take possession of the fort on May 31. Joost Stol led the militia and citizens in proclaiming William and Mary in mid-June. His statement never even mentions Leisler, who by implication became a mere lackey of the great Joost Stol, who would personally negotiate all outstanding questions with King William. The king did receive him once but did not respond to his petition. Stol never did figure out a way to get appropriate action out of the English government. He was playing politics on a level that he had no chance of mastering.

Yet his petition did suggest political objectives similar to the ones articulated by Leisler in June. Of Stol's seven requests put to the English government, the second asked "that his Majestie might be pleased to grant New Yorke a Charter in the like manner and with same or more priviledges as the citty of Boston, being that the contents of that Charter, dost best agree with the humour and nature of those inhabitants, and with the constitution of the said citty." Here again a note of disquieting ambiguity pervades the petition. Boston had no charter. Massachusetts had had one until 1684; New York City had acquired one in 1686. Was Stol talking about municipal or provincial privileges? Like many contemporaries, he probably used "Boston" as a shorthand expression for Massachusetts or even New England. But in that case to request "the same *or more* priviledges" than the Massachusetts charter of 1629 had conferred upon that colony virtually guaranteed almost in-

---

[42] Leisler to Major Nathan Gold, June 12, 1689, in O'Callaghan, *NY Doc. Hist.* II, 14–15.

stant rejection by the English government, which had been trying to tame the pretensions of Massachusetts since 1660 and would impose a new and more limited charter upon the colony in 1691.[43]

For all of the ambiguity of their statements and for all of the ethnic hostilities that they had to encounter within New York City, let us give the Leislerian spokesmen the benefit of the doubt. They probably hoped to acquire a charter that would confer on New York a set of privileges comparable to those contained in the Massachusetts or Connecticut charters. They were even willing to contemplate annexation to Connecticut, and because Leisler occasionally did exercise jurisdiction over East Jersey, they probably expected a continuing connection with that predominantly English province. Despite the angry resentment that pitted ordinary Dutch militiamen against English New Yorkers, the leaders of the movement always intended to keep the colony as an *English* province and saw New Englanders as their natural allies in this process. The English merchants who had agitated for the Charter of Liberties were another matter.

The unspoken assumption behind these preferences and antagonisms was undoubtedly religious. Leisler believed that fellow Calvinists could get along despite ethnic and social differences. He did not trust English merchants whose constitutional principles were similar to or even more generous than his own if their religious preferences were Anglican rather than strict Calvinist.[44]

Stol's failure coincided with the news that William had appointed a new governor, Colonel Henry Sloughter, who was putting together a council of prominent Anti–Leislerians. Much more urgently this time, the Leislerians dispatched a second emissary to London in 1690, Benjamin Blagge, a ship captain and son-in-law of Edsall. Although this exercise in damage control also failed, Blagge's requests are interesting. He begged the king never to let Nicholas Bayard and his colleagues back into power but instead asked him to approve what the Leisler regime had done in William's name. Finally, Blagge urged that the assembly be empowered to elect the council, an arrangement with no exact equivalent anywhere in New England. It was probably the only expedient Blagge could think of to reverse the appointments already made. The Crown ought to reward its true friends, he explained, "and frustrate the wicked designs of your Ma[jes]tys and their, Enemys on the Place." Like the city militia in June 1689, his goal also seems to have been narrowly political rather than broadly constitutional.[45]

---

[43] Representation of Joost Stol, agent for the New York committee of Safety, Nov. 9, 1689, in O'Callaghan, *NY Col. Docs.* III, 629–32, esp. 631 (emphasis added). See also Stol's account of his proceedings, Nov. 16, 1689, *ibid.,* 632–33.
[44] For the fullest explorations of the religious dimensions of Leisler's Rebellion, see Voorhees, "'In Behalf of the True Protestant Religion'"; and Randall H. Balmer, "Traitors and Papists: The Religious Dimensions of Leisler's Rebellion," *New York History* 70 (1989): 341–72.
[45] Petition of Captain Benjamin Blagge to the king, n.d., in O'Callaghan, *NY Col. Docs.* III, 737.

At no point in their two-year struggle did Leislerians offer any theoretical or even legal justification for their constitutional positions. Partly because New York had no printing press, they published very little. Their most significant statement was a two-page pamphlet that appeared in Boston in 1689 and justified the seizure of the fort. Nobody tried to answer Nicholas Bayard's lengthy attack on Leisler's regime that appeared in 1690 in London, where it had tremendous potential for discrediting Leisler in the one place he could be hurt most. The Leislerians also had some exceptionally bad luck. The French captured the vessel containing their first efforts to communicate with the English government, a piece of ill fortune that permitted the Anti–Leislerians to state their case first. For all of these reasons, New York's revolutionary leaders never found a way to explain to the world what they were doing and why they had to do it.[46]

VI

The Leislerians' actions probably conveyed more effective and eloquent messages than any of their formal pronouncements. What they did can tell us much about their constitutional principles.

Leisler was willing to use elections as a legitimating device, but once again he injected a nearly fatal dose of ambiguity into the whole process. With Leisler in *de facto* command in June 1689, the militia ordered county-level elections throughout the province to choose a committee of safety. When it met, it appointed Leisler commander of the fort and began to exercise broad governmental powers over most of the colony. (Some parts, such as Albany, refused to obey.) Leisler also invoked the New York City charter in September and October 1689 to hold new elections and force his opponents, such as Mayor Stephanus Van Cortlandt, to surrender their municipal posts. Elections served Leisler well so long as he had no other source of legitimacy.[47]

This situation changed starting in December 1689 when Leisler accepted a letter from the king addressed to whoever was preserving the peace in

---

[46] *An Account of the Proceedings at New York, 1689* (Boston, 1689), Evans No. 39,248. This pamphlet contains the militia's statements of May 31 and June 3, 1689. Nicholas Bayard, *A Modest and Impartial Narrative of Several Grievances and Great Oppressions that the Peaceable and Most Considerable Inhabitants of their Majesties Province of New-York in America Lye Under, by the Extravagant and Arbitrary Proceedings of Jacob Leysler and his Accomplices* (London, 1690), in Andrews, ed., *Narratives of the Insurrections*, 315–54. For Leisler's discovery that his enemies got to England first, see Leisler to Shrewsbury, June 23, 1690, in O'Callaghan, ed., *NY Col. Docs.* III, 731.

[47] Nicholas Bayard mocked the elections of 1689 by insisting that the turnout was very low. Because Leisler was appealing mostly to settlers from Continental European Protestant backgrounds, they would indeed have found the device of popular elections unfamiliar, and yet it still would have served a legitimating function. Bayard, *A Modest Narrative* (1690), in Andrews, ed., *Narratives of the Insurrections*, 328–29. See also Osgood, ed., *Minutes of the Common Council of the City of New York*, I, 207–08.

New York. Claiming that this document gave him all the powers of a royal lieutenant governor, he dissolved the committee of safety and appointed his own royal council. At that point his government had no elective base at all and with his own people safely in power in New York City, he did not hold elections when they came due under the municipal charter in 1690. In Albany, where the city corporation had resisted him with prolonged success, his eventual triumph meant the overthrow, not just of the officials in power, but of the whole system of government established under the municipal charter of 1686. In November 1689, just before Leisler claimed the prerogatives of a lieutenant governor, his emissary Jacob Milborne had gone to Albany and denounced its charter as "Illegall . . . null & void Since it was graunted by a Popish kings governour & that now ye Power was in the People to choose both new Civill and Military officers as they pleased." Milborne probably was a good deal more radical than Leisler, and his statement contains a formula for a truly popular form of government. But things turned out differently. Once Leisler claimed to be governor, he did use elections in Albany when he reorganized it about a month later, but he also told that touchy community which men he regarded as acceptable choices. There, as in New York City, he was replacing those who had ruled, not introducing a system of annual elections. Instead, elections to Leisler seem to have been a means to an end, not a good in themselves. They were useful so long as they put the right men in office.[48]

As soon as Leisler assumed formal royal powers, he began to encounter ideological resistance based on the rights of Englishmen. As one of their first acts, he and his council proclaimed the laws of 1683 in force throughout the province. At a minimum, this step demonstrated that Leisler accepted the legitimacy of what the assembly of 1683 had done. This action also meant, as Leisler specifically announced, that he had no doubts about the legality of the permanent revenue act and that he had no intention of reviving the disallowed Charter of Liberties, although he was willing to quote it.

A few days after Leisler posted the notice about the revenue act at the customs house, someone tore it down and put in its place a declaration "By the English Freemen of the province of New York." Quoting Magna Carta, it insisted "that no freemen should be any Wise destroyed, but by the Lawfull

---

[48] William III to Francis Nicholson "and in his absence to such as for the time being take care for Preserving the Peace and administering the Lawes in our said Province of New York in America," July 30, 1689, in O'Callaghan, ed., *NY Col. Docs.* III, 606. Leisler's municipal corporation of New York City met several times after its records cease in December 1689, but we do not know how often. For its proceedings, see Osgood, ed., *Minutes of the Common Council of the City of New York,* I, 208–13; David William Voorhees to author, January 23, 1990. For Albany, see Jacob Milborne's speech at a convention at Albany, Novenber 9, 1689; and Jacob Leisler to Captain Joachim Staats, December 28, 1689, in O'Callaghan, ed., *NY Doc. Hist.* II, 113–14, 52–53. See also, Alice P. Kenney, *The Gansevoorts of Albany: Dutch Patricians in the Upper Hudson Valley* (Syracuse: Syracuse University Press, 1969), 16–19.

Judgment of his peers or by the Laws of the Land," and it added passages from a statute of Edward I and the Petition of Right (1628) that affirmed the principle of no taxation without representation. The declaration attacked the revenue act of 1683 as illegal, alleging inaccurately that James had never approved it. The protestors then denounced Leisler's attempt to revive the tax as an assertion of "the unreasonable unlimmited and arbitrary power of the sword against the fundamental rights of the English subjects and contrary to reason Law & Justice" and condemned his government as "the treacherous betrayers of the Rights & priviledges of their Majestyes good Subjects & the Introducers of a miserable brutish Slavery from which his Majesty has Solemnly Given his Royall word to protect and defend us."[49]

Leisler and the council replied quickly. They accused the protestors of a "false construction on the wholesome Lawes of England not regarding An Act of the Freemen represented in Assembly as aforesd Vizt That the Supreame Legislatiue Authority under his Ma[jes]ties &ca shall forever be & reside in a Governr, Councill & the People met in Generall Assembly." Leisler warned that anyone defacing government proclamations would answer at his peril, and a few days later the government arrested two youthful anglicizing Dutchmen, Jacob DeKey, Jr., and Cornelius Depeyster, for the incident at the customs house.[50]

The struggle over English liberties was becoming serious, and Leisler had made an intelligent beginning. When accused of violating Magna Carta and the Petition of Right, he responded by quoting Article One of the Charter of Liberties. The tax was valid because it had been passed by governor, council, and general assembly, as the Charter of Liberties required. By throwing the Charter of Liberties back in the faces of the people who had drafted it, he positioned himself nicely to take the high ground in defense of English liberties, and he forced such opponents as Nicholas Bayard into arguing that the tax was no law because it was passed in exchange for the Charter of Liberties, which James had disallowed. This position could muster great moral force behind it but could not have been sustained as a matter of strict law. The assembly had passed the tax as a separate act, and James had approved it. But the moral argument also demanded some kind of response, and Leisler never gave it.

Thus Leisler, after gaining an initial polemical edge, never followed through with any broader statement of the constitutional principles that his government embodied. He made no attempt to implement the Charter of Liberties for those who regarded it as a binding bargain in exchange for the revenue act, or to revive it for those who conceded the validity of the disallowance. Nor did he suggest any substitute in a region of America that had

[49] C.O. 5/1081/203, British Public Record Office, London. My thanks to David William Voorhees for bringing this text to my attention and for sending me a copy.
[50] Proclamation of December 20, 1689, in O'Callaghan, ed., *NY Doc. Hist.* II, 50–51.

been awash in daring constitutional schemes since the 1660s. As the constitutional debate continued over the next sixteen months, he permitted his opponents to recapture the Charter of Liberties and the form of government it represented. His opponents kept trying to stigmatize him as an enemy of the Charter of Liberties in particular, and English liberties in general. As Leisler jailed even more of his opponents for extended periods without trial, the accusations began to stick.[51]

Nevertheless Leisler did try to invoke the legitimating power of an English assembly. As expenses mounted in the war against New France, he issued writs for an election in February 1690. His New York City writ was addressed "To the military & civill officers of and ye rest of ye Inhabitants of the city & county of N. Yorrck." The intriguing question is whether "ye rest of ye Inhabitants" mandated a general election by the freeholders and freemen, as established in the Charter of Liberties. It most likely did not, and in any case few communities responded at all, probably because Leisler was drawing ever more narrowly upon a constituency of Continental Protestants, for whom the whole procedure was unusual. Even in Queens, where Leisler did get compliance from the preponderantly New England population, the towns interpreted his writ to require indirect elections similar to those used by Dongan in 1683, not the general elections mandated by the reforming assembly of that year. Each town chose a committee of two men, and those individuals then met separately to select the representatives.[52]

Leisler therefore tried again with new writs in April, and they produced better results in the rest of the province. This time, the writ to heavily Dutch Kings County was addressed only to the ruling cadre, and that small group of men made the choice by themselves, a pattern that was quite familiar to Dutch Protestants. This evidence suggests that Leisler never did invite the freeholders and freemen of the province to participate in a true general election, but then the only one that had ever been held in the entire history of New York had been in 1685.[53]

Beyond fighting the war and rendering his regime secure until he could be relieved by William, Leisler had no legislative agenda. The spring session of the 1690 assembly passed the tax he requested along with a law repealing New York City's monopoly on the bolting of flour. But when the assembly

[51] See Bayard, *Modest Narrative* (1690), in Andrews, ed., *Narratives of the Insurrections*, 340–44.

[52] Jamaica town meeting of March 14, 1689/90, in Josephine C. Frost, ed., *Records of the Town of Jamaica, Long Island, New York, 1656–1751* (New York: Long Island Historical Society, 1914), I, 143; Hempstead town meeting of March 17, 1689/90, in Benjamin D. Hicks, ed., *Records of the Town of North and South Hempstead, Long Island, New York* (Jamaica, N.Y.: Long Island Farmer Print., 1896–1904), II, 28. See also, Leisler to Bishop Gilbert Burnet, March 31, 1690, in which he noted that "the people . . . do not convene, according to our writts" for election of the assembly. O'Callaghan, ed., *NY Col. Docs.* III, 702.

[53] For the New York City writs of February and April, see O'Callaghan, ed., *NY Doc. Hist.* II, 73; for Kings County, see "Flatbush Town Records, Miscellaneous, I: 1652 to 1758," 271–73 (St. Francis College Archives, Brooklyn).

took up the question of the legal rights of Leisler's prisoners under English common law, Leisler prorogued it.[54]

The attempt to collect the tax of April 1690 led to a very serious Anti–Leislerian riot in New York City in June. Of several contemporary accounts, the least partisan indicates that the affair began when a large group of Anti–Leislerians assembled a few blocks from where the Leislerian militia were mustering. After denouncing the tax as arbitrary and illegal, they decided that, with the militia busy elsewhere, they might be able to surprise the fort and free the prisoners. Someone then suggested that they first ask Leisler to free the men, which they did when they happened to meet him coming from the fort. To their immense surprise, he agreed to release the prisoners on bail. Then, as the excited crowd moved closer about him, a bystander (probably his son, Jacob, Jr.) concluded that he was being mobbed and charged the throng with drawn sword. In the melée that followed, someone tried to brain Leisler with a carpenter's adze, a potentially fatal blow, but his followers came to his aid and freed him. Leisler's narrow escape convinced him that the whole incident had been an assassination plot, and he confined another long list of prisoners to the fort. This unhappy resolution probably marked the passing of his last chance to reach some minimal understanding with his opponents about the legal rights of all New Yorkers.[55]

Thereafter Leisler seldom relented from a strategy of confrontation with his opponents. He forced the clergy—particularly Henricus Selyns, his most powerful enemy within the Dutch Reformed ministry—to offer prayers of public thanksgiving for his deliverance. The angry exchange between the two men in church on a Sunday morning shocked the worshippers. Leisler denounced Selyns as "a rascal, which created a great sensation in the house of the Lord." Even in the eyes of many of Leisler's own followers, the politics of rage began to seem both grim and unwise.[56]

This growing estrangement became conspicuous when Leisler summoned a new session of his assembly in September. He issued several writs to fill vacancies, and they show that in Albany and New York City he again expected, not the voters, but the municipal corporations—his people by then—to do the actual choosing. Only in Yankee Queens did his writ also summon the "inhabitants" as well, although I have encountered no evidence

---

[54] Leisler to Captain John D'Bruyn *et al.*, in O'Callaghan, *NY Doc. Hist.* II, 238. For the legislation of April 1690, only the title survives. The two measures may have been embodied in one comprehensive act, which would have been a very un-English thing to do when one item was a tax and the other was not. See Lincoln, ed., *Colonial Laws of New York* I, 218.

[55] For this version of the riot, see Lawrence H. Leder, ed., "'. . . Like Madmen through the Streets': The New York City Riot of June 1690," *New-York Historical Society Quarterly* 34 (1955): 405–15. For the Leislerian version, see "Depositions respecting the Riot at New-York, &c.," in O'Callaghan, *NY Col. Docs.*, III, 740–48.

[56] Leder, ed., "'. . . Like Madmen through the Streets,'" 414.

to show whether freeholders in fact participated. The Albany writ, so far as I know, marks the only occasion—after the incident at the customs house in December 1689—in which he accorded some legitimacy to the Charter of Liberties. Calling it the "Charter of privilege," he accepted its apportionment of delegates, but not its mode of election.[57]

By the autumn of 1690, Leisler was in fact well advanced in losing the allegiance of the New Englanders on Long Island, and the second session of the assembly with its aftermath largely completed the process. Earlier in the year, when Easthampton had announced its intention to seek reunion with Connecticut, Leisler had dispatched Edsall to that town to dissuade the community. At a formal level Edsall succeeded, but in practice the situation became a stalemate. When Leisler and his council appointed a full slate of militia officers for the province, they included commissions for only one Suffolk town, Huntington, and for only one person in what was already becoming a secessionist town, Easthampton. So far as I am aware, no evidence survives to show that Leisler's government collected taxes in Suffolk (although it did appoint a collector). The county sent delegates to the first session of Leisler's assembly but apparently not the second.[58]

Surviving records tell us little about the assembly session of September–October 1690, but it was probably stormy. Still smarting from being prorogued in April for daring to raise the question of the common-law privileges of Leisler's prisoners, the delegates chose an English speaker, the rather obscure John Spratt, and the assembly resorted to a venerable parliamentary tactic. It demanded a redress of grievances before voting supplies. As its first item of business, it passed on September 18 "A Bill Confirming to the Inhabitants of this Province the Full Priviledge and Benefitts of his Maj[ties] Laws within this Province." In brief, it demanded trial and due process according to the laws of England for anyone imprisoned for or accused of an offense, and it offered amnesty to all exiles who would return to New York within three weeks of the publication of the law–an effort to win over English merchants who had fled the colony. Nine days later, Leisler finally approved an amended version that made no explicit mention of his prisoners.

The wrangling never paralyzed the proceedings, however, for the assembly passed several other statutes in late September, including an act to explain the April tax. On October 2, the assembly finally voted the new tax that Leisler demanded, and two days later Leisler approved a measure that imposed harsh penalties on anyone refusing to assume office under his government

---

[57] For the writs, see O'Callaghan, *NY Doc. Hist.*, 282–83.

[58] See Samuel Mulford *et al.* to Leisler, Mar. 10, 1689/90, in *NY Doc. Hist.* II, 187. For a list of Leisler's civil and military commissions with dates and recipients, see *ibid.*, 347–54. David William Voorhees has found evidence that Suffolk County sent Richard Kedee and Thomas Harris to the April assembly. Voorhees to author, January 23, 1990. Until now all historians have assumed that Suffolk participated in neither session.

and fines almost as severe on settlers who fled the exposed frontier counties of
Albany and Ulster without permission. This series of incidents says a great
deal. At a minimum, it tells us that even Leisler's own followers believed that
he ought to be much more accommodating on the sensitive question of English liberties.[59]

The tax of October 1690 largely completed the alienation of Yankee Long
Island. In Queens, led by longstanding enemies of Leisler's government,
over one hundred settlers (perhaps a third of the taxpayers in a county of 500
militia) refused to pay the levy, and by the end of the year they were in various stages of having their property distrained. They called this procedure
plunder, and ominous numbers of them took up arms in resistance. Puritan
Westchester, however, remained loyal.[60]

Leisler's regime collapsed a few months later. Quite correctly, he refused
to surrender the fort to Major Richard Ingoldsby when he arrived with his
advance party of redcoats in January 1691 unless Ingoldsby would show
him a direct order from the governor, who had been delayed enroute, or a
commission from William (rather than James). Ingoldsby disdained to
oblige, and the confrontation between them continued for nearly two
months as both sides awaited Governor Sloughter's arrival. Leisler occupied
the fort and a blockhouse. Ingoldsby took possession of the Town House
(seat of the city government) and began to collect several hundred armed
militia, mostly from Queens. Still suspecting that Ingoldsby represented
James and not William, Leisler issued a proclamation on March 10 ordering
his opponents to disperse and an angrier one on March 16. He opened fire
the next day, killing two men—a last act of Leislerian rage. Ominously for
Leisler, Governor Sloughter then arrived on March 19, and Leisler surrendered the fort to him on the twentieth, only to be arrested, tried, and convicted of treason. Leisler and his English son-in-law, Jacob Milborne, arguing that they were answerable only to the king for their public acts, refused
to plead to their indictments. The court condemned them without trial.
When Sloughter refused to allow an appeal to England, Leisler and Milborne
were hanged on May 16.[61]

[59] The text of the contested bill is in O'Callaghan, *NY Doc. Hist.* II, 355. For the statutes of October 2 and 4, see *ibid.,* 356–57, and Lincoln, ed. *Colonial Laws of New York* I, 219–20. For the others,
including the final version of the contested bill, I am indebted to David William Voorhees to author, January 23 and February 23, 1990.
[60] John Clapp to the secretary of state, November 7, 1690, conveying the protests of the freeholders of Hempstead, Jamaica, Flushing and Newtown, in O'Callaghan, ed., *NY Col. Docs.* III,
754–56.
[61] See generally O'Callaghan, ed. *NY Col. Docs.* III, 756–69; O'Callaghan, ed. *NY Doc. Hist.* II,
320–46; NYHS *Coll.* (1868), 299–333; and Lawrence H. Leder, ed., "Records of the Trials of Jacob
Leisler and his Associates," *New-York Historical Society Quarterly* 36 (1952): 431–57. Those who
pleaded not guilty received a jury trial. Leisler and Milborne did not plead and were condemned without a jury.

VII

What larger significance can we give to this struggle? New York, which had the most diverse population of any mainland English colony, also lived under a Continental European form of government almost continuously until 1689. Whether under the Dutch West India Company or under James as duke or king, the settlers had to cope with varying forms of absolutism. In constitutional terms, New York thus became the one mainland colony in which royal (though initially proprietary) prerogative became firmly established decades before the province acquired an elective assembly. Virtually everywhere else, the assembly was older than royal government and confronted the first royal governor with an existing set of legislative privileges. In New York, the assembly had to make room for itself against the resistance of a well entrenched and very powerful prerogative.

Nonetheless, Leisler's Rebellion guaranteed that an assembly would become a permanent part of the governing process in New York. From the summoning of Leisler's contentious deputies in 1690 until the present, an assembly has met every year with the single exception of 1707. From the moment of their return in 1691, the Anti–Leislerians took dramatic steps of their own to guarantee the success of this effort. With several interesting amendments, they reenacted the Charter of Liberties of 1683, this time denying toleration to Catholics and requiring annual sessions of the legislature. They also declared all prior legislation void to gain control of a full agenda, and they began passing revenue acts for quite limited terms.[62]

Things did not work out as they planned. William III disallowed the 1691 charter, much as James had revoked the 1683 version. Even more important, the execution of Leisler and Milborne so brutalized the political environment that Anti–Leislerians found themselves under constant attack on both sides of the Atlantic. To remain in power, they needed the governor's support, and in the process they became measurably more accommodating on issues of prerogative.[63]

[62] *Journal of the Votes and Proceedings of the General Assembly of the Colony of New York (1692–1765)* (New York: Hugh Gaine, 1764–66), I, 8–9; Lincoln, ed., *Colonial Laws of New York* I, 239–42, 244–48, 248–53. For a fuller discussion of the 1691 Charter of Liberties, see Murrin, ed., "The New York Charter of Liberties, 1683 and 1691."

[63] For disallowance of the Charter of Liberties of 1691, see Lincoln, ed., *Colonial Laws of New York* I, 244. On New York politics after Leisler, see Thomas J. Archdeacon, *New York City, 1664–1710: Conquest and Change* (Ithaca, N.Y.: Cornell University Press, 1976), Chap. 6; Patricia U. Bonomi, *A Factious People: Politics and Society in Colonial New York* (New York: Columbia University Press, 1971), Chaps. 1–3; Lawrence H. Leder, *Robert Livingston, 1654–1728, and the Politics of Colonial New York* (Chapel Hill: University of North Carolina Press, 1961), Chaps. 5–12; and Eugene R. Sheridan, *Lewis Morris, 1671–1746: A Study in Early American Politics* (Syracuse University Press, 1981), Chaps. 1–3.

The Leislerian leadership had favored a New–England style charter for the colony as a way of guaranteeing its privileges. Anti–Leislerians had been the main force behind the two Charters of Liberties passed by the assemblies of 1683 and 1691. In securing a legislature that met every year, both sides won. In winning no broader guarantees, they both lost. On this question, their respective positions were much closer together than either realized or could admit. In the face of other disagreements, they found no way to discover how to concur on constitutional questions even when their differences were not large.

Continuing internal divisions and the need to placate the governor also made New York politics far more venal and corrupt after 1691 than was the public life of the colonies in neighboring New England or Pennsylvania. With rival factions bidding for its support, the governorship became the most lucrative office in British North America, a magnet capable of attracting every gentleman of broken fortune who could reach the ear of the duke of Newcastle. Governors also gave away New York real estate in truly enormous grants that undoubtedly retarded the settlement process by comparison with Pennsylvania or even New Jersey. After 1715, smart governors learned that once they had a safe majority in the assembly they could rule nicely for years—provided they did not call a general election. Elections were annual in New England and Pennsylvania, triennial in England from the Glorious Revolution to 1715 and septennial after that. New York had no such protection. Several different governors went from 1716 to 1726 and from 1728 to 1737 without calling new elections. Only in the 1740s did the province get its own Septennial Act. Only in the decade after 1737 did the assembly begin to make significant inroads on the most bloated prerogative in America. Leisler's Rebellion and the struggle it initiated did indeed destroy absolutism in New York, but the upheaval failed to do much to trim royal prerogative. Success in that contest had to wait for another half-century.[64]

VIII

New Yorkers failed to achieve broader constitutional objectives because in the late seventeenth century the politics of rage took precedence over these issues. Behind that rage loomed the threatening visage of Louis XIV, the monarch whose persecution of the Huguenots made it impossible for English Protestants to trust James II, for Dutch Calvinists and New England Puritans

---

[64] Stanley Nider Katz, *Newcastle's New York: Anglo–American Politics, 1732–1753* (Cambridge, Mass: Harvard University Press, 1968), esp. Chap. 2; Beverly McAnear, *The Income of the Colonial Governors of British North America* (New York: Pageant Press, Inc., 1967); and Charles Worthen Spencer, "The Rise of the Assembly, 1691–1760," in Alexander C. Flick, ed., *History of the State of New York* (New York: Columbia University Press, 1933–37), II, 151–99.

in New York to trust Nicholson and his councillors, and for Jacob Leisler to compromise with his opponents on English liberty or avoid bloodshed in his confrontation with Ingoldsby.

This rage also had ideological implications. Continental European Protestant values, religious and political, had to express themselves in unfamiliar English forms. Because the Dutch, English, and French communities all faced internal divisions, the potential for misunderstanding was always enormous. As the political stakes reached a new high in 1689, when everyone agreed that a false step could be fatal, anxiety and dread exploded inexorably into fury.

Both the youthful Nicholson and the middle-aged Leisler (forty-nine in 1689) responded with passion. Nicholson, who believed that he had taken every reasonable precaution to protect the colony from French attack, lost his temper when the militia continued to display its distrust of him and his soldiers. His angry threat to burn the city initiated the process that overturned his government. Leisler, after accepting command of the fort, went through the next year in one towering rage after another. When Philip French arrived in New York City from Boston on June 5, 1689, and objected to being interrogated, a militiaman growled, "Damn you doe not speake one word more or I'l kill you," and led him to Leisler in the fort.[65] Leisler badgered his opponents in person, fiercely and often. "Yo[u']r[e] a Traitour, a Papist, &c," he shouted "in a rage" at Stephanus Van Cortlandt on June 22, "and made the people just ready to knock me in the head," Van Cortlandt complained. A few days later Leisler told Frederick Philipse that "if he should meet [him] again the Divell should take him."[66] Men who had held office for many years became "Roages, Rascalls, and Devills" in an outburst by Leisler on June 25. Nearly everyone who resisted him became a "papist" or a "popish dog." In another confrontation also on June 25, Leisler accosted Nicholas Bayard at the customs house, "cursing and swearing that he would be the death of me," according to Bayard, "sometimes threatening to run mee thorow, to cudgel mee with his kaine, to run mee in the face."[67] Leisler's followers used similar language. They often threatened their opponents with violence—and even death.

On the one occasion when Leisler is known to have remained calm in a dispute with an Anti–Leislerian, the other party found the exchange so singular that he wrote a detailed account of it for Nicholson. In August, Leisler sent a sergeant and two musketeers to summon Captain George McKenzie, one of Nicholson's officers, to the fort. McKenzie refused to admit them to his house. Then, reported McKenzie, "they told me (in a threatening tone),

[65] Deposition of Philip French, June 7, 1689, in O'Callaghan, ed., *NY Col. Docs.* III, 587.
[66] Stephanus Van Cortlandt to Sir Edmund Andros, July 9, 1689, in O'Callaghan, ed., *NY Col. Docs.* III, 595–96.
[67] Nicholas Bayard's journal, June 25, 1689, in O'Callaghan, ed., *NY Col. Docs.,* III, 602, 603.

you must go along with us; I said I would not; and bid them show me their warrant, and they held up their musquetts, which I said was not satisfactory to me, upon which they called me the greatest rogue in the whole country and threatened to pull down the house, which words I regarded not." But the next day while McKenzie strolled conspicuously along the Broad Way, Leisler's men arrested him and took him to the fort, where Leisler and two members of his council (Edsall and Peter Delanoy) interrogated him about a letter they had intercepted that he had sent to former Governor Andrew Hamilton of East Jersey, in which McKenzie had advised Hamilton not to trust Leisler's word on any matter of importance. As McKenzie reported,[68]

> Mr. Leisler said he wondered what wrong he had done me that I should write so of him to wrong his credit, that if he knew he had done me any wrong he would beg pardon for it upon his knees. I answered if I did him wrong I would beg his, but I told him I was provoked first by his calling me a Papist, for so I was told. He answered it was a very great lye for he had never said so. After a little pause he put on a more angry look, and said he knew I was Popishly affected. I answered that is not true. I am as much a protestant as you or any man in the Country. Why, says he, have not I heard you call Father [John] Smith [the Jesuit who ran a school in the city] a very good man? Yes replyed I, and so I do still; he is a very good humoured man, but I never called him so because he was a Papist, and I was so far from haveing any friendship for his principlis [sic], that in all the six yeares I had known New York I never so much as out of curiosity looked into their Chapell. . . . After a great deal of [such] discourse which what I liked not I always contradicted, he at last said I might call him what I pleased, he would pray God to bless me. And then I prayd God might bless him, in which holy sort of complem[en]t we continued a pretty while. And at last [he] said he would never do me any prejudice, and I made answer after the same manner, and so was dismissed very civilly, which I very much wonder at, for he treated vandenburgh (who is one of the troopers) verry far otherwise, forbidding him to ride in the troop, and that if he should see him ahorseback he would shoot him down. It would proove tedious to give an account of all that passed betwixt him and I, but the other Committee men and he too spoke with as much smoothness and civility as I think I have heard, which was pretty strange because new to me.

In a word, the lion had dragged McKenzie to his lair—and did not even roar. It was a unique occasion, or so McKenzie clearly believed.

Even Leisler's strong supporters often tried to calm him. After the confrontation between Leisler and Bayard at the customs house, Peter Delanoy—a member of Leisler's council and a son-in-law of Edsall—took in Bayard overnight to protect him from the wrath of the crowd that Leisler had aroused, while the angry men "watched the house and swore they would kill

---

[68] George McKenzie to Francis Nicholson, August 15, 1689, in O'Callaghan, ed., *NY Col. Docs.* III, 612–14. I have modernized some of the punctuation in this passage.

him."[69] Pierre Daillé, the Huguenot minister of New York who owed many favors to Leisler, "was accustomed to go to Commander Leisler, and exhort him to moderation."[70] Writing from Boston, a Dutch Leislerian reminded his leader, "Sir gustis, with moderation and mersy is becoming all persons in pour [i.e., power],"[71] John Allyn, the secretary of Connecticut, conveyed the same message much more angrily in 1690, after Leisler had arrested Major General Fitz-John Winthrop following the failure of the invasion of Canada. "A prison is not a catholicon for al State Maladyes, though so much used by you," he declared, "nor are you incapable of need of, nor aid from their Majesties subjects in New England, nor could you in any one action have more disobliged al New England."[72] Both sessions of Leisler's assembly had been trying to tell him the same thing. When the rebellion finally crashed around Leisler's head in 1691, Gerardus Beekman, until then a member of the council and loyal supporter, deplored the violence that occurred near the fort in March. He blamed these "base and inhuman actions" upon "the Malise of a Colerick man"—Leisler.[73] Of course, Leisler retained the passionate loyalty of thousands of New Yorkers. The public indignation provoked by his execution would otherwise be inexplicable. But even many of his closest associates believed that his fierce temper too often made things worse, not better.

Yet this rage fit a pattern. It had both a biography and a history behind it. Leisler maintained his Calvinist principles throughout his life at a real personal cost. In the 1670s, he and Milborne endured a long and expensive lawsuit in order to challenge the orthodoxy of Nicholas Van Rensselaer, a minister with rather odd theological views who had been thrust upon the Albany congregation by Governor Andros. Similarly, when the Dutch Reformed Church of New York City insisted on naming Selyns (whose theology was Arminian or Cocceian rather than Calvinist) as pastor in the early 1680s, Leisler left the congregation to worship with the French instead. Yet as late as 1684, this Calvinist commitment did not prevent him from maintaining friendly relations with Catholics. Although Dongan had never hidden his Catholicism, Leisler had not always hated and feared him. He accepted his first high office as a militia captain from Dongan in September 1684 and married his daughter Susannah to Michael Vaughton, a Dongan protégé. At this stage in Leisler's career, only his persistent orthodoxy set

[69] Stephanus Van Cortlandt to Sir Edmund Andros, July 9, 1689, in O'Callaghan, ed., *NY Col. Docs.* II, 596.

[70] Leislerian members of the Dutch Reformed Church of New York to the Classis of Amsterdam, October 21, 1698, in Hugh Hastings and E. T. Corwin, eds., *Ecclesiastical Records of the State of New York* (Albany: James B. Lyon, State Printer, 1901–16), II, 1256. Hereafter cited as *NY Eccles. Recs.*

[71] Isaac Melyn to Leisler, December 11, 1690, in O'Callaghan, ed., *NY Doc. Hist.* II, 316.

[72] John Allyn to Leisler, September 1, 1690, in O'Callaghan, ed., *NY Doc. Hist.* II, 289.

[73] Petition of Gerrardus Beekman to Governor Henry Sloughter, n.d. (probably April 1691), in O'Callaghan, ed., *NY Doc. Hist.* II, 368–69.

him apart from other Dutch settlers who were getting ahead by coming to terms with English rulers and institutions. Indeed, four of Leisler's daughters chose Englishmen as their first husbands, or quite possibly Leisler selected his daughters' mates himself.[74]

Then something happened that left Leisler fearfully alarmed. He never explained what it was, but we can guess with reasonable accuracy. Louis XIV revoked the Edict of Nantes in 1685 and culminated a mass persecution of Huguenots that compelled perhaps 160,000 of them to flee from France, the largest forced migration in early modern European history—larger even than the Loyalist migration from the United States during the Revolution or the flight of the emigres from the French Revolution. The expulsion of the Huguenots was the most chilling atrocity in Western Europe during Leisler's lifetime, and its impact soon destroyed both James II and Leisler, the tolerant absolutist and the heir of an earlier generation of Huguenot exiles.

Leisler, the son of a Huguenot clergyman who had escaped Spanish persecution by fleeing to Frankfort, deeply sympathized with the refugees. He paid John Pell £1675.5.0 sterling for land in New Rochelle which he made available to Huguenots as they arrived in New York, and he also worshipped with them in Pierre Daillé's French church. No doubt he knew that James II, whose own record on religious toleration had been excellent until then, was trying ineffectually to suppress the many accounts of Louis's persecution that circulated in England. In the process, James managed only to compromise himself irreparably in Protestant eyes. To Leisler, the news that James had fled to France meant that, if the exiled king somehow triumphed in New York, his victory would mean ruthless Catholic persecution of Protestants.

The stakes were too high for compromise. The maddening thing about the situation, in Leisler's mind, was that too many settlers, particularly those who held office under James, refused to recognize what was happening. Leisler understood the temptations they faced. He had tasted them and found them delectable, but since the repeal of the Edict of Nantes he had put stern Protestant duty ahead of any public career he might have been building. His enemies did not. Only one explanation made sense. They too must be papists, especially that other son of a persecuted émigré clergyman, Nicholas Bayard, who would not admit the urgency of the situation. He was the worst of the pack. Leisler's Orangist followers shared these convictions. They were as frightened and angry as the Orangist crowd in the Hague that killed the De Witt brothers during the French invasion of The Netherlands in 1672.[75]

---

[74] Voorhees, "'In Behalf of the True Protestants Religion,'" Chap. 5; Edwin R. Purple's genealogy of the Leisler family, *New York Genealogical and Biographical Record* 7 (1876): 145–51; Lawrence H. Leder, "The Unorthodox Domine: Nicholas Van Rensselaer," *New York History* 35 (1954): 166–76; and for the relationship between Vaughton and Dongan, Dongan's report on the state of the Province, *NY Col. Docs.* III, 407–08.

[75] Jon Butler, *The Huguenots in America: A Refugee People in New World Society* (Cambridge, Mass.: Harvard University Press, 1983), esp. Chaps. 1, 2, and 5; J. Thomas Scharf, *History of Westchester*

Leisler was not only enraged, but as he met continued resistance, he was able to sustain his fury for nearly two years. He directed it against Bayard, against Nicholson's other councillors, and against all other recalcitrant officeholders in New York City or elsewhere who would not defer to him as military commander of New York. Only in his gallows speech did he finally concede that wrath, even righteous wrath, is not a subtle political weapon, that he and Milborne had undertaken "great & weighty matters of State affairs requiring at Such an helme more wise & Cunning powerfull Pilotts than either of us ever was." But by forgiving his enemies and dying in an exemplary Christian manner, Leisler only raised the fury of his followers to a new intensity. During the execution, they chanted the seventy-ninth Psalm:[76]

> O God, the heathen are come into thine inheritance; thy holy temple have they defiled; they have laid Jerusalem on heaps.

> The dead bodies of thy servants have they given to be meat unto the fowls of the heaven, the flesh of thy saints unto the beasts of the earth.

> Their blood have they shed like water round about Jerusalem; and there was none to bury them.

> Pour out thy wrath upon the heathen that have not known thee, and upon the kingdoms that have not called upon thy name.

> For they have devoured Jacob, and laid waste his dwelling place.

> Let the sighing of the prisoner come before thee; according to the greatness of thy power preserve thou those that are appointed to die;

> And render unto our neighbours sevenfold into their bosom their reproach, wherewith they have reproached thee, O Lord.

In May 1691, nobody who mattered was thinking of conciliation.

The rhetoric of rage often obscured important constitutional issues even within the Dutch community. Clashes between Orangist principles and the expectations of New York's proto-regents occurred frequently but seldom found articulate expression. Most of the maneuvering over who would proclaim William and Mary as king and queen in June 1689, once official word of their accession finally arrived, involved a classic confrontation between an Orangist military leader and his angry crowd of supporters against the civil officeholders who had compromised their Protestant identities by cooperating smoothly with Catholics.[77]

County, New York, including Morrisana, Kings Bridge, and West Farms, which Have Been Annexed to New York City (Philadelphia: L. E. Preston and Co., 1886), I, 27.

[76] O'Callaghan, ed. *NY Doc. Hist.* II, 376–79, esp. 376; Balmer, *A Perfect Babel of Confusion*, 42–43 (italics removed).

[77] The most thoughtful effort to understand Leisler within the context of Anglo-Dutch politics in general and the office of *stadholder* in particular is Donna Merwick, "Being Dutch: An Interpretation of Why Jacob Leisler Died," *New York History* 70 (1989), 373–404.

Although Leisler never called himself a *stadholder,* he acted like one. He clearly believed that in a military emergency civil officeholders ought to take orders from him as the highest military officer in the colony loyal to William. Whether he ever said, "The Sword must rule and not the Laws," as Bayard claimed, is irrelevant.[78] He made certain that official news about the accession of William and Mary reached him before it got to Mayor Van Cortlandt, and he proclaimed their majesties at the fort before ordering the mayor to do so later in the day as a civil officer obliged to obey the province's military commander. Van Cortlandt refused to concede that Leisler had any legal power over him but tried to make it clear that he approved of William and Mary. Leisler, of course, did not believe him and accused him of favoring the infant prince of Wales. Like the regent class in The Netherlands under Oldenbarnevelt and De Witt, Van Cortlandt, Bayard, Philipse, and their associates faced an angry Orangist uprising that certainly threatened their status. Beyond any doubt, they feared for their lives. So did the English merchants in New York City, many of whom probably saw in the first phase of the uprising a repetition from within of the Dutch reconquest of 1673. The English, explained *Domine* Rudolphus Varick of Long Island, "had been greatly provoked by their losing the fort a second time."[79]

These encounters ended in a final, terrible irony. For all the violence of their rhetoric, the Leislerians did not kill their enemies. When the Anti–Leislerians returned to power, they purged the Orangist terror from which they had suffered by killing Leisler. The men of moderation and flexibility had none when they most needed it. Instead, they bequeathed a heritage of continuing fury and vengeance to New York politics. Louis XIV never conquered New York, but he quite successfully warped the colony's politics for at least a generation.

Except among the badly outnumbered English merchants of New York City and the increasingly peripheral New Englanders, the battle for English constitutional liberties was always subordinate to the struggle within the Dutch community. Had constitutional systems been the most serious issue of 1689, the quarreling parties could have settled their differences. The confrontation between Orangists and proto-regents prevented the question of English liberties from achieving clear focus. Because the disputants literally could not believe how close together they actually were on basic constitutional questions, New York entered the eighteenth century with a crippled constitution that would take another two generations to repair.

---

[78] Bayard, *Modest Narrative* (1690), in Andrews, ed., *Narratives of the Insurrections,* 332.
[79] See the accounts by Van Cortlandt and Bayard of the events of June 22, 1689, in O'Callaghan, ed., *NY Col. Docs.* III, 595–96, 601; Rudolphus Varick to the Classis of Amsterdam, April 9, 1693, in Hastings and Corwin, eds., *NY Eccles. Recs.* II, 1050.

The Pueblo Revolt and Its Aftermath

Ramón A. Gutiérrez

INTRODUCTION

In 1598, Don Juan de Oñate established the first permanent Spanish colony in New Mexico, choosing a location along the banks of the upper Rio Grande River on which to settle the five hundred members of his expedition. The Spanish presence in New Mexico, although it probably never exceeded three thousand individuals, had dramatic consequences for the Pueblo Indians, the area's scattered and ethnically diverse indigenous peoples. Many were killed by the introduction of European epidemic diseases, and others were used by the Spanish to provide labor, clothing, and food. Moreover, Franciscan priests forced Indians to convert to Catholicism, a process that the friars sought to expedite by destroying the icons and rituals important to native religion. Indian resistance to these measures, though answered by the Spanish with considerable violence, continued throughout the seventeenth century.

This selection from Ramón Gutiérrez's acclaimed social history of the Pueblo Indians considers the most famous of these rebellions, the Pueblo Revolt of 1680. As Gutiérrez explains, religious persecution coupled with an especially severe period of drought and famine led Pueblos throughout New Mexico to turn on their Spanish rulers in near unanimity. Gutiérrez pays particular attention to the religious revivalism of Popé, the Tewa medicine man who coordinated the assault, noting his assurances to his followers that the elimination of the Spaniards would restore the social and spiritual customs disrupted by the intruders. Gutiérrez illuminates the depth of native anger over Spanish treatment of Indian religion in his discussion of the Puebloans' careful destruction of Christian symbols. For their part, the Spanish understood the revolt as a clear rejection of Christianity.

Ramón A. Gutiérrez, "The Pueblo Revolt and Its Aftermath," in his *When Jesus Came, the Corn Mothers Went Away: Marriage, Sexuality, and Power in New Mexico, 1500–1846*, 130–40. Reprinted with the permission of the publishers, Stanford University Press. © 1991 by the Board of Trustees of the Leland Stanford Junior University.

> *Although in a matter of weeks the Indians had driven the Spaniards from New Mexico, killing more than four hundred of the province's twenty-five hundred foreigners and displacing the rest, by 1694 the Spanish had subjugated those Pueblos still in rebellion. With the crushing of a large revolt in 1696, Spanish dominion over New Mexico was complete. And yet the reinstitution of Spanish rule saw the easing of Franciscan strictures and official demands on native labor.*

- *With such considerations in mind, should the Pueblo Revolt of 1680 be seen as a success or failure?*
- *How does this episode challenge or confirm standard interpretations of early Indian-European encounters?*

The years 1666 to 1670 were marked by drought and meager maize production. Famine swept the land in 1670, and a decade of pestilence and death followed. The Indian population, which in 1638 had totaled roughly 40,000, by 1670 had fallen to 17,000. To complicate matters, in 1672 hordes of hungry Apaches and Navajos in similarly desperate straits began attacking the kingdom's settlements with unprecedented regularity, killing and stealing, and carrying off whatever food they found. The Puebloans' discontent hardly needed stoking. For years they had resented the Spanish, and now they spoke openly of rebellion. The medicine men told their tribesmen that the reason they suffered so was because their ancient gods were angry. If they offered the katsina gifts and respect, they would surely bless them with rainfall, fertility, and happiness. The first group to openly defy colonial rule were the Tewa, the Indians who had had the closest contact with the Spaniards during the seventeenth century. In 1673 they publicly performed prohibited dances, making offerings to their gods and begging them to return. The medicine men worked feverishly, placing hexes on the Christians and stealing their hearts. Apparently their magic worked. In 1675 alone, Indian witchcraft was blamed for sending seven friars and three settlers to their graves.[1]

Ominous forebodings of events to come were everywhere. In 1672, the Jumano Indians of Abó Pueblo revolted, burning their church and murdering Fray Pedro de Avila y Ayala. Before killing Father Pedro with blows from their tomahawks, the Indians stripped him, placed a rope around his neck, and cruelly flogged him. His naked body was found hugging a cross and an image of the Blessed Virgin Mary. In an act symbolic of the death-blow the Indians believed they had given Christ and the Trinity, three lambs whose throats had been slashed were placed at the martyr's feet. The message was unequivocal. Yet one friar read it as saying that the Franciscans were "like

---

[1] Petition of Fray Francisco de Ayeta, May 10, 1679, *HD*, p. 302; *RBM*, p. 292.

lambs among wolves, and these three lambs gave testimony that the dead father was a lamb." Three years later, in 1675, the Virgin Mary of Toledo appeared to a sickly New Mexican girl, cured her illness, and ordered her to
"arise and announce to this custody that it will soon be destroyed for the
lack of reverence that it shows its priests." The Virgin's apparition sparked a
flurry of high Masses throughout the province and prompted Fray Juan de
Jesús to urge his brother at San Diego de Jémez Mission to cease construction on the colaterals he was building on the church's nave. Time would be
spent best "uniting ourselves with God and preparing to die for our Holy
Faith," Fray Juan de Jesús advised, "for the colaterals will soon end in the
ashes and many of us in death."[2]

Governor Juan Francisco Treviño, who had arrived in the province in
1675, dealt with the widespread Indian sedition by launching a campaign
against idolatry. At Nambé, San Felipe, and Jémez he had known "sorcerers"
hung. Forty-seven medicine men who admitted practicing witchcraft were
arrested, flogged, and sold into slavery. Before these men could be taken out
of the kingdom, the Tewa, armed with clubs and shields, descended on Santa
Fe demanding that Treviño release them, threatening to kill him and all the
colonists if he refused. The governor pleaded: "Wait a while, children, I will
give them to you and pardon them on condition that you forsake idolatry
and iniquity." The Indians stood firm. Treviño capitulated.[3]

The confrontation between Treviño and the Tewa over the medicine men
indicated how radicalized and defiant the Puebloans had become. One of the
men who felt the sting of Treviño's whip was Popé, a San Juan medicine
man. Convinced that the yoke of subjugation could no longer be tolerated,
Popé moved from San Juan to Taos, the northernmost pueblo, to escape the
governor's watchful eye and to plot a provincewide revolt. At Taos, Popé
conferred with the caciques of the surrounding pueblos, with the war chiefs
who had been marginalized by the superior force of the Spaniards, and with
Pueblo dissidents who had escaped the missions' tyranny and taken refuge
among the Apaches.

Popé's genius lay in his brilliant organizational skills and his ability to
inflame the popular imagination through the millenarianism he articulated.
He told the disaffected, the hungry, and the displaced that their ancient gods
would not return bearing gifts of happiness and prosperity until the Christians and their God were dead. Then their sadness and misery would end,
for they would be as they had been at the time of emergence from the

[2] *TM*, vol. 4, pp. 286–87; *RBM*, p. 292; Defouri, *The Martyrs of New Mexico*, pp. 35–37; Petition of
Fray Francisco de Ayeta, May 10, 1679, *HD*, p. 298. Various authors—Vetancurt, Benavides, Defouri—claim that Fray Pedro de Avila y Ayala was killed at Hawikuh. Fray Francisco de Ayeta
said that Fra Pedro died at Abó, and since the two men were in New Mexico at the same time,
I have accepted his account as true. *TM*, vol. 3, pp. 274, 281–82.
[3] Declarations of Luís de Quintana and Diego López, 1681, *RPI*, vol. 2, pp. 289–90, 300. Declaration of Diego López, 1681, *RPI*, vol. 2, p. 301.

underworld. "They would gather large crops of grain, maize with large and thick ears, many bundles of cotton, many calabashes and watermelons," and would enjoy abundant health and leisure. To those elders and chiefs who had been flayed by the friars for their polygamous marriages, or sheared of their hair as fornicators, Popé promised that "who shall kill a Spaniard will get an Indian woman for a wife, and he who kills four will get four women, and he who kills ten or more will have a like number of women." To a people who had seen their agricultural lands usurped and their tribute payments grow onerous over time, Popé offered liberation. When the Spaniards were all dead, he promised, they would "break the lands and enlarge their cultivated fields . . . free from the labor they performed for the religious and the Spaniards."[4]

From Taos Pueblo, Popé sent messengers throughout the kingdom announcing that if the people respected the katsina and called them properly, they would return to usher in a new age. Popé himself regularly called Caudi, Tilini, and Tleume, the katsina who lived in the kiva of the Taos medicine society but "never came out." Finally, after many prayers and offerings, the katsina came out "emit[ting] fire from all the extremities of their bodies." They told Popé that "they were going underground to the lake of Copala" and would return after the Spaniards were gone. The katsina showed Popé how to defeat the Christians and gave him a knotted cord, which he was to circulate to all the pueblos. Those villages that wished to join the rebellion were to untie one knot as a sign of obedience, and by the others would count the days to revolt.[5]

Popé enlisted the caciques of Taos, Picuris, San Lorenzo, Santo Domingo, Jémez, and Pecos, as well as a number of prominent mixed-bloods: Domingo Naranjo from Santa Clara, Nicolás Jonva from San Ildefonso, and Domingo Romero from Tesuque. They met secretly each time a village celebrated its saint's feast day so that their travel to and fro would not provoke suspicion. August 11, 1680, the first night of the new moon, was chosen as the date for the revolt. They knew the settlers would be most vulnerable to attack right before the triennial supply caravan arrived from Mexico City in mid-September with ammunition and horses.[6]

On August 9, 1680, Popé dispatched two messengers to all the pueblos with knotted cords indicating that only two days remained. They told the caciques that a letter from Po-he-yemu, "the father of all the Indians, their great captain, who had been such since the world had been inundated," had arrived

---

[4] Declaration of Jerónimo, a Tigua Indian, January 1, 1682, *RPI,* vol. 2, p. 361. Declaration of Pedro García, a Tagno Indian, August 25, 1680, *RPI,* vol. 1, pp. 24–25. Declaration of Pedro Naranjo, a Queres Indian, December 19, 1681, *RPI,* vol. 2, pp. 246–47.

[5] Declaration of Pedro Naranjo, a Queres Indian, 1681, *RPI,* vol. 2, p. 246.

[6] *Ibid.;* Declaration of Luís de Quintana, 1681, *RPI,* vol. 2, p. 295; J. Sando, "The Pueblo Revolt," *HNAI,* vol. 9, 195; A. Chávez, "Pohe-yemo's Representative."

from the north informing that "all of them . . . should rebel, and that any pueblo that would not agree to it they would destroy, killing all the people."[7]

The caciques of Tanos, San Marcos, and La Cienega opposed the rebellion, and on August 9 informed Governor Antonio de Otermín of its impending approach. Otermín had Popé's messengers arrested and tortured until they revealed what the knotted cords meant. Tesuque's Indians learned of this, and fearing that all might be lost immediately dispatched runners to the confederate pueblos informing them that they should rebel the next day.[8]

August 10, 1680, began for Fray Juan Pío like any Sunday morning. He left Santa Fe on foot to say Mass at Tesuque, accompanied by his armed escort, Pedro Hidalgo. But on this day the pueblo was totally deserted. The friar searched everywhere for the Indians and finally found them a few miles outside the village armed and wearing war paints. "What is this, children, are you mad?," the friar asked. "Do not disturb yourselves; I will help you and will die a thousand deaths for you." Before he could say anything else, a shower of arrows pierced his breast. Pedro Hidalgo would have been killed too had he not been on his horse. He barely escaped, and by ten that morning was back in Santa Fe reporting to the governor. All day emissaries from every part of the kingdom arrived in Santa Fe telling of the massacres they had seen. The Indians' fury had struck the entire province like a bolt of lightning. In one moment a century's work seemed destroyed.[9]

The revolt proceeded as Popé had instructed. First the Indians stole or killed "the principal nerve of warfare," the horses and mules, which the Spaniards had introduced into the province and which had been so instrumental in the conquest and subordination of the Puebloans. Without these beasts of burden, the Spaniards were helpless against mounted Pueblo and Apache warriors. Without horses the Spanish could not communicate rapidly with the centers of authority in New Spain. Indian runners could outrun and outstalk any settler. Whatever technological advantages the Spaniards had on account of their armaments, the Indians offset in numbers. Against roughly 170 colonists capable of bearing arms stood 8,000 or more Indian warriors; a ratio of approximately 1 to 50.[10]

Once the horses were in Indian hands, Popé's forces isolated the settlements in the northern half of the kingdom (the Rio Arriba) from those in the southern half (the Rio Abajo). In the north, all roads to Santa Fe were blocked, and one by one the Spanish settlements were pillaged and razed by

---

[7] Declaration of Luís de Quintana, 1681, *RPI*, vol. 2, p. 295; Otermín Autos, August 9, 1680, *RPI*, vol. 1, pp. 4–5.

[8] Otermín Autos, August 9–10, 1680, *RPI*, vol. 1, pp. 1–6.

[9] Declaration of Pedro Hidalgo, August 10, 1680, *RPI*, vol. 1, pp. 6–7. Otermín Autos, August 10, 1680, *RPI*, vol. 1, pp. 7–9.

[10] Opinion of Cabildo, September 14, 1680, *RPI*, vol. 1, p. 120. Letter of Fray Francisco de Ayeta, 1679, *HD*, p. 299.

the Indians, who scavenged whatever armaments they could. In a few hours 401 settlers and 21 friars were killed. Those who survived gathered at the governor's residence in Santa Fe. The colonists of the Rio Abajo gathered at Isleta.[11]

By August 13, all of the villages in the Rio Arriba had been destroyed and only Santa Fe stood, surrounded by Pueblo and Apache warriors who were ready for a final assault. Grossly outnumbered but stubbornly refusing to admit defeat, Otermín made one last peace overture. Through Juan, a Tano Indian servant turned rebel leader, Otermín implored the caciques "that even though they had committed so many atrocities, still there was a remedy, for if they would return to obedience to his Majesty they would be pardoned." The chiefs jeered and demanded through Juan that

> all classes of Indians who were in our power be given up to them, both those in the service of the Spaniards and those of the Mexican nation of that sub-urb of Analco. He demanded also that his wife and children be given up to him, and likewise that all the Apache men and women whom the Spaniards had captured in war be turned over to them, inasmuch as some Apaches who were among them were asking for them.

Otermín refused, and the battle for Santa Fe began.[12]

For nine days Santa Fe lay under siege. To hasten the colonists' surrender, the rebels cut off their food and water. By August 20th the Indians sensed victory. That night they were heard shouting gleefully: "Now the God of the Spaniards, who was their father, is dead, and Santa María, who was their mother, and the saints . . . were pieces of rotten wood" and that "their own God whom they obeyed [had] never died." Determined that it was better "to die fighting than of hunger and thirst," the colonists at Santa Fe marshalled all their firepower for a final assault on the morning of August 21. The strategy worked. Popé's forces quickly lost 350 men and temporarily were set to flight. At day's end, Otermín and the settlers decided to abandon Santa Fe before the Indians recouped their losses and returned to rout them. Otermín hoped that he would be able to join forces with the settlers of the Rio Abajo, whom he thought were still gathered at Isleta, and return north with them to subdue the apostates. But unbeknownst to him, the refugees at Isleta had already fled south toward El Paso.[13]

The colonists' retreat south from Santa Fe was filled with horrors. In every village they found piles of mutilated bodies strewn amid ashes of still smoldering fires. At Sandía Pueblo the mission's statues were covered with

---

[11] Otermín Autos, October 9, 1680, *RPI*, vol. 1, pp. 194–95; Muster, September 29, 1680, *RPI*, vol. 1, pp. 134–53.

[12] Otermín to Fray Francisco de Ayeta, September 8, 1680, *RPI*, vol. 1, pp. 98–101.

[13] Declaration of Josephe, Spanish-speaking Indian, December 19, 1681, *RPI*, vol. 2, pp. 239–40; Otermín Autos, August 13–20, 1680, *RPI*, vol. 1, p. 13. Otermín Autos, August 13–21, 1680, *RPI*, vol. 1, p. 15. Certification of departure, August 21, 1680, *RPI*, vol. 1, p. 19.

excrement. Two chalices had been discarded in a basket of manure, and the paint on the altar's crucifix had been stripped off with a whip. Feces covered the holy communion table and the arms of a statue of Saint Francis had been hacked off with an ax. At every mission along their route they reported the most unspeakable profanations of Christian *sacra*.[14]

The Christians felt equal revulsion on seeing and hearing of how the friars had died. On that August night of rebellion, the Jémez Indians apprehended Fray Juan de Jesús, bound him naked onto a pig's back and paraded him through the town, heaping all sorts of jeers and blows on him. Then they removed him from the pig, forced him onto his hands and knees and took turns riding atop his back, repeatedly spurring his haunches to prod him forward. When the warriors were ready to kill him, some dissension erupted in their ranks. But showing a fidelity to death and a love for his persecutors that the manuals of martyrdom assured him would win a crown in heaven, Father Juan allegedly said: "Children, I am a poor old man, do not fight, do not kill each other in order to protect me; do what God permits." And so they shoved a sword through his heart and gave him numerous blows. His body was discovered by the Spaniards in some woods near the pueblo.[15]

Though the Christians were aghast at how the Pueblo Indians had manifested their anger, one only has to recall the massive desecration of katsina masks, kivas, and other native sacra that occurred during the Spanish conquest to understand why the Indians retaliated so exactly during the Pueblo Revolt. The tables were now turned in this contest of cultures. The Indians had learned well from their overlords the functions of iconoclasm in political spectacle.

When Otermín's forces finally reached Isleta, the pueblo was deserted. A week earlier, on August 14, news had reached Isleta that all the Spaniards of the Rio Arriba had been killed, and acting on this information, the settlers, under the leadership of Alonso García, had abandoned Isleta and retreated south. The reconquest of New Mexico would have to wait. For the moment, the only succor either refugee group could expect was from the mission supply train they knew was advancing toward New Mexico. News of the revolt reached Fray Francisco de Ayeta's supply caravan on August 25, just south of El Paso. He promptly advanced toward Socorro, and it was near there on September 6 that the Isleta and Santa Fe survivors of the rebellion were finally united. Together they numbered 1,946, of whom approximately 500 were Pueblo and Apache slaves.[16]

The Christians' defeat and departure were cause for great celebration among the Pueblos. Popé and his two captains, Alonso Catiti of Santo

[14] Opinion of the Santa Fe Cabildo, October 3, 1680, *RPI*, vol. 1, pp. 177–78.
[15] Sariñana y Cuenca, *The Franciscan Martyrs*, p. 16; "Carta del Padre Fray Silvestre de Escalante," April 2, 1778, *DHNM*, pp. 305–324; J. Espinosa, *Crusaders of the Rio Grande*, pp. 19–20.
[16] Scholes, "Civil Government," p. 96; *RPI*, vol. 1, pp. 21–65.

Domingo and Luís Tupatu of Picuris, traveled throughout the province ordering everyone to return "to the state of their antiquity, as when they came from the lake of Copola; that this was the better life and the one they desired, because the God of the Spaniards was worth nothing and theirs was very strong." Popé promised that if they lived in accordance with their ancestral laws, there would be endless peace, prosperity, and harmony.[17]

But none of this would be possible so long as there were vestiges of Christianity. Crosses and images of Christ, of the Virgin Mary, and of the saints had to be destroyed. Churches had to be razed and their bells shattered. Men and women were to forget their Christian names and use only native ones. They were to purify themselves by plunging "into the rivers and wash[ing] themselves with amole [a soap-root] . . . washing even their clothing, with the understanding that there would thus be taken from them the character of the holy sacraments." Anyone who spoke Spanish or uttered the name of Jesus or Mary would be punished severely. Men were to abandon the wife they had taken in matrimony "for any one whom they might wish." Everyone was "to burn the seeds which the Spaniards sowed and to plant only maize and beans, which were the crops of their ancestors." All of this was to be done in the presence of the children so that they would learn the ways of the ancients and the meaning of respect.[18]

Within weeks of the Spaniards' defeat, the indigenous sacral topography was restored. "Flour, feathers, and the seed of maguey, maize, and tobacco" were offered to the spirits at pre-conquest shrines. Kivas that had been desecrated and filled with sand were emptied and resacralized. At last the gods who had abandoned their people and allowed them to perish from hunger and sickness returned from the underworld.[19]

The Spanish survivors of the Pueblo Revolt were genuinely confused by what had happened. They thought themselves blameless and self-righteously pinned the entire disaster on the Indians. A visibly shaken Governor Otermín bristled that the devil had ensnared the Indians with idolatries and superstitions to which "their stupid ignorance predisposes them, for they live blindly in their freedom and stupid vices." In the months that followed, Otermín gleaned the whys of the revolt. Answers came from five Indians he captured. From Pedro Nanboa, an 80-year-old Indian, Governor Otermín learned that for more than 70 years the Indians had resented Spanish rule because the Christians had destroyed their religious objects, had

[17] Declaration of Pedro Naranjo, a Queres Indian, December 19, 1681, *RPI,* vol. 2, p. 248.
[18] Declaration of Pedro Naranjo, a Queres Indian, December 19, 1681, *RPI,* vol. 2, p. 248. Declaration of Juan, a Tegua Indian, December 18, 1681, *RPI,* vol. 2, p. 235. Declaration of Josephe, Spanish-speaking Indian, December 19, 1681, *RPI,* vol. 2, p. 239; Declaration of Juan Lorenzo, a Queres Indian, December 20, 1681, *RPI,* vol. 2, 251.
[19] Declaration of Josephe, a Spanish-speaking Indian, and of Juan Lorenzo, a Queres Indian, December 19–20, 1681, *RPI,* vol. 2, pp. 239–40, 249–52. Declaration of Juan Lorenzo, a Queres Indian, December 20, 1681, *RPI,* vol. 2, p. 251.

prohibited their ceremonials, and had humiliated and punished their old men. For this reason the Indians "had been plotting to rebel and to kill the Spaniards and the religious . . . planning constantly to carry it out down to the present occasion."[20]

Two Queres Indians voiced more specific complaints. They objected to the "ill treatment and injuries" they had received from Otermín's constables who "would not leave them alone, [had] burned their estufas [kivas]," and constantly beat them. The Queres had wanted to be "free from the labor they had performed for the religious and the Spaniards." They had grown "weary of putting in order, sweeping, heating, and adorning the church." The Tano Indians agreed. They too had "tired of the work they had to do for the Spaniards and the religious, because they did not allow them to plant or do other things for their own needs." Had the Christians shown them respect there might not have been a rebellion, explained Joseph. Instead, "they beat [us], took away what [we] had, and made [us] work without pay."[21]

The Franciscans pondered the Pueblo Revolt and concluded that the only thing they were guilty of was selfless love for the Indians. Fray Antonio de Sierra wondered why it was that "the Indians who have done the greatest harm are those who have been most favored by the religious and who are most intelligent." What seemed to preoccupy the friars most were the martyrdoms their brothers had suffered. These were not a cause for sadness and tears, but a cause for joy. "We do not mourn the blood shed by twenty-one of our brothers," wrote Fray Juan Alvarez, "for from them there comes to our sacred religion such an access of faith and such honor and glory to God and His church." Fray Francisco de Ayeta was similarly philosophical; that "which the world calls losses, they [are] really the richest treasure of the church."[22]

The viceroy, dignitaries of the Franciscan Order in New Spain, and a few survivors of the Pueblo Revolt gathered at the Cathedral of Mexico City on March 1, 1681, to eulogize New Mexico's martyrs. In his sermon, Doctor Ysidro Sariñana y Cuenca, the cathedral's canon, reflected on how a century's work among "wild beasts," teaching them how to cultivate the soil, clothing their nakedness, and showing them how to live in houses, had

[20] Otermín Auto, September 13, 1680, *RPI,* vol. 1, 122. Declaration of Pedro Nanboa, an Indian, September 6, 1680, *RPI,* vol. 1, p. 61; Declaration of Pedro García, an Indian, September 6, 1680, *RPI,* vol. 1, p. 62.
[21] Declaration of Josephe, Spanish-speaking Indian, December 19, 1681, and Declaration of Juan Lorenzo, a Queres Indian, December 20, 1681, *RPI,* vol. 2, pp. 239–40, 251. Declaration of Pedro Naranjo, a Queres Indian, December 19, 1681, *RPI,* vol. 2, pp. 245–47. Declaration of Juan Lorenzo, a Queres Indian, December 20, 1681, *RPI,* vol. 2, p. 251. Declaration of Pedro García, a Tano Indian, August 25, 1680, *RPI,* vol. 1, pp. 24–25. Declaration of Josephe, Spanish-speaking Indian, December 19, 1681, *RPI,* vol. 2, pp. 239–41.
[22] Sierra Letter to Ayeta, September 4, 1680, *RPI,* vol. 1, p. 59. Letter of Friar Juan Alvarez, et al., to viceroy, October 15, 1680, *RPI,* vol. 1, pp. 203–4. Letter of Ayeta to viceroy, August 31, 1680, *RPI,* vol. 1, p. 53.

ended. The arrows that had sapped the lives of the friars were like a "womb pregnant with darts." Their suffering was "the sure road to life; because the better title corresponding to such deaths is to call them lives," said Sariñana. New Mexico's martyrs had perfectly imitated Christ. Like Christ, they had died because of their Father's love for humanity and because of man's hatred and ingratitude. God did not love the sins of the persecutors, but he loved the patience of the persecuted. He did not love the evil hand that wounded, but he loved the suffering of the wounds. When the arrows of treachery had pierced the martyrs' breasts, when tomahawks had crushed their skulls, and when flames had consumed their bodies, they had been united in mystical marriage with God, a true sign of their perfection. No words captured the mood of that day better than those of St. Ignatius of Antioch: "I am yearning for death with all the passion of a lover. Earthly longings have been crucified; in me there is left no spark of desire for mundane things, but only a murmur of living water that whispers within me, 'Come to Father.'"[23]

The New Mexican survivors of the revolt settled near the Franciscan mission of Our Lady of Guadalupe, which had been established in 1659 near the present-day site of Ciudad Juárez. There the colonists nursed their wounds and sustained themselves on what little food Father Ayeta had procured for the friars and on what could be extracted from the local Indians. For almost a year they waited for orders and reinforcements to arrive from Mexico City. Finally, in the autumn of 1681, Otermín was ready to punish the apostates. His compatriots were not. Many of them had fled further south. Those who had remained wanted no part in the reconquest. Even the friars were cool to the idea. Otermín, aware that news of the Pueblos' victory had spread like an "infection" throughout northern New Spain, knew that if El Paso and New Mexico were abandoned, the entire area north of Parral would be lost. Already the Indians of Nueva Vizcaya were in revolt. Those around El Paso were seething with discontent because of their exploitation by New Mexico's refugees. All across the north, from Sonora to Coahuila, the drums of war could be heard. On the viceroy's orders, Otermín gathered his troops at El Paso (which had been founded earlier that year), forbade the colonists to desert the area, and departed north on November 5, 1681, with 146 soldiers and 112 Indian allies, many of them "mere boys and raw recruits."[24]

Between November 26 and December 4, Otermín's troops marched north, visiting the abandoned villages of Senecu, San Pascual, Socorro, Alamillio, and Sevilleta. On December 5 they reached Isleta Pueblo and conquered its inhabitants with little effort. Otermín gathered the Indians in the

[23] Sariñana y Cuenca, *The Franciscan Martyrs*, pp. 17–18. Staniforth, trans., *Early Christian Writings*, p. 106. I thank Professor Sabine MacCormack for bringing this document to my attention.
[24] Scholes, "Documents," p. 195. The impact of the Pueblo Revolt on other Indian groups in northern New Spain is studied in Forbes, *Apache, Navaho, and Spaniard*, pp. 177–224. *RPI*, vol. 1, p. cxxi, and vol. 2, pp. 32–88, 153–83, 190–201.

plaza, chastized them for their apostasy, and ordered them to erect large crosses for their houses and little ones to wear around their necks. Fray Francisco de Ayeta arrived the next day. He was triumphantly greeted outside the town by Otermín and the Indians, shouting: "Praised be the most holy sacrament and the purity of our Lady, the Virgin Mary, conceived without stain of sin." Ayeta celebrated Mass the next day. He absolved the Indians' apostasy, baptized their infants, and ordered men to take those wives they had been given in matrimony and to burn all their idols. Before the royal standard, the Indians swore vassalage to the King anew, exclaiming: "Long live the king, our Lord Charles II, God Save Him!" Three volleys of musketry were fired, bugles were sounded, and church bells were rung.[25]

Otermín dispatched emissaries from Isleta to the northern pueblos to announce his arrival and peaceful intent. He expected the Indians to hail his return as repentant apostates, weary of their Apache enemies and of their caciques. Nowhere was such a greeting forthcoming. Alameda, Puaray, Sandía, San Felipe, Santo Domingo, and Cochiti were all abandoned before Otermín's troops entered them. The maize bins at each pueblo were well stocked and what corn there was Otermín had destroyed. By Christmas eve Indian hostilities were growing, and knowing that his troops were ill-prepared and poorly provisioned for a major attack, Otermín retreated to Isleta. By the beginning of 1682, the Spaniards were back in El Paso. The expedition had been a resounding failure. Only the southern pueblos had been penetrated. The Tewa Pueblos and those at Taos, Picuris, and Jémez had not been molested. Substantial force would be necessary to reconquer New Mexico.

The jubilation that swept the pueblos at the defeat of the Spaniards was short-lived. According to Juan, a captured Tiwa Indian, by late 1681, people were muttering that Popé had deceived them. They had had "very small harvests, there [had] been no rain, and everyone [was] perishing." Popé's alliance splintered. Civil war erupted at many pueblos among the caciques, the medicine men, and the warriors, each claiming precedence and superior magical powers. In the midst of this chaos, ill-provisioned pueblos began to prey on the granaries of their neighbors. The Queres and the inhabitants of Taos and Pecos waged war against the Tewa and the Tanos. Then the Queres alliance disintegrated and each pueblo declared itself independent. The Tewa and Tanos deposed Popé as their leader because of his excessive demands for women, grain, and livestock. Luís Tupatu replaced him. Around 1683 the Yutes (modern-day Utes) and Apaches waged what must have seemed an endless war against Jémez, Taos, Picuris, and the Tewa.[26]

Widespread hunger and pestilence were followed by another nine years of drought. Legend holds that even the Rio Grande dried up during those

[25] March of the Army from El Paso to Isleta, 1681, *RPI*, vol. 2, pp. 209, 210–12.
[26] Declaration of Juan, a Tigua Indian, December 27, 1681, *RPI*, vol. 2, p. 346. *RPI*, vol. 1, p. cxxxvii; Bancroft, *History of Arizona and New Mexico*, p. 185n.

years and did not carry water again until a virgin was sacrificed to Horned Water Serpent. Taking the decade of drought that preceded and followed the Pueblo Revolt, we can understand the ecological factors that fueled village factionalism and internecine warfare. Pueblo mythology says that such struggles were endemic to their lifeway and always forced them to migrate until they found a safe place to call home.[27]

Between 1682 and 1692, the 50-soldier presidio established in El Paso in 1683 provided the main force for attempts by the Spanish colonists to reconquer New Mexico. It was not until news reached the Spanish crown that French exploratory teams had made incursions into the Mississippi Valley and Texas that efforts were intensified to reestablish Spanish authority over New Mexico and to colonize Texas as a defensive buffer for the silver mines of northern New Spain. The man chosen for the former task was Don Diego de Vargas Zapata Luján Ponce de León, who assumed New Mexico's governorship in 1691. Scion of one Spain's noblest families, the 48-year-old governor was soon to enter Pueblo country to subdue the infidel and make a world safe for Hispanicism, much as his ancestors had done during the reconquest of Spain.[28]

With the Pueblo Revolt, a century of Christian rule came to an abrupt end. Perhaps in the Kingdom of New Mexico, more perfectly than anywhere else in the New World, the Franciscans had created the semblance of that terrestrial theocracy for which they so worked and prayed. Had the pope rather than the king of Spain been the vicar of Christ in the Indies, as the Franciscans steadfastly maintained, the Antichrists of the colony (the governors) would not have polluted the minds and bodies of innocent Indian babes. Unbeknownst to the martyred friars, who believed that their blood would fructify the soil for an abundant harvest of souls, if anything, their deaths thoroughly repudiated clerical rule. When New Mexico's reconquest was achieved, the zeal, the will, and the way for clerics to successfully challenge the primacy of secular rule were gone.

[27] Ibid., p. 186n.
[28] Schroeder, "Rio Grande Ethnohistory," pp. 41–70.

PART IV

Provincial America

"The Extention of His Majesties Dominions": The Virginia Backcountry and the Reconfiguration of Imperial Frontiers

Warren R. Hofstra

INTRODUCTION

Departing from earlier approaches to frontier studies, Hofstra recasts the American frontier into a British imperial context. He offers a political explanation for what has often been described as a primarily social phenomenon— the westward expansion of white, yeomen householders. In Hofstra's account, the band of yeomen communities that stretched across the frontier from Georgia to Maine owed its existence to a new constellation of factors arising out of the Glorious Revolution and affecting the course of North American history for the rest of the eighteenth century. Catholic France, a frequent ally of England in the seventeenth century, was now its greatest rival, ever ready to support and encourage any Native Americans the colonists antagonized. The plantation economies of the Chesapeake made the switch from servant to slave

Warren R. Hofstra, " 'The Extention of His Majesties' Dominions': The Virginia Backcountry and the Reconfiguration of Imperial Frontiers," *Journal of American History*, 84 (March 1998), 1281–1312. Copyright © 1998 Organization of American Historians. Reprinted with permission.

Warren R. Hofstra is professor of history and director of the Community History Project at Shenandoah University in Winchester, Virginia. Portions of this essay were presented at the conference "Americans in Motion: Virginia, the South, Mobility, and the American Dream" at the Virginia Historical Society in Richmond, Virginia, March 11–12, 1994, and at the eleventh Ulster-American Heritage Symposium at the Ulster-American Folk Park in Omagh, Northern Ireland, August 8–11, 1996.

For their helpful comments and vigorous critiques of earlier drafts of this essay, I would like to thank John M. Hemphill II, Kenneth E. Koons, Michael N. McConnell, James H. Merrell, Robert D. Mitchell, Gregory H. Nobles, Daniel K. Richter, Ian K. Steele, Thad W. Tate, and the anonymous reviewers for the *Journal of American History*.

labor, leaving plantation owners with the perpetual fear of slave insurrection. Finally, with the ecclesiastical experimentation of the Restoration period finally put to rest, Protestantism became the fundamental ideological bond of the British Empire.

In these transformed circumstances, white, Protestant yeomen, whether from Britain or Germany, had a special role to play, one they were familiar with from Europe. From Northern Ireland to Transylvania, yeomen similar to those who settled the American backcountry served as military and cultural buffers on the far edges of European empires. Here, they served as a politically reliable bulwark separating coastal planters from French and Indian enemies and cutting off plantation slaves from potential frontier refuges. Their presence benefited the coastal planters in many ways. No French or Indian expedition ever penetrated into Virginia and no maroon communities were established in the mountains, as they were in Jamaica, Panama, Brazil, and elsewhere. Furthermore, as their population grew, Virginia planters profited from the farmers through land speculation. In Hofstra's account, the frontier is no longer a place of individual freedom but a militarized zone shaped by imperial and elite politics.

- *If these are the real forces that determined the destinies of frontier yeomen, what are we to make of the significance of the frontier in American history?*

During the 1730s, in Virginia west of the Blue Ridge, a settlement frontier developed whose society and culture contrasted sharply with those already established in the colony. A large majority of the new western inhabitants, unlike Virginians elsewhere, were non-English, predominantly German and Scotch-Irish. Called "foreign Protestants" and Irish Protestants, they were almost exclusively white—few Africans or African Americans were among them. Settlers practiced dissenting and sectarian faiths, most stressing a common humanity. Elsewhere, not only was Virginia organized under the Church of England but conforming Virginians largely subscribed to the deferential social practice of the established church. Moreover, western settlers were not tobacco producers. They were yeoman farmers instead of planters—smallholders raising grains and livestock, employing family more often than slave labor, practicing handcrafts, and trading locally in the context of community self-sufficiency.[1]

---

[1] "Foreign Protestants" strictly speaking included only immigrants from outside the British Empire, that is, people who were not natural-born subjects of the English monarch, but the term was commonly used for all the non-English peoples of the eighteenth-century backcountry. On economic diversity and cultural pluralism in the Virginia backcountry, see Richard R. Beeman, *The Evolution of the Southern Backcountry: A Case Study of Lunenburg County, Virginia, 1746–1832* (Philadelphia, 1984); Freeman H. Hart, *The Valley of Virginia in the American Revolution, 1763–1789* (Chapel Hill, 1942); James G. Leyburn, *The Scotch-Irish: A Social History* (Chapel Hill,

The initial distinctiveness of the backcountry raises the question: Why did a society develop on the Virginia frontier whose ethnic and religious diversity, mixed economy, and political outlook fundamentally altered the identity of the colony?[2] Although Virginia escaped the violence of the Regulator movements on the Carolina frontier in the 1760s and of the Whiskey Rebellion that rocked western Pennsylvania in the 1790s, the state would cleave in two along the fault lines of frontier settlement during the American Civil War. Conventional answers to the question of backcountry distinctiveness and its genesis have adopted the perspective of those who took up new lands and highlighted their interests. European refugees wanted land, and Virginia let them have it on very attractive terms. Pouring into Pennsylvania after 1720 from straitened circumstances in Europe and frustrated by high land prices and political disputes, German and Scotch-Irish immigrants turned south to the Shenandoah Valley, where land was good and land prices low.[3]

This school of thought derives from a century of frontier scholarship beginning with Frederick Jackson Turner's arguments that the frontier broke down social conventions and that settlers reconstituted polities on increasingly democratic footings. Postulating that, although at first the "wilderness masters the colonist. . . . little by little he transforms the wilderness," Turner rested his thesis on what settlers did on the frontier, not why they were there.

1962); Turk McCleskey, "Across the First Divide: Frontiers of Settlements and Culture in Augusta County, Virginia, 1738–1770" (Ph.D. diss., College of William and Mary, 1990); Robert D. Mitchell, *Commercialism and Frontier: Perspectives on the Shenandoah Valley* (Charlottesville, 1977); Albert H. Tillson Jr., *Gentry and Common Folk: Political Culture on a Virginia Frontier, 1740–1789* (Lexington, Ky., 1991); and Klaus Wust, *The Virginia Germans* (Charlottesville, 1969), 17–199.

[2] For the argument that backcountry distinctiveness contributed to debates between regions of Virginia in the nineteenth century and the state's division during the American Civil War, see Warren R. Hofstra, "The Virginia Backcountry in the Eighteenth Century: The Question of Origins and the Issue of Outcomes," *Virginia Magazine of History and Biography*, 101 (Oct. 1993), 485–508. On regional implications of eighteenth-century backcountry migrations, see David Hackett Fischer, *Albion's Seed: Four British Folkways in America* (New York, 1989), 605–782; Terry G. Jordan and Matti Kaups, *The American Backwoods Frontier: An Ethnic and Ecological Interpretation* (Baltimore, 1989); Robert D. Mitchell, "The Formation of Early American Cultural Regions: An Interpretation," in *European Settlement and Development in North America: Essays on Geographical Change in Honour and Memory of Andrew Hill Clark*, ed. James R. Gibson (Toronto, 1978), 66–90; and Milton Newton, "Cultural Pre-adaptation and the Upland South," *Geoscience and Man*, 5 (June 1974), 143–54. On Virginia, see Charles Henry Ambler, *Sectionalism in Virginia from 1776 to 1861* (1910; New York, 1964).

[3] A classic statement of the position that "settlement of the Southern back country was largely the result of the quest for cheap lands by people from older communities" appears in Oscar Theodore Barck Jr. and Hugh Talmage Lefler, *Colonial America* (1958; New York, 1968), 255–56. For variants of this position, see Carl Bridenbaugh, *Myths and Realities: Societies of the Colonial South* (1952; Westport, 1981), 122; Johanna Miller Lewis, *Artisans in the North Carolina Backcountry* (Lexington, Ky., 1995), 19, 22, 33, 49–50; Mitchell, *Commercialism and Frontier*, 16–19; and Wust, *Virginia Germans*, 28–30.

He convinced generations of Americans that the frontier was the self-creation of those who settled it and that frontier expansion was an American story. The idea that the motive forces of expansion sprang from American conditions fashioned by settlers themselves dominated later interpretations, including Robert D. Mitchell's account of the eighteenth-century Shenandoah Valley, the lone modern survey of the region.[4]

From the perspective of these studies, the question of why Virginia fostered the growth of a society alien to well-established cultural norms is very difficult to answer. Never had Virginia freely distributed land to all takers. Virginia history had been the story of the engrossment of land in larger and larger quantities by social and political elites drawing ever closer in the nexus of kinship, land ownership, and political power. This elite never achieved stronger and more exclusive control over political power, especially the power to distribute land, than when it was creating a backcountry frontier of outsiders. On the very eve of settlement in the Shenandoah Valley, for instance, Lt. Gov. William Gooch defended the practice of elites' engrossing land in the Piedmont to the east of the Blue Ridge. Writing to the Board of Trade, the English administrative body charged with overseeing colonial affairs, he reasoned that "where the greatest Tracts have been granted & possessed" by "men of substance" the "meaner sort of People [have been encouraged] to seat themselves as it were under the Shade & Protection of the Greater." Occasionally the Virginia Council, the appointed upper house of the colony's legislature, which also served as a high court and the governor's advisory board, turned down land petitions by strangers. In May 1741, for example, it denied a request for three thousand acres, explaining that the "Petitioner is not known to any of the Board and therefore [this quantity is] thought too much for so obscure a Person."[5]

According to another school of thought, Virginia's Blue Ridge frontier was developed by land speculators under the patronage of the colonial government. Thomas Perkins Abernethy and Richard Lee Morton argued that

---

[4] Frederick Jackson Turner, "The Significance of the Frontier in American History" in Frederick Jackson Turner, *The Frontier in American History* (New York, 1920), 1–38; Frederick Jackson Turner, "The Old West," *ibid.*, 67–125; Mitchell, *Commercialism and Frontier.*

[5] William Gooch to Board of Trade, April 2, 1729, C.O. 5/1321, Colonial Office Papers (Public Records Office, London, Eng.); Wilmer L. Hall, ed., *Executive Journals of the Council of Colonial Virginia,* vol. V (Richmond, 1945), 50. On the Council's intent to reserve large quantities of land for the social class it represented, see, for example, H. R. McIlwaine, ed., *Executive Journals of the Council of Colonial Virginia,* vol. IV (Richmond, 1930), 430–31. On the control of land granting by those in power and prominence in Virginia, see Sarah S. Hughes, *Surveyors and Statesmen: Land Measuring in Colonial Virginia* (Richmond, 1979), 84–85, 107; Turk McCleskey, "Rich Land, Poor Prospects: Real Estate and the Formation of a Social Elite in Augusta County, Virginia, 1738–1770," *Virginia Magazine of History and Biography,* 98 (July 1990), 449–86; Charles S. Sydnor, *Gentlemen Freeholders: Political Practices in Washington's Virginia* (Chapel Hill, 1952); and Manning C. Voorhis, "Crown Versus Council in the Virginia Land Policy," *William and Mary Quarterly,* 3 (Oct. 1946), 499–514.

Virginia responded to the pressures of eighteenth-century migrations with speculative ventures benefiting the traditional governing elite. In an explicit attack on Turner's concept of a settler-defined frontier, Abernethy asserted that few pioneers

> would have established themselves there had not the speculators paved the way for them. . . . How different would have been the settlement of our early West had it been carried forward by bands of free spirits setting out upon their own initiative, equipped only with the rifle and the axe, to take possession of unoccupied lands, with no thought of speculators or surveyors!

In Morton's assessment the "gentlemen of eighteenth-century Virginia, like those of the seventeenth century, did not wait for obscure backwoods hunters, fur traders, cattlemen, and small farmers to blaze the trails to the West and subdue the forests for them; they were themselves pioneers in those ventures."[6]

From this perspective, as well, it is difficult to explain the origins of backcountry distinctiveness. In the early 1730s the Virginia Council did issue to individuals grants of land west of the Blue Ridge that were unprecedented in size. Grantees were entitled to profit from land sales at prices six times the cost of crown lands elsewhere in Virginia. But whereas the Council and the families that dominated it were the principal recipients of their own largess in distributing Piedmont lands during the 1720s, most of the massive grants issued between 1730 and 1740 west of the Blue Ridge went to men of non-English origin residing outside Virginia and with neither significant ties to the Council nor the social standing to command its attention. Moreover, conditions placed on the grants attracted the immigrant population that made the colony's mountain region economically and socially distinctive. This region lay outside the bounds of any Virginia county. No sheriff's writ ran there, no deeds could be conveyed or property confiscated for debt, and no justice of the peace held jurisdiction over it. Thus no speculator could be assured of profits from land claims. Virginia was not simply responding conventionally to population pressures with land speculation: it was deliberately provoking a migration to its marchlands where a vacuum of local government and colonial authority existed.[7]

---

[6] Thomas Perkins Abernethy, "The First Transmontane Advance," in *Humanistic Studies in Honor of John Calvin Metcalf*, ed. James S. Wilson (New York, 1941), 138; Richard L. Morton, *Colonial Virginia* (2 vols., Chapel Hill, 1960), II, 540; Thomas Perkins Abernethy, *Three Virginia Frontiers* (Baton Rouge, 1940), 29–62. Morton derives his narrative almost exclusively from Abernethy, as do more recent authors; see W. Stitt Robinson, *The Southern Colonial Frontier, 1607–1763* (Albuquerque, 1979), 139–50.

[7] The 1720 act establishing Spotsylvania County located its western boundary along the Shenandoah River. This boundary remained fixed until Orange County was established in 1734 extending westward to the full extent of Virginia claims. Only then were settlements west of the Shenandoah River absorbed within the legal limits of Virginia counties. Although the Northern Neck counties of Stafford and Prince William were unbounded to the west, they never possessed

To explain the movement of peoples to the Virginia frontier during the eighteenth century requires a new perspective that connects the concerns of settlers and the interests of speculators with the geopolitical and imperial forces that defined frontiers and made their settlements both possible and expedient. The buffer settlements of European Protestants that the colonial government established west of the Blue Ridge between 1730 and 1745 were part of a larger effort to check French expansion across the interior of North America, extend English dominion, secure a western periphery destabilized by Indian conflict, and occupy mountain fastnesses otherwise a refuge to runaway slaves. What met the needs of Europeans looking for land and economic competence in property ownership also served the interests of colonial officials. Events in the Virginia backcountry from 1730 to 1750, moreover, reflected imperial responses to developments between 1700 and 1722 when France laid the basis for a continental empire, northern and southern Indians resumed disruptive wars across that continent, and African slavery came to define the southern colonial labor system. English colonial governments sought ways to secure established, plantation regions from the threats posed by those changes. Williamsburg and London therefore provide the perspective for explaining why a society that differed so significantly from Virginia traditions developed on a strategically sensitive frontier and under the auspices of the elite that governed the colony in its own interest.

Developments in Virginia compose a case study of change in the eighteenth-century backcountry, conceived for the first time as extending continuously from Nova Scotia south to the Carolinas and, eventually, to Georgia. As William Gooch and the Virginia Council began issuing orders for land west of the Blue Ridge, the Board of Trade and the governor of South Carolina matured plans to lay out frontier towns surrounding that colony's Low Country plantations. Similarly, the board and the government of New York were negotiating the establishment of a chain of forts and settlements that would extend English control north and west from Albany to the centers of French power along the St. Lawrence River and the Great Lakes. Farther east, on the coasts of present-day Maine and Nova Scotia, colonial agents were formulating additional settlement projects. The distinctiveness of the entire backcountry was in part the inevitable consequence of the cultures immigrant peoples brought to the region. But in reconfiguring frontiers, British officials on both sides of the Atlantic Ocean came to see predominantly white, Protestant, yeoman societies as distinctively advantageous to securing a continental frontier. Elsewhere, as in Virginia, backcountry settlement developed out of a coincidence of interests among settlers,

---

any jurisdiction beyond the Blue Ridge. See William W. Hening, ed., *The Statutes at Large: Being a Collection of All the Laws of Virginia, from . . . 1619 . . .* (13 vols., Richmond, New York, and Philadelphia, 1819–1823), IV, 77–79, 303, 450–51; Fairfax Harrison, *Landmarks of Old Prince William: A Study of Origins in Northern Virginia* (2 vols., Richmond, 1924), I, 311–14.

speculators, and imperial authorities, but the key to the social construction of this frontier lay with the imperatives of empire.[8]

In Virginia those interests and imperatives met in the forces that transformed what Europeans called wilderness or waste land into property. From the viewpoint of imperial officials, land grants west of the Blue Ridge represented the extension of sovereignty over unorganized territory through the authority of the state in the person of the king to fabricate property. From the viewpoint of European immigrants, however, rights to land meant economic competence and independence from the subject relations of feudal society. Once on the land, these men and women established dispersed communities of enclosed or self-contained farms and household economies lacking the centers of power and forms of administrative control English authorities associated with what the Virginia Council described as "the Extention of His Majesties Dominions."[9]

Exercising dominion in Virginia, therefore, depended upon the formation of county government. The justices of the county court represented the authority of the royal governor, who appointed them, and of the king, who appointed the governor. As the institutional center of the county, the court became the local agent for the transformation of waste land into property.[10] It functioned as a criminal court as well as a court of record for property ownership and conveyance and civil court for resolving disputes over property. By establishing roads and thus defining the rights and routes by which

[8] On South Carolina, see C.O. 5/360–64, 388, 400–401, Colonial Office Papers; on New York, see C.O. 5/1052–55, 1085–86, 1092–93, 1124–25, *ibid.*, and on Nova Scotia, C.O. 217/3–7, 218/2, *ibid.* In 1733 the governor of New York, William Cosby, wrote to the duke of Newcastle, the British secretary of state responsible for colonial affairs: "the most effectual way to extend our settlements is to erect Forts in places more advanced towards Canada . . . such a line of frontier Garrisons would keep the French from incroaching upon us . . . and would encourage our Planters to extend their settlements to our advanced Garrisons." See Edmund Bailey O'Callaghan, ed., *Documents Relative to the Colonial History of the State of New-York* (15 vols., Albany, 1853–1887), V, 972. On the coincidence of interests between settlers and surveyors on the Virginia frontier, cf. Turk McCleskey, "Shadow Land: Provisional Real Estate Claims and Anglo-American Settlement in Southwest Virginia," in *From the Good Earth: Interdisciplinary Perspectives on Frontier Communities*, ed. David C. Crass et al. (Knoxville, forthcoming).

[9] H. R. McIlwaine, ed., *Legislative Journals of the Council of Virginia* (1918–1919; Richmond, 1979), 864. On squatting, see Hughes, *Surveyors and Statesmen,* 111, 127; Leonidas Dodson, *Alexander Spotswood: Governor of Colonial Virginia, 1710–1722* (Philadelphia, 1932), 133–56; and Manning C. Voorhis, "The Land Grant Policy of Colonial Virginia, 1607–1774" (Ph.D. diss., University of Virginia, 1940), 87–165.

[10] In 1710 the governor and Council stipulated that grants for more than four hundred acres required an order of council, but headrights (rights to fifty acres of land due free immigrants or their dependents) to land were still acquired at the county courts. Treasury rights (purchased rights to land) were available only from the receiver general of the colony until 1717, when Lt. Gov. Alexander Spotswood proclaimed that they could be purchased from county surveyors. See H. R. McIlwaine, ed., *Executive Journals of the Council of Colonial Virginia*, vol. III (Richmond, 1928), 580–82; Dodson, *Alexander Spotswood,* 135–36; Hughes, *Surveyors and Statesmen,* 107; Voorhis, "Land Grant Policy of Colonial Virginia," 111–12.

people could communicate among properties, the court also encouraged economic development and community formation. For the security of the frontier, militia units were mustered in county commands, and the court swore officers to their commissions.[11]

Insofar as England settled its Virginia frontier through the extension of property rights from the Crown to those taking up land and through the authority of county governments to secure property, facilitate economic development, and provide for the common defense, it was colonial officials, not settlers, who defined the process. Officials could exploit it for their speculative interests, but they also had to act on behalf of the Crown.[12]

The frontier then was an imperial story. In Virginia the creation of the backcountry constituted a narrative of property formation and county organization in an unbounded region. Colonial officials timed this process according to the imperial interests new settlements were intended to fulfill. Procedures varied in other colonies. New York, for example, resisted the privatization of property in the hands of smallholders, and the Carolinas delayed the extension of effective county government to backcountry areas.[13] In all cases, however, the English occupation of the North American interior, for the most part by non-English peoples, served the interests of empire.

The forces that set the European occupation of the Virginia backcountry in motion can be traced to three sets of developments in the interlude between the close of the War of the League of Augsburg in 1697 and the opening of the War of the Spanish Succession five years later. Those developments set the stage upon which imperial officials reconceptualized English frontiers in colonial North America. In its influential report of September 8, 1721, the Board of Trade moved beyond a colony-by-colony consideration of defense

---

[11] On the county as a "militarized social model," see Stephen Saunders Webb, *The Governors-General: The English Army and the Definition of the Empire, 1569–1681* (Chapel Hill, 1979), 437. See also Richard R. Johnson, "The Imperial Webb: The Thesis of Garrison Government in Early America Considered," *William and Mary Quarterly,* 43 (July 1986), 408–30; and a response: Stephen Saunders Webb, "The Data and Theory of Restoration Empire," *ibid.,* 431–59.

[12] By the eighteenth century the power to determine county and parish boundaries resided in the colonial legislature, but it had earlier been a prerogative of the governor, which Spotswood unsuccessfully attempted to revive. See Dodson, *Alexander Spotswood,* 226–27. On the shiring of Ireland in the sixteenth century as analogous to the formation of counties on colonial frontiers, see D. W. Meinig, *The Shaping of America: A Geographical Perspective on 500 years of History,* vol. I: *Atlantic America* (New Haven, 1986), 29.

[13] The refusal of colonial officials to establish adequate county institutions on the frontiers of the Carolina colonies underscores the unsystematic nature of imperial decision making and the variations in colonial administration. That circumstances in Virginia compelled officials to employ the county as an instrument of imperial security goes a long way in explaining the absence of the social discontent that led to the Regulator controversies in the Carolinas. These controversies themselves affirm the importance of county formation to the settlement process.

issues and set forth proposals about the security of English colonies based on a continental reconfiguration of the American backcountry.[14] The implementation of these proposals in the decades after 1720 helps explain events in Virginia and elucidates connections between imperial decision making and the evolution of backcountry society.

The first development occurred in Virginia during the peace of 1697–1702, when a boom in the tobacco economy stimulated investments in land and slaves bringing more than one million acres into private hands and three thousand slaves to the colony. Within two decades the number of slaves brought annually to Virginia approached two thousand, and the black population nearly doubled. Territorial expansion and the continuing threat of war in Europe led to an increased concern for colonial defenses. French Huguenot refugees were established at Manakin Town on the James River beyond the fall line in 1700 and later organized as an infantry company. The colonial Council took steps to improve militia discipline, and the whole legislature, the General Assembly, passed a land act in 1701 that encouraged companies of armed men to take up frontier tracts. Although unsuccessful, these measures helped establish the principle of colonial defense through a combination of military force and induced settlement.[15]

In a second set of developments, the region between English Carolina and Spanish Florida became contested ground for European powers and Native Americans. From 1698 to 1699 France initiated colonizing efforts in the Gulf of Mexico, Spain responded by establishing the presidio of San Carlos de Austria at Pensacola, South Carolina attempted to extend its Indian trade to the Mississippi, and the English colonizer Daniel Coxe endeavored to plant a Huguenot colony at the mouth of that river. Within three years France had extended its grasp on the North American interior with posts and forts at Cahokia and Kaskaskia in the Illinois Country and along the Great Lakes at Detroit. Native Americans strove to keep all these forces at bay. Virginia governors during the ensuing half century fretted increasingly over the possibility of a French commercial link—an imperial "communication"—between outposts in Canada and Louisiana. But the influence among

---

[14] Board of Trade to the king, Sept. 8, 1721, C.O. 324/10, *Colonial Office Papers*.

[15] Warren M. Billings, John E. Selby, and Thad W. Tate, *Colonial Virginia: A History* (White Plains, 1986), 173; James R. Bugg Jr., "The French Huguenot Frontier Settlement of Manakin Town," *Virginia Magazine of History and Biography*, 61 (Oct. 1953), 359–94; John M. Hemphill II, *Virginia and the English Commercial System, 1689–1733: Studies in the Development and Fluctuations of a Colonial Economy under Imperial Control* (New York, 1985), 14–25; Hening, ed., *Statutes*, III, 204–9; H. R. McIlwaine, ed., *Executive Journals of the Council of Colonial Virginia*, vol. II (Richmond, 1927), 172–77; Edmund S. Morgan, *American Slavery, American Freedom: The Ordeal of Colonial Virginia* (New York, 1975), 301, 420–23; Robinson, *Southern Colonial Frontier*, 121–27; U.S. Department of Commerce, Bureau of the Census, *Historical Statistics of the United States: Colonial Times to 1970* (2 vols., Washington, 1975), II, 1168, 1172.

western Indians that France could achieve through trade and the trouble
these Indians could make for Virginia represented a far greater peril to the
colony's security than French military power, at least until 1750.[16]

Thus the French threat magnified the third development of the European peace: the entanglement of the Five Nations of Iroquoia in the imperial
contentions of the Southeast. In separate agreements concluded in Montreal
and Albany in 1701, the Five Nations abandoned violent efforts to engross
the northern peltry trade and adopted instead a policy of neutrality between
France and England. The Five Nations then resumed domestic mourning-
wars against the Cherokees, Catawbas, Creeks, and Yamasees. These conflicts were intended to replenish kinship circles with captives and to vitalize
tribal leadership through opportunities for young warriors to gain stature in
feats of bravery. The Five Nations could also use threats of southern warfare
as a bargaining chip in diplomatic efforts to maintain neutrality with France
and England.[17]

War parties crossing Virginia territory threatened the colony's frontier
inhabitants and disrupted Virginia Indians. Meherrins and Nottoways were
Iroquoian peoples and Saponies, Siouan. Iroquois-speaking Tuscaroras of
Virginia and the Carolinas were linked to the Five Nations and constituted
the sixth when some members moved north between 1713 and 1720.
Saponies associated with Siouan-speaking Catawbas of the Carolinas. Entwined affiliations inevitably drew Virginia Indians into distant wars, and
their tributary agreements with Williamsburg enmeshed the colonial government in those wars. The movement of non-English Europeans into the region west of the Blue Ridge during the next interval in the imperial wars of
England and France, 1713–1744, resulted from attempts by Virginia's governors to resolve the costly conflicts on the colony's frontiers developing out of
Indian hostilities and the French connection.[18]

---

[16] On the four-way struggle between England, France, Spain, and Native Americans for the
Southwest, see Charles M. Andrews, *The Colonial Period of American History*, vol. III: *The Settle-
ments* (New Haven, 1937), 235–36; Verner W. Crane, *The Southern Frontier, 1670–1732* (1928; New
York, 1981), 47–70; W. J. Eccles, *France in America* (East Lansing, 1990), 107–9; Daniel H. Usner
Jr., *Indians, Settlers, & Slaves in a Frontier Exchange Economy* (Chapel Hill, 1992); and David J.
Weber, *The Spanish Frontier in North America* (New Haven, 1992), 147–58.

[17] Richard Aquila, *The Iroquois Restoration: Iroquois Diplomacy on the Colonial Frontier, 1701–1754*
(Detroit, 1983), 205–45; Francis Jennings, *The Ambiguous Iroquois Empire: The Covenant Chain Con-
federation of Indian Tribes with English Colonies from Its Beginnings to the Lancaster Treaty of 1744*
(New York, 1984), 210–12; Michael N. McConnell, *A Country Between: The Upper Ohio Valley and
Its Peoples, 1724–1774* (Lincoln, 1992), 15–17; James H. Merrell, *The Indians' New World: Catawbas
and Their Neighbors from European Contact through the Era of Removal* (Chapel Hill, 1989), 41–42,
78, 89, 97–98, 113–22, 135–36, 159–60, 244–45; Daniel K. Richter, *The Ordeal of the Longhouse: The
Peoples of the Iroquois League in the Era of European Colonization* (Chapel Hill, 1992), 32–38, 236–80;
Ian K. Steele, *Warpaths: Invasions of North America* (New York, 1994), 148–50, 166–67.

[18] Billings, Selby, and Tate, *Colonial Virginia*, 175–76, 179–80, 195–96; Dodson, *Alexander
Spotswood*, 70–111; Merrell, *Indians' New World*, 25, 49–167.

That the southeastern frontier was now contested territory was borne out during the War of the Spanish Succession. Between 1702 and 1710 South Carolina forces eradicated the Spanish mission presence north of Florida and nearly took forts at St. Augustine and Pensacola, while combined Spanish-French expeditions twice attacked the South Carolina capital at Charles Town. New England forces established a second zone of contention on the northern perimeter of English settlement with the capture of Port Royal, the capital of French Acadia, in 1710. The Peace of Utrecht three years later guaranteed continued conflict over these southern and northern frontiers by failing to establish boundaries between English and French claims in North America and by incorporating three thousand French citizens within the new English province of Nova Scotia. The movement of armies through the Rhine Valley as Catholic France fought to destroy the area's strategic importance also unleashed the first refugee movement of foreign Protestants to North America under the aegis of the British Crown.[19]

These distant developments intensified Virginians' fears about frontier upheavals during the Tuscarora War. Angered by English encroachment on their land and enslavement of their people, Tuscaroras attacked Carolina colonists in 1711. The Tuscaroras' northern ties ensured the support of the Five Nations against Catawbas, Creeks, and Cherokees, now allied with the English. Hints of Meherrin participation in some of the worst fighting in North Carolina inflamed fears of a French-inspired, Pan-Indian war that would engulf the English colonial world from the Carolinas to New York.[20] Instead, a South Carolina force defeated the Tuscaroras in March 1713. But for Lt. Gov. Alexander Spotswood and the Virginia government, the conflict carried important lessons about protecting the colony's frontiers. Military units raised in response to the emergency were ineffective and expensive. Rangers often proved too weak to attack Indian counterparts, and many settlers lay beyond what protection rangers could provide. Force alone was clearly not the answer to frontier security.[21]

[19] Crane, *Southern Frontier*, 71–107; Eccles, *France in America*, 110–24; Gregory H. Nobles, *American Frontiers: Cultural Encounters and Continental Conquest* (New York, 1997), 65–73; Robinson, *Southern Colonial Frontier*, 98–107; A. G. Roeber, *Palatines, Liberty, and Property: German Lutherans in Colonial British America* (Baltimore, 1993), 9–14; Ian K. Steele, *Politics of Colonial Policy: The Board of Trade in Colonial Administration, 1696–1720* (Oxford, Eng., 1968), 116–24; Weber, *Spanish Frontier in North America*, 158–60.

[20] Aquila, *Iroquois Restoration*, 209–10; Jennings, *Ambiguous Iroquois Empire*, 262; Nobles, *American Frontiers*, 73; Richter, *Ordeal of the Longhouse*, 238–39; Robinson, *Southern Colonial Frontier*, 107–10; Steele, *Warpaths*, 159–60. The clothing of North Carolina German casualties turned up among the Meherrins in 1711; see McIlwaine, ed., *Executive Journals of the Council of Colonial Virginia*, III, 291.

[21] Billings, Selby, and Tate, *Colonial Virginia*, 179; Dodson, *Alexander Spotswood*, 73–78; McIlwaine, ed., *Executive Journals of the Council of Colonial Virginia*, III, 298, 342; Morton, *Colonial Virginia*, II, 429–32.

Spotswood's response developed in two stages. Blaming the conflict on the "Clandestine" nature of the Indian trade, he defined the first stage in 1714 with colonial legislation granting a monopoly of the trade to the Virginia Indian Company. He also set out to establish a series of Indian and European settlement buffers to protect the settled regions of Virginia. With Nottoways, Meherrins, Saponies, and Tuscaroras he concluded treaties that relocated them along the Roanoke, James, and Rappahannock river peripheries of the colony. He next fixed a community of German miners at Germanna to fortify the forks of the Rappahannock as well as to work nearby iron deposits.[22]

This initial defense policy of regulating the Indian trade and establishing settlement buffers proved a failure. The Virginia Indian Company was never successful, and opposition to its monopoly led to its disallowance in 1717. The Indians refused to observe the settlement treaties, and in May 1718 Spotswood complained to the assembly: "if these Tributarys had all of them Complyed with their Engagements I cannot but think your ffrontiers might have been constantly provided with a Standing Guard at a very moderate Expence." The Germanna colony, however, did serve as a model for the second stage of Spotswood's frontier defense program.[23]

The Yamasee War provided the immediate stimulus for change. The appropriation of their lands and the enslavement of their people to pay off trading debts had angered the Yamasees. They nearly annihilated South Carolina in 1715 before Cherokee support saved the colony.[24] The war fueled fears in South Carolina that behind all the difficulties with the Indians lay the influence of the French, and the Board of Trade soon passed warnings about French expansion on to Spotswood. The governor responded that a communication between Canadian and Mississippi settlements would allow the French to monopolize the trade with western Indians and harass English settlements. He

[22] H. R. McIlwaine, ed., *Journals of the House of Burgesses of Virginia, 1712–1714, 1715, 1718, 1720–1722, 1723–1726* (Richmond, 1912), 47, 79–80, 116; Abernethy, "First Transmontane Advance," 122; Billings, Selby, and Tate, *Colonial Virginia,* 175, 180–81, 185; Dodson, *Alexander Spotswood,* 76–78, 82–99, 228–32; McIlwaine, ed., *Executive Journals of the Council of Colonial Virginia,* III, 363–64, 366, 368; Merrell, *Indians' New World,* 49–91; Morton, *Colonial Virginia,* II, 434–37, 454–55; Roeber, *Palatines, Liberty, and Property,* 101–9; Wust, *Virginia Germans,* 20–25. For copies of the Indian treaties, see C.O. 5/1344, Colonial Office Papers. In 1710 Spotswood had proposed to the Board of Trade a plan to facilitate settlement along the James River for the purpose of encouraging the Indian trade and checking French expansion. Developed before the Tuscarora War and the end of European hostilities, the project entailed neither foreign Protestants as settlers nor motives of defense; see Dodson, *Alexander Spotswood,* 237–38.

[23] McIlwaine, ed., *Journals of the House of Burgesses . . . , 1712. . . . ,* 189; McIlwaine, ed., *Executive Journals of the Council of Colonial Virginia,* III, 396, 400–401.

[24] Aquila, *Iroquois Restoration,* 210–11; Dodson, *Alexander Spotswood,* 99–100; Jennings, *Ambiguous Iroquois Empire,* 248–79; McIlwaine, ed., *Executive Journals of the Council of Colonial Virginia,* III, 400; Merrell, *Indians' New World,* 89; Nobles, *American Frontiers,* 74; Richter, *Ordeal of the Longhouse,* 240–41; Robinson, *Southern Colonial Frontier,* 110–20; Steele, *Warpaths,* 165–66.

stressed the urgency of securing newly discovered passes over the Blue Ridge before the French could exploit them to menace Virginia. Fortifying the passes and establishing the Blue Ridge as a barrier against the assaults of the Indians and the designs of the French soon became the key elements in Spotswood's plan for protecting Virginia's frontier.[25]

In November 1720 the governor challenged the assembly to seize the opportunity of promoting the landed interests of Virginia elites, including himself, and to defend the royal prerogative through what he now termed a "Political Creed." "If a Conscientious discharge of our duty engages us Governours to be Specially mindful of *Great Britains* Interest yet I cannot See why that may not go hand in hand with the prosperity of these plantations." Land granted to Virginians, in other words, could facilitate settlement as a means to secure the colony against the Indians and the French.[26]

The governor then asked the assembly, not to fortify, but to possess the mountain passes. He pointed to the "naked State" of the frontiers and called on the members to give "Encouragement for Extending your Out Settlements to the high Ridge of Mountains [as] the best Barrier that nature could form to Secure this Colony, from the Incursions of the Indians and more dangerous Incroachments of the *French.*" The assembly responded by creating two new counties. Spotsylvania County was to command the northern gap over the Blue Ridge at Swift Run while Brunswick defended Rockfish Gap to the south. Incentives for settling the areas spreading eastward from these gaps included a ten-year remission of local taxes, colonial appropriations for military supplies and public buildings, deferral of land payments, and provision of arms and ammunition at public expense. Spotswood then demonstrated his seriousness about uniting the interests of empire and colonial landowners by obtaining warrants for forty thousand acres of land for himself and petitioning the Crown to exempt everybody who settled in the new counties from quitrents. Rightly concerned that some Virginians would exploit these incentives to engross large speculative tracts in the Piedmont, the Privy Council limited grants to one thousand acres but concurred with the need to secure the mountain passes and granted the quitrent exemption.[27]

[25] Billings, Selby, and Tate, *Colonial Virginia,* 183–84; Crane, *Southern Frontier,* 208–9; Dodson, *Alexander Spotswood,* 238–44; John Fontaine, *The Journal of John Fontaine: An Irish Huguenot Son in Spain and Virginia, 1710–1719,* ed. Edward P. Alexander (Williamsburg, 1972). Spotswood reported the discovery of the passes over the Blue Ridge to the Council on June 12, 1716, but he seriously underestimated the distance to the Great Lakes, suggesting that the center of French power lay only five days march away. See McIlwaine, ed., *Executive Journals of the Council of Colonial Virginia,* III, 428; Dodson, *Alexander Spotswood,* 240–41. For another estimate of the distance to the lakes, see John Hart to Board of Trade, Aug. 8, 1720, C.O. 5/717, Colonial Office Papers.

[26] McIlwaine, ed., *Journals of the House of Burgesses . . . , 1712. . . . ,* 250; Billings, Selby, and Tate, *Colonial Virginia,* 180–94.

[27] McIlwaine, ed., *Journals of the House of Burgesses . . . , 1712. . . . ,* 250; Hening, ed., *Statutes,* IV, 77–79; Billings, Selby, and Tate, *Colonial Virginia,* 192–94; Dodson, *Alexander Spotswood,* 244–49; Voorhis, "Land Grant Policy of Colonial Virginia," 137–48. By the time the Privy Council

Spotswood and the assembly also took decisive steps to end the violence on the Virginia frontier by establishing the Blue Ridge as a barrier between the Five Nations and Indians living in Virginia. Spotswood had already presented the Five Nations with a plan for limiting their travel to a corridor west of the Blue Ridge. He promised that the Virginia Indians would remain to the east. By 1721 all parties had come to terms, and Spotswood traveled to Albany the next year to conclude negotiations personally, making the Albany Treaty the last act of his administration.[28]

By 1722, when Spotswood left office, his administration had hammered out principles that would shape how royal officials established new settlements in Virginia. Spotswood's experiences demonstrated that threats to the colony from the Indians and the French came separately. But trade and diplomacy inextricably linked the fortunes of all nations, Indian and European. Virginia, however, lacked sufficient trade to forge alliances with Native Americans that could secure the colony's frontiers. Military force by itself was also inadequate to safeguard Virginia. Only settlement buffers could accomplish the task. Indians, however, refused to be exploited for this purpose because land to them never entailed dependence on royal authority. Only subject Europeans could be mobilized into settlement buffers through land grants; foreign Protestants seemed most likely to lend themselves to this use. Finally, the Blue Ridge formed a natural barrier against both the French and Indians. Securing it with settlement buffers was a primary objective.

While Governor Spotswood of Virginia pursued the plan of fortifying and settling the Blue Ridge barrier, the Board of Trade conceived its program of defense and security for a continuous English colonial frontier stretching from Nova Scotia to the Carolinas. In that program Spotswood's barrier ridge played a critical role. The compatibility of the board's proposals and Spotswood's actions was a product both of Spotswood's willingness to mesh the imperatives of empire with the interests of Virginia and of the board's procedure of gathering information for its report of September 8, 1721, directly from colonial governors. Just as the Yamasee War had pushed Spotswood and the Virginia government to establish Spotsylvania and Brunswick counties and to negotiate the Albany Treaty, so that conflict raised the issue of colonial defense to the level of imperial decision making.

Wartime disruptions unsettled the proprietary powers governing South Carolina and emboldened the antiproprietary party, which condemned pro-

---

reached its decision on quitrents in 1723 and imposed the one-thousand-acre limit on land grants in the new counties, the Virginia Council had already issued grants there far in excess of the limit and created controversies for years to come.
[28] Aquila, *Iroquois Restoration,* 212–217; Billings, Selby, and Tate, *Colonial Virginia,* 195–96; Dodson, *Alexander Spotswood,* 99–109; Jennings, *Ambiguous Iroquois Empire,* 278–81, 294–98; McIlwaine, ed., *Journals of the House of Burgesses . . . , 1712. . . . ,* 300–301; McIlwaine, ed., *Executive Journals of the Council of Colonial Virginia,* III, 532–34; Richter, *Ordeal of the Longhouse,* 240–43.

prietary misgovernment for the colony's distress. Both sides complained to London. Antiproprietary forces blamed the French for inciting the Yamasees and exploited the threat of French encirclement in arguing for royal government. The proprietors sought the aid of the Privy Council, which instructed the Board of Trade to prepare a report on "the state of the government and the trade" of the plantations. Proprietary government fell in November 1719, but Paris negotiations that same year over imperial boundaries in North America, although unsuccessful, heightened the London government's need for information about all the colonies.[29]

The Board of Trade queried colonial governors and agents and others knowledgeable on colonial affairs about the "number of the Militia" or "forts and places of defense" in each colony, the "number of Indians . . . and how are they inclined," their "strength," and the "strength of your neighbouring Europeans." "What effect," the board wanted to know, "have the French Settlements on the Continent of America upon H.M. Plantations?" The construction of a fort by the French at Niagara and the growing French influence among the Seneca that blocked the Albany trade were major concerns of New York. From William Keith, lieutenant governor of Pennsylvania, the board heard that only in cultivating the Indian trade could the English hope to preserve themselves and break the hold of the French on the interior and its inhabitants. Keith drew heavily upon a paper provincial secretary James Logan had prepared in 1718. Logan had observed that the French have "with great care settled a communication between Canada and the Southern countries" on the Mississippi River. He suggested that "to prevent the designs of the French" the English government must "preserve the Iroquese," "encourage the Government of Virginia to Extend their settlements beyond the mountains," and advise colonial governors to "take special care of the commerce with the Indians." "By these means all the Indians . . . may be very much united to the British interest," he concluded. The board learned from John Barnwell and Joseph Boone, agents for South Carolina, that the "Method of the French" was to "build Forts on their Frontiers." The English ought "to do likewise, not only to preserve Our Trade with the Indians and their Dependance upon Us, but to preserve our Boundaries." Of immediate concern to South Carolina was the exposed region between the Savannah and Altamaha rivers recently vacated by the defeated Yamasees.[30]

[29] Charles M. Andrews, *The Colonial Period of American History*, vol. IV: *England's Commercial and Colonial Policy* (New Haven, 1938), 389; Crane, *Southern Frontier*, 162–86, 206–9, 224–26, 255–57, 287–89; Gary B. Nash, *Red, White, and Black: The Peoples of Early North America* (1974; Englewood Cliffs, 1992), 137–43.

[30] William Popple to agents for the governments on the continent of America, Aug. 10, 1720, C.O. 323/4, Colonial Office Papers. On William Keith's message to the board, see Crane, *Southern Frontier*, 210—31, esp. 223–24. The 1718 report by James Logan appears as an enclosure in Patrick Gordon to Board of Trade, March 15, 1731, C.O. 5/1268, Colonial Office Papers. Dodson, *Alexander Spotswood*, 240–44; Eccles, *France in America*, 115–16; Robinson, *Southern Colonial Frontier*, 139–41.

After deliberating nearly a year, the board on September 8, 1721, forwarded to the king a report on the "state of your Majesty's Plantations on the Continent of America." In most respects the report mirrored the recommendations of colonial governments. About Nova Scotia the board observed that "it is absolutely necessary for your Majesty's service, that these French inhabitants should be removed." In New York the board recommended that forts be built "where they may best serve to secure and enlarge our trade and interest with ye Indians, and break the designs of ye French."[31]

For Virginia, where "strength and security . . . in a great measure, depend upon their Militia; their plantations being usually at too great a distance from one another to be cover'd by forts or towns," the board endorsed Spotswood's "scheme for securing ye passes over the great ridge of mountains." Of greatest concern were the multiple security risks of South Carolina. The first was internal. Economic growth had increased the "number of black slaves who have lately attempted and were very near succeeding in a new revolution." Meanwhile, "frequent massacres committed of late years by the neighboring Indians at the instigation of the French and Spaniards, has diminished the white men." Externally the colony was "exposed in case of a rupture on the one side to the Spaniards, on the other to the French, and surrounded by savages." As remedies, the Board of Trade called for forts on the colony's rivers, more British troops, and the immigration of more "white servants for the future."[32]

Having dealt with each colony separately, the board then addressed common defense and security issues. Because French encirclement threatened all the colonies collectively and the destabilizing influences of Indian conflicts engulfed the inter-colonial interior, the frontier had to be conceived on the scale of the continent. Thus the board called for "making ourselves considerable at the two heads of your Majesty's Colonies north and south; and [for] building of forts, as the French have done, in proper places on the inland frontiers. . . . naturally fortify'd by a chain of mountains, that run from the back of South Carolina as far as New York, passable but in few places." Significantly, the board added that "altho these mountains may serve at present for a very good frontier, we should not propose them for the boundary of your Majesty's Empire in America. On the contrary it were to be wished that the British settlements might be extended beyond them and some small forts be erected on ye great lakes."[33]

---

[31] Board of Trade to the king, Sept. 8, 1721, C.O. 324/10, Colonial Office Papers.

[32] *Ibid.* In 1720 South Carolina experienced its first major slave rebellion, which one correspondent to the colony's London agent described as a "designe to destroy all the white people in the country and then to take the towne [Charles Town] in a full body." See letter to [Joseph] Boone, June 24, 1720, C.O. 5/358, *ibid.,* and Peter H. Wood, *Black Majority: Negroes in Colonial South Carolina from 1670 through the Stono Rebellion* (New York, 1975), 298–99.

[33] Board of Trade to the king, Sept. 8, 1721, C.O. 324/10, Colonial Office Papers. According to Ian K. Steele, "Attention to French expansion [in the report] was new and formed the crucial argu-

Indian relations likewise had to be approached as a matter of imperial interest, and the board reasoned that "the Indian trade, if properly carried on, would greatly contribute to the increase of your Majesty's power and intrest in America." Indians ought to be furnished "at honest and reasonable prices with the several European commodities they may have occasion for," and commerce with Native Americans ought to be extended "westward upon the lakes and rivers behind the mountains [where] forts should be built and garrisons settled in proper places." To implement all its proposals and "render the several provinces on the Continent of America, from Nova Scotia to South Carolina, mutually subservient to each other's support," the board in conclusion recommended that the king "put the whole under the Government of one Lord Lieut. or Captain General" who with two councilors from each colony would possess the power to issue orders to colonial governors "in all cases for your Majesty's service."[34]

Not only did the board reconfigure the North American frontier as a single entity with an interior mountain barrier and zones of contention at northern and southern perimeters, but the periphery of colonial settlement came to be regarded as an area of internal as well as external threat. Any frontier presented a constant temptation to enslaved Africans to rise up and seek asylum beyond the bounds of British authority. Alexander Spotswood placed this construction on the mountains he himself explored when he reported to the Virginia Council in 1721 that "diverse Negro's . . . have lately run away & suspected to be gone towards ye Great Mountains, where it may be hard to apprehd 'em, & if they shou'd encrease there, it might prove of ill consequence to ye Peace of this Colony." Unoccupied areas such as the Shenandoah Valley or the region between the Savannah and Altamaha rivers in South Carolina possessed neither Indian nor European inhabitants to thwart maroons or resist French and Spanish intrusions. The dual responsibilities of colonial militias for resisting invasion and quelling domestic unrest were difficult to reconcile in such areas. Mobilization to the frontier to counter foreign assaults could leave interior areas exposed to slave uprisings. European enemies could also disrupt English societies by liberating escaped slaves, an effect Spain achieved in 1733 when it promised freedom to English bondsmen who reached St. Augustine. Not until 1738 did any black refugees from South Carolina receive freedom in Spanish Florida, but the attraction of Florida helped precipitate the Stono rebellion the following year.[35]

---

ment for all that the Board was proposing. The sense of urgency was increased by the Board's inaccurate account of the strength of the Indian tribes in league with the French." See Steele, *Politics of Colonial Policy*, 165–70.

[34] Board of Trade to the king, Sept. 8, 1721, C.O. 324/10, Colonial Office Papers.

[35] McIlwaine, ed., *Executive Journals of the Council of Colonial Virginia*, III, 549–50. On the Stono rebellion and the appeal of Spanish Florida, see Nash, *Red, White, and Black*, 169–70, 185, 293–95; Wood, *Black Majority*, 303–26.

By the early 1720s, therefore, the Board of Trade had succeeded in re-defining North American frontiers according to the natural and political ge-ography of English, French, Spanish, and Native American settlement. To counter the threats posed by the frontier, the board had developed an arse-nal of weapons including forts, garrisons, British regulars, and manipulation of the Indian trade. But most important for the social construction of the emerging backcountry were the numerous proposals for settling vacant and sensitive areas with dependents of the English Crown.[36] From the perspec-tive of imperial officials in London and the colonial capitals, new immigrants annually increasing in numbers during the late 1710s and 1720s from the north of Ireland and central Europe possessed characteristics ideal for these backcountry buffer settlements. They were white, Protestant, and yeoman.

The Board of Trade and colonial governors made explicit their intention to populate the backcountry with white people. The report of September 1721 had recommended white servant immigration as an antidote to South Carolina's black majority. Eleven years later the board could advise the Privy Council that "it has been the *constant sense* of this Board, that all ye British Colonies and especially the two frontiers, should be peopled as amply and as soon as possible wh. white inhabitants." In the interim the board had en-dorsed numerous proposals for Swiss, German, or Irish settlements in the backcountry from Nova Scotia to the Carolinas. It acted further to entice white settlers to backcountry areas by remitting quitrents and encouraging colonies to offer settlement bounties and land grants to immigrants. In this light the proscription in the Georgia charter against slavery appears less an attempt to create a preserve for the landless poor of Great Britain than an ef-fort to exploit them as a white buffer for the slave property of Carolina planters. In 1734 the Board of Trade advised the secretary of state that "noth-ing can be more conducive to the service of the Crown, and the general in-terest of Great Britain, than that all your Majesty's Colonies in America and particularly the two frontier provinces of Nova Scotia and South Carolina, should be fully peopled with white inhabitants."[37]

---

[36] One of the most ambitious settlement projects came from Jean Pierre Purry, a Swiss who se-cured the support of the Board of Trade and the proprietors of South Carolina for founding a Swiss-German settlement, Purrysburg, in South Carolina during the 1730s. See Crane, *Southern Frontier*, 283–87; Roeber, *Palatines, Liberty, and Property*, 210–11; and C.O. 5/359, 361–65, 383, 387–88, 393, 400–401, Colonial Office Papers. In 1729 Daniel Hintze and others obtained the Board of Trade's approval of a proposal for settling German and Irish Protestants in Nova Sco-tia. See Daniel Hintze to Alured Popple, May 1, 1729, C.O. 5/870, *ibid.*, Board of Trade to Privy Council, May 14, 1729, C.O. 5/916, *ibid.*

[37] Board of Trade to Privy Council, May 26, 1732, C.O. 5/401, Colonial Office Papers (emphasis added); Board of Trade to Lord Harrington, Dec. 5, 1734, C.O. 4/383, *ibid.*; Board of Trade to the king, Sept. 8, 1721, C.O. 324/10, *ibid.* The Board of Trade also drafted instructions to the gover-nor of South Carolina, in 1730 allowing him to grant fifty acres clear of quitrent for ten years to "all white servants men, or women" at the conclusion of their service. See Board of Trade to duke of Newcastle, May 10, 1730, C.O. 5/400, *ibid.* As an inducement for frontier settlement the

Protestantism, too, was a required asset for English buffers against the Catholic monarchies of France and Spain. Imperial wars for territory and trade waged from the seventeenth to the eighteenth centuries were also religious wars between the cultures of Protestantism and Catholicism for the souls, lands, and wealth of the uncommitted. The dangers posed by Catholic inhabitants of an English frontier were made plain in Nova Scotia, where the Acadians threatened English dominion. In 1735 one correspondent of the Board of Trade advised that "it cannot be presumed that the French inhabitants who remain there by virtue of the Treaty [of Utrecht] . . . being all papists would be faithful to your Majesty's interest in case of a warr" and recommended that "it would be highly conducive to the interest of this Kingdom to setle without loss of time a competent number of industreous protestant familys in this said province, which is the northern frontier of your Majesty's Dominions in America." In the case of the Scotch-Irish, English imperialists had earlier organized the plantation of Ireland by large numbers of Scottish Protestants to neutralize a Catholic presence uncomfortably close to English shores. Among German and Swiss Protestants, recent French occupations of the Rhineland had left a legacy of anti-Catholicism and a sympathy for the commercial values and Protestant temper of Great Britain.[38]

Other qualities of white, Protestant immigrants rendered their communities natural buffers against both internal and external threats to the settled areas of English America. Most came from diversified, small-farm economies in Europe and migrated to the English colonies as families seeking the independence that a competence in landholding, family labor, and diversified agriculture could provide. A mentality of competence combined with modest means to encourage the formation of socially and economically integrated communities of middling landholdings averaging usually less than four hundred acres. Slavery was neither alien nor antithetical to these yeoman peoples, but mixed farming on small holdings did not generate a significant demand for bonded labor beyond what could be provided by white indentured servants. Yeoman societies did not produce black majorities. And communities of independent smallholders had long been recognized as the essential element of the best militia forces.[39]

If eighteenth-century backcountry societies were culturally diverse and characterized by freeholding yeoman farm families pursuing an array of

Privy Council approved the remission of quitrents and treasury rights contained in the Virginia act establishing Spotsylvania and Brunswick counties; see W. L. Grant, James Munro, and Almeric W. Fitzroy, eds., *Acts of the Privy Council of England, Colonial Series* (6 vols., 1910–1912; Lichtenstein, Germany, 1966), III, 23.

[38] Memorial of Thomas Coram to the king, May 1, 1735, C.O. 217/7, Colonial Office Papers; Roeber, *Palatines, Liberty, and Property*, 63.

[39] On yeomen and militia, see Webb, *Governors-General*, 452. Approximately 95% of landholdings acquired from the Crown in Augusta County between 1736 and 1779 contained four hundred or fewer acres. See Mitchell, *Commercialism and Frontier*, 66. The same county in 1760 had only

interdependent economic activities, these traits owed as much to the cultures of constituent peoples as to the use made of those cultures by imperial officials engaged in a struggle for colonial security. The qualities that made the backcountry a distinctive region in early America were not, however, the product of an explicit British colonial policy. The report of September 1721 was not a policy paper. But in effecting a continental reconfiguration of North American frontiers, it accomplished for all the British mainland colonies what Spotswood achieved for Virginia in the 1720 land act and the Albany Treaty. Moreover, most of the report's recommendations, with the notable exception of the proposal for a captain general, were eventually realized in practice, not because the board imposed its proposals as policy, but because they represented working assumptions widely shared by officials at all ranks in the British colonial system. Insofar as colonial governors and members of colonial councils also shared those assumptions, they possessed a remarkably free hand in acting on them. Thus imperial efforts varied from colony to colony and from one decade to another. Spotswood's endeavors in Virginia stimulated the westward expansion of plantation culture into that colony's Piedmont. Buffer settlements of predominantly non-English immigrants beyond the Blue Ridge, however, were the work of Spotswood's successor, William Gooch. The steps he took expressed the working assumptions of the report of 1721, the actions of his predecessor in Williamsburg, and his own combined strategy of enlarging English dominion by the extension of property rights in frontier small holdings and the progressive expansion of county government.

On June 8, 1728, William Gooch, in office as lieutenant governor for less than twelve months, informed the Board of Trade that the "great number of Petitions for Land . . . will be an Evidence of the Increase of the colony, and the flourishing Condition of the King's Revenue." It was one year later that this governor defended large grants in Spotsylvania County on the social theory that the "Shade & Protection of the Greater" gave "encouragement to the meaner sort." But from 1730 to 1732 the governor and Council issued nine grants to individuals and groups for a total of 385,000 acres in the Shenandoah Valley outside the bounds of Spotsylvania County. With the exception of William Beverley, an Essex County planter with close ties to the Council, and his partners, none of these grantees were Virginians, English, or the "men of substance" that Virginia governors and the Council had depended upon to organize settlement in the Piedmont. The governor therefore fixed upon them a requirement to recruit and settle one family for every one thousand acres granted. Settlers were to receive patents for their land through the colony's grantees. That these men's ties lay largely among recent immigrants from the

---

60 blacks in a population of more than 6,800. See Chester R. Young, "The Effects of the French and Indian War on Civilian Life in the Frontier Counties of Virginia, 1754–1763" (Ph.D. diss., Vanderbilt University, 1969), 432.

German Palatinate and the north of Ireland practically guaranteed cultural diversity on the Shenandoah Valley frontier. Alexander Spotswood may have established the principle that foreign Protestants made excellent settlement buffers, but Gooch's actions in bringing them into positions customarily reserved for Virginia elites and in locating them outside the limits of established counties, in places where the gentry feared to tread, requires explanation.[40]

By 1730 and the third year of his administration, Gooch was experiencing pressures to expand Virginia's zone of security. Whether or not he read the report of 1721 is unknown. He never explicitly referred to it or its injunction to extend British settlements beyond the mountains with white, Protestant, small-farm buffers. That a Crown appointee would have been unfamiliar with the Board of Trade's thinking on the colonies is unlikely. The pressures that the governor experienced in Virginia were those that shaped the board's recommendations, and Gooch's actions were in tune with the principles of the report. The governor did not notify the Board of Trade of his actions until July 10, 1731, a full year after the first grant had been made, but he justified his efforts in language familiar to the report of 1721. It was, he wrote, "for H.M. interest to encourage such settlements, since by that means we may in a few years get possession of the Lakes, and be in a condition to prevent the French surrounding us by their settlements."[41] Indian troubles were multiplying. A year before Gooch's arrival Senecas had killed a Virginian. The Council pointed out that, if tolerated, such killings would render the Albany Treaty meaningless. Shortly thereafter, Robert Carter, president of the Council and acting governor, warned the Board of Trade of a "threatned invasion from the Western Indians." Gooch had arrived in Virginia in the midst of disputes among Meherrins, Tuscaroras, Saponies, and Catawbas that reflected ethnic conflicts embroiling the backcountry from New York to the Carolinas. By 1729 the governor complained to the Board of Trade that "I every day expect to hear of an Encounter between them which will certainly happen, whenever they meet in their Hunting. . . . But as our Frontier Inhabitants lye at the same time exposed to the barbarous Insults of these Indians, and the foreign Nations they call in to their aid, this in all probability will involve us in continual Skirmishes & Alarms."[42]

[40] Gooch to Board of Trade, June 8, 1728, April 2, 1729, C.O. 5/1321, Colonial Office Papers. On June 13, 1728, the Virginia Council issued orders for land west of the Blue Ridge but explicitly within Spotsylvania County in three tracts to Spotsylvania land speculators. By 1732 no patents had been issued for these lands. See McIlwaine, ed., *Executive Journals of the Council of Colonial Virginia*, IV, 180–81, 271. For the nine grants in the Shenandoah Valley, see *ibid.*, 223–24, 229, 249–50, 253, 270, 295. The purchase of headrights or treasury rights was set aside in those grants. Settlers purchased land directly from the Council's grantees, who then arranged for surveys and patents.
[41] Gooch to Board of Trade, July 10, 1731, C.O. 5/1322, Colonial Office Papers. For instructions to the governor, see Entry Books for Virginia, 1717–1727, C.O. 5/1365, *ibid.*
[42] Robert Carter to Board of Trade, 1727, C.O. 5/1320, *ibid.*; Gooch to Board of Trade, March 26, 1729, Sept. 21, 1727, Feb. 12, 1728, C.O. 5/1321. *ibid.*; McIlwaine, ed., *Executive Journals of the Council of Colonial Virginia*, IV, 125–26, 144–45, 152–53.

The proprietary of the Northern Neck posed another problem. Proprietary rights to the land between the Potomac and Rappahannock rivers had
been established by royal charters during the seventeenth century. By the
1720s, these rights had devolved on Thomas, sixth Lord Fairfax. On June 11,
1729, Fairfax's Virginia agent, who was none less than Robert Carter, petitioned his fellow councilmen "that the governor will not pass any patent or
patents for any lands lying" within proprietary boundaries. Quoting a 1707
instruction that the Virginia governor be "very watchful that his Majesty's
lands be not invaded under any pretence of a Grant to any Proprietor,"
Gooch responded that he "absolutely refused the suspension of granting of
Patents notwithstanding the remonstrances of the proprietor's Agent." A
battle was joined that would soon pit the colony's claim to the entire lower
Shenandoah Valley against the proprietary's and give the governor a powerful motive for granting land there as a confirmation of colonial claims.[43]

Gooch perhaps felt an additional pressure to hasten settlement west of
the Blue Ridge—the possibility that unoccupied mountain lands would become a haven for runaway slaves and a stimulus for slave uprisings.
Spotswood had earlier pointed to this possibility. The English colony of Jamaica lay in the grips of a maroon war that would not be resolved for another decade. Concern for the internal security of black-majority colonies
such as South Carolina had produced the "constant sense" among members
of the Board of Trade that colonial frontiers must be white. Virginia's slave
population had reached thirty thousand, the largest of any in the English
mainland colonies. In June 1729 the governor reported to the board that approximately fifteen refugees from a James River plantation "formed a Design
to withdraw from their master and to fix themselves in the fastnesses of the
neighbouring Mountains." Stealing arms and tools, they settled themselves
in a "very obscure place among the 'Mountains,' where they had already
begun to clear the ground" when they were discovered and forcibly returned
to slavery. "So [was] prevented for this time a design," Gooch observed,
"which might have proved as dangerous to this country, as is that of the negroes of the mountains of Jamaica to the inhabitants of that island." The
governor concluded that "Tho' this attempt has happily been defeated, it
ought nevertheless to awaken us into some effectual measures for preventing the like hereafter." In 1728 the assembly had passed an act "for making
more effectual provision against Invasions and Insurrections," and the gov-

---

[43] McIlwaine, ed., *Executive Journals of the Council of Colonial Virginia*, IV, 205; Gooch to Board of
Trade, June 29, 1729, C.O. 5/1322, Colonial Office Papers. Gooch's reference to the 1707 instruction reflected the Board of Trade's hostility toward proprietary colonies and its support for
the resumption of governments chartered by the Crown. See Steele, *Politics of Colonial Policy*,
60–81. On the Northern Neck proprietary and its struggle with the colony over land rights, see
Stuart Brown, *Virginia Baron: The Story of Thomas 6th Lord Fairfax* (Berryville, 1965), 26–100;
Douglas Southall Freeman, *George Washington: A Biography* (7 vols., New York, 1948–1957), I,
447–525; and Morgan, *American Slavery, American Freedom*, 244–45.

ernor had subsequently commissioned an adjutant to train local militias against slave uprisings. The mountains unfortunately lay beyond the pale of militia organization.[44]

Indian conflicts, French expansion, proprietary claims, and black maroons all increased the pressure on the Gooch administration to strengthen and extend western settlement buffers, but the governor turned to foreign Protestants in response to a proposal for a mountain colony of Swiss farmers. Swiss and German promoters had long voiced an interest in colonizing the Virginia mountains. In 1707 Franz Ludwig Michel, a Swiss merchant, had explored and mapped the lower Shenandoah Valley as the likely setting for an immigrant colony. Two years later he obtained royal orders for land there, but a Swiss nobleman, Christopher, baron de Graffenried, diverted the project to North Carolina. Graffenried's interest in Virginia silver mines, however, led several years later to the immigration of German miners, whom Spotswood appropriated for Germanna.[45]

Gooch's policy of encouraging buffer settlements of foreign Protestants west of the Blue Ridge was apparently stimulated by proposals in the late 1720s from another Swiss entrepreneur, Jacob Stover. Stover had immigrated to New York in 1709 with a group of impoverished Germans and Swiss under the charity of the English Crown. He soon acquired land in Pennsylvania and gained a reputation for developing frontier settlements. After a three-month exploration of the Shenandoah Valley in 1728 or 1729, he proposed a thirteenth mainland colony, named "Georgia," to be settled by German and Swiss immigrants he would recruit. Flattering a monarch with a name indicated Stover's capacity to pull the right strings and to play on fears of the French and the Indians. In proposals to the Board of Trade he pointed out that Georgia would "not only form a strong and sufficient Barrier to all the British Colonies aforesaid against any opposite Interest or Enemy whatsoever but will also secure the Trade Friendship and Correspondence of the said Western or Naked Indians," objectives of the report of 1721. "If it is neglected to extend the bounds of Great Britain beyond these mountains to the West," he warned, "it is probable that the ffrench in a short time may take possession thereof and if so the English Nation will Loose this fine opportunity."[46]

---

[44] Gooch to Board of Trade, June 29, 1729, C.O. 5/1322, Colonial Office Papers, Hening, ed., *Statutes*, IV, 197–204; Bureau of the Census, *Historical Statistics of the United States*, II, 1168. For other reports of slave disturbances by Gooch, see Gooch to Board of Trade, Sept. 14, 1730, Feb. 12, 1731, C.O. 5/1322, Colonial Office Papers. Alison Gilbert Olson argues that Gooch's efforts to stimulate backcountry settlement were motivated by his need for a following among immigrant landowners to counter the political power of Virginia's ruling elite. See Alison Gilbert Olson, *Making the Empire Work: London and American Interest Groups, 1690–1790* (Cambridge, Mass., 1992), 126–30.

[45] Mitchell, *Commercialism and Frontier*, 25–26; Wust, *Virginia Germans*, 17–22.

[46] Petitions of Thomas Gould, John Ochs, Jacob Stover, and Ezekiel Harlan to Board of Trade [1728 or 1729], received March 30, 1731, in "Documents Relating to a Proposed Swiss and German Colony in the Western Part of Virginia," ed. Charles E. Kemper, *Virginia Magazine of History and*

Stover's proposals were rejected on account of objections by Fairfax and other proprietary claimants to western lands, but William Gooch saw the opportunity. Although Gooch understandably discouraged the Board of Trade from carving new colonies out of Virginia territory, he repeatedly urged the commissioners during the early 1730s to resolve the difficulties with the Northern Neck proprietary quickly so that he could get on with establishing the kind of buffer settlements Stover proposed. Thus he wrote to

> demonstrate to your Lordships how soon that part of Virginia on the other side of the great Mountains may be Peopled, if proper Encouragements for that Purpose were given: Most of these Petitioners are Germans and Swissers lately come into Pensilvania, where being disappointed of the quantity of land they expected . . . have chosen to fix their habitations in this uninhabited part of Virginia . . . for by this means a strong Barrier will be Settled between us and the French; and not only so, but if by encouraging more Foreigners to come Hither, we can once gett the Possession of the Lakes, which are not very far distant, we shall be then able to cutt off all Communication between Cannada and Mississippi, and thereby so much weaken the Power of the French as to have little to fear from that Quarter hereafter.[47]

Stover's proposals also contained a strong argument for reversing the theory that new lands could be most effectively settled under the influence of "men of substance." One of Stover's most prominent supporters was William Keith, whose administration in Pennsylvania had ended in 1726. In memorials to the Board of Trade endorsing Stover's plans, Keith contended that "Persons of a low Degree in life who are known amongst their equals to be morally Honest and industrious will sooner persuade a multitude into a Voluntary Expedition of this Nature than those of greater Wealth and Higher Rank who are ever liable to the suspicion and Jealousy of the Vulgar." Whether Gooch heard this argument is unknown, but he did appoint persons of a low degree to stimulate settlement in the Shenandoah Valley. An early land grant in the valley went to a partnership headed by Jost Hite and Robert McKay. McKay had Scotch-Irish origins, and Hite was a Pennsylvania German who had accompanied Stover in the 1709 immigration. After petitioning the Virginia Council on October 21, 1731, that "Families to the number of one

Biography, 29 (April 1921), 183–88, 287–90. On Stover, see Mitchell, *Commercialism and Frontier,* 26–28; and Wust, *Virginia Germans,* 30–32.
[47] Gooch to Board of Trade, May 24, 1734, C.O. 5/1323, Colonial Office Papers. Gooch must have been aware of Jacob Stover's proposals by late 1729 or 1730. In June 1730 the Council awarded Stover a grant of ten thousand acres; see McIlwaine, ed., *Executive Journals of the Council of Colonial Virginia,* IV, 224. The Board of Trade first ordered that materials concerning Stover's proposals to the Crown be sent to Gooch on September 13, 1732; see *Journal of the Commissioners for Trade and Plantations from January 1728–9 to December 1734,* vol. VI (London, 1928), 318–19. On Gooch's desire that the controversy with the Northern Neck proprietary be settled, see Order in Council, Nov. 29, 1733, C.O. 5/1323, Colonial Office Papers; Gooch to Board of Trade, July 10, 1731, Feb. 8, 1733, C.O. 5/1322, 1323, *ibid.*

hundred are desirous to remove from thence [Pennsylvania] & seat themselves on the back of the great Mountains," he received orders for one hundred thousand acres along the Opequon Creek in the lower Shenandoah Valley with instructions to settle the one hundred families in two years. A year earlier, Alexander Ross, an Irish Quaker immigrant from Pennsylvania, had received a similar grant with Morgan Bryan, another Pennsylvanian. Stover himself settled for ten thousand acres on the South Fork of the Shenandoah in return for recruiting ten families.[48]

Gooch's efforts to establish buffer settlements of white, Protestant, yeoman peoples west of the Blue Ridge by relying upon the attractions of property holding had important consequences for the emerging social landscape of the eighteenth-century frontier. Reflecting the aggregate outcome of individual searches for good land, the morphology of Gooch's settlements was, in an immediate sense, the collective expression of those people who took up the land. The governor's policies, for instance, did not require the concentration of population around fortifications, towns, or townships. Nor did early settlements reflect the controlling hand of Abernethy's "speculators or surveyors" or Morton's "gentlemen." Colonial authorities, however, never lost sight of the larger purposes for which backcountry settlements existed. Having drawn people to the Virginia frontier with the allurement of "free" land and allowed for their "disorderly" dispersal, the governor and Council then overlaid the institutions of county government on the frontier incrementally, during two decades, in a pattern that ordered the backcountry according to the interests of the colony and coincidentally with the concerns of settlers.

The first description of settlements in the Shenandoah Valley came from the Philadelphia naturalist John Bartram. On October 22, 1738, while on a botanizing venture for the British scientist Peter Collinson, this meticulous observer stood on the Blue Ridge and described a "fine prospect of A spacious vail & ye next great ridge northward." During the following two days he traveled through the vale and the Opequon Settlement there, noting that it was "very thinly inhabited with [people] that is lately settled there & lives A lazy life & subsists by hunting." By 1735 the Virginia government had issued eighty-seven patents throughout a broad territory stretching forty-five miles south from the Potomac River and occupied by a total of perhaps 160 families. As a later Virginia governor put it, they "scattered for the Benefit of the best Lands."[49]

[48] William Keith to Board of Trade, Aug. 30, 1731, in "Colony West of the Blue Ridge, Proposed by Jacob Stauber and Others, 1731, etc.," ed. Ann V. Strickler Milbourne, *Virginia Magazine of History and Biography*, 35 (April 1926), 185–87; Keith to Board of Trade, April 6, 1730, in "Documents Relating to a Proposed Swiss and German Colony," ed. Kemper, 188–90; McIlwaine, ed., *Executive Journals of the Council of Colonial Virginia*, IV, 253, 224, 229; Mitchell, *Commercialism and Frontier*, 28–31; Wust, *Virginia Germans*, 32–37. The first Shenandoah Valley grants were issued to Isaac and John Van Meter and Jacob Stover on June 17, 1730. Hite later purchased the Van Meter grants. See McIlwaine, ed., *Executive Journals of the Council of Colonial Virginia*, IV, 223–24.
[49] John Bartram, Journal of a Trip to Maryland and Virginia, 1738, folder 14, vol. 1, John Bartram Papers (Historical Society of Pennsylvania, Philadelphia, Pa.); Edmund Berkeley and Dorothy

Open-country neighborhoods of dispersed small farms clustered fanlike around the drainages of Opequon Creek or tributaries such as Mill Creek.[50] Situated within property holdings and reflecting close attention to topography and resources, dwellings for single families stood at one-quarter- to one-half-mile intervals on stream terraces or rudimentary roads. Subsistence farming yielded a familiar patchwork of fields and woodlands. Although by the end of the 1730s many households produced hides, butter, and even linen for market, most families organized the land in a ramshackle pattern of small enclosures, fencing livestock out of planted land around dwellings. "Ye people most of them came from Jersey or Pensilvania," observed Bartram, "sows wheat & oats flax & hemp on ye high ground & hath fine meadows on ye low." Although slavery was not unknown, the large majority of laborers were white, and even by the 1750s blacks constituted less than 4 percent of the population in the Shenandoah Valley.[51]

The process of fabricating property out of waste land revealed most clearly how the world of Opequon evolved as the interests of settlers were made to meet the security needs of colonial authorities. Acknowledging "his Majesty having by his Governour & Council agreed to grant us those Lands upon the Consideration of settling so many Families . . . for the Defence and Extension of the Frontier of his Government," Jost Hite formed "a Guard to protect them agt. small parties of Hostile Indians, while they were surveying & settling in this Rugged Wilderness." According to Lord Fairfax, who objected to Hite's practices as well as colonial claims, Hite and others had sold

---

Smith Berkeley, eds., *The Correspondence of John Bartram, 1734–1777* (Gainesville, 1992), 121–22; Robert A. Brock, ed., *The Official Records of Robert Dinwiddie, Lieutenant-Governor of the Colony of Virginia, 1751–1758.* . . . (2 vols., Richmond, 1883), I, 389. On land patents and settler families, see Land Patent Books, 15, 16, 17 (Library of Virginia, Richmond); Brown, *Virginia Baron*, 74, 163, 166–67; and *Hopewell Friends History, 1734–1934* (Strasburg, Va., 1936), 12–39. Although the lower Shenandoah Valley beginning in the 1730s was called Opequon (after the Opequon Creek), one of the earliest explicit references to "opickin Settlement" appeared in 1744; see *Bringhurst v. Blackburn,* May 1744, Ended Causes, 1743–1909, Frederick County Court Papers (Library of Virginia).

[50] Conrad Arensburg first applied the term "open-country neighborhood" to dispersed, small-farm communities of the Middle Atlantic region and the southern backcountry. See Conrad Arensburg, "American Communities," *American Anthropologist,* 57 (Dec. 1955), 1143–62.

[51] John Bartram, "Trip to Virginia, Western Pennsylvania and Maryland in 1761," folder 66, vol. 1, Bartram Papers. See also Berkeley and Berkeley, eds., *Correspondence of John Bartram,* 536–37. The landscape description for Opequon is derived from Clarence R. Geier and Warren R. Hofstra, "An Archaeological Survey of and Management Plan for Cultural Resources in the Vicinity of the Upper Opequon Creek," 1991 (Virginia Department of Historic Resources, Richmond, Va.); Jordan and Kaups, *American Backwoods Frontier,* 94–134; and Mitchell, *Commercialism and Frontier,* 133–60. The black population in the Shenandoah Valley was calculated from tithable lists provided by Chester R. Young; see Young, "Effects of the French and Indian War," 432, 436. On the produce of the backcountry, see Gooch to Board of Trade, July 3, 1739, C.O. 5/1324, Colonial Office Papers; and Miles Malone, "Falmouth and the Shenandoah: Trade before the Revolution," *American Historical Review,* 40 (July 1935), 693–703.

land "to that person that would give the greatest Price and that too in such Quantities figures and Positions as the several Purchasers thought proper without Regard to form order Custom Usage Equity or Laws of the Colony." Hite, according to Fairfax, "suffered the Purchasers to make their Surveys in what manner they thought best suited their Interest." Hite responded that

> in 1730 when the Country was unsettled, & a Wilderness was to be explored whose Surface was Rocks & Mountains, & it's Inhabitants Wildbeasts or Hostile Indians, without any necessarys, but what were carried with them at great expence; nothing but a preference to the choice lands, would tempt men to become adventurers, and therefore the Governor & Council very properly indulged Mr. Hite & his partners in this prefference.[52]

William Rogers, a migrant from Pennsylvania, testified to the way the quest for good land also produced a landscape of economic competence and family settlement. "When he came up from Pennsylvania," Rogers observed,

> he was an entire Stranger to the methods that he found since used . . . of getting Orders of Council to take up tracts of Land to make sale of and therefore asked no Questions concerning the same but his business being to seek Land in order to make a Settlement for himself and family did make search to find such as he might think would do for him for that purpose and accordingly found a piece he like very well. . . . [Hite] telling him he should have it as he had let others have hertofore.

Surveyors such as Robert Brooke or speculators such as Hite made no attempt to impose a spatial order on settlement. According to the chain carrier John Dixon, when the surveyor "came to the corner of the line wch was to divide between [John] Keywood and [Abraham] Vanmetre he [Vanmeter] was called on by the surveyor, who said to him, 'as you and Keywood has agreed the matter come and set the compass to run this land' upon wch Vanmetre stepped up, and looking through the sight of the compass turned it a small matter, and raising himself up said, 'I believe this will do.' "[53]

The surveying and dispensing of land in the Shenandoah Valley occurred squarely in the path of the Six Nations, whose right to travel west of the Blue Ridge had been defined by the Albany Treaty in 1722. Ensuing conflicts between settlers and Native Americans drove the colony to complete the settlement process and impose its own order on the backcountry by progressively erecting the institutions of county government. While responding

---

[52] *John Hite et al. v. Lord Fairfax et al.*, transcript by Hunter Branson McKay, pp. 1532, 1547, Additional Manuscript 15317 (British Museum, London, Eng.). (I used a copy of the transcript in the Handley Library Archives, Winchester, Va.) Case of the respondents Hite et al. in the appeal of Lord Fairfax, folio 715, folder 100, Clark-Hite Papers (Filson Club, Louisville, Ky.); folio 116, *ibid.* Lord Fairfax referred to colonial legislation requiring that the "breadth of the tract . . . bear at least the proportion of one third part of the length;" see Hening, ed., *Statutes*, IV, 37–42.

[53] *Hite v. Fairfax*, transcript by McKay, pp. 1575, 1791.

to changing circumstances, the colony remained within the assumptions of the 1721 report. Settlers petitioned the Council in April 1734 that "some persons may be appointed as Magistrates to determine Differences and punish Offenders in regard the Petitioners live far remote from any of the established Counties within the Colony." The Council replied by designating Jost Hite and others who administered colonial land grants as justices of the peace "until there be a sufficient Number of Inhabitants on the North West side of the said Mountains to make a County of itself." The qualification that these men "be not Obdlidged to give their Attendance as Justices of the Court of the County of Spotsylvania" was indicative of the caution with which the Council conferred local government on western settlements. Later in 1734 the assembly created Orange County out of the Spotsylvania piedmont and extended it "westerly, by the utmost limits of Virginia" thus incorporating the Shenandoah Valley settlements for the first time within the bounds and protections of Virginia counties.[54]

When the Williamsburg government subsequently established counties exclusively within the Shenandoah Valley, however, it was responding, not to increases in western population, but to Indian conflicts. During the mid-1730s Gooch and the Council sought a negotiated end to the wars of the northern and southern Indians. On May 5, 1736, the Council noted "the dangers which may happen to the Inhabitants of this Country by the Northern Indians Marching through the Frontiers . . . in Order to Attack the Cattawbaws, & other Southern Indians with whom they were at War" and ordered that "the Southern & Northern Indians be severally Invited to meet here next April for setling a peace between those Nations as the best way for securing the quiet of Our Frontier Inhabitants." But the Six Nations refused to treat anywhere except Albany, and the Cherokees declined to travel that far north into the heart of Iroquoia. The war continued unabated, so that in April 1738 inhabitants on the Shenandoah River petitioned the Council for arms and ammunition because the "Northern Indians frequently passing through their plantations Commit frequent Outrages and have lately killed one of their men." In the absence of a county militia, the governor and Council dispatched munitions from Williamsburg and commissioned local leaders to organize the defense. Later that summer a party of Iroquois, after suffering a defeat by the Catawbas on the banks of the upper Potomac, fell upon an English settlement and killed eleven people from three families. Additional petitions followed that next fall, and when the governor faced the assembly on November 1, he complained of "the late Incursions of the *Indians*, and the

[54] McIlwaine, ed., *Executive Journals of the Council of Colonial Virginia,* IV, 318–19; Hening, ed., *Statutes,* IV, 450–51. In addition to Hite, the new Spotsylvania justices included Morgan Morgan, John Smith, Benjamin Borden, and George Hobson. All joined the commission of the peace for Orange County when it first met in January 1735. On Benjamin Borden's land grants, see McIlwaine, ed., *Executive Journals of the Council of Colonial Virginia,* IV, 351, 408–9; and Mitchell, *Commercialism and Frontier,* 31–34.

Murders they have perpetrated on the Inhabitants beyond the great Ridge of Mountains." He reviewed his attempts to "negotiate a Peace between the Northern *Indians,* under the Government of *New-York,* and the *Cattabaws* and *Cherikees"* and concluded that "fresh Hostilities committed by the former, leaving no Hopes of Success, the Safety of That Frontier must depend on your Councils and Assistance."[55]

On November 8 the House of Burgesses took up a measure "For making more effectual provision against Invasions and Insurrections," which the governor signed into law on December 21. That same day he approved "An Act, for erecting two new Counties, and Parishes; and granting certain encouragements to the Inhabitants." In an obvious ploy for the extension of royal authority, the new counties were named Frederick and Augusta after the Prince and Princess of Wales. They incorporated all the land Virginia claimed west of the Blue Ridge, including territory disputed by Fairfax. Inhabitants were "exempted from the paiment of all public, county, and parish levies," and the governor was authorized to "grant letters of naturalization to any such alien" who took the proper oaths and tests. Like religious toleration, which Gooch extended to western dissenters the next year, easing naturalization had long been a cause among foreign immigrants.[56]

The establishment of local government in the two new counties, however, was delayed until ordered by the governor and Council. The administration was in something of a bind. In conflicts with the Indians the best means of defense clearly lay in settlement and county organization. Gooch assured the Board of Trade that "enlarging the frontier Settlements and Strengthening them by proper encouragements for Cohabitation hath always proved the most effectual Method Securing the Country against the Indians." But in a candid explanation for delaying the appointment of a court, Gooch admitted to the board that "because most of the People likely to settle there are illeterate and many of them not yet understanding the English Language, it is left to the Governor and Council to fix the time, when Justices and other officers are to be established." What the administration wanted

[55] McIlwaine, ed., *Executive Journals of the Council of Colonial Virginia,* IV, 370, 414, 383, 398, 404; H. R. McIlwaine, ed., *Journals of the House of Burgesses of Virginia, 1727–1734, 1736–1740* (Richmond, 1910), 320–21; Gooch to Board of Trade, Sept. 20, 1738, C.O. 5/1324, Colonial Office Papers; McIlwaine, ed., *Legislative Journals of the Council,* 864–65; Samuel Hazard, ed., *Minutes of the Provincial Council of Pennsylvania* (16 vols., Harrisburg, 1838–1853), IV, 203–4; *Virginia Gazette,* April 7, June 30, July 21, 1738. William Gooch later claimed that it was the southern Indians, not the northern, who killed the English people on the upper Potomac River; see O'Callaghan, ed., *Documents Relative to the Colonial History of the State of New York,* VI, 171–72.
[56] Hening, ed., *Statutes,* V, 24, 78–80; McIlwaine, ed., *Journal of the House of Burgesses . . . , 1727. . . ,* 386–87. Gooch to the Synod of Pennsylvania, May 28, 1739, as quoted in Morton, *Colonial Virginia,* II, 584. In his petitions to the Crown, Jacob Stover had asserted that "Naturalization for this People as Forreigners is most humbly desir'd, that they may be qualified to Serve Offices and to have a lawfull right to their Lands." See Jacob Stover to Board of Trade, n.d., in "Colony West of the Blue Ridge," ed. Milbourne, 184.

was the power to move quickly, without relying on the legislature, to install local governments and provide for the common defense in case an all-out Indian war engulfed Virginia. But it also needed to buy time in view of doubts about the ability of the new inhabitants to govern themselves. In June 1739 the Council read but declined any action on a petition from more than fifty backcountry inhabitants praying that the "County of Frederica may immediately take place" because the "Difficulty of obtaining Justice" in the distant court of Orange County caused many crimes to go unpunished and encouraged "Persons of a Scandalous life" to settle among them. Efforts by the settlers to establish internal control would not coincide with the colony's need to impose external order for several years to come.[57]

Other Virginians shared both the government's advocacy of backcountry settlement and its mistrust of the settlers. As early as 1728 William Byrd had written that "it therefore concerns his Majesty's Service very nearly, and the Safety of His Subjects in this part of the World, to take Possession of so important a Barrier [the Blue Ridge] in time, lest our good Friends, the French, and the Indians, thro' their Means, prove a perpetual Annoyance to these Colonies." By the mid-1730s, however, he was complaining to his correspondents Collinson and Bartram about the "Scots-Irish . . . who flock over thither in such numbers, that there is not elbowroom for them. They swarm like the Goths and Vandals of old, & will over-spread our continent soon." But hoping to populate his own western lands, Byrd admitted he would be "glad" to tempt Germans "to remove hither."[58]

Within two months of the passage of the militia and county measures, Gooch was explaining to the Board of Trade that he knew "not in what state they [the Cherokees and Catawbas] are in with the Northern Nations, . . . But if Spring tempts them to renew their Hostilitys, and to make the like return of Barbarity through our inhabitants, 'tis not to be imagined that People who have now Arms in their hands, will suffer the Heathens to insult them with Impunity." In July 1739 Gooch received word from the governor of New York that a combined French and Indian force was on its way south to attack Indians friendly to Virginia. New and even more serious difficulties were also developing with the Six Nations. Not only did they now "insist upon it as agreed by the Treaty [of Albany] that as they were not to Pass to the Eastward, the English were not to get to the Westward" of the Blue Ridge, but the Indians also laid exclusive claim "to the Lands on Shenando River." This

[57] Hening, ed., *Statutes*, V, 78–80; Gooch to Board of Trade, Feb. 22, 1739, C.O. 5/1324, Colonial Office Papers; Petition of the Inhabitants of "Frederica" County, item 2, folder 41, Colonial Papers (Library of Virginia): William P. Palmer, Sherwin McRae, Raleigh Colston, and H. W. Flourney, eds., *Calendar of Virginia State Papers and Other Manuscripts, 1652–1781* (12 vols., 1875–1893; New York, 1968), I, 233.

[58] William Byrd, *The History of the Dividing Line betwixt Virginia and North Carolina run in the year of our Lord 1728* (1929; New York, 1967), 240; Marion Tinling, ed., *The Correspondence of the Three William Byrds of Westover, Virginia, 1684–1776* (2 vols., Charlottesville, 1977), II, 492–94, 529–30.

position varied considerably from the colony's understanding that the treaty conferred only rights of travel, not claims to land. When the Iroquois acted on their interpretation, the Gooch administration moved quickly to effect the final stage of settlement organization west of the Blue Ridge.[59]

On July 19, 1742, William Gooch received a warning from Maryland lieutenant governor Samuel Ogle of an alliance of Indians led by the Six Nations against inhabitants in Maryland, Pennsylvania, and Virginia. A subsequent letter explained that the Indians planned to attack "if they did not receive Satisfaccion for certain Lands lying on Susquehanna Chesapeak Ifanandowa [Shenandoah] & parts adjacent belonging (as they say) to them the said Indians for which they have never been paid and are now possessed by the people of Maryland & Virginia." The Indians sought compensation, but "threaten in Case they have not that they are able & will do themselves Justice."[60]

"Justice" swept down on Virginians the following December. Warriors from the Six Nations appeared in Augusta County "in an hostile manner," reported one white official, "killing and carrying off Horses" and stealing provisions. According to the Indians, however, "there was no more Deer to be killed, and they had been Starved to Death if they not killed a Hog now and then." When an armed force confronted the Indians, a fight broke out, and eleven whites and almost as many Indians died. Both sides claimed they were fired upon first. One Virginian thought he saw "some white men (whom we believe to be French) among the Indians." The war Virginians had feared for almost half a century seemed to be upon them.[61]

The governor and Council acted quickly. By the end of December, they had dispatched arms and ammunition to the people of Augusta and ordered the militias of Orange and Fairfax counties to "hold themselves in Readiness to March to their Assistance upon any Emergency or Apprehension of another Attack." But hearing the "Indian side of the Story" and fearing that armed conflict could spread quickly if not checked, George Thomas,

---

[59] Gooch to Board of Trade, Feb. 15, Aug. 1, 1739, C.O. 5/1324, Colonial Office Papers; Board of Trade to duke of Newcastle, Oct. 18, 1739, C.O. 5/1366, *ibid*. In October 1736 the Six Nations solicited the Pennsylvania Council's aid in warning the governors of Maryland and Virginia "that all the Lands on Sasquehannah & at Chanandowa were theirs, & they must be satisfied for them." Uncertain of these claims, however, the Council failed to act, and William Gooch apparently heard nothing of them until five and one-half years later; see Hazard, ed., *Minutes of the Provincial Council of Pennsylvania*, IV, 90–95.

[60] Hall, ed., *Executive Journals of the Council of Colonial Virginia*, V, 94–95, 98. See also Hazard, ed., *Minutes of the Provincial Council of Pennsylvania*, IV, 569–76; and Gooch to Board of Trade, July 31, 1742, C.O. 5/1235, Colonial Office Papers.

[61] James Patton to Gooch, Dec. 18, 23, 1742, enclosure in Gooch to Board of Trade, Feb. 14, 1743, C.O. 5/1325, Colonial Office Papers Hazard, ed., *Minutes of the Provincial Council of Pennsylvania*, IV, 644, 93–95, 630–46; Jennings, *Ambiguous Iroquois Empire*, 354–55; O'Callaghan, ed., *Documents Relative to the Colonial History of the State of New-York*, VI, 230–42; *Pennsylvania Gazette*, Jan. 27, March 31, 1743.

lieutenant governor of Pennsylvania, wrote to Gooch in early 1743 urging caution "that Justice may be done, and the ill Consequences which otherwise might happen to the back parts of most of the British Colonies in America be prevented." In April the Council reconsidered the 1739 petition from back-country inhabitants, and the governor appointed a commission of the peace for Frederick County to be sworn the following October. In early May, Gooch reassured Thomas that "you may depend upon it no fresh Hostilities shall be Exercised against" the Indians. Forces set in motion as early as 1699 had come to bear on this act, which formalized the settlement of the Virginia backcountry.[62]

On October 29, 1745, the Council ordered that a commission of the peace be appointed for Augusta County. Six months earlier the Privy Council had settled the dispute with the Northern Neck proprietary in Fairfax's favor while confirming all colonial grants. Winchester, the county town for Frederick, had already been laid out, and Staunton in Augusta was soon to emerge. And Virginia had, at least temporarily, settled its differences with the Six Nations at the 1744 Treaty of Lancaster. There the Indians were compensated for land claims in the Shenandoah Valley and agreed to restrict travel to the so-called Warriors Path along its length. Gooch could tell the legislature that he had "concluded a Treaty of Peace and Friendship with the *Northern Indians*; and procured for our Inhabitants seated to the Westward of the Mountains, a quiet Possession of all the Lands to which those Nations claimed a Right." A good thing it was, too, because England was by then at war with France. Possessing the land and organizing a county court to secure the rights of property and to provide for its development and for common defense would afford Virginia the best protection the colonial and imperial governments could command. Decades of experience had indicated that county militias, when properly trained, could best secure frontier areas and that those militias were natural to settlement buffers of white Protestant smallholders. If European settlers were for the most part Scotch-Irish or German Palatinates, so much the better, because both groups had long served the interests of European states by occupying the contested areas of national and imperial struggle.[63]

---

[62] Hall, ed., *Executive Journals of the Council of Colonial Virginia*, V, 112–13, 116–17; Hazard, ed., *Minutes of the Provincial Council of Pennsylvania*, IV, 654, 630–55.

[63] H. R. McIlwaine, ed., *Journals of the House of Burgesses of Virginia, 1742–1747, 1748–1749* (Richmond, 1909), 75–76; Hall, ed., *Executive Journals of the Council of Colonial Virginia*, V, 191; Order in Council, April 11, 1745, C.O. 5/1325, Colonial Office Papers. On the negotiations at the Treaty of Lancaster, see enclosure in Gooch to Board of Trade, Dec. 21, 1744, *ibid.*; Jennings, *Ambiguous Iroquois Empire*, 356–65; Francis Jennings, *Empire of Fortune: Crown, Colonies, and Tribes in the Seven Years War in America* (New York, 1988), 10, 39; and McConnell, *Country Between*, 80, 95. For an argument that Celtic peoples were exploited by the English to secure frontiers in both Ireland and North America, see Rodger Cunningham, *Apples on the Flood: The Southern Mountain Experience* (Knoxville, 1987). The immigrant peoples of the backcountry were not unwitting, compliant tools of empire; by resisting militia duty during the Seven Years' War, they demon-

By the mid-1740s the period when speculative interests were muted by the coincidence of settler demands for land and the pursuit of imperial and colonial security was over; new land grants were overtly speculative and firmly controlled by Virginia elites. In 1743 the Virginia Council had denied a petition from James Patton for one hundred thousand acres on the New River but promised the grant if war broke out with France. The Council fulfilled its promise in April 1745, simultaneously granting one hundred thousand acres on the Greenbrier River to Council president John Robinson and others who formed the Greenbrier Company. Only with the Privy Council's endorsement and at the recommendation of the Board of Trade, however, did the Council in 1749 grant the Ohio Company two hundred thousand acres at the strategic forks of the Ohio, surely designing to force the hand of the French in the contest for the Ohio Valley. That same year, 1749, the Council also granted eight hundred thousand acres near Cumberland Gap to the Loyal Company. The members of the land companies, unlike the colony's grantees of the 1730s, were prominent leaders of Virginia's planter class, now eager to take advantage of the speculative possibilities unleashed by earlier settlement activities. That "foreign Protestants" figured significantly as settlers in all these ventures represented nothing new, but the scale of the efforts and their location deep in the contested interior of North America suggest an unprecedented aggressiveness in British plans for territorial conquest.[64]

This essay began with a question about the origins of the eighteenth-century backcountry, its social construction, and the exercise of power at the highest levels of colonial government. Traditional answers depending on the interests of settlers or speculators alone fail to account for the role of the governor and Council of Virginia in establishing a culturally distinctive frontier. A new frontier narrative requires a different perspective encompassing the entirety of British North America and beginning at the onset of the eighteenth century. Faced with potential French encirclement and, more immediate to this story, with real conflict waged by Native Americans across the continent, colonial governors and their councils explored various defensive strategies to secure their frontiers. Most attractive were the opportunities presented by European migrants uprooted by imperial strife and seeking land and opportunity in America. The interests of white Protestant yeoman peoples stimulated

strated that property holding brought not only ecomonic competence but also the liberty to defy authority. See Warren R. Hofstra, "'A Parcel of Barbarian's and an Uncooth Set of People': Settlers and Settlements of the Shenandoah Valley," in *George Washington and the Virginia Backcountry*, ed. Warren R. Hofstra (Madison, 1997), 87–114.

[64] Kenneth P. Bailey, *The Ohio Company of Virginia and the Westward Movement, 1748–1792: A Chapter in the History of the Colonial Frontier* (Glendale, 1939), 17–31; Alfred P. James, *The Ohio Company: Its Inner History* (Pittsburgh, 1959), 1–27; Hall, ed., *Executive Journals of the Council of Colonial Virginia*, V, 134, 172–73, 295–97; Voorhis, "Land Grant Policy of Colonial Virginia," 166–80.

settlement schemes from Nova Scotia to the Carolinas. That speculative interests also helped drive the settlement process is no surprise.

What is new in this story derives from the decades prior to 1730, when colonial experience came to be woven into the process of imperial decision making and forced London officials to conceive a continental frontier and an integrated program for its defense. In Virginia this new way of thinking about the margins of empire assumed material form in the decades after 1730, first in ethnically and economically diverse settlements built upon the institution of private property and then in the incorporation of varied peoples and their dispersed landscape within the polity of the county. Developments in Virginia gained significance through the reconfiguration of colonial frontiers but also through the global conflict they provoked. The settlement activities of the colony forced Native Americans to take a stand during the Seven Years' War in the defense of tribal homelands and to seek the assistance of the French, themselves eager to contend for the Ohio country. These developments thus bear no small responsibility for the British Empire that emerged from the war and the continuing hostilities that empire spawned.

"Baubles of Britain": The American and Consumer Revolutions of the Eighteenth Century*

T. H. Breen

INTRODUCTION

Historians have recently begun to expand their lists of sources to include items other than written documents. Architecture, objects preserved in museums and private collections, and materials recovered through archaeology are all varieties of material culture and can all provide valuable information about the past. "Material culture" refers to things created or modified by humans and, since all humans have culture, to the ways in which things are a part of and reflect human culture. Material culture draws our attention to the connections between the material world and the more abstract one of human culture: human-created objects are embedded in and reflect systems of meanings. Although the essay that follows is based primarily on written documents, its arguments are grounded in many studies of material culture, and the essay explores connections between the material world and a more abstract one.

Timothy H. Breen identifies what he calls the "consumer revolution" of the eighteenth century as a dramatic transformation of the material lives of colonial Americans. Locally made items were rapidly replaced by items manufactured in England, which created a more homogenous and more

T. H. Breen, " 'Baubles of Britian': The American and Consumer Revolutions of the Eighteenth Century," *Past & Present*, 119 (May 1988), pp. 73–104. Reprinted by permission of Oxford University Press (UK) and T. H. Breen.

* Earlier drafts of this essay were presented at "Of Consuming Interests: The Style of Life in the Eighteenth Century," a conference organized by the United States Capitol Historical Society, Washington, D.C., 20 March 1986; and at a workshop for the Anthropology Department, Univ. of Chicago, 19 January 1987. I would especially like to acknowledge the suggestions of Marshall Sahlins, Michael Silverstein, Bernard Cohn, James Oakes and Josef Barton.

English material culture in colonial America. Historians do not doubt that this transformation occurred, but the study of the consumer revolution is still in its infancy and many questions remain. For example, did this earlier, demand-driven consumer revolution cause the later, supply-side Industrial Revolution? Breen asks another question in this essay, about a different revolution. If the loyalty of colonists was maintained through the supply of consumer goods and not through the use of coercion, then what would happen when Britain turned to coercion and colonists denied themselves consumer goods?

Perhaps the primary problem Breen considers is how the highly diverse and different colonists could communicate with one another. What does Breen mean by his claim that the shared world of consumer goods provided a "language" through which colonists could address one another? While these colonists certainly shared the same world of goods, does Breen's claim necessarily mean that they shared a material culture, a material language? Would this finding hold as well for Dutch or German colonists as it does for British colonists?

One of the most penetrating insights in this essay is that since nearly everyone of European descent indulged in the world of consumer goods, they were all forced to pick sides: would they or would they not buy and drink tea? Boycotts profoundly affected the daily lives of free Americans; perhaps the nearest modern-day analogy would be for us to live like the Amish, forsaking "conveniences." The sacrifices made during these boycotts created extra work for many women, and hostility toward pernicious "luxuries" could mask hostility toward the gentry. Speaking through the language of goods could expose fissures in colonial society along the lines of class and gender as easily as it could create solidarity.

Something extraordinary occurred in 1774. Thousands of ordinary American people responded as they had never done before to an urban political crisis. Events in Boston mobilized a nation, uniting for the first time artisans and farmers, yeomen and gentlemen, and within only a few months colonists who had earlier expressed neutrality or indifference about the confrontation with Great Britain suddenly found themselves supporting bold actions that led almost inevitably to independence.

At mid-century almost no one would have predicted such an occurrence. Some two million people had scattered themselves over an immense territory. They seemed to have little in common. In fact contemporary observers concluded that should the colonists ever achieve political independence, they would immediately turn on each other. "In short," declared one English traveller in 1759, "such is the difference of character, of manners, of religion, of interest, of the different colonies, that I think . . . were they left to themselves, there would soon be a civil war from one end of the continent to the other."[1] John Adams agreed. Reflecting in 1818 on the coming of revolution, he marvelled that the Americans had ever managed to unite. Their own separate histories seemed to have conspired against the formation of a new nation. The colonies, Adams explained, had evolved different constitutions of government. They had also experienced:

> so great a variety of religions, they were composed of so many different nations, their customs, manners, and habits had so little resemblance, and their intercourse had been so rare, and their knowledge of each other so imperfect, that to unite them in . . . the same system of action, was certainly a very difficult enterprise.

Very difficult indeed! And yet in 1776 these colonists surprised the world by successfully forming a new nation. In Adams's words, "Thirteen clocks were made to strike together."[2] Somehow Americans had found a means to communicate effectively with each other, to develop a shared sense of political purpose, to transcend what at mid-century had appeared insurmountable cultural and geographic divisions. The mobilization of strangers in a revolutionary cause eroded the stubborn localism of an earlier period. In other words, it was a process that heightened awareness of a larger social identity. In Benedict Anderson's wonderful phrase, these men and women "imagined" a community, a national consciousness which while not yet the full-blown nationalism of the nineteenth century was nevertheless essential to the achievement of political independence.[3]

Efforts to explain this political mobilization have foundered on an attempt to establish the primacy of ideology over material interest.[4] This is not a debate in which the truth lies somewhere between two extremes. Neither the intellectual nor the economic historian can tell us how Americans of different classes and backgrounds and living in very different physical environments achieved political solidarity, at least sufficient solidarity to make good their claim to independence. Economic explanations—those that analyse an individual's political loyalties in terms of poverty or profits, absence of business opportunities or decline of soil fertility—are not only reductionist in

[1] Andrew Burnaby, *Travels through North America* (New York, 1904), pp. 152–3.
[2] *The Works of John Adams*, ed. C. F. Adams, 10 vols. (Boston, 1850–6), x, p. 283, John Adams to Hezekiah Niles, 13 Feb. 1818.
[3] Benedict Anderson, *Imagined Communities: Reflections on the Origin and Spread of Nationalism* (London, 1983); Linda Colley, "Whose Nation? Class and National Consciousness in Britain, 1750–1830," *Past and Present*, no. 113 (Nov. 1986), pp. 97–117; Geoff Eley, "Nationalism and Social History," *Social Hist.*, vi (1981), pp. 83–107; Richard L. Merritt, *Symbols of American Community, 1735–1775* (New Haven, 1966). See also T. H. Breen, "Persistent Localism: English Social Change and the Shaping of New England Institutions," *William and Mary Quart.*, 3rd ser., xxxii (1975), pp. 3–28.
[4] I discuss this historiographic debate in *Tobacco Culture: The Mentality of the Great Tidewater Planters on the Eve of Revolution* (Princeton, 1985), ch. 1. See also Gordon S. Wood, "Rhetoric and Reality in the American Revolution," *William and Mary Quart.*, 3rd ser., xxiii (1966), pp. 3–32.

character but also narrowly focused upon the experiences of specific, often numerically small groups in colonial society. Though we learn, for example, why certain urban workers in Boston or Philadelphia might have been unhappy with parliamentary taxation, we never discover how such people managed to reach out to—indeed even to communicate with—northern farmers and southern planters. In other words, the more we know about the pocket-book concerns of any particular eighteenth-century American community, the more difficult it becomes to understand a spreading national consciousness which accompanied political mobilization.

Intellectual historians encounter a different, though equally thorny set of problems. They transform the American Revolution into a mental event. From this perspective, it does not matter much whether the ideas that the colonists espoused are classic liberal concepts of rights and property, radical country notions of power and virtue or evangelical Calvinist beliefs about sin and covenants. Whatever the dominant ideology may have been, we find that a bundle of political abstractions has persuaded colonists living in scattered regions of America of the righteousness of their cause, driving them during the 1760s and 1770s to take ever more radical positions until eventually they were forced by the logic of their original assumptions to break with Great Britain. Unfortunately, intellectual historians provide no clear link between the everyday world of the men and women who actually became patriots and the ideas that they articulated. We are thus hard-pressed to comprehend how in 1774 wealthy Chesapeake planters and poor Boston artisans—to cite two obvious examples—could possibly have come to share a political mentality. We do not know how these ideas were transmitted through colonial society, from class to class, from community to community.

These interpretive issues—those that currently separate the materialists from the idealists—may be resolved by casting the historical debate in different terms. Eighteenth-century Americans, I shall argue, communicated perceptions of status and politics to other people through items of everyday material culture, through a symbolic universe of commonplace "things" which modern scholars usually take for granted but which for their original possessors were objects of great significance.[5] By focusing attention on the meanings of things, on the semiotics of daily life, we gain fresh insight into the formation of a national consciousness as well as the coming of the American Revolution.[6]

The imported British manufactures that flooded American society during the eighteenth century acquired cultural significance largely within local

[5] See Mihaly Czikszentmihalyi and Eugene Rochberg-Halton, *The Meaning of Things: Domestic Symbols and the Self* (Cambridge, 1981). Though this is a study of contemporary society, it provides historians with valuable insight into how people interpret the material objects of daily life.
[6] See Lynn A. Hunt, *Politics, Culture and Class in the French Revolution* (Berkeley, 1984); Anthony Giddens, *The Constitution of Society: Outline of the Theory of Structuration* (Berkeley, 1984); Marshall Sahlins, *Islands of History* (Chicago, 1985).

communities. Their meanings were bound up with a customary world of face-to-face relations. Within these localities Americans began to define social status in relation to commodities. This was, of course, an expression of a much larger, long-term transformation of the Atlantic world. And though this process differentiated men and women in new ways, it also provided them with a common framework of experience, a shared language of consumption.

But in America something unusual occurred during the 1760s and 1770s. Parliament managed to politicize these consumer goods, and when it did so, manufactured items suddenly took on a radical, new symbolic function. In this particular colonial setting the very commodities that were everywhere beginning to transform social relations provided a language for revolution. People living in scattered parts of America began to communicate their political grievances *through* common imports. A shared framework of consumer experience not only allowed them to reach out to distant strangers, to perceive, however dimly, the existence of an "imagined community," but also to situate a universal political discourse about rights and liberties, virtue and power, within a familiar material culture. In this context the boycott became a powerful social metaphor of resistance, joining Carolinians and New Englanders, small farmers and powerful merchants, men and women in common cause.[7]

This interpretive scheme gives priority neither to ideas nor experience. Some Americans undoubtedly boycotted British imports because of political principle. By denying themselves these goods they expressed a deep ideological commitment. Other colonists, however, gave up consumer items because their neighbours compelled them to do so. They were not necessarily motivated by high principle, at least not initially. But the very experience of participating in these boycotts, of taking part in increasingly elaborate rituals of non-consumption, had an unintended effect. It served inevitably to heighten popular awareness of the larger constitutional issues at stake. In this sense, the boycott for many Americans was an act of ideological discovery. These particular colonists may not have destroyed tea because they were republicans, but surely they learned something fundamental about republican

---

[7] The Swadeshi movement in late nineteenth-century and early twentieth-century India provides some intriguing parallels to the American experience. As C. A. Bayly explains, "After 1905, the import of British-made cloth into India and the ensuing destruction of Indian handicraft production became the key theme of Indian nationalism. In the hands first of Bengali leaders and later of Mahatma Gandhi and his supporters, the need to support *swadeshi* (home) industries and boycott foreign goods was woven through with notions of neighbourliness, patriotism, purity, and sacrifice, all of which provided unifying ideologies more powerful than any single call for political representation or independence:" C. A. Bayly, "The Origins of Swadeshi (Home Industry): Cloth and Indian Society, 1700–1930," in Arjun Appadurai (ed.), *The Social Life of Things: Commodities in Cultural Perspective* (Cambridge, 1986), p. 285. Also Sumit Sarkar, *The Swadeshi Movement in Bengal, 1903–1908* (New Delhi, 1973); Bernard S. Cohn, "Cloth, Clothes and Colonialism: India in the 19th Century" (paper for the Wenner-Gren Foundation, symposium, 1983).

ideas by their participation in such events. Questions about the use of tea in one's household forced ordinary men and women to choose sides, to consider exactly where one stood. And over time pledges of support for non-importation publicly linked patriotic individuals to other, like-minded individuals. Decisions about the consumer goods tied local communities to other communities, to regional movements and, after 1774, to a national association. Neither the consumer revolution nor the boycott movement can in itself explain an occurrence so complex as the American Revolution. That argument would amount to a new form of reductionism. The aim here is more limited: to explore the relation between the growth of national consciousness and the American rejection of the "baubles of Britain."

I

The eighteenth century witnessed the birth of an Anglo-American "consumer society." Though the Industrial Revolution was still far in the future, the pace of the British economy picked up dramatically after 1690. Small manufacturing concerns scattered throughout England began turning out huge quantities of consumer goods—cloth, ceramics, glassware, paper, cutlery—items that transformed the character of everyday life. Merchants could hardly keep up with expanding demand. The domestic market hummed with activity. People went shopping, gawking at the wares displayed in the "bow-windows" that appeared for the first time along urban streets. Advertisements in the provincial English journals fuelled consumer desire, and to those middling sorts who wanted to participate in the market but who did not possess sufficient cash, tradesmen offered generous credit.[8]

Americans were quickly swept up in this consumer economy. These were not the self-sufficient yeomen of Jeffersonian mythology. Eighteenth-century colonists demanded the latest British manufactures. Few would have disagreed with the members of the Maryland general assembly who

[8] The literature on the development of an Anglo-American consumer society during the eighteenth century is quite large. Works that were particularly helpful for this investigation include Charles Wilson, *England's Apprenticeship, 1603–1763* (Cambridge, 1965); Ralph Davis, *A Commercial Revolution in English Overseas Trade in the Seventeenth and Eighteenth Centuries* (London, 1967); Roy Porter, *English Society in the Eighteenth Century* (Harmondsworth, 1982); Harold Perkin, *The Origins of Modern English Society* (London, 1969); Neil McKendrick, John Brewer and J. H. Plumb, *The Birth of a Consumer Society: The Commercialization of Eighteenth-Century England* (Bloomington, 1982); Eric Jones, "The Fashion Manipulators: Consumer Tastes and British Industries, 1660–1800," in Louis P. Cain and Paul J. Uselding (eds.), *Business Enterprise and Economic Change: Essays in Honor of Harold F. Williamson* (Kent, Ohio, 1973), pp. 198–226; Lorna Weatherill, "A Possession of One's Own: Women and Consumer Behaviour in England, 1660–1740," *Jl. Brit. Studies*, xxv (1986), pp. 131–56; Joanna Innes, "Review Article: Jonathan Clark, Social History and England's 'Ancien Regime,'" *Past and Present*, no. 115 (May 1987), pp. 165–200.

once announced, "We want the British Manufactures."[9] In order to pay for what they imported, the Americans harvested ever larger crops of tobacco, rice and indigo. Northern farmers supplied the West Indian plantations with foodstuffs. Economic historians have traditionally concentrated on this flow of American exports or, more precisely, on the production of staple commodities in response to European market conditions. The problem with this perspective is that it depreciates the role of consumer demand in shaping the colonial economy. At a time when the American population was growing at an extraordinary rate, per capita consumption of British imports was actually rising. In other words, more colonists purchased more manufactured goods every year. Since this was a young population—half of the colonists were under the age of sixteen—one must assume that adults were responsible for this exploding demand. Their consumption raised per capita rates for the entire society. After mid-century the American market for imported goods took off, rising 120 percent between 1750 and 1773. Throughout the colonies the crude, somewhat impoverished material culture of the seventeenth century—a pioneer world of homespun cloth and wooden dishes—was swept away by a flood of store-bought sundries.[10]

These ubiquitous items transformed the texture of everyday life in provincial America. Even in the most inaccessible regions people came increasingly to rely on imports. One English traveller discovered to her surprise that in rural North Carolina women seldom bothered to produce soap. It was not a question of the availability of raw materials. Good ashes could be had at no expense. But these rural women were consumers, and they preferred to purchase Irish soap "at the store at a monstrous price."[11] In more cosmopolitan environments, the imports were even more conspicuous. Eighteenth-century Americans situated other men and women within a rich context of

[9] *Archives of Maryland, lix: Proceedings and Acts of the General Assembly of Maryland, 1764–1765*, ed. J. Hall Pleasants (Baltimore, 1942), p. 210.

[10] I have reviewed the literature of consumer behaviour in eighteenth-century America in "An Empire of Goods: The Anglicization of Colonial America, 1690–1776," *Jl. Brit. Studies*, xxv (1986), pp. 467–99. See also John J. McCusker and Russell R. Menard, *The Economy of British America, 1607–1789* (Chapel Hill, 1985), ch. 13; Carole Shammas, "How Self-Sufficient Was Early America?," *Jl. Interdisciplinary Hist.*, xiii (1982), pp. 247–72; Gloria Main, "The Standard of Living in Colonial Massachusetts," *Jl. Econ. Hist.*, xliii (1983), pp. 101–8; Lorena S. Walsh, "Urban Amenities and Rural Sufficiency: Living Standards and Consumer Behavior in the Colonial Chesapeake, 1643–1777," *Jl. Econ. Hist.*, xliii (1983), pp. 109–17; Marc Egnal and Joseph A. Ernst, "An Economic Interpretation of the American Revolution," *William and Mary Quart.*, 3rd ser., xxix (1972), pp. 3–32. An interpretation of the character of the eighteenth-century American economy that differs substantially from the one advanced here can be found in James A. Henretta, "Families and Farms: *Mentalité* in Pre-Industrial America," *William and Mary Quart.*, 3rd ser., xxxv (1978), pp. 3–32.

[11] [Janet Schaw], *Journal of a Lady of Quality . . . 1774 to 1776*, ed. Evangeline W. and Charles M. Andrews (New Haven, 1921), p. 204.

British manufactures. John Adams betrayed this habit of mind when he visited the home of a successful Boston merchant:

> Went over [to] the House to view the Furniture, which alone cost a thousand Pounds sterling. A seat it is for a noble Man, a Prince. The Turkey Carpets, the painted Hangings, the Marble Table, the rich Beds with crimson Damask Curtains and Counterpins, the beautiful Chimny Clock, the Spacious Garden, are the most magnificent of any Thing I have ever seen.[12]

Like other Americans, Adams had obviously developed a taste for British imports.

How does one make sense out of this vast consumer society? There is much that we do not know about eighteenth-century colonial merchandizing. Still, even at this preliminary stage of investigation, it is possible to discern certain general characteristics that distinguished the colonial marketplace at mid-century: an exceptionally rapid expansion of consumer *choice*, an increasing *standardization* of consumer behaviour and a pervasive *Anglicization* of the American market.

Of these three, the proliferation of choice is the most difficult to interpret. We simply do not know what it meant to the colonial consumer to find himself or herself suddenly confronted by an unprecedented level of variety in the market-place. Perhaps it was a liberating experience? Perhaps the very act of making choices between competing goods of different colour, texture and quality heightened the individual's sense of personal independence? After all, the colonial buyer was actively participating in the consumer economy, demanding what he or she wanted rather than merely taking what was offered.

Whatever the psychological impact of this change may have been, there is no question that Americans at mid-century confronted a range of choice that would have amazed earlier generations. A survey of New York City newspapers revealed, for example, that during the 1720s merchants seldom mentioned more than fifteen different imported items per month in their advertisements. The descriptions were generic: cloth, paper, ceramics. But by the 1770s it was not unusual during some busy months for New York journals specifically to list over nine thousand different manufactured goods. And as the number of items expanded, the descriptive categories became more elaborate. In the 1740s New York merchants simply advertised "paper." By the 1760s they listed seventeen varieties distinguished by colour, function and quality. In the 1730s a customer might have requested satin, hoping apparently that the merchant had some in stock. By the 1760s merchants advertised a dozen different types of satin. No carpets were mentioned in the New York advertisements before the 1750s, but by the 1760s certain stores carried carpets labelled Axminster, Milton, Persian, Scotch, Turkey, Weston and Wilton. One could purchase after the 1750s purple gloves, flowered gloves, orange gloves, white gloves, rough gloves, chamois

---

[12] *Diary and Autobiography of John Adams*, ed. L. H. Butterfield, 4 vols. (New York, 1964), i, p. 294.

gloves, buff gloves, "Maid's Black Silk" gloves, "Maid's Lamb Gloves," and even "Men's Dog Skin Gloves." There is no need to continue. Everywhere one looks, one encounters an explosion of choices.

If, as many scholars currently argue, human beings constitute external reality through language, then the proliferation of manufactures during the eighteenth century may have radically altered how Americans made sense out of everyday activities. The consumer market provided them with an impressive new vocabulary, thousands of words that allowed them not only to describe a changing material culture but also to interpret their place within it. Adams demonstrated this point when in his diary he recorded his reactions to the possessions of the wealthy Boston merchant. This language of goods was shared by all who participated in the market. It was not the product of a particular region or class, and thus furnished colonists with a means of transmitting experience across social and geographic boundaries. As we have seen, a visitor could engage the women of North Carolina in a discourse about imported soap. It was a conversation that the women of Virginia and Massachusetts would also have understood.

An example of this kind of cultural exchange occurred in a Maryland tavern in 1744. A travelling physician from Annapolis witnessed a quarrel between an innkeeper and an individual who by his external appearance seemed "a rough spun, forward, clownish blade." The proprietor apparently shared this impression, because she served this person who wore "a greasy jacket and breeches and a dirty worsted cap" a breakfast fit "for some ploughman or carman." The offended customer vehemently protested that he too was a gentleman and to prove his status, pulled a linen hat out of his pocket. He then informed the embarrassed assembly that "he was able to afford better than many who went finer: he had good linnen in his bags, a pair of silver buckles, silver clasps, and gold sleeve buttons, two Holland shirts, and some neat night caps; and that his little woman att home drank tea twice a day." What catches our attention is not the man's clumsy attempt to negotiate status through possessions—people have been doing that for centuries—but rather that he bragged of owning specific manufactured goods, the very articles that were just then beginning to transform American society. He assumed—correctly, in this case—that the well-appointed stranger he encountered in a country tavern understood the language of shirts, buckles and tea.[13]

This expanding consumer world of the mid-eighteenth century led almost inevitably to a *standardization* of the market-place. To be sure, as the previous anecdote suggests, Americans had begun to define status in relation to commodities. In this they were not especially unique. Throughout the Atlantic world choice created greater, more visible marks of distinction. Nevertheless by actually purchasing manufactured imports as opposed to

---

[13] Alexander Hamilton, *Gentleman's Progress: Itinerarium of Dr. Alexander Hamilton*, ed. Carl Bridenbaugh (Chapel Hill, 1948), pp. 13–14.

making do with locally produced objects, by participating in an expanding credit network and by finding oneself confronted with basically the same types of goods which were now on sale in other, distant communities, Americans developed a common element of personal experience.

One can only speculate, of course, why colonial shoppers purchased certain items. They may have been looking for status, beauty, convenience or price. Whatever the justification may have been, the fact remains that people living in different parts of America were exposed to an almost identical range of imported goods. In part, this standardization of the market-place resulted from the manufacturing process; after all, there were only so many dyes and glazes and finishes available during this period. The Staffordshire ceramics, for example, that sold in Charleston were of the same general shapes and colours as the Staffordshireware that sold in the shops of Philadelphia, New York and Boston. Indeed an examination of newspaper advertisements in these colonial ports reveals no evidence of the development of regional consumer taste.[14] British merchants sent to America what they could obtain from the manufacturers; the colonists bought whatever the merchants shipped. It is not surprising, therefore, to discover a Virginian in 1766 exclaiming, "Now nothing are so common as Turkey or Wilton Carpetts."[15] As we have already discovered, carpets of the same description had just made their appearance in the newspaper advertisements in New York and in the home of the Boston merchant described by John Adams.

The standardization of taste affected all colonial consumers. This is an important point. It is easy for modern historians to concentrate on the buying habits of the gentry.[16] Their beautiful homes—many of which are now preserved as museums—dominate our understanding of the character of daily life in eighteenth-century America. This interpretive bias is not a problem peculiar to the colonial period. The consumer behaviour of the wealthy has always been more fully documented than that of more humble buyers. But however much we are drawn to the material culture of the colonial élite, we should realize that the spread of the consumer market transformed the lives of ordinary men and women as fundamentally as it did those of their more affluent neighbours. Though wealthy Americans purchased goods of superior quality, poorer buyers demanded the same general range of imports. Rural pedlars, urban hawkers, Scottish factors responded to this eager

[14] Observations about the character and content of eighteenth-century American advertising found in this essay are based on extensive research in the newspapers of Boston, New York, Philadelphia, Williamsburg and Charleston, carried out by the author and Rebecca Becker of Northwestern University.

[15] John Hemphill, "John Wayles Rates his Neighbors," *Virginia Mag. Hist. and Biography*, lxvi (1958), p. 305.

[16] See Richard L. Bushman, "American High Style and Vernacular Cultures," in Jack P. Greene and J. Pole (eds.), *Colonial British America: Essays in the New History of the Early Modern Era* (Baltimore, 1984), pp. 345–83.

clientele, providing farmers and artisans with easy credit, the ticket to participation in this consumer society. These people became reliant on imported manufactures, so much so in fact that Francis Fauquier, lieutenant-governor of Virginia, could note in 1763, "These imports daily encrease, the common planters usually dressing themselves in the manufactures of Great Brittain [*sic*] altogether."[17]

Tea provides an instructive example of the standardization of consumer taste. Early in the eighteenth century this hot drink became the preferred beverage in gentry households. Polite ladies—perhaps as a device to lure gentlemen away from tavern society—organized elaborate household rituals around the tea service. In fact the purchase of tea necessitated the acquisition of pots, bowls, strainers, sugar-tongs, cups and slop-dishes. One writer in a New York newspaper suggested the need for a school of tea etiquette. The young men of the city, finding themselves "utterly ignorant in the Ceremony of the Tea-Table," were advised to employ a knowledgeable woman "to teach them the Laws, Rules, Customs, Phrases and Names of the Tea Utensils."[18]

Though less well-do-do Americans did not possess the entire range of social props, they demanded tea. As early as 1734 one New Yorker reported:

> I am credibly informed that tea and china ware cost the province, yearly, near the sum of L10,000; and people that are least able to go to the expence, must have their tea tho' their families want bread. Nay, I am told, they often pawn their rings and plate to gratifie themselves in that piece of extravagance.[19]

It did not take long for this particular luxury to become a necessity. "Our people," wrote another New York gentleman in 1762, "both in town and country, are shamefully gone into the habit of tea-drinking."[20] And when Israel Acrelius visited the old Swedish settlements of Delaware at mid-century, he discovered people consuming tea "in the most remote cabins."[21] During the 1750s even the inmates of the public hospital of Philadelphia, the city poor-house, insisted on having bohea tea.[22] All these colonists drank their tea out of imported cups, not necessarily china ones, but rather ceramics that had originated in the English Midlands where they had been fired at very

---

[17] Public Record Office, London, C.O. 5/1330, Francis Fauquier, "Answers to the Queries Sent to Me by the Right Honourable the Lords Commissioners for Trade and Plantation Affairs," 30 Jan. 1763. See also Breen, "Empire of Goods," pp. 485–96.

[18] Cited in Esther Singleton, *Social New York under the Georges, 1714–1776* (New York, 1902), pp. 380–1.

[19] *Ibid.,* p. 375.

[20] William Smith, *The History of the Late Province of New-York . . . 1762* (New York Hist. Soc. Collections, iv, pt. 2, 1829), p. 281.

[21] Cited in Rodis Roth, "Tea Drinking in Eighteenth-Century America: Its Etiquette and Equipage," in *Contributions from the Museum of History and Technology,* paper 14 (U. S. National Museum, ccxxv, Washington, D.C., 1961), p. 66.

[22] Billy G. Smith, "The Material Lives of Laboring Philadelphians, 1750 to 1800," *William and Mary Quart.,* 3rd ser., xxxviii (1981), p. 168.

high temperature and thus made resistant to the heat of America's new favourite drink.

Ordinary Americans adopted tea for reasons other than social emulation. After all, it was a mild stimulant, and a hot cup of tea probably helped the labouring poor endure hard work and insubstantial housing. Nevertheless in some isolated country villages the desire to keep up with the latest consumer fads led to bizarre results, the kind of gross cultural misunderstanding that anthropologists encounter in places where products of an alien technology have been introduced into a seemingly less-developed society.[23] In 1794 a historian living in East Hampton, New York, interviewed a seventy-eight-year-old woman. "Mrs. Miller," he discovered, "remembers well when they first began to drink tea on the east end of Long Island." She explained that none of the local farmers knew what to do with the dry leaves: "One family boiled it in a pot and ate it like samp-porridge. Another spread tea leaves on his bread and butter, and bragged of his having ate half a pound at a meal, to his neighbor, who was informing him how long a time a pound of tea lasted him." According to Mrs. Miller, the arrival of the first tea-kettle was a particularly memorable day in the community:

> It came ashore at Montauk in a ship, (the *Captain Bell*). The farmers came down there on business with their cattle, and could not find out how to use the tea-kettle, which was then brought up to old "Governor Hedges." Some said it was for one thing, and some said it was for another. At length one, the more knowing than his neighbors, affirmed it to be the ship's lamp, to which they all assented.

Mrs. Miller may have been pulling the historian's leg, but whatever the truth of her story, it reveals the symbolic importance of tea in this remote eighteenth-century village.[24]

Standardization of consumer goods created a paradoxical situation. As Americans purchased the same general range of British manufactures—in other words, as they had similar consumer experiences—they became increasingly Anglicized. Historians sometimes refer to this cultural process as "the colonization of taste."[25] The Anglo-American consumer society of the eighteenth century drew the mainland colonists closer to the culture of the mother country. In part, this was a result of the Navigation Acts which channelled American commerce through Great Britain, a legislative constraint that made it difficult as well as expensive for Americans to purchase goods from the Continent. There is no reason to believe, however, that parliament passed these acts in a conscious attempt to "colonize American taste." That

---

[23] See, for example, H. A. Powell, "Cricket in Kiriwina," *Listener*, xlviii (1952), pp. 384–5.

[24] Henry P. Hedges, *A History of the Town of East-Hampton* (Sag-Harbor, 1897), p. 142.

[25] Bayly, "Origins of Swadeshi," pp. 303–11. See also Nicholas Phillipson, "Politics, Politeness and the Anglicisation of Early Eighteenth-Century Scottish Culture," in R. A. Mason (ed.), *Scotland and England, 1286–1815* (Edinburgh, 1987), pp. 226–46.

just happened. And during the eighteenth century this process is easy to trace. For most people, articles imported from the mother country carried positive associations. They introduced colour and excitement into the lives of the colonists. Their quality was superior to that of locally made goods, silverware and furniture being two notable exceptions. It is not surprising that the demand for British manufactures escalated so quickly after mid-century. The market itself created new converts. Advertisements, merchants' displays, news of other people's acquisitions stoked consumer desire and thereby accelerated the spread of Anglicization. Booksellers—just to note one example—discovered that colonial readers preferred an English imprint to an American edition of the same title. "Their estimate of things English was so high," reports one historian, "that a false London imprint could seem an effective way to sell a local publication."[26]

Anglicized provincials insisted on receiving the "latest" English goods. They were remarkably attuned to even subtle changes in metropolitan fashion. "And you may believe me," a young Virginia planter named George Washington lectured a British merchant in 1760, "when I tell you that instead of getting things good and fashionable in their several kinds[,] we often have Articles sent Us that could have been usd [*sic*] by our Forefathers in the days of yore."[27] Washington may have envied his neighbours in Maryland. According to one visitor to Annapolis:

> The quick importation of fashions from the mother country is really astonishing. I am almost inclined to believe that a new fashion is adopted earlier by the polished and affluent American than by many opulent persons in the great metropolis [London] . . . In short, very little difference is, in reality, observable in the manners of the wealthy colonist and the wealthy Briton.[28]

No doubt this man exaggerated, but as he well understood, after mid-century American consumers took their cues from the mother country. Certainly that was the case of the people whom William Smith observed in New York. "In the city of New-York," he wrote in 1762, "through the intercourse with the Europeans, we follow the London fashions."[29] Benjamin Franklin saw this development in a favourable light; at least he did so in 1751. "A vast Demand is growing for British Manufactures," he marvelled, "a glorious market wholly in the Power of Britain."[30] The colonists belonged to an empire of goods. The

---

[26] Stephen Botein, "The Anglo-American Book Trade before 1776: Personnel and Strategies," in William L. Joyce *et al.* (eds.), *Printing and Society in Early America* (Worcester, Mass., 1983), p. 79.
[27] *The Writings of George Washington*, ed. John C. Fitzpatrick, 39 vols. (Washington, D.C., 1931), ii, p. 350, George Washington to Robert Cary and Co., 28 Sept. 1760.
[28] William Eddis, *Letters from America*, ed. Aubrey C. Land (Cambridge, Mass., 1969), pp. 57–8.
[29] Smith, *History of the Late Province of New York*, p. 277.
[30] Benjamin Franklin, "Observations Concerning the Increase of Mankind" (1751), in *The Papers of Benjamin Franklin*, ed. Leonard W. Labaree, 25 vols. (New Haven, 1959 and continuing), iv, p. 229.

rulers of the mother country could well afford to let the Americans drift politically for much of the eighteenth century, following a policy that has sometimes been labelled "salutary neglect." Like Franklin, the ablest British administrators must have sensed that the bonds of loyalty depended upon commerce, upon the free flow of goods, and not upon coercion.[31]

Let me summarize the argument to this point. Before the 1760s most Americans would not have been conscious of the profound impact of consumption upon their society. They were like foot-soldiers who witness great battles only from a narrow, personal perspective and thus cannot appreciate the larger implications of thousands of separate engagements. Of course, the colonists were aware of the proliferation of choice, but for most of them the acquisition of British imports was a private act, one primarily associated with one's own social status within a community or household. Manufactured goods shaped family routines; they influenced relationships within a particular neighbourhood. In symbolic terms these articles possessed local meanings. Certainly before the Stamp Act crisis—a few extreme evangelicals like James Davenport to the contrary notwithstanding—the Americans developed no sustained public discourse about goods.[32]

Nevertheless the totality of these private consumer experiences deeply affected the character of eighteenth-century provincial society, for in a relatively short period following 1740 this flood of British manufactures created an indispensable foundation for the later political mobilization of the American people. Though these highly Anglicized men and women were not fully aware of this shared experiential framework, it would soon provide them with a means to communicate across social and spatial boundaries. Only after political events beyond their control forced them to form larger human collectivities—as was the case after 1765—did they discover that a shared language of goods was already in place.

II

The importation of British goods on such a vast scale created social tensions that the colonists were slow to appreciate. The very act of purchasing these articles—making free choices from among competing possibilities—heightened the Americans' already well-developed sense of their own personal in-

---

[31] See Breen, "Empire of Goods."

[32] D. D. Hall, "Religion and Society: Problems and Reconsiderations," in Greene and Pole (eds.), *Colonial British America*, pp. 337–8. The most famous evangelical of the period, George Whitefield, embraced the latest merchandizing techniques, literally selling the revival to the American people. The crowds flocked to hear Whitefield, while his critics grumbled about the commercialization of religion. One anonymous writer in Massachusetts noted that there is "a very wholesome law of the province to discourage Pedlars in Trade" and it seems high time "to enact something for the discouragement of Pedlars in Divinity also:" *Boston Weekly News-Letter*, 22

dependence. The acquisition of manufactures also liberated them from a drab, impoverished, even insanitary folk culture of an earlier period. But consumption inevitably involved dependency. The colonists came increasingly to rely upon British merchants not only for what they now perceived as the necessities of daily life but also for a continued supply of credit. So long as the Anglo-American economy remained relatively prosperous and stable, it was possible to maintain the fiction of personal independence in a market system that in fact spawned dependence. But those days were numbered. An increasingly volatile international economy coupled with parliament's apparent determination to tax the colonists sparked an unprecedented debate about the role of commerce within the empire. Comfortable relations and familiar meanings were no longer secure. That was the burden of John Dickinson's troubled remark in 1765, "under all these restraints and some others that have been imposed on us, we have not *till lately* been unhappy. Our spirits were not depressed."[33]

As Dickinson's observation suggests, the colonists' experiences as consumers no longer yielded the satisfaction that they had at an earlier time. The rising level of personal debt made the Americans' growing dependence upon British merchants increasingly manifest, and in this context of growing consumer "disappointment," the meaning of imported goods began to shift.[34] A semiotic order was changing. Articles that had been bound up with local cultures, with individual decisions within households, were gradually thrust into public discourse, and during the constitutional crisis with Great Britain these "baubles" were gradually and powerfully incorporated into a general moral critique of colonial society that traced its origins in part to radical country pamphleteers such as John Trenchard and Thomas Gordon and in part to the evangelical preachers of the Great Awakening.[35] In other words, a constitutional crisis transformed private consumer acts into public political statements. Britain's rulers inadvertently activated a vast circuit of private experience and in the process created in the American colonies what they least desired, the first stirrings of national consciousness.

Apr. 1742. For connections between the consumer revolution and the Great Awakening, see Frank Lambert, " 'Pedlar in Divinity': George Whitefield and the Great Awakening, 1737–1745" (Graduate seminar paper, Northwestern Univ., 1987).

[33] John Dickinson, "The Late Regulations Respecting the British Colonies" (1765), in *The Writings of John Dickinson*, ed. Paul Leicester Ford, 2 vols. (Philadelphia, 1895), i, p. 217 (my emphasis).

[34] The psychological implications of economic "disappointment" are imaginatively discussed in Albert O. Hirschman, *Shifting Involvements: Private Interest and Public Action* (Princeton, 1982). See also Tibor Scitovsky, *The Joyless Economy: An Inquiry into Human Satisfaction and Consumer Dissatisfaction* (New York, 1976).

[35] Bernard Bailyn, *The Ideological Origins of the American Revolution* (Cambridge, Mass., 1967); Gordon Wood, *The Creation of the American Republic, 1776–1787* (Chapel Hill, 1969); Edmund S. Morgan, "The Puritan Ethic and the American Revolution," *William and Mary Quart.*, 3rd ser., xxiv (1967), pp. 3–43.

To understand the process of symbolic redefinition one must remember that the merchants of the mother country bore as much responsibility as did the members of parliament for the growing unhappiness of the American consumers. To be sure, during the Stamp Act crisis British merchants petitioned the House of Commons in support of the colonists. But at the same time these businessmen pushed upon the American market more goods and credit than it could possibly absorb. Indeed their aggressive, though short-sighted drive to maximize returns not only substantially increased colonial indebtedness but also alienated American wholesalers who had traditionally served as middlemen between the large British houses and the American shopkeepers.[36] As Governor Francis Bernard of Massachusetts explained to the earl of Shelburne in 1768:

> for some years past the London merchants, for the sake of increasing their profits, have got into dealing immediately [directly] with the retailers . . . Instead of dealing with respectable houses[,] the London merchants are engaged in a great number of little shops, and for the sake of advantages derived from trading with people who cannot dispute the terms . . . they have extended their credit beyond all bounds of prudence, and have . . . glutted this country with goods.[37]

Parliament exacerbated these structural tensions within the American market. Though its efforts to raise new revenues after 1764 did not cripple the colonists' ability to purchase imported goods, parliament did remind the Americans of their dependence. If the colonists continued to purchase items such as glass, paper and paint from British merchants—which seemed quite likely since they could not produce these articles themselves—then the Americans would inevitably have to pay unconstitutional taxes. As Dickinson noted sarcastically in his influential *Letters from a Farmer*, "I think it evident, that we *must* use paper and glass; that what we use *must* be *British*; and that we *must* pay the duties imposed, unless those who sell these articles are so generous as to make us presents of the duties they pay."[38]

Considering the growing ambivalence of the colonists towards consumer goods—these items were immensely desirable, but also raised unsettling questions about economic dependency—it is not surprising that the Stamp Act crisis sparked a boycott of British manufactures.[39] During the anxious months

---

[36] William T. Baxter, *The House of Hancock: Business in Boston, 1724–1775* (Cambridge, Mass., 1945), pp. 239–42; Egnal and Ernst, "Economic Interpretation of the American Revolution;" Breen, *Tobacco Culture*, chs. 3–5.

[37] Cited in William Pencak, *War, Politics and Revolution in Provincial Massachusetts* (Boston, 1981), p. 164.

[38] John Dickinson, *Letters from a Farmer in Pennsylvania* (1768), in *Writings of John Dickinson*, ed. Ford, i, p. 355. Also "The Pitkin Papers," *Colls. Connecticut Hist. Soc.*, xix (1921), p. 74, William Pitkin to Richard Jackson, 14 Feb. 1767.

[39] See Edmund S. and Helen M. Morgan, *The Stamp Act Crisis: Prologue to Revolution* (Chapel Hill, 1953).

of 1764 and 1765 urban Americans endorsed non-importation as the most likely means to bring about the Stamp Act's repeal and alleviate the burden of personal debt. As "Philo Publicus" explained to the readers of the *Boston Gazette*, "We have taken wide Steps to Ruin, and as we have grown more Luxurious every Year, so we run deeper and deeper in Debt to our Mother Country." After observing how extravagantly the people of Boston decorated their parlours, how they piled their sideboards high with silver plate, how they collected costly china, this writer concluded, "I wonder not that my Country is so poor, I wonder not when I hear of frequent Bankruptcies."[40]

The boycott seemed an almost reflexive reaction to constitutional crisis. Of course, in 1765 angry Americans had little other choice. After all, there was no colonial Bastille for them to storm; George III and his hated ministers lived in safety on the other side of the Atlantic. But however circumscribed the range of responses may have been, the boycott served the colonists well. Participation in these protests provided Americans with opportunities to vent outrage against the policies of a distant government—much as Americans and others who boycott South African goods do today—and though it was not clear whether anyone in the mother country actually listened, the very act of publicly denying themselves these familiar imports began to mobilize colonists of different regions and backgrounds in common cause.

The success of this first boycott should not be exaggerated. Most activities were restricted to urban centres, and though non-importation momentarily upset the flow of Anglo-American trade, it did not bring the British economy to its knees. Nevertheless, however limited its economic impact may have been, this initial confrontation reveals a mental process at work which in time would acquire extraordinary significance. As early as 1765 many colonists had begun to realize that patterns of consumption provided them with an effective language of political protest. In that sense, Americans discovered political ideology through a discussion of the meaning of goods, through observances of non-consumption that forced ordinary men and women to declare where exactly they stood on the great constitutional issues of the day. British manufactures thus took on a new symbolic function, and the boycott became a social metaphor of political resistance. If the mainland colonies had not already been transformed into a consumer society, the Stamp Act protesters would have found it extremely difficult to communicate effectively with each other at this moment of political crisis. The purchase of British manufactures was the one experience that most of them shared, and by raising the possibility that they could do without these goods patriotic Americans strained the bonds of Anglicization.

[40] *Boston Gazette*, 1 Oct. 1764. Also Arthur M. Schlesinger, *The Colonial Merchants and the American Revolution, 1763–1776* (Columbia Univ. Studies in History, Economics and Public Law, lxxviii, no. 182, New York, 1918), pp. 63–5; Charles M. Andrews, "Boston Merchants and the Non-Importation Movement," *Trans. Colonial Soc. Massachusetts*, xix (1916–17), pp. 182–91. For a discussion of the cultural meaning of debt in this period, see Breen, *Tobacco Culture*.

Revolution did not occur in 1765. The bonds of empire withstood the challenge, and as soon as parliament repealed the Stamp Act the Americans returned to the import shops. The confrontation with the mother country had eroded but not destroyed the traditional meaning of consumer goods. Newspaper advertisements carried the familiar words "just imported from England," a clear indication that many colonists still took their cultural cues from Great Britain. Until that connection could be severed, independence was out of the question. This does not mean that Americans deserted the political principles that they had mouthed during the Stamp Act protest; most certainly they were not hypocrites. The boycott had provided colonists with a behavioural link between a political ideology and local experience, and when it was abandoned ideas about liberty and representation, slavery and virtue were temporarily dissociated from the affairs of daily life.

The Townshend Act of 1767 returned consumer goods to the centre of American political discourse. This ill-conceived statute levied a duty upon imported glass, paper, tea, lead and paint.[41] Patriotic leaders throughout the colonies advocated a campaign of non-consumption, and though this boycott would ultimately disappoint some of its more fervent organizers, it revealed the powerful capacity of goods in this society not only to recruit people into a political movement but also to push them—often when they were unaware of what was happening—to take ever more radical positions. As in the Stamp Act crisis, imported British manufactures provided a framework in which many colonists learned about rights and liberties.

During the period of protest against the Townshend Act, roughly between 1767 and 1770, colonists began to speak of consumer goods in a highly charged moral language. Of course, these Americans were not the first people to condemn the pernicious effects of luxury and self-indulgence. That concern had vexed moralists for centuries. Nevertheless during the Stamp Act crisis a dominant theme of the political discourse had been debt. The purchase of British manufactures undermined the personal independence of the American consumers and thus made them fit targets for tyrannical conspirators. But after 1767 the thrust of patriotic rhetoric shifted from *private* debt to *public* virtue. By acquiring needless British imports the colonial consumer threatened the liberties of other men and women. "Every Man who will take Pains to cultivate the Cost of Homespun," advised a writer in the *Boston Gazette*, "may easily convince himself that his private Interest, as well as [that of] the Publick, will be promoted by it."[42] In other words, how one spent one's own money became a matter deserving public scrutiny.

The artefacts of a consumer culture took on new symbolic meaning within a fluid political discourse, and before long it was nearly impossible

---

[41] Merritt Jensen, *The Founding of a Nation: A History of the American Revolution, 1763–1776* (New York, 1968), pp. 237–344; Andrews, "Boston Merchants," pp. 191–252.
[42] *Boston Gazette*, 11 Jan. 1768.

for Americans to speak of imported goods without making reference to constitutional rights. The politicization of consumption was clearly evident in the 22 December 1767 instructions of the Boston town meeting to its representatives in the general assembly. We, your constituents, they announced, are worried about "the distressed Circumstances of this Town, by means of the amazing growth of Luxury, and the Embarrassments of our Trade; & having also the strongest apprehensions that our invaluable Rights & Liberties as Men and British Subjects, are greatly affected by a late Act of the British Parliament;" they urged their representatives "to encourage a spirit of Industry and Frugality among the People."[43] Colonists living in different parts of America called for a boycott not just of those few imports specifically taxed by the Townshend Act but, rather, a long list of British manufactures, everything from clocks to carriages, hats to house furniture, even mustard.[44] The lists contained scores of items, a virtual inventory of the major articles of the mid-century consumer culture. The colonists seemed determined to undo patterns of consumption that had taken root in the 1740s, to return perhaps to a simpler period of self-sufficiency, which in fact had never existed, but which in this political crisis seemed the best strategy for preserving liberty. In this social context it made sense for colonial writers to declare: "Save your money and you can save your country."[45]

The Townshend boycotts—ineffective though they may have been in forcing parliament to back down—helped radical colonists to distinguish friends from enemies. Strangers communicated ideology through the denial of consumer goods. Rhetoric was not enough. One had to reveal where one stood. The non-consumption movement forced individuals to alter the character of their daily lives, and as they did so, they formed collectivities of like-minded colonists, acts which inevitably reinforced their own commitment to radical politics. The leaders of Windham, a small village in south-eastern Connecticut, scheduled a town meeting in response to correspondence they had received from Boston. This letter from the outside urged the people of Windham to join in a boycott; in other words, to think of politics in terms that extended far beyond the boundaries of the community. This invitation caused the villagers to take note of their "surprising fondness . . . for the use and consumption of foreign and British manufactures." After a full discussion of the issues, they publicly pledged "to each other that we will discourage and discountenance to the utmost of our power the excessive use of all foreign teas, china ware, spices and black pepper, all British and foreign superfluities and manufactures." This covenant helped the townspeople to sort themselves out. One group of Windham inhabitants was now prepared to

[43] *A Report of the Record Commissioners of the City of Boston Containing the Boston Town Records, 1758 to 1769* (Boston, 1886), pp. 227–8.
[44] *Ibid.*, p. 221. Also "Virginia Nonimportation Resolutions, 1769," in *The Papers of Thomas Jefferson*, ed. Julian P. Boyd, 22 vols. (Princeton, 1953), i, pp. 28–9.
[45] Cited in Andrews, "Boston Merchants," p. 92.

expose another group as "Enemies to their Country," and once this decision had been taken, both sides probably thought more deeply about political loyalties than they had ever done before. And the villagers spread word of their resolution, appointing a committee "to correspond with committees from the several towns in the County in order to render the fore-going proposals as extensive and effectual as may be." The confrontation with British imports was extending the political horizons of ordinary people in this small Connecticut village. Though they could not possibly correspond directly with distant Americans, they expressed their "earnest desire that every town in this Colony and in every Colony in America would explicitly and publicly disclose their sentiments relating to the Non-importation Agreement and the violations thereof."[46] Without question, one encounters in Windham the makings of an "imagined community," the seeds of national consciousness.

By mobilizing people ordinarily excluded from colonial politics, the non-consumption movement of this period greatly expanded the base of revolutionary activities. The Townshend boycott politicized even the most mundane items of the household economy and thereby politicized American women. Decisions about consumption could not be separated from decisions about politics. Within this electric atmosphere mothers and wives and daughters monitored the ideological commitment of the family. Throughout the colonies women altered styles of dress, wove homespun cloth and stopped drinking tea. At one wedding in Connecticut, countrywomen appeared in garments of their own making and insisted upon having "Labrador tea," a concoction brewed from indigenous herbs. Other women in New England participated in spinning and weaving competitions, community rituals of great symbolic complexity. The actual homespun was invested with political significance. But so too were the women themselves. Their efforts at the wheel, like those of Mahatma Gandhi in another era, became local representations of a general ideology that connected the people of these communities—at least in their political imaginations—to unseen men and women in other American communities.[47]

The boycott of consumer goods also drew young people into the political debate. The students of Harvard, Yale and the College of Rhode Island, for example, appeared at commencement during the late 1760s wearing homespun suits.[48] Though such displays irritated royal officials—that was the fun of it—they also transmitted political meanings through non-consumption to other young people. This was an important element in the process of developing a national consciousness. In a society in which the average age was about sixteen, the young could not be taken for granted. A

[46] Cited in Ellen D. Larned, *History of Windham County, Connecticut,* 2 vols. (Worcester, Mass., 1880), ii, pp. 116–19.
[47] Andrews, "Boston Merchants," pp. 193–4. Also Linda K. Kerber, *Women of the Republic: Intellect and Ideology in Revolutionary America* (Chapel Hill, 1980), pp. 38–41.
[48] Andrews, "Boston Merchants," pp. 195–7.

large percentage of the American population in 1776 had not even been born at the time of the Stamp Act crisis, and if college students had not been recruited into the boycott movement, they might not later as adults have appeared at Bunker Hill.

The circle of participation widened to include even the poorer members of colonial society, the kinds of people who were as dependent upon the consumer society as were their gentry neighbours. They collected rags required for the manufacture of "patriotic" paper. Goods—or in this case the denial of goods—were mobilizing an entire populace. Peter Oliver, the Boston loyalist who later wrote an acerbic history of the Revolution, noted that during the protest against the Townshend duties, the city's radicals circulated:

> A Subscription Paper . . . Enumerating a great Variety of Articles not to be imported from *England,* which they supposed would muster the Manufacturers in *England* into a national Mob to support their Interests. Among the various prohibited Articles, were *Silks, Velvets, Clocks, Watches, Coaches & Chariots;* & it was highly diverting, to see the names & marks, to the Subscription, of Porters & Washing Women.[49]

Oliver found the incident amusing, an example of how a few troublemakers had duped the poorer sorts. But the porters and washerwomen of Boston knew what they were doing.[50] Affixing one's signature or mark to a document of this sort was a personal risk that they were willing to accept. Like the village women and the graduating students, these people had been mobilized through goods; it is difficult to see how independence could have been achieved without them.

The protest against the Townshend duties generated group activities that might best be termed "rituals of non-consumption." These were focused moments in the life of a community during which continuing social relations were often, quite suddenly politicized. The spark for these events was usually a letter sent by some external body urging the villagers to support the boycott. In some towns large numbers of men and women took oaths before their neighbours swearing not to purchase certain items until parliament repealed the obnoxious taxes. These ceremonies possessed a curious religious character, much like the covenant renewals in the early Congregational churches of New England. In other communities specially selected committeemen carried subscription papers from house to house.[51] In Boston the "Subscription Rolls, for encouraging Oeconomy, Industry, our own Manufactures, and the disuse of foreign Superfluities" were kept in the office of the

[49] *Ibid.,* p. 197; Peter Oliver, *Origin and Progress of the American Revolution: A Tory View,* ed. Douglass Adair and John A. Schutz (Stanford, 1961), p. 61.
[50] See Alfred F. Young, "George Robert Twelves Hewes, 1742–1840: A Boston Shoemaker and the Memory of the American Revolution," *William and Mary Quart.,* 3rd ser., xxxviii (1981), pp. 561–623.
[51] Andrews, "Boston Merchants," pp. 209–14; Schlesinger, *Colonial Merchants,* ch. 3.

town clerk. According to a notice in the *Boston Gazette,* "The Selectmen strongly recommend this Measure to Persons of *all ranks,* as the most honorable and effectual way of giving *public* Testimony of their Love to their Country, and of endeavouring to save it from ruin."[52] Whether they lived in Boston or an inland village, ordinary colonists were obviously under considerable pressure to sign. But the decision was theirs to make. By pledging to support non-consumption they reaffirmed their moral standing in the community. They demonstrated that they were not "enemies to their country"—a country that in fact they were only just beginning to define.

Perhaps the most effective political ritual associated with non-consumption, at least in New England, was the funeral. More than any other event connected with the life cycle, the funeral in eighteenth-century America had become an occasion of conspicuous consumption. Wealthy families distributed commemorative rings. Gloves were given out, and custom mandated that all attendants wear mourning dress made of the best imported cloth that they could afford. Indeed opulent funerals were in themselves an indication of the spread of the consumer society. "Such was the fashion," one colonist explained, that bereaved families imagined that if they disappointed their friends and neighbours, "they should have made themselves obnoxious to the censures of an ill-natured and malicious world, who would have construed their frugality into niggardliness."[53]

During the protest against the Townshend duties, such extravagant displays suddenly seemed inappropriate. A shift in the symbolic meaning of British imports called forth a change in funeral etiquette. And since these were highly visible events, they inevitably confronted those persons who had not thought deeply about imperial politics with an ideological message. The freeholders and inhabitants of Boston agreed "not to use any Gloves but what are manufactured here, nor any new Garments upon such Occasion but what shall be absolutely necessary."[54] Everywhere one saw signs of retrenchment at funerals, a trend that one anonymous writer declared "affected every true patriot with particular satisfaction."[55] As might be expected, the loyalist historian, Peter Oliver, denounced the politicization of funerals. He saw the hand of the radicals behind these restrictions. "Under Pretence of Oeconomy," he announced, "the Faction undertook to regulate Funerals, that there might be less Demand for English Manufactures." Oliver recognized that expensive funerals had at an earlier time "ruined some Families of moderate Fortune," but from his perspective the patriot funeral raised even greater problems. "One Extreme was exchanged for an-

---

[52] *Boston Gazette,* 30 Nov. 1767 (my emphasis).
[53] *Massachusetts Spy,* 6 Jan. 1774. Also Robert A. Gross, *The Minutemen and their World* (New York, 1976), p. 33.
[54] *Report of the Record Commissioners,* p. 224. Also Andrews, "Boston Merchants," p. 196; Morgan, *Stamp Act Crisis,* pp. 247–8.
[55] *Massachusetts Spy,* 6 Jan. 1774.

other. A Funeral now seemed more like a Procession to a May Fair; and Processions were lengthened, especially by the Ladies, who figured a way . . . to exhibit their Share of Spite, & their Silk Gowns."[56] Funerals had moved from the private to the public realm, and as was recently the case in the black townships of South Africa, they became powerful political statements. It is perhaps not surprising, therefore, that the members of the Continental Congress enthusiastically endorsed this particular means of mobilizing mass support, pledging in September 1774 that:

> on the death of any relation or friend, none of us, or any of our families will go into any further mourning-dress, than a black crape or ribbon on the arm or hat, for gentlemen, and a black ribbon and necklace for ladies, and we will discontinue the giving of gloves and scarves at funerals.[57]

The repeal of the Townshend Acts in 1770 retarded the growth of national consciousness in the American colonies. Parliament's apparent retreat on the issue of taxation revealed the symbolic function that consumer goods had played in the constitutional discourse. As political tensions within the empire eased, these articles no longer carried such clear ideological meanings. Repeal, in fact, unloosed a frenzy of consumption. Though the tax on tea remained, the colonists could not be deterred from buying British manufactures. Between 1770 and 1772 they set records for the importation of foreign goods. Radical leaders such as Samuel Adams warned the Americans that the threat to their political liberties had not been removed. He begged them to continue their resistance, to maintain the boycott. But few listened. Commerce returned to the old channels, and as it did so, goods again became associated with the Anglicization of American society. It is no wonder that Adams grumbled in a letter to his friend Arthur Lee that the colonial newspapers were once again filled with advertisements for "the Baubles of Britain."[58]

The non-importation movement of the late 1760s had in fact been only a partial success. The merchants of Philadelphia accused the merchants of Boston of cheating. People everywhere found it more difficult than they had anticipated to do without the thousands of items imported from the mother country. The most notable successes of the period had been local, something that had occurred within regionally clustered communities. For all the rhetoric, it had proved hard to communicate to very distant strangers.[59] George Mason understood the problem. "The associations," he explained, "almost from one end of this continent to the other, were drawn up in a hurry and formed upon erroneous principles." The organizers of these boycotts had

[56] Oliver, *Origin and Progress of the American Revolution*, p. 62.

[57] "The Association," 20 Oct. 1774, in *Documents of American History*, ed. Henry Steele Commager (New York, 1949), p. 86.

[58] *The Writings of Samuel Adams*, ed. Harry Alonzo Cushing, 4 vols. (New York, 1904–8), ii, p. 267.

[59] Jensen, *Founding of a Nation*, chs. 10–12.

expected parliament to back down quickly, certainly within a year or two, but that had not happened. The results did not discourage Mason, however, for as he explained in December 1770, "had one general plan been formed exactly the same for all colonies (so as to have removed all cause of jealousy or danger of interfering with each other) in the nature of a sumptuary law, restraining only articles of luxury and ostentation together with the goods at any time taxed," the results might have been different.[60] Americans had not yet discovered how to communicate continentally.

In 1773 parliament stumbled upon an element of mass political mobilization that had been missing during the Townshend protest. By passing the Tea Act, it united the colonists as they had never been before. The reason for this new solidarity was not so much that the Americans shared a common political ideology, but rather that the statute affected an item of popular consumption found in almost every colonial household. It was perhaps *the* major article in the development of an eighteenth-century consumer society, a beverage which, as we have seen, appeared on the tables of the wealthiest merchants and the poorest labourers. For Americans, therefore, it was not difficult to transmit perceptions of liberty and rights through a discourse on tea. By transforming this ubiquitous element of daily life into a symbol of political oppression, parliament inadvertently boosted the growth of national consciousness. "Considering the article of tea as the detestable instrument which laid the foundation of the present sufferings of our distressed friends in the town of Boston," the members of the Virginia house of burgesses declared in August 1774, "we view it with horror, and therefore resolve that we will not, from this day, either import tea of any kind whatever, nor will we use or suffer, even such of it as is now at hand, to be used in any of our families."[61] And in the northern colonies, people now spoke of tea-drinkers not simply as enemies of our country—a term which in the 1760s had referred to one's colony or region—but as enemies "to the liberties of America."[62]

The public discourse over tea raised issues about the political effects of consumption that had been absent or muted during the previous decade. The language of goods became more shrill, hyperbolic. During the Stamp Act crisis, colonists associated consumption chiefly with personal debt. After parliament passed the Townshend duties, they talked more frequently in a moral vocabulary. By denying themselves the "baubles" of the mother country, they might thereby preserve their virtue. But in 1774 they spoke of tea as a badge of slavery, as a political instrument designed by distant tyrants to seize their property. "A WOMAN" argued in the *Massachusetts Spy* that:

[60] Kate Mason Rowland, *The Life of George Mason, 1725–1792*, 2 vols. (New York, 1892), i, pp. 148–9.
[61] "Virginia Non-Importation Agreement," 1 Aug. 1774, in *Documents of American History*, ed. Commager, p. 80.
[62] "New York Sons of Liberty Resolutions on Tea," 29 Nov. 1773, *ibid.*, p. 70.

in the present case the use of tea is considered not as a *private* but as a *public* evil . . . we are not to consider it merely as the herb tea, or what has an ill-tendency as to health, but as it is made a handle to introduce a variety of public grievances and oppressions amongst us.

Tea, A WOMAN concluded, is a sign of "enslaving our country."[63] In an impassioned appeal to the citizens of Charleston, South Carolina, one speaker—probably Christopher Gadsden—insisted that a non-importation agreement would "prove a means of restoring our liberty." "Who that has the spirit of a man," he asked:

but would rather forego the elegancies and luxuries of life, than entail slavery on his unborn posterity to the end of time? . . . Nothing but custom makes the curl-pated beau a more agreeable sight with his powder and pomatum, than the tawney savage with his paint and bear's grease. Too long has luxury reigned amongst us, enervating our constitutions and shrinking the human race into pigmies.[64]

And finally, another writer in this period bluntly reminded newspaper readers in New England that "the use of Tea is a political evil in this country."[65]

Throughout America the ceremonial destruction of tea strengthened the bonds of political solidarity. Once again, we must look to local communities for the embryonic stirrings of national consciousness. It was in these settings that a common commodity was transformed into the overarching symbol of political corruption. By purging the community of tea leaves—an import that could be found in almost every American home—the colonists reinforced their own commitment to certain political principles. But they did more. The destruction of the tea transmitted an unmistakable ideological message to distant communities: we stand together. The Boston Tea Party is an event familiar to anyone who has heard of the Revolution.[66] In many villages, however, the inhabitants publicly burned their tea. Everyone was expected to contribute some leaves, perhaps a canister of tea hidden away in a pantry, a few ounces, tea purchased long before parliament passed the hated legislation, all of it to be destroyed in flames that purged the town of ideological sin. "We hear from [the town of] Montague," reported the *Massachusetts Spy*:

that one of the inhabitants having inadvertently purchased a small quantity of tea of a pedlar, several of the neighbours being made acquainted therewith, went to his house and endeavoured to convince him of the impropriety of making any use of that article for the present, while it continues to be a badge of slavery.

[63] *Massachusetts Spy*, 6 Jan. 1774; also *ibid.*, 13, 20 Jan., 25 Aug. 1774.
[64] "To the Inhabitants of the Province of South Carolina, about to Assemble on the 6th of July," 4 July 1774, in *American Archives*, comp. Peter Force, 4th ser., 6 vols. (Washington, D.C., 1837–53), i, p. 511.
[65] *Massachusetts Spy*, 23 Dec. 1773.
[66] See Benjamin Woods Labaree, *The Boston Tea Party* (New York, 1964).

The visiting committee easily persuaded the man "to commit it to the flames." The group then ferreted the pedlar out of the local tavern, seized his entire stock of tea and "carried [it] into the road, where it was burnt to ashes."[67] In Charleston, Massachusetts, the town clerk announced that he would oversee the collection of all tea in the community: "And that the tea so collected, be destroyed by fire, on Friday next at noon day, in the market place." He declared that any persons who failed to participate in this activity "are not only inimicable to the liberty of America in general, but also show a daring disrespect to this town in particular."[68] From Northampton County on Virginia's eastern shore came news that a committee had collected 416 pounds of tea. Moreover "Some gentlemen also brought their Tea to the Court House, and desired it might be publickly burnt, in which reasonable request they were instantly gratified."[69] And from Wilmington, North Carolina, a traveller reported, "the Ladies have burnt their tea in a solemn procession."[70]

The seizure and destruction of tea became an effective instrument of political indoctrination, forcing the ignorant or indifferent people of these communities publicly to commit themselves to the cause of liberty while at the same time reinforcing the patriots' commitment to a radical ideology. The individuals involved were often ordinary men and women. Had they not become associated with tea, they might have remained anonymous colonists, going about their business and keeping their political opinions to themselves. But they were not so lucky. Early in 1774 Ebenezer Withington, a "labourer" living in Dorchester, allegedly found some tea on a road that ran along the ocean. Soon thereafter he was called before a meeting of "Freeholders and other Inhabitants" where Withington confessed in writing before his neighbours that:

> I found said Tea on Saturday, on going round the Marshes; brought off the same thinking no Harm; returning I met some Gentlemen belonging to the Castle [the British fort in Boston Harbour], who asked me if I had been picking up the Ruins? I asked them if there was any Harm; they said no except from my Neighbours. Accordingly, I brought Home the same, part of which I Disposed of, and the Remainder took from me since.

The townspeople decided that Withington had not realized the political significance of his act. The people who had purchased tea from him were warned to bring it to the village authorities immediately for destruction or risk having their names published as enemies of the country.[71] The Dorchester committee —and committees in other towns as well—performed the same political func-

---

[67] *Massachusetts Spy*, 17 Feb. 1774.
[68] *Ibid.*, 6 Jan. 1774.
[69] *American Archives*, comp. Force, 4th ser., i, pp. 1045–6.
[70] [Schaw], *Journal of a Lady of Quality*, p. 155.
[71] *Massachusetts Spy*, 13 Jan. 1774.

tion that local militia units would serve during the Revolution. They provided ideological instruction, and by so doing made it difficult even for the poorest persons either to remain neutral or retain old loyalties.[72]

Sometimes tea sparked an incident that mobilized an entire village. By their own admission, the inhabitants of Truro, an isolated village on Cape Cod, had not kept informed about the gathering political storm in Boston. Then, one day, some tea apparently washed ashore near Provincetown, and the men who discovered it sold small quantities to a few Truro farmers. That purchase precipitated a crisis. A town committee questioned these persons and concluded "that their buying this noxious Tea was through ignorance and inadvertance, and they were induced thereto by the base and villainous example and artful persuasions of some noted pretended friends to government from the neighbouring towns; and therefore this meeting thinks them excusable with acknowledgement."

But individual confession was not sufficient to exonerate the community. The people of Truro had failed to educate themselves about the dangers to their constitutional liberties and, of course, had left themselves vulnerable to scheming persons who peddled tea, the symbol of oppression. The town meeting decided, therefore, to form a special committee which would draft a resolve "respecting the introduction of Tea from Great Britain subject to a duty, payable in America." After deliberating for half an hour, the members of this committee returned with a statement which was at once defensive and radical:

> WE the inhabitants of the town of Truro, though by our remote situation from the centre of public news, we are deprived of opportunities of gaining so thorough a knowledge in the unhappy disputes that subsist between us and the parent state as we could wish; yet as our love of liberty and dread of slavery is not inferior (perhaps) to that of our brethren in any part of the province, we think it our indispensable duty to contribute our mite in the glorious cause of liberty and our country.

People asked immediately what in fact they could do to demonstrate that their ideological hearts were in the right place. "We think," the committee responded, "that most likely method that we can take to aid in frustrating those inhuman designs of administration is a disuse of that baneful dutied article Tea."[73] The inhabitants of this village communicated their political beliefs not only to the radical leaders of Boston and to the members of the Massachusetts general assembly but also to themselves through tea. By dropping this popular import they overcame the peculiarities of local experience and linked up with other Americans, distant strangers whose crucial

[72] On the responsibility of the colonial militias to indoctrinate citizens, see John W. Shy, *A People Numerous and Armed: Reflections on the Military Struggles for American Independence* (New York, 1976), pp. 193–224.

[73] *Massachusetts Spy*, 31 Mar. 1774.

common bond with the farmers of Truro at this moment was their participation in an eighteenth-century consumer society.

During the summer of 1774 patriot spokesmen throughout America called for some form of boycott. Boston's leaders, for example, urged the people of Massachusetts to sign a Solemn League and Covenant pledging to break off "all commercial connection with a country whose political Councils tend only to enslave them."[74] Loyalists castigated this "infernal Scheme." In this atmosphere almost any manufactured article could spark a dispute. The League in fact threatened to bring the political battles of the street into the home, "raising a most unnatural Enmity between Parents & Children & Husbands & Wives."[75] People living in other parts of America now looked to the Continental Congress for guidance. As George Mason had recognized in 1770, a successful boycott required the united and co-ordinated efforts of all the colonists. When the congressional delegates convened in September 1774, they passed legislation almost immediately, creating the Association, a vast network of local committees charged with enforcing non-importation. This was a truly radical act. In an attempt to halt further commerce with Great Britain, Congress authorized every county, city and town in America to establish a revolutionary government.[76] As Henry Laurens explained in September 1774:

> From the best intelligence that I have received, my conclusions are, that So. Carolina, No. Carolina, Virginia, Maryland, Pensylvania [sic], New Jersey, New York, Connecticut, Rhode Island, Massachusets [sic], New Hampshire, one chain of Colonies extending upwards of 1,200 Miles & containing about three Millions of White Inhabitants of whom upwards of 500,000 [are] Men capable of bearing Arms, will unite in an agreement to Import no goods from Great Britain, the West India Islands, or Africa until those Acts of Parliament which Strike at our Liberties are Repealed.[77]

The colonists responded enthusiastically to the call. The committees monitored consumption, identifying local patriots by the garments they wore and by the beverages they drank, and demanding public confessions from those who erred. In Virginia counties everyone was expected to sign the Association, a promise before one's neighbours—almost a statement of one's new birth as a consumer—not to purchase the despised manufactures of the mother country. According to James Madison, these signings were "the method used among us to distinguish friends from foes and to oblige the Common people to a more strict observance of it [the Association]."[78] As in

---

[74] *American Archives*, comp. Force, 4th ser., i, pp. 397–8; Jensen, *Founding of a Nation*, pp. 468–75; Schlesinger, *Colonial Merchants*, pp. 319–26; Gross, *Minutemen*, pp. 47, 50–1.

[75] Oliver, *Origin and Progress of the American Revolution*, p. 104.

[76] Jensen, *Founding of a Nation*, pp. 506–7.

[77] *The Papers of Henry Laurens*, ed. George C. Rogers, Jr., 10 vols. (Columbia, S. C., 1981), ix, p. 552, Henry Laurens to Peter Petrie, 7 Sept. 1774.

[78] *Papers of James Madison*, ed. W. T. Hutchinson and William M. E. Rachal, 3 vols. (Chicago, 1962), i, p. 135, James Madison to William Bradford, 20 Jan. 1775.

earlier boycotts, people sorted themselves out politically through goods. A committee in Prince George's County announced, "That to be clothed in manufactures fabricated in the Colonies ought to be considered as a badge and distinction of respect and true patriotism."[79] The local associations also educated ordinary men and women about the relation between consumer goods and constitutional rights, in other words, about the relation between experience and ideology. A committee in Anne Arundel County, Maryland, helped Thomas Charles Williams understand that by importing tea he had "endangered the rights and liberties of America." Proceedings against Williams were dropped, after he proclaimed that he was "sincerely sorry for his offense."[80] Silas Newcomb of Cumberland, New Jersey, was more stubborn. The members of the local association failed to convince the man of his error in drinking "East-India Tea in his family," and they were finally compelled "to break off all dealings with him, and in this manner publish the truth of the case, that he may be distinguished from the friends of American liberty."[81]

III

The colonists who responded to Boston's call in 1774 were consciously repudiating the empire of goods. Within barely a generation the meaning of the items of everyday consumption had changed substantially. At mid-century imported articles—the cloth, the ceramics, the buttons—had served as vehicles of Anglicization, and as they flooded into the homes of yeomen and gentry alike, they linked ordinary men and women with the distant, exciting culture of the metropolis. By participating in the market-place, by making choices among competing manufactures, the colonists became in some important sense English people who happened to live in the provinces. By taxing these goods, however, parliament set in motion a process of symbolic redefinition, slow and painful at first, punctuated by lulls that encouraged the false hope that the empire of goods could survive, but ultimately straining Anglicization to breaking-point. Americans who had never dealt with one another, who lived thousands of miles apart, found that they could communicate their political grievances through goods or, more precisely, through the denial of goods that had held the empire together. Private consumer experiences were transformed into public rituals. Indeed many colonists learned about rights and liberties through these common consumer items, articles which in themselves were politically neutral, but which in the explosive atmosphere of the 1760s and 1770s became the medium through which ideological abstractions acquired concrete meaning.

[79] *American Archives*, comp. Force, 4th ser., i, p. 494.
[80] *Ibid.*, p. 1061.
[81] *Ibid.*, ii, p. 34.

When the colonists finally and reluctantly decided that they could do without the "baubles of Britain," they destroyed a vital cultural bond with the mother country. "The country," explained James Lovell to his friend Joseph Trumbull in December 1774, ". . . seems determined to let England know that in the present struggle, commerce has lost all the temptations of a bait to catch the American farmer."[82] Lovell may have exaggerated, but he helps us to understand why in 1774 the countryside supported the cities. Consumer goods had made it possible for the colonists to imagine a nation; the Association made it easier for Americans to imagine independence.

[82] Cited in Jensen, *Founding of a Nation*, p. 561.

Markets and Composite Farms in Early America

Richard Lyman Bushman

INTRODUCTION

By studying change over space and time, historians risk seeing the past only in terms of rapid, even revolutionary, transformations. Here the prominent social and cultural historian Richard Bushman warns that this very practice has distorted our understanding of early American agriculture. He argues against the notion that an early-nineteenth-century market revolution transformed American farms from household to market production. Instead, Bushman believes that commerce always played a role in American agriculture. By the eighteenth century, farmers across British North America simultaneously produced for the home and for the market, hence his term composite farm.

Bushman's thesis redefines the transition debate in American history. Determining when America turned from a largely subsistence-based to a commercial-based economy is the wrong question, he insists. Large areas in the Chesapeake, Lower South, and West Indies followed the opposite evolution, increasing household production over time. Bushman replaces time with geography as the key variable in understanding early American economic development. In his model, colonial America's broad spectrum of settlement patterns serves as its distinguishing feature.

Beyond its brilliant survey of early American agriculture, Bushman's essay provides rare insight into how historical paradigms are made and unmade. He implies that all paradigms simplify the past. Indeed, his construct of composite farming may slight changes in American agriculture after the colonial period.

Richard L. Bushman, "Markets and Composite Farms in Early America," *William and Mary Quarterly*, 3d ser., 55 (1998), 351–74. Reprinted by permission of Omohundro Institute of Early American History and Culture, Williamsburg, VA.

Richard Bushman is Gouverneur Morris Professor of History at Columbia University. He wishes to thank Alan Taylor, Claudia Bushman, William Shade, Richard Brown, Edwin Perkins, James Henretta, and Winifred Rothenberg for their criticism and help.

- *Does Bushman's argument otherwise constitute a theoretical break-through?*
- *Or does it simply split differences between the existing paradigms of sub-sistence and commercial agriculture?*
- *If historical paradigms are inherently inadequate at some level, why do historians still use them?*

The market revolution, the interpretive construct that figures so prominently in current historiography of the nineteenth-century, may be distorting our understanding of eighteenth century farm life. The idea of a market revolution requires a "before" to contrast with an "after," and the eighteenth-century "before" of the market revolution clashes with important aspects of colonial farming. On the opening page of a recent collection of essays on the subject, a single sentence sums up what the revolution supposedly wrought. In early nineteenth-century America, the editors say, "a largely subsistence economy of small farms and tiny workshops, satisfying mostly local needs through barter and exchange, gave place to an economy in which farmers and manufacturers produced food and goods for the cash rewards of an often distant marketplace."[1] That statement conceives of colonial farmers producing mainly for themselves, bartering with neighbors to augment their own production, and trading tiny surpluses for store goods. The proponents of a market revolution associate these household producers with the *longue durée* of traditional agriculture and the older moral economy that preceded modernization. Self-contained and entrenched, this eighteenth-century rural economy resisted the invasion of market forces that threatened local production systems.[2]

This picture of eighteenth-century farming is at best only partially true. Beyond doubt many farmers did produce largely for themselves and relied on barter to augment the deficiencies in their household production. They did refer to products sent to market as a surplus, implying that they aimed

[1] Melvyn Stokes and Stephen Conway, eds., *The Market Revolution in America: Social, Political, and Religious Expressions, 1800–1880* (Charlottesville, 1996), 1.

[2] The synthetic study of 19th-century social and political change is Charles G. Sellers, *The Market Revolution: Jacksonian America, 1815–1846* (New York, 1991). For a recent statement of the conventional view see Daniel P. Jones, *The Economic and Social Transformation of Rural Rhode Island, 1780–1850* (Boston, 1992). For examples of the notion of resistance to the market see David P. Szatmary, *Shays' Rebellion: The Making of an Agrarian Insurrection* (Amherst, Mass., 1980), 16–17, and Paul Boyer and Stephen Nissenbaum, *Salem Possessed: The Social Origins of Witchcraft* (Cambridge, Mass., 1974), 86–109. The standard historiographical essay on 18th-century agriculture is Allan Kulikoff, "The Transition to Capitalism in Rural America," *William and Mary Quarterly*, 3d Ser., 46 (1989), 120–44. Two highly influential essays are Michael Merrill, "Cash is Good to Eat: Self-Sufficiency and Exchange in the Rural Economy of the United States," *Radical History Review*, No. 3 (1977), 42–71, and James A. Henretta, "Families and Farms: *Mentalité* in Pre-Industrial America," *WMQ*, 3d Ser., 35 (1978), 3–32.

to feed their families first. Still, other farmers, large and small, grew crops for town consumption and the Atlantic trade. They benefited from extensive marketing systems radiating from the port towns and from Britain. They purchased labor at considerable expense to enlarge production. Many—not just an insignificant minority—prospered. Colonial market farmers figured in their societies as prominently as nineteenth-century cotton planters figured in the South. Eighteenth-century commercial farming cannot be dismissed as incidental while household producers are considered typical.[3] Yet the idea of a market revolution leaves market farmers out of the picture. To claim that the market revolution transformed American society as a whole implies that commercial agriculture amounted to little before the early nineteenth century. How are we to reconcile the reality of colonial market farming with the idea of a market revolution?

The concept of a market revolution hinges on the division of farms into two types, once termed "subsistence" and "commercial" and now more commonly called "household producers" and "market producers." As well as representing individual farms, the types stand for periods, one dominant before the market revolution and the other after. The division goes back to the first serious agricultural histories of the early twentieth century and Percy Wells Bidwell's "Rural Economy in New England at the Beginning of the Nineteenth Century." In Bidwell's narrative, farmers cast off their retrograde habits in the early nineteenth century and entered the modern world. Bidwell's work came out of the agricultural college tradition and the ethos of the United States Department of Agriculture, whose social scientists idealized efficient production for the market and the advanced farmers who maximized production and profits. Under the influence of Frederick Jackson Turner's stages of civilization, Bidwell and John I. Falconer, his co-worker in writing the *History of Agriculture in the Northern United States,* believed that as one journeyed away from urban centers and the orbit of the market, the quality of agriculture declined. Frontier subsistence farmers mercilessly depleted the soil to reap the greatest fruits with minimum effort, while commercial farmers adopted the best fertilizing techniques in the interest of profit. "Farming appeared at its worst on the frontier, where the scarcity of labor and capital favored predatory methods, and at its best in the neighborhood of the

---

[3] For a comprehensive statement on commercial agriculture in the colonies see Jack P. Greene, *Pursuits of Happiness: The Social Development of Early Modern British Colonies and the Formation of American Culture* (Chapel Hill, 1988). For a similar discussion and an attempt to distinguish colonial marketing from market society see Stephen Innes, ed., *Work and Labor in Early America* (Chapel Hill, 1988), 34–39, and Fred Block and Margaret R. Somers, "Beyond the Economistic Fallacy: The Holistic Social Science of Karl Polanyi," in Theda Skocpol, ed., *Vision and Method in Historical Sociology* (Cambridge, 1984), 47–84. Edwin J. Perkins, "The Entrepreneurial Spirit in Colonial America: The Foundations of Modern Business History," *Business History Review,* 43 (Spring 1989), 160–86, makes the case for an entrepreneurial attitude in most segments of the colonial economy.

commercial towns, where ready markets stimulated intensive use of the soil."[4] Life in general improved when the degraded subsistence agriculture of the eighteenth century yielded to progressive commercial farming.[5]

Agricultural historians in the past quarter century have sharply revised this conceptualization of agricultural change but have retained the two-part typology. The rejection of "subsistence" in favor of "household production" signifies the realization that no farm family could provide everything for itself, nor could it survive without exchange. Bettye Hobbs Pruitt's close study of Massachusetts farms in 1771 revealed systematic deficiencies in the resources of individual farms, requiring virtually every farmer to trade hay, fuel, or corn with neighbors, sometimes plowing a field or lending an ox as part of the barter.[6] In addition, a family had to produce a surplus to exchange at the store for salt, molasses, liquor, metal goods, and fancy fabrics plus something more for taxes. This habit of trade and exchange, as Christopher Clark has shown, made families susceptible later on to market involvement and employment in small manufacturing operations when capitalism came to the countryside. Rather than fighting the market, Clark's farmers collaborated in its conquest of rural society. Qualifications of this sort reduce the stark contrast of subsistence and commercial with which agricultural history began in the early twentieth century, but the two-part typology remains. The structure of Clark's sophisticated and subtle study of western Massachusetts agriculture in the first half of the nineteenth century still hangs on a division of farms into local family producers in the eighteenth century and market farmers by the middle of the nineteenth century.[7] There is no escaping some

---

[4] Bidwell, "Rural Economy in New England at the Beginning of the Nineteenth Century," Connecticut Academy of the Arts and Sciences, *Transactions*, 20 (1916), 241–399; Bidwell and Falconer, *History of Agriculture in the Northern United States, 1620–1860* (New York, 1941; orig. pub. 1925), 84 (quotation), 115, 164–65, 198. Somewhat earlier, Orin Grant Libby, writing in a radical tradition, proposed a similar division in "The Geographical Distribution of the Vote of the Thirteen States on the Federal Constitution, 1787–88," *Bulletin of the University of Wisconsin*, 1 (1894), 1–116.

[5] Bidwell and Falconer worked in a tradition going back to 18th-century reformers who scorned the backward ways of traditional farmers and lauded the achievements of improving husbandmen. The great agricultural achievements were the work of rational experimenters, who kept careful records and practiced business principles. See Christopher Grasso, "The Experimental Philosophy of Farming: Jared Eliot and the Cultivation of Connecticut," *WMQ*, 3d Ser., 50 (1993), 516–18, and G. E. Fussell, "The Farming Writers of Eighteenth-Century England," *Agricultural History*, 21 (1947), 1–8. More recent writing neutralizes the judgment about the value of the two types and even reverses Bidwell's and Falconer's preferences. If less progressive than market farmers, household producers are seen to have enjoyed greater independence and cooperated more with their neighbors in the exchange of work and produce.

[6] Pruitt, "Self-Sufficiency and the Agricultural Economy of Eighteenth-Century Massachusetts," *WMQ*, 3d Ser., 41 (1984), 333–64, does not hold with the distinction between subsistence and commercial production.

[7] Clark, *The Roots of Rural Capitalism: Western Massachusetts, 1780–1860* (Ithaca, 1990). Equally subtle and insightful are the essays in Henretta, *The Origins of American Capitalism: Collected Essays* (Boston, 1991).

such conception when the market revolution is used as the master concept for understanding agricultural change.[8]

Although prevalent in recent writings, the two-part typology is not completely stable. Signs of its mutability surface in the market revolution historiography itself. The difficulty in locating the time of transition suggests an uncertainty. "Revolution" implies a sharp break when obvious manifestations of the new order can be seen supplanting the old. But the time of the market revolution is difficult to determine. Clarence Danhof located the transition after 1820.[9] Clark sees commercial relationships changing soon after 1800. James A. Henretta places the crucial period in the 1780s, when farmers and merchants seemed to be gaining greater control over the production process and maximizing profits in the aftermath of the Revolution. Instead of merely exchanging goods with farmers, Henretta finds, merchants began to hire farm families to make shoes or textiles. Entrepreneurial farmers in the Middle States and South hired laborers or rented out slaves and invested in new productive processes in search of greater gain. Up and down the coast he detects calculation, risk taking, and profit maximization governing the economy in the fourth quarter of the century, a time when Clark's household producers remain entrenched in household production.[10]

The reason for the shifting periodization is clear: so much of the old continues into the new, and so much of the new existed amid the old that the time of change can slide back and forth. Eighteenth-century market production is acknowledged as an obvious condition of the colonial economy, and household production most certainly continued into the nineteenth century.[11] The blending and mingling of the two types of farming blur the sharp distinctions that analysis requires. In short, there is more continuity amid change in the nineteenth century than the concept of the market revolution accounts for.

[8] Bidwell's and Falconer's simple typology has been complicated by the addition of the "transition to capitalism" to the discussion, adding an analysis of labor relations and a change in values. See Kulikoff, "Households and Markets: Toward a New Synthesis of American Agrarian History," *WMQ*, 3d Ser., 50 (1993), 342–55. But market farming and the employment of wage labor hired in a labor market do not necessarily go together. Merrill makes a case for separating the transition to capitalism from the market revolution in "Putting 'Capitalism' in Its Place: A Review of Recent Literature," ibid., 52 (1995), 315–26. He argues that market production did not bring farmers under the sway of capitalism. They were affected only when capitalists threatened to drive them off the land. The question of how to distinguish the colonial economy from capitalism has been debated at great length. See Rona S. Weiss, "Primitive Accumulation in the United States: The Interaction between Capitalist and Noncapitalist Class Relations in Seventeenth-Century Massachusetts," *Journal of Economic History*, 42 (1982), 77–82, and Michael A. Bernstein and Sean Wilentz, "Marketing, Commerce, and Capitalism in Rural Massachusetts," ibid., 44 (1984), 171–73.

[9] Danhof, *Change in Agriculture: The Northern United States, 1820–1870* (Cambridge, Mass., 1969).

[10] Clark, *Roots of Rural Capitalism*, chap. 3; Henretta, "The Transition to Capitalism in America," in *The Transformation of Early America: Society, Authority, and Ideology*, ed. Henretta, Michael Kammen, and Stanley N. Katz (New York, 1991), 218–38.

[11] Clark, *Roots of Rural Capitalism*, 273–77.

Winifred Barr Rothenberg has been more successful than anyone in fixing the exact moment of transition. By assembling systematic information about farmers and markets from a sample of a hundred farm account books, she was able to prepare a striking visual display. On one graph she plots the ups and downs of Massachusetts commodity prices as gleaned from the account books. Above and below it she charts New York and Philadelphia commodity prices. By placing a ruler vertically on the page, one can see that around 1780 Massachusetts price fluctuations came into conjunction with price changes in the two other North American markets. Shortly after the Revolution, Massachusetts fell into step with New York and Philadelphia, whereas before the prices in little villages all over the state had risen and fallen independently of the larger market. Rothenberg designates this moment as the time when the national market overtook Massachusetts. Before 1780, farmers may have traded in local marketplaces; after 1780, their trucking was embedded in a market society in which prices of the same goods and services rose and fell together. The farmers may not have immediately produced vast quantities of goods for sale in Boston—though Rothenberg finds the volume of production rising—but the large urban markets hovered over and controlled the economies of remote rural villages from then on. The small town economies were tied into a larger, continental market, making them players in a market economy.[12]

By grounding her analysis in systematic data, Rothenberg nails down the elusive moment of transition better than any of her colleagues. But she does not resolve the problem of the market revolution in its entirety, for she restricts herself to Massachusetts when the arena under consideration is the United States. Returning to her charts of three price indexes, we can see that New York and Philadelphia price fluctuations were already synchronized in 1750. Prices in the two cities were moving together. Were these two places embedded in a market society at midcentury and with them the hinterlands whence their farm commodities came? Rather than fixing the moment of the overall market revolution at 1780, the chart only marks the time when Massachusetts villages joined a game that Philadelphia, New York, and their hinterlands were already playing. Farther south, we know Chesapeake planters responded to international tobacco and grain prices much earlier. At midcentury, Virginia and Maryland planters made a massive shift from tobacco to wheat in response to deviations in prices. If we select the convergence of price fluctuations as the marker of revolutionary change, much of North America was involved in a market society by 1750 or before, and the 1780s market revolution was a New England affair.[13]

---

[12] Rothenberg, *From Market-Places to a Market Economy: The Transformation of Rural Massachusetts, 1750–1850* (Chicago, 1992). Rothenberg creates other indexes of market embeddedness besides wage and commodity prices, including growth of contract labor and increased use of credit instruments.

[13] As an economic historian, Rothenberg defines market economy more precisely than social historians usually do. By her definition, selling a single staple such as tobacco in a world market

To work our way toward a reconceptualization of farmers and markets in the eighteenth century, we cannot have small, backcountry Massachusetts farms stand in for all of North American agriculture. We must look broadly at British North America, beginning with its Atlantic context. We must remember that most of the first English settlers came to the colonies from a country that was undergoing its own transition to commercial agriculture. Keith Wrightson has said of seventeenth-century husbandmen in England that "very few small farmers were isolated from the market, and for most, market opportunities were the first factor to consider in their husbandry."[14] Coming from this society, English migrants undertook to extend market agriculture to the New World, not to set up little subsistence farms. They went in the largest numbers to the colonies where market opportunities were the greatest. In the seventeenth century, more English migrants set sail for the West Indies sugar islands, where the most intensive commercial agriculture in the world prevailed, than shipped for New England, the Middle Colonies, and the Chesapeake combined.[15] Virginia attracted settlers only after it had identified a profitable staple crop. Once tobacco flowed across the Atlantic, large numbers of people came, prompted by the need for labor to grow the crop.[16] These migrants did not need an education in commercial values to prepare them for market production. Even the Puritans who went to Providence Island in the 1630s struggled to find a cash crop.[17]

---

did not in itself establish Virginia in a market economy. That happened only when the prices of many other commodities in Virginia tended to converge with prices in the broader market so that these market prices influenced production in the Chesapeake. Until a local market's prices responded to prices outside itself, "those Smithian processes of output growth, achieved through specialization and division of labor," would not go to work. Her goal, like most economic historians, is to explain changes in rates of growth; ibid., 21. A similar interest in rates of change underlies Daniel Scott Smith, "A Malthusian-Frontier Interpretation of United States Demographic History before c. 1815," in *Urbanization in the Americas: The Background in Comparative Perspective,* ed. Woodrow Wilson Borah, Jorge Enrique Hardoy, and Gilbert Arthur Stelter (Ottawa, 1980), 15–24, with significant qualifications entered by Henretta, "Wealth and Social Structure," in *Colonial British America: Essays in the New History of the Early Modern Era,* ed. Greene and J. R. Pole (Baltimore, 1984), 272–75. Because the market revolution historiography, which is concerned more with individual farm strategies, uses "market economy" more loosely, the looser usage prevails here.

[14] Wrightson, *English Society, 1580–1680* (New Brunswick, N. J., 1982), 134. For a summary of English agricultural conditions in the 17th century see ibid., 128–39, and for some of the literature on the subject see Greene, *Pursuits of Happiness,* 219 n. 3.

[15] The numbers are roughly 190,000 to the West Indies versus 165,500 to the mainland; Nicholas Canny, "English Migration into and across the Atlantic during the Seventeenth and Eighteenth Centuries," in *Europeans on the Move: Studies on European Migration, 1500–1800,* ed. Canny (Oxford, 1994), 64.

[16] Edmund S. Morgan, *American Slavery, American Freedom: The Ordeal of Colonial Virginia* (New York, 1975), 404.

[17] Karen Ordahl Kupperman, *Providence Island, 1630–1641: The Other Puritan Colony* (Cambridge, 1993), chap. 4.

Once tobacco took hold, Chesapeake farmers were as market driven as any farmers in our history before the twentieth century.[18] Lois Green Carr, Lorena S. Walsh, and Gloria L. Main have found very few wool cards, flax hatchels, or looms in Maryland inventories before 1680, suggesting that all cloth was imported.[19] Robert Beverley complained in 1705 that Virginians were too lazy to make their own clothing, but in reality they were so busy with their market crop they had no time for spinning and weaving.[20] The planters were calculating and risk taking, too. The immense growth in Chesapeake tobacco production per worker in the seventeenth century came about only because of their attention to management and improved methods. Equally assiduous Carolina planters experimented with rice, indigo, and hemp production until they produced marketable crops.[21]

The spread of slavery is itself an index of market production. Southern planters purchased slaves primarily to produce market crops. Farm families did not need help in obtaining a subsistence. They could meet their needs without the trouble and expense of slave labor. Yet by 1782, 57 percent of the households in Orange County, Virginia, an upland district adjacent to the Blue Ridge, owned slaves, indicating that farmers there planned for the market. The figures for Lunenburg County on Virginia's Southside are the same.[22] The expansion of slavery, one of the signal economic developments of the first half of the eighteenth century, presumed a vigorous market for southern farm products.

[18] For estimates of the return from tobacco exports see Lois Green Carr, Russell R. Menard, and Lorena S. Walsh, *Robert Cole's World: Agriculture and Society in Early Maryland* (Chapel Hill, 1991), 77–80.

[19] Carr and Walsh, "The Planter's Wife: The Experience of White Women in Seventeenth-Century Maryland," *WMQ*, 3d Ser., 34 (1977), 562; Main, *Tobacco Colony: Life in Early Maryland, 1650–1720* (Princeton, 1983), 73.

[20] Beverley, *The History and Present State of Virginia* (1705), ed. David Freeman Hawke (Indianapolis, 1971), 155. In the 1660s, more than half the expenditures from Robert Cole's Maryland plantation went for imported goods, mainly cloth, clothing, and shoes; Carr, Menard, and Walsh, *Robert Cole's World*, 81.

[21] Peter A. Coclanis, *The Shadow of a Dream: Economic Life and Death in the South Carolina Low Country, 1670–1920* (New York, 1989), 48–110; Rachel N. Klein, *Unification of a Slave State: The Rise of the Planter Class in the South Carolina Backcountry, 1760–1808* (Chapel Hill, 1990), chap. 1; Richard R. Beeman, *The Evolution of the Southern Backcountry: A Case Study of Lunenburg County, Virginia, 1746–1832* (Philadelphia, 1984), 60–80; Roger A. Ekirch, *"Poor Carolina": Politics and Society in Colonial North Carolina, 1729–1776* (Chapel Hill, 1981), 30–33. Joyce E. Chaplin argues that, besides practicing market agriculture, planters in the Lower South absorbed a capitalist and modernist ethic—though not without misgivings—in *An Anxious Pursuit: Agricultural Innovation and Modernity in the Lower South, 1730–1815* (Chapel Hill, 1993).

[22] John Thomas Schlotterbeck, "Plantation and Farm: Social and Economic Change in Orange and Greene Counties, Virginia, 1716 to 1860" (Ph. D. diss., Johns Hopkins University, 1980; University Microfilms, 1988), 30; Philip D. Morgan and Michael L. Nicholls, "Slaves in Piedmont Virginia, 1720–1790," *WMQ*, 3d Ser., 46 (1989), 215, 217; Beeman, *Evolution of the Southern Backcountry,* 165. The figure on proportion of slaveholders seems to hold for most southern wealth holders; Alice Hanson Jones, *Wealth of a Nation to Be: The American Colonies on the Eve of the Revolution* (New York, 1980), tables 7–9.

Eighteenth-century migrants from the Tidewater and Lowcountry into the Piedmont and the Great Valley behind the Blue Ridge may have been cut off from markets for a few years, but they established links with the Atlantic trade with surprising rapidity. Shenandoah Valley farmers were producing for the international market within one generation of settlement.[23] The steep rise in wheat prices after 1745 stimulated a vast increase in production.[24] Wheat was soon pouring out of the Great Valley on its way to grain-deficient Europe. In the same fashion, upcountry South Carolina plunged into tobacco and indigo production in a very few years.[25] In the Chesapeake, Scottish firms established trading posts at the fall line and beyond to pull in tobacco from the Piedmont.[26] Even in the remote hill country, market involvement, varying from district to district and even from farmer to farmer, was not unknown. Slaveowners moved in almost from the beginning, and the percentage of slaveowning farmers steadily increased through the century, indicating that market production was feasible and practiced by at least part of the population. In a single upcountry county, both slaveholders and family farmers worked the soil. Although not to be classed with the Tidewater in the production of market crops, these patchy upcountry regions were not solely the province of household producers detached from the market.[27]

The literature on the Middle Colonies has never made much of a distinction between commercial and noncommercial farming. The demand for wheat in New York and Philadelphia assumed the existence of energetic production to supply that need.[28] Tenant farming, in the cases where rents were actually collected, required production of marketable crops for the same reason as slavery: there had to be a net profit to reward the landowner.[29] The owners of the huge patents along the Hudson River not only collected rent but also sent their agents through the countryside to buy grain for the New York market.[30] By the early eighteenth century, farmers up and down the

[23] Robert D. Mitchell, *Commercialism and Frontier: Perspectives on the Early Shenandoah Valley* (Charlottesville, 1977).

[24] On the wheat market see Paul G. E. Clemens, *The Atlantic Economy and Colonial Maryland's Eastern Shore: From Tobacco to Grain* (Ithaca, 1980), chap. 6.

[25] Klein, *Unification of a Slave State*, 15–36.

[26] Jacob M. Price, *Capital and Credit in British Overseas Trade: The View from the Chesapeake, 1700–1776* (Cambridge, Mass., 1980), and "The Rise of Glasgow in the Chesapeake Tobacco Trade, 1707–1775," *WMQ*, 3d Ser., 11 (1954), 179–99.

[27] Steven Hahn, *The Roots of Southern Populism: Yeoman Farmers and the Transformation of the Georgia Upcountry, 1850–1890* (New York, 1983), chap. 1.

[28] James T. Lemon, *The Best Poor Man's Country: A Geographical Study of Early Southeastern Pennsylvania* (Baltimore, 1972), 27–31.

[29] Lucy Simler, "Tenancy in Colonial Pennsylvania: The Case of Chester County," *WMQ*, 3d Ser., 43 (1986), 558–59; Innes, *Labor in a New Land: Economy and Society in Seventeenth-Century Springfield* (Princeton, 1983), xvi–xvii, 6–9.

[30] Lemon, *Best Poor Man's Country*, chap. 6; Sung Bok Kim, *Landlord and Tenant in Colonial New York: Manorial Society, 1664–1775* (Chapel Hill, 1978), 158.

river had learned to bargain for the best price in the spirit of capitalist calculation.[31] After midcentury, the wheat belt that stretched from central Virginia to New York was producing grain and flour for the West Indies, much
of Europe, and cities along the North American coast.[32] By 1768, the value of
grains and grain products exported from the colonies equaled 80 percent of
the value of tobacco exports and, if the domestic market is taken into account, likely exceeded them.[33]

Considering that this map of colonial agricultural regions is not really
contested, where are the household producers who form the baseline for the
market revolution? They have been imagined as settled around the fringes
of market-farming areas or stuck in the interstices between market farmers,
working poorer lands in otherwise productive counties, and above all concentrated in New England. New England is the heartland of the household
producer; hence the significance of Rothenberg's convergence of price fluctuations in the 1780s. The case for a market revolution rests heavily on an
image of the pretransition New England village that has been part of American lore from at least the nineteenth century.[34] That image was refurbished
by the town studies of the 1970s, which, although they said almost nothing
about the economy in their preoccupation with rural society, drew a picture
of inward-looking communities where people were most concerned for the
preservation of family and the maintenance of social harmony.[35] Backed by
these studies, social historians imagined New England as a land of communal covenants, hostile to the disruptions of trade and competitive individualism, and defensive when the market economy disrupted their lives.

That dominant image of colonial New England, however, does not account for much of the region before 1780. Even in the first years of settlement

---

[31] Cathy Matson, " 'Damned Scoundrels' and 'Libertisme of Trade': Freedom and Regulation in
Colonial New York's Fur and Grain Trades," *WMQ*, 3d Ser., 51 (1994), 408–12.

[32] Customers of two merchants in the Kingston, N. Y., area between 1774–1820 divided into large
producers, who shipped agricultural goods and barrel staves to the New York City market, and
smaller farmers, who sold in a local market, according to Thomas S. Wermuth, " 'To Market, To
Market'; Yeoman Farmers, Merchant Capitalists, and the Development of Capitalism in the
Hudson River Valley, 1760–1820," *Essays in Economic and Business History*, 9 (1991), 20–34. His
data can also be read to show the existence of a thriving local market that absorbed the production of even small farmers. Because Kingston was in close touch with New York City, city
prices would influence the local market.

[33] James F. Shepherd and Gary M. Walton, *Shipping, Maritime Trade, and the Economic Development
of Colonial North America* (Cambridge, 1972), 211–27.

[34] Carolyn Merchant relies on data from inland mountain towns in New England for her analysis of subsistence farms in *Ecological Revolutions: Nature, Gender, and Science in New England*
(Chapel Hill, 1989), 175–85.

[35] This tendency was most pronounced in Michael Zuckerman, *Peaceable Kingdoms: New England
Towns in the Eighteenth Century* (New York, 1970); Kenneth A. Lockridge, *A New England Town:
The First Hundred Years: Dedham, Massachusetts, 1636–1736* (New York, 1970); and, in its 17th-
century sections, Richard L. Bushman, *From Puritan to Yankee: Character and the Social Order in
Connecticut, 1690–1765* (Cambridge, Mass., 1967).

in Massachusetts Bay, farmers at Plymouth found a market for their livestock among the migrants flooding into Boston after 1630. William Bradford lamented the scattering of his little flock as people sought more land to pasture their herds. By 1650, one-fifth of the Massachusetts Bay population was concentrated in Boston, where it could produce only a small part of its own food.[36] The town depended on nearby farmers for wood, meat, and grain. In the Connecticut River valley, William Pynchon presided over a diversified economy with many small manufacturing enterprises supported by commercialized agriculture.[37] Throughout the remainder of the colonial period, cities and towns contained populations that had to be fed and warmed. In the late eighteenth century, 20 percent of the population was not laboring on the land, and the 80 percent who farmed had to produce their food, requiring that a quarter of farm production on average go to market.[38] Farms closest to the bigger towns likely commanded the larger portion of these sales and so sent even larger proportions of their production to market.[39]

In addition to the townsmen themselves, the ships that were essential to New England's balance of trade, fishermen's families, and the visiting British fleets required supplies.[40] Besides provisioning its towns and shipping, New England supplied the West Indies with food after the development of sugar plantations in the 1650s. The primary leg of those complex Atlantic trading voyages was Boston or New London to Barbados or St. Kitts. Cargoes for these voyages were assembled by merchants from the produce and meat flowing in from the New England countryside.[41] Around Narragansett Bay, the mild climate permitted the development of large horse farms manned in part by slave labor and aimed at sales in the sugar islands.[42]

In short, New England had a geography of commercial farming around centers like New London, New Haven, Newport, Boston, Salem, Gloucester,

[36] Darrett B. Rutman, *Winthrop's Boston: Portrait of a Puritan Town, 1630–1649* (New York, 1965), 179.

[37] Innes, *Labor in a New Land,* xvi–xxi, 4–14.

[38] For the proportion of people making their living from farming see John J. McCusker and Menard, *The Economy of British America, 1607–1789* (Chapel Hill, 1985), 248, and Stanley Lebergott, "Labor Force and Employment, 1800–1960," in Conference on Research in Income and Wealth, *Output, Employment, and Productivity in the United States after 1800* (New York, 1966), 117–204.

[39] Karen J. Friedmann, "Victualling Colonial Boston," *Agricultural History,* 47 (1973), 189–205.

[40] On home markets see Max George Schumacher, *The Northern Farmer and His Markets during the Late Colonial Period* (New York, 1975), 105–21.

[41] Rutman, *Winthrop's Boston,* 184–87; Richard Pates, *Yankees and Creoles: The Trade between North America and the West Indies before the American Revolution* (Cambridge, Mass., 1956); Bruce C. Daniels, "Economic Development in Colonial and Revolutionary Connecticut: An Overview," *WMQ,* 3d Ser., 37 (1980), 434–38; Terry Lee Anderson, *The Economic Growth of Seventeenth-Century New England: A Measurement of Regional Income* (New York, 1975).

[42] William Davis Miller, "The Narragansett Planters," American Antiquarian Society, *Proceedings,* 43 (1933), 49–115; Christian McBurney, "The South Kingstown Planters: Country Gentry in Colonial Rhode Island," *Rhode Island History,* 45 (1986), 81–93.

Marblehead, and Newburyport and along the navigable stretches of the major rivers.[43] The first settlers of New England had come with the intention of integrating their settlements into the international economy, and in parts of the countryside they succeeded. Without a substantial measure of market production in the first half of the eighteenth century, the external trade of New England would have looked far different.[44]

These port towns and their immediate hinterlands must have been incorporated into broader markets before 1780. Newport's shipping in the eighteenth century expanded primarily by increasing its coastal trade, which composed 15–30 percent of all trade in the 1720s and 1730s and swelled to 65 percent in the 1760s.[45] Ships sailing between New York and Boston brought back price information that was necessarily conveyed to the merchants' rural suppliers in Rhode Island and southeastern Massachusetts. How could the farmers ringing the port towns have sealed themselves off from knowledge of coastal markets? Households in the hill towns of central and western Massachusetts may have set prices in their local marketplaces, but not farmers driving cattle to markets in Boston or Newport.

The convergence of price fluctuations in Rothenberg's index may reflect the extension of price information from coastal regions into isolated hinterlands rather than a sudden conversion of Massachusetts as a whole. Rothenberg draws information for pre-1765 prices from twenty-two account books. Seven of those books came from Franklin County on the upper Connecticut River at the Vermont border. Would the charts look different if the prices in the sample had been taken solely from the seven account books listed for Essex County just north of Boston and covering the ports of Salem, Gloucester, and Newburyport? Farmers in Essex County would have fallen under the influence of city markets to a degree that those in towns upstream from two falls on the Connecticut River could not realize in 1750. Essex County price fluctuations were far more likely to have converged with Boston-New York-Philadelphia markets before the Revolution than towns buried in the backcountry. The map of market influences in New England was probably as mottled as the map for the colonies as a whole.

If the two-part typology is to be retained, the configuration of New England agriculture suggests a spatial, not a temporal, analysis. Rather than search for the moment in time when the economy converted from local marketplaces to a national market society, the change should be located geo-

---

[43] Christine Leigh Heyrman, *Commerce and Culture: The Maritime Communities of Colonial Massachusetts, 1690–1750* (New York, 1984); Daniel Vickers, "The Northern Colonies: Economy and Society, 1600–1775," in *The Cambridge Economic History of the United States*, ed. Stanley L. Engerman and Robert E. Gallman, I (Cambridge, 1996), 221–22.

[44] Howard S. Russell, *A Long, Deep Furrow: Three Centuries of Farming in New England*, abridged ed. (Hanover, N. H., 1982), 57–65.

[45] Lynne Withey, *Urban Growth in Colonial Rhode Island: Newport and Providence in the Eighteenth Century* (Albany, 1984), 21, 29.

graphically. Along the coast, near port towns, and adjacent to navigable rivers, farmers were attuned to Atlantic markets from the beginning. The Chesapeake was in the grip of the European tobacco market from 1620 on. Boston supplied the West Indies after 1650. New York and Philadelphia shipped grain and flour by the end of the century. The Carolina Lowcountry had identified its staple exports by 1720. As population expanded, farmers farther inland may have been cut off from the markets, but sooner or later they joined the larger economy, sooner in the Shenandoah Valley, later perhaps in the Massachusetts backcountry and in the southern piedmont. Following the logic of the household-market typology, the market can be envisioned as a rising tide that gradually inundated more and more regions, not as a switch turned at some moment for the entire continent.[46]

But should the two-part farm typology be sustained, even in this modified form? Its very simplicity is its strength and its weakness. Simplicity has the advantage of clarity. The household-and-market-production model evaluates hundreds of thousands of farms hundreds of miles apart, in differing climate regions, and following contrasting crop regimes and casts them into two categories based on a single criterion—involvement in market production. That single idea accounts for varied forms of farm behavior from the way women and children were employed to the ethos of farm life. On a grander scale, it provides a master narrative for agriculture during a two-hundred-year period. In the household-to-market-production story, the communal world before the market revolution gives way to individualistic market production afterward. The typology and the narrative gain strength because they satisfy the needs of various systems of thought: the Marxist transition to capitalism, post–World War II modernization theory, and Bidwell and Falconer's spread of progressive agriculture. This simple clear typology performs a lot of work for historians.

Simplicity, however, easily becomes oversimplification. Can all these variegated individual farms be divided conclusively into household producers and market farmers? At the extremes of a thousand-acre tobacco plantation and a newly opened tract in a Berkshire County hill town, the difference may be obvious, but what about the great majority in between? Was a farmer who sent 20 percent of his crop to market a market farmer? Did 30 percent or 40 percent indicate a commitment to profit maximization? Where lies the great divide?[47] It is commonly argued that the motive behind

[46] Kulikoff, "Households and Markets," 342–55, also suggests that different regions passed through the stages of the transition at different times, although this insight has not been absorbed into the historiography that tries to explain many forms of political, social, and religious conflict by a revolution in one brief span.
[47] Daniel Scott Smith, "Malthusian-Frontier Interpretation of United States Demographic History before c. 1815," 15–24, calculates that 20–30% of agricultural production was exported in 1710. He also argues that this proportion declined during the 18th century and that this was part

production rather than its volume makes the difference. Households produced for their own use rather than exchange. Even the extensive barter that went on among neighbors, so it is said, grew out of the intention to produce for family consumption and was qualitatively different from exchange production that passed through storekeepers into broader markets. But that distinction is hard to maintain. Exchanges with storekeepers scarcely differed from exchanges with neighbors. The storekeeper collected labor from farmers as well as grain and meat. Virtually all storekeepers, like artisans, owned land and worked farms on the side. In many instances, they had to have a farm to make the payment useful. In the cash-poor economies of rural New England, farmers often paid in labor, and a farm enabled a storekeeper to use that labor. The storekeeper was simply one more player in the intricate network of village exchange. Daniel Vickers, who has looked carefully at eighteenth-century farm journals, concludes that the "distinction between production for use and production for sale was sometimes recognizable and sometimes not, but it was never a matter of significance."[48] Farmers produced all they could for themselves and then in ingeniously complicated interactions with neighbors and fellow townsmen purchased, bartered, or worked for the rest. Production for exchange with the storekeeper and production for use with their neighbors were indistinguishable.

The presence of storekeepers in the village exchange networks meant that exchange and use production co-existed in most New England villages. In every hamlet with a store, farmers exchanged their products for imported goods. By 1771 in the more settled parts of Massachusetts—in the Connecticut Valley and in all towns east of Worcester—80 percent of the towns had stores; in the mountains west of the Connecticut River and in the hilly middle of the state, 42 percent of the towns did.[49] The stock of these little shops was modest—rum, cloth, salt, iron, buttons, hats—but they provided goods that every farmer wanted and needed. Payment could be made in goods and sometimes in labor, but ultimately the payments had to be transmuted into cash through sale at a market. Carole Shammas's research on colonial imports

---

of a trend continuing into the 19th century as the local market absorbed more and more of farm production. T. H. Breen argues that the sense of commercial exchange was strong enough to sustain an imagined community of buyers and sellers who acted politically in the nonimportation agreements in "Narrative of Commercial Life: Consumption, Ideology, and Community on the Eve of the American Revolution," *WMQ*, 3d Ser., 50 (1993), 471–501.

[48] Vickers, "Competency and Competition: Economic Culture in Early America," *WMQ*, 3d Ser., 47 (1990), 7. Vickers bases his judgment on the study of the Caleb Jackson farm in Rowley, Mass., in the 1790s. The type of farming they practiced was common, however, in New England during the whole of the previous century. He discusses the issue at length in *Farmers and Fishermen: Two Centuries of Work in Essex County, Massachusetts, 1630–1850* (Chapel Hill, 1994), 206–19.

[49] Bushman, "Shopping and Advertising in Colonial America," in Cary Carson, Ronald Hoffman, and Peter J. Albert, eds., *Of Consuming Interests: The Style of Life in the Eighteenth Century* (Charlottesville, 1994), 239–40.

suggests that a substantial amount of trade was going on, even in the inland towns. Colonists on the average may have spent as much as a quarter of their total incomes on imported goods. Every gallon of rum and yard of cloth in a country store represented production for exchange beyond subsistence.[50]

In other words, even in the heartland of communal agricultural villages—the inland New England town—production for use and production for exchange blended imperceptibly. William Cronon has argued that Europeans looked for commodities in the ecosystem from the beginning. Indians thought of the land as supplying food and fuel, meeting their human needs; Europeans looked for "resources," by which they meant things to sell. "The landscape of New England thus increasingly met not only the needs of its inhabitants for food and shelter but the demands of faraway markets for cattle, corn, fur, timber, and other goods whose 'values' became expressions of the colonists' socially determined 'needs.'"[51] In Cronon's reading, nothing else can account for the colonists' exploitation of the land, far in excess of the Indians' more frugal use. European colonists cut trees, fenced land, and ran cattle in volumes that were inexplicable to the Indians. Cronon acknowledges expansion of the market in the seventeenth and eighteenth centuries, but he argues nonetheless that "the abstract concept of the commodity informed colonial decision-making . . . from the start."[52]

How then are we to speak of the vast numbers of middling farmers who produced for their families and yet engaged with the market through storekeepers or drovers and in the nonstaple regions could not differentiate between use and exchange production? Is there a workable way to characterize eighteenth-century farms and relate them to what came after? As Allan Kulikoff notes in a useful essay on the "Transition to Capitalism in Rural America," the European debate "is conceptually clear, dealing with the transition *from* feudalism *to* capitalism," but that clarity fails in America. "Although all agree that feudalism did not reach these shores," Kulikoff writes, "the social order, economic system, or mode of production that preceded capitalism in America is rarely specified." The feudalism-capitalism polarity offers no middle term for American farms through most of our history. "It is evident," Kulikoff concludes, "that the American economy survived for several centuries in a transitional state—clearly not feudal and not yet fully capitalist."[53] But, can we be satisfied with a conceptual scheme that offers no useful description of economic conditions for several centuries? To call this

[50] Shammas, "How Self-Sufficient Was Early America?" *Journal of Interdisciplinary History*, 13 (1982–1983), 247–72.
[51] Cronon, *Changes in the Land: Indians, Colonists, and the Ecology of New England* (New York, 1983), 167.
[52] Ibid., 168.
[53] Kulikoff, "Transition to Capitalism," 133, 140. For an effort to label and describe this transitional farm see Kevin D. Kelly, "The Independent Mode of Production," *Review of Radical Political Economics*, 11 (Spring 1979), 38–48.

time "transitional" is excessively teleological, deriving significance from changes many decades in the future. The term implies that a farm was not what it was but the embryo of something it was going to be.

A realistic understanding of eighteenth-century farming must recognize the porous boundary between household production and market production and all the other complexities of the rural economy in early America. In what can be termed "composite farming," most farmers simultaneously produced for the farm family and for the market.[54] A number of interlocking yet distinguishable economies operated on composite farms. 1) The husbandman devoted a large part of his effort to raising the meat and grain his family needed for their subsistence. 2) The housewife had her own productive system of chickens, dairy products, vegetables and fruits, and sometimes textiles and other products. Housewifery aimed primarily at family sustenance, but like the husbandman's labors could be directed to the market or enter into neighborly exchanges when the opportunity arose.[55] 3) In the South, slaves also produced for their own use and exchange, in a distinguishable economy that was essential to their sustenance.[56] Growing out of these three productive systems were 4) the barter economy with neighbors and 5) the exchange economy for sales outside the community, through storekeepers, drovers, merchant millers, factors, or other agents of continental or international commerce or both.[57] These various economies, interacting with each other and the world beyond, made up the composite farm.[58]

The first priority of these productive units was the family's welfare. Recent scholarship rightly emphasizes household production and the preeminence of family values. The farm family provided for its own needs and for

[54] Other historians have arrived at something near this common sense conclusion. Among them are McCusker and Menard, *Economy of British America*, 297–301; Alan Taylor, *Liberty Men and Great Proprietors: The Revolutionary Settlement on the Maine Frontier, 1760–1820* (Chapel Hill, 1990), 77; and Vickers, "Competency and Competition."

[55] Laurel Thatcher Ulrich, "Martha Ballard and Her Girls: Women's Work in Eighteenth-Century Maine," in *Work and Labor in Early America*, ed. Innes, 70–105; "Housewife and Gadder: Themes of Self-Sufficiency and Community in Eighteenth-Century New England," in *"To Toil the Livelong Day": America's Women at Work, 1780–1980*, ed. Carol Groneman and Mary Beth Norton (Ithaca, 1987), 21–34; and "Wheels, Looms, and the Gender Division of Labor in Eighteenth-Century New England," *WMQ*, 3d Ser., 55 (1998), 3–38; Adrienne D. Hood, "The Material World of Cloth: Production and Use in Eighteenth-Century Rural Pennsylvania," ibid., 53 (1996), 43–66; Joan M. Jensen, *Loosening the Bonds: Mid-Atlantic Farm Women, 1750–1850* (New Haven, 1986).

[56] Philip Morgan, "Work and Culture: The Task System and the World of Lowcountry Blacks, 1700 to 1880," *WMQ*, 3d Ser., 39 (1982), 563–99.

[57] This formulation of the composite farm economy has been worked out by Claudia Bushman for her forthcoming study of John Walker, a 19th-century Virginia small planter.

[58] The multiple economies of the composite farm are close to Kulikoff's judgment that colonial farmers created "dynamic and modern social formations tied to the world market but not fully of it" in *The Agrarian Origins of American Capitalism* (Charlottesville, 1992), 27.

the descent of property down through the generations before taking chances on commercial undertakings. Household producers were cautious about any marketing venture that jeopardized the main enterprise of family support. The eighteenth century's own term for this attitude and the related agricultural practices was "competency."[59] Historians' recognition of the preeminence of family values came in reaction to scholarly work in the post-World War II period that depicts farmers as aggressive entrepreneurs, profit-seeking businessmen with their eyes on the main chance, grasping at every opportunity to make money whether through land speculation or adoption of the latest agricultural craze.[60] Henretta recognized the error in this caricature, which resulted from one of the historiographical enthusiasms of the 1950s. He saw that, because farming was so precarious and markets so remote, farmers had to meet their own needs first and only then send the surplus to market.[61]

Devotion to family sustenance did not imply aversion to market production. Although many farmers lacked the land, the animals, the labor, or the implements to produce in quantity for the market, some fruits of the farm family's labor had to enter exchanges with neighbors, storekeepers, and the tax collector. The family could not survive otherwise. Farm families developed market goods whenever they could. Farmers near to the Pennsylvania and Maryland iron furnaces cut and hauled wood. Connecticut and Long Island farmers grew flax when the Irish linen industry wanted to buy American-grown seed. Between 1736 and 1756, exports of flaxseed from American farms increased sevenfold, becoming Connecticut's second most important commercial activity. Farmers in Massachusetts hill towns hauled sand to the Connecticut Valley when housewives started to sand their floors. They produced broom handles when broom corn production boomed. In Maine, folks hunted pelts and logged. In South Carolina, Eliza Pinckney's ingenious experiments added indigo to the repertoire of commercial crops. Whenever market opportunities arose, people were quick to seize them.[62]

[59] The best explication is Vickers, "Competency and Competition." For the 19th-century South see Gavin Wright, *The Political Economy of the Cotton South: Households, Markets, and Wealth in the Nineteenth-Century* (New York, 1978), 62–74.
[60] Charles S. Grant called the settlers of 18th-century Kent, Connecticut "aggressive opportunists" and entitled one of his chapters "The Drive for Profits" in *Democracy in the Connecticut Frontier Town of Kent* (New York, 1961), 53–54, chap. 3. The same note is struck in Lemon, *Best Poor Man's Country*, xv–xvi.
[61] Henretta, "Families and Farms." For the literature on the debate that followed Henretta's article see Kulikoff, "Transition to Capitalism," 124.
[62] Bernard Bailyn, *Voyages to the West: A Passage in the Peopling of America on the Eve of Revolution* (Cambridge, Mass., 1986), 246–48; Gregory H. Nobles, "Shays's Neighbors: The Context of Rebellion in Pelham, Massachusetts," in *In Debt to Shays: the Bicentennial of an Agrarian Rebellion*, ed. Robert A. Gross (Charlottesville, 1993), 370 n. 20; J. Ritchie Garrison, *Landscape and Material Life in Franklin County, Massachusetts, 1770–1860* (Knoxville, 1991), 79–89; Thomas M. Truxes, *Irish-American Trade, 1660–1783* (New York, 1988), 48, 109–13; Taylor, *Liberty Men and Great*

Market production implied, not the abandonment of family values, but the reverse. Far from going reluctantly to market for fear of undermining their families, farmers went precisely to sustain and advance them.[63] Market production not only raised the level of family comfort but was essential for family perpetuation. In no other way could farmers accumulate land for their children except by selling farm goods. One family farm was not enough for the average American family. If every son was to receive a farm and every daughter an adequate dowry, the farm parents had to acquire property beyond the requirements of day-to-day living. Tabulations of farm property by age of owner show the acreage swelling through a farmer's forties and fifties and then shrinking in his sixties, as he distributed land to his offspring.[64] The accumulation of property for the rising generation required strenuous effort, even with all members working together. That many families only partially succeeded, or failed altogether, does not diminish the significance of land purchases in the overall family economy. The family had to maximize market production at certain points, not to relish the pleasures of profit or even to enjoy more comforts and conveniences, but to provide for their children.[65] Debt increased dramatically after 1720 as older systems of dispersing land at minimal cost gave way to auctions and sales by large speculators.[66] Farmers had to incur debt to buy land for the rising generation; if the fathers did not go in debt, the sons would.[67]

Proprietors, 77; David L. Coon, "Eliza Lucas Pinckney and the Reintroduction of Indigo Culture in South Carolina," *Journal of Southern History*, 42 (1976), 61–76; Coclanis, *Shadow of a Dream*, 56, 61–63. Vickers's Essex farmers mysteriously did not raise more cattle per capita in the decades before the American Revolution, even though the amount of cleared land nearly doubled and the county's port towns needed provisions. His data, however, did not permit him to measure increased production of specialized crops such as hay that Essex farmers produced after the Revolution in response to the same market stimulus; *Farmers and Fishermen*, 211–15, 293–99.

[63] For this family strategy on the frontier see Nobles, "Breaking into the Backcountry: New Approaches to the Early American Frontier, 1750–1800," *WMQ*, 3d Ser., 46 (1989), 655–56, and Taylor, *Liberty Men and Great Proprietors*, chap. 3.

[64] Jackson Turner Main, *Society and Economy in Colonial Connecticut* (Princeton, 1985), 117; Lee Soltow, *Patterns of Wealthholding in Wisconsin since 1850* (Madison, 1971), 42, 46. In Essex County, the dropoff came in a farmer's seventies; Vickers, *Farmers and Fishermen*, 227.

[65] Vickers says that the responsibility to bestow land on children "could be serious enough to provide the organizing principle for a life's work" in *Farmers and Fishermen*, 245. Jackson Turner Main, *Society and Economy in Colonial Connecticut*, 375, says the parents succeeded somehow in acquiring land for children in Connecticut. For the relationship among family values, debt, and market production in a later period see Sue Headlee, *The Political Economy of the Family Farm: The Agrarian Roots of American Capitalism* (Westport, Conn., 1991); for 18th- and 19th-century New England see Merchant, *Ecological Revolutions*, 185–90, and Clark, "Economics and Culture: Opening Up the Rural History of the Early American Northeast," *American Quarterly*, 43 (1991), 279–301.

[66] John Frederick Martin, *Profits in the Wilderness: Entrepreneurship and the Founding of New England Towns in the Seventeenth Century* (Chapel Hill, 1991), argues that profits were being made in land sales from the beginning of New England settlement.

[67] William Cooper went to great effort to find markets for his purchasers, knowing they could never meet the annual 7% interest payment, much less repayment of the principal, without a

Composite farming thus proceeded under the double mandate of providing first for daily living and then for cash to buy the next generation's land. That double purpose resulted in one part of the farm being devoted to the mixed crops necessary for the family's food, clothing, and fuel—a part that was much the same from Maine to Georgia—and another part for market production. In the subsistence portion, all farmers grew corn and maybe another grain crop. They all grazed cattle and let hogs roam in the woods. Woodlots provided fuel and timber for simple construction. More in the North than in the South, they harvested apples for cider. Closer to the house, the women kept kitchen gardens and probably chickens, though these creatures left few tracks in eighteenth-century records. This family provision component of the composite farm looked much the same on all colonial farms.[68]

The market component, the second element of composite farming, distinguished one farm from another going from North to South and even from farm to farm within a single region. In the North, the market component was frequently a "surplus" beyond family production: more pork or beef than the family could eat or cure, or one of the grains, or butter and cheese. Northern farmers also produced potash from burned trees, or barrel staves, or flaxseed, or maple sugar, or tanned hides, or coffins and chairs made in the off-season—all for the market and not an incidental surplus. Fifty percent of the estates in a sample of Essex County farm inventories taken before the Revolution contained looms, shoemaking kits, tan yards, mills, or smithing implements.[69] The returns may have been small and only a fraction of the farm's entire production, but in the family economy by-employments played a critical role.[70]

In the South, the market crops tobacco, indigo, and hemp met no family need and were not surpluses in the New England sense; rice, although consumed in the household, was grown in quantities far exceeding family requirements. But the obvious market orientation of southern planters should not obscure the powerful subsistence component of their agriculture. Vast amounts of labor on tobacco farms went to the production of food, the preparation of cloth, and the practice of crafts to keep the large household in operation.[71]

commercial crop; Taylor, *William Cooper's Town: Power and Persuasion on the Frontier of the Early American Republic* (New York, 1995), 102–10.

[68] This condition is well documented in Lewis Cecil Gray, *History of Agriculture in the Southern United States to 1860* (Washington, D. C., 1933), and Bidwell and Falconer, *History of Agriculture in the Northern United States*. See also Clemens, *Atlantic Economy and Colonial Maryland's Eastern Shore*, 82–83, 172–74, and David Klingaman, "The Significance of Grain in the Development of the Tobacco Colonies," *Journal of Economic History*, 29 (1969), 268–78.

[69] Vickers, *Farmers and Fishermen*, 314.

[70] For an illuminating explication of diversification in Pennsylvania see Mary M. Schweitzer, *Custom and Contract: Household, Government, and the Economy in Colonial Pennsylvania* (New York, 1987), 57–79.

[71] The rice planters may have partially emulated those in the sugar islands in concentrating on their staple and purchasing food from inland growers. They were the exception on the North

Farming for family subsistence may be construed, erroneously, as intrinsically hostile to the market.[72] We assume that commercial farming drove out subsistence production, that as one increased, the other decreased. In reality, commerce seems to have fostered composite farming. Commercial farmers are known to have increased their subsistence production at the same time they were heavily involved in world markets. One striking instance is the creation of mixed farms in the most commercial section of the colonies in the seventeenth century, the Chesapeake tobacco region. Until the end of the nineteenth century, no area in all of North America exceeded the seventeenth-century Chesapeake in its devotion to a single commercial crop. At first, planters raised their own food and cut their own wood but imported leather, cloth, pottery, and iron goods, while the entire labor force concentrated on tobacco production. Near the end of the century, when tobacco prices fell, planters began to divert resources to once-neglected aspects of subsistence.[73] Carville V. Earle's tabulation of implements from estate inventories measures the increasing incidence of spinning wheels, churns, and other tools for family production in the first half of the eighteenth century.[74] These highly commercial farms grew more and more self-sufficient during the eighteenth century.

The reasons for the change in strategy are easily understood. When the returns on a market crop fell, the natural reaction was to reduce costs. If expenditures could be reduced to a minimum, declining prices for the staple would be less painful. If prices fell too far, the planter might be driven to rely entirely on his own production for survival. Not the smallest but the largest planters—the ones most heavily involved in the market—followed this strategy. Their very dependence on market production made them more eager to buffer the ill-effects of falling prices. Only later did smaller farmers follow suit. By the early nineteenth century, agricultural writers advised all farmers to feed their families first before carrying goods to market. In 1841, Henry Colman claimed "it must be considered as an established principle in domestic economy that every farmer should look to his farm for all that his farm can furnish him." Part admonition, part description, Colman had good

---

American continent. See McCusker and Menard, *Economy of British America*, 183–84. For a summary of the literature on South Carolina self-sufficiency see Coclanis, *Shadow of a Dream*, 147, and Philip Morgan, "The Development of Slave Culture in Eighteenth-Century Plantation America" (Ph. D. diss., University College London, 1977), 20–47.

[72] For comments on the blend of use and exchange values and for the best analysis of 18th-century rural cultural values see Vickers, "Competency and Competition."

[73] Carr, "Diversification in the Colonial Chesapeake: Somerset County, Maryland, in Comparative Perspective," in *Colonial Chesapeake Society*, ed. Carr, Morgan, and Jean B. Russo (Chapel Hill, 1988), 342–88; Clemens, *Atlantic Economy and Colonial Maryland's Eastern Shore*, chap. 6; Kulikoff, *Tobacco and Slaves: The Development of Southern Cultures in the Chesapeake, 1680–1800* (Chapel Hill, 1986), 99–104.

[74] Earle, *The Evolution of a Tidewater Settlement System: All Hallow's Parish, Maryland, 1650–1783* (Chicago, 1975), 122–23.

reason to advocate domestic production. "Abandoning self-sufficiency was risky," Gavin Wright observes, "because households had to eat regardless of the outcome of the season's yields and prices."[75]

The composite farm did not disappear as commercial farming increased. Instead, it flourished even in later periods of intense commercialization. Mixed farming protected growers against the terrifying price oscillations that went with market production. Prices could vary 10–20 percent from year to year, and, in addition to market ups and downs, the farmer's own yields could deviate by at least as much. Lower yields might mean higher prices for all farmers, but an individual farmer—a victim of pests or bad weather—could suffer from a decline in both yield and price. How could he survive these wrenching reverses that were almost entirely out of his control? For simple survival, he required a subsistence foundation that would guarantee food and warmth whatever the fluctuations in the market.[76]

The utility of a subsistence base was as important in the nineteenth century as it was in the beginning. The first cotton farmers concentrated almost wholly on their immensely profitable staple until the 1840s, when declining prices brought them to their senses. After the suffering of that decade, they learned to produce the basics for themselves. Heavily commercial farms transmuted into composite farms, prompted by the market itself.[77] In the four decades before the Civil War, John Walker, a planter with fifteen slaves and more than 500 acres in the wheat belt of tidewater Virginia, not only grew corn and hogs to feed his large household but also planted cotton and raised sheep for wool. He hired a woman to spin and weave the fibers and another to cut clothing for his people. He even had a suit made for himself from this homespun cloth. As the years went by, he brought the spinning and weaving and eventually the tailoring on to his own farm, employing a resident weaver. He had his slaves tan leather and make their own shoes. His strategy was to minimize household consumption expenditures at the same time that he was selling wheat in Norfolk, Baltimore, and New York, investing in railroad stock, buying machinery, and renting out a skilled slave in Richmond. Every inch a commercial farmer, Walker worked as hard at producing for family consumption as for the market.[78]

[75] Colman, *Fourth Report: Agriculture of Massachusetts* (1841), quoted in Bidwell and Falconer, *History of Agriculture in the Northern United States*, 255; Wright, *Political Economy of the Cotton South*, 62–74, quotation on 63; Carr and Walsh, "Economic Diversification and Labor Organization in the Chesapeake, 1650–1820," in *Work and Labor in Early America*, ed. Innes, 181–82.

[76] For a discussion of the relationship of markets and self-sufficiency see Rothenberg, *From Market-Places to a Market Economy*, 33, 46–48.

[77] John Hebron Moore, *The Emergence of the Cotton Kingdom in the Old South West: Mississippi, 1770–1860* (Baton Rouge, 1988), 21–27; Alfred Glaze Smith, Jr., *Economic Readjustment of an Old Cotton State: South Carolina, 1820–1860* (Columbia, S. C., 1958), 53–111; Earle, *Geographical Inquiry and American Historical Problems* (Stanford, Calif., 1992), 258–99.

[78] Walker, "Diary," entries for Oct. 27, Nov. 15, Dec. 7, 1825, Jan. 15, June 13, 1827, May 8, 1829, Apr. 1, Nov. 9, 1833, June 6, Nov. 2, 29, 1834, Nov. 5, 1836, in Virginia Historical Society, Richmond, and

As late as the 1850s in the South Carolina tidewater, small yeomen farmers with up to 150 acres of improved land were still producing heavily for themselves and diverting only their surplus production of rice and cotton to the market, according to Stephanie McCurry. In one of the most heavily commercialized regions of the country, the supposed market revolution still had not eliminated household production among farmers with lots of land and slaves. If those farmers remained unaffected, we have reason to question the end of family production everywhere in the nation.[79]

Composite farming was a basic American practice from the seventeenth through the nineteenth centuries and even after then in a modified form. Many changes occurred in farm operations over those years, but the fundamental strategy of producing both for self and for sale persisted.[80] Composite farming weathered the storms of commercial expansion with remarkable durability. No matter how rapidly the urban population grew, American farmers supplied the cities' agricultural needs. No famines, grain shortages, or subsistence crises threatened the nation's well-being. Nor did food prices skyrocket as the urban population soared; at most, prices mildly inflated. American farms produced food to sustain unprecedented urban growth. At the same time, American farmers benefited from commercial sales when they could and lived off the land during bad years. Except on newly opened frontiers, the rural population rarely suffered from hunger. The composite farm was the "transitional" type that carried American farm families through two centuries of social change.

The idea of composite farming enables us to recognize the continuities in the rural economy from the eighteenth to the nineteenth centuries, but does it underestimate the amount of change? If the two-part typology of household production and market farming exaggerates the transformation wrought by a presumed market revolution, does the composite farm flatten out the differences? We know the farmers' world changed in the nineteenth century; how are we to describe what happened? In my opinion—and taste in historical explanation enters in here—the belief in an axial turning point should be abandoned. We have conceived of the market revolution as work-

Southern Historical Collection, University of North Carolina, Chapel Hill. For examples of other farmers see Philip N. Racine, ed., *Piedmont Farmer: The Journals of David Golightly Harris, 1855–1870* (Knoxville, 1990), and Vickers, *Farmers and Fishermen*, 207.

[79] McCurry, *Masters of Small Worlds: Yeoman Households, Gender Relations, and the Political Culture of the Antebellum South Carolina Low Country* (New York, 1995). On the self-sufficiency of individual southern farms in the 19th century see Gallman, "Self-Sufficiency in the Cotton Economy of the Antebellum South," *Agricultural History*, 44 (1970), 5–23, and Raymond C. Battalio and John Kagel, "The Structure of Antebellum Southern Agriculture: South Carolina, A Case Study," ibid., 25–37.

[80] Garrison, *Landscape and Material Life in Franklin County*, 45, 56, 60, 160, finds this true for Franklin County, Mass., in 1855 when commercial production was common. So does Vickers, *Farmers and Fishermen*, 295, for Essex County in the 1830s.

ing a great transformation when the economic organization of the world changed. Conceptually, the market revolution resembles a journey from the Mississippi to the Pacific. At the Continental Divide in the Rocky Mountains, all the rivers flow in another direction. Farmers may have raised the same crops after the market revolution but for wholly different reasons.

Alternatively, we can think of historical change as a journey from North to South rather than from East to West, from Canada to Mexico rather than from the Mississippi to the Pacific. Going south, the landscape, the climate, the topography, the flora and fauna keep changing until at the end we have reached a region at great variance from our starting point, yet never do we cross a boundary where the fundamental geography is reoriented all at once. Change is evolutionary rather than revolutionary.

In practice, the North-South version of historical change gives more weight to the many changes over time than does focusing exclusively on a single big transformation. The market revolution tends to overshadow seventeenth- and eighteenth-century developments that may have affected farmers as much as nineteenth-century events. If the crest of the Rockies is the goal, the foothills fade in importance. But think of the major passages in agriculture before the 1780s. In the seventeenth century, Chesapeake farmers searched for a variety of tobacco that satisfied English taste, worked out a routine for growing and curing it, increased the productivity of labor by a factor of eight or ten, and collaborated with English merchants to sell their product in Britain and on the Continent. Those innovations shaped Chesapeake agriculture for two centuries and led in turn to the introduction of captured Africans to work the plantations, making possible the growth of farming operations four and five times as large as any in the seventeenth century.[81] The purchase of slaves and the expansion into the interior was financed by the emergence of transatlantic and local credit markets that provided the capital to purchase land and develop it, all the while implicating farmers in the debt that shadowed their existence from then until now. Southern planters owed their English agents, and all over the North the number of debt cases per capita rose sharply after 1720, paving the way for the fights over paper money that continued right down to the Populist movement.[82] The increased consumption of amenities and luxuries, the first

---

[81] For changes in the Chesapeake agricultural system from the 17th to the 18th centuries see Menard, "Economic and Social Development of the South," in *Cambridge Economic History of the United States*, ed. Engerman and Gallman, 1:261–73.

[82] Bruce H. Mann, *Neighbors and Strangers: Law and Community in Early Connecticut* (Chapel Hill, 1987), 33; Bushman, *From Puritan to Yankee: Character and the Social Order in Connecticut, 1690–1765* (Cambridge, Mass., 1967), 297; Szatmary, *Shays' Rebellion*, 29; Main, *Society and Economy in Colonial Connecticut*, 212, 215; Herbert Alan Johnson, *The Law Merchant and Negotiable Instruments in Colonial New York, 1664–1730* (Chicago, 1963); Deborah A. Rosen, *Courts and Commerce: Gender, Law, and the Market Economy in Colonial New York* (Columbus, Ohio, 1997), 34–55, 82–85; Peter Charles Hoffer, "Honor and the Roots of American Litigiousness," *American Journal of Legal*

of the consumer revolutions, accounted for a large part of the increasing debt
to storekeepers, and much of the rest was probably the result of land purchases and the improvement of new farms.[83] As the seventeenth-century systems of headrights and town grants gave way to auctions conducted by
provincial governments and purchase from large speculators, land prices
rose in an active market. Between 1750 and 1770, land prices doubled and
tripled.[84] Throughout the eighteenth century, warfare required farmers to
supply the armies without the help of hands recruited to march into battle.
The French and Indian War, with its great influx of British funds, stimulated
the northern economy, and the American Revolution was even more effective because American farmers supplied the armies on both sides.[85]

Although no one denies the reality of these changes, they tend to fade in
the bright light of the later market revolution. We forget that European farmers in North America had to cope with far-reaching and disruptive change
almost from the moment they set foot on these shores.

The emergence of the composite farm can be added to the list of important changes taking place in the eighteenth century. Doubtless the combination of self-sufficiency and modest market production existed in England
and was found in all the early North American colonies. But not until the
drop in tobacco prices in the 1680s did Chesapeake planters adopt the balanced strategy of the composite farm in an effort to buffer market swings. In
the North, the sequence was reversed. The commercial side of the composite farm strategy was weaker in the seventeenth century. After 1700, the demand for New England farm products grew substantially when the French
sugar islands opened up and coastal markets improved.[86] The steep rise in
grain prices after 1750, caused by population growth in Europe, further improved the market for farmers in both North and South, making possible the
balanced blend of commercial and subsistence farming necessary for com-

---

History, 33 (1989), 295–319. On the growth of debt in the Chesapeake see Kulikoff, *Tobacco and
Slaves,* 128.
[83] Carr and Walsh, "Changing Life Styles and Consumer Behavior in the Colonial Chesapeake,"
in *Of Consuming Interests,* ed. Carson, Hoffman, and Albert, 59–166; Carson, "The Consumer
Revolution in Colonial British America," ibid., 483–697.
[84] Mitchell, *Commercialism and Frontier,* 52, 79–80, 83; Perkins, *The Economy of Colonial America,* 2d
ed. (New York, 1988), 57; Main, *Society and Economy in Colonial Connecticut,* 206–07; Kim, *Landlord and Tenant in Colonial New York,* 139–40; Kulikoff, *Tobacco and Slaves,* 132.
[85] McCusker and Menard, *Economy of British America,* 364; Richard Buel, Jr., *Dear Liberty: Connecticut's Mobilization for the Revolutionary War* (Middletown, Conn., 1980).
[86] Jackson Turner Main believes that, in the last quarter of the 17th century, Connecticut farmers
moved into the pattern that was to hold for the remainder of the colonial period; Main, *Society
and Economy in Colonial Connecticut,* 368. For increased agricultural specialization and the
growth of shipping tonnage in 18th-century Connecticut see Daniels, *The Fragmentation of New
England: Comparative Perspectives on Economic, Political, and Social Divisions in the Eighteenth Century* (New York, 1988), chap. 1.

petency. This combination of factors made the eighteenth century the time when the composite farm came into its own in all sections of Britain's North American colonies.[87]

These developments and changes should not be thought of as stages, marked by paradigmatic transitions or shifts in economic regimes. They are better regarded as strands woven into a rope, adding to and changing its character as they started and ended. The nineteenth century brought more than its share of new strands. The growth of large urban populations made a significant impact on farm management. Nearby urban markets, compared to the distant markets of Europe and the Caribbean, presented the surrounding farmers with commercial opportunities unknown earlier, especially in the North. Staples like flour, wheat, and barreled meat that were easily shipped across the Atlantic or into the Caribbean gave way to specialty crops such as the peaches that enriched the Delmarva Peninsula in the mid-nineteenth century, or New England hay for the mushrooming urban horse population in Boston and New York, or cheese, butter, and milk for all the cities and towns, or broom corn and brooms to meet new standards of housekeeping. Farmers changed their methods to make the most of the new opportunities, cultivating all of their land continuously rather than leaving the bulk of it in fallow as they had done traditionally in America. Peter D. McClelland finds the interest in new farm equipment surging between 1815 and 1830, just as urban population growth took off. By the middle of the century, northern farmers were investing large sums in expensive equipment to increase efficiency.[88] During the next half century, elaborate marketing mechanisms were worked out to grade, pack, and distribute farm produce.[89] Meanwhile, manufacturers and factories offered new forms of employment to wives, sons, and daughters. In the South, the entire labor system was overturned as slavery gave way to sharecropping. The decline in world cotton prices at the end of the century blighted the prospects of white and black farmers alike. Amid changes like these, the ambient conditions of farm life constantly modulated even while the basic strategy of composite farming continued. Hal S. Barron calls the period 1870–1930 "the second great transformation," and the rest of the twentieth century has brought still more change—the chemical revolution of pesticides and new fertilizers, the

---

[87] Greene makes a similar argument in *Pursuits of Happiness*, chaps. 3–4. For simultaneous growth in self-sufficiency and market involvement in New York see Rosen, *Courts and Commerce*, 19–29. For New England see Ulrich, "Wheels, Looms, and the Gender Division of Labor in Eighteenth-Century New England," 6, 16; For women's involvement in the market see Gloria Main, "Gender, Work, and Wages in Colonial New England," *WMQ*, 3d Ser., 51 (1994), 39–66.
[88] McClelland, *Sowing Modernity: America's First Agricultural Revolution* (Ithaca, 1997), x, 9. Farmers in the South did not adopt this practice. See Wright, *Political Economy of the Cotton South*, 53–54.
[89] Cronon, *Nature's Metropolis: Chicago and the Great West* (New York, 1991).

biological revolution of hybrids and new varieties, the New Deal's introduction of crop controls and price supports, and the rise of corporate farming.[90] Agricultural change has never ceased.[91]

Among the changes is the phasing out of the composite farm. The strategy of producing for both family and the market gradually eroded over many decades, worn down primarily by demands from the consumer culture.[92] Like so many other changes, subsistence production did not end suddenly, nor was it always in decline. The goods that farmers produced for themselves rose and fell, but generally the subsistence segment of farming diminished over time. In the first years of settlement, farmers already were purchasing metal goods, most ceramics, and finished fabrics. After a surge in home production of cloth in the eighteenth century, northern farm wives gave up spinning and weaving almost entirely in the second and third decades of the nineteenth century, and southern women followed a few decades later. As rural society came to feel embarrassed by its rusticity, farm families required finer clothing and furnishings, more genteel flourishes in houses and gardens, and costly educations for the young. The desire for comforts and conveniences enjoyed in town and the need for legal and medical services added to cash expenditures. Retailers like Montgomery Ward and Sears Roebuck targeted rural customers with their famous catalogues. Finally, in the twentieth century, farmers felt they had to buy an automobile, and rural electrification brought a train of expensive appliances in its wake.[93] As purchases increased, the family provision component of the composite farm failed in its designated purpose. When homegrown and homemade would not suffice, farmers had to maximize their cash returns in order to

[90] Barron, *Mixed Harvest: The Second Great Transformation in the Rural North, 1870–1930* (Chapel Hill, 1997).

[91] Thomas Dublin, "Women and Outwork in a Nineteenth-Century New England Town: Fitzwilliam, New Hampshire, 1830–1850," in Hahn and Jonathan Prude, eds., *The Countryside in the Age of Capitalist Transformation* (Chapel Hill, 1985), 51–70, and see also the other essays in this volume; Cronon, *Nature's Metropolis;* Bushman, "Opening the American Countryside," in *Transformation of Early American History,* ed. Henretta, Kammen, and Katz, 239–56; Danhof, *Change in Agriculture;* Clark, *Roots of Rural Capitalism;* Barron, *Mixed Harvest.*

[92] On the gradual shift to purchasing goods and giving up home production see Jeremy Atack and Fred Bateman, *To Their Own Soil: Agriculture in the Antebellum North* (Ames, Iowa, 1987), 204–08, 272–74.

[93] The coming of consumer culture to the rural North is analyzed in Barron, *Mixed Harvest,* chaps. 5–6. Barron reports an increase in the number of automobiles on U. S. farms from 85,000 in 1911 to 9,724,950 in 1930 when 58% of American farms had at least one car (p. 195). For other aspects of rural consumption see Bushman, "Opening the American Countryside," 239–56; David Paul Blanke, "Sowing the American Dream: Consumer Culture in the Rural Middle West, 1865–1900" (Ph. D. diss., Loyola University, 1996); Susan Strasser, *Satisfaction Guaranteed: The Making of the American Mass Market* (New York, 1989); Mary Neth, *Preserving the Family Farm: Women, Community, and the Foundations of Agribusiness in the Midwest, 1900–1940* (Baltimore, 1995); and Michael L. Berger, *The Devil Wagon in God's Country: The Automobile and Social Change in Rural America, 1893–1929* (Hamden, Conn., 1979).

purchase the desired goods. By World War II, the doom of the composite farm was sealed. Full-blown commercial farming took over.[94]

Composite farming thus is one current in a flow of continual change on the rural landscape. For the purpose of writing agricultural history, it is a conciliatory concept. It overcomes the tension between the hypothesized dominance of household production before the market revolution and the actual existence of extensive market production in the same period. In the multiple economies of the composite farm, subsistence and market production co-existed. The concept does not force a sharp division between farm types but allows for varying shades of market involvement. It accepts that farm families seized on market opportunities while pursuing family goals—and for the very purpose of achieving family stability. It helps us recognize the succession of changes that took place in the rural economy from the beginning of European settlement until now without exaggerating the importance of one short span. We see that great transformations stretch over decades and centuries rather than being crammed into a few years. Above all, the idea of composite farming permits us to understand how farm families coped with continual economic change and managed still to feed themselves and the developing nation.

[94] For a different explanation of the end of self-sufficiency in the South see Wright, *Political Economy of the Cotton South*, 164–76. Wright's figures show that small and medium-sized farms still planted only about half their land in cotton, with the rest presumably devoted to subsistence crops. The same proportions or even larger corn-to-cotton ratios obtained in upcountry Georgia; Hahn, *Roots of Southern Populism*, 150.

Taking the Trade: Abortion and Gender Relations in an Eighteenth-Century New England Village

Cornelia Hughes Dayton

INTRODUCTION

Cornelia Hughes Dayton demonstrates the approach of recent social historians who ingeniously reconstruct the details of everyday, local life in early America. In this essay, she uses the remarkably ample records of a little-known, mid-eighteenth-century Connecticut murder trial to recreate aspects of colonial human interactions previously obscure to historians, especially gender and sexual relations. The vivid story of the liaison between Amasa Sessions and Sarah Grosvenor is fascinating in its own right as an unusually detailed example of intimate personal relations. However, Dayton also insists upon its larger historical significance as an indication of the emergence of the sexual double standard in eighteenth-century New England, the gendering of family reactions to Sarah Grosvenor's death, the possibility of the social acceptability of abortion that did not result in death to the mother, and the ambivalent character of contemporary medical practice.

- *Dayton's essay raises an important methodological question about narrative local history: How far can one generalize on the basis of a unique example?*
- *Even if the Sessions-Grosvenor episode is characteristic of Connecticut, what are its implications for other regions in colonial America?*
- *What confidence can we place in legal depositions taken from family members several years after the incident in question?*

Cornelia Hughes Dayton, "Taking the Trade: Abortion and Gender Relations in an Eighteenth-Century New England Village," *William and Mary Quarterly*, 3d Ser. (1991), pp. 19–49. Reprinted by permission of the author.

*Above all, Dayton forces us to confront the significance of gender relations
in understanding historical change. Until recently, historians ignored gender as a historical factor. Were they wrong?*

In 1742 in the village of Pomfret, perched in the hills of northeastern Connecticut, nineteen-year-old Sarah Grosvenor and twenty-seven-year-old
Amasa Sessions became involved in a liaison that led to pregnancy, abortion,
and death. Both were from prominent yeoman families, and neither a marriage
between them nor an arrangement for the support of their illegitimate child
would have been an unusual event for mid-eighteenth-century New England.
Amasa Sessions chose a different course; in consultation with John Hallowell,
a self-proclaimed "practitioner of physick," he coerced his lover into taking an
abortifacient. Within two months, Sarah fell ill. Unbeknownst to all but Amasa,
Sarah, Sarah's sister Zerviah, and her cousin Hannah, Hallowell made an attempt to "Remove her Conseption" by a "manual opperation." Two days later
Sarah miscarried, and her two young relatives secretly buried the fetus in the
woods. Over the next month, Sarah struggled against a "Malignant fever" and
was attended by several physicians, but on September 14, 1742, she died.[1]

Most accounts of induced abortions among seventeenth- and eighteenth-
century whites in the Old and New Worlds consist of only a few lines in a private letter or court record book; these typically refer to the taking of savin or
pennyroyal—two common herbal abortifacients. While men and women in diverse cultures have known how to perform abortions by inserting an instrument into the uterus, actual descriptions of such operations are extremely rare
for any time period. Few accounts of abortions by instrument have
yet been uncovered for early modern England, and I know of no other
for colonial North America.[2] Thus the historical fragments recording events in

---

[1] The documentation is found in the record books and file papers of the Superior Court of Connecticut: *Rex* v. *John Hallowell et al.*, Superior Court Records, Book 9, 113, 173, 175, and Windham
County Superior Court Files, box 172, Connecticut State Library, Hartford. Hereafter all loose
court papers cited are from *Rex* v. *Hallowell,* Windham County Superior Court Files, box 172, unless otherwise indicated. For the quotations see Security bond for John Hallowell, undated;
Deposition of Ebenezer Grosvenor, probably Apr. 1746; Indictment against John Hallowell and
Amasa Sessions, Sept. 20, 1746; Deposition of Parker Morse.

[2] One such abortion was reported in *Gentleman's Magazine* (London), II, No. 20 (August 1732),
933–934; see Audrey Eccles, *Obstetrics and Gynaecology in Tudor and Stuart England* (London,
1982), 70. On the history of abortion practices see George Devereux, "A Typological Study of
Abortion in 350 Primitive, Ancient, and Pre-Industrial Societies," in Harold Rosen, ed., *Abortion
in America: Medical, Psychiatric, Legal, Anthropological, and Religious Considerations* (Boston, 1967),
97–152; Angus McLaren, *Reproductive Rituals: The Perception of Fertility in England from the Sixteenth Century to the Nineteenth Century* (London, 1984), chap. 4; Linda Gordon, *Woman's Body,
Woman's Right: A Social History of Birth Control in America* (New York, 1976), 26–41, 49–60; and
Edward Shorter, *A History of Women's Bodies* (New York, 1982), chap. 8.

For specific cases indicating use of herbal abortifacients in the North American colonies see
Julia Cherry Spruill, *Women's Life and Work in the Southern Colonies* (New York, 1972; orig.
pub. Chapel Hill, N. C., 1938), 325–326; Roger Thompson, *Sex in Middlesex: Popular Mores in a*

a small New England town in 1742 take on an unusual power to illustrate how an abortion was conducted, how it was talked about, and how it was punished.

We know about the Grosvenor-Sessions case because in 1745 two prominent Windham County magistrates opened an investigation into Sarah's death. Why there was a three-year gap between that event and legal proceedings, and why justices from outside Pomfret initiated the legal process, remain a mystery. In November 1745 the investigating magistrates offered their preliminary opinion that Hallowell, Amasa Sessions, Zerviah Grosvenor, and Hannah Grosvenor were guilty of Sarah's murder, the last three as accessories. From the outset, Connecticut legal officials concentrated not on the act of abortion per se, but on the fact that an abortion attempt had led to a young woman's death.[3]

The case went next to Joseph Fowler, king's attorney for Windham County. He dropped charges against the two Grosvenor women, probably because he needed them as key witnesses and because they had played coverup roles rather than originating the scheme. A year and a half passed as Fowler's first attempts to get convictions against Hallowell and Sessions failed either before grand juries or before the Superior Court on technical grounds. Finally, in March 1747, Fowler presented Hallowell and Sessions separately for the "highhanded Misdemeanour" of attempting to destroy both Sarah Grosvenor's health and "the fruit of her womb."[4] A grand jury endorsed the bill against Hallowell but rejected a similarly worded presentment against Sessions. At Hallowell's trial before the Superior Court in Windham, the jury brought in a guilty verdict and the chief judge sentenced the physician to twenty-nine lashes and two hours of public humiliation standing at the town gallows. Before the sentence could be executed, Hallowell managed

Massachusetts County, 1649–1699 (Amherst, Mass., 1986), 11, 24–26, 107–108, 182–183; and Lyle Koehler, *A Search for Power: The "Weaker Sex" in Seventeenth-Century New England* (Urbana, Ill., 1980), 204–205. I have found two references to the use of an abortifacient in colonial Connecticut court files. Doubtless, other accounts of abortion attempts for the colonial period will be discovered.

[3] Abortion before quickening (defined in the early modern period as the moment when the mother first felt the fetus move) was not viewed by the English or colonial courts as criminal. No statute law on abortion existed in either Britain or the colonies. To my knowledge, no New England court before 1745 had attempted to prosecute a physician for carrying out an abortion.

On the history of the legal treatment of abortion in Europe and the United States see McLaren, *Reproductive Rituals*, chap. 5, Gordon, *Woman's Body, Woman's Right*, chap. 3; James C. Mohr, *Abortion in America: The Origins and Evolution of National Policy, 1800–1900* (New York, 1978); Michael Grossberg, *Governing the Hearth: Law and the Family in Nineteenth-Century America* (Chapel Hill, N. C., 1985), chap. 5; and Carroll Smith-Rosenberg, "The Abortion Movement and the AMA, 1850–1880," in *Disorderly Conduct: Visions of Gender in Victorian America* (New York, 1985), 217–244.

In 1683, a Newport, Rhode Island, woman was whipped for fornication and "Indeavouringe the distruction of the Child in her womb" (Supreme Court Records, Bk. A, 66, Supreme Court Judicial Records Center, Pawtucket; I thank Catherine Osborne DeCesare for alerting me to this case).

[4] Indictment against John Hallowell, Mar. 1746/47.

to break jail. He fled to Rhode Island; as far as records indicate, he never returned to Connecticut. Thus, in the end, both Amasa Sessions and John Hallowell escaped legal punishment for their actions, whereas Sarah Grosvenor paid for her sexual transgression with her life.

Nearly two years of hearings and trials before the Superior Court produced a file of ten depositions and twenty-four other legal documents. This cache of papers is extraordinarily rich, not alone for its unusual chronicle of an abortion attempt, but for its illumination of the fault lines in Pomfret dividing parents from grown children, men from women, and mid-eighteenth-century colonial culture from its seventeenth-century counterpart.

The depositions reveal that in 1742 the elders of Pomfret, men and women alike, failed to act as vigilant monitors of Sarah Grosvenor's courtship and illness. Instead, young, married householders—kin of Sarah and Amasa—pledged themselves in a conspiracy of silence to allow the abortion plot to unfold undetected. The one person who had the opportunity to play middleman between the generations was Hallowell. A man in his forties, dogged by a shady past and yet adept at acquiring respectable connections, Hallowell provides an intriguing and rare portrait of a socially ambitious, rural medical practitioner. By siding with the young people of Pomfret and keeping their secret, Hallowell betrayed his peers and elders and thereby opened himself to severe censure and expulsion from the community.

Beyond depicting generational conflict, the Grosvenor-Sessions case dramatically highlights key changes in gender relations that reverberated through New England society in the eighteenth century. One of these changes involved the emergence of a marked sexual double standard. In the mid-seventeenth century, a young man like Amasa Sessions would have been pressured by parents, friends, or the courts to marry his lover. Had he resisted, he would most likely have been whipped or fined for the crime of fornication. By the late seventeenth century, New England judges gave up on enjoining sexually active couples to marry. In the 1740s, amid shifting standards of sexual behavior and growing concern over the evidentiary impossibility of establishing paternity, prosecutions of young men for premarital sex ceased. Thus fornication was decriminalized for men, but not for women. Many of Sarah Grosvenor's female peers continued to be prosecuted and fined for bearing illegitimate children. Through private arrangements, and occasionally through civil lawsuits, their male partners were sometimes cajoled or coerced into contributing to the child's upkeep.[5]

[5] The story of the decriminalization of fornication for men in colonial New England is told most succinctly by Carol F. Karlsen, *The Devil in the Shape of a Woman: Witchcraft in Colonial New England* (New York, 1987), 194–196, 198–202, 255. Laurel Thatcher Ulrich describes a late eighteenth-century Massachusetts jurisdiction in *A Midwife's Tale: The Life of Martha Ballard, Based on Her Diary, 1785–1812* (New York, 1990), 147–160. For New Haven County see Cornelia Hughes Dayton, "Women Before the Bar: Gender, Law, and Society in Connecticut, 1710–1790" (Ph.D. diss., Princeton University, 1986), 151–186. See also Zephaniah Swift, *A System of Laws of the State of Connecticut*, 2 vols. (Windham, Conn., 1795–1796), I, 209. A partial survey of fornication prosecutions in the

What is most striking about the Grosvenor-Sessions case is that an entire community apparently forgave Sessions for the extreme measures he took to avoid accountability for his bastard child. Although he initiated the actions that led to his lover's death, all charges against him were dropped. Moreover, the tragedy did not spur Sessions to leave town; instead, he spent the rest of his life in Pomfret as a respected citizen. Even more dramatically than excusing young men from the crime of fornication, the treatment of Amasa Sessions confirmed that the sexually irresponsible activities of men in their youth would not be held against them as they reached for repute and prosperity in their prime.[6]

The documents allow us to listen in on the quite different responses of young men and women to the drama unfolding in Pomfret. Sarah Grosvenor's female kin and friends, as we shall see, became preoccupied with their guilt and with the inevitability of God's vengeance. Her male kin, on the other hand, reacted cautiously and legalistically, ferreting out information in order to assess how best to protect the Grosvenor family name. The contrast reminds us yet again of the complex and gendered ways in which we must rethink conventional interpretations of secularization in colonial New England.

Finally, the Grosvenor case raises more questions than it answers about New Englanders' access to and attitudes toward abortion. If Sarah had not died after miscarriage, it is doubtful that any word of Sessions's providing her with an abortifacient or Hallowell's operation would have survived into the twentieth century. Because it nearly went unrecorded and because it reveals that many Pomfret residents were familiar with the idea of abortion, the case supports historians' assumptions that abortion attempts were far from rare in colonial America.[7] We can also infer from the case that the most dangerous abortions before 1800 may have been those instigated by men and performed by surgeons with instruments.[8] But both abortion's frequency

---

Windham County Court indicates that here, too, the local JPs and annually appointed grand jurymen stopped prosecuting men after the 1730s. The records for 1726–1731 show that 15 men were prosecuted to enjoin child support and 21 single women were charged with fornication and bastardy, while only 2 women brought civil suits for child maintenance. Nearly a decade ahead, in the 3-year period 1740–1742, *no* men were prosecuted while 23 single women were charged with fornication and 10 women initiated civil paternity suits.

[6] Such also was the message of many rape trials in the mid- and late 18th century. See Dayton, "Women Before the Bar," 112–143; trial of Frederick Calvert, Baron Baltimore, as reported in the *Connecticut Journal*, New Haven, June 10, 1768, and in other colonial newspapers and separate pamphlets; and the Bedlow-Sawyer trial discussed by Christine Stansell in *City of Women: Sex and Class in New York, 1789–1860* (New York, 1986), 23–30.

[7] For a recent summary of the literature see Brief for American Historians as *Amicus Curiae* Supporting the Appellees 5–7, *William L. Webster et al.* v. *Reproductive Health Services et al.*, 109 S.Ct. 3040 (1989).

[8] In none of the cases cited in n. 2 above did the woman ingesting an abortifacient die from it. If abortions directed by male physicians in the colonial period were more hazardous than those

and the lineaments of its social context remain obscure. Did cases in which older women helped younger women to abort unwanted pregnancies far outnumber cases such as this one in which men initiated the process? Under what circumstances did family members and neighbors help married and unmarried women to hide abortion attempts?

Perhaps the most intriguing question centers on why women and men in early America acted *covertly* to effect abortions when abortion before quickening was legal. The Grosvenor case highlights the answer that applies to most known incidents from the period: abortion was understood as blameworthy because it was an extreme action designed to hide a prior sin, sex outside of marriage.[9] Reading the depositions, it is nearly impossible to disentangle the players' attitudes toward abortion itself from their expressions of censure or anxiety over failed courtship, illegitimacy, and the dangers posed for a young woman by a secret abortion. Strikingly absent from these eighteenth-century documents, however, is either outrage over the destruction of a fetus or denunciations of those who would arrest "nature's proper course." Those absences are a telling measure of how the discourse about abortion would change dramatically in later centuries.

THE NARRATIVE

Before delving into the response of the Pomfret community to Sarah Grosvenor's abortion and death, we need to know just who participated in the conspiracy to cover up her pregnancy and how they managed it. The following paragraphs, based on the depositions, offer a reconstruction of the events of 1742. A few caveats are in order. First, precise dating of crucial incidents is impossible, since deponents did not remember events in terms of days of the week (except for the Sabbath) but rather used phrases like "something in August." Second, the testimony concentrated almost exclusively on events in the two months preceding Sarah's death on September 14. Thus, we know very little about Sarah and Amasa's courtship before July 1742.[10] Third, while the depositions often indicate the motivations and feelings of the principals, these will be discussed in subsequent sections of this article, where the characters' attitudes can be set in the context of their social

---

managed by midwives and lay women, then, in an inversion of the mid-20th-century situation, women from wealthy families with access to, and preferences for, male doctors were those most in jeopardy. For a general comparison of male and female medical practitioners see Ulrich, *A Midwife's Tale*, 48–66, esp. 54.

[9] Married women may have hidden their abortion attempts because the activity was associated with lewd or dissident women.

[10] Conception must have occurred sometime in the months of January through March, most probably in late January. Sarah had been pregnant nearly 7 months at her delivery in early August, according to one version offered later by her sister.

backgrounds, families, and community. This section essentially lays out a medical file for Sarah Grosvenor, a file that unfolds in four parts: the taking of the abortifacient, Hallowell's operation, the miscarriage, and Sarah's final illness.

The case reveals more about the use of an abortifacient than most colonial court records in which abortion attempts are mentioned. Here we learn not only the form in which Sarah received the dose but also the special word that Pomfret residents applied to it. What the documents do not disclose are either its ingredients[11] or the number of times Sarah ingested it.

The chronicle opens in late July 1742 when Zerviah Grosvenor, aged twenty-one, finally prevailed upon her younger sister to admit that she was pregnant. In tears, Sarah explained that she had not told Zerviah sooner because "she had been taking [the] trade to remove it."[12] "Trade" was used in this period to signify stuff or goods, often in the deprecatory sense of rubbish and trash. The *Oxford English Dictionary* confirms that in some parts of England and New England the word was used to refer to medicine. In Pomfret trade meant a particular type of medicine, an abortifacient, thus a substance that might be regarded as "bad" medicine, as rubbish, unsafe and associated with destruction. What is notable is that Sarah and Zerviah, and neighboring young people who also used the word, had no need to explain to one another the meaning of "taking the trade." Perhaps only a few New Englanders knew how to prepare an abortifacient or knew of books that would give them recipes, but many more, especially young women who lived with the fear of becoming pregnant before marriage, were familiar with at least the *idea* of taking an abortifacient.

Sarah probably began taking the trade in mid-May when she was already three-and-a-half-months pregnant.[13] It was brought to her in the form of a powder by Amasa.[14] Sarah understood clearly that her lover had obtained the concoction "from docter hollowel," who conveyed "directions" for her doses through Amasa. Zerviah deposed later that Sarah had been "loath to Take" the drug and "Thot it an Evil," probably because at three and a half months she anticipated quickening, the time from which she knew the

---

[11] Hallowell's trade may have been an imported medicine or a powder he mixed himself, consisting chiefly of oil of savin, which could be extracted from juniper bushes found throughout New England. For a thorough discussion of savin and other commonly used abortifacients see Shorter, *History of Women's Bodies*, 184–188.

[12] Deposition of Zerviah Grosvenor. In a second deposition Zerviah used the word "Medicines" instead of "trade"; Testimony of Zerviah Grosvenor in Multiple Deposition of Hannah Grosvenor et al.: hereafter cited as Testimony of Zerviah Grosvenor. Five times out of 8, deponents referred to "the trade," instead of simply "trade" or "some trade."

[13] So her sister Zerviah later estimated. Testimony of Rebecca Sharp in Multiple Deposition of Hannah Grosvenor et al.

[14] After she was let into the plot, Zerviah more than once watched Amasa take "a paper or powder out of his pocket" and insist that Sarah "take Some of it." Deposition of Zerviah Grosvenor.

law counted abortion an "unlawful measure."[15] At the outset, Sarah argued in vain with Amasa against his proposed "Method." Later, during June and July, she sometimes "neglected" to take the doses he left for her, but, with mounting urgency, Amasa and the doctor pressed her to comply. "It was necessary," Amasa explained in late July, that she take "more, or [else] they were afraid. She would be greatly hurt by what was already done." To calm her worries, he assured her that "there was no life [left] in the Child" and that the potion "would not hurt her."[16] Apparently, the men hoped that a few more doses would provoke a miscarriage, thereby expelling the dead fetus and restoring Sarah's body to its natural balance of humors.

Presumably, Hallowell decided to operate in early August because Sarah's pregnancy was increasingly visible, and he guessed that she was not going to miscarry. An operation in which the fetus would be removed or punctured was now the only certain way to terminate the pregnancy secretly.[17] To avoid the scrutiny of Sarah's parents, Hallowell resorted to a plan he had used once before in arranging a private examination of Sarah. Early one afternoon he arrived at the house of John Grosvenor and begged for a room as "he was weary and wanted Rest."[18] John, Sarah's thirty-one-year-old first cousin, lived with his wife, Hannah, and their young children in a homestead only a short walk down the hill but out of sight of Sarah's father's house. While John and Hannah were busy, the physician sent one of the little children to fetch Sarah.[19]

The narrative of Sarah's fateful meeting with Hallowell that August afternoon is best told in the words of one of the deponents. Abigail Nightingale had married and moved to Pomfret two years earlier, and by 1742 she

[15] Deposition of John Grosvenor; Deposition of Zerviah Grosvenor; Testimony of Zerviah Grosvenor in Multiple Deposition of Hannah Grosvenor et al. "Unlawful measure" was Zerviah's phrase for Amasa's "Method." Concerned for Sarah's well-being, she pleaded with Hallowell not to give her sister "any thing that should harm her"; Deposition of Zerviah Grosvenor. At the same time, Sarah was thinking about the quickening issue. She confided to a friend that when Amasa first insisted she take the trade, "she [had] feared it was too late"; Deposition of Abigail Nightingale.

[16] Deposition of Zerviah Grosvenor; Testimony of Zerviah Grosvenor.

[17] Hallowell claimed that he proceeded with the abortion in order to save Sarah's life. If the powder had had little effect and he knew it, then this claim was a deliberate deception. On the other hand, he may have sincerely believed that the potion had poisoned the fetus and that infection of the uterine cavity had followed fetal death. Since healthy babies were thought at that time to help with their own deliveries, Hallowell may also have anticipated a complicated delivery if Sarah were allowed to go to full term—a delivery that might kill her. On the operation and variable potency of herbal abortifacients see Gordon, *Woman's Body, Woman's Right*, 37, 40; Shorter, *History of Women's Bodies*, 177–188; and Mohr, *Abortion in America*, 8–9.

[18] Testimony of Hannah Grosvenor in Multiple Deposition of Hannah Grosvenor et al. Hannah may have fabricated the account of Hallowell's deception to cover her own knowledge of and collusion in Hallowell and Session's scheme to conceal Sarah's pregnancy.

[19] Deposition of Zerviah Grosvenor. Hallowell attended Sarah overnight at John Grosvenor's house once in July; Multiple Deposition of Sarah and Silence Sessions.

had become Sarah's close friend.[20] Several weeks after the operation, Sarah attempted to relieve her own "Distress of mind" by confiding the details of her shocking experience to Abigail. Unconnected to the Grosvenor or Sessions families by kinship, and without any other apparent stake in the legal uses of her testimony, Abigail can probably be trusted as a fairly accurate paraphraser of Sarah's words.[21] If so, we have here an unparalleled eyewitness account of an eighteenth-century abortion attempt.

This is how Abigail recollected Sarah's deathbed story:

> On [Sarah's] going down [to her cousin John's], [Hallowell] said he wanted to Speake with her alone; and then they two went into a Room together; and then sd. Hallowell told her it was necessary that something more should be done or else she would Certainly die; to which she replyed that she was afraid they had done too much already, and then he told her that there was one thing more that could easily be done, and she asking him what it was; he said he could easily deliver her. but she said she was afraid there was life in the Child, then he asked her how long she had felt it; and she replyed about a fortnight; then he said that was impossible or could not be or ever would; for that the trade she had taken had or would prevent it: and that the alteration she felt Was owing to what she had taken. And he farther told her that he verily thought that the Child grew to her body to the Bigness of his hand, or else it would have Come away before that time, and that it would never Come away, but Certainly Kill her, unless other Means were used.[22] On which she yielded to his making an Attempt to take it away; charging him that if he could perceive that there was life in it he would not proceed on any Account. And then the Doctor openning his portmantua took an Instrument[23] out of it and Laid it on the Bed, and she asking him what it was for, he replyed that it was to make way; and that then he tryed to remove the Child for Some time in vain putting her to the Utmost Distress, and that at Last she observed he trembled and immediately perceived a Strange alteration in her body and thought a bone of the Child was broken; on which

[20] On Abigail's husband, Samuel, and his family see Clifford K. Shipton, *Biographical Sketches of Those Who Attended Harvard College in the Classes 1731–1735* (Boston, 1956), IX, 425–428; Pomfret Vital Records, Barbour Collection, Conn. State Lib. All vital and land records cited hereafter are found in the Barbour Collection.

[21] Hearsay evidence was still accepted in many 18th-century Anglo-American courts; see J. M. Beattie, *Crime and the Courts in England, 1660–1800* (Princeton, N. J., 1986), 362–376. Sarah's reported words may have carried special weight because in early New England persons on their deathbeds were thought to speak the truth.

[22] Twentieth-century obstetrical studies show an average of 6 weeks between fetal death and spontaneous abortion; J. Robert Willson and Elsie Reid Carrington, eds., *Obstetrics and Gynecology*, 8th ed. (St. Louis, Mo., 1987), 212. Hallowell evidently grasped the link between the 2 events but felt he could not wait 6 weeks, either out of concern for Sarah's health or for fear their plot would be discovered.

[23] A 1746 indictment offered the only other point at which the "instrument" was mentioned in the documents. It claimed that Hallowell "with his own hands as [well as] with a certain Instrument of Iron [did] violently Lacerate and . . . wound the body of Sarah"; Indictment against John Hallowell, endorsed "Ignoramus," Sept. 4, 1746.

she desired him (as she said) to Call in some body, for that she feared she was a dying, and instantly swooned away.[24]

With Sarah's faint, Abigail's account broke off, but within minutes others, who would testify later, stepped into the room. Hallowell reacted to Sarah's swoon by unfastening the door and calling in Hannah, the young mistress of the house, and Zerviah, who had followed her sister there. Cold water and "a bottle of drops" were brought to keep Sarah from fainting again, while Hallowell explained to the "much Surprized" women that "he had been making an Attempt" to deliver Sarah. Despite their protests, he then "used a further force upon her" but did not succeed in "Tak[ing] the Child . . . away."[25] Some days later Hallowell told a Pomfret man that in this effort "to distroy hir conception" he had "either knipt or Squeisd the head of the Conception."[26] At the time of the attempt, Hallowell explained to the women that he "had done so much to her, as would Cause the Birth of the Child in a Little time." Just before sunset, he packed up his portmanteau and went to a nearby tavern, where Amasa was waiting "to hear [the outcome of] the event."[27] Meanwhile, Sarah, weak-kneed and in pain, leaned on the arm of her sister as the young women managed to make their way home in the twilight.

After his attempted "force," Hallowell fades from the scene, while Zerviah and Hannah Grosvenor become the key figures. About two days after enduring the operation, Sarah began to experience contractions. Zerviah ran to get Hannah, telling her "she Tho't . . . Sarah would be quickly delivered." They returned to find Sarah, who was alone "in her Father's Chamber," just delivered and rising from the chamber pot. In the pot was "an Untimely birth"—a "Child [that] did not Appear to have any Life In it." To Hannah, it "Seemed by The Scent . . . That it had been hurt and was decaying," while Zerviah later remembered it as "a perfect Child," even "a pritty child."[28] Determined to keep the event "as private as they Could," the two women helped Sarah back to bed, and then "wr[ap]ed . . . up" the fetus, carried it to the woods on the edge of the farmstead, and there "Buried it in the Bushes."[29]

---

[24] Deposition of Abigail Nightingale.

[25] Joint Testimony of Hannah and Zerviah Grosvenor in Multiple Deposition of Hannah Grosvenor et al.; Deposition of Hannah Grosvenor; Deposition of Zerviah Grosvenor.

[26] Deposition of Ebenezer Grosvenor.

[27] Deposition of John Grosvenor; Deposition of Hannah Grosvenor; Deposition of Ebenezer Grosvenor.

[28] Testimony of Hannah Grosvenor, Alexander Sessions, and Rebecca Sharp in Multiple Deposition of Hannah Grosvenor et al. In a second statement Hannah said that "the head Seemed to be brused"; Deposition of Hannah Grosvenor.

[29] Testimony of Rebecca Sharp, Hannah Grosvenor, and Alexander Sessions in Multiple Deposition of Hannah Grosvenor et al.; Testimony of Silence Sessions in Multiple Deposition of Sarah and Silence Sessions.

On learning that Sarah had finally miscarried and that the event had evidently been kept hidden from Sarah's parents, Amasa and Hallowell may have congratulated themselves on the success of their operation. However, about ten days after the miscarriage, Sarah grew feverish and weak. Her parents consulted two college-educated physicians who hailed from outside the Pomfret area. Their visits did little good, nor were Sarah's symptoms—fever, delirium, convulsions—relieved by a visit from Hallowell, whom Amasa "fetcht" to Sarah's bedside.[30] In the end, Hallowell, who had decided to move from nearby Killingly to more distant Providence, washed his hands of the case. A few days before Sarah died, her cousin John "went after" Hallowell, whether to bring him back or to express his rage, we do not know. Hallowell predicted "that She woul[d] not live."[31]

Silence seems to have settled on the Grosvenor house and its neighborhood after Sarah's death on September 14. It was two and a half years later that rumors about a murderous abortion spread through and beyond Pomfret village, prompting legal investigation. The silence, the gap between event and prosecution, the passivity of Sarah's parents—all lend mystery to the narrative. But despite its ellipses, the Grosvenor case provides us with an unusual set of details about one young couple's extreme response to the common problem of failed courtship and illegitimacy. To gain insight into both the mysteries and the extremities of the Grosvenor-Sessions case, we need to look more closely at Pomfret, at the two families centrally involved, and at clues to the motivations of the principal participants. Our abortion tale, it turns out, holds beneath its surface a complex trail of evidence about generational conflict and troubled relations between men and women.

THE POMFRET PLAYERS

In 1742 the town of Pomfret had been settled for just over forty years. Within its central neighborhood and in homesteads scattered over rugged, wooded hillsides lived probably no more than 270 men, women, and children.[32] Dur-

---

[30] Joint Testimony of Hannah and Zerviah Grosvenor in Multiple Deposition of Hannah Grosvenor et al.; Deposition of Parker Morse of Woodstock, Apr. 1746. Although Pomfret had had its own resident physician (Dr. Thomas Mather) since 1738, Sarah's family called in young Dr. Morse of Woodstock, who visited twice (he later admitted he was not much help), and a Dr. Coker of Providence (who I assume was Theodore Coker). On Mather see Ellen D. Larned, *History of Windham County, Connecticut* (Worcester, Mass., 1874), I, 354. On Morse: Shipton, *Biographical Sketches*, IX, 424. On Coker: ibid., VIII, 19, and Eric H. Christianson, "The Medical Practitioners of Massachusetts, 1630–1800: Patterns of Change and Continuity," in *Medicine in Colonial Massachusetts, 1620–1820*, Publications of the Colonial Society of Massachusetts, LVII (Boston, 1980), 123.

[31] Deposition of John Grosvenor.

[32] I am using a list of 40 heads of household in the Mashamoquet neighborhood of Pomfret in 1731, presuming 5 persons to a household, and assuming a 2.5% annual population growth. See

ing the founding decades, the fathers of Sarah and Amasa ranked among the ten leading householders; Leicester Grosvenor and Nathaniel Sessions were chosen often to fill important local offices.

Grosvenor, the older of the two by seven years, had inherited standing and a choice farmstead from his father, one of the original six purchasers of the Pomfret territory.³³ When the town was incorporated in 1714, he was elected a militia officer and one of the first selectmen. He was returned to the latter post nineteen times and eventually rose to the highest elective position—that of captain—in the local trainband. Concurrently, he was appointed many times throughout the 1710s and 1720s to ad hoc town committees, often alongside Nathaniel Sessions. But unlike Sessions, Grosvenor went on to serve at the colony level. Pomfret freemen chose him to represent them at ten General Assembly sessions between 1726 and 1744. Finally, in the 1730s, when he was in his late fifties, the legislature appointed him a justice of the peace for Windham County. Thus, until his retirement in 1748 at age seventy-four, his house would have served as the venue for petty trials, hearings, and recordings of documents. After retiring from public office, Grosvenor lived another eleven years, leaving behind in 1759 an estate worth over £600.³⁴

Nathaniel Sessions managed a sizable farm and ran one of Pomfret's taverns at the family homestead. Town meetings were sometimes held there. Sessions was chosen constable in 1714 and rose from ensign to lieutenant in the militia—always a step behind Leicester Grosvenor. He could take pride in one exceptional distinction redounding to the family honor: in 1737 his son Darius became only the second Pomfret resident to graduate from Yale College, and before Sessions died at ninety-one he saw Darius elected assistant and then deputy governor of Rhode Island.³⁵

Larned, *History of Windham County*, I, 342, and Bruce C. Daniels, *The Connecticut Town: Growth and Development, 1635–1790* (Middletown, Conn., 1979), 44–51. Pomfret village had no central green or cluster of shops and small house lots around its meetinghouse. No maps survive for early Pomfret apart from a 1719 survey of proprietors' tracts. See Larned, *History of Windham County* (1976 ed.), I, foldout at 185.

³³ Leicester's father, John Grosvenor, a tanner, had emigrated from England about 1670 and settled in Roxbury, Mass., whence the first proprietors of Pomfret hailed. John died in 1691 before he could resettle on his Connecticut tract, but his widow, Esther, moved her family to their initial allotment of 502 acres in Pomfret in 1701. There she lived until her death at 87 in 1738, known in the community as a woman of energy and "vigorous habits," "skillful in tending the sick," and habitual in "walking every Sunday to the distant meeting-house." See Daniel Kent, *The English Home and Ancestry of John Grosvenor of Roxbury, Mass.* (Boston, 1918), 10–13, and Larned, *History of Windham County*, I, 353–355.

³⁴ Kent, *The English Home of John Grosvenor*, 10–13; Larned, *History of Windham County*, I, 200–202, 204, 208–209, 269, 354, 343–344; Charles J. Hoadly and J. Hammond Trumbull, eds., *The Public Records of the Colony of Connecticut, 1636–1776*, 15 vols. (Hartford, Conn., 1850–1890), V–IX; Inventory of Leicester Grosvenor, Oct. 29, 1759, Pomfret District Probate Court Records, II, 260.

³⁵ Larned, *History of Windham County*, I, 201, 204, 206, 208–209, 344; Ellen D. Larned, *Historic Gleanings in Windham County, Connecticut* (Providence, R. I., 1899), 141, 148–149; Francis G. Sessions,

The records are silent as to whether Sessions and his family resented the Grosvenors, who must have been perceived in town as more prominent, or whether the two families—who sat in adjoining private pews in the meetinghouse—enjoyed a close relationship that went sour for some reason *before* the affair between Sarah and Amasa. Instead, the signs (such as the cooperative public work) of the two fathers, the visits back and forth between the Grosvenor and Sessions girls) point to a long-standing friendship and dense web of interchanges between the families. Indeed, courtship and marriage between a Sessions son and a Grosvenor daughter would hardly have been surprising.

What went wrong in the affair between Sarah and Amasa is not clear. Sarah's sisters and cousins knew that "Amasy" "made Sute to" Sarah, and they gave no indication of disapproving. The few who guessed at Sarah's condition in the summer of 1742 were not so much surprised that she was pregnant as that the couple "did not marry."[36] It was evidently routine in this New England village, as in others, for courting couples to post banns for their nuptials after the woman discovered that she was pregnant.

Amasa offered different answers among his Pomfret peers to explain his failure to marry his lover. When Zerviah Grosvenor told Amasa that he and Sarah "had better Marry," he responded, "That would not do," for "he was afraid of his Parents . . . [who would] always make their lives [at home] uncomfortable."[37] Later, Abigail Nightingale heard rumors that Amasa was resorting to the standard excuse of men wishing to avoid a shotgun marriage—denying that the child was his.[38] Hallowell, with whom Amasa may have been honest, claimed "the Reason that they did not marry" was "that Sessions Did not Love her well a nough for [he] saith he did not believe it was his son and if he Could Cause her to gitt Red of it he would not Go near her again."[39] Showing yet another face to a Grosvenor kinsman after Sarah's death, Amasa repented his actions and extravagantly claimed he would "give All he had" to "bring Sarah . . . To life again . . . and have her as his wife."[40]

---

comp., *Materials for a History of the Sessions Family in America; The Descendants of Alexander Sessions of Andover, Mass., 1669* (Albany, N. Y., 1890), 34–35, hereafter cited as Sessions, *Sessions Family.* Nathaniel's inheritance from his father Alexander of Andover (d. 1687) was a mere £2.14.5.

[36] Deposition of Hannah Grosvenor; Deposition of Ebenezer Grosvenor; Deposition of Anna Wheeler, Nov. 5, 1745; Deposition of Zerviah Grosvenor; Testimony of Zerviah Grosvenor.

[37] Deposition of Zerviah Grosvenor; Testimony of Zerviah Grosvenor.

[38] Deposition of Abigail Nightingale. Contradicting Amasa's attempt to disavow paternity were both his investment in Hallowell's efforts to get rid of the fetus and his own ready admission of paternity privately to Zerviah and Sarah.

[39] Deposition of Ebenezer Grosvenor. Hallowell revealed this opinion in an Aug. 1742 conversation with Sarah's 28-year-old cousin Ebenezer at Ebenezer's house in Pomfret. In a study of 17th-century Massachusetts court records Roger Thompson finds evidence that when pregnancy failed to pressure a couple into marriage, it was often because love "had cooled"; Thompson, *Sex in Middlesex,* 69.

[40] Testimony of John Shaw in Multiple Deposition of Hannah Grosvenor et al.

The unusual feature of Amasa's behavior was not his unwillingness to marry Sarah, but his determination to terminate her pregnancy before it showed. Increasing numbers of young men in eighteenth-century New England weathered the temporary obloquy of abandoning a pregnant lover in order to prolong their bachelorhood or marry someone else.[41] What drove Amasa, and an ostensibly reluctant Sarah, to resort to abortion? Was it fear of their fathers? Nathaniel Sessions had chosen Amasa as the son who would remain on the family farm and care for his parents in their old age. An ill-timed marriage could have disrupted these plans and threatened Amasa's inheritance.[42] For his part, Leicester Grosvenor may have made it clear to his daughter that he would be greatly displeased at her marrying before she reached a certain age or until her older sister wed. Rigid piety, an authoritarian nature, an intense concern with being seen as a good household governor—any of these traits in Leicester Grosvenor or Nathaniel Sessions could have colored Amasa's decisions.

Perhaps it was not family relations that proved the catalyst but Amasa's acquaintance with a medical man who boasted about a powder more effective than the herbal remedies that were part of women's lore. Hallowell himself had fathered an illegitimate child fifteen years earlier, and he may have encouraged a rakish attitude in Amasa, beguiling the younger man with the promise of dissociating sex from its possible consequences. Or the explanation may have been that classic one: another woman. Two years after Sarah's death, Amasa married Hannah Miller of Rehoboth, Massachusetts. Perhaps in early 1742 he was already making trips to the town just east of Providence to see his future wife.[43]

What should we make of Sarah's role in the scheme? It is possible that she no longer loved Amasa and was as eager as he to forestall external pressures toward a quick marriage. However, Zerviah swore that on one occasion before the operation Amasa reluctantly agreed to post banns for their nuptials and that Sarah did not object.[44] *If* Sarah was a willing and active

---

[41] For one such case involving two propertied families see Kathryn Kish Sklar, "Culture Versus Economics: A Case of Fornication in Northampton in the 1740's," *The University of Michigan Papers in Women's Studies* (1978), 35–56. For the incidence of illegitimacy and premarital sex in families of respectable yeomen and town leaders see Dayton, "Women Before the Bar," 151–186, and Ulrich, *A Midwife's Tale*, 156.

[42] Two years later, in Feb. 1744 (9 months before Amasa married), the senior Sessions deeded to his son the north part of his own farm for a payment of £310. Amasa, in exchange for caring for his parents in their old age, came into the whole farm when his father died in 1771. Pomfret Land Records, III, 120; Estate Papers of Nathaniel Sessions, 1771, Pomfret Probate District. On the delay between marriage and "going to housekeeping" see Ulrich, *A Midwife's Tale*, 138–144.

[43] Sessions, *Sessions Family,* 60; Pomfret Vit. Rec., I, 29.

[44] The banns never appeared on the meetinghouse door. Sarah may have believed in this overdue betrothal. She assured her anxious sister Anna that "thay designed to mary as soone as thay Could and that Sessions was as much Concarned as she." Deposition of Zerviah Grosvenor; Testimony of Zerviah Grosvenor; Deposition of Anna Wheeler.

participant in the abortion plot all along, then by 1745 her female kin and friends had fabricated and rehearsed a careful and seamless story to preserve the memory of the dead girl untarnished.

In the portrait drawn by her friends, Sarah reacted to her pregnancy and to Amasa's plan first by arguing and finally by doing her utmost to protect her lover. She may have wished to marry Amasa, yet she did not insist on it or bring in older family members to negotiate with him and his parents. Abigail Nightingale insisted that Sarah accepted Amasa's recalcitrance and only pleaded with him that they not "go on to add sin to sin." Privately, she urged Amasa that there was an alternative to taking the trade—a way that would enable him to keep his role hidden and prevent the couple from committing a "Last transgression [that] would be worse then the first." Sarah told him that "she was willing to take the sin and shame to her self, and to be obliged never to tell whose Child it was, and that she did not doubt but that if she humbled her self on her Knees to her Father he would take her and her Child home." Her lover, afraid that his identity would become known, vetoed her proposal.[45]

According to the Pomfret women's reconstruction, abortion was not a freely chosen and defiant act for Sarah. Against her own desires, she reluctantly consented in taking the trade only because Amasa "So very earnestly perswaided her." In fact, she had claimed to her friends that she was coerced; he "would take no denyal."[46] Sarah's confidantes presented her as being aware of her options, shrinking from abortion as an unnatural and immoral deed, and yet finally choosing the strategy consistent with her lover's vision of what would best protect their futures. Thus, if Amasa's hubris was extreme, so too was Sarah's internalization of those strains of thought in her culture that taught women to make themselves pleasing and obedient to men.

While we cannot be sure that the deponents' picture of Sarah's initial recoil and reluctant submission to the abortion plot was entirely accurate, it is clear that once she was caught up in the plan she extracted a pledge of silence from all her confidantes. Near her death, before telling Abigail about the operation, she "insist[ed] on . . . [her friend's] never discovering the Matter" to anyone.[47] Clearly, she had earlier bound Zerviah and Hannah on their honor not to tell their elders. Reluctant when faced with the abortionist's powder, Sarah became a leading co-conspirator when alone with her female friends.

One of the most remarkable aspects of the Grosvenor-Sessions case is Sarah and Amasa's success in keeping their parents in the dark, at least until

---

[45] Deposition of Abigail Nightingale. I have argued elsewhere that this is what most young New England women in the 18th century did when faced with illegitimacy. Their parents did not throw them out of the house but instead paid the cost of the mother and child's upkeep until she managed to marry. Dayton, "Women Before the Bar," 163–180.

[46] Deposition of John Grosvenor; Deposition of Abigail Nightingale. Amasa Sessions, "in his prime," was described as "a very strong man," so it is possible that his physical presence played a role in intimidating Sarah. See Sessions, *Sessions Family,* 31.

[47] Deposition of Abigail Nightingale.

her final illness. If by July Sarah's sisters grew suspicious that Sarah was "with child," what explains the failure of her parents to observe her pregnancy and to intervene and uncover the abortion scheme? Were they negligent, preoccupied with other matters, or willfully blind?[48] Most mysterious is the role of forty-eight-year-old Rebecca Grosvenor, Grosvenor's second wife and Sarah's stepmother since 1729. Rebecca is mentioned only once in the depositions,[49] and she was not summoned as a witness in the 1745–1747 investigations into Sarah's death. Even if some extraordinary circumstance—an invalid condition or an implacable hatred between Sarah and her stepmother—explains Rebecca's abdication of her role as guardian, Sarah had two widowed aunts living in or near her household. These matrons, experienced in childbirth matters and concerned for the family reputation, were just the sort of older women who traditionally watched and advised young women entering courtship.[50]

In terms of who knew what, the events of summer 1742 in Pomfret apparently unfolded in two stages. The first stretched from Sarah's discovery of her pregnancy by early May to some point in late August after her miscarriage. In this period a determined, collective effort by Sarah and Amasa and their friends kept their elders in the dark.[51] When Sarah fell seriously ill from the aftereffects of the abortion attempt and miscarriage, rumors of the young people's secret activities reached Leicester Grosvenor's neighbors and even one of the doctors he had called in.[52] It is difficult to escape the conclusion that by Sarah's death in mid-September her father and stepmother had learned of the steps that had precipitated her mortal condition and kept silent for reasons of their own.

Except for Hallowell, the circle of intimates entrusted by Amasa and Sarah with their scheme consisted of young adults ranging in age from nineteen to thirty-three.[53] Born between 1710 and 1725, these young people had

[48] Like his wife, Leicester was not summoned to testify in any of the proceedings against Hallowell and Sessions.

[49] Zerviah testified that, a day or two after Sarah fell sick for the first time in July, the family heard "that Doctor Hallowell was at one of our Neighbors [and] my Mother desired me to go and Call him." Deposition of Zerviah Grosvenor.

Sarah's mother had died in May 1724, when Sarah was 11 months old. Perhaps Sarah and Zerviah had a closer relationship with their grandmother Esther (see n. 33 above) than with their stepmother. Esther lived in their household until her death in 1738, when Zerviah was 17 and Sarah 15.

[50] Laurel Thatcher Ulrich, *Good Wives: Image and Reality in the Lives of Women in Northern New England, 1650–1750* (New York, 1982), chap. 5, esp. 98.

[51] In Larned's account, the oral legend insisted that Hallowell's "transaction" (meaning the abortion attempt) and the miscarriage were "utterly unsuspected by any . . . member of the household" other than Zerviah. *History of Windham County,* I, 363.

[52] Deposition of Parker Morse.

[53] Within days of Sarah's miscarriage, the initial conspirators disclosed their actions to others: Hallowell talked to 2 of Sarah's older male cousins, John (age 31) and Ebenezer (age 28), while Zerviah confessed to Amasa's brother Alexander (age 28) and his wife Silence. Anna Wheeler

grown up just as the town attracted enough settlers to support a church, militia, and local market. They were second-generation Pomfret residents who shared the generational identity that came with sitting side by side through long worship services, attending school, playing, and working together at children's tasks. By 1740, these sisters, brothers, cousins, courting couples, and neighbors, in their visits from house to house—sometimes in their own households, sometimes at their parents'—had managed to create a world of talk and socializing that was largely exempt from parental supervision.[54] In Pomfret in 1742 it was this group of young people in their twenties and early thirties, *not* the cluster of Grosvenor matrons over forty-five, who monitored Sarah's courtship, attempted to get Amasa to marry his lover, privately investigated the activities and motives of Amasa and Hallowell, and, belatedly, spoke out publicly to help Connecticut juries decide who should be blamed for Sarah's death.

That Leicester Grosvenor made no public move to punish those around him and that he avoided giving testimony when legal proceedings commenced are intriguing clues to social changes underway in New England villages in the mid-eighteenth century. Local leaders like Grosvenor, along with the respectable yeomen whom he represented in public office, were increasingly withdrawing delicate family problems from the purview of their communities. Slander, illegitimacy, and feuds among neighbors came infrequently to local courts by mid-century, indicating male householders' growing preference for handling such matters privately.[55] Wealthy and ambitious families adopted this ethic of privacy at the same time that they became caught up in elaborating their material worlds by adding rooms and acquiring luxury goods. The "good feather bed" with all of its furniture that Grosvenor bequeathed to his one unmarried daughter was but one of many marks of status by which the Grosvenors differentiated themselves from

---

(age 33), Sarah's older sister, knew of Sarah's pregnancy before the abortion operation and thus must have guessed or secured information about the miscarriage. As we have seen, Sarah would soon confess privately to Abigail Nightingale, recently married and in her 20s. Others in the peer group may also have known. Court papers list 7 witnesses summoned to the trials for whom no written testimony survives. At least 4 of those witnesses were in their 20s or early 30s.
[54] The famous "bad books" incident that disrupted Jonathan Edwards's career in 1744 involved a similar group of unsupervised young adults ages 21 to 29. See Patricia J. Tracy, *Jonathan Edwards, Pastor: Religion and Society in Eighteenth-Century Northampton* (New York, 1980), 160–164. The best general investigation of youth culture in early New England is Thompson's *Sex in Middlesex*, 71–96. Thompson discusses the general ineffectiveness of parental supervision of courtship (pp. 52–53, 58–59, 69–70). Ellen Rothman concludes that in New England in the mid- to late 18th century "parents made little or no effort to oversee their children's courting behavior"; Rothman, *Hands and Hearts: A History of Courtship in America* (New York, 1984), 25.
[55] Helena M. Wall, *Fierce Communion: Family and Community in Early America* (Cambridge, Mass., 1990); Bruce H. Mann, *Neighbors and Strangers: Law and Community in Early Connecticut* (Chapel Hill, N. C., 1987).

their Pomfret neighbors.[56] But all the fine accoutrements in the world would not excuse Justice Grosvenor from his obligation to govern his household effectively. Mortified no doubt at his inability to monitor the young people in his extended family, he responded, ironically, by extending their conspiracy of silence. The best way for him to shield the family name from scandal and protect his political reputation in the county and colony was to keep the story of Sarah's abortion out of the courts.

THE DOCTOR

John Hallowell's status as an outsider in Pomfret and his dangerous, secret alliance with the town's young adults may have shaped his destiny as the one conspirator sentenced to suffer at the whipping post. Although the physician had been involved in shady dealings before 1742, he had managed to win the trust of many patients and a respectable social standing. Tracking down his history in northeastern Connecticut tells us something of the uncertainty surrounding personal and professional identity before the advent of police records and medical licensing boards. It also gives us an all-too-rare glimpse into the fashion in which an eighteenth-century country doctor tried to make his way in the world.

Hallowell's earliest brushes with the law came in the 1720s. In 1725 he purchased land in Killingly, a Connecticut town just north of Pomfret and bordering both Massachusetts and Rhode Island. Newly married, he was probably in his twenties at the time. Seven months before his wife gave birth to their first child, a sixteen-year-old Killingly woman charged Hallowell with fathering her illegitimate child. Using the alias Nicholas Hallaway, he fled to southeastern Connecticut, where he lived as a "transient" for three months. He was arrested and settled the case by admitting to paternity and agreeing to contribute to the child's maintenance for four years.[57]

---

[56] Leicester Grosvenor's Will, Jan. 23, 1754, Pomfret Dist. Prob. Ct. Rec., I, 146. For recent studies linking consumption patterns and class stratification see Richard L. Bushman, "American High-Style and Vernacular Cultures," in Jack P. Greene and J. R. Pole, eds., *Colonial British America: Essays in the New History of the Early Modern Era* (Baltimore, 1984), 345–383; T. H. Breen, "'Baubles of Britain': The American and Consumer Revolutions of the Eighteenth Century," *Past and Present*, 119 (May 1988), 73–104; and Kevin M. Sweeney, "Furniture and the Domestic Environment in Wethersfield, Connecticut, 1639–1800," in Robert Blair St. George, ed., *Material Life in America, 1600–1860* (Boston, 1988), 261–290.

[57] Killingly Land Records, II, 139; *Rex* v. *John Hallowell and Mehitable Morris,* Dec. 1726, Windham County Court Records, Book I, 43, and Windham County Court Files, box 363. Hallowell paid the £28 he owed Mehitable, but there is no evidence that he took any other role in bringing up his illegitimate namesake. Just before his death, Samuel Morris, the maternal grandfather of John Hallowell, Jr., out of "parentiall Love and Effections," deeded the young man a 300-acre farm "for his advancement and Settlement in the World"; Killingly Land Rec., IV, 261.

Hallowell resumed his life in Killingly. Two years later, now referred to as "Dr.," he was arrested again; this time the charge was counterfeiting. Hallowell and several confederates were hauled before the governor and council for questioning and then put on trial before the Superior Court. Although many Killingly witnesses testified to the team's suspect activities in a woodland shelter, the charges against Hallowell were dropped when a key informer failed to appear in court.[58]

Hallowell thus escaped conviction on a serious felony charge, but he had been tainted by stories linking him to the criminal subculture of transient, disorderly, greedy, and manually skilled men who typically made up gangs of counterfeiters in eighteenth-century New England.[59] After 1727 Hallowell may have given up dabbling in money-making schemes and turned to earning his livelihood chiefly from his medical practice. Like two-thirds of the male medical practitioners in colonial New England, he probably did not have college or apprentice training, but his skill, or charm, was not therefore necessarily less than that of any one of his peers who might have inherited a library of books and a fund of knowledge from a physician father. All colonial practitioners, as Richard D. Brown reminds us, mixed learned practices with home or folk remedies, and no doctor had access to safe reliable pharmacological preparations or antiseptic surgical procedures.[60]

[58] Hallowell was clearly the mastermind of the scheme, and there is little doubt that he lied to the authorities when questioned. According to one witness, Hallowell had exclaimed that "If he knew who" had informed anonymously against him, "he would be the death of him tho he ware hanged for it the next minit"; Letter of Joseph Leavens, Sept. 1727, Windham Sup. Ct. Files, box 170. The case is found in ibid.; Sup. Ct. Rec., bk. 5, 297–298; and *Public Records Conn. Colony*, VII, 118. One associate Hallowell recruited was Ephraim Shevie, who had been banished from Connecticut for counterfeiting four years earlier. See Kenneth Scott, *Counterfeiting in Colonial America* (New York, 1957), 41–45.

[59] The authority on counterfeiting in the colonies is Kenneth Scott. His 1957 general book on the subject emphasizes several themes: the gangs at the heart of all counterfeiting schemes, the ease with which counterfeiters moved from colony to colony (especially between Connecticut and Rhode Island), "the widespread co-operation between" gangs, "the readiness of [men of all ranks] . . . to enter such schemes," the frequent use of aliases, the irresistible nature of the activity once entered into, and "the extreme difficulty of securing the conviction of a counterfeiter"; *Counterfeiting in Colonial America*, esp. 123, 35, 10, 36. See also Scott's more focused studies, *Counterfeiting in Colonial Connecticut* (New York, 1957), and *Counterfeiting in Colonial Rhode Island* (Providence, R. I., 1960).

For an illuminating social profile of thieves and burglars who often operated in small gangs see Daniel A. Cohen, "A Fellowship of Thieves: Property Criminals in Eighteenth-Century Massachusetts," *Journal of Social History*, XXII (1988), 65–92.

[60] Richard D. Brown, "The Healing Arts in Colonial and Revolutionary Massachusetts: The Context for Scientific Medicine," in Col. Soc. Mass., *Medicine in Colonial Massachusetts*, esp. 40–42. For detailed analysis of the backgrounds and training of one large sample of New England practitioners see Christianson, "Medical Practitioners of Massachusetts," in ibid., 49–67, and Eric H. Christianson, "Medicine in New England," in Ronald L. Numbers, ed., *Medicine in the New World: New Spain, New France, and New England* (Knoxville, Tenn., 1987), 101–153. That the majority of colonial physicians made "free use of the title 'doctor'" (ibid., 118) and simply "taught

In the years immediately following the counterfeiting charge, Hallowell appears to have made several deliberate moves to portray himself as a sober neighbor and reliable physician. At about the time of his second marriage, in 1729, he became a more frequent attendant at the Killingly meetinghouse, where he renewed his covenant and presented his first two children for baptism.[61] He also threw himself into the land and credit markets of northeastern Connecticut, establishing himself as a physician who was also an enterprising yeoman and a frequent litigant.[62]

These activities had dual implications. On the one hand, they suggest that Hallowell epitomized the eighteenth-century Yankee citizen—a man as comfortable in the courtroom and countinghouse as at a patient's bedside; a man of restless energy, not content to limit his scope to his fields and village; a practical, ambitious man with a shrewd eye for a good deal.[63] On the other hand, Hallowell's losses to Boston creditors, his constant efforts to collect debts, and his farflung practice raise questions about the nature of his activities and medical practice. He evidently had clients not just in towns across northeastern Connecticut but also in neighboring Massachusetts and Rhode Island. Perhaps rural practitioners normally traveled extensively, spending many nights away from their wives and children.[64] It is also possible, however, either that Hallowell was forced to travel because established doctors from leading families had monopolized the local practice or that he chose to recruit patients in Providence and other towns as a cover for illicit activities.[65] Despite his land speculations and his frequent resort to litigation, Hallowell was losing money. In the sixteen years before 1742, his creditors

themselves medicine and set up as doctors" is reiterated in Whitfield J. Bell, Jr., "A Portrait of the Colonial Physician," *Bulletin of the History of Medicine*, XLIV (1970), 503–504.
[61] Hallowell's sons, baptized between 1730 and 1740, were named Theophilus, Bazaleel, Calvin, and Luther. Killingly Vital Records, I, 3, 24; Putnam First Congregational Church Records, I, 5–7, 14–15. Hallowell may have been one of the "'horse-shed' Christians" whom David D. Hall describes as concerned to have their children baptized but more interested in the men's talk outside the meetinghouse than in the minister's exposition of the Word. Hall, *Worlds of Wonder, Days of Judgment: Popular Religious Belief in Early New England* (New York, 1989), 15–16.
[62] Between 1725 and 1742, Hallowell was a party to 20 land sales and purchases in Killingly; he also assumed 2 mortgages. During the same period he was involved in county court litigation an average of 3 times a year, more often as plaintiff than defendant, for a total of 46 suits.
[63] For example, in early 1735 Hallowell made a £170 profit from the sale of a 60-acre tract with mill and mansion house that he had purchased 2 months earlier. Killingly Land Rec., IV, 26, 36.
[64] Evidence of Hallowell's widespread clientele comes from his 1727–1746 suits for debt, from his traveling patterns as revealed in the depositions of the abortion case, and from a petition written in 1747 on his behalf by 14 male citizens of Providence. They claimed that "Numbers" in Rhode Island "as well as in the Neighbouring Colonies" had "happily experienc'd" Hallowell's medical care. Petition of Resolved Waterman et al., Oct. 1747, Connecticut Archives, Crimes and Misdemeanors, Series I, IV, 109.
[65] For a related hypothesis about the mobility of self-taught doctors in contrast to physicians from established medical families see Christianson, "Medical Practitioners of Massachusetts," in Col. Soc. Mass., *Medicine in Colonial Massachusetts*, 61.

secured judgments against him for a total of £1,060, while he was able to collect only £700 in debts.[66] The disjunction between his ambition and actual material gains may have led to Hallowell in middle age to renew his illicit money-making schemes. By supplying young men with potent abortifacients and dabbling in schemes to counterfeit New England's paper money, he betrayed the very gentlemen whose respect, credit, and society he sought.

What is most intriguing about Hallowell was his ability to ingratiate himself throughout his life with elite men whose reputations were unblemished by scandal. Despite the rumors that must have circulated about his early sexual dalliance, counterfeiting activities, suspect medical remedies, heavy debts, and shady business transactions,[67] leading ministers, merchants, and magistrates welcomed him into their houses. In Pomfret such acceptance took its most dramatic form in September 1739 when Hallowell was admitted along with thirty-five other original covenanters to the first private library association in eastern Connecticut. Gathering in the house of Pomfret's respected, conservative minister, Ebenezer Williams, the members pledged sums for the purchase of "useful and profitable English books." In the company of the region's scholars, clergy, and "gentlemen," along with a few yeomen— all "warm friends of learning and literature"—Hallowell marked himself off from the more modest subscribers by joining with thirteen prominent and wealthy signers to pledge a sum exceeding £15.[68]

Lacking college degree and family pedigree, Hallowell traded on his profession and his charm to gain acceptability with the elite. In August 1742 he shrewdly removed himself from the Pomfret scene, just before Sarah Grosvenor's death. In that month he moved, without his wife and children, to Providence, where he had many connections. Within five years, Hallowell had so insinuated himself with town leaders such as Stephen Hopkins that fourteen of them petitioned for mitigation of what they saw as the misguided sentence imposed on him in the Grosvenor case.[69]

Hallowell's capacity for landing on his feet, despite persistent brushes with scandal, debt, and the law, suggests that we should look at the fluidity

---

[66] These figures apply to suits in the Windham County Court record books, 1727–1742. Hallowell may, of course, have prosecuted debtors in other jurisdictions.

[67] In Dec. 1749, Samuel Hunt, "Gentleman" of Worcester County, revoked the power of attorney he had extended to Hallowell for a Killingly land sale. Hunt claimed that the physician had "behaved greatly to my hindrance [and] Contrary to the trust and Confidence I Reposed in him." Killingly Land Rec., V, 151.

[68] Larned, *History of Windham County,* I, 356–359.

[69] The petition's signers included Hopkins, merchant, assembly speaker, and Superior Court Justice, soon to become governor; Daniel Jencks, judge, assembly delegate, and prominent Baptist; Obadiah Brown, merchant and shopkeeper; and George Taylor, justice of the peace, town schoolmaster, and Anglican warden. Some of the signers stated that they had made a special trip to Windham to be "Earwitnesses" at Hallowell's trial. The petition is cited in n. 64 above.

of New England's eighteenth-century elite in new ways.[70] What bound sons of old New England families, learned men, and upwardly mobile merchants and professionals in an expanded elite may partly have been a reshaped, largely unspoken set of values shared by men. We know that the archetype for white New England women as sexual beings was changing from carnal Eve to resisting Pamela and that the calculus of accountability for seduction was shifting blame solely to women.[71] But the simultaneous metamorphosis in cultural images and values defining manhood in the early and mid-eighteenth century has not been studied. The scattered evidence we do have suggests that, increasingly, for men in the more secular and anglicized culture of New England, the lines between legitimate and illegitimate sexuality, between sanctioned and shady business dealings, and between speaking the truth and protecting family honor blurred. Hallowell's acceptability to men like minister Ebenezer Williams and merchant Stephen Hopkins hints at how changing sexual and moral standards shaped the economic and social alliances made by New England's male leadership in the 1700s.[72]

WOMEN'S TALK AND MEN'S TALK

If age played a major role in determining who knew the truth about Sarah Grosvenor's illness, gender affected how the conspiring young adults responded to Sarah's impending death and how they weighed the issue of blame. Our last glimpse into the social world of eighteenth-century Pomfret looks at the different ways in which women and men reconstructed their roles in the events of 1742.

An inward gaze, a strong consciousness of sin and guilt, a desire to avoid conflict and achieve reconciliation, a need to confess—these are the impulses expressed in women's intimate talk in the weeks before Sarah died. The central female characters in the plot, Sarah and Zerviah Grosvenor, lived for six weeks with the daily fear that their parents or aunts might detect Sarah's

[70] For discussions of the elite see Jackson Turner Main, *Society and Economy in Colonial Connecticut* (Princeton, N. J., 1985), esp. 317–366, and Joy B. and Robert R. Gilsdorf, "Elites and Electorates: Some Plain Truths for Historians of Colonial America," in David D. Hall, John M. Murrin, and Thad W. Tate, eds., *Saints and Revolutionaries: Essays on Early American History* (New York, 1984), 207–244.

[71] Ulrich, *Good Wives*, 103–105, 113–117.

[72] Compare the 17th-century case of Stephen Batchelor (Charles E. Clark, *The Eastern Frontier: The Settlement of Northern New England, 1610–1763* [New York, 1970], 43–44) with 18th-century Cape Cod, where ministers retained their posts despite charges of sexual misconduct (J. M. Bumsted, "A Caution to Erring Christians: Ecclesiastical Disorder on Cape Cod, 1717 to 1738," *William and Mary Quarterly*, 3d Series, XXVIII [1971], 413–438). I am grateful to John Murrin for bringing these references to my attention. For a prominent Northampton, Mass., man (Joseph Hawley) who admitted to lying in civil and church hearings in the 1740s and yet who suffered no visible damage to his career see Sklar, "A Case of Fornication," *Mich. Papers in Women's Studies* (1978), 46–48, 51.

condition or their covert comings and goings. Deposing three years later, Zerviah represented the sisters as suffering under an intensifying sense of complicity as they had passed through two stages of involvement in the concealment plan. At first, they were passive players, submitting to the hands of men. But once Hallowell declared that he had done all he could, they were left to salvage the conspiracy by enduring the terrors of a first delivery alone, knowing that their failure to call in the older women of the family resembled the decision made by women who committed infanticide.[73] While the pain and shock of miscarrying a five-and-one-half-month fetus through a possibly lacerated vagina may have been the experience that later most grieved Sarah, Zerviah would be haunted particularly by her stealthy venture into the woods with Hannah to bury the shrouded evidence of miscarriage.[74]

The Grosvenor sisters later recalled that they had regarded the first stage of the scheme—taking the trade—as "a Sin" and "an Evil" not so much because it was intended to end the life of a fetus as because it entailed a protracted set of actions, worse than a single lie, to cover up an initial transgression: fornication.[75] According to their religion and the traditions of their New England culture, Sarah and Zerviah knew that the proper response to the sin of "uncleanness" (especially when it led to its visible manifestation, pregnancy) was to confess, seeking to allay God's wrath and cleanse oneself and one's community. Dire were the consequences of hiding a grave sin, so the logic and folklore of religion warned.[76] Having piled one covert act upon another, all in defiance of her parents, each sister wondered if she had not ventured beyond the pale, forsaking God and in turn being forsaken.

Within hours after the burial, Zerviah ran in a frenzy to Alexander Session's house and blurted out an account of her sister's "Untimely birth" and the burying of the fetus. While Alexander and Silence Sessions wondered if Zerviah was "in her right mind" and supposed she was having "a very bad fit," we might judge that she was in shock—horrified and confused by what she had done, fearful of retribution, and torn between the pragmatic strategy of silence and an intense spiritual longing to confess. Silence took her aside and demanded, "how could you do it?—I could not!" Zerviah, in despair, replied, "I don't Know; the Devil was in us." Hers was the characteristic refuge of the defiant sinner: Satan made her do it.[77]

---

[73] See Ulrich, *Good Wives*, 195–201, and Cornelia Hughes Dayton, "Infanticide in Early New England," unpub. paper presented to the Organization of American Historians, Reno, Nev., Mar. 1988.

[74] Burying the child was one of the key dramatic acts in infanticide episodes and tales, and popular beliefs in the inevitability that "murder will out" centered on the buried corpse. For two 18th-century Connecticut cases illustrating these themes see ibid., n. 31. For more on "murder will out" in New England culture see Hall, *Worlds of Wonder*, 176–178, and George Lyman Kittredge, *The Old Farmer and His Almanack . . .* (New York, 1920), 71–77.

[75] Testimony of Zerviah Grosvenor.

[76] Hall, *Worlds of Wonder*, 172–178.

[77] Testimony of Silence Sessions in Multiple Deposition of Sarah and Silence Sessions; Testimony of Alexander Sessions in Multiple Deposition of Hannah Grosvenor et al.; Testimony of Silence

Sarah's descent into despondency, according to the portrait drawn in the women's depositions, was not so immediate. In the week following the miscarriage she recovered enough to be up and about the house. Then the fever came on. Bedridden for weeks, yet still lucid, she exhibited such "great Concern of mind" that Abigail, alone with her, felt compelled to ask her "what was the Matter." "Full of Sorrow" and "in a very affectionate Manner," Sarah replied by asking her friend "whether [she] thought her Sins would ever be pardoned?" Abigail's answer blended a reassuringly familiar exhortation to repent with an awareness that Sarah might have stepped beyond the possibility of salvation. "I answered that I hoped she had not Sinned the unpardonable Sin [that of renouncing Christ], but with true and hearty repentance hoped she would find forgiveness." On this occasion, and at least once more, Sarah responded to the call for repentance by pouring out her troubled heart to Abigail—as we have seen—confessing her version of the story in a torrent of words.[78]

Thus, visions of judgment and of their personal accountability to God haunted Sarah and Zerviah during the waning days of summer—or so their female friends later contended. Caught between the traditional religious ethic of confession, recently renewed in revivals across New England, and the newer, status-driven cultural pressure to keep moral missteps private, the Grosvenor women declined to take up roles as accusers. By focusing on their own actions, they rejected a portrait of themselves as helpless victims, yet they also ceded to their male kin responsibility for assessing blame and mediating between the public interest in seeing justice done and the private interests of the Grosvenor family. Finally, by trying to keep the conspiracy of silence intact and by allowing Amasa frequent visits to her bedside to lament his role and his delusion by Hallowell, Sarah at once endorsed a policy of private repentance and forgiveness *and* indicated that she wished her lover to be spared eventual public retribution for her death.

Talk among the men of Pomfret in the weeks preceding and following Sarah's death centered on more secular concerns than the preoccupation with sin and God's anger that ran through the women's conversations. Neither Hallowell nor Sessions expressed any guilt or sense of sin, as far as the record shows, *until* Sarah was diagnosed as mortally ill.[79] Indeed, their initial accounts of the plot took the form of braggadocio, with Amasa (according to Hallowell) casting himself as the rake who could "gitt Red" of his

---

Sessions; Hall, *Worlds of Wonder,* 174. Alexander and Silence may have had in mind their brother Amasa's interests as a criminal defendant when they cast doubt on Zerviah's reliability as the star prosecution witness.

[78] Deposition of Abigail Nightingale.

[79] Testimony of Zerviah Grosvenor; Deposition of John Grosvenor. Abigail Nightingale recalled a scene when Sarah "was just going out of the world." She and Amasa were sitting on Sarah's bed, and Amasa "endeavour[ed] to raise her up &c. He asked my thought of her state &c. and then leaning over her used these words: poor Creature, I have undone you[!]"; Deposition of Abigail Nightingale.

child and look elsewhere for female companionship, and Hallowell boasting of his abortionist's surgical technique to Sarah's cousin Ebenezer. Later, anticipating popular censure and possible prosecution, each man "Tried to Cast it" on the other. The physician insisted that "He did not do any thing but What Sessions Importuned him to Do," while Amasa exclaimed "That he could freely be Strip[p]ed naked provided he could bring Sarah . . .To life again . . . , but Doct. Hollowell had Deluded him, and Destroyed her."[80] While this sort of denial and buck-passing seems very human, it was the antithesis of the New England way—a religious way of life that made confession its central motif. The Grosvenor-Sessions case is one illustration among many of how New England women continued to measure themselves by "the moral allegory of repentance and confession" while men, at least when presenting themselves before legal authorities, adopted secular voices and learned self-interested strategies.[81]

For the Grosvenor men—at least the cluster of Sarah's cousins living near her—the key issue was not exposing sin but protecting the family's reputation. In the weeks before Sarah died, her cousins John and Ebenezer each attempted to investigate and sort out the roles and motives of Amasa Sessions and John Hallowell in the scheme to conceal Sarah's pregnancy. Grilled in August by Ebenezer about Sarah's condition, Hallowell revealed that "Sessions had bin Interseeding with him to Remove her Conseption." On another occasion, when John Grosvenor demanded that he justify his actions, Hallowell was more specific. He "[did] with her [Sarah] as he did . . . because Sessions Came to him and was So very earnest . . . and offered him five

[80] Deposition of Ebenezer Grosvenor; Testimony of John Shaw in Multiple Deposition of Hannah Grosvenor et al. See also Deposition of John Grosvenor. For discussions of male and female speech patterns and the distinctive narcissistic bravado of men's talk in early New England see Robert St. George, "'Heated' Speech and Literacy in Seventeenth-Century New England," in David Grayson Allen and David D. Hall, eds., Seventeenth-Century New England, Publications of the Colonial Society of Massachusetts, LXIII (Boston, 1984), 305–315; Dayton, "Women Before the Bar," 248–251, 263–283, 338–341; and John Demos, "Shame and Guilt in Early New England," in Carol Z. Stearns and Peter N. Stearns, eds., Emotion and Social Change: Toward a New Psychohistory (New York, 1988), 74–75.
[81] On the centrality of confession see Hall, Worlds of Wonder, 173, 241. The near-universality of accused men and women confessing in court in the 17th century is documented by Gail Sussman Marcus in "'Due Execution of the Generall Rules of Righteousnesse': Criminal Procedure in New Haven Town and Colony, 1638–1658," in Hall, Murrin, and Tate, eds., Saints and Revolutionaries, esp. 132–133. For discussions of the increasing refusal of men to plead guilty to fornication (the most frequently prosecuted crime) from the 1670s on see Thompson, Sex in Middlesex, 29–33; Karlsen, Devil in the Shape of a Woman, 194–196, 198–202; and Dayton, "Women Before the Bar," 168–169. On the growing gap between male and female piety in the eighteenth century see Mary Maples Dunn, "Saints and Sisters: Congregational and Quaker Women in the Early Colonial Period," American Quarterly, XXX (1978), 582–601. For the story of how the New England court system became more legalistic after 1690 and how lawyerly procedures subsequently began to affect religious practices and broader cultural styles see Mann, Neighbors and Strangers, and John M. Murrin, "Anglicizing an American Colony: The Transformation of Provincial Massachusetts" (Ph.D. diss., Yale University, 1966).

pounds if he would do it." "But," Hallowell boasted, "he would have twenty of[f] of him before he had done." John persisted: did Amasa know that Hallowell was attempting a manual abortion at John's house on that day in early August? Hallowell replied that Amasa "knew before he did anything and was at Mr. Waldo's [a Pomfret tavernkeeper] to hear the event."[82]

John and Ebenezer, deposing three or four years after these events, did not mention having thrown questions at Amasa Sessions at the time, nor did they explain why they did not act immediately to have charges brought against the two conspirators. Perhaps these young householders were loath to move against a male peer and childhood friend. More likely, they kept their information to themselves to protect John's wife, Hannah, and their cousin Zerviah from prosecution as accessories. They may also have acted, in league with their uncle Leicester, out of a larger concern for keeping the family name out of the courts. Finally, it is probable that the male cousins, partly because of their own complicity and partly because they may have believed that Sarah had consented to the abortion, simply did not think that Amasa's and Hallowell's actions added up to the murder of their relative.

Three years later, yet another Grosvenor cousin intervened, expressing himself much more vehemently than John or Ebenezer ever had. In 1742, John Shaw at age thirty-eight may have been perceived by the younger Grosvenors as too old—too close to the age when men took public office and served as grand jurors—to be trusted with their secret. Shaw seems to have known nothing of Sarah's taking the trade or having a miscarriage until 1745 when "the Storys" suddenly surfaced. Then Hannah and Zerviah gave him a truncated account. Shaw reacted with rage, realizing that Sarah had died not of natural causes but from "what Hallowell had done," and he set out to wring the truth from the doctor. Several times he sought out Hallowell in Rhode Island to tell him that "I could not look upon him otherwise Than [as] a Bad man Since he had Destroyed my Kinswoman." When Hallowell countered that "Amasa Sessions . . . was the Occasion of it," Shaw's fury grew. "I Told him he was like old Mother Eve When She said The Serpent beguild her; . . . [and] I Told him in my Mind he Deserved to dye for it."[83]

Questioning Amasa, Shaw was quick to accept his protestations of sincere regret and his insistence that Hallowell had "Deluded" him.[84] Shaw

<hr>

[82] Deposition of Ebenezer Grosvenor; Deposition of John Grosvenor. Although a host of witnesses testified to the contrary, Hallowell on one occasion told Amasa's brother "That Sessions never applied to him for anything, to cause an abortion and that if She was with Child he did not Think Amasa knew it"; Testimony of Alexander Sessions in Multiple Deposition of Hannah Grosvenor et al.

[83] Testimony of John Shaw in Multiple Deposition of Hannah Grosvenor et al. One of these confrontations took place in the Providence jail, probably in late 1745 or early 1746.

[84] It is interesting to note that Sessions claimed to have other sources for strong medicines: he told Shaw that, had he known Sarah was in danger of dying, "he tho't he could have got Things that would have preserved her Life"; ibid.

concluded that Amasa had never "Importuned [Hallowell] . . . to lay hands on her" (that is, to perform the manual abortion). Forged in the men's talk about the Grosvenor-Sessions case in 1745 and 1746 appears to have been a consensus that, while Amasa Sessions was somewhat blameworthy "as concerned in it," it was only Hallowell—the outsider, the man easily labeled a quack—who deserved to be branded "a Man of Death." Nevertheless, it was the stories of *both* men and women that ensured the fulfillment of a doctor's warning to Hallowell in the Leicester Grosvenor house just before Sarah died: "The Hand of Justice [will] Take hold of [you] sooner or Later."[85]

THE LAW

The hand of justice reached out to catch John Hallowell in November 1745. The warrants issued for the apprehension and examination of suspects that autumn gave no indication of a single informer or highly placed magistrate who had triggered the prosecution so long after the events. Witnesses referred to "those Stories Concerning Amasa Sessions and Sarah Grosvenor" that had begun to circulate beyond the inner circle of Pomfret initiates in the summer of 1745. *Something* had caused Zerviah and Hannah Grosvenor to break their silence.[86] Zerviah provided the key to the puzzle, as she alone had been present at the crucial series of incidents leading to Sarah's death. The only surviving account of Zerviah's belated conversion from silence to public confession comes from the stories told by Pomfret residents into the nineteenth century. In Ellen Larned's melodramatic prose, the "whispered" tale recounted Zerviah's increasing discomfort thus: "Night after night, in her solitary chamber, the surviving sister was awakened by the rattling of the rings on which her bed-curtains were suspended, a ghostly knell continuing and intensifying till she was convinced of its preternatural origin; and at length, in response to her agonized entreaties, the spirit of her dead sister made known to her, 'That she could not rest in her grave till her crime was made public.' "[87]

Embellished as this tale undoubtedly is, we should not dismiss it out of hand as a Victorian ghost story. In early modern English culture, belief persisted in both apparitions and the supernatural power of the guiltless victim to return and expose her murderer.[88] Zerviah in 1742 already fretted over her

[85] Ibid. Shaw here was reporting Dr. [Theodore?] Coker's account of his confrontation with Hallowell during Sarah's final illness. For biographical data on Coker, see n. 30 above.

[86] Testimony of Rebecca Sharp, Zebulon Dodge, and John Shaw in Multiple Deposition of Hannah Grosvenor et al.; Deposition of Ebenezer Grosvenor.

[87] Larned reported that, according to "the legend," the ghostly visitations ceased when "Hallowell fled his country." *History of Windham County*, I, 363.

[88] For mid-18th-century Bristol residents who reported seeing apparitions and holding conversations with them see Jonathan Barry, "Piety and the Patient: Medicine and Religion in Eighteenth

sin as an accomplice, yet she kept her pledge of silence to her sister. It is certainly conceivable that, after a lapse of three years, she could no longer bear the pressure of hiding the acts that she increasingly believed amounted to the murder of her sister and an unborn child. Whether Zerviah's sudden outburst of talk in 1745 came about at the urging of some Pomfret confidante, or perhaps under the influence of the revivals then sweeping Windham County churches, or indeed because of her belief in nightly visitations by her dead sister's spirit, we simply cannot know.[89]

The Pomfret meetinghouse was the site of the first public legal hearing into the facts behind Sarah Grosvenor's death. We can imagine that townsfolk crowded the pews over the course of two November days to watch two prominent county magistrates examine a string of witnesses before pronouncing their preliminary judgment.[90] The evidence, they concluded, was sufficient to bind four people over for trial at the Superior Court: Hallowell, who in their opinion was "Guilty of murdering Sarah," along with Amasa Sessions, Zerviah Grosvenor, and Hannah Grosvenor as accessories to that murder.[91] The inclusion of Zerviah and Hannah may have been a ploy to pressure these crucial, possibly still reluctant, witnesses to testify for the crown. When Joseph Fowler, the king's attorney, prepared a formal indictment in the case eleven months later, he dropped all charges against Zerviah and Hannah. Rather than stand trial, the two women traveled frequently during 1746 and 1747 to the county seat to give evidence against Sessions and Hallowell.

The criminal process recommenced in September 1746. A grand jury empaneled by the Superior Court as its Windham session first rejected a presentment against Hallowell for murdering Sarah "by his Wicked and Diabolical practice." Fowler, recognizing that the capital charges of murder and

---

Century Bristol," in Roy Porter, ed., *Patients and Practitioners: Lay Perceptions of Medicine in Pre-Industrial Society* (Cambridge, 1985), 157.

[89] None of the depositions produced by Hallowell's trial offers any explanation of the 3-year gap between Sarah's death and legal proceedings. Between 1741 and 1747, revivals and schisms touched every Windham County parish except Pomfret's First Church, to which the Grosvenors belonged; see Larned, *History of Windham County*, I, 393–485, esp. 464.

[90] One of the magistrates, Ebenezer West, had been a justice of the county court since 1726. The other, Jonathan Trumbull, the future governor, was serving both as a county court justice and as an assistant. The fact that the 2 men made the 24-mile trip from their hometown of Lebanon to preside over this Inferior Court, rather than allow local magistrates to handle the hearing, may indicate that one or both of them had insisted the alleged crime be prosecuted.

[91] Record of the Inferior Court held at Pomfret, Nov. 5–6, 1745. Hallowell was the only one of the 4 persons charged who was not examined at this time. He was in jail in Providence for debt. Apprehended in Connecticut the following March, he was jailed until the Pomfret witnesses could travel to Windham for a hearing before Trumbull and West. At the second hearing, the magistrates charged Hallowell with "murdering Sarah . . . *and* A Bastard Female Child with which she was pregnant" (emphasis added). See Record of an Inferior Court held at Windham, Apr. 17, 1746.

accessory to murder against Hallowell and Sessions were going to fail before jurors, changed his tack. He presented the grand jury with a joint indictment against the two men not for outright murder but for endangering Sarah's health by trying to "procure an Abortion" with medicines and "a violent manual operation"; this time the jurors endorsed the bill. When the Superior Court trial opened in November, two attorneys for the defendants managed to persuade the judges that the indictment was faulty on technical grounds. However, upon the advice of the king's attorney that there "appear reasons vehemently to suspect" the two men "Guilty of Sundry Heinous Offenses" at Pomfret four years earlier, the justices agreed to bind them over to answer charges in March 1747.[92]

Fowler next moved to bring separate indictments against Hallowell and Sessions for the "highhanded misdemeanor" of endeavoring to destroy Sarah's health "and the fruit of her womb." This wording echoed the English common law designation of abortion as a misdemeanor, not a felony or capital crime. A newly empaneled grand jury of eighteen county yeomen made what turned out to be the pivotal decision in getting a conviction: they returned a true bill against Hallowell and rejected a similarly worded bill against Sessions.[93] Only Hallowell, "the notorious physician," would go to trial.[94]

On March 20, 1747, John Hallowell stepped before the bar for the final time to answer for the death of Sarah Grosvenor. He maintained his innocence, the case went to a trial jury of twelve men, and they returned with a guilty verdict. The Superior Court judges, who had discretion to choose any penalty less than death, pronounced a severe sentence of public shaming and corporal punishment. Hallowell was to be paraded to the town gallows, made to stand there before the public for two hours "with a rope visibly hanging about his neck," and then endure a public whipping of twenty-nine lashes "on the naked back."[95]

Before the authorities could carry out this sentence, Hallowell escaped and fled to Rhode Island. From Providence seven months after his trial, he audaciously petitioned the Connecticut General Assembly for a mitigated sentence, presenting himself as a destitute "Exile." As previously noted,

[92] Indictment against Hallowell, Sept. 4, 1746; Indictment against Hallowell and Sessions, Sept. 20, 1746; Pleas of Hallowell and Sessions before the adjourned Windham Superior Court, Nov. [18], 1746; Sup. Ct. Rec., bk. 12, 112–117, 131–133.

[93] Sup. Ct. Rec., bk. 12, 173, 175; Indictment against John Hallowell, Mar. 1746/47; *Rex v. Amasa Sessions*, Indictment, Mar. 1746/47, Windham Sup. Ct. Files, box 172. See William Blackstone, *Commentaries on the Laws of England* (Facsimile of 1st ed. of 1765–69) (Chicago, 1979), I, 125–126, IV, 198.

[94] Larned, *History of Windham County*, I, 363.

[95] Even in the context of the inflation of the 1740s, Hallowell's bill of costs was unusually high: £110.2s.6d. Sessions was hit hard in the pocketbook too; he was assessed £83.14s.2d. in costs.

fourteen respected male citizens of Providence took up his cause, arguing that this valued doctor had been convicted by prejudiced witnesses and hearsay evidence and asserting that corporal punishment was unwarranted in a misdemeanor case. While the Connecticut legislators rejected these petitions, the language used by Hallowell and his Rhode Island patrons is yet another marker of the distance separating many educated New England men at mid-century from their more God-fearing predecessors. Never mentioning the words "sin" or "repentance," the Providence men wrote that Hallowell was justified in escaping the lash since "every Person is prompted [by the natural Law of Self-Preservation] to avoid Pain and Misery."[96]

In the series of indictments against Hallowell and Sessions, the central legal question became who had directly caused Sarah's death. To the farmers in their forties and fifties who sat as jurors, Hallowell clearly deserved punishment. By recklessly endangering Sarah's life he had abused the trust that heads of household placed in him as a physician.[97] Moreover, he had conspired with the younger generation to keep their dangerous activities secret from their parents and elders.

Several rationales could have been behind the Windham jurors' conclusion that Amasa Sessions ought to be spared the lash. Legally, they could distinguish him from Hallowell as not being immediately responsible for Sarah's death. Along with Sarah's male kin, they dismissed the evidence that Amasa had instigated the scheme, employed Hallowell, and monitored all of his activities. Perhaps they saw him as a native son who deserved the chance to prove himself mature and responsible. They may have excused his actions as nothing more than a misguided effort to cast off an unwanted lover. Rather than acknowledge that a culture that excused male sexual irresponsibility was responsible for Sarah's death, the Grosvenor family, the Pomfret community, and the jury men of the county persuaded themselves that Sessions had been ignorant of the potentially deadly consequences of his actions.

[96] Petition of John Hallowell, Oct. 1747, Conn. Archives, Crimes and Misdemeanors, Ser. 1, IV, 108; Petition of Resolved Waterman et al., ibid., 109. Specifically, Hallowell and his supporters asked that his sentence be reduced to a fine in an amount "adequate to his reduced Circumstances." Such requests for reduced sentences were increasingly submitted by convicted felons in 18th-century Connecticut, and some were granted. See ibid., Ser. 1 and 2. Rumors of bankruptcy had haunted Hallowell since he moved to Providence in 1742. As a physician and shopkeeper, between 1742 and 1750 he won a net of £325 in frequent county court litigation (including two substantial executions against Dr. Theodore Coker). However, two 1743–1744 Superior Court judgments against him totalling over £4000 spelled financial ruin. His name last appears in Connecticut records in 1749, and in Rhode Island, as far as I can tell, in 1750. Three of his sons settled in Providence as mariners. These conclusions are based on an analysis of Rhode Island Census records, and the Record books and indices of the Providence County Court of Common Pleas and of the Supreme Court at the Judicial Records Center, Pawtucket.
[97] Note Blackstone's discussion of the liability of "a physician or surgeon who gives his patient a potion . . . to cure him, which contrary to expectation kills him." *Commentaries*, IV, 197.

MEMORY AND HISTORY

No family feud, no endless round of recriminations followed the many months of deposing and attending trials that engaged the Grosvenor and Sessions clans in 1746 and 1747. Indeed, as Sarah and Amasa's generation matured, the ties between the two families thickened. In 1748 Zerviah married a man whose family homestead adjoined the farm of Amasa's father. Twenty years later, when the aging Sessions patriarch wrote his will, Zerviah and her husband were at his elbow to witness the solemn document. Amasa, who would inherit "the Whole of the Farm," was doubtless present also.[98] Within another decade, the third generation came of age, and despite the painful memories of Sarah's death that must have lingered in the minds of her now middle-aged siblings, a marriage directly joining the two families finally took place. In 1775 Amasa's third son, and namesake, married sixteen-year-old Esther Grosvenor, daughter of Sarah's brother, Leicester, Jr.[99]

It is clear that the Grosvenor clan was not willing to break ranks with their respectable yeoman neighbors and heap blame on the Sessions family for Sarah's death. It would, however, be fascinating to know what women in Pomfret and other Windham County towns had to say about the outcome of the legal proceedings in 1747. Did they concur with the jurors that Hallowell was the prime culprit, or did they, unlike Sarah Grosvenor, direct their ire more concertedly at Amasa, insisting that he too was "a Bad man?" Several decades later, middle-class New England women would organize against the sexual double standard. However, Amasa's future career tells us that female piety in the 1740s did not instruct Windham County women to expel the newly married, thirty-two-year-old man from their homes.[100]

Amasa, as he grew into middle age in Pomfret, easily replicated his father's status. He served as militia captain in the Seven Years' War, prospered in farming, fathered ten children, and lived fifty-seven years beyond Sarah Grosvenor. His handsome gravestone, inscribed with a long verse, stands but twenty-five feet from the simpler stone erected in 1742 for Sarah.

After his death, male kin remembered Amasa fondly; nephews and grandsons recalled him as a "favorite" relative, "remarkably capable" in his prime and "very corpulent" in old age. Moreover, local storytelling tradition and the published history of the region, which made such a spectacular

[98] Killingly Land Rec., III, 99; Estate papers of Nathaniel Sessions, 1771, Pomfret Prob. Dist. Although Zerviah bore five daughters, she chose not to name any of them after the sister she had been so close to. In 1747, the final year of the trials, Sarah's much older sister, Anna, gave birth to a daughter whom she named Sarah.
[99] Pomfret Vit. Rec., II, 67.
[100] Carroll Smith-Rosenberg, "Beauty, the Beast and the Militant Woman: A Case Study in Sex Roles and Social Stress in Jacksonian America," *American Quarterly*, XXIII (1971), 562–584. There were branches of the Female Moral Reform Society in several Connecticut towns.

ghost story out of Sarah's abortion and death, preserved Amasa Sessions's reputation unsullied: the name of Sarah's lover was left out of the tale.[101]

If Sarah Grosvenor's life is a cautionary tale in any sense for us in the late twentieth century, it is as a reminder of the historically distinctive ways in which socialized gender roles, community and class solidarity, and legal culture combine in each set of generations to excuse or make invisible certain abuses and crimes against women. The form in which Sarah Grosvenor's death became local history reminds us of how the excuses and erasures of one generation not unwittingly become embedded in the narratives and memories of the next cultural era.

---

[101] Sessions, *Sessions Family*, 31, 35; Larned, *History of Windham County*, I, 363–364. Indeed Larned referred to the Grosvenor and Sessions families only obliquely, characterizing them as among Pomfret's "proudest," "first and wealthiest families." The only principal in the case whom she identified directly was the culprit Hallowell.

Social Transactions between Whites and Blacks

Philip D. Morgan

INTRODUCTION

In today's world, relations between races occur largely in public places, away from the home and often away from one's neighborhood. During the eighteenth century, the opposite was true: relations between races occurred largely in private spaces, in the home and on the plantation. Philip D. Morgan examines this world of "continual, inescapable, face-to-face encounters" between the races. One caveat should be kept in mind: the concept of race has no basis in biology or any other science. Race is a culturally and historically created idea, and it has no reality outside the cultural systems that endow it with meaning.

The following selection represents half of a chapter from Morgan's book, Slave Counterpoint. *The book as a whole addresses the development of black culture—or perhaps more accurately black cultures—in the eighteenth-century Chesapeake of Virginia and Maryland and the Low Country of South Carolina, which were the two principal slave societies in the area that would become the United States. Morgan does not discuss the sugar plantations of the British Caribbean, the third large slave system in Britain's American colonies. The Chesapeake and the Low Country were given shape by two different principal crops, tobacco and rice respectively, and by two different systems of slave labor, the gang system and the task system. Morgan offers a stern corrective to studies that generalize about* the slave system *or* African American *culture in the singular, regardless of region or time. Morgan examines topics as diverse as diet, housing, ecology, work, kinship, and religion to give us a rich portrait of these changing cultures. Unlike many previous studies of slavery, Morgan does not focus explicitly on slave resistance; he sees the formation of coherent black cultures as the ultimate form of resistance.*

Philip D. Morgan, *Slave Counterpoint: Black Culture in the Eighteenth-Century Chesapeake and Low-country*, 1998, pp. 377–412. Copyright © 1998 by The University of North Carolina Press. Published for the Omohundro Institute of Early American History and Culture. Used by permission of the publisher and the author.

This selection focuses on two aspects of relations between slaves and slaveowners: violence and sex. Morgan draws extensively on written accounts of encounters between masters and slaves to illustrate the variety of forms these interactions could take. The stories that Morgan recounts are full of vivid details that help us imagine what these encounters were like, which can be quite disturbing. These black cultures formed in the midst of such violence, and the interaction between slave and master shaped both black and white cultures in countless ways.

- *How significant were regional and temporal differences?*
- *How does Morgan explain them?*
- *Why was miscegenation more acceptable in the Low Country?*

I know not which to pity the most—the master or the slave.
— Francis Asbury

Transactions between masters and bondpeople were enormously wide-ranging. Many a white child came into the world in the arms of a black nurse; many a master went out of it on the backs of black pallbearers.[1] Masters' dependence on and exploitation of their slaves was both comprehensive and far-reaching, from the most public to the most private of activities, from the most elemental to the most tangential of roles. Conversely, the slave's existence was inextricably shaped by the master's will and power. However hard they struggled to break free, slaves could never escape the long shadow cast by the master. This mutual dependence took a frightening toll on everyone. Nothing and no one escaped the effects of slavery, an institution forged in the heat of continual, inescapable, face-to-face encounters.

From public places to private spaces, slaves were ubiquitous. They could intrude on society's most elevated ceremonial occasions. In 1719, celebrations of the anniversary of the king's coronation in Williamsburg involved the firing of the great guns; unfortunately, the slave gunner lost his arm. The privacy of the home was no more sacrosanct. Janet Schaw took pleasure in getting up early because there would be no "yelping Negroes with their discording voices to grate my ears and disturb my thoughts." A South Carolina resident advised against building stairs of cedar, for the wood was "too brittle . . . at least where Negroes go up and down." He also noted composing a letter to the loud snores of his waiting man. Slaves gave their masters no peace.[2]

---

[1] For the role of black nurses and midwives, see Chapter 6. For black pallbearers, see will of Philip Rootes, Aug. 13, 1746, in Beverley Fleet, ed., *Virginia Colonial Abstracts*, IV, *King and Queen County Records concerning Eighteenth Century Persons* (Baltimore, 1961), 79; and will of William Sanders, Aug. 4, 1775, Guignard Family Papers, USC.

[2] Petition of John Tyler to the Governor, May 6, 1721, Colonial Papers, VSL; [Janet Schaw], *Journal of a Lady of Quality . . .* , ed. Evangeline Walker Andrews and Charles McLean Andrews (New Haven, Conn., 1923), 169; *Laurens Papers*, IV, 98, X, 222.

Whites even encountered slaves in their dreams. According to one minister, a woman of his acquaintance who had a withered arm dreamed three nights successively that if she applied to a Methodist preacher her arm would be restored. Blocking her path, however, was "a Negro Man (as she thought) who, by persuasion, threats and lyes turn'd her back." Conversely, the slave in Lachlan Bain McIntosh's religious vision played a more positive role—a portent of the master's fate. The apparition of Jesus Christ first spoke to McIntosh's slave, July, telling July that he would soon die. It then pointed to McIntosh, saying he would be "call'd" the following day. More prosaically, Frederick George Mulcaster, a young Scottish planter in East Florida, had a wish-fulfillment reverie, in which he was standing "in a Hall and beneath me was Indigo Rice Cotton etc., in great abundance [and] at my command my slaves . . . instantly gathered the crop and put it on Board Vessels." Most dramatically, when nine of Landon Carter's slaves fled to the British in 1776, both he and his daughter dreamed about them. In the father's case, he envisioned them "most wretchedly meager and wan," begging him to intercede for a pardon on their behalf. Carter had to dream on, for the slaves never returned.[3]

Just as blacks invaded the masters' unconscious world, so they intruded on their everyday world. Slaveowners populated their figures of speech with slaves: humble as slaves, yellow as a mulatto, looking skyward "like a Negro weeding corn," sleeping in one's clothes "like a Negro." These derogatory similes reveal the impact of blacks on the everyday consciousness of whites. Blacks also inscribed themselves on the landscape. Masters named fields and quarters after slaves and transferred African locations to North America. John Ball (or one of his ancestors) named an area within his plantation as Gold Coast Hill; Cumberland County, Virginia, had its Guinea Road, Little Guinea Neck, Great Guinea Creek, Angola Road, and Angola Creek. Even a slave's features made an impression. Henry Laurens was so taken with the appearance of his gardener that he had his picture drawn; a newly arrived guest at Mount Vernon, in contrast, promptly turned on his heels, "disgusted" at seeing "an old Negroe there resembling his own Image." Whether their impact was pleasing or not, slaves could at least take satisfaction in registering their presence.[4]

[3] Marjorie Moran Holmes, "The Life and Diary of the Reverend John Jeremiah Jacob" (master's thesis, Duke University, 1941), 135; Memoranda Book, Sept. 22, 1807, Lachlan Bain McIntosh Papers, GHS, cited by J. E. Chaplin, "An Anxious Pursuit: Innovation in Commercial Agriculture in South Carolina, Georgia, and British East Florida, 1740–1815" (Ph.D. diss., The Johns Hopkins University, 1986), 144; F. George Mulcaster to [?], Nov. 6, 1768, Manigault Family Papers, USC; Jack P. Greene, ed., *The Diary of Colonel Landon Carter of Sabine Hall, 1752–1778*, 2 vols. (Charlottesville, Va., 1965), 1064 (hereafter cited as *Carter Diary*).
[4] *Laurens Papers*, III, 553 (humble), V, 702 (picture); Josiah Smith to George Austin, Jan. 30, 1773, Josiah Smith Letterbook, UNC (yellow); Sam Briggs to Randolph Barksdale, July 22, 1789, Peter Barksdale Letters, Duke (skyward); John C. Fitzpatrick, ed., *The Writings of George Washington from the Original Manuscript Sources, 1745–1799*, 39 vols. (Washington, D.C., 1931–1944), I, 17 (sleeping);

For the master, much of his self-image depended on the possession of slaves. According to William Byrd II, slaves served to "blow up the pride" of "white people." This was as true of the urban tradesmen who owned one or two slaves as of the great planter. Timothy Ford observed that many Charleston mechanics "bear nothing more of their trade than the name," precisely because they were the proud owners of slaves. They were always "followed by a negro carrying their tools," and barbers were "supported in idleness and ease by their negroes who do the business." Gentlemanly status was equally predicated on slaveowning. Ford found that "a person can no more act or move without an attending servant than a planet without its satellites." A gentleman out riding without servants was a contradiction in terms. Slaves formed the advance guard, the "ensigns" of a gentleman's "rank and dignity." Indeed, a recent immigrant to South Carolina in 1749 discovered that "they say here when they talk of a Man's being Rich he has so many Negroes."[5]

Because social respect was inextricably connected to slaveownership, wealthy families made sure their young children had slaves at an early age. In 1728, Robert "King" Carter proposed to buy three slave girls to distribute to each of his three male grandchildren. In 1792, Robert Stafford, a two-year-old boy living on Cumberland Island, Georgia, received a mulatto slave boy named Peter, also about two years of age, from his uncle. According to Johann Schoepf, at age fifteen, a well-bred Virginian acquired "a horse and a negro," the two adjuncts of gentlemanly self-presentation, "with which he riots about the country, attends every fox-hunt, horse race, and cock-fight, and does nothing else whatever." In Baltimore County, Maryland, slaveowners who deeded slaves as gifts routinely picked black boys of roughly the same age as their sons, "perhaps hoping," Charles Steffen notes, "to groom a lifelong companion and trusted servant." Whites learned to command at an early age.[6]

Account or Planting Book, 1780–1784, Apr. 2, 1781, John Ball, Jr., Papers, Duke; Cumberland County Court Order Book, 1758–1762, 286, 1774–1778, 483, 524, 1779–1784, 21, 166, VSL; Donald Jackson and Dorothy Twohig, eds., *The Diaries of George Washington*, 6 vols. (Charlottesville, Va., 1976–1979), I, 222. See also Darrett B. Rutman and Anita H. Rutman, *A Place in Time: Middlesex County, Virginia, 1650–1750* (New York, 1984), 164, 166; and Mechal Sobel, *The World They Made Together: Black and White Values in Eighteenth-Century Virginia* (Princeton, N.J., 1987), 93–94.

[5] Marion Tinling, ed., *The Correspondence of the Three William Byrds of Westover, Virginia, 1684–1776*, 2 vols. (Charlottesville, Va., 1977), II, 488; Joseph W. Barnwell, ed., "Diary of Timothy Ford, 1785–1786," *SCHM*, XIII (1912), 142, 189–190; James Steuart to Thomas Steuart, Oct. 17, 1749, GD38/2/7/96, Steuart of Dalguise Muniments, Scottish Record Office, Edinburgh. See also Henry Melchior Muhlenberg, *The Journals of Henry Melchior Muhlenberg*, trans. and ed. Theodore G. Tappert and John W. Doberstein, 2 vols. (Philadelphia, 1942–1958), II, 664; and John Hammond Moore, ed., "The Abiel Abbot Journals: A Yankee Preacher in Charleston Society, 1818–1827," *SCHM*, LXVIII (1967), 68.

[6] Robert "King" Carter to [?], May 21, 1728, Robert Carter Letterbook, 1727–1728, VHS; John E. Ehrenhard and Mary R. Bullard, *Stafford Plantation, Cumberland Island National Seashore, Georgia:*

Countless observers realized that youthful command took an emotional toll on whites as well as blacks. Charles Wesley was strongly opposed to the practice of giving a white child a slave of the same age "to tyrannize over, to beat and abuse out of sport." Similarly, John Lambert noted that South Carolina planters appropriated one or two young slaves to each of their children so that white Carolinians "are nurtured in the strongest prejudices against the blacks, whom they are taught to look upon as beings almost without a soul, and whom they sometimes treat with an unpardonable severity." The process by which young white children learned to dehumanize blacks began early. For Elkanah Winchester, "Little children are taught, from their cradles, . . . to exercise the most brutal cruelties upon [slaves] without the least pity"; for the duc de La Rochefoucauld-Liancourt, "The little white man learns, even before he can walk, to tyrranize over the blacks." But the most powerful indictment came from Thomas Jefferson. In a famous passage, he described how "the parent storms, the child looks on, catches the lineaments of wrath, puts on the same airs in the circle of smaller slaves, gives a loose to his worst of passions, and thus nursed, educated, and daily exercised in tyranny, cannot but be stamped by its odious peculiarities." George Mason was right on the mark when he observed, "Every Master is born a petty tyrant."[7]

But there was a more benign side to contact between some white children and slaves. In the 1770s, William Richardson, a South Carolina slaveowner, advised his wife to keep a close eye on their four-year-old son, Billy, because "some of the little Negroes that Billy is fond of playing with, go often down to the Pond to play and that it is not impossible that some accident . . . may happen." Billy obviously liked playing with black children, and his father countenanced the fraternization, provided it was monitored. A few years earlier, Richardson's young daughter Nancy pleaded "in favour" of three household slaves who were about to be punished. Her appeal had the desired ef-

Archaeological Investigations of a Slave Cabin (Tallahassee, Fla., 1981), 4; Johann David Schoepf, *Travels in the Confederation [1783–1784]*, trans. and ed. Alfred J. Morrison, 2 vols. (Philadelphia, 1911), II, 95; Charles G. Steffen, *From Gentlemen to Townsmen: The Gentry of Baltimore County, Maryland, 1660–1776* (Lexington, Ky., 1993), 88. See also *Laurens Papers*, IV, 363; and Robert Carter to Priscilla Mitchell, Dec. 25, 1786, Robert Carter Letterbook, VII, 165, Duke.

[7] *The Journal of the Rev. Charles Wesley* . . . (Taylors, S.C., 1977 [London, 1909]), 68; John Lambert, *Travels through Lower Canada and the United States of North America, in the Years 1806, 1807, and 1808*, II (London, 1810), 393; Elhanan Winchester, *The Reigning Abominations, Especially the Slave Trade* . . . (London, 1788), 24 (see also 22); François Alexandre Frédéric, duke de La Rochefoucault Liancourt, *Travels through the United States of North America* . . . , 2 vols. (London, 1799), I, 557; Adrienne Koch and William Peden, eds., *The Life and Selected Writings of Thomas Jefferson* (New York, 1944), 278; Max Farrand, ed., *The Records of the Federal Convention of 1787*, rev. ed., 4 vols. (New Haven, Conn., 1937), II, 370. See also diary of Jonathan Evans, July 24, 1797, UNC; *Laurens Papers*, III, 356; Kenneth Roberts and Anna M. Roberts, trans. and eds., *Moreau de St. Méry's American Journey [1793–1798]* (Garden City, N.Y., 1947), 54; Tinling, ed., *The Correspondence of the Three William Byrds*, I, 32, II, 682.

fect. Due to depart for an English school, a young Richard Henry Lee had daily fights with "a stout negro boy" in preparation for his anticipated boxing bouts with English youths. A young white man and his slave even went to their deaths together: a planter's son, accompanied by a slave, traveled by canoe down the Ashley River to Charleston, where he was to attend school. Neither completed the journey. Their bodies were ultimately found, "sticking in the Mud in the said River, their Arms clasping one another."[8]

Whether the contacts between white and black children were benign or malignant, there can be no doubt that growing up in a slave society meant learning to rely on slaves. In fact, adult masters clearly proclaimed their dependence on their slaves—particularly where money was involved. In claiming compensation for the loss of his "valuable waterman," one humble Virginia master had no hesitation in declaring that he had thereby been "deprived of his chief support in maintaining a large Family." Similarly, the mainstay of a South Carolina resident was his capable house painter and glazier, who had become "the chief support of [his] poor Family wch without such assistance must soon be reduced to Indigence and want."[9]

But eighteenth-century masters were even willing to declare their dependence on their slaves gratuitously, publicly, even humiliatingly. Thus, a South Carolina master, in advertising for his runaway slave, managed to strike a note of maudlin self-pity and exaggerated anger that would be humorous were it not pathetic. "As this inhuman creature, when she went away," the master whined, "left myself extreme ill in one bed, her mistress in another, and two of my children not one able to help the other, she must be conscious of some very atrocious crime." Similarly, a Virginia master grew self-righteous because his slave had become "very idle during my present Indisposition" and then had run away in order to seek freedom, "though he has lived little short of it with me, having been too much indulged." Masters did not hide their misplaced trust.[10]

As masters relied on slaves, so slaves returned the favor. The set-piece that seemed to convey the depths of the slaves' attachment to their masters was the scene—the stuff of which plantation legends are made—when the long-absent patriarch returned home to the warm greetings of joyful dependents. Even if such occasions are interpreted as ritualized events, with a

[8] Emma B. Richardson, "Letters of William Richardson, 1765–1784," *SCHM*, XLVII (1946), 17, 10; Richard H. Lee, *Memoir of the Life of Richard Henry Lee, and His Correspondence with the Most Distinguished Men in America and Europe . . .* , 2 vols. (Philadelphia, 1825), I, 7; *SCG*, Jan. 22, 1737, cited in Peter A. Coclanis, *The Shadow of a Dream: Economic Life and Death in the South Carolina Low Country, 1670–1920* (New York, 1989), 111.

[9] Legislative Petitions, Gloucester County, Dec. 23, 1800, VSL; petition of Michael Jeans, South Carolina Council Journal, Jan. 12, 1743, CO5/441, fols. 448–449, PRO; petition of Col. John Thomas, Journal of South Carolina House of Representatives, Feb. 3, 1783, SCDAH.

[10] Stephen Hartley, *SCG*, Oct. 13, 1757; James Mercer, *VaG* (P and D), Mar. 19, 1772. See also Thomas Ringgold, *Md Gaz*, Mar. 20, 1755; Gabriel Jones, *VaG* (P and D), June 30, 1774; Robert Brent, *VaG* (D and H), Nov. 18, 1775.

certain amount of role-playing on all sides—William Drayton, for example, lightheartedly asked of a friend who had just returned home how he found "being kiss'd and Slabber'd" by the "Masters, Misses, Negroes, Dogs and Cats of your Family"—some receptions seem too effusive to be explained away as a set of cynical maneuvers. Henry Laurens, for instance, was obviously moved by the welcome he received when he returned to his Charleston home in 1774 after an absence of three years in Europe:

> I found no body here but three of our old Domestics Stepney Exeter, and big Hagar, these drew tears from me by their humble and affectionate Salutes and congratulations my Knees were Clasped, my hands kissed my very feet embraced and nothing less than a very, I can't say fair, but *full* Buss of my Lips would satisfy the old Man [Stepney] weeping and Sobbing in my Face—the kindest enquiries over and over again were made concerning Master Jacky, Master Harry, Master Jemmy [Laurens's children, still in Europe]—they encircled me held my hands hung upon me I could scarcely get from them—Ah said the old Man, I never thought to see you again, now I am happy—Ah, I never thought to see you again.

As much as he tried to make a joke about the "fair" kiss on his lips, Laurens was clearly moved. He finally broke his "way through these humble *sincere friends* thanking them a thousand times for such marks of their affection and proceeded to Broad Street."[11] These were, of course, urban domestics, hardly typical eighteenth-century slaves.

Yet fifteen years later, much the same happened in the depths of the Virginia countryside when Thomas Jefferson returned from France. According to his daughter Martha, Jefferson's slaves "collected in crowds" around his carriage well before it reached Monticello, "and almost drew it up the mountain by hand." The shouts of greeting reached a climax when they reached the top. And when Jefferson stepped from the carriage, "they received him in their arms and bore him to the house, crowding around and kissing his hands and feet—some blubbering and crying—others laughing." Black folklore was a little at variance with Martha's account. According to the "lips of old family servants who were present as children," the carriage horses had been unharnessed and the vehicle dragged to the front door at Monticello by "strong black arms." Jefferson was literally borne back home on the strong backs of his slaves.[12]

Similar welcomes greeted humble planters, too. When Devereux Jarratt, a common planter and minister, returned home, "his brothers and their

---

[11] William Henry Drayton to Peter Manigault, Nov. 16, 1756, Manigault Family Papers; *Laurens Papers*, X, 2–3 (my emphasis).
[12] Sarah N. Randolph, *The Domestic Life of Thomas Jefferson* (Charlottesville, Va., 1871), 152–153. For similar homecomings, see St. George Tucker's Journal to Charlestown, Apr. 14, 1777, Tucker-Coleman Papers, typescript, CW; William Moultrie, *Memoirs of the American Revolution*, 2 vols. (New York, 1802), II, 355–356; Robert Dawidoff, *The Education of John Randolph* (New York, 1979), 52.

wives, and all the black people on the plantation, seemed overjoy'd" at his coming. Edmund Botsford, another minister of humble status, encountered an effusive reception when reunited with his slave. As Botsford described it, his "poor negro was almost frantic upon seeing once more his kind master. He jumped, hallowed, fell down, embraced his master's feet, and in every possible way gave vent to his joy." Homecomings were opportunities for slaves to display their attachment to masters, whether the estates were large or small.[13]

As these scenes suggest, many slaves identified closely with their masters. When Landon Carter had his son's weaver whipped, the slave invoked the protection of his own master, who "would not have let him be served so." Similarly, fugitive Peter's destination was predictable, for "he often told the other Negroes that if ever [his present master] used him ill he would go to his old mistress . . . and be protected." Slaves allied with masters not just for protection but in opposition to outsiders. A gang of slaves ridiculed a tenant recently discharged by their master; do not worry, they mocked, if our master's horses eat your grain, because it no longer belongs to you. Imagine the bombshell when a slave disclosed to his master that a "Friend" had seduced his master's wife; the frenzied slaveholder, with the assistance of his slaves, promptly cut off the cuckolder's ears. A Virginia master and his slaves even went on a rampage together, killing one white man and wounding another. The affinity of slave and master knew no bounds.[14]

The supreme test of slave loyalty, however, came during the Revolutionary war. Many slaves during this long, drawn-out conflict had opportunities to throw off their allegiance to masters and decamp to the British. Many did. However, most did not—for a variety of reasons, most strategic—and a significant minority went further and actively demonstrated their allegiance. Thus a Georgia loyalist recalled that her father was able to escape from patriot forces when a favorite slave "contrived to amuse the soldiers in different ways" in order to delay them. One Lowcountry plantation was spared a visit from enemy because a neighbor's slave "disuaded [the British] from it by saying it was not worth while, for it was only a plantation belonging to an old decrepit gentleman, who did not live there; so they took his word for it and proceeded on." The slave received "many blessings" from the owners "for his consideration and pity." A slave driver exhibited such fidelity that "during

---

[13] Devereux Jarratt, *The Life of the Reverend Devereux Jarratt . . . Written by Himself . . .* (New York, 1969 [orig. publ. Baltimore, 1806]), 42; Charles D. Mallary, *Memoirs of Elder Edmund Botsford* (Charleston, S.C., 1832), 58.

[14] Greene, ed., *Carter Diary*, 845; William Gregory, *VaG* (P and D), May 4, 1769; Anne King Gregorie, ed., *Records of the Court of Chancery of South Carolina, 1671–1779* (Washington, D.C., 1950), 123; *SCG*, July 24, 1738; J. F. Mercer to R. Sprigg, Aug. 6, 1794, Mercer Family Papers, VHS. For a series of slave crimes that seemed to have been instigated by masters, see trial of Dick, July 26, 1748, and related episodes, Accomac County Court Order Book, 1744–1753, 265, 283, 332–333, 339, VSL (Philip Schwarz first alerted me to this case).

the invasion of the country [he] never went off with the British, and had the address to prevent any going who were under his care."[15]

Because slaveholders' expectations concerning the loyalty of their slaves were not high on the eve of the Revolutionary war, they suffered no "moment of truth" akin to the trauma, the deep shock experienced by slaveholders during the Civil War, when so many slaves proved faithless. In fact, if anything, the reverse was true in the earlier civil war. Revolutionary slaveholders were generally surprised and gratified by their slaves' actions, even though only a minority could be said to have demonstrated "loyalty." An advertisement offering a South Carolina gang of forty slaves for sale suggests the sense of wonder, for what made them valuable was "that not one ever quitted their owner," even when the state "was in confusion, and invested by the British Army." Similarly, a Lowcountry manager informed his absentee employer that his two plantations had suffered remarkably little: not a single slave had been lost "either per force or by their own acord but on the contrary they have behaved exceeding well, faithfully attending to their work, though pinched by cold." In gratitude for "their fidelity," the manager planned to reward them with an extra suit of summer clothing and a personal visit, for "the poor Creatures I am told are desirous of seeing Me." These claims of loyalty may smack of a desperate need to believe in the slaves' constancy, but clearly the behavior of some slaves provided confirmation. If the overwhelming response of mid-nineteenth-century slaveholders to their slaves' actions in the Civil War was one of betrayal, that of late-eighteenth-century slaveholders was one of surprise.[16]

Masters and slaves depended on one another, and the burdens of that dependence were enormous. Masters often succumbed to the corrupting temptations of untrammeled power; slaves were frequently drawn into a tragic complicity in their own fate. At one end of the scales was the raw horror of an institution that condoned cruelty, violence, rape, and even murder; at the other was the tragic involvement of many slaves in their own oppression. Many masters tried to treat their slaves humanely, but their efforts were doomed to fail, for at bottom the relationship violated humanity. Conversely, many slaves acted generously toward their masters, but "ten thousand recollections," to

[15] Elizabeth Lichtenstein Johnston, *Recollections of a Georgia Loyalist*, ed. Rev. Arthur Wentworth Eaton (London, 1901), 45; Caroline Gilman, ed., *Letters of Eliza Wilkinson . . .* (New York, 1839), 13 (see also 67–71); Colcock and Gibbons, *SCG and GA*, June 10, 1783. See also John Postele to Major Hyrne, June 2, 1781, South Carolina, Peter Force Collection, series 7E, box 62, LC; *Laurens Papers*, XI, 223–224, 254.
[16] Frances-Susanna Pinckney, *Gaz of State of SC*, Nov. 27, 1783; Josiah Smith to George Appleby, June 5, 1783, Smith Letterbook. See also Maurice A. Crouse, ed., "Papers of Gabriel Manigault, 1771–1784," *SCHM*, LXIV (1963), 2; M. Pope to J. Jacob, Aug. 25, 1775, British Museum transcripts, LC; Anne Deas, ed., *Correspondence of Mr. Ralph Izard, of South Carolina . . .*, I (New York, 1844), 154. For slaveowners during the Civil War, see Eugene D. Genovese, *Roll, Jordan, Roll: The World the Slaves Made* (New York, 1974), 97–112; and Leon F. Litwack, *Been in the Storm So Long: The Aftermath of Slavery* (New York, 1979), esp. chaps. 1–3.

use Jefferson's words, "of the injuries they have sustained" inevitably corroded their magnanimity, creating unfathomable depths of bitterness. Masters
and slaves created a world that "could shimmer with mutual affection or . . .
shatter in mutual antagonism." Plantations were arenas of shared companionship and intense warfare, friendly cooperation and savage conflict.[17]

VIOLENCE

Because slavery bound whites and blacks together in bitter antagonism, violence was always an important part of their relationship. Yet whites were
often complacent about the prospect of collective slave violence, and this
was evident not just in their response to potential rebellions but in their
policing of slaves and in the access slaves had to firearms. Eighteenth-
century American slave societies were not police states constantly on the
brink of violent rebellion. Sporadically, however, white fears about potential
slave rebelliousness assumed near-hysterical proportions. The fury of slaveowners lay just below the surface like a smoldering volcano, always about to
erupt. Thus rhythm—long periods of laxity alternating with short bursts of
frenzy—needs explanation. The everyday violence committed by masters on
their slaves and occasional acts of retaliation by slaves will help provide the
answers by exposing the raw nerves of slavery.

Eighteenth-century masters never doubted that slaves were capable
of violence or that they might rebel. As it happened, however, no Anglo-
American mainland region had to face a large-scale slave insurrection in the
eighteenth century. The one incident that came close was the Stono revolt of
1739, in which about sixty slaves in South Carolina killed approximately
twenty whites and destroyed much property. By New World standards,
however, this was a small-scale revolt of short duration. In spite of the lack
of prolonged or widespread slave rebelliousness, both Chesapeake and
Lowcountry slave societies experienced periods of sheer panic when an insurrection seemed imminent. At the prospect of collective slave violence,
eighteenth-century public opinion oscillated between protracted stretches of
near-complacency and brief spasms of near-paranoia.[18]

An incident that occurred in Virginia at the end of the eighteenth century
neatly captures this divided state of mind. Passing the door of a magistrate
in Madison, Virginia, Charles Janson, a stranger, heard the justice's raised
voice "and the strokes of the cow-skin" being applied to one of the slaves of

---

[17] Thomas Jefferson, *Notes on the State of Virginia*, ed. William Peden (Chapel Hill, N.C., 1954),
138; Elizabeth Fox-Genovese, *Within the Plantation Household: Black and White Women of the Old
South* (Chapel Hill, N.C., 1988), 27.
[18] Peter H. Wood, *Black Majority: Negroes in Colonial South Carolina from 1670 through the Stono Rebellion* (New York, 1974), chap. 12; John K. Thornton, "African Dimensions of the Stono Rebellion," *AHR*, XCVI (1991), 1101–1113.

the justice of the peace. At every blow, the magistrate "urged the obstinate creature to confess to something which he appeared anxious to discover." Eventually the justice extracted the information he feared: "The negroes were planning an insurrection." As the neighboring whites assembled in a state of armed readiness, their "fears were wrought up to a high degree of alarm." Their anxieties were understandable, Janson observed, for "we counted our ranks at twelve or fifteen" whereas the slaves "could form a phalanx of as many hundreds within the circle of a few miles."

Six whites paid a visit to a quarter some two miles away, where the leaders of the insurrection were supposedly to be found. As his companions entered the loghouse, Janson stood guard outside and saw a slave appear on the roof and jump to safety. Within the quarter were an old couple and their daughter. The man who made his escape was the girl's lover. These were hardly the leaders of a conspiracy. Returning empty-handed, Janson found that other raiding parties had been more successful. After a "strict examination" of various captured slaves, however, Janson concluded, "Nothing appeared to confirm our suspicions." When asked why they had been out so late, some slaves replied that they had been out hunting raccoons and opossums; others had been visiting their friends and relations. Janson "really believed" their stories. The magistrate did not, because "he had never known an instance of so many being out of their quarters at such a time." Janson responded that it was between two and three o'clock in the morning and, perhaps, no search of this nature had ever been conducted before. But the magistrate prevailed, and the slaves were severely flogged.

Four or five nights later, Janson was at the house of a friend, Mr. Gilpin, a newcomer to the area, when they "were greatly alarmed by an uncouth Singing of the negroes about a mile distant." They listened attentively "and fancied the noise drew near." While the host's family slept, "in great consternation we sallied out, myself with my loaded gun and Mr Gilpin with his mounted bayonet. We first ascended a rising ground to determine with more precision from what quarter the alarm proceeded. Convinced that our surmises were just, apprehending an attack, and conceiving that it was the negro war-song," the two headed for the local tavern to raise an alarm. The party playing cards were "greatly surprised" at seeing the armed men. And when they heard the reason, "they burst into a laugh, informing us that it was only a harvest-home of the negroes, in one of the quarters." The two would-be heroes "now felt ashamed," although their neighbors "greatly commended [their] activity," for which they became more respected in the community.

This sequence of events provides a revealing glimpse into the swirling, conflicting maelstrom that engulfed so many slaveholding communities when a slave insurrection seemed imminent. At one moment, local residents believed the worst. Only an outsider, it seems, thought otherwise. However unjustified, the floggings served their purpose. Not only were blacks given a sharp lesson, but whites reaffirmed their solidarity. After all, the whippings were "executed by the white men, in turns." A few days later, the outsider again found himself out of step with community opinion. With the recent incident fresh in his mind, he was only too susceptible to new fears. This time, the locals were skeptical. They scoffed at his alarm. The outsider had not yet adjusted to the rhythms of the slaveholding community: first, a short burst of intense suspicion, more than likely out of proportion to the real dangers; second, a cathartic show of force; and, finally, a return to normalcy or near-complacency. To the passerby, there seemed no logic to this process; to a slaveowning community, such inconsistencies were second nature.[19]

A similar inconsistency was the hallmark of contemporary observations about the potential rebelliousness of slaves. Eighteenth-century whites knew that their slaves were not truly submissive. And yet they could still sound a note of complacency—particularly if they were Virginians. Thus William Byrd, who could be positively apocalyptic about the prospect of a slave rebellion, yet spoke confidently of harboring no fears where slaves were concerned. Byrd and other Virginians pinpointed a major reason for their assurance. In the words of Charles Steuart, black numbers were "not so large as to give any uneasiness, and the country is under so proper regulation that we have no apprehension of an Insurrection." Even after Lord Dunmore had, as Archibald Cary put it, pointed "a dagger to [the whites'] throats, thro' the hands of their slaves," this Virginia patriot could still claim, "We have, however, no apprehension on that score."[20]

For Arthur Lee, this blithe self-confidence would only hasten the day of doom. He explained himself as follows:

> Since time, as it adds strength and experience to the slaves, will sink us into perfect security and indolence, which debillitating our minds, and enervating our bodies, will render us an easy conquest to the feeblest foe. Unarm'd already and undisciplined, with our Militia laws contemned, neglected or perverted, we are like the wretch at the feast; with a drawn sword depending over his head by a Single hair; yet we flatter ourselves, in opposition to the force of reason and conviction of experience, that the danger is not imminent.[21]

But the sword never fell. And the opinions of eighteenth-century whites concerning the dangers presented by their slaves came to alternate between even longer periods of complacency and even shorter bursts of fear.

The uneven performance of Chesapeake patrols is symptomatic of the fluctuating nature of white concern. On his appointment as a patroller in

---

[19] Charles William Janson, *The Stranger in America* (London, 1807), 402–405. See also Bertram Wyatt-Brown, *Southern Honor: Ethics and Behavior in the Old South* (New York, 1982), chap. 15, which judiciously probes insurrectionary scares.

[20] For Byrd's comments, see Chapter 5, n. 25; Charles Steuart to Walter Tullideph, Sept. 23, 1751, microfilm, CW; Archibald Cary to R. H. Lee, Dec. 24, 1775, Lee Family Papers, UVa.

[21] Richard K. MacMaster, ed., "Arthur Lee's 'Address on Slavery': An Aspect of Virginia's Struggle to End the Slave Trade, 1765–1774," *VMHB*, LXXX (1972), 156–157.

Princess Anne County, Virginia, in 1767, Edward James received orders "at least one night in every week to visit all negro Quarters," to break up all "unlawful Assemblys," and to apprehend all slaves who lacked a pass. In spite of these extensive responsibilities, James claimed for only thirteen nights' work in 1767 and but two nights' labor in 1768. Not exactly a rigorous policing system; rather, a highly irregular one. The same general laxness and alternating annual rhythms are evident elsewhere. In 1755, twelve Middlesex County whites patrolled an average of nine nights each; the following year, six patrollers averaged three nights each. In 1757, the Sussex County patrol met just about once a week, but only from the beginning of July to the end of September. On some nights, they "found several Negroes," presumably slaves wandering off their plantations without passes; at other times, they whipped slaves by their owners' "consent." In 1763, the same county patrol met less than once a week, but over a longer period—from April to early November. Each night they traveled on average to about seven slave quarters. This spotty itinerary and half-yearly activity—during late fall, winter, and early spring, patrollers stayed at home—indicates a less than draconian police system.[22]

Most of the time, policing was no more diligent in South Carolina. In 1756, a provincial grand jury confidently reported, "In several parts of the country the people have not been mustered these two years, and few will take trouble to ride patrol in any part of the country." This complaint was only a pointed variation on a persistent refrain: grand juries warned of "the want of a patrol duty being duly done" or an "almost total neglect of patrol duty." Yet, as in the Chesapeake, an extraordinary incident could galvanize a community, as happened at Christmastime in 1765, when some Charleston blacks, in the words of Henry Laurens, "mimick'd their betters in crying out 'Liberty.'" As a result, Laurens reported, patrols rode "day and Night for 10 or 14 days in most bitter weather," although, as it happened, "there was Little or no cause for all that bustle."[23]

Whites were no more consistent in their attitude toward slaves' possession of firearms. Certainly, masters denied guns to most of their slaves, and both Virginia and South Carolina passed laws restricting bondpeople's access to guns. Nevertheless, the Virginia law of 1723 banning guns to slaves made an exception for frontier regions. And the South Carolina law of 1722

---

[22] Order from Edward H. Moseley, *County Lieutenant,* Oct. 4, 1767, and County of Princess Anne to Edward James, 1767 and 1768, Edward Wilson James Papers, UVa; Middlesex County Orders, 1752–1758, 324–325, 383–385, VSL; Freemans and Payne Patrol Accounts, July 7–Sept. 29, 1757, Sussex County Court Papers, 1758, VSL; Patrol Journal, Apr. 30–Nov. 6, 1763, ibid., 1763–1764.
[23] Charleston Grand Jury presentments, *SCG,* May 1, 1756; for succeeding complaints, see Court of General Sessions, Mar. 15, 1758, Apr. 22, 1769, Jan. 21, 1771, Oct. 19, 1773, SCDAH; Provincial Grand Jury presentments, *SCG,* June 2, 1766; *SC and AGG,* Jan. 29, 1768; and *Laurens Papers,* V, 53–54. See also Senate Presentments, Nov. 26, 1799; Liberty County, Ga., 1787, Duke. For more on lax policing in Charleston, see Philip D. Morgan, "Black Life in Eighteenth-Century Charleston," *Perspectives in American History,* N.S., I (1984), 217–221.

permitted a plantation owner to license one slave to carry a gun for the hunting of game and vermin and the slaughtering of cattle. Even this stipulation was unnecessary if a white man accompanied the slave when hunting. In addition, the legislature made an exception where the slave carried his master's arms either to and from muster or to and from a plantation. Moreover, no limit was placed on those slaves' "keeping off rice-birds and other birds in the day time within the plantation," provided the guns were lodged at night in the master's dwelling. Slave watchmen on Lowcountry plantations usually carried guns.[24]

Even more important, slaves had much greater access to guns than statutes allowed. In the Chesapeake, one county court fined several masters for selling weapons to their slaves. Two of Landon Carter's slaves took "Guns loaded with small shot" to catch a runaway, and one of them shot the fugitive in the leg. On another occasion, Carter complained that hogs were jumping over his fences, even though he had "guns out every night after them." Slaves with guns did not always do their master's bidding. One slave faced trial for shooting a horse and cow and wounding a white man; another faced excommunication from his church for shooting his master's dog. Perhaps the best insight into the general distribution of arms among Chesapeake slaves was a discovery made by Eastern Shore residents on the eve of the Revolution. They collected about "eighty Guns, some Bayonets, swords, etc." from their slaves.[25]

It was public policy in early South Carolina to arm slaves. In principle, the colony never abandoned the enlistment of slaves, and, even as late as

[24] William Waller Hening, *The Statutes at Large: Being a Collection of All the Laws of Virginia . . .* , 13 vols. (Richmond, Va., and Philadelphia, 1809–1823), III, 459, IV, 131, XII, 182; Thomas Cooper and David J. McCord, eds., *The Statutes at Large of South Carolina*, VII (Columbia, S.C., 1837), 345, 353–354, 372–373, 422. In North Carolina, licensing was the law. Thus, a planter petitioned his county court "to grant him Liberty for his Negro slave by name Derry to Carry a gun on his own Plantation" (application of James Hathaway, Mar. 13, 1804, Chowan County Slave Papers, NCDAH).

[25] Lancaster County Court Order Book, no. 7, 1721–1729, 140, cited in Robert Anthony Wheeler, "Lancaster County, Virginia, 1650–1750: The Evolution of the Southern Tidewater Community" (Ph.D. diss., Brown University, 1972), 143; Greene, ed., *Carter Diary*, 289, 613; Granville County Court, Oct. 4, 1776, Treasurer's and Comptroller's Records, Miscellaneous Group, box 8, NCDAH; Court of Oyer and Terminer, Apr. 23, 1784, Executive Papers, box 34, VSL; minutes of Black Water Baptist Church, Southampton County, June 21, 1793, photostat, VSL; Committee of Inspection for Dorchester County, Maryland, May 23, 1775, Gilmor Papers, IV, 14, MHS. Only about 1% of runaway slaves in either Virginia or South Carolina had weapons. Between 1736 and 1790, 16 advertisements for Virginia fugitives mention that they carried weapons (15 guns, 1 sword). One group of six slaves was "armed with Guns"; another group of twelve stole "some guns"; Peter took along a gun of "uncommon large size," George a brace of pocket pistols, and Prince a brass-barreled holster pistol: Robert King et al., *VaG* (Hunter), May 24, 1751 (group of six); John Payne, *Maryland Journal, and the Baltimore Advertiser*, June 27, 1780 (group of 12); William Gregory, *VaG* (P and D), May 4, 1769 (Peter); Hamilton Ballantine, ibid. (D and N), May 22, 1779 (George); James Marsden, ibid. (Purdie), Aug. 21, 1778 (Prince).

1747, the assembly passed a law to draft slaves during emergencies, but, in practice, slaves were never mobilized after 1715. Yet the private arming of slaves continued well past this date. In Charleston, numbers of slaves were often seen carrying firearms. In 1754, at one muster, slaves carried home their masters' firearms, "which they charged and discharged several times as they went along the streets to the great Terror of many Ladies." Thirteen years later, the city grand jury complained that masters let their slaves keep their guns "during divine service." In 1772, the same body observed more generally that "Negroes were being allowed to . . . carry Fire-Arms." On the frontier, the private enlistment of slaves was still necessary. In 1788, Edward Rutledge noted that Indians had raided various outlying Georgia planta-tions and that the farmers had in turn "armed their Negroes."[26]

The chief reason for whites' complacency toward potential slave vio-lence, the ineffectiveness of patrols and watches, and the use of firearms by slaves was the overwhelming coercive powers available to individual mas-ters and the white community in general. In an emergency, masters could de-pend on a large adult white male population to come to their rescue. White supremacy was a more effective authority than any patroller or watchman could ever be. The best witnesses to the formidable array of masters' powers were the slaves themselves. The few extant narratives of eighteenth-century slaves speak eloquently of the barbarities they suffered.

James Carter, born a slave in Virginia, began the "Small Jernal" of his life by recounting the tragedy that befell his brother Henry. Raised in the "Fam-ily of Mrs. Lucy Armistead of Caroline County," Henry Carter reached age twenty-two before being sold to George Buckner. So cruel was Buckner's reputation that Henry immediately ran off. Discovered crossing a river, Henry was stoned to death by an overseer. James recorded in touching detail

[26] Wood, *Black Majority*, 124–130; Cooper and McCord, eds., *Statutes at Large*, IX, 645–663. In 1743, the South Carolina Council debated a plan for the defense of the province in the case of invasion, in which blacks were to be armed and enlisted in companies that were always two-thirds white (South Carolina Council Journal, no. 10, Apr. 14, 1743, 158); 12 years later, the same body thought it might be a good idea, in case of Indian attacks, to arm "the most Trusty of our Slaves" (ibid., Mar. 7, 1755); Parish Transcripts, box 3, NYHS; *SCG*, Oct. 17, 1754; presentments of the Grand Jury of Charlestown, *SCG and CJ*, Nov. 17, 1767, and *SCG*, Jan. 25, 1772; William L. McDowell, Jr., ed., *Documents Relating to Indian Affairs, May 21, 1750–August 7, 1754*, Colonial Records of South Carolina, 2d Ser. (Columbia, S.C., 1958), 370 (my thanks to James Merrell); Ed-ward Rutledge, Jr., to John Rutledge, Apr. 8, 1788, Rutledge Papers, UNC. Between 1732 and 1782, 26 advertisements for South Carolina fugitives mention that they carried guns (also in three cases a cutlass and in another a Dutch knife). Tim, an "Angolan," was captured with a gun; London, another African, carried a gun, a shot pouch, and some powder and shot; and a group of four took three guns and a cutlass. Sometimes the descriptions of the weapons were highly specific: Nero, a "Coromantee," had "a holster pistol of Wilford's make," and Bob had "one of Wilson's fowling-pieces." Workhouse, *SCG*, Sept. 13, 1742 (Tim); Arthur Bull, ibid., July 24, 1755 (London); John Forbes, ibid., Aug. 20, 1763 (group of four); John Mouret, *SC and AGG*, June 5, 1777 (Nero); John Brailsford, ibid., Dec. 3, 1779.

how his family scoured the riverbanks until they found his brother's body, which they brought home for a family burial.[27]

David George, born in Surry County, Virginia, about 1740, began the account of his life by recalling the cruelties visited on his family:

> My oldest sister was called Patty: I have seen her several times so whipped that her back has been all corruption, as though it would rot. My brother Dick ran away, but they caught him, and brought him home; and as they were going to tie him up, he broke away again; then they hung him to a cherry-tree in the yard, by his two hands, quite naked, except his breeches, with his feet about half a yard from the ground. They tied his legs close together, and put a pole between them, at one end of which one of the owner's sons sat, to keep him down, and another son at the other. After he had received 500 lashes, or more, they washed his back with salt water, and whipped it in, as well as rubbed it in with a rag; and then directly sent him to work in pulling off the suckers of tobacco. I also have been whipped many a time on my naked skin, and sometimes till the blood has run down over my waist band; but the greatest grief I then had was to see them whip my mother, and to hear her, on her knees, begging for mercy.[28]

The punishments were harsh enough, but the humiliation was even worse.

Boston King was rather more fortunate than either Carter or George. Both his parents held responsible posts on Richard Waring's South Carolina plantation. His father was a driver much "beloved by his master," his mother a nurse and seamstress. King's hardships began when he was apprenticed to a tradesman in Charleston. He assumed charge of the artisan's tools, and, whenever they were lost or misplaced, his master "beat [him] severely, striking [him] upon the head, or any other Part without mercy." When the workshop was burglarized, the master blamed King, whom he flogged "in a most unmerciful manner," so that he was unable to work for a fortnight. On another occasion, the craftsman "tortured" King "most cruelly," and he missed work for three weeks. Only when his owner intervened did King's treatment improve.[29]

If life in Charleston could be cruel, a Lowcountry plantation could be a living hell. Warwick Francis's reminiscences of the barbarities suffered by slaves in the South Carolina countryside are gruesome in the extreme. He first recounted how Dr. Aron Jelot tied a slave boy

---

[27] Linda Stanley, ed., "James Carter's Account of His Sufferings in Slavery," *Pennsylvania Magazine of History and Biography*, CV (1981), 335–339.

[28] "An Account of the Life of Mr. David George, from Sierra Leone in Africa . . . ," *Baptist Annual Register*, I (1790–1793), 473. George gave his birthplace as Essex, but this was probably a transcription error, because the other details he mentioned suggest that he was born in the part of Surry that later became Sussex County: Grant Gordon, *From Slavery to Freedom: The Life of David George, Pioneer Black Baptist Minister* (Hantsport, Canada, 1992), 7–11.

[29] "Memoirs of the Life of Boston King, a Black Preacher," *Methodist Magazine*, XXI (1798), 105–107.

on a wooden spit so near the fire that it Scorch him well and basted with Salt
and Water the same as you would a pigg. I have seen this same Aron Jelot
took a pinchers and clap it to a mans tooth the Soundest in his head about
one hour and a half and then draw it out the two persons was his own
Slaves. I have seen the same A Jelot shoot a man Down the same as You
would a Buck. This was about Nine or ten o'clock at night. I have also seen
Joseph Belseford in the same County chain two of his slaves and make them
Walk on a plank at a mill pond and those 2 got drownd and the said Joseph
Belseford gave a man 360 lashes and then wash them down with Salt and
Water and after that took brand that he branded his Cattel with and make
the Brand red hot and put it on his buttocks the same as you would brand
a creater.

I have seen John Crimshire oversear on Barnet Elicot [or Elliot] estate a
man whose name is Tom had 300 Lashes and put on the pickit with his Left
Hand tied to his left toe behind him and his Right hand to post and his Right
foot on the pickets till it worked through his foot. John Draten I have Seen
him take his Slave and put them in a tierce and nailed spikes in the tierce
and Roale down a Steep hill.

The crueltity and punishment of the Slave which I have seen would not
permit me to make mention but for Lashes 300 or 400 a[nd] to be Washed
Down with Salt and Water is but Slite punishment[.] Many poor Women
which I have Seen likely to be Deliver the child and oblige to wear a mouth
peace and Lock out the Back part of it the keys the Driver keeps and are
obliged to Worke all Day and at Night Put in Clos Houses.

I have Seen them with a thim Screw Screwed till the Blood gushed out
of their Nails. This I have Seen at Isaac Macpersons . . . this is what I have
said I am an Eye Witness to it it is not what I have heard. Time will not permit me to go further.

A number of the planters Francis mentioned lived in the Stono region of
South Carolina, lending his account a ring of authenticity.[30]

The physical appearance of many runaway slaves also points to widespread cruelties practiced on individual plantations. About two hundred
slave fugitives advertised in colonial South Carolina newspapers were
branded, usually with the master's initials but occasionally with his sur-
name. Masters applied brands most commonly to the breast or shoulder, but
slaves were also branded on the forehead, cheek, and buttocks. About another hundred runaways went off with iron clogs (weighing, in some instances, about eight to twelve pounds) or spurs on their legs, iron collars or
pot hooks (often with three or more protruding prongs) around their necks,
their arms pinioned together, their hands cuffed, or their head in an iron con-
traption. Finally, another seventy-five bore the marks of a whipping, had

[30] Testimony of Warwick Francis, 1812, Paul Cuffee Collection, New Bedford Public Library,
Mass. (reprinted in Ellen Gibson Wilson, *The Loyal Blacks* [New York, 1976], 23–24). Francis lived
in the Horse-Savannah/Stono area of Colleton County, where Barnard Elliott, John Drayton,
and Isaac McPherson all resided.

some toes removed, had cropped ears, or had been castrated. In all, at least one in seventeen of the fugitives advertised in colonial South Carolina newspapers exhibited the physical scars of oppression. A similar proportion of Virginia runaways displayed maltreatment. But whippings accounted for about half of the physical scars and brandings for another third. Rare were the Virginia runaways who had irons fastened to their legs or an iron collar attached to their neck. No Virginia runaway slave was described as suffering castration, although a few had lost toes or had had their ears cropped.[31]

Slaves suffered so much personal violence at the hands of masters that they might be expected to have reciprocated. Yet, just like large-scale insurrections, prosecutions of slaves for crimes of violence, ranging from assault to murder, were infrequent. A study of slave trials in Richmond County, Virginia, from 1721 to 1776 reveals that only 4 of 55 cases involved murder and attempted murder and in just 2 cases were the victims white. My analysis of slave trials in eight Virginia counties from 1710 to 1785 indicates that acts of violence by slaves against whites numbered only 47 of a total of 449 prosecutions. The most comprehensive study of eighteenth-century slave crime—Philip Schwarz's investigation of all Virginia county court cases involving slaves—concludes that "less than one-tenth of 1 percent" of Virginia's slave population in the mid-eighteenth century "resorted to killing white people." More whites than blacks were found guilty of murdering white people. Acts of violence by slaves that ended up in court were rare, crimes against property far outnumbered crimes against persons, and most slave crime was committed individually rather than collectively. All of this might seem to support the contention that masters had little to fear from their slaves.[32]

Some contemporaries said as much. St. George Tucker asserted that the murder of a master or mistress was a highly unusual event in eighteenth-century Virginia. Such crimes occurred so seldom that he was "inclined to

---

[31] Among South Carolina runaways, I count 188 brandings, 70 leg irons, 14 chains, padlocks, spurs, or collars, 2 arms pinioned, 1 handcuffs, 1 headpiece, 61 whip marks, 3 toes removed, 3 castrations, 1 broken arm, and 1 gunshot wound. In all, this number represents just over 6% of all colonial South Carolina's advertised fugitives. Among Virginia fugitives, I count 40 whippings, 26 brandings, 10 leg irons or iron collars, 2 toes removed, and 5 ears cropped, representing about 7% of Virginia's advertised runaways. Presumably, not all masters mentioned the physical scars of their slave runaways. Yet, the fugitive population probably included a disproportionately large number of slaves who had experienced physical punishment. It is difficult, therefore, to know how representative this group is of the larger population.

[32] Gwenda Morgan, "The Hegemony of the Law: Richmond County, 1692–1776" (Ph.D. diss., The Johns Hopkins University, 1980), 145–146. My sample is based on a study of York, Essex, Middlesex, Richmond, Caroline, Chesterfield, Charles City, Louisa, and Elizabeth City County court orders; Philip J. Schwarz, *Twice Condemned: Slaves and the Criminal Laws of Virginia, 1705–1865* (Baton Rouge, La., 1988), 144–145. See also Rutman and Rutman, *A Place in Time*, 486; Arthur P. Scott, *Criminal Law in Colonial Virginia* (Chicago, 1930), 321; Gerald W. Mullin, *Flight and Rebellion: Slave Resistance in Eighteenth-Century Virginia* (New York, 1972), 61–62; Thad W. Tate, *The Negro in Eighteenth-Century Williamsburg* (Charlottesville, Va., 1972), 99–102.

believe as many cases happen in England of masters or mistresses murdered by their servants, as in Virginia." The duc de La Rochefoucauld-Liancourt, who visited South Carolina in 1796, reported, "Lawyers and judges have informed me that the white inhabitants commit more criminal offences, in proportion to their numbers, than the negroes." Although he acknowledged that "some masters may perhaps, from avaricious motives, shelter their slaves from punishment," he judged: "This can only take place in regard to crimes perpetuated in the midst of plantations. Few people assaulted, robbed or injured by the negroes would refrain from prosecuting them, merely to save their masters."[33]

Reassuring though such reflections and statistics might prove, a murder did not, as Eugene Genovese has pointed out, "have to occur often: one nearby, perhaps no closer than a neighboring county and perhaps only once in a decade to make a deep impression on masters as well as slaves." The unpredictability of such occurrences was particularly disturbing. A "most shocking murder" committed in Orangeburg, South Carolina, by a slave belonging to John Meyer was found sufficiently newsworthy to be publicized in the *London Gazette*. Apparently, the slave murdered Mrs. Meyer, the Meyers' daughter of sixteen years, and a suckling infant. He then dressed himself in his master's best clothes and set fire to the house. John Meyer, who was away in Charleston at the time, could think of no reason for his slave's behavior. Virginians must have pondered the same question when they learned that the sole slave belonging to Benjamin Hyde suddenly turned on his master, killing him and his whole family. Or they might have paused over a notice in the *Virginia Gazette* of 1778 reporting that eight Elizabeth County slaves strangled their master in bed and were "two hours about it." No one was safe. In 1780, the minister of Wappetaw congregation in South Carolina was murdered by one of the parsonage slaves.[34]

To travel any distance in the Anglo-American plantation colonies was to have one's complacency shaken, even if momentarily. In 1765, a Frenchman arrived in Williamsburg to be greeted by the spectacle of three slaves hanging from the gallows. In 1771, when Oliver Hart passed through Amherst County, Virginia, the local news was of a horrid murder committed some years earlier. A slave had killed four people outright and wounded another two. Hart even saw "some of the Blood still remaining on one of the Doors." Three years later, near Piscataway, Maryland, Nicholas Cresswell saw one-quarter of a slave

[33] St. George Tucker to Belknap, June 29, 1795, Massachusetts Historical Society, *Collections*, 5th Ser., III (1877), 409; La Rochefoucault Liancourt, *Travels*, I, 566.
[34] Genovese, *Roll, Jordan, Roll*, 616–617; *London Gazette*, May 10, 1763, in Belfast Newspaper file, USC; Albemarle Parish Register, Sussex County, Virginia, Jan. 14, 1754, in *WMQ*, 1st Ser., XIV (1905–1906), 3; *VaG* (P and D), Nov. 6, 1778; Josiah Smith to Rev. J. J. Zubly, Aug. 22, 1780, Smith Letterbook. See also Schwarz, *Twice Condemned*, 137–164; and Marion Dargan, "Crime and the Virginia Gazette, 1736–1775," *University of New Mexico Bulletin*, Sociological Series, II, no. 1 (May 31, 1934), 3–61, esp. 13–15.

body chained to a tree. The man had murdered his overseer. In 1781, at the Guilford County court house in North Carolina, William Feltman saw a slave head stuck on a sapling on one side of the road, and the man's right-hand side on a sapling on the opposite side. Talking with the residents could be even more alarming. A traveler in Virginia in 1800 met a gentleman who assured him "that more than 500 Masters and overseers had been murdered by the negroes within the limits of his knowledge and memory." It is impossible to reconcile this hearsay observation with the recorded prosecutions of murders committed by slaves and other contemporary observations. It was undoubtedly an exaggeration, but it is evidence of at least one white person's perceptions.[35]

A white person probably had more reason to fear for personal safety in South Carolina than in Virginia. Between 1735 and 1755, when Virginia's slave population was at least twice as large as South Carolina's, the number of compensations for executed slaves was half as large. Between 1786 and 1815, compensations for executed slaves in South Carolina were a little more than half of those in Virginia, but the disproportion in the size of the two black populations was widening rather than diminishing. A dominating black majority, more isolated plantations, and less acculturated slaves all contributed to a more threatening environment in the Lowcountry than in the Chesapeake.[36]

The knife-edge that Lowcountry planters trod between economic gain and personal safety is captured well in the comments of an East Florida planter who was rapidly building up his estate in the 1760s. "I am sensible the progress ought to be gradual," he reflected judiciously, "that there should (with a view to safety) be an addition of strength of whites, before I can venture to increase the number of Negros." At the same time, the imperative to buy more slaves was almost impossible to resist, because "the life of the settlement and the profits arising from it must depend upon the Negro." The situation of William Bartram, who also established a plantation

---

[35] "Journal of a French Traveller in the Colonies, 1765," part 1, *AHR*, XXVI (1920–1921), 745; Oliver Hart diary, Dec. 1, 1769 (see also Jan. 16, 1770), Oliver Hart Papers, USC; Nicholas Cresswell, *The Journal of Nicholas Cresswell, 1774–1777* (New York, 1924), 20; William Feltman, *The Journal of Lieut. William Feltman . . .* (Philadelphia, 1853), 30; Miscellaneous MSS, HSP, June 10, 1800, II, 7, microfilm, CW.

[36] Compare John Donald Duncan, "Servitude and Slavery in Colonial South Carolina, 1670–1776" (Ph.D. diss., Emory University, 1972), 708–710, with Timothy Everett Morgan, "Turmoil in an Orderly Society: Colonial Virginia, 1607–1754: A History and Analysis" (Ph.D. diss., College of William and Mary, 1976), 290. For the early national years, compare Larry Darnell Watson, "The Quest for Order: Enforcing Slave Codes in Revolutionary South Carolina, 1760–1800" (Ph.D. diss., University of South Carolina, 1980), 99, and Philip D. Morgan, "Black Society in the Lowcountry, 1760–1810," in Ira Berlin and Ronald Hoffman, eds., *Slavery and Freedom in the Age of the American Revolution* (Charlottesville, Va., 1983), 117, with Schwarz, *Twice Condemned*, 56. Schwarz's early national Virginia figure is for all executions, whereas the corresponding figure for South Carolina is just for compensations for executions. The South Carolina figures, therefore, are artificially low.

in East Florida in the 1760s, was a vivid reminder of these dangers. According to Henry Laurens, who visited Bartram, here was "a gentle mild Young Man, no Wife, no Friend, no Companion, no Neighbor, no Human inhabitant within nine miles of him," except for his slaves, and one of them threatened his life.[37]

The precariousness of life in the Lowcountry is suggested in some particularly gruesome and graphic incidents. One South Carolina master described how his "stout young Negroe man" armed himself with a "Scymeter," broke into his house, threatened to get a gun, and defied anyone to take him alive. The master managed to shoot the slave, but he could be forgiven for being uneasy thereafter. Beaufort residents were no doubt reassured when a slave was gibbeted for the murder of Charles Perry. Before his execution, however, the slave "disclosed a scene equally shocking," one in which he and eight other blacks had planned to murder two other of the town's "Gentlemen" and make off with a schooner to Saint Augustine. A notice in the *South-Carolina Gazette* asked the owner to retrieve his gun and shot pouch taken from a slave, who "was gibeted last spring for murdering people near the Congarees." No wonder a Lowcountry resident might say, "Instances of Negroes murdering, scorching, and burning their own masters or overseers are not rare."[38]

The response of whites to the prospect of slave violence has been aptly likened to listening to static on an old radio. The background noise was always present; it would never quite go away. Similarly, whites were never free from anxiety, never entirely convinced of their slaves' intentions. Fear always lurked beneath the surface of these brittle societies. And yet Anglo-American planters could also go for long periods without paying the noise much attention. The listener could even get accustomed to the static, essentially not notice its presence. Whites congratulated themselves on the control they exercised over their slaves, were generally lax about patrolling, and often appeared recklessly complacent. Yet, if the static became louder or if the listener got a headache, the noise could become overwhelming and drown out all other sounds. Indeed, the hearer might become obsessive about it. In the same way, once whites fixated on the prospect of slave violence, they became prey to all sorts of imaginary fears. Perhaps this helps explain why insurrectionary scares came in clusters.[39]

[37] Richard Oswald to James Grant, Mar. 15, 1767, bundle 295, Papers of Governor James Grant of Ballindalloch, sometime Governor of East Florida, in ownership of Sir Evan Macpherson-Grant, Bart., Ballindalloch Castle Muniments, Scotland; Francis D. West, "John Bartram and Slavery," *SCHM*, LVI (1955), 116; *Laurens Papers*, V, 153–154.

[38] South Carolina Commons House Journal, Dec. 18, 1766; *SCG*, Aug. 29, 1754; Peter Taylor, ibid., Sept. 1, 1759; "Johann Martin Bolzius Answers a Questionnaire on Carolina and Georgia," trans. and ed. Klaus G. Loewald et al., *WMQ*, 3d Ser., XIV (1957), 234.

[39] Robert M. Weir, *Colonial South Carolina: A History* (Millwood, N.Y., 1983), 202. Insurrectionary scares clustered in the 1740s and 1790s. See Winthrop D. Jordan, *White over Black: American Attitudes toward the Negro, 1550–1812* (Chapel Hill, N.C., 1968), 110–122, 391–399.

SEX

Wherever whites and blacks congregated, sexual liaisons resulted. Even mundane, daily encounters had a sexual dimension. Slaves, after all, in contrast to whites, often wore little or no clothing. Admittedly, their seminudity might well have impressed a passing visitor more than their masters, who no doubt accustomed themselves to such things; but it is doubtful whether the shock registered by travelers could be ignored entirely. William Feltman, for instance, was surprised that the feelings of Virginia women were not hurt when they were attended by virtually naked "young boys of about Fourteen and Fifteen years Old." Feltman added, "I can Assure you It would Surprize a person to see these d——d black boys how well they are hung." In an imaginary dialogue with a Virginia mistress, Benjamin Henry Latrobe expressed similar sentiments. "What do you think, Madam," inquired the visitor, "of the naked little boys and girls running about every plantation. What do you think of the Girls and Women, waiting upon your daughters in presence of Gentlemen with their bosoms uncovered. What think you of the known promiscuous intercourse of your servants, the perpetual pregnancies of your young servant girls, shamefully exhibited to your children, who well know, that marriage exists not among them?" The mistress of the plantation quickly dismissed the questions. "Oh but who minds the blacks," she argued. "Our Girls never think of these things."[40] To shrug off pertinent questions so hastily may suggest unease. One wonders, for example, Did white men "never think of these things"? Moreover, the conversation ignored the most obvious demonstration of the relevance of these questions—the presence of mulattoes.

The proportion of mulattoes in the black population provides a clue, albeit a rough one, to the incidence of interracial sex. Unfortunately, reliable statistics on the mulatto population are unavailable for the eighteenth century. The only listing that differentiates between "Negroes" and "Mulattoes" is the Maryland census of 1755. Apparently, 8 percent of Maryland's slaves were of mixed racial origin in that year. Great significance cannot be attached to this figure, for British colonists were notoriously indiscriminate about degrees of racial intermixture. They were inclined to lump slaves of mixed racial ancestry with other blacks. One colonial planter even described his slave as a "Mulatto or Negro man." For what they are worth, contemporary perceptions suggest quite large mulatto populations. An observer of mid-eighteenth-century Virginia reckoned that "the country swarms with mulatto bastards"; Johann Bolzius thought it all too common in midcentury South Carolina for "white men [to] live in sin with Negresses" so that mulatto children abounded "in large numbers"; and a generation later Ebenezer

---

[40] Military Journal of Lt. William Feltman, June 22, 1781, HSP, as cited by Jordan, *White over Black*, 159; Edward C. Carter II et al., eds., *The Virginia Journals of Benjamin Henry Latrobe, 1795–1798*, I (New Haven, Conn., 1977), 225.

Hazard judged that "the number of Mulattoes in the four southernmost states" is clear "proof of a viciated taste in their inhabitants." But, if, as seems likely, there were proportionately more mulattoes in the eighteenth century than later, the difference cannot be measured precisely.[41]

What also seems clear, though equally impervious to precise measurement, is that mulattoes formed a higher proportion of the black population in the Chesapeake than in the Lowcountry. The more evenly matched black and white populations of the Chesapeake provided more opportunities for racial intermixture than the heavily imbalanced black-white ratios of the Lowcountry. The duc de La Rochefoucauld-Liancourt, who visited both regions in the late eighteenth century, had no doubts about the difference. "In Virginia," he noted, "mongrel negroes are found in greater number than in Carolina and Georgia." He attributed this in part to "the superior antiquity of the settlement of Virginia."[42] In fact, however, the proportion of mulattoes among the Chesapeake's black population was probably higher in the earlier as opposed to the later part of the eighteenth century.

Restrictions on interracial sex promulgated in the Chesapeake in the middle to late seventeenth century were not immediately effective. In 1671, Norfolk County court ordered Francis Skiper, a white resident, to pay levies and tithes on his wife, "shee being a negro," but apparently eschewed any other legal harassment. A generation later, a mulatto slave woman petitioned for her freedom on the grounds that she had lived "without disguise" with a white man, had borne a child by him, had had herself and her child baptized, and had been promised marriage by her white lover before his death. Her petition was granted. A number of Virginia whites also petitioned their council to repeal a prohibition on interracial marriage in the late seventeenth century. In early-eighteenth-century Maryland, a white woman persisted in her common law marriage to a slave, despite the penalties, and bore him seven children. In the first decade of the eighteenth century, a Northern Neck planter, Stephen Loyde, openly recorded the birthdates of his two illegitimate children. As he noted in his diary, both were born "of Rachel a negro woman." Late in the century, Robert Carter of Nomini Hall took an

[41] Robert V. Wells, *The Population of the British Colonies in America before 1776: A Survey of Census Data* (Princeton, N.J., 1975), 146, 149; Julien Legge's deed of sale, Apr. 19, 1755, Miscellaneous Records, KK, 163, SCDAH; Peter Fontaine to Moses Fontaine, Mar. 30, 1757, Maury Papers, as cited in Robert E. Brown and B. Katherine Brown, *Virginia, 1705–1786: Democracy or Aristocracy?* (East Lansing, Mich., 1964), 68; "Bolzius Answers a Questionnaire," trans. and ed. Loewald et al., *WMQ*, 3d Ser., XIV (1957), 235; H. Roy Merrens, ed., "A View of Coastal South Carolina in 1778: The Journal of Ebenezer Hazard," *SCHM*, LXXIII (1972), 190. About 1 in 6 of 251 fugitives, who came primarily from the Lowcountry to Spanish Florida in the late 18th century, were listed as mulattoes. Mulattoes are known to have taken flight more readily than the broader population, but perhaps the high proportion also owes something to a precise interest in racial origins among Spanish investigators. See Jane Landers, "Spanish Sanctuary: Fugitives in Florida, 1687–1790," *Florida Historical Quarterly*, LXII (1984), 296–313, esp. 307.
[42] La Rochefoucault Liancourt, *Travels*, II, 82.

interest in the legal status of Thomas Clarke, a mulatto, then detained in servitude. This led Carter to reconstruct the history of the Clarke family in Westmoreland County. It happened that Thomas was the grandson of Sarah Clarke, a white woman who came to Westmoreland as an indentured servant in 1729. She gave birth to "two Mulatto bastard Children during her servitude," both of whom were free by 1775. Thomas was the eldest son of Sarah's daughter.[43]

However, by midcentury, the incidence of interracial sex, particularly between black men and white women, but perhaps also between white men and black women, seems to have declined, as social sanctions against the practice gradually took effect. Thus, sixteen white women were convicted of bearing mulatto bastards in Prince George's County, Maryland, in the 1720s and 1730s; but this number was more than halved in the next two decades. Too much should not be read into individual plantation listings, but the difference between the number of mulattoes among William Fitzhugh's slaves at the turn of the century (8 of 51) and those belonging to Robert "King" Carter a generation later (3 of 734) is striking. In the late-eighteenth-century Chesapeake, a traveler reported that a man's reputation could be ruined by fathering a mulatto child. He "would be scorned, dishonored; every house would be closed to him; he would be detested." Another traveler noted that public opinion was firmly against miscegenation, so much so that "no white man is known to live regularly with a black woman." The intensity of social disapproval against miscegenation contradicts Joel Williamson's assertion that colonial Virginia "supported conditions nearly ideal for the proliferation of a large mulatto population."[44]

Public condemnation was often the fate reserved for those who committed infractions of the new moral code. In this racially charged sexual atmosphere, well in evidence by the early eighteenth century, one white woman accused another of being "a Negro whore and Negros strumpet [who] . . . would have Jumpt over nine hedges to have had a Negroe." In 1767, the

---

[43] Norfolk County Wills and Deeds E (Orders), Aug. 15, 1671, 73, VSL, cited in Kathleen M. Brown, *Good Wives, Nasty Wenches, and Anxious Patriarchs: Gender, Race, and Power in Colonial Virginia* (Chapel Hill, N.C., 1996), 126; Legislative Petitions, Lancaster County, 1697, as cited in Philip Alexander Bruce, *Economic History of Virginia in the Seventeenth Century: An Inquiry into the Material Conditions of the People . . .* , II (New York, 1896), 110; H. R. McIlwaine, ed., *Legislative Journals of the Council of Colonial Virginia*, I (Richmond, Va., 1918), 262; Allan Kulikoff, *Tobacco and Slaves: The Development of Southern Cultures in the Chesapeake, 1680–1800* (Chapel Hill, N.C., 1986), 387; Letterbook of Stephen Loyde, July 3, 1709, Aug. 15, 1710, Tayloe Family Papers, VHS; Robert Carter Daybook, Jan. 18, 1775, XIII, 65–66, Duke.

[44] Kulikoff, *Tobacco and Slaves*, 386–387, 395; Richard Beale Davis, ed., *William Fitzhugh and His Chesapeake World, 1676–1701* (Chapel Hill, N.C., 1963), 378–379, 381–382; inventory of Robert "King" Carter, November 1733, VHS; Ferdinand-M. Bayard, *Travels of a Frenchman in Maryland and Virginia*, ed. and trans. Ben C. McCrary (Williamsburg, Va., 1950), 20; Robert Sutcliffe, *Travels in Some Parts of North America . . .* (New York, 1811), 53; Joel Williamson, *New People: Miscegenation and Mulattoes in the United States* (New York, 1980), 35.

Reverend Patrick Lunan of Nansemond County found himself roundly condemned for drinking, quarreling, fighting, swearing, "exposing his private
parts" to public view, and, last but not least, his solicitation of "Negro and
other women to commit the crimes of fornication and adultery with him."
Two years later, when Mary Skinner bore a black child, her husband, a prominent gentleman of Calvert County, Maryland, proclaimed his disgust at her
"pollut[ing]" his bed. In 1785, the members of the Hartwood Baptist Church
in Stafford County, Virginia, registered their strong displeasure at the behavior of Susan Leftrage. In their eyes, "such an Evil person" had to be excom-
municated and expelled from membership because she had "swerved intirely
from the line of truth and brought public scandal on our holy profession by
commiting fornication by cohabiting with a negro." Ten years later, Captain
James West of Maryland called off his proposed marriage to Peggy Whitaker
when he discovered that Peggy's sister had a mulatto or black husband.[45]

As these incidents suggest, cases of interracial cohabitation or marriage,
though never numerous in the eighteenth-century Chesapeake, recurred. In
spite of a Virginia law that stipulated six months' imprisonment and fine of
ten pounds for any white person entering into an interracial marriage, some
whites went ahead and faced the consequences. In 1738, a Northampton
County white, Tamar Smith, served the prison term and paid the fine so that
she could marry a mulatto man, Edward Hitchens. A half-century later,
when Robert Ayres, a Methodist circuit rider, passed by Old Town, Virginia,
he met a white woman who had married a black slave. In 1764, Bolling Stark
acknowledged the disappearance of his slave man Bob, "decoyed away by a
white woman who, it seems had a child by him, and who disappeared about
the time he runaway." John Custis so favored his mulatto child, Jack, born of
slave woman "young Alice," that he threatened to disinherit his only legitimate son in Jack's favor. Perhaps his respect for community opinion prevailed, for he did not carry out his threat, although he did provide for Jack's
manumission and for his "handsome" maintenance.[46]

[45] *Anne Batson* v. *John Fitchet and wife Mary*, Northampton County Loose Papers, 1731, as cited in
Douglas Deal, "A Constricted World: Free Blacks on Virginia's Eastern Shore, 1680–1750," in
Lois Green Carr, Philip D. Morgan, and Jean B. Russo, eds., *Colonial Chesapeake Society* (Chapel
Hill, N.C., 1988), 279–280; complaint against Rev. Patrick Lunan, Fulham Palace Papers, miscellaneous typescripts, CW; Walter Skinner, *Md Gaz*, Oct. 12, 1769; Hartwood Baptist Church, June
25, 1785, VBHS; William Faris diary, Dec. 31, 1795, MHS, as cited in Daniel Blake Smith, *Inside
the Great House: Planter Family Life in Eighteenth-Century Chesapeake Society* (Ithaca, N.Y., 1980),
132n.
[46] J. Douglas Deal, *Race and Class in Colonial Virginia: Indians, Englishmen, and Africans on the Eastern Shore during the Seventeenth Century* (New York, 1993), 180; journal of Robert Ayres, Apr. 9,
1788, microfilm, Duke; Bolling Stark to George MacMurdo, Dec. 15, 1764, Maxwell, MacMurdo,
and Newhall Family Papers, box 3, National Library of Scotland, Edinburgh; Josephine Zuppan,
"The John Custis Letterbook, 1724 to 1734" (master's thesis, College of William and Mary, 1978),
34–35; Ivor Noel Hume, *All the Best Rubbish* (New York, 1974), 189; Sobel, *The World They Made
Together*, 150–152.

Affectionate interracial unions also occurred among the Wright family in piedmont Virginia. In 1779, Thomas Wright bought a 390-acre plantation in Bedford County. Among his slaves was a "very black" woman, Sylvia, who had already given birth to two children and was pregnant with another. Almost a year after moving to the new plantation, Sylvia bore Thomas Wright's mulatto son Robert. Thomas Wright and Sylvia lived together openly as man and wife, and she gave birth to three more mulatto children between 1784 and 1793. Thomas was said to be "much attached" to Sylvia. He eventually freed her, her children (including those not his), and provided for her after his death. Thomas's attitude toward his children was equally loving. In 1791, Thomas decided to free "his Robin," as he called eleven-year-old Robert, told friends that the boy would be his heir, and gave him a horse to ride to school, where his closest companions were white boys. The proud father even boasted that his son—usually described as a "light" or "bright" mulatto—was one of the "strongest negro fellows" in the county. After Thomas's death in 1805, Robert Wright inherited his father's plantation and six adult slaves, and a year later married a white woman. Robert's marriage was contrary to law but aroused no controversy among his neighbors. Although the marriage did eventually fail, it was happy for the first eight years, with Robert "kind and affectionate" to his wife and she bringing him "great domestic comfort and felicity." Three white male neighbors declared that Robert "allways treated his wife with kindness." As Thomas Buckley puts it, the story of the Wright family suggests "a level of openness in interracial sexual relationships and a degree of white acceptance of miscegenation that challenge historical generalizations and traditional stereotypes."[47]

Of course, there were always masters who preyed on slave women. William Byrd II approached slave and servant women indiscriminately. One night he asked a slave girl to kiss him; another time, he felt the breasts of a black girl; even as a sixty-seven-year-old he could be found "playing the fool with Sally." Virginia masters learned these lessons at a young age. In the spring of 1774, Robert Carter's eighteen-year-old son Ben reportedly took a young maid named Sukey into the stable "and there for a considerable time lock'd" themselves together. Six months later, the Carter household "whispered" with rumors that Ben had broken into the nursery in order to "commit fornication with Sukey (a plump, sleek, likely Negro Girl about sixteen)."[48]

[47] Thomas E. Buckley, S.J., "Unfixing Race: Class, Power, and Identity in an Interracial Family," *VMHB*, CII (1994), 349–380 (quotations on 350, 354, 355, 363).
[48] Louis B. Wright and Marion Tinling, eds., *The Secret Diary of William Byrd of Westover, 1709–1712* (Richmond, Va., 1941), 90, 425; Wright and Tinling, eds., *William Byrd of Virginia: The London Diary (1717–1721), and Other Writings* (New York, 1958), 484; Maude Woodfin, ed., and Marion Tinling, trans., *Another Secret Diary of William Byrd of Westover, 1739–1741: With Letters and Literary Exercises, 1696–1726* (Richmond, Va., 1942), 157, 168; Hunter Dickinson Farish, ed., *Journal and Letters of Philip Vickers Fithian, 1773–1774: A Plantation Tutor of the Old Dominion* (Williamsburg, Va., 1957), 115, 241–243, 246, 248.

The life of Thomas Jefferson offers insight into the twisted web created by sexual relations between generations of blacks and whites. After his third wife died in 1761, John Wayles, Jefferson's father-in-law, allegedly took Elizabeth, or Betty, Hemings, the mulatto child of an English sea captain and an African woman, as his concubine. Apparently, Wayles and Hemings had six children between 1762 and 1773, this last the year of Wayles's death at the age of fifty-eight. Jefferson's refusal to defend himself against the scurrilous attacks concerning his connection to the Hemings family seemingly stems from his reluctance to reveal that they were his own beloved wife's half-brothers and half-sisters. Furthermore, Sally Hemings, the last child born to John Wayles and Betty Hemings in 1773, probably became the mistress of Peter Carr, Jefferson's favorite nephew and surrogate son. It seems likely that their intimacy, begun when both were in their early twenties, lasted at least fifteen years and resulted in five children. Peter Carr's marriage to Hetty Smith, the daughter of a prominent Baltimore family, in the same year that Sally conceived their second child might have fostered jealousy on Sally's part, which later led her to repudiate Carr's paternity of her children. Such, in Douglass Adair's words, were the "circumstances that knotted the lives of the Wayles, the Hemingses, the Carrs, and the Jeffersons into the tangled web of love and hatred, of pride and guilt, of love and shame." And such may well explain Jefferson's explosive condemnation of slavery, especially his description of the "whole commerce between master and slave" as the "perpetual exercise of the most boisterous passions." In spite of Jefferson's oft-stated aversion to miscegenation and regardless of his possible personal involvement, he headed a household and a family in which interracial sex had been and was still commonplace. He lived, as Lucia Stanton notes, "surrounded by its examples."[49]

Precisely because community disapproval of miscegenation was so intense by the second half of the eighteenth century, Virginians tended to respond calmly rather than hysterically to alleged rapes committed by slaves on white women. Before 1740, the eight Virginia slaves tried for rape were all convicted, but, from 1740 to 1785, 30 percent of the fifty-one slaves tried for rape were found not guilty, and another 12 percent were punished only with a whipping. Of the sixty rape sentences (by black men on white women) that came before the Virginia executive in the late eighteenth and early nineteenth centuries, almost half included either recommendations for mercy from the justices or petitions for pardon from the community. In 1803, the justices of King and Queen County, who had sentenced a slave for rape, recommended a pardon on the grounds that the victim "by her own confes-

---

[49] I have relied heavily on the highly judicious and insightful "Jefferson Scandals," in Douglass Adair, *Fame and the Founding Fathers: Essays by Douglass Adair,* ed. Trevor Colbourn (New York, 1974), 160–191; and Lucia Stanton, " 'Those Who Labor for My Happiness': Thomas Jefferson and His Slaves," in Peter S. Onuf, ed., *Jeffersonian Legacies* (Charlottesville, Va., 1993), 147–180, esp. 152, 173–174. I think the case for the paternity of Sally's children is stronger for Peter Carr than for Jefferson, although I realize that definitive proof is lacking.

sion" acknowledged having three mulatto children "begotten by different negro men." Perhaps sexism outweighed racism here, but it does indicate that the alleged sexual aggressiveness of black men did not automatically rule out other considerations—particularly gender and class concerns, for naturally all the alleged victims were women, and most appear to have been lower-class—in late-eighteenth-century Virginia.[50]

Miscegenation was probably even less widespread in the Lowcountry than in the Chesapeake, but more commonly accepted. This seeming paradox is simply explained. South Carolina's black majority made for fewer sexual contacts across racial lines than Virginia's white majority. At the same time, South Carolinians viewed open concubinage quite casually precisely because it presented little danger to fundamental social distinctions. The chasm between white and black opened wide in South Carolina, and the presence of a small mulatto population was unlikely to bridge it. A matter-of-fact acceptance of interracial unions explains why a leading South Carolina planter petitioned to act as the guardian of a mulatto slave child who had been granted "her Freedom and fifteen Negroes" by her white father. It also explains why the white heirs of Benjamin Williamson decided to manumit three mulatto children whom they openly acknowledged to be Williamson's "Issue."[51]

Visitors to the Lowcountry were shocked by the openness with which white men consorted with black women. In 1737, a Swiss settler in South Carolina railed at the "swinishness" of his neighbors, for "if a white man has a child by a black woman, nothing is done to him on account of it." Thirty years later, a New Englander observed that "the enjoyment of a negro or mulatto woman is spoken of as quite a common thing: no reluctance delicacy or shame is made about the matter." Some visitors, however, adapted rapidly to the region's mores. "I assure you," wrote one recently arrived Englishman to his friend at home, that "one is obliged to be exceeding Severe with the Sooty race, from a native Obstinacy and Idleness which pervades them[.] Its true there are exceptions for some deserve every attention that can be paid them." No wonder Francis Bayard believed that the inhabitants of the Carolinas and Georgia were "less scrupulous" about interracial affairs than their Chesapeake counterparts.[52]

[50] Schwarz, *Twice Condemned*, 39, 82, 157, 206; James Hugo Johnston, *Race Relations in Virginia and Miscegenation in the South, 1776–1860* (Amherst, Mass., 1970), 257–260. In an atmosphere somewhat rawer and cruder than Virginia, whites did not always act calmly. Thus, when Phill was convicted of raping a white woman in North Carolina in 1762, he was sentenced not only to be hanged but then to have "his private parts cut off and thrown in his face": Marvin L. Michael Kay and Lorin Lee Cary, *Slavery in North Carolina, 1748–1775* (Chapel Hill, N.C., 1995), 85.

[51] Petition of James Coachman, June 6, 1770, William Bull Papers, Duke; indenture agreed to between the heirs of Benjamin Williamson, June 18, 1774, and subsequent deed of manumission, Nov. 21, 1774, Miscellaneous Records, WW, 77–78. See also deposition of Paul Trapier, Mar. 24, 1784, ibid., VV, 63.

[52] R. W. Kelsey, "Swiss Settlers in South Carolina," *SCHM*, XXIII (1922), 90; Mark Antony De Wolfe Howe, ed., "Journal of Josiah Quincy, Junior, 1773," Mass. Hist. Soc., *Proceedings*, XLIX

This casualness is not to say that there was universal acceptance of inter-racial unions in the eighteenth-century Lowcountry. In 1743, the grand jury of South Carolina emphatically denounced "the too common practice of CRIMI-NAL CONVERSATIONS with Negro and other slave wenches in this Province, as an Enormity and Evil." But these criticisms were often class-related. In 1763, for example, Henry Laurens dismissed an overseer for his "familiarity" with a slave woman in part because it was "wrong and unwarrantable in itself" but, more important, it seems, because it was "extremely offensive to me and very hurtful to my Interest, as it must tend to make a good deal of Jealousy and disquiet among my Negroes." Seven years later, Laurens revealed the ex-tent of his moral scruples when he reemployed an overseer who had previ-ously given in his notice "for no other Cause but my kind and friendly Ad-monition against keeping a Wench in the House in open Adultery." Similarly, a Georgia planter was apparently less upset that his overseer had engaged in sexual relations with his slaves than that during his "four month stay he in-fected every negroe wench on the plantation with a foul, inveterate and highly virulent disease." Another social group that sometimes elicited criti-cism for dalliances with black women was ministers. In 1756, the vestry of Saint Helena Parish accused their clergyman of "indecent familiarities" with Mrs. Cattell's "Negro Wench." A vestryman in Saint Bartholomew Parish op-posed more clerical power because it might lead his rector to "stay at home drinking his Bottle with his negroe woman" instead of officiating at church.[53]

On the whole, however, interracial sex in the Lowcountry was not just countenanced but rather regarded with amusement. Lowcountry residents could afford to be flippant about racial intermixture. Black slaves were in a firmly subordinate position, and the mulatto population was never likely to be sizable. A supporter of the plan by the governor of East Florida to pur-chase slaves pointed out that a "few likely young wenches must be in the parcell, and should their Husbands fail in their duty, I dare say my friend Sweetinham and other publick spirited Young Men, will be ready to render such an essential service to the Province as to give them some help." The public mood of Charleston concerning miscegenation is captured in a num-ber of lighthearted contributions to the local newspaper in the 1730s. Some seventy years later, the mood had changed little, for John Davis met some gentlemen on his travels who were "laughing over their nocturnal adven-tures in Mulatto Alley at Charleston."[54]

(1915–1916), 463; L. Dalton to Mr. Gibbs, 1796, Miscellaneous MSS, LC; Bayard, *Travels of a Frenchman*, 20. See also John S. Ezell, ed., and Judson P. Wood, trans., *The New Democracy in America: Travels of Francisco de Miranda in the United States, 1783–84* (Norman, Okla., 1963), 14.
[53] *SCG*, Mar. 28, 1743; *Laurens Papers*, III, 248, VII, 376, 380; Kenneth Baillie, Sr., *Ga Gaz*, Sept. 26, 1765; A. S. Salley, Jr., *Minutes of the Vestry of St. Helena's Parish, South Carolina, 1726–1812* (Co-lumbia, S.C., 1919), 78–83; Florence Gambrill Geiger, ed., "St. Bartholomew's Parish as Seen by Its Rectors, 1713–1761," *SCHM*, L (1949), 192.
[54] John Graham to James Grant, July 19, 1765, bundle 401, Papers of Governor James Grant of Ballindalloch; Jordan, *White over Black*, 146–150; Wood, *Black Majority*, 234–238; Duncan, "Slav-

The Lowcountry capital undoubtedly saw the most openly displayed interracial liaisons in British North America. As was to be expected of a port, prostitutes (most of whom were probably black) were widely available. A runaway slave man, for example, was said to be "intimate with abundance of black prostitutes" in town, and a slave woman was thought to be harbored in "these houses where sailors frequent." Visitors to Charleston were generally appalled at the level of racial intermixture. Johann Bolzius longed "to get out of this sinful city . . . [where] the Europeans commit dreadful excesses with the Negro girls" with "little or no shame." Henry Muhlenberg found "many slaves who are only half black, the offspring of those white Sodomites who commit fornication with their black slave women." The one visitor who is on record as being surprised by the relative "privacy" with which interracial "conversations" were conducted was from the West Indies, where concubinage was both extensive and even more openly countenanced than in South Carolina.[55]

If Charlestonians generally adopted a relaxed, tolerant view of miscegenation, the privileges that some black women assumed for their favors were far more disturbing. Sexual exploitation of black women produced no unease; the aspirations of these same black women proved profoundly disquieting. Ebenezer Hazard drew precisely this implication from Charleston's "black dances," to which "many of the first gentlemen (so called) attend" and at which many of the black women "dress elegantly, and have no small acquaintance with polite behaviour." During the Revolutionary war, a Charlestonian found no better illustration of the "shame and perfidy [to which] the officers of that once great nation (Britain) has arriv'd" than their attendance at "an Ethiopian Ball," where female slaves "dress'd up in the most pompous manner." In 1795, a public investigation followed a "Negro dance" that the Charleston Guard discovered. Most unsettling was the presence of a white magistrate; indeed, as one of the black women was taken into custody, she handed him "her Head Dress and Bonnet and desired him to take Care of it for her."[56]

The expectations of black women in Charleston extended far beyond the dance floor. More tangible benefits could be realistically entertained from their liaisons with whites. George Dick, a mariner, left all his property to Jenny Dick, a free black who lived with him as his servant, and to Alexander

---

ery and Servitude," 284; John Davis, *Travels of Four Years and a Half in the United States of America* . . . (Bristol, 1803), 355.

[55] James Reid, *SCG*, Nov. 14, 1761; Margaret Peronneau, *SC and AGG*, Oct. 15, 1779; George Fenwick Jones, "John Martin Boltzius' Trip to Charleston, October 1742," *SCHM*, LXXXII (1981), 101; Muhlenberg, *Journals of Muhlenberg*, I, 58; G. Moulton to [?], Jan. 23, 1773, Add. MSS 22677, 75, BL.

[56] Merrens, "A View of Coastal South Carolina in 1778," *SCHM*, LXXIII (1972), 190; Daniel Stevens to John Wendell, Feb. 20, 1782, Mass. Hist. Soc., *Procs.*, XLVIII (1915), 342; depositions of Peter S. Ryan, William Johnson, James Allison, James McBride, and Henry Moses, Nov. 7, 1795, General Assembly, Governor's Messages, no. 650, Nov. 24, 1795, 9–30, SCDAH.

Dick, his natural son. Abraham Newton, a self-styled Charleston "gentle-man," bequeathed his whole estate to Rose Peronneau, a free black woman, because of the "very great Care, Tenderness and Attention" she displayed in tending him through an illness. The mulatto mistress of Captain Davis of Sa-vannah "had the custody of all his Cash, as well as Books." She was instru-mental in having one of Davis's employees, a ship's master, fired. If a slave mother gained nothing for herself, she might yet entertain hopes for her chil-dren. In the early eighteenth century, a mulatto slave woman bore a white butcher a daughter. The slave's mistress, a Mrs. Frost, refused to sell the girl to the butcher, who died in 1740. But his plans for his progeny did not expire with him, though they had to wait twenty-six years, until Frost died, before his executors could purchase his daughter, set her free, and bestow on her £350, the balance of his estate. If her mother was still alive, she might have taken solace from having a daughter who was free.[57]

Black women in the rural Lowcountry occasionally benefited from their intimate relations with whites. In 1749, a planter in Saint Bartholomew Parish bequeathed to his "friend," James Bond, the right to purchase his three enslaved children. Two years later, Bond, styling himself a "planter," bought the Negro woman Peggy and her three children from his friend's es-tate for a thousand pounds. Two years after this purchase, Bond freed his family out of his "love and affection" for them and acknowledged that Peggy had been his wife "for many years past." In 1756, Bond made his will, stipulating that his estate should be divided into four equal parts and en-trusting this task to his wife, Peggy. Another marriage of a slave woman to a white man was recognized in a manumission document. A mulatto slave woman named Elizabeth who belonged to Captain Thomas Broughton was permitted to "intermarry with one Henry Clusteny by whom she had Issue one Daughter," also named Elizabeth. In 1754, the wife gained her freedom because of "her good and faithful services, the request of Elizabeth [and] the desire of her husband."[58]

---

[57] Will of George Dick, Oct. 24, 1773, Charleston County Wills, XV, 1771–1774, 609–610, SCDAH; will of Abraham Newton, Apr. 8, 1790, ibid., XXIII, 1786–1793, 635; William Stephens, *A Journal of the Proceedings in Georgia Beginning October 20, 1737 . . .* , in Allen D. Candler, comp., *The Colonial Records of the State of Georgia,* IV (Atlanta, Ga., 1906), 344–345; Robert Raper to Thomas Boone, Mar. 5, 1770, Robert Raper Letterbook, West Sussex Record Office, England, microfilm, SCHS. See also Elias Ball's deed of sale to William Ellis, July 9, 1746, and William Ellis's deed of manumission to William, Oct. 28, 1746, Miscellaneous Records, GG, 75–76; and Michael Dougherty's deed of manumission to Isaac Dougherty, June 14, 1758, ibid., LL, 53.

[58] Will of John Peter, Jan. 2, 1749, Will Book, NN, 164; Tabitha Peter's sale of Negroes to James Bond, May 2, 1751, Miscellaneous Records, II, 182; James Bond's deed of manumission, Feb. 14, 1753, ibid., 381–382; and will of James Bond, Dec. 4, 1756, Will Book, RR, 518. I find no manu-mission document for a James Bond. I therefore assume that he is white, especially given the wording of John Peter's will (Nathaniel Broughton's deed of manumission, Oct. 19, 1754, Mis-cellaneous Records, KK, 290–291). The only reference to a Henry Clusteny notes that he lives at Mrs. Child's plantation, perhaps as the overseer (Charlestown Gaol, *SCG,* Oct. 12, 1738).

In the Chesapeake, such favors were perhaps less common and certainly less openly acknowledged. An exception was Ryland Randolph, who, in the 1780s, freed his house servant Aggy and her two children on account of his "great affection" for them. He bequeathed them "all his Household furniture of every kind including Gold and Silver," provided for their passage to England, and established a trust fund of three thousand pounds sterling for them. Not even acknowledged members of his family were so generously treated. Far more typical, no doubt, was the fate that befell a slave woman who had five children by an Alexandria merchant. Nicholas Cresswell, who visited the household in 1776, marveled at the man's callousness in seeing "his own flesh and blood in this horrid situation," daily "wanting the common necessaries of life." Johann Schoepf caustically remarked on the "great-mindedness of the Virginians" who failed to "speak of the cases, not rare, of mulattoes out of negresses by gentlemen, who then sell their own children to others as slaves."[59]

Most sexual contacts between whites and blacks, in other words, reflected only physical needs and opportunities in societies where whites possessed a disproportionate share of power. This was nowhere more blatantly expressed than by John Ross, a resident of East Florida, who in 1766 bought a black woman and child for seventy pounds. In justifying his purchase, he reproached his father for suspecting him "of any other connexion with such a wench than that of having got some children by her." After all, he continued in jocular vein, "I am not yet old enough for dotage, although my head and beard are become pretty gray." However, the son then explained that he would like to have the purchase price transferred to his account "not because I would choose, if it were in my power to give either the mother or children their freedome at present—but only because I would wish to have that in my power as soon as possible, for fear of accidents, I mean to myself." In short, Ross's apparent callousness masked at least a measure of responsibility to his New World family. And, in fact, he made good on his promises, for, in 1782, he freed his two daughters, paid for their passage to Scotland, where they were educated at his expense and under the eye of their paternal grandfather.[60] Personal sentiment insinuated even the most heartless relationship.

Miscegenation always gave rise to a tangled web of competing emotions and tensions. Slaves themselves might even take the initiative in forcing this to the attention of whites. In 1775, a mulatto girl accused her master, Mr. Walton, a Baptist of Southside Virginia, of "offering the Act of uncleaness" to her. She "often hinted to [her master's] Daughters that [he] was the Father" of her prospective child. When Walton attempted to correct her for making this

[59] Will of Ryland Randolph, Henrico County Wills, 1781–1787, 179, cited in Gerald Steffens Cowden, "The Randolphs of Turkey Island: A Prosopography of the First Three Generations, 1650–1806" (Ph.D. diss., College of William and Mary, 1977), 462; Cresswell, *Journal*, 165; Schoepf, *Travels in the Confederation*, II, 92–93.
[60] John Ross to his father, March 1776, Leith Ross Muniments, Scottish Record Office, Edinburgh.

allegation, "she faced him in it, and declared she believed he was the father of it, if any one was; tho' she knew not that any person had carnal knowledge of her but supposed it might be done while she was asleep but that she knew of his coming and offering such things at times to her." Even more damning was the testimony she gave "at the time of her extremity in childbearing [when] she was charged by the midwives then to own the truth and clear her Master, if clear, and as her extremity was more than common, they told her it might be a Judgement of God upon her, and that she might die; but all could not prevail upon her she confidently affirmed what she had said she then said." However, when the child was born, it proved to be "a negro without any doubt." Even then, four white members of Walton's church still doubted him, and some weeks passed before they "relinquished" their "difficulties" concerning the case.[61]

If miscegenation was a source of tension in slave societies, too often it resulted in tragedy. Ben, a Virginia slave, was one such victim. In the late eighteenth century, Ben took a neighboring planter's house servant for his wife; like many another slave husband in the Chesapeake, he visited her weekly. Then, for no apparent reason, Ben was barred from seeing his spouse. It soon became common knowledge that her master allowed a neighboring white man to visit her. Some time later, these two whites had a disagreement; and Ben, seeing an opportunity, applied to see his wife again. In return for renewing the old arrangement, the master of Ben's wife encouraged him to harm his white usurper. Ben stole his master's gun and shot his white rival. The pathology of slavery also seems evident in the early-eighteenth-century trial of "old Caesar," charged with the attempted rape and buggery of a four-year-old white girl.[62]

Children suffered from the tensions to which the issue of interracial sex gave rise. In 1754, a thirteen-year-old South Carolina slave boy was convicted of "having carnally and unlawfully known" a ten-year-old white girl. At the trial it was accepted that this encounter had occurred with the girl's consent. However, the court felt that an example had to be set, even of a boy of such tender years. It is debatable whether any serious sexual misdemeanor occurred in this instance. In any event, the master whose property was at stake did not rest his case on this possibility. Rather, he claimed that the girl had already "been Injured by others." He was then challenged to support his "allegation . . . of the Girl's having been deflowered by any other Negro," so that the governor might reduce the punishment of his slave.[63]

The capacity of slavery to poison the relations of otherwise decent men and women was nowhere more evident than in the realm of sex. Some sexual encounters were marked by tenderness, esteem, and a sense of responsibility,

---

[61] Minutes of Meherrin Baptist Church, Lunenburg County, 1775, photostat, VSL.
[62] Executive Papers, *Commonwealth v. Ben*, Jan. 12, 1801, VSL; trial of "old Caesar," Nov. 3–4, 18, 1724, Spotsylvania County Court Order Book, 1724–1730, 29, 36–37, VSL.
[63] South Carolina Council Journal, Apr. 16, 1754. The outcome of this case is unknown.

but most were exploitative and unspeakably cruel—nothing more than rapes by white men of black women—a testament to the ugliness of human relations when people are treated as objects. Similarly, although some whites took a relaxed view of miscegenation, most saw it as potentially explosive, because it threatened to close the gap between the free and the enslaved and produced a group of people whose position was deeply ambiguous. Love and cruelty, affection and callousness, composure and frenzy—such were the contradictory strands in the twisted emotional knot that bound whites and blacks in the sexual arena.

PART V

Mid-Century Crises and Transformations

Gracia Real de Santa Teresa de Mose: A Free Black Town in Spanish Colonial Florida

Jane Landers

INTRODUCTION

If Philip D. Morgan's chapter in this volume represents the mainstream experience of African Americans in the eighteenth century, then this essay by Jane Landers represents the unusual and exceptional. Gracia Real de Santa Theresa de Mose was a fort and village just north of St. Augustine, the capital of Colonial Spanish Florida. Mose was occupied by former slaves who escaped their South Carolina plantations and sought freedom in Spanish Florida. Freedom came at a price: the free blacks had to convert to claim sanctuary, and the Spanish governors expected them to form a militia to protect Florida from the slaveholders to the North, both of which many escapees did with enthusiasm. During the Stono Rebellion, discussed in John Thornton's essay, a group of South Carolina slaves attempted to depart for Mose. What factors kept more slaves from trying?

As seen by archaeologist Kathleen Deagan more than two hundred years after its abandonment, Mose could almost have been inhabited by converted Indians—the artifacts are very similar. Archaeology can be strangely perceptive at times. Many Indian nations found a place in the

Jane Landers, "Gracia Real de Santa Teresa de Mose: A Free Black Town in Spanish Colonial Florida," *American Historical Review,* 95 (1990), pp. 9–30. Copyright © 1990 American Historical Association. Reprinted by permission of American Historical Association and by Jane Landers.

This research was funded by the Spain/Florida Alliance, the Florida Legislature, the Program for Cultural Cooperation between Spain's Ministry of Culture and United States' Universities, and the Department of History of the University of Florida. An earlier version of this article was awarded the President's Prize by the Florida Historical Society. Dr. Kathleen Deagan was the principal investigator for the Ft. Mose Archaeological project of the Florida Museum of Natural History, and Mr. Jack Williams permitted her team to excavate on his property. I would like to thank Jim Amelang, Bertram Wyatt-Brown, Cheryl Cody, David Colburn, Susan Kent, Helen Nader, John J. TePaske, Eldon Turner, and Peter Wood for their comments, criticisms, and encouragement. I am also indebted to my anonymous readers and the *AHR* staff for their suggestions and editing.

colonial world on the edges of empires. They offered military service to one empire or the other and played off imperial rivalries to secure their position. These Indians were free, yet not full citizens of the empires they defended. The inhabitants of Mose inhabited a similar niche and had a similar status. Readers can use the essays by David Weber, Ramón Gutiérrez, and Gregory Dowd in this volume to determine the similarities and differences between the free blacks of Mose and these various Indian groups. What kinds of relationships existed between Africans and Indians in colonial America?

When the English first began to colonize the Americas, they thought of themselves as liberators of Spanish slaves. In the 1570s, Sir Francis Drake offered freedom to a group of runaway African slaves called Cimarrons, and he hoped to fight the Spanish Empire with an army of liberated slaves. By the 1750s, Spain had become the liberator of British slaves, and Spanish governors hoped to fight the British Empire with an army of liberated slaves.

- *What accounts for this ironic reversal of roles?*
- *This reading implies that race relations were more fluid and less rigid in the Spanish Empire. Do you agree?*
- *What accounts for the differences between Spanish and British attitudes toward race, if there are any such differences?*

For too long, historians have paid little attention to Spain's lengthy tenure in the South.[1] As a result, important spatial and temporal components of the American past have been overlooked. Recent historical and archaeological research on the free black town of Gracia Real de Santa Teresa de Mose, located in northeast Spanish Florida, suggests ways in which Spanish colonial records might illuminate these neglected aspects of the Southern past.[2] Because of this black town's unusual origins and political and military significance, Spanish bureaucrats documented its history with much care.

---

[1] An early classic that examined the triracial Southern frontier was Verner W. Crane, *The Southern Frontier, 1670–1732* (New York, 1981), but, as Peter Wood noted in his historiographic review, "'I Did the Best I Could for My Day': The Study of Early Black History during the Second Reconstruction, 1960–1976," *William and Mary Quarterly,* 3d ser., 35 (1978): 185–225, few scholars followed Crane's lead. The difficulty of the sources deterred some from crossing the cultural and linguistic frontier into Florida, but Latin Americanists have also neglected what were the northern boundaries of the Spanish empire. The "Borderlands" school pioneered by Herbert Bolton produced a number of important studies, but these focused primarily on the southwestern areas of the present-day United States. See Herbert E. Bolton, *The Spanish Borderlands, A Chronicle of Old Florida and the Southwest* (Toronto, 1921); and Herbert E. Bolton and Mary Ross, *The Debatable Land* (Berkeley, Calif., 1925). For a review of these borderland studies, see David Weber, "John Francis Bannon and the Historiography of the Spanish Borderlands," *Journal of the Southwest,* 29 (Winter 1987): 331–63.

[2] Scholars who have attempted to explore the African experience in northern America through Spanish sources include John TePaske, "The Fugitive Slave: Intercolonial Rivalry and Spanish

Gracia Real de Santa Teresa de Mose, hereafter referred to as Mose, was born of the initiative and determination of blacks who, at great risk, manipulated the Anglo-Spanish contest for control of the Southeast to their advantage and thereby won their freedom. The settlement was composed of former slaves, many of West African origin, who had escaped from British plantations and received religious sanctuary in Spanish Florida. Although relatively few in number (the community maintained a fairly stable size of about 100 people during the quarter-century between 1738 and 1763, while St. Augustine's population grew from approximately 1,500 people in the 1730s to approximately 3,000 by 1763), these freedmen and women were of great contemporary significance.[3] By their "theft of self," they were a financial loss to their former owners, often a serious one.[4] Moreover, their flight was a political action, sometimes effected through violence, that offered an example to other bondsmen and challenged the precarious political and social order of the British colonies. The runaways were also important to the Spanish colony for the valuable knowledge and skills they brought with them and for the labor and military services they performed.[5] These free blacks are also historiographically significant; an exploration of their lives sheds light on questions long debated by scholars, such as the relative severity of slave systems,

Slave Policy, 1687–1764," in Samuel Proctor, ed., *Eighteenth-Century Florida and Its Borderlands* (Gainesville, Fla., 1975), 1–12; Jack D. L. Holmes, "The Role of Blacks in Spanish Alabama: The Mobile District, 1780–1813," *Alabama Historical Quarterly,* 37 (Spring 1975): 5–18; Gilbert Din, "Cimarrones and the San Malo Band in Spanish Louisiana," *Louisiana History,* 21 (Summer 1980): 237–62; Jack D. Forbes, "Black Pioneers: The Spanish-Speaking Afroamericans of the Southwest," *Phylon,* 27 (1966): 233–46; Peter Stern, "Social Marginality and Acculturation on the Northern Frontier of New Spain" (Ph.D. dissertation, University of California, Berkeley, 1984); and Kimberly Hanger, "Free Blacks in Spanish New Orleans—The Transitional Decade, 1769–1779" (Masters thesis, University of Utah, 1985). Gwendolyn Midlo Hall has a detailed study of Africans in colonial Louisiana forthcoming that is drawn from Spanish as well as French sources.

[3] Theodore G. Corbett, "Migration to a Spanish Imperial Frontier in the Seventeenth and Eighteenth Centuries: St. Augustine," *Hispanic American Historical Review,* 54 (August 1974): 419–20. Corbett noted that St. Augustine, the largest of the borderland settlements, also had the most blacks, slave and free, in the Spanish borderlands. As late as 1763, St. Augustine was larger than any other town in the southern colonies except Charleston. See Theodore G. Corbett, "Population Structure in Hispanic St. Augustine, 1629–1763," *Florida Historical Quarterly,* 54 (July 1975–April 1976): 268.

[4] Peter Wood, *Black Majority; Negroes in Colonial South Carolina from 1670 through the Stono Rebellion* (New York, 1974), 239–68; Philip D. Morgan, "Colonial South Carolina Runaways: Their Significance for Slave Culture," in *Slavery and Abolition,* 6 (December 1985): 57–78; Darrett Rutman and Anita Rutman, *A Place in Time: Middlesex County, Virginia, 1650–1750* (New York, 1984), 180–87.

[5] The role of Africans as cultural agents is discussed in Wood, *Black Majority,* 35–63, 95–130. Also see Daniel Littlefield, *Rice and Slaves, Ethnicity and the Slave Trade in Colonial South Carolina* (Baton Rouge, La., 1981), 98–99. Wood also pointed out that "in literally every conflict in eighteenth-century South Carolina there were Negroes engaged on both sides"; Wood, *Black Majority,* 128–29.

the varieties of slave experiences, slave resistance, the formation of a Creole culture, the nature of black family structures, the impact of Christianity and religious syncretism on African-American societies, and African-American influences in the "New World."[6]

Although a number of historians have alluded to the lure of Spanish Florida for runaway slaves from the British colonies of South Carolina and Georgia, few have examined what became of the fugitives in their new lives or the implications of their presence in the Spanish province.[7] The Spanish policy regarding fugitive slaves in Florida developed in an ad hoc fashion and changed over time to suit the shifting military, economic, and diplomatic interests of the colony as well as the metropolis. Although the Spanish crown preferred to emphasize religious and humane considerations for freeing slaves of the British, the political and military motives were equally, if not more, important. In harboring the runaways and eventually settling them in their own town, Spanish governors were following Caribbean precedents and helping the crown to populate and hold territory threatened by foreign encroacl ment.[8] The ex-slaves were also served by this policy. It offered them a refuge within which they could maintain family ties. In the

[6] Frank Tannenbaum, *Slave and Citizen* (New York, 1946). Tannenbaum's early view that institutional protections benefited slaves in Hispanic areas was challenged by scholars who found economic determinants of slave treatment more significant. See Eugene Genovese, "The Treatment of Slaves in Different Countries: Problems in the Application of the Comparative Method," in Laura Foner and Eugene Genovese, eds., *Slavery in the New World* (Englewood Cliffs, N.J., 1969), 202–10; Marvin Harris, *Patterns of Race in the Americas* (New York, 1964). Historians who have reviewed Spanish racial prejudice and discriminatory regulations include Lyle McAlister, "Social Structure and Social Change in New Spain," *Hispanic American Historical Review,* 43 (April 1963): 349–70; Magnus Mörner, *Race Mixture in the History of the Americas* (Boston, 1967); and Leslie B. Rout, Jr., *The African Experience in Spanish America, 1502 to the Present* (Cambridge, 1976). On the varieties of slave experiences, see Sidney M. Mintz and Richard Price, *An Anthropological Approach to the Afro-American Past: A Caribbean Perspective* (Philadelphia, 1976). On resistance in Latin America, see Richard Price, ed., *Maroon Societies, Rebel Slave Communities in the Americas* (Garden City, N.Y., 1973). On the formation of Creole cultures, see Charles Joyner, *Down by the Riverside, A South Carolina Slave Community* (Urbana, Ill., 1984). On black families, see Ira Berlin, "Time, Space, and the Evolution of Afro-American Society on British Mainland North America," *AHR,* 85 (June 1980): 44–78. On black religion and African cultural retentions in the "New World," see Robert Farris Thompson, *Flash of the Spirit: African and Afro-American Art and Philosophy* (New York, 1984); and Margaret Washington Creel, *"A Peculiar People": Slave Religion and Community-Culture among the Gullahs* (New York, 1988). For an interesting comparison of African and British world views and attitudes, see Mechal Sobel, *The World They Made Together: Black and White Values in Eighteenth-Century Virginia* (Princeton, N.J., 1987).

[7] Irene Wright, "Dispatches of Spanish Officials Bearing on the Free Negro Settlement of Garcia Real de Santa Teresa de Mose," *Journal of Negro History,* 9 (1924): 144–93; TePaske, "Fugitive Slaves"; Luis Arana, "The Mose Site," *El Escribano,* 10 (April 1973): 50–62; Kenneth Wiggins Porter, *The Negro on the American Frontier* (New York, 1971); Jane Landers, "Spanish Sanctuary; Fugitive Slaves in Florida, 1687–1790," *Florida Historical Quarterly,* 62 (September 1984): 296–313; Larry W. Kruger and Robert Hall, "Fort Mose: A Black Fort in Spanish Florida," *The Griot,* 6 (Spring 1987): 39–48.

[8] Lyle N. McAlister, *Spain and Portugal in the New World, 1492–1700* (Minneapolis, Minn., 1984), 133–52.

highly politicized context of Spanish Florida, they struggled to maximize their leverage with the Spanish community and improve the conditions of their freedom. They made creative use of Spanish institutions to support their corporate identity and concomitant privileges.[9] They adapted to Spanish values where it served them to do so and thereby gained autonomy. They also reinforced ties within their original community through intermarriage and use of the Spanish mechanism of godparenthood *(compadrazgo)*. Finally, they formed intricate new kin and friendship networks with slaves, free blacks, Indians, "new" Africans, and whites in nearby St. Augustine that served to stabilize their population and strengthen their connections to that Hispanic community.[10]

That runaways became free in Spanish Florida was not in itself unusual. Frank Tannenbaum's early comparative work shows that freedom had been a possibility for slaves in the Spanish world since the thirteenth century. Spanish law granted slaves a moral and juridical personality, as well as certain rights and protections not found in other slave systems. Among the most important were the right to own property, which in the Caribbean evolved into the right of self-purchase, the right to personal security, prohibitions against separating family members, and access to the courts. Moreover, slaves were incorporated into the Spanish church and received its sacraments, including marriage. Slaves in the Hispanic colonies were subject to codes based on this earlier body of law.[11] Eugene Genovese and others have persuasively argued that the ideals expressed in these slave codes should not be accepted as social realities, and it seems obvious that colonials observed these laws in their own fashion—some in the spirit in which they were written and others not at all.[12] Nevertheless, the acknowledgement of a slave's humanity and rights, and the lenient attitude toward manumission embodied in Spanish law and social practices, made it possible for a significant free black class to exist in the Spanish world.[13]

[9] On corporate privileges of the Spanish militias, see Lyle N. McAlister, *The "Fuero Militar" in New Spain, 1764–1800* (Gainesville, Fla., 1957); Herbert S. Klein, "The Colored Militia of Cuba: 1568–1868," *Caribbean Studies*, 6 (July 1966): 17–27; Allan J. Kuethe, "The Status of the Free Pardo in the Disciplined Militia of New Granada," *Journal of Negro History*, 56 (April 1971): 105–15; Roland C. McConnell, *Negro Troops of Antebellum Louisiana—A History of the Battalion of Free Men of Color* (Baton Rouge, La., 1968).

[10] On the function and meaning of godparents, see George M. Foster, "Cofradia and Compadrazgo in Spain and Spanish America," *Southwestern Journal of Anthropology*, 9 (1953): 1–28; Sidney W. Mintz and Eric Wolf, "An Analysis of Ritual Co-Parenthood (Compadrazgo)," *Southwestern Journal of Anthropology*, 6 (1950): 341–67.

[11] Tannenbaum, *Slave and Citizen*.

[12] Genovese, "Treatment of Slaves"; Mörner, *Race Mixture*; Rout, *African Experience*. For a study of the law in practice, see Norman A. Meiklejohn, "The Observance of Negro Slave Legislation in Colonial Nueva Granada" (Masters thesis, Columbia University, 1968).

[13] Hanger, "Free Blacks"; David W. Cohen and Jack P. Greene, eds., *Neither Slave nor Free, The Freedmen of African Descent in the Slave Societies of the New World* (Baltimore, Md., 1972); Landers,

Although the Spanish legal system permitted freedom, the crown assumed that its beneficiaries would live among the Spaniards, under the supervision of white townspeople *(vecinos)*. While the crown detailed its instructions regarding the physical layout, location, and function of white and Indian towns, it made no formal provisions for free black towns. But Spanish colonizers throughout the Americas were guided by an urban model. They depicted theirs as a civilizing mission and sought to create public order and righteous living by creating towns. Urban living was believed to facilitate religious conversion, but, beyond that, Spaniards attached a special value to living a *vida política,* believing that people of reason distinguished themselves from nomadic "barbarians" by living in stable urban situations.[14] Royal legislation reflected a continuing interest in reforming and settling so-called vagabonds of all races within the empire. The primary focus of reduction efforts was the Indians, but, as the black and mixed populations grew, so too did Spanish concerns about how these elements would be assimilated into "civilized" society. The "two republics" of Spaniards and Indians gave way to a society of castes, which increasingly viewed the unforeseen and unregulated groups with hostility. Spanish bureaucrats attempted to count these people and to limit their physical mobility through increasingly restrictive racial legislation. Officials prohibited blacks from living unsupervised or, worse, among the Indians. Curfews and pass systems developed, as did proposals to force unemployed blacks into fixed labor situations.[15] The crown also recognized with alarm the increased incidence of *cimmaronage,* slaves fleeing Spanish control. Communities of runaway blacks, mulattos, Indians, and their offspring were common to all slaveholding societies, but they challenged the Spanish concept of civilized living, as well as the hierarchical racial and social order the Spaniards were trying to impose. Despite repeated military efforts, the Spaniards were no more successful than other European powers at eradicating such settlements.[16]

"Spanish Sanctuary"; Ira Berlin, *Slaves without Masters—The Free Negro in the Antebellum South* (New York, 1974), 108–32; Lyman L. Johnson, "Manumission in Colonial Buenos Aires," *Hispanic American Historical Review,* 59 (1979): 258–79; Frederick Bowser, "Free Persons of Color in Lima and Mexico City: Manumission and Opportunity, 1580–1650," in Stanley Engerman and Eugene D. Genovese, eds., *Slavery in the Western Hemisphere: Quantitative Studies* (Princeton, N.J., 1974), 331–68.

[14] Richard Morse elegantly analyzed the concept of the *ciudad perfecta* and Spanish efforts to reproduce it in the New World in his chapter, "A Framework for Latin American Urban History" in Jorge Hardoy, ed., *Urbanization in Latin America: Approaches and Issues* (Garden City, N.Y., 1975), 57–107.

[15] Richard Konetzke, "Estado y sociedad en las Indias," *Estudios Americanos,* 3 (1951): 33–58; Rolando Mellafe, *Negro Slavery in Latin America* (Berkeley, Calif., 1975), 109–17.

[16] Meiklejohn, "Observance of Negro Slave Legislation," 103–14, 295–306; Carlos Federico Guillot, *Negros rebeldes y negro cimarrones: Perfil afroamericano en la historia del Nuevo Mundo durante el siglo XVI* (Buenos Aires, 1961); Miguel Acosta Saignes, *Vida de los esclavos negros en Venezuela* (Caracas, 1967), 249–84; R. K. Kent, "Palmares: An African State in Brazil," *Journal of African*

Black Labor

Paradoxically, it was in this context of increasing racial animosity that Spanish officials legitimized free black towns. These towns appeared in the seventeenth and eighteenth centuries in a region described by one scholar as the "Negroid littoral"—the sparsely populated and inhospitable coastal areas of the Caribbean.[17] Faced with insurmountable problems and lacking the resources to "correct" them, the Spanish bureaucracy proved flexible and adaptable. When maroon communities such as those described by Colin Palmer and William Taylor in Mexico were too remote or intractable to destroy, the Spaniards granted them official sanction.[18] The Spanish governor of Venezuela once chartered a free black town to reward pacification of lands held by hostile Indians.[19] Mose was established as a buffer against foreign encroachment and provides a third model of free black town formation.[20]

The experience of the residents of Mose was in many ways shaped by Caribbean patterns. Declining Indian populations, a Spanish disdain for manual labor, and the defense requirements of an extended empire had created an early demand for additional workers. Blacks cleared land and planted crops, built fortifications and domestic structures, and provided a wide variety of skilled labor for Spanish colonists. By the sixteenth century, they had become the main labor force in Mexican mines and on Caribbean plantations. Also by that time, the Spanish had organized them into militia companies in Hispaniola, Cuba, Mexico, Cartagena, and Puerto Rico.[21] In Florida, too, Spaniards depended on Africans to be their laborers and to supplement their defenses. Black laborers and artisans helped establish St. Augustine, the first successful Spanish settlement in Florida, and a black and mulatto militia was formed there as early as 1683.[22]

Florida held great strategic significance for the Spanish: initially, for its location guarding the route of the treasure fleets, later, to safeguard the mines of Mexico from the French and British. The colony was a critical component

---

History, 6 (1965): 161–75; Carlos Larrazábal Blanco, *Los negros y la esclavitud en Santo Domingo* (Santo Domingo, 1967).

[17] Leon Campbell used this term in his article, "The Changing Racial and Administrative Structure of the Peruvian Military under the Later Bourbons," *The Americas,* 32 (July 1975): 117–33.

[18] Colin Palmer, *Slaves of the White God-Blacks in Mexico, 1570–1650* (Cambridge, 1976); William Taylor, "The Foundation of Nuestra Señora de Guadalupe de los Morenos de Amapa," *The Americas,* 26 (April 1970): 442–46.

[19] Richard Konetzke, *Colección de documentos para la historia de la formación social de Hispano-América, 1493–1810,* 3 vols. (Madrid, 1953–58), 2: 118–20.

[20] For a later example of a buffer town, see John Hoyt Williams, "Trevegó on the Paraguayan Frontier: A Chapter in the Black History of the Americas," *Journal of Negro History,* 56 (October 1971): 272–83; and Germán de Granda, "Origin, función y estructura de un pueblo de negros y mulatos libres en el Paraguay del siglo XVIII (San Agustin de la Emboscada)," *Revista de Indias,* 43 (enero–junio 1983): 229–64.

[21] Klein, "Colored Militia"; Kuethe, "Status of the Free Pardo."

[22] Roster of Black and Mulatto Militia for St. Augustine, September 20, 1683, Santo Domingo (hereafter cited as SD), 266, Archivo General de Indias: Seville (hereafter cited as AGI).

in Spain's Caribbean defense, and, when British colonists established Charles Town in 1670, it represented a serious challenge to Spanish sovereignty.[23] No major response by the weakened Spanish empire was feasible, but, when the British incited their Indian allies to attack Spanish Indian missions along the Atlantic coast, the Spaniards initiated a campaign of harassment against the new British colony. In 1686, a Spanish raiding party including a force of fifty-three Indians and blacks attacked Port Royal and Edisto. From the plantation of Governor Joseph Morton, they carried away "money and plate and thirteen slaves to the value of [£]1500." In subsequent negotiations, the new governor of Carolina, James Colleton, demanded the return of the stolen slaves as well as those "who run dayly into your towns," but the Spaniards refused.[24] These contacts may have suggested the possibility of a refuge among the enemy and directed slaves to St. Augustine, for, the following year, the first recorded fugitive slaves from Carolina arrived there. Governor Diego de Quiroga dutifully reported to Spain that eight men, two women, and a three-year-old nursing child had escaped to his province in a boat. According to the governor, they requested baptism into the "True Faith," and on that basis he refused to return them to the British delegation that came to St. Augustine to reclaim them.[25] The Carolinians claimed that one of Samuel de Bordieu's runaways, Mingo, who escaped with his wife and daughter (the nursing child), had committed murder in the process. Governor Quiroga promised to make monetary restitution for the slaves he retained and to prosecute Mingo, should the charges be proven.[26] Quiroga housed these first runaways in the homes of Spanish townspeople and saw to it that they were instructed in Catholic doctrine, baptized and

[23] Crane, *Southern Frontier*, 3–17; John Jay TePaske, *The Governorship of Spanish Florida, 1700–1763* (Durham, N.C., 1964), 3–6; Verne E. Chatelain, *The Defenses of Spanish Florida, 1565–1763* (Washington, D.C., 1941).

[24] Letter from Mr. Randolph to the Board, June 28, 1699, in A. S. Salley, *Records of the British Public Records Office Relating to South Carolina, 1698–1700* (Columbia, S.C., 1946), 4: 89; Crane, *Southern Frontier*, 31–33.

[25] "William Dunlop's Mission to St. Augustine in 1688," *South Carolina Historical and Genealogical Magazine*, 34 (January 1933): 1–30; Diego de Quiroga to the king, February 2, 1688, cited in Wright, "Dispatches," 150. Morton's stolen male slaves included Peter, Scipio, Doctor (whose name suggests a specialized function or skill), Cushi, Arro, Emo, Caesar, and Sambo. The women included Frank, Bess, and Mammy. Sambo was the Hausa name for a second son, while in Mende or Vai it meant "disgrace." Cushi may have been "Quashee," the Twi day-name for Sunday, which also came to signify "foolish" or "stupid." For a discussion of slave naming, see Wood, *Black Majority*, 181–86, among others. The men who stole the canoe were named Conano, Jesse, Jacque, Gran Domingo (Big Sunday), Cambo, Mingo, Dicque, and Robi. Wood suggests that forms of the name Jack derived from the African day-name for Wednesday, Quaco. Names of the two women and the little girl were not given. The owners of the fugitives who escaped in the canoe were: Samuel de Bordieu, Mingo, his wife and daughter; John Bird, two men; Joab Howe, one man; John Berresford, one woman; Christopher Smith, one man; Robert Cuthbert, three men. "William Dunlop's Mission," 4, 26, 28.

[26] "William Dunlop's Mission," 25.

married in the church. He put the men to work as ironsmiths and laborers on the new stone fort, the Castillo de San Marcos, and employed the women in his own household. All were reportedly paid wages: the men earned a peso a day, the wage paid to male Indian laborers, and the women half as much.[27]

Florida's governors enjoyed considerable autonomy. Their dual military and political appointments, the great distance from the metropolis, and an unwieldy bureaucracy contributed to their ability to make their own decisions. In unforeseen circumstances, they improvised. But, as fugitives continued to filter into the province, the governors and treasury officials repeatedly solicited the king's guidance. Eventually, the Council of the Indies reviewed the matter and recommended approving the sanctuary policy shaped by the governors. On November 7, 1693, Charles II issued the first official position on the runaways, "giving liberty to all . . . the men as well as the women . . . so that by their example and by my liberality others will do the same."[28]

The provocation inherent in this order increasingly threatened the white Carolinians. At least four other groups of runaways reached St. Augustine in the following decade, and, despite an early ambiguity about their legal status, the refugees were returned to their British masters only in one known example.[29] Carolina's changing racial balance further intensified the planters' concerns. By 1708, blacks outnumbered whites in the colony, and slave revolts erupted in 1711 and 1714. The following year, when many slaves joined the Yamassee Indian war against the British, they almost succeeded in exterminating the badly outnumbered whites. Indians loyal to the British helped defeat the Yamassee, who with their black allies headed for St. Augustine. Although the Carolina Assembly passed harsh legislation designed to prevent further insurrections and control the slaves, these actions and subsequent negotiations with St. Augustine failed to deter the escapes or effect the reciprocal return of slaves. British planters claimed that the Spanish policy, by drawing away their slaves, would ruin their plantation economy. Arthur Middleton, Carolina's acting governor, complained to London that the Spaniards not only harbored their runaways but sent them back in the company of Indians to plunder British plantations. The Carolinians set

[27] Royal officials to the king, March 3, 1689, cited in Wright, "Dispatches," 151–52.
[28] Royal edict, November 7, 1693, SD 58–1–26 in the John B. Stetson Collection (hereafter cited as ST), P. K. Yonge Library of Florida History, University of Florida, Gainesville (hereafter cited as PKY). Also see "William Dunlop's Mission," 1–30.
[29] The various petitions of Carolina fugitives gathered together by Governor Manuel de Montiano are found in SD 844, fols. 521–46, microfilm reel 15, PKY. They mention groups arriving in 1688, 1689, 1690, 1697, 1724, and 1725. Governor Joseph de Zuñiga reported that his predecessor, Governor Laureano de Torres y Ayala, on August 8, 1697, returned six blacks and an Indian who had escaped from Charlestown that year, "to avoid conflicts and ruptures between the two governments." Joseph de Zuñiga to the king, October 10, 1699, SD 844, microfilm reel 15, fol. 542, PKY.

up patrol systems and placed scout boats on water routes to St. Augustine, but slaves still made good their escapes on stolen horses and in canoes and piraguas.[30]

In 1724, ten more runaway slaves reached St. Augustine, assisted by English-speaking Yamassee Indians. According to their statements, they were aware that the Spanish king had offered freedom to those seeking baptism and conversion.[31] The royal edict of 1693 was still in force, and Governor Antonio de Benavides initially seems to have honored it. In 1729, however, Benavides sold these newcomers at public auction to reimburse their owners, alleging that he feared the British might act on their threats to recover their losses by force. Some of the most important citizens of St. Augustine, including the royal accountant, the royal treasurer, several military officers, and even some religious officials, thus acquired valuable new slaves.[32] Others were sold to owners who took them to Havana. In justifying his actions, Benavides explained that these slaves had arrived during a time of peace with England and, further, that he interpreted the 1693 edict to apply only to the original runaways from the British colony.[33]

Several of the reenslaved men were veterans of the Yamassee war in Carolina, and one of these, Francisco Menéndez, was appointed by Governor Benavides to command a slave militia in 1726. This black militia helped defend St. Augustine against the British invasion led by Colonel John Palmer in 1728, but, despite their loyal service, the Carolina refugees still remained enslaved.[34] Meanwhile, the Spaniards continued to send canoes of Carolina fugitives and Yamassee Indians north in search of British scalps and live slaves. Governor Middleton charged that Governor Benavides was profiting by the slaves' sale in Havana, a charge that seems well founded.[35]

Perhaps in response to continued reports and diplomatic complaints involving the fugitives, the crown issued two new edicts regarding their treatment. The first, on October 4, 1733, forbade any future compensation to the British, reiterated the offer of freedom, and specifically prohibited the sale of

---

[30] Wood, *Black Majority,* 304–05. For a new overview of the broader demographic context, see Peter H. Wood, "The Changing Population of the Colonial South: An Overview by Race and Region, 1685–1790," in Peter H. Wood, Gregory A. Waselkov, and M. Thomas Hatley, eds., *Powhatan's Mantle: Indians in the Colonial Southeast* (Lincoln, Neb., 1989), 35–103.

[31] Memorial of the Fugitives, 1724, SD 844, fol. 530, microfilm reel 15, PKY.

[32] Governor Antonio de Benavides to the king, November 11, 1725, cited in Wright, "Dispatches," 164–66. The noted citizens who acquired the slaves filed various memorials to record their concerns about British threats to come take the slaves and the fact that British forces outnumbered Spanish. Memorial, August 26, 1729, SD 844, fols. 550–62. Governor Benavides then authorized their auction and gave the proceeds to a British envoy, Arthur Hauk. Accord, June 27, 1730, SD 844, fols. 564–66, microfilm reel 15, PKY.

[33] Consulta by the Council of the Indies, April 12, 1731, cited in Wright, "Dispatches," 166–72.

[34] Petition of Francisco Menéndez, November 21, 1740, SD 2658, AGI. On the role of the black militia in 1728, see TePaske, *Fugitive Slave,* 7.

[35] Governor Arthur Middleton, June 6, 1728, British Public Record Office Transcripts, 13: 61–67, cited in Wood, *Black Majority,* 305.

fugitives to private citizens. The second edict, on October 29, 1733, commended the blacks for their bravery against the British in 1728; however, it also stipulated that they would be required to complete four years of royal service prior to being freed. But the runaways had sought liberty, not indenture.[36] Led by Captain Menéndez of the slave militia, the blacks persisted in attempts to secure complete freedom. They presented petitions to the governor and to the auxiliary bishop of Cuba, who toured the province in 1735, but to no avail.[37] When Manuel de Montiano became governor in 1737, their fortunes changed. Captain Menéndez once more solicited his freedom, and this time his petition was supported by that of a Yamassee cacique named Jorge. Jorge related how Menéndez and three others had fought bravely for three years in the Yamassee rebellion, only to be sold back into slavery in Florida by a "heathen" named Mad Dog. Jorge condemned this betrayal of the blacks whom he stated had been patient and "more than loyal," but he did not blame Mad Dog, for he was an "infidel" who knew no better. Rather, he held culpable the Spaniards who had purchased these loyal allies.[38] Governor Montiano ordered an investigation and reviewed the case. On March 15, 1738, he granted unconditional freedom to the petitioners. Montiano also wrote the governor and captain general of Cuba, attempting to retrieve eight Carolinians who had been taken to Havana during the Benavides regime. At least one, Antonio Caravallo, was returned to St. Augustine, against all odds.[39]

Governor Montiano established the freedmen in a new town, about two miles north of St. Augustine, which he called Gracia Real de Santa Teresa de Mose.[40] The freedmen built the settlement, a walled fort and shelters described by the Spaniards as resembling thatched Indian huts. Little more is known about it from Spanish sources, but later British reports add that the fort was constructed of stone, "four square with a flanker at each corner, banked with earth, having a ditch without on all sides lined round with

[36] Royal edict, October 4, 1733, SD 58–1–24, ST; Royal edict, October 29, 1733, SD 58–1–24, ST.

[37] Memorial of the Fugitives, SD 844, fols. 533–34, included in Manuel de Montiano to the king, March 3, 1738, SD 844, microfilm reel 15, PKY.

[38] Memorial of Chief Jorge, SD 844, fols. 536–37, *ibid.* Jorge claimed to be the chief who had led the Yamassee uprising against the British. Jorge stated that he and the rest of the Yamassee chiefs commonly made treaties with the slaves, and that he now wanted to help Menéndez and the three others who fought along with him become free. Mad Dog sold them into slavery for some casks of honey, corn, and liquor *(aguardiente)*.

[39] Decree of Manuel de Montiano, March 3, 1738, SD 844, fols. 566–75, microfilm reel 15, PKY. The eight slaves who were sold to Havana included "Antonio, an English slave from San Jorge [the Spanish name for Charlestown], another of the same name, Clemente, Andres, Bartholome Chino [the term for a mixed-blood], Juan Francisco Borne, Juan (English), Jose, who's other name is Mandingo, all of whom are from San Jorge."

[40] Montiano to the king, February 16, 1739, SD 844, microfilm reel 15, PKY. The name is a composite of an existing Indian place name, Mose, the phrase that indicated that the new town was established by the king, Gracia Real, and the name of the town's patron saint, Teresa of Avilés, who was the patron saint of Spain.

prickly royal and had a well and house within, and a look-out." They also confirm Spanish reports that the freedmen planted fields nearby.[41] The town site was said to be surrounded by fertile lands and nearby woods that would yield building materials. A river of salt water "running through it" contained an abundance of shellfish and all types of fish.[42] Montiano hoped the people of Mose could cultivate the land to grow food for St. Augustine, but, until crops could be harvested, he provided the people with corn, biscuits, and beef from government stores.[43]

Mose was located at the head of Mose Creek, a tributary of the North River with access to St. Augustine, and lay directly north of St. Augustine, near trails north to San Nicholas and west to Apalache. For all these reasons, it was strategically significant, Governor Montiano surely considered the benefits of a northern outpost against anticipated British attacks. And who better to serve as an advanced warning system than grateful ex-slaves carrying Spanish arms? The freedmen understood their expected role, for, in a declaration to the king, they vowed to be "the most cruel enemies of the English" and to risk their lives and spill their "last drop of blood in defense of the Great Crown of Spain and the Holy Faith."[44] If the new homesteaders were diplomats, they were also pragmatists, and their own interests were clearly served by fighting those who would seek to return them to chattel slavery. Mose also served a vital objective of Spanish imperial policy, and, once Governor Montiano justified its establishment, the Council of the Indies and the king supported his actions.[45]

Since Spanish town settlement implied the extension of *justicia*, the governor assigned a white military officer and royal official to supervise the establishment of Mose. Mose was considered a village of new converts comparable to those of the Christian Indians, so Montiano also posted a student priest at the settlement to instruct the inhabitants in doctrine and "good customs."[46] Although the Franciscan lived at Mose, there is no evidence that the white officer did. It seems rather that Captain Menéndez was responsible for governing the settlement, for, in one document, Governor Montiano referred to the others as the "subjects" of Menéndez. The Spaniards regarded Menéndez as a sort of natural lord, and, like Indian caciques, he probably exercised

---

[41] *St. Augustine Expedition of 1740: A Report to the South Carolina General Assembly Reprinted from the Colonial Records of South Carolina with an introduction by John Tate Lanning* (Columbia, S.C., 1954), 25.

[42] Report of Antonio de Benavides, SD 58–2–16/45, bundle 5725, ST.

[43] Purchases and Payments for 1739, Cuba 446, AGI.

[44] Manuel de Montiano to the king, February 16, 1739, SD 845, fol. 700, SD 845, microfilm reel 16, PKY. Fugitive Negroes of the English plantations to the king, June 10, 1738, SD 844, microfilm reel 15, PKY.

[45] Council of the Indies, October 2, 1739, cited in Wright, "Dispatches," 178–80; Council of the Indies, September 28, 1740, SD 845, fol. 708, microfilm reel 16, PKY.

[46] Manuel de Montiano to the king, February 16, 1739, SD 845, fol. 701, microfilm reel 16, PKY.

considerable autonomy over his village.[47] Spanish titles and support may have also reinforced Menéndez's status and authority. Whatever the nature of his authority, Menéndez commanded the Mose militia for over forty years, and his career supports Price's contention that eighteenth-century maroon leaders were military figures well-versed in European ways and equipped to negotiate their followers' best interests.[48]

As new fugitives arrived, the governor placed these in Menéndez's charge as well. A group of twenty-three men, women, and children arrived from Port Royal on November 21, 1738, and were sent to join the others at the new town. Among the newcomers were the runaway slaves of Captain Caleb Davis of Port Royal. Davis was an English merchant who had been supplying St. Augustine for many years, and it is possible that some of the runaways had even traveled to St. Augustine in the course of Davis's business. Davis went to the Spanish city in December 1738 and spotted his former slaves, whom he reported laughed at his fruitless efforts to recover them.[49] The frustrated Davis eventually submitted a claim against the Spanish for twenty-seven of his slaves "detained" by Montiano, whom he valued at 7,600 pesos, as well as for the launch in which they escaped and supplies they had taken with them. He also listed debts incurred by the citizens of St. Augustine. Among those owing him money were Governors Antonio Benavides, Francisco Moral Sánchez, and Manuel de Montiano, various royal officials and army officers, and Mose townsmen Francisco Menéndez and Pedro de Leon.[50] There is no evidence Davis ever recouped his losses.

In March 1739, envoys from Carolina arrived in St. Augustine to press for the return of their runaway slaves. Governor Montiano treated them with hospitality but referred to the royal edict of 1733, which required that he grant religious sanctuary.[51] In August, an Indian ally in Apalache sent word to Montiano that the British had attempted to build a fort in the vicinity, but that the hundred black laborers had revolted, killed all the whites, and hamstrung their horses before escaping. Several days later, some of the blacks encountered the Indians in the woods and asked directions to reach the Spaniards.[52] The following month, a group of Angola slaves revolted near Stono, South

---

[47] Manuel de Montiano to the king, September 16, 1740, SD 2658, AGI. Montiano's successor also stated that the townspeople of Mose were "under the dominion of their Captain and Lieutenant." Melchor de Navarrete to the Marqués de Ensenada, April 2, 1752, cited in Wright, "Dispatches," 185.

[48] Evacuation report of Juan Joseph Eligio de la Puente, January 22, 1764, SD 2595, AGI; Price, *Maroon Societies*, 29–30.

[49] Manuel de Montiano to the king, February 16, 1739, SD 845, fol. 700, microfilm reel 16, PKY; "Journal of William Stephens," cited in Wood, *Black Majority*, 307.

[50] Claim of Captain Caleb Davis, September 17, 1751, SD 2584, AGI.

[51] Manuel de Montiano to the king, March 13, 1739, Manuscript 19508, Biblioteca Nacional, Madrid.

[52] Letter of Manuel de Montiano, August 19, 1739, "Letters of Montiano, Siege of St. Augustine," *Collections of the Georgia Historical Society* (Savannah, Ga., 1909), 7: 32.

Carolina, and killed more than twenty whites before heading for St. Augustine. They were apprehended before reaching their objective, and retribution was swift and bloody. But officials of South Carolina and Georgia blamed the sanctuary available in nearby St. Augustine for the rebellion, and relations between the colonies reached a breaking point.[53] With the outbreak of the War of Jenkins' Ear, international and local grievances merged. In January 1740, Governor James Oglethorpe of Georgia raided Florida and captured Forts Pupo and Picolata on the St. John's River west of St. Augustine. These initial victories enabled Oglethorpe to mount a major expeditionary force, including Georgia and South Carolina regiments, a vast Indian army, and seven warships for a major offensive against the Spaniards.[54]

The free black militia of Mose worked alongside the other citizenry to fortify provincial defenses. They also provided the Spaniards with critical intelligence reports.[55] In May, one of Oglethorpe's lieutenants happened across five houses occupied by the freedmen and was able to capture two of them.[56] Unable to protect the residents of Mose, Governor Montiano was forced to evacuate "all the Negroes who composed that town" to the safety of St. Augustine. Thereafter, the Mose militia continued to conduct dangerous sorties against the enemy and assisted in the surprise attack and recapture of their town in June.[57] The success at Mose was one of the few enjoyed by the Spaniards. It is generally acknowledged to have demoralized the combined British forces and to have been a significant factor in Oglethorpe's withdrawal. British accounts refer to the event as "Bloody Mose" or "Fatal Mose" and relate with horror the murder and mutilation (decapitation and castration) of two wounded prisoners who were unable to travel. They do not say whether Spaniards, Indians, or blacks did the deed. Although Spanish sources do not even mention this incident, atrocities took place on both sides. Both Spanish and British authorities routinely paid their Indian allies for enemy scalps, and at least one scalp was taken at "Moosa," according to British reports.[58]

[53] "The Stono Rebellion and Its Consequences," in Wood, *Black Majority*, 308–26.

[54] TePaske, *Governorship*, 140.

[55] On January 8, 1740, Montiano sent Don Pedro Lamberto Horruytiner "with 25 horsemen from his company, 25 infantry and 30 Indians and free Negroes (of those who are fugitives from the English Colonies) to scout the country." Manuel de Montaino to the king, January 31, 1740, SD 2658, AGI. On January 27, 1740, Montiano sent Don Romualdo Ruiz del Moral out on a similar mission accompanied by "25 horsemen, 25 Indians, and 25 free Negroes." Montiano wrote, "The difficulty of getting information in our numerous thickets, lagoons and swamps, is so great as to make the thing almost impossible." Manuel de Montaino to the king, January 31, 1740, "Letters of Montiano," 7: 36.

[56] *St. Augustine Expedition*, 23. One was the escaped slave of Mrs. Parker, and the other claimed to have been carried away from Colonel Gibbs by the Indians.

[57] Manuel de Montiano to the king, January 17, 1740, SD 2658, AGI. For Montiano's account of Oglethorpe's siege and the victory at Mose, see Manuel de Montiano to the king, August 9, 1740, SD 845, fols. 11–26, microfilm reel 16, PKY; and "Letters of Montiano," 7: 54–62.

[58] Mills Lane, ed. *General Oglethorpe's Georgia: Colonial Letters, 1738–1743*, II (Savannah), 447. For more accounts of atrocities, see *St. Augustine Expedition of 1740*, 47; TePaske, *Governorship of*

Cuban reinforcements finally relieved St. Augustine in July. Shortly thereafter, Oglethorpe and his troops returned to Georgia and Carolina.[59] Governor Montiano commended all his troops to the king but made the rather unusual gesture of writing a special recommendation for Francisco Menéndez. Montiano extolled the exactitude with which Menéndez had carried out royal service and the valor he had displayed in the battle at Mose. He added that, on another occasion, Menéndez and his men had fired on the enemy until they withdrew from the castle walls and that Menéndez had displayed great zeal during the dangerous reconnaissance missions he undertook against the British and their Indians. Moreover, he acknowledged that Menéndez had "distinguished himself in the establishment, and cultivation of Mose, to improve that settlement, doing all he could so that the rest of his subjects, following his example, would apply themselves to work and learn good customs."[60]

Shortly thereafter, Menéndez petitioned for remuneration from his king for the "loyalty, zeal and love I have always demonstrated in the royal service, in the encounters with the enemies, as well as in the effort and care with which I have worked to repair two bastions on the defense line of this plaza, being pleased to do it, although it advanced my poverty, and I have been continually at arms, and assisted in the maintenance of the bastions, without the least royal expense, despite the scarcity in which this presidio always exists, especially in this occasion." He added, "my sole object was to defend the Holy Evangel and sovereignty of the Crown," and asked for the proprietorship of the free black militia and a salary to enable him to live decently (meaning in the style customary for an official of the militia). He concluded that he hoped to receive "all the consolation of the royal support . . . which Christianity requires and your vassals desire." Several months later, Menéndez filed a second, shorter petition.[61] It was customary for an illiterate person to sign official documents with an X, and for the notary or witnesses to write underneath, "for ——, who does not know how to write." Both these petitions, however, were written and signed in the same hand and with a flourish, so it would seem that at some point Menéndez learned how to write in Spanish—perhaps when he was the slave of the royal accountant whose name he took.[62] Despite his good services, appropriate behavior and rhetoric, there is no

Spanish Florida, 143; Larry E. Ivers, *British Drums on the Southern Frontier, The Military Colonization of Georgia 1733–1749* (Chapel Hill, N.C., 1974). This account is written from British sources and therefore is inaccurate on many aspects of the Spanish history. Ivers seriously undercounts St. Augustine's population, glamorizes Oglethorpe's role, and fails to recognize the role of blacks at Mose and throughout the Anglo-Spanish conflict.

[59] TePaske, *Governorship of Spanish Florida*, 144.
[60] Manuel de Montiano to the king, January 31, 1740, SD 2658, AGI.
[61] Memorial of Francisco Menéndez, November 21, 1740, SD 2658, AGI. Memorial of Francisco Menéndez, December 12, 1740, *ibid*.
[62] The proprietary royal accountant for St. Augustine was Don Francisco Menéndez Márquez. The Menéndez Márquez family is the subject of several works by Amy Turner Bushnell. See

evidence of a response, and the noted royal parsimony made such payment unlikely.

Nevertheless, the runaways form Carolina had been successful in their most important appeal to Spanish justice—their quest for liberty. Over the many years, they persevered, and their leaders learned to use Spanish legal channels and social systems to advantage. They accurately assessed Spain's intensifying competition with England and exploited the political leverage it offered them. Once free, they understood and adapted to Spanish expectations of their new status. They vowed fealty and armed service, establishing themselves as vassals of the king and deserving of royal protection. Governor Montiano commended their bravery in battle and their industry as they worked to establish and cultivate Mose. They were clearly not the lazy vagabonds feared by Spanish administrators, and the adaptive behavior of Menéndez and his "subjects" gained them at least a limited autonomy.

Such autonomy is evident in both the black and Indian militias that operated on St. Augustine's frontiers. Their role in the defense of the Spanish colony has not yet been appreciated. They were cavalry units that served in frontier reconnaissance and as guerrilla fighters. They had their own officers and patrolled independently, although Spanish infantry officers also commanded mixed groups of Spanish, free blacks, and Indians on scouting missions.[63] The Florida garrison was never able to maintain a full contingent, and these militias constituted an important asset for the short-handed governors.[64] Because England and Spain were so often at war during his administration, Governor Montiano probably depended on the black troops more than did subsequent Florida governors.

When the Spaniards mounted a major retaliatory offensive against Georgia in 1742, Governor Montiano once again employed his Mose militia. Montiano's war plans called for sending English-speaking blacks of the Mose militia to range the countryside gathering and arming slave recruits, which suggests that he placed great trust in their loyalty and ability, as well, perhaps, as in their desire to punish their former masters.[65] Bad weather, mishaps, and confusion plagued the operation, and several hundred of the Spanish forces were killed

---

"The Menéndez Márquez Cattle Barony at La Chua and the Determinants of Economic Expansion in Seventeenth-Century Florida," *Florida Historical Quarterly*, 56 (April 1978): 407–31; and *The King's Coffers, Proprietors of the Spanish Florida Treasury, 1565–1702* (Gainesville, Fla., 1981).

[63] Manuel de Montiano to the king, January 22, 1740, "Letters of Montiano," 7: 32–42. Indian militias continued to serve Florida's governors, and in 1759 Cacique Bernardo Lachiche commanded a unit of twenty-eight men, by election of the other caciques. Report of Don Lucas de Palacio on the Spanish, Indian and Free Black Militias, April 30, 1759, SD 2604, AGI.

[64] Although St. Augustine was allotted a troop complement of 350 men, Montiano had only 240 men fit for service in St. Augustine when the siege of 1740 ended. Manuel de Montiano to the king, August 9, 1740, SD 846, fol. 25 V, microfilm reel 16, PKY.

[65] Manuel de Montiano to the captain general of Cuba, Don Juan Francisco de Güemes y Horcasitas, March 13, 1742, SD 2593, AGI; TePaske, *Governorship of Spanish Florida*, 146–52.

at Bloody Marsh on Saint Simon's island. By August, the Spaniards had returned to St. Augustine. Oglethorpe mounted two more attacks on St. Augustine in 1742 and 1743, but neither did major damage. An uneasy stalemate developed, punctuated occasionally by Indian and corsair raids.[66]

Corsairing was practiced by both the British and the Spanish during the
1740s and 1750s, and St. Augustine became a convenient base of operations
for privateers commissioned by Spain. The capture and sale of prizes provided badly needed species and supplies for war-torn Florida, which had
not received government subsidies in 1739, 1740, 1741, and 1745 and which
struggled under the additional burden of maintaining the large number of
Cuban reinforcements that had arrived in 1740.[67] Corsairing ships were
manned by volunteers, some of whom were drawn from the free black community, for, as Governor Garcia noted, "without those of 'broken' color,
blacks, and Indians, which abound in our towns in America, I do not know
if we could arm a single corsair solely with Spaniards."[68] Unfortunately,
when these men were captured, the British presupposed them by their color
to be slaves and sold them for profit.

When the British ship *Revenge* captured a Spanish prize in July 1741,
found aboard was a black named "Signior Capitano Francisco," who was
"Capt. of a Comp'y of Indians, Mollattos, and Negroes that was att the Re-
taking of the Fort [Mose] att St. Augus'ne formerly taken Under the Command of that worthless G——— O———pe who by his treachory suffered so
many brave fellows to be mangled by those barbarians." His captors tied
Francisco Menéndez to a gun and ordered the ship's doctor to pretend to cas-
trate him (as Englishmen at Mose had been castrated), but while Menéndez
"frankly owned" that he was Captain of the company that retook Mose, he
denied ordering any atrocities, which he said the Florida Indians had committed. Menéndez stated that he had taken the commission as privateer in
hopes of getting to Havana, and from there to Spain, to collect a reward for
his bravery. Several other mulattoes on board were also interrogated and substantiated Menéndez's account, as did several of the whites, but "to make
Sure and to make him remember that he bore such a Commission," the British
gave him 200 lashes and then "pickled him and left him to the Doctor to take
Care of his Sore A–se." The following month, the *Revenge* landed at New
Providence, in the Bahamas, and her commander, Benjamin Norton, who was
due the largest share of the prize, vehemently argued before the Admiralty
Court that the blacks should be condemned as slaves. "Does not their Complexion and features tell all the world that they are of the blood of Negroes
and have suckt Slavery and Cruelty from their Infancy?" He went on to describe Menéndez as "this Francisco that Cursed Seed of Cain, Curst from the

---

[66] TePaske, *Governorship of Spanish Florida*, 152–55.
[67] TePaske, *Governorship of Spanish Florida*, 100–05.
[68] Fulgencio García de Solís to the king, August 25, 1752, SD 845, fols. 81–112, microfilm reel 17,
PKY.

foundation of the world, who has the Impudence to Come into this Court and plead that he is free. Slavery is too Good for such a Savage, nay all the Cruelty invented by man . . . the torments of the World to Come will not suffice." No record of Francisco's testimony appears in this account, but the Court ordered him sold as a slave, "according to the Laws of the plantation."[69] However, as we have seen, Menéndez was a man of unusual abilities. Whether he successfully appealed for his freedom in British courts as he had in the Spanish, was ransomed back by the Spanish in Florida, or escaped is unknown, but, by at least 1752, he was once again in command at Mose. This incident illustrates the extreme racial hatred some British felt for Spain's black allies, as well as the grave dangers the freedmen faced in taking up Spanish arms. Other blacks captured as privateers in the same period were never returned.[70]

Although unsuccessful, Governor Oglethorpe's invasion in 1740 had wreaked havoc in Spanish Florida. Mose and the other outlying forts had been destroyed, along with many of the crops and animals on which the community subsisted. For the next twelve years, the townspeople of Mose lived among the Spanish in St. Augustine. This interlude was critical to the integration of the Carolina group into the larger and more diverse society in the city. Wage lists in treasury accounts and military reports from this period show that they performed a variety of valuable functions for the community. Free blacks labored on government projects, were sailors and privateers, tracked escaped prisoners, and helped forage food for the city. In the spring, they rounded up wild cattle for slaughter and wild horses for cavalry mounts.[71] They probably led lives much like those of free blacks in other Spanish colonial ports and may have engaged in craft production, artisanry, and the provision of services.[72] Although certain racial restrictions existed, they were rarely enforced in a small frontier settlement such as St. Augustine, where more relaxed personal relations were the norm. Everyone knew everyone else, and this familiarity could be a source of assistance and protection for the free blacks of Mose, who had acquired at least a measure of acceptability.[73]

[69] "Account of the Revenge," in John Franklin Jameson, ed., *Privateering and Piracy in the Colonial Period: Illustrative Documents* (New York, 1923), 402–11. My thanks to Charles Tingley for providing this source.
[70] Report of Captain Fernando Laguna, October 7, 1752, SD 846, fols. 84–108, microfilm reel 17, PKY.
[71] Michael C. Scardaville and Jesus María Belmonte, "Florida in the Late First Spanish Period: The Griñán Report," *El Escribano*, 16 (1979): 10.
[72] Works that provide information on the life and labor of blacks in colonial Spanish America include: Jorge Juan and Antonio de Ulloa, "Eighteenth-Century Spanish American Towns—African and Afro-Hispanic Life and Labor in Cities and Suburbs," in Anne Pescatello, ed., *The African in Latin America* (New York, 1975): 106–11; Greene and Cohen, *Neither Slave nor Free;* and Louisa Schell Hoberman and Susan Migden Socolow, eds., *Cities and Society in Colonial America* (Albuquerque, N. Mex., 1986).
[73] Michael P. Johnson and James L. Roark's work, *Black Masters: A Free Family of Color in the Old South* (New York, 1984), demonstrates how personalism might mediate race relations even in a

Parish registers reflect the great ethnic and racial diversity in Spanish Florida in these years. Because there were always fewer female runaways, the males of that group were forced to look to the local possibilities for marriage partners—either Indian women from the two outlying villages of Nuestra Señora de la Leche and Nuestra Señora de Tholomato, or free and slave women from St. Augustine. Interracial relationships were common, and families were restructured frequently when death struck and widowed men and women remarried. The core group of Carolina fugitives formed intricate ties among themselves for at least two generations. They married from within their group and served as witnesses at each other's weddings and as godparents for each other's children, sometimes many times over. They also entered into the same relationships with Indians, free blacks, and slaves from other locations. Some of these slaves eventually became free, which might suggest mutual assistance efforts by the black community. The people of Mose also formed ties of reciprocal obligation with important members of both the white and black communities through the mechanism of ritual brotherhood (*compadrazgo*). A few examples should serve to illustrate the complex nature of these frontier relationships.

Francisco Garzia and his wife, Ana, fled together from Carolina and were among the original group freed by Governor Montiano. Francisco was black, and Ana, Indian. As slaves in St. Augustine, they had belonged to the royal treasurer, Don Salvador Garzia. Garzia observed the church requirement to have his slaves baptized and properly married, for the couple's children are listed as legitimate. Francisco and Ana's daughter, Francisca Xaviera, was born and baptized in St. Augustine in 1736, before her parents were freed by the governor. Her godfather was a free mulatto, Francisco Rexidor. This man also served as godfather for Francisco and Ana's son, Calisto, born free two years later. Garzia died sometime before 1759, for in that year his widow, Ana, married a black slave named Diego. Calisto disappeared from the record and presumably died, while Francisca Xaviera married Francisco Díaz, a free black from Carolina. Their two children, Miguel Francisco and María, were born at Mose, and Francisco Díaz served in the Mose militia.[74]

---

more rigid caste society, but free blacks always had to balance carefully their legal rights against the social limits accepted in their community. For other examples of upwardly mobile slaves from Spanish Florida, see Jane Landers, "Black Society in Spanish St. Augustine, 1784–1821" (Ph.D. dissertation, University of Florida, Gainesville, 1988).

[74] In 1738, Francisco and Ana were the slaves of Don Salvador Garzía, SD 844, fols. 593–94, microfilm reel 15, PKY. Baptism of Francisca Xaviera, August 30, 1736, and baptism of Calisto, October 23, 1738, Black Baptisms, Cathedral Parish Records, Diocese of St. Augustine Catholic Center, Jacksonville (hereafter cited as CPR), microfilm reel 284 F, PKY. Marriage of the widowed Ana García Pedroso to Diego, the slave of Don Juan Joseph Eligio de la Puente, January 14, 1759, Black Marriages, CPR, microfilm reel 284 C, PKY. Baptism of Miguel Francisco, January 29, 1753, Black Baptisms, CPR, microfilm reel 284 F, PKY. Mose militia list, included in evacuation report of Juan Joseph Eligio de la Puente, January 22, 1764, SD 2595, AGI.

Juan Jacinto Rodríguez and his wife, Ana María Menéndez, were also among the first Carolina homesteaders at Mose. Shortly after the town was founded, their son Juan married Cecilia, a Mandingo from Carolina who was the slave of Juan's former owner, cavalry Captain Don Pedro Lamberto Horruytiner. Cecilia's sister-in-law, María Francisca, had served as godmother at Cecilia's baptism two years earlier. María Francisca married Marcos de Torres, a free and legitimate black from Cartagena, Colombia, during the time the Mose homesteaders lived in St. Augustine. Marcos de Torres and María Francisca had three children born while they lived in town, and María Francisca's brother, Juan, and his wife, Cecilia, served as the children's godparents. After Marcos de Torres died, María Francisca and her three orphaned children lived with her parents at Mose. In 1760, the widowed María Francisca married the widower, Thomas Chrisostomo.[75]

Thomas and his first wife were Congo slaves. Thomas belonged to Don Francisco Chrisostomo, and his wife, Ana María Ronquillo, to Juan Nicolás Ronquillo. The couple married in St. Augustine in 1745. Pedro Graxales, a Congo slave and his legitimate wife, María de la Concepción Hita, a Caravalí slave, were the godparents at the wedding. By 1759, Thomas was a free widower living alone at Mose. The next year, he and María Francisca were wed. By that time, Thomas's godfather, Pedro Graxales, was also living at Mose as a free man, but Pedro's wife and at least four children remained slaves in St. Augustine.[76]

A simple bicultural encounter model will not suffice to explain the extent of cultural adaptation at Mose and the formation of this African-Hispanic community.[77] Many of its members were born on the western coast of Africa and then spent at least some time in a British slave society before risking their lives to escape. Some had intimate contact for several years with the Ya-

---

[75] In 1738, Juan Jacinto Rodríguez and Ana María Menéndez were the slaves of Petronila Pérez, SD 844, fol. 594, PKY. They were married as slaves on October 9, 1735, CPR, 284 C, PKY. After Juan Jacinto died, Ana María married the free black, Antonio de Urisa, of the Lara nation on April 26, 1740, *ibid.* Juan Jacinto and Ana María's daughter, María Francisca, was baptized on October 11, 1736, while she was still the slave of Petronila Pérez, CPR, 284 F, PKY. Juan Lamberto Horruytiner married Cecilia Horruytiner on July 12, 1739, CPR, 284 C, PKY. Baptism of Cecilia, September 9, 1737, CPR, 284 F, PKY. Marriage of María Francisca to Marcos de Torres, August 20, 1742, CPR, 284 C, PKY. Baptism of their daughter, María, May 20, 1743, and their son Nicholás de la Concepción, January 10, 1746, CPR, 284 F, PKY. María Francisca and the children were living in her parents' home at the time of the 1759 census. Census of Father Gines Sánchez, February 12, 1759, SD 2604, AGI. Marriage of Thomas Chrisostomo and María Francisca, December 15, 1760, CPR, 284 C, PKY.
[76] Marriage of Thomas Chrisostomo and Ana María Ronquillo, February 28, 1745, *ibid.* Baptism of Pedro Graxales, December 9, 1738, CPR, 284 F, PKY. Marriage of Pedro Graxales, Congo slave of Don Francisco Graxales, and María de la Concepción Hita, Caravalí slave of Don Pedro de Hita, January 19, 1744, CPR, 284 C, PKY. Baptisms of their children, María, November 4, 1744; Manuela de los Angeles, January 1, 1747; Ysidora de los Angeles, December 22, 1748; Joseph Ynisario, April 4, 1755; and Juana Feliciana, July 13, 1757, CPR, 284 F, PKY.
[77] Mintz and Price, "Anthropological Approach."

massee Indians and fought other non-Christian Indian groups before reaching Spanish Florida. At least thirty-one became slaves of the Spanish prior to achieving free status. Once free, they associated closely with the remnants of the seven different Indian nations aggregated into the two outlying Indian towns. From 1740 until 1752, the Mose group lived within the city of St. Augustine; after that time, they were forcibly removed to a rebuilt settlement. Meanwhile, new infusions of Africans continued to be incorporated into the original Mose community through ties with godparents. Many historians now agree that, although the ex-slaves did not share a single culture, their common values and experiences in the Americas enabled them to form strong communities, as they did in Spanish Florida. Ira Berlin, Steven F. Miller, and Leslie F. Rowland have argued that British slaves understood their society "in the idiom of kinship" and that, for slaves, "familial and communal relations were one."[78] The Spaniards also viewed society as an extension of family structures. The institution of the extended kinship group *(parentela)*, which included blood relations, fictive kin, and sometimes even household servants and slaves, and the institution of *clientela*, which bound powerful patrons and their personal dependents into a network of mutual obligations, were so deeply rooted in Spain that, according to one scholar, they might have been the "primary structure of Hispanic society." Thus African and Spanish views of family and society were highly compatible, and each group surely recognized the value that the other placed on kinship.[79]

Despite the relationships that developed between people of St. Augustine and the Mose settlers, there were objections to their presence in the Spanish city. Some complaints may have stemmed from racial prejudice or ethnocentrism. To some of the poorer Spanish, the free blacks represented competition in a ravaged economy. Indians allied to the British remained hostile to the Spaniards and raided the countryside with regularity. Plantations were neither safe nor productive. Havana could not provide its dependency with sufficient goods, and the few food shipments that reached St. Augustine were usually ruined. British goods were cheaper and better, and the governor was forced to depend on enemy suppliers for his needs. War and corsair raids on supplies shipped from Havana further strained the colony's ability to sustain its urban population. As new runaways continued to arrive, they only exacerbated the problem.[80] Finally, Melchor de Navarrete, who succeeded

---

[78] Licenses for Slaves Imported into St. Augustine, 1762–1763, Cuba 472, AGI. Ira Berlin, Steven F. Miller, and Leslie S. Rowland, "Afro-American Families in the Transition from Slavery to Freedom," *Radical History Review*, 42 (1988): 89.

[79] For a concise description of the importance of the extended family, *parentela*, and the system of personal dependency, *clientela*, in Spain, see McAlister, *Spain and Portugal*, 39–40.

[80] TePaske, *Governorship*, 227–29. TePaske described the chronic financial shortages of Florida, saying that "poverty and want characterized life in Florida and pervaded all aspects of life." Father Juan Joseph de Solana also described Florida as a destitute colony, impoverished, despite its natural resources, by the continual attack of Indians loyal to the British. Father Juan Joseph

Montiano in 1749, decided to reestablish Mose. He reported his achievements in converting the newcomers, remarking that he withheld certificates of freedom until the supplicants had a satisfactory knowledge of doctrine. Navarrete also claimed to have resettled all the free blacks from Carolina at Mose.[81]

Governor Fulgencio García de Solís, who served from 1752 to 1755, refuted his predecessor's claims, stating that persistent illnesses among the blacks had prevented their relocation. When García attempted to remove the freedmen and women to Mose, he faced stubborn resistance. The governor complained that it was not fear of further Indian attacks but the "desire to live in complete liberty" that motivated the rebels. He "lightly" punished the two unnamed leaders of the resistance and threatened worse to those who continued to fight the resettlement. He fortified the town to allay their fears and finally effected the resettlement. In a familiar litany, he alluded to "bad customs," "spiritual backwardness," and "pernicious consequences" and condemned not only the original Mose settlers but also "those who have since fled the English colonies to join them." He was determined that they would have "no pretext which could excuse them" from living at Mose and sought to isolate them from "any dealings or communication with . . . the town within the walls."[82] The Spanish association of urbanization with the advance of civilization traditionally had as its corollary the idea that those living outside a city's boundaries were lacking in cultural and spiritual attainments. In his official papers, García evidenced a much lower opinion of the free blacks than had Governor Montiano, and by removing them "beyond the walls" he made a visible statement about their supposed inferiority.

García was no doubt angered by the rebellion he faced, and he was probably correct in contending that it actually arose from the free black desire to live in "complete liberty." The crown had many times reiterated its commitment to their freedom, and, after living in St. Augustine for thirteen years and repeatedly risking their lives in its defense, the free blacks surely recognized the eviction for the insult it represented. Possibly, after García's interim term ended, there was greater interaction between the peoples of St. Augustine and its satellite, as later governors did not display his antipathy toward the free blacks.[83] Governor García may also have been disturbed by the presence and influence of unacculturated Africans (*bozales*) among the

---

de Solana to Bishop Pedro Agustin Morel de Sánchez, April 22, 1759, SD 516, microfilm reel 28 K, PKY.

[81] Melchor de Navarrete to the Marqués de Ensenada, April 2, 1752, cited in Wright, "Dispatches," 184–86.

[82] Fulgencio García de Solís to the king, November 29, 1752, SD, microfilm reel 17, PKY. Also, Fulgencio García de Solís to the king, December 7, 1752, cited in Wright, "Dispatches," 187–89.

[83] Governors Alonso Fernandez de Heredia and Lucas de Palacio both requested special financial assistance for the townspeople of Mose, citing their poverty. Aiteso de Heredía to Julian de Arriaga, April 7, 1756, cited in Wright, "Dispatches," 193–94; the king to Locas de Palacio, April 21, 1759, *ibid.*, 195.

latecomers. The "bad customs" that he alleged had so troubled his predecessors and himself might have been African cultural retentions. In 1744, Father Francisco Xavier Arturo baptized Domingo, a Caravalí slave, in ex-
tremis, with the comment that his "crudeness" prevented his understanding
Christian doctrine.[84] Four years later, Miguel Domingo, a Congo slave, received a conditional baptism, because he told the priest that he had been
baptized in his homeland, and continued to pray in his native language.[85]

Peter Wood's analysis of slave imports into South Carolina during the
late 1730s determined that 70 percent of those arriving during this brief period came from the Congo-Angola region.[86] St. Augustine's church registers
suggest a similar preponderance there but within a broader context of considerable ethnic diversity. The Spanish often recorded the nation of origin for
the Africans among them, and, although these designations are troublesome
and must be used with caution, they offer at least a general approximation
of the origins of those recorded. One hundred and forty-seven black marriages were reported from 1735 to 1763, and fifty-two of those married were
designated as Congos—twenty-six males and twenty-six females. The next
largest group was the Caravalís, including nine males and nineteen females.
The Mandingos constituted the third largest group and had nine males and
four females. Also represented in the marriage registers were the Minas,
Gambas, Lecumis, Sambas, Gangas, Araras, and Guineans.[87]

Governor García was required by royal policy to grant sanctuary to
slave refugees, but he was not required to accommodate them in St. Augustine, and he did not. The chastened freedmen built new structures at Mose,
including a church and a house for the Franciscan priest within the enclosed
fort, as well as twenty-two shelters outside the fort for their own households.
A diagram of the new fort, which had one side open on Mose Creek, shows
the interior buildings described by Father Juan Joseph de Solana but not the
houses of the villagers.[88] The only known census of Mose, from 1759,
recorded twenty-two households with a population of sixty-seven individuals. Mose had almost twice as many male as female occupants, and almost a
quarter of its population consisted of children under the age of fifteen. Thirteen of the twenty-two households belonged to nuclear or nuclear extended
families, and fifty villagers, or 75 percent of the total population, lived with
immediate members of their families. There were no female-headed households at this outpost, and nine households were composed solely of males.
At the time of the census, four men lived alone, Francisco Roso, Antonio Caravallo, Thomas Chrisostomo, and Antonio Blanco, but at least two of these

[84] Baptism of Miguel, 1744, CPR, 284 F, PKY.
[85] Baptism of Miguel Domingo, January 26, 1748, CPR, 284 F, PKY.
[86] Wood, *Black Majority*, 302.
[87] Dr. Kathleen Deagan, Florida Museum of Natural History, University of Florida, Gainesville,
provided these figures.
[88] In a map drawn by Pablo Castello, 1763, 833 B, PKY.

men, Roso and Chrisostomo, had family members among the slaves in St. Augustine. A third all-male household consisted of a father, Francisco de Torres, and his son, Juan de Arranzate. Francisco's wife and Juan's mother, Ana María, was a slave in St. Augustine. Pedro Graxales was also separated from his slave wife and their children but had a younger man, Manuel Rivera, attached to his household. Three other all-male households included a total of eleven men living together, at least three of whom had slave wives in St. Augustine.[89] Although spouses lived separately, parish registers record that children continued to be born of these unions and attest that family ties were maintained. Father Solana reported that some members of the Mose community were permitted to live in St. Augustine even though they continued to serve in the Mose militia. Several of those men appear on 1763 evacuation lists for Mose.[90]

The people of Mose were remarkably adaptable. They spoke several European and Indian languages, in addition to their own, and were exposed to a variety of subsistence techniques, craft and artistic traditions, labor patterns, and food ways. We know that the freedmen and women of Mose adopted certain elements of Spanish culture. For example, since their sanctuary was based on religious conversion, it was incumbent on them to exhibit their Catholicism. Their baptisms, marriages, and deaths were faithfully recorded in parish registers. But studies of other Hispanic colonies show that religious syncretism was widespread and tolerated by the church. Following centuries-old patterns set in Spain, Cuba's blacks organized religious brotherhoods by nations. They celebrated Catholic feast days dressed in traditional African costumes and with African music and instruments.[91] Because St. Augustine had such intimate contact with Cuba and blacks circulated between the two locations, it would not be surprising to find that Africans in Florida also observed some of their former religious practices.

Kathleen Deagan, of the Florida Museum of Natural History, currently directs an interdisciplinary team investigating Mose. In addition to locating

[89] Census of Gines Sánchez, February 12, 1759, SD 2604, AGI. Marriage of Francisco Roso, free Caravalí and María de la Cruz, Caravalí slave of Don Carlos Frison, January 8, 1743, CPR, 284 C, PKY; Baptism of Carlos Roso, November 4, 1743, CPR, 284 F, PKY. Marriage of Francisco Xavier de Torres, Mandingo, to Ana María, Mandinga slave of Josepha de Torres, February 1, 1752, CPR, 284 C, PKY. Others with slave wives in St. Augustine were Joseph de Peña, Caravalí, married to Ana María Ysquierdo, Conga slave of Don Juan Ysquierdo, January 29, 1743, *ibid.;* Juan Francisco de Torres, married to María Guillen slave of Joseph Guillen, January 21, 1743, *ibid.;* Joseph Fernández, Mandingo, married to Ana María, Caravalí slave, December 1, 1756, *ibid.;* Juan Baptista married to María de Jesus, August 17, 1757, *ibid.*
[90] Report of Father Juan Joseph de Solana to Bishop Pedro Agustin Mocel de Sánchez, April 22, 1759, SD 516, microfilm reel 28 K, PKY; Evacuation report of Juan Joseph Eligio de la Puente, January 22, 1764, SD 2595, AGI.
[91] Fernando Ortiz, "La Fiesta Afro-Cubana del 'Dia de Reyes,'" *Revista Bimestre Cubana,* 15 (January–June 1920): 5–16.

and excavating the site, this group is exploring the process of cultural adaptation at Mose to determine what mixture of customs and material culture its residents adopted and what in their own traditions might have influenced Spanish culture.[92] One suggestive find is a hand-made pewter medal that depicts St. Christopher on one side and a pattern resembling a Kongo star on the other.[93] Other recovered artifacts include military objects such as gunflints, a striker, and musket balls; and domestic articles such as metal buckles, a thimble, and pins, clay pipe bowls—of both local and European design—metal buttons, bone buttons—including one still in the process of manufacture—amber beads (perhaps from a rosary); and a variety of glass bottles and ceramic wares. Many of the latter are of English types, verifying documentary evidence of illicit, but necessary, trade with the enemy.

Preliminary analysis of faunal materials from the site indicates that the diet at Mose approximated that of indigenous villages and supports documentary evidence that the Indian and black villages resembled each other in many respects. Mose's villagers incorporated many estuarine resources and wild foods into their diet. The fish were net-caught, perhaps using African techniques. The people at Mose also caught and consumed deer, raccoon, opossum, and turtle to supplement the corn and beef occasionally provided them from government stores.[94]

Although noted for its poverty and the misery of its people, Mose survived as a free town and military outpost for St. Augustine until 1763, when, through the fortunes of war, Spain lost the province to the British. The Spanish evacuated St. Augustine and its dependent black and Indian towns, and the occupants were resettled in Cuba. The people of Mose left behind their meager homes and belongings and followed their hosts into exile to become homesteaders in Matanzas, Cuba—consigned once more to a rough frontier. The crown granted them new lands, a few tools, and a minimal subsidy, as well as an African slave to each of the leaders of the community; however, Spanish support was never sufficient, and the people from Mose suffered terrible privations at Matanzas. Some of them, including Francisco Menéndez,

---

[92] Kathleen Deagan analyzes elements and patterns of cultural exchange and adaptation in several works. See *Artifacts of the Spanish Colonies of Florida and the Caribbean, 1500–1800* (Washington, D.C., 1987); *Spanish St. Augustine: The Archaeology of a Colonial Creole Community* (New York, 1983); *St. Augustine: First Urban Enclave in the United States* (Farmingdale, N.Y., 1982); and *Sex, Status and Role in the Mestizaje of Spanish Colonial Florida* (Gainesville, Fla., 1974). On African-American archaeology, see Theresa Singleton, *The Archaeology of Slavery and Plantation Life* (Orlando, Fla., 1985); and Leland Ferguson, "Looking for the 'Afro' in Colono-Indian Pottery," in Robert L. Schuyler, ed., *Archaeological Perspectives on Ethnicity in America: Afro-American and Asian American Culture History* (Farmingdale, N.Y., 1980), 14–28.

[93] On Kongo-American connections, see Thompson, *Flash of the Spirit*, 112–15.

[94] Personal communication from Kathleen Deagan, October 1989. On African fishing techniques in the colonial southeast, see Peter H. Wood, "'It was a Negro Taught Them': A New Look at African Labor in Early South Carolina," *Journal of Asian and African Studies*, 9 (July and October 1974): 167–68.

eventually relocated in Havana, which offered at least the possibility of a better life, and this last diaspora scattered the black community of Mose.[95]

Located on the periphery of St. Augustine, between the Spanish settlement and its aggressive neighbors, Mose's interstitial location paralleled the social position of its inhabitants—people who straddled cultures, pursued their own advantage, and in the process helped shape the colonial history of the Caribbean as well as an African-American culture. In 1784, Spain recovered Florida, and many Floridanos, or first-period colonists, returned from Cuba. It is possible that among these were some of the residents of Mose. During its second regime, however, the weakened Spanish government made no effort to reestablish either Indian missions or the free black town of Mose. Free blacks took pivotal roles on interethnic frontiers of Spanish America such as Florida, serving as interpreters, craftsmen, traders, scouts, cowboys, pilots, and militiamen. The towns they established made important contributions to Spanish settlement. They populated areas the Spaniards found too difficult or unpleasant, thereby extending or maintaining Spanish dominion. They buffered Spanish towns from the attacks of their enemies and provided them with effective military reserves.

Although there were other towns like Mose in Latin America, it was the only example of a free black town in the colonial South. It provides an important, and heretofore unstudied, variant in the experience of African-born peoples in what was to become the United States. Mose's inhabitants were able to parlay their initiative, determination, and military and economic skills into free status, an autonomy at least equivalent to that of Spain's Indian allies in Florida, and a town of their own. These gains were partially offset by the constant danger and deprivation to which the townspeople of Mose were subjected, but they remained in Mose, perhaps believing it their best possible option. Despite the adversities of slavery, flight, wars, and repeated displacements, the freedmen and women of Mose managed to maintain intricate family relationships over time and shape a viable community under extremely difficult conditions. They became an example and possibly a source of assistance to unfree blacks from neighboring British colonies, as well as those within Spanish Florida. The Spanish subsequently extended the religious sanctuary policy confirmed at Mose to other areas of the Caribbean and applied it to the disadvantage of Dutch and French slaveholders, as well as the British.[96] The lives and efforts of the people of Mose

---

[95] Evacuation Report of Juan Joseph Eligio de la Puente, January 22, 1764, SD 2595, AGI. Accounts of the royal treasury of Matanzas, 1761–82, SD 1882, AGI. At least one family attempted to recover the losses of the evacuation, but they were denied on the basis of their color. Petition of María Gertrudis Roso, September 25, 1792, SD 2577, AGI.

[96] Slaves escaped from Guadaloupe to Puerto Rico in 1752, and the case was still before the Council of the Indies twenty years later; Consulta, July 19, 1772. Slaves from the Danish colonies of Santa Cruz and Santo Thomas also fled to Puerto Rico in 1767, and eventually the governments signed a convention; Consulta, July 21, 1777. Slaves from the Dutch settlement at Esquibo

thus took on international significance. Moreover, their accomplishments outlived them. The second Spanish government recognized religious sanctuary from 1784 until it bowed to the pressures of the new U.S. government and its persuasive secretary of state, Thomas Jefferson, and abrogated the policy in 1790. Before that escape hatch closed, several hundred slaves belonging to British Loyalists followed the example of the people of Mose to achieve emancipation in Florida.[97] Thus the determined fugitives who struggled so hard to win their own freedom inadvertently furthered the cause of freedom for others whom they never knew.

---

fled to Guyana, October 22, 1802; Documents relating to fugitive slaves, Indiferente General 2787, AGI.

[97] See Landers, "Spanish Sanctuary." Upon registering themselves and obtaining work contracts, slaves escaped from British colonists were freed by the second Spanish government; Census Returns, 1784–1814, East Florida Papers, PKY, microfilm reel 323 A; Royal decree, included in Captain General Luis de las Casas to Governor Manuel Vicente de Zéspedes, July 21, 1790, East Florida Papers, PKY, microfilm reel 1.

African Dimensions
of the Stono Rebellion

John K. Thornton

INTRODUCTION

Early American scholars have long studied the history of early modern Europe, especially England. In this essay, John Thornton demonstrates how early Americanists might profit similarly from knowledge of African history. He could not apply the methodology to a more significant event. The Stono Rebellion in September 1739 was the most violent slave uprising ever in Britain's mainland American colonies; approximately sixty black slaves and twenty-five whites in South Carolina died. Moreover, the rebellion influenced global imperial politics, taking place on the eve of war between Britain and Spain.

Since the late seventeenth century, Spanish Florida had promised freedom to escaped slaves who were willing to accept Catholicism. In 1738 the Spanish governor also established Gracia Real de Santa Teresa de Mose, *the first community of free blacks in what is now the United States. Thornton argues that the Kongolese heritage among leaders of the Stono Rebellion made them particularly susceptible to Spanish appeals. Catholic missionaries from Portugal had converted Africans in the kingdom of Kongo (in modern Angola) in the sixteenth century. Thus Kongolese slaves in South Carolina had religious as well as personal reasons for wanting to reach Florida.*

Thornton's analysis of an exceptional event also informs our understanding of the everyday realities of slave life in the Lower South. Note, in particular, his depiction of the rich cultural diversity within America's

John Thornton, "African Dimensions of the Stono Rebellion," *American Historical Review*, 96 (1991), pp. 1101–13. Copyright © 1991 American Historical Association. Reprinted by permission of American Historical Association and by John Thornton.

I would like to thank the Carter Woodson Institute of the University of Virginia, whose support for the years 1984–1985 began the project from which this essay is drawn. I also benefited from a grant for additional research from the National Endowment for the Humanities, Summer Stipend (1988) on European military encounters with non-European Atlantic societies in the Columbian era. Finally, thanks to Joseph C. Miller, Linda M. Heywood, Michael Birkner, and Susan Mackielwicz for their comments on earlier versions.

slave population. Increasing awareness of this diversity is forcing histori-
ans to reconsider age-old historical categories. For example, should scholars
refer to African slaves, whenever possible, by their respective group and re-
gional identities as they now do for native Americans and Europeans?
Writing from the perspective of the slaves, Thornton describes confronta-
tions during the Stono Rebellion as "military engagements."

- *Should historians refer to slave revolts as wars instead of rebellions?*
- *What challenges might internal cultural differences have posed for Amer-*
  ica's slave communities?
- *How does Thornton suggest that these differences helped to undermine the*
  Stono Rebellion?

African Background

The Stono Rebellion of 1739 was one of the largest and costliest in the history
of the United States. In studying it, historians have generally not appreciated
the extent to which the African background of the participants may have
shaped their decision to revolt or their subsequent actions. This essay addresses this upheaval in South Carolina in terms of its African background
and attempts to show that understanding the history of the early eighteenth-
century kingdom of Kongo can contribute to a fuller view of the slaves' motivations and actions.

In some ways, the failure to consider the African background of the revolt is surprising, since a number of historians have recently explored the
possibility of African religions, cultures, and societies playing an important
role in other aspects of South Carolina life. Peter Wood, author of the richest
examination of Stono, was one of the pioneers in considering African competence at rice growing as important in shaping the decisions of slave buyers, a point followed up in great detail by Daniel Littlefield.[1] Wood also argued that the African origins of the slaves can do much to explain a range of
behaviors, from health patterns to language.[2] Tom Shick showed that African
concepts of health and healing influenced the development of folk medicine
in South Carolina, and Margaret Washington Creel explained religious development in terms of African religion and religiosity.[3]

Historians have yet to apply the same sort of approach to the Stono Rebellion. Scholars of the United States interested in the African background of
American history have usually sought general information about African

---

[1] Peter B. Wood, *Black Majority: Negroes in Colonial South Carolina from 1670 through the Stono Rebellion* (New York, 1974), 56–62; Daniel Littlefield, *Rice and Slaves: Ethnicity and the Slave Trade in
Colonial South Carolina* (Baton Rouge, La., 1981).

[2] Wood, *Black Majority*, 63–91, 167–91.

[3] Tom W. Shick, "Healing and Race in the South Carolina Low Country," in Paul Lovejoy, ed.,
Africans in Bondage: Studies in Slavery and the Slave Trade (Madison, Wis., 1986), 107–24; Margaret
Washington Creel, *A Peculiar People: Slave Religion and Community Culture among the Gullahs*
(New York, 1988).

culture by reading the accounts of modern anthropologists and ethnologists, which are not always helpful for understanding specific historical situations. Appreciating the African roots of the Stono Rebellion, for example, requires a specific understanding of the kingdom of Kongo between 1680 and 1740 rather than simply a broad understanding of African culture. Historians of Africa, who have access to this type of specific information, have, unfortunately, rarely used it in a way helpful to their colleagues in U.S. history.[4]

Although the Stono Rebellion was very important in the history of South Carolina, it was not well documented. Only one eyewitness account is extant, supplemented by several secondhand reports.[5] Many English residents of South Carolina, including the anonymous author of the best account, believed that the revolt was somehow precipitated by Spanish propaganda and was part of the larger set of tensions that led to war between England and Spain in 1740. English officials reported a number of Spanish vessels acting suspiciously in English waters, and some Spaniards, including priests, were reported to have made surreptitious visits to South Carolina.[6] Among other things, these Spaniards were believed to be stirring up the slaves, offering freedom to any who would run away, as indeed many did.[7]

The actual rebellion broke out on Sunday (normally a slaves' day off), September 9, 1739, led by a man named Jemmy and including a core of some twenty "Angolan" slaves. The Spanish were suspected in the uprising because, according to the account, the slaves were Catholics, and "the Jesuits have a mission and school in that Kingdom [Angola] and many Thousands of the Negroes profess the Roman Catholic Religion." In addition to the sentiments of a common religion, many slaves could speak Portuguese, which was "as near Spanish as Scotch is to English,"[8] thus increasing their receptivity to Spanish offers and propaganda.

The rebels seized a store of firearms and marched off on a trail of destruction and killing, with two drums and banners flying, which attracted a

---

[4] The problem is compounded by linguistic difficulties: to do historical studies of eighteenth-century Angola, the most important African source of slaves for South Carolina before Stono, one needs to consult sources written in Portuguese and Italian, very few of which are available in translation and many of which are unpublished or have only been published in recent years.

[5] See "An Account of the Negroe Insurrection in South Carolina" (undated, *ca.* 1740), in Allen D. Candler and William J. Northern, eds., *Colonial Records of the State of Georgia* (1904–16; rpt. edn., New York, 1970), 22/2: 232–36. The most useful secondhand accounts are "A Ranger's Report of Travels with General Oglethorpe, 1739–42" (diary), in William D. Merenes, ed., *Travels in the American Colonies* (New York, 1916), 222–23; and William Stephens, *A Journal of the Proceedings in Georgia, Beginning October 24, 1737 . . .* , 2 vols. (London, 1742), 2: 128–30 (this journal was also reprinted in Candler and Northern, *Colonial Records*, vol. 4). This last document is closest in time, dated September 13, 1739, just four days after the revolt.

[6] Some of these events are reported in Stephens, *Journal*, 2: 77, 78. In retrospect, Stephens was glad that earlier they had stopped a priest on the Georgia coast; 130.

[7] The earlier incidents are detailed in Wood, *Black Majority*, 309–12; on runaways in Spanish Florida, see Jane Landers, "Gracia Real de Santa Teresa de Mose: A Free Black Town in Spanish Colonial Florida," *AHR*, 95 (February 1990): 9–30.

[8] Candler and Northern, "Account of Negroe Insurrection," 233.

large crowd of slaves. Having reached over sixty in number, they paused at a large field and "set to dancing, Singing and beating Drums to draw more Negroes to them." Shortly afterward, now numbering ninety, they met a force of militia, and a battle resulted. The slaves were dispersed, though not without "acting boldly" and leaving some dead.[9] The slaves were not finished, however, for they re-formed and continued toward the Spanish possessions around St. Augustine, one body of about ten fleeing until caught by mounted troops the next day.[10] A week later, another group fought a pitched battle with pursuing militia about thirty miles south of the initial skirmish.[11]

While the immediate causes of the revolt clearly lay in the difficult conditions of slavery in South Carolina, detailed in Wood's analysis of the colony and the revolt,[12] several elements in the eyewitness account suggest that, along with English mistreatment and Spanish promises, the African background of the slaves contributed to the nature of the revolt. A study of the African background supports the following interpretation: first, South Carolina slaves were in all likelihood not drawn from the Portuguese colony of Angola (as the account implies) but from the kingdom of Kongo (in modern Angola), which was a Christian country and had a fairly extensive system of schools and churches in addition to a high degree of literacy (at least for the upper class) in Portuguese. In its creole form, Portuguese was also a widely used language of trade as well as the second language of educated Kongolese. The Kongolese were proud of their Christian and Catholic heritage, which they believed made them a distinctive people, and thus Kongolese slaves would have seen the Spanish offers in terms of freedom of religion (or rather, freedom of Catholic religion) as additionally attractive beyond promises of freedom in general.

Second, throughout the eighteenth century, Kongo was disturbed by sporadic and sometimes lengthy civil wars, which resulted in the capture and sale of many people, no small number of whom would have been soldiers with military training. Significant changes in the organization and training of armies that were occurring at the same time had increased the number of soldiers trained in the use of firearms, thus increasing the likelihood that such soldiers would be enslaved. These ex-soldiers might contrast with the untrained villagers often netted by slave raids, judicial enslavement, or other means by which slaves ended up being sold to the Americas. Former soldiers might have provided the military core of the rebels, who fought on after their first engagement and generally gave a good account of themselves.

[9] Candler and Northern, "Account of Negroe Insurrection," 234–35; Stephens, *Journal*, 128.
[10] Stephens, *Journal*, 129, 235.
[11] Andrew Leslie to Philip Bearcroft, January 7, 1740, quoted in Stephens, *Journal*, 318–19; see also Frank Klingberg, *An Appraisal of the Negro in Colonial South Carolina* (Washington, D.C., 1941), 80.
[12] Wood, *Black Majority*, 271–320.

From patterns of the English slave trade to central Africa, we know it is unlikely that the "Kingdom of Angola" to which the author of the main account of the Stono Rebellion referred was the Portuguese colony known as Angola, largely because the colony sent its slaves on Portuguese and Brazilian ships to Brazil and not to English shipping bound for North America.[13] Rather, the author surely meant the general stretch of central Africa known to English shippers as the Angola coast. This area included coastal parts of modern Zaire, Congo-Brazzaville, and Gabon as well as Angola. The English slave trade, conducted in this period by the Royal African Company, fixed its operations on the northern part of the coast, especially at the town of Kabinda, just north of the mouth of the Zaire River.[14] The importance of Kabinda is underscored by the fact that, according to company records, every central African voyage the company undertook in the 1720s gave Kabinda as its destination.[15] Kabinda was the capital of an independent state, which, lying as it did against a sparsely inhabited interior, did not procure many slaves itself but served as an export station for suppliers coming from the south. Since Kabinda's first line of supply was its southern neighbor across the Zaire, the "Angolans" of the Stono Rebellion most likely came from Kongo. Eighteenth-century visitors such as James Barbot often left from Kabinda to visit other ports along the Kongo coast to the south or up the Zaire River to the town of Nzari (Zaire).[16] Accounts of the 1760s refer to a brisk trade in Kongo's province of Mbula lying on the Zaire and upstream of Nzari, which supplied English, French, and Dutch merchants (probably based at Kabinda) as well.[17]

The possibility that people from other parts of central Africa were involved in the rebellion cannot be completely ruled out, however, since Kabinda was also served by the Vili trading network. Centered in the kingdom of Loango, farther north up the coast, Vili traders had built a series of towns since at least the mid-seventeenth century under a disciplined cara-

---

[13] For a full discussion of the legal strictures as well as the substantial smuggling, see Joseph C. Miller, *Way of Death: Merchant Capitalism and the Angolan Slave Trade, 1730–1830* (Madison, Wis., 1988), 245–83.

[14] A general survey of the English trade of this coast is presented in Phyllis Martin, *The External Trade of the Loango Coast, 1576–1870* (Oxford, 1972), 75–130.

[15] David Galenson, *Traders, Planters, and Slaves: Market Behavior in Early English America* (Cambridge, 1986), 164–65.

[16] James Barbot, "Abstract of a Voyage to the Kongo River and Kabinda in 1700," in Thomas Astley, ed., *A New General Collection of Voyages and Travels . . .* , 5 vols. (London, 1746), 3: 202–09.

[17] Cherubino da Savona, "Breve ragguaglio del 'Regno di Congo, e sue Missione' scritto dal Padre Cerubino da Savona, Missionario Apostolico Capuccino" (MS of 1775), fols. 42, 44; mod. edn. in Carlo Toso, ed., "Relazioni inedite di P. Cherubino Cassinis da Savona sul 'Congo e sue Missioni,'" *L'Italia francescana*, 45 (1975): 136–214. A French translation is available, Louis Jadin, "Aperçu de la situation du Congo en 1760 et rite d'élection des rois en 1775, d'après le P. Cherubino da Savona, missionnaire au Congo de 1759 à 1774," *Bulletin, Institute historique belge de Rome*, 35 (1963): 343–419.

van system across Kongo that supplied many of their slaves,[18] but they also contacted suppliers outside Kongo. The Vili engaged in trade with Portuguese Angola despite colonial attempts to prohibit it, and they dealt extensively with Matamba, Angola's independent eastern neighbor.[19] In eastern Kongo, they contacted the merchants of Kongo's marquisate of Nzombo, whose operations extended to the east and included many non-Kongolese.[20] Nzombo merchants capitalized on the expansion of the Lunda empire in the second quarter of the eighteenth century to supply slaves to the Vili, although, before 1740, such slaves would not have been available in large numbers.[21] Likewise, Vili merchants operating to the east and north of Kongo could buy slaves at the busy markets around the Malebo Pool, which was served by merchants originating higher up the Zaire River.[22]

Thus merchants based at Kabinda would buy slaves from an extensive area of central Africa. Nevertheless, the majority enslaved in the period between about 1710 and 1740 were probably from Kongo. First of all, the kingdom was the principal supplier to Kabinda-based merchants and to Vili merchants as well. Second, the eastern regions served by merchants in Nzombo and the Malebo Pool were not as fully engaged in the slave trade in the early eighteenth century as they would become by mid-century, especially after the arrival of Lunda armies in the Kwango region around 1750. Third, the southern regions were jealously guarded by the Portuguese authorities, who sought to block trade northward with a fort at Nkoje built in 1759 specifically to stop Vili traders.[23] Even though the Portuguese could not stop northbound trade completely—it continued to reach Kabinda by overland or

[18] For a detailed discussion on trading networks in Angola and its eastern regions, see Miller, *Way of Death,* 207–83.

[19] See Martin, *External Trade,* 130; Miller, *Way of Death,* 200–03.

[20] On the Nzombo traders, see da Savona, "Breve ragguaglio," 136–214.

[21] For an assessment of the Lunda expansion, see John Thornton, "The Chronology and Causes of Lunda Expansion to the West, ca. 1700–1852," *Zambia Journal of History,* 1 (1981): 1–13. Kongo (presumably Nzombo) participation in the trade of Lunda slaves was noted in 1756 by the Portuguese traveler Manuel Correia Leitão, "Relação brêve summário da viagem que eo, o sargento-mor dos moradores do Dande fiz as remotas partes de Cassange e Olos . . . 15 de agosto de 1756," in Gastão Sousa Dias, "Uma viagem a Cassange nos meados do século XVIII," *Boletim da Sociedade de Geográfia de Lisboa,* 56 (1938): 19–20, 25. Note that Cherubino da Savona had Lunda (Mollua) as one of Kongo's neighbors by 1760; da Savona, "Breve ragguaglio," fol. 41v.

[22] A description of the Malebo Pool markets in the late seventeenth and early eighteenth centuries can be found in Luca da Caltanisetta, "Relatione del Viaggo e Missione fatta per me Fra' Luca da Caltanisetta . . . nel 1691 al . . ." (MS of 1701), fols. 55–60v; published in Romain Rainero, ed., *Il Congo agli inizi del settecento nella relazione di P. Luca da Caltanisetta* (Florence, 1974); French translation, François Bontinck, *Diaire congolaise, 1690–1701* (Brussels, 1970). See also Marcellino d'Atri, "Giornate Apostoliche fatte da me Fra Marcellino d'Atri, Predicator Cappuccino nelle messioni de Regni d'Angola e Congo . . . 1690" (MS of 1708), fols. 306–34; mod. edn., Carlo Toso, *L'anarchia Congolese nel Sec. XVII: La relazione inedita di Marcellino d'Atri* (Genoa, 1984). For the history of the commercial group upriver, see Robert Harms, *River of Wealth, River of Sorrow: The Central Zaire Basin in the Era of the Slave and Ivory Trade* (New Haven, Conn., 1981).

[23] Miller, *Way of Death,* 277–78, 582–85.

coastal routes and French, English, and Dutch merchants based on the north coast—they probably did limit it considerably.

The background of trade points strongly to a Kongo origin of the Stono slaves, but it is their adherence to Catholicism that confirms it. Only two countries in central Africa were Christian: Kongo and the Portuguese colony of Angola. Missionaries based in Angola did some work in eastern areas outside colonial control, such as Matamba, but they were limited by a shortage of missionaries in the eighteenth century.[24] Even in the best of times, these missions were typically of short duration and did not lead to the establishment of a long-lasting, permanent church organization.[25] In eastern Angola, moreover, admission of missionaries and acceptance of baptism was usually linked to surrender to Portugal, which slowed missionary work and restricted mass conversions.[26] The slaves from the east of Kongo, supplied by Nzombo or Vili merchants, were definitely not Christians according to the Italian Capuchin missionary in Kongo, Cherubino da Savona, who referred to them as "heathens."[27]

Of these two Christian countries, Angola was unlikely to export slaves to English ships, especially Christian slaves who would surely have been drawn from areas under direct Portuguese control, where Portuguese restrictions were strongest. That Christian slaves in English hands would be from Kongo is substantiated by complaints of the Spanish Governor Antonio de Salas of New Granada (Colombia) to the Spanish crown in 1735. He stated that English merchants representing the South Sea Company (drawing on the same sources as the English supplying South Carolina) were introducing "black Christians of the Congo" into Cartagena.[28]

These same "black Christians of the Congo" were the leading rebels of the Stono Rebellion, susceptible to Spanish and Catholic propaganda. They came from a culture well disposed toward Catholics. The Kongolese of the eighteenth century regarded their Christianity as a fundamental part of their national identity,[29] since the kingdom was voluntarily converted with the

[24] See, for example, Anselmo da Castelvetrano, "Relatione dello stato in cui presentemente si trovano le Missioni Cappuccini in Regno di Congo," October 14, 1742, Scritture riferite nel Congregazioni Generali, vol. 712, fols. 296–305, Archivio "De Propaganda Fide" (Rome). Also, *ibid.,* Acta, vol. 112 (1742), fol. 422. On the general state of the Capuchin mission, and other ecclesiastical bodies in Kongo and Angola, see Graziano Saccardo [da Leguzzano], *Congo e Angola, con la storia del missione dei Cappuccini,* 3 vols. (Venice, 1982–84), vol. 2, *passim.*
[25] An extreme example comes from Kasanje in the 1660s; see Giovanni Antonio Cavazzi, "Missione Evangelica al Regno di Congo" (MS of 1665), Book 3, MSS Araldi Family (Modena).
[26] Beatrix Heintze, "Luso-African Feudalism in Angola? The Vassal Treaties of the Sixteenth to Eighteenth Centuries," *Revista Portuguesa de História,* 18 (1980): 111–31.
[27] da Savona, "Breve ragguaglio," fol. 42.
[28] Documents cited and quoted in Jorge Palacios Preciado, *La Trata de negros por Cartagena de Indias* (Tunja, 1973), 349.
[29] John K. Thornton, "Demography and History in the Kingdom of Kongo, 1550–1750," *Journal of African History,* 18 (1977): 507–50. See the revealing comments of Luca da Caltanisetta, "Rela-

baptism of King Nzinga Nkuwu as João I in 1491, not linked to submission to Portugal as many of the eastern Angolan conversions were. It had independent relations with Rome and its own internally developed church and school system.[30]

This locally rooted Christian tradition is sometimes regarded as less than orthodox. Most modern scholars have pointed out that the Kongolese simply added Christian labels to their indigenous beliefs. Foreign clergy who worked in Kongo in the seventeenth and eighteenth centuries often regarded them as "Christians in name only," although some other accounts praise them as model Christians.[31] But, whatever modern scholars or some eighteenth-century priests thought, the Kongolese regarded themselves as Christians. The elite carefully maintained chapels and sent their children to schools, and the ordinary people learned their prayers and hymns, even in the eighteenth century, when ordained clergy were often absent.[32] Even those priests who doubted the orthodoxy of the Kongolese did not doubt their sincerity, since, as priests, they were often surrounded by crowds of people singing hymns or demanding their children be baptized. The high wooden crosses that marked Kongolese chapels could still be seen in the twentieth century.[33] These observations by travelers in Africa were seconded by occasional clerical observations in the Americas, where Kongolese slaves were well known to be Christians.[34] The same was true in Spanish Florida, for, in 1748, a free Kongolese, Miguel Domingo, told the priest at Garcia Real de Santa Teresa de Mose that he had been baptized and continued to pray in Kikongo, probably using prayers like those printed in the Kikongo catechism of 1624.[35]

---

tione del Viaggio," fols. 15, 25v. See the French translation by Bontinck, *Diaire congolaise*, for supporting references to Christianity, especially the rigorous following of the sacraments (particularly marriage) as distinctively Kongolese attributes.

[30] For the origin and development of Christianity in Kongo, see John Thornton, "The Development of an African Catholic Church in the Kingdom of Kongo, 1491–1750," *Journal of African History*, 25 (1984): 147–49.

[31] Hilton, *Kingdom of Kongo*, 179–98; Wyatt MacGaffey, *Religion and Society in Central Africa: The Bakongo of Lower Zaire* (Chicago, 1986), 198–211; Andrea da Pavia, "Viaggio Apostolico alla Missione" (MS *ca.* 1690), MS 3165, Biblioteca Nacional de Madrid; da Savona, "Breve ragguaglio," *passim;* Rafael Castello de Vide, "Viagem do Congo do Missionário Fr. Raphael de Castello de Vide, hoje Bispo do São Tomé" (MS of 1788), MS Vermelho, 296 fol. 77 and *passim,* Academia das Ciênças (Lisbon).

[32] For example, see the account of da Savona, "Breve ragguaglio," fols. 42v, 43, 45, 45v. Also see Castello de Vide, "Viagem do Congo," fols. 53, 64, and *passim.*

[33] François Bontinck, "Les Croix du bois dans l'ancien royaume de Kongo," *Miscellanea historiae pontificiae,* 50 (1983): 199–213.

[34] In addition to the correspondence of Antonio de Salas cited above, see John Thornton, "On the Trail of Voodoo: African Christianity in Africa and the Americas," *The Americas,* 44 (1988): 268–69.

[35] Landers, "Gracia Real de Santa Teresa de Mose," 27, citing a baptismal register entry of January 26, 1748. The catechism text was reprinted with French translation and annotation by

In many ways, acceptance of the Portuguese language as the official language of the kingdom of Kongo paralleled the acceptance of Christianity.
The author of the account of the Stono Rebellion believed that the slaves
were especially open to Spanish propaganda because some could speak its
Iberian sister language, and at least some Kongolese slaves could indeed do
this. Almost from the start of European contacts, the Kongolese developed
literacy in Portuguese: the first letter composed by a literate Kongolese dated
from 1491.[36] Schools developed rapidly in Kongo, and by the seventeenth
century there was a school in every major provincial capital.[37] Literacy was
more or less restricted to the upper class, but the fact that Kongo's archives
and official documents were written in Portuguese helped create a general
familiarity with the language among the ordinary people.[38]

More important for the people, undoubtedly, was the dominance of Portuguese in the language of trade, not just in Kongo but in the whole of west-
central Africa.[39] The status of Portuguese (or rather, creole Portuguese) as a
trade language did not mean that all, or even most, Kongolese could speak
Portuguese; in fact, governors of Angola complained that even citizens of the
colony seemed to prefer African languages to Portuguese at home.[40] But it
did mean that among any sizable group of Kongolese slaves there were
likely to be bilingual speakers. During an earlier period, Jesuit missionaries

---

François Bontinck and D. Ndembe Nsasi, *Le Catéchisme kikongo de 1624: Réédition critique* (Brussels, 1978). Italian clergy introduced a new edition in 1650, and copies were extant in the nineteenth century.

[36] See Rui da Pina's untitled account (in an early sixteenth-century Italian translation), fol.
99rb–100vb, photographically reproduced in Francisco Leite da Faria, "Uma relação de Rui de
Pina sobre o Congo escrita em 1492," *Studia*, 19 (1966), which quotes a letter of the king of
Kongo written about September or October 1491. The author of the letter is likely to have been
a Kongolese who had visited Portugal between 1488 and 1491, "a black Christian who knew
how to read and write, who began to teach the young men *(moços)* of the Court and children of
the nobility, which is a great number"; Rui da Pina, *Cronica del Rey D. Joham I (ca.* 1515), cap. 63,
excerpted in António Brásio, ed., *Monumenta Missionaria Africana*, 1st ser., 14 vols. (Lisbon,
1952–81), 1: 136.

[37] For a summary of Capuchin educational work, see Saccardo [da Leguzzano], *Congo e Angola*,
1: 402–15.

[38] On literacy, see John Thornton, *The Kingdom of Kongo: Civil War and Transition, 1641–1718*
(Madison, Wis., 1983), 67–68; Anne Hilton, *The Kingdom of Kongo* (Oxford, 1985), 79–83, 205, 217;
Susan H. Broadhead, "Beyond Decline: The Kingdom of the Kongo in the Eighteenth and Nine-
teenth Centuries," *International Journal of African Historical Studies*, 12 (1979): 633–35.

[39] Jean-Luc Vellut, "Relations internationales au moyen-Kwango et d'Angola dans la deuxième
moitié du XVIIIᵉ siècle," *Etudes d'histoire africaine*, 1 (1970): 82–89.

[40] This was a constant complaint of mid-eighteenth-century governors; see, for example, Memorial of Francisco Innocencio de Sousa Coutinho, 1765, Fundo Geral, Códice 8554, fol. 28, Biblioteca Nacional de Lisboa. This and other complaints ought to be taken as indications of the
failure of the Portuguese government to replace Kimbundu as the language of the colony, rather
than that Kimbundu and not Portuguese were known, for Sousa Coutinho took Brazil, a completely Lusophonic country (in his opinion), as a model.

in America had routinely used bilingual Kongolese as catechists.[41] Thus, in the context of colonial South Carolina, Spanish agents were quite likely to be able to communicate with others who knew no Portuguese.

The slaves fought well in the various military engagements that made up the Stono Rebellion. This may have been a result of their bravery and desperation, or they may have acquired military skills as soldiers of the colonies. In the Americas, slaves did sometimes serve in the colonial militia, and they may have been trained there. Wood examined the issue, however, and pointed out that militia service for slaves, while common in the earlier periods, had been phased out by the 1720s. By that time, South Carolina had already passed strong restrictions against slaves possessing firearms, and slaves no longer served in the militia, although many probably still had access to guns for hunting.[42]

Military service in Africa may well have served a more important role than occasional militia service or hunting. Considering that many slaves were first captured in wars, it is reasonable to assume that some of the rebels had been soldiers.[43] Of course, not every person enslaved during military action in Kongo was a soldier. Often, armed forces raided villages, carrying off civilians who would then be sold into slavery. Luca da Caltanisetta, traveling in Kongo, noted one such example that took place on February 10, 1701: "The Mani Lumbo [a title] returned with 58 slaves captured by order of the king; he had destroyed a *libata* [village] of one of his vassals, accused of treason . . . [A]mong these slaves were many free people, some inhabitants of the *libata* . . . and others who were just there on business."[44] In another incident, da Caltanisetta recorded the poignant tale of a woman who was already a slave but whose master decided to sell her to a trader with connections to the Atlantic trade. Once the woman heard of his plans, she killed her baby and then herself rather than be deported.[45] Obviously, incidents like these could be multiplied. There were many other ways to become enslaved—kidnapping, judicial punishment, or indebtedness. Any of these methods might capture a civilian with no knowledge of military affairs at all. Soldiers were only captured in wars, wars that ranged armies against each other. However, eighteenth-century Kongo had plenty of wars.

Before 1665, Kongo was a centralized kingdom, one in which there was a great deal of internal order. If Kongolese were enslaved, it would be as a result of external attack, not internal disorder; consequently, relatively few

---

[41] This use had religious implications; see Thornton, "On the Trail of Voodoo," 271–73.

[42] Wood, *Black Majority*, 127.

[43] Wood, *Black Majority*, 126–27, proposed that African soldiers may have been brought to the Americas and cited the use of firearms in Africa, although the evidence relates to the Gold Coast rather than Angola.

[44] da Caltanisetta, "Relatione del Viaggio," fol. 99v.

[45] da Caltanisetta, "Relatione del Viaggio," fol. 20v.

Kongolese were enslaved before the mid-seventeenth century.[46] After 1665, all this changed, as civil wars raged almost constantly for the next forty-four years. While the causes and development of the wars need not concern us here,[47] it is enough to note that fairly large-scale engagements between Kongolese armies were commonplace. Some of the differences that lay behind the civil wars were patched up when most contenders recognized King Pedro IV between 1709 and 1716 and brought a formal restoration of the kingdom, but intermittent wars broke out after that.[48] Unfortunately, the documentary record that affords substantial information about Kongo in the late seventeenth and early eighteenth centuries dries up after about 1720. Nevertheless, several incidents in the 1730s are clearly indicative of major wars during that period. For example, a Capuchin priest, Angelo Maria da Polinago, visiting Kongo's coastal principality of Nsoyo in 1733, noted that he was prevented from traveling to the southern areas (in the duchy of Mbamba) because of a major war in that area.[49] Soldiers captured in this war, or others like it that are not documented, would certainly be exported, via Kabinda to Spanish Cartagena or to South Carolina by the English companies.

Some features of the account of the Stono Rebellion suggest that Kongolese soldiers taken as slaves in this and other, undocumented, wars of the 1730s were among the rebels at Stono. For example, the rebels quickly seized a supply of guns and apparently handled them well.[50] The utility of guns in a revolt is directly proportional to the skill with which the rebels are capable of using them, and this, in turn, is dependent on training. Presumably, those unfamiliar with guns might have sought other weapons, such as knives, axes, or agricultural tools, and passed up a raid on an armory. Because the colonial militia did not provide much in the way of firearms training, the possibility of an African source of training seems more likely.

Kongolese soldiers would certainly have had training with modern weapons. By the early eighteenth century, guns were becoming more and more common on African battlefields, and skill in their use was being passed on to a larger and larger group of soldiers. A military revolution was altering war in Kongo and other parts of Africa, increasing the size of armies, and replacing the hand-to-hand combat of lances, swords, and axes with the missile combat of muskets.

[46] Thornton, *Kingdom of Kongo*, xiv–xv. Slaves in the New World known as "Congos" were typically transshipped through the country from farther east and exported either through Kongo ports or by Angola-based merchants who crossed Kongo to buy slaves.

[47] For a detailed account, see Thornton, *Kingdom of Kongo*, 69–96.

[48] See Thornton, *Kingdom of Kongo*, 97–113; for a general discussion of the late eighteenth century and the pattern of wars, see Broadhead, "Beyond Decline," 635–36.

[49] Angola Maria da Polinago to Dorotea Sofia di Neoburgo, August 16, 1733, Raccolta manuscritti, busta 49, Viaggi, fol. 3, Archivio di Stato, Parma.

[50] Candler and Northern, "Account of Negroe Insurrection," 233.

Good descriptions of war in seventeenth-century Kongo make clear that, in general, firearms were not important in Angolan wars before 1680.[51] Rather, the musketeers who served were fairly small in number and, moreover, tended to be drawn from an elite of *mestiços*, racially mixed Kongolese with some Portuguese ancestry. At the battle of Mbwila in 1665, Kongo assembled only 360 musketeers under a *mestiço* commander, out of an army of many thousands.[52] Donigio Carli da Piacenza, an Italian Capuchin traveler, likewise met only some twenty musketeers in the service of the powerful duke of Mbamba in 1668, all *mestiços*.[53] Then, such soldiers were not only rare but had social connections that made their enslavement and sale to the Atlantic world improbable.

But this situation changed during the late seventeenth and early eighteenth centuries. In all probability, African generals decided to include more musketeers because of improvements in technology, dating from the 1680s, which saw the replacement of the matchlock musket by the more reliable flintlock weapon. In Europe, armies were altered dramatically; the masses of pikemen who had dominated seventeenth-century wars exchanged their pikes for muskets with fixed bayonets to serve the same purpose. Soldiers armed in this way prevailed over the European battlefield until well into the nineteenth century.[54] Many African armies seem to have rearmed at about the same time. Ray Kea has shown how armies on the Gold Coast rearmed and swiftly changed battlefield tactics during this period.[55] Unfortunately, the sources do not allow us to trace developments in Angola with the detail that can be shown in West Africa. Nevertheless, mid-eighteenth-century sources that describe battles fought by the Portuguese-led Angolan army, and its African opponents in southern Kongo, include the musketeer as a prominent force on the battlefield.[56] He was perhaps significant much earlier. The thousands of soldiers who fell in to greet a Capuchin visitor to Kongo's coastal province of Sonyo in 1694 were already equipped with muskets.[57] In

[51] For a general survey of the situation, see John Thornton, "The Art of War in Angola, 1595–1680," *Comparative Studies in Society and History*, 30 (1988): 373–75.
[52] Thornton, *Kingdom of Kongo*, 75.
[53] Dionigio Carli da Piacenza, *Viaggio del P. Michelangelo de' Guattini da Reggio et del P. Dionigi de' Carli da Piacenza al regno del Congo* (Reggio, 1671).
[54] Theodore Ropp, *War in the Modern World* (New York, 1962), 37–60.
[55] Ray Kea, *Settlements, Trade and Polities on the Seventeenth-Century Gold Coast* (Baltimore, Md., 1982), 154–68.
[56] Alexandre Elias da Silva Corrêa, *História de Angola* (MS *ca.* 1789), 2 vols. (Lisbon, 1937), 1: 48–62, a general account of techniques of war in the 1770s illustrating an event (of 1774) based on contemporary records as preserved in a recension of the "Catálogo dos Governadores de Angola." For further textual history, see Joseph C. Miller and John Thornton, "The Chronicle as Source, History and Hagiograpy: The *Catálogo dos Governadores de Angola*," *Paideuma*, 33 (1987): 359–90.
[57] Filippo Bernardi da Firenze, "Ragguaglio del Congo, cioè viaggi fatti da' missionarij apostolici cappuccini della provincia di Toscana a' regni del Congo, Angola, Matamba, ecc . . ." (1711),

1701, Prince António Baretto da Silva of Sonyo felt a sufficient need for firearms that he wrote the pope, asking for a dispensation on the ruling that Prince António not sell slaves to English and Dutch "heretics" in order to arm his soldiers with the muskets they imported.[58]

During the 1730s, however, this military revolution was still incomplete, especially in areas such as south Kongo, where access to firearms imports was restricted by distance, price, and Portuguese policy. When Anton Felice Tomassi da Cortona visited the duke of Mbamba in Kongo's southern interior in 1734, he found the duke's military retinue still contained archers and lancers as well as numerous musketeers, more than Dionigio Carli had noted fifty years earlier.[59] Although muskets were not yet the only weapon used, muskets had passed from the prerogative of a small, racially mixed elite to the hands of more people, and the trend toward an increasing use of muskets was clear. By the 1780s, the musket was the most important weapon in use in warfare. In 1781, Father Raphael de Castello de Vide saw the royal army assemble for war, composed, he believed, of "more than thirty thousand men, armed with powder and ball,"[60] a phrase suggesting a virtually exclusive reliance on muskets. Indeed, other military units that the priest traveled with were armed with muskets as well.[61]

Not only were muskets used by a greater percentage of soldiers than before but the use of trained military forces had also spread to outlying areas and led to recruitment of more soldiers among the population. At its height, Kongo's army was centralized: the authorities in the capital (São Salvador) had most of the soldiers, while the provincial nobility possessed relatively small guard units.[62] But after the civil wars began in Kongo, armed retinues became essential in even small provinces and towns. Tomassi da Cortona noted that the duke of Mbamba had a fairly large standing army in 1734, and his contemporary, Angelo Maria da Polinago, observed that even the small marquisate of Kitombo mustered a considerable force of soldiers to greet him in 1733.[63] Thus, although the size of any given army probably fell dur-

---

Archivio Provinciale de' Cappuccini da Provincia di Toscana, Montughi Convent, Florence, p. 619.

[58] Prince António Baretto da Silva to Pope Clement XI, October 4, 1701, Scritture refirite nelli Congressi, Africa-Congo, vol. 3, fols. 288–88v, Archivio "De Propaganda Fide."

[59] Anton Felice Tomassi da Cortona to his brother, Anibal Tomassi, November 20, 1734, Papers of the Tomassi Family, Cortona, fol. 2. Luca da Caltanisetta also noted that arrows were still used along with muskets in the last years of the seventeenth century; "Relatione del Viaggo," fol. 17 (incident of 1694).

[60] Castello de Vide, "Viagem do Congo," fol. 118.

[61] Castello de Vide, "Viagem do Congo," fol. 93.

[62] Thornton, *Kingdom of Kongo*, 42.

[63] Tomassi da Cortona to Anibal Tomassi, November 20, 1734, Tomassi Papers, fol. 2; Angelo Maria da Polinago to Dorotea Sofia Neoburgo, August 16, 1733, Raccolta manoscritti, busta 49, Viaggi, fol. 2, Archivio di Stato, Parma.

ing the period 1665 to 1740, as a result of the decentralization of power the total number of people under arms and receiving military training with firearms probably rose.[64]

In addition to handling firearms in a way that suggests military training, the Stono rebels also gave other indications of an African military background. For example, they marched under banners like the unit flags that African armies flew in their campaigns,[65] and they used drums to encourage the rebels. Of course, such behavior might simply have been imitative of colonial militias in which Africans may still have served or at the very least observed. Far more significant was the fact that the rebels danced.[66] Their dancing need not have been simply a reflection of the joy of the prospect of freedom or the result of drunkenness. Although European and Euro-American armies and militias marched, flew flags, and beat drums as they approached combat, they did not dance. Military dancing was a part of the African culture of war. In African war, dancing was as much a part of military preparation as drill was in Europe. Before 1680, when soldiers fought hand to hand, dancing was a form of training to quicken reflexes and develop parrying skills. Dancing in preparation for war was so common in Kongo that "dancing a war dance" (*sangamento*) was often used as a synonym for "to declare war" in seventeenth-century sources.[67]

Dancing was less useful in the period after 1680, since hand-to-hand combat was largely replaced by missile tactics with muskets. However, Africans did not use bayonets on their muskets; they needed swords and other hand-to-hand weapons for those times when close fighting was required. One Portuguese commander who fought in the late eighteenth century in southern Kongo, after praising his opponents' skill with muskets and their nearly universal use of the weapon, noted that they retained the "arma

[64] Miller has argued that firearms were less important in central Africa than proposed here. His main basis for this is the conclusion that firearms imports were insufficient to arm more than about 20,000 soldiers in the whole of central Africa (*Way of Death,* 86–94), even though he estimated that as many as 60,000 guns were imported per year. This low number derives from a pessimistic judgment of the capacity of Africans to repair defective imports or maintain existing weapons. I believe Miller is wrong in part because of the eyewitness evidence of large armies armed with muskets cited in previous notes and also on the grounds that his estimates of imports, number of serviceable weapons at any time, repair capacities of African smiths, and average life span of weapons are all considerably too low.
[65] Candler and Northern, "Account of Negroe Insurrection," 234. Wood proposed a religious interpretation for the banners, *Black Majority,* 316, n. 30, even though no eighteenth-century source mentions the sort of cultic devotion to flags that he suggested. Unit flags were commonplace, however, in seventeenth-century armies; see Thornton, "Art of War," 366–67; and Castello de Vide mentioned them as always being a part of any force in the later eighteenth century; de Vide, "Viagem do Congo," fols. 93, 96.
[66] Candler and Northern,"Account of Negroe Insurrection," 234.
[67] It is so used, for the seventeenth century, even in sources by Europeans; see Mateus Cardoso, "Relação do alevamento de Dom Afonso, irmão del Rey Dom Alvaro III de Congo" (January 1622), Assistencia Portugal, vol. 55, fol. 115v, Archivum Romanum Societatis Iesu (Rome).

r hand-to-hand fighting.[68] Thus dancing may have been important even after guns became the principal weapons to ensure that soldiers still honed their skill in hand-to-hand fighting, or it may have survived just as close-order drill survives in modern armies, where it has little combat utility, as a distinctive element of military life. Luca da Caltanisetta still described the musketeer armies of the prince of Nsoyo in 1691 as dancing in preparation for war, and Castello de Vide noted dancing before battle in 1781.[69]

The African military background can also shed some light on the tactics of the Stono rebels. At first glance, they do not appear to have been very soldierly, standing in a disorderly group and dispersing after a brief engagement. Many rapidly fled to their masters' homes, and only a small determined core persisted, fighting several more encounters with the colonial militia in the days after the first battle.[70] It is most likely that, by the time the colonial forces met the rebels, their numbers had been swelled by a large number of slaves who had no military experience but hoped that the rebels would succeed and deliver them from slavery. When the real fighting began, these hangers-on might have been the ones who dispersed quickly, hoping to get back to their masters' farms before they were missed.[71]

But the tactics of the core of the rebels, perhaps those twenty Angolans who started the revolt and a few others, who had all the guns, disorderly as they seemed, are consistent with a central African model. Europeans' ideas of a proper military formation were based on the necessity, created by cavalry, of maintaining close order at all times. Indeed, the European musketeer of the eighteenth century was a converted pikeman, just as his musket with bayonet was a combination pike and missile weapon.[72] In central Africa, where there was never a large or effective cavalry, the musketeer was more

[68] Paulo Martins Pinheiro de Lacerda, "Noticia da campanha e paiz do Mosul, que conquistou o Sargento Mor Paulo Martins Pinheiro de Lacerda" (1790–91), *Annaes Maritímos e Colonais*, 6 (1846): 129–30. Miller, *Way of Death*, 91, n. 57, cited this account as evidence that the Kongo possessed few guns and still fought with their traditional weapons. In fact, he pointedly praised their skill with firearms in a way that suggests it was their principal weapon, noting the use of the "arma blanca" as a secondary weapon. The use of musket fire is also clear in other accounts by Pinheiro de Lacerda, which describe the actual battles of the same campaign in greater detail; see Angola, Caixa 76, doc. 28 (May 20, 1791), Arquivo Histórico Ultramarino (Lisbon); and doc. 34, service record of Felix Xavier Pinheiro de Lacerda (his son), enclosure by Paulo Martins Pinheiro de Lacerda.

[69] da Caltanisetta, "Relatione del Viaggo," fols. 9, 25v; Castello de Vide, "Viagem do Congo," MS Vermelho 296, fols. 98, 119, Academia das Cienças. He also witnessed a *sangamento* in a village, which he compared to these military dances, and was told that the people were in fact dancing to make war on the Devil; fol. 137.

[70] Documents summarized in Wood, *Black Majority*, 318–20.

[71] Candler and Northern, "Account of Negroe Insurrection," 235.

[72] William H. McNeill, *The Pursuit of Power: Technology, Armed Force and Society since 1000* (Chicago, 1982), 125–39. When fighting with Native Americans, and even during the colonial

likely to be a converted skirmisher. Central African musketeers in the seventeenth century often opened engagements with random fire from covered positions to weaken enemy infantry. This infantry was armed with swords and battle axes intended for hand-to-hand fighting that would resolve the battle.[73] But, unlike Europeans, who retained the hand-to-hand aspects of pike warfare, central Africans greatly reduced their close fighting in favor of skirmishing tactics, which replaced the shock encounters of heavily armed infantry. Eighteenth-century battles tended to be drawn-out affairs in which units attacked the enemy, withdrew, maneuvered, and in general avoided hand-to-hand combat.[74]

Thus the Stono rebels were not revealing their rude origins when they fought in the way they did. Instead, their tactical behavior was perfectly consistent with tactics of the battlefields of Kongo. They withdrew after a brief encounter, relocated, and fought several battles over a protracted period, a pattern typical of Angola.

We can see the Stono Rebellion from a new angle if we consider the African contribution as well as the American one. The combination of evidence certainly suggests that the slaves' Christianity and the religious appeal of Spanish propaganda may have played a role in the revolt. Likewise, though less certain, the slaves' probable military experience in Africa could also have influenced their behavior and their ultimate fate.

---

wars, colonial militias sometimes abandoned these principles, however, much to the chagrin of their professional leaders or opponents.

[73] Thornton, "Art of War," 363, 374.

[74] The best description involves a southern Kongo army fighting Portuguese-led forces in the mid-eighteenth century; Silva Corrêa, *História de Angola*, 2: 48–62. See the interesting description of tactics in Pinheiro de Lacerda, "Noticia da campanha," 131–32.

"Pedlar in Divinity": George Whitefield and the Great Awakening, 1737–1745

Frank Lambert

INTRODUCTION

Historians typically recognize George Whitefield as America's first mass celebrity. The distinction is deeply ironic, for the evangelical Anglican preacher was not born in America but in England. Whitefield sparked the immense transatlantic religious revivals of the mid-eighteenth century known in America as the Great Awakening. An amateur actor, he developed an electrifying sermon style and issued dramatic appeals for an immediate sense of sin, guilt, and conversion in his listeners. Anxious followers gathered by the thousands in England, Scotland, and America to hear Whitefield's call for a spiritual "new birth."

More important, according to Frank Lambert, the drama of Whitefield's oratory transferred to the printed page. Print capitalism has aided insurgent religious movements since the Protestant Reformation. But Lambert establishes that Whitefield carried the relationship to dizzying new heights. The preacher "peddled" spiritual wares, from serialized sermons and journals to evangelical books and newspapers. His merchandising prowess prepared the ground for mass religious conversions in numerous locales. In short, Whitefield built his ministry on the partnership of medium and message.

Lambert revises the dated historical view that the Great Awakening was a reaction to new secular forces, including the market economy. The reality, he shows, was more complex: even critics of the eighteenth-century consumer revolution could not escape its pervasive influence.

Frank Lambert, " 'Pedlar in Divinity': George Whitefield and the Great Awakening, 1737–1745" in *Journal of American History*, 77 (1990), pp. 812–837. Copyright © 1990 Organization of American Historians. Reprinted with permission.

Frank Lambert is an instructor in the Department of History at Northwestern University. He wishes to thank T. H. Breen, whose encouragement and guidance sustained the project from conception to completion. He also wishes to thank James Oakes and Robert H. Wiebe for their helpful suggestions.

- *Does evidence of commercialism within religious revivals make them any less authentic?*
- *Or is Lambert correct in suggesting that ministers merely sought the most powerful vehicle available to deliver their message?*

Whether a hero or a huckster or both, George Whitefield was undoubtedly a master publicist who understood the new dynamics of communication in the commercialized Atlantic world.

When the Anglican evangelist George Whitefield arrived at Lewis Town, Pennsylvania, on October 30, 1739, he brought with him more than his zeal to declare the necessity of a spiritual new birth. His cargo in the hold of the *Elizabeth* contained boxes of evangelical books and pamphlets, including Benjamin Jenks's *Prayers and Offices of Devotion for Families*, John Flavel's *Husbandry Spiritualised*, Isaac Watts's *Divine Songs*, William Law's *A Practical Treatise Upon Christian Perfection*, John Norris's *A Treatise Concerning Christian Prudence*, 200 copies of the *Country-parson's advice to his parishioners*, and 150 volumes of the *Book of Common Prayer*. He also transported cartons of his own printed sermons, journals, letters, and prayers. These items represented just part of the apparatus he employed to generate religious enthusiasm in the intercolonial revivals known as the Great Awakening.[1]

Whitefield's shipload of consumer merchandise symbolizes his immersion in a thoroughly commercialized society, one that provided him with the means of constructing a new religious discourse—modern revivalism. Recent works have illuminated how Whitefield and other evangelicals shaped the Great Awakening. One imaginative volume has focused on Whitefield's innovations in rhetoric and social communication that challenged local distinctions and authority relations. Case studies have explored the revivalist's audiences, in particular those factors influencing the colonists' attitudes toward the awakening—a complex interaction of age, gender, church membership, and social standing. And one landmark in early American historiography has indicated that commerce—long viewed as destructive of traditional values, including piety—served as a means of promoting community and religion. However, Whitefield's appropriation of new commercial techniques to publicize the revivals has only been alluded to (often in passing) without systematic development. What was new about Whitefield

---

[1] George Whitefield, *An Account of Money, Receiv'd and Expended by the Rev. Mr. Whitefield, for the Poor of Georgia* (London, 1739); George Whitefield, *Journals* (London, 1960), 360. Benjamin Jenks, *Prayers and Offices of Devotion for Families, and for particular Persons upon most Occasions* (London, 1697); John Flavel, *Husbandry Spiritualised* (London, 1669): Isaac Watts, *Divine Songs* (London, 1680); William Law, *A Practical Treatise Upon Christian Perfection* (London, 1726); John Norris, *A Treatise Concerning Christian Prudence* (London, 1710); *The Country-parson's advice to his parishioners* (London, 1680).

was the skill as an entrepreneur, an impresario, that made him a full-fledged forerunner to evangelists like Charles Grandison Finney and Billy Graham.[2]

One recent writer asserted that "crowds materialized out of nowhere to hear [Whitefield] speak in the most stirring terms about the 'New Birth,'" adding an offhanded acknowledgment that "word" of Whitefield's successes "prepared" new regions to receive him. However, by applying means from the world of commerce to publicize his meetings, Whitefield generated large, enthusiastic crowds. Like the rest of us, the evangelist constructed his social reality with the elements at hand, and in the mid-eighteenth century, commercial language and techniques abounded, affording him a new way of organizing, promoting, and explaining his evangelical mission. Thus, the spreading market enabled him to conceive of organizing a revival spanning the Atlantic, making "the whole world his parish."[3] Improvements in marketing organization and practices provided the means of relieving the suffering of "strangers at a distance," transforming mere awareness of distant needs into a moral imperative to deliver spiritual and material aid.[4] In Whitefield's case, that meant preaching the gospel to the "uttermost parts of the earth," including the wilderness of Georgia. Drawing upon the experience of enterprising merchants selling their wares at great distances, Whitefield prepared remote auditors to receive the spoken word through advance publicity, especially that of newspaper advertising. And he employed a com-

---

[2] On rhetoric, see Harry S. Stout, *The New England Soul: Preaching and Religious Culture in Colonial New England* (New York, 1986). Case studies include Harry S. Stout and Peter S. Onuf, "James Davenport and the Great Awakening in New London," *Journal of American History*, 70 (Dec. 1983), 556–78; Peter S. Onuf, "New Lights in New London: A Group Portrait of the Separatists," *William and Mary Quarterly*, 37 (Oct. 1980), 627–43; and James Walsh, "The Great Awakening in the First Congregation of Woodbury, Connecticut," *ibid.*, 28 (Oct. 1971), 543–62. On commerce, see Christine L. Heyrman, *Commerce and Culture: The Maritime Communities of Colonial Massachusetts, 1690–1750* (New York, 1984). Whitefield's awareness of the importance of press coverage anticipates that of Charles Finney and Billy Graham. Finney advocated the use of "all appropriate means," including "blaz[ing] away in the newspapers," to promote his revivals. See William G. McLoughlin, Jr., *Modern Revivalism: Charles Grandison Finney to Billy Graham* (New York, 1959), 87. After William Randolph Hearst ordered his Los Angeles reporters to "puff Graham" because of the evangelist's anticommunist message, Graham acknowledged that "God uses the press in our work," adding "it has been one of the most effective factors in sustaining public interest through the years." See Marshall Frady, *Billy Graham: A Parable of American Righteousness* (Boston, 1979), 201.

[3] Stout, *New England Soul*, 189. On the cultural construction of social reality, see Roger Chartier, *Cultural History: Between Practices and Representations*, trans. Lydia G. Cochrane (Ithaca, 1988), 1–14. Whitefield, *Journals*, 439; John Gillies, ed., *The Works of the Reverend George Whitefield* (6 vols., London, 1771–1772), I, 312; John Gillies, ed., *Memoirs of the Reverend George Whitefield* (Middletown, 1838), 88.

[4] On the market's effects on intellectual categories and perceptions, see Thomas L. Haskell, "Capitalism and the Origins of the Humanitarian Sensibility, Part 1," *American Historical Review*, 90 (April 1985); and Thomas L. Haskell, "Capitalism and the Origins of the Humanitarian Sensibility, Part 2," *ibid.* (June 1985).

mercial vocabulary to convey the necessity of the New Birth to his listeners who themselves thought in categories of market exchange.

An argument that advance publicity and self-promotion alone explain the Grand Itinerant's attraction of unprecedented crowds is unfounded and reductionist. However, an examination of his promotional strategies does provide a new understanding not only of Whitefield's success but also of the diffusion of commercialism throughout mid-eighteenth-century society. It indicates a need to view the Great Awakening in a larger context, as part of an evangelical stirring that occurred throughout the Atlantic world. And such a study points toward a reexamination of the relation between commerce and religion, challenging the interpretation that the two were antithetical, suggesting instead a creative tension whereby evangelists such as Whitefield, while preaching against a selfish preoccupation with the pursuit of wealth, employed the tools of trade to promote the gospel.

Contemporaries observed and commented on the extent and importance of Whitefield's advance publicity. Opponents and supporters alike remarked on the evangelist's use of print to promote his work. In early 1740, the antirevivalist, Timothy Cutler, an Anglican minister in Boston, complained in a letter to the bishop of London that Whitefield's "Journals, Sermons, and Pamphlets are reprinted and eagerly bought here," adding that "the enthusiastic Notions [were] very much kindled . . . and propagated by his Writings, dispersed everywhere." Six months after the evangelist's departure from New England in October 1740, Cutler lamented that the "ill effects of Mr. Whitefield's visit might to some measure have worn off could we have been preserved from his Writings, and those of his Converts and Followers now spread all over our Country." As a tribute to Whitefield's success in employing print to disseminate his message, Cutler requested a shipment of "orthodox" books to neutralize enthusiastic influence.[5]

Thomas Prince, Jr., the prorevivalist editor of the Boston magazine Whitefield inspired, the *Christian History*, recounted the advance publicity that prepared New Englanders for the evangelist's trip in 1740. Prince recalled the succession of written works that arrived in Boston in the months preceding Whitefield's arrival. First Whitefield mailed copies of his journals and printed sermons to prominent ministers such as Benjamin Colman and Jonathan Edwards. Then Boston newspapers furnished New Englanders accounts of the preacher's successes in the middle and southern colonies— self-promoting reports written by Whitefield himself or his traveling companion William Seward, a London stockjobber, and transmitted through Benjamin Franklin's intercolonial newspaper network. Then supporters such as the Reverend Josiah Smith, heeding Whitefield's plea to "take up [their] pen[s]" on behalf of the revival, published glowing testimonials

[5] William S. Perry, ed., *Historical Collections Relating to the American Colonial Church* (4 vols., Hartford, 1870), II, 350–60.

extolling Whitefield's evangelism and humanitarianism—works that recommended the itinerant to New Englanders. Thus when Whitefield began his services, Bostonians, indeed, "were prepared to embrace him."[6]

By 1739 Whitefield had discovered that "the meanest instruments," especially the press, promoted the gospel by "excit[ing] people's curiosity, and serv[ing] to raise their attention." He explained to Colman his motives for publishing accounts of the revivals, expressing his confidence that "our Lord's cause might be promoted thereby." Whitefield believed that his mission was so great that his publicity should exceed that of "the world." Admonishing his business agent for mishandling the release of a promotional pamphlet, Whitefield wondered, "when will the children of light be as wise in their generation as the children of the world?" His opponents, however, chafed under Whitefield's control of the press. One antirevivalist complained that Whitefield so dominated the newspapers in Philadelphia in 1740 that "printers would not publish anything for [opponents of the revival] and that the press [was] shut against them," a charge Whitefield denied even as he supplied a steady stream of self-serving articles to the publishers.[7]

In the first year of Whitefield's public ministry, press coverage helped elevate him and his revival to an unprecedented level of popular acceptance. While Whitefield was not yet ordained as an Anglican minister and little known outside his hometown of Gloucester, England, he became the best-known evangelist in the Atlantic world in large part because of newspaper advertising, which interpreted his preaching as a second Reformation. The evangelical bookseller, James Hutton, recorded Whitefield's emergence as the dominant figure in the early stirrings of the revival. In 1737 Whitefield came from Oxford to London "amongst other young awakened preachers," not yet distinguished from the zealous band of aspirants to the ministry. Meanwhile John Wesley, Whitefield's mentor, who had traveled as a missionary to the new colony of Georgia, had written requesting his assistance in Savannah. Whitefield had accepted, forgoing "some advantageous proposals, which were designed to hold him back in England." Hutton reported that "notice of this was given in the papers, with some prominence . . . which brought together great numbers." A wealthy businessman who promoted charity schools—Seward—had placed that advertisement in the London newspapers. Seward introduced Whitefield to the readers as "a young gentleman of distinguished piety, very eminent in his profession, and a considerable fortune [going] voluntarily to preach the gospel in Georgia." Hutton noted that because Seward presented Whitefield as undertaking "a cause . . . without

[6] "Accounts of the Rev. Mr. Whitefield," *Christian History,* Jan. 5, 1744/1745; "Accounts of the Rev. Mr. Whitefield Continued," *ibid.,* Jan. 12, 1744/1745.
[7] *Pennsylvania Gazette,* May 1, May 8, 1740; Gillies, ed., *Works of Whitefield,* I, 291, II, 180; Whitefield, *Journals,* 407.

selfish interest, everybody ran after him." Hutton further observed that Seward "also had the result [of Whitefield's performance] put in, viz. that much money was collected at the preaching" for charity schools. For Hutton, it was the "novelty of the thing"—the bold advertising of Whitefield and his success—that attracted "many hundred people... curious to hear this Whitefield." The bookseller noted that the other young revivalists also "preached in a more than ordinarily earnest way," but Whitefield, benefiting from the prominent publicity, "was everywhere made known," and emerged as the leading evangelical preacher.[8]

Although the London clergy had long employed newspapers to publicize charity sermons, under Seward's guidance Whitefield transformed mere notices into advertisements rivaling those promoting the latest consumer goods. Typical ecclesiastical entries in the *London Daily Advertiser* announced sermons by presenting the bare essentials: who was to preach, for what charity, in which church, and at what time. And rarely did the ministers provide the press with a report of the services, such as the number attending and the amount collected. By contrast, Seward "sold" Whitefield to the readers, complete with advertising "puffs," appealing details designed to pique interest. Seward's paid advertisements appeared on the front page in the form of news articles written by a third party. The format recounted recent successes and announced upcoming events. In describing Whitefield's performance at St. Swithin's church in September 1737, Seward reported that the evangelist preached an *"excellent"* charity sermon before a *"crowded"* congregation whose contributions were *"remarkable."* He noted that Whitefield's sermon on the *"greatness* of the charity of the poor widow's mites" inspired the auditors to contribute over five pounds including "no less than 800 halfpence." He concluded by announcing Whitefield's next sermon as a continuation of the evangelist's *"truly pious"* undertaking to promote the *"good effects* [charity schools] have on the lower ranks of the people." Seward employed similar language in promoting his own stockjobbing business. His advertisement of November 11, 1739, for instance, announced that he offered for sale shares "in a *new method,* much *more advantageous* to the purchaser than they can *possibly* be bought *any other way."* Whether publicizing sermons or securities, London's daily newspapers provided a powerful means of self-presentation, a lesson Whitefield learned and applied even after Seward's death in October 1740.[9]

---

[8] "James Hutton's Account of 'The Beginning of the Lord's Work in England to 1746,'" *Proceedings of the Wesley Historical Society,* 15 (1926), 183–84; *London Daily Advertiser,* Sept. 19, 1737.

[9] For a typical sermon notice, see, for example, *London Daily Advertiser,* Sept. 24, 1737. Ibid., Sept. 28, 1737, Nov. 11, 1737 [italics added]; "A List of Deaths in the Year 1740," *Gentleman's Magazine,* 10 (Nov. 1740), 571. Whitefield had dispatched Seward to England to raise funds for a school for Negroes. Seward accompanied evangelist Howell Harris on a preaching tour through Wales, where a mob attacked them. Seward died in October 1740 from being hit in the eye by a stone.

Noting that following the press coverage "there was no end of the people flocking to hear the Word of God," Whitefield developed a sustained advertising campaign to promote his charity sermons in London prior to departing on his second American trip. Early in 1739, while collecting for an orphan house he had founded in Georgia, Seward placed two or three notices per week in the *London Daily Advertiser*, relying also on verbal communication at the services to publicize upcoming meetings. However, because of an embarrassing episode, Whitefield's "press agent" announced in the May 3 edition that "daily notice [would] be given in [the] paper." Although Whitefield had announced at a Sunday sermon when and where he would preach over the next few days, many people, including several "persons of distinction," awaited the evangelist at the wrong site. Thenceforward, daily newspaper advertising became a standard feature of Whitefield's publicity until his sailing for America almost three months later.[10]

Whitefield also benefited from the extensive advertising of his printed works, which both contributed to his growing popularity and resulted from his spreading fame. Booksellers recognized Whitefield as an author who had "made sermons, once a drug, a vendible commodity." Consequently, enterprising publishers vied with each other to exploit the lucrative demand for the evangelist's writings. In one issue of the *Daily Advertiser*, for instance, a printseller advertised a portrait of Whitefield, "neatly engrav'd from a drawing taken by an excellent painter," and on the same page, a bookseller advertised two of the evangelist's sermons plus a collection of prayers "recommended by George Whitefield." In the summer of 1738, competition between publishers over which had the right to publish Whitefield's first journal resulted in a windfall of publicity. The rivals, Thomas Cooper and James Hutton, advertised their editions on the same pages of the *Daily Advertiser* for a full week. They also engaged in a front-page debate over whose edition offered the more faithful rendering of Whitefield's manuscript. While no evidence points to Seward's involvement, someone as zealous and shrewd as he must have placed a copy of Whitefield's diary in the hands of the non-Methodist Cooper. The itinerant had mailed the document to Hutton, at the time an ardent supporter. Whatever the case, the competing advertisements heightened interest in the journals, increasing their sales and thus promoting the revival.[11]

By the beginning of 1738, colonial newspapers reprinted Whitefield's advertisements, almost two years before his preaching tour that triggered the Great Awakening. Philadelphia's *American Weekly Mercury* included

---

[10] William Seward, *Journal of a Voyage From Savannah to Philadelphia, and from Philadelphia to England, in 1740* (Boston, 1740), 16–22; *London Daily Advertiser*, May 3, 1739.

[11] Josiah Smith, *The Character, Preaching, etc., of the Reverend Mr. George Whitefield, Impartially Represented and Supported, in a Sermon, Preach'd in Charleston, South-Carolina, March 26th 1740* (Boston, 1740); *London Daily Advertiser*, Dec. 25, 1737. For the competing editions of Whitefield's journal, see *ibid.*, Aug. 3–8, 1738.

Seward's initial report of Whitefield's success at St. Swithin's, complete with the superlatives describing the evangelist's preaching and fund raising. The *Williamsburg Virginia Gazette* highlighted the revivalist's commitment to go to Georgia and his attraction of "so great a concourse of people." William Parks, the Williamsburg editor, may have selected the report about Whitefield because it stood out from the blander announcements of other Anglican clergymen. Or, he may have received the advertisement through Whitefield's expanding letter-writing network, a transatlantic chain of correspondence by which evangelicals circulated revival news, recommended devotional literature, and exchanged successful strategies. A year later, Whitefield provided Parks with material—sermons, pamphlets, newspaper reports, and journals—to reprint in his newspaper or to publish and sell through his bookstore. Whatever the case, press coverage on both sides of the Atlantic prepared men and women to receive the spoken word from this extraordinary evangelist.[12]

Upon arriving in America in October 1739, Whitefield continued to promote his revivals through vigorous newspaper coverage. Though Whitefield's associates, John Syms and James Habersham, handled "press relations" while traveling with the itinerant, Seward proved the most aggressive and effective agent. In his own journal, published in 1740 in England and America, the zealous businessman recorded his role in newspaper reporting and press relations. Successive entries during 1740 reveal the nature and extent of his activities. "April 27. Wrote paragraph for the News, of our Brother's Preaching, etc., particularly the following to be published in New York. April 29. Wrote and examined sundry things for the Press; Particularly Mr. Whitefield's Letter. . . . May 2. Call'd at Mr. Franklin's the Printer."[13]

While advance men and merchants performed the role of press agents, Whitefield himself exercised direct control over press coverage. After he dispatched Seward to England in April 1740 to raise money, the itinerant reported his own performances and successes, producing third-person accounts of his latest preaching tour in the middle colonies, complete with puffs. He opened a typical report with a statistical account of his activities, indicating he was on shore thirty-three days, traveled "hundreds" of miles, preached fifty-eight sermons, attracted crowds of up to twenty thousand, and collected "near 500 pounds sterling." Then, assessing the power of the revival, he wrote, "Great and visible effects followed his preaching. There was never such a general awakening, and concern for the things of God known in America before." He closed by announcing his intention to visit New England in the fall and return to Philadelphia afterwards. Thus, Whitefield advertised his revivals under the guise of a newspaper article—just the

---

[12] *American Weekly Mercury*, Jan. 24, 1738; *Williamsburg Virginia Gazette*, Dec. 30, 1737–Jan 6, 1738; Whitefield, *Journal*, 372.
[13] Seward, *Journal*, 16–22.

kind of "objective" third-party report Josiah Wedgwood instructed his associates to secure to promote pottery sales because he considered it the most powerful of advertisements.[14]

Although print runs remained small for mid-eighteenth-century newspapers, seldom numbering more than a few hundred, improvements in marketing and distribution meant that Whitefield could reach a wide audience. Parliament's failure to renew the Licensing Act of 1694 prompted a proliferation of newspapers in London. The first daily was published in 1702, and by 1740 London boasted of "three dailies, five weeklies, seven thrice a week, and three thrice a week halfpenny posts, or fifty-three issues of various papers per week." And the number of provincial and colonial newspapers mushroomed as well. But the number of subscribers does not indicate the readership of newspapers and books. Coffeehouses, which sprang up throughout England in the half century before Whitefield's revivals, operated as circulating libraries where gentlemen gathered to read the latest newspapers and books. And entrepreneurial booksellers offered books for loan as well as for sale, enabling those who could not afford the purchase price to read the latest works. In Whitefield's evangelical circles, religious societies and itinerant preachers served a similar function, widening the readership of evangelical papers and books. By the mid-1740s, after their well-publicized theological split, both Whitefield and John Wesley maintained "book rooms" that distributed their works through their separate "connexions."[15]

Most of the fourteen colonial newspaper publishers played important roles in promoting Whitefield's revivals, advertising his writings, and soliciting contributions. As the major intercolonial event in 1740–1741, Whitefield's revival enjoyed extensive coverage. For example, 60 percent of the *Pennsylvania Gazette's* issues of that period devoted space to Whitefield, often including reports of his successes and itineraries, reprints of his publications, and advertisements for his writings. And though Whitefield conducted most of his preaching tours in northern cities, the *Virginia Gazette* carried stories of the evangelist in a third of its issues. But, more than frequency, the space allotted Whitefield within single editions attested to the widespread interest he generated. For instance, during 1740, Andrew Bradford often devoted the entire front page of the *American Weekly Mercury* to the evangelist's letters,

---

[14] Gillies, ed., *Works of Whitefield*, I, 179. See Neil McKendrick, "Josiah Wedgwood and the Commercialization of the Potteries," in *The Birth of a Consumer Society: The Commercialization of Eighteenth-Century England,* ed. Neil McKendrick, John Brewer, and J. H. Plumb (Bloomington, 1982), 99–144.

[15] Louis Wilfrid Moffit, *England on the Eve of the Industrial Revolution: A Study of Economic and Social Conditions from 1740 to 1760 with Special reference to Lancashire* (London, 1925), 246–47. On the establishment of one circulating library, see Benjamin Franklin, *Autobiography,* ed. Larzer Ziff (New York, 1959), 70. For Whitefield's book operations, see "London Tabernacle Minutes, 1743–7," in *Two Calvinistic Methodist Chapels, 1743–1811,* ed. Edwin Welch (London, 1975), 1–19. For John Wesley's book operation, see Luke Tyerman, *The Life and Times of the Rev. John Wesley, M.A.: Founder of the Methodists* (3 vols., New York, 1872), II, 176–79.

journals, endorsements, and testimonials. In seventeen of fifty-two issues of the *South Carolina Gazette* published between the summers of 1740 and 1741, the lead story was a heated controversy pitting Whitefield and his supporters against his opponents. The disputes centered on whether Whitefield's "enthusiasm" was acceptable behavior for an Anglican minister. Its persistence as a news item suggests revival controversy was good business for the newspaper.[16]

No one was a more aggressive Whitefield promoter than Franklin. Though differing in religious views, Franklin and Whitefield enjoyed a lasting and profitable relationship that satisfied both men—the publisher sold more newspapers and books, and the evangelist reached a wider audience. Franklin sent sermons, pamphlets, and journals through his intercolonial booksellers' network, insuring fast and widespread dissemination. And Franklin's newspaper coverage of the revival was so favorable and extensive he was forced to print a defense against charges of editorial bias in the *Pennsylvania Gazette*. But the printer's support went beyond publishing. He helped Whitefield raise money through an effective subscription by which evangelicals covenanted to make installment payments to underwrite the revival. He also defended the preacher's integrity when opponents accused Whitefield of misappropriating funds donated for the orphan house. However, Whitefield also helped Franklin. From 1739 to 1741, Franklin published 110 titles—as many as he printed during the previous seven years. Almost all the increase came from Whitefield. The itinerant's works sold well. Franklin projected sales of two hundred for an expensive four-volume collection of two volumes each of sermons and journals, but actual sales exceeded the forecast by more than 25 percent. And according to Franklin's ledgers, Whitefield's words generated more revenue in some cities, for example, Charleston, South Carolina, and Newport, Rhode Island, than did his popular *Poor Richard's Almanac*.[17]

Desiring a vehicle dedicated to the propagation of his revivals, in 1741 Whitefield assumed management of the London-based evangelical magazine, the *Weekly History*. His action inspired similar periodicals in Scotland and New England. In taking this initiative Whitefield responded to an expressed desire among evangelicals for a periodical dedicated to their cause. One subscriber noted that the "polite world have their Spectators, Tatler's, Guardian's, and Comedies," adding that "the Children of God also [should have] their proper entertainment, their weekly amusement, their divine miscellany, and the historical account of the progress of their Lord's kingdom." Whitefield responded to such demands by supplying the editor, John Lewis,

[16] See, for example, *American Weekly Mercury*, Nov. 6, 13, 29, Dec. 6, 13, 20, 1739. For the controversy, see, for example, *South Carolina Gazette*, May 17, June 26, July 5, 12, 19, Aug. 1, 23, Sept. 13, 20, 26, Oct. 2, 16, 30, Nov. 6, 1740.
[17] Franklin, *Autobiography*, ed. Ziff, 109–11; *Pennsylvania Gazette*, July 24, 1740; L. W. Labaree, ed., *The Papers of Benjamin Franklin* (27 vols., New Haven, 1959–1988), III, 143.

"fresh matter every week," including sermons, journals, and letters. But by 1742 the evangelist had assumed editorial control and determined the magazine's contents and format. And the paper became the official organ of the Whitefield Methodists, as the Calvinist branch of the movement became known. In the autumn of 1743, the paper assumed a new title, describing its purpose and scope: *Christian History or General account of the Progress of the Gospel in England, Scotland, and America as far as the Reverend Mr. Whitefield, his fellow-labourers and Assistants are Concerned.*[18]

Whether Whitefield published his magazine or other printed matter such as sermons, he considered the reader as a consumer. He wrote for a mass audience that included the poor. In a letter to his fellow evangelist, William Hervey, Whitefield disclosed his plans to sell four sermons for just sixpence, noting that he wrote "for the poor, you for the polite and noble." Thus while Hervey selected for one of his works "a very neat paper, with an elegant type," Whitefield instructed his printer to reduce the paper costs for a sermon "designed for the poor . . . [because] the poor must have them cheap." The evangelist also expressed his consciousness of the reader as he contemplated the length of his printed works. In explaining the brevity of one pamphlet, he noted, "I wrote short, because I know long compositions generally weary the reader." His sensitivity to readers as consumers resulted in the wide diffusion of his works throughout the Atlantic world, attested to by booksellers, followers, and opponents alike.[19]

Whitefield promoted his revivals through the widespread distribution of sermons and journals. The significance of the evangelist's printed sermons is of particular interest because of Franklin's well-known criticism of them. Focusing on the heated controversy the published discourses sparked, Franklin believed the itinerant's sermons gave advantage to his enemies. The printer pointed out that they could not attack "unguarded expressions and erroneous opinions" delivered in oration. But his critics dissected his writings, leading Franklin to conclude, "I am of the opinion if he had never written anything, he would have left behind him a much more numerous and important sect." However, Whitefield did not desire to create another denomination or church nor to swell the ranks of an existing denomination. Indeed, he incurred the wrath of the Scottish evangelist, Ebenezer Erskine, by refusing to join the Presbyterian church. Whitefield's intention was to replace the "bad books" written by such rationalists as John Tillotson, archbishop of Canterbury, for example, with "good books" adhering to Calvinist tenets, thus strengthening Calvinist tendencies within the Anglican communion. Whitefield encouraged his followers to display the badges of their New Birth

[18] Letter to editor, *Weekly History,* July 6, 1741, p. 3; "Postscript," *ibid.,* April 25, 1740, p. 3; Gillies, ed., *Works of Whitefield,* II, 90.
[19] Gillies, ed., *Works of Whitefield,* II, 141, 479; Luke Tyerman, *The Oxford Methodists: Memoirs of the Rev. Messrs. Clayton, Ingham, Gambold, Hervey, and Broughton, with Biographical Notices of Others* (New York, 1873), 250; Gillies, ed., *Works of Whitefield,* II, 265.

through material goods—the books they carried and the dress they wore. He exhorted them to "put on [their] cockades" that men and women would know them "to be Christ's." His own books could be displayed as just such cockades. And his written sermons advertised the kind of discourse auditors could expect at his services.[20]

To thousands, the printed sermons also had important symbolic significance. They represented the principles of the revival—the primacy of the individual in salvation, renunciation of unconverted ministers, and emotional experience as the basis of religion. Opponents like Charles Chauncy and Timothy Cutler of Boston noted the symbolic nature of the sermons, crediting their ubiquitous presence with perpetuating religious "enthusiasm."[21] Printed sermons in Whitefield's revivals were analogous to consumer goods displayed by the followers of the radical English politician, John Wilkes. Pro-Wilkes potters sold mugs, punch bowls, and other ceramic articles adorned with the candidate's political slogans. Mercers marketed such Wilkite clothing as coats with special buttons, cuffs, and handkerchiefs. Other merchandise symbolizing the radical cause included tobacco pipes, candlesticks, and tankards.[22] All of these goods served as visible means by which supporters identified with and participated in a movement.

Whitefield disseminated his sermons in large numbers, with publishers eager to satisfy the demand during the revival's peak years. From the first year of his ministry in 1737, the evangelist's discourses sold well. Of his sermon on the necessity of a new birth, the evangelist noted, "This sermon sold well to persons of all denominations, and was dispersed very much both at home and abroad." As he provided his bookseller, Hutton, a steady supply of homilies for publication he observed that they "were everywhere called for." On his first landing in Philadelphia, Whitefield authorized Franklin's rival, the publisher Bradford, to print two of his sermons when Bradford forecast sales of one thousand, a significant press run for any publication in the mid-eighteenth century. In the spring of 1740, the itinerant reported to a London supporter that "God is pleased to give a great blessing to my printed sermons. They are now in the hands of thousands in these parts." And Cutler lamented to the bishop of London, "His Journals, Sermons, and Pamphlets are reprinted and eagerly bought here."[23]

---

[20] Franklin, *Autobiography*, ed. Ziff, 111; Gillies, ed., *Works of Whitefield*, I, 277, VI, 406–7. For Whitefield's polemic against Tillotson, see George Whitefield, *A Letter from the Reverend Mr. George Whitefield to a Friend in London, Shewing the fundamental error of a book entitled The Whole Duty of Man* (Charles-Town, S.C., 1740). For his view of goods as badges, see George Whitefield, *Eighteen Sermons Preached by the Late George Whitefield* (Springfield, Mass., 1808), 249.

[21] See, for example, Perry, ed., *Historical Collections*, II, 350.

[22] See John Brewer, "Clubs, Commercialization, and Politics," in *Birth of a Consumer Society*, ed. McKendrick, Brewer, and Plumb, 238–39.

[23] Whitefield, *Journals*, 86–89, 360; Gillies, ed., *Works of Whitefield*, I, 167; Perry, ed., *Historical Collections*, II, 348.

Through his publications, Whitefield did more than publicize his revivals. For some people, his writings represented the primary means of receiving his message. While traveling through the southern colonies in 1739,
the evangelist noted the difficulty of holding revivals among a sparse and
scattered population. Though he conducted services, the absence of sizable
towns and difficulty of travel limited the crowds. While in Virginia, the
evangelist preached in Williamsburg, unaware of a small group of evangelicals just sixty miles away in Hanover County who were unable to come to
hear him preach. The lay leader of the group, Samuel Morris, observed that
Whitefield's "fame was much spread abroad, as a very warm and alarming
Preacher, which made such of us in Hanover as had been awakened, very
eager to see and hear him." Despite Morris's eloquent statement of the efficacy of Whitefield's promotional campaign, the group did not hear him.
They procured, however, from a Scottish traveler a "book of his sermons
preached in Glasgow and taken from his mouth in short Hand."[24] Thus
Whitefield's publications circulated through unexpected routes and with
surprising consequences.

Through reading Whitefield's sermons, the Virginians spread the revival. Acting as a surrogate preacher, Morris began to read the sermons
aloud at meetings attended by ten to twelve faithful souls. While the writings of reformers like Martin Luther had introduced the members to "the
Way of Justification," the "Concern was not very extensive." But when Morris read Whitefield's works, "many were convinced to seek deliverance with
the greatest solicitude." As the readings continued, the group grew too large
to meet in homes and built its first meetinghouse. Unable to find a suitable
pastor—that is, one who was evangelical and Calvinist—these dissenting
evangelicals continued to rely on Whitefield's printed sermons. "When the
report of these Sermons and the Effects occasioned by reading them was
spread Abroad," Morris reported, he was invited to several places to read
them, and "by this Means the concern was propagated." Through the aid of
Whitefield's printed sermons, the group survived and evolved into the first
Presbyterian church in Virginia.[25]

By preceding the oral message with the printed word, Whitefield's journals were effective in raising expectations for the revivals.[26] Upon reading

---

[24] Samuel Davies, "The State of Religion Among the Protestant Dissenters in Virginia" [1751] in
The Great Awakening: Event and Exegesis, ed. Darrett Rutman (New York, 1970), 46–51.
[25] Ibid.
[26] In mid-eighteenth-century Anglo-America orality had status only in ground prepared by
print. If the Great Awakening had not occurred in a print culture, it would not have extended
to the masses it reached. For the contrary argument that the revivalists participated in a popular, oral culture as opposed to an elite, print culture, see Harry S. Stout, "Religion, Communications, and the Ideological Origins of the American Revolution," *William and Mary Quarterly,*
34 (Oct. 1977), 519–41; and Stout, *New England Soul.* See also Rhys Isaac, "Dramatizing the Ideology of Revolution: Popular Mobilization in Virginia, 1774 to 1776," *William and Mary Quarterly,* 33 (July 1976), 357–85. Isaac contrasts personal oral communication in a traditional face-to-

Whitefield's journals, Benjamin Colman wrote, "I lov'd and honour'd [you] from the first sight I had of your Journal to Gibraltar." He continued, "when I read your Journals, my Heart tells me, if God were not with you of a Truth, neither could your bodily Strength hold out and less the Powers of your Mind." Thomas Prince, editor of Boston's evangelical magazine, the *Christian History*, recalled that in 1738 New Englanders began reading about the remarkable success of the evangelist in "his first two Journals." In the weeks before the first Boston preaching tour, lengthy journal extracts in the newspapers traced the revival's northward progress.[27]

Whitefield disseminated his journals in various forms and through several media. The evangelist and his assistants circulated his latest journals through the letter-writing network. Often he mailed extracts from the version in process to give his supporters a current account of the revival. And on occasion the evangelist even read from his journals to religious societies. He also sent copies to newspapers where they sometimes appeared in successive issues on the front page. Eager to print anything with Whitefield's name on it, book publishers facilitated the dispersion of the journals. Though all sixteen printed versions emanated from Boston and Philadelphia presses, they radiated through an intercolonial bookseller network. Franklin published the seven journals in a two-volume set and distributed it to other printers and booksellers in Massachusetts, Connecticut, Rhode Island, Pennsylvania, Delaware, Maryland, Virginia, and South Carolina. He also issued an eighth volume for a regional audience, covering only Whitefield's travels in the environs of Philadelphia.[28] Franklin's colonywide network was a new scheme in America, just as Whitefield's open-air preaching was novel. These two innovators naturally joined their intercolonial interests to serve each other.

Not only did Whitefield exploit a wide variety of printed forms, he also employed several merchandising techniques to promote his evangelical activities. One marketing strategy Whitefield favored was serial publication of his sermons and journals. Introduced by imaginative publishers earlier in the eighteenth century, "this method of weekly publication allure[d] multitudes to peruse books, into which they would otherwise never have looked." Through serialization, Whitefield increased demand two ways. First, the low price for each segment made it affordable for a larger group of people than could purchase the two-volume collection. Second, the serialized journals created a heightened sense of anticipation as readers followed the evangelist's progress toward their own communities. From 1737 through 1741, the formative years of his transatlantic revivals when promotion was most

face society with impersonal print media in a modern society, arguing that the latter made possible a level of withdrawal that promoted individualism.

[27] Benjamin Colman, *Three Letters to the Rev. Mr. George Whitefield* (Philadelphia, 1739), 5; *Christian History*, Jan. 5, 12, 19, 1744/1745.

[28] *American Weekly Mercury*, Aug. 14, 1740; *Pennsylvania Gazette*, Nov. 15, 1739.

needed, he wrote and published seven different volumes. At the end of the first, describing events from his departure to his arrival at Savannah, he wrote, "I . . . close this part of my Journal," setting the stage for an ongoing account. He also serialized his spiritual autobiography. In 1740, during his second passage to America, he wrote for publication the first part of his life, *A Short Account of God's dealings with the Reverend Mr. George Whitefield*, designed to inform the reader of important events and influences up to those described in his first journal. At the close of the first of two volumes, he wrote, "I shall hereafter relate God's further dealings with my soul, and how He led me into my present way of acting." Advertisements for subsequent volumes of both the journals and the autobiography emphasized the "latest edition" or "most recent account."[29] About every six months, the itinerant sent new editions to his publishers on both sides of the Atlantic.

Whitefield increased publication sales through a variety of creative pricing schemes. Seeking widespread distribution in a mass market, Whitefield instructed his publisher to "print so as to sell cheap." In the preface to his hymnal, he made explicit the connection between price and purchaser, "As the generality of those who receive the Gospel are commonly the poor of the flock, I have studied cheapness, as well as conciseness." However, raising money for the orphanage through a private subscription for a collection of sermons, the itinerant set a high price of four shillings. Recognizing that merchants such as Thomas Noble of New York bought hundreds of books and sermons for free distribution to those who could not afford them, Whitefield and his booksellers offered quantity discounts. The sermon on the new birth sold for "six pence; or two guineas per hundred for those who give them away," the latter terms representing a 16 percent discount. Through his London printer, Lewis, Whitefield offered a cash discount to encourage early payment on subscription sales. Through flexible pricing Whitefield expanded the market for his publications, facilitating widespread publicity.[30]

Whitefield best displayed his merchandising acumen in efforts to increase the *Weekly History's* sagging circulation and bolster its anemic revenue. After Whitefield returned to London in 1741, the magazine's management began to reflect his consumer-driven mentality. Late in 1742, editor Lewis announced, "we purpose to begin next in a more commodious manner as we are likely to be furnished with more materials," no doubt from the evangelist himself. The editor pledged "to let our readers have more reading for their money" by removing the large title, resulting in "much [more] room

[29] Whitefield, *Journals*, 70, 152; George Whitefield, *A Short Account of God's dealings with the Reverend Mr. George Whitefield, late of Pembroke College, Oxford. From his infancy, to the time of his entering into Holy Orders* (Glasgow, 1741).

[30] Gillies, ed., *Works of Whitefield*, II, 77; George Whitefield, *A Collection of Hymns for Social Worship More Particularly design'd for the Use of the Tabernacle Congregation in London* (London, 1756), n.p.; Gillies, ed., *Works of Whitefield*, I, 508; George Whitefield, *Nature and Necessity of Our new Birth in Christ Jesus, in order to Salvation* (London, 1738), 1; *Weekly History*, Sept. 18, 1742.

for useful reading." And for consumer convenience, the magazine would be made available in pocket size, perhaps an innovation Whitefield borrowed from Franklin, who produced a pocket-sized version of his almanac. And Lewis promised home delivery, dispensing the magazine at "people's houses, at the price of one penny."[31] Through such imaginative merchandising, Whitefield and his associates reversed the fortunes of the publication, which survived well past the revival's decline.

Whitefield was an innovator in advertising. Merchants who viewed markets as restricted to a fixed number of customers did not advertise to create consumer demand. Instead, they merely provided information about the availability of their goods and the terms of sale. However, English capitalists in the eighteenth century expanded both domestic and foreign markets and advertised in order to exploit what they considered to be an elastic consumer demand. With a similar view, Whitefield sought to generate interest in his revivals through aggressive advertising. Opponents protested "the various methods taken up by Mr. Whitefield and his adherents, for trumpeting abroad his fame, and magnifying his person and performance."[32]

Whitefield recognized that negative as well as positive publicity could generate interest in his revivals. Especially during his first three American trips, the evangelist engaged in polemics to differentiate his message of the new birth from what he considered to the the "stirrings of dry bones," rattling from unconverted ministers. In a published letter to the students at Harvard and Yale, he charged both colleges with allowing their "light [to] become darkness." That incendiary tract attacking cherished institutions sparked a heated exchange of supporting and opposing publications. Whitefield wrote of the debate, "A few mistaken, misinformed good old men are publishing halfpenny testimonials against me." However, Whitefield agreed with Colman that such opponents had done him "a real service" by giving the evangelist's friends an opportunity "to publish testimonials in [his] favour." Whitefield recorded in his journal that opponent's charges served in the end to benefit him and the revival because they kept readers' attention focused on him.[33]

On occasion, Whitefield and his associates manipulated the news to publicize the revival. William Seward wrote an account of a dancing school's closing in Philadelphia and attributed its demise to Whitefield's charge that its activities were "inconsistent" with the gospel. Franklin inserted the unedited article in the May 1, 1740, *Pennsylvania Gazette,* sparking a dispute that dominated the paper's front page for the entire month. The school's proprietor accused Franklin of biased coverage and Seward of planting the story

---

[31] *Weekly History,* Nov. 13, 1742.
[32] See Daniel Boorstin, "Advertising and American Civilization," in *Advertising and Society,* ed. Yale Brozen (New York, 1974). *South Carolina Gazette,* June 18, 1741.
[33] Gillies, ed., *Works of Whitefield,* I, 296, II, 76; Whitefield, *Journals,* 373.

to "spread his master's fame."[34] That astute observation proved accurate as the story was reprinted from Boston to Charleston.

Testimonials and endorsements were key elements in Whitefield's advertisement program. They introduced and recommended him to a local community. For instance, when he first arrived in Boston in 1740, he brought with him a strong testimonial from Josiah Smith, a Harvard-educated minister in Charleston, South Carolina. Smith, a friend of Colman, testified to the positive changes Whitefield's preaching had wrought in Charleston. He extolled the itinerant's oratorical prowess and pronounced his theology orthodox. Whitefield delivered the document to Colman and another leading clergyman, Thomas Cooper. Both Colman and Cooper wrote their own endorsements of the evangelist as a preface to Smith's testimony and published the whole as a pamphlet promoting the revival. Whitefield continued to benefit from the testimony by reprinting it in the *Christian Weekly* and circulating it throughout the letter-writing network.[35]

Whitefield's writings initiated a chain of events leading to unsolicited endorsements. A New Yorker in 1739 "read two or three of Mr. Whitefield's Sermons and Part of his Journal, and from thence . . . obtain'd a settled opinion he was a good man." Inspired by what he read, the man attended one of the revival services. After he heard Whitefield, he wrote a strong endorsement of the itinerant's theology and oratory. Philadelphia and Boston newspapers published the endorsement, further extending the influence of a single testimonial.[36]

How Whitefield managed the revival's funds illustrates a final important commercial influence on his ministry. After announcing his intention to evangelize in America, the itinerant preached a series of charity sermons in England, collecting donations of more than a thousand pounds for the orphanage John and Charles Wesley had suggested for Georgia. At the prompting of a merchant, Whitefield bought consumer goods, which he transported on the *Elizabeth,* intending to sell them in America where demand for English merchandise ran high. Upon arriving in Philadelphia, he advertised his wares, conducted an auction, and made a profit sufficient to finance his preaching tour. On a subsequent fund-raising journey, Whitefield purchased a five-hundred-acre plantation in South Carolina with donations he collected in Charleston. Using slave labor, he hoped to generate a surplus to provide working capital for the orphanage. Thus Whitefield the entrepreneur significantly shaped the contours of the ministry of Whitefield the evangelist.[37]

Whitefield exploited the growing consumer demand to help finance the revivals. He found opportunities for profits at almost every level of the distribution chain. As a producer of raw materials for English textile manufac-

[34] *Pennsylvania Gazette,* May 1, May 8, 1740.
[35] *Christian History,* Jan. 12, 19, 1744/1745.
[36] *Christian History,* Jan. 5, 12, 19, 1744/1745; *American Weekly Mercury,* Dec. 20, 1739.
[37] Gillies, ed., *Works of Whitefield,* III, 464–65, II, 90.

tories and provisions for the West Indies market, the master of the Georgia orphanage generated 20 percent of the institution's revenues from such exports. His superintendent, James Habersham, who by the 1750s had become one of Savannah's wealthiest merchants, placed the orphanage schooner in the service of the expanding coastal trade to realize additional earnings from shipping fees. And at the Tabernacle, Whitefield's London headquarters, a bookkeeper managed the evangelist's book-selling business, preparing a weekly report of revenues from the sales of printed material throughout the Atlantic evangelical community.[38]

As a tireless fund raiser, Whitefield not only funded his evangelical and humanitarian interests, he amassed an estate in excess of £3,300—exclusive of his lands and buildings in England and America. Such a sum was significant in 1770 when an artisan's house and lot in Savannah cost £250 and a teacher at the Georgia orphan house received an annual stipend of £50.[39]

Whitefield's extensive application of the new merchandising techniques set him apart from his evangelical predecessors and contemporaries. Although the revivalist exploited the power of newspaper publicity to "spread his fame" abroad, even his early colleagues in English pietism, John and Charles Wesley, rejected advertising as a means of promoting their religious enterprises, viewing it as a tasteless "sounding [of] a trumpet."[40] What influenced Whitefield to employ innovations from the marketplace? How and from whom did the evangelist learn the commercial strategies he employed so successfully?

Whitefield's initial inspiration for appropriating commercial means to promote his revivals stemmed from his family's involvement in the market. His father was a wine merchant in Bristol before moving to Gloucester, where he purchased the Bell Inn, whose income placed the elder Whitefield's name near the top of the town's tax rolls. After his father died during George's childhood, the youngster's mother married a man who traded in hardware, who immediately assumed ownership of the tavern. There, George worked as a "common drawer," under both his stepfather and, after the latter's death, his brother Richard, who gained title to the business. Before his departure to begin his studies at Oxford University, Whitefield ran the tavern in his brother's absence for almost a year. In addition to his direct experience in running a local business, Whitefield had at least a glimpse into overseas trade. He spent several months in Bristol with his older brother, James, who was a ship's captain trading in the American and West Indies

[38] E. Merton Coulter, ed., *The Journal of William Stephens, 1741–1745* (Athens, Ga., 1958), 81–83, 197; Welch, ed., *Two Calvinistic Methodist Chapels*, 12.

[39] "The Letters of the Hon. James Habersham, 1756–1775," *Collections of the Georgia Historical Society*, 6 (1904), 110, 119, 123.

[40] Whitefield, *Journals*, 86–89; Thomas Jackson, ed., *The Journal of Charles Wesley* (2 vols., London, 1849), I, 159.

markets. James sold English manufactured goods, Barbados rum, and mus-covado, or raw sugar, at his store on the Charleston, South Carolina, wharf. Indeed, his advertisements appeared in the *South Carolina Gazette* before those of his evangelist brother. James gave financial support to the young minister, but his more important contribution may have been the knowledge he imparted regarding the world of commerce.[41]

Whitefield's childhood friends introduced him to the spreading world of book selling and newspaper publishing. Gabriel Harris, whose father owned Gloucester's most prominent book store, remained a faithful supporter throughout Whitefield's ministry. As a youngster, Whitefield spent consid-erable time in the Harris home and gained the approbation of the elder Har-ris, who provided both books and money toward George's studies at Pem-broke College at Oxford. He helped promote the young minister by sending one of Whitefield's early sermon manuscripts to an older clergyman, who not only liked the discourse but also paid Whitefield a guinea for the docu-ment. Whitefield also associated with Robert Raikes, whose father founded the town's first newspaper, the *Gloucester Journal*. After assuming control of the paper following his father's death, Raikes attended Whitefield's first public sermon and wrote a favorable report in the next edition. At White-field's urging, Raikes published extracts from William Law's treatises on practical piety in six successive issues during 1737. Whitefield noted that "God was pleased to give [the reprints] His Blessing."[42] Thus, Whitefield's early friendships introduced him to the print trade, which would later be-come the most important agent of his advertising and publicity.

Beyond the influence of family and friends in Gloucester, Whitefield was shaped by the spreading commercialized society itself—the world of Daniel Defoe and Bernard Mandeville—where "more [people] than ever was known in former years . . . [engaged] in buying and selling." Because of ris-ing incomes and easy credit, consumers on both sides of the Atlantic had the means to purchase the new consumer goods coming on the market. As the cost of food declined throughout the 1730s and 1740s, the English enjoyed greater purchasing power. And, by the American Revolution, the colonists' per capita income matched that of the British. Further, American merchants made available "a large amount of credit extended for the purchase of all kinds of commodities and services for consumption purposes."[43]

By the second quarter of the eighteenth century, household producers throughout the English countryside turned out "small consumer goods on an unprecedented scale" to meet the demand of a very large and growing

---

[41] Whitefield, *Journals*, 40, 61. For James Whitefield's advertisements, see, for example, *South Carolina Gazette*, Feb. 15, 1739.

[42] Whitefield, *Journals*, 63.

[43] Neil McKendrick, "Introduction," in *Birth of a Consumer Society*, ed. McKendrick, Brewer, and Plumb, 2; Wilbur C. Plummer, "Consumer Credit in Colonial Philadelphia," *Pennsylvania Mag-azine of History and Biography*, 46 (Oct. 1942), 390.

market. Defoe noted in 1722 that 120,000 people were employed in the woolen and silk manufactures of Norwich alone. Most worked out of their country homes, spinning yarn or operating looms. They sold their goods through merchants not only in London and the provinces but throughout the Atlantic world as well. One visitor to Maryland observed that "the quick importation of fashions from the mother country is really astonishing. I am almost inclined to believe that a new fashion is adopted earlier by the polished and affluent American than by many opulent persons in the great metropolis." Lorena Walsh's examination of probate inventories in the Chesapeake Bay area revealed that by the 1730s, "middling families got into the act [of consuming] and by the 1750's, even the poorer sorts were finding a wide variety of non-essentials increasingly desirable." Carole Shammas estimated that by 1774, "the average American spent over one quarter of his or her budget on imports from outside his or her colony of residence."[44]

Consumer demand spurred enterprising merchants to restructure the marketplace, creating institutions Whitefield found useful in promoting his religious enterprises. The scope and nature of advertising changed. Print capitalists published newspapers throughout provincial England and colonial America and made their readers aware of the latest London fashions. Generic descriptions of products, such as cloth, paper, and ceramics, characterized advertisements in the 1720s, but by the 1750s, New York advertisers publicized the availability of "purple gloves, rough gloves, chamois gloves, buff gloves, 'Maid's Black Silk' gloves, 'Maid's Lamb Gloves,' and even 'Men's Dog Skin Gloves.'" Retailers introduced "bright, glass-fronted and bow-windowed" shops, "enabling English householders to obtain goods from the length and breadth of the country." And Scottish merchants extended the retail network to the sparsely populated Virginia countryside. In 1743 Francis Jerdone, a merchant in Hanover County, observed, "There are 25 stores within 18 miles round me . . . and 4 or 5 more expected next year from some of the [British] outports." Middlemen became more important links in the lengthening distribution chain, as their warehouses and credit smoothed the flow of goods from manufacturers to final consumer. A new breed of wholesalers, traveling merchants, carried with them goods worth upwards of a thousand pounds sterling, supplied country shops with goods in bulk (called "whole pieces"), and gave "large credit" to shopkeepers. And as they had for centuries, itinerant hawkers and peddlers continued to sell their wares directly to consumers in London and beyond. Communications improvements enabled merchants to expand the flow of goods to the widening

---

[44] Daniel Defoe, *A Tour through England and Wales,* ed. Ernest Rhys (London, 1927), 62; William Eddis, *Letters from America,* ed. Aubrey C. Land (Cambridge, Mass., 1969), 57–58; Lorena Walsh, "Urban Amenities and Rural Sufficiency: Living Standards and Consumer Behavior in the Colonial Chesapeake, 1643–1777," *Journal of Economic History,* 43 (March 1983), 111; Carole Shammas, "How Self-Sufficient Was Early America?" *Journal of Interdisciplinary History,* 13 (Autumn 1982), 266.

market. English businessmen raised funds through subscriptions to build the canals and turnpikes necessary to make exchanges easier and to mobilize demand.[45]

Consumer demand also prompted businessmen to develop new merchandising techniques that Whitefield applied to the propagation of religion. Prior to the mid-eighteenth century, many manufacturers were content to remain at home and "let the orders come to them." But by 1780 William Hutton, observing business practices in Birmingham, could write, "The merchant stands at the head of the manufacturer . . . [and] travels the whole island to promote the sale; a practice which would have astounded our forefathers." The brass manufacturer Matthew Boulton and the potter Josiah Wedgwood pioneered many of the aggressive sales strategies that characterized what Neil McKendrick has called the "birth of a consumer society." Boulton seized such special occasions as royal birthdays to conduct spectacular London sales "to boost demand and to win the attention of the fashion spreaders." Advertisements included familiar references to royal patronage to "milk the effects of social emulation." But advertising alone was insufficient in warding off competitors who sought their share of the growing consumer demand. Wedgwood concluded that "various means must be unremittingly made use of to awake, and keep up the attention of the world to the fine things we are making." He and other entrepreneurs employed a range of selling ploys that sound anachronistically modern, including market research, product differentiation, giveaways to promote sales, advanced credit, three-tier discount schemes, solicited puffs, and even "false attacks organized to provide the opportunity to publicize the counter-attack."[46]

The new commercialism produced a language of goods that extended to human endeavors beyond the business world. John Brewer has claimed that Wilkes "cribbed from the tradesman's copybook" to fund his campaign and capture votes.[47] And George Whitefield linked religion and commerce to or-

---

[45] T. H. Breen, "'Baubles of Britain': The American and Consumer Revolutions of the Eighteenth Century," *Past and Present*, 119 (May 1988), 80; Roy Porter, *English Society in the Eighteenth Century* (New York, 1982), 206; T. H. Breen, "An Empire of Goods: The Anglicization of Colonial America, 1690–1776," *Journal of British Studies*, 25 (Oct. 1986), 492; Defoe, *Tour through England*, ed. Rhys, 207–8.

[46] Neil McKendrick, "The Commercialization of Fashion," in *Birth of a Consumer Society*, ed. McKendrick, Brewer, and Plumb, 66–67, 72–73; McKendrick, "Josiah Wedgwood," 141. On the new commercialism in England, see Porter, *English Society in the Eighteenth Century*; Harold Perkin, *Origins of Modern English Society* (London, 1969); Charles H. Wilson, *England's Apprenticeship, 1603–1763* (Cambridge, Eng., 1965); Ralph Davis, *A Commercial Revolution: English Overseas Trade in the Seventeenth and Eighteenth Centuries* (London, 1967); and Lorna Weatherill, "A Possession of One's Own: Women and Consumer Behavior in England, 1660–1740," *Journal of British Studies*, 25 (April 1986), 131–56. On the new commercialism in colonial America, see Breen, "Baubles of Britain'"; and Breen, "Empire of Goods." See also "Toward a History of the Standard of Living in British North America," *William and Mary Quarterly*, 45 (Jan. 1988), 116–70.

[47] Brewer, "Clubs, Commercialization, and Politics," 231–62, esp. 232.

ganize and promote the transatlantic revivals. The young Anglican's message of the necessity of a spiritual new birth was not new. Jonathan Edwards of Northampton, Massachusetts, had sounded a similar theme in the regional awakening he led in 1735. Whitefield's innovation lay in the commercialization of his revivals. Although the eighteenth-century English world underwent significant demographic and economic change, churches clung to tradition. The norm was a settled ministry serving local parishioners who gathered at fixed times for worship. With a commercialized perspective strengthened by his familiar association with merchants, Whitefield developed a different vision—one informed by patterns of thought gleaned from the expanding market.[48] Like the merchants who generated their own consumer demand by planting colonies and advertising their wares at home and abroad, Whitefield applied the latest marketing strategies to create and exploit a transatlantic audience for evangelicalism.

Whitefield heightened his familiarity with the world of commerce as he immersed himself in the Atlantic market to promote and fund his favorite charity, the Georgia orphan house (which he called Bethesda). Whitefield sharpened his entrepreneurial skills as he sought a commercial enterprise to make the orphanage self-sustaining. Throughout the 1740s, Whitefield's correspondence reflected his preoccupation with such mundane matters as profits from book sales, bills of exchange to settle transatlantic accounts, and the high cost of labor. Whitefield tried to keep track of funds being raised and disbursed on both sides of the Atlantic. While in Charleston in 1745, for instance, he requested his London agent, John Syms, to send "a short sketch of my accompts that I may know how my affairs stand." To balance his books, the evangelist sought to increase his revenue and decrease his expenses. Whitefield wrote Boston supporters concerning his latest publications, expressing his expectation that "some profit will accrue to me from my sermons, etc." But to improve their profitability, Whitefield urged a trusted Bostonian to "make what bargain with [the printers] you think proper" to reduce printing costs. Whitefield also fretted over reducing expenditures, at one point proposing smuggling and illegally introducing slavery into Georgia as a way to lower Bethesda's labor costs. To a South Carolina planter, Whitefield expressed his opinion that although Georgia prohibited slavery, "no notice [was] taken of Negroes at all." Therefore, he suggested if the planter would "give [him] a Negro, [he would] venture to keep him, and if he should be seized" the itinerant would buy him again. Like merchants of the day, Whitefield relied on credit to operate in overseas trade. He, for

[48] See Haskell, "Capitalism and the Origins of the Humanitarian Sensibility, Part 1"; Haskell, "Capitalism and the Origins of the Humanitarian Sensibility, Part 2"; and Linda Colley, "Whose Nation? Class and National Consciousness in Britain, 1750–1830," *Past and Present*, 113 (Nov. 1986), 97–117. Benedict Anderson, *Imagined Community: Reflections on the Origin and Spread of Nationalism* (London, 1983).

example, drew bills on William Seward's brother, Benjamin, a London merchant, to remit funds to Syms to satisfy British suppliers. Thus, Whitefield's own experience in the market influenced his favorable attitude toward merchants and their role in propagating the gospel.[49]

Whitefield deepened his immersion in the commercial culture through consumption—purchases for himself as well as those for Bethesda. Unlike some of the radical revivalists, such as James Davenport of Long Island, who preached against spreading consumerism, Whitefield not only did not condemn consumption, he enjoyed material possessions.[50] After securing the orphan house's financial position in the mid-1750s, the evangelist spent more freely on himself. Concluding that his "one-horse chaise [would] not do for [him]," Whitefield ordered a closed four-wheeled carriage with improved springs to make his trips over England's rough roads more comfortable. It cost "thirty or forty pounds," equivalent to the annual income of some of the lesser clergy. After taking delivery, the itinerant indicated he "like[d] the purchase exceedingly well." And he cherished a handsome watch adorned with a beautiful gold case, though he covered it with leather so the "delicacy [would] not offend." Whitefield also delighted in personal gifts his supporters gave him, including books, horses, and even a slave. One of his most treasured gifts was a slave whom his co-laborer William Hervey purchased for him at a cost of thirty pounds sterling. To remember the donor, Whitefield named the servant Weston, after Hervey's parish, Weston-Flavel. At times, Whitefield even demonstrated great anxiety over his personal goods. While in America in 1746, he wrote successive letters to his mother, brother-in-law, and finally his agent, Syms, requesting that his "padlocked chest . . . [and] portable furniture" be sent to Charleston. The letters expressed a growing sense of urgency by one attached to his possessions.[51]

Contrary to the interpretations of many contemporaries and historians alike, Whitefield viewed commerce and revivalism as compatible. Edwin S. Gaustad, agreeing with Perry Miller's thesis that there was a steady decline in the vitality of colonial Puritanism as third- and fourth-generation laymen and clergymen alike turned from the faith of their spiritual forefathers to the pursuit of profits and pleasure, argued that the "thriving West Indian trade . . . brought a measure of prosperity to the New England colonies" that led to such evils as pride and economic oppression. As a result of the expansion of the market, "God became less respected as man became more respectable."

---

[49] John W. Christie, ed., "Newly Discovered Letters of George Whitefield, 1745–1746," *Journal of the Department of History of the Presbyterian Historical Society*, 32 (June 1954), 73, 171, 183, 248, 76–77, 251–52.

[50] *Boston Weekly Post Boy*, March 28, 1743.

[51] Gillies, ed., *Works of Whitefield*, III, 232–34; "Letters of the Hon. James Habersham," 138–39; Tyerman, *Oxford Methodists*, 277–78; Christie, ed., "Newly Discovered Letters," 252–55; *Whitefield, Journals*, 48, 296.

Writing on the Great Awakening in the major seaports, Gary Nash concluded that the awakening became "class specific," embraced by the laboring poor and shunned by the merchant elites of colonial cities. However, many merchants did support Whitefield and the early Methodists. Whitefield and John Wesley counted among their most ardent supporters in Bristol, for example, businessmen attracted not only by their proclamation of the Puritan ethic but also by their energy, dedication, and organization—qualities essential to mercantile success. And, Whitefield enjoyed no greater acceptance and support than that accorded him by the Brattle Street Church in Boston, a congregation dominated by merchants. Discovering a creative tension between profits and piety, Whitefield's entrepreneurial evangelism accommodated Christians who pursued their callings in the marketplace.[52]

Not only did Whitefield view commerce and religion as compatible, he maintained that trade was an essential feature of the divine economy. He argued that God would have deemed creation incomplete if his human creatures lacked company. Therefore, the Almighty made it impossible that "communities be kept up, or commerce carried on, without society." Indeed, "Providence seem[ed] wisely to have assigned a particular product to almost each particular Country, on Purpose, as it were to oblige us to be social." Whitefield concluded that the mutual dependence of commerce and society demonstrated that "the one great end of [human] existence," consisted in individuals' being useful to each other in social life.[53] Toward that end, he determined to share his "particular product"—his evangelical message—with the widest possible audience through the means at hand.

Whitefield's acquaintance with the spreading market influenced his conception of evangelism. It provided him the language to define his "business" as that of propagating the gospel to a parish that encompassed the whole world. It also shaped his view that merchants were necessary to the spread of evangelical religion. Whitefield held that Christian merchants were called to their vocation, arguing that their success in profitable trade promoted soul winning by generating the funds necessary to conduct the transatlantic revivals. Whitefield expressed his regard for honorable exchange through the liberal sprinkling of commercial metaphors in his sermons and correspondence. In one self-conscious application of mercantile imagery, Whitefield thanked God for converting one supporter into a "Christian merchant, and teaching him the art of trafficking for the Lord."[54]

[52] Edwin S. Gaustad, *The Great Awakening in New England* (New York, 1957), 15; Gary Nash, *The Urban Crucible: Social Change, Political Consciousness, and the Origins of the American Revolution, 1760–1800* (Princeton, 1979), 198–232; Geoffrey E. Milburn, "Piety, Profit, and Paternalism: Methodists in Business in the North-East of England, c. 1760–1920," *Proceedings of the Wesley Historical Society,* 44 (Dec. 1983), 45–46.
[53] J. E. Crowley, *This Sheba, Self: The Conceptualization of Economic Life in Eighteenth-Century America* (Baltimore, 1974), 112.
[54] Gillies, ed., *Works of Whitefield,* I, 316; II, 134.

As his ministry progressed in partnership with supporters from the world of commerce, Whitefield inserted commercial language more frequently into his discourses. Employing the vocabulary of trade and finance, the revivalist assured one merchant that the trader's "all [was] insured, and [he would] receive [his] own with good usury at the great day." He encouraged the businessman to "spend and be spent for Christ's people," declaring evangelism to be a "glorious employ." Departing for his fifth visit to America in 1754, Whitefield exhorted his followers to be "laudably ambitious, and get as rich as [they could] towards God." He declared the "bank of heaven . . . a sure bank" on which he had "drawn thousands of bills . . . and never had one sent back protested." Before embarking on his last American journey, Whitefield lamented losing "the sale of some gospel goods at Gravesend market-place" and urged his fellow laborers to "meet with thousands of moneyless customers" to "sell" the gospel. Then, referring to his own mission to the colonies, the evangelist voiced his desire for a fruitful "trading voyage [wherein he would] sail into harbour with a well full and choice cargo of heavenly wares."[55]

Whitefield's use of commercial language sounded exactly like what ministers such as Cotton Mather and Benjamin Colman had preached a generation before the awakening. What was new about Whitefield was not his appropriation of the language of the market, but his adaptation of marketing techniques. Yet, Whitefield's commercialization of religion need not suggest a secular orientation. Rather it indicates a zeal for propagating the gospel through the most powerful means available. Therefore, he intuitively and self-consciously appropriated merchandising strategies for igniting the transatlantic revivals.

Whitefield profited from a close association with businessmen. They followed the revivalist for a variety of reasons and provided him with valuable merchandising assistance. His major benefactor, Seward, an ardent supporter of charity schools as a means of elevating the "poorer sorts," recognized Whitefield's ability to solicit funds. James Hutton suggested that while Whitefield's "chief object was at the time to convert souls," Seward and others sought merely "to get money for their schools." However, Seward demonstrated his commitment to the cause of broadcasting the need for the New Birth. Not only did he leave his lucrative business as a stockjobber to travel to America with Whitefield, he played a major role in financing and publicizing Whitefield's revivals. In Philadelphia in 1739, he purchased a sloop and gave it to the evangelist, enabling the preacher and fellow travelers to itinerate between Savannah and Boston at their convenience. At Whitefield's request, Seward bought five thousand acres on the forks of the Delaware River to establish a school for Negroes and a community for English evangelicals. He also gave monetary and spiritual encouragement to the

---

[55] *Ibid.*, II, 134, III, 397, 404.

religious societies that formed the nucleus of the itinerant's informal organization in towns throughout Britain and America. As a respected member of the evangelical community, Seward extended the evangelist's letter-writing network, corresponding with sympathetic business associates about Whitefield's successes and needs. From Philadelphia, for example, he sent letters to "Savannah, Charleston, Frederica, Virginia, Cape Fear, New Brunswick, and New York," enclosing both newspaper accounts and Whitefield's latest publications.[56]

Whitefield, shaped by the world of trade, also influenced lay followers in their business enterprises. James Lackington, a successful London bookseller, traced his initial encouragement in business to the early Methodist revivals of Whitefield and Wesley. While attending a revival meeting in the 1740s, Lackington underwent a conversion experience, which "caused [him] to embrace every opportunity to learn to read." His determination to read evangelical works led him to collect religious books, the foundation for the modest initial inventory of his first bookstore. Whitefield and Wesley encouraged evangelical entrepreneurs by inviting them to advertise their wares in evangelical magazines and by advancing them interest-free loans. Lackington "borrowed five pounds" from one of the Methodist society's funds, adding that the advance "was of great service" in increasing his stock.[57]

In a more direct way, Whitefield helped Habersham launch a successful commercial career, resulting in his becoming one of Savannah's leading merchants. Habersham accompanied Whitefield to Georgia on his first American trip and remained to lay the foundation for the orphan house. Just as Bethesda was "the means of first bringing [Whitefield] out" as an evangelist, it provided the enterprising Habersham the means of beginning his trading business. As he engaged in the coastal and West Indies trade on behalf of the orphanage, he also traded on his own account. By 1744 Habersham had left the orphan house and formed a partnership that participated in the transatlantic trade, exporting tobacco and rice and importing English manufactures. The link between commerce and evangelical religion stands in bold relief in the relationship between Whitefield and Habersham. On the initial voyage to Georgia, Whitefield taught Habersham the Bible and Latin so he would be effective in teaching the orphans. Then in the 1750s, Habersham, by that time a savvy businessman, taught Whitefield how to solve Bethesda's financial difficulties. Beset by funding problems exacerbated by the war with the Spanish, Whitefield turned to Habersham to devise a plan to reduce the orphan house's expenses and increase its revenues.[58] As a result of his plan, the orphanage became self-sustaining.

---

[56] "James Hutton's Account of 'The Beginning of the Lord's Work,'" 207; Seward, *Journal*, 10; Whitefield, *Journals*, 89, 361; Seward, *Journal*, 10.

[57] *Memoirs of the Forty-Five First Years of the Life of James Lackington* (London, 1794), 59, 129.

[58] Gillies, ed., *Works of Whitefield*, III, 309, 452.

Printers supported Whitefield in part because he was good business. As the revival spread in the colonies, Whitefield and American booksellers profited from the commercial appeal of the evangelist's publications, fostered by his well-publicized successes—huge crowds, numerous conversions, and liberal contributions. Each year from 1739 through 1745, American publishers released more works by Whitefield than by any other writer. The total number of publications printed in the colonies increased by 85 percent from 1738 to 1741, with most of the increase attributable to the Grand Itinerant. In the peak revival year, 1740, Whitefield wrote or inspired thirty-nine titles, or 30 percent of all works published in America. For many printers, Whitefield's writings constituted a significant proportion of their business. For instance, from 1739 to 1742, one of the largest publishers in the colonies, Daniel Henchman of Boston, spent more than 30 percent of his printing budget producing the evangelist's books. Whitefield not only profited from the sale of his works, he also benefited from Henchman's and Franklin's generous contributions to Bethesda. However, the relationship between business and theology was a complicated one with both commerce and religion influencing decisions. Hutton, who had printed most of Whitefield's early works, refused to produce further writings after 1741, when he sided with Wesley's rejection of Whitefield's Calvinism. Although he had, according to Whitefield, "made hundreds" from the revivalist's publications, Hutton forswore future profits, refusing to print religious matters "except what [he] believed and approved."[59]

Whitefield shared with the new merchants of the consumer revolution both similar strategies and a common view of the market as elastic. Improvements in communications and marketing enabled traders to escape the "cosseted constraints" of local markets and sell their goods to strangers at great distances. And the increased disposable income of urban consumers resulting from falling agricultural prices in the first half of the eighteenth century prompted merchants to consider means of selling consumer goods to the middling and even poorer people, not just the better sort. In a similar way, Whitefield discovered in the new merchandising techniques vehicles for conveying the necessity of a new birth to people far beyond the confines of a single local parish, or the entire Anglican church, or even the very boundaries of Britain itself. Although he subscribed to the Calvinist doctrine of election, Whitefield believed that God used the "meanest instruments" to awaken sinners to his grace. Thus, the evangelist felt compelled to employ

[59] Charles Evans, *American Bibliography: A Chronological Dictionary of All Books, Pamphlets, and Periodicals Printed in the United States of America from the Genesis in 1639 down to and including the year 1820* (Chicago, 1904), 122–98; Rollo G. Silver, "Publishing in Boston, 1726–1757: The Accounts of Daniel Henchman," *Proceedings of the American Antiquarian Society*, 66 (April 1957), 17–36; "James Hutton's Account of 'The Beginning of the Lord's Work,'" 212.

every means—even those "the world" used to merchandise its baubles—to deliver the gospel to all people.[60]

As Whitefield succeeded in generating unprecedented crowds, he raised the ire of those who opposed his violation of traditional ecclesiastical boundaries and clerical conduct. The eminent Boston rationalist, Charles Chauncy, protested the way Whitefield hawked religion like a traveling salesman peddling his wares, objecting especially to the itinerant's giving "Public Notice" of his preaching activities. An anonymous writer to the *Boston Weekly News-Letter* proposed a remedy for the evangelist's blatant commercial activities in the name of religion. The correspondent wrote that as there was "a very wholesome law in the province to discourage Pedlars in Trade," the time had arrived "to enact something for the discouragement of Pedlars in Divinity also."[61] These outcries point to one of the greatest ironies of the Great Awakening: the Calvinist Whitefield embraced mass marketing. While Chauncy and other proto-Unitarians rejected Whitefield's Calvinism as narrow and decidedly unenlightened, they also denounced his innovative, rational adaptations of the latest commercial means to propagate his message to vast audiences.

---

[60] Brewer, "Clubs, Commercialization, and Politics," 198; Whitefield, *Journals*, 372.
[61] Charles Chauncy, *A Letter From a Gentleman in Boston to Mr. George Wishart, concerning the state of religion in New England* (Edinburgh, 1742); *Boston Weekly News-Letter*, April 22, 1742.

The Indians' Great Awakening, 1745–1775

Gregory Evans Dowd

INTRODUCTION

At the end of the Seven Years' War, Indians living between the Appalachian Mountains and the Mississippi River stood at a pivotal historical intersection. French withdrawal from North America following military defeat by the English robbed Ohio Valley and Great Lakes Indians of their primary trading partner and political arbiter. The British, viewed by many eastern Indians as a common enemy, seemed to produce an endless stream of land speculators, squatters, and missionaries. They were an unwelcome and ineffective substitute for the French. At the same time, Ohio Valley natives struggled to manage their polyglot, multiethnic communities of displaced eastern Indians as well as the chronic problems of epidemic disease and alcohol abuse. Some Indian leaders tried to make the best of a terrible situation by accommodating English demands to host Christian missionaries and make ever more land cessions. Other natives were appalled by such compromises and instead called for a pan-Indian resurgence. View eighteenth-century developments through their eyes, argues Gregory E. Dowd, and you will see a population searching to recover sacred power.

Demonstrating rare sensitivity toward the conjunction of Indian religion and politics as well as toward periodization (the chronological bounding of historical developments), Dowd chronicles the "nativistic" revolt against "accommodationist" policies and British influence. Dowd submits that over the course of the eighteenth century, a burgeoning sense of crisis and impotence gave rise to a host of visionary prophets, foremost among them the Delaware Neolin, who announced that their peoples' dilemmas stemmed less from English might than from their own lack of sacred power.

Power—the ability to control others—could be recovered only if the Indians followed a series of rituals and rejected a series of taboos, according to instructions sent by the Great Spirit through his chosen. Long ago, this Spirit had created the Indians separate from whites and blacks. Now he demanded that they adhere to his distinct blueprint for their lives. They had to abandon "evil ways," such as overhunting and drinking, revive select dormant traditions, and adopt what were in fact new behaviors, such as the southeastern custom of imbibing the emetic "black drink." The visionaries defined these actions as quintessentially "Indian" across time, space, and ethnic boundaries. The Spirit also banned English goods, Christianity, liquor, and cooperation with colonial officials, because they polluted Indian purity. The consequences of ignoring such messages, the prophets warned, were continued powerlessness, catastrophic disaster, and a torturous afterlife similar to the Christian Hell. Fate lay in Indian hands, not in those of encroaching colonists. Dowd argues that this pastel of rituals and ideas underlay Pontiac's famous campaign to join the eastern Indian nations in a military alliance against the British presence in the Ohio Valley and Great Lakes region. Without his forces' widespread sense that they were in the process of restoring sacred power and without rituals that transcended ethnic loyalties, Pontiac would never have gained such a following.

Dowd makes several contributions in this piece. Not only does he reinterpret a critical historical event, but he also raises several methodological issues. Dowd prods us to cast a wider net in our consideration of Indian geographical and cosmological worlds. By using intellectual currents as his unit of analysis rather than a political or ethnic group, he is able to transcend the tribal narratives that typically confine students of Indian history. He shows that the nativists' shared ideas about race, religion, and ritual developed over the course of several decades as Indians created an extensive network linking diverse native villages, colonial towns, and Christian missions. Furthermore, his exploration of the ideology of native resistance suggests that just as we cannot fully comprehend the Indians' social landscape within tribal limits, neither can we understand historical behavior unless we take the natives' historical worldviews as seriously as their economic and political concerns.

The questions raised by Dowd's research are as important as its conclusions.

- *Was the nativists' geographical vision shared by less-notable Indians, or is Dowd falling into the common trap of using the activities of great men to stand for those of the rest of society?*
- *Similar to the pan-Indian movement discussed in the piece by Gutiérrez, Pontiac's campaign wound up in defeat and division. What do these defeats tell us about centripetal and centrifugal forces in native societies?*

- *Given English-America's advantages in population, technological prowess, and political organization, was there any real chance that Indians could successfully halt white expansion?*
- *If the answer to the previous question is "no," what is the value in studying Indian resistance movements?*

In 1749, Captain Pierre-Joseph Céloron de Blainville, an envoy of the government of New France, undertook a claims-staking journey down the Allegheny and Ohio rivers. Céloron nailed metallic plaques, emblems of his king's claim, to stout trees. But because he knew that Upper Ohio Indians had different ideas about sovereignty, he staked the claim unceremoniously, almost on the sly. After he left, local Shawnees tore down "and trampled underfoot with contempt" the symbols of French ownership.[1] Céloron's voyage dramatized the great issue of Ohio country possession; but the journal he left does more: it provides us with a glimpse into the dynamic social and political world of the region's Indians.

Céloron described complicated interactions among Indian peoples. In early August 1749, he stopped at the village of Chiningue (Logstown), twenty miles downstream from the forks of the Ohio. Though nominally an Ohio Iroquois (or "Mingo") town, Delawares and Shawnees also peopled the village, and "besides these three nations," according to the journal "there are in the village some Iroquois from Sault St. Louis, from the Lake of Two Mountains; some Nepassingues, Abenakes, Ottawas and other nations." Filled with peoples nominally allied with the British as well as with dissidents from the nominal allies of France, the grouping, in Céloron's view, formed "a very bad village." Later that month, Céloron approached Sonioto, where the Indians displayed their lack of intimidation by firing a thousand rounds into the air as the French flotilla appeared. Sonioto, like Chiningue, was a polyglot village; predominantly Shawnee and Mingo, it had "added to it thirty men [Caughnawaga Mohawks] of the Sault St. Louis."[2]

These villages of mixed ethnicity, located on strategic paths between the Southeast, the Ohio River, and the Great Lakes, were centers of Indian trade and diplomacy. In 1752, for example, the Virginian William Trent recorded in his diary that a Cherokee embassy from the southern Appalachians had visited the Ohioan Shawnees, Delawares, and Mingos to request that they convince the English to reopen a trade in the Cherokee villages. The Cherokees, desperate for ammunition, had long been under attacks from the Creeks of the Gulf Plains. They explained to their northern hosts that if the English failed to reopen a Cherokee trade, many, even thousands, of Cherokees

---

[1] Captain Raymond to La Jonquière, Fort Miami, January 5, 1750, *Ill. Hist. Coll.* 19: 155–56. It is noteworthy that the more famous lead plates were buried and hidden from view.
[2] Jean Pierre Joseph de Céloron, "Journal of Captain Celoron," in *Fort Pitt and Letters from the Frontier*, 2nd ed., ed. Mary C. Darlington (New York, 1971), 35, 42–45.

would be forced to retreat northward to the Ohio. Two years later, a group of Cherokees did establish a temporary settlement near the Shawnees in 1755, bringing the worlds of the Ohio and the Southeast closer together.[3]

Such relations between the Ohio country and the Southeast were not new in the mid-eighteenth century, although they would intensify in the coming years. The Ohio Shawnees had a long history of interaction with southeasterners, particularly the Creeks. The Shawnees had dwelled along the Ohio River until the Five Nations Iroquois invasion of the late 1630s, an event that signaled the beginning of a remarkable Shawnee diaspora.[4] Under strong Iroquoian attacks, the Shawnees had fled to the south and east, pretty much abandoning the Ohio country. By 1685, the scattered Shawnees were tilling the soil and hunting for white-tailed deer in Tennessee, Georgia, and Alabama, establishing close relations with Cherokees and Creeks. By 1690, other Shawnees, now at peace with the Five Nations Iroquois, inhabited eastern Pennsylvania among the Unami- and Munsee-speaking peoples who would come to be called the Delawares. Turmoil in the Southeast accompanying the colonization of the Carolinas constricted the Shawnees to widely separated enclaves in Alabama among the Creeks and in Pennsylvania among the Delawares and Iroquois.[5] The resulting close relations between Creeks and Shawnees, on the one hand, and Delawares and Shawnees, on the other, would be particularly important in the development of militant religious nativism. The far-flung networks possessed by the Shawnees provided immense opportunities for communication among borderland Indians in the mid and late eighteenth century. They also gave the Shawnees their critical influence in the militant, sixty-odd year quest for Indian unity that germinated as Céloron made his descent.

The Shawnees, though remarkable in the extent of their migrations and acquaintances, were not unique in their promotion of far-ranging alliances. What is more, like other peoples, as subsequent chapters will demonstrate,

[3] Helen Hornbeck Tanner, "Cherokees in the Ohio Country," *Journal of Cherokee Studies* 3 (1978): 95. William Trent, *Journal of Captain William Trent from Logstown to Pickawillany, A.D. 1752*, ed. Alfred T. Goodman (New York, 1971), 103; George Croghan to James Hamilton, Shippensburg, November 12, 1755, in *Penn. Archives*, 1st ser., 2:483–85.

[4] James Bennet Griffin, *The Fort Ancient Aspect* (Ann Arbor, Mich., 1943), 207, 308; Helen Hornbeck Tanner, "The Greenville Treaty," in *Indians of Ohio and Indiana Prior to 1795*, ed. Helen Hornbeck Tanner and Erminie Wheeler-Voegelin (New York, 1974), 1:65–67; Erminie Wheeler-Voegelin, "Ethnohistory of Indian Use and Occupancy in Ohio and Indiana Prior to 1795," in ibid., 1:173–76; Jerry Eugene Clark, "Shawnee Indian Migration: A System Analysis" (Ph.D. diss., University of Kentucky, Lexington, 1974), 22. Charles Callender, "Shawnee," in *Northeast: Handbook of North American Indians*, ed. William C. Sturtevant (gen. ed.) and Bruce Trigger (Washington, D.C., 1978), 15:622–35, is more tentative about centering the Shawnees in Ohio.

[5] George Henry Loskiel, *History of the Mission of the United Brethren among the Indians in North America* (London, 1794), 127; Callender, "Shawnee," 622; [Charles Thomson,] *An Enquiry into the Causes of the Alienation of the Delaware and Shawanese Indians from the British Interest* (London, 1759), 25; Tanner, "The Greenville Treaty," 65.

Shawnee villages often divided among themselves over the issue of war or peace with the Anglo-Americans. That qualification is important, indeed central, to the story, but, the qualification notwithstanding, the Shawnees would be among the most obvious promoters of pan-Indian action from the Seven Years' War to the age of their most famous compatriot, Tecumseh.

No people, however, not even the Shawnees, could compete in 1749 with the French when it came to Eastern Woodlands diplomacy. No event would intensify intertribal relations as would the Seven Years' War, an event for which Céloron's voyage would prove a precipitant.

THE SEVEN YEARS' WAR AND INDIAN IDENTITY

The Seven Years' War involved Indians from the St. Lawrence River to the Mississippi Delta, demanding deep changes in the diplomatic relations among and the social relations within Indian peoples, changes that would shape history for a generation. Over the course of the war's active North American phase, from 1754 to 1760, Indians of the Great Lakes, the Ohio country, and even the Southeast met, both with one another and with the French, to plan for their common defense, strengthening relations and seeking the development of widespread networks along which ideas would regularly be exchanged. Those networks penetrated even such peoples allied with Britain as the Cherokees. The ideas they conducted concerned not just strategy but also identity and power.

Understandings of power, particularly those expressed in war ritual and ceremony, were traded actively among the members of the different peoples who fought shoulder to shoulder in the conflict. Early in the war, in 1755, on the eve of British Major General Edward Braddock's spectacular defeat on the Monongahela River, the French officer Daniel de Beaujeu at Fort Duquesne, now Pittsburgh, employed Indian ceremony when he sought to raise a fighting force among the Ottawas, Chippewas, Hurons, Mingos, Shawnees, and Potawatomis. He "began the Warsong and all the Indian Nations Immediately joined him except the Poutiawatomis of the Narrows [Detroit] who were silent." The Potawatomi hesitation sent the Indians into conference, and the Potawatomis, probably at the urging of the Mingos and Shawnees, marched to victory with the rest the next day. By the end of the following winter, the local Delawares and Shawnees had sent symbolic war belt after war belt to the surrounding peoples, and many responded, causing one observer to claim that the Ohioans had "caused all those Nations to chant the war [song] during the whole of the winter."[6] Many among the Iro-

[6] [M. Roucher,] "Account," Fort Duquesne, July 6, 1755, excerpted and translated in Paul E. Kopperman, *Braddock at the Monongahela* (Pittsburgh, 1977), 266–72; "Abstract of Dispatches from Canada," in *DRCHSNY*, 10:423.

quois, Catawbas, Cherokees, Chickasaws, and other peoples did not join in the chorus. But factions among most Eastern Woodlands nations did, and the peoples who sang together did so in fact, not just in metaphor. As in the sharing of war belts, the singing of the war song suggests a growing identification of the peoples with one another. So it was also toward the end of the conflict in the Ohio region. In 1758, Indians from throughout the Ohio and Great Lakes countries shared in powerful ceremonies after defeating British forces under James Grant, stalling—though not frustrating—General John Forbes's and Colonel Henry Bouquet's ultimately successful campaign against Fort Duquesne. Outside the walls of the French fort the warriors of different nations dressed scalps "with feathers and painted them, then tied them on white, red, and black poles. . . . Immediately after they began to beat their drums, shake their rattles, hallow and dance."[7]

The presence of French posts, where ammunition was dispensed and where raids were often organized, drew Indians from distant regions together against a common enemy. When a band of Tiogan Delawares, three years before they saw the battle of the celestial horses with which this book opened, traveled from their eastern Appalachian slopes to Montreal, seeking assistance from the French, they kept company with Ottawas from Michigan. Also at Montreal that month were Chippewas from Lake Superior, Foxes, Sauks, Menominees, and Potawatomis, as well as a number "from a Nation so far away that no Canadian interpreter understands their language." Commerce occurred among these Indians as well as between them and the French. The exchanges were not always harmonious, but the fact of the common British enemy did make for friendships and alliances.[8] The Seven Years' War, terribly violent though it was, opened an opportunity for the elaboration of intertribal relations. The memory of the unions shaped by alliance with France would persist long after France departed.

The departure of France from North America left the Indians more dependent than ever on the British for goods. To break that dependence without recourse to New France was for the militants the challenge of the 1760s. One strategy adopted to meet that challenge had been suggested by the extensive cooperation of Indian peoples with the armies of France and New France. New diplomatic and military ventures would have to be undertaken without the coordination provided by an imperial power, but some wondered at the possibilities of assistance from the sacred powers. Outside of but influenced by the old networks, a nativistic movement formed. It took on a strong religious dimension, one whose full range of attributes had already begun to find expression in the Susquehanna and Ohio valleys.

[7] Howard H. Peckham, ed., "Thomas Gist's Indian Captivity," *PMHB* 80 (1956): 293–94.
[8] Louis Antoine de Bougainville, *Adventure in the Wilderness: The American Journals of Louis Antoine de Bougainville, 1756–1760* (Norman, Okla., 1964), 117–21; M. De Vaudreuil to M. de Moras, Montreal, July 13, 1757, in *DRCHSNY*, 10:588–90.

NORTHEASTERN ORIGINS, 1737–1775

A nativistic movement that would last a generation to become the religious underpinning of militant pan-Indianism first developed most clearly in the polyglot communities on the Upper Susquehanna. Refugees from earlier dispossessions in New Jersey and eastern Pennsylvania, these peoples began again to fall back before the Anglo-American advance of the 1750s and 1760s. The movement accompanied refugees as they fled northwest and then west from the Susquehanna to the headwaters of the Allegheny, from whence it descended upon the Ohio country. Here it found inviting souls among the already established refugees who inhabited the polyglot villages that had been so suspicious of Céloron. Laid low during the Seven Years' War, the Indians provided the movement with deep basins of support. The Ohio River issued from mountain springs, snows, and rains. The currents of nativism issued from the reckonings of the several thousand souls, and from the many prophets who gave those souls voice.[9] Because the movement roughly coincided with British America's Christian revival, I have chosen to call it the Indians' Great Awakening. But it was not a "revival" of a religious spirit that had lain, somehow, dormant. In its most important aspect, it was an "awakening" to the idea that, despite all the boundaries defined by politics, language, kinship, and geography, Indians did indeed share much in the way of their pasts and their present. It was an awakening to the notion that Indians shared a conflict with Anglo-America, and that they, as Indians, could and must take hold of their destiny by regaining sacred power.

Between 1737 and 1775, a time of economic dislocation and much warfare in the Susquehanna and Ohio valleys, a cluster of men and women came into direct contact with the usually remote Master of Life. Styled "prophets" by the least hostile of their Christian observers and "impostors" by others, these people differed from the more common shamans or conjurers only in the level of their experience. Although their spiritual encounters may have represented departures from, or elaborations upon, more ordinary shamanistic experiences, they were not new phenomena in the mid-eighteenth century. Over a full century before, Hurons reported spiritual encounters that

---

[9] Four works examine the prophets of the mid-eighteenth century: James Mooney, "The Ghost Dance Religion and the Sioux Outbreak of 1890," in *Fourteenth Annual Report of the Bureau of American Ethnology*, pt. 2 (Washington, D.C., 1896), which suggests that the Delaware Prophet's movement may have been directly related to the Shawnee Prophet's movement of the nineteenth century; Melburn Delano Thurman, "The Algonquian Prophetic Tradition," chapter 7 of his "The Delaware Indians: A Study in Ethnohistory" (Ph.D. diss., University of California, Santa Barbara, 1973), and Charles Hunter, "The Delaware Nativist Revival of the Mid-Eighteenth Century," *Ethnohistory* 18 (1971): 39–49, both of which push Mooney's suggestion further by bringing to light several of the Delaware prophets who surrounded Neolin between 1760 and 1775; and Anthony F. C. Wallace, "New Religions among the Delaware," *Southwestern Journal of Anthropology* 12 (1956): 1–21, which, unlike the other works, emphasizes discontinuity.

led them to perform new ceremonies.[10] Indian myths, moreover, are replete with similar journeys to the sky world.

In its mid-eighteenth-century manifestations prophetic nativism first appears, mildly, in the 1737 journals of Pennsylvania's Indian agent, Conrad Weiser. Weiser found starving Shawnees and Onondaga Iroquois at the Susquehanna River town of Otseningo discussing the recent visions of "one of their seers." In "a vision of God," the seer learned that God had "driven the wild animals out of the country" in punishment for the crime of killing game for trade in alcohol. The seer convinced his listeners that if they did not stop trading skins for English rum, God would wipe them "from the earth." Weiser did not dwell on the matter; we do not learn of any ensuing reformation.[11] But by 1744, the Susquehanna Valley, increasingly populated by polyglot refugees from dispossession in the East, swelled again with prophecy.

That year, lower down the river, the Presbyterian missionary David Brainerd encountered religious nativists among the Delawares and Shawnees. He reported that "they now seem resolved to retain their pagan notions and persist in their idolatrous practices." Beset by disease, the Indians looked to the sacred powers "to find out why they were then so sickly." Among the inhabitants of one Delaware town Brainerd met "a devout and zealous reformer, or rather restorer of what he supposed was the ancient religion of the Indians." Like the seer at Otseningo, the holy man claimed that his people "were grown very degenerate and corrupt," and he emphatically denounced alcohol. But he also claimed that his people must revive what he believed were the ceremonies of their ancestors. Although the sight of the Delaware holy man stirred "images of terror" in Brainerd's mind, the shaman did not reveal any hostility toward Anglo-Americans, and Brainerd admitted that "there was something in his temper and disposition that looked more like true religion than anything I ever observed amongst other heathens."[12]

Neither Weiser's "seer" nor Brainerd's "reformer" mounted a political challenge discernible in the record. They did stand against the alcohol trade and therefore against a most visible and physical form of dependence upon Europeans. That is all. But Weiser's mission of 1737 was part of an effort to firm up an alliance between Pennsylvania and the Six Nations, an alliance that was political. The upshot of his mission and of several ensuing years of Pennsylvanian negotiation with the Six Nations did affect prophecy. The

---

[10] Bruce G. Trigger, *Children of Aataentsic: A History of the Huron People to 1660* (Montreal, 1976), 2:592–94; James P. Ronda, "Black Robes and Boston Men: Indian-White Relations in New France and New England, 1524–1701," in *The American Indian Experience: A Profile*, ed. Philip Weeks (Arlington Heights, Ill., 1988), 16.

[11] Paul A. W. Wallace, *Conrad Weiser, 1696–1760, Friend of Colonist and Mohawk* (Philadelphia, 1945), 88.

[12] David Brainerd, *The Life of David Brainerd*, ed. Jonathan Edwards and Philip E. Howard, Jr. (1749; Chicago, 1949), 233–34, 236–38.

upshot was that a large group of Delawares lost their homes on the Delaware River and reluctantly migrated to new homes, under Six Nations supervision, on the Susquehanna. By the early 1750s, these and other Susquehanna Valley refugees began to demonstrate, politically and spiritually, against both Six Nations authority and Anglo-American expansion. The obvious political developments are treated as such elsewhere.[13] Let us briefly explore their religious dimension.

The first of the prophets to mount a political challenge was a young Delaware woman. Noted in 1751 by Brainerd's younger brother, John, she lived in the increasingly militant Susquehanna River town of Wyoming, which was choked with refugees. We know little of her, not even her name; indeed the Indians "seemed somewhat backward to tell" John Brainerd about her at all. But the scanty evidence is tantalizing. Her vision "was a confirmation of some revelations they had had before." She had been told by the "Great Power that they should destroy the poison from among them." The woman worried about the sickness and death of so many of her people and blamed it on that "poison," probably a witch bundle, allegedly held by "their old and principal men." The evidence, though thin, suggests a challenge to the local leadership of the town of Wyoming, a leadership bound to the powerful Six Nations Iroquois to the north and, through their cooperation, to the British colonies. Her people would attack that bondage openly and violently during the Seven Years' War.[14]

The people of this Delaware village asserted their Indian identity. They drew distinctions that separated Indians from blacks and whites. The distinctions, they felt, were God-given. Rejecting Presbyterian attempts to establish a mission among them, they explained, "God first made three men and three women, viz: the indians, the negro, and the white man." Because Europeans were produced last, "the white people ought not to think themselves better than the Indians." Moreover, the Bible was for Europeans alone; since God gave no such book "to the Indian or negro, and therefore it could not be right for them to have a book, or be any way concerned with that way of worship."[15]

This idea of the separate creation of Indians, blacks, and whites, an idea that sanctioned separate forms of worship, was widely reported in the Susquehanna and Ohio regions, where it became commonplace. On the eve of the American Revolution, it would be shared as well by the southern Indians, who described it to Anglo-Americans.[16] The notion of the separate cre-

---

[13] Francis Jennings, *The Ambiguous Iroquois Empire* (New York, 1984), 309–46; and his *Empire of Fortune: Crowns, Colonies, and Tribes in the Seven Years War in America* (New York, 1988), 262–67, 271–80.
[14] The Reverend John Brainerd to Ebenezar Pemberton, 1751, in *Life of John Brainerd*, ed. Thomas Brainerd (Philadelphia, 1865), 233–34.
[15] John Brainerd to Pemberton, 1751, in *Life of John Brainerd*, 234–35.
[16] Contrast with William G. McLoughlin, "A Note on African Sources of American Indian Racial Myths," in *Cherokee Ghost Dance: Essays on the Southeastern Indians, 1789–1861*, ed. William G. McLoughlin (Macon, Ga., 1984), 253–60.

ation gave legitimacy to the Indians' way of life. It explicitly challenged not only those Indians who had converted to Christianity but also those few who had grown too close to the Anglo-Americans. It played in harmony with the Wyoming woman's dissent from the accommodating leadership of her village. Claiming that only Indian ways could lead Indians to salvation, the theology of separation implicitly attacked Indian clients of the Anglo-Americans.

The notion had radical implications for Indian identity. Attachments to the older, local, linguistic, and lineage-oriented conceptions of one's people now competed with a decidedly innovative pan-Indianism. The notion reflected the growing cooperation of militant factions from different peoples in political efforts to unite Indians against the Anglo-American menace. It also reflected the heightening of local tensions, as Indians who rejected nativism and urged accommodation with the British found themselves accused of abomination.

The year after the younger Brainerd first encountered this separatist theology, a group of Munsee Delawares settled a new town some seventy miles up the winding Susquehanna. Munsees increasingly identified with their Unami Delaware–speaking cousins, and like many Unamis they had maintained friendly relations with the Moravians and Quakers. This particular group of Munsees displayed a marked ambivalence toward both Christianity and nativism. Its leader, Papoonan, had once been "a drunken Indian." At the age of about forty-five he "underwent a sorrowful period of reformation, including a solitary sojourn in the woods & a vision following the death of his father." Like other Indian prophets, Papoonan emerged from the vision with a message of love and reformation. He preached against the use of alcohol, as would most prophets, and he preached that the Master of Life, angered by the sins of the Indians, had met them with punishing visitations.

Unlike many of the other prophets, Papoonan refused to countenance war—a stand he may have absorbed from the Moravians and Quakers. The prophet once told a Pennsylvanian that in his heart he knew "the Quakers are Right." He and his followers remained at peace with Pennsylvania throughout the 1750s, and toward the end of the war they sought out Quakers to mediate their talks with the suspicious British authorities.

But even sincere protestations of friendship and interest in Christianity could not mask Papoonan's frustration with the social changes wrought by the Indian-Anglo trade. Recognizing the increasing importance in Indian society of access to British trade goods, Papoonan aimed his message primarily at the greedy. His own people, he worried, "grow proud & Covetous, which causes God to be Angry & to send dry & hot Summers & hard Winters, & also Sickness among the People."[17] He also aimed the message at

[17] "Remarks made by a Person [Anthony Benezet?] who accompanied Papoonhoal and other Indians on their way home as far as Bethlehem, July, 1760," Huntington MSS, 8249, Henry E.

Anglo-Americans, telling the Pennsylvania Provincial Council that their raising of the prices of manufactured goods created tensions: "You alter the price that you say you will give for our Skins, which can never be right; God cannot be pleased to see the prices of one & the same thing so often alter'd & Changed." While challenging the greed of British colonists, Papoonan, like other prophets, urged his followers to purify themselves of similar greed by "adhering to the ancient Customs & manners of their Forefathers." He and his followers resisted, for a time, Christian efforts to establish missions among them, for they were "much afraid of being seduced & [brought] off from their ways by the White People."[18]

In spite of its attempt to live in peace, Papoonan's community could not escape the massive troubles that surrounded it. Christian Frederick Post found the villagers troubled and quarrelsome in 1760. The town still existed as a native, non-Christian religious community the following year, but as Pontiac's War of 1763 embroiled the region, Papoonan, who held to the peace, lost influence. British colonial lynch mobs, having killed neutral Indians in the Paxton Massacre, forced Papoonan to flee with others to the safety of barracks under Quaker protection in Philadelphia. At the war's end, he was there numbered among the "Christian Indians." Some among his followers invited the Moravian missionaries to come among them. Others went off to join the nativistic communities that were, by then, abundant on the Upper Ohio.[19] It would not be the last failure of studied neutrality.

Further up the Susquehanna, not far from what is now New York State, Wangomend, or the Assinsink Prophet, experienced his first visions in the early 1750s, probably in 1752, the year Papoonan settled his new town. Unlike Papoonan, this Munsee showed open hostility toward the British. Indeed his message closely resembles the separatist beliefs of the Unami Delaware woman downstream at Wyoming who received her visions the previous year. The Assinsink Prophet encouraged the Indians to abandon British ways, emphatically denouncing rum drinking. He employed a chart on which "there is Heaven and a Hell and Rum and Swan hak [Europeans] and Indiens and Ride [Red] Strokes for Rum."[20] As late as 1760, his fellow

---

Huntington Library, San Marino, California; [Anthony Benezet,] *Some Observations on the Situation, Disposition, and Character of the Indian Natives of This Continent* (Philadelphia, 1784), 24; "Relation by Frederick Post of Conversation with Indians, 1760" *Penn. Archives,* 1st ser., 3:743; Edmund A. De Schweinitz, *The Life and Times of David Zeisberger* (Philadelphia, 1871), 427.

[18] "Council at the State House in Philadelphia, Friday, July 11, 1760," Pennsylvania Council Minutes, Huntington MSS, 8249, Huntington Library; Christian Frederick Post, "Journal, 1760," May 19, on microfilm at American Philosophical Society, Philadelphia.

[19] "Relation by Christian Frederick Post," 743; Wallace, "New Religions among the Delaware," 8–9; "Journal Kept at Fort Augusta, 1763," *Penn. Archives,* 2nd ser., 7:439; John Heckewelder, *Narrative of the Mission of the United Brethren* (Philadelphia, 1820), 90–92.

[20] Hunter, "The Delaware Nativist Revival," 42–43, argues convincingly that Wangomend and the Assinsink Prophet were one and the same; Zeisberger supplies the 1752 dating: David Zeisberger, "1769 Diary," 79, translated typescript in Miscellaneous File, Ethnohistory Archive;

villagers manifested their enmity toward the colonists when they prevented a Pennsylvania peace delegation from passing west into the Ohio country.

Wangomend, like other Susquehanna country prophets, introduced or reintroduced ceremonies in an effort to gain power. Post reported that the prophet had revived "an Old quarterly Meeting," during which the participants recited the "Dreams and Revelations everyone had from his Infancy, & what Strength and Power they had received thereby." The meeting, which lasted all day and all night, involved walking, singing, dancing, and, finally, cathartic weeping. The people of the town paid close attention to visions and dreams, not only their own but those of others. When news of the collective vision that opened this book came from Munsee Tioga, miles upstream, the Assinsink Munsees also sought to discover its meaning. Prophecy in the Susquehanna and Ohio countries was not a local affair.

Following the Seven Years' War, refugee Munsee and Unami Delawares fled the Susquehanna for the Ohio, and the Assinsink Prophet was among them.[21] There he undoubtedly encountered, if he had not done so previously, the thoroughly compatible teachings of another advocate of Indian separation from Britain, the Delaware Prophet, Neolin. The Ottawa warrior Pontiac would claim inspiration from Neolin for his siege of Detroit in 1763, and Neolin would rapidly emerge as the spiritual leader of a militant movement with political overtones. But it is important to recall that he neither invented nor was solely responsible for the spiritual quest for unity.

THE DELAWARE PROPHET, NEOLIN

One night in the eighteen months or so of only relative calm that followed the French evacuation of the Upper Ohio Valley, Neolin sat alone by his fire, "musing and greatly concerned about the evil ways he saw prevailing among the Indians." Strangely, a man appeared and "told him these things he was thinking of were right" and proceeded to instruct him in religion. By the fall of 1761 Neolin had gained a considerable following as he relayed the will of the Master of Life to the Delawares. Like the Assinsink Prophet, he employed a pictographic chart. Neolin drew a path from earth to heaven, along "which their forefathers use'd to assend to Hapiness." The path, however, was now blocked by a symbol "representing the White people." Along the right side of the chart were many "Strokes" representing the vices brought by Europeans. Through these strokes the Indians now "must go, ye Good Road being Stopt." Hell was also close at hand, and "there they are

"John Hays' Diary and Journal of 1760," ed. William A. Hunter, *Pennsylvania Archaeologist* 24 (1954): 76–77, also quoted in Wallace, "New Religions among the Delaware," 9.

[21] Post, "Journal, 1760," May 23, May 24; "John Hays Diary," 77; Hunter, "The Delaware Nativist Revival," 43; Zeisberger, "1769 Diary," 79.

Led irrevocably."[22] The programs offered by the Assinsink Prophet and Neolin were identical in many particulars. Each preached strenuously against the use of rum, chief among "ye vices which ye Indians have learned from ye White people," and which each depicted on his chart as strokes through which the difficult way to heaven now led.[23]

Neolin not only drew a cosmographic distinction between Anglo-Americans and Indians, he preached a rejection of dependence on the British through the avoidance of trade, the elaboration of ritual, and the gradual (not the immediate) abandonment of European-made goods. In 1763, Delaware councils agreed to train their boys in the traditional arts of warfare, and to adopt, for seven years, a ritual diet that included the frequent consumption of an herbal emetic, after which they would be purified of the "White people's ways and Nature."[24] The ritual brewing, drinking, and vomiting of this tea became a regular feature of Ohio Valley nativism in the 1760s. Very common in the Southeast, "black drink" may have been introduced to the Delawares by their Shawnee neighbors, well connected with the Cherokees and Creeks. The practice repelled missionaries and other visitors to the Ohio country. Shawnees drank and spewed the beverage with such literal enthusiasm that one of their towns, Wakatomica, was known to traders in the late 1760s as "vomit town."[25] Wakatomica became a center of

[22] Charles Beatty, *Journals of Charles Beatty, 1762–1769,* ed. Guy Soulliard Klett (University Park, Penn., 1962), 65; see also Charles Beatty, *The Journal of a Two Months Tour with a View of Promoting Religion* (Edinburgh, 1798), for a fairly faithful, though polished, revision of the original journals; James Kenny, "Journal of James Kenny, 1761–1763," *PMHB* 37 (1913): 171.

[23] Kenny, "Journal," 171; Wallace, "New Religions among the Delaware," 9. "John Hays Diary," 77, suggests the similarity between the two charts in n. 111. On abstention from alcohol, see John Heckewelder, *History, Manners, and Customs of the Indian Nations Who Once Inhabited Pennsylvania, and the Neighboring States* (1819; Philadelphia, 1876), 292–93; [Robert Navarre,] "Journal of Pontiac's Conspiracy," in *The Siege of Detroit in 1763, the Journal of Pontiac's Conspiracy and John Rutherford's Narrative of a Captivity,* ed. Milo Quaife (Chicago, 1958), 14; Neyon de Villiers to d'Abbadie, Fort Chartres, December 1, 1763, in *Ill. Hist. Coll.,* 10:51.

[24] That Neolin preached a gradual abandonment, a point missed by scholars, is implied in his suggestion that boys be trained "to ye use of the Bow & Arrow for Seven Years," and that the people were, "at ye Expiration of ye Seven Years, to quit all Commerce with ye White People & Clothe themselves with Skins." See Kenny, "Journal," 188.

[25] De Schweinitz, *Life and Times of Zeisberger,* 383; Heckewelder, *Narrative of the Mission,* 104–5, refers to Wangomend's advocacy of "purging the body"; Zeisberger, "1767 Diary," translated typescript in Miscellaneous File, Ethnohistory Archive, 608–609a; Zeisberger, "1769 Diary," 6; John Ettwein, "Some remarks and annotations concerning the Traditions, Customs, languages &c. of the Indians in North America, from the memoirs of the Rev. David Zeisberger and other Missionaries of the United Brethren. Sent to General Washington by Rev. John Ettwein, Bethlehem, March 28, 1788," Miscellaneous Papers, Historical and Philosophical Society of Ohio, on microfilm in Ethnohistory Archive; William L. Merrill, "The Beloved Tree, *Ilex Vomitoria* among the Indians of the Southeast and Adjacent Regions," in *Black Drink: A Native American Tea,* ed. Charles Hudson (Athens, Ga., 1979), 40–82. For early use of emetics among the New England Peoples, close cultural cousins of the Delawares, see William S. Simmons, *Spirit of the New England Tribes: Indian History and Folklore, 1620–1984* (Hanover, N.H., 1986), 40.

resistance to Anglo-American expansion and cultural influence. Here is where the Delaware Prophet took refuge, in fact, when British troops threatened to invade his hometown on the Tuscarawas River in 1764.[26]

Neolin's message clearly entailed armed resistance to Anglo-American expansion. As early as 1761, Neolin predicted that "there will be Two or Three Good Talks and then War." Neolin's words struck a chord among Indians who suffered from or looked with foreboding upon three major threats to their economics: the disappearance of game, land encroachments by settlers (now well under way on the Monongahela), and the British abandonment of customary presentations of gunpowder to the Indians. Like the seer at Otseningo, Neolin explained the exhaustion of the deer herds as the Great Spirit's punishment for the Indians' embrace of Anglo-American vices. He berated Indians for allowing the colonists to establish settlements west of the Appalachians and for the Indians' humiliating dependence: "Can ye not live without them?" And he threatened continued disaster if they did not both reform and revolt: "If you suffer the English among you, you are dead men. Sickness, smallpox, and their poison will destroy you entirely."[27]

The prophet's message spread among the nations. When the French commander of Fort Chartres (Illinois) learned of the prophet late in 1763, he wrote that Neolin "has had no difficulty in convincing all his own people, and in turn all red men, that God had appeared to him." Commandant Neyon de Villiers was "perfectly convinced of the effect that it has had on the Potawatomi."[28] In 1764, the Wyandots of Sandusky, militants who associated closely with the Shawnees and Delawares, openly joined the crusade against the English. The combined Shawnee, Delaware, and Wyandot inhabitants of Sandusky declared that they had no fear of English numbers. Of the English they claimed that one Indian was "as good as a thousand of them, and notwithstanding they are but *Mice* in Comparison to them, they will bite as hard as *they* can." In addition to the Potawatomis, Wyandots, Shawnees, and Delawares, the prophet's message raised spirits among the Miamis, Senecas, Ottawas, Chippewas, and beyond.[29]

Many spin-off revivals occurred, just as Neolin's had spun off from the earlier Susquehanna episodes. A Delaware of Kuskuski visited Heaven in

---

[26] Reuben Gold Thwaites and Louise Phelps Kellogg, *Documentary History of Dunmore's War, 1774* (Madison, Wis., 1905), 153n; Bouquet to Lieut. Francis and Col. Clayton, Fort Pitt, September 23, 1764, in *The Papers of Colonel Henry Bouquet*, ed. Sylvester K. Stevens and Donald H. Kent (Harrisburg, Penn., 1943), 13, pt. 2:142.

[27] Kenny, "Journal," 171; Randolph Downes, *Council Fires on the Upper Ohio* (Pittsburgh, 1949), 105–6; Wilbur Jacobs, *Wilderness Politics: Diplomacy and Indian Gifts* (Lincoln, Neb., 1950), 183–85; [Navarre,] "Journal of Pontiac's Conspiracy," 14–15; De Villiers to D'Abbadie, December 1, 1763, in *Ill. Hist. Coll.*, 10:51.

[28] *Ill. Hist. Coll.*, 10:51–52.

[29] Major Gladwyn to Johnson, Detroit, June 9–11, 1764, in *The Papers of Sir William Johnson*, ed. James Sullivan, Alexander C. Flick, Almon W. Lauber, Milton W. Hamilton, 14 vols. (Albany, 1921–1965), 11:228; "Indian Conference," May 25, 1764, ibid., 11:206, hereafter cited as *Johnson Papers*.

1762. He used charts in his ministry and communicated with the Great Spirit through intermediaries, or, as James Kenny put it, through "a little God." A great chief of the Ottawas, Katapelleecy, had personal encounters with the Great Spirit in 1764. In the heart of the Six Nations country an Onondaga received revelations critical of the Anglo-Americans and laced with separation theology on the eve of Pontiac's War.[30] With no end in sight to the British threat, these prophets, despite their many innovations, offered a solution to Indian problems that came out of Indian traditions. Reform the world through ritual; recapture sacred power. The message took hold.

PROPHETIC RESISTANCE, 1760–1775

In the spring of 1763, thirteen of the British posts that stood north of the Ohio and the Potomac and west of the Susquehanna, in the heartland of religious nativism, came under devastating Indian attacks. From Senecas in New York to Chippewas in Minnesota and the Indians of Illinois, militant factions joined in a struggle to remove the British from posts so recently French. By 1765 this war, commonly known as Pontiac's War, had ended, and only four of the posts remained, most notably Detroit and Pitt.

Prophecy has long been acknowledged as having had a role in Pontiac's War, a colorful but incidental role. Generally, the prophet's message is a historian's addendum to a list of substantive causes of the war: British abuses in the trade, colonial encroachments on Indian land, Jeffrey Amherst's orders curtailing the customary dispensing of gifts to Indians, and French encouragement to the Indians.[31] A common view is that Neolin's message was a slogan employed by militants to attract warriors. Howard Peckham, calling Neolin a "psychopathic Delaware," sees the prophet as providing a justification for Pontiac's attack on the British at Detroit. Suggesting that Pontiac manipulated "the Prophet's message slightly to support his own ambitions," Peckham implies that the Ottawa leader was too sophisticated to have believed in the prophet's visions, but used prophecy to inspire his more gullible followers.[32]

Pontiac, however, portrayed himself as a true believer in the nativistic movement, and there seems little reason to doubt his claim.[33] Even addressing the Catholic French he spoke in prophetic terms. Visiting Fort Chartres

[30] Kenny, "Journal," 173; "Journal of Captain Thomas Morris of His Majesty's XVII Regiment of Infantry," in *Early Western Travels*, ed. Reuben Gold Thwaites (Cleveland, 1904), 1:309–10; Indian Conference, Johnson Hall, September 8–10, 1762, in *Johnson Papers*, 10:505–6.

[31] Francis Parkman, *The Conspiracy of Pontiac and the Indian Uprising of 1763* (1851; Boston, 1898), 1:180–84.

[32] Howard Peckham, *Pontiac and the Indian Uprising* (Chicago, 1961), 98, 116; Thurman, "The Delaware Indians," 160, also sees Pontiac as an "empirical" leader.

[33] See Gregory E. Dowd, "The French King Wakes Up in Detroit: 'Pontiac's War' in Rumor and History," *Ethnohistory* 34 (1990): 254–78.

in 1764 to reject de Villiers's request that he stop the war, Pontiac declared that the Master of Life "put Arms in our hands, and it is he who has ordered us to fight against this bad meat that would come and infest our lands." He warned the French not to speak of "Peace with the English," for in doing so they went "against the orders of the Master of Life."[34] Indeed, there is other evidence that Pontiac acted upon Neolin's initiative. Robert Navarre, a pro-British *habitant* who knew Pontiac at Detroit, said of Neolin's message that it "contains in blackest aspect the reason of the attack upon the English." Fort Pitt's Captain Simeon Ecuyer had it on the authority of Detroit's Major Henry Gladwyn that the Delawares and Shawnees were the *"canaille* who stir up the rest to mischief."[35]

But the extent of the prophet's influence on Pontiac or of Pontiac's influence on the war that now bears his name is less important for an understanding of Indian militancy than is the spiritual nature of militancy itself. The Delaware Prophet was not the single leader of the movement any more than was Pontiac. Both drew upon widespread beliefs in their efforts to confront the problems of 1763. The Delaware Prophet, and many other prophets who preceded and followed him, provided Indians with an explanation for their misfortunes that squared well with their traditions: Indian abominations, including cooperation with the British, caused their loss of sacred power. Construed in this manner, the disturbance could be rectified by ritual and by steadfast, united opposition to British expansion.

When the Indians failed to drive the British from Fort Detroit and Fort Pitt, when smallpox—deliberately disseminated in hospital blankets by Fort Pitt's British officers—broke out among the Ohio peoples, and when British columns marched within striking distance of Indian towns, the military unity of the Indians temporarily collapsed and the war ended. But neither prophetic nativism nor the idea of unity collapsed with it. Prophets and diplomats grew more active.

PROPHECY IN DEFEAT

Following the logic of nativism—that proper behavior could restore Indian power—it would be reasonable to expect the British victory of 1765 to have disproved prophecy and ended the Indians' Great Awakening. Neolin's followers did indeed face a crisis as they were forced to submit to Henry Bouquet's forces. Responding to the crisis in January 1765, Neolin had another vision, the last in the record. He approached veteran Indian agent George

[34] "A council in Illinois, Pontiac addresses Mons. Neyon de Villiers, April 15, 17, 1764," enclosed in Farmer to Gage, December 21, 1764, Thomas Gage Papers [selected], William Clements Library, on microfilm at the Ethnohistory Archive.
[35] [Navarre,] "Journal of Pontiac's Conspiracy," 8; Ecuyer to Bouquet, May 29, 1763, quoted in Parkman, *The Conspiracy of Pontiac,* 2:7.

Croghan with it in April, for it required British action. Like Papoonan at the end of the Seven Years' War, Neolin requested that the British send out Quaker negotiators. The Great Spirit had recently permitted Neolin to negotiate with Britain, but only through the Quakers. Still, recovering from smallpox, without ammunition, and with a British army poised to strike their villages, the Indians were in no position to bargain. Croghan, an agent of the Pennsylvania Proprietors, suspected that his employers' political opponents in the "Quaker Party" lay behind the Indian request, and he refused it. Delaware delegates yielded to British power and signed a treaty of peace in April, but in their villages they were "in great Confusion amongst themselves and without any order in their Council," as factionalism prevailed.[36]

Such divisions plagued Indians throughout the period. Even during the war, nativists found parties of Indians ranged against them. Roman Catholic Hurons under the baptized leader, Teata, confronted militants: "We do not know what the designs of the Master of Life toward us may be. Is it He who inspires our brothers, the Ottawas to war?"[37] Mingos and Genese Senecas sided with the militants against the wishes of the seat of Iroquois accommodation, the Onondaga Council, which eventually neutralized the militant Senecas by providing Sir William Johnson, Britain's Northern Superintendent of Indian Affairs, with Iroquois troops. And even among Neolin's people, the division between nativism and accommodation was pronounced: "The Capts and Warriors of the Delaware pay no regard to their Chiefs who advised them not to accept the Hatchet."[38]

Paradoxically, it was precisely these divisions that permitted the survival of the nativist movement for unity. Nativism depended upon its Indian opponents. Infighting extended the life of the movement. Nativists could attribute the failure of Native American arms not to British numbers, technology, or organization, but to the improper behavior of the accommodating Indians. As long as nativists faced serious opposition within their own communities, they could explain Indian defeat as the consequence of other Indians' misdeeds.

For years following the collapse of armed Indian rebellion in 1765, militant prophets continued to attract followers, and internal animosities mounted within the villages. The young people, wrote George Henry Loskiel, "began to despise the counsel of the aged, and only endeavored to get into favor with these preachers, whose followers multiplied very fast."[39] One of the best known of these "preachers" was the Assinsink Prophet,

[36] "Journal of Transactions with the Indians at Fort Pitt," in *Pennsylvania Colonial Records* (Harrisburg, Penn., 1852), 9:254–56; Croghan to Gage, Pittsburgh, May 12, 1765, Gage Papers, on microfilm at the Ethnohistory Archive.
[37] [Navarre,] "Journal of Pontiac's Conspiracy," 63.
[38] Johnson to Lords of Trade, May 11, 1764, in *DRCHSNY*, 7:624–26; entry for June 16, 1763, in "William Trent's Journal at Fort Pitt, 1763," ed. Albert T. Volwiler, *MVHR* 11 (1924–25): 399.
[39] Loskiel, *History of the Mission*, 38.

Wangomend. Wangomend had long preached that there were fundamental differences between Indians and Anglo-Americans. Like his counterparts at the Susquehanna town of Wyoming in the 1750s and like his contemporary Neolin, whom he outlasted as a prophet, he spoke of separate paths to heaven for Indians and Anglo-Americans, and he drew the paths "on the ground, showing the way for the Indians to be much more direct" than that for the Christians. God, he later said, "has created them and us for different purposes. Therefore, let us cling to our old customs and not depart from them."[40] Wangomend did not preach alone. At Goshgoshunk on the Allegheny River, where the Moravian missionary David Zeisberger encountered him in 1767, elderly women also saw the Indians' misfortunes as the result of "having changed their ancient way of living, in consequence of what the white men had told them, and this white preacher (Zeisberger) was saying to them."[41]

Wangomend attended to a variety of voices, not only that of the Great Spirit. One vision, which was most likely Wangomend's, suggests his concern for the depleted condition of game. While out hunting, he came across a buck that spoke to him, warning the Indians "not to have so much to do with the whites, but cherish their own customs and not to imitate the manners of the whites, else it would not go well with them."[42] Like the medicine bear of the Cherokee myth, this buck was probably the "deer master," the manitou that controlled the supply of game and made certain that hunters behaved properly.

Wangomend's erratic career lasted to the very eve of the American Revolution. For a time, after the failure of one of his prophecies to come true and in the face of a swell of Munsee conversions to the Moravian's religion in the summer of 1770, he despaired and tried to become a Moravian Christian, but within a year he abandoned the attempt, resumed his own mission, and led an intensive witch-hunt in an effort to rescue his people from abomination. As late as 1775, as the American Revolution broke out in the East, Wangomend still sought to rid his people of evil, proposing a witch-hunt at a Delaware council at Goshgoshunk.[43]

[40] David Zeisberger, "The Diaries of David Zeisberger Relating to the First Missions in the Ohio Basin," ed. Archer Butler Hulbert and William Nathaniel Schwarze, *Ohio Archaeological and Historical Quarterly* 21 (1912): 28. Quotations from Zeisberger's 1767 material derive from this translation, which is more accessible to the researcher. This translation and the 1767 material in the Ethnohistory Archive are substantively quite similar. See also Zeisberger, "1767 Diary," 610 a; and Zeisberger, "1769 Diary," 23.
[41] Heckewelder, *Narrative of the Mission*, 102–3; De Schweinitz, *Life and Times of Zeisberger*, 340.
[42] Zeisberger, "Diaries . . . Relating to the First Missions in the Ohio Basin," 24–25; Zeisberger, "1767 Diary," 608–9.
[43] Heckewelder, *History, Manners, and Customs of the Indian Nations*, 293–95; Heckewelder, *Narrative of the Mission*, 108, 112, 135–36; Jungmann, "Diaries of Brother Jungmann, 1771," 202–4, typescript in Miscellaneous File, Ethnohistory Archive; Zeisberger, "1769 Diary," 62–63, 74, 125, 172; David Zeisberger Diary, 1772–81, in MAB, reel 8, box 141, 15:11.

Such accusations made him many enemies, a fact that both troubled his career and made it possible, for he could only preach reformation against a convincing backdrop of corruption. We know so much of Wangomend largely because he, of all the Ohio prophets, had the most direct contact with a determined group of Moravian Brethren, a group that had attracted about one hundred, mostly Munsee, Delawares to its Ohio mission between 1769 and 1782, a significant accomplishment considering that the Delaware population at this time may have been as low as two and a half thousand.

With every twenty-fifth Delaware attending to the Moravian Brethren, and with others attending to the likes of Wangomend, Delaware fissures deepened. Nativist sentiment surfaced regularly in the two major Unami Delaware towns, Kuskuski and Newcomer's, into the early 1770s. Like other advocates of Indian separation, these nativists stressed the distinction between Indians and the eastern settlers. One, visiting the Moravian Munsees in 1771, laid out his categories of understanding before Zeisberger. Christianity, the nativist said, was "for the white people. . . . God has made different kinds of men and has made each kind for a different purpose." The Indian clearly worried that to worship in the Christian manner was to violate the cosmic order. Another Indian, claiming to be a literate ex-Christian, told his townspeople "that he has read the Bible from beginning to end and that it is not written in it that the Indians should live like white people, or that they should change their lives." The nativists of Kuskuski never threatened the mission with violence, but they worried at its success and sought to convince the Christian converts to return to the nativist fold. One nativistic "new preacher" used images of Anglo-American society as the symbols of danger to Indians, declaring that the Moravians sought to have the Indians "transported as slaves, where they would be harnessed to the plough, and whipped to work."[44]

A prophet at Delaware Newcomer's town, so named by the English for its leader, not only accused the Moravians of plotting to enslave the Delawares but claimed that worse catastrophes awaited all the people if Moravian successes continued: in three and a half years "there would be a terrible flood . . . and until then nothing which they would plant would grow." Drawing on Indian traditions that regarded fasts as a means of rectifying disorders caused by an improper mixing of categories, this prophet recommended a diet of only corn and water for four months to forestall the disaster.[45]

The people of Newcomer's town pondered these developments in the midst of a terrible epidemic. Some of them had sought answers in the faith of the Moravians, others joined the Moravians seeking powers to supple-

[44] Zeisberger, "1769 Diary," 22, 144, 150; Heckewelder, *Narrative of the Mission*, 116.
[45] Zeisberger, "1769 Diary," 167–70.

ment their own beliefs, but still others shunned the Christians as they intensified their efforts to rectify the disturbances that had left them so vulnerable to harm. As the sickness persisted, the village council hit upon a solution
that may well have been proposed by its famous resident, Neolin. Drawing
upon their ideas about the power of fasts to enable humans to cross into
other dimensions, the council decided to raise two boys as prophets. For two
years the children would receive daily emetics, and they would eat only corn
and water. After this preparation, "they would become very spiritualized
and have many visions, revelations and dreams, they would even possess a
special spirit and strength." Whether any boys underwent this preparation
is not known, but the idea was not completely new. Eight years before, Neolin had proposed a variant: all the boys were to "Live intirely on dry'd Meat
& a Sort of Bitter Drink made of Roots & Plants & Water." Now, in 1770, the
town council, by underfeeding two of the village children, sought to create
prophets to help them meet future disasters.[46]

The drive for purity so vividly represented by the regular purges and
fasts that the nativists endured found expression in another form of purge,
the witch-hunt. Witches and witch bundles, or "poison," became chief objects of nativistic wrath as Indians felt a loss of power to resist disease, want,
and Anglo-American expansion. Indians saw witches as inherently evil beings who enjoyed killing; to discover witches and "poison" among them
would be to understand their calamities. In 1772, a council at Kuskuski suspected that one of the Moravian Indians possessed such a bundle, the
"strong poison by which many Indians are killed."[47]

Although the witchcraft accusations against Indians well connected
with the colonists resulted in little violence during the early 1770s, they did
contribute to growing divisions within the villages of the Unamis and Munsees. While nativists urged unity in the face of the Anglo-American threat,
Delaware councils divided. The nativistic Indians of Newcomer's town
squared off against a faction led by the accommodation-minded Delaware
war captain, Chief White Eyes.[48] This fracture among the Delawares would
prevent the Shawnees and Mingos from obtaining much Delaware support
in their attempts to prevent the Anglo-American capture of Kentucky during
what has come to be called "Lord Dunmore's War," after the royal governor
of aggressive Virginia.

---

[46] Zeisberger, "1769 Diary," 81, 132; Beatty, *The Journal of a Two Months Tour*, 23–30; Kenny, "Journal," 188.

[47] Zeisberger, "1767 Diary," 603; Zeisberger, "1769 Diary," 28, 81; John George Jungmann, "Diaries," 217. Thurman, "The Delaware Indians," 150, points to similiarities between the witch-
hunts of the 1760s and 1770s and those of the Shawnee Prophet.

[48] De Schweinitz, *Life and Times of Zeisberger*, 416–18; Dunmore to Dartmouth, Williamsburg, December 24, 1774, Draper MSS, 15 J 48.

THE SCIOTO CONFERENCES AND DUNMORE'S WAR,
1767–1775

Currents of nativism ran as deeply among the Shawnees as they did among the Delawares. Because there were no Christian missionaries settled among them, however, we have fewer records. This emptiness is itself revealing, for Moravians, Presbyterians, and Baptists all attempted to preach to this militant people but were not allowed. Instead, the Shawnees welcomed the preaching of Delaware nativists, even after Neolin's powers had waned.

One of these Delaware prophets, Scattameck, became a vessel for the sacred at Newcomer's town in 1771. Like previous visionaries, he strongly recommended that the Indians drink "Beson (medicinal herbs and roots), in order to cleanse themselves from sin." Two other Delaware "preachers" supported Scattameck. The Shawnees "received the tidings with joy and sent the message on to the Delamattenoos [Miamis]." According to Zeisberger, Scattameck claimed that adherence to the ritual would bring the Indians a good crop even if "they planted but little." Zeisberger held this teaching responsible for a famine among the Shawnees, but the Indians apparently saw the matter differently. Despite their hunger, the missionary noted, "the idea continues and has not been recalled . . . the matter remains unchanged."[49]

Scattameck, following the other prophets, invoked the doctrine of Indian separateness. During one vision he learned that Europeans and Indians did not share the path to salvation, that the son of the Great Spirit desired that Indians "should come to him by another way than that used by the white people."[50] This separatist notion, although informed by the Christian notion of salvation as a coming to God, nonetheless was clearly and consciously anti-Christian, and it continued to resonate among nativists.

The Baptist minister David Jones found his mission to the five Shawnee towns in 1772 and 1773 mired in thick Shawnee nativism. During these early childhood years of the great future nativist, Tecumseh, Jones encountered an enthusiasm to match his own. After he entered the village of Chillicothe, Shawnees brought Jones to Red Hawk, from whom Jones requested permission to preach. Red Hawk refused in separatist terms, arguing that Indians should live and worship in their own manner: "When God, who first made us all, prescribed our way of living, he allowed the white people to live one way, and Indians another way."[51] Jones failed to gather a Shawnee audience.

The Baptist noticed that the Indians entertained suspicions that his object was to promote their enslavement, that "the white people had sent me as a spy." The Shawnees' rumors were not far off the mark, for Jones actually

---

[49] David Zeisberger, Diary, 1772–81, in MAB, reel 8, box 141, May 7, 1772, 12:3, January 1, 1773, 13:7–8.

[50] Ibid., reel 8, box 141, January 1, 1773, 13:7–8.

[51] David Jones, *A Journal of Two Visits Made to Some Nations of Indians on the West Side of the River Ohio in the Years 1772 and 1773* (Burlington, N.J., 1774), 64, and viii.

was reporting on the land for speculators. David Zeisberger, who had no designs on Indian land, was shocked by reports of Jones's views on the subject. Jones openly criticized Indians for allowing the land to "lay waste," he accused them of being a "lazy people," and he declared that "in a few years the land would be taken from the Indians by the whites." If the customarily hospitable Indians needed any excuse, Jones had supplied it, and they sent him packing; but not without first sending spirits against him, and perhaps having some fun at his expense. Three Shawnees, wearing spiritually endowed masks, accosted the missionary; according to Jones, "the foremost stooped down by a tree and took sight as if he designed to shoot at me: but I could see that he only had a pole in his hand."[52]

Even Zeisberger, certainly more discreet and less self-interested than Jones, the missionary-land agent, became an object of the Shawnees' suspicion. Attempting to preach to them in 1773, he was discouraged by Chief Gischenatsi of Wakatomica, where ritual vomiting continued. Europeans, argued the headman, "always profess to have great wisdom and understanding from above, at the same time, they deceive us at will, for they regard us as fools." The spiritual wisdom and justice of such seemingly good British subjects as Zeisberger, the chief argued, was merely a scheme to "deceive the Indians, to defraud them of their lands."[53] He turned Zeisberger away.

Among the Mingos, the Iroquois inhabitants of the Upper Ohio region and close allies of the Shawnees and Delawares, the story was much the same. At Dyonosongohta, not far downstream from the village where, a generation later, the Seneca Handsome Lake would have his visions, Zeisberger heard an Indian insist that the "Indians are men, even as are the whites, but God has created them differently." When Zeisberger asked the Indian if he had heard that God had come to earth as a human and died on the cross, the Seneca Mingo quipped, "then the Indians are certainly not guilty of His death, as the whites are."[54] Christian doctrine must have struck nativists as odd. It provided them with more evidence of the abomination of whites: here were a people who admitted to having killed their God. Toward the end of the eighteenth century, Quaker missionaries would hear Senecas of the same region express similar sentiments.

The nativist conviction that Indians were one people under God, at least equal to but quite different from Anglo-Americans, had serious diplomatic consequences. It certainly provided a measure of unity during Pontiac's War, and it continued to influence Indians even beyond their defeat in that struggle. For militants who sought to oppose Anglo-American expansion with armed resistance, it provided justification in their struggles against leaders who cooperated with the British. It also gave an opportunity,

[52] Ibid., 72, 78; Zeisberger, Diary, MAB, reel 8, box 141, October 7, 1772, 12:4.
[53] Zeisberger, Diary, MAB, reel 8, box 141, September 19, 1773, 13:17–18.
[54] Zeisberger, "Diaries . . . Relating to the First Missions in the Ohio Basin," 14–15; Zeisberger, "1767 Diary," 601–2.

through cooperation with the militants of other Indian peoples, to nullify the authority of leading advocates of accommodation. The popularity of the doctrine meant that dissenters from one village or people could find a ready home among the nativists of another.

Stirred by the promise of sacred power, but conscious of their earthly need for numbers, militant Shawnees sent messengers out to surrounding peoples. They took tentative steps close on the heels of Pontiac's War, inviting the Great Lakes area Indians to a "general congress" at one of their villages in 1767. Determined to defend their lands, Shawnee and Mingo nativists continued to insist on their independence from the "protection" of the Six Nations Iroquois, a powerful people who were well connected with the British, and who had British support in their dubious claim to lands in the Ohio country and beyond. Of the supposed Iroquois sovereignty over the Ohio country and its inhabitants, Red Hawk declared in 1770 that "their power extends no further with us." Angry at the Iroquois-British Treaty of Fort Stanwix in 1768, which ceded Shawnee hunting ground south of the Ohio to Britain, Red Hawk and others sought to raise an anti-British Indian confederacy.[55] Although Shawnees directed much of their anger at the Six Nations "for giving up so much of the Country to the English without asking their Consent," they had the support of many Iroquoian Mingos, who also had long hunted in the Kentucky country.[56] Beginning in 1769, militant Shawnees joined by the "Delawares and other Northern Tribes," courted the Cherokees and the Creeks far to the south, as they had during the Seven Years' War and Pontiac's War. In February 1769, some Cherokees and Creeks agreed to visit the "very large Council House" that the Shawnees had just built on the Scioto. The Shawnees also invited the Indians who remained in pockets along the Susquehanna to come live with them in the Ohio country, "where they have Lands for them which the Six Nations can not Sell to the English." The Treaty of Fort Stanwix had put a final end to serious Six Nations' claims to leadership over the Ohioans, whose nativists now considered the Six Nations councillors as "Slaves of the White People."[57]

British official correspondence in the period betrays a fear that the militants might accomplish their objective, forming a new, militant confederacy. In 1770, when the British learned that the Shawnees and Delawares had recruited Cherokees and Creeks as participants in another pan-Indian confer-

---

[55] McKee to Croghan, Fort Pitt, February 20, 1770, in *Johnson Papers*, 7:404–8; Thomas Gage to Earl of Shelburn, New York, October 10, 1767, CO 5/85, f. 205, PRO.

[56] "Journal of Alexander McKee," enclosed in McKee to Johnson, Ostega, September 18, 1769, in *Johnson Papers*, 7:184. The famous Mingo, Logan, lived near the Shawnees in a Mingo settlement at the mouth of the Scioto River. He was apparently married to a Shawnee woman. Draper MSS, 14 J 10–11.

[57] "Journal of Alexander McKee," in *Johnson Papers*, 7:184–85; Thomas Gage to William Johnson, April 1, 1771, in *Johnson Papers*, 8:58; Gage to Earl of Hillsborough, New York, September 9, 1769, CO 5/87, f. 157; John Stuart to Governor Botetourt, Charleston, January 13, 1770, CO 5/71, f. 61; Croghan to Gage, Philadelphia, January 1, 1770, CO 5/88, f. 44, PRO.

ence held that year at Shawnee villages in the Scioto Valley, they doubted that the Indians could actually form a general confederacy, but worried about the matter nonetheless. Indeed the British commander of American forces, Thomas Gage, considered the prospect "a very dangerous Event."[58]

The Scioto conference achieved a notable success. Although it did not have the power to end the desultory hostilities that had long simmered between the Cherokees and the peoples of the Great Lakes and Illinois, the conference stood strongly in favor of such a peace. George Croghan observed that "all the Western tribes over the Lakes, and about Lake Michigan, as well as the Ouabache [Wabash] Indians had unanimously agreed to make peace with the Cherokees and other Southern Indians." British Southern Superintendent of Indian Affairs John Stuart later learned that some Cherokees had accepted a "painted Hatchet" from the "Shawanese, Delawares, and other Tribes of the Western Confederacy."[59]

The possibility of Shawnee-Cherokee cooperation was undergirded by a fact of which the British were well aware: both the Shawnees and the Cherokees hunted in the Kentucky lands "ceded" by the Six Nations to Great Britain. John Stuart, learning that the Shawnees had revealed the extent of the cession to the Cherokees, was relieved to learn that most Cherokees would not believe it was true, "for I had never mentioned it to them." But notwithstanding Stuart's misleading silence, interregional Indian diplomacy intensified, and it caused alarm among the English. Traders, fearing property losses in an uprising, countermanded their orders for supplies and prepared to flee Cherokee country while they awaited the Scioto conference's results. British General Thomas Gage recognized that the Shawnees, if successful in recruiting the southern nations to militancy, would completely isolate the Six Nations (and with them the most influential Briton among the northern Indians, Sir William Johnson), "against whom they have been much exasperated, on account of the Boundary Treaty, held at Fort Stanwix." Stuart, Johnson's counterpart in the South, complained that his job among the southern Indians would be easier if the Shawnees, whom he wryly called "the Northern and Western Gentry," would stay out of the Southeast. Even religious notions may have circulated with the Indian diplomats, for it was in 1770 that the Cherokees first voiced the theology of separation. Bargaining for a good price

[58] John Stuart to Earl of Hillsborough, Charleston, May 2, 1770, CO 5/71, f. 105; Gage to Hillsborough, New York, August 18, 1770, CO 5/88, f. 122, PRO.
[59] For the peace with the Cherokees, see George Croghan to Thomas Gage, September 20, 1770; Gage to John Stuart, New York, October 16, 1770; Gage to Stuart, New York, November 20, 1770, all in the Papers of General Thomas Gage, William Clements Library, University of Michigan, Ann Arbor (hereafter cited as Gage MSS). See also John Stuart to George Germain, Pensacola, August 23, 1776, CO 5/77, f. 126; Croghan to Gage, Philadelphia, January 1, 1770, CO 5/88, f. 44; Gage to Hillsborough, New York, November 12, 1770, ibid., f. 174, PRO. For Shawnee messengers to Creeks, see Stuart, "Talk to the Headman and Warriors of the Upper Creek Nation," Charleston, November 25, 1770, Gage MSS; for messengers to Cherokees, see Croghan to Gage, September 20, 1770, and John Stuart to Gage, Charleston, December 12, 1770, Gage MSS.

in a land cession to Britain, the accommodationist Attakullaculla may have borrowed the phrase from the militants when he declared that "There are three Great Beings above, one who has the Charge of the White, one of the Red, and one of the Black people." Although the Indians' Great Being gave them the land, "the white people seem to drive us from it."[60]

In 1771, the Shawnees repeated their previous year's efforts with another conference at Scioto. That year ceremonial belts, strings of beads, symbolic war hatchets, and dried scalps circulated between the Ohio country and the Southeast as Shawnees and Mingos exchanged proposed strategies with militants among the Creeks and Cherokees. Such widespread militancy encouraged dissident Cherokees to speak out against the recent Cherokee land cession made with Stuart at the Treaty of Lochaber (October 1770). Although the cession was carried out, Cherokee militants continued to develop their plans for a broad-based opposition to Anglo-American expansion. In the cession's wake, militants, joined by the northerners, created such disturbances among the Cherokees that prudent traders fled to the South Carolina settlements, "where Pannick Spread with amazing Rapidity."[61]

The efforts on the part of Indians of the Ohio country, particularly the Shawnees, to "establish what they call a general Peace," threatened the English with the prospect of another major Indian war. Rumors of proposed attacks on the English mingled with reports that "the Rogue Mankiller," a leading Cherokee militant, had recently led a party of Cherokees against a small British party near the confluence of the Mississippi and Ohio, killing the colonists, and taking the last man, an African-American slave, alive. On the party's return to the Cherokee towns, it presented the nation with the scalps, but the Cherokees were not prepared formally to go to war and rejected the offer. They continued to be divided over their policy toward Anglo-America. Such divisions similarly plagued both the Creeks, who awaited messages from the Northern Shawnees, and the northern Indians themselves, particularly the Mingos, who remained angry at their Six Nations kinfolk for the Stanwix cession.[62]

---

[60] Stuart to Gage, March 12, 1771, Charleston; Gage to Stuart, New York, October 16, 1770; Gage to Stuart, New York, May 17, 1771; Stuart to Gage, Charleston, December 12, 1770; Stuart to Gage, Charleston, February 8, 1771; Gage to Stuart, New York, September 19, 1770, Gage MSS; copy of the Report of the General Meeting with the Principal Chiefs and Warriors of the Cherokee Nation with John Stuart, Lochaber, October 18–20, 1770, CO 5/72, f. 22, PRO.

[61] George Galphin to John Stuart, February 19, 1771; "Convention of the Overhill Cherokee Chiefs and Beloved Men . . . at Taquah . . . March 3, 1771; Alexander Cameron to Stuart, March 19, 1771 (abstract); Stuart to Gage, Charleston, April 29, 1771; Gage to Stuart, New York, June 11, 1771; Stuart to Gage, Pensacola, August 31, 1771; Stuart to Gage, Mobile, December 14, 1771; Gage to Stuart, New York, February 17, 1772, Gage MSS; Governor Wright to Hillsborough, Savannah, February 28, 1771, CO 5/661, f. 25; John Stuart to Hillsborough, Charleston, March 5, 1771, CO 5/72, f. 165, PRO.

[62] Alexander Cameron to John Stuart, Lochaber, August 9, 1772; Stephen Forester to Stuart, Tuccabatchies, September 7, 1772; Stuart to Gage, Charleston, September 7, 1772; Gage to Stuart,

The militants labored to form their confederacy well into the year 1773. General Gage, who thought them "ingenious and Sound Polititians," noted that the Six Nations had failed to stop the Shawnee "Contrivers" of "a general Union of all the Western & Southern Nations."[63] But militant unity remained limited; the results of their efforts fell short of the militants' expectations. By 1773, the militants had not consolidated enough authority to meet the threat posed by the Anglo-American settlement of Kentucky. To gather members from many nations together to discuss pan-Indian resistance was not to form a union; they had yet to win over key village councils. Since 1767 many Delaware chiefs, particularly White Eyes, had advocated the avoidance of confrontation with the Anglo-Americans. Tensions increased in many Delaware towns. White Eyes left the nativistic Newcomer's town and set up his own village to avoid daily strife. Croghan wrote that many chiefs, some even among the Shawnees, opposed the confederacy and "has Tould thire Warrers that itt wold End in there Ruin Butt the Worrars Say they May as well Dey Like Men as be Kicked about Like Doggs."[64] Such division added urgency to the militants' quest for support among other Indian peoples, but it imposed clear limits upon their efforts to organize on a grand scale.

The test came in 1773, when white frontiersmen slew the Shawnee wife and children of the Mingo chief, Logan. No militant himself, Logan retaliated, and other Shawnees and Mingos joined in the fray. These border incidents triggered Dunmore's War (1773–1774), the central issue of which soon became the British claim to Kentucky. Militant Shawnees and Mingos, protesting not merely the murders but also the invasion of their lands by hunters and squatters, won the support of some Delawares, Wyandots, Miamis, Ottawas, and even a party of Cherokees,[65] but they had substantial support from no nation. Suffering from want, and not wishing to become embroiled in another Pontiac's War, most Indian councils held the peace. Lacking numbers, the militants still attempted to resist the British conquest of Kentucky. They persisted in their calls for assistance, but they could count only on the justice of their cause and the sacred powers that could be invoked through ritual.

Explaining the matter to British agent and once-adopted Shawnee Alexander McKee in March 1774, a Shawnee pointed to the Virginians' new

---

New York, September 30, 1772; David Taitt to Stuart, Little Tallassies, October 19, 1772; Gage to Stuart, New York, December 20, 1772, Gage MSS.

[63] Gage to Johnson, New York, April 1, 1771, in *Johnson Papers,* 8:58; Gage to Frederick Haldimand, New York, June 3, 1773, in Haldimand Papers, British Museum Additional Manuscripts, 21665, pt. 3, ff. 141–42, photostats in the Library of Congress, Washington, D.C.

[64] Croghan to Johnson, September 18, 1769, in *Johnson Papers,* 7:182.

[65] Major Arthur Campbell to Colonel William Preston, July 9, 1774, Draper MSS, 3 QQ 58; "Colonel Fleming's Orderly Book," Draper MSS 2 ZZ 72; "Conference at Fort Pitt," Draper MSS, 4 J 103.

settlements. "We have had many disagreeable Dreams this winter about this matter, and what we have seen and been witnesses to since we came here seems to confirm our fears." The British colonies had clearly intended war. To resist, the militants could only put a hearty trust in ritual. Shortly after their narrow but critical defeat at Point Pleasant, in what is now West Virginia, Zeisberger learned that the Indians had prepared for the battle with "the warrior beson, which they use when going to war, in order that they may be successful." Another medicine, probably a sacred bundle, was "thought to be capable of preserving them from arrow and ball." According to Zeisberger, the bearer of the bundle was killed in the battle, but neither "disagreeable dreams" nor militant nativism died with him.[66]

The serious failure of both ritual and pan-Indianism in Dunmore's War did not kill the idea of Indian unity and the networks that supported it. McKee had noted in 1774 that the plan for unity "had been on foot for many years," and it was not surrendered. Throughout 1774 and 1775, militant northerners and southerners exchanged delegations.[67] Northern nativists could still attribute their defeat in Dunmore's War to the misconduct of those among their own people who had not defended their lands. But more important to the survival of militancy was the opening presented by events across the Alleghenies in the British colonies. With the American Revolution, the nativists' English-speaking enemies divided against themselves, providing the militants with an opportunity to cooperate with leaders who favored the British in a new struggle against the Anglo-American settlers. Breeches within many Indian communities temporarily closed, religious nativism became submerged beneath a broader movement against Anglo-America, and the largest, most unified Native American effort the continent would ever see erupted with the American Revolution.

[66] Zeisberger, Diary, MAB, reel 8, file 141, October 11, 1774, 15:3; David Zeisberger, "History of the Northern American Indians," ed. Archer Butler Hulbert and Nathaniel Schwarze, *Ohio Archaeological and Historical Society Publications* 19 (1910): 127; "Extract from the Journal of Alexander McKee," March 8, 1774, CO 5/75, f. 142, PRO.

[67] "Extract from the Journal of Alexander McKee, Sir William Johnson's Resident on the Ohio, March 8, 1774," CO 5/75, ff. 142–47; John Stuart to Earl of Dartmouth, Charleston, August 2, 1774, ibid., f. 165; Alexander Cameron to John Stuart, Lochaber, February 23, 1775, CO 5/76, f. 91.